DYNAMIC PHYSICAL EDUCATION
FOR ELEMENTARY SCHOOL CHILDREN

FIFTEENTH EDITION

ROBERT P. PANGRAZI
Arizona State University

PEARSON
Benjamin Cummings

San Francisco   Boston   New York
Cape Town   Hong Kong   London   Madrid   Mexico City
Montreal   Munich   Paris   Singapore   Sydney   Tokyo   Toronto

Senior Acquisitions Editor: Deirdre Espinoza
Development Manager: Claire Alexander
Project Editor: Marie Beaugureau
Editorial Assistant: Amy Yu
Senior Marketing Manager: Sandra Lindelof
Production Supervisor: Beth Masse
Managing Editor: Deborah Cogan
Manufacturing Buyer: Stacy Wong
Project Coordination and Composition: Elm Street Publishing Services, Inc.
Cover and Interior Design: Hespenheide Design
Cover Photo Credits: Rubberball/Super Stock, Inc.

Photo credits can be found on page 750.

ISBN 0-8053-7908-8

www.aw-bc.com

10 9 8 7 6 5 4 3 2—QWD—10 09 08 07

Dedication

To my wife Deb whom I love and respect.
She is not only a valued professional colleague, but a special friend and companion
who has enriched my life.
I regard Deb as a silent author who has contributed much to this textbook.

To my son and daughter, Charles and Connie, and their wonderful families.
I appreciate the joy and love they deliver on a regular basis.

To Dr. Victor P. Dauer, my late co-author, who taught and mentored me
throughout my career and continues to guide my thinking and writing efforts.

Robert P. Pangrazi

About the Author

Robert P. Pangrazi received his B.A., M.S, and Ph.D. from Washington State University. He is a Professor Emeritus at Arizona State University, where he was a Professor for 31 years in the Department of Kinesiology. He is an educational consultant giving guidance to a number of companies including Gopher Sport, Walk4Life, and the United States Tennis Association. Bob travels the country to give workshops on teaching methods and regularly conducts training sessions in schools and universities. He has served as a fifth grade teacher, elementary physical education specialist, university professor, researcher, and administrator. He has many devoted students who have gone on to teach and follow his methods.

Bob is an AAHPERD Honor Fellow and a Fellow in the American Academy of Kinesiology and Physical Education. He is a Fellow in the North American Society of Health, Physical Education, Recreation, Sport, and Dance Professionals and was honored by the National Association for Sport and Physical Education

(NASPE) with the Margie Hanson Distinguished Service Award.

In addition to *Dynamic Physical Education for Elementary School Children,* Bob has written *Dynamic Physical Education Curriculum Guide: Lesson Plans for Implementation* (Benjamin Cummings) and *Dynamic Physical Education for Secondary School Children* with Paul W. Darst (Benjamin Cummings). He co-edited *Toward a Better Understanding of Physical Fitness and Activity: Selected Topics* for The President's Council on Physical Fitness and Sports with Charles Corbin, and has also written nearly 100 journal articles.

Bob is quick to point out that what he enjoys in life is teaching, regardless of the age of students. He has been quick to point out to college students that a class of first grade physical education students do not care about their teacher's academic record—what is important is being able to make learning enjoyable and exciting for them. In his spare time, Bob enjoys hiking, mountain biking, working out, and playing the guitar and piano.

Brief Contents

PART I

Instruction and Program Implementation

PART II

Teaching the Objectives of Physical Education

Contents

Preface

The fifteenth edition of *Dynamic Physical Education for Elementary School Children (DPE)* represents a major revision. New chapters have been added and others have received major revisions. Readers should know that there have been numerous changes based on the input of many reviewers and the evolving nature of the profession. Three of the new chapters represent the increasing emphasis that physical activity and health are receiving because of the national concern about childhood obesity. The third new chapter focuses on integrating academic concepts into physical education classes. In an attempt to broaden the base of activities taught in physical education, the book also provides a new focus on cooperative and lifetime activities. More information about each of these chapters is provided in the following discussion.

GENERAL ORGANIZATION OF THE TEXT

The 30 chapters in *DPE* continue to be grouped into two major parts—*Instruction and Program Implementation* and *Teaching the Objectives of Physical Education*. Part I, *Instruction and Program Implementation*, contains the theory and requisite knowledge a teacher needs to develop a quality program. The chapters in Part I are separated into three sections that help students understand the need for quality physical education programs in schools, how to be a quality instructor, and an understanding of school procedures including the need for integrating academic content. When combined with the Internet websites included at the end of each chapter, the *Instructor's Resource Manual*, the *Media Manager*, and instructional videotapes, college and university instructors have a rich tool chest of ideas for helping pre-service and in-service teachers think, reflect, and improve the act of teaching.

Part I, *Instruction and Program Implementation*, contains the knowledge necessary to become an effective teacher. The chapters in this part are designed to teach students how to implement a program that is based on the National Association for Sport and Physical Education (NASPE) standards.

Part I Instruction and Program Implementation

Section 1   Understanding the Need for Physical Education
Chapter 1   Elementary School Physical Education
Chapter 2   Teaching Children in the Physical Education Environment

Section 2   The Instructional Process
Chapter 3   Preparing a Quality Lesson
Chapter 4   Curriculum Development
Chapter 5   Improving Instructional Effectiveness
Chapter 6   Management and Discipline
Chapter 7   Children with Disabilities

Section 3   Program Implementation
Chapter 8   Evaluation
Chapter 9   Legal Liability, Supervision, and Safety
Chapter 10 Facilities, Equipment, and Supplies
Chapter 11 Integrating Academic Concepts

Section 1 offers a brief history of the profession and sets the framework for the entire text by listing and explaining the NASPE standards. Chapter 2 helps teachers understand children and their needs in a physical education setting.

Section 2 focuses on successful instruction. This section shows how to plan a quality lesson, view the importance of a curriculum, and teach it effectively. Management and discipline are always the constructs under which teachers will succeed or fail, and Chapter 6 offers much practical information for successfully teaching youngsters in an activity setting. Chapter 7 shows teachers how to adapt and modify activities for all students in their classes.

Part II, *Teaching the Objectives of Physical Education*, is filled with instructional activities. No text on the market offers teachers a greater variety of evidence-based activities, and the emphasis on this revision has been to add even more activities. This portion of the text is separated into four sections that are filled with activities and strategies designed to help teachers accomplish the NASPE standards that define a quality physical education program.

Section 4 contains many activities and techniques for teaching personal health skills, including methods for teaching students how to develop and maintain an active and healthy lifestyle. This section includes new chapters on the need to promote physical activity among students and how to create an active and healthy school environment.

Section 5 brings together methods and activities for teaching fundamental motor skills. Movement concepts, fundamental motor skills, and body management skills encompass the majority of content in this section. Now pre-service and in-service teachers can identify activities and strategies that will improve student competencies in this important skill area.

Section 6 is designed to improve specialized motor skills among students of diverse backgrounds. Chapters on manipulative skills, rhythmic movement skills, gymnastic skills, cooperative skills (a new chapter), and game skills offer in-depth coverage for the development of a personalized set of specialized skills.

Finally, Section 7 focuses on developing sport skills including a new chapter on lifetime activities. These chapters contain many skills, drills, and lead-up activities. These chapters use the paradigm of teach the skill properly, practice it in a drill, and apply in a lead-up game that assures success.

As an added organizational aid, each section is color-coded for ease of reference. Each chapter in a section contains a tab in the outside margin that shows the chapter number and corresponds with the color code for that section. This makes it easy to find a desired section or chapter quickly.

DPE is written for classroom teachers and physical education teachers based on the author's experience as both a physical education and a classroom teacher. Material is written and illustrated with many examples that make it easy to understand regardless of the degree of background in physical education. All activities in the text are listed in progression from the easiest activity to the most difficult. This enables teachers to plan a lesson that incorporates proper sequencing of skills. The accompanying lesson plan book, *Dynamic Physical Education Curriculum Guide: Lesson Plans for Implementation,* Fifteenth Edition, organizes the activities listed in *DPE* into a 36-week curriculum guide that features lesson plans for an academic year. The *Curriculum Guide* offers a section that identifies academic concepts that can be taught within a physical education lesson. This makes it easy for the physical educator to show classroom teachers and administrators how physical activities contribute to academic outcomes of the school. Additionally, the new NASPE content standards that guide each lesson plan have been added to the fifteenth edition. The *Curriculum Guide* offers three sets of plans for students at differing developmental levels. *DPE* and the *DPE Curriculum Guide* are used in a large number of schools as the foundation for a curriculum that is supplemented with local district materials and activities.

ESSENTIAL COMPONENTS OF QUALITY PROGRAMS AND NASPE NATIONAL STANDARDS FOR PHYSICAL EDUCATION

Across the country, a wide variety of differing areas of instructional emphasis characterize physical education programs. Some view these differences as an outcome of diverse and differing points of view while others think all programs should follow one model. My own point of view is that difference is part of the American culture. However, even when large differences exist, similarities mark quality programs. Therefore, in Chapter 1 I have identified what I believe to be eight key **essential components of quality programs.** This approach allows programs to maintain their uniqueness while ensuring a quality program. These essential components are listed at the start of each chapter, and the components that are particularly relevant to each chapter are highlighted, so it is possible to see how they contribute to a comprehensive physical education program.

With the age of accountability upon education, it has become vitally important to determine what should be taught and what youngsters should know when they leave the school environment. The American Alliance for Health, Physical Education, Recreation, and Dance (AAHPERD) and the NASPE have done much to make physical educators aware of the need for content standards. The six **NASPE national standards for physical education** identified in Chapter 1 reflect the development of a program that stresses lifetime activity, competency in a wide variety of physical skills, the need for strong social and personal responsibility skills, and the knowledge needed to maintain personal wellness. These standards are placed at the start of each chapter to illustrate how they guide the content and development of this text. The standards that are particularly relevant to each chapter are highlighted.

The inclusion and integration of essential components and content standards are an important feature in this text. For example, by looking at the NASPE standards on the opening page of Chapter 12, Promoting and Monitoring Physical Activity, you can see that this chapter offers activities that help students meet Standards 2–4 and 6. These features are designed to help pre-service and in-service teachers understand *why* they are teaching activities and to assist them in developing quality physical education programs that help children become active for life. Information and instructional activities in *DPE* are included only if they contribute to the standards or essential components found in Chapter 1.

NEW FEATURES

The fifteenth edition of *DPE* reflects a number of other significant changes based on feedback from peer reviewers and users of *DPE* and changes in the field of physical education. This edition of *Dynamic Physical Education for Elementary School Children* provides teachers with a sound foundation for establishing a well-rounded, comprehensive physical education program. What follows is a highlight of key changes made to this edition:

- Chapter 1 has an expanded section on justifying a physical education program. Discussion of the Child Nutrition and WIC Reauthorization Act of 2004 and how it impacts the profession is included. The revised NASPE standards replace the physical education standards that were found in the previous edition of *DPE.*

- Chapter 4 now focuses on developing a curriculum. This chapter is sandwiched between the lesson planning (Chapter 3) and improving instructional effectiveness (Chapter 5) chapters. This makes it easy for teachers to see how these three chapters form the basis for planning a quality physical education program.

- Chapter 6 maintains its focus on the importance of knowing how to effectively manage and discipline students. Reviewers felt the need to separate these important areas so teachers could better understand when to manage students and when to discipline students. A new section on peer mediation has been added so teachers can teach students to help each other solve some of their interpersonal problems.

- Based on reviewers' comments, Chapter 7, Children with Disabilities, has been changed. The treatment of specific disabilities was removed. Reviewers felt such issues were better covered in an adapted physical education class. Thus, more emphasis was given to inclusion and modifying activities for greater student success.

- Chapter 11, Academic Integration, is a new chapter. This chapter focuses on showing physical education teachers how they can integrate academic concepts into physical education lessons. The need for integrating concepts is discussed and a step-by-step approach is offered. The chapter offers all new instructional activities that can be throughout the physical education curriculum.

- Chapter 12, Promoting and Monitoring Physical Activity, is a new chapter that reflects the national concern for youth obesity. One of the best antidotes for this problem is to increase the volume of activity students accumulate throughout the day. Using pedometers to monitor program accountability is discussed in detail. Developing a walking program to increase activity outside of school is also offered in this chapter.

- Chapter 14, Active and Healthy Schools, is a new chapter that shows how to change the environment of the school so students increase their activity levels and improve their nutrition and eating habits. This is important for setting a healthy foundation for students as they grow to be active adults. This chapter discusses the many components of an operational active and healthy school environment.

- Chapter 16 combines introductory activities and fundamental motor skills. Since the core of most introductory activities is based on fundamental motor skills, I present these activities together.

- Cooperative activities appeal to elementary school youngsters. Chapter 21 is virtually a new chapter with many new cooperative activities. A section on how to present the activities to students has been added as well. Parachute activities have been moved to this chapter because they demand a cooperative effort by students. Reviewers felt relays should be removed from the text due to their tendency to allow for periods of inactivity by waiting students, so they are no longer part of *DPE.*

■ For many adults, lifetime activities are the skills they use to stay active. Chapter 23 is a new chapter that offers a number of activities that can be used to maintain an active lifestyle. This activity-based chapter includes walking, orienteering, tennis, racquetball, badminton, and Frisbee units.

QUALITY CONTROL AND FIELD TESTING

A tradition that continues in this edition of *DPE* is to assure that all activities have been field-tested with children. I continue to teach elementary school children and evaluate new activities based in part on student reception and instructional effectiveness. A number of experts have been involved in evaluating and helping with this text to ensure the content is accurate and on the cutting edge. Chapter 19, Rhythmic Movement Skills, was enhanced by Jerry Poppen, an expert physical educator; Paul James, Wagon Wheel Records; Dr. Barbara Cusimano, Oregon State University; and Deb Pangrazi, elementary school physical education resource teacher for the Mesa, Arizona, Public Schools. John Spini, current coach of the women's gymnastics team at Arizona State University, evaluated and contributed to Chapter 20, Gymnastic Skills. Dr. Carole Casten, California State University, Dominguez Hills, contributed the material for the section on rhythmic gymnastics. Dr. Virginia Atkins Chadwick, Fresno State University, and Dr. Julian Stein, George Mason University, evaluated and contributed to Chapter 7, Children with Disabilities. Jim Roberts, a Mesa, Arizona, physical education specialist, field-tested the materials for developing responsible behavior. In addition, the authors are indebted to the Mesa School District elementary school physical education specialists in Mesa, Arizona, who have field-tested the activities and offered numerous suggestions and ideas for improvement. Dr. Steven Hogan, director of physical education and athletics, and Deb Pangrazi, resource teacher, lead this stellar group of nearly 90 specialists. All of these individuals have unselfishly contributed their energies and insights to assure that quality activities and teaching strategies are part of this textbook. The result of this continued field testing is a book filled with activities, strategies, and techniques that work.

SUPPLEMENTARY MATERIALS

Available with the fifteenth edition of *Dynamic Physical Education for Elementary School Children* is a complete package of supplements that offer students and instructors alike an integrated and comprehensive set of learning and instructional tools.

Dynamic Physical Education Curriculum Guide: Lesson Plans for Implementation, **Fifteenth Edition** (0-8053-7909-6) has been developed concurrently with the text and offers a framework for implementing a developmentally appropriate curriculum. The lesson plans are presented in three developmental levels, allowing for a greater range of activity and ensuring that presentations are closely aligned to the maturity and experience of students. The plans are filled with activities and outcomes that enable teachers to plan and understand *why* various activities are being taught. The lesson plans offer a framework for planning comprehensive lessons rather than preempting teachers from planning duties. As mentioned above, the curriculum guide offers sections on academic integration and content standards for each of the more than 110 individual lesson plans.

Lecture and Lesson Plan Videos: Four videos have been developed for *Dynamic Physical Education for Elementary School Children.* Two new 20-minute videos have been developed for this edition.

■ **Pedometers and Physical Activity** (0-8053-0403-7) is a new video that features using pedometers in a physical education setting. How to use pedometers, a number of instructional activities for students, and promoting physical activity outside of the school environment are all covered in this video.

■ **Active and Healthy Schools** (0-8053-0263-8) is a second brand new video that focuses on how to create an Active and Healthy School environment. This video shows the steps physical educators can implement to change the environment of an elementary school so increased physical activity and healthy eating habits are promoted. Schools that follow the illustrated steps will be able to meet the wellness plan that is mandated by the Child Nutrition and WIC Reauthorization Act of 2004.

■ **Planning a Quality Lesson: How to Use the DPE Curriculum Guide** (0-8053-5708-4) shows how to plan an effective and fun lesson for your elementary school students.

■ **Quality PE in the Four-Part Lesson Format** (0-8053-5709-2) shows complete lessons, taught to Developmental Level I and Developmental Level II students, modeling successful teaching techniques.

Media Manager CD-ROM (0-8053-7925-8) This all new ancillary includes PowerPoint lecture slides for each chapter of the book, completely updated for the Fifteenth Edition by Brett Christie of Sonoma State University, all of the art and photos from the book, video clips, and student outcomes.

The **Instructor's Resource Manual** (0-8053-7924-X), by Dr. Carole Casten, California State University, Dominguez Hills, is closely correlated to the text. For each chapter, it provides a chapter summary, desired student outcomes, a discussion of the main concepts of the chapter, ideas for presenting the content, discussion topics, suggested written assignments, and a cooperative learning project.

The **Test Bank,** by Mike Ernst, California State University, Dominguez Hills, is available in printed (0-8053-7918-5) and computerized (0-8053-8167-8) format. It offers true/false, multiple-choice, matching, and essay questions for every chapter of the book. Answers and page references are provided for all but the essay questions. The 1,500 test questions are all included in the computerized test bank. Using this cross-platform CD-ROM, instructors can create tests, edit questions, and add their own material to the existing test bank.

Transparency Acetates (0-8053-7838-3) Important figures from the text are available in an easy-to-use format for lecture presentations.

Companion Website: A Website (www.aw-bc.com/pangrazi) has been developed to complement the text. Features for instructors include PowerPoint® slides. Content for students includes learning objectives, quizzes, and Internet links.

Online Courses: In addition to offering Blackboard (0-8053-7917-7), we also offer CourseCompass (0-8053-7922-3) our nationally hosted online course management system. All CourseCompass and Blackboard courses offer pre-loaded content including testing and assessment, Web links, illustrations, and photos. To view a demonstration of any course, go to http://cms.awlonline.com.

ACKNOWLEDGMENTS

Useful textbooks are the result of cohesive teamwork among the publishing company, reviewers, and the author. This edition I want to acknowledge the in-depth help from a friend and fellow professional: Dr. Aaron Beighle, a faculty member at the University of Kentucky, who played an important role in helping with this revision. He has contributed much to the academic integration, cooperative skills, and lifetime activities chapters. His insight, hard work, and understanding of the instructional process have helped to make this edition more useful to teachers.

I am indebted to the professional group at Benjamin Cummings for their major contributions to this text. Deirdre Espinoza, Senior Acquisitions Editor, has given ongoing support and encouragement. I am particularly indebted to Marie Beaugureau, Project Editor, who coordinated the development and completion of this text with efficiency and thoughtfulness. She has an outstanding sense of organization and her hard work and dedication are greatly appreciated. I also appreciate the efficiency and competency of Beth Masse, Production Supervisor. Eric Arima, Production Editor, and all the others at Elm Street Publishing Services did a wonderful job handling the production of the text. To these and many other individuals at Benjamin Cummings who go unnamed, please accept a hearty thank you.

A sincere note of thanks goes to the following reviewers who provided valuable feedback that helped guide the author's efforts throughout the project: Rhonda Clements, Manhattanville College; Cloyce D. Cox, Howard Payne University; Lydia Crain, University of Arizona; Suzanna Rocco Dillon, Wayne State University; Molly Hare, Indiana State University; Patricia E. Keiffner, University of Louisville; Linda Rikard, George Mason University; Sharon Schneider, Hofstra University; and Virginia Trummer, University of Texas, San Antonio.

Instruction and Program Implementation

Understanding the Need for Physical Education

Section 1 contains the basic information needed to teach children in the physical education setting. A basic understanding of physical education in the United States and the evolution of physical education offers some perspective for teachers. Physical education is an integral part of the development of educated and healthy students. National content standards guide the development and integration of physical education into the school curriculum. There are essential components to be found in quality physical education programs and these are identified and discussed in this section. A basic understanding of the growth and development characteristics of youngsters is covered in detail. Key points that ensure all children are given equal opportunity to learn motor skills offer necessary information to teachers. Finally, guidelines for safely engaging children in physical activity are listed so that teachers can feel confident as they lead children toward an active lifestyle.

After reading this section, you should have the knowledge necessary to implement a comprehensive program that is safe, based on the needs of children, and organized around national physical education standards.

CHAPTER 1

Elementary School Physical Education

SUMMARY

Physical education is that phase of the general educational program that contributes to the total growth and development of each child, primarily through movement experiences. Program objectives provide the framework and direction for the physical education curriculum. Systematic and properly taught physical education can help achieve the major content standards, including movement competence, maintaining physical fitness, learning personal health and wellness skills, applying movement concepts and skill mechanics, developing lifetime activity skills, and demonstrating positive social skills. Modern programs of physical education have been influenced by cultural and educational factors related to games, sports, fitness, educational movement, perceptual-motor competency, federal mandates, value and attitude development, the Surgeon General's report, and the nationwide emphasis on physical activity.

ESSENTIAL COMPONENTS OF QUALITY PROGRAMS

▶ I. **Organized around content standards**

II. Student-centered and developmentally appropriate

III. Physical activity and motor skill development form the core of the program

IV. Teaches management skills and self-discipline

V. Promotes inclusion of all students

VI. Focuses on process over product

VII. Promotes lifetime personal health and wellness

VIII. Teaches cooperation and responsibility and promotes sensitivity to diversity

NATIONAL STANDARDS FOR PHYSICAL EDUCATION*

▶ 1. **Demonstrates competency in motor skills and movement patterns needed to perform a variety of physical activities.**

▶ 2. **Demonstrates understanding of movement concepts, principles, and tactics as they apply to the learning and performance of physical activities.**

▶ 3. **Participates regularly in physical activity.**

▶ 4. **Achieves and maintains a health-enhancing level of physical fitness.**

▶ 5. **Exhibits responsible personal and social behavior that respects self and others in physical activity.**

▶ 6. **Values physical activity for health, enjoyment, challenge, self-expression, and/or social interaction.**

*National Association for Sport and Physical Education (NASPE), 2004.

OUTCOMES

▪ Justify the need for a quality physical education program in the elementary school setting based on the health benefits it can offer children.

▪ Cite the NASPE national standards for physical education.

▪ List program objectives and recognize the distinctive contributions of physical education.

▪ Describe the educational reasons for including physical education as part of the elementary school experience.

▪ Define physical education and its role in the elementary school experience.

▪ Articulate how various pedagogical influences changed the course of elementary school physical education programs.

▪ Identify essential components of a quality physical education program.

▪ Verbally portray how a variety of societal influences and federal mandates impacted elementary school physical education.

WHAT IS PHYSICAL EDUCATION?

Physical education means many things to many people. Physical education professionals often describe it as essential subject matter dedicated to learning in the psychomotor domain and committed to developing lifetime physical activity patterns. However, some individuals mistakenly consider physical education to be the same as athletics or competitive sports. Some perceive physical education to be recess or free-time play. Suffice it to say that while some view it as a meaningful subject matter area, others report having less than satisfactory physical education experiences, if they had physical education at all.

So, what is physical education? It is part of the total educational program that contributes, primarily through movement experiences, to the total growth and development of all children. *Physical education* is defined as education through movement. It is an instructional program that gives attention to all learning domains: psychomotor, cognitive, and affective. No other area of the curriculum is designed to help children learn motor and lifetime activity skills. This makes physical education a necessary component of the total school curriculum. It is not enough to educate children academically; they must also be educated physically. Too often, physical educators try to do all things for their students, including improving their academic skills. Certainly, whenever possible, it is important to do so. However, physical education programs should always place the majority of emphasis on the learning of physical skills. If students, particularly the unskilled, don't receive quality instruction in physical education, there is little opportunity for them to learn these skills as adults. Unskilled youngsters often have little opportunity to learn new skills as compared to those who are skilled. For example, there are all types of opportunities for skilled youngsters to participate in Little League, gymnastics clubs, and sport clubs. However, for the unskilled youngster, physical education may be the only place that offers an opportunity to learn new skills. Therefore, a strong physical education program emphasizes helping all youngsters succeed regardless of ability or skill level.

THE EVOLUTION OF ELEMENTARY SCHOOL PHYSICAL EDUCATION

A number of concerns, historical events, and pedagogical influences have significantly impacted elementary school physical education programs. Often these programs are created as responses to events that are publicized by the press and other interested parties. The many changes that have occurred in elementary school physical education programming clearly point out how the public's needs and concerns shape the direction of U.S. education.

The German and Swedish Influence

During the nineteenth century in both Germany and Sweden, physical education systems that centered on body development were established in the schools. Around the middle of that century, German and Swedish immigrants to the United States introduced these concepts of physical education. The German system favored a gymnastic approach and required a good deal of equipment and special teachers. The Swedish system incorporated an exercise program into the activity presentations. The physical education program in many of the schools that adopted this system consisted of a series of structured exercises that children could perform in the classroom. The need for equipment and gymnasiums posed problems for the schools that followed these systems, and many economy-minded citizens questioned the programs. A combination of games and calisthenics evolved and became the first scheduled physical education activity offered in some U.S. schools. The Swedish system was structured and formal and often not suited to the needs of elementary school children.

The Emphasis on Games and Sports

When about one-third of the American men drafted in World War I were rejected as physically unfit for military service, the result was a new demand for physical education in the schools. State educational authorities legislated minimum weekly time requirements for physical activity in school programs. In many states, these laws established physical education as part of the school curriculum. The laws were, however, quantitative in nature, and little attention was given to program quality.

Training programs designed for soldiers during World War I placed an emphasis on games and sports and proved more effective than strict calisthenics. This shift to the use of games and sports for physical development spawned school programs with similar emphasis. John Dewey, professor of philosophy at Columbia University, had a profound impact on educational theory during the mid-twentieth century. Since two of Dewey's cardinal aims of education stressed attention to physical activities, the teaching of games and sports in schools received impetus. These aims, the promotion of health and the worthy use of leisure time, became school curricular responsibilities. The school was deemed responsible for molding social change, and a high value was placed on games and sports.

Programs stressing sports and games primarily appeared in the secondary schools. Elementary school programs were merely diluted models of these secondary programs; they literally could have been described by answering the question, "What games are we going to play today?" During the Great Depression, equipment was difficult to secure, and physical education teachers were almost nonexistent. Physical education was relegated to a minor role, and in many schools was eliminated entirely.

During World War II, many new training programs for special groups appeared. Research proved the efficacy of physical fitness development, hospital reconditioning programs, and other innovative approaches. An improvement in the quality of physical education programs might have been expected after the war, but unfortunately, little positive effect trickled down to elementary school programs.

National Concern about Physical Fitness

A renewed emphasis on fitness occurred in the 1950s, following the publication of comparative studies of fitness levels of U.S. and European children that were based on the Kraus-Weber tests. A study by Kraus and Hirschland (1954) that compared strength and flexibility measurements of 4,000 New York–area schoolchildren with a comparable sample of Central European children had far-reaching results. The press became concerned about the comparative weakness of U.S. children, and, as a consequence of this publicity, the fitness movement was born. One result of the uproar was the establishment of the President's Council on Physical Fitness and Sports, an agency established to promote physical fitness, not only among schoolchildren but also among citizens of all ages. Recently, the Council has begun to focus on increasing the activity of youngsters rather than just promoting fitness. This emphasis is manifested in a forthcoming award program for individuals who participate in regular physical activity and show the ability to maintain a physical activity regimen over an extended period of time.

Pedagogical Influences

Changes in physical education can be implemented from within the profession by teachers and professionals who see a need for different instructional methods and programs. The changes are often stimulated by dissatisfaction with the status quo and a desire to make physical education a more "needed" part of the school curriculum. The following are some of the major approaches that have influenced the course of elementary school physical education.

MOVEMENT EDUCATION

Movement education originated in England and was incorporated into U.S. programs during the late 1960s. To some degree, it was a revolt against structured fitness programs, which included calisthenics presented in a formal, command style. The demanding fitness standards advocated by the President's Council led some teachers to teach for fitness outcomes rather than to present a balanced physical education program that also taught skills and concepts. This practice created a backlash among some physical educators, who felt that creativity, exploration, and cognition should also be focal points of the profession.

Movement education programs shifted some of the responsibility for learning to children. The methodology featured problem solving and an exploratory approach. Adopting movement education led to the rejection of physical fitness-oriented activities, especially calisthenics, which were labeled *training* and not education. Controversy arose regarding the application of movement principles to the teaching of specific skills, particularly athletic skills. There was a tendency to apply the exploration methodology to all phases of instruction without examining the effectiveness of such practices. Regardless of the questions raised, movement education resulted in better teaching methodology and increased emphasis on instruction focused on the individual. In addition, movement education offered an opportunity for diversity of movement through creative instructional methods and allowed students of all ability levels to find success.

PERCEPTUAL-MOTOR PROGRAMS

The focus of perceptual-motor programs was corrective in nature and attempted to remedy learning difficulties attributed to a breakdown in perceptual-motor development. Theorists held that children progressed through growth and developmental stages from head to foot (cephalocaudally) and from the center of the body outward (proximodistally) in an orderly fashion. When disruptions, lags, or omissions occurred in this process, certain underlying perceptual-motor bases failed to develop fully and impaired the child's ability to function correctly in both the physical and the academic settings.

Perceptual-motor programs flourished because of concern for slow academic learners, sometimes called *slow* or *delayed* learners. Some children identified as academically subpar demonstrated motor problems involving such movement factors as coordination, balance and postural control, image of the body and its parts, and relationships involving time and space. Perceptual-motor programs attempted to remediate these shortcomings and gave physical education teachers hope that their profession would be viewed as an integral part of a child's academic success. Unfortunately, when researchers examined the effectiveness of such programs, it was apparent that perceptual-motor activities did not improve academic achievement. Today, few perceptual-motor programs designed to replace physical education programs exist. However, the contribution of perceptual-motor programs in today's physical education programs is the integration of perceptual-motor principles into skill-learning sequences (such as using both sides of the body, practicing balance skills, and so forth).

CONCEPTUAL LEARNING

Conceptual understanding (that is, the application of abstract ideas drawn from experience) plays an important part in physical education. In the process of movement, children learn to distinguish between near and far, strong and weak, light and heavy, and high and low. Physical education gives children an opportunity to experiment with and establish an understanding of such movement concepts.

An example of a conceptual approach to physical education is the *Fitness for Life* program by Corbin and Lindsey (2005). Students spend time receiving information in a lecture situation and then utilize the information on themselves or on peers in a laboratory (physical education) setting. Emphasis is placed on information, appraisal procedures, and program planning. Students are expected to understand the "how, what, and why" of physical activity and exercise. They learn to use diagnostic tests in areas such as cardiovascular endurance, muscular strength and endurance, flexibility, body composition, and motor ability.

Conceptual learning is an important part of the physical education program. However, some teachers believe that using an academic approach focused solely on knowledge and cognitive growth instead of on physical skills and activity will place physical education on par with other academic areas. Others believe that when student knowledge is increased, attitudes and behaviors will change, causing physical activity to be incorporated into the student's lifestyle. Neither of these beliefs has been proved to date. Increasing a person's knowledge does not ensure a change in behavior any more than reading and gaining knowledge about how to play tennis will make a skilled tennis player. Students must experience and learn physical skills and understand their conceptual components. Physical activity is, and must remain, the core component of physical education because it is the only place in the school setting where physical skills are taught and learned.

VALUE AND ATTITUDE DEVELOPMENT (AFFECTIVE DOMAIN LEARNING)

During the 1990s, the American public expressed concern about the lack of moral values among its youth. The political views of many U.S. leaders who emphasize law and order have created greater pressure on the schools to teach morals and values. In an annual Gallup Poll of the public's attitudes toward schools, lack of discipline often heads the list of major problems. Discipline problems also rank as one of the major concerns of teachers. There is growing pressure on the schools to teach values, responsibility skills, and moral education.

Values, feelings, beliefs, and judgments have received more attention in the schools and in physical education classes in particular. Public concern about crime among professional athletes has also increased parents' demand for help with responsibility training. Such issues as alcohol and substance abuse, sex education, and AIDS awareness are being introduced in the elementary school years in an attempt to prevent students from developing problems later in life. Awareness programs are becoming more common in schools with physical educators who are often called on to conduct appropriate district-approved programs.

Federal Mandates

From time to time, citizens' concerns about their children have led to legislation that has impacted physical education curriculum and instruction. The following legislative mandates in particular continue to impact physical cal education programs throughout the United States.

TITLE IX: EQUAL OPPORTUNITY FOR THE SEXES

Title IX of the Educational Amendments Act of 1972 has had a significant impact on most secondary school physical education programs. Title IX has had a lesser effect on elementary school physical education because the majority of programs at this level have long been coeducational. Title IX rules out separation of sexes and calls for all offerings to be coeducational. The law is based on the principle that school activities and programs are of equal value for both sexes and that students should not be denied access to participation on the basis of gender. Legal ramifications have forced schools to provide equal access to physical education activities for both boys and girls. Organizing separate competitions for the sexes is permissible, provided that mixed participation in an activity can be determined to be hazardous. In principle, the law also dictates that the most qualified teacher, regardless of gender, provides instruction.

Title IX also relates to the elimination of sexism and sex-role typing. Human needs and opportunities must be given precedence over traditional sexual stereotypes of masculinity and femininity. Appreciation for the physical abilities of the opposite sex is learned at an early age. Segregating children by sex in elementary school physical education classes is indefensible because it takes away the opportunity for children to learn that gender differences are small in the desire to perform well athletically.

PL 94-142: EQUAL RIGHTS FOR STUDENTS WITH DISABILITIES

Public Law 94-142 has given hope for a full education to the 3.5 to 4 million youngsters in the United States with disabilities. This federal law mandates that all youngsters have the right to a free and public education and are educated in the least restrictive educational environment possible. No longer can children with disabilities be assigned to segregated classes or schools unless a separate environment is determined by due process to be in the child's best interest. A 1990 amendment, Public Law 101-476 (also known as IDEA—Individuals with Disabilities Education Act), continues with the objective of providing handicapped individuals with the least restrictive environment in the school setting.

Mainstreaming is a term used to identify the practice of placing children with disabilities into classrooms with able children. These laws have resulted in degrees of mainstreaming (full or partial), allowing many children with disabilities to participate in regular physical education classes. The law, which is considered commendable and morally sound, often necessitates changing the structure and educational procedures of the school as well as the viewpoints and attitudes of school personnel. Many teachers do not have the educational background, the experience, or the inclination to handle children with disabilities in addition to children without disabilities. The answer is not to ignore the problem but to provide teachers with knowledge and constructive approaches that allow them to function successfully with children who have disabilities. If children with disabilities are to function in society when they become adults, they deserve and need the opportunity to participate with able youngsters.

In addition to the mainstreaming of students into regular education classes, the law mandates the preparation of a specific learning program for each disabled student, called an *individualized educational program* (IEP). Establishing the child's due process committee, developing the IEP, and monitoring that program in the best interest of the student is a process of considerable challenge and magnitude. IEPs can be used for able children as well, and help to make education more personal and individual.

CHILD NUTRITION AND WIC REAUTHORIZATION ACT OF 2004

Nationally, there is widespread concern about the health status of Americans, particularly related to physical activity and nutrition. The number of overweight Americans has increased rapidly during the past 15 years. Today, statistics show that over 60 percent of Americans are overweight or obese (National Center for Health Statistics, 2004). Much of this increase has been attributed to a decrease in physical activity patterns and an increase in the amount of calories consumed. Obviously, childhood problems with weight management and proper nutrition have put physical activity square in the eye of the public.

Physical education programs must place their focus on improving the health status of students, particularly with respect to their eating habits and physical activity. In the Child Nutrition and WIC Reauthorization Act of 2004, the U.S. Congress established a new requirement that all school districts with a federally funded school meals program develop and implement wellness policies that address nutrition and physical activity by the start of the 2006–7 school year. This Act offers an excellent opportunity for physical educators to implement physical activity and eating behavior programs into their classes. Changing activity and eating behaviors takes the efforts of an entire community. Physical educators can make this an opportunity to change the environment of the school rather than focus on a minor curriculum change. Making changes in the school environment will require the efforts of parents, classroom teachers, administrators, and students. If implemented correctly, there is a strong possibility that this mandate will lead physical education programs to a prominent role in the total school curriculum.

Contemporary Social Influences

A NATIONWIDE CONCERN FOR HEALTH AND WELLNESS

The Surgeon General's report on *Physical Activity and Health* (U.S. Department of Health and Human Services [USDHHS], 1996) outlined clearly the health benefits of physical activity for all ages. The contributions of physical activity to health and wellness have been widely disseminated, and efforts have been undertaken to promote physical activity among all segments of the population. Today's educators are centering increased attention on integrating physical activity into a healthful living style. This focus is pushing physical educators to develop programs that teach more than fitness and skill activities. Wellness is a broader concept than physical fitness. It is a dynamic state of well-being that implies living fully and deriving the most from life.

Eating wisely, controlling weight, dealing with tension, understanding body (muscular) movement, getting sufficient sleep, controlling posture, keeping in shape, and dealing with forthcoming challenges (such as potential use of alcohol and drugs, and the danger of contracting AIDS or other infectious diseases) impact wellness. For example, the problem of weight control merits special attention in the elementary school. Unless lifestyle is changed at an early age, obese children usually become obese adults. Recent research shows that activity and inactivity track into adulthood, meaning that active children become active adults (Raitakari et al., 1994).

Human wellness is an area where physical education can have a lifelong impact on students. It is most effectively presented when classroom teachers and physical education specialists work together. Identifying wellness as a common goal for all schoolchildren makes physical education an integral and vital part of the total school curriculum. Wellness instruction teaches concepts that help students develop and maintain an active lifestyle. Understanding the principles of fitness, the importance of daily physical activity, and the benefits of physical fitness increases the odds that students will stay active throughout their lives (Dale, Corbin, & Cuddihy, 1998).

A DEMAND FOR "BACK-TO-BASICS" SCHOOLS

Basic schools were designed as a response to a perceived decline in academic performance. Basic schools stress discipline and cognitive learning, often at the expense of the arts and physical education. To increase academic rigor, the school day is lengthened and physical education and performing arts are dropped to allow more time for "the three Rs." A demand for uninterrupted academic time often makes it impossible to schedule physical education time for youngsters. To combat this trend, physical education programs must demonstrate that they are instructional in nature and of high quality, and make unique contributions to the school curriculum. In 1983, the National Commission on Excellence in Education presented a critical review of the total process of U.S. education in *A Nation at Risk* (Gardner, 1983). In the report, physical education was not included as part of a basic education. Whether the omission was deliberate or happenstance is open to question. In the past, other deliberations and reports have included physical education as a part of basic instruction. It is possible that the school experiences of commission members in the physical education area were largely of an unorganized fun-and-games approach, and that they perceived little need for such recreation. This attitude illustrates the importance of educating the public about the need for a quality physical education program in the quest to develop well-rounded students.

To conform to the concept of basic education, this text delineates fundamental content standards to be accomplished in physical education. Content standards are written in measurable terms so that teachers and schools are held accountable for helping students reach a predetermined level of achievement. Even though accountability is a desirable concept, some abuse can occur when teachers are rewarded based solely on student achievement levels. Some teachers may turn to the use of memorization, drill, and rote learning and may encourage practice solely in areas in which students will be tested. In physical education, this often means teaching only fitness test activities so students score well on a mandated physical fitness test. This approach can result in an inferior and narrow program that satisfies the accountability concerns of the school, but does little to give students a well-rounded education.

A NATIONAL FOCUS ON PHYSICAL ACTIVITY

The document entitled *Healthy People 2000: National Health Promotion and Disease Objectives* (U.S. Public Health Service, 1990) focused on the role of physical activity in improving the health of all Americans. A majority of the three hundred physical activity target goals are specifically directed toward improving the health status of U.S. children and youth. The goals focus on decreasing health risks and emphasizing preventative approaches to a healthy lifestyle. Several of the objectives in the physical activity area emphasize an increase in the amount of light to moderate activity (that is, activity similar in intensity to brisk walking) among children age six and older. For years, emphasis was placed on fitness goals and high-intensity activity. The *Healthy People* report places more emphasis on moderate and regular physical activity. Much of the emphasis on improving the health status of youth is accomplished through a quality physical education program. The focus of the document is on the health benefits of exercise and activity for all students in contrast to systems that only reward students who are physically gifted.

A successor to *Healthy People 2000* is *Healthy People 2010* (USDHHS, 2000). Two major goals addressed in this document are to: (1) increase the years of healthy life; and (2) eliminate health disparities. These major goals are supported by enabling goals concerned with promoting healthy behaviors, protecting health, achieving access to quality health care, and strengthening community prevention. The objectives are grouped into a number of focus areas similar to those in *Healthy People 2000*. New focus areas include disability, low income, race and ethnicity, chronic diseases, and public health infrastructure.

The release of the Surgeon General's report on *Physical Activity and Health* (USDHHS, 1996) documented many health benefits achieved through moderate and regular activity. The report showed that people of all ages, both male and female, benefit from regular physical activity. Never before has a body of research been compiled to show the strong need for activity and fitness in the lives of youth. Activity programs are an absolute requisite for healthy youngsters.

THE CURRENT STATUS OF PHYSICAL EDUCATION IN THE UNITED STATES

The differences in perceptions of physical education are no doubt a result of the wide variety of experiences offered under the physical education umbrella. Though professionals consider true physical education to be nothing less than a quality instructional program conducted by a physical education specialist, for many this is not the actual experience. Most states and districts require physical education in their schools. However, the SHPPS 2000 report shows that when physical education requirements by grade are analyzed carefully, each grade shows a decline from about 50 percent in grades 1–5 to about 5 percent in grade 12 (Burgeson et al., 2001). Because many states and schools allow exemptions from physical education classes, the actual percentage of kids receiving instruction is even less. Few children in America receive daily physical education instruction. Only about 8 percent of elementary schools provide daily physical education for their students. When physical education is taught in these grade levels, a "specialist" often teaches it, though many people having this designation do not hold valid credentials. In fact, only 17 percent of states require elementary level physical education teachers to be certified in physical education (USDHHS, 1994). Classroom teachers often teach physical education and because these teachers have wide ranges of interests and qualifications, instruction often varies dramatically among schools.

A common picture of elementary school physical education might look something like this: Youngsters go to school and receive about 25 hours of overall instruction weekly. Out of the 25 hours, physical education may be scheduled for 30 to 60 minutes a week in a school that cares about physical education. This amounts to 2–4 percent of the total instructional time devoted to the health and wellness of students. Instruction may be carried out by a physical education specialist, classroom teacher, or paraprofessional. Often, up to four classes are sent to physical education at once so that the student-to-teacher ratio is 120 to 1 with one or two paraprofessionals sent to help. Small wonder that obesity and hypokinetic disease have become rampant throughout the United States. Many of America's schools do not value physical education and do little to ensure that all children receive daily physical education instruction as a minimum.

THE NEED FOR PHYSICAL EDUCATION PROGRAMS

During the past decade, the interest in the benefits derived from an active lifestyle has spawned a wide assortment of health clubs, a vast array of books and magazines concerning exercise and fitness, a weekly smorgasbord of distance runs and triathlons, streamlined exercise equipment, and apparel for virtually any type of physical activity. Unfortunately, most of this interest and lifestyle change has occurred among middle- and upper-class Americans. Little change in activity patterns has occurred in lower-middle- and lower-class families.

The nation's enthusiasm for physical activity has not trickled down to elementary school youngsters. A statement issued by the American Academy of Pediatrics (1991) reported that children from the ages of 2 to 12 watch about 25 hours of television per week, more time than they spend in school receiving instruction. Another study (Anderson et al., 1998) showed that children who watched four or more hours of television per day had significantly greater BMI compared to children watching fewer than two hours per day. Health goals for the nation for the year 2010 (USDHHS, 2000) are based on increasing daily levels of physical activity. Many of the goals directly target schools, or programs that can take place within the school setting. These goals emphasize reducing inactivity and increasing light to moderate physical activity. The need is clear: Implement physical education programs to teach youngsters how to live an active and healthy lifestyle. What evidence is available that shows the benefits of a quality physical education program?

1. The percentage of youth who are overweight has more than tripled in the past 30 years (USDHHS, 2002). A recent study has suggested that the prevalence of obesity is more strongly related to decreases in energy expenditure than to increases in energy intake (Jebb & Moore, 1999). The school environment discourages physical activity. Students are asked to move slowly, sit still, and walk, rather than run, everywhere they go, which results in a decrease in energy expenditure. A 30-minute physical education class can offer 1,200 to 2,000 steps of moderate to vigorous physical activity to counteract the effects of an inactive day (Beighle & Pangrazi, 2000; Morgan, Pangrazi, & Beighle, 2003). This is a substantial contribution to the daily energy expendi-

ture of students, particularly those who are inactive. For example, for a student who is averaging 8,000 steps a day, a quality physical education class could increase the number of steps by 20 percent. This would increase the number of steps to 10,000, which is a substantial increase in physical activity.

2. A positive experience in physical education classes will encourage youngsters to be active as adults. In a survey sponsored by the Sporting Goods Manufacturers Association (2000), 60 percent of respondents ages 18 to 34 reported that a positive experience in physical education classes encouraged them to be active later in life. On the other hand, of those respondents who said they were sedentary, only 10 percent said their physical education classes encouraged them to be active.

3. Overweight children grow into overweight adults. Studies (Guo et al., 1994; Must et al., 1992) show that adolescent weight is a good predictor of adult obesity. A study by Whitaker et al. (1997) showed that the risk of obesity persisting into adulthood is much higher among adolescents than younger children. The chance for childhood obesity persisting into adulthood increases from 20 percent at four years of age to 80 percent by adolescence (Guo & Chumlea, 1999). This supports the case for dealing with overweight children in elementary school, before the problem becomes much more difficult to rectify. Since a quality program encourages active behavior, it makes sense that a program be in place to help youngsters understand the importance of proper weight management and an active lifestyle.

4. A quality physical education program educates youngsters physically but does not detract from their academic performance in school. An argument often used is that spending time on physical education will lower the academic performance of students because they have less time to study and learn. To the contrary, studies have shown that students who spend time in physical education classes do equally well or better in academic classes. Two major studies that looked at this issue are the Three Rivers study (Trudeau et al., 1998) and a SPARK-related activity program study (Sallis et al., 1999). In both cases, students received the health benefits of physical education without any negative impact on their academic performance.

5. Physical education gives students the skills they need to be active as adults. One commodity that youngsters have in contrast to adults is the time to practice and learn new skills. Few adults learn an entire new set of physical skills. More often than not, they practice and enhance skills they learned earlier in childhood. Since many adults like to participate in activities that require a requisite skill level (e.g., golf, tennis, racquetball, etc.), learning such skills during their school years makes it more likely that they will feel able and competent to participate in later life.

6. Physical activity (which most often occurs in physical education classes) provides immediate and short-term health benefits for children (Bar-Or, 1995). For obese children, increased physical activity results in a reduction of the percentage of body fat. Additionally, increased activity reduces blood pressure and improves the blood lipid profile for high health-risk children. Finally, evidence shows that weight-bearing activities performed during the school years offer bone mineral density benefits that carry over into adulthood (Bailey et al., 1996).

7. Active children become active adults. Telama et al. (1997) looked at retrospective and longitudinal tracking studies and concluded that the results "indicate that physical activity and sport participation in childhood and adolescence represent a significant prediction for physical activity in adulthood." The relationship is low but still indicates that activity during youth has an impact on adult activity levels. Another study (Raitakari et al., 1994) showed how strongly inactivity patterns track. In that study, the probability of an inactive 12-year-old remaining sedentary at age 18 was 51–63 percent for girls and 54–61 percent for boys. This clearly delineates the legacy given to youth when we place them into an inactive school environment.

THE CONTENT OF PHYSICAL EDUCATION

Whether speaking of academic class settings or physical education, a key to providing proper education includes following agreed-upon guidelines, or standards, that have been shown to ensure that children obtain the right kind of education. Content standards are the framework of a program; they determine the focus and direction of instruction. Standards specify the content of the program, what students should know and be able to perform. Standards express what knowledge students should possess and how they should demonstrate that knowledge when they exit a developmental level. The establishment of standards can make a significant contribution to the overall goal of school and U.S. society: the development of a well-rounded individual capable of contributing to a democratic society. Quality programs are driven by standards that move children toward high-level achievement.

Physical education content standards are taught nowhere else in the school curriculum. Should these standards not be accomplished in physical education classes, children will leave school without a well-developed set of physical skills. A positive result of efforts to identify standards is that there is now general agreement among most professionals about what a physical education program should accomplish. The National Association for Sport and Physical Education (NASPE) (2004) recently identified six major content standards for physical education that provide a basis for describing a physically educated person. Generally, experts agree on the major content of the standards that constitute categories of emphasis for physical education instruction. Many school districts have developed similar sets of standards that allow room for program individuality.

The standards not only give direction to instruction but also form the framework for assessment and accountability in the program. NASPE (go to the Website http://member.aahperd.org/template.cfm to view the publications) also offers a series of assessment publications that offer a wide range of strategies for identifying student progress toward the standards. There is a range of strategies recommended in the assessment series including teacher observations, written tests, student logs, student projects, student journals, class projects, and portfolios. The assessment strategies offer teachers examples of many forms of assessment, with the expectation that each teacher will modify and select assessment tools that are meaningful in his or her setting.

NASPE CONTENT STANDARDS FOR PHYSICAL EDUCATION

In the following section, each of the six NASPE national standards is reviewed and includes references to chapters that offer instructional activities and strategies designed to reach these strategies. Note that each chapter in this text also opens with a table showing how activities in the chapter contribute to the desired standards. A detailed discussion of what teachers can expect students to learn follows each standard. Also included are two levels of outcomes for each standard: a set for children at Developmental Level I (see page 52–53 for an in-depth discussion of developmental levels) and a set for youth at Developmental Levels II and III (grades 3–6).

> **Standard 1:** Demonstrates competency in motor skills and movement patterns needed to perform a variety of physical activities.

Standard 1 focuses on skill competency. All people want to be skilled and competent performers. The elemen-

tary school years are an excellent time to teach motor skills because children have the time and predisposition to learn them. The types and range of skills presented in physical education should be unlimited; youngsters need the opportunity to encounter and learn as many different physical skills as possible. Because youngsters vary in genetic endowment and interest, they should have the opportunity to learn about their personal abilities in many types of skills and settings. Major areas of movement competence and motor skill development are described next.

MOVEMENT CONCEPTS SKILLS

Youngsters need to learn about the classification of movement concepts (Chapter 15), which includes body and space awareness, qualities of movement, and relationships. It is not enough for them to learn only skills; youngsters need to perform these skills in a variety of settings. This standard ensures children will be taught how movement concepts are classified and is designed to give children an increased awareness and understanding of the body as a vehicle for movement and the acquisition of a personal vocabulary of movement skills.

FUNDAMENTAL MOTOR SKILLS

Fundamental skills enhance the quality of life. This group of skills is sometimes labeled "basic" or "functional" skills. The designation *fundamental skills* is used because the skills are requisite for children to function fully in the environment. Fundamental skills are divided into three categories: locomotor, nonlocomotor, and manipulative skills.

Locomotor Skills

Locomotor skills (Chapter 16) are used to move the body from one place to another or to project the body upward, as in jumping and hopping. These skills also include walking, running, skipping, leaping, sliding, and galloping.

Nonlocomotor Skills

Nonlocomotor skills (Chapter 16) are performed in place, without appreciable spatial movement. These skills are not as well defined as locomotor skills. They include bending and stretching, pushing and pulling, balancing, rolling, curling, twisting, turning, and bouncing.

Manipulative Skills

Manipulative skills (Chapter 17) are developed through handling some type of object. Most of these skills involve the hands and feet, but other parts of the body can

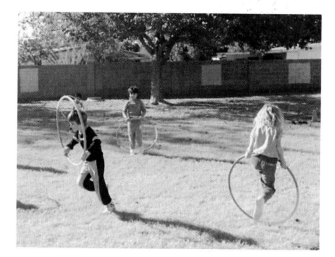

FIGURE 1.1 Developing manipulative skills.

also be used. Manipulation of objects leads to better hand-eye and foot-eye coordination, which is particularly important for tracking items in space. Manipulative skills form the basis of many game skills. Propulsion (throwing, striking, striking with an implement, kicking) and reception (catching) of objects are important skills that can be taught by using beanbags and various balls. Rebounding or redirecting an object in flight (such as a volleyball) is another useful manipulative skill. Continuous control of an object, such as a wand or a hoop, is also a manipulative activity.

SPECIALIZED MOTOR SKILLS

Specialized skills are used in various sports and other areas of physical education, including apparatus activities, tumbling, dance, and specific games. Specialized skills receive increased emphasis beginning with Developmental Level II activities. In developing specialized skills, progression is attained through planned instruction and drills. Many of these skills have critical points of technique, and teaching emphasizes correct performance.

Body Management Skills

Efficient movement of the body (Chapter 18) demands integration of a number of physical traits, including agility, balance, flexibility, and coordination. In addition, youngsters need to develop an understanding of how to control their bodies while on large apparatus such as beams, benches, and jumping boxes.

Rhythmic Movement Skills

Individuals who excel in movement activities possess a strong sense of rhythmic ability. Rhythmic movement (Chapter 19) involves motion with a regular and pre-

dictable pattern. The aptitude to move rhythmically is basic to skill performance in all areas. A rhythmic program that includes dance, rope-jumping, and rhythmic gymnastics offers a variety of activities to help students attain this objective. Early experiences center on functional and creative movement forms. Instruction begins with and capitalizes on locomotor skills that children already possess: walking, running, hopping, and jumping. Rhythmic activities provide a vehicle for expressive movement.

Gymnastic Skills

Gymnastic activities (Chapter 20) make a significant contribution to the overall physical education experience for children in elementary schools. Gymnastic activities develop body management skills without the need for equipment and apparatus. Flexibility, agility, balance, strength, and body control are outcomes that are enhanced through participation in gymnastics. Basic gymnastic skills such as body rolling, balancing, inverted balances, and tumbling are learned in a safe and progressive manner.

Game Skills

Games (Chapter 22) are a laboratory where children can apply newly learned skills in a meaningful way. Many games develop large-muscle groups and enhance the ability to run, dodge, start, and stop under control while sharing space with others. Through games, children experience success and accomplishment. Social objectives encountered through games are the development of interpersonal skills, acceptance of rule parameters, and a better understanding of oneself in a competitive and cooperative situation.

FIGURE 1.2 Learning body management skills.

Sport Skills

Sport skills (Chapters 24–30) are learned in a context of application, using an approach of teaching skills, drills, and lead-up activities. Students learn the basic skills and then practice them doing different drills. After the skills have been learned and practiced, they are applied in lead-up activities. Lead-up activities reduce the number of skills youngsters have to use to be successful, thereby increasing their chance for successful participation. Sport skills involve proper techniques, so the cognitive aspect of learning is important as well.

Outcomes for Developmental Level I Students:

a. Apply movement concepts such as body and space awareness, relationships, and qualities of movement to a variety of locomotor and body management skills.

b. Move efficiently using a variety of locomotor skills such as walking, running, skipping, and hopping.

c. Combine locomotor and nonlocomotor skills into movement themes, for example, supporting body weight, forming bridges, and receiving and transferring weight.

d. Perform body management skills on the floor and on apparatus including benches, balance beams, individual mats, and jumping boxes.

e. Use a variety of manipulative skills such as tossing, throwing, catching, and kicking.

f. Move rhythmically in a variety of settings including fundamental rhythms, creative rhythms, and simple folk dances.

g. Perform simple gymnastic skills such as animal walks, body rolling, simple balances, and inverted balances.

h. Use a variety of locomotor skills in low-organized game settings such as running, dodging, evading, and stopping.

Outcomes for Developmental Levels II and III Students:

a. Perform specialized sport skills with mature form such as throwing, catching, dribbling with foot and hand, kicking and striking, batting, punting, and passing.

b. Use sport skills in a variety of activities such as volleyball pass, basketball dribble, and batting a softball.

c. Perform a wide variety of gymnastic skills including tumbling, inverted balances, individual stunts, and partner stunts.

d. Perform body management skills on a variety of apparatus including benches, balance beams, and climbing ropes.

e. Move rhythmically in a variety of settings including folk, square, and line dances, rope-jumping, and rhythmic gymnastics.

f. Apply a wide variety of locomotor and manipulative game skills in low-organized game settings.

g. Incorporate specialized sport skills in a variety of sport lead-up games.

> **Standard 2:** Demonstrates understanding of movement concepts, principles, and tactics as they apply to the learning and performance of physical activities.

Standard 2 addresses developing knowledge about various aspects of physical activity. The school years are the years of opportunity—the opportunity to experience and learn many different types of physical activities and skills. Related to this standard is the opportunity to learn basic concepts of movement (Chapter 15). Movement concepts help students understand what, where, and how the body can move. Again, emphasis is placed on experiencing the diversity of human movement. Allied to this experience is learning the correct mechanics of skill performance (Chapter 3). Students leave school knowing about stability, force, leverage, and other factors related to efficient movement.

Instruction is focused on teaching youngsters to be self-directed learners who can evaluate their performance and self-correct their skill technique. Accepting the premise that motor skills are only learned through repetition and refinement (two of the three Rs of physical education) is necessary if youngsters are to become competent performers. Because much adult activity is done alone, students need to learn how to warm up for activity and cool down when finished. Understanding simple principles of motor learning (Chapter 3) such as practice, arousal, and refinement of skills will be knowledge that serves students in future experiences.

Outcomes for Developmental Level I Students:

a. Understand a vocabulary of basic movement concepts such as personal space, qualities of movement, body awareness, and the relationship of movements.

b. Understand words that describe a variety of relationships with objects, such as *around, behind, over, through,* and *parallel.*

c. Implement space awareness concepts and control of movements when performing locomotor movements in a group setting.

d. Understand basic mechanics of skill performance when performing specialized skills such as throwing, kicking, striking, and catching.

e. Appreciate the value of practice in learning motor skills.

Outcomes for Developmental Levels II and III Students:

a. Find information regarding skill performance improvement including asking friends and coaches, self-evaluation, and learning to monitor personal accomplishments.

b. Know the importance of repetition and refinement for learning specialized motor skills.

c. Understand how warm-up and cool-down prevent injuries.

d. Incorporate the mechanics of skill performance into a variety of settings.

e. Use simple strategies when participating in a variety of lead-up games (modified rules, equipment, and number of participants).

> **Standard 3:** Participates regularly in physical activity.

Standard 3 is concerned with the performance of physical activity. The basic premise of this standard is that active children mature into active adults (Raitakari et al., 1994). Specifically, learning how to monitor personal activity levels, how to plan meaningful activity programs, and how to make informed decisions about physical activity are important outcomes. The PLAY program (Arizona Department of Health Services, 2004) and the Activitygram (Cooper Institute, 2004) are examples of programs designed to reward youngsters for monitoring and participating in daily physical activity. Youngsters need to learn where they can participate within their community and how they can join clubs, YMCAs, and sport programs. Chapter 12 offers information on these programs and ways to increase physical activity levels of children.

The basic considerations for lifetime activity are several. Sallis (1994) classifies in four categories the factors that influence people to be active: psychological, social, physical environmental, and biological. A major role of physical education is to foster those factors that are often referred to as determinants of active living. Psychological determinants are among the most powerful. For example, students must derive enjoyment through physical activity if they are expected to participate as adults. Enjoyment increases when there is an adequate level of proficiency in a favored activity. Learning new motor skills demands time and an opportunity to practice, things that are difficult for most adults to find. Childhood is one of the few times in life when there is

adequate free time to develop skill proficiency. Since most adults do not participate in activities unless they have an adequate level of perceived competence, learning skills becomes a priority of childhood. Another psychological factor is the rational basis for play. This can be established through activity orientations that are transferable to other situations. Such activities include a variety of games suitable for small groups and sports activities adapted to local situations.

Social and environmental influences also affect lifetime activity patterns. These factors include having family and peer role models, receiving encouragement from significant others, and having opportunities to participate in activities with others in one's social group. Physical environmental factors include adequate programs and facilities, adequate equipment and supplies, safe outdoor environments, and available opportunities near home and at school. Included are adequate school opportunities such as recess, physical education, intramural games, recreation programs, and sports. Finally, biological factors include age, gender, and ethnic and/or socioeconomic status. For more details concerning determinants of physical activity, refer to Sallis' (1994) work.

A NASPE publication, *Physical Activity for Children: A Statement of Guidelines* (2004), outlines why youngsters need daily physical activity. It is the first document to offer a recommendation for how much activity youngsters need (a minimum of 60 minutes per day). The publication discusses the physical activity pyramid and the importance of participating in different types of physical activity, including lifestyle activity, active aerobics, active sports and recreation, flexibility, and muscle fitness exercises. The document offers support and direction for teachers who need to offer justification for increasing the amount of daily physical activity for children.

Outcomes for Developmental Level I Students:

a. Show willingness to try different physical activities.

b. Understand how activities must be enjoyable for each individual if they are to be used throughout one's life span.

c. Monitor the amount of time spent in short bouts of activity; for example, "I played tag for five minutes."

d. Set aside time for play outside of school each day.

Outcomes for Developmental Levels II and III Students:

a. Show a willingness to try many different activities and to identify those activities best suited to them.

b. Demonstrate the ability to set physical activity goals in terms of time and type of activity.

c. Find opportunities for play outside of school such as after-school sports, intramurals, and private clubs and organizations.

d. Use a pedometer to monitor daily activity in terms of steps or accumulated time.

e. Maintain an activity log showing the different types and amounts of physical activity accumulated each day.

> **Standard 4:** Achieves and maintains a health-enhancing level of physical fitness.

Standard 4 is concerned with physical fitness. Physical fitness instruction (Chapter 13) for elementary school children concentrates on the process of their participating in daily physical activity rather than being concerned about the product of fitness (how many repetitions, how fast, or how far). Giving students an opportunity to offer input about their fitness program and make personal activity choices prepares them for a lifetime of activity. When students accept responsibility for participating in regular activity, fitness becomes an authentic learning experience that may last a lifetime. Positive experiences in physical activity are a must. Meeting this standard means helping students develop positive attitudes that carry over into adulthood. Little is gained if students develop high physical fitness levels in the elementary school years but leave school with a strong dislike of physical activity.

A portion of each physical education period should be allotted to having children learn about and experience fitness. It is not enough for them to learn the facts of fitness; there must be a participatory experience in the elementary school years. This is not to say that knowledge is unimportant, but that it is not enough.

FIGURE 1.3   Fitness is a participatory experience.

Many people know the facts of fitness but do not stay active because they have not learned the activity habit. Students must participate in physical fitness activity; the best way to learn the amount of effort necessary to maintain personal fitness is to experience it. Too often, fitness has been seen solely as an aerobic experience. Today, it is clear that aerobics are important, but maintenance of strength and flexibility is equally vital. Fitness routines that incorporate interval training (alternating aerobic activities with strength and flexibility activities) show students that the best lifetime fitness experience is a balanced one. Teaching students how to correctly perform calisthenics gives them a series of activities they can perform in adulthood. In fact, after weight lifting, calisthenics are the most popular form of strength development for adults (Fitness Products Council, 1999).

Meeting this standard also implies that students will leave elementary school understanding the basic facts of fitness. Such concepts as the FIT principle (frequency, intensity, and time) can be taught in short question-and-answer episodes. Because each individual has unique needs and because programs must be developed according to these needs, an understanding of genetic diversity among people (such as differences in muscle type, cardiorespiratory endurance, and motor coordination) is requisite for helping students understand their physical capabilities. Understanding concepts such as how to exercise properly, how much activity is enough, and how to safely participate in activity helps create a positive mind-set in youngsters. Finally, students learn to personally evaluate their fitness levels in a semiprivate setting. Doing self-testing on health-related fitness and charting physical activity offer students evidence about whether they are in the healthy fitness zone on the Fitnessgram and Activitygram evaluation (Cooper Institute, 2004).

Outcomes for Developmental Level I Students:

a. Participate daily in at least 60 minutes of physical activity in and out of the school environment.

b. Monitor the basic physiological changes that occur when being active (increased rate of breathing, increased heart rate, and perspiration).

c. Participate in activities that develop muscular strength and endurance (for example, climbing ropes, hanging activities, and supporting the body weight with arms and hands).

d. Perform a variety of flexibility activities.

e. Identify how personal body composition and different body types impact physical performance.

Outcomes for Developmental Levels II and III Students:

a. Participate daily in at least 60 minutes of moderate to vigorous physical activity in and out of the school environment.

b. Engage in a variety of activities that develop muscular strength, ranging from exercises to climbing.

c. Perform activities that increase and maintain flexibility.

d. Know basic elements of safe participation in activities (including safe exercises, overtraining, muscle soreness, and inherent risk of activities).

e. Monitor the intensity of exercise by counting heart and breathing rates.

f. Understand that all health-related fitness components (body composition, muscular strength and endurance, flexibility, and cardiorespiratory endurance) need to be given attention for total physical fitness.

g. Evaluate personal health-related physical fitness and interpret the meaning of the results.

h. Understand the basic principles of training such as frequency, intensity, and time.

Standard 5: Exhibits responsible personal and social behavior that respects self and others in physical activity.

Standard 5 addresses the need for responsible behavior. Physical education classes offer a unique environment for learning effective social skills. Children have the opportunity to internalize and practice the merits of participation, cooperation, competition, and tolerance. Some terms, such as *citizenship* and *fair play,* help define the desired social atmosphere. Through listening, empathy, and guidance, children learn to differentiate between acceptable and unacceptable ways of expressing feelings. Youngsters must develop an awareness of how they interact with others, and how the quality of their behavior influences others' responses to them.

Responsible behavior (Chapter 6) implies behaving in a manner that doesn't negatively impact others. Hellison (2003) and others have developed methodology for teaching responsible behavior. It is generally accepted that if responsible behavior is to be learned, it must be taught through experiences where such behavior is reinforced on a regular basis. Accepting consequences for one's behavior is learned and needs to be valued and reinforced by responsible adults. Responsible behavior occurs in a hierarchy of behavior from irresponsible to caring and behaving in a responsible manner. Physical education classes are an excellent setting for teaching responsibility because most behavior is highly visible during them. Youngsters in a competitive setting may react openly in an irresponsible fashion, offering instructors a "teachable moment" to discuss such unacceptable behavior. Additionally, youngsters have to learn to win and lose in an acceptable manner and to assume responsibility for their performances. Accepting the consequences of one's behavior is a lesson that arises regularly in a cooperative/competitive environment.

Conflicts must be solved in a nonviolent manner (Chapter 6) that allows all parties to maintain self-esteem and dignity. Physical education offers an excellent opportunity to apply conflict-resolution skills because misbehavior is easily observed. Students are taught to solve conflicts and disagreements in a peaceful and nonthreatening manner. Many diversity and gender issues (Chapter 5) arise in activity settings, and insightful and caring instruction can destroy negative stereotypes. Learning about the similarities and differences among cultures and how all people share common values and beliefs is an important outcome.

The organization of the lesson, the types of activities presented, teachers' views of students who are less successful, and the treatment of children with disabilities send implied messages to students (the hidden curriculum). When teachers and parents respond to children in a caring fashion, they teach youngsters that they are loved, capable, and contributing people. If children believe they belong, are loved and respected, and that their successes outweigh their failures, they will be on the road to developing a desirable self-concept.

Cooperation precedes the development of competition, which makes it an important behavior to teach in elementary physical education settings. Without cooperation, competitive games cannot be played. The nature of competitive games demands cooperation, fair play, and respect for teammates, and when these are not present, the joy of participation is lost. Cooperative games teach children that all teammates are needed to reach group goals.

Outcomes for Developmental Level I Students:

a. Participate in a variety of multicultural activities.

b. Understand how different individuals make a variety of contributions to the group.

c. Explain simple differences and similarities among activities played in different cultural and ethnic backgrounds.

d. Show empathy for the concerns and limitations of peers.

FIGURE 1.4   Learning to cooperate to achieve group goals.

e. Resolve conflicts in an acceptable nonviolent manner.

f. Follow rules and procedures in physical activity settings.

g. Participate safely by observing safety procedures for equipment and apparatus.

h. Understand and follow the rules of low-organized games.

i. Cooperate in a group setting and be willing to take turns and help others.

j. Show the ability to behave responsibly when differences of opinion occur.

k. Play willingly with all students regardless of race, gender, or disability.

Outcomes for Developmental Levels II and III Students:

a. Understand how sports, games, and dance play a central role in modern-day cultures.

b. React in a positive manner toward individuals who have cultural or ethnic differences, or who have limitations.

c. Demonstrate a willingness to participate with peers regardless of diversity or disability.

d. Enjoy and interact with peers in a variety of physical activity settings.

e. Resolve conflicts in an acceptable nonviolent manner.

f. Reveal the ability to create and modify rules to better meet the needs of the group.

g. Understand that cooperative skills must be developed before competitive games can be played.

h. Understand how sports and games impact issues of gender and diversity.

i. Recognize the benefits (social and physical) derived from participation in group games and activities.

j. Show a willingness to follow rules, procedures, and safety guidelines in all physical activity settings.

k. Behave in a caring and helping manner toward all peers.

> **Standard 6:** Values physical activity for health, enjoyment, challenge, self-expression, and/or social interaction.

Standard 6 focuses on how much the student values physical activity, and whether the student has the knowledge necessary to make thoughtful decisions that impact her or his health and wellness (Chapter 14). Meeting this standard does not have to turn physical education into a sedentary fact-learning experience. Instruction should be integrated into activity and skill development sessions. Simple principles about nutrition, stress, substance abuse, and safety can be woven into daily instruction so children have an opportunity to learn about healthy lifestyles.

Wellness implies developing a lifestyle that is balanced in all phases with *moderation* the keyword. Wellness is predicated on developing a clear understanding of choices and alternatives that lead to making wise decisions. Students cannot make meaningful choices for wellness if they don't understand the consequences of their decisions. Wellness instruction involves studying the wisdom of past generations and integrating it into the lifestyles of current and future generations. In elementary school, basic wellness instruction covers how the skeletal, muscular, and cardiorespiratory systems function. In addition, students study lifestyle alternatives that impact wellness including basic facts about nutrition, weight control, stress and relaxation, substance abuse, and safety.

Outcomes for Developmental Level I Students:

a. Explain why physical activity is important for good health.

b. Try new activities and persist in learning them.

c. Tell others how physical activity makes them feel good.

d. Know that everybody should be active at least 30 minutes a day.

Outcomes for Developmental Levels II and III Students:

a. Make meaningful decisions about personal wellness by gathering information, considering the alternatives, and understanding the consequences that accompany such choices.

b. Know what types of physical activity are important for wellness.

c. Understand factors that are detrimental to good health such as substance abuse and stress.

d. Understand how physical activity is important for weight management.

e. Understand the importance of safety, particularly in activity settings such as bicycling, swimming, playing sports, and walking.

f. Identify some examples of proper eating habits.

ESSENTIAL COMPONENTS OF A QUALITY PHYSICAL EDUCATION PROGRAM

Physical education teachers need to know the essential components of a quality physical education program. In other words, they need to know the critical elements that should be included to ensure youngsters receive a quality physical education experience. The following components interlock to form a comprehensive physical education program that will be valued by parents, teachers, and students. Each of the components is described briefly in this section. In-depth coverage is offered in the chapters referenced under each point. Figure 1.5 illustrates the essential components of a quality physical education program.

I. **Quality physical education programs are organized around NASPE national standards that offer direction and continuity to instruction and evaluation.** A quality program is driven by a set of content standards. These standards are defined by a number of competencies youngsters are expected to accomplish. Standards are measurable so that both teachers and students know when progress has been made. Previously in this chapter you read about a comprehensive set of physical education content standards. Chapter 8 offers a number of evaluation strategies for checking to see if you and your students are meeting the standards.

II. **Quality programs are student-centered and based on the developmental urges, characteristics, and interests of students.** Youngsters learn best when the skills and activities they must learn match their physical and emotional development. Including activities in the program because they match the competencies of the teacher is not a criterion. Teachers have to teach new activities outside their comfort zone if they are going to present a comprehensive program. See Chapter 4 to learn about the urges, characteristics, and interests of children and how they impact the creation of a quality physical education program. Chapter 5 offers many ideas for understanding and teaching to the personal needs of students. A quality program focuses on the successes of students so that there is motivation to continue. Developing a positive set of behaviors toward physical activity is a key goal of physical education. Chapter 5 also discusses essential elements of teaching and how to positively reinforce youngsters during learning situations.

III. **Quality physical education programs make physical activity and motor skill development the core of the program.** Physical education is the only place in the total school curriculum where instruction is focused on teaching motor skills. Physical education is a unique discipline that focuses on physical activity to ensure the physical development of students. It is mandatory that the program focus on skill development and quality physical activity. Chapters 2 and 12 explain the importance of physical activity for the optimal growth and development of youngsters.

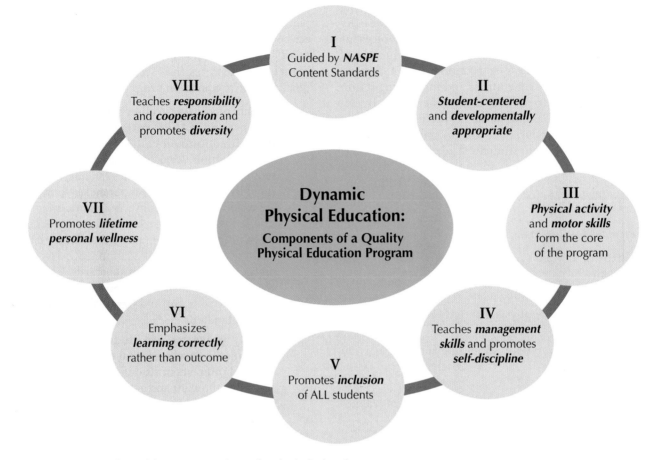

FIGURE 1.5   Essential components of a quality physical education program.

IV. **Quality physical education programs teach management skills and self-discipline.** Physical education teachers are usually evaluated based on how students in their classes behave. Administrators and parents look to see that students are on task and receiving many opportunities to learn new skills. When a class is well managed and students work with self-discipline, the experience compares to classroom instruction, bringing credibility to the program. Chapter 6 offers many different methods for managing a classroom and promoting self-discipline.

V. **Quality programs emphasize inclusion of all students.** Instruction is designed for students who need help the most—less skilled youngsters and children with disabilities. Students who are skilled and blessed with innate ability have many opportunities to learn. They have the confidence to take private lessons, join clubs, and play in after-school sports programs. Unskilled youngsters or children with disabilities lack confidence and often are un-

able to help themselves. Physical education is most likely the last opportunity youngsters will have to learn skills in a caring and positive environment. Instructional progressions designed to facilitate youngsters whose ability places them in the lower 70 percent of the class ensure a positive experience for all. Students who aren't naturally gifted must be made to feel successful if they are expected to enjoy and value physical activity. See Chapter 7 for dealing with youngsters who have disabilities and modifying activities so all children can be successful.

VI. **Quality physical education programs focus instruction on the process of learning skills rather than on the product or outcome of the skill performance.** When youngsters are learning new motor skills, performing the skill correctly is more important than the outcome of the skill. Youngsters need to learn proper techniques first and then focus on the product of the skill performance. Translated, this means it is more important to teach a youngster to catch a beanbag properly than to worry about how many he catches or misses. Chapter 3 offers strategies for optimizing skill learning. Chapter 8 helps explain when to focus on the process or product evaluation of motor skills.

VII. **Quality physical education programs teach lifetime activities that students can use to promote their health and personal wellness.** Quality physical education programs prepare youngsters to participate in activities that they can perform when they become adults. If a program is restricted to team sports, the program will be of little value to the majority of adults. Participation in sports activities declines rapidly with age. Less than 5 percent of adults above the age of 30 report playing a team sport (USDHHS, 1996). By far, walking is the activity most often reported in adulthood. Other activities such as stretching exercises, bicycling, strength development exercises, jogging, swimming, and aerobics are also popular with adults. Quality physical education looks to the future and offers activities that youngsters can enjoy and use as adults. Chapter 12 offers information about the importance of teaching lifetime physical activity skills in a physical education setting. Chapter 14 offers instructional strategies for teaching wellness and developing a healthy lifestyle.

VIII. **Quality physical education programs teach cooperation and responsibility and help students develop sensitivity to diversity and gender issues.** Cooperative skills have to precede competitive skills. Students have to agree to follow rules in order to enjoy group activities. The majority of fights and physical violence occur when youngsters are in a physical activity setting. Physical education is an effective laboratory for students to learn to behave responsibly because behavior is so observable to others. Situations in physical activity give rise to the need to resolve conflicts in a peaceful manner. Chapter 6 presents ways to teach youngsters responsible behavior and conflict-resolution techniques. Students need to learn about similarities and differences between cultures. Competitive activities such as the Olympics often bring cultures together and offer students the opportunity to see different cultures compete with respect and dignity. Coeducational activities help students understand how activities cut across gender and stereotypes. When gender differences occur in physical activities, it is an excellent time to point out that individuals differ

regardless of race or gender. Chapter 5 offers a number of strategies for dealing with gender and diversity issues.

REFLECTION AND REVIEW QUESTIONS

How and Why

1. How have your perceptions of physical education changed based on your understanding of its evolution?
2. How does physical education fit into a school's curriculum?
3. How can the nationwide focus on health, wellness, and physical activity influence the lives of children?
4. How do the NASPE national standards help teachers?
5. Why is it important to understand the essential components of physical education?

Content Review

1. Are physical education programs and physical education teachers necessary? Defend your answer.
2. Why is physical education a unique component of the total school curriculum?
3. What has been the evolution of physical education?
4. What contributions have different pedagogical approaches made to the evolution of physical education?
5. How have federal mandates influenced physical education?
6. What are the content standards and what role do they play in physical education?
7. What are the essential components of a quality physical education program and what is the significance of each?

FOR MORE INFORMATION

References and Suggested Readings

AAHPERD. (1986). *Physical activity and well being.* Waldorf, MD: American Alliance.
AAHPERD. (1990). *Professional preparation of the specialist teaching physical education to children.* Reston, VA: Author.
American Academy of Pediatrics. (1987). Physical fitness and the schools. *Pediatrics, 80*(3), 449–450.
American Academy of Pediatrics. (1991). *Sports medicine: Health care for young athletes.* 2nd ed. Elk Grove Village, IL: Author.

Anderson, R. E., Crespo, C. J., Bartlett, S. J., Cheskin, L. J., & Pratt, M. (1998). Relationship of physical activity and television watching with body weight and level of fatness among children: Results from the Third National Health and Nutrition Examination Survey. *Journal of the American Medical Association, 279,* 938–942.

Arizona Department of Health Services. (2004). *PLAY: Promoting lifetime activity for youth.* Phoenix, AZ: Author.

Bailey, D. A., Faulkner, R. A., & McKay, H. A. (1996). Growth, physical activity, and bone mineral acquisition. *Exercise and Sport Science Reviews, 24,* 233–266.

Bar-Or, O. (1995). Health benefits of physical activity during childhood and adolescence. *Physical Activity and Fitness Research Digest, 2*(4), 1–6.

Beighle, A., & Pangrazi, R. P. (2000). The validity of six pedometers for measuring the physical activity of children. Unpublished manuscript.

Burgeson, C. R., Wechsler, H., Brener, N. D., Young, J. C., & Spain, C. G. (2001). Physical education and activity: Results from the school health policies and programs study (SHPPS) 2000. *Journal of School Health, 71*(7), 279–293.

Cooper Institute. (2004). *Fitnessgram/Activitygram test administration manual.* 3rd ed. Champaign, IL: Human Kinetics Publishers.

Corbin, C., & Lindsey, R. (2005). *Fitness for life.* 5th ed. Champaign, IL: Human Kinetics Publishers.

Dale, D., Corbin, C. B., & Cuddihy, T. F. (1998). Can conceptual physical education promote physically active lifestyles? *Pediatric Exercise Science, 10,* 97–109.

Fitness and Lifestyle in Canada. (1983, May). *Canada fitness survey.* Ottawa, Canada. (Report funded by Fitness Canada.)

Fitness Products Council. (1999). *U.S. participation in fitness activities, 1987–1998.* North Palm Beach, FL: Sporting Goods Manufacturers Association.

Gardner, D. P. (Chair). (1983). A nation at risk: The imperative for educational reform. A report to the nation and the Secretary of Education, U.S. Department of Education. The National Commission on Excellence in Education. *Chronicle of Higher Education, 26*(10), 11–16.

Gortmaker, S. L., Must, A., Sobol, A. M., Peterson, K., Colditz, G. A., & Dietz, W. H. (1996). *Archives of Pediatric Adolescent Medicine, 150,* 356–362.

Guo, S. S., & Chumlea, W. C. (1999). Tracking of body mass index in children in relation to overweight in adulthood. *American Journal of Clinical Nutrition, 70,* 145S–148S.

Guo, S. S., Roche, A. F., Chumlea, W. C., Gardner, J. D., & Siervogel, R. M. (1994). The predictive value of childhood body mass index values for overweight at age 35 y. *American Journal of Clinical Nutrition, 59,* 810–819.

Hellison, D. (2003). *Teaching responsibility through physical activity.* 2nd ed. Champaign, IL: Human Kinetics.

Jebb, S. A., & Moore, M. S. (1999). Contribution of a sedentary lifestyle and inactivity to the etiology of overweight and obesity: Current evidence and research issues. *Medicine and Science in Sports and Exercise, 31,* S534–S541.

Kraus, H., & Hirschland, R. P. (1954). Minimum muscular fitness tests in school children. *Research Quarterly, 25,* 178–187.

Morgan, C. F., Pangrazi, R. P., & Beighle, A. (2003). Using pedometers to promote physical activity in physical education. *Journal of Physical Education Recreation and Dance, 74*(7), 33–38.

Must, A., Jacques, P. F., Dallal, G. E., Bajema, C. J., & Dietz, W. H. (1992). Long-term morbidity and mortality of overweight adolescents: A follow-up of the Harvard Growth Study of 1922 to 1935. *New England Journal of Medicine, 327,* 1350–1355.

National Association for Sport and Physical Education. (2004). *Moving into the future: National standards for physical education.* 2nd ed. Reston, VA: Author.

National Association for Sport and Physical Education. (2004). *Physical activity for children: A statement of guidelines.* 2nd ed. Reston, VA: Author.

National Center for Health Statistics. (2004). *Health, United States, 2004 with chartbook on trends in the health of Americans.* Hyattsville, MD: CDC.

Raitakari, O. T., Porkka, K. V. K., Taimela, S., Telama, R., Rasanen, L., & Viikari, J. S. A. (1994). Effects of persistent physical activity and inactivity on coronary risk factors in children and young adults. *American Journal of Epidemiology, 140,* 195–205.

Ross, J. G., Pate, R. P., Corbin, C. B., Delpy, L. A., & Gold, R. S. (1987). What's going on in the elementary physical education program? *JOPERD, 58*(9), 78–84.

Sallis, J. F. (1994). Influences on physical activity of children, adolescents, and adults or determinants of active living. *Physical Activity and Fitness Research Digest, 1*(7), 1–8.

Sallis, J. F., McKenzie, T. L., Kolody, B., Lewis, M., Marshall, S., & Rosengard, P. (1999). Effects of health-related physical education on academic achievement: Project SPARK. *Research Quarterly for Exercise and Sport, 70,* 127–134.

Sporting Goods Manufacturers Association. (2000, May/June). *Fitness and sports newsletter.*

Telama, R., Yang, X., Laakso, L., & Viikari, J. (1997). Physical activity in childhood and adolescence as predictors of physical activity in young adulthood. *American Journal of Preventative Medicine, 13,* 317–323.

Trudeau, F., Laurencelle, L., Tremblay, J., Rajic, M., & Shephard, R. J. (1998). A long-term follow-up of participants in the Trois-Rivieres semi-longitudinal study of growth and development. *Pediatric Exercise Science, 10,* 366–377.

U.S. Department of Health and Human Services. (1994). *School health policies and programs study.* Atlanta, GA: U.S. Department of Health and Human Services, Centers for Disease Control and Prevention, National Center for Chronic Disease Prevention and Health Promotion.

U.S. Department of Health and Human Services. (1996). *Physical activity and health: A report of the surgeon general.* Atlanta, GA: U.S. Department of Health and Human Services, Centers for Disease Control and Prevention, National Center for Chronic Disease Prevention and Health Promotion.

U.S. Department of Health and Human Services. (2000). *Healthy people 2010: National health promotion and disease objectives.* Washington, DC: U.S. Government Printing Office.

U.S. Department of Health and Human Services. (2002). *Prevalence of overweight among children and adolescents: United States, 1999.* Centers for Disease Control and Prevention, National Center for Health Statistics.

U.S. Public Health Service. (1990). *Healthy people 2000: National health promotion and disease objectives.* Washington, DC: U.S. Government Printing Office.

Whitaker, R. C., Wright, J. A., Pepe, M. S., Seidel, K. D., & Dietz, W. H. (1997). Predicting obesity in young adulthood from childhood and parental obesity. *New England Journal of Medicine, 337,* 869–873.

Websites

American Alliance for Health, Physical Education, Recreation, and Dance
www.aahperd.org

American Heart Association
www.americanheart.org

Centers for Disease Control and Prevention
www.cdc.gov

Public Law 94-142
http://asclepius.com/angel/special.html

Title IX
www.ed.gov/pubs/TitleIX

C H A P T E R

2

Teaching Children in the Physical Education Environment

ESSENTIAL COMPONENTS OF QUALITY PROGRAMS

I. Organized around content standards

▶ **II. Student-centered and developmentally appropriate**

III. Physical activity and motor skill development form the core of the program

IV. Teaches management skills and self-discipline

V. Promotes inclusion of all students

VI. Focuses on process over product

▶ **VII. Promotes lifetime personal health and wellness**

VIII. Teaches cooperation and responsibility and promotes sensitivity to diversity

NATIONAL STANDARDS FOR PHYSICAL EDUCATION*

1. Demonstrates competency in motor skills and movement patterns needed to perform a variety of physical activities.

▶ **2. Demonstrates understanding of movement concepts, principles, and tactics as they apply to the learning and performance of physical activities.**

3. Participates regularly in physical activity.

4. Achieves and maintains a health-enhancing level of physical fitness.

5. Exhibits responsible personal and social behavior that respects self and others in physical activity.

6. Values physical activity for health, enjoyment, challenge, self-expression, and/or social interaction.

*National Association for Sport and Physical Education (NASPE), 2004.

SUMMARY

Physical activity positively impacts the growth and development of children. Research supports the value of an active lifestyle for optimum growth and development. There is a positive correlation between the incidence of certain health disorders and a sedentary lifestyle. Lifetime involvement in physical activity often depends on early participation and gratification gained from such participation. Developing motor skills at an early age provides the tools needed to be physically active throughout life. Guidelines for safe participation in physical activity, including weight lifting, running, exercising in heat, and fitness testing, are delineated.

OUTCOMES

- Describe the need for physical activities.

- Cite stages of the growing child.

- Understand the relationship between physical activity and the development of muscular strength and endurance and skeletal growth.

- Define aerobic capacity and discuss its relationship to health and physical activity.

- Understand how body composition impacts the health and well-being of an individual.

- Discuss the role organized youth sports should play in the proper growth and development of children.

- Identify guidelines to follow for exercising children safely.

- Describe the proper approach to distance running and weight training for preadolescent children.

This chapter offers an overview of the impact of physical activity on the growing child. Many of the studies cited in this chapter offer excellent justification for including physical education in the total school curriculum. For example, the high numbers of overweight youth, the need for skill competency so children have tools to be active for a lifetime, and the long-term effects of physical activity are strong arguments for a well-taught, well-organized physical education program.

THE GROWING CHILD

Growth patterns are generally controlled by genetic makeup at birth. Although an unhealthy environment can have a negative impact on proper growth and development, this section examines maturation patterns that are common to the majority of youngsters. All youngsters follow a general growth pattern; however, each child's timing is unique. Some children are advanced physically for their chronological age, whereas others are slow maturers. Only when aberration from the norm is excessive is there cause for concern.

Growth Patterns

Teachers and parents should notice if youngsters are maturing normally. When heights and weights are plotted on a graph from year to year, a distance curve can be developed. These curves (Figure 2.1) give an indication of how tall and heavy children are expected to be during a specific year of life. Another way to examine

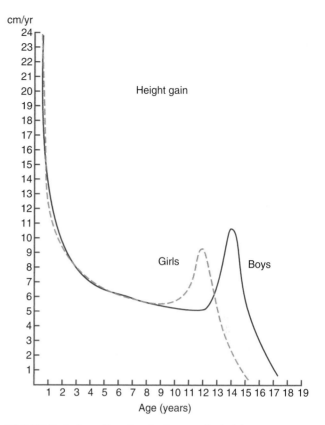

FIGURE 2.2 Growth velocity curve for height.

(From Tanner, J. M., Whitehouse, R. H., & Takaishi, M. (1966). *Archives of Diseases in Childhood, 41*, 466.)

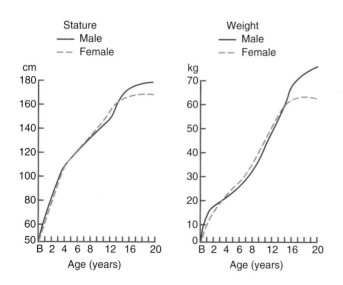

FIGURE 2.1 Distance curves for height and weight.

(From Malina, R. (1975). *Growth and development: The first twenty years in man*, p. 19. Minneapolis: Burgess.)

growth patterns is to look at a velocity curve, which reveals how much a child grows on a year-to-year basis (Figure 2.2). Children go through a rapid period of growth from birth to age five. From age six to the onset of adolescence, growth slows to a steady but increasing pattern. A general rule of thumb in regard to motor learning is that when growth is rapid, the ability to learn new skills decreases. Because the rate of growth slows during the elementary school years, this is an excellent window for children to learn motor skills.

During adolescence, rapid growth occurs until adulthood is reached. During the elementary school years, boys are generally taller and heavier. Girls reach the adolescent growth spurt first, and grow taller and heavier during the sixth- and seventh-grade years. Boys quickly catch up and grow larger and stronger. Growth charts based on a large sample of children have been developed by the National Center for Health Statistics (Figures 2.3 and 2.4, pages 26 and 27). These tables can be consulted to identify both stature (height) and weight percentiles for children ages 2 through 20. The tables offer an opportunity to visualize marked differences between children in a so-called normal population.

FIGURE 2.3 2 to 20 years: Boys' stature-for-age and weight-for-age percentiles.

Developed by the National Center for Health Statistics in collaboration with the National Center for Chronic Disease Prevention and Health Promotion (2000).

Young children have relatively short legs for their overall height. The trunk is longer in relation to the legs during early childhood. The ratio of leg length (standing height) to trunk length (sitting height) is similar for boys and girls through age 11. The head makes up one-fourth of the child's total length at birth and about one-sixth at age six. Figure 2.5 (page 28) illustrates how body proportions change with growth. Because K–2 students have short legs in relation to their upper bodies, they are "top heavy" and fall more easily than adults do. This high center of gravity will gradually lower and give children increased stability and balance.

Body Physique

A child's physique (somatotype) affects the quality of his or her motor performance. Sheldon, Dupertuis, and McDermott (1954) developed the original scheme for

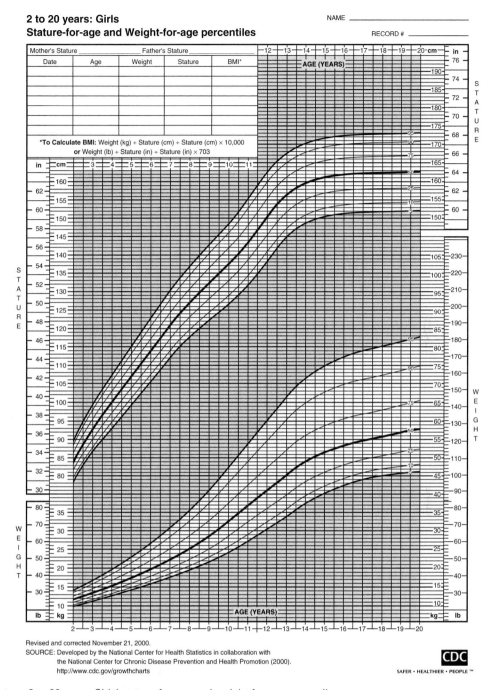

2 to 20 years: Girls
Stature-for-age and Weight-for-age percentiles

FIGURE 2.4 2 to 20 years: Girls' stature-for-age and weight-for-age percentiles.

Developed by the National Center for Health Statistics in collaboration with the National Center for Chronic Disease Prevention and Health Promotion (2000).

somatotyping, identifying three major physiques: *mesomorphy, ectomorphy,* and *endomorphy*. Rating is assessed from standardized photographs on a 7-point scale, with 1 being the least expression and 7 the most expression of the specific component. The ratings of each component give a total score that results in identification of an individual's somatotype. A similar system of classification for children (Petersen, 1967) is available for teachers who are interested in understanding the body physiques of children.

In general, children who possess a mesomorphic body type perform best in activities requiring strength, speed, and agility such as most team sports. The *mesomorph* is characterized as having a predominance of muscle and bone and is often labeled "muscled." The *ectomorph* is identified as being extremely thin, with a

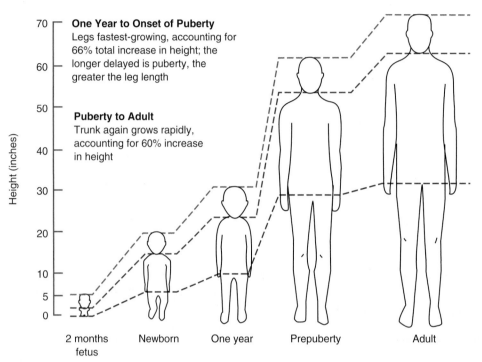

Changing Bodily Proportions

Conception to Birth
Head fastest-growing structure,
completing 70% of its total growth

Birth to One Year
Trunk fastest-growing, accounting for
60% total increase in height

One Year to Onset of Puberty
Legs fastest-growing, accounting for
66% total increase in height; the
longer delayed is puberty, the
greater the leg length

Puberty to Adult
Trunk again grows rapidly,
accounting for 60% increase
in height

Height (inches)

2 months fetus   Newborn   One year   Prepuberty   Adult

FIGURE 2.5   Changing body proportions from conception to adulthood.

(From Whipple, D. (1966). *Dynamics of development: Euthenic pediatrics*, p. 122. New York: McGraw-Hill.)

minimum of muscle development, and is characterized as "skinny." These children may be less proficient in activities requiring strength and power, but able to perform well in aerobic endurance activities such as jogging, cross-country running, and track and field. The third classification is the *endomorph*, characterized as soft and round, with an excessively protruding abdomen. These children may perform poorly in many areas, including aerobic and anaerobic skill-oriented activities. The overweight child is generally at a disadvantage in all phases of physical performance. Somatotype classification illustrates how dramatically children differ in body physique and necessitates that instruction accommodate individual differences.

Skeletal Maturity

Teachers often speak about the *maturity* of students. Physical maturity has a strong impact on the performance of children in physical education. Maturity is usually measured by comparing chronological age with

skeletal age. Ossification (hardening) of the bones occurs in the center of the bone shaft and at the ends of the long bones (growth plates). The rate of ossification gives an accurate indication of a child's rate of maturation. Maturation rate can be identified by X-raying the wrist bones and comparing the development of the subject's bones with a set of standardized X rays (Gruelich & Pyle, 1959; Roche, Chumlea, & Thissen, 1988). Children whose chronological age is beyond skeletal age are said to be late (or slow) maturers. If skeletal age is ahead of chronological age, children are labeled early (fast) maturers.

Studies examining skeletal age (Gruelich & Pyle, 1959; Krahenbuhl & Pangrazi, 1983) consistently show that a five- to six-year variation in skeletal maturity exists in a typical classroom of youngsters. For example, a class of third graders who are all 8 years old chronologically would range in skeletal age from 5 to 11 years. This means that some youngsters are actually 5-year-olds skeletally and are trying to compete with others who are as mature as 11-year-olds. Effective programs have to

FIGURE 2.6 Children the same age vary in size and maturity.

offer activities that are *developmentally appropriate* and suited to youngsters' level of maturity.

Early maturing children of both sexes are generally heavier and taller for their age than are average- or late-maturing students. Overweight children (endomorphs) are often more mature for their age than are normal-weight children and carry larger amounts of muscle and bone tissue. However, these overweight children also carry a greater percentage of body weight as fat tissue (Malina, 1980), which decreases their motor performance. The motor performance of boys is related to skeletal maturity in that a more mature boy usually performs better on motor tasks (Clarke, 1971). For girls, however, motor performance appears not to be related to physiological maturity, and Malina (1978) found that late maturation is commonly associated with exceptional motor performance. Physical education programs often ask students to learn at the same rate even though this practice may be detrimental to the development of students who are maturing at a faster or slower rate. Students do not mature at the same rate and are not at similar levels of readiness to learn (Figure 2.6). Offering a wide spectrum of developmentally appropriate activities helps ensure that youngsters will be successful regardless of the maturity factor.

Muscular Development and Strength

In the elementary school years, muscular strength increases linearly with chronological age (Beunen, 1989; Malina, 1980). A similar yearly increase occurs until adolescence, at which time a rapid increase in strength occurs. When differences in strength between the sexes are adjusted for height, there is no difference in lower body strength from ages 7 through 17. When the same adjustment between the sexes is made for upper body strength, however, boys have more upper extremity and trunk strength (Malina, 1980). Boys and girls can participate on somewhat even terms in activities demanding leg strength, particularly if their size and mass are similar. On the other hand, in activities demanding arm or trunk strength, boys have an advantage, even if they are similar to the girls in height and mass. When pairing children for activities, students should not be paired with someone who is considerably taller and heavier (or more mature) and therefore stronger.

MUSCLE FIBER TYPE AND PERFORMANCE

The number of muscle fibers an individual possesses is genetically determined. An increase in muscle size is accomplished by an increase in the size of each muscle fiber. The size of the muscles is determined primarily by the number of fibers and secondarily by the size of the fibers. An individual is therefore somewhat muscularly limited by genetic restrictions.

Skeletal muscle tissue contains a ratio of fast-contracting fibers (fast twitch [FT]) to slow-contracting fibers (slow twitch [ST]) (Saltin, 1973). The percentage of fast- versus slow-contracting fibers varies from muscle to muscle and among individuals. The percentage of each type of muscle fiber is determined during the first weeks of postnatal life (Dubowitz, 1970). Most individuals possess a 50–50 split; that is, half of the muscle fibers are FT and half are ST. A small percentage of people have a ratio of 60 to 40 (in either direction), and researchers have verified that some people possess an even more extreme ratio.

What is the significance of variation in the ratio of muscle fiber type? ST fibers have a rich supply of blood and related energy mechanisms. This results in a slowly contracting, fatigue-resistant muscle fiber that is well suited to endurance-type (aerobic) activities. In contrast, FT fibers are capable of bursts of intense activity but are subject to rapid fatigue. These fibers are well suited to activities demanding short-term speed and power (for example, pull-ups, standing long jump, and shuttle run). ST fibers facilitate performance in the mile run or other endurance-oriented activities.

Surprisingly, elementary-age children who do best in activities requiring FT fibers also do best in distance running (Krahenbuhl & Pangrazi, 1983). Muscle fiber metabolic specialization does not occur until adolescence; this fact is a strong argument for keeping all youngsters involved in varied physical activities throughout the elementary years. A youngster who does poorly in elementary school may do quite well during and after adolescence, when a high percentage of ST fibers will aid in the performance of aerobic activity. On the other hand, the same child may do poorly in a physical education program dominated by team sports that demand quickness and strength. Designing a program that incorporates activities using a range of physical attributes (that is, endurance, balance, and flexibility) is essential.

Relative Strength and Motor Performance

Strength is an important factor in performing motor skills. A study by Rarick and Dobbins (1975) identified and weighted factors that contribute to the motor performance of children. The factor identified as most important was strength in relation to body size (*relative strength*). High levels of strength in relation to body size helped predict which students were most capable of performing motor skills. Deadweight (fat) was the fourth-ranked factor in the study and was weighted negatively. Overweight children were less proficient at performing motor skills. Deadweight has a negative impact on motor performance because it reduces relative strength. Overweight children may be stronger than normal-weight children in absolute terms, but are less strong when strength is adjusted for body weight. This lack of strength in relationship to body size causes overweight children to find a strength-related task (such as a push-up or pull-up) much more difficult than the task would seem to normal-weight children. The need for varied

and personalized workloads is important to ensure all youngsters the opportunity for success in strength-related activities. Strength is an important part of a balanced fitness program and offers youngsters a better opportunity to find success in a variety of motor development activities.

Aerobic Capacity: Children Are Not Little Adults

Maximal aerobic power is an individual's maximum ability to use oxygen in the body for metabolic purposes. The oxygen uptake of an individual, all other factors being equal, determines the quality of endurance-oriented performance. Maximal aerobic power is closely related to lean body mass, which explains the differences in performance between boys and girls. When maximum oxygen uptake is adjusted per kilogram of body weight, it shows little change for boys (no increase) and a gradual decrease for girls (Bar-Or, 1983). This decrease in females is due to an increase in body fat and a decrease in lean body mass. When maximal oxygen uptake is not adjusted for body weight, it increases in similar amounts on a yearly basis for both boys and girls through age 12, even though boys have higher values as early as age 5.

Adults interested in increasing endurance-based athletic performance train extensively to increase aerobic power. A frequently asked question is whether similar training will increase the aerobic performance of children. A meta-analysis by Payne & Morrow (1993) analyzed 28 studies dealing with the impact of exercise on aerobic performance in children. The results showed that training caused little, if any, increase in aerobic power in prepubescent children. If there is improvement in running performance in young children, Bar-Or (1983) postulates that it may occur because they become more efficient mechanically or improve in anaerobic metabolism. Another theory is that young children are active enough to make intergroup differences negligible (Corbin & Pangrazi, 1992).

Even though children demonstrate a relatively high oxygen uptake, they do not perform up to this level because they are not economical in running or walking activities. An 8-year-old child running at 180 meters per minute is operating at 90 percent of maximal aerobic power, whereas a 16-year-old running at the same rate is operating at only 75 percent of maximum. This explains why young children are less capable than adolescents and adults at competing over long distances, even though they can maintain a slow speed for long distances (Bar-Or, 1983).

Children exercising at a certain workload perceive the activity to be easier than do adults working at a similar level. Youngsters were asked to rate their perceived exertion at different percentages of maximal heart rate

(Bar-Or & Ward, 1989) and usually rated the exertion to be less stressful than did adults. Youngsters also demonstrate a rapid recovery rate after strenuous exercise. This implies that teachers should not judge workloads for children based on their own perceptions of the difficulty of an activity. Teachers also should use a child's rapid recovery rate to full advantage. Exercise bouts can be interspersed with restful episodes of stretching and nonlocomotor movements. This type of interval training is a particularly effective training method to use with children because it allows them to exercise aerobically and recover.

Overweight Children and Physical Performance

Overweight children seldom perform physical activities on par with leaner children (Bar-Or, 1983). In part, this is due to the greater metabolic cost of the overweight child's exercise. Overweight children require a higher oxygen uptake capacity to perform a given task. Being oveweight takes a great toll on a child's aerobic power because such children must perform at a higher percentage of their maximal oxygen uptake (Figure 2.7). Usually, their maximal uptake values are lower than those of lean children. This gives overweight children less reserve capacity and causes them to perceive higher exertion (Bar-Or & Ward, 1989) when performing a task. These reactions contribute to the common perception among teachers that "overweight children don't like to run." Teachers must understand that asking overweight children to run as far and as fast as normal-weight children is unrealistic. The task is more demanding for the overweight child. Overweight children have to work harder than normal-weight children to accomplish the same tasks and thus need adjusted workloads. There is no acceptable premise, physiological or psychological, for asking all children to run the same distance regardless of ability or body type.

Workloads should be based on time rather than distance. Lean and efficient runners should be expected to move farther than overweight youngsters during a stipulated time period. All children *should not* have to do the same workload. Just as one would not expect kindergarten children to perform the same workload as that of fifth graders, it is unreasonable to expect overweight children to be capable of workloads similar to those of lean, ectomorphic youngsters. *Exercise programs for overweight subjects should be designed to increase caloric expenditure rather than to improve cardiovascular fitness* (Rowland, 1991). The intensity of the activity should be secondary to the amount of time the student is involved in some type of moderate activity.

TEACHING SPECIALIZED MOTOR SKILLS

The majority of children will participate in some type of sport activity, if for no other reason than their parents want them to do so. Physical educators can offer expert advice to parents and community leaders. Since these programs may be administered by persons who have little understanding of young, immature children, it is important that teachers step forward and share their knowledge.

Allow Students to Learn All Skills and Play All Positions

Allow youngsters to play all positions when teaching sport skills. If the best athletes are always assigned to skilled positions, it becomes a situation of the rich getting richer and the poor getting poorer. Because all children deserve equal opportunity to learn sport skills, it should be a mandate to teachers that all children play all positions and receive similar amounts of practice time. In addition, reinforcement schedules need to be similar for children regardless of their current skill level. Children participate in activities that offer them

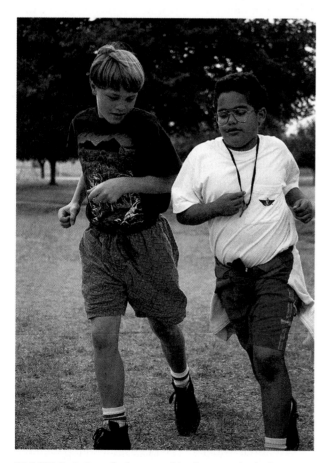

FIGURE 2.7   Body composition impacts physical performance.

reinforcement; it is easy for them to become discouraged if little encouragement and praise are given when they are trying to learn new skills and positions.

Teachers must understand that maturity plays an important role in dictating how youngsters learn motor skills. One of the reasons for helping children learn all skills and play all positions is that it will give them the opportunity to be successful when they reach maturity. For example, should the teacher identify a youngster as a pitcher or a right fielder, or as a lineman or a quarterback? Often, these questions are answered for youngsters when teachers make judgments and force them to play a certain position. Many times, such judgments are based on the maturity of the individual rather than the actual skill level. In a study by Hale (1956), skeletally mature athletes were found to be playing in the skilled positions in the Little League World Series. Chronologically, all players were 11 years old, with a skeletal age range similar to that described earlier. The most mature were pitchers and catchers, and the least mature played at less skilled positions. This study points out how skeletally mature children receive more opportunity to throw at an early age (through pitching and catching). These youngsters obviously have the chance to become better throwers due to the large number of opportunities they receive when throwing in games and practice. In contrast, children who are immature play right field and receive limited throwing or catching opportunities. Because these less mature children receive much less throwing practice, it is improbable that they will ever have the chance to close the skill gap and develop adequate skill competency.

Ensure Success for All Students

The willingness to try new experiences and participate in activities is driven by how people feel about their ability level—their *perceived competence.* Perceived competence becomes more specific as students mature. Young students think they are good and competent at everything. As they become older (third or fourth grade), they start to realize that other students are better in some areas. If these students are not given the chance to succeed in class, low perceived competence about their ability to perform physical skills is the result. This "learned helplessness" (Harter, 1978) eventually results in the students' disliking and dropping out of physical education and future physical activity. There is a strong possibility that they will leave school with negative feelings about developing an active lifestyle. Dropping out of physical education commonly occurs in middle school and high school, when students have the opportunity to make a choice. Unfortunately, it is quite possible that the process of feeling incompetent begins in the elementary school years. Elementary school youngsters are often characterized as gifted (or not gifted) at a young age. This creates a self-fulfilling prophecy, with those students identified as gifted receiving more feedback and being expected to reach higher levels of performance. Less able students receive less feedback and expectations remain low.

Assume All Youngsters Have the Ability to Achieve

Even though teachers and parents make early judgments about the potential of students, it is difficult to identify outstanding athletes in the elementary school years. In a study by Clarke (1968), athletes identified as outstanding in elementary school were seldom outstanding in junior high school, and predictions based on elementary school performance were correct only 25 percent of the time. Most people would not risk discouraging a youngster if they knew they were going to be wrong 75 percent of the time. However, youngsters are often labeled at an early age, even though three out of four such predictions are incorrect. Treat all children as if they have the potential to become successful. It is not the purpose of a physical education program to develop athletes, but rather to help *all* students develop their physical skills within the limits of their potential. The program should not be presented in such a fashion that it allows the athletically gifted to excel and prosper at the expense of the less talented youngsters.

Understand That Starting Young Doesn't Ensure Excellence

There is no evidence to support the idea that starting a child's participation in sports at a young age ensures the child will become an outstanding athlete (Figure 2.8). In fact, many professional athletes did not even play their sport of excellence until the high school years. One reason that many parents and coaches push to have children start competing in a sport at an early age is that this competition offers the perception that a better athlete has been developed by the age of eight or nine. The participating child may seem extremely gifted compared with the nonparticipant, because he or she has been practicing skills for four or five years. Naturally, the "early starter" looks advanced compared with a child who has not been in an organized program. In most cases, however, a child who is genetically gifted quickly catches up to and surpasses the "early superstar" in one to three years. As Shephard (1984) states, "Any advantage that is gained from very prolonged training probably lies in the area of skill perfection rather than in a fuller realization of physical potential."

Children who have been in documented programs for many years may burn out at an early age. A docu-

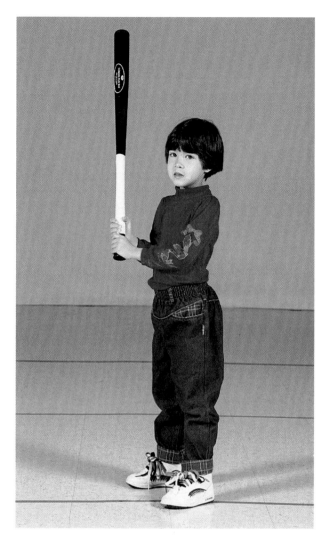

FIGURE 2.8   An early start does not guarantee success.

other children participating and practicing sport skills in an organized setting. They worry that their children will be unable to "catch up" if they do not get them involved in a similar program immediately. Even though this is not true, parents need reassurance, and they need facts. Physical educators can help parents find programs that minimize pressure and focus on skill development. A key is to find programs that allow the child to participate regardless of ability, and to have fun while playing. Children consider having fun and improving their skills to be more important than winning (Athletic Footwear Association, 1990). Many children drop out of sport activities but would probably continue to participate if given the opportunity (Petlichkoff, 1992). Unfortunately, some programs become elitist and start eliminating and "cutting" less gifted players. It is difficult to justify this approach at the elementary school level. All children should be given the opportunity to participate if they choose to do so.

Another reason given for starting children at a young age is tied to the commodity that only children have—free time. Parents know they have little time in their lives to learn new skills. They feel their youngsters have an abundance of free time that can be devoted to practice. Unfortunately, if the child shows promise, greater emphasis is placed on increasing practice time since it becomes necessary "to ensure that all this talent is not lost." It is important to remind parents that life includes more than athletic development and that many youngsters have been maimed by an excessive emphasis on sports at the expense of intellectual and social development. Participation in an activity should be self-selected and student-driven rather than motivated by external factors. Similarly, students should have the opportunity to withdraw from participation in an activity if they choose. Withdrawal should be child-controlled rather than externally controlled (Gould, 1987). In other words, participants should not be forced out of the program due to cost, limitation of participants, or injury. On the other hand, if youngsters choose to withdraw, they should be allowed that opportunity without pressure.

GUIDELINES FOR EXERCISING CHILDREN SAFELY

As is usually the case with most things, moderation is the way to ensure that children are safe and grow up enjoying physical activity. Moderate exercise, coupled with opportunities to participate in recreational activity, helps develop a lasting desire to move. Some adults are concerned that a child may be harmed physiologically by too much activity. To date, there is no evidence that a healthy child is harmed through vigorous activity

mented program is one in which extrinsic rewards are offered. Examples of such rewards are trophies, published league standings, ribbons, and excessive parental involvement. Evidence shows that extrinsic motivation may ultimately decrease intrinsic motivation, particularly in children age seven and older. Researchers (Thomas & Tennant, 1978; Whitehead & Corbin, 1991) found that younger children (age five) perceived a reward as a bonus, thus adding to the joy of performing a throwing motor task. This effect decreased with age, and by age nine the reward was seen as a bribe; intrinsic motivation was undermined. There is no substitute for allowing young children to participate in physical activity for the sheer enjoyment and excitement involved in moving and interacting with peers.

If starting youngsters early can create early burnout, why do parents feel pressured to force their child into a sport program? One explanation is that they constantly compare their children to other children. Parents see and exercise. Children can withstand a gradual increase in workload and are capable of workloads comparable to those of adults when the load is adjusted for height and size. Fatigue causes healthy children to stop exercising long before any danger to health occurs (Shephard, 1984). In addition, the child's circulatory system is similar in proportion to that of an adult and thus is not at a disadvantage during exercise.

Exercising in the Heat

Caution should be used when exercising youngsters in hot weather. The arrival of summer does not mean that exercise must stop, but certain measures should be taken to avoid heat-related illness. Children are not little adults and do not adapt to extremes of temperature as effectively as adults do for the following physiological reasons (American Academy of Pediatrics, 2000; Bar-Or, 1983):

1. Children have higher surface area/mass ratios than those of adults. This allows a greater amount of heat to transfer between the environment and the body.

2. When walking or running, children produce more metabolic heat per unit mass than adults produce. Youngsters are not as efficient in executing movement patterns, so they generate more metabolic heat than do adults performing a similar task.

3. Sweating capacity is not as great in children as in adults, resulting in a lowered ability to cool the body.

4. The ability of the blood to convey heat from the body core to the skin is reduced in children due to a lower cardiac output at a given oxygen uptake.

These physiological differences place children at a distinct disadvantage compared with adults when exercising in an ambient air temperature that is higher than the skin temperature. Individuals do acclimatize to warmer climates. However, children appear to adjust to heat more slowly (up to twice as long) than do adults (Bar-Or, 1983). Also, children do not instinctively drink enough liquids to replenish fluids lost during exercise. The American Academy of Pediatrics (2000) offers the following guidelines for exercising children during hot days:

1. The intensity of activities that last 15 minutes or more should be reduced whenever relative humidity and air temperature are above critical levels. Table 2.1 shows the relationship between humidity and air temperature and when activity should be moderated.

2. At the beginning of a strenuous exercise program or after traveling to a warmer climate, the intensity and duration of exercise should be restrained ini-

TABLE 2.1	Weather guide: When the humidity and air temperature exceed the corresponding levels, intense activity should be curtailed.
Humidity Level (%)	**Air Temperature (°F)**
40	90
50	85
60	80
70	75
80	70
90	65
100	60

tially and then increased gradually over a period of 10 to 14 days so that the students can acclimatize to the effects of heat. When such a period is not available, the length of time for participation should be curtailed.

3. Children should be hydrated 20 to 30 minutes before strenuous activity (Figure 2.9, page 35). During the activity, periodic drinking (e.g., 150 milliliters of cold tap water every 20 minutes for a child weighing 40 kilograms) should be enforced.

4. Clothing should be lightweight and limited to one layer of absorbent material to facilitate evaporation of sweat and to expose as much skin as possible. Sweat-saturated garments should be replaced by dry ones. Rubberized sweat suits should never be used to produce weight loss.

The academy identifies children with the following conditions as being at a potentially high risk for heat stress: overweight, febrile (feverish) state, cystic fibrosis, gastrointestinal infection, diabetes insipidus, diabetes mellitus, chronic heart failure, caloric malnutrition, anorexia nervosa, sweating insufficiency syndrome, and mental retardation.

Distance Running

An often-asked question is how much and how far children should be allowed to run, particularly in a competitive or training setting. The answer is difficult to agree on because parents, teachers, and coaches seldom see the long-term effects of excessive running. The American Academy of Pediatrics Executive Committee (1990) identifies some of the concerns:

FIGURE 2.9   Water is mandatory for participation in strenuous activity in the heat.

Psychologic and social problems for the child runner can result from spending long hours in training and setting unrealistic goals. This is similar to the effects of participation in other competitive sports, in which the child may be submitted to inappropriate pressures. A prepubertal child should be allowed to participate for the enjoyment of running without fear of parental or peer rejection or pressure. (p. 290)

A position taken by the International Athletics Association Federation (IAAF) Medical Committee was reprinted in 1983. In part, it states, "The danger certainly exists that with over-intensive training, separation of the growth plates may occur in the pelvic region, the knee, or the ankle. While this could heal with rest, nevertheless definitive information is lacking whether in years to come harmful effects may result." In view of these concerns, it is the opinion of the Committee that training and competition for long-distance track and road-running events should not be encouraged. Up to the age of 12, it is suggested that not more than 800 meters (one-half mile) should be run in competition. An increase in this distance should be introduced gradually—with, for example, a maximum of 3,000 meters (nearly two miles) in competition for 14-year-olds.

FITNESS TESTING CONSIDERATIONS

Teachers often test children at the start of the school year in the one-mile run/walk or other high-effort aerobic tests. This practice should be discouraged, since many children may not have ample conditioning to par-

ticipate safely in the activity. In addition, in many parts of the country, the start of the school year is hot and humid, adding to the stress placed on the cardiovascular system. A recommendation is to test only at the end of the school year after youngsters have had the opportunity to be conditioned. If this is not possible, at least allow youngsters four to six weeks to condition themselves. Rowland (1990) recommends starting with a one-eighth-mile run/walk and gradually building to a one-mile run/walk over a four-week period.

A strongly recommended alternative is to eliminate the mile run and substitute the PACER aerobic fitness test (see page 158). The PACER can be administered indoors and does not require running to exhaustion. As a cardiovascular fitness measure, the PACER is as accurate as the mile run and produces much less emotional stress for participants.

Resistance Training

Resistance training for preadolescent children has generated concern among educators. Many worry about safety and stress-related injuries, while others question whether such training produces significant strength gains. Accepted thinking for years was that prepubescents are incapable of making significant strength gains because they lack adequate levels of circulating androgens. Evidence is continuing to build that contradicts this point of view (Faigenbaum, 2003). A study by Cahill (1986) demonstrated significant increases in strength among 18 prepubescent boys. A study by Servedio et al. (1985) showed significant strength gains in shoulder flexion. Weltman et al. (1986) conducted a 14-week, three-times-a-week program using hydraulic resistance training (circuit training using ten different stations) in 6- to 11-year-old boys. Results showed an 18–37 percent gain in all major muscle groups. Strength can be increased through weight training in prepubescent youngsters; however, the way prepubescent children gain strength differs from adolescents and adults (Tanner, 1993). In preadolescent children, it appears that strength gains occur from motor learning rather than muscle hypertrophy. Youngsters develop more efficient motor patterns and recruit more muscle fibers, but show no increase in muscle size (Ozmun, Mikesky, & Surburg, 1994).

Note that the term *resistance training* is used here to denote the use of barbells, dumbbells, rubber bands, or machines as resistance. This is in sharp contrast to *weight lifting* or *power lifting,* which is a competitive sport for the purpose of determining maximum lifting ability. There is agreement among experts that weight *training* is acceptable for children, but weight *lifting* is highly undesirable and may be harmful. In a statement of strength training recommendations, the American Orthopaedic Society for Sports Medicine (AOSSM) (Duda, 1986) states, "(1) competition is prohibited, and (2) no maximum lift should ever be attempted." In addition, AOSSM recommends a physical exam, proper supervision by knowledgeable coaches, and emotional maturity on the part of the participating youngster. The American Academy of Pediatrics (2001) recommends that preadolescents and adolescents avoid competitive weight lifting, power lifting, bodybuilding, and maximal lifts until they reach skeletal maturity.

Safety and prevention of injury are paramount considerations for those interested in weight training for children. It is questionable whether weight training is an appropriate activity for a typical group of children in a physical education class. When injuries were reported, most occurred due to inadequate supervision, lack of proper technique, or competitive lifting. The majority of weight lifting injuries were caused by the major lifts, the power clean, the clean and jerk, the squat lift, or the dead lift (Tanner, 1993). These lifts often are competitive and performed in an uncontrolled (ballistic) manner; they should not be used with preadolescent children. If knowledge and expertise are limited, weight training programs for children should be avoided. A knowledgeable instructor is required to provide an effective and safe program.

The long-term effects of strength training in children have not been studied. In addition, many experts worry about highly organized training programs that place emphasis on relative gains in strength. A weight training program should be one component of a comprehensive fitness program for children. The National Strength and Conditioning Association (NSCA) (1985) recommends that 50–80 percent of the prepubescent athlete's training must include a variety of different exercises such as agility exercises (basketball, volleyball, tennis, and tumbling) and endurance training (distance running, bicycling, and swimming).

When a variety of physical activities is experienced in elementary school physical education, there is little need for weight training within the school curriculum. There are many ways to enhance strength in children besides using weights, which may present a safety issue. For a number of alternative ways to develop strength, see the text by Roberts (1996). However, weight training is acceptable on an individual basis with parental approval in a club setting. If a decision is made to develop a weight training program for children, it should be done in a thoughtful and studied manner. Focus on the correct lifting technique instead of the amount of weight lifted. Proper supervision and technique are key ingredients in a successful program. Program prescription guidelines recommended by AOSSM and NSCA are as follows:

1. Training is recommended two or three times a week on nonconsecutive days for 20- to 30-minute periods. High repetitions at low resistance appear to be most safe for elementary school-age children.

2. No resistance should be applied until proper form is demonstrated. Six to 15 repetitions equal one set; one to three sets per exercise should be done.

3. Weight or resistance is increased in one- to three-pound increments after the prepubescent does 15 repetitions in good form.

4. Maximal lifts should not be performed until youngsters are at least 16 to 17 years old.

REFLECTION AND REVIEW QUESTIONS

How and Why

1. How have your views of what is appropriate for children changed as a result of reading this chapter?

2. Why is it important for physical education teachers to understand "The Growing Child"?

3. How might physical education be different for an overweight child as compared to a leaner peer?

4. Should children under nine years old be permitted to play youth sports?

5. Is fitness testing in elementary physical education an appropriate practice? Defend your answer.

Content Review

1. What impact do growth patterns, body physique, and skeletal maturity have on skill acquisition and performance?

2. What is the importance of physical activity for children?

3. What are the influences of muscular development and strength on physical activity for children?

4. Is training designed to improve aerobic capacity appropriate for children? Explain.

5. What can be done to maximize the youth sport experience for all children?

6. What is the relationship between physical activity and intelligence?

7. How do adults and children differ with respect to exercising in the heat? Discuss guidelines for exercising students in the heat.

FOR MORE INFORMATION

References and Suggested Readings

American Academy of Pediatrics. (1990). *Policy statement: Risks in distance running for children,* 86(5). (Reaffirmed January 1994).

American Academy of Pediatrics. (2000). Policy statement: Climatic heat stress and the exercising child and adolescent. *Pediatrics,* 106(1), 158–159.

American Academy of Pediatrics. (2001). Policy statement: Strength training by children and adolescents. *Pediatrics,* 107(6), 1470–1472.

Athletic Footwear Association. (1990). *American youth and sports participation.* North Palm Beach, FL: Author.

Bar-Or, O. (1983). *Pediatric sports medicine for the practitioner.* New York: Springer-Verlag.

Bar-Or, O., & Ward, D. S. (1989). Rating of perceived exertion in children. In O. Bar-Or (Ed.), *Advances in pediatric sport sciences. Vol. III.* Champaign, IL: Human Kinetics.

Beunen, G. (1989). Biological age in pediatric exercise research. In O. Bar-Or (Ed.), *Advances in pediatric sport sciences. Vol. III.* Champaign, IL: Human Kinetics.

Cahill, R. R. (1986). Prepubescent strength training gains support. *The Physician and Sportsmedicine,* 14(2), 157–161.

Clarke, H. H. (1968). Characteristics of the young athlete: A longitudinal look. *Kinesiology Review,* 3, 33–42.

Clarke, H. H. (1971). *Physical motor tests in the Medford boys' growth study.* Englewood Cliffs, NJ: Prentice-Hall.

Corbin, C. B., & Pangrazi, R. P. (1992). Are American children and youth fit? *Research Quarterly for Exercise and Sport,* 63(2), 96–106.

Dubowitz, V. (1970). Differentiation of fiber types in skeletal muscle. In E. J. Briskey, R. G. Cassens, & B. B. Marsh (Eds.), *Physiology and biochemistry of muscle as a food, Vol. 2.* Madison: University of Wisconsin Press.

Duda, M. (1986). Prepubescent strength training gains support. *The Physician and Sportsmedicine,* 14(2), 157–161.

Faigenbaum, A. V. (2003). Youth resistance training. *Research Digest,* Series 4, Number 3. Washington, DC: President's Council on Physical Fitness and Sports.

Gould, D. (1987). Understanding attrition in children's sport. In *Advances in pediatric sport sciences. Vol. 2. Behavioral issues.* Champaign, IL: Human Kinetics.

Gruelich, W., & Pyle, S. (1959). *Radiographic atlas of skeletal development of the hand and wrist.* 2nd ed. Stanford, CA: Stanford University Press.

Hale, C. (1956). Physiological maturity of Little League baseball players. *Research Quarterly,* 27, 276–284.

Harter, S. (1978). Effectance motivation revisited. *Child Development,* 21, 34–64.

International Athletics Association Federation. (1983). Not kid's stuff. *Sports Medicine Bulletin,* 18(1), 11.

Krahenbuhl, G. S., & Pangrazi, R. P. (1983). Characteristics associated with running performance in young boys. *Medicine and Science in Sports,* 15(6), 486–490.

Malina, R. M. (1978). Physical growth and maturity characteristics of young athletes. In R. A. Magill, M. H. Ash, & F. L. Smoll (Eds.), *Children and youth in sport: A contemporary anthology.* Champaign, IL: Human Kinetics.

Malina, R. M. (1980). Growth, strength, and physical performance. In G. A. Stull & T. K. Cureton (Eds.), *Encyclopedia of physical education, fitness, and sports.* Salt Lake City, UT: Brighton.

Malina, R. M., & Bouchard, C. (1991). *Growth, maturation, and physical activity.* Champaign, IL: Human Kinetics.

National Strength and Conditioning Association. (1985). Position paper on prepubescent strength training. *National Strength and Conditioning Association Journal,* 7(4), 27–31.

Ozmun, J. C., Mikesky, A. E., & Surburg, P. R. (1994). Neuromuscular adaptations following prepubescent strength training. *Medicine and Science in Sports and Exercise,* 26(4), 510–514.

Pate, R. R., Dowda, M., & Ross, J. G. (1990). Associations between physical activity and physical fitness in American children. *American Journal of Diseases of Children,* 144, 1123–1129.

Payne, V. G., & Morrow, J. R., Jr. (1993). Exercise and VO$_2$ max in children: A meta-analysis. *Research Quarterly for Exercise and Sport,* 64(3), 305–313.

Petersen, G. (1967). *Atlas for somatotyping children.* The Netherlands: Royal Vangorcum Ltd.

Petlichkoff, L. M. (1992). Youth sport participation and withdrawal: Is it simply a matter of fun? *Pediatric Exercise Science,* 4(2), 105–110.

Rarick, L. G., & Dobbins, D. A. (1975). Basic components in the motor performances of children six to nine years of age. *Medicine and Science in Sports,* 7(2), 105–110.

Roberts, S. O. (with Pillarella, D.). (1996). *Developing strength in children: A comprehensive guide.* Reston, VA: American Alliance for Health, Physical Education, Recreation, and Dance.

Roche, A. F., Chumlea, W. C., & Thissen, D. (1988). *Assessing the skeletal maturity of the hand-wrist: Fels method.* Springfield, IL: Thomas.

Rowland, T. W. (1990). *Exercise and children's health.* Champaign, IL: Human Kinetics.

Rowland, T. W. (1991). Effects of obesity on aerobic fitness in adolescent females. *American Journal of Disease in Children,* 145, 764–768.

Sallis, J. F., & McKenzie, T. L. (1991). Physical education's role in public health. *Research Quarterly of Exercise and Sport,* 62, 124–137.

Saltin, B. (1973). Metabolic fundamentals of exercise. *Medicine and Science of Sports, 5,* 137–146.

Servedio, F. J., Bartels, R. L., Hamlin, R. L., Teske, D., Shaffer, T., & Servedio, A. (1985). The effects of weight training, using Olympic style lifts, on various physiological variables in prepubescent boys [Abstract]. *Medicine and Science in Sports and Exercise, 17,* 288.

Sheldon, W. H., Dupertuis, C. W., & McDermott, E. (1954). *Atlas of men: A guide for somatotyping the adult male at all ages.* New York: Harper & Row.

Shephard, R. J. (1984). Physical activity and child health. *Sports Medicine, 1,* 205–233.

Smoll, F. L., & Smoll, R. E. (1996). *Children and youth in sport.* Dubuque, IA: Brown and Benchmark.

Tanner, S. M. (1993). Weighing the risks: Strength training for children and adolescents. *The Physician and Sportsmedicine, 21*(6), 105–116.

Thomas, J. R., & Tennant, L. K. (1978). Effects of rewards on changes in children's motivation for an athletic task. In F. L. Smoll & R. E. Smoll (Eds.), *Psychological perspectives in youth sports.* New York: Hemisphere.

Weltman, A., Janney, C., Rians, C. B., Strand, K., Berg, B., Tippitt, S., Wise, J., Cahill, B. R., & Katch, F. I. (1986). The effects of hydraulic resistance strength training in pre-pubertal males. *Medicine and Science in Sports and Exercise, 18,* 629–638.

Whitehead, J. R., & Corbin, C. B. (1991). Effects of fitness test type, teacher, and gender on exercise intrinsic motivation and physical self-worth. *Journal of School Health, 61,* 11–16.

Websites

Children and Physical Activity
www.cdc.gov/nccdphp/dash/presphysactrpt/index.htm
www.kidsource.com/kidsource/content4/promote.phyed.html
www.americanheart.org/presenter.jhtml?identifier=4596

Children's Health
www.aap.org/

Fitness Tests
www.cooperinst.org/ftgmain.asp
www.indiana.edu/~preschal

Overweight
www.cdc.gov/nccdphp/dnpa/obesity/index.htm
www.familyhaven.com/health/fitkids.html

The President's Challenge and the Presidential Active Lifestyle Award
www.presidentschallenge.org

Strength Training and Children
www.acsm.org/pdf/YSTRNGTH.pdf

Youth Sports
www.nays.org/
http://kidshealth.org/parent/nutrition_fit/
www.betterbodz.com/kid/myth.html

The Instructional Process

This section is intended to help teachers plan and implement a quality physical education program. Planning is integral to program and instructional success. Planning includes designing effective lessons, incorporating essential elements of instruction, and reflecting on the implementation of planned lessons. Communicating and personalizing lessons to better meet the needs of all students is reviewed in this section. At the top of the list of teachers' concerns is being able to effectively manage and discipline students. An entire chapter focuses on teaching responsible behavior, maintaining desirable behavior, and decreasing undesirable behavior. Developing meaningful class rules and implementing consequences when such rules are not followed are also part of an effective instructional system. Physical education programs have to include children with disabilities, and many ideas for helping students find success regardless of their personal limitations are covered.

After reading this section, you should be able to plan effective lessons, implement a fair and rational discipline system, and communicate with students in personal and group settings.

3

Preparing a Quality Lesson

ESSENTIAL COMPONENTS OF QUALITY PROGRAMS

   I. Organized around content standards

  II. Student-centered and developmentally appropriate

 III. Physical activity and motor skill development form the core of the program

 IV. Teaches management skills and self-discipline

   V. Promotes inclusion of all students

 VI. Focuses on process over product

 VII. Promotes lifetime personal health and wellness

VIII. Teaches cooperation and responsibility and promotes sensitivity to diversity

NATIONAL STANDARDS FOR PHYSICAL EDUCATION

1. Demonstrates competency in motor skills and movement patterns needed to perform a variety of physical activities.

2. **Demonstrates understanding of movement concepts, principles, and tactics as they apply to the learning and performance of physical activities.**

3. Participates regularly in physical activity.

4. Achieves and maintains a health-enhancing level of physical fitness.

5. **Exhibits responsible personal and social behavior that respects self and others in physical activity.**

6. Values physical activity for health, enjoyment, challenge, self-expression, and/or social interaction.

*National Association for Sport and Physical Education (NASPE), 2004.

SUMMARY

Effective teachers are able to use more than one style of teaching and may, in fact, use several styles during a particular lesson. In this chapter, planning strategies associated with quality instruction are described in detail. A number of preinstructional decisions must be made that influence the quality of the lesson. Quality teachers know how to regulate instructional space and how to use formations to maximize learning. Instructors need to understand the influence that developmental patterns, arousal, feedback, and practice have on learning skills. A productive class environment demands consistent monitoring of student performance, an emphasis on safety, and a method for keeping students on-task. A comprehensive lesson plan format is offered to encourage effective planning.

OUTCOMES

- Describe various teaching styles and the best time to use each style to increase student learning.

- Describe the role of planning in preparing for quality instruction.

- Understand the relationships between instruction and the developmental and experiential level of the students.

- List preinstructional decisions that must be made before the actual delivery of the lesson.

- Know the basic mechanical principles required for efficient performance of motor skills.

- Cite effective ways to use equipment, time, space, and formations in the instructional process.

- Understand how to optimize skill learning. Include discussions of developmental patterns, arousal, feedback, practice sessions, and skill progression.

- Understand the rationale for the four components of a lesson and describe characteristics of each.

- Know how to improve the quality of instructional presentations through reflection and critique.

Planning is a critical part of teaching that ensures a quality lesson. Preinstructional decisions, which determine how the lesson will be presented, are discussed here and in Chapter 5. They include choosing a teaching style, using equipment effectively, utilizing class time, arranging for teaching space, and properly employing instructional formations. Planning also involves designing and implementing lesson plans that are both flexible and meaningful. On an average day, teachers must make many unexpected decisions. So, the job can be made much easier if as many decisions as possible are made prior to the actual lesson presentation. Preinstructional decisions are as important as the content of the lesson. Failing to carefully plan this phase of the lesson can diminish the content presentation.

CHOOSE FROM A VARIETY OF TEACHING STYLES

One of the first steps to take when planning for instruction is to decide on the teaching styles that will be most effective for each skill. A teaching style provides direction for presenting information, organizing practice, providing feedback, keeping students engaged in appropriate behavior, and monitoring progress toward goals or objectives. Teaching styles are usually defined in terms of planning and setup of the environment, the instructional approach used, the students' responsibilities during the lesson, and expected student outcomes. Successful instructors are able to incorporate a variety of teaching styles (Harrison, Blakemore, & Buck, 2001; Mosston & Ashworth, 2002; Rink, 2002; Siedentop & Tannehill, 2000).

There is no single "best" or universal teaching style. Even though some educators endorse their favorite approaches, evidence does not suggest that one style is more effective than another. A repertoire of styles that can be used with different objectives, students, activities, facilities, and equipment is the mark of a master teacher. Many variables have to be considered when selecting an appropriate teaching style, including:

1. The objectives of the lesson such as skill development, activity promotion, knowledge, and social behaviors.
2. The activities to be taught such as body management skills, manipulative skills, or rhythmic movement skills.
3. The students, including their individual characteristics, interests, developmental levels, socioeconomic status, motivation, and background.
4. The size of the class.
5. The equipment and facilities available for instruction.
6. The unique abilities, skills, and comfort of the teacher.

The use of a different teaching style in an appropriate setting often improves the environment for students and teachers and increases the effectiveness of the program. A new or modified teaching style is not a panacea for all the ills of every school environment or setting, and a teaching style cannot be selected without considering a number of variables. Teachers can use combinations of styles in a lesson or unit plan; they do not have to adopt just one style at a time. Figure 3.1 shows a continuum of teaching styles based on the degree of control and decision-making exercised by the teacher and students. At one end of the continuum (Direct), the teacher makes instructional decisions exclusively. At the other end (Free exploration), children make the majority of decisions about their learning. Along the continuum there is a gradual shift in decision-making and responsibility for learning.

Direct Style

The direct style is the most teacher-controlled approach. The teacher provides instruction to either the entire class or to small groups and guides the pace and direction of the class. Direct teaching often begins with an explanation and demonstration of skills to be developed. Students are

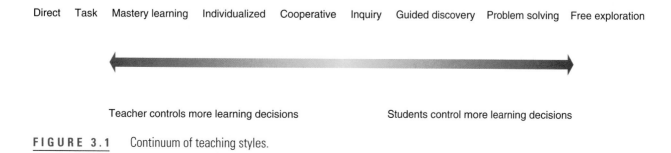

Direct   Task   Mastery learning   Individualized   Cooperative   Inquiry   Guided discovery   Problem solving   Free exploration

Teacher controls more learning decisions   Students control more learning decisions

FIGURE 3.1   Continuum of teaching styles.

organized into partners, small groups, or squads for practice. While students practice, the teacher actively moves around the area correcting errors, praising, encouraging, and asking questions. Independent practice follows and is supervised by an actively involved teacher. Throughout the class, students can be brought together for evaluative comments and instruction, or to focus on another skill. Students spend most of the class time engaged in predetermined subject matter aimed at reaching established goals. Direct instruction makes the teacher the major demonstrator, lecturer, motivator, organizer, disciplinarian, director, and corrector of errors.

The direct teaching style has been disliked by some teachers who identify it with Mosston and Ashworth's (2002) command style in which all actions performed by students are commanded by a teacher signal or demonstration. The direct teaching style has more flexibility and variations than the command style. The direct style, like any other type of instruction, can be effective or ineffective depending on how it is used and administered. The direct style is an effective strategy for teaching physical skills, especially when there is the possibility of an inherent hazard or accident with inexperienced students. The direct teaching format offers organization and close teacher supervision that is useful for activities such as raquet skills, striking skills, and gymnastics. Students are offered little freedom to explore until they understand and demonstrate personal responsibility. The direct style is also useful when discipline is a problem because it places more control in the hands of the teacher. The direct style is useful for beginning teachers with new students, new content preparations, large classes, or difficult-to-manage classes.

The direct teaching style emphasizes creating a controlled class environment that is safe for students. Effective use of the direct style minimizes time children spend passively watching, listening to a lecture-demonstration, or waiting in line. A challenge when using this style is offering activities that meet the needs of all students. Higher-skilled and lower-skilled students may be hindered when learning activities are too easy and unchallenging, or too difficult. This can be avoided, however, by offering learning tasks of varying difficulty.

Task (Station) Style

The task style of teaching involves arranging and presenting learning tasks at several learning areas or stations. Students rotate between learning stations and practice a variety of assigned tasks. Each station contains a number of tasks that students practice with a minimum of teacher direction. For example, students might spend five minutes at stations practicing four or five defined tasks. A cue or signal to rotate to a new station is given after time has elapsed. This style provides more freedom than does the direct approach because students make decisions to practice different tasks.

Using the task style allows teachers to move off center stage and away from being the central figure in the instructional process. Instruction focuses on visiting learning stations and interacting with students who need help. Less time is spent directing and managing the group as a whole. This approach requires more preparation time for planning and designing tasks. Adequate facilities, equipment, and instructional signs are necessary to keep students productive and working on appropriate tasks. The following guidelines are useful when selecting, writing, and presenting tasks:

1. Select tasks that cover the basic skills of an activity.
2. Select tasks that provide students with success and challenge. Create tasks that are developmentally appropriate. The most skilled student should be challenged, and the least skilled student should be successful.
3. Avoid tasks that carry a high safety risk.
4. Tape task cards on the wall, strap them to boundary cones, or place them on the floor. Another alternative is to provide a task sheet for each student to carry station to station and take home for practice after school.
5. Write tasks so they are easy to comprehend. Use teaching cues or phrases that students have learned previously. Effective task descriptions explain what the skill is and how to do it (see the example in Figure 3.2). Periodically check to see if students understand and practice the tasks when unsupervised.
6. Incorporate a combination of instructional equipment that offers feedback and motivation, such as targets, cones, hoops, ropes, and stopwatches.

The task style of instruction can utilize a variety of grouping patterns. Students can work alone, with a partner, or in a small group. The partner or reciprocal grouping pattern is useful with large classes, limited amounts of equipment, and skills where partners can time, count, record, or analyze each other. For example, one partner dribbles through a set of cones while the other is timing and recording. In a group of three students, one student bounces and catches a ball off the wall, another analyzes the form with a checklist, and the third counts and records the number of catches. The social aspect of being able to work on tasks with a partner or friend is a form of cooperative learning discussed later. Arrange learning tasks so students experience success frequently at first and become challenged by later objectives. Objectives can be modified daily or repeated, depending on the progress of the class.

Some teachers are uncomfortable when first using the task style because it implies less order and control compared to direct instruction. With proper planning,

Name_____Class_____Grade _____

Your expected outcome is to master five of the following individual rope-jumping steps. You must be able to complete a minimum of ten consecutive jumps when doing one of the steps. Please ask a friend to approve your performance before asking for instructor approval.

Approved by a friend	Approved by teacher	Skill to be completed
		Side Swing. Swing the rope, held with both hands, to one side of the body. Switch and swing the rope on the other side of the body.
		Double Side Swing and Jump. Swing the rope once on each side of the body. Follow the second swing with a jump over the rope. The sequence should be swing, swing, jump.
		Running in Place. When the rope passes under the feet, shift the weight alternately from one foot to the other, raising the nonsupport foot in a running position.
		Spread Legs Forward and Backward. Start in a stride position with weight equally distributed on both feet. As the rope passes under the feet, jump into the air and reverse the position of the feet.
		Side Straddle Jump. Alternate a regular jump with a straddle jump. The straddle jump is performed with the feet spread to shoulder width.
		Cross Legs Sideways. When the rope passes under the feet, spread the legs in a straddle position (sideways) to take the rebound. As the rope passes under the feet on the next turn, jump into the air and cross the feet with the other foot forward. Then repeat with the other foot forward and continue this alternation.
		Toe-Touch Forward. Swing the right foot forward as the rope passes under the feet and touch the right toes on the next count. Then alternate, landing on the right foot and touching the left toes forward.
		Toe-Touch Backward. Same as the Toe-Touch Forward, but touch the toes of the free foot to the back at the end of the swing.
		Shuffle Step. Push off with the right foot and sidestep to the left as the rope passes under the feet. Land with the weight on the left foot and touch the right toes beside the left heel. Repeat the step in the opposite direction.

FIGURE 3.2   Task card: Advanced individual rope-jumping steps.

organization, and supervision, however, it offers an opportunity for students to practice a variety of tasks. Students often find the task style motivating because of the variety of learning tasks and self-paced learning. If students do not behave in a responsible manner, it may be necessary to practice self-management skills that focus on freedom, flexibility, and opportunities to make decisions.

Mastery Learning (Outcomes-Based) Style

Mastery learning is an instructional strategy that takes a general program outcome and breaks it into smaller parts, providing a progression of skills. These subskills are the focus of learning and are written as tasks that must be mastered before students are allowed to attempt more complex skills. The number of subskills depends on the complexity of the outcome. If mastery is not achieved, corrective activities are offered to help students learn in different ways, such as alternative instructional materials, peer tutoring, or any other learning activity that meets personal preferences. (For an in-depth discussion of mastery learning, see Guskey, 1985.)

The following steps are used to implement the mastery style:

1. The outcome or movement competency is divided into sequenced, progressive units.

2. Necessary (prerequisite) competencies are evaluated.

3. Skill objectives for each of the successive learning units are established.

4. Students informally evaluate themselves to determine whether they are ready for formal testing by the teacher or a peer.

5. When a student is ready for formal evaluation, the teacher (or a peer) determines *pass* or *fail* for a particular outcome. If the performance of the outcome is satisfactory, the youngster moves to the next learning unit.

6. If the evaluation is not satisfactory, practice continues, incorporating alternatives or corrective measures.

The following outline demonstrates how a soccer lesson might be broken down to teach the target outcomes for dribbling, trapping, and kicking using the mastery learning style.

▶ DRIBBLING OUTCOMES

1. Dribble the ball a distance of ten yards, three consecutive times, making each kick travel no more than five yards.

2. Dribble the ball through an obstacle course of six cones over a distance of ten yards in 20 seconds or less.

3. With a partner, pass the ball back and forth five times while running for a distance of 20 yards, two consecutive times.

▶ TRAPPING OUTCOMES

4. When the ball is rolled to you by a partner five yards away, trap it four of five times, using the instep method with the right and then the left foot.

5. Repeat outcome 4 using the sole of the foot.

6. With a partner tossing the ball, trap four of five shots using the chest method.

▶ KICKING OUTCOMES

7. Kick the ball to your partner, who is standing five yards away, five consecutive times with the right and left inside-of-the-foot push pass.

8. Repeat outcome 7 using the instep kick. Loft the ball to your partner.

9. Kick four of five shots that enter the goal in the air from a distance of ten yards.

Mastery learning is useful because students can move at an individualized pace and master preliminary skills needed to reach the outcomes. It offers a continuum of outcomes youngsters can practice in their spare time. For this reason, the style is well suited for students with disabilities or those who are low-skilled. However, because the style requires self-direction on the part of

the students, some students may take longer to acquire the discipline necessary to use this instructional format. Consider the amount of freedom, flexibility, and choice your students can handle and yet be productive. When first introducing students to this style, use it sparingly and take time to teach the importance of self-management skills to students.

A rotational scheme utilizing small groups at learning stations can be implemented within this style. After an adequate amount of time, each group rotates to a new station. Another alternative is to allow students to rotate to any learning area they need to practice. A variety of grouping patterns (individually, with a partner, or with a small group) can be used depending on available facilities, equipment, objectives, and student choice. During the lesson, the teacher or peers can monitor successful completion of objectives. If class size is small, and the number of objectives also is small, it may be possible for a teacher to do all of the monitoring. Otherwise, a combination of procedures is recommended. Student involvement in the monitoring process enhances their understand-

Name: _____

Instructor approved	Peer reviewed	Skill
_____	_____	1. Toss and catch with both hands.
_____	_____	2. Toss and catch with right hand.
_____	_____	3. Toss and catch with left hand.
_____	_____	4. Toss and catch with the back of both hands (create soft home).
_____	_____	5. Toss, do a half turn, and catch with both hands.
_____	_____	6. Toss, do a heel click, and catch with both hands.
_____	_____	7. Place beanbag on foot, kick in the air, and catch.
_____	_____	8. Place beanbag on foot, kick in the air, and catch behind back.
_____	_____	9. Put beanbag between feet, jump up with beanbag, and catch.
_____	_____	10. Toss overhead, move to another spot, and catch.
_____	_____	11. Toss overhead, take three skipping steps, and catch.
_____	_____	12. Toss overhead, lay down, and catch with hands.

FIGURE 3.3 Performance objectives: Manipulative skills using beanbags.

ing of the objectives and shares learning responsibility. Monitors can use a performance chart to check objectives at each learning station or carry a master list from station to station. Another approach is to develop a performance sheet for each student that combines teacher and peer monitoring (Figure 3.3). Peers monitor simple objectives while the teacher monitors more difficult ones. Students can also privately monitor themselves on the performance objectives. Try experimenting with several monitoring approaches depending on the activity, the number of objectives, the students' abilities, the size of the class, and the available equipment and facilities.

Individualized Style

The individualized style is based on the concept of student-centered learning through an individualized curriculum. This style uses a variety of teaching strategies designed to allow students to progress at an individual rate. Each student's needs are diagnosed and a program is prescribed to address those needs. Objectives are stated in behavioral terms. Students are required to learn cognitive factors before moving to psychomotor tasks.

Certain materials and hardware are necessary to establish the learning environment for individualized instruction, such as reference books, wall charts, and cards for recording student progress. Other useful equipment includes slide and overhead projectors, cassette tape recorders, videotape players, screens, and chalkboards. A learning center that includes materials, equipment, and software to direct the learning process can be established. An example of a learning center is shown in Figure 3.4. The individualized style of teaching basically follows five steps:

1. *Diagnosis.* Assessment is made to determine each student's level of cognitive and psychomotor knowledge.

2. *Prescription.* Each student is given a learning package based on his or her current level of knowledge.

3. *Development.* The student works on tasks in the learning package until he or she is able to perform them. Self-testing goals are offered, and the student decides whether to proceed to final evaluation.

4. *Evaluation.* The student goes to the teacher for final evaluation. Both psychomotor and cognitive progress are evaluated at this point.

5. *Reinforcement.* If a student completes the tasks successfully, the teacher gives positive reinforcement, records the data on the student's progress chart, and prescribes a new learning package based on the student's needs. If the student does not perform the task successfully, possible alternatives for reaching the objective are offered. The evaluation process offers an opportunity to counsel each student and reinforce critical points.

Learning packages form the core of the individualized style. The learning package is a student contract that provides an inventory of skills students need to accomplish in a meaningful sequence. The learning package consists of the following parts:

1. The content classification statement describes the task or concept to be learned. This could be a psychomotor task (such as demonstrating the cartwheel) or a cognitive task (such as learning how to absorb force).

2. The purpose section explains what the package will do for the learner (for example, "This contract

FIGURE 3.4   Organization of a learning center.

provides you with activities that will enable you to perform a cartwheel").

3. The learning objectives identify what is to be learned, under what conditions the learning will take place, and how the student will perform when learning has occurred.

4. The diagnostic test (pretest) determines the student's knowledge and skill level. The student is given a cognitive test as well as psychomotor tasks to perform for assessment.

5. The learning activities section offers different ways to learn a skill, concept, or activity. In each contract, different choices should be available. Students can select any of the strategies to enhance learning. The following are examples of learning strategies: viewing and analyzing transparencies, listening to audiotapes for instruction in cognitive tasks, reading books that describe the task (referenced in advance by the instructor), viewing videotapes that offer demonstration and explanation of a skill to be performed, or studying charts that break down a skill into components. Students can ask other students who have successfully completed the activity to help them practice.

6. The self-test phase helps students decide whether they are ready for an evaluation given by the teacher. Students can ask their peers to evaluate whether they are ready for the final test.

7. The final evaluation is an observable measure of the student's achievement. The teacher judges psychomotor achievements, and cognitive learning is measured by a written exam.

The individualized style allows students to control the rate of learning and to receive personalized feedback about progress. Teacher control is dictated by the design of learning packages and the size of learning increments. Students are encouraged to investigate different approaches to learning through written material, various audiovisual media, and contacts with peers. Examining the learning process itself is a valuable experience that students can use later to learn new activities or skills. Individualized instruction is an effective style to use for some of the following reasons:

- Students, parents, and administrators know exactly what is expected and accomplished by students.

- Self-direction enhances the motivational level of most students.

- Students at most competency levels find success and challenge with objectives.

- Students progress through the objectives at their own rate.

- Students choose and sequence learning activities.

- Students have some choice concerning the grouping arrangement of skill practice (such as alone, with a partner, or in a small group).

- Students accept a greater degree of responsibility for learning.

- Teachers have greater freedom to give individual attention and offer feedback.

Despite its many advantages, the individualized style of instruction also has its problems. Most notably, the preparation for this style can be time-consuming; a teacher must develop performance objectives for each student and revise them accordingly over the course of the class. In addition, the teacher must develop an efficient system for monitoring student progress. Finally, incorporating the individualized style of instruction requires an adjustment period for teachers and students, who are usually more used to—and more comfortable with—the direct approach.

Cooperative Learning (Reciprocal) Style

When students compete against each other for a grade or another measure of success, they strive for a goal that only a few students can achieve. In competitive situations, students perceive that they can reach their goals only if other students in the class fail (Johnson & Johnson, 2003). Cooperative learning is a style that focuses on the importance of people working together to accomplish common goals. In cooperative learning, students are assigned to groups where each member works to reach common goals. In cooperative activities, individuals seek outcomes that are beneficial to themselves and to the group. A resource for cooperative learning is the text by Johnson, Johnson, and Holubec, *Circles of Learning: Cooperation in the Classroom* (1990). Reciprocal teaching (Mosston & Ashworth, 2002) is another form of cooperative learning.

A strong research base (Slavin, 1990) suggests that cooperative learning helps foster constructive relationships among students. Emphasis is placed on joint rather than individual outcomes, and peers are given the opportunity to work with each other regularly. Because students are expected to foster the success of their peers rather than wish for their failure, this style has the potential to enhance the social and psychological growth of students.

When using this style, learners are assigned a project or goal to complete as a team. Youngsters are grouped heterogeneously (that is, by mixing race, ability, or socioeconomic level) so there is diversity within the cooperative unit. Usually, there are two to five students in each group. They work through the assignment until all group members understand and complete it. The very nature of cooperative learning helps students realize that they cannot achieve the goal alone, that success occurs only when all members of the group reach the goal. The accomplishments of a group are successful if the outcomes are meaningful and cooperation and participation by all group members have occurred. A number of roles can be assigned to group members, including:

- A performer, who does the skills or tasks.
- A recorder, who keeps track of statistics, trials, or key points made by the group.
- A coach, who provides skill feedback to the performer or times practice trials.
- A presenter, who communicates key points to the rest of the class.
- A motivator, who encourages and provides general and positive feedback to all group members.

Cooperative learning is most successful when students switch roles often and stated group tasks proceed from simple to complex. Teachers need to monitor the groups to ensure all members contribute, but the responsibility for success truly lies with the students' ability to cooperate. Selected activities should require the knowledge and efforts of all members of the group. If students feel cooperation is not necessary to complete the task, the style is not effective. It must be clear that all members of the team are needed, even if in varying amounts of involvement. The tasks can be cognitive or psychomotor skills. The following are examples of class activities that could be used with the cooperative learning style:

- Design a fitness routine that requires each member of the group to design one or two exercises for inclusion. The overall routine must show balance (exercise all body parts) and be appropriate for the entire group.
- Modify a sport or game to make it more inclusive. The goal is to redesign the game so all students can play successfully.
- Have each member of the group design a drill that enhances skill learning and ensures that all members of the group improve. The drills must be cohesive and focus on a single skill to be learned (throwing, rope-jumping, etc.).
- Break down a folk dance into various parts so that it is easier to learn. Each member of the group is responsible for teaching one of the parts. The group must determine how the parts will be put together (taught to the rest of the class).

Inquiry Style

The inquiry style of teaching is process-oriented rather than product-oriented, thereby placing greater impor-

tance on the learning process than on the final product or outcome. During this type of instruction, students are cognitively active as they experience learning situations that require them to inquire, speculate, reflect, analyze, and discover.

The teacher, on the other hand, plays the role of guiding and directing students, rather than commanding or telling. Students are challenged to discover their own answers and solutions. The teacher assumes responsibility for stimulating student curiosity about the subject matter. A combination of questions, problems, examples, and learning activities leads students toward one or more final solutions. This process follows a consistent and logical sequence so that students can move from one step to the next after a certain amount of thinking. It may be necessary to modify questions and learning activities if students become frustrated or bored. The instructional environment is one of open communication where students feel comfortable experimenting and inquiring without fear of failure.

Advocates of inquiry methods of instruction feel this style should have a more prominent place in educational methodology—including in physical education—fearing that too many of today's approaches only emphasize listening, absorbing, and complying (Mosston & Ashworth, 2002). Proponents of this style believe it enhances students' ability to think, improves creativity, creates a better understanding of the subject matter, enhances individual self-concept, and develops lifelong learning patterns. Some educators argue that students who do not experience inquiry methods are dormant, unchallenged, and unused, but little evidence is available to support such claims.

Critics of the inquiry method, however, point out some problems with the approach: Too much time is spent on one subject or topic; a focus is on trivial or nonessential learning; most motor skills have a best way to be performed that should be quickly explained; students already know the answers; and the instruction is difficult to plan because each class has a wide range of knowledge and ability.

Regardless of the pros and cons, there is little doubt that students need to be involved to a greater degree in the learning process. Guided discovery and problem solving are two types of inquiry that give the learner more control over the direction and content of the learning process. These styles are effective when the goal is to immerse students in the process of uncovering new and better methods for performing motor skills.

Guided Discovery (Convergent) Style

Guided discovery is used when there is a predetermined choice or result that the teacher wants students to discover. Consider teaching the concept of opposition (Example: A right-handed thrower should place the feet in a stride position with the left foot forward). Using guided discovery, students are given different foot patterns for experimentation, with the goal of selecting the best pattern. They practice right-handed throwing with the following limitations: feet together, feet in a straddle position, feet in a stride position with the left foot forward, and feet in a stride position with the right foot forward. After practicing the four different foot positions, students choose the position that seems best in terms of throwing potential.

Guided discovery is effective when the teacher is interested in having children discover the most suitable movement response when developing a new skill. This allows youngsters to try different ways of accomplishing the task and helps them learn why some solutions work better than others. The following are examples of skill techniques that can be explored to discover the best solutions:

1. Placement of the hands when catching.
2. Angles of release for distance throwing with different implements such as the shot put, discus, football, and softball.
3. Batting stance and foot pattern alterations for hitting the baseball or softball to various fields.
4. Ready position for sport skills.
5. Stopping and starting quickly.
6. The best place to enter in long rope-jumping skills.
7. The role of a person's center of gravity and momentum in performing activities in gymnastics such as the forward roll.

Problem-Solving (Divergent) Style

The problem-solving style involves input, reflection, choice, and response. The problem is structured so that there is no one prescribed answer. When there is just one answer, problem solving becomes guided discovery. Problems selected vary from simple ones for primary-level children to more complex problems for intermediate-level children. A simple problem might be expressed as, "What are the different ways you can bounce a ball and stay in your personal space?" Emphasis may or may not be placed on a best way. A more complex problem involving deeper thought might be, "What is the most effective way to position and move your feet while guarding an opponent in basketball?" The solution could use an individual, partner, or group approach. The following are steps to problem solving:

- *Present the problem.* Present students with a problem in the form of a question or statement that provokes thought and reflection. No demonstration or explanation of appropriate responses is given, because students generate solutions.

- *Determine procedures.* Ask students to think about the procedures necessary for arriving at a solution. With younger children, problems are simple and this phase is minimal. It is important, however, because assessment of how to proceed toward a solution has cognitive value.

- *Experiment and explore.* In experimentation, have students try different solutions, evaluate them, and make a choice. In exploration, the goal is to seek breadth of activity. Self-direction is important, and the teacher acts in an advisory role—answering questions, helping, commenting, and encouraging, but not providing solutions.

- *Observe, evaluate, and discuss.* Give all children the opportunity to offer a solution and to observe what others have discovered. Have students use various kinds of achievement demonstrations—by individuals, by small groups, by squads, or by part of the class. Discussion centers on justifying a particular solution.

- *Refine and expand.* After having the students observe solutions that others have selected and evaluate the reasoning behind the chosen solutions, give all children the opportunity to rework their movement patterns, incorporating ideas from others.

Children learn that problems can be solved and that they are able to find solutions. To do so, they must be equipped with techniques to proceed under self-direction toward a sound solution.

Problem solving works best when teaching concepts, relationships, strategies, and proper use of skills for specific solutions. One of the more difficult procedures in the problem-solving style, however, is designing problems that students have not previously solved. On the surface, this sounds simple, but a student who knows the answer or secures the solution ahead of time may pass it on to the rest of the class, and the process of exploring and solving will be lost.

Free-Exploration Style

Free exploration is the most child-centered style of learning. Guidance by the teacher in the free-exploration style is limited to the selection of the instructional materials to be used and the designation of the area to be explored. Two directives might be: "Today, for the first part of the period, you may select any piece of equipment and see what you can do with it," or "Get a jump rope and try creating a new activity." No limits are imposed on children except those dictated by safety. If necessary, forewarn or remind students how to use equipment safely. This style is used effectively to introduce new equipment, concepts, and ideas to children so they generate new ideas and responses. It often works best with young children who are experiencing activities and situations for the first time.

With free exploration, the teacher should avoid demonstrations and praising certain results too early because these can lead to imitative and noncreative behavior. This does not mean, however, that the teacher remains uninvolved. The teacher should move among students—encouraging, clarifying, and answering questions individually. Concentrate on motivating effort, since the student is responsible for being a self-directed learner. It is wise to offer students the opportunity for self-direction in small doses, increasing the time as they become more disciplined. Exploratory opportunities should be offered frequently because this phase of learning takes advantage of the child's love of movement experimentation and allows the free exercise of natural curiosity. Self-discovery is a necessary and important part of learning, and students should have this concept reinforced by experiencing the joy of creativity.

OPTIMIZE SKILL LEARNING

Helping students effectively learn motor skills requires that teachers understand a few basic principles of motor learning. Teaching motor skills is not a difficult task when teachers understand the basic tenets of proper performance techniques.

Understand Developmental Patterns

The learning and development of motor skills varies among children of similar chronological age. However, the *sequence* of skill development in youngsters is similar and progresses in an orderly fashion. Three development patterns typify the growth of primary-grade children:

1. Development, in general, proceeds from head to foot (cephalocaudal); that is, coordination and management of body parts occur in the upper body before they are observed in the lower. For example, children develop throwing skills before kicking competency.

2. Development occurs from inside to outside (proximodistal). Children control their arms before they control their hands. They can reach for objects before they can grasp them.

3. Development proceeds from general to specific. Gross motor movements are learned before fine motor coordination and refined movement patterns. As children learn motor skills, nonproductive movement is gradually eliminated. When learners begin to eliminate wasteful and tense movements and are able to concentrate on repro-

ducing a smooth and consistent performance, motor learning is occurring.

Know the Effect of Arousal

Arousal is the level of excitement that stress produces (Schmidt & Wrisberg, 2004). The level of arousal can have a positive or negative impact on motor performance. The key to proper arousal is to find the "just right" amount. With too little arousal, a youngster will be uninterested in learning. Too much arousal will fill a youngster with stress and anxiety, resulting in a decrease in motor performance. The more complex a skill, the more likely it is that arousal may disrupt learning. On the other hand, if a skill is simple, such as skipping or running, a greater amount of arousal can be tolerated without causing a reduction in skill performance. Optimally, youngsters should be aroused to a level at which they are excited and confident about participation.

Competition affects the arousal level of children. When competition is introduced in the early stages of skill learning, stress and anxiety reduce a child's ability to learn. On the other hand, if competition is introduced after a skill has been overlearned, it can improve the level of performance. Since most elementary school youngsters have not overlearned skills, teachers should avoid competitive situations when teaching skills. For example, assume the objective is to practice basketball dribbling. The teacher places youngsters in squads and runs a relay requiring that they dribble to the opposite end of the gym and return. The first squad finished is the winner. The result: Instead of concentrating on dribbling form, students are more concerned about winning the relay. They are overaroused and determined to run as quickly as possible. Dribbling is done poorly (if at all), the balls fly out of control, and the teacher is dismayed by the result. Unfortunately, competitiveness overaroused the youngsters, who had not yet overlearned dribbling.

Offer Meaningful Skill Feedback

Feedback is important in the teaching process because it impacts what is to be learned, what should be avoided, and how the performance can be modified. Skill feedback is any kind of information about a movement performance. There are two types of skill feedback, intrinsic and extrinsic. *Intrinsic feedback* is internal, inherent to the performance of the skill, and travels through the senses such as vision, hearing, touch, and smell. *Extrinsic feedback* is external and comes from an outside source such as a teacher, a videotape, a stopwatch, and so on. Skill feedback should be encouraging (or constructive), given frequently, delivered publicly so all students benefit, and contingent on performance or (preferably) effort.

KNOWLEDGE OF RESULTS

Knowledge of results is extrinsic feedback given after a skill has been performed. It is a requisite for learning new motor skills and is usually verbal information about performance. Knowledge of results provides information about an incorrect or unsuccessful performance. Learners need feedback about performance errors so they can adjust the practice trials that follow. This type of feedback need not be negative, but rather a statement of fact telling whether the skill performance resulted in a successful outcome.

Knowledge of results originates externally from a teacher, peer, or other source. It is an external variable most often controlled by the teacher to stimulate effective skill performance. Knowledge of results is critical in the early stages of learning motor skills. After performers start to master a skill, they can self-analyze their performance and develop a personal system of internal feedback rather than depend on knowledge of results.

KNOWLEDGE OF PERFORMANCE

This feedback is similar to knowledge of results in that it is verbal and extrinsic in nature and occurs after the performance. Knowledge of results focuses on the outcome of a skill, whereas knowledge of performance relates to the process of the skill performance. When using this type of feedback, refer to specific components of the learner's performance. For example, "I like the way you kept your chin on your chest," or "That's the way to step toward the target with your left foot."

Knowledge of performance can increase a youngster's level of motivation because it provides feedback about improvement. Many youngsters become frustrated because they find it difficult to discern improvement. Feedback provides a lift and a rededication to continued practice. Knowledge of performance is a strong reinforcer, particularly when an instructor mentions something performed correctly. This feedback motivates youngsters to repeat the same pattern, ultimately resulting in improved performance. The most important aspect of this feedback is that it provides information for future patterns of action.

Make performance feedback short, content-filled, and concise. It should tell the youngster exactly what was correct or incorrect (for example, "That was excellent body rotation"). Concentrate on one key point to avoid confusing the youngster. Imagine a young student who is told, "Step with the left foot, rotate the trunk, lead with the elbow, and snap the wrist on your next throw!" Such excessive feedback would confuse anyone trying to learn a new skill.

If choosing between knowledge of results and knowledge of performance, focus on knowledge of performance. Knowledge of results relies solely on the performance outcome and doesn't consider whether the skill was performed correctly. A youngster who manages to throw a ball into a basket might believe that the skill performance was performed correctly even though the technical points of the throw were performed incorrectly. The goal of elementary school physical education is to teach skills correctly, with less emphasis placed on the outcome of the skill performance. In contrast, strong emphasis is placed on product (performance) rather than on process (technique) when youngsters choose to enter the competitive world of athletics.

A final point about knowledge of performance: Allow time for youngsters to internalize the feedback. Often, teachers tell a youngster something and at the same time ask them to "try it again." It is possible that the same mistake will be repeated because the youngster did not have time to concentrate on the feedback. Offer knowledge of performance feedback and move to another youngster. Follow up on your feedback at a later time. This allows the child a chance to relax, internalize the feedback, and modify future practice attempts.

Design Effective Practice Sessions

Practice is a key part of learning motor skills. It is not enough that students receive the opportunity to practice; they must practice with emphasis on quality of movement (practicing correctly). This section explains how to design practice sessions that optimize motor skill learning.

FOCUS PRACTICE ON PROCESS

The emphasis of practice often goes in two sometimes conflicting directions—product or process. Product- or performance-based practice has the teacher asking students to do the best they can and then reinforcing those who reach the desired outcome (product). Process-based practice, however, has the teacher encouraging students to learn the skill correctly without concern for the outcome. This leads to a product-process conflict. Students who think the teacher is interested in the product will be less willing to concentrate on proper technique. Focus practice on learning a skill correctly by placing emphasis on technique and by encouraging experimentation. Emphasis on the outcome decreases a student's willingness to take risks and to learn new ways of performing a skill.

A way to minimize this conflict is to make sure students know the focus of the practice session. In most cases, it is best for elementary school children to focus on technique since they are learning new motor patterns. Excessive pressure to perform without mistakes can stifle students' willingness to try (especially less gifted children). If it is necessary to evaluate a skill outcome, the teacher should tell students why the outcome is important and say that "we will practice doing our best today."

USE MENTAL PRACTICE TECHNIQUES

Mental practice involves practicing a motor skill in a quiet, relaxed environment. The experience involves thinking about the activity and its related sounds, colors, and other sensations. Students visualize themselves doing the activity successfully and at regular speed. Images of failure should be avoided (Schmidt & Wrisberg, 2004). Mental practice stimulates children to think about and review the activity they are to perform. Some experience or familiarity with the motor task is requisite before the performer can derive value from mental practice. Mental practice is used in combination with regular practice, not in place of it. Before having students perform the task, prompt them to mentally review the critical factors and sequencing of the act.

DECIDE ON WHOLE VERSUS PART PRACTICE

Skills can be taught by the whole or part method. The whole method refers to the process of learning the entire skill or activity in one dose. The part method breaks down a skill into a series of parts and then combines the parts into the whole skill. For example, in a rhythmic activity, each section of a dance is taught and then put together. A simple gymnastics routine might be broken into component parts and put back together for the performance.

Whether to use the whole or part method depends on the complexity and organization of the skills to be learned. Complexity refers to the number of serial skills or components there are in a task. Organization defines how the parts are related to each other. High organization means the parts of the skill are closely related to each other, making separation difficult. An example of a highly organized and complex skill is throwing, which would be difficult to practice without going through the complete motion. A low-organized skill is a simple folk dance, in which footwork and arm movements can be rehearsed separately. Generally, if the skills are high in complexity but low in organization, they can be taught in parts. If complexity is low but organization high, the skills must be taught as a whole. A final consideration is the duration of the skill. If the skill is of short duration, such as throwing, batting, or kicking, trying to teach the skill in parts is probably counterproductive. Imagine trying to slow down kicking in order to teach it part by part. The performer would not develop proper pattern and timing.

When skill components are learned separately, students have to learn how to put the parts together. Practice time should be allowed for sequencing. For example, in a gymnastics routine, students might perform the activities separately, but find difficulty sequencing them because they have not learned how to modify each activity based on the previous one. Teaching a skill in parts is best used when it optimizes learning.

DETERMINE THE LENGTH AND DISTRIBUTION OF PRACTICE SESSIONS

Short practice sessions usually produce more efficient learning than do longer sessions. This is due to both physical and mental fatigue (boredom). The challenge is to try to offer as many repetitions as possible within short practice sessions. Use varied approaches, challenges, and activities to develop the same skill in order to maintain motivational levels. For example, using many different types of beanbag activities helps maintain motivation but still focuses on tossing and catching skills.

Another way to determine the length of practice sessions is to examine the tasks being practiced. If a skill causes physical fatigue, demands intense concentration, or has the potential to become tedious, practice sessions should be short and frequent, with an adequate rest between intervals. Stop practice when youngsters become bored or tired, and play a game until they regain their enthusiasm to learn.

Practice sessions that are spread out over many days are usually more effective than sessions crowded into a short time span. The combination of practice and review is effective for youngsters because activities can be taught in a short unit and practiced in review sessions throughout the year. In the initial stages of skill learning, it is particularly important that practice sessions be distributed in this way. Later, when success in skill performance increases motivational levels, individual practice sessions can be lengthened.

USE RANDOM PRACTICE TECHNIQUES

There are two ways to organize the presentation of activities to be taught. The first is *blocked practice*, where all the trials of one task are completed before moving on to the next task. Since blocked practice is effective during the first stages of skill practice, learners find rapid improvement because they are practicing the same skill over and over. As a result, learners are often motivated to continue practicing. A drawback to blocked practice is that it makes learners believe they are more skilled than they actually are. When the skill is applied in a natural setting, performance level lowers, causing some youngsters to feel discouraged.

The other method is *random practice*, where the order of multiple task presentations is mixed and no task is practiced twice in succession. Goode and Magill (1986) showed that random practice was the most effective approach to use when learning skills. Blocked practice gave the best results during the acquisition phase of skill learning; however, students who learned a skill using random practice demonstrated a much higher level of retention.

Random practice results in better retention because the students are mentally generating solutions. When the same task is practiced over and over, youngsters not only become bored, but they also don't think about how to solve the problem. Since the same motor program is used over and over to complete the task, little effort or thinking is required. In contrast, students using random practice forget the motor program used and have to consciously re-create the solution to be successful. Because youngsters become bored quickly when doing the same task over and over, random practice helps minimize this side effect.

OFFER VARIABLE PRACTICE EXPERIENCES

Motor tasks are usually grouped into classes of tasks. For example, throwing is a collection of a class of movements. Throwing a ball in a sport can be performed in many different ways; the ball can travel at different speeds, different trajectories, and varying distances. Even though throwing tasks are all different, the variations have fundamental similarities. Movements in a class usually involve the same body parts and have similar rhythm but can be performed with many variations. These differences create the need for variable practice in a variable setting.

Practice sessions should include a variety of skills in a movement class with a variety of situations and parameters in which the skill is performed. If a skill to be learned involves one fixed way of performing it (a "closed" skill), such as placekicking a football or striking a ball off a batting tee, variability is much less important. However, most skills are "open," and responses are somewhat unpredictable, which makes variability in practice the usual mode of operation (catching or batting a ball moving at different speeds and from different angles). Motor skills should be practiced under a variety of conditions so students can respond to a wide variety of novel situations.

Teach Skills in Proper Progression

Skill progression involves moving the learning process through ordered steps from the least challenging to the most challenging facets of an activity. Most motor skills can be ordered in an approximate hierarchy from simple to complex. Instructional progression includes reviewing previously learned steps before proceeding to new material and learning prerequisite skills before trying more difficult activities.

DEVELOPMENTAL LEVELS AND PROGRESSION

Children learn skills in a natural progression, but not at the same rate. Encourage youngsters to progress at a rate that is best suited for them. This usually means that all children will be learning a similar class of skills (throwing or striking, for instance) but will progress at different rates and practice different skills within the category. This premise forms the basis for presenting a "developmentally appropriate physical education program" (Barrett, Williams, & Whitall, 1992).

Placing activities into developmental levels makes it easier to present activities that are appropriate to the maturity and developmental level of students. Understand that placing activities in levels serves as a general guideline for instruction. Some youngsters may be gifted or in need of special instruction. In that case, present activities that best suit the individual regardless of the recommended level. Since schools group children by chronological age and grade rather than by developmental level, Table 3.1 shows how developmental levels roughly equate with grades and ages. To help plan lessons in which skills are presented in proper sequence, activities in Chapters 15–30 have been placed in order of difficulty, from beginning to advanced. For instructional and lesson planning purposes, the accompanying lesson plan book *Dynamic Physical Education Curriculum Guide: Lesson Plans for Implementation* (Pangrazi, 2007) places the activities into developmental level lesson plans.

Developmental Level I activities (used most often with kindergarten through second-grade children) are the least difficult and form the foundation for more complex skills. Most of these skills are performed individually or with a partner so as to increase the success of primary-grade children. Examples are tossing and catching, striking a stationary object, and playing games that simply incorporate fundamental locomotor movements. The number of complex decisions to make while performing the skill is minimized so youngsters can concentrate on the skill at hand. As youngsters mature and progress into *Developmental Level II* (usually grades 3–4), the tasks be-

TABLE 3.1	Equating developmental levels to grades and ages	
Developmental Level	**Grades**	**Ages**
I	K–2	5–7
II	3–4	8–9
III	5–6	10–11

Level	Typical Grades	Level of Difficulty	Individual or Group?	Examples and Characteristics
I	K–2	Least difficult; foundation for more complex skills; much concentration required to perform skills	Mostly individual; sometimes with a partner	Tossing and catching; striking a stationary object; games that incorporate basic locomotor skills
II	3–4	More difficult; skills are performed in a more consistent manner; less concentration required	Often individual or in small groups; groups and teams introduced	Specialized skills and variation in environmental factors (e.g., speeds and size of objects)
III	5–6	Advanced individual and specialized skills and activities; skills often performed automatically without thinking; students able to perform well in group activities	Emphasis on playing with others and utilizing skills in cooperative and competitive settings	Sport and game situations; cognitive decisions and strategies are involved; more emphasis on manipulative activity, less on movement concept activities

TABLE 3.2   Characteristics of activities for Developmental Levels I, II, and III

3

come more difficult and many are performed individually or within small groups. Environmental factors such as different speeds of objects, different sizes of objects, and games requiring locomotor movements and specialized skills (throwing, catching, and so on) are introduced at this level. In *Developmental Level III* (grades 5–6), students use skills in a number of sport and game situations. Simple skills previously learned are sequenced into more complex motor patterns. Cognitive decisions about when to use a skill and how to incorporate strategy into the game are integrated into the learning experiences at this level. See Table 3.2 for a quick comparison of typical activities for the three developmental levels. The placement of activities into developmental levels is a general rule of thumb. **There will always be exceptions.** Expect to make exceptions to meet the developmental needs of students.

INTEGRATE MECHANICAL PRINCIPLES INTO INSTRUCTION

When planning for skill instruction, mechanical principles need to be considered an integral part of skill performance. It is best to teach young children the proper way to perform a skill so that they won't have to unlearn incorrect motor patterns later. Many teachers have experienced the difficulty of changing a performer's motor patterns after a skill has been learned incorrectly. Stability, force, leverage, motion, and direction are concepts that are best learned when they accompany a skill being taught. A discussion of each is covered in the following sections.

Stability

Stability reflects balance and equilibrium, which affect the performance of many sport skills. A stable base is necessary when one applies force to a projectile or absorbs force. Instability is useful in some activities, such as when a rapid start is desired. Introduce the following concepts:

1. The size of the base of support needs to be increased for greater stability. The base must be widened in the direction of the force being applied or absorbed.

2. The body's center of gravity must be moved lower, or closer to the base of support, when stopping quickly or applying/absorbing force (as when pushing/pulling). Lowering the center of gravity is accomplished by bending the knees and hips (Figure 3.5).

3. The center of gravity should be kept over the base of support (within the boundaries of the base) for

FIGURE 3.5   Lowering the center of gravity while pulling.

FIGURE 3.6   Ready position.

stability and balance. When the center of gravity passes beyond the boundaries of the base of support, balance is lost. In most activities, students should keep the head up and eliminate excessive body lean. The ready position (Figure 3.6) is an example of a stable position used in many sport activities.

4. "Free" or non-weight-bearing limbs should be used as counterbalances to aid stability. The ready position and fast starts are used in many physical activity settings and illustrate how stability and instability (used in fast starts) can enhance performance.

Force

Force is a measure of the push or pull that one object or body applies to another. Force is necessary to move objects of various types and sizes. The larger the object to be moved, the greater the amount of force required to cause the movement. Generating large forces usually requires the involvement of large muscle groups and a greater number of muscles than does the generation of a smaller force. Torque is the twisting or turning effect that force produces when it acts eccentrically with re-

spect to a body's axis of rotation. Concepts to remember when teaching children include the following:

1. When resisting or applying force, the bones on either side of the major joints should form a right angle to each other. A muscle is most effective at causing rotation when it pulls at a 90-degree angle.

2. To generate greater force, body parts are activated in a smooth, coordinated manner. For example, in throwing, the hips and trunk are rotated first and followed in sequence by the upper arm, lower arm, hand, and fingers.

3. More force is generated when more muscles are used. Muscles are capable of generating high levels of force when the contraction speed is low. For example, lifting a very heavy object rapidly is impossible.

4. Force should be absorbed over a large surface area and over as long a period of time as possible. An example of absorbing force over a large surface area is a softball player rolling after a dive through the air to catch a ball. The roll absorbs the force with the hands and the large surface area of the body.

5. The follow-through in striking and throwing activities is necessary to ensure maximum application of force and gradual reduction of momentum. An example is the continued swing of the baseball bat after striking the ball.

Leverage and Motion

Body levers amplify force into motion. Levers offer a mechanical advantage so that less effort is needed to accomplish tasks. Motion occurs after force has been applied or when force is absorbed. A simple lever is a bar or other rigid structure that can rotate about a fixed point to overcome a resistance when force is applied. Levers serve one of two functions: (a) They allow resistance greater than the applied force to be overcome, or (b) they serve to increase the distance or the speed at which resistance can be moved. The following are characteristics of levers and the effects they have on movement:

1. The three types of levers in the body are first-, second-, and third-class levers (Figure 3.7). Most of the body's levers are third-class levers; they have the point of force (produced by the muscles) between the fulcrum (the joint) and the point of resistance (produced by the weight of the object to be moved).

2. Most of the levers in the body are used to gain a mechanical advantage for speed, not to accomplish heavy tasks.

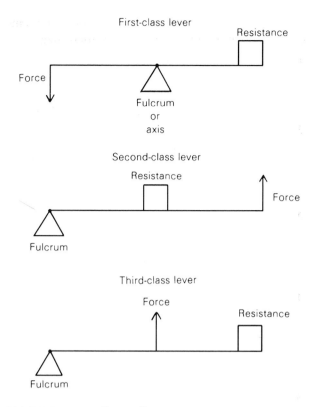

First-class lever

Resistance

Force

Fulcrum
or
axis

Second-class lever

Resistance

Force

Fulcrum

Third-class lever

Force

Resistance

Fulcrum

FIGURE 3.7   Types of levers.

3. A longer force arm (distance from joint to point of force application) allows greater resistance to be overcome (Figure 3.8). This concept is useful when manipulating an external lever. For example, to pry open a paint can, force is applied to the screwdriver away from the rim rather than near the paint can. This allows the screwdriver to act as a longer lever.

4. A longer resistance arm (distance from joint to point of resistance) allows greater speed to be generated (Figure 3.9). Raquets and bats are extensions of the arm; that is, they offer longer resistance arms for applying greater speed. The longer the raquet or bat, therefore, the greater the speed generated. Longer levers are more difficult to rotate, which is why young baseball players are encouraged to choke up to make the bat easier to

Force

Resistance

Force arm

Fulcrum

FIGURE 3.8   Longer force arm.

Force

Resistance arm

Resistance

Fulcrum

FIGURE 3.9   Longer resistance arm.

swing and control. Even though the lever is shortened, bat velocity (at point of contact with the ball) is probably not much reduced. The important result is that performance improves through increased quality contacts.

Motion and Direction

The majority of skills in physical activities are associated with propelling an object. The following concepts of motion and direction are basic to throwing, striking, and kicking skills learned in physical education:

1. The angle of release determines how far an object will travel. Theoretically, the optimum angle of release is 45 degrees. The human body has various limitations, however, that cause the optimum angle of projection to be well below 45 degrees. For example, the angle of projection for the shot put is 40 to 41 degrees; for the running long jump, it is 20 to 22 degrees.

2. A ball rebounds from the floor or from the racket at the same angle at which it is hit. However, various factors such as rotation applied to the ball, the type of ball, and the surface contacted by the ball can modify the rebound angle.

3. In most throwing situations, the propelled object should be released at a point tangent to the target. During throwing, for example, the arm travels in an arc, and the ball must be released when the hand is in line with the target.

CONSIDER THE LEARNING ENVIRONMENT

The environment where youngsters experience physical education can have an impact on the effectiveness of instruction and learning. Factors such as space, equipment, and safety are important in the process of planning a quality experience. Environmental factors can be controlled entirely by the teacher, in contrast to student response and interest. There is little excuse for not considering and planning for these variables.

Predetermine Your Space Needs

A common error is to take a class to a large practice area, give students a task to accomplish, and fail to define or limit the space in which it should be performed. The class spreads out in an area so large it is impossible to communicate and manage the class. The skills being practiced and the ability of the teacher to control the class dictate the size of the space. Delineating a small area for participation makes it easier to control a class because students can see and hear better. As students become more responsive, the size of the area can be enlarged. Regardless of the size of the space, delineate the practice area. An easy way is to set up cones around the perimeter of the area. Chalk lines, evenly spaced equipment, or natural boundaries can also serve as restraining lines. A factor affecting the size of the practice area is the amount of instruction needed. When students are learning a closed skill and need constant feedback and redirection, it is important for them to stay near the instructor. Establish a smaller area where students can move in closer for instruction, and then return to the larger area for practice.

Available space is often divided into smaller areas to maximize student participation. An example is a volleyball game where only ten students can play on one available court. In most cases, it is more effective to divide the area into two courts to facilitate a greater number of students. A related consideration when partitioning space is safety. If the playing areas are too close together, players from one area might run into players in the other area. A softball setting is unsafe if a player on one field can hit a ball into another play area.

Use Equipment Efficiently

Equipment can be a limiting factor. Before beginning the lesson, determine how much equipment is available since this will determine the structure of the lesson. For example, if there are only 16 paddles and balls for a class of 30, some type of sharing or station work will have to be organized. Know exactly what equipment is available and how much is in working condition. It is an embarrassing experience to roll out a cart of playground balls only to find that half of them are not inflated.

How much equipment is enough? If it is individual-use equipment such as raquets, bats, and balls, there should be one piece of equipment for each student (Figure 3.10). If it is group-oriented equipment such as gymnastics apparatus, there should be enough to ensure waiting lines of no more than four students. Some teachers settle for less equipment because they teach as they have been taught. An often-observed example involves an instructor teaching volleyball with plenty of available equipment: Rather than having students prac-

FIGURE 3.10 All students must have a piece of equipment.

tice individually (each with a volleyball) against the wall or with a partner, they divide the class into two long lines and use one or two balls. The majority of equipment remains on the sidelines, leaving students to spend more time waiting in line than practicing skills.

If equipment is limited, it is necessary to adapt instruction for the time being. Be careful about accepting limited equipment without offering a voice of dissatisfaction. Some administrators characterize physical educators as being good people and always willing to "make do." Communicate with the educational leader regularly by explaining that instruction is much more effective when necessary equipment is available. Speak with parent-teacher groups about conducting fundraisers to purchase necessary equipment. Math teachers are not expected to teach math without a book for each student and physical educators cannot teach without adequate equipment. If you settle for less, you end up with less.

What are temporary alternatives when equipment is lacking? One solution is to teach using the task style. This involves dividing students into small groups so each group has enough equipment. For example, in a softball unit, have some students practice fielding, others batting, others pitching, and so on. Another approach is to divide the class in half and allow one group to work on one activity while another is involved in an unrelated activity. For example, due to a shortage of paddles and balls, one-half of the class can be involved in raquet skill practice while the other half is playing half-court basketball. This approach is less educationally sound and increases managerial and instructional demands. Another method is the peer-review approach. While one student practices an activity, a peer offers feedback and evaluation. The peers share equipment and take turns being involved in practice and evaluation. A final method is to do what is most commonly done—design drills that involve standing in line and waiting for a turn. This is unacceptable from an educational standpoint.

Effectively distributing equipment is a key component of a quality lesson. Usually, the most effective method for distributing individual equipment is to place it around the perimeter of the area. It requires some setup time prior to the lesson, but makes it easy for students to acquire a piece of equipment without confusion. Efficient equipment distribution reduces the time spent on a task that is not related to learning. Large apparatus should be arranged in the safest possible formation so that all pieces are visible from all angles. The initial setup of equipment also depends on the focus of the lesson. For example, the height of the basket may be reduced to emphasize correct shooting form. The height of the volleyball net may be lowered to allow spiking. Nets may be placed at different heights to allow different types of practice. Equipment and apparatus should always be modified to best suit the needs of the learner. There is nothing sacred about a ten-foot basket or a regulation-sized ball. If modifying the equipment improves the quality of learning, go ahead and do so.

Ensure a Safe Environment

Do not underestimate the importance of a safe environment. Injuries are inevitable in physical education classes, but if they are due to poor planning and preparation, you may be found liable and responsible for such injuries (see Chapter 9). You are expected to foresee hazardous situations that might result in student injury. Rules dictating safe and sensible behavior need to be taught and practiced. For example, if students are in a tumbling unit, they need instruction and practice in absorbing momentum and force. Have them practice safety procedures such as taking turns, spotting, and following directions.

Another component of a safe environment is a written curriculum that guides instructional presentations in proper progression. A written curriculum offers evidence to a safety committee or court of law that proper progression and sequencing of activities were used in the lesson presentation. In addition, proper progression of activities gives students confidence because they develop the skills needed to perform safely before moving on to the next level of difficulty.

Conduct safety inspections at regular intervals. If an apparatus has not been used for some time, inspect it prior to the lesson to ensure that you will not have to stop a lesson to fix the equipment. Equipment such as tumbling mats, beanbags, and benches should be kept clean to prevent the spread of disease.

In spite of the foregoing precautions, accidents can happen. All activities in physical education have a certain degree of risk because students are moving. One of the most important outcomes of a physical education program is to offer students an opportunity to take calculated risks and overcome fear. When students feel adequate safety precautions are in place, they are less hesitant to learn new activities that involve risk.

CHOOSE AN INSTRUCTIONAL FORMATION

Appropriate formations or arrangements facilitate learning experiences. Different formations are needed for activities done in place (nonlocomotor), activities where children move (locomotor), and activities in which balls, beanbags, or other objects are thrown, kicked, caught, or otherwise received (manipulative). Select a formation based on ensuring maximum activity for all students. When small groups are used, try to place no more than four students in a squad. This minimizes the amount of time students spend standing and waiting for a turn.

Mass or Scattered Formation

Youngsters scatter throughout the area so that each student has a personal space. This formation is useful for in-place activities and when individuals need to move in every direction. Place emphasis on not bumping into, colliding with, or interfering with classmates. Scattered formation is basic to such activities as wands, hoops, individual rope-jumping, and individual ball skills.

Squad Formation

In squad formation, members stand about three feet apart in a column. In extended squad formation, the squad column is maintained with more distance (10 to 15 feet) between members. Figure 3.11 shows regular and extended squad formations.

Regular Ⓛ **X X X X X**

Extended Ⓛ **X X X X X X**

FIGURE 3.11   Regular and extended squad formations.

Partner Formation

Partner formation is useful for reciprocal teaching, where partners help each other learn new skills. Catching and receiving activities can be practiced if each pair has a projectile. Keeping pairs aligned is necessary if space is limited or objects are being caught and thrown (Figure 3.12).

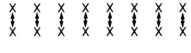

F I G U R E 3 . 1 2 Partner formation.

Lane or File

The lane, or file, formation is commonly used with locomotor activity (Figure 3.13). Students at the front of the lane move as prescribed and take their place at the rear of the lane.

X X X X
X X X X
X X X X
X X X X
X X X X
X X X X

F I G U R E 3 . 1 3 Lane, or file, formation.

Line and Leader

Line-and-leader formation (Figure 3.14) is often used for throwing and catching skills. The leader passes back and forth to each line player in turn. Placing students in a semicircle-and-leader formation (Figure 3.15) can be used to make the distance from the leader equal for all players.

X X X X X X
Ⓛ

F I G U R E 3 . 1 4 Line-and-leader formation.

F I G U R E 3 . 1 5 Semicircle-and-leader formation.

Double Line

The double-line formation can be used for passing and kicking. Figure 3.16 shows a zigzag formation in which the ball is passed from one line to the next.

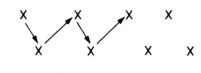

F I G U R E 3 . 1 6 Double-line formation.

Regular Shuttle Formation

The regular shuttle formation (Figure 3.17) is used for practicing passing and dribbling skills on the move. It is often used for hockey, soccer, basketball, and football ball-carrying skills. The player at the head of one line dribbles toward, or passes to, the player at the head of the other line. Each player keeps moving forward and takes a place at the end of the other half of the shuttle.

F I G U R E 3 . 1 7 Regular shuttle formation.

Shuttle Turn-Back Formation

Shuttle turn-back formation (Figure 3.18) is used for passing, kicking, and volleying for distance. The player at the head of one shuttle line passes to the player at the head of the other. After passing, players go to the back of their line.

F I G U R E 3 . 1 8 Shuttle turn-back formation.

Simultaneous Class Movement

There are times when certain activities require that the entire class move simultaneously. Without some structure and organization, this has the potential to become chaotic. For such activities, the following formations can be useful.

Children can start on opposite sides of the gym and exchange positions (Figure 3.19). On signal, they cross to the opposite side of the area, passing through the opposite line without contact.

You could also have children start on opposite sides of the gym, move toward the center, and then go back. A dividing line can be formed with ropes, wands, or cones to mark the center (Figure 3.20).

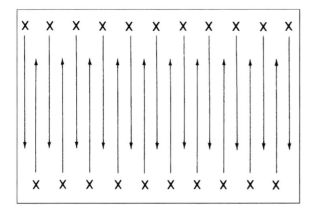

FIGURE 3.19 Exchanging positions on opposite sides.

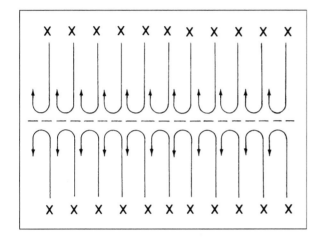

FIGURE 3.20 Moving to center and back on opposite sides.

Finally, children can start on each of four sides of the play area and alternately exchange sides (Figure 3.21). The children in one pair of opposite sides exchange first and then the others exchange. This formation is useful for class demonstrations—one-half of the class demonstrates while the other half observes and evaluates.

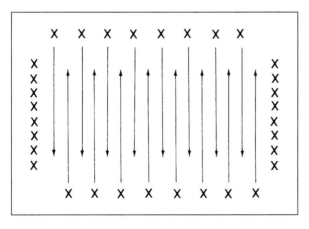

FIGURE 3.21 Exchanging on four sides.

CHAPTER 3 | Preparing a Quality Lesson

DESIGN A LESSON PLAN FORMAT

Written lesson plans vary in form and length, depending on the activity and the background of the teacher. A written plan ensures that thought has been given to the lesson before children enter the activity area. It helps avoid spur-of-the-moment decisions that disrupt the unity and progression of instruction. Lesson plans can and should be modified when needed, but a written plan gives focus and direction to instruction. Progression is more apt to occur in a lesson when instruction is based on activities presented in previous lesson plans. Notes and changes can be written on the lesson plans to give direction for future modifications of the curriculum.

A standardized lesson plan format allows teachers and substitute teachers to interchange plans within a school district. Include the following basic information in your lesson plan:

1. *Objectives.* Design and list instructional objectives for the purpose of accomplishing content standards. Writing effective objectives is discussed in the next chapter.

2. *Equipment required.* Identify amounts of materials and supplies required and how the equipment will be distributed.

3. *Instructional activities.* List actual movements and skill experiences to be taught. Place the activities in proper developmental sequence. You do not need to describe activities in detail but give enough description so they can be easily recalled.

4. *Teaching hints.* Include organizational tips and important learning cues including how equipment is arranged, how students are grouped, and what teaching cues are proper. If needed, list text and video references for in-depth information.

A common format is the four-part lesson plan. Figure 3.22 on pages 60–62 is an example of a lesson plan taken from the accompanying curriculum guide by Pangrazi (2007). This curriculum contains a year's supply of lesson plans for each of the three developmental levels. Each lesson includes an introductory or warm-up activity, fitness activities, lesson focus, and closing activity. Using four parts prepares youngsters for the activity, ensures moderate to vigorous activity, teaches skills, and implements the skills in a game setting.

Lesson planning takes time. Comprehensive lesson plans are best written when you have time to plan and reflect. Lesson plans give direction to the day's lesson and may include many more activities than can be taught in a typical period. Many teachers use a four-by-six-inch card to write down the actual activities they are teaching. The size of the card and the brevity of information are much

Movement Skills and Concepts (7)
Twisting, Turning, Stretching, and Relaxing Movements
Level I—Week 26

Objectives:

To apply movement concepts such as body and space awareness, relationships, and qualities of movement to a variety of locomotor and body management skills.

To combine locomotor and nonlocomotor skills into movement themes, e.g., supporting body weight, bridges, and receiving and transferring weight.

NASPE Content Standards:

Introductory Activity: 1, 3, 5
Fitness Activity: 4
Lesson Focus: 1, 3, 6
Game: 1, 5

Equipment Required:

Music for Animal Movements
Teacher's choice of equipment for introductory activity and manipulative skills in the lesson focus

Instructional Activities	Teaching Hints

Introductory Activity—Creative and Exploratory Opportunities

Put out enough equipment for all children to have a piece. Allow them to explore and create activities while moving. Another alternative is to have students work with a piece of equipment with a partner or small group.

Ask students to move and be active without being told what to do. Encourage independent thinking.

Fitness Development Activity—Animal Movements and Fitness Challenges

1. Puppy Dog Walk—30 seconds.
2. Freeze; perform stretching activities.
3. Measuring Worm Walk—30 seconds.
4. Freeze; perform abdominal development challenges.
5. Frog Jump—30 seconds.
6. Freeze; perform push-up position challenges.
7. Elephant Walk—30 seconds.
8. Freeze; perform stretching activities.
9. Bear Walk—30 seconds.
10. Freeze; perform abdominal challenges.
11. Crab Walk—30 seconds.
12. Freeze and perform stretching and relaxing activities.

Tape alternating segments (30 seconds in length) of silence and music to signal duration of exercise. Music segments indicate performing animal movements while intervals of silence announce doing the fitness challenges.

A variation is to place animal movement signs throughout the area and instruct students to move from sign to sign, performing the appropriate animal movement each time they reach a new sign.

Lesson Focus—Movement Skills and Concepts (7)

Fundamental Skill: Twisting

1. Glue your feet to the floor. Can you twist your body to the right and to the left? Can you twist slowly, quickly? Can you bend and twist at the same time? How far can you twist your hands back and forth?
2. Twist two parts of the body at the same time. Try three. More?
3. Twist one part of the body in one direction and another in a different direction.
4. Try to twist the upper half of your body without twisting the lower part. How about the reverse?
5. Seated on the floor, find what parts of the body you can twist.
6. Try to twist one part of the body around another. Can you do this?
7. Balance on one foot and twist your body. Can you bend and twist in this position?
8. Show different shapes that can be made using twisted body parts.

Select a few activities from each of the categories so students receive a variety of skills to practice. When possible, integrate the manipulative skill activities with fundamental skill activities. A common error is to teach all the activities from one category. The reason for multiple groups of activities is to provide variety and enhance motivation.

Teach youngsters the difference between a twist and a turn. Twisting is rotating a selected body part around its own long axis. Twisting involves movement around the body part itself while turning focuses on the space in which the body turns. Turning here involves movement of the entire body.

FIGURE 3.22 Example of a lesson plan.

Fundamental Skill: Turning

1. Turn your body left and right with quarter and hair turns. Turn clockwise and counterclockwise.
2. (Post compass directions on the walls—north, south, east, and west.) Face the correct direction on call. Also face some in-between directions—northwest, southeast, etc.
3. Stand on one foot and turn around slowly, quickly, with a series of small hops.
4. Cross your legs with a turn and then sit down. Can you get up without moving your feet too much?
5. When you hear the signal, turn completely around once. Next time turn the other way. Now try with two full turns; three.
6. Lie on your tummy and turn yourself around in an arc. Try a seated position.

Emphasize maintaining balance while performing turning activities.

Perform twisting and turning movements in both directions. Also, try the movements in sitting position or on tummy.

Fundamental Skill: Rocking

1. Rock in many different ways. Which part of the body is used to rock the highest?
2. Select a part of the body and show me how you can rock smoothly and slowly. How about quickly and smoothly?
3. Rock like a rocking chair.
4. Lie on your back and rock. Point both hands and feet toward the ceiling and rock on the back.
5. Lie on your tummy and rock. Rock as high as you can. Hold your ankles and make giant rocks.
6. Rock in a standing position. Try forward, sideways, and diagonal rocking directions.
7. Select a position where you can rock and twist at the same time.
8. Lie on your back, with knees up and rock side to side.

Make rocking a smooth and steady rhythm. It should be a controlled movement.

Rocking is usually best done when the body surface is rounded. Discuss how the body can be rounded to make rocking easier.

Manipulative Skill: Student's Choice

Select one or more manipulative activities that need additional developing with respect to the children's needs and progress. During the week's work, a different activity might be scheduled each individual day.

Since equipment was placed out for the introductory activity, use it for the manipulative skill.

Movement Concept: Stretching and Curling

1. While on your feet, show us a stretched position. A curled position.
2. Go very slowly from your stretched position to the curled one you select. Go rapidly.
3. Keeping one foot in place (on a spot), show how far you can stretch in different directions.
4. Show us a straight (regular) curled position. A twisted curled position. A tightly curled position.
5. Select three different curled positions. On signal, go from one to the other rapidly. Repeat with stretch positions.
6. Explore and show the different ways that the body can support itself in curled positions.

Stretching and curling are somewhat opposite movements.

Encourage stretching through the full range of movement. The stretch is done slowly and smoothly.

Encourage holding the stretch for six to ten seconds.

Movement Concept: Tension and Relaxation

1. Make yourself as tense as possible. Now relax.
2. Take a deep breath, hold it tight. Expel the air and relax.
3. Tense and reach as high as you can; slowly relax and drop to the floor.
4. Show how you can tense different parts of the body.
5. Tense one part of the body and relax another. Shift the tenseness to the relaxed part and vice versa.
6. Press your fingers hard against your tensed abdominal muscles. Take your fists and beat lightly against the tensed position. Relax. Repeat.
7. Move forward, stop suddenly in a tensed position. Relax. Repeat.

Relaxation activities are an excellent way to finish the lesson. Help youngsters learn to recognize when a limb and muscles are relaxed.

A quiet atmosphere facilitates relaxing. Soft voices encourage students to "wind down."

FIGURE 3.22 (continued)

Closing Activity

Midnight

Supplies: None

Skills: Running, dodging

A safety line is established about 40 feet from a den in which two or three players, the foxes, are standing. The others stand behind the safety line and ask, "What time is it, Mr. Fox?" One of the foxes is designated to answer in various fashions, such as "one o'clock," four o'clock," etc. When the fox says a certain time, the class walks forward that number of steps. For example, if the fox says, "six o'clock" the class has to move forward six steps. The fox continues to draw the players toward him. At some point, the fox answers the question by saying, "Midnight" and chases the others back to the safety line. Any player who is caught becomes a fox in the den and helps to catch others.

Twins (Triplets)

Supplies: None

Skills: Body management

Youngsters are scattered throughout the area with a partner (twin). Commands are given such as, "Take three hops and two leaps" or "Walk backward four steps and three skips." When the pairs are adequately separated, the leader calls out, "Find your twin!" Players find their twin and stand frozen toe to toe. The goal is to not be the last pair to find each other and assume the frozen position. Ensure students move away from each other during the movements. One alternative is to find a new twin each time. Another variation is to separate twins in opposite ends of the playing area.

Variation: The game is more challenging when played in groups of three (triplets). When using this variation, new partners should be selected each time.

FIGURE 3.22 (continued)

---

easier to refer to while teaching. The four major parts in a lesson plan consist of the following.

Introductory (Warm-Up) Activity

The introductory (warm-up) activity lasts two to three minutes and sets the tone for the rest of the lesson. If you are able to shape a class into a well-behaved group during the introductory activity, such behavior is easier to maintain throughout the remainder of the lesson. The first part of the lesson provides an opportunity to review class management skills such as stopping on signal, running under control, and so on. Starting a lesson is a difficult phase of teaching that can be made easier by practicing management skills. An effective rule of thumb is to run and freeze your class three times. If all students are with you after three freezes, proceed to teach an introductory activity (Chapter 16). On the other hand, if students are not well managed at that point, skip the introductory activity and practice management skills. The premise for making this decision is that management skills take priority over physical development skills. It is impossible to teach if youngsters are not paying attention to you. Learning to respect others takes top billing in any educational setting and moves skill learning to a lesser priority.

Introductory activities serve several purposes in the lesson format including the following:

- Students engage in immediate activity when they enter the activity area. Youngsters want to move immediately rather than have to sit down, be quiet, and listen to instructions. Offer vigorous activity first; then give instructions or discuss learning objectives while they recover from vigorous activity.

- They serve as a physiological warm-up, preparing students for physical activity.

- This part of the lesson can be used for anticipatory set (Chapter 5, page 84) or to review previously learned skills. Anticipatory set prefocuses on the skill and cognitive objectives of the lesson.

Fitness Activity

The second part of the lesson is designed to enhance health-related fitness and promote lifetime physical activity. A variety of exercises is used so students experience the wide range of options available for maintaining an active lifestyle. This portion of the lesson teaches youngsters the type and amount of activity necessary to maintain a healthy lifestyle. Talking about the importance of a healthy lifestyle is not enough; it must be experienced. Students are taught how to determine their personal workloads with an implied expectation that they will do their best. Forcing all students to do the same amount of activity fails to consider the genetic and personality differences inherent in a class of students. Physical fitness and activity are discussed in detail in Chapter 13.

Lesson Focus

For many adults, physical skills are the tools they use to participate in a physically active lifestyle. The lesson focus is designed to teach physical skills. It contains learning experiences designed to help students meet program content standards. Repetition and refinement of physical skills in a sequential and success-oriented setting characterize the lesson focus. This portion of the lesson (15 to 25 minutes) teaches students skills that are necessary to function comfortably in a lifestyle that features physical activity. Emphasis is placed on instruction that teaches the process of performing skills correctly. Chapters 15–30 are filled with many instructional units presented in the lesson focus.

Closing Activity

The closing activity brings closure to the lesson through evaluation of the day's accomplishments—stressing and reinforcing skills learned, revisiting performance techniques, and checking cognitive concepts. The closing activity may be a game that uses skills developed in the lesson focus or simply a low-organized game or activity children enjoy (see Chapter 22 for a variety of games). If a lesson is demanding or spirited, focus closing activities on relaxation and winding down so that students return to the classroom in a calmer state of mind. Taking a few minutes to relax may calm teachers and students and create goodwill between classroom teachers and physical education specialists.

At times the closing activity is minimized or deleted entirely. For example, if a game or activity is the focus of the lesson, more time might be needed for instruction. Whether a game is played or not, avoid disciplining a class by suggesting, "We will not have a game if you don't quiet down." Closing activities are a useful part of the lesson and should not be used to bribe youngsters to behave. Doing so may cause youngsters to leave physical education classes with negative feelings.

REFLECTIVE TEACHING

Teaching is a full-time job. Teachers who excel and impact the lives of their students put a great deal of time and energy into their teaching. All who teach physical education work hard to reach physical education outcomes. But it is easy to identify a truly outstanding teacher who seems to get students to perform at a high level. One of the elements that is apparent in all great teachers is their level of caring and thinking. They spend a great deal of time thinking about the lessons they have presented in order to find new and better ways to get students to respond. This process is often referred to as reflection, the process of sitting back and asking the question, "How could I have done better so students would have learned more?"

Many things make teaching difficult, for example, the weather, having to teach outside, having a limited amount of equipment, not knowing how certain youngsters will respond to your discipline techniques, etc. There are no simple answers to be found. What works one time may not work the next. Some teachers like to put in an eight o'clock to three o'clock day, and there had better not be anyone in their way when the "clock strikes three." These teachers will teach the same way and the same thing year after year without change. It is often said that these teachers have been "teaching 20 years and have 1 year of experience." That approach is the opposite of reflecting and trying to improve.

Quality teachers find time to reflect on all factors related to their lessons. Most teachers admit that their first lesson of the week is not as polished and effective as one taught near the end of the week. A lesson taught during the first period of the week does not include all the finer points learned through trial and error. Instruction improves when teachers reflect on why some things worked and others didn't. Leave time at the end of the day to reflect and note ways the lesson can be improved. Try keeping a portfolio related to inspiration and insight you uncover during the reflection process. Write down personal growth indicators and situations that offer evidence you are growing professionally. Continue to reflect and see it as a dynamic and ongoing process. Examine Figure 3.23, page 64 for a list of questions that aid the reflection process. Add other questions that are specific and related to your professional growth.

REFLECTION AND REVIEW QUESTIONS

How and Why

1. Why is it important for teachers to understand and use a variety of teaching styles?

Planning

- Did I prepare ahead of time? Mental preparation prior to a lesson ensures flow and continuity in a lesson.

- Did I understand the "whys" of my lesson? Knowing why you are teaching something will give you greater strength and conviction in your presentation.

- Did I state my instructional goals for the lesson? Students are more focused if they know what they are supposed to learn.

- Did I plan the lesson so students can participate safely, such as areas for running; no slippery spots, broken glass, or objects to run into; adequate room for striking activities; etc.?

Equipment

- Was my equipment arranged prior to class? Proper equipment placement reduces management time and allows more time for instruction and practice.

- Did I use enough equipment to keep all students involved and assured of maximum practice opportunities?

- Did I notify the principal about equipment that needs to be repaired or replaced? On a regular basis, do I record areas where equipment is lacking or insufficient in quantity? Do I inform the principal of these shortcomings?

- Did I select equipment that is appropriate for the developmental level of the students, i.e., proper size and types of balls, basketball hoop height, hand implements?

Methodology

- Did I constantly move and reposition myself during the lesson? Moving allows you to be close to more students so you can reinforce and help them. It usually reduces behavior problems.

- Did I teach with enthusiasm and energy? Energy and zest rub off on students.

- Did I try to show just as much energy for the last class of the day as I did for the first class of the day? Did I work just as hard on Friday as I did at the start of the week?

- Did I keep students moving during lesson transitions? Did I plan my transitions carefully so little time was needed to proceed to the next part of the lesson?

Instruction

- Was I alert for children who were having trouble performing the activities and needed some personal help? Youngsters want to receive relevant but subtle help.

- Did I praise youngsters who made an effort or improved? Saying something positive to children increases their desire to perform at a higher level.

- Did I give sufficient attention to the personalization and creativity of each student? Everybody feels unique and different and wants to deal with learning tasks in a personal manner.

- Did I teach for quality of movement or just offer a large quantity of activities in an attempt to keep students on task? Repetition is a necessary part of learning new skills.

Discipline/Management

- Did I teach students to be responsible for their learning and personal behavior? Students need to learn responsibility and self-direction skills.

- Did I evaluate how I handled discipline and management problems? Did I preserve the self-esteem of my students during behavior correction episodes? What are some ways I could have handled situations better?

- Did I make positive calls home to reinforce students who are really trying and working hard?

Assessment

- Did I bring closure to my lesson? This gives feedback about the effectiveness of instruction. It also allows students a chance to reflect on what they have learned. Did I ask for answers in a way that allows me to quickly check that all students understand?

- Did I evaluate the usefulness of activities I presented? Did I make changes as quickly as possible to ensure my lessons were improving and better meeting the needs of my students?

- Did I communicate with teachers and the principal about things that need to be improved or better understood? For example, did I say something about classes arriving late, teachers arriving late to pick up their class, schedule problems that cause excessive work, etc.?

FIGURE 3.23 Questions that aid the reflection process.

2. How can knowledge of motor learning help teachers maximize student learning in physical education?

3. Why are mechanical principles taught in elementary physical education? How might these principles help teachers and students?

4. How does the college learning environment differ from an appropriate learning environment for elementary physical education?

5. How did your elementary physical education learning environment differ from that advocated in this chapter?

Content Review

1. Identify what variables must be considered when choosing a teaching style.

2. Describe the teaching styles used in physical education. Include comments on the effective use of the different styles.

3. Discuss the basic tenets of motor learning required to "optimize skill learning."

4. Explain several mechanical principles and how they are used in elementary physical education.

5. Describe four instructional formations. How can these formations be used?

6. Identify the four parts of a lesson. Discuss the characteristics of each part and its significance.

7. State several issues that physical education teachers must address when preparing to teach.

FOR MORE INFORMATION

References and Suggested Readings

Barrett, K. R., Williams, K., & Whitall, J. (1992). What does it mean to have a "developmentally appropriate physical education program"? *The Physical Educator, 49*(3), 113–117.

Byra, M., & Jenkins, J. (2000). Matching instructional tasks with learner ability: The inclusion style of teaching. Teaching style E. *Journal of Physical Education, Recreation, & Dance, 71*(3), 26–30.

Dyson, B. & Grineski, S. (2001). Using cooperative learning structures in physical education. *Journal of Physical Education, Recreation, & Dance, 72*(2), 28–31.

Gabbard, C. (2004). *Lifelong motor development.* 4th ed. San Francisco: Benjamin Cummings.

Gallahue, D. L., & Donnelly, F. C. (2003). *Developmental physical education for all children.* 4th ed. Champaign, IL: Human Kinetics Publishers.

Goode, S., & Magill, R. A. (1986). The contextual interference effects in learning three badminton serves. *Research Quarterly for Exercise and Sport, 57,* 308–314.

Graham, G., Holt/Hale, S. A., & Parker, M. (2001). *Children moving.* 5th ed. Mountain View, CA: Mayfield.

Guskey, T. R. (1985). *Implementing mastery learning.* Belmont, CA: Wadsworth.

Harrison, J. M., Blakemore, C. L., & Buck, M. M. (2001). *Instructional strategies for secondary physical education.* 5th ed. Boston: McGraw-Hill.

Johnson, D. W., & Johnson, F. (2003). *Joining together: Group theory and group skills.* 8th ed. Boston: Allyn & Bacon.

Johnson, D. W., Johnson, R. T., & Holubec, E. J. (1990). *Circles of learning: Cooperation in the classroom.* 3rd ed. Edina, MN: Interaction.

Metzler, M. W. (2000). *Instructional models for physical education.* Boston: Allyn and Bacon.

Mosston, M., & Ashworth, S. (2002). *Teaching physical education.* 5th ed. San Francisco: Benjamin Cummings.

Nichols, B. (1994). *Moving and learning: The elementary school physical education experience.* 3rd ed. St. Louis: McGraw-Hill.

Pangrazi, R. P. (2007). *Dynamic Physical Education Curriculum Guide: Lesson Plans for Implementation.* 15th ed. San Francisco: Benjamin Cummings.

Rink, J. E. (2002). *Teaching physical education for learning.* 5th ed. Boston: WCB/McGraw-Hill.

Schmidt, R. A., & Wrisberg, C. (2004). *Motor learning and performance.* 3rd ed. Champaign, IL: Human Kinetics Publishers.

Siedentop, D., & Tannehill, D. (2000). *Developing teaching skills in physical education.* 4th ed. Mountain View, CA: Mayfield Publishing Co.

Slavin, R. (1990). Research on cooperative learning: Consensus and controversy. *Educational Leadership, 47*(4), 52–55.

Websites

Physical Education Teaching and Curriculum Information (Styles Information)
  www.pecentral.com
  www.pelinks4u.org
  www.pe4life.org
  http://reach.ucf.edu/~pezone/
  www.masterteacher.com/

Research for Education and Learning
  www.mcrel.org

Research on Teaching Physical Education
  www.UnlockResearch.com

Teaching Styles and Learning Styles
  www2.ncsu.edu/unity/lockers/users/f/felder/public/
    Learning_Styles.html

4

Curriculum Development

ESSENTIAL COMPONENTS OF QUALITY PROGRAMS

▶ **I. Organized around content standards**

▶ **II. Student-centered and developmentally appropriate**

▶ **III. Physical activity and motor skill development form the core of the program**

IV. Teaches management skills and self-discipline

▶ **V. Promotes inclusion of all students**

▶ **VI. Focuses on process over product**

▶ **VII. Promotes lifetime personal health and wellness**

VIII. Teaches cooperation and responsibility and promotes sensitivity to diversity

NATIONAL STANDARDS FOR PHYSICAL EDUCATION*

▶ **1. Demonstrates competency in motor skills and movement patterns needed to perform a variety of physical activities.**

2. Demonstrates understanding of movement concepts, principles, and tactics as they apply to the learning and performance of physical activities.

3. Participates regularly in physical activity.

4. Achieves and maintains a health-enhancing level of physical fitness.

5. Exhibits responsible personal and social behavior that respects self and others in physical activity.

6. Values physical activity for health, enjoyment, challenge, self-expression, and/or social interaction.

*National Association for Sport and Physical Education (NASPE), 2004.

SUMMARY

This chapter offers a systematic approach for developing a curriculum and suggests formats for organization and evaluation. A written curriculum gives direction to the instructional program. A sequence of steps is offered for planning, designing, and implementing a comprehensive curriculum. The concepts of scope, sequence, and balance help ensure that the curriculum will meet the needs of all students.

OUTCOMES

▪ Define scope, sequence, and balance as each relates to curriculum development.

▪ List elements common to a quality curriculum.

▪ Delineate your philosophy of physical education for children.

▪ List environmental factors that impact curriculum development.

▪ Specify the seven-step approach in developing a quality curriculum.

▪ Specify the needs, characteristics, and interests of children and be able to explain how these age and maturity factors influence program development.

▪ Describe the difference between content standards and student-centered objectives.

▪ Cite the three learning domains and discuss characteristics of each.

urriculum is a framework of child-centered physical activities that promote physical activity and
skill development. A curriculum is a delivery system that gives sequence and direction to the learning
experiences of students. The curriculum includes a set
of beliefs and goals that evolves from a theoretical
framework or value orientation. *Value orientation* is a
set of personal and professional beliefs that provides a
basis for determining curricular decisions. Most often,
physical educators have several value orientations, and
physical education programs reflect a blend of different
values. For example, a chosen model might include participating in physical activities throughout one's lifetime,
developing sport skills, acquiring fitness knowledge, improving social skills, acquiring disciplinary knowledge,
or a combination of orientations.

When developing or revising an existing curriculum, the value orientation of the physical education staff
toward the existing curriculum and toward proposed
changes is a necessary consideration (Jewett, Bain, &
Ennis, 1995). Determining the value orientation of the
curriculum involves consideration of three major components: the subject matter to be learned, the students
for whom the curriculum is being developed, and the society that has established the schools. Priorities in curriculum vary depending on the value orientations of the
physical educators involved in the planning. Physical educators who place highest priority on subject matter
mastery include an emphasis on sports, dance, outdoor
adventure activities, physical fitness activities, and
aquatic activities. This orientation places strong emphasis on students learning skills and gaining knowledge so
they have the opportunity to learn the subject matter and
continue active participation for a lifetime. In contrast,
instructors who favor a student-centered approach prize
activities that develop the individual student. They emphasize helping students find activities that are personally meaningful. Other physical educators see student
autonomy and self-direction as the most important
goals. They focus instruction and curricula on lifetime
sport skills and nontraditional activities, such as cooperative games and group activities, in an attempt to foster
problem-solving and interpersonal skills.

The examples above illustrate a few of the different
value orientations of physical educators. Usually, most
curricula are put together by committee and therefore
reflect a number of value orientations. Teachers need to
know the value orientations that drive their curriculum
so there is consistency in instructional goals. Finding
common ground among value orientations makes it
easier for a staff to present lessons that teach common
goals and objectives. Before accepting a new teaching
position, ask yourself the following questions about the
school's curriculum. If you answer "no" to most of
the questions that follow, it could be difficult to work

comfortably in such a setting because it conflicts with
your value orientation.

- Will the curriculum express a point of view about
  subject matter that is consistent with mine?
- Does the curriculum express a point of view about
  student learning that I believe?
- Does the curriculum express a point of view about
  the school's role in accomplishing social-cultural
  goals that is similar to my beliefs?
- Can I implement the instructional strategies I value
  within this model?

DESIGNING A QUALITY CURRICULUM

The steps that follow offer a sequential approach for
constructing a meaningful, well-planned curriculum
guide. The first four steps focus on designing a framework that guides selection of activities for the curriculum. These steps are often ignored because the focus
is on activities that are easily implemented regardless
of whether they contribute to content standards. The result is a curriculum with little direction, a situation similar to building a house or skyscraper without blueprints.

Step One: Develop a Guiding Philosophy

The initial step in curriculum design is to define a philosophy of physical education that reflects the educators' beliefs. A philosophical statement defines how
physical education fits into the total school curriculum
and what it will accomplish for each student. The following is an example of a philosophical platform for
physical education.

Physical education is that portion of the child's
overall education that is accomplished through
movement. It is education about and involving
movement. Physical education must be largely an
instructional program if it is to acquire a full partnership in the child's overall education. Only high-
quality programs based on developmental goals
with demonstrable and accountable outcomes
achieve this respect. The overriding goal of U.S.
education—to develop an individual who can live
effectively in a democracy—guides the development
of this program. Although physical education stresses
psychomotor goals, it also contributes to cognitive
and affective learning domains. Three major and
unique contributions of physical education to the
total school curriculum are:

1. *To develop personal activity and fitness habits.*
   The program teaches children the conceptual

framework under which personal fitness and lifetime activity habits are developed. This implies teaching the concept of human wellness (that is, teaching students how to maintain a vibrant and functional lifestyle throughout adulthood). Emphasis is placed on lifetime activity and personal habits that can be used in adulthood.

2. *To develop and enhance movement competency and motor skills.* Movement competency is rooted in developing a broad base of body management skills. The focus is on developing motor skills in a positive and nurturing environment. Personal competency in a wide variety of skills is an overriding theme of instruction.

3. *To gain a conceptual understanding of movement principles.* Moving efficiently requires learning basic concepts of movement and understanding anatomical and mechanical principles. Physical education instruction integrates knowledge and skill performance to develop students who know how to move.

Step Two: Define a Conceptual Framework for the Curriculum

A conceptual framework is a series of statements that characterize the desired curriculum. These concepts establish criteria that will be used to select activities and experiences included in the curriculum. The framework not only directs the selection of activities but also reflects beliefs about education and the learner. Following are examples of conceptual statements that define a child-centered, developmental curriculum:

■ *Curriculum goals and objectives are appropriate for all youngsters.* This implies a balanced curriculum that covers fundamental skills, sport skills, games, rhythms and dance, gymnastics, and individual and dual activities. Emphasis is placed on developing a broad foundation of motor skills for all students.

■ *Activities in the curriculum are selected based on their potential to help students reach national and local content standards.* The elementary school years are a time of experimentation, practice, and decision-making with all movement possibilities. The criterion for inclusion of activities is not based on whether teachers or students prefer certain activities. Rather, activities are included in the curriculum because they contribute to student progress toward content standards.

■ *The curriculum helps youngsters develop lifelong physical activity habits and understand basic fitness concepts.* Regardless of the philosophy of the curriculum, it should be designed so youngsters leave school with active lifestyle habits. Fitness is an important component of the curriculum and should be varied, positive, and educational. The fitness program is experiential, that is, students participate in fitness activities rather than just learn the facts of fitness. A meaningful curriculum helps students learn activities that can be used throughout their life span. Graduates immersed in the curriculum should leave school knowing how to live an active lifestyle and being able to pursue physical fitness goals that are related to good health.

■ *The curriculum includes activities that enhance cognitive and affective learning.* Children are whole beings and need to learn more than just how to perform physical skills. They must understand skill performance principles and develop cognitive learning related to physical activity and wellness. Affective development, the learning of cooperative and social skills, can be fostered through group activities, and these skills are every bit as important as physical skills.

■ *The curriculum provides experiences that allow all children to succeed and feel satisfaction.* Quality programs focus on minimizing failure and emphasizing success. Activities that emphasize self improvement, participation, and cooperation encourage development-perceived competence, the feeling that "I am capable of performing well." Physical education instruction focuses on learning, without labeling students as winners or losers.

■ *The curriculum is planned and based on an educational environment that is consistent with other academic areas in the school.* Physical education teachers need the same working conditions as other teachers in the school setting. Class sizes similar to those of classroom teachers (20 to 35 students) and an assigned teaching area (such as a gym or multipurpose room) are needed for physical education instruction. Enough equipment for maximum activity and participation implies one piece of individual equipment for each youngster and ample apparatus to limit long lines and waiting for a turn. A daily program ensures maximum opportunity for learning and retention.

■ *Activities in the curriculum are presented in an educationally sound sequence.* Progression is the soul of learning and the curriculum should reflect progression vertically (between developmental levels) and horizontally (within each level and within each activity).

■ *The curriculum includes an appropriate means of assessing student progress.* Student assessment includes health-related fitness, physical activity assessment, skill development, cognitive learning, and attitude development toward physical activity. Any assessment program should enhance the effectiveness of the curriculum and should help teachers individualize instruction, communicate with parents, and identify youngsters with special needs.

Step Three: Consider Environmental Factors

Environmental factors are conditions within the community and school district that limit or extend the scope of the curriculum. Examples of environmental factors are the amount and type of equipment, budget size, and cultural makeup of the community. Other factors—such as the support of school administrators—can affect the type of scheduling or amount of required physical education in the school. Different communities may value certain types of activities or experiences for their children. Although environmental factors need to be examined carefully, they should not circumvent or limit curriculum scope and sequence. Rather, these factors should give direction to the curriculum development process. A well-designed curriculum is a goal, direction, and destination for the future, a high road to instructional success. Consider various environmental factors and try to use them to enhance the creativity and scope of the curriculum.

Following are examples of environmental factors that limit the development of a quality curriculum. Although these factors can sometimes be limiting, they can be handled creatively to ensure that the curriculum is effectively implemented. Think big; develop a comprehensive and ideal curriculum that is as varied, broad, and creative as possible. Seek to expand and develop the curriculum beyond these limiting factors.

SCHOOL ADMINISTRATORS

The support of school administrators has a significant impact on the curriculum. It is important to communicate program goals to administrators. Like the general public, administrators may have misconceptions about physical education and its contribution to the overall education of students. In most cases, administrators will support physical education if they perceive that the program is built on sound educational principles that are documented and evaluated.

THE COMMUNITY: PEOPLE AND CLIMATE

Occupations, religions, educational levels, cultural values, and physical activity habits within the community are factors that might affect curriculum development. Parents have a strong influence on the activity interests and habits of their children. The geographical location and the climate of the area are also important factors for consideration. The terrain (mountains, deserts, plains, and so on), combined with the weather conditions particular to each area, has an effect on people's activity interests. Extremely hot or cold climates influence markedly what activities are included in the curriculum and at what time of the year they should be scheduled.

FACILITIES AND EQUIPMENT

Available teaching facilities dictate which activities can be offered. Facilities include on-campus as well as off-campus areas in the neighboring community. Off-campus facilities might be a community swimming pool or park. Equipment must be available in quality and quantity. One piece of equipment per child is necessary if students are to learn at an optimum rate. Equipment can be purchased with school funds or with special funds raised through student performance programs. Some types of equipment can be constructed by school maintenance departments or as industrial arts projects. Another less desirable alternative is to ask students to bring equipment, such as jump ropes, soccer balls, and foam balls, from home. Once this precedent is set, administrators may fail to fund the program properly because they feel the physical educator can always find a way to "just get by."

LAWS AND REQUIREMENTS

Laws, regulations, and requirements at the national, state, and local levels may restrict or direct a curriculum. Programs must conform to these laws. Examples of two national laws affecting physical education programs are Title IX of the Educational Amendments Act of 1972 and Public Law 94-142. Title IX enforces equal opportunities for both sexes, and PL 94-142 mandates equal access to educational services for students with disabilities (see Chapter 7). Individual states also may have various laws that affect physical education programming.

SCHEDULING

The schedule or organizational pattern of the school has an impact on curriculum development. How many times per week classes meet, how long class periods last, and who teaches the classes are factors to consider. Many scheduling alternatives exist: daily, two or three times per week, every other week, and other variations. Regardless of the various parameters, most elementary schools put together a scheduling committee that consists of a number of classroom teachers, specialists in areas such as art and music, and the physical education teacher.

Consider several factors when developing schedules. Most often, 30 minutes is the amount of time scheduled for physical education classes. Some teachers prefer 40 minutes for upper-grade youngsters; however, such periods are long for primary-grade children. On the other end of the spectrum, periods can be too short. Some schools try to compress periods for primary-grade children to 20 minutes. A short period makes it difficult to present a balanced and complete lesson. Another important issue is how many periods a physical education teacher should teach per day. Physical education teachers should not be expected to have more contact time with students than classroom teachers do. Teaching physical education is demanding, and it is unfair to expect physical education specialists to teach all day without relief. An acceptable workload is eight or nine 30-minute periods per day with at least 5 minutes of passing time between classes so that teachers can rearrange equipment, talk to students, and take care of personal matters. It is difficult to teach with classes scheduled back-to-back. Teachers need time to prepare for the next lesson. Passing time also avoids the situation where a class has to wait for the current class to finish.

Another important consideration is scheduling classes by developmental levels; for example, all Developmental Level I children should be scheduled within a particular block of time. Because physical education is equipment- and planning-intensive, scheduling by developmental level helps reduce the time needed for preparation and for placement or removal of equipment.

BUDGET AND FUNDING

The amount of funding allocated for purchasing new equipment and replacing old supplies impacts the quality of the curriculum. Physical educators deserve parity in funding with other school program areas. Students are not expected to learn to read and write without materials and supplies. In similar fashion, they cannot learn physical skills without the necessary equipment and supplies.

Step Four: Determine Content Standards and Student Objectives

Content standards determine the direction of the program as dictated and desired by the state, district, or individual school. Such standards are fixed goals for learning. They determine what students should know and be able to do when they complete their schooling. Student progress is dictated by how students compare to the fixed standards rather than how they compare to other students. Content standards determine what criteria will be used to select instructional activities for the curriculum. The National Association for Sport and Physical Education (NASPE) has identified six national

standards that are used to guide content in this textbook. See Chapter 1 for an in-depth discussion of each standard.

1. Demonstrates competency in motor skills and movement patterns needed to perform a variety of physical activities.
2. Demonstrates understanding of movement concepts, principles, and tactics as they apply to the learning and performance of physical activities.
3. Participates regularly in physical activity.
4. Achieves and maintains a health-enhancing level of physical fitness.
5. Exhibits responsible personal and social behavior that respects self and others in physical activity.
6. Values physical activity for health, enjoyment, challenge, self-expression, and/or social interaction.

WRITE STUDENT-CENTERED INSTRUCTIONAL OBJECTIVES

After defining content standards, instructional objectives are written. Objectives dictate the specific activities students will need to learn throughout the school year. Student-centered objectives are usually written in behavioral terms. Behavioral objectives contain three key characteristics: (a) a desired behavior that is observable; (b) a behavior that is measurable; and (c) a criterion for success that can be measured. Objectives are written for all three of the learning domains—psychomotor, cognitive, and affective. A description of each domain follows.

1. *Psychomotor domain.* This domain (Corbin, 1976) is the primary focus of instruction for physical educators. The seven levels in psychomotor domain taxonomy are movement vocabulary, movement of body parts, locomotor movements, moving implements and objects, patterns of movement, moving with others, and movement problem solving. This graduated list progresses according to the developmental level of learners. Children learn the vocabulary of movement before proceeding to simple body part movements. More complex movements are taught to enable youngsters to participate in activities with others and to solve personal movement dilemmas.
2. *Cognitive domain.* The cognitive domain was defined by Bloom (1956) and includes six major areas: knowledge, comprehension, application, analysis, synthesis, and evaluation. The focus of the cognitive domain for physical education is knowing rules, health information, safety procedures, and so on, and being able to understand and apply such knowledge. As students mature, they learn to

analyze different activities, develop personalized exercise routines (synthesis), and evaluate their fitness levels.

3. *Affective domain.* The affective domain (Krathwohl et al., 1964) deals with feelings, attitudes, and values. The major categories of learning in this area are receiving, responding, valuing, organizing, and characterizing. The affective domain changes more slowly than do the psychomotor and cognitive domains. How teachers treat students and the feelings students develop toward physical education are ultimately more important than the knowledge and skill developed in physical education programs.

Behavioral objectives are time-consuming to write. Some teachers become bogged down and discouraged because the number of objectives appears overwhelming. A text edited by Chepko and Arnold (2000) offers a wide variety of behavioral objectives and sample assessment activities based on content standards. This text expedites the task of writing a standards-based curriculum. The following are examples of behavioral objectives related to the NASPE content standards listed in Chapter 1:

Psychomotor Domain

1. Move efficiently using a variety of locomotor skills such as walking, running, skipping, and hopping.
2. Perform body management skills on a variety of apparatus including climbing ropes, benches, and balance beams.

Cognitive Domain

1. Understand words that describe a variety of relationships with objects such as *around, behind, over, through,* and *parallel.*
2. Understand how warm-up and cool-down prevent injuries.

Affective Domain

1. Show empathy for the concerns and limitations of peers.
2. Demonstrate a willingness to participate with peers regardless of diversity or disability.

Step Five: Select Child-Centered Activities

When selecting activities for a child-centered curriculum, a clear understanding of children is requisite. The task of designing a program that flows with children and doesn't run contrary to their urges, characteristics, and interests requires a clear view of their nature. It makes little sense to gather activities for instruction if they are not developmentally appropriate or do not appeal to children. The major criterion to follow when selecting activities for the curriculum is, "Do the activities contribute to content standards and student-centered objectives?" This approach contrasts with selecting activities because they are fun or because you enjoy them. Some teachers fail to include activities in the curriculum if they lack confidence or feel incompetent. This results in a curriculum that is designed for the teacher's benefit rather than students'. If an activity contributes to content standards, it is necessary to develop requisite instructional competency. Imagine a math teacher choosing not to teach fractions or multiplication tables to students because of feelings of incompetence. It is your responsibility to learn to teach new activities so students experience and learn all requisite physical skills.

As many activities as possible that contribute to content standards should be gathered in the planning stage. The greater the number of activities considered, the more varied and imaginative the final program. In this step, place emphasis on brainstorming, creating, and innovating without restriction. The finished curriculum will be deficient if it is limited at this step. Later steps will offer an opportunity to delete inappropriate activities.

KNOW THE BASIC URGES OF CHILDREN

A basic urge is a desire to do or accomplish something. All children have similar urges, which are hereditary or environmentally influenced. Basic urges are linked closely to societal influences and are affected by teachers, parents, and peers. Usually, basic urges are similar among youngsters of all ages and are not affected by developmental maturity. These urges provide direction for creating child-centered experiences.

The Urge for Movement

Children have an insatiable appetite for moving, performing, and being active. They run for the sheer joy of running. For them, activity is the essence of living. Design a physical education program that takes advantage of this craving for movement.

The Urge for Success and Approval

Children like to achieve and have their achievements recognized. They wilt under criticism and disapproval, whereas encouragement and friendly support can promote growth and development. Failure can lead to frustration, lack of interest, and inefficient learning. Successes should far outweigh failures, and students should achieve a measure of success during each class meeting. Activities in the curriculum should be organized and presented in a manner that ensures that students will find an adequate amount of success.

The Urge for Peer Acceptance and Social Competence

Peer acceptance is a basic human need. Children want others to accept, respect, and like them. Teach and encourage peer acceptance in physical education and the overall school environment. Learning to cooperate with others, being a contributing team member, and sharing accomplishments with friends are important outcomes of the program for students.

The Urge to Cooperate and Compete

Children want to work and play with other children. They find satisfaction in being a needed part of a group and experience sadness when others reject them. Cooperation needs to be taught prior to competitive experiences since competition is impossible when people choose not to cooperate or follow the rules. Often, the joy of being part of a group far outweighs the gains from peer competition.

The Urge for Physical Fitness and Attractiveness

Boys and girls are eager to be fit, active, and attractive. Youngsters who have any type of disability suffer much humiliation. The opportunity to improve personal skills often helps students overcome subpar strength, lack of physical skill, inadequate physical fitness, and obesity.

The Urge for Adventure

The drive to participate in something different, adventurous, or unusual impels children to participate in interesting new activities. Youngsters are motivated by new and exciting activities and teaching methodologies. When youngsters want to know, "What are we going to do today?," they hope for something new and exciting. This urge is one of the reasons that physical education units in elementary schools should not be longer than two to three weeks in length.

The Urge for Creative Satisfaction

Children like to try different ways of doing things, to experiment with different implements, and to find creative ways of accomplishing goals. Finding different ways to express themselves physically satisfies the urge for creative action.

The Urge for Rhythmic Expression

Physical education should offer a variety of rhythmic activities that students can learn well enough to achieve satisfaction. Emphasize the natural rhythm involved in all physical activity, be it walking, running, or skipping. Many effective and beautiful sport movements can be done rhythmically, including shooting layups, jumping rope, and running hurdles.

The Urge to Know

Young people are naturally curious. They are interested not only in what they are doing but also in why they are doing it. Knowing why is a great motivator. It takes little time or effort to share with a class why an activity is performed and the contributions it makes to physical development.

UNDERSTAND THE CHARACTERISTICS AND INTERESTS OF CHILDREN

The urges of children represent broad traits that are typical of children regardless of age, sex, or race. In contrast, characteristics and interests are age- and maturity-specific attributes that influence learning objectives. The characteristics and interests chart (Table 4.1) provides information that influences appropriate selection and sequencing of curriculum activities. The information in the chart is broken down by the three learning domains—psychomotor, cognitive, and affective—and is grouped by developmental levels, which are discussed in the next section.

Step Six: Organize Selected Activities into Instructional Units

After appropriate activities that contribute to content standards have been selected, design a delivery system that ensures all activities are taught. Activities are most often grouped by grade level or developmental level. Developmental levels are used to group activities and units of instruction in this textbook because such grouping allows for greater variation of skill development among students. Even though this developmental skill continuum is common to all youngsters, there are large variations among children. Placing activities in developmental levels offers activities that are appropriate for the maturity and developmental levels of all youngsters. On occasion, it may be necessary to move to a higher or lower developmental level to accommodate youngsters. Table 4.2 on page 76 shows how developmental levels roughly equate with grades and ages. The following section describes characteristics of learners at each level and identifies skills and competencies typical of children in each of the levels. Refer back to Table 3.2 in Chapter 3 for a summary of characteristics of activities at the three developmental levels.

Developmental Level I

For the majority of children, activities used in Developmental Level I are appropriate for kindergarten through second grade. Most activities for younger children are

TABLE 4.1   Characteristics and interests of children

Characteristics and Interests	Program Guidelines
Developmental Level I	
Psychomotor Domain	
Noisy, constantly active, egocentric, exhibitionistic. Imitative and imaginative. Want attention.	Include vigorous games and stunts, games with individual roles (hunting, dramatic activities, story plays), and a few team games or relays.
Large muscles more developed; game skills not developed.	Challenge with varied movement. Develop specialized skills of throwing, catching, and bouncing balls.
Naturally rhythmic.	Use music and rhythm with skills. Provide creative rhythms, folk dances, and singing movement songs.
May become suddenly tired but soon recover.	Use activities of brief duration. Provide short rest periods or intersperse physically demanding activities with less vigorous ones.
Hand-eye coordination developing.	Give opportunity to handle different objects such as balls, beanbags, and hoops.
Perceptual abilities maturing.	Give practice in balance—unilateral, bilateral, and cross-lateral movements.
Pelvic tilt can be pronounced.	Give attention to posture problems. Provide abdominal strengthening activities.
Cognitive Domain	
Short attention span.	Change activity often. Give short explanations.
Interested in what the body can do. Curious.	Provide movement experiences. Pay attention to educational movement.
Want to know. Often ask *why* about movement.	Explain reasons for various activities and the basis of movement.
Express individual views and ideas.	Allow children time to be creative. Expect problems when children are lined up and asked to perform the same task.
Begin to understand the idea of teamwork.	Plan situations that require group cooperation. Discuss the importance of such.
Sense of humor expands.	Insert some humor in the teaching process.
Highly creative.	Allow students to try new and different ways of performing activities; sharing ideas with friends encourages creativity.
Affective Domain	
No gender differences in interests.	Set up same activities for boys and girls.
Sensitive and individualistic; self-concept very important.	Teach taking turns, sharing, and learning to win, lose, or be caught gracefully.
Accept defeat poorly. Like small-group activity.	Use entire class group sparingly. Break into smaller groups.
Sensitive to feelings of adults. Like to please teacher.	Give frequent praise and encouragement.
Can be reckless.	Stress safe approaches.
Enjoy rough-and-tumble activity.	Include rolling, dropping to the floor, and so on, in both introductory and program activities. Stress simple stunts and tumbling.
Seek personal attention.	Recognize individuals through both verbal and nonverbal means. See that all have a chance to be the center of attention.
Love to climb and explore play environments.	Provide play materials, games, and apparatus for strengthening large muscles (e.g., climbing towers, climbing ropes, jump ropes, miniature challenge courses, and turning bars).

(continued)

TABLE 4.1	Characteristics and interests of children *(continued)*
Characteristics and Interests	**Program Guidelines**

Developmental Level II

Psychomotor Domain

Characteristics and Interests	Program Guidelines
Capable of rhythmic movement.	Continue creative rhythms, singing movement songs, and folk dancing.
Improved hand-eye and perceptual-motor coordination.	Give opportunity for manipulating hand apparatus. Provide movement experience and practice in perceptual-motor skills (right and left, unilateral, bilateral, and cross-lateral movements).
More interest in sports.	Begin introductory sport and related skills and simple lead-up activities.
Sport-related skill patterns mature in some cases.	Emphasize practice in these skill areas through simple ball games, stunts, and rhythmic patterns.
Developing interest in fitness.	Introduce some of the specialized fitness activities to third grade.
Reaction time is slow.	Avoid highly organized ball games that require and place a premium on quickness and accuracy.

Cognitive Domain

Characteristics and Interests	Program Guidelines
Still active but attention span longer. More interest in group play.	Include active big-muscle program and more group activity. Begin team concept in activity and relays.
Curious to see what they can do. Love to be challenged and will try anything.	Offer challenges involving movement problems and more critical demands in stunts, tumbling, and apparatus work. Emphasize safety and good judgment.
Interest in group activities; ability to plan with others developing.	Offer group activities and simple dances that involve cooperation with a partner or a team.

Affective Domain

Characteristics and Interests	Program Guidelines
Like physical contact and belligerent games.	Include dodging games and other active games, as well as rolling stunts.
Developing more interest in skills. Want to excel.	Organize practice in a variety of throwing, catching, and moving skills, as well as others.
Becoming more conscious socially.	Teach need to abide by rules and play fairly. Teach social customs and courtesy in rhythmic areas.
Like to perform well and to be admired for accomplishments.	Begin to stress quality. Provide opportunity to achieve.
Essentially honest and truthful.	Accept children's word. Give opportunity for trust in game and relay situations.
Do not lose willingly.	Provide opportunity for children to learn to accept defeat gracefully and to win with humility.
Gender difference still of little importance.	Avoid separation of genders in any activity.

individual in nature and center on learning movement concepts through theme development. Children learn about movement principles, and educational movement themes are used to teach body identification and body management skills. By stressing the joy and personal benefits of physical activity, positive behaviors can be developed that last a lifetime.

Developmental Level II

Developmental Level II activities are usually appropriate for the majority of third- and fourth-grade children. In Developmental Level II activities, refinement of fundamental skills occurs and the ability to perform specialized skills begins to surface. Practicing manipulative skills enhances visual-tactile coordination. This is a time

TABLE 4.1   Characteristics and interests of children *(continued)*

Characteristics and Interests	Program Guidelines
Developmental Level III	
Psychomotor Domain	
Steady growth. Girls often grow more rapidly than boys.	Continue vigorous program to enhance physical development.
Muscular coordination and skills improving. Interested in learning detailed techniques.	Continue emphasis on teaching skills through drills, lead-up games, and free practice periods. Emphasize correct form.
Differences in physical capacity and skill development.	Offer flexible standards so all find success. In team activities, match teams evenly so individual skill levels are less apparent.
Posture problems may appear.	Include posture correction and special posture instruction; emphasize effect of body carriage on self-concept.
Sixth-grade girls may show signs of maturity; may not wish to participate in all activities.	Have consideration for their problems. Encourage participation on a limited basis, if necessary.
Sixth-grade boys are rougher and stronger.	Keep genders together for skill development but separate for competition in certain rougher activities.
Cognitive Domain	
Want to know rules of games.	Include instruction on rules, regulations, and traditions.
Knowledgeable about and interested in sport and game strategy.	Emphasize strategy, as opposed to merely performing a skill without concern for context.
Question the relevance and importance of various activities.	Explain regularly the reasons for performing activities and learning various skills.
Desire information about the importance of physical fitness and health-related topics.	Include in lesson plans brief explanations of how various activities enhance growth and development.
Affective Domain	
Enjoy team and group activity. Competitive urge strong.	Include many team games, relays, and combatives.
Much interest in sports and sport-related activities.	Offer a variety of sports in season, with emphasis on lead-up games.
Little interest in the opposite gender. Some antagonism may arise.	Offer coeducational activities with emphasis on individual differences of all participants, regardless of gender.
Acceptance of self-responsibility. Strong increase in drive toward independence.	Provide leadership and followership opportunities on a regular basis. Involve students in evaluation procedures.
Intensive desire to excel both in skill and in physical capacity.	Stress physical fitness. Include fitness and skill surveys both to motivate and to check progress.
Respect for teammates a concern for both teachers and students.	Establish and enforce fair rules. With enforcement include an explanation of the need for rules and cooperation if games are to exist.
Peer group important. Want to be part of the gang.	Stress group cooperation in play and among teams. Rotate team positions as well as squad makeup.

when children explore, experiment, and create activities without fear. While these activities do not stress conformity, children learn the how and why of activity patterns. Cooperation with peers receives more emphasis through group and team play. Initial instruction in sport skills begins in Developmental Level II, and a number of lead-up activities allow youngsters to apply newly learned skills in a small-group setting.

Developmental Level III

Developmental Level III activities place more emphasis on specialized skills and sport activities. The majority of activities at this level are used with fifth- and sixth-grade students. Football, basketball, softball, track and field, volleyball, and hockey are added to sport offerings. Students learn and improve sport skills while participating in cooperative sport lead-up games. Less

TABLE 4.2	Equating developmental levels to grades and ages	
Developmental Level	**Grades**	**Ages**
I	K–2	5–7
II	3–4	8–9
III	5–6	10–11

emphasis is placed on movement concept activities, and a larger percentage of instructional time is devoted to manipulative activity. Adequate time is set aside for the rhythmic program and for the program area involving apparatus, stunts, and tumbling.

After assigning activities to developmental levels, the activities in each instructional unit are organized in order of difficulty, starting with the easiest to master and finishing with the most difficult. Organizing activities in progression (a) helps children be successful because the easiest activities are taught first, (b) ensures that safety and liability factors are met, since the activities are presented in proper sequence, and (c) aids teachers in finding a starting point for sound instruction.

Another element that should be included in the unit of instruction is a list of teaching hints that encompass safety, teaching for quality, dispersing equipment properly, and instructional cues that enhance motor skill development. An accompanying curriculum and lesson plan text by Pangrazi (2007) incorporates activities in this textbook and places them into lesson plans by developmental level. The lesson plans contain activity progressions, teaching hints, and learning objectives that help minimize the demands of planning. In addition to the weekly lesson plans, a yearlong curriculum is offered for each of the three developmental levels.

Table 4.3 illustrates the parallel listing of the four parts of the lesson in the yearly curriculum. This plan ensures that youngsters learn many ways of warming up for activity and approximately 15 different types of fitness activity. In addition, they are exposed to 20 to 25 lesson activities that focus on skill development and 60 to 80 low-organized game activities.

WEEKLY UNITS

Organizing the curriculum into weekly activity units is a common approach. When using this approach, instruction focuses on the same activity over an entire week. The weekly plan has three major advantages. First, one comprehensive lesson plan will suffice for the week and keep planning duties manageable. The objective is to move children along the path of learning at an optimal rate. What cannot be covered one day is taught in the next lesson. Second, less orientation instruction is needed after the first day. Safety factors, teaching hints,

and key points need only a brief review each day and equipment needs are similar from day to day. Third, progression and learning sequences are evident; both teacher and children can see improvement.

Activities in the lesson focus section of the lesson plans begin with skills all students can perform and progress to a point where further instruction and skill practice are necessary because students are challenged. Starting each lesson with basic activities ensures that all students begin with success. This is critical for developing positive attitudes toward new activities. If the first thing youngsters experience is failure, the rest of the unit will be a tough sell. Build instructional sequences for each day based on the preceding lesson. Keep the length of units of instruction to one or two weeks so students do not become bored or discouraged. Long units force children who are unskilled or who dislike the activity to have to live with failure for long periods of time. If more time is needed for a specific unit, add another week or two later in the year. Use a game activity to provide a change of pace when the motivational level of the class (and, in turn, of the teacher) appears to be waning.

Another approach to yearly planning is to use the movement theme approach. This approach takes a set of skills or movements and offers a wide variety of activities for instruction related to the same skill. A wide variety of equipment is needed since the same skills are taught using different activities and equipment.

CHECK THE SCOPE, SEQUENCE, AND BALANCE OF THE CURRICULUM

An important step in creating a quality program is to review and monitor the scope, sequence, and balance of the curriculum. These are important concepts that ensure that the curriculum is comprehensive and varied.

Scope is the yearly content of the curriculum. Scope is also referred to as the horizontal articulation of the curriculum. Monitoring the scope of the curriculum ensures that the entire content of the program will be covered in a systematic and accountable fashion. In elementary school physical education, the scope of the curriculum is broad; many activities are presented rather than in-depth coverage of a few activities. The reason for this is that student interest wanes if units are too long. Also, elementary school physical education is designed to help students learn about all the available types of physical activity.

Sequence, or vertical articulation, of the curriculum defines the skills and activities to be covered on a year-to-year basis. Sequence ensures that youngsters receive different instruction and activities at each developmental level. Of particular importance is the articulation of program material throughout elementary, middle, and senior high school programs.

Balance ensures that all objectives in the program receive adequate coverage. When reviewing the scope

TABLE 4.3 An example of a yearly plan: Developmental Level II

Week	Introductory Activity	Fitness Development Activity	Lesson Focus Activity	Game Activity
1	Move and freeze on signal	Teacher/leader movement challenges	Orientation	Back to Back Whistle Mixer
2	Fundamental movements and stopping	Teacher/leader exercises	Manipulative skills using wands and hoops	Hand Hockey Cageball Kickover Home Base
3	Move and assume pose	Teacher/leader exercises	Throwing skills (1)	Whistle Mixer Couple Tag Partner Stoop
4	Creative routines	Hexagon Hustle	Football-related activities	Football End Ball Five Passes
5	Four-corners movement	Hexagon Hustle	Manipulative skills using playground balls	Bounce Ball One Step
6	Run, stop, and pivot	Circuit training	Fundamental skills using tug-of-war ropes and relays	Nonda's Car Lot Indianapolis 500
7	European running	Circuit training	Stunts and tumbling skills (1)	Whistle Mixer Competitive Circle Contests Alaska Baseball
8	Magic number challenges	Astronaut drills	Soccer-related activities (1)	Circle Kickball Soccer Touch Ball Diagonal Soccer Soccer Take-Away
9	New leader	Astronaut drills	Soccer-related activities (2)	Soccer Touch Ball Diagonal Soccer Dribblerama Bull's-Eye
10	Group over and under	Aerobic fitness	Fundamental skills using parachutes	Nine Lives Box Ball
11	Bend, stretch, and shake	Aerobic fitness	PE games Recreational activities	Addition Tag Alaska Baseball Recreational Activities
12	Fastest tag in the West	Walk, trot, and jog	Walking and jogging skills	Recreational Activities
13	Jumping and hopping patterns	Challenge course fitness	Rhythms (1)	Whistle March Arches Home Base
14	Group tag	Walk, trot, and jog	Long rope-jumping skills	Fly Trap Trades Fox Hunt
15	Fleece ball fun	Challenge course	Stunts and tumbling skills (2)	Partner Stoop Crows and Cranes
16	Ball activities	Challenge course	Rhythms (2)	Fox Hunt Steal the Treasure Addition Tag
17	Partner leaping	Aerobic fitness and partner resistance	Basketball-related activities (1)	Birdie in the Cage Dribblerama Captain Ball Basketball Tag

(continued)

		Fitness		
Week	Introductory Activity	Development Activity	Lesson Focus Activity	Game Activity
18	Bridges by three	Aerobic fitness and partner resistance	Basketball-related activities (2)	Captain Ball Five Passes Around the Key
19	Locomotor and manipulative activity	Exercise to music	Throwing skills (2)	In the Prison Snowball Center Target Throw Target Ball Throw
20	Yarnball fun	Exercise to music	Fundamental skills using benches	Cageball Kickover Squad Tag
21	Low organizational games	Continuity drills	Hockey-related activities (1)	Circle Keepaway Star Wars Hockey Lane Hockey Circle Straddleball
22	Following activity	Continuity drills	Hockey-related activities (2)	Modified Hockey Lane Hockey
23	Moving to music	Aerobic fitness	Manipulative skills using paddle and balls	Steal the Treasure Trees
24	Stretching activities	Stretching activities	Track and field skills (1)	Potato Shuttle Relay Shuttle Relays
25	Stretching activities	Stretching activities	Track and field skills (2)	Circular Relays Shuttle Relays One-on-one contests
26	Move and perform task	Walk, trot, and jog	Manipulative skills using beanbags	Crows and Cranes Galloping Lizzie
27	Long rope routine	Parachute fitness	Rhythms (3)	Jump the Shot Beachball Batball Club Guard
28	Squad leader movement	Parachute fitness	Stunts and tumbling skills (3)	Trades Beachball Batball
29	European running with equipment	Exercise to music	Individual rope-jumping	Loose Caboose Wolfe's Beanbag Exchange Tag
30	Marking	Circuit training	Volleyball-related skills (1)	Beachball Volleyball Informal Volleyball
31	Tag games	Hexagon Hustle	Volleyball-related skills (2)	Beachball Volleyball Shower Service Ball
32	Combination movement patterns	Continuity drills	Rhythms (4)	Alaska Baseball Addition Tag
33	European running with variations	Aerobic fitness	Manipulative skills using Frisbees	Frisbee Keepaway Frisbee Golf
34	Tortoise and hare	Aerobic fitness	Fundamental skills using balance beams	Hand Hockey Nonda's Car Lot
35	Move and perform task	Parachute exercises	Softball-related activities (1)	Throw It and Run Two-Pitch Softball Hit and Run
36	Walk, trot, and sprint	Teacher/leader exercises	Softball-related activities (2)	Beat Ball Kick Softball In a Pickle

TABLE 4.3 An example of a yearly plan: Developmental Level II *(continued)*

and sequence of the curriculum, adhering to balance avoids a skewing toward one particular area. To ensure balance, major areas of emphasis are determined based on program objectives. These areas can be allotted a percentage of program time based on the characteristics and interests of students. This determination reveals to administrators, teachers, and parents the direction and emphasis of the program. All areas have a proportionate share of instructional time, and the percentage of time allotted to each area reflects its needs and characteristics.

Another phase of balance is alternating units based on the type of student interaction required, that is, individual, dual (partner), and small-group or large-group activities. Team sports require organization in a large group, whereas a movement concepts lesson is individual in nature. Learning to catch is a partner activity, whereas a lead-up game requires small groups. The *Dynamic Physical Education Curriculum Guide* (Pangrazi, 2007) is balanced in this manner. Individual units are followed by a small-or large-group activity, etc. Balance ensures that children do not have to stay with one type of activity too long. It gives them a chance to experience the types of physical activity they enjoy on a regular basis.

Step Seven: Evaluate and Modify the Curriculum

Evaluation schedules and suggested techniques for modifying the curriculum are an integral part of the curricular structure. A number of sources can supply evaluative data: pupils, teachers, consultants, parents, and administrators. The type of data desired can vary. Achievement test scores can supply hard data to compare pre-assessments and post-assessments with those of other programs. Subjective assessments might include likes and dislikes, value judgments, problem areas, and needed adjustments. The evaluation schedule can select a limited area for assessment, or assessment can be broadened to cover the entire program. Collecting information is only the first step; the information must be translated into action. Modification of possible program deficiencies is based on sound educational philosophy. If the program has weak spots, identifying the weaknesses and determining the causes are important steps to take.

A pilot or trial project can be instituted if the new curriculum represents a radical change. One school in the district might be chosen to develop a pilot program. Site selection should offer the program a strong opportunity to succeed, for success depends in large part on the educational climate of the school. In some cases, the experimental program might be implemented with only one class in a school. Enthusiastic, skilled direction is necessary for such projects. Much information can be

derived from this pilot process before an entire program is implemented throughout the school system.

REFLECTION AND REVIEW QUESTIONS

How and Why

1. What is your value orientation for physical education? How will this influence your teaching?

2. Why have a curriculum?

3. Who should be involved in the curriculum development?

4. What issues must be considered by curriculum designers?

5. How are the needs, interests, and characteristics of elementary students today the same as or different from what they were 30 years ago?

Content Review

1. List and discuss the seven steps for designing a quality physical education curriculum.

2. State what environmental factors can impact a curriculum. Discuss your answers.

3. Define and discuss the importance of standards and student objectives.

4. Explain the importance of student-centered objectives.

5. Explain the role of the scope, sequence, and balance of a curriculum.

6. Discuss the three learning domains. Explain each.

7. List the components that are common to quality physical education curricula.

8. State what needs, characteristics, and interests of children must be considered when designing a physical education curriculum. Include comments regarding the impact of age and maturity on program development.

FOR MORE INFORMATION

References and Suggested Readings

Barrett, K. R., Williams, K., & Whitall, J. (1992). What does it mean to have a "developmentally appropriate physical education program"? *The Physical Educator, 49*(3), 113–117.

Bloom, B. S. (Ed.). (1956). *Taxonomy of educational objectives, the classification of educational goals, handbook I: The cognitive domain.* New York: David McKay.

Chepko, S., & Arnold, R. K. (Eds.). (2000). *Guidelines for physical education programs, K–12: Standards, objectives and assessments.* Boston: Allyn and Bacon.

Corbin, C. B. (1976). *Becoming physically educated in the elementary school.* Philadelphia: Lea & Febiger.

Gabbard, C. (2004). *Lifelong motor development.* 4th ed. San Francisco: Benjamin Cummings.

Gallahue, D. L., & Donnelly, F. C. (2003). *Developmental physical education for all children.* 4th ed. Champaign, IL: Human Kinetics Publishers.

Graham, G., Holt/Hale, S. A., & Parker, M. (2004). *Children moving.* 6th ed. Boston: McGraw-Hill.

Jewett, A., Bain, L., & Ennis, K. (1995). *The curriculum process in physical education.* Dubuque, IA: Wm. C. Brown and Benchmark.

Kirchner, G., & Fishburne, G. J. (1998). *Physical education for elementary school children.* 10th ed. Boston: WCB/McGraw-Hill.

Krathwohl, D. R., Bloom, B. S., & Masia, B. B. (1964). *Taxonomy of educational objectives, handbook II: Affective domain.* New York: David McKay.

Lambert, L. T. (1999). *Standards-based assessment of student learning: A comprehensive approach.* Reston, VA: National Association for Sport and Physical Education.

Melograno, V. J. (1996). *Designing the physical education curriculum.* 3rd ed. Champaign, IL: Human Kinetics.

Mosston, M., & Ashworth, S. (2002). *Teaching physical education.* 5th ed. San Francisco: Benjamin Cummings.

National Association for Sport and Physical Education (NASPE). (2004). *Moving into the future: National standards for physical education.* Reston, VA: American Alliance for Health, Physical Education, Recreation and Dance.

Pangrazi, R. P. (2007). *Dynamic physical education curriculum guide: Lesson plans for implementation.* 15th ed. San Francisco: Benjamin Cummings.

Rink, J. E. (2002). *Teaching physical education for learning.* 5th ed. Boston: WCB/McGraw-Hill.

Siedentop, D., & Tannehill, D. (2000). *Developing teaching skills in physical education.* 4th ed. Mountain View, CA: Mayfield Publishing Co.

Wuest, D., & Lombardo, B. (1994). *Curriculum and instruction: The secondary school physical education experience.* St. Louis, MO: Mosby.

Websites

Learning Domains

http://coe.sdsu.edu/eet/Articles/BloomsLD/index.htm
http://officeport.com/edu/blooms.htm

Physical Education Curriculum Information

www.pecentral.com
www.pelinks4u.org
www.pe4life.org
www.masterteacher.com

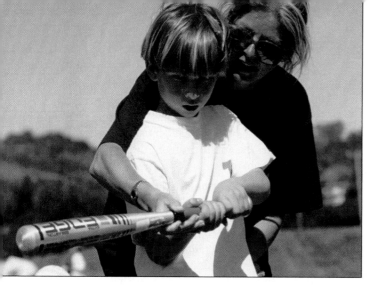

Improving Instructional Effectiveness

ESSENTIAL COMPONENTS OF QUALITY PROGRAMS

▶ **I. Organized around content standards**

II. Student-centered and developmentally appropriate

III. Physical activity and motor skill development form the core of the program

IV. Teaches management skills and self-discipline

▶ **V. Promotes inclusion of all students**

▶ **VI. Focuses on process over product**

VII. Promotes lifetime personal health and wellness

▶ **VIII. Teaches cooperation and responsibility and promotes sensitivity to diversity**

NATIONAL STANDARDS FOR PHYSICAL EDUCATION*

1. Demonstrates competency in motor skills and movement patterns needed to perform a variety of physical activities.

2. Demonstrates understanding of movement concepts, principles, and tactics as they apply to the learning and performance of physical activities.

3. Participates regularly in physical activity.

4. Achieves and maintains a health-enhancing level of physical fitness.

5. **Exhibits responsible personal and social behavior that respects self and others in physical activity.**

6. Values physical activity for health, enjoyment, challenge, self-expression, and/or social interaction.

*National Association for Sport and Physical Education (NASPE), 2004.

SUMMARY

Some instructional elements in quality lessons cut across all presentations regardless of the students' ages or grades, or lesson content. Diversity and gender are two areas that particularly impact instruction in physical education. A number of strategies for enhancing diversity and reducing gender stereotyping are outlined in this chapter. Instructional effectiveness can be improved by using instructional cues, demonstration, modeling, and feedback. Communication with students clearly increases by offering one or two key points while simultaneously demonstrating the desired behavior. Listening skills are as important as speaking skills when trying to establish meaningful relationships with students. Instructional cues—words or phrases—can be used as quick and efficient communication regarding proper technique in the performance of a particular skill or movement. Feedback to students can be delivered in various ways, including positive, negative, and corrective. Over time, positive feedback is the most effective means for developing positive attitudes toward activity. Instruction is best when it is personalized and offers something of value to each individual.

OUTCOMES

- Know how to teach for the promotion of diversity in physical education classes.

- Understand how gender stereotypes can be minimized.

- Identify various ways to effectively communicate with youngsters in a physical education learning environment.

- Understand the procedures needed to develop effective instructional cues.

- Cite various ways to enhance the clarity of communication between the teacher and the learner.

- Identify essential elements of instruction and discuss the manner in which each relates to the learning environment.

- Describe the value of nonverbal behavior in the physical education setting.

- Describe various demonstration and modeling skills that facilitate an environment conducive to learning.
- Understand how instructional cues can be used to increase student performance.
- Articulate techniques that supply youngsters with meaningful feedback regarding performance.
- Describe various ways to personalize instruction within the physical education setting.

Quality instructors create a positive atmosphere for learning. They may not know more about skills and activities than less capable teachers, but they are able to apply a set of effective instructional skills. This chapter deals with instructional techniques that all teachers can master. Becoming an effective teacher demands an inward look in order to see one's teaching personality and how it impacts learning. How teachers interact with students, in large part, influences how those students feel.

CHARACTERISTICS OF A QUALITY LESSON

Regardless of the teaching style used, an effective learning environment is characterized by a set of instructional behaviors that occur regularly. These behaviors do not describe a specific method or style but allow significant room for individual approaches to teaching content. The focus is less on what the teacher does and more on what students do. For example, any style of teaching that produces high rates of student-engaged time and positive attitudes toward the subject matter is considered an effective learning environment. Evidence from teacher effectiveness research (Brophy & Good, 1986; Evertson, 1989; Siedentop & Tannehill, 2000) indicates that, regardless of the teacher's instructional style, an educational environment is most effective when the following elements are present:

1. **Students are engaged in appropriate learning activities for a large percentage of class time.** Effective teachers use class time wisely. They plan carefully and insist on appropriate learning activities that deal with the subject matter. Students need time to learn; effective teachers ensure that students use class time to receive information and practice skills. Developmental learning activities are matched to students' abilities and contribute to overall class objectives.

2. **The learning atmosphere is success oriented, with a positive, caring climate.** Teachers who develop a supportive atmosphere foster learning and positive student attitudes toward school. Appropriate social and organizational behavior needs to be supported by teachers. Students and teachers must feel positive about working and learning in the physical education environment.

3. **Students are given clear objectives and receive high rates of information feedback from the teacher and the environment.** Students need to know what they are going to be held accountable for in the physical education class. Class activities are arranged so that students spend large amounts of time learning the required objectives. Instructional activities have a clear-cut tie to the class objectives. Positive and corrective feedback is regularly offered. The environment is designed so that students receive feedback on learning attempts even if the teacher is not available.

4. **Student progress is monitored regularly and students are held accountable for learning in physical education.** Students are expected to make progress toward class objectives. Students are able to assess and record their progress toward objectives. Students know exactly what is expected of them and how the expectations are tied to the accountability system. Rewards are available for small steps of progress toward larger goals.

5. **Low rates of management time and smooth transitions from one activity to another characterize the environment.** Effective teachers are efficient managers of students. Students move from one learning activity to another smoothly and without wasting time. Time-saving procedures are planned and implemented efficiently. Students spend little time waiting during instructional activities. Equipment is organized to facilitate smooth transitions. Instructional procedures are all tightly organized with little wasted time.

6. **Students spend a limited amount of time waiting in line or in other unproductive behaviors.** Effective environments are characterized by high rates of time engaged in subject matter. In physical education, this means high rates of time spent practicing, drilling, and playing. Physical education is activity-based and students learn by practicing the activity, not by waiting in line for an opportunity.

7. **Teachers are organized and have high but realistic expectations for student achievement.** Structure learning activities that challenge students. Activities must not be too easy or too difficult. Students need success and challenge from learning activities, and a balance of both is key to quality teaching. Expect students to learn, and hold them accountable for their progress.

8. **Teachers are enthusiastic about what they are doing and are actively involved in the instructional process.** Students need an enthusiastic model—someone who incorporates physical activity into his or her lifestyle. Active involvement means active supervision, enthusiasm, and high interaction rates with students. These characteristics enhance learning regardless of the teaching style used; they are important for ensuring student achievement and positive attitudes.

INCORPORATE ESSENTIAL ELEMENTS OF INSTRUCTION

Learning occurs when a well-planned curriculum is presented in a sound instructional manner. Education is effective when both a quality curriculum and able instruction are smoothly meshed. The curriculum is a critical component of the educational process; however, when the curriculum is poorly taught, student progress is limited. Hunter (1994) identified a set of essential elements for effective instruction, as shown in Figure 5.1. This section takes Hunter's approach to instruction and adapts it to physical education.

Design Measurable Student Outcomes

Educational outcomes give a lesson direction and meaning. Outcomes that are stated clearly let learners know what needs to be accomplished. Learning is enhanced when youngsters help select and set personal and group objectives. Discussions and teaching aids such as movies, videotapes, posters, and speakers can help

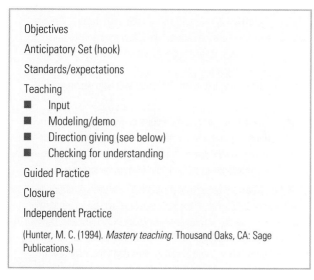

Objectives

Anticipatory Set (hook)

Standards/expectations

Teaching
- Input
- Modeling/demo
- Direction giving (see below)
- Checking for understanding

Guided Practice

Closure

Independent Practice

(Hunter, M. C. (1994). *Mastery teaching.* Thousand Oaks, CA: Sage Publications.)

FIGURE 5.1 Hunter's essential elements for effective instruction.

teachers and students work toward desirable objectives. Learning outcomes are characterized as follows:

- *First, outcomes must define observable behavior.* Teachers and students must know when an outcome is reached. If an objective is not clearly stated, neither party knows when it has been reached. Attainment in physical education is easier than in some other areas because most activities are overt and easy to observe.

- *Second, objectives must identify clearly and specifically the content to be learned.* Teachers and students will be comfortable when both parties clearly understand what is expected. Problems arise when students have to guess what the teacher wants them to learn. Students have a right to know what is expected and what they need to accomplish to reach the stated outcome. Stated outcomes help ensure that learning has occurred and that students know more than they did prior to reaching the desired outcomes. If outcomes are ambiguous or nonexistent, students have no way of knowing if they have improved or learned anything.

Develop outcomes for the three learning domains—psychomotor, cognitive, and affective. Psychomotor domain outcomes are defined most commonly in physical education and cover areas such as learning physical skills and developing health-related physical fitness. Cognitive outcomes for physical education aim toward knowledge and comprehension of skill performance principles and precepts related to fitness and activity. Affective outcomes focus on attitudes and behaviors such as learning to cooperate with peers on a team or behave in a responsible manner. Figure 5.2 provides examples of measurable student outcomes.

Determine the Instructional Entry Level

Entry level is defined as, "At what skill level do I begin instructing my class?" Instruction in a new activity should always begin with a successful experience or students will be turned off and see the rest of the unit as a negative experience. Selecting the level of difficulty for skill instruction is challenging because a class of students presents a wide variation in ability and maturation level. An important step in determining a proper instructional entry level is to formulate a desired terminal outcome (one that is just beyond the grasp of the most skillful student in the class). Ask yourself, "When this lesson is over, where do I want the students to be?" Then, develop a progression of essential learning activities that lead to the terminal outcome.

A way to determine entry level is to move through a progression of activities (easy to most difficult) until a

Psychomotor

"The student will demonstrate four ways to perform a forward roll."

"Using a jump rope, the student will be able to perform three consecutive forward crossover moves."

Cognitive

"The student will show an understanding of soccer rules by explaining when a corner kick is awarded."

"The student will demonstrate knowledge and understanding of rhythmic gymnastic routines by diagramming a sample floor routine for balls."

Affective

"After participating in physical activity, the students will be able to express their personal satisfaction in their accomplishments."

"The students will be able to share how they feel about participating in physical activities with friends."

F I G U R E   5 . 2   Examples of measurable outcomes.

number of students have difficulty performing them successfully. This accomplishes two things: It offers a review of skills (review makes students feel successful) and gives the instructor a general estimate of the students' ability levels. Another approach is to let students self-determine an entry level that they feel is best suited for them. For example, when using balance beams, use task charts listing skills students are to perform on the beam. Students then pick activities they feel competent in performing and progress at their own rate through the tasks. Instruction and learning are effective when students find an entry level that is appropriate for them.

Use Anticipatory Set

Anticipatory set refers to a technique designed to focus students on an upcoming instructional concept. The opening instructional sequence in a lesson is one of the more difficult sequences. Students are somewhat tentative about a new unit and need to be focused and prepared to move into the "learning mode." Use anticipatory set to "mentally warm up" a class. Anticipatory sets are most effective when they tie into students' past learning experiences. For example, in a basketball unit, asking students to identify why they are missing so many shots encourages them to think about technique. Instructional focus might involve discussing hand placement, keeping the eyes on the basket, or keeping the shooting elbow in. Anticipatory set is also used to reveal the skill level of students in the class. For

example, asking students, "What are three things we have to remember when tossing and catching bean-bags?" reveals whether they know the basic tenets of catching skills. Identifying what students know is necessary for designing an effective lesson.

Another type of anticipatory set is sharing with students the desired outcome. Tell students what they are going to learn and why it is important. Few people care about learning if the outcome is not stated or is thought to be unimportant. The more convinced students are about the importance of learning something, the more motivated they will be to participate.

It is not always necessary to use anticipatory set, but there should be a reason for omitting it. If students already know the necessary information, there is little value in taking time for anticipatory set. On the other hand, at the beginning of a lesson, after an interruption, or when choosing to move to a new objective, anticipatory set is effective. Examples of anticipatory sets are shown in Figure 5.3.

Deliver Meaningful Skill Instruction

Instruction is the cornerstone of learning because it is the way information is shared with students. Such information can include the definition of the skill; the elements or parts of the skill; and when, why, and how the skill should be used. The following are suggestions for effective instruction:

1. *Limit instruction to one or two key points.* It is difficult for anyone to remember a series of instructions.

- "On Monday we practiced the skills of passing, dribbling, and shooting layins. Yesterday we used those skills in a game of three-on-three. Take a few moments to think about the problems you had with dribbling or passing skills. (Allow time for thought and discussion.) Today we are going to use some drills that will help you improve in these areas."

- "Think of activities that require body strength and be ready to name some when called upon. (Allow time for thinking and discussion.) This week we are going to learn some activities that will help us become stronger."

- "What is it called when we move quickly in different directions? Think of as many activities as you can that require agility, and be ready to share with the class. (Allow time for thinking and discussion.) This week we are going to learn how to do Tinikling. This rhythmic activity will improve your agility level."

F I G U R E   5 . 3   Examples of anticipatory sets.

Telling students a number of points related to skill performance leaves them baffled and frustrated. In a series of points, most learners remember the first and the last points. Strong emphasis on one or two key points makes it easier for students to focus their concentration.

2. *Refrain from lengthy skill descriptions.* When instructions last longer than 30 to 60 seconds, students become listless because they can't comprehend and remember all of the input. Develop a pattern of short, concise presentations alternated with practice sessions. Short practice sessions offer an opportunity to refocus on key points of a skill many times.

3. *Present information in its most basic, easy-to-understand form.* If a class does not understand the presentation, you, not your students, have failed. Check for understanding (discussed further in the next section) to see if students comprehend the material.

4. *Separate management and instructional episodes.* Consider the following instructions during the presentation of a new game: "In this game, we will break into groups of five. Each group will get a ball and form a small circle. On the command 'Go,' the game will start. Here is how you play the game. . . ." A lengthy discussion of game rules and conduct follows. Because the instructions are long, students forget what they were asked to do earlier. Or, they think about whom they want in their group rather than the game rules. Instead, move the class into game formation (management) and then discuss the activity to be learned (instruction). This serves two purposes: It reduces the length of the episode, and makes it easier to conceptualize how the game is played.

Monitor Student Performance

Monitoring class performance ensures that students stay on-task and practice activities correctly. Effective monitoring involves being in a position where eye contact is made with all students. Students generally stay on-task when they know someone is watching them. Try to be unpredictable when positioning yourself throughout the teaching area. If students know where you like to stand to teach and observe, some of them will move away from you. You will find students who enjoy being nearby and students who like to move as far away as possible. Random positioning ensures contact and proximity with all students in the class.

A common but false assumption held by teachers is that they must move to the same area when giving instructions. The assumption is that students listen only when the teacher is on or near this "instructional spot." Not only is this incorrect, but it sometimes results in some rather negative consequences. Students who choose to exhibit deviant or off-task behaviors usually move as far away from the instructor as possible. If you always instruct from the same place, some of these students will try to move to a position that is difficult to observe. In addition, you won't move near students who need or want attention. Deliver instruction from the perimeter of the area and vary your location regularly.

Teacher movement coupled with effective observation keeps students on-task. Moving into position to observe skill performance enhances your ability to improve student learning. For example, if you are observing kicking, stand to the side rather than behind the student. When observing student performance, avoid staying too long with a single group of students or the rest of the class will begin to move off-task. Give a student one or two focus points and then move to another student.

Because teacher movement affects instructional effectiveness, it needs to be planned. To facilitate coverage, divide the instructional area into four (or more) equal areas and make an attempt to move into the far corner of each area a certain number of times. Try to give instructions and reinforcement from all four quadrants of the area. Ask a student to chart your movement if you are interested in reaching a personal goal. (See Figure 8.14, page 166, for an example of a chart for recording different teacher behaviors.)

Use Instructional Cues

Instructional cues are keywords that quickly and efficiently communicate proper technique and performance of skills and movement tasks. Children require a clear understanding of critical skill points because motor learning and cognitive understandings are developed simultaneously. Teaching activities without instructional cues can result in ineffective learning if students do not clearly understand proper technique and key points of performance. When using instructional cues, consider the following points:

DEVELOP PRECISE CUES

Make cues short, descriptive phrases that call attention to key points of skill technique. Cues must be precise and accurate. They should guide learners and enhance the quality of learning. Cues make it easier for learners to remember a sequence of new motor patterns. Study an activity and design cues that focus student learning on correct skill technique.

All teachers occasionally have to teach activities that they know little about. To develop cues in areas of less expertise, self-study must be conducted. Many textbooks and media aids delineate key points of skills. For example, *Teaching Cues for Basic Sport Skills for Elementary and Middle School Students* (Fronske & Wilson, 2002) offers teaching cues for a wide variety of physical activities. Other avenues of information are teachers who have strengths in different activities. Videotape an activity and analyze points of performance where students are having the most difficulty.

USE SHORT, ACTION-ORIENTED CUES

Effective cues are short and to the point. To avoid confusing and overwhelming the learner, choose a small number of cues to be presented during each lesson. Design cues that contain keywords and are short. Meaningful cues encourage the learner to focus on one phase of a skill during practice. For example, if a student is learning to throw, offer a cue such as, "Begin with your throwing arm farthest from the target." This cue reminds the student not to face the target, which precludes trunk rotation in later phases of the throw. Other examples of throwing cues are:

"Step toward the target."

"Keep your eye on the target."

"Shift your weight from the rear to the front foot."

To examine the effectiveness of cues, see if they communicate the skill as a whole. Have all the critical points of throwing been covered, or is the skill incorrect in certain phases? With most skills, the performance can be broken down into three parts: preparation, action, and recovery. Focus on one phase of a skill at a time, as most beginners can best concentrate on only one thing at a time. Action-oriented words are effective with children, particularly if the words have an exciting sound. For example, "*Pop up* at the end of the forward roll," "*Twist* the body during the throw," or "*Explode* off the starting line." In other situations, let the voice influence the effectiveness of the cue. For example, if a skill is to be done smoothly and softly, speak in a soft tone and ask students to "let the movement *floooooow*" or to "move *smooooooothly* across the balance beam." The most effective cues use voice inflections, body language, and action words to signal the desired behavior.

INTEGRATE CUES

Integration of cues involves putting the parts of a skill together so that learners can focus on the skill as a whole. Integrated cues depend on prior cues used during the presentation of a skill and assume the understanding

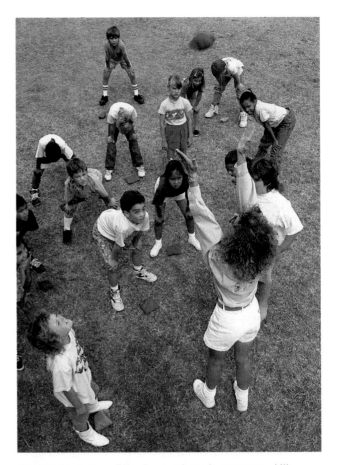

FIGURE 5.4   Effective teachers demonstrate skill techniques.

of concepts from earlier phases of instruction. Examples of integrated cues are:

"Step, rotate, throw."

"Run, jump, and forward roll."

"Stride, swing, follow through."

The first integrated cue ("Step, rotate, throw") reminds students to sequence parts of the skill. The second set of words ("Run, jump, and forward roll") helps young children remember a sequence of movement activities. Integrated cues help learners to remember proper sequencing of skills and to form mental images of the performance.

Enhance Instruction by Demonstrating Skills

A quick and effective way to present a physical activity is to demonstrate it (Figure 5.4). Effective demonstration accentuates critical points of performance. While demonstrating, simultaneously verbalize key focal points so students know what to observe. Both teachers and students

CHAPTER 5 | Improving Instructional Effectiveness **87**

- Students are in partners spread out about 20 yards apart; one partner has a football. "When kicking the football, take a short step with your kicking foot, a long step with the other foot, and kick (*demonstrate*). Again, short step, long step, kick (*teaching cue*)."

- "Listen to the first verse of this schottische music. I'll do the part of the schottische step we just learned starting with the second verse (*demonstrate*). Ready, step, step, step, hop (*teaching cue*). When I hit the tambourine, begin doing the step."

- "Today we are going to work on developing fitness by moving through the challenge course. Move through the course as quickly as you can, but do your best at each challenge; quality is more important than speed. Travel through the course like this (*demonstrate*). Move under the bar, swing on the rope, and so forth (*teaching cue*). When I say go, start at the obstacle nearest you."

FIGURE 5.5 Combining demonstration and teaching cues.

can demonstrate instructional activities. Regardless of who does it, in the early stages of learning it is important that the demonstration be clear and unambiguous.

Teachers cannot be expected to demonstrate all physical activities. Even skilled teachers need to devise an alternative plan for activities they cannot perform. Through reading, study, and analysis of movement, it is possible to develop an understanding of how to present activities. If performing an activity is impossible, know what key points of the activity should be emphasized. Use visual aids and media to enhance instruction.

When possible, slow down the demonstration and present it step-by-step. Many skills can be videotaped and played back in slow motion. The replay can be stopped at critical instances so students can emulate a position or technique. For example, in a throwing unit, freeze at a point that illustrates the position of the arm. Have students imitate moving the arm into proper position based on the stop-action pose. Figure 5.5 offers examples for combining teaching cues and demonstration.

Use Students to Demonstrate Skills

If you can't demonstrate a skill, find a student who can help. Be sure students can correctly demonstrate the desired skill so that they will not be embarrassed in front of the class. Usually, it is possible to find a capable student by verbally asking the class to perform the desired skill. Identify a student who is correctly performing the skill during the practice session and ask if

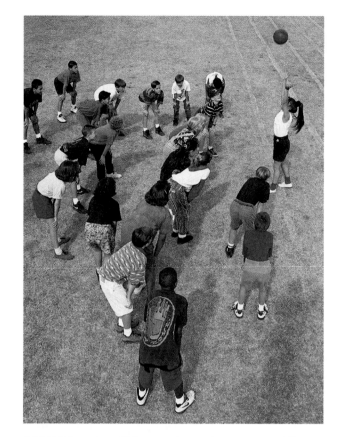

FIGURE 5.6 Using a student to demonstrate a skill.

he would be willing to demonstrate. Most students will not volunteer to demonstrate unless they feel able. While the student demonstrates the skill, identify key points of the action.

Student demonstration interjects original ideas into the lesson sequence (Figure 5.6). It also helps to build self-esteem if youngsters can successfully demonstrate. If you are unsure about students' abilities to demonstrate, ask them to try the activity while all other students are engaged. If they are successful, have them demonstrate. If not, let them know you will call on them at another time. At opportune times, stop the class and let children volunteer to show what they have done. Make comments about demonstrations positive in nature. If a demonstration is unsatisfactory, go on to another child without comment or reprimand, saying only, "Thank you, Janet. Let's see what Carl can do." Or redirect the class to continue practicing. Ensure that all students who want to be selected are given an opportunity at one time or another.

Check for Understanding

Checking to see if students comprehend instructional content is necessary to monitor student progress. Students are effective at displaying an exterior that says they understand even when they do not. Additionally, a common (but poor) habit of teachers is to ask periodically, "Does everybody understand?" It appears they are checking for understanding; however, this seldom is the case. More often than not, teachers do not even wait for a response. Further, it takes a brave and confident student to admit to a lack of understanding in front of the entire class. Therefore, it is important to find a quick and easy way to check for understanding without causing student embarrassment. The following are suggestions for monitoring student understanding:

1. *Use hand signals.* Examples might be: "Thumbs-up if you understand," or "If you think this demonstration is correct, balance on one foot," or "Raise the number of fingers to signal which student you think did a correct forward roll." If the signals are given quickly and without comment, students will signal quickly and privately without embarrassment. Signaling with the head down and the eyes closed can be used if the situation is touchy or embarrassing.

2. *Ask questions that can be answered in choral response.* Some students may mouth an answer even though they do not know the correct response. An indicator of the number of students who understand can be estimated by the intensity of the group response. A strong response by the class indicates that the majority of youngsters understand.

3. *Direct a forthcoming check to the entire class rather than to a specified student.* For example, "Be ready to demonstrate the grapevine step." This encourages all members of the class to focus on the activity, knowing they may be called on to demonstrate. Even though it does not ensure that everyone understands, it increases the possibility that students will think about the skill check.

4. *Use peer-checking methods.* Have students pair up and evaluate each other's performance using a checklist you have designed. More than one evaluation can be made by different students to help ensure the validity of the scoring.

5. *Use tests and written feedback to monitor cognitive concepts.* For example, written tests can be used to see if students can diagram and explain the options of an offense or a defense. Asking students to list safety precautions for an activity ensures student understanding. Use some restraint when administering written instruments—an excess of written assessments will take a great deal of time away from skill practice. Use these instruments when the information cannot be gathered more efficiently with other methods.

Offer Guided Practice

Guided practice helps ensure that students are performing a skill correctly. Practice does not necessarily make perfect if it is incorrect practice. Correct practice develops correct skill patterns, whereas incorrect practice ingrains mistakes. Guided practice helps a class move through each step of a skill correctly. During the early phases of guided practice, small amounts of information are presented. New skills build on previously learned skills so that students can see the importance of prerequisite learning.

Offer practice sessions as quickly as possible after students have been taught a skill. Allow them to get a "feel" for the skill as a whole before they work on parts of it. This opportunity to perform the skill before practicing smaller components enables the learner to see how the parts fit together. During guided practice sessions, monitor group responses and offer feedback to ease the pain of learning new activities. Make feedback specific, immediate, and focused on the skill being practiced. Make sure that drills and lead-up activities guarantee all students the same amount of practice. If anyone has to receive less practice, make it the skilled performer.

Bring Closure

Closure is a time to review learning that has taken place during the lesson. Closure helps increase retention because students review what they have learned. Focus closure discussions on what has been learned rather than on just naming activities practiced. Closure is not simply a recall of activities that were completed, but a discussion of the application of skills and knowledge learned through practice.

Closure can be an opportunity to show how movement patterns in different skills are similar to each other. Often, students do not realize that a movement pattern is parallel to one learned earlier. Discussing what was learned focuses students on what they should be learning through practice. Use closure as a time to remind a class to tell their parents and others what they have learned. How many times do parents ask, "What did you learn at school today?" only to hear the reply, "Nothing"? The following prompts are ways to initiate closure discussions:

"Describe two or three key components of skill performance to your partner."

"Demonstrate the proper skill when I (or a peer) give you a verbal cue."

"Use a closing activity that requires implementation of learned skills."

"Describe and demonstrate a key point for a new skill learned in the lesson."

An additional note about closure is in order here. Often teachers line up students at the end of the lesson in preparation for their return to the classroom. They then conduct closure, asking a number of questions. Unfortunately, students are close to each other, giving rise to an opportunity to disrupt the class by talking and bothering others. Leave the class spaced out in the teaching area and conduct closure. When it is time to line up, it can be done quickly and the opportunity for disruptive behavior will be reduced.

PROVIDE INSTRUCTIONAL FEEDBACK

Delivering student feedback is an important part of instruction. Used properly, feedback enhances a student's self-concept, improves the focus of performance, increases the rate of on-task behavior, and improves student understanding. Consider the following points to enhance the quality of your instructional feedback.

Types of Feedback

Much of the feedback delivered by teachers is corrective with a focus on rectifying or improving student performance. Outright negative feedback (such as, "That was a lousy throw") should always be avoided. Instead, corrective feedback should be offered with the intent of correcting a problem. Some corrective feedback is expected by students; however, when it is the only feedback offered, it creates a negative environment. A danger of overusing corrective feedback is that it will create a climate where students worry about making errors for fear the instructor will embarrass or belittle them. In addition, many youngsters surmise that no matter what they do correctly, they are never recognized for their effort.

Try to focus feedback on positive student performance. A positive atmosphere makes it easier for students to accept a challenge and to risk error or failure. Positive feedback also makes it easier to feel good about students because it focuses on their strengths. This is not to suggest that corrective feedback should never be used; Siedentop and Tannehill (2000) suggest that a four to one ratio of positive to corrective feedback is desirable. If your physical education experiences have been in a setting where most feedback is corrective, you may think it is the best way to teach, even though it isn't. It is usually necessary for most teachers to consciously increase positive feedback and decrease negative feedback given to students.

Use Meaningful Feedback Statements

It is easy to develop patterns of interaction that are positive, yet habitual. For example, statements such as, "Nice job," "Way to hustle," "Much better," "Right on," and "Great move" are often used repetitiously. When used habitually, students may "tune out" and fail to feel the positive nature of the comments. These general comments also contain little specific information or value content, thus allowing for misinterpretation. For example, after a student performs a forward roll, a "Nice job" comment is delivered. You, the teacher, were pleased with the performance because the student's head was tucked. However, the student thought you were pleased because her legs were bent. Nonspecific feedback can easily result in an incorrect behavior being reinforced.

Adding specific information or value to feedback improves desired student behavior (Figure 5.7). The value content of a feedback statement tells students why it is important to perform a skill in a certain manner. Students clearly understand why their performance was positive and can build on the reinforced behavior. Examples of positive feedback with value content are:

FIGURE 5.7 Delivering meaningful feedback.

"Good throw. When you look at your target, you are much more accurate."

"Excellent catch. You bent your elbows while catching, which created a soft home for the ball."

"That's the way to stop. When you bend your knees, you always stop under control."

Examples of feedback with specific content are as follows:

"That's the way to tuck your head on the forward roll."

"Wow! Everybody was dribbling the ball with their heads up."

"I'm impressed with the way you kept your arms straight."

Distribute Feedback Evenly

Feedback should be evenly distributed to all students by moving systematically from student to student, assuming there are no major discipline problems. This approach fosters contact with students a number of times during the lesson. In addition, it keeps students on-task because they know the teacher is moving and "eyeballing" everybody regularly. If skills are complex and refinement is a goal, it is better to take more time with individual students. This involves watching a student long enough to offer specific and information-loaded feedback. The result is high-quality feedback to fewer students.

When offering instructional feedback to a student, avoid scrutiny of the student at the completion of the feedback. Many students become tense when you tell them how to do something and then watch to see if they do it exactly as they were instructed. Students will be more willing to try new ways of performing if allowed to practice without close observation. Observe carefully, offer feedback, move on to another student, and recheck progress later.

Effective Feedback: Positive, Focused, and Immediate

Often feedback is group-oriented; that is, it is delivered to the entire class. This is an expedient method, but it also allows the most room for misinterpretation. Some students may not understand the feedback while others may not listen because it does not seem relevant. Sometimes feedback is directed to a youngster in such a way that other students hear it. Negative or corrective feedback that "ripples" through the class can be a debilitating experience for youngsters. Direct negative or corrective feedback personally to an individual so only you and the

student can hear it. This avoids resentment that might build due to being humiliated in front of peers.

Focus feedback on the desired refinement of a task. For example, if you want students to "give" while catching a ball thrown by a partner, avoid giving feedback about the quality of the throw. If catching is the focus, feedback should be on catching, as in, "Rachel is reaching out and giving with her hands when she catches the ball." It is not necessary to have students observe each other as they accomplish the desired outcome. Observing other students is effective only if the performer is capable of showing the skill correctly. If this approach is used exclusively, less skilled (or shy) performers will never have an opportunity to receive class feedback. Instead, tell the class how well a student is doing and move on; for example, "Mike always keeps his head up when dribbling." An added note: Students in Developmental Levels I and II are willing to be praised in front of other students. However, some older students will dislike being singled out. In this case, make feedback personal in nature.

Offer feedback to students as soon as possible after a correct performance. When feedback is delayed, allow opportunity for immediate practice so that students can apply the feedback information. Little is gained if students are told how to improve but are not given a chance to practice before leaving class. Few, if any, students remember points given in previous classes. If the end of class is approaching, it is probably best to limit feedback to situations that can be practiced immediately. Write down points of emphasis that you want to teach at the next class meeting.

Nonverbal Feedback

Nonverbal behavior is another way to deliver feedback. Nonverbal feedback is effective because it is easily interpreted by students and often perceived as more meaningful than words. Beginning teachers often have a difficult time coordinating their feelings and words with body language. They may be pleased with student performance, yet carry themselves in a less-than-pleased manner (with a frown on their face and their hands on their hips, for example). They may want to be assertive but take a submissive stance. For instance, when undesirable behavior occurs, an unsure teacher might place his hands in his pockets, stand in a slouched position, and back away from the class. These nonverbal behaviors signal anything but assertiveness and send students a mixed message.

Many types of nonverbal feedback can be used to encourage a class: the thrust of a finger into the air to signify "you're number 1," thumbs-up, high fives, shaking hands, and so on (Figure 5.8). In contrast to the positive nonverbal behaviors, negative nonverbal behaviors

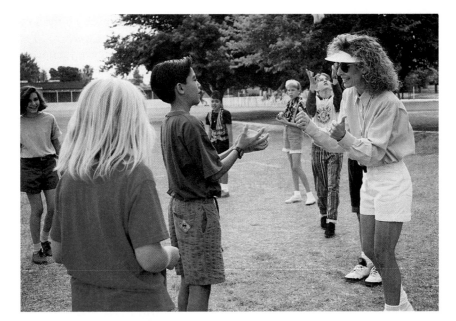

FIGURE 5.8   Using nonverbal communication.

can be delivered, including hands on the hips, finger to the lips, frowning, and staring. Effective use of nonverbal feedback increases the validity and strength of verbal communication.

When using nonverbal feedback, find out how the customs and mores of different cultures impact the response of youngsters to different types of gestures. For example, Hmong and Laotian children may be touched on the head only by parents and close relatives. A teacher who pats the child on the head for approval is interfering with the child's spiritual nature. The okay sign, touching thumb and forefinger, is an indication of approval in the United States. However, in several Asian cultures it is a "zero," indicating the child is not performing properly. In many South American countries, the okay sign carries a derogatory sexual connotation. Ask for advice when using nonverbal gestures with youngsters from other cultures.

To make nonverbal feedback more convincing, practice it in front of a mirror and attempt to display different emotions. Another way is to display a variety of behaviors to someone who does not know you well. If this person can identify the emotions and see them as convincing, you are an effective nonverbal communicator.

Videotape recorders are effective tools for self-analysis. Analyze how you look when under stress, when disciplining a student, when praising, and so on. It may be possible that you exhibit distracting or unassertive nonverbal behaviors such as playing with the whistle, slumping, putting your hands in your pockets, or shuffling your feet. Just as verbal feedback must be practiced and critiqued, so must nonverbal behavior.

CONSIDER THE PERSONAL NEEDS OF STUDENTS

If teaching only involved presenting physical activities to students, it would be a rather simple endeavor. The uniqueness of each student in a large class is a factor that makes teaching complex and challenging. This section focuses on ways to make instruction meaningful and personal. Teachers who are able to make each student feel important impact the lives of their students. Understanding the diversity of classes, encouraging student creativity, and allowing students to make educational decisions are some of the ways to make a lesson feel as if it were specifically designed for each student.

Teach for Diversity

Multicultural education allows all students to reach their potential regardless of the diversity among learners. Four major variables of diversity influence how teachers and students think and learn: race/ethnicity, gender, social class, and ability. Multicultural education creates an educational environment in which students from a variety of backgrounds and experience come together to experience educational equality (Manning & Baruth, 2004). Multicultural education assumes that children come from different backgrounds and helps them make sense of their everyday lives. It emphasizes the contributions of various groups that make up our country, and focuses on how to learn rather than on what to learn.

Current trends in growth in the United States are causing changes in classrooms. Children who were previously excluded from classes because of language, race, economics, and abilities are now learning together. Teaching now requires a pluralistic mind-set and the ability to communicate across cultures. It is the responsibility of educators to teach children to live comfortably and to prosper in this diverse and changing world. It is important that students celebrate their own culture while learning to integrate into the diversity of the world. For most students, classroom interaction between teachers and students is the major part of multicultural education they will receive. There are a number of things teachers can do to teach and value diversity:

1. Help students learn about the similarities and differences among cultures.
2. Encourage students to understand that people from similar cultures share common values, customs, and beliefs.
3. Make children aware of acts of discrimination and teach them ways to deal with inequity and prejudice.
4. Help youngsters develop pride in their family's culture.
5. Teach youngsters ways to communicate effectively with other cultures and races and with the other gender.
6. Instill respect for all people regardless of race/ethnicity, gender, social class, and ability.

How teachers perceive students strongly impacts their performance. Teachers who effectively teach for diversity hold high expectations for all students, including ethnic minority children and youth. Research shows that teachers tend to have lower expectations for ethnic minority youth (Vasquez, 1988). These low expectations occur in interpersonal interactions and in how students are placed in opportunities for enrichment and personal growth. At-risk youth need a rich curriculum that allows no room for failure and provides the necessary support for success.

Teachers have to know and educate themselves so they better understand the needs of all students. Diversity implies differences within and between cultures. Learning about other cultures ensures that working with students will be done with an increased understanding of past experiences each student has had. When working with different cultures, the focus should be on understanding the culture and the individuals. This contrasts with learning about a culture and then stereotyping its members as "all the same." It is important

to gather information about the cultures that are diverse and different from the teacher's. Teachers almost always teach like they have been taught and often with inadequate knowledge about other cultures. Fuller (2001) offers a number of questions to seek answers for when working with a different group or culture:

1. **What is their history?** Certainly few teachers can become experts in the history of all the cultures of the students they teach. However, they can recognize and be familiar with major events and important names within the cultures.
2. **What are their important cultural values?** Different cultures interact and discipline students in different ways. Ask parents and students how they work with children and what values are particularly important in their households.
3. **Who are influential individuals in their group?** Students will identify with local individuals who are held in high esteem in their community. Teachers who are aware of these important people will have insight into their students by knowing the role models they admire.
4. **What are their major religious beliefs?** Many groups belong to similar religions that drive many of their beliefs. Often, many values of children in a community area will be driven by religious beliefs.
5. **What are their important political beliefs?** Important political issues are often discussed at home. By making an effort to learn about these issues, teachers show they are interested in how their students live in their community.
6. **What political, religious, and social days do they celebrate?** Students will discuss these important days and expect teachers to understand why they celebrate them. Talking about these days with students creates goodwill and makes students feel like their culture is valued.

Increasing instructional focus on cooperative learning is strongly recommended. This offers students the opportunity to work together toward common goals and to feel positive about the different contributions of each member of the group. Diversity can also be increased through discussion sessions. The greater the number of students who participate, the better will be the chance for diverse and different points of view. When students are involved in discussions, they are usually attentive and participating in the learning process. Students are motivated by different approaches because they come from varied backgrounds. Getting to know students will increase the possibility of being able to effectively help them learn.

Some teaching tips that can help increase instructional effectiveness in a diverse setting follow:

- At the start of the school year (and at regular intervals thereafter), speak about the importance of encouraging and respecting diversity.

- When using group activities, insist that groups be diverse with regard to race, gender, and nationality.

- Be aware of how you speak about different groups of students. Do you refer to all students alike? Do you address boys and girls differently? Develop a consistent style for addressing all students regardless of their differences.

- Encourage all students to participate in discussions. Avoid allowing some students from certain groups to dominate interaction. Use a random method of picking students so that all have an equal chance of contributing.

- Treat all students with respect and expect students to treat each other with dignity. Intervene if a student or group of students is dominating.

- When a difficult situation arises over an issue with undertones of diversity, take a time-out and ask students to evaluate their thoughts and ideas. Allow all parties time to collect their thoughts and plan a response.

- Make sure evaluations and grades are written in gender-neutral or gender-inclusive terms.

- Encourage students to work with different partners every day. Students need to get to know other students in order to appreciate their differences.

- Invite to class guest speakers who represent diversity in gender, race, and ethnicity even if they are not speaking about multicultural or diverse issues.

- When students make comments that are sexist or racist, ask them to restate their ideas in a way that is nonoffensive to others. Teach students that it is all right to express one's opinion but not in an inflammatory manner.

- Use rotating leaders when using groups. Give all students the opportunity to learn leadership skills.

GENDER DIFFERENCES

Teachers play a large role in how children learn to behave. Adults model gender-specific behaviors for children and youngsters, who, in turn, copy the behavior. Research shows that teachers tend to treat boys and girls differently (Grossman & Grossman, 1994). For example, teachers pay more attention to boys and give boys more encouragement. Teachers give more praise for achievement to boys and call on girls less often than they call on boys. Teachers also respond to inappropriate behavior from boys and girls in different ways. Aggression is tolerated more in boys than in girls. However, disruptive talking is tolerated more in girls than in boys. Boys are reprimanded more than girls, and teachers use more physical means of disciplining boys.

The expectations a teacher has for boys and girls strongly impact how they interact in different ways with them. For example, teachers expect boys to be more active and more precocious and not to be as good academically. As a result, teachers pay closer attention to boys, and when boys do well, they are more likely to get positive attention. Girls, on the other hand, are expected to be more reserved and to do well academically, so they tend to be overlooked when they are doing "what they are supposed to do." When they misbehave, teachers see this as an aberration and are more negative to the female than they might be to the male. This is a common, yet unacceptable, pitfall among teachers. It takes a concerted effort to overcome these biases.

Some physical education teachers believe that girls aren't able to perform at a level similar to boys, even though research shows otherwise. Particularly in elementary school, differences in strength, endurance, and physical skills are minimal. An effective physical education environment helps all youngsters find success. Using the following teaching behaviors minimizes stereotyping by gender:

- Reinforce the performances of all students regardless of gender.

- Provide activities that are developmentally appropriate and allow all students to find success.

- Design programs that ensure success in coeducational experiences. Boys and girls can challenge each other to achieve higher levels if the atmosphere is positive.

- Don't use and don't accept students' stereotypical comments such as, "You throw like a girl."

- Include activities in the curriculum that cut across typical gender stereotypes such as rhythms are for girls, football is for boys.

- Arrange activities so the more aggressive and skilled students do not dominate. Little is learned if students are taught to be submissive or to play down their ability.

- Arrange practice sessions so that all students receive equal amounts of practice and/or opportunity to participate. Practice sessions should not give more practice opportunities to the skilled while the unskilled stand aside and observe.

- Expect all boys and girls to perform equally well. Teacher expectations communicate much about a student's ability level. Students view themselves through the eyes of their teacher.

Encourage Creative Responses

An effective lesson includes more than planned experiences. Offering students an opportunity to create and modify new experiences is an important part of the total learning environment. Effective lessons include opportunities for creative expression and student input regarding lesson implementation.

By encouraging creativity in the classroom, a teacher helps students develop habits of discovery and reflective and abstract thinking. Self-discovered concepts are often better retained and retrieved for future use. To encourage creativity, set aside time for youngsters to explore (Figure 5.9). For example, offer a hoop and the challenge, "See how many movements can be done with it." Offer creative opportunities during appropriate segments of the instructional sequence. Ask children to add on to a movement progression just presented or to expand it in a new direction. Make the lesson plan flexible enough to allow for creativity at teachable moments. Stimulate creativity with a show-and-tell demonstration. After a period of exploration, allow youngsters to demonstrate movement patterns they have created.

Allow Students to Make Educational Decisions

Decision-making is a large part of behaving in a responsible manner, but responsibility is a learned skill that takes practice. Part of the decision-making process is learning consequences that are tied to decisions and the impact those decisions have on others. Cognitive development of students can be enhanced by allowing them to be an integral part of the lesson—choosing content, implementing the lesson, and assessing each other's techniques and development. When students are allowed to make decisions at a young age, incorrect decisions

FIGURE 5.9 **FIGURE 5.9**   Creating different movement variations.

result in much less serious consequences and offer an opportunity to learn. If youngsters are always told how to behave when they are young, they may not know how to make serious decisions that impact their future as they age. Offer youngsters the opportunity to make decisions and choose from various alternatives, even if at times they make poor choices. The following are strategies that can be used to help youngsters learn to make decisions in a safe environment:

1. *Limit the number of choices.* This strategy retains ultimate control for the teacher, but gives students a chance to decide, in part, how the outcome is reached. Use this technique when learners have had little opportunity in the past to make decisions. If you have a new class and know little about the students, limit their choices. For example, permit students the choice of practicing either a drive or a pass shot in a hockey unit. The desired outcome is that students practice striking skills, but they can decide which striking skill to practice.

2. *Let students modify activities.* Allowing student modification of skills reduces pressure because it is no longer necessary to make exceptions and listen to student complaints that "it is too hard to do" or "I'm bored." Modification allows learners to change activities to suit their personal skill level. There are many ways to modify activities; some examples are:

   a. Use a slower-moving family ball rather than a handball.

   b. Increase the number of fielders in a softball game.

   c. Lower the basket in a basketball unit.

   d. Decrease the length of a distance run or the height of hurdles.

3. *Offer open-ended tasks.* This approach offers wide latitude for making decisions about the content of the lesson. Students decide how the task should be accomplished. You decide the educational outcome and students determine the means to reach it. For example:

   a. "Develop a game that requires four passes before a shot on goal."

   b. "Plan a floor exercise routine that contains a forward roll, a backward roll, and a cartwheel."

   c. "Design a rope-jumping routine that involves a long rope, four people, and two pieces of manipulative equipment."

The problem-solving approach has no predetermined answers. Students apply principles they have learned previously and transfer them to new situations. Ultimately, the problem is solved through a movement response that has been guided by cognitive involvement.

Develop Positive Affective Skills

The performing arts (physical education, music, and drama) offer opportunities for affective domain development. They offer occasions to learn to share, express feelings, set personal goals, and function independently. Teamwork—learning to be subordinate to a leader, as well as being a leader—is learned. Effective instruction includes teaching the whole person rather than just physical skills. It is disappointing to hear a teacher say, "My job is just to teach skills. I'm not going to get involved in developing attitudes. That's someone else's job." Physical education offers an opportunity to develop positive attitudes and values. Much is lost when youngsters leave physical education with well-developed physical skills but negative attitudes toward physical activity and participation. Ponder the following situations:

1. A teacher asks everyone to run a mile, knowing overweight students will run slowest. Many faster students who finish first will hurry the slower students to finish—an embarrassing situation. Obese students cannot change the outcome of the run even if they want to. Failure and belittlement for these students occur every time they have to run. Small wonder such students hate physical activity.

2. Students are asked to perform skills in front of the class. Lesser skilled students feel unsure and perform more poorly because of the pressure. Many of them vow to never perform these skills again.

3. A student pitches in a softball game only to find she is unable to throw strikes. The teacher refuses to remove her from the situation and admonishes the student to "concentrate!" This student may never want to pitch again.

Few people have positive feelings about an activity if they are embarrassed or fail miserably. How youngsters feel about a subject affects their motivation to learn. Therefore, when planning, analyze whether the lesson will result in experiences that enhance the development of positive attitudes and values.

Students have to sense that you care about their feelings and that you try to avoid placing them into embarrassing situations. It is not a sign of weakness to care about students. Knowingly placing students into embarrassing situations is never justified and results in negative student attitudes. It is not the content of the lesson plan but the attitude of the teacher that fosters positive feelings toward activity. The attitudes and values that students form are based in part on how they were treated by teachers and peers. To enhance the affective domain, how you teach is as important as what you teach. Students must be acknowledged as human beings with needs and concerns and should be treated in a courteous and nonderogatory manner. Discover how students feel by asking them. If you ask, however, you must be ready to accept that the feedback may not be positive. Learn to listen without taking it personally or making negative judgments about students when they are honest. Concern for others' feelings creates an atmosphere that is conducive to the constructive development of positive attitudes and values.

Personalize Instruction

Even though most instruction is conducted as a group activity, it is obvious that the ability levels of students vary widely. As students mature, the range of ability increases because many students participate in extracurricular activities such as Little League baseball, YBA basketball, and private tutoring in gymnastics. This range of experiences demands that tasks be modified so that all students find success. The following are some ways to personalize instruction to accommodate developmental differences among youngsters:

1. *Modify the conditions.* Modify tasks and activities to help all children experience success. For example, if students are learning to catch, move partners closer together, have them use a slower-moving object such as a beach ball or a balloon, increase the size of the target, change the size of boundaries or goal areas, allow students to toss and catch individually, or increase the size of the striking implement. An optimum ratio of minimum error and maximum success is a goal. When students find little success they will exhibit off-task behavior in an attempt to draw attention away from their subpar performance. Such behavior indicates that the error rate is too high and learning is stymied.

2. *Use self-competition.* As surprising as it sounds, if the success rate is too high, students become bored. When teaching individual activities, encourage students to set personal goals for themselves. For example, ask youngsters to see if they can beat their personal best performance. Challenges can be offered by asking students to accomplish higher levels of performance, using a faster-moving object, increasing the distance to the goal, or decreasing its size. Students respond best to challenges that are personal and slightly above their current skill level. Try to avoid holding all students to a single standard of performance.

3. *Offer different task challenges.* All students do not have to work on the same tasks simultaneously. Offer a number of tasks of varying complexity so that students can find personal challenges. Task cards and station teaching allow students to learn at an optimum rate. When difficult skills are listed on task cards, ensure that there is a balance of less demanding tasks as well. For example, students who have limited upper body strength might find inverted balances

to be difficult, if not impossible. Include some activities using the legs so all students can achieve some success as they work on balance skill challenges.

EMPLOY EFFECTIVE COMMUNICATION SKILLS

Communicating with a learner—indeed, with all learners—is critical, and communication skills can always be improved. For children to learn essential information, communication must occur in a manner that encourages students to listen. Quality instructors seem able to create a positive atmosphere for learning. They may not know more about skills and activities than less able teachers, but they often know how to communicate effectively. Meaningful feedback helps students learn when skills are performed correctly or need refinement.

Students want to communicate openly and honestly with adults. Behavior used when talking to students can help keep relationships strong. When talking with students, assume a physical pose that expresses interest and attention. Kneel at times so that youngsters do not always have to look up. Check to see if facial and verbal cues reinforce your interest and concern. Some of the following suggestions can help to establish a positive bond with students and create a learning environment enjoyed by everyone.

1. *Speak about the behavior of students, not about their personal character.* The following is an example of speaking about a student's behavior: "Talking when I am talking is unacceptable behavior." Such feedback identifies behavior that can be improved upon and avoids questioning the self-worth of the student. This approach helps students feel you are interested in helping rather than belittling them. In contrast, saying something like, "Why do you always have to act like a fool?" reflects on the child's character and undermines his or her self-esteem. It is also nonspecific, making it difficult to determine what behavior you are reprimanding. Focus on specific misbehavior and then identify the type of behavior that should be displayed.

2. *Understand the child's point of view.* Imagine if someone embarrassed you in front of a class. How would you feel if you were inept and trying to learn a new skill with others watching? These and other emotions make listening difficult for youngsters. Unrestrained feedback can stress a youngster and increase behavior problems. When suggesting ways to improve performance, do so in a private manner (so that other youngsters can't hear you) and allow the student to practice without your scrutiny. Asking

students to try something new and then watching over them until they do it correctly can be intimidating and cause resentment.

3. *Identify your feelings about the learner.* At times, mixed messages are sent to students. You may be unhappy with a student because of a previous incident, yet be unwilling to confront that student. Instead, you might offer unkind or sarcastic feedback about a skill performance out of frustration with the student. This negative interaction resulted from pent-up feelings over a previous issue. Usually, when you have negative feelings toward a student, that student may not be able to understand your unhappiness. Communicate how you feel (even though it is negative), but make sure such communication is directed at correctable behavior in a caring manner.

4. *Accentuate the positive.* When teaching key instructional points of a skill, accent positive performance points rather than incorrect actions. For example, stress that children "land lightly," rather than saying, "Don't land so hard." An easy way to emphasize key points positively is to say, "Do this because . . . ." If there are several different and acceptable ways to perform movement patterns, be explicit with your points.

5. *Speak precisely.* Limit the use of open-ended directives and substitute precise goals. Instead of saying, "How many times can you . . . ?" or "See how many times you can . . . ," give children a definite target goal. Use directives such as, "See if you can . . . five times without missing," or "Show me five different ways to . . . ." Encourage youngsters to set personal target goals.

6. *Optimize speech patterns.* Avoid sermonizing at the least provocation. Sermons seldom work in the teaching environment. Excessive reliance on certain words and phrases—"Okay," "All right," and the irritating "and uh"—are unappealing to children. Acquire a broad vocabulary of effective phrases that indicate approval and good effort. A common list used by teachers shows one hundred ways to say, "Good job." Also, a period of silence can be effective; it allows students time to internalize and digest the information.

7. *Conduct lengthy discussions in a classroom setting.* Whenever possible, hold lengthy discussions in the classroom. Students expect to physically move in the activity area, whereas they have learned to sit and interact cognitively in the classroom. Presenting time-consuming explanations in the classroom before students go to the activity area makes maximum use of activity time. Rules can be explained, procedures and responsibilities outlined, and

formations illustrated on the chalkboard. Limit discussions in the activity area to 30 to 60 seconds.

8. *Respect student opinion.* Avoid humiliating a child who gives a wrong answer. There are a number of ways to deal with this issue. Pass over inappropriate answers by directing attention to more appropriate responses. Alternatively, suggest that the student has offered a good answer, but that the question was not asked correctly. Ask the student to "save that answer" and then go back to that student when the answer is correct for another question. When injecting your personal opinion into the question-and-answer process, label it as such and avoid overemphasizing its worth in comparison to student opinion. Try not to be stunned, show surprise, or take offense if children comment negatively in response to a query asking for candid opinions about an activity or procedure. When opinions are honest, some are bound to be negative.

Be a Good Listener

Listening skills are more difficult to learn than are speaking techniques. Teachers are trained to impart knowledge to students and have practiced speaking for years. Many students view teachers as people who speak but do not listen. Poor communication often occurs because of a breakdown in listening. There is truth in the adage, "You were given two ears and one mouth so you could listen twice as much as you speak." Each of the following promotes effective listening skills:

1. *Be an active listener.* Active listeners convince the speaker they are interested in what the speaker is saying. Much of this is done through nonverbal behavior such as eye contact, nodding the head in agreement, facial expressions, and moving toward the speaker (Figure 5.10).

2. *Listen to the hidden message of the speaker.* Young children sometimes find it difficult to clearly express their feelings. The words expressed may not signal what the child is actually feeling. For example, a child may say, "I hate P.E." Most children do not hate all phases of physical education, and most likely something more immediate (such as jumping rope) is the problem. Try acknowledging their feelings with a response such as, "You sound angry; are you having a problem you want to discuss?" This helps students realize that their feelings are important and gives them an opportunity to clarify concerns. It prevents the teacher from internalizing students' anger (or frustration) and responding in an emotionally charged manner, such as "I don't want to hear that; now get back on-task!"

3. *Paraphrase what the student said.* Paraphrasing is restating in your own words what was said to you, including your interpretation of the other person's feelings. For example, you might respond, "Do I hear you saying you are frustrated and bored with this activity?" If the paraphrasing is correct, it makes the student feel validated and understood. If the interpretation is incorrect, the student has an opportunity to restate his or her concern.

4. *Let students know you value listening.* Teachers who listen to students learn about their students' feelings. Let students know you will listen and then do something about what they say. If you are a good listener, you will hear things that are not always positive. For example, students may state honestly which activities they enjoy and which they do not. They may express how they felt when they were criticized. This communication can be constructive if it is not taken personally. Even though it may not be valid criticism of the program or your procedures, it opens the door to good communication. A word of caution: If you find it difficult to accept such feedback, it is best to ask students to keep their comments to themselves. Avoiding such interactions is necessary if their feedback will affect your confidence.

FIGURE 5.10   Being an active listener.

REFLECTION AND REVIEW QUESTIONS

How and Why

1. State whether the characteristics of a quality lesson were present for all students in your elementary physical education classes as a child.

2. Using teacher talk, state five meaningful feedback statements. Use statements other than those presented in this chapter and discuss why your statements are meaningful.

3. Describe how you can promote diversity in your classes. Why is this important?

4. Discuss your strengths and weaknesses with respect to communicating.

Content Review

1. List the characteristics of a quality elementary physical education lesson. Explain each.

2. Explain the importance of several essential elements of instruction.

3. State the key components of instructional feedback. Discuss each.

4. Discuss what methods can be used to make instruction personal and meaningful for students.

5. Discuss several important communication skills for teachers.

FOR MORE INFORMATION

References and Suggested Readings

Banks, J. A. (2003). *Teaching strategies for ethnic studies.* 7th ed. Boston: Allyn and Bacon.

Bennett, C. L. (2003). *Comprehensive multicultural education: Theory and practice.* 5th ed. Boston: Allyn and Bacon.

Brophy, J., & Good, T. (1986). Teacher behavior and student achievement. In M. Wittrock (Ed.), *Handbook of research on teaching.* New York: Macmillan.

Cushner, K. H. (2003). *Human diversity in action: Developing multicultural competencies for the classroom.* 2nd ed. Boston: McGraw-Hill.

Evertson, C. (1989). Classroom organization and management. In M. Reynolds (Ed.), *Knowledge base for the beginning teacher.* Washington, D.C.: American Association of Colleges for Teacher Education.

Fronske, H. (2005). *Teaching cues for sport skills for secondary school students.* 3rd ed. San Francisco: Benjamin Cummings.

Fronske, H., & Wilson, R. (2002). *Teaching cues for basic sport skills for elementary and middle school students.* San Francisco: Benjamin Cummings.

Fuller, M. L. (2001). Multicultural concerns and classroom management. In C. A. Grant & M. L. Gomez (Eds.), *Campus and classroom: Making schooling multicultural.* Upper Saddle River, NJ: Prentice Hall.

Gordon, A., & Browne, K. W. (1996). *Guiding young children in a diverse society.* Boston: Allyn and Bacon.

Grant, C. A. (Ed.). (1995). *Educating for diversity: An anthology of multicultural voices.* Boston: Allyn and Bacon.

Grossman, H., & Grossman, S. H. (1994). *Gender issues in education.* Boston: Allyn and Bacon.

Harrison, J. M., Blakemore, C. L., & Buck, M. M. (2001). *Instructional strategies for secondary physical education.* 5th ed. St. Louis: McGraw-Hill.

Hunter, M. C. (1994). *Mastery teaching.* Thousand Oaks, CA: Sage Publications.

Hunter, M. C. (1995a). *Motivation theory for teachers.* Thousand Oaks, CA: Corwin Press.

Hunter, M. C. (1995b). *Teach for transfer.* Thousand Oaks, CA: Corwin Press.

Koppelman, K., & Goodhart, L. (2005). *Understanding human differences: Multicultural education for a diverse America.* Boston: Allyn and Bacon.

Manning, M. L., & Baruth, L. G. (2004). *Multicultural education of children and adolescents.* 4th ed. Boston: Allyn and Bacon.

Melograno, V. J. (1996). *Designing the physical education curriculum.* 3rd ed. Champaign, IL: Human Kinetics.

Mosston, M., & Ashworth, S. (1994). *Teaching physical education.* 4th ed. New York: Macmillan.

Pang, V. O. (2005). *Multicultural education: A caring-centered, reflective approach.* 2nd ed. Boston: McGraw-Hill.

Rink, J. E. (2002). *Teaching physical education for learning.* 3rd ed. Boston: WCB/McGraw-Hill.

Siedentop, D., & Tannehill, D. (2000). *Developing teaching skills in physical education.* 4th ed. Mountain View, CA: Mayfield Publishing Co.

Tiedt, P. L., & Tiedt, I. M. (2002). *Multicultural teaching: A handbook of activities, information, and resources.* 6th ed. Boston: Allyn and Bacon.

Vasquez, J. (1988). Contests of learning for minority children. *Educational Forum,* 52(3), 243–253.

Wardle, F., & Cruz-Janzen, M. I. (2004). *Meeting the needs of multiethnic and multiracial children in schools.* Boston: Allyn and Bacon.

Websites

Activity Cues
www.pecentral.org/climate/monicaparsonarticle.html

Communication
http://crs.uvm.edu/gopher/nerl/personal/comm/e.html
http://nonverbal.ucsc.edu/
www.pecentral.org/climate/monicaparsonarticle.html
www.bizmove.com/skills/m8g.htm

Elements of Instruction
www.humboldt.edu/~tha1/hunter-eei.html

Enhancing Teacher Effectiveness
www.hcc.hawaii.edu/intranet/committees/FacDevCom/
guidebk/teachtip/enhance.htm

Multicultural Education
www.ncrel.org/sdrs/areas/issues/educatrs/leadrshp/
le4pppme.htm

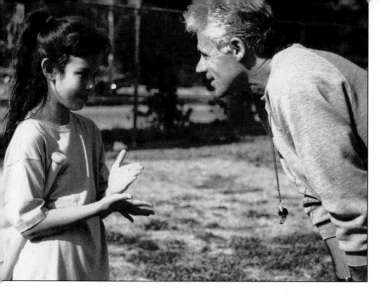

6

Management and Discipline

ESSENTIAL COMPONENTS OF QUALITY PROGRAMS

  I. Organized around content standards

 II. Student-centered and developmentally appropriate

III. Physical activity and motor skill development form the core of the program

▶ IV. **Teaches management skills and self-discipline**

  V. Promotes inclusion of all students

 VI. Focuses on process over product

VII. Promotes lifetime personal health and wellness

▶ VIII. **Teaches cooperation and responsibility and promotes sensitivity to diversity**

NATIONAL STANDARDS FOR PHYSICAL EDUCATION*

1. Demonstrates competency in motor skills and movement patterns needed to perform a variety of physical activities.

2. Demonstrates understanding of movement concepts, principles, and tactics as they apply to the learning and performance of physical activities.

3. Participates regularly in physical activity.

4. Achieves and maintains a health-enhancing level of physical fitness.

▶ 5. **Exhibits responsible personal and social behavior that respects self and others in physical activity.**

6. Values physical activity for health, enjoyment, challenge, self-expression, and/or social interaction.

*National Association for Sport and Physical Education (NASPE), 2004.

SUMMARY

Management and discipline are requisite parts of effective instruction. Management requires designing and implementing a preventive approach to discipline. This chapter presents effective class management skills that improve the efficiency and productivity of instruction. Dealing with behavior involves two major parts: The first part requires modifying and maintaining acceptable behavior; the second part is an approach to decrease unacceptable behavior. Procedures such as time-out, reprimands, and removal of privileges are described. Ways to minimize the use of criticism and punishment are reviewed, and specific recommendations are listed.

OUTCOMES

▪ Describe the role of the teacher as it pertains to managing children in a physical education setting.

▪ Implement management and discipline skills that result in a positive and constructive learning environment.

▪ Identify techniques used to start and stop the class; organize the class into groups, formations, and squads; and prepare youngsters for activity.

▪ Cite acceptable and recommended procedures for dealing with inappropriate behavior.

▪ Describe techniques to increase or decrease specific behaviors.

▪ Explain the role of teacher reaction in shaping and controlling student behavior.

▪ Design or modify games that are effective in changing the behavior of children.

▪ Know the shortcomings of criticism and punishment when used to change and improve student behavior.

▪ Understand the legal ramifications associated with expelling a student from school.

Successful teachers effectively manage student behavior. Management skills may vary among teachers in emphasis and focus, but collectively they characterize quality teaching. Effective teachers make three assumptions: Teaching is a profession, students are in school to learn, and the teacher's challenge is to promote learning. These assumptions imply a responsibility to teach a diverse group of students, both those who accept instruction and those who do not. Competent teachers maintain faith in students who have not yet found success and expect them to do so eventually. The majority of children in a class are relatively easy to teach, but causing low-aptitude and indifferent students to make appreciable gains is the result of effective instruction.

EFFECTIVE MANAGEMENT AND DISCIPLINE: A COORDINATED APPROACH

Managing student behavior is a difficult task. Teachers often question themselves in terms of their ability to control and manage a classroom. A class of children is really a group of individuals, each of whom must be uniquely treated and understood. Some teachers question the importance of effective management and discipline. The most basic of reasons to use management and discipline is that doing so allows children to learn effectively without encroaching on the rights of others. U.S. society is based on freedom partnered with self-discipline. Americans have much personal freedom as long as they do not encroach on the rights of others. In similar fashion, children can enjoy freedom as long as their behavior is consistent with educational objectives and does not prevent other students from learning.

Most children choose to cooperate and participate in the educational setting. In fact, the learner is largely responsible for allowing the teacher to teach. No one can be taught who chooses not to cooperate. Effective management of behavior means maintaining an environment in which all children have the opportunity to learn. Students who choose to be disruptive and off-task infringe on the rights of students who choose to cooperate. When a teacher has to spend a great deal of time working with youngsters who are disorderly, students who want to learn are shortchanged.

A smoothly functioning class is a joy to watch. Teachers behave in ways that promote positive student behavior and, in turn, students perform in a positive and caring manner. Management and discipline techniques are interrelated and one impacts the other. Throughout this chapter, *management* is defined as organizing and controlling the affairs of a class. It refers to how students are organized, started and stopped, grouped, and arranged during class. Effective management means that students are moved quickly, called by their names, moved into instructional formations, and taught in an efficient manner, etc. *Discipline* is defined as changing student behavior when it is unacceptable. When things don't go smoothly, and some students decide not to follow the management requests of the teacher, discipline techniques are required to create a constructive teaching environment. In a nutshell, effective management implies that students follow class procedures and when such class procedures are not followed, discipline techniques must be used.

It is unrealistic to believe that it is possible to work with children without having some type of discipline problem. There are a number of steps that lead to a well-managed and disciplined class. Each of these steps will be discussed in detail throughout the remainder of this chapter.

1. Use proper teaching behaviors.
2. Define class procedures, rules, and consequences.
3. Incorporate efficient management skills.
4. Teach acceptable student behavior.
5. Use behavior management to increase acceptable behavior.
6. Decrease unacceptable behavior with discipline.

USE PROPER TEACHING BEHAVIORS

In a well-managed class, teacher and students assume dual responsibility for learning. Presentations and instructional strategies used are appropriate for the capabilities of students and the nature of activity sequences. How teachers teach, more than the characteristics of a particular teaching style, determines what students learn. Effective class management and organizational skills create an environment that gives students freedom of choice in harmony with class order. When a skillful instructor prevents problems before they occur, less time is spent dealing with deviant behavior.

Be aware of the impact your behavior has on students. What students learn reflects your personality, outlook, ideals, and background. Recognize your personal habits and attitudes that affect youngsters negatively. A basic requisite is the ability to model the behavior you desire from students. This means hustling if you demand that students hustle. It means listening carefully to students or performing fitness activities from time to time. Modeling acceptable behavior has a strong impact on students. The phrase "Your actions speak louder than your words" has significant implications.

Develop an Assertive Communication Style

It is important to hear yourself speak to students. Taping a class session will help you identify the approach you take when interacting with your class. How you communicate is often revealed when you are under pressure or are unsure of yourself. At this point, teachers who are not assertive may become aggressive or passive in trying to get students "back in line." Generally, there are three ways a teacher communicates when dealing with management and discipline scenarios. Each style is discussed in detail here with the obvious goal being that teachers learn to develop and use an assertive style of communication when dealing with management and discipline issues.

PASSIVE COMMUNICATOR

A passive teacher "hopes" to make all children happy in order to avoid becoming upset at them. Passive means trying to avoid all conflict and please others. Directly or indirectly the passive teacher is constantly saying, "Like me, appreciate what I do for you." Many passive teachers want to be perfect so that everybody will like them and students will behave perfectly. When students behave like students and go off-task, Mr. Passive becomes upset and angry. A common pattern is for the passive teacher to let behavior slide until "he can't take it anymore." Then he loses composure and lashes out at the class in anger. When the anger subsides, Mr. Passive wants to make up and again starts the cycle of letting things go and trying to be liked. This cycle is often repeated.

Passive teachers often turn over their power to students, particularly the least cooperative students. For example, they will say things like, "We are not going to start until everyone is listening!" Interpreted concretely, students may hear, "This is great. We don't have to start until we are finished with our conversation." Passive teachers also ignore unacceptable behavior and hope it will disappear. Ignoring seldom causes behavior to disappear; rather, it becomes worse over time. Passive teachers often say things but never follow through. For example, "If you do that one more time, I am going to call your parents." When there is no follow-through or it is impossible to follow through, the words are empty and meaningless and students soon learn disrespect for the teacher. Another common trait of a passive teacher is that she asks questions that result in meaningless information. For example, "What did you do that for?" Or "Why are you doing this?" Or "Don't you know better than that?" None of these questions will elicit useful information and the teacher will soon become frustrated and angry at all of the "I don't know" responses.

AGGRESSIVE COMMUNICATOR

An aggressive responder wants to overpower others by coming on strong. Aggressive people feel it is a competition that they must win at all costs whenever communication occurs. A common trait of aggressive communicators is that they use the word "You" all the time. A number of statements keep students feeling defensive and attacked. Examples are, "You never listen to me; you are always the one in trouble; you are the problem here; you are always talking." Aggressive responders often think that they have all the answers and attempt to express others' viewpoints. For example, they may say to a student, "You think that because you did that last year, you can do it in my class." Obviously, no one knows what another person is thinking, and it serves no purpose to communicate this way.

Aggressive communicators often use the words "always" and "never." These are labeling words. They make students feel as if they are bad people who always behave in certain ways or never do anything right. Words that generalize and label create problems in communication and often result in alienation, rather than respect for a teacher. Aggressive communicators often see students as personally attacking them and focus on labeling the student rather than dealing with the behavior. Often, they don't reveal how they feel about things and are unwilling to express their own thoughts. If students never know how a teacher feels, it is likely they will not develop much empathy for their instructor. A good rule of thumb is this: Any statement about the student rather than your own feelings or thoughts will give your communication an attacking and aggressive quality.

ASSERTIVE COMMUNICATOR

An assertive responder does not beg, plead, or threaten. Rather, he or she uses a straightforward approach to express feelings and expectations. Assertive people are not afraid to say what they want and do not worry about what others will think of them. Teachers who want to be liked are quite concerned about what their students think. An assertive teacher wants what is best for students and doesn't worry about what they think. Assertiveness comes across to students as a "no-nonsense" approach that needs to be followed. The approach is clear and direct and very concrete (requiring little interpretation to be carried out). For example, an assertive teacher might say to a student who has been talking out of turn, "It upsets me when you talk while I am talking." This teacher is expressing feelings and making it clear what the unacceptable behavior is. Now the teacher follows that statement with an assertive statement that expresses the acceptable behavior—i.e., "That is your second warning; please go to time-out."

Assertive communication places great emphasis on clarity without anger. High emotion is not part of assertive responding; rather, it turns assertion into aggressiveness.

An excellent way to make messages more assertive is to use the word "I" instead of "you." Talking about your own feelings and emotions will make the messages sound much more reasonable and firm. For example, "When you are playing with your equipment while I am talking, it bothers me and makes me forget what I planned on saying. Please leave your equipment alone when I talk." Such messages always identify the behavior that is disruptive or annoying, offer how you feel, and direct the student to behave in a proper manner. An excellent reference on discipline is *Conscious Discipline* by Bailey (2001). This is a valuable reference if you are unsure of how to become an assertive communicator.

Create a Personal Behavior Plan

One of the key elements of a management approach is to understand and plan for how you will behave when disciplining students. Serious misbehavior can cause some teachers to become angry, others to feel threatened, and others to behave in a tyrannical manner. Part of your behavior plan will be to remind yourself how you should act when misbehavior occurs. Personal behavior plans usually include the following points:

1. *Maintain composure.* Students don't know your trigger points unless you reveal them. If you "lose it," students lose respect for you and believe you are an ineffective teacher.

2. *Acknowledge your feelings when student misbehavior occurs.* Do you feel angry, threatened, challenged, or fearful? How do you typically respond when a student defies you?

3. *Design a plan for yourself when such feelings occur.* For example, count to ten before responding, or take five deep breaths. Avoid dealing with the student misbehavior until you are aware of how you feel.

4. *Know the options you have for dealing with the deviant behavior.* Talking with students is best done after class if it is going to take more than a few seconds. Limited-time options are: quietly warn the student; quietly remove the student from class; or quietly send another student for help if the situation is severe.

Be a Leader, Not a Friend

Students want a teacher who is knowledgeable, personable, and a leader. They are not looking for a new friend; in fact, most students feel uncomfortable if they perceive that you want to be "one of them." Let students know what they will learn during the semester. Don't look to be a part of their personal discussions. There must be a comfortable distance between you and your students. This is not to say that you shouldn't be friendly and caring; it is important to be concerned about students as long as your concern is expressed in a professional manner. Being a leader means knowing where to direct a class. You are responsible for what is learned and how it is presented. Student input is important, but ultimately, it is your responsibility to lead a class to acceptable objectives.

Communicate High Standards

Students respond to your expectations. If you expect students to perform at high levels, the majority of them will strive to do so. A common and accurate expression is, "You get what you ask for." If you expect students to perform to the best of their abilities, they probably will do so. On the other hand, if you act as if you don't care whether they try, most students will do as little as possible.

Understand Why Students Misbehave

A number of situations cause students to misbehave. Some of these causes are listed in Figure 6.1. Understanding these reasons and being able to identify them when they occur will help you anticipate and prevent

- The student may be testing the teacher.
- The student may have some type of learning disability that causes the behavior problem.
- The student may be looking for reinforcement from the teacher.
- The student may have low self-esteem, which causes the student to misbehave while trying to become the center of attention.
- The student may not understand the directions given.
- The student may be bored and unchallenged by the activities.
- Performing the activities may result in continuous failure, so the student misbehaves to avoid revealing a lack of ability.
- Parents may deal with their children in a manner completely unlike the methods used in physical education.
- The teacher may not like the student, thus forcing the student to be combative and angry.
- Failure in other subjects may carry over to physical education.

FIGURE 6.1 Typical causes of misbehavior.

many behavior problems. There are times when students misbehave because they didn't understand the instructions. Give instructions and then proceed with the activity. If some students don't perform correctly, it may be that they didn't understand. Clarify the instructions and proceed. This two-tiered approach usually ensures that directions are clear and that ample opportunity is given for all to understand.

Deliver Negative Feedback Individually

When negative feedback is delivered, it should be done privately and personally to individual students. Few people want to have negative comments delivered globally for others to hear. In addition, all students should not be punished for the behavior of a few misbehaving youngsters. Negative feedback directed to a group can have contrary results. If you criticize the entire group, there is a strong possibility that you will lose the respect and admiration of students who were behaving properly.

Avoid Feedback that Offers the Possibility for Backlash

Some verbal types of interactions may work in the short term but cause long-term negative consequences. The following types of feedback often work immediately but cause greater problems over the long haul. If students become resentful, they may have a tendency to be deviant when the teacher is not around. Some examples:

- *Preaching or moralizing.* The most common example of moralizing is telling students they "should know better than that!" Students make mistakes because they are young and learning. A part of learning is making mistakes. Correct mistakes in a quiet and caring manner.

- *Threatening.* Threats are ultimatums given in an attempt to terminate unacceptable behavior even though you know the ultimatum will be impossible to carry out. For example, the threat, "If you do not stop that, I'm going to kick you out of class" sounds tough, but is usually impossible to enforce. You are not in a position to expel students, and some students are aware of your inability to carry out the threat. If students hear enough idle threats, they will start to tune out and their respect for you will gradually wane.

- *Ordering and commanding.* If you are bossy, students begin to think they are nothing more than pawns to be moved around the area. Use patterns of communication that ask students to carry out tasks. Courtesy and politeness are requisites for effective teacher-student relationships.

- *Interrogating.* When there is a problem (such as a fight between students), an initial reaction is to figure out who started the fight rather than deal with the feelings of the combatants. Little is gained by trying to solve "who started it." Students often shirk the blame and suggest it was not their fault. Try calmly saying, "You know fighting is not accepted in my class. You must have been very angry to place yourself in this situation." This encourages youngsters to talk about their feelings rather than place blame. It also communicates a caring and concerned attitude toward youngsters even when they do something wrong.

- *Refusing to listen.* This commonly manifests itself as, "Let's talk about it some other time." At times, during instruction, this response is necessary. However, if you always refuse to listen, students will avoid interaction with you and believe you don't care.

- *Labeling.* Labeling is characterized by telling children, "Stop acting like babies" or "You're behaving like a bunch of first graders." On an individual level, it might sound like, "You're always the troublemaker." This is degrading and dehumanizes youngsters. Often, labeling is done with the intent of improving performance. In actuality, it is usually destructive and leaves youngsters with negative feelings.

DEFINE CLASS PROCEDURES, RULES, AND CONSEQUENCES

Effectively managing a class depends on letting students know what you expect of them. They want to know what routines they are going to follow. Without guidelines and routines, students have to guess what the teacher wants on a day-to-day basis. This leads to uneasiness and incorrect guesses. The following example illustrates the need for guidance: Students are outside in a physical education lesson. The teacher tells them not to get too far away so they can hear all the directions. Sure enough, some students stray beyond a distance the teacher deems acceptable and the students are disciplined. Unfortunately, the wrong party was disciplined; it should have been the teacher who was disciplined because he didn't set up clear guidelines. How are students to judge what is too far away? What if they felt they could hear the directions? Can the teacher be consistent in applying this rule when even he doesn't know how far is too far? If cones had been set up around the perimeter of the area and students had been told to stay inside the cones, the problem would have been eliminated for both the teacher and students. Carry out the following steps at the start of the school year and reinforce them on a regular basis throughout the year.

Step One: Determine Routines for Students

Being assertive is important. Students feel best when they know what your expectations are. Students expect to follow established routines. Explain your routines so that students understand why the chosen procedures are used. Examples of routines that teachers often use are:

1. How students are supposed to enter the teaching area.
2. How the teaching area is defined.
3. Where and how they should meet—in sitting squads, moving and freezing on a spot, in a semicircle, and so on.
4. What they should do if equipment is located in the area.
5. What signal is used to freeze a class.
6. How they procure and put away equipment.
7. How they will be grouped for instruction.

Once these routines are established and practiced, it is easier for both teacher and students to work together comfortably.

Step Two: Determine Rules and Procedures for the School Year

Rules are an expected part of the school environment. Most teachers want students to be respectful to them and to other students. It is reasonable to expect students to behave. If you can't manage students, you can't teach them. School administrators usually judge your effectiveness by how well you manage students. Accept the fact that managing students is a necessary and important part of teaching; in fact, it is requisite for the delivery of content. When creating your rules, select general categories rather than specific behavior. For example, "Respect your neighbor" means many things, from not pushing to not swearing at another student. Post rules in the teaching area where all students can easily read them. The following are examples of general rules:

- *Stop, look, and listen.* This implies freezing on signal, looking at the instructor, and listening for instructions.
- *Take care of equipment.* This includes caring for equipment and distributing, gathering, and using it properly.
- *Respect the rights of others.* This includes behavior such as not pushing others, leaving others' equipment alone, not fighting or arguing, and not physically or emotionally hurting others.

The number of rules should be minimized. Try not to exceed three to five rules; more than this number makes it difficult for students to remember all the details and makes you appear overly strict. Numerous rules also make students rule-specific. A youngster may choose to chew gum in the multipurpose room because the rule is "No gum-chewing in the halls." When students become rule-specific, they do not learn to think about right and wrong and the spirit of the rule; rather, they often look for exceptions to the rule. Rules are general guidelines for acceptable behavior rather than negative statements telling students what they can't do. Consider the following points when designing rules:

- Select major categories of behavior rather than a multitude of specific rules.
- Identify observable behavior. This makes it easy to determine whether a person is following a rule and does not involve subjective judgment.
- Make rules reasonable for the age level of students. Meaningful rules cut across all ages and can be used throughout the elementary school years.
- Limit the number of rules (three to five).
- State rules briefly and positively. It is impossible to write a rule that covers all situations and conditions. Make the rule brief, yet broad.

Step Three: Determine Consequences When Rules Are Not Followed

When rules are broken, students must learn to accept the consequences of their behavior. List and post consequences in a prominent place in the teaching area. Discuss the rules with students to make sure they understand and see the necessity of having behavior guidelines. Having agreed-upon rules and consequences involves students in the development of an environment that, in part, they have designed. One of the best ways to earn students' respect is to treat them all in a fair and caring manner. Most students are willing to accept the consequences of their misbehavior if they think they will be treated in a manner consistent with and equal to how other students were treated. Animosity occurs when students sense that you play favorites. It is common for physical education teachers to favor gifted athletes and students who are physically attractive. Be aware of such behavior and prevent its occurrence. One reason for defining consequences prior to misbehavior is that it allows you to administer the consequences equitably. When a student chooses to break a rule, apply the consequences without judging the character of or making a derogatory statement about the student. It is the student's misbehavior that has triggered the consequences.

Step Four: Share Your Rules with Parents, Teachers, and Administrators

It is not enough to share your rules with students. If the saying, "It takes a village to raise a child" is valid, it makes sense to be sure all parties know and understand your rules. A newsletter to parents at the start of the year explaining your program and your approach to class management will set the tone for students immediately. Parents will have little complaint if their child has a problem; routines, rules, and consequences were clearly explained in the newsletter. Sharing your rules with classroom teachers and administrators also helps clarify what your expectations are. Classroom teachers will then be able to reinforce your approach. Principals will also clearly understand what you expect; when the two of you are on the same page, it will be easier to work together to achieve common goals.

Step Five: Have the Class Practice Rules Systematically

Rules stipulate expected class behavior. If a rule is in place for proper care of equipment, students need the opportunity to practice how the teacher wants equipment handled. If a rule requires students to stop and listen, practice such behavior and reinforce a proper response. Student behavior is not always correct, regardless of rules. It is common to hear teachers tell students, "I told you before not to do that." This assumes that telling students once will result in perfect adherence to rules. Obviously, this is not the case. Continue to allow time for students to practice acceptable behavior throughout the school year.

INCORPORATE EFFICIENT MANAGEMENT SKILLS

Class management skills are prerequisites to effective instruction. Moving and organizing students quickly and efficiently requires comprehension of various techniques coupled with student acceptance of those techniques. If a class is unmanageable, it is unteachable. Most students enjoy a learning environment that is organized and efficient and allows a maximum amount of class time to be devoted to learning skills.

Teach class management skills in a manner similar to physical skill teaching. All skills need to be learned through practice and repetition until they become second nature. Viewing class management skills in this light makes it easier to have empathy for students who do not perform well. Just as students make mistakes when performing physical skills, some will perform management skills incorrectly. A simple, direct statement, such as, "It appears that you forgot how to freeze quickly. Let's practice," is much more constructive than indicting a class for its carelessness and disinterest.

Deliver Instruction Efficiently

If students are not listening when instructions are given, little learning will occur. Deliver instructions in small doses, focusing on one or two points at a time. Instructions should be specific and seldom last longer than 20 to 30 seconds. An effective approach is to alternate short instructional episodes with periods of activity. This contrasts with the common practice of delivering long and involved technical monologues on skill performance only to find that many students have forgotten most of the information by the time practice begins. In a series of spoken items, people usually remember only the first and the last; thus, most students will be able to integrate and concentrate on only one or two points during skill practice. Minimizing the amount of content per instructional episode helps eliminate students' frustration and allows them to focus on stated goals. This is not to suggest that information should not be delivered to students, but that the "tell it all at the start" style should be replaced by the more effective "input, practice, feedback" model.

When giving instructions, tell students "when before what." Tell the class when to perform an activity before stating what the activity is. An effective way to implement "when before what" is to use a keyword, such as *Begin!* or *Start!* to start an activity. For example, "When I say *Start!* I'd like you to . . ." or, "When I say *Go!* I want you to jog to a beanbag, move to your own space, and practice tossing and catching." Since the keyword is not given until all directions have been issued, students have to listen to all instructions before starting.

Stop and Start a Class Consistently

The most basic and important management skill is being able to start and stop a class. Many teachers like to have students assume a specific position when they stop (Figure 6.2). Freezing in the ready position with hands on knees helps keep students' hands in their own space so they don't distract other students. Pick a consistent signal you want to use to stop a class. It does not matter what the signal is, as long as it always means the same thing. Using both an audio signal (such as a whistle blast) and a visual signal (such as raising the hand overhead) is useful because some youngsters may not hear the audio signal when engrossed in activity. Whereas a loud audio signal is used to stop a class, a voice command should be used to start the class. (See the previous discussion on keywords.) Regardless of the signal used to indicate a stop, it is best to select a different signal from the one used to start the class. If children do not respond to the signal to stop, take time to practice the procedure. Reinforce youngsters when they perform management behavior properly. Often, skill performance is reinforced but correct management behavior is not. Behavior that is not reinforced regularly will not be performed well.

Expect 100 percent compliance when students are asked to stop. If some students stop and listen to directions and others do not, class morale will degenerate. Students begin to wonder why they have to stop but other students don't. Scan the class to see if all students are stopped and ready to respond to the next set of directions. If you settle for less than full attention, students will fulfill those expectations.

Move Students into Groups and Formations Quickly

It is necessary to move students into small groups and instructional formations on a regular basis. Simple techniques can be used to accomplish this in an enjoyable and rapid fashion. Regardless of the technique used when finding partners and grouping, students should match up with someone near them rather than running and looking for their best friend. Place some rubber marking spots in the center of the area and call it the "friendship spot." Students who don't have a partner nearby run to the friendship spot, raise their hands, and look for a partner. After identifying a partner, they move out of the friendship spot area. This approach will keep students from running around and looking for a partner and feeling "left out."

FINDING PARTNERS

Use the activity Toe to Toe (see page 556) to teach children to find partners quickly. The goal of the game is to get toe to toe with a partner as fast as possible. Other challenges are to get elbow to elbow or shoulder to shoulder or to look into the eyes of a partner. Students without a partner must go to the center of the teaching area (marked by a cone or rubber marking spot) and find someone else without a partner. This gives students a designated spot to locate themselves, as opposed to feeling unwanted while running around the area looking for a partner. Place emphasis on rapid selection of the nearest person to keep children from looking for a favorite friend or telling someone that "he is not wanted" as a partner. If students insist on staying near a friend, tell the class to move throughout the area and find a different partner each time "toe to toe" is called. Another effective idea is to require them to find a different partner each time they are asked to find a partner. By asking them to take the person nearest them and find a different partner each time, they will meet many more students.

FIGURE 6.2 Class in freeze position.

Other suggestions for finding partners are to ask students to find a partner wearing the same color, with a birthday during the same month, with a phone number that has two similar numbers in it, and so on. To arrange students in equal-sized groups, place an equal number of different-colored beanbags or hoops on the floor. Ask students to move throughout the area and on signal sit on a beanbag. All students with a red beanbag are in the same group, those with green beanbags make up another group, and so on.

DIVIDING A CLASS IN HALF

To divide a class into two equal groups, have students get toe to toe with a partner. For Developmental Level I students, have one partner sit down while the other remains standing. Those standing are asked to go to one area, after which those sitting are then moved to the desired location. With Developmental Levels II and III students, one partner can raise a hand. Move the students with their hands up to one side of the area.

CREATING SMALL GROUPS

Another activity for arranging students in groups of a selected size is Whistle Mixer (see page 568). When the whistle is blown a certain number of times, students form groups corresponding to the number of whistle blows and sit down to signify that they have the correct number in their group. Students left out go to the "friendship spot," find the needed number of members, and move to an open area. When this skill is mastered, students will be able to move quickly into groups with the correct number of students. The use of hand signals to show the desired number of students in the group will make it easier for all students to recognize.

CREATING CIRCLES OR SINGLE-FILE LINES

An effective technique for moving a class into a single-file line or circle is to have students run randomly throughout the area until a signal is given. On the signal to "fall in," students continue jogging, move toward the perimeter of the area, and fall in line behind someone until a circle is formed. They jog in the same direction as the teacher; this avoids some students running one direction and others moving in the opposite direction. As long as students continue to move behind another person, a circle will form automatically. Either you or a student leader can lead the line into an acceptable formation or position.

Another method of moving a class into formation is to ask students to get into various formations without talking. Youngsters can use visual signals but cannot ask someone verbally to move. Have groups hustle to see how quickly they can form the acceptable formation.

Another method is to hold up a shape drawn on a large card to signal the acceptable formation. Young students learn to visualize various shapes through this technique.

Use Squads to Expedite Class Organization

Some teachers find that placing students into squads helps them manage a class effectively. Squads offer a place for students to meet, keep certain students from being together, group students into prearranged teams of equal ability, and make it easier to learn students' names. The following are guidelines for using squad formation to maximize teaching effectiveness:

1. Squads or groups shouldn't be selected in a manner that embarrasses a child who might be chosen last. In all cases, avoid using an "auction" approach, where student leaders look over the group and pick those whom they favor. A fast way to group youngsters into squads is to use the Whistle Mixer technique described previously.

2. A designated location should be used for assembling students into squad formation. On signal, children move to the designated area, with squad leaders in front and the rest of the squad behind.

3. Squads provide opportunities for leadership and following among peers. Use squad leaders so that youngsters have an opportunity to learn leadership skills. Examples of leadership activities are moving squads to a specified location, leading squads through exercises or introductory activities, and appointing squad members to certain positions in sport activities.

4. The composition of squads can be predetermined. It may be important to have equal representation of the sexes on each squad. Squad makeup may be determined by ability level so that you can quickly organize games with teams of similar ability. Squads can also be used to separate certain students so they don't have the opportunity to disrupt the class. In order for students to get to work with all students in the class, change squad members on a regular basis.

5. In most cases, an even number of squads should be formed. This allows the class to be broken quickly into halves for games. Having a class of 30 students divided into six squads of five members each places a small number of students on each piece of apparatus and makes for less waiting in line for group activities.

6. The use of squads should be an exciting activity, not an approach that restricts movement and creativity. For example, place numbered cones in different locations around the activity area. When students

enter the gym, instruct them to find their squad number and assemble. The numbers can be written in a different language or hidden in a mathematical equation or story problem. Another method is to distribute task cards specifying how the squads are arranged. The first squad to follow instructions correctly can be awarded a point or given acknowledgment from the rest of the class. Examples of tasks for squads might be arranging the members in a circle, sitting with their hands on their heads, or arranging themselves in crab positions in a straight line facing northwest. Task cards can also be used to specify an introductory activity or to tell students where to move for the fitness development activity.

7. An effective way to use squads is "Home Base." Place a number of marking spots on the floor throughout the area. When "Home Base" is called, the captains quickly find the closest spot and their respective squad members line up behind them. If an even number of squads has been created, half of the spots can be put in one half of the area and half in the opposite half. When "Home Base" is called, the class will quickly divide in half. This is handy for station teaching as well; place a spot at each of the teaching stations and call "Home Base." A squad will be lined up at each station.

Know Students' Names

Effective class management requires learning the names of your students. Praise, feedback, and correction go unheeded when students are addressed as, "Hey, you!" Develop a system to expedite the task of learning names. One approach is to memorize three or four names per class period. Write the names on a note card, and identify those students at the start and throughout the period. At the end of the period, identify the students again. Once the first set of names has been memorized, a new set can be learned. The next time the class meets, those names learned previously can be reviewed and new students identified.

Tell students you are trying to learn their names. Asking students to say their name before performing a skill or answering a question can help you learn students' names. Once a name is learned, you may precede the question or skill performance with the student's name. For example, say, "Mary, it's your turn to jump."

Another effective way to learn names is to take a photograph of each class in squads and identify students by matching names to the picture. Identification is easier with students in squads, because they will be in the same location. Identify a few students whose names you know and a few you do not know before the start of the period. Set personal goals by calculating the percentage of students whose names you know after each period.

Establish Pre- and Post-Teaching Routines

Children appreciate the sense of security that comes from knowing what to do from the time they enter the instructional area until they leave. Effective teaching demands that a number of procedures be routinely handled. The following are situations that occur before and after teaching and need to be planned for prior to the lesson.

NONPARTICIPATION

An efficient system should be devised for identifying children who should not participate in the lesson. This decision is best made before children arrive at the lesson area and by someone (nurse or classroom teacher) other than the physical education teacher. This avoids a situation in which the physical education teacher encourages students to participate even though they are not supposed to do so. A note from the classroom teacher or school nurse, listing the names and health problems of those who are to sit out or to take part in modified activity, can be delivered as children enter the room. Accept the information at face value. This avoids the time-consuming procedure of questioning students on the sidelines to determine what the problem is and what the solution should be. A student with a note from home or from a physician should never be allowed to participate without parental permission.

ENTERING THE TEACHING AREA

Nothing is more difficult than trying to start a class that has not entered the teaching area in a quiet, orderly fashion. Meet your class at the door before they enter the area. Explain how the class should enter the area and what they are supposed to do. Another successful approach is to have the class enter the area and begin jogging around the area. When told to freeze, the day's activities are described. Another, less desirable method is to have youngsters enter the area and sit in squads behind their respective cones or floor markers. Instruction starts when all students are in position. Regardless of the method used, students should enter the area under control and knowing where they are supposed to meet.

When a classroom teacher allows students to "straggle" in late, or brings the entire class in late, it disrupts the instructional process. Discuss the problem of tardiness with the teacher and try to find a solution. Try designating a couple of responsible students in each class to remind the classroom teacher that physical education begins in five minutes. Another solution is to have a designated area away from the teaching area where classes can assemble, and request that they line up at the gym door as soon as the entire group is ready. Allowing students to filter in one by one is disconcerting and a sure bet to irritate any physical education teacher. Resolve this problem quickly even if it requires asking the school's administrator to intervene.

STARTING THE LESSON

Students enter the activity area expecting to move. Take advantage of their desire to move by having them participate in some activity before discussing the content of the lesson. Youngsters will be more willing to listen after they have participated in vigorous activity. Allow students to try an activity before offering instruction on points of technique. Students listen to instruction better after they have tried an activity and found it difficult to perform correctly. Having them try an activity before you give instruction allows an opportunity to assess the performance level of the students.

CLOSING THE LESSON

A regular routine for closing the lesson is beneficial. It allows time for closure of the instructional content and a procedure for leaving the teaching area. This may involve lining up at the door, returning to squads, or kneeling in a semicircle. Using a routine at the end of the lesson tends to calm and quiet youngsters, which is appreciated by classroom teachers picking up their class. Another way to calm students is to take a few minutes for relaxation activities.

EQUIPMENT PROCEDURES

Make students responsible for securing the equipment they use. Teach students how you want them to get the equipment and return it at the end of the lesson. This minimizes the amount of equipment rearrangement you will have to do. Place your equipment around the perimeter of the teaching area so it is easily accessible for all students. Using students to assist in distributing and gathering equipment before and after school allows an opportunity to work closely with students who need special attention.

DEALING WITH STUDENT BEHAVIOR PROBLEMS

Youngsters who misbehave during class need to be talked with after class. This makes it critical to schedule a minimum of five minutes of passing time between classes. Scheduling classes back-to-back makes it

impossible to talk with students, rearrange equipment, and take care of personal matters. If time between classes is not available, a "meeting appointment" form should be given to the classroom teacher and student. This reminds both parties of the student's obligation to meet with you at the end of the school day.

Use Equipment Effectively

When using small equipment such as balls, hoops, and jump ropes, be sure that every youngster has a piece for personal use. When large equipment or apparatus is used, establish as many stations or groups as possible. For a class of 30, a minimum of six benches, mats, or jumping boxes should be available so that students have only a short wait in line. One way to avoid students' standing and waiting for a turn is to use return activities (see Chapter 18) where students are asked to perform a task or tasks on their return to their squad.

Teach students where the equipment is to be placed during instruction. Equipment should be placed in the same (home) position when the class is called to attention. For example, beanbags are placed on the floor, basketballs between the feet, and jump ropes folded and placed behind the neck. Placing the equipment in home position avoids the problem of youngsters striking one another with the equipment, dropping it, or practicing activities when they should be listening. To avoid students' playing with the equipment when it is placed on the floor, ask students to take a giant step away from it.

Distribute equipment to students as rapidly as possible. When students have to wait in line for a piece of equipment, time is wasted and behavior problems occur. For example, a common practice is to assign student leaders to get the equipment for their squad. This approach results in many students sitting and waiting. A better and faster method is to have the equipment placed around the perimeter of the area (Figure 6.3). On signal, youngsters move to acquire a piece of equipment, take it to their personal space, and begin practicing an assigned skill. This approach takes advantage of the natural urge to try the equipment and reinforces students who procure equipment quickly. The reverse procedure is used to put equipment away. Certainly, any method beats the often-used practice of placing the equipment in the middle of the area in a container and telling students to "run and get a ball." This approach raises the chances that youngsters will be aggravated or hurt.

Regardless of the method used to acquire equipment, clearly state what students are supposed to do with it once they have a piece of equipment. Waiting for all students to get a piece of equipment before allowing anybody to use it places control in the hands of the slowest and least cooperative students. The students who have hustled to get their equipment have to wait while the

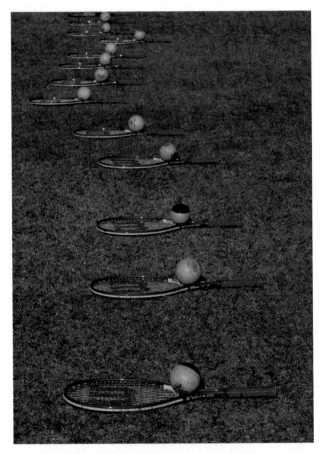

FIGURE 6.3   Equipment around the perimeter.

slowpokes take their time. Avoid this problem by allowing students to start practicing once they get their equipment. Interact with those students who are slow and less cooperative while the others are practicing.

TEACH ACCEPTABLE STUDENT BEHAVIOR

There are a number of ways to teach youngsters to behave in a socially acceptable manner. Teaching acceptable behavior has always been a basic premise of why schools were implemented by societies in the first place. When a program that focuses on behavior is implemented by a school, it shows parents and students that this is an important school outcome. There are a number of programs used in the physical education setting that focus on acceptable and responsible behavior. Each is discussed below.

Responsibility through Physical Activity

Concern about student behavior and lack of discipline has increased the need to teach responsible behavior to students. Hellison (2003) developed strategies and programs for teaching responsibility skills in a physical education setting. A basic premise for learning responsible behavior is that it must be planned for, taught, and reinforced. Responsible behavior takes time and practice to learn, much like any other skill. Hellison (2003) suggests a hierarchy of responsible behavior. The ideas described in this section subscribe to the idea that there are different levels of responsible behavior that can be learned. Teaching responsible behavior as described here involves five levels of behavior. Each is defined below, followed by examples of typical student behavior at each level.

Level 0: Irresponsibility Level 0 students are unmotivated and undisciplined. Their behavior includes discrediting other students' involvement and interrupting, intimidating, manipulating, and verbally or physically abusing other students and perhaps the teacher.

Behavior examples:

- At home: Blaming brothers or sisters for problems; lying to parents.
- On the playground: Calling other students names; laughing at others.
- In physical education: Talking to friends when the teacher is giving instructions; pushing and shoving when selecting equipment.

Level 1: Self-Control Students at this level do not participate in the day's activity or show much mastery or improvement. These students control their behavior enough that they do not interfere with other students' right to learn or the teacher's right to teach.

Behavior examples:

- At home: Refraining from hitting a brother or sister even though angry.
- On the playground: Standing and watching others play; not getting angry at others because they did something to upset them.
- In physical education: Waiting until an appropriate time to talk with friends; having control and not letting others' behavior bother them.

Level 2: Involvement These students show self-control and are involved in the subject matter or activity.

Behavior examples:

- At home: Helping clean up the dishes after dinner; taking out the trash.
- On the playground: Playing with others; participating in a game.
- In physical education: Listening and performing activities; trying even when they don't like an activity; doing an activity without complaining or saying, "I can't."

Level 3: Self-Responsibility Level 3 students take responsibility for their choices and for linking these choices to their own identities. They are able to work without direct supervision, eventually taking responsibility for their intentions and actions.

Behavior examples:

- At home: Cleaning up without being asked.
- On the playground: Returning equipment after recess.
- In physical education: Following directions; practicing a skill without being told; trying new activities without encouragement.

Level 4: *Caring* Students behaving at this level are motivated to extend their sense of responsible behavior by cooperating, giving support, showing concern, and helping.

Behavior examples:

- At home: Helping take care of a younger brother or sister or a pet.
- On the playground: Asking others (not just friends) to join them in play.
- In physical education: Helping someone who is having trouble; helping a new student feel welcome; working with all students; showing that all people are worthwhile.

Responsible behavior is taught using a number of strategies. Post the levels of responsibility in the teaching area. Explain the different levels of behavior and identify acceptable behaviors at each level. After students have received an introduction to responsible behavior, implement the program by reinforcement of acceptable behavior and redirection of inappropriate behavior. The program is based on this two-pronged approach: (1) Catch students using responsible behavior and reinforce them; and (2) Redirect students behaving at Level 0 by asking, "At what level are you performing and what level would be more acceptable?" An example is the following discussion between teacher and student:

You see a student behaving at Level 0 and open dialogue with the student in a nonconfrontational and nonadversarial manner:

"Johnny, it appeared you were making fun of someone. . . ."

"I wasn't making fun of anyone!"

"Maybe not, but if you were, what level of behavior would it be?"

"Zero!"

"Is that the kind of person you want to be or the level of behavior you want to show?"

"No!"

"If you were at Level 0, do you think you could make some changes? Perhaps you could move to Level 1 and have self-control even if someone else makes you mad or even if you do not like that person."

STRATEGIES FOR INCREASING RESPONSIBLE BEHAVIOR

Teacher feedback forms the core of the responsibility approach; however, there are many strategies for increasing responsible behavior in the instructional setting. The following are some strategies that can be used:

- ***Model acceptable behavior.*** How you interact with students encourages responsible behavior. Students do not care about how much you know until they know how much you care. Treat youngsters with dignity and respect and follow through with responsible action and words. In return, expect students to treat you and others with the same dignity and respect.

- ***Use reinforcement.*** Give students specific feedback about the quality of their behavior. If corrective feedback is given, make sure it identifies the acceptable level of behavior. If you are reinforcing acceptable behavior, be specific in identifying why the behavior is acceptable and stating that you appreciate such acts. In some cases, it may be beneficial to identify a super citizen or give a "happygram" for special behavior.

- ***Offer time for responsibility and reflection.*** Allow time for students to think about the attitudes and behaviors associated with each of the levels. Ask the students to fill out a self-responsibility checklist at different times of the year. See Figure 6.4 for an example of a checklist.

- ***Allow student sharing.*** Offer students a chance to give their opinions about responsible behavior. Accept all students' feelings as important. Focus on ways to encourage higher levels of responsible behavior. Brainstorming with your students to identify consequences of high and low behavior is an effective approach. Another practice is to ask different students to give examples of responsible behavior at different levels. Allow students time to share how they feel when someone uses a high- or low-level behavior around them.

- ***Encourage goal setting.*** Help students set goals for responsible behavior they want to exhibit. This can be done at the start of the lesson by asking students to tell a partner the behavior they want to use today. At the end of the lesson, partners evaluate each other to see if the behavior was exhibited. Examples of behaviors are listening, hustling, following directions, being courteous, and complimenting others.

- ***Offer opportunities for responsibility.*** There are a number of times when students can be given responsibility in a class setting. Being a group leader, team captain, referee, score keeper, rule maker, or dispute resolver are roles that encourage students to exhibit high-level behavior. Since responsible

---

My Self-Responsibility Checklist

Name: _____

Date: _____

Self-Control:

_____   I did not call others names.

_____   I had self-control when I became mad.

_____   I listened when others were talking.

_____   Other (describe) _____

Involvement:

_____   I listened to all directions before starting.

_____   I was willing to try all activities.

_____   I tried activities even when I didn't
                 like them.

_____   Other (describe) _____

Self-Responsibility:

_____   I followed directions without being told more
                 than once.

_____   I did not blame others.

_____   I worked on activities by myself.

_____   Other (describe) _____

Caring:

_____   I helped someone today.

_____   I said something nice to someone.

_____   I asked someone to do something with me.

_____   Other (describe) _____

F I G U R E   6 . 4   Example of a responsibility checklist.

positions affect other students, effective leaders have to behave responsibly.

■ *Allow student choice.* Responsible behavior is best learned when students make choices. The natural consequences of self-selected choices are often the best teachers. Students can make choices about games they choose to play, fitness activities they select, and friends they choose. Discussion about how to make meaningful health choices (see Chapter 14) is an important phase of learning to make responsible choices.

TEACHER-DIRECTED CONFLICT RESOLUTION

Conflict between students often results in aggression and violence. About one in seven children is either a bully or a victim (Beane, 1999). Nobody wants to create a world where the strong dominate and the weak live in fear and submission. Conflict is a part of daily life, and youngsters should understand that it is necessary to deal with conflict in an effective manner. Students can learn ways to respect others' opinions and feelings while maintaining their own worth and dignity.

There are a number of ways to solve conflicts, but the most common methods involve three types of behavior—dominating, appeasing, and cooperating. Students who use the dominating style are often unsure about their standing in the group. They want things to be done in their way but are afraid others will reject them. They often lack confidence and try hard to get others to accept their way of doing things. Youngsters who are appeasers lack confidence but want to be accepted by others. They do not like conflict and are willing to set aside their feelings in order to placate others.

Neither the dominating nor the appeasing approach for solving conflicts is effective in the long run. No one likes to be dominated or placed in the position of having to appease others. Conflict resolution can help students learn to solve conflicts in a peaceful manner with no apparent losers. This approach takes a cooperative approach to solving problems. Cooperation often builds positive feelings between students and leads to better group cohesiveness. The following are steps typically used to resolve conflicts (Gordon & Browne, 1996). These steps are effective with younger children or children without experience in conflict resolution. If children are experienced in conflict resolution, they may be able to carry out the steps without instructor intervention.

1. *Stop the aggressive behavior immediately.* Students in conflict are separated immediately and given an opportunity to cool down. Time-out boxes are often an excellent place to send students to relax and unwind.

2. *Gather data about what happened and define the problem.* Find out what happened, who was involved, and how each youngster is feeling. Ask open-ended questions such as, "What happened?" and "How did you feel about . . .?" so that youngsters can talk freely about the problem.

3. *Brainstorm possible solutions.* Keep in mind that brainstorming is a nonjudgmental process where all solutions are accepted regardless of their perceived value. Encourage youngsters to think of as many options as possible by asking open-ended questions such as, "How could we solve this problem?" or "What other ways could we deal with this?"

4. *Test the solutions generated through brainstorming.* Ask a question such as, "What solutions might work best?" Help students understand the implications of the solutions and how the solutions can be implemented. Accept solutions that may differ from your way of solving the problem.

5. *Help implement the plan.* Walk students through the solution so that they develop a perception of the approach. Guide them through the steps by asking, "Who goes first?" and "Who will take the next step?" As the solution is implemented, there may be a need to change it, which can be agreed on by the involved students.

6. *Evaluate the approach.* Observe to make sure the plan is accomplishing the accepted outcome. Encourage students to change the plan if necessary.

The conflict-resolution process takes practice and time. It demands that you play certain roles and take an objective approach to resolution. The conflict-resolution process demands certain behaviors from the instructor. Good listening to both parties is necessary. Both sides of the problem must be explored and students must feel as though the process was equitable. Blame is not assessed in this process. Placing blame only encourages defensive behavior such as appeasing or being aggressive. Students must trust that the process will be fair and objective and that they will receive a fair shake if they deal with the issue cooperatively.

Peer Mediation

Peer mediation is similar to conflict resolution except that it is student-directed. Disputes and conflicts are resolved between students with a neutral peer acting as a moderator in the process. In peer mediation, the goal is to work out differences constructively. Mediation gets students involved in the problem-solving process, either as mediators or disputants, and teaches them a way of handling conflicts. A text by Cohen (2005) is an excellent resource for a step-by-step approach to student peer mediation.

Students are trained to help their classmates identify the problems behind the conflicts and to find solutions. Peer mediation is not about finding who is right or wrong. Instead, students are encouraged to move beyond the immediate conflict and learn how to get along with each other. Peer mediators ask the disputing students to tell their stories and ask the students questions for clarification. The mediators help the students identify ways to solve the conflict.

A key component to any mediation process is letting each student tell his or her own story so that he/she feels as if someone understands his/her perspective. Common situations involving name-calling, spreading rumors, bumping into students in the hallways, and bullying are often best resolved through peer mediation. There are two parts to the mediation process: establishing ground rules and following the steps of mediation.

GROUND RULES

All parties (including the mediator) participate in reviewing and agreeing to the ground rules to be followed. When there is agreement on the ground rules, mediation begins. Basic ground rules that must be agreed to are:

- *The problem will be solved.* Participants have to agree that a solution will be found in the session. It is not acceptable to leave without solving the problem.

- *The truth will be told.* Students must agree to tell the truth regardless of the impact it has on the situation. Since students will be solving the problem without adult supervision and the session will be confidential, telling the truth will not result in negative consequences.

- *The full story will be heard without interruption.* Each party must be able to tell their side of the story without interruption. Each person should feel as though their side of the story is completely and fairly presented.

- *All parties will act in a respectful manner.* Students need to learn to state their case without excessive emotion and anger.

- *All discussion will be confidential.* Both the arbitrator and the parties in conflict agree not to discuss the situation with nonparticipants.

- *The solution will be implemented.* Both parties will carry out the agreement regardless of whom the solution favors.

MEDIATION STEPS

After agreeing to the ground rules, mediation led by a trained peer begins. The problem is not discussed during the creation of ground rules. The mediation steps are about solving the actual problem and doing so in a manner dictated by the ground rules students agreed to follow. The following are steps to finding a mediated solution:

- *Tell your story or grievance.* Each student now has a chance to tell their side of the story. This should be an opportunity to "lay it on the table" and feel like the problem is clearly understood by both the other party and the mediator.

- *Verify the story.* The mediator and the other party have the opportunity to ask questions to clarify and verify the story. The mediator is responsible for trying to find out exactly what happened and how each party feels.

- *Discuss the conflict.* The mediator conducts a discussion about the situation and the emotions involved.

- *Brainstorm solutions to the problem.* All parties discuss ways the problem might be solved. Emphasis is placed on the need to find solutions that resolve the situation for both parties.

- *Discuss and implement the agreed-upon solution.* Both parties agreed previously to follow ground rules they developed. One of the rules was to solve the problem. Therefore, it is not acceptable to leave without a solution.

- *Sign a contract.* After agreeing to a solution, the offended parties must sign a contract agreeing to carry out the solution.

USE BEHAVIOR MANAGEMENT TO INCREASE ACCEPTABLE BEHAVIOR

Positive discipline focuses on reinforcing acceptable behavior. The premise is that the plan should be to focus on the positive attributes of a youngster. Increasing positive behavior may help reduce negative behavior because the student will receive increased feedback and attention. Lavay et al. (2006) provide an excellent resource for taking a systematic approach to positive behavior management. The purpose of this section is to present an action plan for modifying and maintaining acceptable behavior. There are three phases to such a program: (1) increasing acceptable behavior; (2) prompting acceptable behavior; and (3) sharing acceptable behavior. The focus of a discipline program is on positive and constructive approaches designed to teach children responsible behavior. One note here: It is usually best to try and think of behavior in terms of *acceptable* and *unacceptable* rather than *positive* and *negative*. Unacceptable and acceptable speak only to the behavior, not the child. Positive and negative behavior can easily be interpreted by the child as good and bad. This starts to characterize the child as good or bad, which is never an effective or constructive approach to improving student behavior.

Increase Acceptable Behavior

"Catch them doing what you want them to do" is the secret to increasing acceptable behavior. Behavior that is followed by appropriate positive reinforcement will occur more often in the future. This principle is the key for increasing acceptable behavior. The strength of this simple principle is that it focuses on positive, acceptable educational outcomes. Key points for implementing the principle lie in deciding what to use as reinforcers, selecting those that effectively reinforce individuals, and properly using the reinforcers.

SOCIAL REINFORCERS

Teachers most often use this class of reinforcers. Your positive behavior is the reinforcement given when students perform acceptable behavior. Most children have been involved in an environment filled with social reinforcers prior to attending school. Parents use praise, physical contact, and facial expressions to acknowledge acceptable behavior in their children. The following are examples of reinforcers that can be used with students in a physical education setting:

Words of Praise

Great job.	Nice going.
Exactly right.	I really like that job.
Perfect arm placement.	That's the best one yet.
Way to go!	Nice hustle.

Physical Expressions

Smiling	Winking
Nodding	Holding a clenched fist overhead
Giving thumbs-up	Clapping

Physical Contact

Handshake	High five

Find out what type of social reinforcers students are accustomed to responding to in the school setting. Certain reinforcers may embarrass students or make them feel uncomfortable. For example, some students may not want to be touched even to the point of receiving a high five. Some students, particularly those of the opposite sex, may interpret a hug or pat on the back incorrectly. If unsure, ask the school administrator to clarify the acceptable social reinforcers to which students respond positively.

ACTIVITY REINFORCERS

Various types of activities that children enjoy can be used as reinforcement. An effective way to determine activities that can be used as reinforcers is to observe children. Free time always ranks high among children's preferences. Some examples of activities that might be used to reinforce a class are free time to practice a skill, the opportunity to play a game, extra time in physical education class, and the opportunities to help administer equipment, act as a teacher's aide, be a teacher in a cross-aged tutoring situation, or be a team captain.

Students might be given special privileges such as being "student of the day," getting to choose the game to play, or having lunch with the teacher.

TOKEN REINFORCERS

Many teachers feel a need to offer some type of token as a reinforcer. It may be points, gold stars, certificates, or trophies. Physical education is closely related to athletic competition, where awards are often given to winners. This causes some teachers to believe that tokens should be used to motivate children in physical education. The less favorable aspect of giving tokens (ribbons or certificates) is that when they are given only to winners, losers become less likely to be motivated to perform in the future. Some teachers give participation certificates or ribbons to all students; however, this gives the token little reinforcement value. In addition, there is evidence that extrinsic rewards may actually decrease a child's intrinsic desire to participate (Greene & Lepper, 1975; Whitehead & Corbin, 1991). Token reinforcers work best with primary-grade children. Young children are motivated by the tokens they receive. However, after the age of nine, students begin to see tokens as a form of bribery to behave in a certain manner. Generally, it is best to use token reinforcers only if it appears that social reinforcers are ineffective.

SELECTING REINFORCERS

A common question among teachers is, "How do I know what will be reinforcing to my students?" It is impossible to know what will reinforce a student until it is administered. Fortunately, there are a lot of things to which most children will respond, such as praise, attention, smiles, games, free time, and privileges. A practical way to identify effective reinforcers is to observe children during free time, analyzing the things they enjoy doing. Another simple solution is to ask them what they would like to do. Most youngsters will tell you that they would like more recess, free time, or other enjoyable activity.

USING SOCIAL REINFORCERS

Effective use of social reinforcers requires praise and making positive statements. You may feel uncomfortable when learning to administer positive reinforcement to youngsters because such behavior feels inauthentic. A common complaint from teachers learning how to reinforce is, "I do not feel real and children think I'm a fake." Any change in communication patterns feels uncomfortable at first. Trying new ways of communicating with a class requires a period of adjustment. New patterns of praise and reinforcement often feel contrived and insincere (fortunately, most students don't know the difference), and there is no way to avoid the discomfort. Teachers who are unwilling to experience

the uneasiness of learning will usually remain unchanged. The assumption that patterns of speech learned as a child are effective in an instructional setting is false. Teachers are made, not born, and they find success through hard work and dedication. If practiced regularly, new behavioral patterns will become a natural part of your repertoire after a period of time.

Praise is effective when it refers to specific behavior exhibited by a youngster. This contrasts with general statements such as, "Good job" or "You are an excellent performer." General and nonspecific statements do not tell the youngster what was done well. They leave it to the student to try to identify what you had in mind. If the student's thoughts do not align with your intent, incorrect behavior is reinforced. To improve the specificity and effectiveness of feedback, describe the behavior to be reinforced rather than judge it. For example, compare the following:

> *Describing:* "I saw your excellent forward roll, James; you tucked your head just right."
>
> *Judging:* "That's a poor job. I do not see why you cannot do better."

In the first example, the youngster is identified and the specific behavior performed is reinforced. In the second situation, it is impossible to identify what is poor or to whom the feedback is directed. In most cases, if a question can be asked about delivered praise or criticism (such as what was good, or why was it a poor performance), the feedback is nonspecific and open to misinterpretation. To increase acceptable behavior, verbally or physically describe what made the performance effective, good, or noteworthy. This reinforces the student and communicates to the rest of the class what behavior is expected by the instructor.

THE PREMACK PRINCIPLE

The Premack principle (Premack, 1965) is often used unknowingly to motivate students. This principle states that a highly desirable activity can be used to motivate students to learn an activity they enjoy to a lesser degree. In practice, this principle allows students to participate in a favorite activity if they perform a less enjoyable one. The Premack principle is often referred to as the "Eat your peas before you get dessert" rule. An activity that children enjoy is used to motivate youngsters to participate in activities they are reluctant to perform. The following are examples of the Premack principle:

- "You may shoot baskets [preferred] after you complete the passing drill [less desirable]."
- "When everybody is quiet [less desirable], we will begin the game [preferred]."
- "Those who raise their hand [less desirable] will be selected to answer the question [preferred]."

Prompt Acceptable Behavior

Prompts are used to remind students to perform acceptable behavior. They encourage development of new patterns of behavior. There are a number of ways to prompt children in the physical education setting. The most common are the following:

1. *Modeling.* You or a student performs the acceptable behavior with the expectation that the other students will respond in similar fashion. For example, placing your piece of equipment on the floor when stopping the class will remind the class to do likewise. Modeling is an effective prompt for acceptable behavior because young students emulate their teacher.

2. *Verbal cues.* This is a common method of prompting—using words such as "Hustle" and "Keep going." The purpose is to remind students about acceptable behavior. Usually, verbal cues are used to maintain the pace of the lesson, increase the intensity of the performance, or motivate youngsters to stay on task.

3. *Nonverbal cues.* Many physical cues are given through body language to communicate concepts such as "Hustle," "Move over here," "Great performance," "Quiet down," and so on. When teaching skills, nonverbal physical cues can prompt youngsters by moving them into proper position, helping them through the correct pattern, or placing body parts in proper alignment.

Prompts should not be used to the point at which students will not perform without them. The goal is to remove the prompt so that behavior is self-motivated. This process is called fading and involves gradual removal of the prompt. It is likely that you will use prompts at opportune times; however, the major purposes of prompting are to implement new behavior patterns and to increase the occurrence of acceptable behavior. The weakest (least intrusive) prompt possible should be used to stimulate the behavior. For example, it is possible to give students a long lecture about the importance of staying on-task. However, this approach is time-consuming and overreactionary. It is not suited to multiple (repetitive) use and is ineffective in the long run. Select a cue that is closely identified with the acceptable skill and that is short and concise.

In addition to these points, be sure that the prompt identifies the task being prompted. For example, if you prompt the class to "hustle" and the prompt is not tied to an acceptable behavior, there may be confusion. Some children may think your prompt means to perform the skill as fast as possible; others may think it means to stop what they are doing and hustle to the teacher. Tie the prompt to the acceptable behavior in a consistent manner and make sure that students clearly understand the meaning of your prompt.

Shape Acceptable Behavior

Shaping techniques can be used to build new acceptable behavior. When acceptable behavior does not exist, shaping—using extinction and reinforcement—is used to create new behavior. Two principles are followed when shaping behavior.

1. *Differential reinforcement is used to increase the incidence of acceptable behavior.* Reinforce responses that reach a predetermined criterion and ignore those that do not meet the criterion (extinction). An example of this principle involves asking a class to put their equipment down quickly. You decide that students should put the equipment on the floor within five seconds. Using differential reinforcement, reinforce the students whenever they meet the five-second criterion and ignore their performance when it takes longer than five seconds.

2. *The criterion that must be reached for reinforcement to occur is increased.* In this step, you gradually shift the criterion standard toward the desired goal. For example, if the acceptable behavior is for the class to become quiet within 5 seconds after a signal has been given, it might be necessary to start with a 12-second interval. Why the longer interval? In all likelihood, it is not reasonable to expect that an inattentive class will quiet down quickly. If a 5-second interval is selected initially, there is a strong possibility that you and your students will be frustrated by the lack of success. In addition, this stringent standard of behavior will not be achieved very often, resulting in very few opportunities to reinforce the class. The result is a situation in which both you and the class feel they have failed. To avoid this possibility of failure, gradually move toward the acceptable behavior goal. In this case, start with 12 seconds until the class reaches this goal. Next, shift to a 10-second interval and ask the class to perform to this new standard. The process is gradually repeated until the desired behavior is reached.

Changing behavior can also be accomplished in a similar manner by taking a systematic approach to behavior modification. Figure 6.5 offers a step-by-step plan for changing unacceptable behavior.

DECREASE UNACCEPTABLE BEHAVIOR WITH DISCIPLINE

Most effective techniques for improving class behavior are designed to guide the student away from behavior

Changing behavior can be done if teachers are willing to experiment and be patient. Teachers want to change behavior quickly and on the spot and at times make incorrect decisions because they don't have time to think of an effective solution. In-class misbehavior can be temporarily stopped, but may often go unchanged for the future. Realize that change will require long-term action that must be planned ahead of time. The following steps can be used to develop a plan for changing behavior:

- Identify a single behavior that needs to be changed, improved, or strengthened. Don't pick more than one behavior as it will make it much more difficult to monitor change.

- Identify a behavior that will be substituted for the behavior to be changed.

- Determine what positively reinforces the student. Have a discussion with the student to see what is reinforcing.

- Decide whether a negative reinforcer is needed to give momentum to the change process.

- Develop a plan for getting the desired behavior to occur. This will generate a behavior that can be reinforced and used to replace the undesirable behavior.

- Put the plan into effect and set a time frame for evaluation of the plan. Decide what modifications are needed to make the plan more effective. This modification may demand a different set or schedule of reinforcers or negative consequences. If an entirely different plan is needed (because the behavior hasn't decreased or changed), make such changes and proceed.

- Continue evaluating and modifying the plan.

FIGURE 6.5 A plan for changing misbehavior.

that is disrupting the class. Corrective feedback and the use of consequences can be effective means for decreasing unacceptable behavior. Such consequences are actions that follow misbehavior and teach students that their behavior results in some action from the teacher.

Use Corrective Feedback

First, as described above, try using positive reinforcement to increase acceptable behavior with the hope that it will replace unacceptable behavior. For example, if a skilled youngster is always criticizing less able youngsters, ask that student to help others and serve as a student assistant. The intent is to teach the youngster to deliver positive and constructive feedback rather than criticism. An effective rule of thumb before choosing to use corrective feedback is to reinforce the acceptable behavior twice. For example, assume a youngster is slow to stop on signal, while the majority of other students are stopping and listening properly. Ask the class to move and freeze again. Reinforce students who are on-task. (This doesn't work with students who are older; public reinforcement is usually not acceptable to Developmental Level III students.) If the result is not acceptable, try it again. Many times, with primary-grade children, the misbehaving students will emulate those who are being reinforced. If not, it may be necessary to use corrective feedback. Corrective feedback should be clear and specific. Students must know exactly what it is they are to stop and what acceptable behavior they are to start. Use corrective feedback as soon after the misbehavior as possible, just as positive reinforcement should be delivered immediately following the acceptable behavior.

When students are disciplined or corrected, they may respond in a negative manner, causing class disruption if such feedback is not delivered correctly. The following steps will prevent teacher-student conflicts from occurring in front of other students. Whether delivering corrective feedback or consequences, use these steps to avoid embarrassing students and yourself.

1. *Do not address the student publicly.* Buy some time for talking with the student privately by giving the class a task to perform. It may be as simple as jogging around the area. This leaves you in control and allows time to discuss the situation with the misbehaving student.

2. *Isolate the student and yourself.* Don't correct a student where others can hear what you are saying. The problem is a private matter between you and the student.

3. *Deal with one student at a time.* Often, a couple of students are misbehaving together. Separate them and deal with their unacceptable behavior one-on-one.

4. *State your position once; repeat it once if you believe the student didn't understand.* Don't argue or try to prove your point. Take no more than 10–15 seconds to tell the student the unacceptable behavior and what acceptable behavior you would like to see.

5. *Deliver and move away.* Avoid eyeballing the student when delivering corrective feedback. Such behavior is confrontational to older students. Stand beside them and softly deliver your feedback. Walk away after you have delivered the feedback. Don't eyeball a student after you have reprimanded him as you may see things you don't want to see. To get yourself back on track, positively reinforce

one or two students who are performing the acceptable behavior.

6. *Don't threaten or bully the student.* It builds resentment in students and may cause greater problems at a later time.

7. *Avoid touching the student when correcting behavior.* Even if you have positive intentions, it can send mixed messages. Some students don't want to be touched and will aggressively pull away and make a scene in front of the class.

8. *Don't curse or raise your voice excessively.* Don't be sarcastic. Instead deliver clearly what you desire from the student in terms of acceptable behavior.

When corrective feedback fails to cause an acceptable change in behavior, consequences must be used. Students need to understand that unacceptable behavior will bring consequences. Becoming responsible for one's behavior may be one of the most, if not *the* most, important social behaviors learned from the school experience. Consequences that can be used to decrease unacceptable behavior include reprimands, removal of positive consequences, and time-out.

TRY REPRIMANDS

This is a common approach used to decrease unacceptable behavior. If done in a caring and constructive manner, reprimands can serve as effective reminders to behave.

- Identify the unacceptable behavior, state briefly why it is unacceptable, and communicate to students what behavior is acceptable. For example, "You were talking while I was speaking. It bothers other students, so please listen to me."

- Don't reprimand in front of other students. Not only does it embarrass students, it also can diminish their self-esteem. When students feel belittled, they may lash out and react in a manner more severe than their original behavior.

- Speak about behavior, not the person, when reprimanding. Ask the behavior to stop rather than telling a student that "You are always causing problems in this class." Avoid general and negative statements related to the personality of the student.

- After reprimanding and asking for acceptable behavior, reinforce it when it occurs. Be vigilant in looking for the acceptable behavior since reinforcing such behavior will cause it to occur more often in the future.

REMOVE POSITIVE CONSEQUENCES

This is a common approach used by parents, so many students are familiar with it. The basic approach is to remove something positive from the student when misbehavior occurs. For example, have students give up some of their free time due to misbehavior or lose points related to a grade. Or don't allow them to participate in an activity that is exciting to them. For removal of positive consequences to be effective, make sure students really want to be a part of the removal activity. It doesn't work to keep a student out of a game if the student doesn't like the game. A few key principles should be followed when using this technique:

- Be sure that the magnitude of the removal fits the crime. In other words, children who commit a minor infraction shouldn't have to miss recess for a week.

- Be consistent in removal, treating all students and occurrences the same. Students believe teachers are unfair if they are more severe with one student than another. In addition, a student penalized for a specific misbehavior should receive the same penalty for a later repetition.

- Make sure students understand the consequences of their misbehavior before the penalties are implemented. This avoids applying penalties in an emotional, unthinking manner. If students know what the consequences will be, they are making the choice to accept the consequences when they choose to misbehave.

- Chart a student's misbehavior to see if the frequency is decreasing. Regardless of the method used, if the behavior is not decreasing or is increasing, change methods until a decrease in frequency occurs.

USE TIME-OUT

The time-out procedure is an equitable technique for dealing with youngsters in a manner that is consistent with society. Rules are clearly posted and consequences are clear and easy to comprehend. Time-out is an effective approach for dealing with unacceptable behavior that occurs randomly on an individual basis. The time-out approach moves youngsters out of the class setting and places them into a predesignated area when they misbehave. *Time-out means time out from reinforcement.* It does not imply that the student is a "bad person," but rather that unacceptable behavior has occurred and there is a need for a time-out to reconsider and redirect their misbehavior. When placing students in time-out, communicate to children that they are acceptable individuals, but their misbehavior is unacceptable.

Being placed in time-out communicates to youngsters that they have disrupted the class and must be removed so that the rest of the class can participate without interruption. It is also acceptable for children to voluntarily use the time-out area as a "cooling off" spot if they become angry, embarrassed, or frustrated.

6

If youngsters have been placed in the time-out area for fighting or arguing, they should be placed at opposite ends of the area so that the behavior does not escalate. In addition, mandate that they stay in their half (or quadrant) of the teaching area until the next meeting of the class. This prevents recurring agitation between the two combatants and the possibility of increased hostility.

The implementation of this plan should be discussed with students so that they know exactly what constitutes acceptable and unacceptable behavior and what consequences will occur when they behave in an unacceptable manner. Post a list of acceptable behavior (rules) and consequences for unacceptable behavior, as discussed above, in the teaching area.

Time-out does not serve as a deterrent if the youngster is reinforced by being placed in time-out. Time-out means receiving *as little* reinforcement as possible. If class participation is a negative experience for students, taking them out of class will be a positive rather than a negative consequence. The physical location for time-out must be considered to make it effective. For example, if a student who is not participating properly is sent to the office, as the teacher thinks this will be a good location for time-out, the student may find some of her friends in the office; as a result, this student not only gets to avoid participation, she also gets to visit with friends. Another example: Being a spectator in our society is highly reinforcing. People are willing to pay high prices to watch others play sports or act. Sitting on the side of the teaching area and looking on as a spectator may be a more reinforcing experience than participating in class activities. If you put someone in time-out, make sure he is not facing the class and interacting with peers (Figure 6.6). *Remember—If students don't enjoy being in class, time-out does not work.*

CONSEQUENCES FOR UNACCEPTABLE BEHAVIOR

Just as with rules, consequences for unacceptable behavior should be listed and posted in the area. Each of the consequences should be discussed until there is general class consensus that the rules are fair and necessary. A possible set of consequences for unacceptable behavior follows.

First Misbehavior: The student is warned quietly that the unacceptable behavior must stop. At times, students are not aware that they are bothering others, and a gentle reminder will refocus the youngster. In terms of teacher talk, private conversation with the student would be as follows: "John, you were talking while I was talking. That is unacceptable behavior. I will appreciate you listening in the future. This is your first warning."

Second Misbehavior: The student goes to one of the four time-out spots and stays there until ready to return and behave in an acceptable manner. Place time-out stations in each of the four corners of the instructional area. When outdoors, delineate the instructional area with four

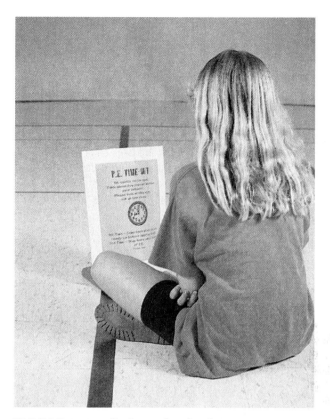

FIGURE 6.6   Student assigned to time-out.

cones and place a time-out sign on each cone. It is acceptable for the student to go to the time-out area and return immediately to physical education class, but the assumption is that the student has agreed to behave properly.

A point here is necessary. Some teachers want to have students stay in the time-out area for five minutes before returning. That is fine if you have a way to keep track of the time. However, it is difficult to manage when a number of students go to time-out at different times. Another method used by some teachers is the "You can return when I say you can return" method. The problem with this approach is that it can become arbitrary or you may forget and leave a student in time-out longer than you had planned. Also, if a student is a chronic offender, you may leave her in time-out longer for the same behavior than you would a student who seldom misbehaves. That sends a message that you have favorites and like some students better than others. An effective behavior management system should be fair and consistent.

Third Misbehavior: The student goes to the time-out area for the remainder of the period. Each time a student starts a new class, he should receive a fresh start on the consequences. It is fairly common to hear a teacher tell a student at the start of class, "If you do one thing wrong, you are going to time-out for the rest of the period." This student is then treated differently than all the other students. It will make it difficult to establish a positive relationship with a student if he feels you are unfair or uncaring.

If the unacceptable behavior continues each time the class meets, most schools have an in-school suspension program to deal with severe behavior. In-school suspension requires the student to leave his or her class of students and move into another room of students (of a different grade level). This ensures that the student will receive little, if any, reinforcement. The foregoing steps assume that you have communicated with the student about her unacceptable behavior and how she is expected to behave.

If these consequences are ineffective, the next alternative is to discuss with the principal more serious consequences. The last alternative is to call the parents in for a conference with you and the principal. Discretion must be used when deciding to call parents. There is a strong possibility that it will further alienate you from the student because of parental pressure and punishment at home. Another possibility is that parents will disagree with your assessment. If parents can't or won't support you, it may be a better option not to call the parents but to deal with the behavior in a school setting. Along the same lines, don't ask the principal to solve all your problems with misbehaving students. The principal will soon come to believe that you cannot effectively manage students. Ultimately, this will erode the principal's confidence in your teaching ability.

Implement Behavior Contracts with Older Students

A behavior contract is a written statement specifying certain student behaviors that must occur for students to earn certain rewards or privileges. The contract is drawn up after a private conference to decide on the appropriate behaviors and rewards. It is agreed upon and signed by the student and teacher. This approach allows students to make decisions that will improve their own behavior.

The behavior contract may be a successful strategy for intermediate-grade students with severe behavior problems. Every attempt should be made to find activities in physical education class (such as Frisbee play, jump rope games, aerobics, or basketball) that are naturally rewarding. If this is not possible, different types of rewards may have to be used. For example, a student who is interested in music could be allowed to spend some time selecting CDs or tapes to be used for class during the next week. As behavior improves and the student's attitude becomes more positive, rewards should be switched to physical education activities. The contract is gradually phased out over a period of time as the youngster gains control of the behavior and can participate in normal class environments.

Contracts can be written for a small group of students or for an entire class with similar problems, but teachers must be careful about setting up a reward system for too many students. The system can become too complex or time-consuming to supervise properly. The contract is best used with a limited number of students who have severe problems. Examples of behavior contracts are shown in Figures 6.7 and 6.8. The contract in Figure 6.8 can be used with an individual, a small group, or an entire class of students.

Incorporate Behavior Games for Overall Class Behavior

Behavior games are an effective strategy for changing class behavior in the areas of management, motivation, and discipline. These activities use the shaping technique and are useful in changing whole-class behavior (in contrast to individual-student behavior). If you are having problems in any of these areas, a well-conceived behavior game may turn the situation around in a short period. These games can be organized so a group of students compete against each other or against an established criterion. The goal of the game is to use group contingencies to develop behaviors that enhance the learning environment and to eliminate behaviors that detract from the environment (Darst & Whitehead, 1975; Paese, 1982).

The list below provides an example of a behavior game used successfully with sixth graders in an effort to improve management behaviors.

1. The class is divided into four to six squads. Each squad has a designated color for identification. Four boundary cones with appropriate colors are arranged to mark a starting area.
2. The rules of the game are as follows:

Date: _____

I, _____, agree to follow the rules listed below:

1. Listen when the teacher is talking.

2. Do not touch others during class.

If all the rules are followed during physical education class, I will earn 10 minutes of basketball activity for myself and a friend after school on Thursday anytime between 3:00 and 3:45.

Signed: _____, Student

Signed: _____, Teacher

FIGURE 6.7 Individual behavior contract.

Group Behavior Contract

Our squad agrees to follow the rules listed below:

1. Listen when the teacher is talking.

2. Take care of the equipment.

3. Treat others as we would like to be treated.

One point is earned each time the music stops and every member of the squad is following the rules. No points are awarded if one or more members of the squad are not following the rules. Each point is worth 1 minute of free activity time to be awarded every other Friday.

Signed: Squad Number _____   _____

_____   _____

_____   _____

_____   _____

FIGURE 6.8   Group behavior contract.

a. Each squad member has to be ready for activity and in proper position at a designated starting time. *Reward:* Two points.

b. Each squad member has to move from one activity to another activity within the specified time (10, 20, or 30 seconds) and begin the appropriate behavior. *Reward:* One point for each activity.

c. Each point earned is rewarded with one minute of free activity time on Friday. Free activity time includes basketball, Frisbee playing, rope-jumping, or any other activity popular with students.

d. The squad with the most points for the week earns a bonus of five points.

3. The allotted time for each management episode (10, 20, or 30 seconds) is explained, and a "go" signal is given. At the end of the allowed time, the signal for "stop" is given and points are awarded for appropriate behavior.

4. Successful squads are praised and their points recorded on a small card. The unsuccessful squads are not hassled or criticized, just reminded that they did not earn a point.

5. On Fridays, the appropriate squads are awarded the special free-time activities while the other squads continue with the regularly scheduled class activities.

6. The game is slowly phased out (faded) as students begin to manage themselves more quickly.

Research used to evaluate behavior games showed the following results:

- The use of group contingencies and free-time activities reduced overall class management time.
- The free-time activities were within the physical education curriculum objectives and served as a break from regular activities.
- The free-time activities gave the teacher an opportunity to interact with students on a personal level.
- Students enjoyed the competition and the feeling of success when they behaved appropriately.
- Students enjoyed the free times with novelty activities.
- The positive approach of the game seemed to improve the overall teaching-learning atmosphere. Students were more attentive and cooperative.
- Teachers estimated that more time was available for instruction because of the reduction in management time.

A key point to keep in mind when designing behavior games is to structure them so that any student or squad is able to win the game. Each game need not generate one winner and many losers. All participants should be able to win. Be aware that one or two students may find it reinforcing to cause their team to lose the behavior game. They will try to break every game rule to make sure that their team loses consistently. In these cases, hold a special team discussion with a vote to eliminate those students from the team and the game. These students are then sent to a time-out area or to in-school suspension. They can be asked to sit out for the duration of the behavior game.

Another effective behavior game can be used to help students persist at learning activities in a station-type approach. Often, four to six learning stations are used for instruction. Performance objectives or learning tasks are posted at each station for students to practice. However, it may be that some students are not motivated and do not use their time productively until you rotate to the station where they are working. Overall, the environment is not productive, and you quickly get tired of hassling unmotivated students. A possible solution to this situation is the following game:

1. Divide the class into four to six squads. Let the students pick a name for their squad.

2. Set up the learning stations with the activities to be practiced. An equal number of squads and learning stations is necessary.

3. Program a cassette tape with popular music. Intersperse short gaps of silence throughout the tape.

4. Inform students that if everyone in their squad is properly engaged in practicing the appropriate task, a point will be awarded to the squad at each gap in the music. If one or more persons are not engaged, the point will not be awarded.

5. Exchange points for minutes of time in selected activities such as Frisbee play, juggling, or rope-jumping. Fridays can be designated as reward days, when the accumulated time is used.

6. Change the music regularly. Also change and slowly increase the intervals between gaps until the gaps are eliminated. The music then serves as a discriminative cue for future practice time.

Students enjoy exercising and practicing skills while listening to music. The music enhances the motivational level and productivity of the environment. Students can be allowed to bring their own music as a special reward for productive behavior. (Make sure the music is not offensive to others due to sexual, ethnic, or religious connotations.)

USE CRITICISM SPARINGLY

Use criticism and punishment with caution and good judgment. Criticism is sometimes used with the belief that it will improve the performance of students. Some teachers make scolding and criticism the behavior control tools of choice because these tools give the impression that the results are effective and immediate. Usually, misbehavior stops and the assumption is that the situation has been rectified. Unfortunately, this is not always the case. Criticism and punishment lend a negative air to the instructional environment and have a negative impact on both student and teacher. The old saying, "It hurts me more than you" is often the case. The majority of teachers feel uncomfortable when they

must criticize or punish students. It makes them feel as though they cannot handle students and that the class is incorrigible. This feeling of incompetence leads to a destructive cycle where students feel negative about the instructor and the instructor feels negative about the students. In the long run, this is the debilitating impact of criticism and punishment.

As mentioned above, another negative aspect of criticism is that it does not offer a solution. In a study by Thomas, Becker, and Armstrong (1968), a teacher was asked to stop praising a class. Off-task behavior increased from 8.7 percent to nearly 26 percent. When the teacher was asked to increase criticism from 5 times in 20 minutes to 16 times in 20 minutes, more off-task behavior was demonstrated. On some days the percentage of off-task behavior increased to more than 50 percent. When attention is given to off-task behavior and no praise is offered for on-task accomplishment, off-task behavior increases dramatically. Using criticism makes teachers feel effective (students respond to the request of the criticism), but students do not actually change. In fact, the students are reinforced (they receive attention from the teacher) for their off-task behavior. In addition, since their on-task behavior is not praised, it decreases. The net result is exactly the opposite of what is desired.

MAKE PUNISHMENT A LAST RESORT

The question of whether punishment should be used in an educational setting is a difficult one. Punishment can have negative side effects because fear is the primary motivator. Consider the long-term need for punishment. If the long-term effects of using punishment are more beneficial than not using it, it is unethical not to use punishment. In other words, if a child is going to be in a worse situation because punishment was not used to deter self-destructive behavior, it is wrong not to use it. It may be necessary to punish a child for protection from self-inflicted harm (for example, using certain apparatus without supervision). It may be necessary to punish children so that they learn not to hurt others. Punishment in these situations will cause discomfort to teacher and child in the short run, but it may allow the student to participate successfully in society later.

Most situations in the educational setting do not require punishment because they are not as severe as those described above. A major reason for avoiding punishment is that it can have negative side effects. When children are punished, they learn to avoid the source of punishment. It forces them to be more covert in their actions. They spend time finding ways to be devious without being caught. Instead of encouraging students to discuss problems with teachers and parents, punishment teaches them to avoid these individuals for fear of being punished. Another side effect is that it teaches children to be aggressive toward others. Children who have been physically or emotionally punished by parents act in similar fashion to others. The result is a child who is secretive and aggressive with others—certainly less-than-desirable traits. Finally, if punishment is used to stop certain behavior, as soon as the punishment stops the behavior will return. Thus, little has been learned; the punishment has just led to short-term change.

If it is necessary to use punishment, remember the following points:

1. *Be consistent and make the punishment "fit the crime."* Students quickly lose respect for a teacher who treats others with favoritism. They view the teacher as unfair if punishment is extreme or unfair. Peers quickly side with the student who is treated unfairly, causing a class morale problem for the instructor.

2. *Offer a warning signal, as discussed previously.* This may prevent excessive use of punishment, as students often behave after receiving a warning. In addition, they probably view the teacher as caring and fair.

3. *Do not threaten students.* Offer only one warning. Threats have little impact on students and make them feel that you cannot handle the class. One warning gives students the feeling that you are not looking to punish them and are fair. Follow through; do not challenge or threaten students and then fail to deal with the behavior.

4. *Make sure the punishment follows the misbehavior as soon as possible.* It is much less effective and more often viewed as unfair when it is delayed.

5. *Punish quietly and calmly.* Do not seek revenge or be vindictive. If responsible behavior is expected from students, be sure you reprimand and punish in a responsible manner. Studies (O'Leary & Becker, 1968) show that quiet reprimands are more effective than loud ones.

One more point related to punishment: Try to avoid developing negative feelings toward a student because you internalize the misbehavior. Being punitive when handling deviant behavior destroys any chance for a worthwhile relationship with the student. Misbehavior should be handled in a manner that contributes to the development of responsible, confident students who understand that people who function effectively in society must adjust to certain limits. Forget about past bouts of deviant behavior and approach the student in a positive fashion at the start of each class. If this is not done, students will feel labeled, making behavioral change more difficult. Students may also learn to live up to the teacher's negative expectations.

If punishment is used, make sure that only those youngsters who misbehave are punished. Punishing an entire class for the deviant behavior of a few youngsters is unfair and may trigger unacceptable side effects. Students become hostile toward those who caused the loss of privileges, and this peer hostility lowers the level of positive social interaction with the students who have misbehaved.

EXPULSION: LEGAL CONSIDERATIONS

If serious problems occur, discuss the problems with the classroom teacher and principal. Many times, deviant behavior is part of a larger, more severe problem that is troubling a child. A cooperative approach may provide an effective solution. A group meeting involving parents, classroom teacher, principal, counselor, and physical education specialist may open avenues that encourage understanding and increase productive behavior.

Legal concerns involving the student's rights in disciplinary areas are an essential consideration. While minor infractions may be handled routinely, expulsion and other substantial punishments can be imposed on students only after due process. The issue of student rights is complicated, and most school systems have established guidelines and procedures for dealing with students who have been removed from the class or school setting. Youngsters should be removed from class only if they are disruptive to the point of interfering with the learning experiences of other children and if all other means of altering behavior have not worked. Sending a child out of class is a last resort and means that both teacher and student have failed.

REFLECTION AND REVIEW QUESTIONS

How and Why

1. How would you respond to a child who consistently misbehaves?

2. How does it make you feel when a professor knows your name?

3. How might pre- and post-teaching routines change depending on the school?

4. Why is it important for teachers to know their own trigger points? What are your trigger points?

5. What rules would you have in your classes?

6. What types of emotions might you feel when placing a child in time-out?

7. As an adult, how does criticism make you feel?

Content Review

1. What class management skills are necessary to be an effective teacher?

2. What is the importance of using efficient instruction, a consistent stop signal, and moving students into formation quickly in an effective lesson?

3. How can knowing the names of students help teachers?

4. What types of routines do successful teachers establish?

5. What is the effective use of equipment?

FOR MORE INFORMATION

References and Suggested Readings

Bailey, B. A. (2001). *Conscious discipline.* Oviedo, FL: Loving Guidance, Inc.

Beane, A. (1999). *The bully free classroom.* Minneapolis: Free Spirit Publishing.

Canter, L., & Canter, M. (1997). *Assertive discipline: Positive behavior management for today's classroom.* Santa Monica, CA: Lee Canter and Associates.

Charles, C. M. (1989). *Building classroom discipline.* 3rd ed. New York: Longman.

Cohen, R. (2005). *Students resolving conflict.* Tucson: Good Year Books.

Curwin, R. L., & Mendler, A. N. (1988). *Discipline with dignity.* Washington, DC: Association for Supervision and Curriculum Development.

Darst, P. W., & Whitehead, S. (1975). Developing a contingency management system for controlling student behavior. *Pennsylvania JOPER,* 46(3), 11–12.

Gordon, A., & Browne, K. W. (1996). *Guiding young children in a diverse society.* Boston: Allyn and Bacon.

Greene, D., & Lepper, M. R. (1975). Turning play into work: Effects of adult surveillance and extrinsic rewards on children's internal motivation. *Journal of Personality and Social Psychology,* 31, 479–486.

Hellison, D. (2003). *Teaching responsibility through physical activity.* 2nd ed. Champaign, IL: Human Kinetics Publishers.

Lavay, B. W., French, R., & Henderson, H. L. (2006). *Positive behavior management in physical activity settings.* 2nd ed. Champaign, IL: Human Kinetics Publishers.

Nelson, J. (1996). *Positive discipline.* New York: Ballantine.

O'Leary, K. D., & Becker, W. C. (1968). The effects of intensity of a teacher's reprimands on children's behavior. *Journal of School Psychology,* 7, 8–11.

Paese, P. (1982). Effects of interdependent group contingencies in a secondary physical education setting. *Journal of Teaching in Physical Education,* 2(1), 29–37.

Premack, D. (1965). Reinforcement theory. In D. Levine (Ed.), *Nebraska symposium on motivation.* Lincoln: University of Nebraska Press.

Siedentop, D., & Tannehill, D. (2000). *Developing teaching skills in physical education.* 4th ed. Mountain View, CA: Mayfield Publishing Co.

Thomas, D. R., Becker, W. C., & Armstrong, M. (1968). Production and elimination of disruptive classroom behavior by systematically varying teachers' behavior. *Journal of Applied Behavior Analysis,* 1, 35–45.

Whitehead, J. R., & Corbin, C. B. (1991). Effects of fitness test type, teacher, and gender on exercise intrinsic motivation and physical self-worth. *Journal of School Health,* 61, 11–16.

Wolfgang, C. H. (1996). *The three faces of discipline for the elementary school teacher.* Boston: Allyn and Bacon.

Websites

Classroom Management
www.pecentral.org/climate/disciplinelinks
    .html#classroombehaviormanagementsites
www.honorlevel.com/techniques.html

Management Styles
http://education.indiana.edu/cas/tt/v1i2/what.html

7

Children with Disabilities

ESSENTIAL COMPONENTS OF QUALITY PROGRAMS

▶ **I. Organized around content standards**

▶ **II. Student-centered and developmentally appropriate**

III. Physical activity and motor skill development form the core of the program

IV. Teaches management skills and self-discipline

▶ **V. Promotes inclusion of all students**

▶ **VI. Focuses on process over product**

VII. Promotes lifetime personal health and wellness

▶ **VIII. Teaches cooperation and responsibility and promotes sensitivity to diversity**

NATIONAL STANDARDS FOR PHYSICAL EDUCATION*

▶ **1. Demonstrates competency in motor skills and movement patterns needed to perform a variety of physical activities.**

2. Demonstrates understanding of movement concepts, principles, and tactics as they apply to the learning and performance of physical activities.

3. Participates regularly in physical activity.

4. Achieves and maintains a health-enhancing level of physical fitness.

▶ **5. Exhibits responsible personal and social behavior that respects self and others in physical activity.**

▶ **6. Values physical activity for health, enjoyment, challenge, self-expression, and/or social interaction.**

*National Association for Sport and Physical Education (NASPE), 2004.

SUMMARY

Federal law requires every state to develop a plan for identifying, locating, and evaluating all children with disabilities. Due process for students and parents is an important requisite when conducting formal assessment procedures. Mainstreaming involves the practice of placing children with disabilities into classes with able youngsters. Moving a child to a less restrictive learning environment is based on achievement of specified competencies that are required for moving into the new environment. The most common types of disabilities and ways to modify activities for successful participation are discussed. Programs for children with weight problems, motor deficiencies, and postural problems are detailed in a step-by-step manner.

OUTCOMES

▩ Understand the implications of PL 94-142 and IDEA for physical education.

▩ Explain due process guidelines associated with assessment procedures.

▩ Develop a plan for identifying, locating, and evaluating all children with disabilities.

▩ Cite standards associated with assessment procedures for special children.

▩ Identify essential elements of an individualized education program and list the stages of development.

▩ List guidelines for successful inclusion of students.

▩ Describe ways of modifying activities for inclusion.

▩ Describe characteristics of specific impairments and ways to modify learning experiences in physical education to accommodate children with disabilities.

▩ Locate nationally validated programs to assist in the screening, assessment, and curriculum development for children with special needs.

▩ Indicate a step-by-step approach used to develop a success profile for obese youngsters in elementary school.

▩ Describe the attributes of good posture and explain its importance in successful physical performance.

Providing a quality educational experience for all students is the responsibility of the educational system. It should be the goal of all professionals to view this responsibility as an ethical and professional duty rather than something that is required by law. It is the appropriate thing to do for all children—and all children come to school with varying ability levels, disabled or not. Dr. Claudine Sherrill in her text (2004) states that "in a sense, all good physical education is adapted physical education."

The Education for All Handicapped Children Act (Public Law 94-142) was passed by Congress in 1975. It was the 142nd act of legislation passed by the 94th Congress. This legislation introduced new requirements, vocabulary, and concepts into physical education programs across the United States. These concepts include individualized education programs (IEPs), mainstreaming, least restrictive environments, zero reject, and progressive inclusion. The purpose of the law is clear and concise:

> It is the purpose of this act to assure that all handicapped children* have available to them . . . a free appropriate public education which emphasizes special education and related services designed to meet their unique needs, to assure that the rights of handicapped children and their parents or guardians are protected, to assist States and localities to provide for the education of all handicapped children, and to assess and assure the effectiveness of efforts to educate handicapped children.

In short, the law requires that all youth with disabilities, ages 3 to 21, receive a free and appropriate education in the least restrictive environment. The law includes youngsters in public and private care facilities and schools. Youth with disabilities who can learn in regular classes with the use of supplementary aids and services must be educated with youngsters who are able. Physical education is the only specific area mentioned in PL 94-142. The law indicates that the term *special education* "means specially designed instruction, instruction in physical education, home instruction, and instruction in hospitals and institutions." A 1997 amendment, Public Law 105-17 (also known as *IDEA*—Individuals with Disabilities Education Act), continues with the objective of providing handicapped individuals with the least restrictive environment in the school setting. The Individuals with Disabilities Education Act states, "Physical education services, specially designed if necessary, must be made available to every child with a disability receiving a free appropriate public education." Autism and traumatic brain injury have been added to the list of handicapping conditions that should receive the least restrictive environment. IDEA provides that an individual transition plan be developed no later than age 16 as a component of the IEP process. Rehabilitation and social work services are included as related services.

To comply with PL 94-142, secondary schools must locate, identify, and evaluate all students who might have a disability. A screening process must be followed by a formal assessment procedure. An assessment must be made and an IEP developed for each student before placement into a special program can be made. The law states who will be responsible for developing the IEP and what the contents of the IEP will include.

The passage of PL 94-142 shows that a strong commitment has been made to equality and education for all Americans. Prior to 1970, these students had limited access to schools. They certainly did not have an equal opportunity to participate in school programs. The government also ensured that funding would be made available to provide quality instruction. The law authorizes a payment to each state of 40 percent of the average per-pupil expenditure in U.S. elementary and secondary schools, multiplied by the number of youngsters with disabilities who are receiving special education and related services. The federal mandate reveals the concern of the public for comprehensive education programs for all students regardless of disability.

LEAST RESTRICTIVE ENVIRONMENT

PL 105-17 uses the term *least restrictive environment* to help determine the best placement arrangement of students with disabilities. This concept refers to the idea that not all individuals can do all of the same activities in the same environment. However, the concept of zero reject entitles everyone of school age to some aspect of the school program. No one can be totally rejected because of a disability. The focus should be on placing students into settings that offer the best opportunity for educational advancement. It is inappropriate to place a youngster in an environment where success is impossible. However, it would be debilitating to put a student into a setting that is more restrictive than necessary. Special educators speak about many experiences that offer a variety of opportunities from participation in regular physical education classes to physical education in a full-time special school. Figure 7.1 shows a series of options that might be available for physical education.

The least restrictive environment also varies depending on the unit of instruction and the teaching style. For example, for a student in a wheelchair, a soccer

---

*The term *handicapped* is used in PL 94-142 to include youngsters who are mentally retarded, hard of hearing, deaf, speech impaired, visually handicapped, seriously emotionally disturbed, orthopedically impaired, other health impaired, deaf-blind, multihandicapped, or specific learning disabled. The phrase *students with disabilities* is used throughout this chapter to identify youngsters with such conditions.

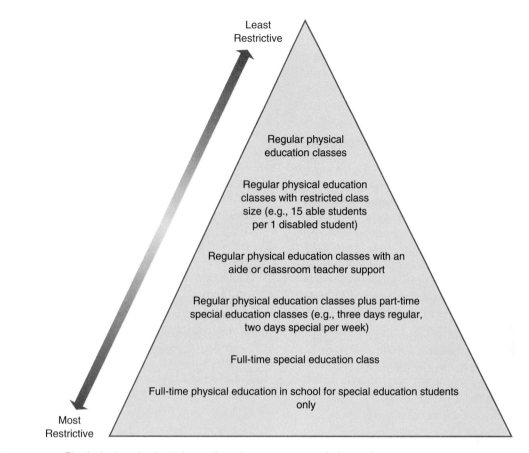

FIGURE 7.1 Physical education inclusion options, least to most restrictive environments.

activity might be very restrictive, whereas in basketball or Frisbee activities, the environment would be less restrictive. For a student with emotional disabilities, the direct style of instruction might be the least restrictive environment, while a problem-solving method with group cooperation may be too difficult and would end up being more restrictive. Consistent and regular judgments need to be made since curriculum content and teaching styles change the type of environment the student enters. It is shortsighted to place students into a situation and then forget about them. Evaluation and modification of environments need to be ongoing. The concept of "progressive inclusion" focuses on the idea that students make progress as a result of educational experiences. Thus, students with disabilities should have the opportunity to progress to the least restrictive environments and experience more and more of the mainstream of our schools and their programs.

Mainstreaming

Physical educators usually speak in terms of mainstreaming rather than least restrictive environments. Mainstreaming means that students with disabilities must have

opportunities to integrate with other students in public schools. Prudent placement in a least restrictive educational environment means that the setting must be as normal as possible (normalization) while ensuring that the student can fit in and achieve success in that placement. The placement may be mainstreaming but is not confined to this approach. There are several categories of placement relative to physical education classes.

1. *Full mainstreaming.* Students with disabilities function as full-time members of a regular school routine. They go to all classes with able students. Within the limitations of their disability, they participate in physical education with able peers. An example may be auditory-impaired students who with a minimal amount of assistance are able to participate fully.
2. *Mainstreaming for physical education only.* Students with disabilities are not members of the regular academic classes in the secondary schools but can still participate in physical education with able peers. This setting may include students with emotional disabilities who are grouped in the classroom and are separated into regular physical education classes.

3. *Partial mainstreaming.* Students participate in selected physical education experiences but do not attend on a full-time basis because they can be successful in only a few of the offerings. Their developmental needs are usually met in special classes.

4. *Special developmental classes.* Students with disabilities are in segregated special education classes.

5. *Reverse mainstreaming.* Able students are brought into a special physical education class to promote intergroup peer relationships.

Segregation should be maintained only when it is in the best interests of the student.

The purpose of segregated programs is to establish a level of skill and social proficiency that will eventually enable the special student to be transferred to a less restricted learning environment. The goal of the process is to place students in the least restrictive environment, where they can benefit most. Students with disabilities working on their own have often been denied opportunities to interact with peers and to become a part of the social and academic classroom network.

Students with disabilities need contact with support personnel during mainstreaming. Even though the physical education teacher is responsible for the mainstreamed students during class time, these students may still require access to special education teachers, school psychologists, and speech therapists. Support personnel may view physical education as a time to get rid of their students; however, they are a source of information and support for the physical education teacher in charge.

SCREENING AND ASSESSMENT

Screening is a process that involves all students in a school setting and is part of the "child find" process. It is often conducted at the start of the school year and is performed districtwide. The physical educator usually conducts screening tests, which may include commonly used test batteries (such as the Fitnessgram). In most situations, screening tests may be administered without parental permission and are used to make initial identification of students who may need special services.

Assessment is conducted after screening evaluations have been made. Assessment is usually conducted after "child find" screening by referring identified students to special education directors. Assessment is performed by a team of experts, which may include the physical education specialist. Due process for students and parents is an important requisite when conducting formal assessment procedures. Due process assures parents and children that they will be informed of their rights and that they have the

opportunity to challenge educational decisions they feel are unfair or incorrect.

Due Process Guidelines

To ensure that due process is offered parents and students, the guidelines discussed here must be followed:

- *Written Permission* A written notice must be sent to parents stating that their child has been referred for assessment. The notice must explain that the district requests permission to conduct an evaluation to determine if special education services are required for their child. Also included in the permission letter must be the reasons for testing and the titles of the tests to be used. Before assessment can begin, the letter must be signed by the parents and returned to the district.

- *Interpretation of the Assessment* The results of the assessment must be interpreted in a meeting with parents. Persons who are knowledgeable about the test procedures must be present to answer questions parents may ask. At the meeting, parents must be told whether their child has any disabilities and what services will be provided for the child.

- *External Evaluation* If parents are not satisfied with the results of the assessment, they may request an evaluation outside the school setting. The district must provide a list of agencies that can perform such assessment. If the results differ from the school district evaluation, the district must pay for the external evaluation. However, if the results are similar, parents must pay for the external testing.

- *Negotiation and Hearings* If parents and the school district disagree on the results of the assessment, the district is required to try to negotiate the differences. When negotiations fail, an impartial hearing officer listens to both parties and renders an official decision. This is usually the final review; however, both parties do have the right to appeal to the state department of education, which must render a binding and final decision. Civil action through the legal system can be pursued should the district or parents still disagree with this action. However, few cases ever reach this level of long-term disagreement, and educators should not be hesitant to serve the needs of children with disabilities based on this concern.

- *Confidentiality* As is the case with other student records, only parents of the child or authorized school personnel can review the student's records. Review by other parties can be done only after written permission has been given by the parents of the child under review.

Procedures for Ensuring Assessment Standards

PL 94-142 requires that assessment is held to certain standards to ensure fair and objective results. The following areas are specifically delineated.

SELECTION OF TEST INSTRUMENTS

Test instruments used must be valid examinations that measure what they purport to measure. Thus, when selecting instruments, it must be clear to all parties how the tests were developed and how they will measure correctly the area of possible disability. More than one test procedure must be used to determine the student's status. Both formal and informal assessment techniques should be used to ensure that the results measure the student's impairment rather than simply reflect the student's shortcomings.

It is an unfortunate situation that children must be labeled as disabled in order to reap the benefits of a special education program. The stigmatizing effect of labels and the fallibility of various means of testing students create a dilemma that must be faced. Although current pedagogical practices discourage labeling, it is double-talk, because school districts have to certify the disability (to receive funding) through which the child is classified.

ADMINISTRATION PROCEDURES

Many disabilities interfere with standard test procedures. For example, many students have communication problems and thus must be tested in a manner that ensures that their motor ability is measured rather than their lack of communication skills. Many students have visual and hearing disabilities that prevent using tests that rely on these faculties.

A probability of misdiagnosis and incorrectly classifying children as mentally retarded can occur with certain ethnic groups such as Native Americans, African Americans, and Spanish-speaking children. Some of these youngsters may be victims of a low standard of living and be only environmentally retarded and in need of cultural enrichment. This is subtle discrimination, but it must be replaced with the understanding that children differ because of culture, poverty, migrancy, and language. Many of the tests are based on white middle-class standards. Minority children should be carefully assessed to determine the validity of the testing procedure.

TEAM EVALUATION

A number of experts should be used for assessment. Emphasis should be placed on a multidisciplinary team to help ensure that all facets of the child will be reviewed and evaluated. Evaluation professionals must be well trained and qualified to administer the various tests. It is the responsibility of the school district to ensure that this occurs.

DEVELOPING AN INDIVIDUALIZED EDUCATION PROGRAM

PL 94-142 requires that an IEP be developed for each child with a disability receiving special education and related services. The IEP must be developed by a committee as stipulated by the law. The committee must include the following members: a local education association representative who is qualified to provide and supervise the administration of special education, the child's parents, the teachers who have direct responsibility for implementing the IEP, and, when appropriate, the student. Other individuals may be included at the discretion of the parents or the school district.

This program identifies the child's unique qualities and determines educationally relevant strengths and weaknesses. A plan is then devised based on the diagnosed strengths and weaknesses. Figure 7.2 on pages 130–131 is an example of a comprehensive IEP form. The IEP must contain the following material:

1. Current status of the child's level of educational performance.
2. A statement of long-term goals and short-term instructional objectives.
3. A statement of special education and related services that will be provided to the youngster. Also, a report as to the extent the youngster will be able to participate in regular educational programs.
4. The dates for initiation of services and anticipated duration of the services.
5. Appropriate objective criteria for determining on an annual basis whether the short-term objectives are being reached.

Developing and sequencing objectives for the student are the first steps in formulating the IEP. Short-range and long-range goals should be delineated, and data collection procedures and testing schedules established to monitor the child's progress. Materials and strategies to be used in implementing the IEP should also be established. Finally, methods of evaluation to be used are selected to monitor the student's progress and the effectiveness of the program. Movement to a less restrictive environment is based on achievement of specified competencies that are necessary to function in the new environment.

INDIVIDUALIZED EDUCATION PLAN

☐ Initial Placement
☐ Re-evaluation
☐ Change of Placement
☐ Review

A. **STUDENT INFORMATION:**

Student Name _____ Student No. _____ Home School _____
              Last   First   Middle

Date of Birth _____ Chronological Age ___ (M___ or F___) Present Placement/Grade _____
Parent/Guardian Name(s) _____ Receiving School _____
Home Address _____ Program Recommended _____
            Street   City/State   Zip

Home Phone _____ Work Phone _____ Starting Date _____
Emergency Phone _____ Three (3) Year Re-evaluation Due Date ___/___/___
Primary Language (Home) _____ (Child) _____ Interpreter Needed: Yes ___ No ___

B. **VISION SCREENING RESULTS:** Pass ___ Fail ___   **HEARING SCREENING RESULTS:** Pass ___ Fail ___
Date: _____ Comments: _____   Date: _____ Comments: _____

C. **REQUIRED OBSERVATION(S):** (All categories other than regular teacher)

_____ By: _____ _____ By: _____ _____ By: _____
Date(s)   Name(s)   Date(s)   Name(s)   Date(s)   Name(s)

D. **SUMMARY OF PRESENT LEVELS OF PERFORMANCE:**

Educational: _____

_____

Behavioral: _____

E. Additional justification. See comments _____ See addendum _____
                         Initial   *Initial*

F. **PLACEMENT RECOMMENDATION INDICATING LEAST RESTRICTIVE ENVIRONMENT:**
Related services needed: Yes ___ No ___ (*List below.)

Placement Recommendation	Person Responsible	Amount of Time (Range)	Entry Date On/About	Review Reports On/About	Projected Ending Date	IEP Review Date
Primary:						
*Related Services:						

Transportation Needed? Yes ___ No ___ (If Yes, submit MPS Special Education Transportation Request Form.)

Describe extent student will participate in regular program: _____

_____

Page 1 of ___

FIGURE 7.2   Example of an individualized education plan (IEP).

The IEP must contain a section determining whether specially designed physical education is needed. If not, the child should be held to the same expectations as the peer group. A child who needs special physical education might have an IEP with specified goals and objectives and might be mainstreamed in regular physical education with goals that do not resemble those of classmates.

Continued and periodic follow-up of the child is necessary. Effective communication between special and regular teachers is essential, because the child's progress needs careful monitoring. At the completion of the designated time period or school year, a written progress report is filed along with recommendations for action during the coming year or time period. A program for the summer months can be an excellent prescription to ensure that improvement is maintained. Records should be complete so that information about the youngster's problem and the effects of long-term treatment is always available.

INDIVIDUALIZED EDUCATION PLAN

REPORT OF MULTIDISCIPLINARY CONFERENCE
Date Held _____

Student Name _____ Student No. _____

G. PROGRAM PLANNING:

Long-Term Goals:	Short-Term Objectives (Goals):

H. EVALUATION:

Evaluation criteria are described in the Individual Implementation Plan (IIP) which is available in the classroom file.

I. PLACEMENT COMMITTEE:

The following have been consulted or have participated in the placement and IEP decisions:

Names of Members	Position	Present (Initial)	Oral Report	Written Report	Signatures
	Parents/Guardian				
	Parents/Guardian				
	School Administrator				
	Special Ed Administrator				
	School Psychologist				
	Nurse				
	Teacher(s) Receiving				
	Teacher(s) Referring				
	Interpreter				

Dissenting Opinion: Yes _____ No _____ If Yes, see comments _____ *Initial* _____ See addendum _____ *Initial* .

J. PARENT (OR GUARDIAN) STATEMENT:

We agree to the placement recommended in this IEP. Yes _____ No _____

We give our permission to have our child counseled by the professional staff, if necessary. Yes _____ No _____

We understand that placement will be on a continuing trial basis and we will be contacted if any placement changes are contemplated. We are aware that such placement does not guarantee success; however, in order to help our child, we accept the responsibility to cooperate in every way with the school program. We acknowledge that we have been notified of and have received a copy of our due process rights pertaining to Special Education placement and have a basic understanding of these rights. We acknowledge that we have received a copy of the completed IEP Form.

_____   _____
Parent or Guardian Signature   Date

COMMENTS: _____
_____
_____
_____
_____
_____
_____
_____

Page 2 of _____

FIGURE 7.2 (continued)

A SYSTEMATIC APPROACH TO SUCCESSFUL MAINSTREAMING

Mainstreaming is a moral issue. Educators have the responsibility to see that all students have the opportunity to take part in activity and related social experiences. All parents desire the best experiences for their youngsters, and the goal of teachers is to help facilitate this desire.

The issue is not whether to mainstream but how to mainstream effectively. The physical educator has to teach a number of students, some with disabilities and diverse impairments. Learning strategies that the instructor is familiar with and has been using successfully may not be appropriate for students with disabilities. Attitudinal change is important since the teacher must accept the student as a full-fledged participant and assume the responsibilities that go along with special education.

FIGURE 7.3   Successful mainstreaming of youngsters with disabilities.

Few disagree that mainstreaming increases the difficulty of offering instruction for all students; however, teachers who support it show their concern for the human spirit regardless of a student's condition.

Determine How to Teach

The success or failure of the mainstreaming process depends largely on the interaction between the teacher and the student with a disability. There is no foolproof, teacher-proof system. Purposes and derived goals are perhaps more important to students with disabilities than to so-called "normal" peers. Proper levels of organic fitness and skill are vital for healthful living. Such levels enable students with disabilities to compete with peers. It is important to accept responsibility for meeting the needs of students, including those with disabilities that permit some degree of mainstreaming. Teachers need to be able to judge when referral for special assistance or additional services is in order. Physical education teachers must be able to: (1) analyze and diagnose motor behavior of students with disabilities; (2) provide appropriate experiences for remediation of motor conditions needing attention; and (3) register data as needed on the student's personal record. Record keeping is important. Set aside a short period, perhaps five minutes between classes, to accomplish the task promptly. When time between classes is short, the teacher can use a portable tape recorder for recording evaluative comments during class time.

To work successfully with students with disabilities, teachers have to understand specific impairments and how they affect learning. Also, it is necessary to know how to assess motor and fitness needs and how to structure remediation to meet those needs. Keep a number of alternative strategies in reserve in case the original method fails. Make use of the special education specialist when possible because they see the child in a number of settings. When giving explanations and directions, couch them in terms that all students can understand. Be sure that students with disabilities understand what is to be accomplished before the learning experiences begin, especially when working with the hearing impaired. Concentrate on finding activities where students can excel. Avoid placing students with disabilities in situations where they could easily fail. Offer participative opportunities that make the best use of their talents. Stress the special objectives of those with disabilities. Obvious increments of improvement toward terminal objectives are excellent motivators for both students and teachers. Let youngsters know that you as a teacher are vitally interested in their progress.

Determine What to Teach

This step involves reviewing the existing physical education curriculum and determining how it will impact students who have differing needs. An important consideration is whether certain activities completely exclude certain students. Many students with disabilities have severe developmental lags that will work against successful integration if the curriculum is not modified. On the other hand, if the student is going to be included, he must be able to accomplish a portion of the program. It also may be that certain activities are limiting and inclusion is not in the best interest of the student. A compromise must be reached where the physical education teacher has made changes in their curriculum and mainstreamed students realize that there may be activities that are not suited to their participation. It should be the intent and responsibility of the teacher to try and individualize activities as much as possible so youngsters with disabilities are smoothly integrated.

Find Ways to Modify Instruction and Activities for Student Success

Students may need additional consideration when participating in group activities, particularly when the activity is competitive. Much depends on the physical condition of the student and the type of disability. Students like to win in a competitive situation, and resentment may result if a team loss is attributed to the presence of a student with a disability. Equalization helps reduce this source of friction. Rules can be changed for everyone so that the student with a disability has a chance to contribute to group success. On the other hand, all students need to recognize that everyone has a right to play.

Be aware of situations that devalue the student socially. Avoid using the degrading method of having captains choose teams from a group of waiting students. Elimination games should be changed so that points are scored instead of players being eliminated. Determine the most desirable involvement for students with disabilities by analyzing participants' roles in game and sport activities. Assign a role or position that will make the experience as natural or normal as possible.

Students with disabilities have to build confidence in their skills before they will want to participate with others. Individual activities give them a greater amount of practice time without the pressure of failing in front of peers. The aim is to make students with disabilities less conspicuous and not set apart from able classmates. Using students with disabilities as umpires or score keepers should be a last resort. Overprotectiveness benefits no one and prevents the special student from experiencing challenge and personal accomplishment. Avoid the tendency to underestimate students' abilities.

There are many instructional modifications that can be made that will not be obvious to other students but will improve the opportunity for special students to succeed. For example, factors such as teaching styles, verbal instructions, demonstrations, and the elimination of distractions might easily be manipulated in a manner that improves the lesson for all.

A REFLECTION CHECK

Making modifications to the lesson impacts many people: the youngsters with differing needs, the other students in the class, and the teacher. It is relatively easy to modify activities, but it can be quite difficult to make modifications that add to the total environment rather than create unsafe conditions or reduce the educational value of the experience. When thinking about ways to accommodate all students, take some time to reflect on the total experience. The following questions should be considered as you formulate modifications:

1. Do the changes allow the student with differing needs to participate successfully yet still be challenged?

2. Does the modification make the setting unsafe for the student with differing needs as well as for those students without disabilities?

3. Does the change negatively impact the quality of the educational experience? Is learning seriously hampered because of the change that was made?

4. Does the change cause an undue burden on the teacher? This is important because many teachers come to resent students with differing needs because they feel the burden is too great. Certainly, change needs to be made, but it has to be reasonable for all parties.

Activities need to be modified because all students have differing needs. In fact, when teachers seldom or never modify activities, they probably are not meeting the needs of many students. Effective teachers always examine an activity and know that it is their responsibility to make the environment better for all students. The idea of "doing the most good for the most students" is a good adage to follow. The following are ways to modify activities that may help all students.

MODIFICATIONS FOR STUDENTS LACKING STRENGTH AND ENDURANCE

1. *Decrease or increase the size of the goal.* In basketball, the basket can be lowered; in soccer, the goal might be enlarged.

2. *Modify the tempo of the game.* For example, games might be performed using brisk walking rather than running. Another way to modify tempo is to stop the game regularly for substitution. Using autosubstitutions can be an excellent method: Students determine when they are fatigued, and they ask a predetermined substitute to take their place.

3. *Reduce the weight and/or modify the size of the projectile.* A lighter object will move more slowly and

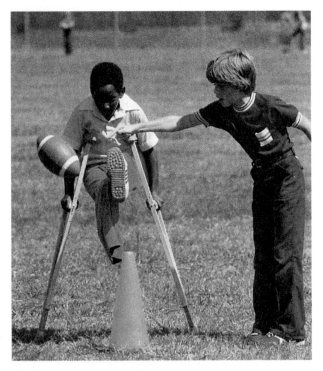

FIGURE 7.4   Modifying an activity for successful participation.

inflict less damage upon impact. A larger object will be easier for students to track visually and catch.

4. *Reduce the distance that a ball must be thrown or served.* Options are to reduce the dimensions of the playing area or to add more players to the game. In serving, others can help make the serve playable. For example, in volleyball, other teammates can bat the serve over the net as long as it does not touch the floor.

5. *In games that are played to a certain number of points, reduce the number required for a win.* For example, volleyball games could be played to 7 or 11 points, depending on the skill and intensity of the players.

6. *Modify striking implements by shortening and reducing their weight.* Racquets are much easier to control when they are shortened. Softball bats are easier to control when the player "chokes up" and selects a lighter bat.

7. *If possible, slow the ball down by letting out some air.* This will reduce the speed of rebound and make the ball easier to control in a restricted area. It will also keep the ball from rolling away from players when it is not under control.

8. *Have students play the games in a different position.* Some games may be played in a sitting or lying position, which is easier and less demanding than standing or running.

9. *Provide matching or substitution.* Match a student on borrowed crutches with a student on braces. Two players can be combined to play one position. A student in a desk chair with wheels can be matched against a student in a wheelchair. Permit substitute runners.

10. *Allow students to substitute skills.* For example, a student may be able to strike an object but may lack the mobility to run, in which case another student can be selected to run.

MODIFICATIONS FOR STUDENTS LACKING COORDINATION

1. *Increase the size of the goal or target.* Increasing the size of a basketball hoop will increase the opportunity for success. Another alternative is to offer points for hitting the backboard near a hoop. Since scoring is self-motivating, modification should occur until success is ensured.

2. *Offer protection when appropriate.* The lack of coordination will make the student more susceptible to injury from a projectile. Use various types of protectors (such as glasses, chest protectors, or face masks).

3. *When teaching throwing, allow students the opportunity to throw at maximum velocity without concern for accuracy.* Use small balls that can be grasped easily. Fleece balls and beanbags are easy to hold and release.

4. *Use a stationary object when teaching striking or hitting.* The use of a batting tee or tennis ball fastened to a string can offer the student an opportunity for success. In addition, a larger racquet or bat and "choking up" on the grip can be used.

5. *Make projectiles easily retrievable.* If a great deal of time is spent on recovering the projectile, students will receive few practice trials and feel frustrated. Place them near a backstop or use a goal that rebounds the projectile to the shooter.

6. *When teaching catching, use a soft, lightweight, and slow-moving object.* Beach balls and balloons are excellent for beginning catching skills since they allow the student to track their movement visually. In addition, foam-rubber balls eliminate a student's fear of being hurt by a thrown or batted projectile.

MODIFICATIONS FOR STUDENTS LACKING BALANCE AND AGILITY

1. *Increase the width of rails, lines, and beams when having students practice balance.* Having students carry a long pole will help minimize rapid shifts of balance and is a useful lead-up activity.

2. *Have students increase the width of their base of support.* Students should be taught to keep their feet spread at least to shoulder width.

3. *Emphasize use of many body parts when teaching balance.* The more body parts in contact with the floor, the easier it is to balance the body. Beginning balance practice should emphasize controlled movement using as many body parts as possible.

4. *Have students increase the surface area of the body parts in contact with the floor or beam.* For example, walking flat-footed is easier than walking on tiptoe.

5. *Have students lower their center of gravity.* This offers more stability and greater balance to the youngster. Place emphasis on bending the knees and leaning slightly forward.

6. *Make sure that surfaces offer good friction.* Floors and shoes should not be slick or students will fall. Carpets or tumbling mats will increase traction.

7. *Provide balance assistance.* A barre, cane, or chair can be used to keep the student from falling.

8. *Teach students how to fall.* Students with balance problems will inevitably fall. Offer practice in learning how to fall so that they gradually learn how to absorb the force.

Determine What Support and Aid Are Necessary

When a student is deemed ready for placement, consultation between the physical education teacher and the special education supervisor is of prime importance. In a setting where emotions and feelings run high, it is important to ensure that communication and planning occur on a regular basis. The reception and acceptance of students cannot be left to chance. A scheduled plan has to be instituted before the student is mainstreamed. Special and physical education professionals must discuss the needs of the student and the physical education teacher, and develop realistic expectations. It is quite possible that the special education teacher will have to participate in the physical education class to ensure a smooth transition. The thrust should center on what students can do rather than on what they cannot do. Any approach that has lowered expectations when treating students is dehumanizing.

Full information about the needs of the student is due the physical education teacher before the student participates. Physical education teachers must feel able to tell the support personnel what kind of help they

FIGURE 7.5 Using sign language can meet the needs of a student with an auditory impairment.

need. Negative feelings toward students with differing needs will occur if the physical educator feels students are dropped into their class before they've been asked what kind of help they need to integrate the students properly. This procedure should also be implemented when the student moves from one mainstreaming situation to another. Both able students and students with disabilities need opportunities to make appropriate progress.

Teach Tolerance to All Students

An important part of the physical education experience is for all students to understand the problems related to being disabled. Fully able students need to learn to understand, accept, and live comfortably with persons with disabilities. They should recognize that students with disabilities are functional and worthwhile individuals who have innate abilities and can make significant contributions to society. The concept of understanding and appreciating individual differences is one that merits positive development and should concentrate on three aspects:

1. Recognizing the similarities among all people: their hopes, rights, aspirations, and goals.

2. Understanding human differences and focusing on the concept that all people are disabled. For some, disabilities are of such a nature and severity that they interfere with normal living.

3. Exploring ways to deal with those who differ without overhelping, and stressing the acceptance of all students as worthwhile individuals. People with disabilities deserve consideration and understanding based on empathy, not sympathy.

Integrate Students with Differing Needs into the Class Setting

Once the mainstreamed student, able students, and teacher have undergone preliminary preparation, consideration can be given to integrating the disabled youngster into the learning environment. When correctly implemented, mainstreaming allows the student to make educational progress, achieve in those areas outlined in the IEP, learn to accept limitations, observe and model appropriate behavior, and become socially accepted by others. Guidelines for successful integration of students with disabilities into physical education follow.

1. Help students with disabilities meet target goals specified in the IEP and participate in the regular program of activities. This may demand the use of resources beyond the physical education class, including special work and homework.

FIGURE 7.6 Youngsters with disabilities can find the joy of participation.

2. Build ego strength; stress abilities. Eliminate established practices that unwittingly contribute to embarrassment and failure.

3. Foster peer acceptance by accepting each student as a functioning, participating member of the class.

4. Concentrate on the student's physical education needs and not on the disability. Give strong attention to fundamental skills and physical fitness qualities.

5. Provide continual monitoring and assess periodically the student's target goals. Anecdotal and periodic record keeping are implicit in this guideline.

6. Be constantly aware of students' feelings and anxiety concerning their progress and integration. Provide positive feedback as a basic practice.

POSTURE

The physical education program should include vigorous physical activities that lead to fitness and strengthening of the muscle groups that maintain proper body alignment. Strengthening the abdominal wall and the musculature

7

Correct posture	Fair posture	Poor posture
Head up, chin in, head balanced above the shoulders with the tip of the ear directly above the point of the shoulders, eyes ahead Shoulders back and easy, chest up Lower abdomen in and flat Slight and normal curves in the upper and lower back Knees easy Weight balanced with toes pointed forward	Head forward slightly Chest lowered slightly Lower abdomen in but not flat Back curves increased slightly Knees back slightly Weight a little too far back on the heels	Head noticeably forward, eyes generally down Chest flat or depressed Shoulder blades show winged effect Abdomen relaxed and prominent Back curves exaggerated Knees forced back in back-kneed position Pelvis noticeably tilted down Weight improperly distributed

FIGURE 7.7 Characteristics of correct, fair, and poor posture.

of the upper back and neck helps maintain proper body alignment. Enough flexibility of the various body segments must be attained so that children are able to move their body with ease and proper postural alignment.

The maintenance of correct posture contributes to physical attractiveness and wellness. *Posture* refers to the habitual or assumed alignment and balance of the body segments while the body is standing, walking, sitting, or lying down. Posture is a reflection of the inner self. Appropriate posture radiates a positive self-image; improper posture (e.g., slouching) may reflect fatigue or a lack of confidence.

The association of posture with good health is justified. The antigravity muscles, those that help support the body against the forces of gravity, must be exercised regularly to accomplish body support with ease and without undue fatigue. From a mechanical standpoint,

the musculature involved in correct posture must be balanced to hold the bones and joints properly. Faulty alignment can cause undue strain on supporting muscles and ligaments, which leads to early fatigue, muscle strain, and progressive displacement of postural support. In extreme cases, pain may result, and the position and function of vital organs, primarily those located in the abdomen, can be affected adversely.

What Is Correct Posture?

Posture varies with the individual's age, gender, and body type. Very young children often toe out while standing and walking to provide a wider, more stable base. Standing position exhibits an exaggerated lumbar curve and rounded shoulders, which are normal at this developmental stage. By age six or seven, however, the

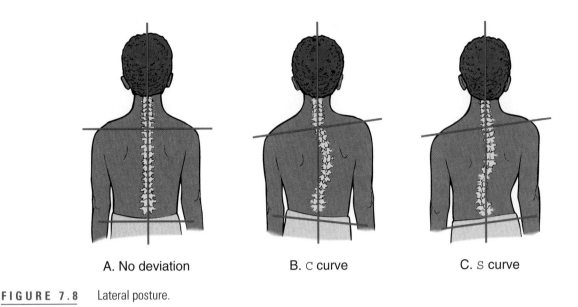

A. No deviation   B. c curve   C. s curve

FIGURE 7.8   Lateral posture.

lumbar curve lessens and the prominent abdominal protrusion begins to disappear. At this stage, the feet and toes generally point ahead. The educational process should assist the child in making the transition from the normal exaggerated curves of young children to proper adult posture in adolescence. The basic components of posture are illustrated in Figure 7.7 on page 137.

Lateral Deviations in Posture

The last section reviewed the forward-backward plane of body movement, generally assessed from the side. The body also must be in balance in the lateral plane, as viewed from either front or back. The spinal column viewed from the back should show a straight, vertical line that divides the body into two symmetrical halves (Figure 7.8A).

A deviation occurs when this vertical line becomes either a single (*C*) curve (Figure 7.8B) or a multiple (*S*) curve (Figure 7.8C). Such deviations are coupled with one or more of the following body adjustments: (a) one shoulder higher than the other, (b) head tilts to one side, (c) hips not level, and (d) weight carried more on one leg than on the other. Marked deviations are noticeable, but moderate deviations are difficult to detect, especially when the body is clothed.

One way in which lateral curvature (scoliosis) can be detected is to have children bend forward and touch their toes. A serious curvature is indicated when the ribs protrude on one side. Early attention to lateral curvature is important because it generally gets worse with age. By the time youngsters reach high school, the curvature is probably well established and difficult to remedy.

Evaluating Posture

Because elementary school teachers are responsible for detecting and reporting their students' physical problems, a program of posture evaluation can help identify posture problems. Evaluation can be done through observation, both formal and informal, and with measurement devices. A referral system should be established for individuals who exhibit marked posture deviations.

Posture Check Method. For youngsters with posture problems, the application of the posture check can be an educational experience. Two methods of recording are presented: an individual form (Figure 7.9) and a class form (Figure 7.10). Teachers may prefer using the class form, which includes all of the class, but the individual form is easier for parents and administrators to interpret. The class form is more adaptable to class analysis and comparisons. Each item is rated 1, 2, or 3 on an ascending scale. By averaging the rating numbers, a mean rating is obtained for each child.

Informal Observation. Formal posture evaluation is an analysis of an assumed posture, which is not necessarily the posture children use in daily living. To offset this testing effect, posture checks can be made informally when young people are participating in classroom and physical education activities. Teachers should notice how each child walks, stands, or sits when not conscious of an observer. The teacher can make notes and supplement the formal posture check.

Ear-Shoulder Method. In normal posture, the lobe of the ear is directly above the point of the shoulder. Any departure from this relationship indicates a degree of back and shoulder roundedness and can be used as a measure of general posture deviation. When one body area is out of alignment, other body segments compensate

Posture Check Report

Name _____ Grade _____ School _____

Date _____ Check made by _____

Side View

Head

Erect, chin in _____   Somewhat forward _____   Markedly forward _____

Upper Back

Shoulders back _____   Slightly rounded _____   Rounded _____

Lower Back

Slight natural curve _____   Moderately curved _____   Hollowed _____

Abdomen

Flat _____   Slightly protruded _____   Protruding _____

Knees

Relaxed _____   Slightly back _____   Hyperextended _____

Feet

Pointed ahead _____   Pointed out somewhat _____   Pointed out _____

Front and Back View

Shoulders

Level _____   Slightly uneven _____   Considerably uneven _____

Hips

Level _____   Slightly uneven _____   Considerably uneven _____

Backs of Ankles and Feet

Heels and ankles straight _____   Turned out somewhat _____   Pronated _____

Remarks

FIGURE 7.9   Individual posture check form.

proportionally. For example, if the head is forward, other parts of the body protrude to counterbalance the poor alignment. If one measures the degree by which the head is forward, then one has an estimate of general posture. Measurement can be made with a wand or pointer and can be expressed in terms of the number of inches the earlobe is positioned from the vertical line above the shoulder point. (In a deviated posture, the earlobe is usually forward, if anything.)

Videotaping and Self-Evaluation. An effective way to identify obvious posture problems is to videotape and play back pictures of children standing, walking, and performing other actions. In this way, they can observe themselves and make their assessments using the posture check report.

Referral. A perceptive teacher observing children in study or play can screen children who need attention because of poor posture. Make referrals to the nurse, principal, or an appropriate agency for help. After a program has been established, the teacher can help by encouraging the child to fulfill the prescribed remedial exercises.

Class Posture Check

Class _____   School _____

Date _____   Teacher _____

Code
Meets good postural standards   1
Slight but definite deviation   2
Marked deviation   3

Name	Side View						Front and Back Views			Remarks
	Head and Neck	Upper Back	Lower Back	Abdomen	Knees	Feet	Level of Shoulders	Level of Hips	Feet and Ankles	
1.										
2.										
3.										

FIGURE 7.10   Class posture check form.

Posture and the Instructional Process

Posture is both a practice and a subject. The teacher's emphasis should be on hints, reminders, and encouragement during all phases of the program. Even the simplest movements present postural challenges that give opportunities for incidental teaching. Strong postural implications can be derived from exercises when the children understand the "why" of the movement. Values and advantages of correct posture should be stressed. Emphasis should be placed on helping children accept responsibility for their own posture. Nagging and overzealousness can have negative results. The following are examples of cues for correct posture:

> Feet: "Feet forward. Weight on entire foot."
>
> Lower back and abdomen: "Tuck the seat under. Flatten the tummy."
>
> Upper body: "Shoulder blades flat. Chest high. Raise chest."
>
> Neck and head: "Stand tall. Head high. Eyes ahead."
>
> Walking: "Feet forward. Eyes ahead. Arms relaxed."
>
> Sitting: "Seat back. Sit erect. Bend forward at the hips when working."

REFLECTION AND REVIEW QUESTIONS

How and Why

1. How do you feel about teaching individuals with disabilities?

2. Why is it important for children with disabilities to participate in physical education?

3. Do all children have disabilities? Explain your answer.

4. How can teachers generate parental and social support for children with disabilities?

5. How does our society look at obese children? Are these assumptions accurate?

Content Review

1. Identify what implications PL 94-142 and IDEA have for physical education teachers.

2. Discuss the screening and assessment procedures for evaluating students.

3. Describe how individualized educational programs are developed. Include comments on who is involved and what the IEP contains.

4. Describe inclusion and mainstreaming. Discuss guidelines for successful inclusion.

5. Identify methods of modifying activities for inclusion.

6. Identify several disabilities and techniques for modifying activities to accommodate these disabilities.

7. Explain the process of designing programs for obese children with motor deficiencies.

8. State why posture is an important topic for physical education teachers.

FOR MORE INFORMATION

References and Suggested Readings

Auxter, D., Pyfer, J., & Huettig, C. (2005). *Principles and methods of adapted physical education and recreation.* 10th ed. Boston: McGraw-Hill.

Bennett, T., Bruns, D., & Deluca, D. (1997). Putting inclusion into practice: Perspectives of teachers and parents. *Exceptional Children,* 64(1), 115–132.

Block, M. E. (2000). *A teacher's guide to including students with disabilities in regular physical education.* 2nd ed. Baltimore: Paul H. Brookes Publishing Co.

Block, M., Oberweiser, B., & Bain, M. (1995). Using classwide peer tutoring to facilitate inclusion of students with disabilities in regular physical education. *The Physical Educator,* Late winter, 47–56.

Block, M., & Vogler, E. V. (1994). Inclusion in regular physical education: The research base. *Journal of Health, Physical Education, Recreation, and Dance,* 65(1), 40–44.

Bouchard, C., Tremblay, A., Despres, J. P., Nadeau, A., Lupien, P. J., Theriault, G., Dussault, J., Moorjani, S., Pinault, S., & Fourmier, G. (1990). The response to long-term overfeeding in identical twins. *New England Journal of Medicine,* 322, 1477–1482.

Brustad, R. J. (1993). Who will go out and play? Parental and psychological influences on children's attraction to physical activity. *Pediatric Exercise Science,* 5, 210–223.

Burton, A., & Miller, D. (1998). *Movement skill assessment.* Champaign, IL: Human Kinetics.

Cooper Institute. (2004). *Fitnessgram activitygram test administration manual.* 3rd ed. Champaign, IL: Human Kinetics.

Davis, R. W. (2002). *Inclusion through sports: A guide to enhancing sport experiences.* Champaign, IL: Human Kinetics.

DePauw, K. (1996). Students with disabilities in physical education. In S. Silverman & C. Ennis (Eds.), *Student learning in physical education.* Champaign, IL: Human Kinetics.

DePauw, K., & Goc Karp, G. (1994). Integrating knowledge of disability throughout the physical education curriculum: An infusion approach. *Adapted Physical Activity Quarterly,* 11, 3–13.

Dobbins, D. A., Garron, R., & Rarick, G. L. (1981). The motor performance of educable mentally retarded and intellectually normal boys after covariate control for differences in body size. *Research Quarterly,* 52(1), 6–7.

Dunn, J. M. (1997). *Special physical education: Adapted, individualized, developmental.* Madison: Brown & Benchmark.

Education for All Handicapped Children Act of 1975, Pub. L. No. 94–142.

Eichstaedt, C. B., & Kalakian, L. H. (1993). *Developmental/Adapted physical education: Making ability count.* New York: Macmillan.

Epstein, L. H., et al. (1984). The modification of activity patterns and energy expenditure in obese young girls. *Behavior Therapy,* 15(1), 101–108.

Foster, G. D., Wadden, T. A., & Brownell, K. D. (1985). Peer-led program for the treatment and prevention of obesity in the schools. *Journal of Consulting and Clinical Psychology,* 53(4), 538–540.

Harter, S. (1985). *Manual for the self-perception profile for youth.* Denver: University of Denver.

Horvat, M., et al. (2003). *Developmental/adapted physical education: Making ability count.* 4th ed. San Francisco: Benjamin Cummings.

Jansma, P., & French, R. (1994). *Special physical education: Physical activity, sports, and recreation.* Englewood Cliffs, NJ: Prentice Hall.

Lavay, B., & DePaepe, J. (1987). The harbinger helper: Why mainstreaming in physical education doesn't always work. *Journal of Health, Physical Education, Recreation, and Dance,* 58(7), 98–103.

Lieberman, L., & Houston-Wilson, C. (2002). *Strategies for inclusion: A handbook for physical educators.* Champaign, IL: Human Kinetics.

Lohman, T. G. (1987). The use of skinfold to estimate body fatness on children and youth. *Journal of Physical Education, Recreation, and Dance,* 58(9), 98–102.

Sherrill, C. (2004). *Adapted physical activity, recreation and sport.* 6th ed. Boston: WCB/McGraw-Hill.

Simon, J., & Smoll, F. (1974). An instrument for assessing youth's attitude toward physical activity. *Research Quarterly,* 45(4), 407–415.

Ulrich, D. A. (1983). A comparison of the qualitative motor performance of normal, educable, and trainable mentally retarded students. In R. L. Eason, T. L. Smith, & F. Caron (Eds.), *Adapted physical activity.* Champaign, IL: Human Kinetics.

U.S. Department of Health and Human Services. (1995). *Asthma & physical activity in the school.* (NIH Publication No. 95-3651). Washington, DC: National Institutes of Health.

Vogler, E. (2000). Students with disabilities in physical education. In S. Silverman & C. Ennis (Eds.), *Student learning in physical education.* 2nd ed. Champaign, IL: Human Kinetics.

Wilmore, J. H. (1994). Exercise, obesity, and weight control. *Physical Activity and Fitness Research Digest,* 1(6), 1–8.

Winnick, J. P. (2005). *Adapted physical education and sport.* 4th ed. Champaign, IL: Human Kinetics.

Winnick, J. P., & Short, F. X. (1999). *The Brockport physical fitness test manual.* Champaign, IL: Human Kinetics.

Yun, J., Shapiro, D., & Kennedy, J. (2000). Reaching IEP goals in the general physical education class. *Journal of Physical Education, Recreation, and Dance,* 71(8), 33–37.

Websites

Adapted Physical Education
www.pecentral.org
www.palaestra.com
www.pelinks4u.org/sections/adapted/adapted.htm
www.twu.edu/inspire

Adapted P.E. Assessment Tools
www.pecentral.org/adapted/adaptedinstruments.html

Children's Disabilities Information
www.childrensdisabilities.info

Inclusion Programs That Work
www.ed.gov/pubs/EPTW/eptw12/index.html
www.palaestra.com/Inclusion.html
http://clerccenter2.gallaudet.edu/KidsWorldDeafNet/
    e-docs/IDEA/section-1.html#historyofidea

Legal Issues
http://asclepius.com/angel/special.html
www.ed.gov/offices/OSERS/Policy/IDEA/the_law.html

National Standards
www.cortland.edu/apens/

SECTION 3

Program Implementation

Physical education teachers need to know more than simply how to teach an effective class. Teachers who do not follow established school procedures or seek support for their program will have limited success. Evaluating students is receiving greater emphasis as schools focus on achieving state and national standards. Even though physical education instructors may evaluate their students differently than classroom teachers, a system for fair and unbiased evaluation must be in place. Schools are responsible for students when they are in the care of teachers, and most teachers are expected to supervise students before and after school, during recess, and at lunch. Thus, teachers must have a clear understanding of their duties, and how to protect themselves from lawsuits and other liability claims. Supervisors must know the guidelines for supervising in a safe and legal manner. Another important topic in creating a physical education curriculum is learning what facilities, equipment, and supplies are needed to implement a quality program. Also included in this section is a chapter on integrating academic subject matter into a physical education program.

After reading this section, you should understand how to evaluate students and place them into a safe environment, know how school policies impact the program, be able to secure equipment and facilities needed to implement a quality program, and understand how to integrate some academic subject matter into particular physical activities.

CHAPTER **8**
Evaluation

CHAPTER **9**
Legal Liability, Supervision, and Safety

CHAPTER **10**
Facilities, Equipment, and Supplies

CHAPTER **11**
Integrating Academic Concepts

Evaluation

ESSENTIAL COMPONENTS OF QUALITY PROGRAMS

▶ **I. Organized around content standards**

▶ **II. Student-centered and developmentally appropriate**

▶ **III. Physical activity and motor skill development form the core of the program**

IV. Teaches management skills and self-discipline

▶ **V. Promotes inclusion of all students**

▶ **VI. Focuses on process over product**

▶ **VII. Promotes lifetime personal health and wellness**

VIII. Teaches cooperation and responsibility and promotes sensitivity to diversity

NATIONAL STANDARDS FOR PHYSICAL EDUCATION*

▶ 1. **Demonstrates competency in motor skills and movement patterns needed to perform a variety of physical activities.**

2. Demonstrates understanding of movement concepts, principles, and tactics as they apply to the learning and performance of physical activities.

3. Participates regularly in physical activity.

4. Achieves and maintains a health-enhancing level of physical fitness.

5. Exhibits responsible personal and social behavior that respects self and others in physical activity.

6. Values physical activity for health, enjoyment, challenge, self-expression, and/or social interaction.

*National Association for Sport and Physical Education (NASPE), 2004.

SUMMARY

There are many types of evaluation, but all evaluation is done to improve instruction and increase learning. Ways to evaluate student learning include the use of checklists, logs, tests, and scoring rubrics. A grading system that communicates student progress to parents is difficult to design. There are many reasons for giving grades and just as many reasons for avoiding grading in elementary schools. A student progress report can be a useful approach for helping parents understand their child's progress in physical education. Growth in instructional effectiveness occurs when teachers choose to self-evaluate their instruction. A program checklist can be used to score the total physical education setting.

OUTCOMES

- Differentiate between formal and informal evaluation.
- Explain and understand the differences between process and product evaluation.
- Cite a number of ways to assess student learning.
- Know the advantages of a progress report for parents.
- Describe arguments for and against grading in physical education.
- Identify methods of instructional analysis of teacher behavior.
- Identify ways to self-evaluate instructional behavior.
- Recognize the key elements of an effective physical education evaluation form.

ASSESSMENT AND EVALUATION

The purpose of evaluation is to determine whether progress is being made toward objectives. Evaluation should review all phases of education including pupil progress, teacher performance, and program effectiveness. Evaluation can be formal or informal and can focus on individual or group progress. For the sake of clarity, this chapter looks at evaluation as a multifaceted approach that includes **assessment** (student performance), **institutional evaluation** that evaluates whether the school (or district or state) is reaching desired student outcomes, and **instructional effectiveness** as measured by quantifying teacher behavior. A related area to be evaluated is the actual physical education program, and an instrument for this purpose is included at the end of the chapter.

ASSESSMENT OF STUDENT PERFORMANCE

Assessment is defined as the collection of information about student performance. Traditionally, assessment in physical education has been directed at functions of compliance (i.e., participation, attendance, effort) and not on components that reflect student learning (Lund, 1993). Even when performance is considered, it is done in ways that are suspect in recording true learning. Matanin and Tannehill (1994) suggest the use of ongoing, daily assessments to obtain measures that reliably reflect student learning. The purpose of assessment in this chapter will be to obtain knowledge about student performance that can be used for grading and measuring student accountability. As professionals, physical education teachers tend to perform informal assessments daily when they help students improve skill performance. The important issue becomes how they use this information to evaluate or even grade students since there are few formal assessment tools available for physical education that target student performance (Lund, 1993; Matanin & Tannehill, 1994).

Within the field of physical education, assessment is a difficult issue. Classes are often bigger than traditional classroom settings, the area covered is more expansive, and there is often no permanent record of work completed (like a written example of work for an English class) for teachers to take home and thoroughly inspect. With these types of obstacles stacked against physical education teachers, what are they to do that will allow them to produce a quality assessment routine for students? The assessment process is crucial in providing feedback to students, teachers, and parents. Collecting data allows teachers to make judgments about student performance based on certain criteria.

Many components are evaluated in physical education. A major part of assessment is examining the skill learning and development that occur through the instructional process. Even though skill development is a primary focus of physical education, it is not enough; students need to learn about strategy, skill performance techniques, and positive attitudes toward physical activity.

Written exams can evaluate whether students have requisite knowledge for successful participation. Finally, the area of attitudes and values is important to the program. Students will choose not to participate if their attitudes and values have not developed concurrently with skills and knowledge.

Using assessment instruments serves a number of purposes (Strand & Wilson, 1993). Some of the more common reasons for assessment include the following.

Grading. Performance on established instruments offers objective data for grading. Communicating with students and parents is more effective when an objective and systematic tool has been used for assessment. Parents and students can see how the students compare to others and are given a realistic view of their performance in relation to other students or established criteria. Grades based on objective data carry more credibility and respect both inside and outside the profession.

Motivation. Nothing motivates individuals more than improvement. When improvement can be documented through assessment, it is evidence that effort has been rewarded. It is difficult to know the extent (or lack) of improvement if assessment is not a part of the program. Another factor that motivates students is the teacher's setting reachable goals. It is difficult to know what is reasonable and reachable if students are unaware of their performance level and ability.

Diagnosis. Assessment often reveals problems or deficiencies. When teaching an entire class, it is difficult to gauge the ability and progress of each student. Often more energy is placed on monitoring student behavior than student performance. Assessment will focus energy on progress of individual students and reveal those students who are deficient or performing skills incorrectly.

Placement and Equalization. At times, it is effective to group students homogeneously—that is, placing students with equal ability in groups. On the other hand, a peer-tutoring method can be used if assessment reveals skilled performances and students having problems. Student assessment helps teachers place students with peer helpers and equalizes small groups when it enhances learning.

Program Assessment. Assessment of students can reveal the effectiveness of the program and the relevancy of objectives. If all students pass the assessment, it may mean that the goals of the program are too low. If many fail, the quality of instruction may be inadequate or the standard of performance may be out of reach. Over time, assessment of students can give direction to the program as objectives and instructional strategies are modified to increase student success.

Program Support. Results of regular assessment can be used to validate and support the program. The data gained through assessment is objective and can reveal what students are expected to learn and how effectively they are learning. Accountability is a buzzword among educators as schools try to document what students are learning, in order to gain public support. When administrators need to make cutbacks in programs, they usually ask faculty members to justify continuation of their programs. Data gained through consistent assessment of students are strong and effective ways to defend the program.

Assessment: Process of Learning or Product Outcomes?

Physical education is different from academic areas because it demands physical performance. In academia, once a student masters a skill, she no longer thinks abut that skill and begins to concentrate on new skills. The ability to add numbers or read words stays with people throughout life once it is mastered. However, in physical education, skills are learned only to be lost if not practiced. It is never possible to say in physical education that a skill or fitness level will be maintained at a high level if it isn't used. Therefore, it becomes important to look at physical education in a slightly different perspective. Two types of outcomes pertain to students: process of learning and product. The *process of learning outcomes* relate to the performance of movement patterns and skills with emphasis on correct technique. The form used to execute the movement is the point of assessment rather than the outcome of the skill performed. In contrast, *product outcomes* focus on performance in terms of measurable increments of what learners accomplish. For example, if product outcomes were applied to ball skills, emphasis would be placed on how many times the ball is caught without a miss. On the other hand, process outcomes would focus on the techniques of catching properly. Following are key points to consider when thinking about the type of outcomes you want for your students.

DEVELOP ATHLETES OR TEACH ALL STUDENTS?

Should elementary school physical education focus on product outcomes or should it emphasize the process of learning skills correctly? Should physical education experiences be designed to develop high-quality performances or should they focus on teaching all students the proper way to perform skills? Physical education has a unique role in the elementary school curriculum. Nowhere else can students receive skill instruction and the opportunity to learn the benefits of lifetime activity. Academics can teach character, knowledge, social skills, and the like, but only physical education can accomplish unique physical skill and activity outcomes. Physical education doesn't have to be like academics; in fact, it is important because it is different.

IS PERFECTION POSSIBLE IN PHYSICAL EDUCATION?

Physical education doesn't have an absolute and exact product. Cognitive knowledge is based on the building-block theory—that new learning is based on previously acquired facts. For example, basic math facts are necessary to perform higher-level math manipulations. Physical education differs in that the same set of skills is learned and refined throughout the school years. For instance, the skill of throwing is taught in elementary school and continues to be repeated and refined each year thereafter. After the basic skill is learned, little new is taught about throwing; instead, emphasis is placed on repetition and refinement of the skill.

Perfection (of skill performance) does not occur in physical education, or sport for that matter. This contrasts with most academic areas that demand accuracy and correctness. New knowledge is based on previously learned information, which is based on a commonly accepted body of information. This is not so with physical education, because correct performance is impossible to predict and errors are expected. Even the best athletes miss half of the baskets they shoot or make an out in baseball about 70 percent of the time. Often, however, physical educators teach as though perfection were a realistic and reasonable goal. This causes youngsters to believe that focusing on the outcome (such as making a basket) is more important than performing the skill correctly. Teachers encourage such thinking when they reinforce skill attempts that are correct while failing to comment on a student's quality of performance.

SKILL REFINEMENT OR SKILL PERFORMANCE?

Skill refinement is not synonymous with performance improvement. Teachers have been taught to evaluate the effectiveness of their teaching based on how many students reach product benchmarks, such as the number of baskets made or jumping rope a number of times without a miss. Many teachers have written such outcomes, thinking they will be able to get all students to reach them. Unfortunately, they promise a product that may not be achievable. For example, when adults hire a professional instructor to improve their golf swing, they do so without guarantees. Creditable golf pros will not guarantee a reduction in golf scores. Rather, they will assure their pupils that they can improve their swing, which, over time, *may* result in improved scores. They are unable to control the genetic makeup or the psychological willingness of individuals to change, practice, and improve. What the golf pro will guarantee is that she will teach with enthusiasm, be knowledgeable of the latest techniques, and devote the time and energy necessary to help refine her students' skills. Teachers can teach youngsters how to perform skills properly, but can't guarantee that all students will be high-level performers.

WINNING OR FEELING GOOD?

The ultimate goal of physical education is to graduate students who feel competent and willing to perform skills throughout a lifetime of activity. Leaving students a legacy of knowing how to live an active lifestyle may be more important than their being able to make 10 to 15 free throws or hit 20 successful tennis serves. In addition, students benefit from being taught to value effort more than victory. Something is lost for many participants when winning dictates success. The process of doing one's best is an important issue in physical education. It is possible, but not common, to find students who participate in an activity without worrying about winning and losing. In many areas in the school curriculum, emphasis is placed on cooperative learning. Physical education can benefit by such an approach. Evidence shows that cooperative learning improves self-esteem and attitude toward school and can temper the negative aspects of competition (Johnson, Johnson, & Holubec, 1990). Activity and participation can be enhanced through the joy of working together.

Consider the product-versus-process of learning conflict and how it relates to a teacher's view of the instructional environment. A product-oriented teacher shows less concern for how students feel about learning, or about the technique and form used when performing skills. In a game of Frisbee Golf, for example, the focus is on the outcome of the game—winning or losing. The process-oriented teacher, on the other hand, is more concerned that students develop proper techniques of skill performance and positive attitudes toward the activity. Winning or losing is secondary to the learning experience. Most teachers find themselves somewhere between the two viewpoints and place varying amounts of emphasis on process and product. A reminder is in order here: Physical education teachers are not coaches (who focus on winning) in the physical education setting. They are coaches when they work in the athletic arena. Quality teachers and coaches are able to separate the two domains to ensure that proper outcomes are reached in both arenas.

ASSESSING STUDENT OUTCOMES

Assessment of student performance is an important issue that can be accomplished in many different ways. Informal assessment is often done on the spot when a teacher corrects or reinforces a student's performance. A number of more formal, yet alternative assessments are becoming popular because teachers are expected to assess and report student progress toward program standards (Chepko & Arnold, 2000).

Many of the techniques that follow can be used to measure learning in the three major learning domains. The domains are briefly described here; see Chapter 4 for more information.

Psychomotor Domain. This area is related to learning motor skills. Students are most often assessed in this domain because the focus of physical education is skill development. Figure 8.1 below is an example of a way to evaluate skills in the psychomotor domain.

Cognitive Domain. The cognitive domain focuses on understanding concepts of movement performance and related fitness and activity knowledge. It is most often evaluated with written tests. Figure 8.2 on page 148 is an example of a knowledge test related to pedometers.

Affective Domain. This domain is related to responsibility and attitudes toward physical education and physical activity. It is how a student feels and how a student behaves. The affective domain deals with a set

Student Name	Elbows are flexed in preparation to catch.	Hands adjust to the flight of the ball.	Contact is made with the hands. Elbows are flexed.	Force of the ball is absorbed by the hands and arms.
Jon				
Mike				
Mary				
Aaron				
Deb				

FIGURE 8.1 Checklist rubric for scoring catching skills.

Pedometer Knowledge Test

Name: _____

1. Pedometers measure physical activity. What two ways do the pedometers we use in class measure our physical activity?

2. Where should the pedometer be placed to ensure that it will measure accurately?

3. What are the two rules we learned about using pedometers in physical education?

4. What types of physical activity will a pedometer measure?

5. If two people are walking together and one person is tall and the other is short, who will have the most steps on their pedometer when they reach the end of their walk?

FIGURE 8.2   Evaluating the cognitive domain: Pedometer knowledge.

of internal constructs, so it is often best to allow students to self-evaluate themselves. It is important to know how students feel about the physical education experience. Figure 8.3 is an example of an instrument that Developmental Level II students can use to show their attitudes toward physical education activities.

A number of tools can be used for student assessment, but a caution should be stated about using any of these tools. They are not standardized instruments that can be used to evaluate the institutional effectiveness of the program. Those instruments can be found in the next section of this chapter. In most cases, each teacher decides what elements he wants to include in his assessment tools. However, that does not make them valid or reliable instruments; it takes much work and testing before such assumptions can be made. What the tools do offer is a listing of skills and behaviors each teacher believes students should learn in her classes. By monitoring such behavior in students, teachers have a systematic approach to collecting information that lets students and their parents know whether expected outcomes have been met.

Checklist Rubrics

A checklist rubric is a rating scale that lists multiple criteria related to a task or motor skill performance. This rubric is most often used to evaluate skill performance outcomes. The criteria are techniques students should use when performing skills. A basic question common to most assessments is, "Can the child perform the stated motor pattern using proper techniques?" Employing this type of assessment requires accurate knowledge of the related critical elements. Videotaping is useful for viewing the skill performance a number of times and in slow motion. For example, a nine-year-old youngster at the expected developmental level should be able to demonstrate all four components when catching. If a child of this age exhibits only two of the components, a developmental deficiency is indicated. Figure 8.1 is an example of a checklist rubric for catching skills. This rubric lists four critical elements required for all catching skills. In most cases, the degree of the quality of behavior is not judged. Rather, the behavior is marked as present or absent.

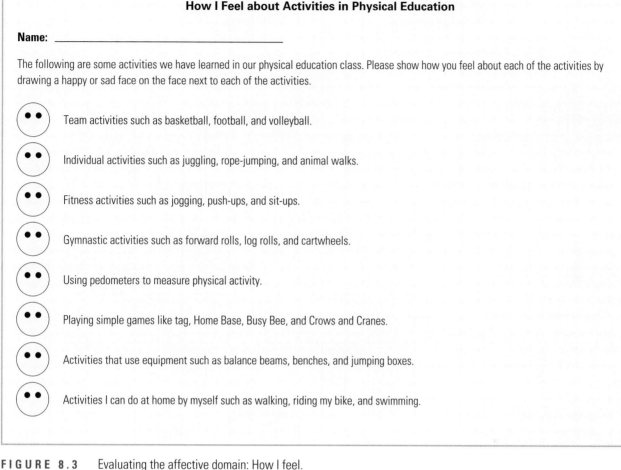

FIGURE 8.3   Evaluating the affective domain: How I feel.

Observation Checklists

Another means of assessing student progress is to use an observation checklist. Observation checklists are commonly used for assessing skill performance. Criteria governing proper technique for the motor skills are listed, and the child's performance is checked against these points. Limiting coverage to two or three of the critical points of technique is usually best. Ratings for each point can be on a 3-point scale: above developmental level, at developmental level, and below developmental level. These can be numbered 3, 2, and 1, respectively, which provides a point scale for ease of recording. The record sheet can also be organized so that achievement levels are listed and the evaluator circles the appropriate number. Figure 8.4 on page 150 is an example of an observation checklist for some of the fundamental locomotor skills.

Rating Scales

Rating scales have long been used as a system for reporting progress to students and parents. A class roster with skills listed across the top of the sheet is a common method used for recording class progress. It gives a graphic indication of those students who may be in need of special help. If grading is based on the number of activities students master, the checklist can deliver this information. Rating scales are usually most effective when skills are listed in the sequence in which they should be learned. In this way, instruction is designed to address diagnosed needs. To avoid disrupting the learning process, it is best to record student progress informally while students are practicing. Figure 8.5 on page 151 is a sample checklist for rope-jumping.

Anecdotal Record Sheets

A record sheet that contains student names and has room for comments about student behavior can be used to assess student progress. Anecdotal records of student progress can be reinforcing to both student and teacher, as it is often difficult to remember how much progress has been made over time. With anecdotal records,

Class _____   Grade _____   Date _____

Scoring:
3 = above developmental level
2 = at developmental level
1 = below developmental level

Student's Name	Running			Jumping			Hopping			Skipping		
	Arm Action	Leg Action	Composite	Arm Action	Leg Action	Composite	Arm Action	Leg Action	Composite	Arm Action	Leg Action	Composite

FIGURE 8.4   Observation checklist for locomotor skills.

Rope-Jumping Checklist

Student	Jump in Place	Jump, Turn Both Ends	Jump, Pendulum Swing	Slow Time	Fast Time	Alternate-Foot Step	Swing Step Forward	Rocker Step	Spread Legs, Forward	Toe-and-Heel Touch	Shuffle Step	Cross Arms	Cross Arms, Backward	Double Jump	

FIGURE 8.5   Sample skill checklist.

teachers can inform students of their initial skill level compared with their present performance.

Another use for anecdotal record sheets is to monitor behavior in the affective domain. For example, some students may be asked to behave in certain ways because they are exhibiting behavior problems. Teachers can write short notes about how these students behaved each day. This leads to a documented record of how long the behavior has occurred and when it started to improve (or not improve). This information can be shared with parents or students.

A tape recorder is useful for recording anecdotal information. Comments can be recorded during observation and transcribed later. This process makes it easier to learn the names and behavior patterns of students and can lead to an increased understanding of student performance. Observations should be recorded at the start of the unit and compared with observations made later in the semester. A sample anecdotal record sheet is illustrated in Figure 8.6 on page 152.

Student Logs

Intermediate-grade youngsters are capable of maintaining a log that indicates their progress toward a goal over time. Assume students want to increase the amount of physical activity they accomplish each day. Teacher and students can cooperatively design goals that will help

the students become more active. Another approach is to ask students to develop behaviors they need to accomplish to reach their goals. The log should include goal behaviors they have accomplished over time—including decisions and choices made, time spent on goal behaviors, and a reflection area to record their perceptions of the experience.

Students can share their experiences and feelings about things they have tried. The logistics of activities each student has tried can be shared. Examining how well the stated outcomes were reached is the most common way to evaluate logs. For example, for students who wanted to increase their activity outside of school, a high score would go to youngsters who were active for 30 minutes five days a week. An acceptable score would go to students who were active three days a week. An unacceptable score would go to those who were active one day or less.

Student Self-Assessments

Students in the intermediate grades are capable of self-evaluation. They can be given lists of performance objectives and told to make judgments about their achievement. If more objectivity is desired, students can evaluate each other, or groups of two or three students can evaluate one another. Self-evaluation reduces the amount of teacher evaluation time, allowing the teacher more time for instruction. The ability to evaluate oneself

---

Anecdotal Record Sheet

Class _Ms. Massoney_   Date _2/14_

Bob: Is making progress on the backward jump. Sent a jump rope home with him for practice.

Gene: Seems to be discouraged about rope-jumping. Called parents to see if there is a problem outside of school.

Linda: Discussed the need for helping others. She is going to be a cross-aged tutor for next two weeks, as her performance in batting is excellent.

F I G U R E 8 . 6   Sample anecdotal record sheet.

and the desire to be evaluated are important outcomes of any effective program.

Student self-assessments are particularly useful for affective domain behavior. They can be used to monitor how students feel about certain activities or about their behavior. Having students assess themselves forces a look inward that may help both the teacher and student understand why the behavior is occurring. It is also possible to learn about activities students enjoy and how they behave when they don't like an activity. Figure 8.7 shows an example of a self-assessment form.

Written Tests

Written tests are administered to check the cognitive learning that has accompanied physical skill learning. The tests can be true/false or multiple choice for ease of correction. On the other hand, short-answer or essay questions encourage students to apply knowledge to different situations. The reading level of students must be considered when composing tests or it will be difficult to tell whether it is a comprehension or knowledge test. Oral presentation of questions is often best for younger students. Even though it seems apparent, bear in mind that written tests give little, if any, indication of how a youngster will perform a motor skill. Be careful not to grade just on written tests that examine cognition since physical education is primarily based on becoming skilled physically.

GRADING

There is wide variation in physical education grading policies in elementary schools, ranging from no grading

to grading with letter grades similar to high school classes. Effective points can be made on each side of the issue of whether to grade or not to grade, and there is no definitive answer. If a decision is made to grade, a more difficult question arises: What type of grading approach should be used? For an in-depth review of grading systems and ideas for evaluation, the text by Lacy and Hastad (2007) is recommended.

Points against Using a Grading System

- Grades are difficult to interpret between teachers and schools. A single-letter grade means one thing to one teacher and another to a different teacher. When a student moves to a different school, the meaning of the grade might not transfer, and teachers at the new school may view the grade differently.

- Physical education does not place emphasis on content and product. Rather, it judges success by improvement on skills. Grades in academic areas reflect achievement and accomplishment; because grades in physical education reflect improvement and effort, they may be interpreted incorrectly.

- Often, physical education classes in elementary schools only meet once or twice a week. Regularly testing for grade requirements is time-consuming and takes away from learning opportunities. Physical educators in this setting are trying to squeeze as much learning as possible into a minimal amount of time, and grading reduces their instructional time.

- Physical education is diverse and broad in nature. Instruction covers all three learning domains— i.e., skill development, attitude formation, and content knowledge. Trying to grade all three of these areas is difficult and demands a great deal

Responsible Behavior Checklist

Name: _____

Please rate yourself on your personal behavior during the times you were playing in games this week. Answer the questions fairly and as accurately as possible.

My Level of Responsible Behavior*	0	1	2	3	4
1. I encouraged others and said things such as, "Nice job," "Good hustle," "Excellent catch," etc. Explain why you gave yourself this rating:					
2. I won or lost gracefully. I didn't get angry or put down others. Explain why you gave yourself this rating:					
3. I followed the rules without trying to cheat. I was willing to abide by the referee's decisions. Explain why you gave yourself this rating:					
4. I did my best to get all my teammates involved in the game. Explain why you gave yourself this rating:					
5. I was willing to play in games even when it wasn't my favorite activity. Explain why you gave yourself this rating:					
*0 indicates you never behaved this way. 4 indicates you always behaved this way.					

FIGURE 8.7   Student self-assessment. Evaluating the affective domain: Responsible behavior.

of time. In addition, which of these three domains is most important, and can any of them be overlooked?

- Grading usually occurs in areas where standardized instruments have been developed. Fitness testing is the major area in elementary physical education where a variety of standardized tests has been developed. Due to the dearth of standardized tests in other areas, excessive attention is given to fitness testing.

- Physical education emphasizes physical fitness and skill performance. Performance in these areas is strongly controlled by genetics, making it difficult for every child to achieve, even when he "gives it his best effort." In addition, when grades are given for physical fitness performance, some youngsters feel discouraged because they trained and still did not reach standards of high performance.

Points for Using a Grading System

- Giving grades makes physical education similar to other academic areas in the school curriculum. This gives physical education credibility and gains respect from parents, teachers, and administrators.

- Grades communicate to parents the performance of students. Parents have a right to know how their youngsters perform in physical education. Grades are used by teachers in other areas and are easily understood and interpreted by parents; therefore, they should be used in physical education.

- When grades are not given, academic respect is lost. Physical education already suffers from the misguided perception that physical educators don't teach anything, they just "roll out the ball." Lack of a grading system may make it appear to others that little learning is occurring.

- A grading system provides accountability. When grades are given, administrators and parents often assume that teaching and student accomplishment have occurred.
- A grading system rewards skilled students. Students are rewarded in academic areas for their intelligence and performance and should be similarly rewarded for accomplishment in physical education settings.

If You Choose to Grade, Consider the Following . . .

If the decision is made to implement a grading system, more difficult issues follow. There are different ways to grade, and many issues have to be examined before developing a grading approach. Consider the following points when determining how you will assign grades.

EDUCATIONAL OUTCOMES VERSUS ADMINISTRATIVE TASKS

There is general agreement that physical education should help students achieve in a number of areas including skill development, personal values, and cognitive development. Some grading systems assign weight to each of these areas when compiling a grade. Regardless of the amount of emphasis given to each area, the final grade depends on accomplishment of educational objectives. This contrasts with grading on completion of administrative tasks where students earn a part or all of their grade by attendance, participation, and attitude. This latter approach grades students on tasks that have little to do with accomplishment of physical education objectives. Furthermore, these tasks are usually documented at the beginning of the period and will serve little in holding students accountable for their in-class performances.

Consider the conflicts arising when students are graded on achievement of educational objectives versus accomplishment of administrative tasks. Assume a student in a math class regularly forgets to bring a pencil and is tardy but earns an A grade on all math exams. Does this student earn a final grade of A, or is the student penalized for doing poorly on administrative tasks (tardiness, and so on) and given a C grade? Reverse the situation and assume the student has an outstanding attitude, is never tardy, and always brings the proper supplies to class. At the end of the semester, the student has earned a C grade on exams yet performed all administrative tasks at a high level. Does this student receive a final grade of A? If grades in other curricular areas of the school are earned through accomplishment of educational objectives or performance of administrative tasks, it is probably wise to follow suit in the physical education area.

ATTITUDE VERSUS SKILL PERFORMANCE

Another area of concern when grading is whether attitude or skill performance should be the focal point. Those who emphasize attitudes stress the importance of students leaving school with warm and positive feelings toward physical activity. These educators state their beliefs in the following manner: "I am not concerned about how many skills my students learn; I just want them to walk out of my class with positive feelings about physical activity." The assumption is that students who feel positive about physical activity will be willing to be active throughout their lifetimes. These teachers assign grades based on the process of trying rather than on reaching skill outcomes. Students who receive higher grades may not be the most skilled but have shown good behavior and a positive attitude throughout the semester.

Teachers who reside in the product camp focus primarily on student accomplishment and see effort as something that is laudable but not part of the grading process. Their philosophy might be stated as follows: "I don't really care whether students like me or physical education. What is ultimately important is their performance. After all, the students who are best in math earn the highest grades, so why should it be any different in physical education?" Teachers who focus on performance give the highest grade to the best performer, regardless of other factors. Less skilled students, no matter how hard they try, will not receive an above-average grade.

This is a difficult problem to resolve in physical education and is always hotly debated. One point of view is that students should learn from the grading system how society works. People are not rewarded in life based on how hard they try, but, rather, on their performance. For example, if real estate agents try hard but never sell a house, they don't make any money. The payoff is for selling houses, not for trying hard to sell houses. An opposing viewpoint is that many people in society are rewarded for effort, so "doing your best" should be rewarded.

A solution to consider is to grade on performance while teaching in a manner that focuses on students' attitudes toward physical activity and skill learning. Much is to be said for teaching in a manner that helps students develop a positive attitude toward activity. Attitude development depends largely on how teachers present the material rather than on how students perform skills. Help students understand that they also perform differently from each other in math or science and receive a respectively higher or lower grade.

RELATIVE IMPROVEMENT

Some physical educators believe that effort, or "just doing the best that you can," should be the most important factor in assigning grades. To reward effort, these teachers base student grades on the amount a student improves. This involves pre-testing and post-testing to determine the amount of progress made throughout the grading period. This approach contrasts with basing the grade on absolute performance; it is quite possible that the best performer in the class will not receive the highest grade because of lack of improvement.

Grading on improvement is time-consuming and requires that the same test be given at the beginning and end of the semester or unit. The test may or may not be a valid reflection of what has been learned in the class and may not be sensitive enough to reflect improvement made by both poor and outstanding performers. Testing at the beginning of a unit can be discouraging and demoralizing if a student performs poorly in front of peers. It can also be hazardous in some activities, such as gymnastics or archery, that require intensive instruction to prevent accident or injury.

Another factor to consider is the issue of performing for a grade. Students learn quickly that if they perform too well on the pre-test, they will be penalized at post-test time. It is thus important to perform at a low level in order to demonstrate a higher degree of improvement on the post-test. A related problem is that improvement is sometimes easier at beginning levels of skill than at high levels of performance. Most teachers are aware of the rapid improvement beginners make before reaching a learning plateau. A skilled performer may be at a level where improvement is difficult to achieve. Lack of improvement in this situation results in a skilled performer receiving a lower grade than a beginner.

GRADING ON POTENTIAL OR EFFORT

Some teachers choose to grade on whether students reach their potential. Such teachers may lower a student's grade because the student did not reach his potential due to a lack of effort in the teacher's opinion. On the other hand, a grade may be raised because the teacher felt a student didn't have much ability but did reach her potential. In other words, the teacher decides what a student's potential performance level should be and then assigns a grade based on whether the student reached this level. The grade a student receives depends on the teacher's subjective perception of that student's genetic abilities and limitations. How can any teacher really know the absolute potential of any student? This approach results in students being assigned a grade based on an unknown factor: potential.

This approach often depends on the teacher's feelings about the student in question. It is based on intangibles, and may result in a grade being assigned because the student is "just like her brothers or sisters." When grades are based on the teacher's subjective beliefs rather than on criteria that can be measured and evaluated, grades become difficult to defend. How would a parent react to a teacher's statement that "your youngster received a failing grade because he just didn't live up to his potential"? To be defensible, grading systems need to be based on tangible data gleaned from observable behavior and performance.

NEGATIVE VERSUS POSITIVE GRADING

To make the grading system defensible and concrete, some teachers have used point systems. In most point systems, both performance objectives and administrative factors are listed as grade components. A student earns a grade through performance, attitude, and knowledge. Point systems can become a negative influence if handled incorrectly. For example, some teachers give students 100 points at the start of the semester and then "chip off" points for various unsatisfactory levels of performance. A student may lose points for not trying, not performing, or not knowing answers on a test. Students soon realize that energy should be spent on concentrating on negative behaviors that lose points rather than on educational objectives.

This contrasts with a system that rewards positive behavior. When the student performs well, points are assigned and the student can earn her grade through self-direction. In a negative system, teachers make all the judgments about points lost and receive in turn the negative feelings of the student. In a positive system, students can behave in a positive manner to earn points. Teachers are constantly rewarding positive behavior, which fosters positive feelings toward physical education and teachers. Rewarding positive behavior makes students feel that the teacher cares about their welfare and growth.

A negative system tends to focus teachers on what students cannot do, rather than on what they should or can do. Energy is spent on "policing" students and threatening to take away points if they do not behave. Students do not respond well to this approach, since a loss of points does not require an immediate change in behavior and a redirection. The loss of points results in a reduction of the final grade, a consequence that is usually six to nine weeks away. Few students respond positively to grade leverage through a negative system. Students who care about their grades are performing well in the first place. Threatening to lower the grade of a student who does not like physical education or school in general only further alienates the student and is based on a system of negative reinforcement. The grading system should positively encourage students to perform.

Progress Report for Physical Education

Student: _____   Class: _____

Students are expected to learn a wide variety of skills in physical education. The following areas reflect major program standards. Expectations are that your child will perform at or above developmental level (compared with other students the same age). If you are interested in discussing the progress of your child, please arrange a meeting with the physical education instructor.

Physical Education Assessment

Program Standards	Developmental Level Performance		
	Above	**At**	**Below**
Exhibits motor skills and movement competence			
Is able to monitor and maintain physical fitness			
Understands human movement principles			
Uses lifestyle habits that foster wellness			
Possesses lifetime physical activity skills			

Social Skills and Responsible Behavior Assessment

Students are graded on social skills and responsible behavior in physical education classes. Rewards and consequences are recorded daily. Grades are based on how students perform in these areas.

O = Outstanding   Exhibits effort and a positive attitude about participating in physical activities on a regular basis. Cooperates with classmates and receives no more than one behavior consequence during the nine-week grading period.

S = Satisfactory   Willingly attempts activities. Puts forth average effort, displays a positive attitude, cooperates with classmates, and receives two to five behavior consequences during the nine-week grading period.

N = Needs Improvement   Consistently exhibits off-task behavior and/or a negative attitude. Has difficulty cooperating with classmates. Parents are notified by midterm of the grading period if their child is in jeopardy of receiving a grade of "N."

Program Standards	O	S	N
Develops quality social skills			
Exhibits responsible behavior			

Instructor's Comments

FIGURE 8.8   Sample progress report.

LETTER GRADES VERSUS A STUDENT PROGRESS REPORT

Letter grades tell parents very little about the performance of their youngsters in physical education. Many times the grade is a reflection of student behavior while the parents interpret it as an indicator of their student's physical skill level. A letter grade doesn't communicate progress or performance related to other students at a similar developmental level. A student progress report takes more time to compile, but gives parents much more information and helps to communicate the goals of the program.

Figure 8.8 is an example of a progress report that could be used to share information with parents. The seven areas of evaluation represent the seven major content standards of the program (see Chapter 1). If desired, some of the specific benchmarks under each standard could also be included. Note that program standards are divided into two major areas: (1) physical education skills and (2) social skills and responsible behavior. Most teachers want an opportunity to separate behavior and skill performance when grading. This progress report allows students to be rewarded for effort and proper behavior regardless of their skill and physical ability. An advantage to evaluating a student based on developmental level is that it gives parents an idea of how their child is performing compared to others of similar development and maturity. This report helps parents understand the skill performance of other children who are similar developmentally or who are above, at, or below their child's skill level. This feedback may help temper unrealistic expectations of parents and coaches who do not have the perspective of seeing many children at similar developmental levels.

Since completing a progress report takes more time than assigning letter grades, such a report can't be sent home as often as a simple letter grade. Most elementary school teachers are responsible for 350 to 600 or more students. Completing a progress report for each student four times a year would be an unrealistic expectation because of the inordinate amount of time it takes to complete one. A solution is to offer a comprehensive and meaningful progress report once a year or once every second or third year. This approach alerts teachers to students they will have to grade for the forthcoming year and allows them time to review these youngsters in detail throughout the year.

EVALUATING INSTITUTIONAL OUTCOMES

Institutional outcomes are those goals that the state, school district, superintendent, school board, and parents want to reach. In other terms, they are referred to as "accountability outcomes" or "What is it that the physical education program should contribute to the total school environment?" To evaluate institutional goals, it is necessary to use a test that is valid and respected both in and out of the school setting. The best examples of tests for measuring institutional outcomes in schools today are the "high-stakes" tests used for measuring math, science, and reading outcomes. In some cases, students are not allowed to graduate if they don't pass these exams. It is a poor reflection on the institution if a large number of students don't pass, so the tests become an important catalyst for change.

Health-Related Fitness

Physical fitness testing has occurred for decades in physical education. Some experts argue for placing less emphasis on fitness testing and more on activity evaluation (Pangrazi, 2004). Currently the Fitnessgram System (Cooper Institute, 2004) is a popular test used to measure health-related physical fitness and is the recommended test for the AAHPERD. The test items have been checked for validity and reliability. The Fitnessgram offers a variety of fitness test items so teachers can develop a customized test battery. The focus of the Fitnessgram is on teaching students about the importance of activity for good health. Students are not compared to one another but are given feedback about their fitness and whether it meets the minimum standard for good health.

The Fitnessgram is based primarily on exercise behaviors rather than on students' attempts to demonstrate that they are the "best." The Fitnessgram program acknowledges and commends performance; however, it places its highest priority on the development and reinforcement of health-related behaviors that are attainable by all students. These behavior programs are used to commend participants for any of the following activities: completion of exercise logs, achievement of specific and personalized goals, and fulfillment of a contractual agreement (with a responsible adult). A new text that is helpful for understanding fitness and activity topics is *Toward a Better Understanding of Physical Activity and Fitness: Selected Topics, Volume II* (Corbin, Pangrazi, & Franks, 2004).

FITNESSGRAM TEST ITEMS

The suggested test items in the Fitnessgram are briefly described in this section. Other test items are included in the manual to give teachers a choice of designing a different test battery. A comprehensive test administration manual, related materials, and software can be ordered from Human Kinetics, P.O. Box 5076, Champaign, IL 61825-5076 (www.Fitnessgram.net).

Aerobic Capacity. The PACER (Progressive Aerobic Cardiovascular Endurance Run) test is an excellent alternative to the mile run—it involves a 20-meter shuttle run and can be performed indoors. The test is progressive and starts out at a level that allows all youngsters to be successful and gradually increases in difficulty. The objective of the PACER is to run back and forth across the 20-meter distance within a specified time limit that gradually decreases. The 20-meter distance is not intimidating to youngsters (compared to the mile) and avoids the problem of trying to teach students to pace themselves rather than run all-out and fatigue rapidly.

Body Composition. Body composition is evaluated using percent of body fat, which is calculated by measuring the triceps and calf skinfolds or body mass index (calculated using height and weight).

Abdominal Strength. The curl-up test uses a cadence (one curl-up every three seconds). The maximum limit is 75. Students lie in a supine position with their knees bent at a 140-degree angle. The hands are placed flat on the mat alongside the hips. The objective is to gradually sit up and move the fingers down the mat a specified distance.

Upper Body Strength. The push-up test is done to a cadence (one every three seconds) and is an excellent substitute for the pull-up. A successful push-up is counted when the arms are bent to a 90-degree angle. This item allows many more students to experience success as compared to the pull-up and flexed-arm hang. Other alternative test items are the modified pull-up, the pull-up, and the flexed-arm hang.

Trunk Extensor Strength and Flexibility. The trunk lift test is done from a face-down position. This test involves lifting the upper body 6 to 12 inches off the floor using the muscles of the back. The position must be held until the measurement can be made.

Flexibility. The back-saver sit and reach is similar to the traditional sit-and-reach test except that it is performed with one leg flexed so that students aren't encouraged to hyperextend. Measurement is made on both the right and left legs.

CRITERION-REFERENCED HEALTH STANDARDS

A major reason for doing health-related fitness evaluation is to provide students, teachers, and parents with information about good health. The Fitnessgram (Cooper Institute, 2004) uses *criterion-referenced health standards* that represent good health instead of traditional percentile rankings. These standards represent a level of fitness that offers some degree of protection against diseases resulting from sedentary living. The Fitnessgram uses an approach that classifies fitness performance into two categories: needs improvement and healthy fitness zone (HFZ). All students are encouraged

to score in the HFZ; however, there is little advantage to scoring beyond the healthy fitness zone. Criterion-referenced health standards do not compare students against each other as do percentile rankings. Instead, youngsters are taught to be concerned with personal fitness and minimizing possible health problems through trying to score within the healthy fitness zone.

Criterion-referenced health standards for aerobic fitness are based on a study by Blair et al. (1989). A significant decrease in risk of all-cause mortality occurred when people were active enough to avoid classification in the bottom 20 percent of the population. The risk level continues to decrease as fitness levels increase, but not significantly when compared to moving out of the least active group. The aerobic performance minimums (mile run or PACER) for the Fitnessgram HFZ require achieving a fitness level that is above the least active portion (bottom 20 percent) of the population.

Criterion-referenced health standards for percent of fat are calculated from equations reported by Slaughter et al. (1988). Detailed information on the development of these equations and other issues related to the measurement and interpretation of body composition information is available in Lohman (1992). Williams et al. (1992) reported that students with body fat levels above 25 percent for boys and 30–35 percent for girls are more likely to exhibit elevated cholesterol levels and hypertension. The lower limit for the Fitnessgram HFZ corresponds to these levels of body fat. In other words, students who have higher levels of body fat may be at risk for future health problems.

Criterion-referenced health standards have not been established for abdominal strength, upper body strength, or flexibility. For example, it is difficult to determine whether a lack of upper body strength is important for quality health. Instead, criterion-referenced training standards are used for these areas of fitness. The lower limit represents a performance level that youngsters should be able to accomplish if they are reasonably active and exercise. These standards reflect how many push-ups active students should be able to perform. Stated another way, these standards reflect a reasonable expectation for students who are sufficiently active.

EFFECTIVE USES OF FITNESS TESTS

Fitness tests are designed to evaluate and educate students about the status of their physical fitness. In spite of continued research and improvement, fitness tests have limitations and usually show low validity (that is, they do not measure what they purport to measure). Therefore, how the tests are used becomes an important issue. There are three major ways to use fitness tests: (1) to teach personal self-testing, (2) to establish personal-best fitness performances, and (3) to evaluate institutional fitness goals. The personal self-testing program is most strongly advocated in the elementary school physical education program. It can be done in the least amount of time, is educational, and can be done in an unthreatening manner. In addition, little instructional time is lost, and students learn how to evaluate their fitness, a skill that will serve them for a lifetime. Many people have experienced fitness testing many times, but few people ever learn how to evaluate their personal fitness level.

Personal Self-Testing. The personal self-testing program is an approach that is student-centered and concerned with the process of fitness testing, and emphasizes learning to self-evaluate. When using this technique, students can work individually or find a friend with whom they would like to self-test. Partners evaluate each other and develop their own fitness profiles. The goal is to learn the process of fitness testing so that students will be able to evaluate their health status during adulthood. Students are asked to do their best, but the teacher does not interfere in the process. The results are the property of the student and are not posted or shared with other students. The personal self-testing program is an educational endeavor; it also allows for more frequent evaluation because it can be done quickly, privately, and informally.

Figure 8.9 on page 160 is an example of a self-evaluation Fitnessgram form that can be used by students. It contains a column to check off whether the minimum criterion-referenced health standard for each test item has been met. The purpose of recording the data is to help students learn to self-evaluate without the stigma of others viewing or knowing about it. A final note: It is acceptable for some students to choose not to be tested on a certain item because they fear embarrassment (skinfolds) or failure (PACER). It is worse for them to be tested and embarrassed than not to be tested at all.

Personal-Best Testing. The personal-best testing approach appeals to gifted performers and to students who are motivated to achieve a maximum performance. The objective is to achieve a maximum score in each of the test items. This approach has been used for years with most fitness tests. In addition, several awards (President's Council on Physical Fitness and Sports, 2004) are issued to high-level performers. This is a formal testing program as compared to the self-testing approach discussed previously. Test items must be performed correctly, following test protocol to the letter. It also requires a considerable amount of time to administer.

Personal-best testing is an elective program that requires maximal performance and usually is not motivating to less capable students. Some students are threatened and fear the embarrassment of failing to perform well in front of peers. A way to avoid embarrassing students who are less capable is to administer the test outside of class time. Testing opportunities can be offered after or before school and on a weekend when school is not in session. As another elective option, some city recreation departments offer fitness testing opportunities outside the physical education program. This approach is much less threatening; students can choose to participate in the personal-best testing session or decide to entirely avoid such situations.

Institutional Evaluation. The institutional evaluation program involves examining the fitness levels of students to see if the institution (school) is reaching its desired objectives. Institutional objectives are closely tied to the physical education curriculum. If the curriculum being taught to students is adequate and the goals are meaningful, the majority of students should be able to reach institutional goals. A common approach for institutional goal setting is to establish a percentage of the student body that must meet or exceed criterion-referenced health standards for a fitness test. If the percentage is below established institutional standards, it may indicate that the curriculum needs to be modified in order to meet the objective.

Since this type of testing impacts teachers and curriculum offerings, it is done in a formal and standardized manner. A common approach is to train a team of parents to administer tests throughout the system. This ensures accuracy and consistency across all schools in the district. Each test item is reviewed separately, since it is possible that objectives are reached for some but not all of the items. To avoid testing all students every year, some districts evaluate only during entry level years—i.e., the seventh and ninth grades. This minimizes the amount of formal testing youngsters have to endure during their school career.

Physical Activity

Another way to evaluate the effectiveness of the institution is to monitor the amount of physical activity students accumulate on a daily basis. Fortunately, today there are accurate instruments available for measuring the amount of physical activity students accumulate (for an in-depth discussion of physical activity monitoring and promotion, see Chapter 12). Using pedometers to measure the physical activity levels of youth is now an accepted instructional and research methodology (Beighle, Pangrazi, & Vincent, 2001; Crouter et al., 2003; Kilanowski et al., 1999). Walk4Life pedometers (www.walk4life.com) have a function that measures activity time. Every time a person moves, the pedometer starts accumulating time. When the person stops moving, the timing function stops. This function shows the total hours and minutes of activity time accumulated throughout the day. This is useful for students and parents

My Personal Fitness Record

Name _____ Age _____ Grade _____ Room _____

	Score	HFZ*
Body Composition		
Calf (leg) Skinfold		
Triceps (arm) Skinfold	+	
Total (leg and arm)	=	
Cardiovascular Endurance PACER		
Abdominal Strength Curl-Ups		
Upper Body Strength Push-Ups		
Back Strength Trunk Lift		
Lower Back Flexibility Sit and Reach	L R	
Upper Body Flexibility Shoulder Stretch	L R	

* HFZ means you have scored in the Healthy Fitness Zone. You have achieved or passed the minimum fitness standard required for good health and feeling good. Regardless of whether you scored in the HFZ for all the tests, you must maintain an active lifestyle for good health. Try to accumulate at least 60 minutes of activity every day.

You do not have to share the results of your personal fitness record. It is for your information and should help you determine your health status. Ask your teacher if you need ideas for increasing your physical activity level. You are learning the process of evaluating your fitness. The scores recorded may not be accurate.

FIGURE 8.9 Fitnessgram form: My Personal Fitness Record.

because most activity recommendations are expressed in terms of minutes per day (see Chapter 12).

There are a number of ways to gather institutional data with pedometers. Research has shown that gathering four days of physical activity will give an accurate indication of a student's average activity level. A set of pedometers can be rotated between classrooms to establish the average level of activity for each classroom. Goals for classes and schools can be established using this objective data set. Physical activity is a more achievable outcome measure (as compared to physical fitness outcomes) for elementary school students. Students can

be monitored for four days at the start of the year and again near the end of the year. A factor that makes monitoring physical activity an excellent outcome is that all students can become more active. Contrast this with physical fitness where most of the performance in elementary school students is controlled by their genetic endowments and physical growth. Most pre-test/post-test fitness gains shown in elementary school are due to youngsters becoming eight to nine months older.

Another spin-off of monitoring physical activity is that an award system for active children can be implemented. The President's Council on Physical Fitness and Sports has developed an award for students who accumulate at least 60 minutes of physical activity almost every day for six weeks. The award, called the Presidential Active Lifestyle Award, looks like the Presidential Physical Fitness Award (President's Challenge, 2005). Students can sign up and log their activity into the Website on a daily basis at www.presidentschallenge.org. This is an excellent way to promote physical activity outside the school day.

Children's Attraction to Physical Activity (CAPA)

The CAPA instrument is used to assess the attraction of children ages 8 to 12 to physical activity (Brustad, 1993). This instrument has been used for research purposes and validated by Brustad (1993). The CAPA is a 15-item pencil-and-paper instrument that assesses the extent of children's interest in physical activity by giving them two opposing points of view from which to select. Children first choose which point of view describes them and then select the strength of that feeling ("sort of true" or "really true") for each of the 15 items. The instrument is scored on a 1-to-4-point scale with 4 reflecting the most positive attraction to physical activity. Figure 8.10 on page 162 shows the CAPA instrument.

The CAPA can be used to evaluate how students feel about physical activity. Since this is a standardized instrument, the results can be used to see whether the physical education program is having a positive impact on the affective domain of students. Schools and classrooms can be compared to see how students feel about physical activity. If attitudes toward physical activity are low, strategies for improvement can be implemented by teachers and parents to enhance the students' feelings.

EVALUATING INSTRUCTIONAL EFFECTIVENESS

A key to improving teaching ability is being able to gather meaningful feedback about your own instructional behavior. It is often difficult to find someone capable of offering evaluative feedback. Principals and curriculum supervisors may be too busy to evaluate teaching regularly, or they may not possess the skills necessary for systematically evaluating teaching behavior. This accentuates the importance of finding ways for self-evaluating teaching as a primary avenue for improvement. Without regular and measurable means of evaluation, improving the quality of teaching becomes next to impossible. Teachers have long been told to talk less, move more, praise more, learn more names, and increase student practice time—all without documented methods of

measurement. This section offers methods for evaluating teaching behavior that are observable and therefore measurable. If readers desire in-depth information on this topic, the texts *Developing Teaching Skills in Physical Education* (Siedentop & Tannehill, 2000) and *Analyzing Physical Education and Sport Instruction* (Darst, Zakrajsek, & Mancini, 1989) are excellent resources.

The do-it-yourself approach to evaluation is recommended because feedback that is reviewed in the privacy of one's office is easier to digest and is less threatening. You can set personal goals and chart your performance privately. When you choose to evaluate your teaching procedures, you are making a commitment to change. This attitude is in contrast to the resistance that some teachers feel when principals and supervisors evaluate them and dictate change. Instructors often doubt the validity of the latter process and find reasons for not changing.

The first steps to self-improvement are to decide what teaching behavior to evaluate and the best possible way to record and monitor the data. Evaluating a single teaching behavior when starting to evaluate your instructional effectiveness is preferable, since recording more than one variable at a time can be frustrating and confusing. After determining the behavior to change, design a coding form to facilitate recording the data.

Coding sheets are best designed for a specific teaching behavior. Areas on the sheet are provided for the recording teacher's name, the date, the focus and content of the lesson, the grade level and competency of the students, the duration of the lesson, and a short description of the evaluation procedure. Maintaining a consistent format for the coding sheets will make it easier to compare your performance throughout the year. Appropriate coding forms for gathering data on a number of teaching behaviors are offered in the next section. These forms are examples that can be modified to meet the specific needs of the instructor. Effective teachers usually make self-evaluation an ongoing, integral part of their teaching.

There are many ways to gather data about your teaching. For example, students who are not participating can gather the data; another teacher can gather the data easily; or the data can be gathered from an audiotape or a videotape. Most teachers feel comfortable evaluating their own teaching performance. Daily teaching behavior is least affected when outside observers are not present, making self-evaluation techniques more likely to reveal actual instructional patterns.

Instructional Time

It is important to know the amount of instruction you offer students. To analyze instructional time, the number

What I Am Like

Please look at the sample question first. Choose only one answer to each question. There are no right or wrong answers. Simply choose the statement you think is most true for you.

Really true for me	Sort of true for me	**Sample**			Really true for me	Sort of true for me
↓ A	↓ B	Some kids like to eat ice cream more than anything else.	BUT	Other kids like other foods more than ice cream.	↓ C	↓ D

	Really true for me	Sort of true for me				Really true for me	Sort of true for me
1.	A	B	Some kids have more fun playing games and sports than anything else.	BUT	Other kids like doing other things.	C	D
2.	A	B	Some kids don't like to exercise very much.	BUT	Other kids like to exercise a whole lot.	C	D
3.	A	B	Some kids get told by other kids that they are not very good at games and sports.	BUT	Other kids are told that they are good at games and sports.	C	D
4.	A	B	Some kids get teased by other kids when they play games and sports.	BUT	Other kids don't get teased when they play games and sports.	C	D
5.	A	B	Some kids think that the more exercise they get the better.	BUT	Other kids think that it is not good to get too much exercise.	C	D
6.	A	B	Some kids don't enjoy exercise very much.	BUT	Other kids enjoy exercise a whole lot.	C	D
7.	A	B	Some kids try hard to stay in good shape.	BUT	Other kids don't try hard to stay in good shape.	C	D
8.	A	B	Some kids don't like getting out of breath when they play hard.	BUT	Other kids don't mind getting out of breath when they play hard.	C	D

FIGURE 8.10   Children's Attraction to Physical Activity (CAPA) instrument.

	Really true for me	Sort of true for me				Really true for me	Sort of true for me
9.	A	B	Some kids think it is very important to always be in good shape.	BUT	Other kids don't think it is so important to always be in good shape.	C	D
10.	A	B	For some kids, games and sports is their favorite thing.	BUT	Other kids like other things more than games and sports.	C	D
11.	A	B	Some kids are popular with other kids when they play games and sports.	BUT	Other kids are not very popular with others when they play games and sports.	C	D
12.	A	B	Some kids look forward to playing games and sports.	BUT	Other kids don't look forward to playing games and sports.	C	D
13.	A	B	Some kids really don't like to exercise.	BUT	Other kids do like to exercise.	C	D
14.	A	B	Some kids feel bad when they run hard.	BUT	Other kids feel good when they run hard.	C	D
15.	A	B	Some kids *don't* like to run very much.	BUT	Other kids do like to run a whole lot.	C	D

Source: Brustad, R. J. (1996). Attraction to physical activity in urban schoolchildren: Parental socialization and gender influences. *Research Quarterly for Exercise and Sport, 67*, 316–323.

FIGURE 8.10   (continued)

of instructional episodes and the length of each episode are recorded. The average length of an instructional episode can be evaluated, as well as the percentage of the lesson that was used for instruction. Generally, episodes should be short and frequent, with an attempt made to limit each episode to 30 seconds or less.

HOW TO DO IT

1. Design a form for duration recording.
2. Have a colleague or a nonparticipating student turn on the stopwatch every time you begin an instructional episode; or record the lesson using an audiotape recorder and time the instructional episodes at the end of the day. Establish consistency in identifying

the difference between instructional and management episodes.
3. Total the amount of time spent on instruction.
4. Convert the amount of time to a percentage of the total lesson time by dividing the total lesson time into the time spent on instruction. The average length of an instructional episode can be determined by dividing the amount of instructional time by the number of instructional episodes. Figure 8.11 on page 164 is an example of a form that could be used.

Management Time

Management time is defined as episodes that occur when students are moved into various formations, when equipment is gathered or put away, and when directions are given relative to these areas. Disciplining a class is another example of time used for management. As a rule of thumb, if you are talking and not giving instructions, you are managing students. Figure 8.12 is an example of a form that can be used to record the amount of management time.

The length of each episode can be recorded by an observer. These data are useful for analyzing how much of the lesson time is devoted to management. You may be alerted to inefficient organizational schemes or realize that students are not responding quickly to explanations and requests.

HOW TO DO IT

1. Design a form to gather the desired data.
2. Record the lesson with an audiotape recorder. Time the episodes of management and note the length of each episode on the form.
3. Total the amount of management time and divide it by the length of the period to determine the percentage of management time in the lesson.

4. Total the number of episodes and divide this number into the amount of time devoted to management to find the average length of a management episode.

Practice Time (Time on Task) and Dead Time

To learn physical skills, students must have an opportunity for productive skill practice. Physical education programs have a finite amount of scheduled time per week. Practice time, or time on task, has also been referred to as ALT-PE. This is an acronym for Academic Learning Time in Physical Education. Practice time is the amount of time students spend practicing skills that result in accomplishment of program objectives. Gathering data to show the amount of time students are involved in productive, on-task activity can reveal whether there is adequate time for students to learn skills. In a well-regarded school district, the authors found that the average amount of activity time per 50-minute period was only 9 to 12 minutes. It is possible that more learning could occur if practice time were increased.

Instructional Time

Teacher _Charlene Darst_ Observer _B. Pangrazi_

Class _1st period_ Grade _5th_ Date and Time _3/22 - 9:05_

Lesson focus _Basketball_ Comments _1st class meeting of unit_

Starting time _9:30_ Ending time _10:00_ Length of lesson _30 min_

15	10	8	35	17	1:03	31	9	8
14	21	10	21	43	7			

Total instruction time _5 min 12 sec_

Percentage of class time devoted to instruction _17%_

Number of episodes _15_ Average length of episodes _31.5 sec_

FIGURE 8.11 Sample form for calculating instructional time.

Management Time

Teacher _Don Hicks_   Observer _Connie Orlowicz_

Class _6th period_   Grade _3rd_   Date and Time _10/29 – 1:30_

Lesson focus _Manipulative skills_   Comments _____

Starting time _1:30_   Ending time _2:00_   Length of lesson _30 min_

55	10	21	20	35	18	29	10	10	21	9	19	21
11												

Total management time _4 min 49 sec_

Percentage of class time devoted to management _16%_

Number of episodes _14_   Average length of episodes _20.6 sec_

FIGURE 8.12   Sample form for calculating management time.

Duration recording is best for evaluating practice time. A student or fellow teacher observes the lesson and times when students are involved in practicing skills. Figure 8.13 on page 166 shows the results of duration recording for practice time. Strive to increase the amount of time devoted to skill practice by using more equipment, implementing drills that demand a minimum of standing in line, or streamlining the amount of verbal instructions given.

The amount of dead time in a lesson also can be measured. Dead time occurs when students are off-task or are doing something unrelated to practice, management, or instruction. Examples might be standing in line waiting for a turn, doing nothing because instructions were not understood, or waiting for the ball to come to them during game play.

HOW TO DO IT

1. Design a form for collecting the data (Figure 8.14).
2. Identify a student who will be timed when practicing. This is a critical step. The student chosen should

be neither exceptional nor below par and should give a realistic picture of the amount of practice time allotted. If evaluation of dead time is desired, then time when that student is not involved in on-task practice, management, or instructional activity. Another way to calculate dead time is to subtract the combined amounts of time used for practice, management, and instruction (assuming all have been timed) from the total length of the lesson.

3. Turn on the stopwatch when the student is involved in practice (or dead) activity. Stop the watch when the student stops (or starts) practicing. Record the amount of practice (or dead) time. Time all practice (or dead) episodes.

4. Total the amount of time devoted to student practice (in minutes) and divide it by the length of the lesson. This is the percentage of practice time in a lesson. Total the amount of dead time and divide it by the length of the lesson to compute the percentage of dead time.

Teacher: Debbie Massoney School: Whittier Elementary		
Parts of the lesson	**Practicing**	**Inactive, off-task, listening**
Introductory activity	1.5 min	0.5 min
Fitness development	6.5 min	1.5 min
Lesson focus	10.0 min	4.0 min
Game	5.0 min	1.0 min
Total	23.0 min	7.0 min

FIGURE 8.13 Results of a duration recording for practice time.

Response Latency

Response latency is the amount of time it takes for students to respond when commands or signals are given. Response latency occurs when instructions are given to begin or stop an activity. An observer records the amount of time that elapses between the moment a command is given to start or stop an activity and the moment the students actually begin or stop. The amount of elapsed time is the response latency.

The average duration of response latency can be calculated. A certain amount of response latency should be expected. However, most instructors have a strong feeling about the amount of latency they are willing to tolerate. After more than a five-second response latency, teachers usually become uneasy and expect the class to stop or start.

HOW TO DO IT

1. Develop a form for gathering the data (Figure 8.15).

2. Have a nonparticipating student or colleague time the response latency that occurs when the class is asked to stop (start). The clock should run from the time the command to stop (start) is given until the next command is given or until the class is involved in productive behavior. Starting and stopping latency are two separate behaviors that must be recorded separately.

3. Tally the number of response latency episodes and divide this number into the total amount of time devoted to response latency to calculate the average episode length.

Practice Time

Teacher Eugene Petersen   Observer P. W. Darst

Class 2nd period   Grade 4th   Date and Time 11/15 – 9:15

Lesson focus Gymnastics skills   Comments week two

Starting time 9:25   Ending time 10:00   Length of lesson 35 min

35	10	2:04	25	29	1:39	17	55	34
43	1:55	1:01	33	10	10	18	1:17	4:50
24	39	31	34					

Total practice time 20 min 13 sec

Percentage of class time devoted to practice 57.8%

Number of episodes 22   Average length of episodes 55.1 sec

FIGURE 8.14 Sample form for collecting data on practice time.

Response Latency

Teacher _Jim Roberts_   Observer _Bob Pangrazi_

Class _2nd period_   Grade _2nd_   Date and Time _2/5 – 9:00_

Lesson focus _Movement concepts_   Comments _____

Starting time _9:05_   Ending time _9:35_   Length of lesson _30 min_

Starting Response Latency

3	7	5	9	15	3	3	4	9	7	5	3	
2	4	10	7									

Stopping Response Latency

10	12	9	8	8	15	8	6	2	9	10	11	15
14	5	5	13									

Total amount of starting response latency _1 min 42 sec_

Percentage of class time devoted to response latency _5.7%_

Number of episodes _16_   Average length of episodes _6 sec_

Total amount of stopping response latency _2 min 41 sec_

Percentage of class time devoted to stopping response latency _8.9%_

Number of episodes _17_   Average length of episodes _9.5 sec_

FIGURE 8.15 Sample form for evaluating response latency.

Student Performance

Some classes have a greater percentage of students performing at optimum level than others. The percentage of students performing the desired task is an excellent indicator of a well-managed class. The placheck (planned activity check) observation technique (Siedentop & Tannehill, 2000) is an excellent way to monitor the percentage of students who are on-task.

Placheck recording is a technique used to observe group behavior at different times during a lesson. At regular intervals, the observer scans the class from the left to the right side of the instructional area and records the number of students who are not performing the predefined behavior. (Recording the smaller number of students exhibiting a behavior is easier. For example, if you are interested in identifying the percentage of students on-task, generally it is easier to record the number of students *not* on-task.) Each student in the class is observed one time only during a scan. The observer does not go back and change the decision, even if the student changes behavior during the interval. Intervals should last for ten seconds and be randomly spaced throughout the lesson, with eight to ten observation intervals. Signals to scan the class should be recorded on a tape recorder at random intervals to cue the observer.

The placheck is used to monitor behavior that is "yes or no" in nature. In other words, students either are performing the desired behavior or are doing

Student Performance

Teacher _Albert Santillan_   Observer _Ms. Estfan_

Class _8th period_   Grade _6th_   Date and Time _5/5 - 2:30_

Lesson focus _Rhythmic movement skills_   Comments _____

Starting time _2:30_   Ending time _3:00_   Length of lesson _30 min_

Active/Inactive

On-Task/Off-Task

5	4	12	7	3	3	2	5	6	5
4	3								

Effort/Noneffort

Number of plachecks _12_

Total number of students _30_

Average number of students not on desired behavior _4.9_

Average percentage of students not on desired behavior _16%_

FIGURE 8.16   Sample form for placheck observation.

something else. Examples of areas that might be evaluated are on-task behavior, active behavior, or effort in performing an activity. Once the results are determined, a goal can be set to increase the percentage of students involved in the desired observable behavior.

HOW TO DO IT

1. Design a form for recording the desired data. Figure 8.16 is a sample form for placheck observation and can be used to identify three different types of student performance. The data gathered in Figure 8.16 evaluate on-task and off-task student behavior.

2. Place eight to ten "beeps" at random intervals on a tape recording to signal when to conduct a placheck.

3. Have the observer scan the area in a specified and consistent direction from left to right each time the tape-recorded signal is heard. The class is scanned for seven to ten seconds while the observer records the number of students who are engaged in the desired behavior.

4. Convert the data to a percentage by dividing the total number of students into the number of unproductive students and then multiplying the result by 100. Four to six plachecks spaced throughout a class period will yield valid information about class conduct.

Instructional Feedback

Teacher _____   Observer _____

Class _____   Grade _____ Date and Time _____

Lesson focus _____   Comments _____

Starting time _____ Ending time _____   Length of lesson _____

Interactions unrelated to skill performance	+										
	−										
General instructional feedback	+										
	−										
Corrective instructional feedback											
First names											
Nonverbal feedback	+										
	−										

Ratio + to −/nonskill related _____

Ratio + to −/skill related _____

FIGURE 8.17 Sample form for feedback observation.

Instructional Feedback

Feedback given to students strongly affects the instructional presentation. It is possible to define and measure feedback so that meaningful goals for improvement can be established. The process of changing interaction patterns can create some discomfort, but ultimately it will pay dividends. The following areas can be evaluated to give direction for implementing useful change.

PRAISE AND CRITICISM

When students are involved in activity, feedback related to student performance should be administered. Feedback can be positive and constructive, or negative and critical in nature. It is easy to ask a student or peer to record the occurrence of praise and criticism. The results can be tallied and evaluated at the end of the day. The number of instances and the ratio of positive to negative comments are then calculated. With this information, goals can be set for increasing the number of comments per minute and modifying the ratio of positive to negative comments.

GENERAL VERSUS SPECIFIC FEEDBACK

Feedback to students can be general or specific. "Good job," "Way to go," and "Cut that out" are examples of general feedback. General feedback can be positive or negative; it does not specify the behavior being reinforced. In contrast, specific feedback identifies the student by name and reinforces an actual behavior; it also might be accompanied with a valuing statement. An example is, "Michelle, that's the way to keep your head tucked! I really like that forward roll!" To evaluate this area, general and specific feedback instances are tallied. Feedback can be positive or negative, and this distinction can be made as part of the tallying process.

The use of first names is important in personalizing feedback and directing it to the proper individual. The number of times first names are used can be totaled. Valuing statements can also be evaluated. Data gathered in these categories are divided by the length of the lesson (in minutes) to render a rate per minute. Figure 8.17 is an example of a form that can be used to tally behaviors described in this section.

CORRECTIVE INSTRUCTIONAL FEEDBACK

Effective teachers inspire students to achieve higher levels of performance. Part of this process involves giving performers meaningful corrective feedback. Corrective feedback focuses on improving the performance of the participant. Corrective instructional feedback should be specific so that performers know what they must correct. An example of corrective instructional feedback is, "You struck the soccer ball much too high. Try to strike it a little below center." This type of feedback tells the student what was incorrect about the skill attempt and how to perform the skill correctly.

NONVERBAL FEEDBACK

Much performance feedback is given nonverbally. Nonverbal communication is meaningful to students and may be equal to or more effective than verbal forms of communication. Examples of nonverbal feedback after a desired performance are a pat on the back, a wink, a smile, a nod of the head, the thumbs-up sign, and clapping the hands. Nonverbal feedback can also be negative: a frown, shaking the head in disapproval, walking away from a student, and laughing at a poor performance.

A student or another instructor can tally the number of positive and negative nonverbal behaviors exhibited by a teacher. Students are often better at evaluating the instructor in this domain, because they are keenly aware of the meaning of the instructor's nonverbal mannerisms.

HOW TO DO IT

1. Design a form to collect the data. Figure 8.17 is an example of such a form.
2. Audiotape a lesson for playback and evaluation at a later time.
3. Record the data to be analyzed. It is usually best to take one category at a time when beginning. For example, analyze the use of first names during the first playback, and then play the tape again to evaluate corrective feedback.
4. Convert the data to a form that can be generalized from lesson to lesson (i.e., rate per minute, rate per lesson, or ratio of positive to negative interactions).

Active Supervision and Student Contact

Effective instructors actively supervise students. Active supervision means moving among students and offering them personalized feedback. The number of times

an instructor becomes personally involved with a student can be counted. One-on-one feedback differs from total class interaction and offers insight into each student's behavior and concerns.

Allied to this area is the relationship between teacher movement and active supervision. Many instructors establish a particular area in the gymnasium where they feel most comfortable teaching. Before instruction begins, they move to this area. This consistent movement pattern can cause students to drift to different areas, depending on their feeling about the activity or the instructor. Students who like the instructor will move closer, whereas students who dislike the teacher or are uneasy about the activity may move as far away as possible. This results in a configuration in which the better performers are near the instructor and the students who may be somewhat less able are farther away and more difficult to observe.

The teacher can avoid these problems by moving throughout the teaching area. A way to evaluate movement is to divide the area into quadrants and tally the number of times you move into each quadrant. A tally in the quadrant is made when you speak to a student or the class as a whole. Do not make a tally for just passing through a quadrant. The amount of time spent in each quadrant can also be evaluated. Try to spend similar amounts of time in each area. When students cannot predict where you will be next, they have a greater tendency to remain on-task.

Movement related to the use of lesson time can be determined by the amount of time the teacher stays in a quadrant. The length of time a teacher stays in a quadrant can be recorded in a corresponding location on the form. At the end of the lesson, the amount of time the teacher has spent in each quadrant can then be analyzed. Another technique is to code the type of behavior that occurs each time the instructor moves into a new quadrant. For example, an "M" might signify management activity, an "I" instructional activity, and a "P" practice time. This approach reveals the location and amount of time spent on each behavior.

HOW TO DO IT

1. Develop a coding form similar to the one in Figure 8.18.
2. Ask a nonparticipating student or a colleague to record the desired data on active supervision. An alternative is to videotape the lesson and evaluate it at a later time.
3. Evaluate the data by calculating the number of moves per lesson, and the number of moves during instruction, management, and practice.

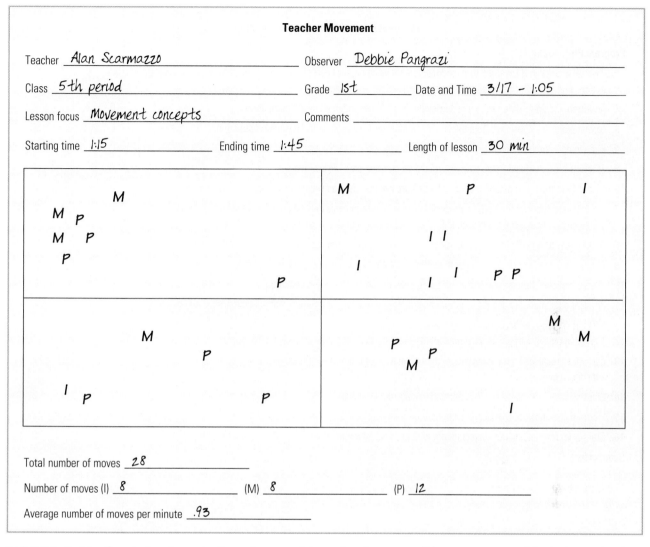

FIGURE 8.18 Sample form for evaluating active supervision and student contact (M = management activity, I = instructional activity, P = practice time).

EVALUATING YOUR PROGRAM

Your program should be evaluated regularly to ensure that it is achieving stated program goals. Evaluation instruments reflect program philosophy and objectives of individual districts. Figure 8.19 (pages 172–174) is a sample instrument that may be adapted for your own use, depending on district needs and goals. This instrument can be used to expose serious program deficiencies and operational difficulties. The results, including program strengths and weaknesses, can be shared with administrators or used by teachers to evaluate a program they have developed. The instrument can also be used to compare programs or to identify effective programs.

In the sample instrument, evaluative statements are written as a set of standards that, when met, ensure an effective program. The four areas listed for evaluation are: (1) philosophy of the program; (2) instructional procedures; (3) curricular offerings; and (4) facilities, equipment, and supplies. The entire instrument can be used, or any of the four areas can be evaluated individually. Read each statement, determine the extent to which there is compliance with the accepted standard, and circle the appropriate scale score. Comments can be made at the end of each section. Rate and assign points on the following basis: A rating of 2 represents full compliance (the program meets the standard fully without deficiencies), 1 represents partial compliance with room for improvement, and 0 represents no compliance (the deficiency is serious and a detriment to an effective program).

Physical Education Program Evaluation

Program Philosophy

1. Physical education is regarded by the administration as an integral part of the total curriculum and is dedicated to the same curricular goal, the fullest possible development of each pupil for living in a democracy.	0	1	2
2. A written and up-to-date sequential curriculum is available and used by all instructors.	0	1	2
3. Lesson plans are developed from the course of study and are used as the basis for instruction.	0	1	2
4. A meaningful progression of activities is evident between developmental levels.	0	1	2
5. Students are scheduled in the physical education program on a regular basis.	0	1	2
6. Music, field trips, and extracurricular activities are not accepted as substitutes for physical education.	0	1	2
7. Students are excused from physical education on a long-term basis only when they can submit a physician's statement indicating the medical condition and the duration of the excuse.	0	1	2
8. Appropriate arrangements are made for students with medical, religious, or temporary health excuses.	0	1	2
9. A nurse, teacher, or staff member with suitable first aid training is available in case of accident.	0	1	2
10. The budget specified for physical education equipment and supplies is adequate.	0	1	2
11. Physical education demonstration programs are offered regularly for purposes of public relations and general information.	0	1	2
12. The minimum amount per class of time allotted for physical education activity is 30 minutes.	0	1	2
13. Each class receives physical education instruction a minimum of three times per week, excluding recess and supervised play.	0	1	2
14. Class sizes are the same as those allotted to classroom teachers.	0	1	2
15. Program activities are coeducational in nature.	0	1	2
16. Classroom teachers do not keep students from physical education classes for disciplinary reasons.	0	1	2

Comments:

Instructional Procedures

1. The teacher is prepared prior to the class. A written set of instructional activities is carried into the lesson on a small note card.	0	1	2
2. Equipment is correctly arranged around the perimeter of the activity area prior to class.	0	1	2
3. Proper procedures are used for acquiring and putting away equipment.	0	1	2
4. The instructor constantly moves and repositions him-/herself so all students are in the line of sight. Instruction is conducted from different areas in the activity area.	0	1	2
5. Children in need receive special help during the lesson. The level of instruction is geared to the needs of students who lack skill.	0	1	2
6. Students understand why they are practicing skills.	0	1	2
7. There is an adequate level of teacher enthusiasm and energy. Teacher movement and personal involvement are evident.	0	1	2
8. Positive encouragement is given to all students. Youngsters are encouraged to do their best.	0	1	2
9. Students are directed to be responsible for their learning and personal behavior. Content instruction is stopped when there is a need to improve behavioral skills.	0	1	2

FIGURE 8.19 Sample evaluation form for physical education program (0 = no compliance; 1 = partial compliance; 2 = full compliance).

10. Instruction is focused on developing quality skills rather than on changing activities often in an attempt to keep students on-task. Adequate opportunity is given for repetition and refinement of skills.	0	1	2
11. Closure of the lesson is a positive experience. Students are encouraged to evaluate their level of responsibility. The pitfall of nagging students about their poor class performance is avoided.	0	1	2
12. Discipline and management problems are handled effectively. The self-esteem of students is preserved during behavior correction episodes.	0	1	2
13. Disciplinary measures in physical education instruction do not include physical punishment.	0	1	2
14. Procedures for dealing with accidents, including administration of first aid, reporting, and follow-up, are in written form.	0	1	2
15. Knowledge of liability concerns related to physical education instruction and programming is evident.	0	1	2
16. Facilities, equipment, and activity areas that could be liabilities are reported in writing to appropriate administrators.	0	1	2
17. Bulletin boards, charts, pictures, and other visual materials are posted and used in the instructional process.	0	1	2
18. Teaching aids such as instructional signs, videotapes, and posters are used to enrich and supplement instruction.	0	1	2

Comments:

Curricular Offerings

1. The physical education program provides learning experiences to help each child attain the following:			
a. Refinement of motor skills and movement competence	0	1	2
b. Development of lifestyle habits that foster wellness	0	1	2
c. Ability to monitor and maintain physical activity	0	1	2
d. Understanding and applying human movement principles	0	1	2
e. Enjoyment of a lifetime of physical activity	0	1	2
f. Acquisition of quality social skills	0	1	2
g. Ability to demonstrate responsible behavior	0	1	2
2. All children are considered important and the program is adjusted to suit the maturity and skill levels of youngsters.	0	1	2
3. Each lesson has a portion of time (seven to ten minutes) devoted to physical fitness activities.	0	1	2
4. The physical education program emphasizes and allocates enough time at the appropriate grade level for each of the following areas:			
a. Educational movement concepts	0	1	2
b. Fundamental skills, including locomotor, nonlocomotor, manipulative, and specialized skills	0	1	2
c. Rhythmic activities	0	1	2
d. Gymnastics activities	0	1	2
e. Games and relays	0	1	2
f. Sports and lead-up activities	0	1	2
5. Both indoor and outdoor teaching stations are available for physical education instruction.	0	1	2
6. Units of instruction last no longer than three weeks and include skill instruction.	0	1	2

Comments:

FIGURE 8.19   (continued)

Facilities, Equipment, and Supplies	0	1	2
1. Facilities include teaching stations that allow all students a minimum of three classes per week.	0	1	2
2. Outdoor facilities include the following:	0	1	2
a. A physical education instructional area that is isolated from playground activities	0	1	2
b. Areas where different age groups can play without interference from each other	0	1	2
c. Areas for court games	0	1	2
d. Cement or asphalt spaces marked with a variety of game patterns	0	1	2
e. Backstops and goals for softball, soccer, and basketball	0	1	2
f. Suitable fencing for safety and control	0	1	2
g. Outdoor playground equipment, including climbing apparatus, turning bars, and tetherball areas	0	1	2
3. The outdoor area is free from rocks, sprinkler heads, and other hazards that might cause injury.			
4. Indoor facilities meet the following standards:	0	1	2
a. Clean, sanitary, and free from hazards	0	1	2
b. Well lighted, well ventilated, heated, cooled, and treated for proper acoustics	0	1	2
c. Surfaced with a nonslip finish and painted game area lines	0	1	2
5. There is periodic inspection of all facilities and equipment, both indoor and outdoor, and a written report is filed with appropriate administrators.	0	1	2
6. Storage facilities are adequate for supplies and portable equipment.	0	1	2
7. An office that is located near the instruction area is provided for the physical education instructor.			
8. Basic supplies are sufficient in the following areas:	0	1	2
a. Manipulative equipment (one piece for each child): fleece balls, small balls, beanbags, wands, hoops, and jump ropes	0	1	2
b. Sport and game balls: softballs, footballs, volleyballs, basketballs, soccer balls, floor hockey sticks and pucks, tetherballs, and cageballs in sufficient numbers	0	1	2
c. Sport and game supplies: cones, pinnies, track and field standards, jumping pits, and hurdles	0	1	2
d. Testing equipment: measuring tapes, stopwatches, calipers to measure skinfold thickness, and specialized apparatus	0	1	2
9. Sufficient materials are available for a varied rhythmic program: CD/tape player, tapes and CDs, tom-toms, and tambourines.			
10. Capital-outlay items for the indoor facility include the following:	0	1	2
a. Minimum of six tumbling mats (four by eight feet or larger)	0	1	2
b. Individual mats (one per student)	0	1	2
c. Sufficient climbing apparatus so that at least one-half of the class can be active at one time. Apparatus should include wall bars, chinning bars, horizontal bars, climbing ropes on tracks, and ladders.	0	1	2
d. Balance-beam benches (at least six)	0	1	2
e. Jumping boxes (at least eight)	0	1	2
f. Basketball goals, volleyball nets, hockey goals	0	1	2
g. Equipment carts (at least two)			

Comments:

F I G U R E 8 . 1 9   (continued)

8

REFLECTION AND REVIEW QUESTIONS

How and Why

1. In a music or art class, would you want to be evaluated based on the product or the process? Why? How does this relate to your grading as a physical education teacher?

2. How is giving a child "on the spot" feedback regarding performance a form of evaluation?

3. How are you evaluated as a college student? Do you feel you are evaluated fairly? Explain your answer.

4. How can progress reports be more effective tools for communicating with parents?

5. Would you rather self-evaluate a lesson using videotape or have a peer evaluate you during the lesson? Why?

6. Why might the ability to be self-critical be important for physical education teachers and physical education curriculum designers?

Content Review

1. Discuss the significance of focusing on the process in physical education. Include comments about how physical education and other academic areas differ with respect to evaluation.

2. Identify and describe several methods of assessing performance outcomes.

3. Describe the advantages and disadvantages of a grading system.

4. State the steps to implementing a grading system.

5. Explain how teachers can use self-evaluation.

6. Identify and explain four areas of teaching that can be evaluated. Within your comments, describe how to assess the specific areas.

7. List the elements of a physical education program evaluation form.

FOR MORE INFORMATION

References and Suggested Readings

Block, M. E., Lieberman, L. J., & Connor-Kuntz, F. (1998). Authentic assessment in adapted physical education. *Journal of Physical Education, Recreation, and Dance,* 69(3), 48–55.

Brustad, R. J. (1995). Who will go out and play? Parental and psychological influences on children's attraction to physical activity. *Pediatric Exercise Science,* 5, 210–223.

Brustad, R. J. (1996). Attraction to physical activity in urban schoolchildren: Parental socialization and gender influences. *Research Quarterly for Exercise and Sport,* 67, 316–323.

Chepko, S., & Arnold, R. K. (Eds.). (2000). *Guidelines for physical education programs: Grades K–12 standards, objectives, and assessments.* Boston: Allyn and Bacon.

Cooper Institute. (2004). *Fitnessgram/Activitygram test administration manual.* M. Meredith & G. Welk (Eds.). 3rd ed. Champaign, IL: Human Kinetics.

Darst, P. W., Zakrajsek, D. B., & Mancini, V. H. (1989). *Analyzing physical education and sport instruction.* 2nd ed. Champaign, IL: Human Kinetics.

Johnson, D. W., Johnson, R. T., & Holubec, E. J. (1990). *Circles of learning: Cooperation in the classroom.* Edina, MN: Interaction.

Lacy, A., & Hastad, D. (2003). *Measurement and evaluation in physical education and exercise science.* 4th ed. San Francisco: Benjamin Cummings.

Lambert, L. T. (1999). *Standards-based assessment of student learning: A comprehensive approach.* Reston, VA: National Association for Sport and Physical Education.

Lund, J. (1993). The role of accountability and assessment in physical education. In J. Rink (Ed.), *Critical crossroads: Middle secondary school physical education* (pp. 102–112). Reston, VA: National Association for Sport and Physical Education.

Matanin, M., & Tannehill, D. (1994). Assessment and grading in physical education. *Journal of Teaching in Physical Education,* 13, 395–405.

Safrit, M. J., & Wood, T. (1995). *Introduction to measurement in physical education and exercise science.* 3rd ed. Boston: McGraw Hill.

Siedentop, D., & Tannehill, D. (2000). *Developing teaching skills in physical education.* 4th ed. Mountain View, CA: Mayfield Publishing Co.

Strand, B. N., & Wilson, R. (1993). *Assessing sport skills.* Champaign, IL: Human Kinetics.

Zhu, W., Safrit, M. J., & Cohen, A. (1999). *FitSmart test user manual.* Champaign, IL: Human Kinetics.

Websites

FitnessGram/ActivityGram
www.fitnessgram.net

Physical Education Assessment Ideas and Grading Information
www.pecentral.org/assessment/assessment.html
www.pelinks4u.org
www.pe4life.org

President's Council on Physical Fitness and Sports
www.fitness.gov
www.presidentschallenge.org

Self-Assessment/Reflection
www.utexas.edu/academic/cte/getfeedback
www.coe.ufl.edu/school/proteach/pathwiselesson/pathwise.htm

Video as an Assessment Tool
http://teaching.berkeley.edu/bgd/videotape.html

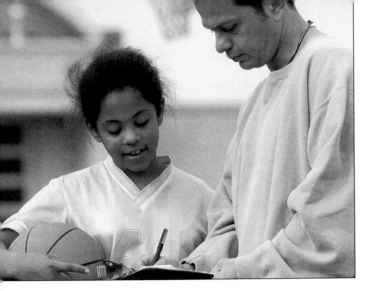

9

Legal Liability, Supervision, and Safety

ESSENTIAL COMPONENTS OF QUALITY PROGRAMS

I. Organized around content standards

▶ **II. Student-centered and developmentally appropriate**

III. Physical activity and motor skill development form the core of the program

IV. Teaches management skills and self-discipline

V. Promotes inclusion of all students

VI. Focuses on process over product

VII. Promotes lifetime personal health and wellness

VIII. Teaches cooperation and responsibility and promotes sensitivity to diversity

NATIONAL STANDARDS FOR PHYSICAL EDUCATION*

1. Demonstrates competency in motor skills and movement patterns needed to perform a variety of physical activities.

2. Demonstrates understanding of movement concepts, principles, and tactics as they apply to the learning and performance of physical activities.

3. Participates regularly in physical activity.

4. Achieves and maintains a health-enhancing level of physical fitness.

▶ **5. Exhibits responsible personal and social behavior that respects self and others in physical activity.**

6. Values physical activity for health, enjoyment, challenge, self-expression, and/or social interaction.

*National Association for Sport and Physical Education (NASPE), 2004.

SUMMARY

This chapter explains the various legal terms and situations associated with physical education and describes instructional and administrative procedures common to the responsible and prudent conduct of the physical education program. It is a teacher's legal responsibility to create a safe environment in which risk and the opportunity for injury are minimized and to provide a standard of care that any reasonable and prudent professional with similar training would apply under the given circumstances. Safety instruction is designed to prevent accidents and should be included in lesson plans to ensure coverage. A comprehensive safety checklist is included to be sure that beginning teachers understand how to establish an accident-free environment.

OUTCOMES

- Define *tort, negligence, liability, malfeasance, misfeasance, nonfeasance,* and other terms common to legal suits brought against educators.

- List major points that must be established in order to determine negligence on the part of the teacher.

- Explain how to examine all activities, equipment, and facilities for possible hazards and sources of accidents.

- Identify common defenses against negligence.

- Describe supervisory responsibilities expected of all teachers.

- List guidelines for the proper supervision of instruction, equipment, and facilities.

- Describe aspects of sport programs that often give rise to lawsuits.

- Understand how to ensure safety, focusing on prevention.

- Outline an emergency care plan.

School district personnel, including teaching and nonteaching members, are obligated to exercise ordinary care for the safety of students. This duty is manifested as the ability to anticipate reasonably foreseeable dangers and the responsibility to take necessary precautions to prevent problems from occurring. Failure to do so may cause the district to be the target of lawsuits.

Compared with other subject matter areas, physical education is particularly vulnerable to accidents and resultant injuries. More than 50 percent of all accidents in the school setting occur on the playground and in the gymnasium. Even though schools cannot be held financially accountable for costs associated with treatment of injuries, they can be forced to pay these expenses if the injured party sues and wins judgment. Legal suits are conducted under respective state statutes. Principles underlying legal action are similar, but certain regulations and procedures vary among states. You should acquire a copy of the legal liability policy for your district. Districts usually have a written definition of situations in which teachers can be held liable.

All students have the right to freedom from injury caused by others or due to participation in a program. Courts have ruled that teachers have the duty to protect their students from harm. Teachers must offer a standard of care that any reasonable and prudent professional with similar training would apply under the given circumstances. A teacher is required to exercise the teaching skill, discretion, and knowledge that members of the profession in good standing normally possess in similar situations. Lawsuits usually occur when citizens believe that this standard of care was not exercised.

Liability is the responsibility to perform a duty to a particular group. It is an obligation to perform in a particular way that is required by law and enforced by court action. Teachers are bound by contract to carry out their duties in a reasonable and prudent manner. Liability is always a legal matter. Before one can be held liable, it must be proved in a court of law that negligence occurred.

TORTS

In education, a *tort* is concerned with the teacher-student relationship and is a legal wrong that results in direct or indirect injury to another individual or to property. *Black's Law Dictionary* (Garner, 1999) defines a tort as

> a private or civil wrong or injury, other than breach of contract, for which the court will provide a remedy in the form of an action for damages. Three elements of every tort action are: existence of legal duty from defendant to plaintiff, breach of duty, and damage as proximate result.

As the result of a tort, the court can give a monetary reward for damages that occurred. The court can also give a monetary reward for punitive damages if a breach of duty can be established. Usually, the court rewards the offended individual for damages that occurred due to the negligence of the instructor or other responsible individual. Punitive damages are much less common.

NEGLIGENCE AND LIABILITY

Liability is usually concerned with a breach of duty through negligence. A situation that gave rise to injury can be examined by lawyers to establish if liability can be determined. Four major points must be examined to decide if a teacher is negligent.

Determination of Liability

1. *Duty.* The first point considered is that of duty owed to the participants. Did the school or teacher owe students a duty of care that implies conforming to certain standards of conduct? When examining duty or breach of duty, the court looks at reasonable care that a member of the profession in good standing would provide. In other words, to determine a reasonable standard, the court uses the conduct of other teachers as a standard for comparison.

2. *Breach of duty.* A teacher must commit a breach of duty by failing to conform to the required duty. After it is established that a duty was required, it must be proved that such duty was not performed. Two situations are possible: (a) the teacher did something that was not supposed to be done (for example, putting boxing gloves on students to resolve their differences), or (b) the teacher did not do something that should have been done (for example, failing to teach an activity using proper progressions).

3. *Proximate cause.* The failure of the teacher to conform to the required standard must be the proximate cause of the resulting injury. It must be proved that the injury was caused by the teacher's breach of duty. It is not enough to prove simply that a breach of duty occurred. It must simultaneously be shown that the injury was a direct result of the teacher's failure to provide a reasonable standard of care. The plaintiff's expert will try to convince the court that there was a requisite standard that was not met. In contrast, the defendant's expert will try to show that the teacher met the proper standard of care.

4. *Damages.* Actual harm must occur if liability is to be established. If no injury or harm occurs, there is no liability. It must be proved that the injured party

is entitled to compensatory damages for financial loss or physical discomfort. Actual damages can be physical, emotional, or financial, but the court will only award financial remuneration.

Foreseeability

A key to the issue of negligence is foreseeability. Courts expect that a trained professional is able to foresee potentially harmful situations. Was it possible for the teacher to predict and anticipate the danger of the harmful act or situation and to take appropriate measures to prevent it from occurring? If the injured party can prove that the teacher should have foreseen the danger involved in an activity or situation (even in part), the teacher will be found negligent for failing to act in a reasonable and prudent manner. This points out the necessity of examining all activities, equipment, and facilities for possible hazards and sources of accident.

> ### A Case of Foreseeability?
>
> A common game (unfortunately) in many school settings is bombardment, or dodgeball. During the game, a student is hit in the eye by a ball and loses vision in that eye. Was this a foreseeable accident that could have been prevented? Were the balls being used capable of inflicting severe injury? Were students aware of rules that might have prevented this injury? Were the abilities of the students somewhat equal, or were some capable of throwing with such velocity that injury was predictable? Were all students forced to play the game? These questions would likely be considered in court in an attempt to prove that the teacher should have been able to predict the overly dangerous situation.

TYPES OF NEGLIGENCE

Negligence is defined by the courts as conduct that falls below a standard of care established to protect others from unreasonable risk or harm. Several types of negligence can be categorized.

Malfeasance

Malfeasance occurs when a teacher does something improper by committing an act that is unlawful and wrongful, with no legal basis (often referred to as an *act of commission*). Malfeasance can be illustrated by the following incident: A male student has misbehaved on numerous occasions. In desperation, the teacher gives the student a choice of punishment—a severe spanking in front of the class or running many laps around the field. The student chooses the former and suffers physical and emotional damage. Even though the student was given a choice whereby he could have avoided the paddling, the teacher is still liable for any physical or emotional harm caused.

Misfeasance

Misfeasance occurs when a teacher follows proper procedures but does not perform according to the required standard of conduct. Misfeasance is based on performance of the proper action, but not up to the required standard. It is usually the subpar performance of an act that might otherwise have been lawfully done. An example would be a teacher's offering to spot a student during a tumbling routine and then not doing the spotting properly. If the student is injured due to a faulty spot, the teacher can be held liable.

Nonfeasance

Nonfeasance is based on lack of action in carrying out a duty. This is usually an *act of omission*: The teacher knew the proper procedures but failed to follow them. Teachers can be found negligent if they act or fail to act. Understanding and carrying out proper procedures and duties in a manner befitting members of the profession are essential. In contrast to the misfeasance example, nonfeasance occurs when a teacher knows that it is necessary to spot certain gymnastic routines but fails to do so. Courts expect teachers to behave with more skill and insight than parents do (Strickland, Phillip, & Phillips, 1976). Teachers are expected to behave with greater competency because they have been educated to give students a higher standard of professional care than have parents.

> ### Does Student Size Make a Difference?
>
> Students are playing a game of Diagonal Soccer. When their numbers are called, three students from each team run to the center to try and get the ball first and gain scoring advantage. One of the students is a small student who weighs about 70 pounds. A student on the other team is mature and weighs nearly 160 pounds. As they approach the ball, the larger student basically runs over the smaller student, knocking him down and causing a head injury. Within two weeks, the student has a seizure and the parents plan to sue. Should the students have been matched for size? Should they have been matched for maturity and ability? Does gender make a difference? Could the game have been modified to avoid this injury? Is the teacher guilty of malfeasance?

Contributory Negligence

The situation is different when the injured student is partially or wholly at fault. Students are expected to exercise sensible care and to follow directions or regulations designed to protect them from injury. Improper behavior by the injured party that causes the accident is usually ruled to be *contributory negligence,* because the injured party contributed to the resulting harm. This responsibility is directly related to the maturity, ability, and experience of the child. For example, most states have laws specifying that a child under seven years of age is incapable of contributory negligence (Baley & Matthews, 1988).

I Told Them, But They Did It Anyway!

A physical education instructor teaching a class of fourth-grade students has thorough softball hitting and related safety rules and has marked out restraining lines that are easy for students to see. During class, students are engaged in a number of softball stations. One of the students runs through the restricted area and is hit by an aluminum baseball bat. Who is to blame? Was the student old enough to know better? Were there too many stations being taught at the same time? Should the teacher have foreseen that an accident might happen even if students were prewarned? Are aluminum or wood bats an appropriate choice for physical education classes? Is there an assumption of risk in all physical education activities causing these situations to happen from time to time?

Comparative or Shared Negligence

Under the doctrine of comparative negligence, the injured party can recover only if found to be less negligent than the defendant (the teacher). Where statutes apply, the amount of recovery is generally reduced in proportion to the injured party's participation in the circumstances leading to the injury.

COMMON DEFENSES AGAINST NEGLIGENCE

Negligence must be proved in a court of law. Many times, teachers are negligent in carrying out their duties, yet the injured party does not take the case to court. If a teacher is sued, some of the following defenses are used in an attempt to show that the teacher's action was not the primary cause of the accident.

Act of God

The act of God defense places the cause of injury on forces beyond the control of the teacher or the school. The defense is made that it was impossible to predict an unsafe condition, but through an act of God, the injury occurred. Typical acts would be a gust of wind that blew over a volleyball standard or a cloudburst of rain that made a surface slick. The act of God defense can be used only in cases in which the injury still would have occurred even if reasonable and prudent action had been taken.

Proximate Cause

This defense attempts to prove that the accident was not caused by the negligence of the teacher. There must be a close relationship between the breach of duty by the teacher and the injury. This is a common defense in cases dealing with proper supervision. Imagine that a student is participating in an activity supervised by a teacher. When the teacher leaves the playing area to get a cup of coffee, the student is injured. The defense lawyer will try to show that the accident would have occurred regardless of the teacher's location.

Assumption of Risk

Clearly, physical education is a high-risk activity when compared with most other curriculum areas. The participant assumes the risk accompanying the activity when choosing to be part of that activity. The assumption of risk defense is seldom used by physical education teachers because students are not often allowed to choose to participate or not participate. An instructor for an elective program who allows students to choose desired units of instruction might find this a better defense than one who teaches a totally required program. Athletic and sport club participation is by choice, and players must assume a greater risk in activities such as football and gymnastics.

Contributory Negligence

Contributory negligence is often used by the defense in an attempt to convince the court that the injured party acted in a manner that was abnormal. In other words, the injured individual did not act in a manner that was typical of students of similar age and maturity. The defense attempts to demonstrate that the activity or equipment in question had been used for years with no record of accident. A case is made based on the manner of presentation—how students were taught to act in a safe manner—and on the premise that the injured student acted outside the parameters of safe conduct. A key point in this defense is whether the activity was suitable for the age and maturity level of the participants.

AREAS OF RESPONSIBILITY

A two-tiered approach for analyzing injuries is useful for determining responsibility. The first tier includes duties the administration must assume in support of the program. The second tier defines duties of the instructor or staff member charged with teaching or supervising students. Each party has a role to fill, but some overlap occurs. The following example illustrates the differences:

A student is hurt while performing a tumbling stunt. A lawsuit ensues, charging the teacher with negligence for not following safe procedures. The administration could also be included in the suit, being charged with negligence for hiring an incompetent (not qualified) instructor. Two levels of responsibility should be considered when delegating responsibility because:

1. They identify different functions and responsibilities of the teaching staff and administration.

2. They provide a framework for reducing injuries and improving safety procedures.

3. They provide perspective for following legal precedents.

For the responsibilities that are described in the following sections, both administrative and instructional duties are presented.

Supervision

All activities in a school setting must be supervised, including recess, lunchtimes, and field trips. The responsibilities of the school are critical if supervision is to function properly.

ADMINISTRATION

Two levels are identified in supervision: general and specific. General supervision (for example, playground duty) refers to broad coverage when students are not under direct control of a teacher or a designated individual. A plan of supervision should be made, designating the areas to be covered and including where and how the supervisor should rotate. This plan, kept in the principal's office, should cover rules of conduct governing student behavior. Rules should be posted prominently on bulletin boards, especially in classrooms. In addition to the plan, administrators must select qualified personnel, provide necessary training, and monitor the plan properly.

The general supervisor is concerned primarily with student behavior, focusing on the student's right to a relaxing recreational experience. Supervisors should observe the area, looking for breaches of discipline, particularly when an individual or group "picks on" another youngster. The supervisor needs to look for protruding sprinkler heads, broken glass, and debris on the play area. If it becomes necessary to leave the area, a qualified substitute must be found to prevent the area from being unsupervised.

INSTRUCTIONAL STAFF

General supervision is necessary during recess, before and after school, during lunch hour break, and during certain other sessions when instruction is not offered. The supervisor should know the school's plan for supervision as well as the emergency care procedures to follow in case of an accident. Supervision is a positive act that requires the supervisor to be actively involved and moving throughout the area. The number of supervisors should be determined by the type of activity, the size of the area, and the number and age of the students.

Specific supervision requires the instructor to be with a certain group of students (a class). An example is spotting students who are performing challenging gymnastic activities. If certain pieces of apparatus require special care and proper use, the teacher should post rules and regulations near the apparatus (for upper-grade children). Students should be made aware of the rules and should receive appropriate instruction and guidance in applying the rules. When rules are modified, they should be rewritten in proper form. There is no substitute for documentation when the need to defend policies and approaches arises.

When teaching, arrange and teach the class so that all students are in view. This implies supervising from the perimeter of the area. If you are at the center of the student group with many students behind you, it will be impossible to supervise a class safely and effectively. Equipment and apparatus should not go unsupervised at any time when left accessible to students in the area. An example is leaving equipment on the playing field between classes. If other students in the area have easy access to the equipment, they may use it in an unsafe manner, and the teacher can be found liable if an injury occurs.

Do not agree to supervise activities for which you are unqualified to anticipate possible hazards. If this situation arises, send a written memo to the department head or principal stating this lack of insight and qualification. Maintain a copy for your files.

Merriman (1993) offers five recommendations to ensure that adequate supervision occurs:

1. The supervisor must be in the immediate vicinity (within sight and hearing of the students).

2. If required to leave, the supervisor must have an adequate replacement before departing. Adequate replacements do not include paraprofessionals, student teachers, custodial help, or untrained teachers.

3. Supervision procedures must be preplanned and incorporated into daily lessons.

4. Supervision procedures should include what to observe and listen for, where to stand for the most effective view, and what to do if a problem arises.

5. Supervision requires that age, maturity, and skill ability of participants always be considered, as must be the inherent risk of the activity.

I Know We Had a Supervisor Out There!

At lunch, students have 20 minutes of free time to play on the activity field or in the gymnasium. One teacher is assigned to supervise the students on the playing field and one supervises the gym. The playing field is large and there is an injury opposite where the teacher is standing. The teacher hustles to the aid of the student. While the teacher is attending the student, a fight breaks out and goes unnoticed by the teacher because she is busy with the injured student. A smaller student is severely beaten by a larger student. Is the teacher liable because she did not see the fight? Can one teacher adequately supervise a playground full of students? Is the administrator the one who is responsible because only one teacher was assigned to supervise? Did the teacher have a way to communicate with the front office to ask for additional help?

Instruction

Instructional responsibility rests primarily with the teacher, but administrative personnel have certain defined functions as well.

ADMINISTRATION

The administration should review and approve the curricular plan. The curriculum should be reviewed regularly to ensure that it is current and updated. Be sure that activities included in the curriculum are based on contributions they make to the growth and development of youngsters. It makes little sense in a court of law to say that an activity was included "for the fun of it" or "because students liked it." Instead, make sure that activities in the curriculum meet program objectives.

Administrators are obligated to support the program with adequate finances. The principal and higher administrators should visit the program periodically. Familiarity with program content and operation obviates the possibility that practices occur without adequate administrative supervision.

INSTRUCTIONAL STAFF

With regard to instruction, teachers have a duty to protect students from unreasonable physical or mental harm. This includes avoiding any acts or omissions that might cause such harm. Teachers are educated, experienced, and skilled in physical education and must be able to foresee situations that could be harmful.

The major area of concern involving instruction is whether all students receive adequate instruction before or during activity participation. Adequate instruction means (1) teaching children how to perform activities correctly and use equipment and apparatus properly, and (2) teaching youngsters necessary safety precautions. If instructions are given, they must be correct and understandable and include proper technique, or the instructor can be held liable. The risk involved in an activity must be communicated to the learner.

The ages and maturity levels of students play an important role in the selection of activities. Younger students require more care, instructions that are easy to comprehend, and clear restrictions in the name of safety. Some students have a lack of appropriate fear, and the teacher must be aware of this when discussing safety factors. A very young child may have little concern about performing a high-risk activity if an instructor is nearby. This places much responsibility on the teacher to give adequate instruction and supervision.

Careful planning is a necessity. Written curriculum guides and lesson plans can offer a well-prepared approach that withstands scrutiny and examination by other teachers and administrators. Written lesson plans should include proper sequence and progression of skill. Teachers are on defensible grounds if they can show that the progression of activities was based on presentations designed by experts and was followed carefully during the teaching act. District and state guidelines enforcing instructional sequences and restricted activities should be checked closely.

Proper instruction demands that students not be forced to participate. If a youngster is required to perform an activity unwillingly, you may be open to a lawsuit. In a lawsuit dealing with stunts and tumbling (Appenzeller, 1970), the court held the teacher liable when a student claimed that she was not given adequate instruction in how to perform a stunt called a "roll over two." The teacher was held liable because the student claimed she was forced to try the stunt before adequate instruction was offered. Gymnastics and tumbling are areas in which lawsuits are frequent due to a lack of adequate instruction. Posting the proper sequence of skills and lead-up activities may be useful to ensure that they have been presented properly. Tread the line carefully

The Need for a Curriculum and Lesson Plan

A former gymnast who is now an elementary school physical education teacher decides to teach her classes gymnastics. The school does not have a curriculum guide, and the teacher does not write lesson plans. The teacher decides to have students try a headspring over a tumbling mat. A student is seriously hurt (severe neck injury that causes paralysis) and the parents of the student file a 1.5 million dollar lawsuit. What argument would you use to defend yourself in this situation? Would it help if you could say that gymnastics was part of the school curriculum? What if the plaintiff's lawyer brings in an expert witness who says the instructional sequence was inappropriate? Can you show your written lesson plan that delineates the proper instructional sequence based on what expert instructors recommend? Can you be an expert in every activity you teach, or do you need to rely on other experts for the proper sequence of activities to teach?

between helpful encouragement and forcing students to try new activities.

The following points help ensure safe instruction:

1. Sequence all activities in units of instruction and develop written lesson plans. Problems occur when snap judgments are made under the daily pressure and strain of teaching.

2. Scrutinize high-risk activities to ensure that all safety procedures have been implemented. If in doubt, discuss the activities with experienced teachers and administrators.

3. Make sure activities used in the curriculum are within the developmental limits of the students. Since the range of maturity and development of youngsters in a class is usually wide, activities may be beyond the ability level of some students.

4. When students' grades are based on the number of activities in which they participate, causing some students to feel forced to try all activities, make it clear to students that the choice to participate belongs to them. When they are afraid of getting hurt, they can elect not to perform an activity.

5. Include in written lesson plans necessary safety equipment. The lesson plan should detail how equipment should be arranged, how the mats should be placed, and where the instructor will carry out supervision.

6. If a student claims injury or brings a note from parents asking that the student not participate in physical activity, honor the request. Excuses are almost always given at the start of the period, when the teacher is busy with many other duties (such as getting equipment ready, taking roll, and opening lockers). It is difficult to make a thoughtful judgment during this time. The school nurse is qualified to make these judgments when they relate to health and should be expected to make such decisions. If the excuses continue over a long period of time, the teacher or nurse should schedule a conference with the parents to rectify the situation.

7. Make sure activities included in the instructional process are in line with the available equipment and facilities. An example is the amount of space available. If a soccer lead-up activity is brought indoors because of inclement weather, it may no longer be a safe and appropriate activity.

8. If spotting is required for safe completion of activities, make sure the instructor or trained students always perform the spotting. Teaching students how to spot is as important as teaching them physical skills. Safe conduct is learned.

9. If students are working independently at stations, distribute carefully constructed and written task cards to help eliminate unsafe practices.

10. Have a written emergency care plan posted in the gymnasium. This plan should be approved by health care professionals and should be followed to the letter when an injury occurs.

For teachers who incorporate punishment as a part of the instructional process, the consequences of its use should be examined carefully before implementing it. Physical punishment that brings about permanent or long-lasting damage is certainly indefensible. The punishment used must be in line with the physical maturity and health of the student involved. A teacher's practice of having students perform laps when they have misbehaved might go unchallenged for years. However, what if an asthmatic student or a student with congenital heart disease is asked to run and suffers injury or illness? What if the student is running unsupervised and is injured from a fall or suffers heat exhaustion? In these examples, defending such punitive practices would be difficult. Making students perform physical activity for misbehavior is indefensible under any circumstance. If a child is injured while performing physical punishment, teachers are usually found liable and held responsible for the injury.

Running for Punishment—The Right Choice?

Youngsters are participating in a physical education class and are unruly. They are talking when they shouldn't and are generally not cooperating. The teacher, in a fit of controlled anger, tells two students to go run laps around a large field until they decide to behave. It is a hot fall day and after 15 minutes of running, one of the students falls and goes into convulsions on the far side of the field (a third of a mile away from the teacher). The teacher doesn't see the child go down until a student tells him about it. Is this malfeasance? Is running an acceptable choice for punishment? Were the weather conditions considered? Did the youth have some preexisting health condition? Were the students under the watchful eye of the teacher or out of sight? Could you defend yourself in this situation?

EQUIPMENT AND FACILITIES

School responsibility for equipment and facilities is required for both noninstructional and class use.

Administration

The principal and the custodian should oversee the fields and playground equipment that are used for recess and outside activities. Students should be instructed to report broken and unsafe equipment, as well as hazards (glass, cans, rocks), to the principal's office. If equipment is faulty, it should be removed from the area. A regular inspection of equipment and facilities, preferably by the physical education specialist, should be instituted, perhaps weekly. If a specialist is not employed, the inspection will have to be performed by the principal or the custodian. Results of the inspection should be filed with the school district safety committee. Replacement of sawdust, sand, or other shock-absorbing material should be done regularly. Administrators should have a written checklist of equipment and apparatus for the purpose of recording scheduled safety inspections. Note the date of inspection and be sure that inspection occurs at regular intervals. If a potentially dangerous situation exists, post rules or warnings so that students and other teachers are made aware of the risk.

Proper installation of equipment is critical. Climbing equipment and other equipment that must be anchored should be installed by a reputable firm that guarantees its work. When examining apparatus, inspection of the installation is important. Maintenance of facilities is also important. Grass should be kept short, and the grounds inspected for debris. Holes in the ground should be filled, and loose gravel removed. Hazards found on playing fields need to be repaired and eliminated. A proper finish that prevents excessive slipping should be used on indoor floors. Shower rooms should have a roughened floor finish applied to prevent falls when the floors are wet.

Safe participation in an activity can be enhanced by the selection of equipment and facilities. Choice of apparatus and equipment should be based on the growth and developmental levels of students. For example, allowing elementary school children to use a horizontal ladder that was designed for high school students may result in a fall that causes injury. The legal concept of an *attractive nuisance* implies that some piece of equipment or apparatus, usually left unsupervised, was so attractive to children that they could not be expected to avoid using it. When an injury occurs, even though students may have been using the apparatus incorrectly, teachers and school administration are often held liable because the attractive nuisance should have been removed from the area when unsupervised.

Instructional Staff

Indoor facilities are of primary concern to physical education instructors. Even though the administration is charged with overall responsibility for facilities and equipment, including periodic inspection, the instructor should make a regular safety inspection of the instructional area. If corrective action is needed, the principal or other designated administrator should be notified in writing. Verbal notification is not enough, since it offers little legal protection to the instructor.

Arrange facilities in a safe manner. Often, the side- and end lines of playing fields for sports such as football, soccer, and field hockey are placed too close to walls, curbings, or fences. The boundaries should be moved to allow adequate room for deceleration, even though the size of the playing area is reduced. In the gymnasium, students should not run to a line that is close to a wall. Another common hazard is placing basketball hoops too close to the playing area. The poles that support the baskets must be padded.

Proper use of equipment and apparatus is important. Regardless of the state of equipment repair, if it is misused, it may result in an injury. Give students instruction in the proper use of equipment and apparatus before the students use them. All safety instruction should be included in the written lesson plan to ensure that all points are covered.

Equipment should be purchased on the basis of quality and safety as well as potential use. Many lawsuits occur because of unsafe equipment and apparatus. The liability for such equipment may rest with the manufacturer, but this has to be proved, which means that the teacher must state, in writing, the exact specifications of the desired equipment. The process of bidding for lower-priced items may result in the purchase of less safe equipment. If teachers have specified proper equipment in writing, however, the possibility of their being held liable for injury is reduced.

THE SPORTS PROGRAM

A common problem with elementary school sports programs for school administrators is providing qualified coaches. The administration should set minimum requirements for coaches and ensure that incompetent individuals are removed from coaching duties. When students are involved in extracurricular activities, teachers (coaches) are responsible for the safe conduct of activities. The following areas often give rise to lawsuits if they are not handled carefully.

Mismatched Opponents

A common error that gives rise to lawsuits is mismatching students on the bases of size and ability. Just because the competitors are the same gender and choose to participate does not absolve the instructor of liability if an injury occurs. The question that courts examine is whether an effort was made to match students according to height, weight, and ability. Courts are less understanding about mismatching in the physical education setting compared with an athletic contest, but mismatching is a factor that should be avoided in any situation.

Waiver Forms

Participants in extracurricular activities should be required to sign a responsibility waiver form. The form should explain the risks involved in voluntary participation and discuss briefly the types of injuries that have occurred in the past during practice and competition. Supervisors should remember that waiver slips do not waive the rights of participants, and that teachers and coaches still can be found liable if injuries occur. The waiver form should communicate clearly, however, the risks involved and may be a strong "assumption of risk" defense.

Medical Examinations

Participants must have a medical examination before participating. Records of the examination should be kept on file and should be identified prominently when physical restrictions or limitations exist. It is common to "red dot" the folders of students who have a history of medical problems. Students must not be allowed to participate unless they purchase medical insurance, and evidence of such coverage should be kept in the folders of athletic participants.

Preseason Conditioning

Preseason conditioning should be undertaken in a systematic and progressive fashion. Starting the season with a mile run for time makes little sense if students have not been preconditioned. Be aware of guidelines dealing with heat and humidity. For example, in Arizona, guidelines advise avoiding strenuous activity when the temperature exceeds 85 degrees Fahrenheit and the humidity exceeds 40 percent. When these conditions are exceeded, running is curtailed to 10 minutes and active games to 30 minutes. Students should be hydrated prior to activity, with drinking water available on demand.

Transportation of Students

Whenever students are transported, teachers are responsible for their safety both en route and during the activity. Transportation liability can be avoided by not providing transportation, but instead requiring participants to meet at the site of the event (Pittman, 1993). If the school must provide transportation, licensed drivers and school-approved vehicles should always be used. Travel plans should include official approval from the appropriate school administrator. One special note: If the driver receives pay or reimbursement for the trip, the possibility of the driver being held liable for injury increases dramatically. To make the matter worse, many insurance policies do not cover drivers who receive compensation for transporting students. When teachers transport students and receive reimbursement, a special insurance rider that provides liability coverage for this situation should be purchased.

SAFETY

The major thrust of safety is to prevent situations that cause accidents. It is estimated that more than 70 percent of injuries in sport and related activities could be prevented through proper safety procedures. On the other hand, some accidents occur despite precautions, and proper emergency procedures should be established to cope with such situations. The U.S. Consumer Product Safety Commission conducted a comprehensive study of injuries received in sport and related activities (1992).

This study involved a network of computers in 119 hospital emergency rooms that channeled injury data to a central point. The sports and activities that produced the most injuries were, in order, football, touch football, baseball, basketball, gymnastics, and skiing. The facility that produced the most disabling injuries was the swimming pool.

Learning to recognize potential high-risk situations is an important factor in preventing accidents. Teachers must possess a clear understanding of the hazards and potential dangers of an activity before they can establish controls. Instructors must not assume that participants are aware of the dangers and risks involved in various activities. Students must be told of all dangers and risks before participation.

Guidelines for Safety

1. In-service sessions in safety should be administered by experienced and knowledgeable teachers. Department heads may be responsible for the training, or outside experts can be employed to undertake the responsibility. Giving in-district credit to participating teachers offers strong evidence that the district is concerned about using proper safety techniques.

2. Medical records should be reviewed at the start of each school year. Students with disabilities should be identified and noted within each class listing before the first instructional day. If necessary, the teacher or school nurse can call the doctors of students with disabilities or students with activity restrictions to inquire about the situation and discuss special needs. Physical education teachers should be notified by the classroom teacher or school nurse about youngsters who have special conditions such as epilepsy or temporary problems caused by taking medication.

3. Throughout the school year, safety orientations should be conducted with students. Discussions should include potentially dangerous situations, class conduct, and rules for proper use of equipment and apparatus. Teachers should urge students to report any conditions that might cause an accident.

4. Safety rules for specific units of instruction should be discussed at the onset of each unit. Rules should be posted and regularly brought to the attention of students. Posters and bulletin boards can promote safety in an enjoyable and stimulating manner.

5. If students are to serve as instructional aides, they should be trained. Aides must understand the techniques of spotting, for example, and must receive proper instruction if they are to be a part of the educational process. Use caution with student aides because teachers are still responsible even if an aide performs a duty incorrectly.

6. Instructional practices need to be monitored for possible hazards. For example, students in competitive situations should be matched by size, maturity, and ability. Proper instruction necessary for safe participation should occur prior to an activity. Instructors should receive a competence check to be sure that they are adequately trained to give instruction in various activities. The instructional area should be properly prepared for safe participation; if the area is lacking necessary apparatus and safety devices, instruction should be modified to meet safety standards.

7. An inventory of equipment and apparatus should include a safety checklist. Whenever necessary, send equipment in need of repair to proper agents. If the cost of repair is greater than 40 percent of the replacement cost, discarding the equipment or apparatus is usually a more economical choice.

8. When an injury occurs, it should be recorded and a report placed in the student's file. An injury report should also be filed by type, such as ankle sprain or broken arm. The report should list the activity and the conditions, in order to facilitate analysis at regular intervals. Analysis may show that injuries are occurring regularly during a specific activity or on a certain piece of equipment. This process can give direction for creating a safer environment or for defending the safety record of a sport, activity, or piece of equipment.

9. Teachers need up-to-date first aid and CPR certification. Administrators should be sure that teachers meet these standards and should provide training sessions when necessary.

The Safety Committee

Safety should be publicized regularly throughout the school, and a mechanism should exist that allows students, parents, and teachers to voice concerns about unsafe conditions. A safety committee can meet at regular intervals to establish safety policies, rule on requests to allow high-risk activities, and analyze serious injuries that have occurred in the school district. This committee should develop safety rules that apply districtwide to all teachers. It may determine that certain activities involve too high a risk for the return in student benefit. Acceptable criteria for sports equipment and apparatus may be established by the committee.

Include one or more high-level administrators, physical education teachers, health officers (nurses), parents, and students on the safety committee. School administrators are usually indicted when lawsuits occur; because they are held responsible for program content and curriculum, their representation on the safety

Student Accident Report

_____ **School**

In all cases, this form should be filed through the school nurse and signed by the principal of the school. The original will be forwarded to the superintendent's office, where it will be initialed and sent to the head nurse. The second copy will be retained by the principal or the school nurse. The third copy should be given to the physical education teacher if the accident is related.

Name of injured _____ Address _____

Phone _____ Grade _____ Home room _____ Age _____

Parents of injured _____

Place of accident _____ Date of accident _____

Hour _____ A.M. P.M. Date reported _____ By whom _____

Parent contact attempted at _____ A.M. P.M. Parent contacted at _____ A.M. P.M.

Describe accident, giving specific location and condition of premises _____

_____

Nature of injury _____
(Describe in detail)

Care given or action taken by nurse or others _____

_____

Reason injured person was on premises _____
(Activity at time—i.e., lunch, physical education, etc.)

Staff member responsible for student supervision at time of accident _____

_____

Is student covered by school-sponsored accident insurance? _____ Yes _____ No

Medical Care Recommended _____ Yes _____ No

Where taken after accident _____
(Specify home, physician, or hospital, giving name and address)

By whom _____ **At what time** _____ A.M. P.M.

Follow-up by nurse to be sent to central health office

Remediative measures taken _____
(Attach individual remarks if necessary)

School _____ Principal _____

Date _____ Nurse _____

On the back of this sheet, list all persons familiar with the circumstances of the accident, giving name, address, telephone number, age, and location with respect to the accident.

FIGURE 9.1   Sample accident report form.

committee is important. Students on the committee may be aware of possible hazards, and parents may often voice concerns overlooked by teachers.

The Emergency Care Plan

Before any emergency arises, teachers should prepare themselves by learning about special health and physical conditions of students (Gray, 1993). Most schools have a method for identifying students with special health problems. If a student has a problem that may require treatment, a consent-to-treat form should be on file in case the parent or guardian is unavailable. Necessary first aid materials and supplies should be available in a kit and be readily accessible.

Establishing procedures for emergency care and notification of parents in case of injury is of utmost importance in providing a high standard of care for students. To plan properly for emergency care, all physical education teachers should have first aid training. *First aid* is the immediate and temporary care given at an emergency before a physician is available. Its purposes are to save life, prevent aggravation of injuries, and alleviate severe suffering. If there is evidence of life-threatening bleeding or if the victim is unconscious or has stopped breathing, the teacher must administer first aid. When already-injured persons may be further injured if they are not moved, then moving them is permissible. As a general rule, however, an injured person should not be moved unless absolutely necessary. If there is an indication of back or neck injury, the victim's head must be immobilized and should not be moved without the use of a spine board. Remember, the purpose of first aid is to save life. The emergency care plan should consist of the following steps:

1. *Administer first aid to the injured student as the first priority.* Treat only life-threatening injuries. The school nurse should immediately be called to the scene of the accident. Emergency care procedures should indicate whether the student can be moved and in what fashion. It is critical that the individual applying first aid avoid aggravating the injury.

2. *Notify parents as soon as possible when emergency care is required.* Each student's file should list home and emergency telephone numbers where parents can be reached. If possible, the school should have an arrangement with local emergency facilities so that a paramedic unit can be called immediately to the scene of a serious accident.

3. *Release the student to a parent or a designated representative.* Policies for transportation of injured students should be established and documented.

4. *Promptly complete a student accident report while the details of the accident are clear.* Figure 9.1 is an example of an accident form that covers the necessary details. The teacher and principal should both retain copies, and additional copies should be sent to the administrative office.

PERSONAL PROTECTION: MINIMIZING THE EFFECTS OF A LAWSUIT

In spite of proper care, injuries do occur, and lawsuits may be initiated. Two courses of action are necessary to counteract the effects of a suit.

Liability Insurance

Teachers may be protected by school district liability insurance. Usually, however, you must purchase your own policy. A common way many physical education professionals purchase liability insurance at a reasonable cost is to join AAHPERD. As a member, a group liability policy can be purchased for a modest amount. Most policies provide for legal services to contest a suit and will pay indemnity up to the limits of the policy (liability coverage of $500,000 is most common). Most policies give the insurance company the right to settle out of court. Unfortunately, when this occurs, some people may infer that the teacher was guilty even though the circumstances indicate otherwise. Insurance companies usually settle out of court to avoid the excessive legal fees required to try to win the case in court.

Record Keeping

The second course of action is to keep complete records of accidents. Many lawsuits occur months or even years after the accident, when memory of the situation is fuzzy. Accident reports should be filled out immediately after an injury occurs. Take care to provide no evidence, oral or written, that others could use in a court of law. Do not attempt in the report to make a diagnosis or to specify the supposed cause of the accident.

If newspaper reporters probe for details, avoid describing the accident beyond the basic facts. When discussing the accident with administrators, only the facts recorded in the accident report should be discussed. Remember that school records can be subpoenaed in court proceedings. The point here is not to dissemble, but to be cautious and avoid self-incrimination.

Safety and Liability Checklists

The following checklists can be used to monitor the physical education environment. Any situations that deviate from safe and legally sound practices should be rectified immediately.

SUPERVISION AND INSTRUCTION

1. Are teachers adequately trained in all of the activities that they are teaching?

2. Do all teachers have evidence of a necessary level of first aid training?

3. When supervising, do personnel have access to a written plan of areas to be observed and responsibilities to be carried out?

4. Have students been warned of potential dangers and risks and advised of rules and the reasons for the rules?

5. Are safety rules posted near areas of increased risk?

6. Are lesson plans written? Do they include provisions for proper instruction, sequence of activities, and safety? Are all activities that are taught listed in the district curriculum guide?

7. When a new activity is introduced, are safety precautions and instructions for correct skill performance always communicated to the class?

8. Are the activities taught in the program based on sound curriculum principles? Could the activities and units of instruction be defended on the basis of their educational contributions?

9. Do the methods of instruction recognize individual differences among students, and are the necessary steps taken to meet the needs of all students regardless of gender, ability, or disability?

10. Are substitute teachers given clear and comprehensive lesson plans so that they can maintain the scope and sequence of instruction?

11. Is the student evaluation plan based on actual performance and objective data rather than on favoritism or arbitrary and capricious standards?

12. Is appropriate dress required for students? This does not imply uniforms, only dress (including shoes) that ensures the safety of all students.

13. When necessary for safety, are students grouped according to ability level, size, or age?

14. Is the class left unsupervised when the teacher visits the office, lounge, or bathroom? Is one teacher ever asked to supervise two or more classes at the same time?

15. If students are used as teacher aides or to spot other students, are they given proper instruction and training?

EQUIPMENT AND FACILITIES

1. Is all equipment inspected regularly, and are the inspection results recorded on a form and sent to the proper administrators?

2. Is a log maintained recording the regular occurrence of inspections, the equipment in need of repair, and the times repairs were made?

3. Are "attractive nuisances" eliminated from the gymnasium and playing field?

4. Are specific safety rules posted on facilities and near equipment?

5. Are the following inspected periodically?
   a. Playing field for the presence of glass, rocks, and metal objects
   b. Fasteners holding equipment such as climbing ropes, horizontal bars, or baskets
   c. Goals for games such as football, soccer, and field hockey, to be sure that they are fastened securely
   d. Padded areas, such as goal supports

6. Are mats placed under apparatus from which a fall is possible?

7. Are playing fields arranged so participants will not run into each other or be hit by a ball from another game?

8. Are landing pits filled and maintained properly?

EMERGENCY CARE

1. Is there a written procedure for emergency care?

2. Is a person who is properly trained in first aid available immediately following an accident?

3. Are emergency telephone numbers readily accessible?

4. Are telephone numbers of parents available?

5. Is an up-to-date first aid kit available? Is ice immediately available?

6. Are health folders that list restrictions, allergies, and health problems of students maintained?

7. Are health folders reviewed by instructors on a regular basis?

8. Are students who participate in extracurricular activities required to have insurance? Is the policy number recorded?

9. Is there a plan for treating injuries that involve the local paramedics?

10. Are accident reports filed promptly and analyzed regularly?

TRANSPORTATION OF STUDENTS

1. Have parents been informed that their students will be transported off campus?

2. Are detailed travel plans approved by the site administrator and kept on file?

3. Are school vehicles used whenever possible?

4. Are drivers properly licensed and vehicles insured?

5. If teachers or parents use their own vehicles to transport students, are the students, drivers, and car owners covered by an insurance rider purchased by the school district?

REFLECTION AND REVIEW QUESTIONS

How and Why

1. Should teachers have professional insurance?

2. How can effective classroom management help teachers avoid legal issues?

3. How can teachers protect themselves from lawsuits?

4. Why is a safety and liability checklist important?

Content Review

1. Define a tort.

2. Identify four major points that must be established to determine if a teacher is negligent. Also, discuss the importance of foreseeability.

3. List and explain types of negligence.

4. Describe the common defenses against negligence.

5. Discuss the importance of supervision and instruction when examining responsibility.

6. Identify who is responsible for equipment and facilities. Explain your answer.

7. List some issues related to sports programs that often result in lawsuits.

8. Briefly describe several guidelines for safety in physical education.

9. Explain the importance of an emergency care plan and discuss the steps in the plan.

FOR MORE INFORMATION

References and Suggested Readings

Appenzeller, H. (1993). *Managing sports and risk management strategies.* Durham, NC: Carolina Academic Press.

Appenzeller, H. (Ed.). (1998). *Risk management in sport: Issues and strategies.* Durham, NC: Carolina Academic Press.

Appenzeller, H. (2003). *Managing sports and risk management strategies.* 2nd ed. Durham, NC: Carolina Academic Press.

Baley, J. A., & Matthews, D. L. (1988). *Law and liability in athletics, physical education, and recreation.* Boston: Allyn and Bacon.

Blucker, J. A., & Pell, S. W. (1986). Legal and ethical issues. *Journal of Physical Education, Recreation, and Dance, 57,* 19–21.

Dougherty, N. J. (Ed.). (2002). *Principles of safety in physical education and sport.* 3rd ed. Reston, VA: AAHPERD.

Dougherty, N. J., Golberger, A. S., & Carpenter, A. S. (2002). *Sport, physical activity, and the law.* Champaign, IL: Sagamore Publishing.

Gallup, E. M. (1995). *Law and the team physician.* Champaign, IL: Human Kinetics.

Garner, B. A. (Ed.). (1999). *Black's law dictionary.* 7th ed. St. Paul, MN: West Group.

Gray, G. R. (1993). Providing adequate medical care to program participants. *Journal of Physical Education, Recreation, and Dance, 64*(2), 56–57.

Hart, J. E., & Ritson, R. J. (2002). *Liability and safety in physical education and sport: A practitioner's guide to the legal aspects of teaching and coaching in elementary and secondary schools.* 2nd ed. Reston, VA: AAHPERD.

Institute for the Study of Educational Policy, Law Division. (1986). *School athletics and the law.* Seattle: University of Washington Press.

Kaiser, R. A. (1984). *Liability and law in recreation, parks, and sports.* Englewood Cliffs, NJ: Prentice-Hall.

Merriman, J. (1993). Supervision in sport and physical activity. *Journal of Physical Education, Recreation, and Dance, 64*(2), 20–23.

Pittman, A. J. (1993). Safe transportation—A driving concern. *Journal of Physical Education, Recreation, and Dance, 64*(2), 53–55.

Strickland, R., Phillip, J. F., & Phillips, W. R. (1976). *Avoiding teacher malpractice.* New York: Hawthorn.

U.S. Consumer Product Safety Commission. (1992). *Handbook for public playground safety.* Washington, DC: U.S. Government Printing Office.

van der Smissen, B. (1990). *Legal liability and risk management of public and private entities.* Cincinnati, OH: Anderson.

Websites

Legal Issues and Physical Education
www.kin.sfasu.edu/finkenberg/kin511/Liability.html
www.nils.com/rupps/comparative-negligence.htm

Playgrounds
www.cpsc.gov/CPSCPUB/PUBS/playpubs.html
www.parenthoodweb.com/articles/phw506.htm
www.playdesigns.com

School Safety and Security
www.schoolsecurity.org

10

Facilities, Equipment, and Supplies

ESSENTIAL COMPONENTS OF QUALITY PROGRAMS

   I. Organized around content standards

▶ **II.** **Student-centered and developmentally appropriate**

  III. Physical activity and motor skill development form the core of the program

  IV. Teaches management skills and self-discipline

   V. Promotes inclusion of all students

  VI. Focuses on process over product

 VII. Promotes lifetime personal health and wellness

VIII. Teaches cooperation and responsibility and promotes sensitivity to diversity

NATIONAL STANDARDS FOR PHYSICAL EDUCATION*

1. Demonstrates competency in motor skills and movement patterns needed to perform a variety of physical activities.

2. Demonstrates understanding of movement concepts, principles, and tactics as they apply to the learning and performance of physical activities.

3. Participates regularly in physical activity.

4. Achieves and maintains a health-enhancing level of physical fitness.

5. Exhibits responsible personal and social behavior that respects self and others in physical activity.

6. Values physical activity for health, enjoyment, challenge, self-expression, and/or social interaction.

*National Association for Sport and Physical Education (NASPE), 2004.

SUMMARY

Chapter 10 presents procedures associated with the design, purchase, maintenance, and construction of physical education facilities, equipment, and supplies. The term *equipment* refers to items that are more or less fixed in nature. Equipment has a relatively long life span, needs periodic safety checks, and requires planned purchasing. Supplies are nondurable items that have a limited period of use. When resources are limited, much equipment can be constructed. A comprehensive section on how to build equipment and supplies is offered.

OUTCOMES

■ Identify standards to follow in the construction of outdoor and indoor physical education facilities.

■ Understand that safety is an essential consideration in facility design.

■ Illustrate floor lines and markings that enhance management potential and increase ease of instruction.

■ List essential equipment and supplies for physical education in the elementary school.

■ List recommended equipment for outdoor and indoor physical education areas.

■ Outline a systematic plan for the storage of physical education equipment and supplies.

■ Describe procedures for the care and repair of physical education equipment and supplies.

■ Be able to construct selected physical education equipment and supplies.

The facilities for physical education are often classified into two categories: outdoor and indoor. Usually, outdoor space provides enough room for several classes to work simultaneously. When weather conditions require frequent use of indoor space, a minimum of one indoor teaching station for every eight classrooms is needed. In addition, to meet the needs of students with disabilities (as required by Public Law 94-142), another indoor play area, separate from but close to the regular indoor facility, is needed.

Physical education facilities should be planned in terms of maximum projected enrollment. Too often, planning is done in terms of the present situation. Later, when classrooms are added to the school, they are added without a change in physical education areas. What was previously an adequate arrangement now becomes a scheduling problem. Adding physical education facilities is difficult because of generally escalating costs and the relatively high cost of physical education facilities in comparison to the cost of adding regular classroom space.

OUTDOOR FACILITIES

Standards for outdoor play areas call for a minimum of ten acres for the school, with an additional acre for each one hundred pupils in the maximum projected enrollment. Parking areas, cycle racks, and entry roads are in addition to these standards. The outdoor areas should include field space for games, a track, hard-surfaced areas, apparatus areas, play courts, age-group-specific play areas, covered play space, and a jogging trail.

Fields should be leveled, drained, and turfed, because grass is the most usable field surface. An automatic sprinkler system is desirable, but sprinkler heads must not protrude and become safety hazards. Automatic installations permit sprinkling during the evening and night so that the fields are not too soggy for play the next day.

A hard-top area should be marked for a variety of games such as tetherball, volleyball, and basketball. Four-square courts, hopscotch layouts, and circles for games are examples of other markings that can be put on these surfaces. Simple movement pattern courses can also be marked. Some administrators prefer a hard surface for the entire play area, because this eliminates the mud problem and the need for sprinkling and in general lowers maintenance costs. Hard surfaces are used when play space is limited and when the number of students makes keeping a turf surface in adequate condition difficult.

As a minimum, space should be provided for a track, and it should be placed in an area where it will not interfere with other activities. For schools where a permanent installation is not practical, a temporary track can be laid out each spring (see page 703).

Separate play spaces for different age groups should be included in the planning. Such areas should contain apparatus designed for each age group. The play area for primary-level children should be well away from areas where footballs and softballs are used.

Small, hard-surfaced play courts can be located strategically near the edges of the outdoor area, thus spreading out the play groups. These courts, approximately 40 by 60 feet, can be equipped for basketball or volleyball or both. A covered shed can be divided for use by different age groups. Climate conditions would dictate the need for such facilities.

A jogging trail can stimulate interest in jogging. Small signs indicating the distances covered and markers outlining the trail are all that are needed. Stations with exercise tasks can be placed at intervals. For example, a station could instruct students to accomplish a specified number of push-ups or sit-ups. Such a circuit is popularly called a *parcourse.*

An area set aside as a developmental playground is an important part of the total play space. The area should contain equipment and apparatus and should be landscaped to have small hills, valleys, and tunnels for children. A recommended approach is to divide the playground into various developmental areas so that children must use different body parts in different areas of the play space. For example, one area might contain a great deal of climbing equipment to reinforce arm-shoulder girdle development, and another area might challenge the leg and trunk regions. Equipment and apparatus should be abstract in nature, leaving creation and imagination to the children. Apparatus can be manipulated and changed to suit the needs and desires of the youngsters.

SAFETY ON THE PLAYGROUND

Studies by the U.S. Consumer Product Safety Commission (1997) show that the majority of injuries (60 to 70 percent) are caused when children fall from apparatus and strike the underlying surface. The type of surface under the equipment is a major factor affecting the severity of injuries associated with falls from apparatus. Injuries range from minor bruises to skull fractures, concussions, and brain damage. Falls onto paved surfaces result in a disproportionately high number of severe injuries. Some deaths also have resulted from such falls.

Slides offer a high potential for accidents. The greatest number of injuries occurs from falls over the side, from the platform, and from the ladder. Roughhousing, improper usage, and slipping are the most prominent causes of accidents. Rules should be established so that only one person is on the platform, with the next user waiting at the base of the ladder.

Concrete, asphalt, and other paved surfaces placed under apparatus require little or no maintenance, which is often the reason for their installation and use. However, hard surfaces do not provide injury protection from the impacts of accidental falls and therefore are unsuitable for use. Organic materials such as pine bark nuggets, pine bark mulch, shredded hardwood bark, and cocoa shell mulch are recommended. Other materials are wood chips, shredded tires, and sand. If hard surfaces are already in place, outdoor interlocking tiles or dense synthetic turf may be placed over the existing base.

If loose, organic materials are used, a six-inch layer of material to cushion the impact of falling should be a minimum. Frequent leveling, grading, and replacement of the material is necessary, as children will move the material away from the impact areas. The material should be screened to eliminate insects, animal excrement, and concealed sharp objects. Unfortunately, organic materials decompose, become pulverized and dusty, and mix with dirt, which causes a loss of their cushioning properties. In rainy or humid weather, they can absorb moisture and pack down, resulting in a loss of resiliency. Finally, materials that will not become firm during freezing temperatures must be selected.

The choice of materials needs to be based on local conditions and the availability of necessary funds. As important as the selection of the proper material is continuous and correct maintenance. Allied to proper maintenance is the need for a checklist of proper procedures to be followed. This form should be filled out and dated on a regular basis.

OUTDOOR APPARATUS AND EQUIPMENT

The continued emphasis on physical fitness should dictate the selection of outdoor equipment. Equipment that offers "sit-and-ride" experiences (swings, merry-go-rounds, and teeter-totters) does not meet this criterion. A second criterion is safety. Each piece of equipment should minimize the potential for injury. As a general rule, if equipment has moving parts, its potential for injury is increased. This section offers suggestions for equipment based on their potential to develop various components of fitness. The categories can be useful if you want to establish a challenge course that develops all parts of the body. Outdoor equipment should stimulate children's creative drives and their desire to move.

Equipment for Upper Body Development

Most children do not receive enough activity that develops upper body strength. In order to develop arm-shoulder girdle strength on the playground, youngsters need the opportunity to climb and swing, and to elevate their bodies. Climbing is important for physical development and for helping children learn to overcome the fear of new situations. The following are examples of equipment that could be used to develop arm-shoulder girdle strength:

- Large telephone cable spools fastened securely so they will not move or tip over. Youngsters can climb on and jump off the spools.
- Climbing poles placed next to platforms that children can reach by climbing the poles.
- Logs and clean railroad ties, positioned vertically, with handholds or handles placed in strategic locations for climbing.
- Climbing ropes attached to tracks (tracks can be locked up in a storage area when school is not in session).
- Tires attached to telephone poles or logs for climbing through and around.
- Jungle gyms attached securely.
- Horizontal ladders placed in a variety of combinations and forms. Arched ladders are quite popular and allow children to reach the rungs easily. Uniladders, consisting of a single beam with pegs on each side, offer a different ladder challenge to children.
- Logs anchored vertically with handholds provided for climbing.

Equipment for Lower Body Development

Equipment and apparatus for enhancing lower body development should encourage youngsters to use locomotor movements throughout the available space. Allow enough distance and area to ensure movement. Suggestions for lower body development are the following:

- Large spaces, which encourage free movement and running games, provided.
- Railroad ties anchored vertically at varying heights and distances, which encourage children to walk, run, hop, and jump from one to the other.
- Used automobile tires fastened on the ground in different patterns to stimulate moving in and out, around, and over the tires using different movements.
- Stairways and platforms provided for climbing on and jumping off.

- Stepping stones placed to encourage movement patterns. Stones can be placed so that they encourage oppositional patterning while moving.

- Miniature challenge courses provided that contain tires to move over and through, sand pits provided to run and jump into, and poles or cones arranged for moving around and dodging.

Equipment for Balance Skills

Balance is improved through regular practice. Many pieces of equipment can be used to challenge youngsters' balance skills. Youngsters should be encouraged to move under control while practicing balance. The following are suggestions for offering balance challenges:

- Balance beams made of four-by-four-inch beams can be permanent installations. They can be arranged in various patterns but should not be more than 12 to 18 inches above the ground.

- Logs, anchored securely, can be used as balance beams.

- Balance beams that start with a width of 6 inches and progress in difficulty to 1½ inches can be included.

- Wooden ladders secured six inches above the ground can offer students opportunities to walk on the rungs and rails.

Equipment for Sport Skills

BASKETBALL GOALS

Outdoor basketball goals may or may not be combined with a court. Youngsters play a lot of one-goal basketball, and a regulation court is not needed for this game. The goals should be in a surfaced area, however. Outdoor baskets for elementary school use should be eight to nine feet above the ground. The lowered height sometimes poses a problem, because children can jump up and grasp the front of the rim, which may damage or tear the basket loose. Strong construction that withstands such abuse is one solution. Some schools have reverted to the 10-foot-high basket, thus putting it out of reach of most children.

VOLLEYBALL STANDARDS

Volleyball standards should have flexible height adjustments, including a low height of 30 inches for use in paddleball.

SOFTBALL BACKSTOPS

Softball backstops can be either fixed or portable.

TETHERBALL COURTS

Tetherball courts should have fastening devices for the cord and ball so that they can be removed from the post for safekeeping. The immediate playing area should be surfaced.

TRACK AND FIELD EQUIPMENT

Jumping standards, bars, and pits should be available. These must be maintained properly.

INDOOR FACILITIES

The gymnasium must be well planned for maximum use. The combination gymnasium-auditorium-cafeteria facility leaves much to be desired and creates more problems than it solves. Although it may be labeled a "multipurpose room," a better description is probably "multiuseless." The cafeteria poses a particular problem. The gymnasium must be vacated before the lunch hour so that chairs and tables can be set up, and the facility is not available again for physical education activities until it has been cleaned, which usually involves mopping. This eliminates noontime recreational use, thus leaving little play area for children during inclement weather. In extreme cases, a lack of help postpones gymnasium use for the early part of the afternoon, until the custodian has completed cleaning chores. Special programs, movies, and other events necessitating chairs and the use of the area also complicate the situation.

The gymnasium should be located in a separate wing connected to the classrooms by a covered corridor. It should provide ready access to play areas. Isolating the gym from the rest of the school minimizes the noise problem and allows after-school and community groups to use the facilities without access to other parts of the school. The indoor facility should be planned in such a way that athletic contests can be scheduled there at times, but the primary purpose of the gymnasium is not to be an athletic facility. Consideration for spectators should not be a major planning concern. Only after basic physical education needs have been met should the needs of spectators be considered.

In the gymnasium, markings and boundaries should be put on the floor to outline convenient areas for the more common activities. The markings should be painted on the floor after the first or second sealer coat has been applied. A finish coat should then be

FIGURE 10.1 Floor markings to maximize gymnasium use.

applied on top of the line markings. Figure 10.1 is an example of how floor markings can maximize the usefulness of a facility.

Temporary lines needed occasionally during the year can be applied with pressure-sensitive tape. These tapes are, however, difficult to remove completely and are likely to take off the finish when removed. A hardwood (preferably maple) floor is recommended for the gymnasium. Other surfaces limit community use and create both safety and maintenance problems.

For safety reasons and for rebound practice, walls should have a smooth surface at a distance of eight to ten feet up from the floor. Walls and ceilings should have acoustical treatment. When planning a new facility, a recess for each set of ropes on tracks is an excellent feature. Insulation should conform to modern health standards, and older buildings should be scrutinized for unacceptable insulation materials such as asbestos fibers and certain formaldehyde-based plastics.

The lighting should be of sufficient intensity, and fixtures should be recessed to prevent damage. Lights should be arranged so that they can be serviced from the floor. Exposed beams should be available for attaching

apparatus, and all walls should have electrical outlets. A permanent overhead public address system is desirable, permitting permanent installation of a record, tape, or CD player for easy and quick access. When planning a new facility, the player can be recessed.

Windows should be placed high on the long sides of the gymnasium. Protection from glare and direct sun should be provided.

If baskets and backboards need to be raised and lowered often, a motor-driven system eliminates laborious hand cranking. The system switch should be activated with a key.

Adequate storage space must be given careful thought. The storage space needed for the equipment and instructional supplies used in present-day physical education is considerable, and the area should be designed so that the materials are readily available.

One problem frequently associated with a combination auditorium-gymnasium facility is the use of the physical education storeroom for bulky auditorium equipment such as portable chairs on chair trucks, portable stages, lighting fixtures, and other paraphernalia for dramatic productions. Unless the storage facility is quite large—and most are not—an unworkable and cluttered facility is the result. The best solution is two separate storerooms for the dual-purpose facility, or at least one very large storeroom.

A separate storage area of cabinets is essential for outside groups who use the facility. These groups should not have access to the regular physical education supply room. If they are permitted to use school equipment, the equipment should be checked out to the group and later checked in again.

Many storage areas in European schools have doors on tracks, similar to U.S. overhead garage doors. This design has a number of advantages, the main one being that the overhead opening makes the handling of large apparatus much easier.

Most architects are unaware of the storage needs of a modern physical education program. Teachers can only hope that the architects designing new schools will be persuaded to allow for sufficient storage. For the physical education specialist, an office–dressing room is desirable. The office should contain a toilet and a shower.

If contract or task styles of teaching are important in the instructional process, an area to house instructional materials is also desirable. This should be a place where children can go to search through materials and view loop films and videotapes as they complete their learning packets.

EQUIPMENT AND SUPPLIES

As mentioned, equipment refers to items of a more or less fixed nature. Supplies are those nondurable items that have a limited period of use. To illustrate the difference, a softball is listed under supplies, but the longer-lasting softball backstop comes under the category of equipment. Equipment needs periodic replacement, and budget planning must consider the life span of each piece of equipment. Supplies generally are purchased on a yearly basis. It is important to have adequate financing for equipment and supplies and to expend funds wisely.

If the objectives of the physical education program are to be fulfilled, instructional materials must be available in sufficient quantity. Enough equipment should be present so that children do not waste practice time waiting for turns.

Policies covering the purchase, storage, issuance, care, maintenance, and inventory of supplies are necessary if maximum return on the allotted budget is to be realized. Program features should be decided first, and a purchasing plan should then be implemented based on these features. Having a minimal operational list of instructional supplies stabilizes the teaching process.

Equipment constructed by the school staff should be considered. Quality must not, however, be sacrificed. Articles from home (including empty plastic jugs, milk cartons, old tires, and the like) should be regarded as supplementary materials. Care must be taken so that the administration does not look for the cheap or no-cost route to securing supplies and thus sacrifice valuable learning experiences when the program requires an appreciable investment.

Some articles can be constructed adequately at the school or in the home, and these merit consideration for the sake of economy. Such items as yarn balls, hoops, Lummi sticks, balance beams, and bounding boards can be made satisfactorily by school staff, parents, and in some instances students. For other articles, the administration must be reminded that constructed equipment is usually a temporary solution only, undertaken in the early phases of a program when equipment costs are high and cannot all be met immediately.

PURCHASING POLICIES

The purchase of supplies and equipment involves careful study of need, price, quality, and material. The safety of the children who will use the equipment is of vital concern. Quantity buying by pooling the funds of an entire school district generally results in better use of the tax dollar. However, cooperative purchasing may require compromises on equipment type and brand to satisfy different users in the system. If bids are requested, careful specifications are necessary. Bids should be asked for only on specified items, and "just as good" merchandise should not be accepted as a substitute.

One individual within a school should be made responsible for the physical education supplies and for keeping records of equipment, supplies, and purchasing. Needs will vary from school to school, and it is practical for school district authorities to deal with a single individual at each school. Prompt attention to repair and replacement of supplies is possible under this system. The individual designated should also be responsible for testing various competing products to determine which will give the best service over time. Some kind of labeling or marking of materials is needed if this is to be accomplished.

An accurate inventory of equipment should be undertaken at the start and end of each school year. Through a sound inventory system, the durability of equipment and supplies and an accounting of supplies lost or misplaced can be established. The ordering of supplies and equipment should be done by the end of the school year or earlier, if possible. A delivery date in August should be specified so that orders can be checked and any necessary adjustments made before the school year begins.

Most equipment of good quality will last from seven to ten years, thus keeping replacement costs to a minimum. The policy of some purchasing agents of selecting low-cost items with little regard for quality is financially unsound. Budgetary practices should include an allotment for the yearly purchase of instructional supplies as well as for major replacement and procurement costs for large items, which are usually staggered over a number of years. Once sufficient equipment and supplies have been procured, budget considerations should be for replacement and repair only.

INDOOR EQUIPMENT

Several principles should govern the choice of indoor equipment. First, a reasonable variety and amount of equipment should be available to keep children active. Included should be items to facilitate arm-shoulder girdle development (for example, climbing ropes, climbing frames, ladders, and similar apparatus). A criterion for selection is that most, if not all, indoor equipment should be of the type that the children themselves can carry, assemble, and disassemble. A regular trampoline, for example, would not meet this criterion.

Mats for Tumbling and Safety

Mats are basic to any physical education program. Enough mats must be available to provide a safe floor for climbing apparatus. At least eight should be present. The light folding mats are preferable because they are easy to handle and store (Figure 10.2). They stack well and can be moved on carts. Mats should have fasteners so that two or more can be joined. The covers should be plastic for easy cleaning. (The one objection to plastic covers is that they are not as soft as the type of mat cover used for wrestling.) Mats should be four feet wide and seven or eight feet long. Heavy hand-me-down mats from the high school program may prove counterproductive, because they are difficult to handle and bulky to store.

Other mats that might be considered are thick, soft mats (somewhat similar to mattresses) and inclined mats. Soft mats are generally four or more inches thick and may entice the timid to try activities that they otherwise would avoid. Inclined mats are wedge-shaped and provide downhill momentum for rolls.

Individual Mats

A supply of 30 to 35 individual mats is used for the primary-level program. The mats, which can be 20 by 40 inches or 24 by 48 inches, are useful for practicing many

FIGURE 10.2 Tumbling mats stored on wall with Velcro fasteners.

movement experiences and introductory tumbling activities.

Tape/CD Player

A portable combination tape and CD player with remote control is the most affordable and versatile choice for the physical education program.

Balance-Beam Benches

Balance-beam benches have double use. They can serve as regular benches for many types of bench activity, and, when turned over, they can be used for balance-beam activities. Wooden horses or their supports can serve as inclined benches. Six benches are a minimum for class activity.

Balance Beams

A wide beam (4 inches) is recommended for kindergarten and first grade. Otherwise, a 2-inch beam can be used. Balance beams with alternate surfaces (two and four inches) can be constructed from common building materials.

Chinning Bar

The chinning bar is especially useful for physical fitness testing and in body support activities. The portable chinning bar installed in the gymnasium doorway is an acceptable substitute.

Climbing Ropes

Climbing ropes are essential to the program. At least eight ropes should be present, but having more than eight

FIGURE 10.3   Climbing ropes on tracks.

allows for better group instruction. Climbing rope sets on tracks are the most efficient to handle (Figure 10.3). With little effort or loss of time, the ropes are ready for activity. Ropes on tracks are available in a variety of materials, but good-quality manila hemp seems to be the most practical. Ropes should be either 1½ or 1¾ inches in diameter.

Quality climbing ropes made of synthetic fibers are appearing on the market. The best are olefin fiber ropes, which are nonallergenic and have nonslip qualities, thus forestalling the problem of slickness, a characteristic of plastic ropes and even of older cotton ropes. Climbing ropes on tracks and other large apparatus can be purchased from Gopher Sport, 220 24th Avenue NW, P.O. Box 998, Owatonna, MN 55060-0998; phone: 1-800-533-0446 or www.gophersport.com.

Volleyball Standards

Volleyball standards should adjust to various heights for different grade levels and games.

Supply Cart

A cart to hold supplies is desirable. Other carts can be used for the audio equipment and for regular and individual mats.

Jumping Boxes

Small boxes used for jumping and for allied locomotor movements extend the opportunities to work on basic movement skills. Boxes should be 8 and 16 inches high (Figure 10.4). If the boxes are made about 16 by 16 inches with a rubber skid-proof surface on the bottom, they will be stable. Holes drilled through the sides provide fingerholds for ease of handling. Eight boxes, four of each size, are a minimum number for the average-sized class. Jumping boxes can be purchased from Gopher Sport.

Horizontal Ladder Sets

Horizontal ladders that fold against the wall make an excellent indoor equipment addition. The ladder may be combined with other pieces of apparatus in a folding set.

Other Indoor Items

A portable chalkboard is desirable, as is a wall screen for displaying visual aids. A large bulletin board and a wall chalkboard should be located near the main entrance to the gym. The wall chalkboard permits the display of announcements or notes. An audiovisual cart or stand for projectors is helpful. It should contain sufficient electrical cord to reach wall outlets.

FIGURE 10.4   First graders using 16-inch jumping boxes.

Priority	Material and Supplies	Quantity
1	8½ in. inflatable rubber playground balls	36
1a	8 in. foam balls (can be substituted for playground balls)	36
1b	8 in. polyurethane-coated foam balls (a substitute for playground balls; they are much more durable and give a true bounce. They can be used for all types of sport activities.)	36
2	6 in. × 6 in. beanbags, assorted colors	72
3	Jump ropes (plastic segments for beginners and speed ropes for experienced jumpers)	
	7 ft length	36
	8 ft length	36
	9 ft length	18
	16 ft length (long rope-jumping)	12
4	Hoops (solid or segmented)	
	30 in diameter	36
	36 in diameter	36
5	Wands (36 in. length, ¾ in. diameter hardwood)	36
6	Game cones (12 in. bright orange vinyl)	20
7	Tambourine, single head double ring	1
8	Plastic racquets (sized for elementary children)	36
9	Foam balls for racquet skills (2½ in.)	36
10	Fleece balls (3–4 in. diameter)	36
11	Floor hockey sticks and pucks—36 of each	36
12	Whiffle balls (use for throwing, hockey, softball, etc.)	36
13	Individual mats (23 in. × 48 in. × ½ in.)	36
14	Partner tug-of-war ropes (handles on both ends made with nylon webbing or garden hose and ⅜ in. nylon rope)	18
15	Juggling scarves	108
16	Beach balls (18 in. to 20 in. diameter)	36
17	Soccer balls (junior size or trainers)	18
18	Basketballs (junior size)	18
19	Footballs (junior size or foam rubber)	18
20	Volleyballs (lightweight trainer balls)	18
21	Softballs (extra soft)	18
22	Softball bats (wood or aluminum)	3
23	Frisbees, (9 in. to 10 in. diameter)	36
24	Magic stretch ropes	12
25	Cageball (24 in.)	1
26	Pinnies (four colors—12 each)	48
27	Ball bags (nylon see-through mesh)	12
28	Team tug-of-war rope (¾ in. × 50 ft nylon with sealed ends)	1
29	Stopwatches (digital)	6
30	Batons (for track and field relays)	12
31	Scooterboards, 12 in. with handles	18
32	Bowling pins	30
33	Lummi sticks	72

F I G U R E 1 0 . 5 Basic equipment and supplies needed for quality physical education.

Priority	Capital-Outlay Items	Quantity
1	Tumbling mats (4 ft × 8 ft × 1¼ in. thick; four sides of Velcro fasteners)	12
2	Cassette tape player	1
3	Parachute and storage bag (28 ft diameter)	1
4	Electric ball pump	1
5	Heavy-duty equipment (ball) carts	4
6	Balance-beam benches (12 ft length)	6
7	Jumping boxes (8 in. height)	6
8	Jumping boxes (16 in. height)	6
9	Audiovisual cart with electrical outlet (for tape player, etc.)	1
10	Sit-and-reach box (measure flexibility)	2
11	Utility gym standards (for volleyball nets, etc.)	2
12	Field marker (for chalking lines)	1

FIGURE 10.5   (continued)

Rebound nets for throwing and kicking have excellent utility. They do, however, pose storage problems. Substitute goals for basketball and related games can be designed. One suggested goal is four feet square, with the rim five feet above the ground. Beginners can find success with this goal design. The frame can be made of one-inch pipe or plastic (PVC) tubing.

EQUIPMENT AND SUPPLIES FOR PHYSICAL EDUCATION

Knowing what equipment to obtain for your program and where to find it can be an obstacle, but it doesn't need to be a major obstacle. Figure 10.5 identifies the equipment, supplies, and capital-outlay items needed to teach a quality physical education program. The items are listed by priority in two categories: materials and supplies, and capital outlay. Priority is based on cost, need, and versatility of the equipment. The first piece of equipment listed (playground balls) can be used to teach the most units, therefore giving it the highest priority. The quantity of equipment is also listed to ensure that the proper amount is ordered to facilitate a normal class size. Some of the equipment can be constructed, as described later in this chapter.

The majority of listed equipment is available from Gopher Sport. The author has worked closely with this company to develop a *Dynamic Physical Education* equipment list. This list offers all the equipment and teaching materials needed to implement a high-quality program. Equipment has been field-tested and is shipped quickly with an unconditional guarantee. If you are not satisfied with any Gopher purchase for any reason, at any time, contact Gopher and they will replace it, credit your account, or refund your money. For a current catalog or more information, call 1-800-533-0446 or fax a request to 1-800-451-4855.

STORAGE PLANS

When a class goes to the gymnasium for physical education, the teacher has a right to expect sufficient supplies to be available to conduct the class. A master list stipulating the kinds and quantities of supplies in storage should be established. A reasonable turnover is to be expected, and supply procedures should take this into account. Supplies in the storage facility should be available for physical education classes and for organized after-school activities. The supplies should not be used for games played during recess or for free play periods; each classroom should have its own supplies for such purposes. A system should be established for the storage of equipment and supplies. "A place for everything and everything in its place" is the key to good housekeeping. Bins, shelves, and other assigned areas where supplies and equipment are to be kept should be labeled.

Both teachers and students must accept responsibility for maintaining order in the storage facility. Squad leaders or student aides can assume major responsibility. At the end of each week, the teacher in charge of the storage area can assign older children to help tidy the area, put any stray items back in place, and repair or replace articles as needed. A principal will be more favorably

FIGURE 10.6 Portable ball cart.

inclined toward purchase requests when obvious care is taken of instructional materials.

Some schools use small supply carts of the type pictured in Figure 10.6. The carts hold those articles used most frequently. They take up some additional space but save students time in accessing needed items. The carts can be built inexpensively to meet specific needs, or commercially manufactured equipment carriers can be purchased. A cart that holds the audio equipment and carts that store and move mats and balls are helpful.

An off-season storage area, where articles not in present use can be kept, should be established. Equipment not in current use should be kept in this separate area, perhaps under lock and key.

CARE, REPAIR, AND MARKING

A definite system should be developed for repairing supplies and equipment. A quick decision must be made whether to repair an item locally or to send it out of the area for repair. If the repair process is lengthy and not cost efficient, using the article until it can no longer be salvaged may be preferable to being deprived of its use. An area should be established for equipment needing repair, so that all articles to be repaired are evident at a glance.

Balls must be inflated to proper pressures. This means using an accurate gauge and checking the pressures periodically. The inflation needle should be moistened before inserting it into the valve. Children should kick only those balls made specifically for kicking (soccer balls, footballs, and playground balls).

Cuts, abrasions, and breaks in rubber balls should be repaired immediately. In some cases, repairs can be made with a vulcanized patch such as those used for repair of tire tubes. In other cases, a hard-setting rubber

preparation is of value. In some instances, repair may be beyond the scope of the school, and the ball should be sent away for repair.

For off-season storage, balls should be deflated somewhat, leaving just enough air in them to retain their shape. Leather balls should be cleaned with an appropriate conditioner.

Mats are expensive, and proper care is needed if they are to last. A place where they can be stacked properly must be provided, or if the mats have handles, they should be hung from those. A mat truck is another storage option if there is space for storing the truck. The newer plastic or plastic-covered mats should be cleaned periodically with a damp, soapy cloth.

For small items, clean plastic ice-cream buckets make adequate storage receptacles. Most school cafeterias have these and other containers that can be used in the storage room to keep order. Small wire or plastic baskets also make good storage containers.

All equipment and supplies should be marked. This is particularly important for equipment issued to different classrooms. Marking can be done with indelible pencil, paint, or stencil ink. Few marking systems are permanent, however, and re-marking at regular intervals is necessary. Sporting goods establishments have marking sets. An electric burning pencil works well but must be used with caution so as not to damage the equipment being marked.

Rubber playground balls come in different colors, and assignment to classrooms can be made on the basis of color. A code scheme with different-colored paints can be used also. It is possible to devise a color system in which the year of issue is designated. This offers the opportunity to document equipment usage and care.

CONSTRUCTING EQUIPMENT AND SUPPLIES

This section is divided into two parts. The first part offers recommendations for sources and materials needed to construct equipment and supplies. The second part provides diagrams and specifications for building equipment in an economical manner. If the recommended equipment can be described adequately without an illustration, it is included in the first part.

Recommendations for Constructing Equipment and Supplies

The supply of balls can be augmented with tennis balls or sponge balls. Discarded tennis balls from the high school tennis team are useful. Holes can be poked in the tennis balls if they are too lively for young children to handle. Sponge balls are inexpensive and with care last indefinitely.

A good supply of ropes for jumping is essential. We are partial to the newer, plastic-link jump ropes; these ropes have good weight, come in attractive colors, can be shortened easily (by removing links), and can be purchased with color-coded handles. The handles provide good leverage for turning. However, ropes can also be made from cord. Heavy sash cord or hard-weave polyethylene rope is suitable. The ends should be whipped, heated, or dipped into some type of hardening solution to prevent unraveling. The lengths can be color coded with dye or stain. Developmental Level I students use mostly 7-foot ropes, with a few 6- and 8-foot ropes. Developmental Levels II and III students use mostly 8-foot ropes, with a few 7- and 9-foot ropes. Instructors will require 9- or 10-foot ropes.

Enough ropes should be available in the suggested lengths to provide each child with a rope of the correct length. The supply of ropes should include eight to ten long (14- to 16-foot) ropes for long-rope-jumping activities. A jump-the-shot rope can be made by tying an old, completely deflated volleyball on one end of a rope.

Beanbags are made easily. High-quality, bright-colored muslin is suitable as a covering. Some teachers have asked parents to save the lower legs of worn-out denim jeans; this material wears extremely well and is free. Other instructors prefer a beanbag with an outer liner that snaps in place to allow for washing. Another idea is to sew three sides of the beanbag permanently. The fourth side is used for filling and has an independent stitch. The beans can be removed through this side when the bag is washed. Beanbags should be about 4 by 4 inches or 6 by 6 inches and can be filled with dried beans or peas, wheat, rice, or even building sand.

For games requiring boundary markers, pieces of rubber matting can be used; small sticks or boards, painted white, are also excellent. A board 1 by 2 inches across and 3 or 4 feet in length makes a satisfactory marker.

Tetherballs should have a snap-on fastener for easy removal.

Schools near ski areas may be able to get discarded tow ropes. These make excellent tug-of-war ropes.

Bowling pins or clubs can be turned in the school shop, or suitable substitutes can be made. For example, pieces of 2-by-2-inch lumber cut short (6 to 10 inches) stand satisfactorily. Lumber companies usually have dowels 1 to 1½ inches in diameter. Sections of these dowels make a reasonable substitute for clubs. Broken bats also can be made into good substitute clubs.

White shoe polish has numerous marking uses and can be removed from the floor with a little scrubbing.

Three-pound coffee cans make excellent targets. Empty half-gallon milk cartons also have a variety of uses.

Inner tubes can be cut in strips and used as resistance exercise equipment. The tube should be cut crosswise in one-inch-wide strips.

Old bowling pins can be obtained from most bowling alleys free of charge. Because the standard pins are too large for children to handle easily, cutting two to four inches off the bottom is recommended. Parallel cuts through the body of the pin provide shuffleboard disks. For kindergarten and first-grade children, improvised balls can be made from crumpled newspaper bound with cellophane tape. Papier-mâché balls are also useful. Light foam-rubber cubes can be trimmed to make interesting objects for throwing and catching.

Bamboo for making tinikling poles can sometimes be procured from carpet stores, which use the poles to give support to the center of a carpet roll. Plastic tinikling sticks are available commercially.

Diagrams and Specifications for Constructing Equipment and Supplies

Safety standards should apply to all school-constructed equipment; the construction and the materials used should not create any safety hazards. The design must be educationally sound and utilitarian.

BALANCE BEAM

The balance beam is used for many kinds of activities. Two types of stands for a 2-by-4-inch beam are shown in Figure 10.7 on page 202. The beam can be placed with the wide or the narrow side up, depending on the skill of the performer. If the beam is longer than eight feet, a third stand should be placed in the middle. Care must be taken to sand and apply multiple coats of finish to the beam to prevent splintering and cracking.

BALANCE-BEAM BENCH

The balance-beam bench is a versatile piece of equipment. Its dimensions can be modified depending on the age of the users (Figure 10.8 on page 202). It should be made of hardwood or hardwood plywood and should be well finished. Hooks can be fastened to the underside of the bench to provide even more uses for this important piece of apparatus.

BALANCE BOARDS

Many styles of balance board can be constructed, depending on the materials available and individual needs (Figure 10.9 on page 202). Glue a piece of rubber matting to the top of the board to prevent slipping and place it on an individual mat or on a piece of heavy rubber matting. A square board is easier to balance than a round one, for its corners touch the floor and give more stability.

FIGURE 10.7 Balance beam with stand.

BATTING TEE

Ideally, the batting tee should be adjustable to accommodate batters of various heights (Figure 10.10). Constructing an adjustable tee takes time, however, and the results are not always satisfactory. An alternative is to make several nonadjustable tees of different heights.

Materials:

One piece of one-inch pipe, 24 to 28 inches long

One piece of radiator hose, 8 to 12 inches long, with an inside diameter of 1¹/₂ inches

One block of wood, 3 by 12 by 12 inches

One pipe flange for one-inch pipe, to be mounted on the block

Screws and hose cement

Directions: Mount the flange on the block and screw the pipe into the flange. Place the radiator hose on the pipe. Paint as desired. To secure a good fit for the radiator hose, take the pipe to the supply source. If the hose is to remain fixed, then secure it with hose cement.

An alternative method is to drill a hole in the block and mount the pipe directly in the hole with mastic or good-quality glue. Note that 1-inch pipe has an outside diameter of approximately 1 inch, allowing the hose to fit properly over it.

FIGURE 10.8 Balance-beam bench.

BLOCKS AND CONES

Blocks with grooves on the top and on one of the sides are excellent for forming hurdles with wands. A 4-by-4-inch board cut in lengths of 6, 12, and 18 inches yields a variety of hurdle sizes. Cones can be notched and used in place of the blocks (Figure 10.11).

BOWLING PINS

Bowling alleys give away old pins, which can be used for many purposes. Some suggested uses are as field and gymnasium markers, for bowling games, and for relays. The bottom 2 inches of the pin should be cut off, and the base sanded smooth (Figure 10.12). Pins can be numbered and decorated with decals, colored tape, or paint.

FIGURE 10.9 Styles of balance board.

1½-in. radiator hose, 8–12 in. long (to be obtained at any service station; take pipe along to get good fit)

Hose can be adjusted for size of batter by sliding pipe up and down.

1-in. pipe, 24–28 in. long Screw into flange, which then is screwed onto the block of wood.

Batting tee (3 ft behind home plate)

Pipe flange

3 x 12 x12-in. block of wood

3 in.   12 in.   12 in.

FIGURE 10.10 Batting tee construction.

Blocks 4 x 4 x 12 in. or 4 x 4 x 18 in.

Down position

Notches cut ½ x ½ in. by table saw

Up position

Wand

Wand

Cones

Wand

Cut a ½-in. notch on each side of top lip of cone.

FIGURE 10.11 Blocks and cones.

13 in.

Mystic tape

Numeral

2 in.

Cut off.

FIGURE 10.12 Bowling pin.

FIGURE 10.13   Conduit hurdle construction.

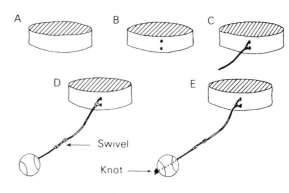

FIGURE 10.14   Footsie construction.

CONDUIT HURDLES

Conduit hurdles are lightweight and easy to store. Because they are not weighted and fall over easily, children have little fear about hitting them. The elastic bands can be moved up and down to create different heights and different challenges. Conduit can be purchased at most electrical supply houses.

Materials:

One piece of $\frac{1}{2}$-inch electrical conduit pipe, ten feet long

One piece of 1-inch stretch elastic tape

Wood doweling, $\frac{1}{2}$ inch in diameter

Directions: Bend the piece of conduit to the following dimensions: Uprights should be 30 inches high, the base should be 30 inches wide, and the sides of the base should be 15 inches long. A special tool for bending the conduit usually can be purchased from the supply house where the conduit was bought. Sew loops on each end of the elastic tape so that the tape will slide over the ends of the hurdles with a slight amount of tension. If necessary, short pieces of doweling can be put into the ends of the conduit to raise the height of the hurdle (Figure 10.13).

FOOTSIES

Footsies can be made economically by the children and provide an excellent movement challenge. The activity requires coordination of both feet to keep the footsie rotating properly.

Materials:

Plastic bleach bottle, half-gallon size

One piece of $\frac{1}{8}$-inch clothesline-type rope

Old tennis ball

Large fishing swivel, preferably with ball bearings

Directions: Cut a circular strip about two inches wide out of the bottom of a bleach bottle. Cut two holes in the strip about 1 inch apart. Thread a 3-foot piece of clothesline through the holes, and tie a knot on the outside of the strip. Cut the clothesline in half and tie the swivel to each end of the cut cord. The swivel prevents the rope from becoming twisted.

Puncture the tennis ball with an ice pick, making two holes directly across from each other. Thread the line through the holes with a piece of wire or a large crochet hook. Tie a large knot near the outer hole so that the line cannot slip back through (Figure 10.14).

GYM SCOOTERS

Scooters are easily constructed from readily available materials and can be made in many sizes and shapes. The casters should be checked to make sure that they do not mark the floor. Scooters have many activity applications and can also be used to move heavy equipment.

Materials:

One piece of 2-inch yellow pine board, 12 by 12 inches

Four ball-bearing casters with 2-inch wheels of hard rubber

Protective rubber stripping, four feet in length

Cement

Screws and paint

Directions: Actual dimensions of the board are around $1\frac{5}{8}$ by $11\frac{5}{8}$ inches. Two pieces of three-quarter-inch plywood glued together can be substituted. Cut and round the corners, smoothing them with a power sander. Sand all edges by hand, and apply two coats of paint. Fasten the four casters approximately $1\frac{1}{2}$ inches diagonally in from the corners. A rubber strip fixed around the edges with staples and cement (Figure 10.15) will cushion the impact of the scooter on other objects.

FIGURE 10.17 Weighted hurdle and high-jump rope construction.

FIGURE 10.15 Gym scooter construction.

HOOPS

Hoops can be constructed from one-half-inch plastic water pipe (PVC), which unfortunately is available in drab colors only. The cost savings of using the pipe are, however, great. Hoops can be constructed in different sizes. A short piece of doweling, fixed with a power stapler or tacks, can be used to join the ends together (Figure 10.16). An alternative joining method is to use special pipe connectors. Weather-stripping cement helps make a more permanent joint.

HURDLE AND HIGH-JUMP ROPE

The weighted hurdle and high-jump rope is ideal for beginning hurdlers and high jumpers who may fear hitting the bar. The rope can be hung over the pins of the high-jump standards; the weights keep the rope fairly taut.

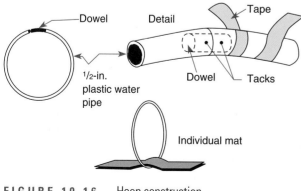

FIGURE 10.16 Hoop construction.

Materials:

One piece of $\frac{3}{8}$-inch rope, 10 feet long

Two rubber crutch tips (number 19)

Tacks (number 14) and penny shingle nails

Sand

Directions: Drive a carpet tack through the rope approximately three-quarters inch from each end. Drive three nails into the bottom of each of the two rubber crutch tips. Place the rope ends inside the crutch tips and fill the tips with sand. Tape shut the top of the tips (Figure 10.17).

INDIVIDUAL MATS

Individual mats can be made from indoor-outdoor carpeting that has a rubber backing. This prevents the mat from sliding on the floor and offers some cushion. The mats also can be washed easily when they become soiled. Mats of different colors are preferable, because they can be used for games, for color tag, and for easy division of the class according to mat color. Carpet stores often have small pieces and remnants that they will sell cheaply or give away.

Another type of individual mat is designed to fold (Figure 10.18). These mats are useful for aerobic dance classes because they are lighter and easier to handle than the carpet mats. The major drawback is that the folding mats are more expensive.

JUMPING BOXES

Jumping boxes are used to develop a wide variety of body management skills. The dimensions can be varied to satisfy individual needs, but 8- and 16-inch boxes seem to be the most useful.

FIGURE 10.18   Folding individual mat.

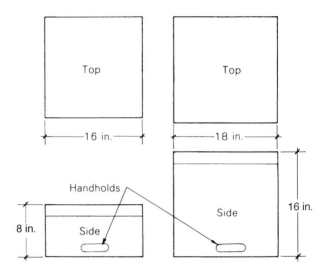

FIGURE 10.19   Jumping box construction.

Materials:

¾-inch marine plywood

Wood screws, paint, and glue

Carpet pad remnants

Naugahyde or similar material to cover box top

Upholstery tacks

Directions: Cut the four sides to similar dimensions and then sand them together to make sure they are exactly the same size. Use a countersink and drill the screw holes, apply glue at the joints, and screw the sides together. When the box is assembled, sand all edges to remove any sharpness. Paint the boxes, preferably with a latex-based paint, because it does not chip as easily as oil-based enamel. If handholds are desired, drill holes and then cut them out with a saber saw (Figure 10.19). Covering is optional; if desired, cut a carpet pad remnant to match the size of the top of the box, and cover with a piece of Naugahyde. The Naugahyde should overlap about four inches on each side of the box so that it can be folded under to make a double thickness and then tacked down.

JUMPING STANDARDS

Jumping standards are useful for hurdling, jumping, and over-and-under activities. Many shapes and sizes are possible (Figure 10.20).

Materials:

Two pieces of ¾-inch plywood 25 inches long, cut as shown

Two blocks of wood, 2 by 4 by 6 inches

Glue and paint

Broomstick, 48 inches long

Directions: The wood blocks should be mortised lengthwise, about one inch deep. After the uprights have been cut to form, set them with glue into the

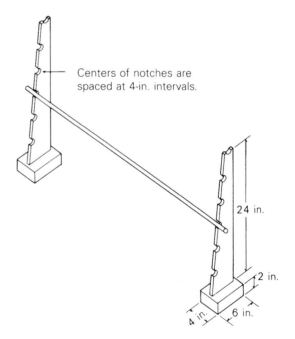

Centers of notches are spaced at 4-in. intervals.

FIGURE 10.20   Jumping standard construction.

blocks—making sure that the uprights are plumb. Paint as desired. Small circles of various colors can be placed at each of the corresponding notches of the uprights for quick positioning of the crosspiece.

LADDER

A ladder laid on the floor or on a mat provides a floor apparatus for various movement experiences and has value in remedial programs and programs for exceptional children. Sizes may vary (Figure 10.21).

Materials:

Two straight-grained 2-by-4-inch timbers, 9½ feet long

Ten 1¼-inch or 1½-inch dowels, 20 inches long

Glue

Paint or varnish

Directions: Round the ends and sand the edges of the timbers. Center holes for the ladder rungs 12 inches apart, beginning 3 inches from one end. Cut the holes for the rungs one-sixteenth inch smaller than the diameter of the rungs. Put glue in all the holes on one timber, and drive in all the rungs. Next, glue the other timber in place. Varnish or paint the ladder.

LUMMI STICKS

Lummi sticks are excellent tools for developing rhythmic skills. The sticks can also be used as relay batons.

Materials:

1-inch doweling, in 12-inch lengths

Paint and varnish

Directions: Notches and different colors are optional, but these decorations do make the sticks more attractive.

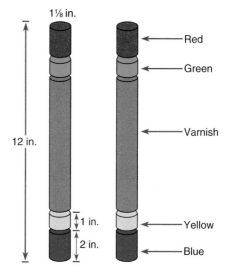

FIGURE 10.22 Lummi stick construction and decoration.

If desired, use a table saw to cut notches one-eighth inch wide and one-eighth inch deep. Round off the ends and sand the entire stick. Paint and varnish the stick as shown in Figure 10.22.

MAGIC ROPES

Magic or stretch ropes can be made by stringing together 25 to 30 large rubber bands (Figure 10.23). Common clothing elastic also can be used to make the ropes. Some teachers have had success with shock cord, which usually can be purchased at a boating marina or hardware store. Bungee cord of the proper length may also be used. Similar to shock cord, it may be purchased at many sports equipment outlets.

OUTDOOR BASES

There are many satisfactory methods for constructing bases. They can be made from heavy canvas by folding the canvas over three or four times and stitching it together. Heavy rubber matting can be cut to size. More permanent bases can be made from outdoor plywood and painted (Figure 10.24).

FIGURE 10.21 Ladder construction.

FIGURE 10.23 Magic rope construction.

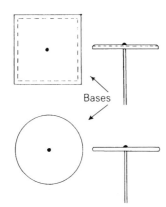

FIGURE 10.24 Outdoor base construction.

Materials:

Exterior ³/₄-inch plywood

One ¹/₂-inch carriage bolt, 14 inches long

Paint

Directions: Cut the plywood into 12-by-12-inch squares. Bevel and sand the top edges. Drill a ¹/₂-inch hole in the center of the base and then paint the base. When the paint has dried, place the carriage bolt into the center hole and drive it into the ground. More holes can be used to make the base more secure. Large spikes can be substituted for the carriage bolt.

PADDLES

Paddles can be made in many sizes and with different thicknesses of plywood (Figure 10.25). Usually, ¹/₄-inch plywood is recommended for kindergarten through grade 2, and ³/₈-inch plywood for grades 3 through 6. Paddles can be painted or varnished, and the handles taped to give a better grip. Holes can be drilled into the paddle area to make it lighter and to decrease air resistance. Good-quality plywood, perhaps marine plywood, is essential.

For hitting a foam-rubber ball or a newspaper ball, nylon-stocking paddles can substitute quite effectively for wooden paddles. Because of their light weight, they do not cause injuries. They are therefore excellent for primary-age children. A badminton birdie can be used with the paddle for various activities such as hitting over a net, and for many individual stunts.

Materials:

Old nylon stocking

Wire coat hanger

Masking tape or athletic tape

String or wire

Directions: Bend the hanger into a diamond shape. Bend the hook into a loop, which becomes the handle of the paddle (Figure 10.26). Pull the stocking over the hanger, beginning at the corner farthest from the handle, until the toe of the nylon is as tight as possible against the corner point of the hanger. Hold the nylon at the neck of the hanger and stretch it as tight as possible.

Tie the nylon securely with a piece of heavy string or light wire. Wrap the rest of the nylon around the handle to make a smooth, contoured surface. Complete the paddle by wrapping tape around the entire handle to prevent loosening.

PADDLE TENNIS NET SUPPORTS

The advantage of paddle tennis net supports is that they stand by themselves on the floor and still provide proper net tension. The stands come apart easily and quickly and can be stored in a small space. For lengths up to eight feet or so, a single center board, with holes on each end, can be used, thus eliminating the need for bolting two pieces together (Figure 10.27).

FIGURE 10.25 Paddle construction.

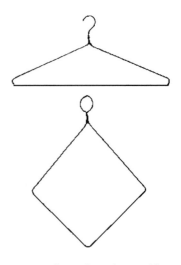

FIGURE 10.26 Frame for nylon-stocking paddle.

FIGURE 10.27 Paddle tennis net support construction.

Materials:

Two broomsticks or ³⁄₄-inch dowels, 2 feet long

Two 1-by-4-inch boards, 2 feet long

One or more additional 1-by-4-inch boards

Glue

Directions: For the upright supports, drill a hole ³⁄₄ inch in diameter in the center of each one-by-four-inch board. Drive the dowel into the hole, fixing it with glue. The dowels can be notched at intervals for different net heights.

The length of the crosspiece depends on how much court width is to be covered. If a single crosspiece is to be used, holes should be bored into each end. The holes should be big enough (⁷⁄₈ inch) so that the dowel slides through easily. If the crosspiece is in two halves, ¼-inch bolts are needed to bolt the halves together, as indicated in the diagram.

PARTNER TUG-OF-WAR ROPES

Partner tug-of-war ropes can be made from garden hose and ropes (Figure 10.28). The cheaper, plastic garden hose (⁵⁄₈ inch in diameter) works much better than the more expensive rubber hose. The plastic hose then does not crease as easily and gives the hands more protection. The white, soft, braided nylon rope (³⁄₈ inch in diameter) offers adequate strength and is much easier to handle than other types of rope. A bowline knot should be used, because it does not slip and tighten around the hands. The ends of the nylon rope should be melted over a flame to prevent them from unraveling.

PLASTIC MARKERS AND SCOOPS

One-gallon plastic jugs filled halfway with sand and recapped make fine boundary markers. The markers can be painted different colors to signify goals, boundaries, and division lines. The jugs also can be numbered and used to designate different teaching stations. Plastic

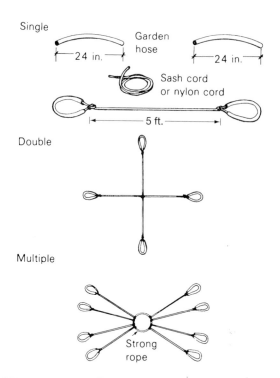

FIGURE 10.28 Partner tug-of-war construction.

bottles can be cut down to make scoops (Figure 10.29), which have many activity possibilities.

RINGS, DECK TENNIS (QUOITS)

Deck tennis is a popular recreational net game that requires only a ring as basic equipment. The rings can be made easily by the students and are useful for playing catch and for target throwing. They can be fashioned from heavy rope by braiding the ends together, but the construction method illustrated in Figure 10.30 on page 210 is easier. Weather-stripping cement helps strengthen the joints.

FIGURE 10.29 Plastic marker and scoop.

FIGURE 10.30   Ring construction.

FIGURE 10.32   Sit-and-reach box.

RING TOSS TARGET

Many ring toss targets can be made from 1-by-4-inch lumber and old broom or mop handles. They can be made to hang on the wall or to lie flat on the ground. The quoits constructed from garden hose are excellent for throwing at the targets. The target pegs can be painted different colors to signify different point values.

Materials:

Two 1-by-4-inch boards, 18 to 20 inches long

Five pegs, 6 inches long (old broom handles)

Screws and paint

Directions: Glue and screw the one-by-four-inch boards together, as shown in Figure 10.31. Bore the proper-sized holes in the boards with a brace and bit, and glue or screw the pegs into the holes. Note that two blocks must be screwed on the ends of the board placed on top so that the target stands level. Paint the base and the sticks, and, if desired, number the sticks according to point value.

SIT-AND-REACH BOX

Sit-and-reach boxes are used for measuring flexibility in the Fitnessgram (Figure 10.32). The basic sit-and-reach box is a 12-inch cube with a top that is 21 inches long. Sit-and-reach boxes for the Fitnessgram require that the top of the box be calibrated in inches. The 9-inch mark is lined up with the side of the box where the feet are placed.

TIRE STANDS

Tire stands keep tires in an upright position (Figure 10.33). The upright tires can be used for movement problems, over-and-through relays, and vaulting activities, and as targets. Tires are much cleaner and more attractive when they are painted both inside and out.

Materials:

Two 1-by-6-inch boards, 24 inches long, for side pieces

Two 1-by-6-inch boards, 13 inches long, for end pieces

Four $^3/_8$-inch carriage bolts, 2 inches long

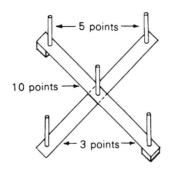

FIGURE 10.31   Ring toss target construction.

FIGURE 10.33   Tire stand construction.

Glue, screws, and paint

One used tire

Directions: Cut the ends of the side boards at a 70-degree angle. Dado each end piece with two grooves ³/₄ inch wide and ¹/₄ inch deep. The distance between the grooves is determined by the width of the tire. Round off the corners and sand the edges. Glue and screw the stand together. Install the tire in the frame by drilling two three-eighths-inch holes in each side of the frame and in the tire. Secure the tire inside the frame with the bolts. Paint both the tire and the frame a bright color. Note that the frame dimensions will vary according to the size of the tire, making it necessary to adjust the frame dimensions to the tire.

TRACK STARTER

The track starter simulates a gun report. If many starters are made, the children can start their own races.

Materials:

Two 2-by-4-inch boards, 11 inches long

Two small strap hinges

Two small cabinet handles

Directions: Cut the boards to size, and sand off any rough edges. Place the two blocks together, and apply the two hinges with screws. Add the two handles on the outside of the boards. Open the boards and then slam them together quickly to obtain a loud bang (Figure 10.34).

WANDS

Handles from old brooms or mops make excellent wands (Figure 10.35). The handles may have different diameters, but this is not an important factor. The ends can be sanded, and the wands painted different colors. If noise is a concern, rubber crutch tips can be placed on the wand ends.

⅝-in. or ¾-in. doweling

Lengths: grades K–1 = 30 in., 2–3 = 36 in., 4–6 = 42 in. or 1 m

FIGURE 10.35 Wand dimensions.

YARN BALLS

Yarn balls can be used to enhance throwing and catching skills and for many games. They have advantages over balls in that they do not hurt when they hit a child, and they can be used in the classroom or in other areas of limited space. Yarn balls can be made by the older children or by the PTA. Two construction methods are offered here; both work well. When possible, wool or cotton yarns should be used, because the balls will then shrink and become tight when soaked in hot water or steamed. Nylon and other synthetic yarns are impervious to water and do not shrink and bond.

Materials for Method One:

One skein of yarn per ball

One piece of box cardboard, 5 inches wide and about 10 inches long

Strong, light cord for binding

Directions for Method One: Wrap the yarn 20 to 25 times around the 5-inch-wide dimension of the cardboard. Slide the yarn off the cardboard, and bind it in the middle with the cord to form a tied loop of yarn. Continue this procedure until all of the yarn is used up and tied in looped bunches. Next, take two of the tied loops and tie them together at the center, using several turns of the cord. This forms a bundle of two tied loops, as illustrated in Figure 10.36. Continue tying the bundles together until all are used. Now cut the loops and trim the formed ball. The cutting should be done carefully so that the yarn lengths are reasonably even, or considerable trimming will be needed.

FIGURE 10.36 Yarn ball, method one.

(Track starter illustration)

Handle

Hinges

FIGURE 10.34 Track starter.

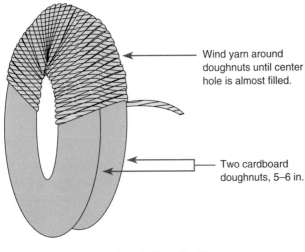

Wind yarn around doughnuts until center hole is almost filled.

Two cardboard doughnuts, 5–6 in.

FIGURE 10.37   Yarn ball, method two.

Materials for Method Two:

Two skeins of yarn per ball

Two cardboard doughnuts, 5 or 6 inches in diameter

Strong, light cord for tying

Directions for Method Two: Make a slit in the doughnuts so that the yarn can be wrapped around the cardboard (Figure 10.37). Holding strands from both skeins, wrap the yarn around both doughnuts until the center hole is almost completely filled with yarn. Lay the doughnut of wrapped yarn on a flat surface, insert a pair of scissors between the two doughnuts, and cut around the entire outer edge. Carefully insert a double strand of the light cord between the two doughnuts and catch all of the individual yarn strands around the middle with the cord. Tie the cord as tightly as possible with a double knot. Remove the doughnuts, and trim the ball if necessary.

REFLECTION AND REVIEW QUESTIONS

How and Why

1. Do the school facilities in your area meet the standards of outdoor facilities?

2. How might teachers have to adapt because of the many "non-PE" uses of the indoor physical education facilities?

3. Why would "homemade" equipment be necessary for some schools? Identify equipment that can be made by teachers.

4. How can teachers ensure appropriate maintenance of equipment?

Content Review

1. Present several standards for outdoor facilities. Include comments regarding playgrounds.

2. Identify four pieces each of outdoor equipment for upper body development, lower body development, and balance skills.

3. Discuss the standards for indoor facilities for physical education.

4. Discuss the difference between equipment and supplies. Provide examples of each.

5. List several pieces of equipment that are primarily used indoors.

6. Discuss the importance of purchasing policies, storage plans, and maintenance for equipment.

FOR MORE INFORMATION

References and Suggested Readings

Dougherty, N. J. (Ed.). (2002). *Principles of safety in physical education and sport.* 3rd ed. Reston, VA: AAHPERD.

Hart, J. E., & Ritson, R. J. (2002). *Liability and safety in physical education and sport: A practitioner's guide to the legal aspects of teaching and coaching in elementary and secondary schools.* 2nd ed. Reston, VA: AAHPERD.

McIntyre, S., & Goltsman, S. M. (1997). *Safety first checklist: Audit & inspection program for children's play areas.* Berkeley, CA: MIG Communications.

Morrison, M. L. (1993). *Evaluating and improving playground safety: A playground inventory and assessment system.* Pittsburgh: Injury Prevention Works.

Raatma, L. (1999). *Safety on the playground.* Mankato, MN: Bridgestone Books.

U.S. Consumer Product Safety Commission. (1997). *Handbook for public playground safety* (Publication No. 325). Washington, DC: Author.

Werner, P. H., & Simmons, R. A. (1990). *Homemade play equipment for children.* Reston, VA: American Alliance for Health, Physical Education, Recreation, and Dance.

Websites

Equipment
www.gophersport.com

Making Physical Education Equipment
www.pecentral.org/preschool/
   prekhomemadeequipmentmenu.html
http://igreen.tripod.com/gerpe/id18.html

Playground Safety
www.cpsc.gov/CPSCPUB/PUBS/playpubs.html
www.playgroundsafety.org

11

Integrating Academic Concepts

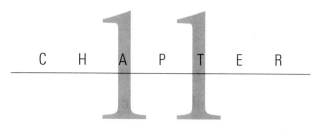

ESSENTIAL COMPONENTS OF QUALITY PROGRAMS

▶ **I. Organized around content standards**

▶ **II. Student-centered and developmentally appropriate**

▶ **III. Physical activity and motor skill development form the core of the program**

  IV. Teaches management skills and self-discipline

▶ **V. Promotes inclusion of all students**

  VI. Focuses on process over product

  VII. Promotes lifetime personal health and wellness

  VIII. Teaches cooperation and responsibility and promotes sensitivity to diversity

NATIONAL STANDARDS FOR PHYSICAL EDUCATION*

1. Demonstrates competency in motor skills and movement patterns needed to perform a variety of physical activities.

▶ **2. Demonstrates understanding of movement concepts, principles, and tactics as they apply to the learning and performance of physical activities.**

3. Participates regularly in physical activity.

4. Achieves and maintains a health-enhancing level of physical fitness.

5. Exhibits responsible personal and social behavior that respects self and others in physical activity.

6. Values physical activity for health, enjoyment, challenge, self-expression, and/or social interaction.

*National Association for Sport and Physical Education (NASPE), 2004.

SUMMARY

Integrating academic concepts into physical education involves incorporating concepts learned in the classroom into the physical education lesson in an effort to reinforce the concepts or teach them from a different perspective. Although research findings do not suggest that increasing the physical activity levels of children increases their academic performance, integrating academic content into physical education may help clarify concepts students are having difficulty with or simply strengthen the children's understanding of a concept. In addition, by assisting classroom teachers through integrating academic content, physical education teachers build goodwill with classroom teachers and improve the overall climate of the schools to the extent that all teachers will be working toward the betterment of all students.

OUTCOMES

- Define integrating academic concepts and explain its importance.

- Understand the role of integrating academic concepts in physical education.

- Explain the benefits and limitations of integrating academic concepts in physical education.

- Discuss the relationship between physical activity and learning.

- Present models of integration of academic concepts and discuss how they can be used.

- Describe several activities that integrate either math, language arts, science, and/or social studies into a quality physical education lesson.

INTEGRATING ACADEMIC CONCEPTS INTO PHYSICAL EDUCATION

During their time in school, students are often taught concepts that combine two seemingly unrelated academic areas. Reading about the habitats of animals combines reading (language arts) and biology (science). Students calculating the distance from their town to the state capital use concepts from both math and social studies. Instruction that combines academic concepts from more than one subject area is referred to as *integration,* which is instruction designed to integrate two or more concepts from different areas to enhance learning. Other terms to describe this process are *interdisciplinary, multidisciplinary,* and *cross-disciplinary.* Although each of these has specific definitions, for the purpose of this chapter and book, the term *integration* is used throughout.

Physical education offers an outstanding setting for integration of academic concepts with minimal impact on the integrity of the physical education curriculum. For instance, teachers often have students time their stretching exercises by counting from one to ten. To integrate a foreign language, teachers can have students count in that different language; to integrate spelling, students can be told to spell out vocabulary words for the week; and to integrate math, teachers can instruct their students to skip-count by fours. All of these examples are simple adjustments to common instructions that physical education teachers use. However, these adjustments do require planning.

While it is clear that academic concepts can be integrated into a quality physical education curriculum, physical education instruction should not be centered on academic integration. Academic integration is a secondary outcome for physical education in contrast to the six primary NASPE outcomes discussed in Chapter 1. It is important to remember that physical education is the only area in the school where youngsters are taught how to care for the physical side of their bodies. Integrate academic concepts when possible, but not at the expense of physical activity and the health of students.

When integrating academic concepts, a series of instructional activities is planned to ensure that physical education outcomes are reached. The teacher then determines the academic concepts that can be integrated with slight alterations to the lessons. When teaching academic concepts through physical activity, the teacher has an academic concept in mind and then teaches the concept through physical activity. For example, math relays are commonly used when integrating physical education and math. In this activity, teams of five to six students, one student at a time, run the length of the gym, retrieve a flash card, and bring it back to the team. After all members finish, the class uses the numbers from the flash cards and creates the largest number possible. However, with only a few of the students active at any given time during the activity, the activity is not a quality physical education experience. When integrating academic content into the physical education curriculum, it is important to maintain the integrity of the physical education program. In addition, integration should occur *after* a solid, well-planned, quality physical education program has been established.

WHY INTEGRATE ACADEMIC CONCEPTS?

Education is always seeking strategies and research to support methods for effectively teaching concepts. One such method is integration. Purcell-Cone, Werner, Cone, and Woods (1998) provide studies supporting the use of integration in a variety of subjects; however, much of the research has shown mixed results. Thus more research in this area is needed before conclusions can be drawn. Although there are relatively few studies to support the integration of academic content into physical education as an effective strategy for teaching, many experts believe this practice should be promoted. To this end, countless journals, books, and workshops have highlighted activities and ideas for integration. Several of these are listed in the "References and Suggested Readings" section at the end of this chapter.

Related to the need for research on the effectiveness of integration is the need for research on the impact of physical activity on learning. Researchers in this area want to know if physically active children learn better and perform better academically than physically inactive children. In a statistical review of numerous studies on children, Sibley and Etnier (2003) conclude that physical activity and cognition are positively related and that physical activity may aid in cognitive development. Tomporowski (2003) suggests that physical activity may improve cognitive performance. This paper also suggests that behavior improves following activity bouts. Similarly, Pellegrini, Huberty, and Jones (1995) found that recess spread throughout the day, which allows short and regular bouts of physical activity, may help children's attention and behavior. Although the impact of physical activity on learning in children is not as clear as some believe, evidence supports that, either directly or indirectly, physical activity may contribute to academic learning.

If the research is not definitive, why incorporate academic concepts into the physical education lesson? In short, integration serves as a marketing tool for physical educators. In an area of accountability where classroom teachers are under great pressure to increase academic achievement by increasing high-stakes test scores, physical educators can build goodwill with classroom teachers by offering to supplement the classroom content. This shows classroom teachers that physical educators are team players and are concerned with student learning. Integrating also facilitates the need for classroom teachers to observe or visit the physical education setting to see how concepts are being integrated. Lastly, if physical educators are integrating academic content and showing an interest in the classroom, classroom teachers may be inclined to integrate physical activity into their classroom instruction. If this situation arises, the physical educator should assist classroom teachers with ideas and strategies for teaching physically active students. Specifically, classroom teachers may need assistance with management strategies and equipment.

Integration in physical education has benefits and limitations. The benefits include building goodwill in the school, helping students who are kinesthetic learners, teaching content in a new setting through a different method, demonstrating that physical educators are educators too, and increasing the activity level of students when classroom teachers integrate physical activity into their instruction. The limitations most often cited are finding the time to develop the lessons, planning for integration that does not sacrifice the physical education lesson, and feeling uncomfortable teaching outside an area of expertise. These are legitimate concerns; however, with some practice and the belief that integration can supplement classroom learning, physical education teachers can create effective integration activities.

TYPES OF INTEGRATION

Several models can be used when planning academic integration activities. These models range from the physical education teacher working alone to a group of teachers working together to develop learning experiences in a variety of settings. The individual model involves the physical education teacher working individually to develop ideas for integrating academic content. For example, the teacher may want to integrate concepts related to levers during a throwing lesson. This requires the teacher to review information on levers and how they relate to throwing and to determine how to integrate the concepts into the lesson without sacrificing time for activity and the learning of throwing skills.

For the partner model, the physical education teacher collaborates with a classroom teacher. This collaboration can be as simple as the physical education teacher asking the classroom teacher for the vocabulary words for the week. The model can also be as complex as two teachers developing a yearly calendar that has similar concepts taught during the same time. For example, a physical education lesson involving a Hispanic dance could be taught during the same week as a geography lesson on Mexico. During the physical education lesson, the teacher could use Spanish terms during instruction and have students count in Spanish while stretching. Although these changes do not compromise the physical education curriculum, they serve to enrich the educational experience and reinforce academic concepts learned in other areas.

Group collaboration usually involves a group of classroom teachers from a common grade level and the physical educator. In this model, a considerable amount of planning is involved that usually centers on a theme. Teachers take the theme and generate learning activities that cut across academic areas. One example is an Olympics theme. For a set period, a majority of the activities that students engage in are related to the Olympics. Specific countries are chosen and each class represents a country. In social studies, students learn about the cultures, geography, economy, people, and/or government of their country and the others being represented. For math, students calculate distances between cities in the countries and the population of all of the countries involved, determine the average population of the countries, and graph the number of Olympic medals each country earned during the most recent Olympics. During language arts, students read about their country and write a summary of their readings, write letters to pen pals in that country, and learn common phrases from their country's language. For science, concepts associated with the environment of all the countries, their weather, plants and animals, and inventions are covered. The technology teacher helps students research their country online. The music teacher teaches songs, anthems, and dances from each country while the art teacher helps students create the country's flags or draw posters advertising the Olympics. A school assembly can serve as the opening ceremonies where students report about their countries, sing their national anthems, and display their flags. During physical education, students participate in activities related to the Olympics, and the history of these activities in the Olympics is discussed. Track and field, gymnastics, volleyball, rhythmic gymnastics, basketball, tennis, badminton, and hockey are all activities that are included in most physical education curricula already and could be included in lessons taught during this time. Other examples involving the group model are a Viking theme, a Civil War theme, and an ancient Rome theme. Although planning is necessary, students will have truly exciting and educational experiences that they will likely remember for a lifetime.

HOW TO INTEGRATE ACADEMIC CONTENT

As stated earlier, integrating academic content must be carefully and thoughtfully planned to ensure that the activity is a quality learning experience and to maintain the integrity of the physical education curriculum. The following list is a series of steps for initiating integration in physical education, learning what to integrate, and learning how to enhance the effectiveness of the integration activities.

Decide on the Integration Model

If the individual model is used, it is important that the teacher do a considerable amount of research to determine what to teach, at what level it should be taught, how to teach it, and what lessons to teach it in. If the partner model is selected, a potential teacher to partner with must be determined. It is important that the partner teacher be equally interested in what is being taught in physical education. Ideally, the classroom teacher will also be interested in strategies for teaching academic concepts through physical activity in the classroom. Choosing the group model will require the physical education teacher to select teachers who are generally interested in all of the activities, not just those they are teaching.

Ask about Students Who Could Use Additional Support

Approach the classroom teacher to find out what concepts students are having trouble with in the classroom. It may be that physical education offers an excellent opportunity to teach the same concept with a different strategy, namely, teaching the concept with movement.

Ask Teachers What Concepts They Will Be Teaching

Take an interest in what concepts classroom teachers are teaching. Making such an effort makes you seem like an interested and supportive party who wants to help their students reach academic outcomes. Many classroom teachers can provide a calendar containing concepts being taught in the coming weeks. From this calendar, you can generate integration ideas. The classroom teachers often can mention concepts that could be taught through physical education.

Ask How Concepts Are Being Taught

Once the academic concepts to be integrated are established, it is important to find out how these concepts are being taught. Using key terms or similar ideas and slightly modifying them may be helpful when teaching the integrated material. Conversely, teaching a concept differently than how the classroom teacher teaches it may help some students learn the concept better. If this is the case, discuss it with the classroom teacher. In some cases, teaching the same concept with two different methodologies or perspectives may confuse youngsters rather than help them learn.

Show Classroom Teachers What Is Being Taught during Physical Education

Invite the classroom teacher to a lesson involving integration. This serves two purposes. First, the classroom teacher can provide feedback concerning the integration activity that you might use to make the activity more effective. Inviting the classroom teacher also exposes the teacher to physical education. Often, classroom teachers have little knowledge of what is being taught during physical education. Having them observe a lesson will show them that physical education is educational and makes an important contribution to the school curriculum.

Reflect

When reflecting about your lessons, it is important to evaluate integration activities as well. Questions that you can ask are the following: Did the integration activity sacrifice any of the activity planned for the physical education lesson? Could I have integrated the concept with less interference? Did the students understand the academic content? How could I change the integrated activity to make it more effective? Would the integrated concept fit better in another part of the lesson or in another lesson?

ACADEMIC INTEGRATION ACTIVITIES

The remainder of this chapter presents ideas for integrating academic concepts into physical education instruction. All of the activities are designed to be implemented with the *Dynamic Physical Education Curriculum Guide* (2007) lessons. They teach a variety of academic concepts while maintaining physical education outcomes. In fact, many of the activities are simple modifications to traditional activities. Each state and academic area has standards pertaining to what students should learn. In addition, each class, student, and teacher will be learning academic content in a different manner. Therefore, presenting all the activities that could be implemented to teach each of the objectives in each academic area is not possible. Also, keep in mind that the purpose of integrating academic content into physical education is to supplement and enhance what is being taught in the classroom rather than replace it.

Instructional activities in this chapter are organized into four academic areas: math, language arts, science, and social studies. These are the primary academic content areas in most elementary school curricula. Each academic area is then subdivided into "Integration Tips" and "Activities." Integration tips are simple strategies that teachers may use to teach academic content in physical education. For example, rather than saying, "Freeze," a teacher might say, "Fifteen degrees Fahrenheit" to signal a freeze and to reinforce that water freezes when below 32 degrees Fahrenheit. Integration tips are not specific to a lesson; they can be used in a variety of lessons. For each integration activity that follows, these four components are listed: the academic concept, the PE concepts, the PE lesson part where the concept should be integrated, and the supplies necessary to teach the concept. The academic concept is the general concept or concepts being taught or reinforced through the activity. For specific standards and objectives related to the four academic areas, refer to the Websites provided at the end of the chapter. The PE concept provides the general physical education concepts being taught during the activity. The PE lesson part shows where the integration activity can be taught during a four-part lesson. If the activity is part of a lesson focus, ideas for the types of lessons are provided. For more information about these lessons and ideas for integration, see the *Dynamic Physical Education Curriculum Guide* (2007) that accompanies this text.

Math

During the early elementary years, students learn math concepts such as number recognition and meaning, counting, shapes, addition, subtraction, measuring, and patterns. As they progress through the grades, students learn numbers through one million, multiplication, division, fractions, percent, degrees, geometry, and statistics. To familiarize themselves with elementary math, physical educators can read elementary school math books and examine the *Principles and Standards for School Mathematics,* published by the National Council of Teachers of Mathematics (2000). This provides mathematics standards and expectations and is comparable to the National Association for Sport and Physical Education's *National Standards for Physical Education* (2004).

INTEGRATION TIPS

Counting (Skipping Numbers)

Any time counting is used during a lesson (e.g., keeping score, timing a stretch), instruct students to count by a given number. For example, rather than saying that one goal equals 1 point, say that each goal is worth 3 points. Thus, as the number of goals accumulates, students must count by threes.

Math Terms

Many mathematical terms such as *diameter* and *perimeter* can easily be integrated into many physical education lessons. For example, rather than instructing students, "Jog around the outside of the gym floor," tell them, "Jog around the perimeter of the gym." When discussing the influence the size of a ball has on throwing, instead of saying, "Is a bigger ball easier to throw or harder to throw?," say, "If a ball has a larger diameter, is it easier to throw? Remind me what *diameter* means before you answer." These examples allow math terms to be integrated without interfering with the physical education lesson.

Degrees and Fractions

In many physical education lessons, students are told, "Turn facing away from the teacher" or "Turn all the way around." Early in physical education experiences, these basic terms are necessary; however, as students become older, more challenging directions can be used to teach math concepts. For example, have students turn "360 degrees" or "180 degrees" before catching a beanbag or when dismounting from a balance bench. Similarly, incorporate fractions by having students make a half turn or a three-quarter turn. For further challenge, you could instruct students to make a ¼ turn or a $^{36}/_{2}$ turn.

Estimating

Because numbers are often used during physical education, estimating can be naturally integrated into a variety of lessons. The following are just two examples. Messy Back Yard is a game in which students attempt to rid their backyard (side of the court) of yarn balls by throwing them over the net to the other team's side. Meanwhile, the other team tries to rid its side as well. After a set amount of time, the teacher stops the game, and yarn balls on each side are counted. To teach estimation, before counting the number of balls on each side, the teacher can instruct children to estimate how many balls are on each side and keep that number in their heads. When the teacher announces the actual number, the children then self-assess their estimates. Another example is to ask students to estimate how many times they can toss their beanbags a certain height and catch them in 30 seconds. This activity can be repeated two or three times to allow students to make adjustments to their estimates.

Measurement

Measurement is often included during the physical education lesson. Concepts related to measuring distance, height, weight, and time can all be integrated into physical education lessons. During a jumping lesson, students can be asked to jump as far as they can and then quickly measure the distance of their jump using tiles on the floor (Figure 11.1). Floor tiles are generally 12 inches square. Track and field lessons also offer numerous opportunities for students to measure. Students can time each other in a run, measure the length of a person's long jump, or measure the height of a high jump.

ACTIVITIES

► **MYSTERY NUMBER**

Math Concepts: Number recognition and number sequencing

PE Concepts: Locomotor skills, spacing, sequencing skills

PE Lesson Part: Introductory activity

Supplies: Laminated signs with numbers or sequences of numbers

The teacher holds one of the laminated signs in the air so that the students can see it and she cannot. The students are instructed to perform their favorite locomotor skill the same number of times indicated on the sign. When they finish they should stop and then pick a different locomotor skill and perform it the same number of times. For example, if the sign has the number 8 on it, a child may choose to walk eight steps, stop, and then skip eight times. The teacher, by watching the students, tries to determine the mystery number.

FIGURE 11.1   Checking the length of the long jump.

FIGURE 11.2   Number challenge sign.

For older students, a sequence of numbers is placed on the sign. For example, a sign could read "7, 3, 15." For each number, students choose a locomotor movement and perform it. One student may choose to gallop 7 times, walk 3 steps, and jump 15 times. When these are completed, the students start over with a different sequence of 7, 3, 15. Again, the teacher tries to determine the number sequence on the card. If desired, specific locomotor movements can be provided for each number, as shown in Figure 11.2.

► **SHAPES**

Math Concept: Shape recognition

PE Concepts: Locomotor skills, low-organized games

PE Lesson Part: Game activity

Supplies: Different-colored laminated circles, squares, triangles, and rectangles

Each student stands in a circle with a laminated shape on the floor in front of him or her. When the teacher calls out a specific shape, all students with that shape step back out of the circle and begin running around the circle in a designated direction. Their goal is to get back to their shape as quickly as possible. As soon as all runners have returned to their position, the teacher calls out another shape. While the runners are running, the remainder of the class is responsible for running in place and cheering on the runners. To add some challenge for older students, rather than say, "Triangle," the number of sides of the shape ("Three") can be used as the signal. As a variation, rather than shapes, the color of the shape can be used. When the teacher says, "Red," all students with a red shape are runners. Because this activity involves movement of light intensity, it works well as a game following a vigorous activity such as individual rope-jumping.

SYMMETRY ASYMMETRY

Math Concepts: Symmetric and asymmetric balance

PE Concepts: Nonlocomotor skills, balance, body awareness

PE Lesson Part: Lesson focus (gymnastics)

Supplies: Tumbling mats

During a gymnastics lesson students are often asked to perform balances while meeting various challenges (e.g., balancing on two body parts; balancing on three body parts, one being a hand, etc.). For this activity, students are asked to perform a symmetric or asymmetric balance with a specific challenge. Examples include a symmetric balance with only three body parts touching the mat or an asymmetric balance with both feet flat on the mat.

BODY NUMBERING

Math Concept: Number recognition

PE Concepts: Nonlocomotor skills

PE Lesson Part: Lesson focus (movement concepts)

Supplies: None

When teaching nonlocomotor skills such as bending, ask students to make the shape of a number with their bodies. This can be accomplished while lying on the floor or standing. Students can also work together to form a larger number.

HUMAN PENCIL (SHAPES AND NUMBERS)

Math Concept: Number recognition

PE Concepts: Spacing, locomotor skills

PE Lesson Part: Lesson focus (movement concepts)

Supplies: None

Tell students that the gym floor is one big piece of paper and that they are human pencils. Ask students to walk

and make a circle, a triangle, and a square. Following this activity, ask questions such as, "How many turns did you make to create a triangle?" Since they already know how to make a circle, as a transition to making numbers, ask students to skip and make the number 0. Next, have them make numbers or a sequence of numbers using a variety of locomotor skills. For an added challenge, give number problems such as 2 + 2 and have the students "write" the answer as human pencils.

PEDOMETER RECORDING

Math Concept: Place values

PE Concepts: Importance of physical activity, measuring physical activity, logging physical activity

PE Lesson Part: Lesson focus

Supplies: Pedometers, pedometer recording card, pencils

One effective use of pedometers is to have students record their physical education steps. Using the card in Figure 11.3 on page 220, students record their data and learn the place values of the numbers. Although the number of steps children accumulate will vary depending on the lesson, in a 30-minute physical education lesson, most students will accumulate between 1,500 and 2,000 steps. By recording their data on a place value card, students learn ones, tens, hundreds, and thousands.

COMPUTING AVERAGE NUMBER OF STEPS

Math Concept: Computing an average

PE Concept: Tracking physical activity

PE Lesson Part: Lesson focus

Supplies: Pedometer recording card, pedometers, pencils

For older children, after they have recorded several days of physical education data, ask them to compute the average number of steps they take during physical education. Because this activity is sedentary, it is best either to coordinate with the classroom teacher so he can complete the activity in the classroom or to have this activity as one station in a circuit. When students reach this station, they compute their average of previous physical education classes and then begin working on a task assigned by the teacher or the station sign.

NUMBER WIZARD

Math Concept: Positive and negative numbers

PE Concepts: Locomotor skills, low-organized games

PE Lesson Part: Game activity

Supplies: None

Name: _____   Teacher: _____

Day:

Pedometer Steps

Thousands	Hundreds	Tens	Ones
☐	☐	☐	☐

_____

Thousands	Hundreds	Tens	Ones
☐	☐	☐	☐

_____

FIGURE 11.3   Pedometer data card with place values.

The entire class stands on a line in the middle of the teaching area, and the teacher explains that the gym floor is going to be their number line. The line they are standing on is zero. One child, designated the "Number Wizard," stands in the middle of the line. The Number Wizard calls out either a positive or a negative number. For a positive number, all students take that many steps forward. For a negative number, all students take that many steps backward. Throughout the game the entire class remains in a straight line. When the Number Wizard yells, "Zero," the class attempts to get back to zero before being tagged by the Number Wizard. Children who are tagged join the Number Wizard.

 ODDS

Math Concept: Odd and even numbers

PE Concepts: Chasing, fleeing, locomotor skills, spacing, low-organized games

PE Lesson Part: Introductory activity or game activity

Supplies: None

Partners stand facing each other on a line. One partner is designated "odd" and the other "even." Similar to Rock, Paper, Scissors, students place one fist in the palm of the other hand. The game is played one-on-one and begins with both players hitting the palms of their hands twice, saying, "Math rocks"; on the third strike, rather than a fist they extend one to five digits. Both partners should have one hand out in front. The partners quickly count the number of fingers on both hands. If the total

is odd, the person designated "odd" chases her partner. If she can tag him before he takes three steps, she gets a point. If the total number of fingers is even, the "even" person becomes the chaser.

ODDS AND EVENS

Math Concept: Odd and even numbers

PE Concepts: Low-organized games, chasing, fleeing, locomotor skills

PE Lesson Part: Game activity

Supplies: Large die (optional)

This game is played with the same rules as Crows and Cranes (page 561) except that teams are "Odds" and "Evens." To start, the teacher calls out a team name to identify who will be chased. For added challenge, the teacher also calls out actual numbers and students must determine if they are odd numbers or even numbers. Finally, the teacher calls out math equations. Students must then solve the equation and decide if the solution is odd or even. If available, a large die can be rolled to determine the number rather than the teacher calling it out.

FIVE DOLLARS

Math Concept: Counting money

PE Concepts: Throwing, catching, scoring, cooperation, rolling

PE Lesson Part: Game activity

Supplies: One tennis ball

This game is played outside in groups of three to four students. One person is designated the "Bank Teller" and the remainder of the group stands 30 to 50 feet away. The Bank Teller throws a ball into the air toward the rest of the group. If the ball is caught in the air, the person who catches it gets one dollar. Catching the ball after one bounce is worth 75 cents; after two bounces, 50 cents; after three bounces, 25 cents. If the ball is rolling, no money is awarded. Once the ball is caught or picked up after rolling, it is rolled to the Bank Teller, who throws the ball again. This process continues with each person counting his or her money. The first person to earn five dollars becomes the Bank Teller. As in softball, players should be encouraged to call for the ball to avoid collisions.

BEANBAG MATH

Math Concepts: Addition, subtraction, multiplication, division

PE Concept: Tossing

PE Lesson Part: Lesson focus (movement concepts), game activity

Supplies: Beanbags, Frisbees

The Frisbees are marked and set up as in Figure 11.4, approximately five feet from the tossing line. Students

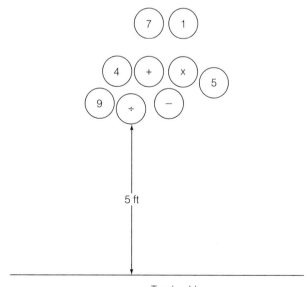

5 ft

Tossing Line

FIGURE 11.4 Beanbag Math Frisbee setup.

work with a partner to create a math equation that results in a specific number (goal), which the teacher designates. Alternating beanbag tosses, the first toss is to a numbered Frisbee. Next, the second partner tosses to a Frisbee marked with a math operation sign to determine what math operation will be used. The third toss goes to a numbered Frisbee. For example, if the first toss lands in a Frisbee numbered 9, the second in the "×" Frisbee, and the third in a Frisbee numbered 5, the partners would now have 45 points. If the teacher sets the goal at 50 points, the easiest way to get to 50 would be to toss to the "+" Frisbee and then the "5" Frisbee. Depending on the desired length of the game, the teacher may pick a large or a small goal. Students must reach the designated goal exactly. Moving the tossing line back will add difficulty to the activity, particularly as the partners get closer to the goal. Additional challenge can be offered by making the goal a negative number. It is important to review cues and provide instruction relative to tossing during this activity.

Language Arts

In the elementary years, students explore language and learn to express ideas by writing, speaking, listening, and communicating nonverbally. Concepts such as giving and following directions, reading, learning vocabulary, thinking critically, taking notes, spelling, and interacting with others are taught. The National Council of Teachers of English and the International Reading Association have published the *National Standards for English Language Arts* (2004), which is an excellent source of what concepts are being taught in language arts in elementary schools.

INTEGRATION TIPS

Reading

Reading is just one of the areas in language arts that can be integrated into physical education. An effective strategy for integrating reading without sacrificing activity time is to use instruction signs. Figures 11.5, 11.6, and 11.7 are examples of instruction signs that require reading. Figure 11.5 on page 222 involves simple word recognition. Once students read the word, they perform the skill while moving to one of the many other signs placed on the floor throughout the teaching area. Figure 11.6 on page 222 requires reading and comprehension of several sentences. These types of signs work well at stations. At each station, students must read the sign and then perform the activity. Figure 11.7 on page 223 requires reading and following more complex instructions. Again, in station format, students move from station to station reading and following instructions. The effective use of instructional signs efficiently integrates reading into physical education and allows the teacher to move about the teaching area, helping those who need assistance. The instructional signs shown here (and many more) are available from DeLynn Designs, 7435 S. Rita Lane, Tempe, AZ 85283 (dlpangra@hotmail.com).

Spelling

Often in physical education, students are asked to count to a given number to determine the length of time to stretch. This can be used to teach skip-counting as discussed earlier; this can also be a great time to teach the spelling of physical education terms or terms being used

FIGURE 11.6   Volleyball sign.

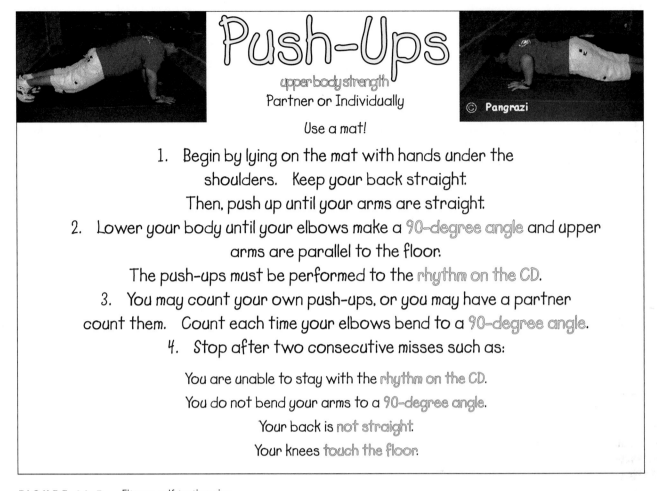

FIGURE 11.7   Fitness self-testing sign.

in the classroom (e.g., spelling words or vocabulary words from a specific content area). Instructions to implement spelling could be, "Fourth graders, choose your favorite lower body stretch that we have learned in physical education. Instead of counting today, we are going to spell words as we stretch. I checked with Ms. Panko and I know you are studying Antarctica, so let's spell it." The teacher then slowly starts the class spelling with a counting tempo.

Parts of Speech

Physical education is full of action words like *skip, run, throw, roll, tap,* etc., which offers an excellent chance to teach about verbs. An effective strategy is to quiz students following a bout of instructions. After saying, "Everyone jump," briefly stop and ask, "What was the verb in that sentence?" If the students do not immediately respond with "Jump," quickly say, "It was *jump*; remember, verbs show action." The key to this strategy is to allow students to take no more than five seconds to determine the verb. As this process continues, students learn which words are verbs and begin responding quickly. This same process can be used to teach other parts of speech (e.g., nouns, adverbs, adjectives, and prepositions).

Antonyms and Synonyms

Physical education offers many contrasting and similar words, thereby offering an excellent opportunity for teaching antonyms and synonyms. During a locomotor lesson, you can ask students to skip at a slow level. Next, ask them to skip at the level that is the antonym for *slow.* As part of a nonlocomotor activity in which you tell students, "Stretch to make yourself large," ask for examples of synonyms for *large.* If students have not learned the words *antonym* and *synonym,* use the words *opposite* and *same.*

Using Foreign Languages

Because many students are kinesthetic learners, reinforcing terms they are learning in a foreign language class may be effective in helping them learn those terms. Students can count in different languages. Key terms for the lesson such as *ball, bounce, roll,* or *jump* can be translated and used during instruction. Rather than say, "Hustle and get a tennis ball," the teacher could say, "Hustle and get a *pelota de tenis.*" Also, the foreign language term for the activity (e.g., *gymnastics* is *gymnastique* in French and *gymnasia* in Spanish) can be used when the activity is introduced and referred to during the lesson. By working with the foreign language teacher, key terms being learned in the classroom can be integrated into physical education instructions. For example, if students are learning the terms in a foreign language for the English words *above, below, in front of,* and *behind,* these can easily be included in physical education instruction.

Peer Teaching

For Developmental Level III students, peer teaching can be an effective tool to help students learn the language concepts of listening and verbal instruction. Peer teaching simply involves one student teaching another a skill using the cues and strategies learned in class. At the conclusion of a softball unit, for example, one student may be asked to teach his partner how to throw using the cues that were discussed in class. Students can also assess their teaching skills by using a self-assessment sheet like that shown in Figure 11.8. This process requires partners to use the skills of listening and speaking.

ACTIVITIES

► BODY SPELLING

LA Concept: Spelling

PE Concepts: Spacing, nonlocomotor skills

PE Lesson Part: Lesson focus (movement concepts, gymnastics), game activity

Supplies: None

Working in groups of four to five, students are given the task of using their bodies to make letters to spell out words provided by the teacher. Students can make the words standing or lying on the ground (see Figure 11.9). For younger students, short words are used and each child is usually one letter of the word. For example, to spell *dog,* one child would be the *D,* one the *O,* and one the *G.* With older students, longer words can be used; however, the entire group may have to make each letter. That is, to spell *locomotor,* the entire group would make an *L,* then an *O,* and so on. Classroom vocabulary words or physical education terms work well for this activity.

☐ Nonthrowing side to the target

☐ Arm up with elbow high

☐ Step with front foot.

☐ Rotate hips and throw hard!

FIGURE 11.8 Peer teaching sheet.

FIGURE 11.9 Making letters.

ALPHABET FREEZE

LA Concept: Letter recognition

PE Concepts: Body awareness, spacing, nonlocomotor skills

PE Lesson Part: Introductory activity, game activity

Supplies: None

Students begin the activity by moving about the teaching area. When the teacher says, "Alphabet freeze," the students select a letter and freeze in the shape of that letter. The activity continues with the stipulation that students must select a different letter with each freeze. The teacher may also choose the letter by saying, "Alphabet freeze—*A*," and all students freeze while forming an *A* with their bodies. The teacher may also designate whether students should freeze in a standing position or on the ground.

LETTER TAG

LA Concept: Letter recognition

PE Concepts: Body awareness, spacing, nonlocomotor skills

PE Lesson Part: Introductory activity, game activity

Supplies: None

This game is played in the fashion of Frozen Tag (page 556). If a youngster is tagged, she freezes in the shape of any letter. To unfreeze her, a classmate must either say the letter or make the letter with her (Figure 11.10). The teacher can also designate the letter shape that students must freeze as; in this case, the student must make the letter to unfreeze a classmate.

SPELLING TOSS

LA Concept: Spelling

PE Concepts: Tossing

PE Lesson Part: Lesson focus (movement concepts), game activity

Supplies: Frisbees or Poly spots marked with various letters, beanbags

The letters are placed five to ten feet away from the tossing line, as shown in Figure 11.11 on page 226. Students then spell words by tossing their beanbags onto the letters in the appropriate order. If *T, S, P, I,* and *E* were the letters available, students could spell *steps, pet, step, pie, pies, sit,* or *pit.* It is important that safe tossing techniques be reinforced during this activity.

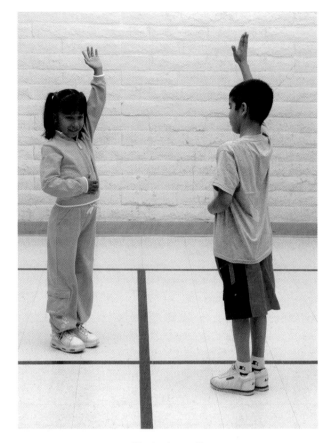

FIGURE 11.10 Playing Letter Tag.

HUMAN PENCIL (SPELLING)

LA Concept: Spelling

PE Concepts: Locomotor skills, spacing

PE Lesson Part: Lesson focus (movement concepts)

Supplies: None

Students are instructed to spell a specific word using locomotor skills. They are pencils and the entire teaching area floor is their paper. Teachers may wish to lead into the activity with the following instructions: "Show me how you would walk to make an *O*." "Now show me how you would walk to spell *cat*." "Okay, now show me how you can skip and spell *education*. I know that is one of your spelling words this week."

NOUNS AND VERBS

LA Concept: Parts of speech

PE Concepts: Chasing, fleeing, locomotor skills, low-organized games

PE Lesson Part: Game activity

Supplies: None

5–10 ft

Tossing Line

 FIGURE 11.11 Spelling Toss Frisbee diagram.

This game is played in the fashion of Crows and Cranes (page 561), except that teams are called "Nouns" and "Verbs." To assist students in learning the game, begin by simply using "Noun" or "Verb" as the chase word. Then call out nouns or verbs as the chase word. Use caution when choosing chase words. Many words such as *jump* can be either a noun or a verb. Students who skateboard are likely to think of a jump, whereas other students may think of jumping like they learned in physical education. Early on, when calling out the chase word, it may be helpful to point the direction in which students should be moving to help students who are having difficulty determining if a word is a noun or a verb.

▶ **IN A LINE**

LA Concept: Alphabetizing
PE Concept: Cooperation
PE Lesson Part: Game activity
Supplies: None

The activity begins with the entire group standing on a line. The challenge is for the students to get in alphabetical order by first name; however, the group must have at least one foot on the line at all times. Once students achieve this, their final challenge is to get into alphabetical order by their last names without speaking. They may use

gestures, but they must keep one foot on the line at all times. During this activity, students can become creative by using letters on their shirts, shoes, or jewelry. However, it is important that the teacher let them establish such strategies on their own.

▶ **LANGUAGE LION SAYS**

LA Concepts: Listening, following directions
PE Concepts: Nonlocomotor skills, locomotor skills, manipulative skills, fitness challenges
PE Lesson Part: Introductory activity, game activity
Supplies: None

This is played just as Simon Says but with "Language Lion" as the leader. Commands that tie in physical education movements should be used throughout. Typically, in Simon Says, the students remain in one position. For Language Lion Says, students should be moving throughout the teaching area. At the end of the game, the teacher can briefly comment, "When most students think of language arts, they think of words that we write or say. However, an important part of language is being able to listen, and playing Language Lion Says helped all students practice their listening skills."

Science

Elementary students are often fascinated by science. Thus, teaching concepts such as the senses, animals, the environment, the solar system, climate, matter, energy, force, and plants are often met with great enthusiasm. By reviewing the *National Science Education Standards* (1996) published by the National Research Council, physical education teachers can learn the content being taught in elementary science and more effectively generate creative ways to integrate science concepts into physical education.

INTEGRATION TIPS

Freeze Signal

Successful teachers have an effective signal that freezes the class. One strategy for teaching Developmental Level III students about temperature is to use "Thirty-two degrees Fahrenheit" as the freeze signal since water freezes at 32 degrees. Similarly, 0 degrees Celsius could be used. Once students learn this concept, teachers can say any number less than 32 degrees Fahrenheit or 0 degrees Celsius to signal the students to freeze. For example, "Eleven degrees Fahrenheit" means to freeze.

Body Part Identification

One skill students learn in science is the ability to identify body parts. Since taking care of the body through physical activity is an important component of physical education, body part identification can be integrated. Some teachers simply have students copy them by saying, "Touch your eyes, your nose, your femur, your triceps." This not only teaches body parts, but it also works on listening skills. Also, touching a specific body part can be the "Go" signal. For example, the teacher can say "When I touch my humerus bone, hustle to the line on the east side of the gym" and then immediately touch her humerus or touch other bones to check for student understanding.

Influence of Physical Activity on the Body

During a vigorous lesson such as jogging/walking or individual rope-jumping, children often need a quick break. These breaks offer a great opportunity to teach the influence of physical activity on the body. Concepts such as increased heart rate and why it happens, sweating and why it happens, why we get tired, and many others can quickly be discussed during short breaks. Using this strategy throughout the year can be an effective method for teaching these concepts.

ACTIVITIES

▶ MUSCLE AND BONE TAG

Science Concept: Muscle and bone identification

PE Concepts: Fleeing, chasing, locomotor skills, low-organized games

PE Lesson Part: Introductory activity, fitness development, game activity

Supplies: None

This tag game starts with five people chosen by the teacher as taggers. If they tag someone, they "give up the tag" and the tagged person becomes the tagger. Before the game, the teacher designates a bone or muscle that is the "base." If a child touches the predetermined bone or muscle and repeats its name three times, he is safe from being tagged for five seconds. He may only use his base once per game, and taggers may not stand by him waiting for the five seconds to expire. This is called the "no guarding" rule.

▶ PONIES IN THE STABLE

Science Concept: Animal habitats

PE Concepts: Locomotor skills, low-organized games, spacing

PE Lesson Part: Game activity

Supplies: One Poly spot per student

Students are in scattered formation with a Poly spot at their feet. When given the signal, they begin galloping around the teaching area. When the teacher says, "Ponies in a stable" they quickly find a spot and stand on it. To teach other animal habitats, the game could be called "Frogs on a Lily Pad," "Rabbits in a Burrow," or "Gorillas in the Jungle." For each of these games, the children's locomotor movement should be consistent with the animal.

▶ PALM PUSH

Science Concept: Force, pushing, pulling

PE Concepts: Balance, body awareness

PE Lesson Part: Introductory activity, fitness development, lesson focus (gymnastics), game activity

Supplies: None

Players face each other, standing approximately 12 inches apart. They place the palms of their hands together and must keep them together throughout the game. The object of the game is to get the opponent to move one of her feet. Following a few rounds, the teacher then asks a few brief questions: "How does force affect this game?" "Is it better to have a lot of force or not much?" "How could you use a little bit of force and still move your opponent off balance?"

▶ FINGER FENCING

Science Concept: Force, pushing, pulling

PE Concepts: Balance, body awareness

PE Lesson Part: Lesson focus (gymnastics), game activity

Supplies: None

Partners start balanced on one foot facing each other with index fingers hooked. The object is to push or pull the opponent off balance. See Figure 11.12 on page 228 for the starting position. If a person causes her opponent to lose his balance, she receives a point and they start over. After a few minutes of play the teacher stops the class to discuss strategies related to pushing and pulling. "Is pushing better or is pulling the best?" "Can you use both?" Be sure that partners are matched by size for this game.

FIGURE 11.12   Finger fencing.

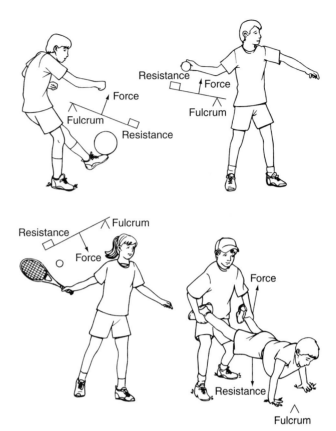

FIGURE 11.13   Levers in physical education.

▶ **LEVERS**

Science Concept: Levers, force

PE Concepts: Throwing, striking with a racquet, cooperation

PE Lesson Part: Lesson focus (throwing skills, racquet activities, tennis, softball, soccer)

Supplies: Racquets, yarn balls, playground balls

Since many motions and activities used in physical education involve levers (see Figure 11.13 for activities that can be used to teach about levers), the concept of levers can easily be integrated into a variety of lessons. As a break from skills involving throwing, kicking, or racquet skills, have students get a partner and assume the wheelbarrow position. Ask questions such as: "What part of your body is making a lever?" "What part was making a lever when we were throwing? Or kicking? Or using the racquet?" Allow students to perform a variety of skills that have been learned in physical education and then asks, "What type of levers are those?" A large picture similar to Figure 11.14 on page 229 may help students answer this question.

▶ **SCIENCE OF THROWING**

Science Concepts: Trajectory and distance, weight and distance

PE Concepts: Cooperation, throwing

PE Lesson Part: Lesson focus (throwing skills, softball)

Supplies: Tennis balls, yarn balls

Introduce three trajectories in which a ball can be thrown such as straight up, straight out, or up and out. In an open space, have students experiment with the distance a tennis ball travels when thrown at these three different trajectories. Then challenge the students to throw the yarn balls using the three trajectories (Figure 11.15 on page 229). Follow this activity with a brief discussion regarding the influence trajectory and the weight of the ball had on distance traveled. After the discussion, allow time for more throwing so that students can experiment.

▶ **IT "MATTERS"**

Science Concepts: Changes in matter, states of water

PE Concepts: Locomotor skills, spacing

PE Lesson Part: Introductory activity

Supplies: None

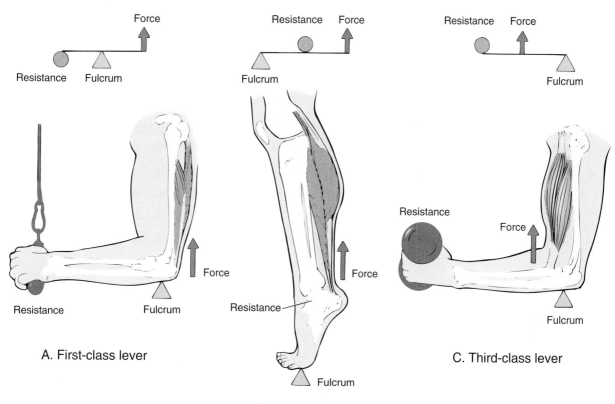

Force
Resistance   Fulcrum

A. First-class lever

Resistance   Force
Fulcrum

Force
Resistance

B. Second-class lever

Resistance   Force
Fulcrum

Resistance
Force
Fulcrum

C. Third-class lever

FIGURE 11.14   Types of levers in human joints.

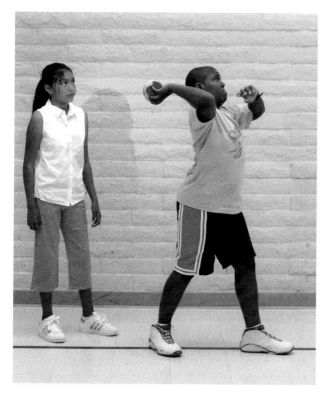

FIGURE 11.15   Checking the trajectory of the throw.

Students begin by moving around the teaching area. Challenge the class to keep moving but in half of the space. Further compress the space by asking the class to move in half of that space, or one-quarter of the original space. Remind the class that the goal is to not touch anyone. Next, ask the students to recall what they know about molecules of water when it is in a solid, liquid, or gas state. After the brief discussion, have the class move like gas molecules, solid molecules, and liquid molecules.

▶ **BOUNCE REBOUNCE**

Science Concepts: Forces, influence of weight on reaction, action and reaction

PE Concepts: Volleying, bouncing, dribbling, catching, passing

PE Lesson Part: Lesson focus (playground ball activities, basketball, volleyball)

Supplies: One playground ball and one balloon per student

Begin the activity by having students bounce or dribble a playground ball in general space. Ask them to experiment by applying different forces to the ball to see how that influences the bouncing. After a brief discussion about how increased force makes the ball bounce higher, have students trade their playground balls for balloons. Next have students volley the balloon using different amounts of force. Challenge students to bounce the balloon as if it were the playground ball. Freeze the class and ask them what would happen if they struck the playground ball with the same force and why. Ask: "Why does the playground ball bounce back up better than the balloon?" Next, have partners stand side by side while bouncing the ball off the wall to each other. After each pass they should take one step away from each other. Ask them: "What happens to your pass? What happens if you pass it like you did when you were close together?" Conclude with the notion that the ball bounces off the wall and the floor at the same angle that it hits them. This concept is of particular importance when teaching a bank shot and dribbling during a basketball unit.

> ### ANIMALS MOVE

Science Concept: Animal locomotion

PE Concepts: Animal movements, spacing

PE Lesson Part: Introductory activity

Supplies: None

The game begins with the teacher calling out different animals and a method of movement. For instance, the teacher might call out, "Horses fly. Birds crawl. Salmon swim." When the leader states a correct relationship, the class must move accordingly. In this example, students make a swimming movement. When an incorrect relationship is given, the children should not move. Games should be kept short so that all children have a chance to lead.

Social Studies

Social studies includes geography, history, government, economics, and other areas. At the elementary level, concepts such as directions, family, rules and laws, the geography of different regions, U.S. history, state history, political systems, cultures, and community are taught. These and many other concepts taught in social studies are presented in *Expectations of Excellence: Curriculum Standards for Social Studies* (1994).

INTEGRATION TIPS

Directions

Directions are an important part of geography and can easily be taught throughout a physical education curriculum. The first step is to place large north, south, east, and west signs on the appropriate walls. Early in the curriculum, teachers can simply refer to lines using a direction. For instance, "When I say, 'Go', hustle to the line by the south wall." Initially it may be helpful to point to the line as well. As students mature, instruction can refer to the "southwest wall" or "the cone closest to the northeast basket." If teaching outside, students can be taught to use the sun to determine direction. In order to do this, students need to know only the time of day and the direction from which the sun rises. These concepts will be especially useful if orienteering is taught later in the year to older students.

Games from Other Countries

The physical education curriculum is filled with activities from other countries. When teaching these activities, simply take a few minutes to discuss the country, show where it is on a map, and talk about the languages spoken there.

Class Greeting

Prepare a list of greetings that are used in other countries. Each week have a greeting of the week to use when the class arrives. The students should then attempt to determine the country in which the greeting is used. Gestures such as bowing or handshaking can also be used.

Conversation

Often in physical education, students work on skills with partners. During these activities, remind students to concentrate on the skills, but also teach them how to have conversations. Discuss appropriate questions, how to ask questions, or what to say if you say something wrong. These skills are often assumed to be learned by children, and are often neglected. Social time during physical education is important, and physical education is a great time to teach social skills.

Cooperative Activities

Cooperation is an important component of community, family, and relationships. See Chapter 21, "Cooperative Activities," for numerous activities that teach cooperative skills such as communicating, sharing, and listening.

ACTIVITIES

▶ **RULES**

SS Concept: The need for rules and laws

PE Concepts: Classroom management skills

PE Lesson Part: Introductory activity

Supplies: None

Early in the school year, rules for physical education are established. This is an excellent time to discuss the importance of rules outside of physical education and outside of school. During the activity, the importance of following directions is discussed. To have students practice this, a variety of instructions are given with one set leading to a game. An example of a series of instructions follows:

"When I say, 'Toe-to-toe,' quickly get toe-to-toe with the person closest to you. Toe to toe (pause). Thank you for doing that quickly. Now one partner remains standing while the other sits. If you are standing, please report to the line by the south wall. If you are sitting, please report to the line by the north wall."

After these directions, the teacher has the class play a game. Following the game, the teacher asks, "What would have happened if the class had decided not to follow directions?" It is important to teach students early in the year that following rules leads to more enjoyment for everybody.

▶ **GOING ON A TRIP**

SS Concepts: Urban, suburban, rural, and state history, geography of the world

PE Concepts: Spacing, locomotor movements, manipulative skills

PE Lesson Part: Lesson focus (movement concepts), game activity

Supplies: Vary

This activity is limited only by the teacher's and students' imaginations. Trips through a city, county, region, state, country, continent, or geographic location such as the mountains or a jungle can be created. If exploring Kentucky, students can pretend to move like horses over rolling hills by galloping at different levels. If going on an expedition through a jungle, students move like gorillas, panthers, monkeys, and birds. When visiting an urban area, students have to read street signs (made by the teacher), know where to cross the street, and know how to obey street crossing rules. Students can also learn traffic laws while

driving their cars (scooter boards) on a predetermined path.

▶ **MOVING ACROSS THE UNITED STATES (OR STATE OR COUNTY)**

SS Concepts: Geography, history, famous people

PE Concepts: Jumping rope, locomotor skills, tracking physical activity

PE Lesson Part: Lesson focus (individual rope-jumping, long rope-jumping, walking and jogging skills)

Supplies: Pedometers, jump ropes, maps, tracking sheets

One important use of pedometers in physical education is to teach students to track their physical activity levels across a number of different lessons. Using cards similar to those in Figure 11.16 on page 232, students track their number of strides during each lesson. Then, using their stride length, they calculate the distance they traveled in miles. The teacher totals the distance traveled by the entire class. Prior to teaching this activity, the teacher determines a route across a given area and tracks the class's progress across a map. It may be best to start with the school's town or county and then progress to larger areas such as states or well-known trails. As the class moves across the route, historic facts related to students' present location can be discussed, a dance that was originated in a nearby town taught, or historic figures from the area studied. In order to plan the activity, the route must be predetermined and the physical education teacher should collaborate with other teachers in the school. Because calculating distance traveled may take students more than a few minutes, this assignment can be completed in the classroom. The book *Pedometer Power* (Pangrazi, Beighle, & Sidman, 2003) has more examples regarding the implementation of this activity.

▶ **HOW DO I GET THERE?**

SS Concepts: Travel, evolution of transportation, rural and urban settings

PE Concept: Locomotor skills

PE Lesson Part: Introductory activity, lesson focus (movement concepts)

Supplies: None

For this activity, students are asked to demonstrate how they would travel to a specific place if they lived during

Pedometer number 8			PE Steps		
Teacher	**Day 1**	**Day 2**	**Day 3**	**Day 4**	**Day 5**
Edmondson					
Brockhagen					
Casson					
Yniguez					
Panko					
Jackson					
Jones					

FIGURE 11.16   Physical education step card.

a given time in history. For example, the teacher could say, "If I lived in the 1700s and wanted to get to my neighbor's house, show me how I could get there." The teacher then points out students who are walking, jogging, skipping, or galloping like a horse, which would have been methods of travel during this time. Depending on their age, some students will pretend to drive a car. This is a teachable moment for discussing the modes of transportation available in the 1700s and the distances between neighbors during this time. This activity can be implemented throughout the year to correspond with the time history classes are studying in the classroom.

One method of teaching students about different cultures is to teach them about the greetings of various cultures and have them experience these greetings. As students move about the teaching area, the teacher calls out a method of greeting (e.g., shaking hands, bowing, curtsying, or giving a high five). The students then move about performing this greeting with as many people as possible before the teacher gives another locomotor movement. The teacher briefly explains to students the countries from which various greetings originate. For older children, the teacher simply calls out the country and has the class respond with the appropriate greeting.

 GREETINGS

SS Concepts: Cultures, courtesy
PE Concept: Locomotor movements
PE Lesson Part: Introductory activity
Supplies: None

COURTESY TAG

SS Concept: Citizenship
PE Concepts: Low-organized games, body management, locomotor skills, chasing, fleeing
PE Lesson Part: Introductory activity, game activity
Supplies: None

This game is played similar to Frozen Tag (page 556). Several students are designated taggers. When tagged by a tagger, the tagged person must freeze. While frozen, the student stands with his hands raised, calling out, "Please help me!" He must say, "Please." When not frozen, players move around giving high fives to the players who are frozen. After getting a high five, the frozen player must say, "Thank you" and the other player must say, "You are welcome" before the frozen player can reenter the game. To add variety to the game, the teacher can designate a specific greeting (see the previous activity) that frozen students must perform with unfrozen students before reentering the game. As with all tag games, the game is stopped often and new taggers are selected.

▶ **TRADES**

SS Concept: Occupations and their roles in the community

PE Concepts: Low-organized games, fleeing, chasing, locomotor skills

PE Lesson Part: Game activity

Supplies: None

Described on page 567, this is an excellent game to teach students about different occupations. Following each round, teachers can quickly discuss the selected occupations and how those occupations contribute to the community.

REFLECTION AND REVIEW QUESTIONS

How and Why

1. Why should physical education teachers integrate academic content into their lessons?

2. How can physical education teachers go about integrating academic content?

3. Why might physical education teachers be apprehensive about integrating academic content?

Content Review

1. Discuss the models of integration available to physical educators.

2. Explain some of the issues a physical educator should consider when deciding whether to integrate academic content.

3. List and discuss strategies teachers should use when integrating academic content into physical education.

4. Discuss several ways to integrate math into physical education.

5. Explain three strategies or activities that can be used to integrate science into physical education.

6. Provide four ways to integrate language arts into physical education.

7. Describe several methods of integrating social studies into physical education.

FOR MORE INFORMATION

References and Suggested Readings

Blaydes-Madigan, J. (2004). *Thinking on your feet.* 2nd ed. Murphy, TX: Action Based Learning.

Christie, B. A. (2000). Topic Teamwork: A collaborative integrative model for increasing student-centered learning in grades K–12. *Journal of Physical Education, Recreation, and Dance, 71*(8), 28–32.

Cook, G. (1994). Topics and themes in interdisciplinary curriculum. *Middle School Journal, 25*(3), 40.

Jensen, E. (2000). *Brain based learning.* San Diego: Brain Store Publishing.

National Association for Sport and Physical Education (2004). *Moving into the future national standards for physical education.* Reston, VA: McGraw-Hill.

National Council for the Social Studies (1994). *Expectations of excellence: Curriculum standards for Social Studies.* Alexandria, VA: Scorpio Educational Communications.

National Council of Teachers of English and International Reading Association (2004). *Standards for the English language Arts.* http://www.ncte.org/store/books/standards/105977.htm.

National Council of Teachers of Mathematics (2000). *Principles and standards for school mathematics.* http://standards.nctm.org/.

National Science Teachers Association (1996). *National science education standards.* http://www.nsta.org/standards.

Pangrazi, R. P. (2007). *Dynamic physical education curriculum guide: Lesson plans for implementation,* 15th ed. San Francisco: Benjamin Cummings.

Pangrazi, R. P., Beighle, A., & Sidman, C. (2003). *Pedometer power.* Champaign, IL: Human Kinetics.

Pellegrini, A. D., P. D. Huberty, & I. Jones (1995). The effects of recess timing on children's playground and classroom behaviors. *American Educational Research Journal, 32*(4), 845–864.

Placek, J. H. (2003). *Interdisciplinary curriculum in physical education: Possibilities and problems.* In S. J. Silverman & C. D. Ennis (Eds.), *Student learning in physical education: Applying research to enhance instruction* (pp. 255–271). Champaign, IL: Human Kinetics.

Purcell-Cone, T., Werner, P., Cone, S. L. & Woods, A. M. (1998). *Interdisciplinary teaching through physical education.* Champaign, IL: Human Kinetics.

Sibley, B. A. & Etnier, J. L. (2003). The relationship between physical activity and cognition in children: A meta-analysis. *Pediatric Exercise Science, 15*(3). 243–256.

Tomporowski, P. D. (2003). Cognitive and behavioral responses to acute exercise in youths: A review. *Pediatric Exercise Science, 15,* 348–359.

11

Werner, P. (Ed.). (2003). Interdisciplinary learning [Special section]. *Teaching Elementary Physical Education,* 14(4).

Werner, P. (Ed.). (2003). The integrated curriculum [Special section]. *Teaching Elementary Physical Education,* 10(1).

Websites

Language Arts Standards
www.ncte.org

Math Standards
http://standards.nctm.org

Science Standards
www.nap.edu/readingroom/books/nses/html

Social Studies Standards
www.socialstudies.org/standards

P A R T

II

Teaching the Objectives of Physical Education

SECTION 4

Personal Health Skills

Nothing is more important to parents than the health of their children. A major contribution physical education can make to schools is maintaining and improving the health of students. This section includes activities and concepts that should be included in every lesson taught in physical education. The approach to personal health takes a three-pronged approach: understanding physical fitness, promoting physical activity, and learning how to develop and maintain a healthy lifestyle. For elementary school children, developing positive attitudes about physical activity and fitness and learning active lifestyle habits is an important goal. Particularly since these attitudes and habits may carry over into adulthood. Many schools require that health and wellness be taught in physical education and this section offers many health and wellness related activities that can be implemented during quality physical education lessons.

After reading this section, you will know how to teach youth the basics of physical fitness, help them develop strong physical activity habits, and give them the knowledge necessary for good health.

12

Promoting and Monitoring Physical Activity

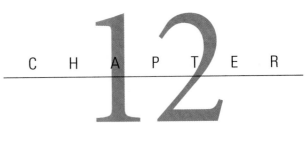

SUMMARY

This chapter explains the differences between physical fitness and physical activity and how different students will choose one outcome over the other based on their personal needs. The Physical Activity Pyramid gives students a concrete explanation of how they should plan for and incorporate physical activity into their daily lifestyles. The focus is on adding at least 60 minutes or more of moderate to vigorous activity to their daily routine.

Pedometers are an important tool for teachers and students in promoting adequate amounts of physical activity. Pedometers are accurate when students learn how to find the best placement point on their body. Goal setting can be easily done using pedometers that measure either steps or activity time. Students can set personal goals that are within reach to ensure continued motivation. Guidelines for teachers are offered for using pedometers in physical education classes. Finally, teachers are urged to use pedometers to measure the effectiveness of their physical education programs. Showing an increase in physical activity outside the school environment may be one of the most positive aspects of a quality physical education program.

Walking is the "real" lifestyle activity. It can be done anywhere with a minimum of equipment, and the vast majority of students are capable of walking for activity. Walking is also an effective tool for teaching students to deal with weight management issues. A school-wide walking program can be implemented to help create an "active school." Many walking activities are included for use in and outside of physical education classes.

ESSENTIAL COMPONENTS OF A QUALITY PROGRAMS

▶ **I. Organized around content standards**

▶ **II. Student-centered and developmentally appropriate**

▶ **III. Physical activity and motor skill development form the core of the program**

IV. Teaches management skills and self-discipline

▶ **V. Promotes inclusion of all students**

VI. Focuses on process over product

▶ **VII. Promotes lifetime personal health and wellness**

VIII. Teaches cooperation and responsibility and promotes sensitivity to diversity

NATIONAL STANDARDS FOR PHYSICAL EDUCATION*

1. Demonstrates competency in motor skills and movement patterns needed to perform a variety of physical activities.

▶ 2. **Demonstrates understanding of movement concepts, principles, and tactics as they apply to the learning and performance of physical activities.**

▶ 3. **Participates regularly in physical activity.**

▶ 4. **Achieves and maintains a health-enhancing level of physical fitness.**

5. Exhibits responsible personal and social behavior that respects self and others in physical activity.

▶ 6. **Values physical activity for health, enjoyment, challenge, self-expression, and/or social interaction.**

*National Association for Sport and Physical Education (NASPE), 2004.

OUTCOMES

■ Describe why activity is just as effective as fitness for ensuring health.

■ Know the different parts of the physical activity pyramid and why each level is important for optimal health.

- Understand how to identify moderate to vigorous physical activity.
- Know how to incorporate pedometers into physical education lessons.
- Help students learn where to place the pedometer for highest accuracy.
- Help students design personal goals for activity.
- Understand why pedometers can be used to measure program activity outcomes.
- Express the role of physical activity in maintaining proper body weight.
- Implement a school-wide walking program.

Physical activity or physical fitness? Which of these outcomes should physical education focus upon in the quest to better serve students? The answer is that it depends on each student's needs and desire. For too long, physical educators determined that they knew what was best for all students regardless of their condition, age, maturity, or ability. In the 1950s youth fitness became a national issue of concern. As is often the case, educational leaders focused on fitness testing in an attempt to solve the problem of low fitness levels. Fitness testing was mandated and most adults clearly remember having their fitness levels evaluated twice a year. The issue was simple: Tests showed that children were unfit, and getting them fit would result in a fit society. Fifty years later, when teachers are asked to show a measure of accountability for their programs, the majority will fall back on fitness testing. Sadly, this approach to children's health has been a failure. Today's youth are showing the same deficits in personal health as their parents did years earlier. The percentage of youth who are overweight has more than tripled in the past 30 years (U.S. Department of Health and Human Services [USDHHS], 2002), and fitness levels show little if any improvement. Students who are overweight, unskilled, or not predisposed to physical fitness may try to avoid physical education classes when they are old enough to make personal choices. It is becoming clear that physical education is not meeting the needs of those who need it most—the children who are otherwise inactive. Could it be that fitness testing youth in front of others twice a year and labeling those who don't score adequately as unfit has undermined their desire to be active? Is it possible that schools are failing the youth we want to help the most?

It is clear that students have different needs and are driven by different personal goals. Some students want to develop their personal fitness to the highest level possible in order to improve their skill performance (skill-related fitness). Others want to improve their appearance. However, the vast majority of students want to enjoy moderate to vigorous activity and are not concerned about achieving a high fitness level. They will probably mature into adults who want to be active but are motivated by appearance and health rather than performance. They will be better served by developing a lifestyle that includes physical activity on a daily basis. To separate these areas, physical fitness and physical activity in this text have a separate chapter. **Physical activity** is defined as bodily movement that is produced by the contraction of skeletal muscle and that substantially increases energy expenditure (National Association for Sport and Physical Education [NASPE], 2004). *Physical activity* is an umbrella term that looks at the process of moving. Such movement can take on different forms such as exercise, sports, and leisure activity. This chapter focuses on moderate to vigorous physical activity that can be performed throughout life by people of all ages and ability.

In contrast, **physical fitness** is a set of attributes that people have or achieve in relation to their ability to perform physical activity (USDHHS, 1996). Whereas physical activity is a process-oriented outcome related to behavior and lifestyles, physical fitness is a product-oriented outcome with an emphasis on achieving a higher state of being. Physical fitness has a strong genetic component that regulates the level of fitness that can be achieved. The vast majority of adults choose not to achieve a high level of physical fitness but may be more receptive to living an active lifestyle and maintaining health-related fitness. In similar fashion, most students who are nonathletes are not interested in the product of physical fitness but are receptive to learning to enjoy their bodies through lifestyle physical activities. Therefore, Chapter 12 focuses on the process of being physically active for good health, while Chapter 13 will help students learn how to develop a higher state of skill-related physical fitness.

PHYSICAL ACTIVITY FOR CHILDREN

The National Association for Sport and Physical Education (NASPE) has developed activity guidelines for elementary school children (2004). The guidelines call for 60 minutes or more of physical activity (total volume) for children and youth. Adult recommendations (30 minutes a day) are based primarily on the energy expenditure necessary to reduce risk of chronic disease associated with what is commonly called "aerobic or cardiovascular fitness." It is important that children and youth gain experience in all areas of physical activity and for all parts of health-related physical fitness, not just aerobic or cardiovascular fitness. Such a recommendation requires an additional time commitment. The four major activity guidelines are briefly described below. For in-depth detail about the physical activity guidelines for children, see the NASPE document (2004).

> **Guideline 1:** Children should accumulate at least 60 minutes, and up to several hours, of *age-appropriate* physical activity on all or most days of the week. This daily accumulation should include moderate and vigorous physical activity of which the majority is intermittent in nature.

Sixty minutes is the minimum amount of daily activity recommended for children. It is becoming increasingly clear that much more than 60 minutes of activity is needed. For example, using data collected with a pedometer that measures activity time and steps, 60 minutes of physical activity equates to slightly fewer than 5,000 steps. The President's Council on Physical Fitness and Sports (2005) has established the Presidential Active Lifestyle Award threshold of 11,000 and 13,000 steps for girls and boys, respectively. This makes it obvious that 60 minutes is a minimal level that youth should accumulate on a daily basis. Physical activity minutes accumulated each day should include some moderate activity equal in intensity to brisk walking and some vigorous activity of greater intensity than brisk walking. For children, most activity will come in intermittent activity bursts ranging from a few seconds to several minutes in length alternated with rest periods. Continuous vigorous physical activity of several minutes in length **should not** be expected for most children, nor should it be a condition for meeting the guidelines.

> **Guideline 2:** Children should participate in several bouts of physical activity lasting 15 minutes or more each day.

Much of a child's daily activity will be in short bursts and accumulated throughout the waking hours. However, if optimal benefits are to accrue, much of the activity should be accumulated in bouts of 15 minutes or more. Examples of physical activity bouts are recess, physical education, play periods, and sports practices. One of the key points for this guideline is that a 15-minute recess is vital to the health and development of children. It is indefensible to eliminate recess and time for physical activity—a trend all too common in today's schools. To be clear, these bouts of 15 minutes or more are not expected to be continuous activity such as jogging a track. Instead, they should include physical activity and opportunity for social development.

> **Guideline 3:** Children should participate each day in a variety of age-appropriate physical activities designed to help them achieve optimal health, wellness, fitness, and performance benefits.

Different levels of physical activity are described in the Physical Activity Pyramid (see Figure 12.1 on page 242). It is recommended that children select from all of the first three levels of activities in the pyramid each week. A section on the types of physical activity follows later in the chapter.

> **Guideline 4:** Extended periods (of two hours or more) of inactivity are discouraged for children, especially during the daytime hours.

Research suggests that people (including children) who watch excessive amounts of television, play computer games, work on computers for extended periods of time, or engage in other low-energy-expenditure activities will likely fail to meet Guidelines 1, 2, and 3 (Gordon-Larsen, McMurray, & Popkin, 2000). In general, extended periods (two hours or more in length) of sedentary behavior (in and out of school) are discouraged. Because many positive things can happen during times of relative inactivity (homework; studying; learning to read, write, and think; and family time), some periods of relative inactivity may be necessary in a typical day. There is evidence to show that reducing the average amount of daily sedentary time is effective in counteracting weight problems in children (Epstein et al., 1995). It is important that children be active when opportunities to be active are available such as before and after school, at appropriate times during school, and on weekends.

Moderate to Vigorous Activity

What is moderate-to-vigorous-intensity activity? Experts roughly agree on what constitutes light, moderate, and vigorous physical activity. METS (resting metabolic rate) are used to quantify activity. One MET equals calories expended at rest (resting metabolism). Two METS is activity that is twice as intense. Three METS requires three times the energy as compared to being at rest, and so on. Activities of three METS or fewer are considered to be light activities. Examples are strolling (slow walking), slow stationary cycling, stretching, golfing with a motorized cart, fishing (sitting), bowling, carpet sweeping, and riding a mower (Pate et al., 1995). Moderate activities range in the area of four to six METS. Examples of moderate activities are shoveling, sweeping, and walking at 2.5 mph. Activity that expends more than six times the energy expended at rest (more than six METS) is considered to be vigorous (high intensity) in nature. Examples of activity at this level are brisk walking, running, stair-climbing, and rope-jumping. A study by Harrell et al. (2005) showed that children burn more calories at rest and while exercising than do adults. If using a standard adult MET table, the values should be increased somewhat (because values for adults are lower than for children) to compensate for the energy expenditure differences between adults and children.

Moderate to vigorous activity of all types is beneficial to students and adults because it contributes to health. For years, students have been told that aerobic activity must be performed in one long, continuous bout to be beneficial. It is now known that activity can be beneficial even if accumulated in several shorter bouts throughout the day. For example, 15 minutes of walking and 15 minutes of aerobic dance done at different times of the day or three 10-minute intervals of continuous cycling done throughout the day meet the physical activity prescription. Table 12.1 shows differences between intermittent and continuous physical activity.

Expending calories in activity that equals 60 minutes of moderate to vigorous activity (walking briskly) each day (1,000 to 2,000 kcal per week) achieves health benefits similar to performance-related fitness training. (See Chapter 13.) The lifestyle activity prescription for children (Table 12.2) covers a broad range of moderate to vigorous activities including those that can be done as part of work or normal daily routines as well as during free time. Frequency, intensity, and time are used to define lifestyle activity, but they differ from physical fitness prescription, which requires high-intensity activity (training zone heart rates). These recommendations are useful because even though they do not require intense physical activity, health benefits are still achieved. Many

TABLE 12.2	Lifestyle activity prescription for children
Frequency	Daily, with frequent activity sessions (three or more) per day
Intensity	Moderate to vigorous activity. Alternating bouts of vigorous activity with rest periods as needed or moderate continuous activity such as walking or riding a bike to school. Examples of activity include walking, playing running games, doing chores at home, and climbing stairs.
Time	Duration of activity necessary to expend more than 6 to 8 kcal/kg/day. Equal to calories expended in 60 minutes or more of active play or moderate sustained activity, which may be distributed over three or more activity sessions.

people remain sedentary or drop out of activity because they believe that exercise is only beneficial when it is vigorous, high-intensity activity. The new recommendations make it easier for sedentary people to see the value in participating in moderate activity.

THE PHYSICAL ACTIVITY PYRAMID

The Physical Activity Pyramid (Figure 12.1) is a prescription model for good health that helps students understand how much and what type of activity they need. The activity pyramid offers a visual approach to activity prescription. It is useful because people have become confused in recent years by scientific reports concerning the amount of physical activity necessary to produce health and fitness benefits. The Physical Activity Pyramid helps students understand the different categories of activity. Each category is required for good health and total body fitness.

The primary reason for arranging the pyramid into six categories and four levels is associated with the benefits that result from each activity type. Those activities having broad general health and wellness benefits for large numbers of people are placed at the base of the pyramid.

Lifestyle activity is placed at the base of the pyramid because scientific evidence indicates that inactive people who begin regular exercise have the most to gain. The Surgeon General's report on physical activity and health (USDHHS, 1996) points out that our nation could reap great health and economic benefits if the 24 percent of the U.S. population who are totally sedentary would begin modest amounts of regular physical activity. Further, those who are only occasionally active could benefit by meeting the standards for lifestyle activity suggested in Level 1 of the pyramid. The benefits

TABLE 12.1	Different types of physical activity	
Intensity of Activity	**Intermittent**	**Continuous**
Moderate	Playing one-wall handball	Walking to a destination at 2.5 mph
	Playing catch with a friend	
	Raking the leaves or vacuuming	Hiking
		Riding a bike
	Playing four-square	Skateboarding
Vigorous	Playing tag games	Jogging
	Rope-jumping	Track activities
	Playing softball or football	Soccer
		Swimming

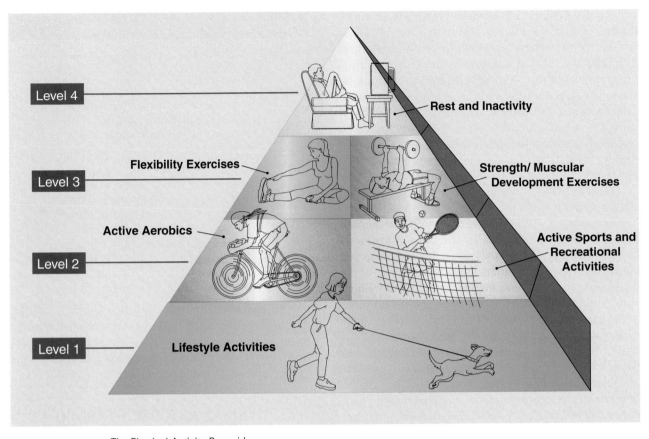

FIGURE 12.1   The Physical Activity Pyramid.

at this level are wide ranging and include a reduced risk of various diseases such as heart disease, diabetes, and cancer. The extra calories expended in doing these activities are also useful in controlling body fat and reducing the risk of obesity. Wellness benefits include increased functional capacity as well as improved quality of life.

Level 2 contains more vigorous activities. Scientific reports suggest that for those people who are already active, active aerobics and active sports and recreation provide health and fitness benefits in addition to those provided by regular lifestyle activity. For those with little free time, regular activity from Level 2 can substitute for lifestyle activity, though participation at both levels is encouraged. Like lifestyle activities, the activities at this level provide broad general health benefits. It is for this reason that these activities are placed at Level 2. It should be noted that the more vigorous nature of the activities makes them difficult for some people to perform, and for this reason they may not be as appealing as activities at Level 1.

Level 3 exercises are designed to build flexibility and muscle fitness. Performing exercises of either type builds physical fitness that contributes to improved performance in various jobs and in active sports. Muscle fitness

has also been associated with reduced risk of osteoporosis (Shaw and Snow-Harter, 1995), and both types of exercises when prescribed and performed appropriately are thought to contribute to reduced rate of injury and less risk of back problems (Plowman, 1993).

It is obvious why rest and inactivity are at the top of the pyramid (Level 4). In general, they do not provide physical activity benefits, but rest does contribute to health.

A secondary reason guiding the placement of activities is frequency of the activity. As the level in the pyramid increases, the frequency of participation decreases. Those activities at Level 1 should be performed daily. Those at Levels 2 and 3 can be performed fewer days per week, and inactivity (Level 4), not rest, should be limited on all days of the week.

Activity Recommendations for Children

LEVEL 1: LIFESTYLE PHYSICAL ACTIVITIES

At the base of the Physical Activity Pyramid is lifestyle physical activity. Lifestyle physical activities are those people can do as part of their everyday work or daily routine. Examples of such activities are yard work and delivering the mail. Of course, there are ways of doing lifestyle physical activity other than working at an active job. For example, someone who sits at a desk for most of the day can get lifestyle activity by walking or riding a bicycle to work rather than driving a car. Other lifestyle physical activities can be done in or around the home. For example, raking the leaves, walking to the store, and carrying the groceries are lifestyle activities. Housework that requires using the large muscles of the body is also lifestyle physical activity.

The greatest portion of accumulated minutes of physical activity for children of this age usually comes from lifestyle activities. Lifestyle activities for this age include active play and games involving the large muscles of the body. Climbing, tumbling, and other activities that require lifting the body or relocating the body in space are desirable activities when they can be performed safely. Activities are typically intermittent in nature rather than continuous. These activities normally involve few rules and little formal organization. Lifestyle activities such as walking to school, when appropriate, and being involved in chores around the home are also appropriate.

LEVEL 2: ACTIVE AEROBICS

The second level of the pyramid includes active aerobic activities. Aerobic activities are those performed at a pace for which the body can supply adequate oxygen to meet the demands of the activity. Because lifestyle activities meet this criterion, they are aerobic in nature. Examples of popular moderate-to-vigorous active aerobics are jogging, brisk walking, moderate-to-vigorous swimming, and biking. Participation in some aerobic activities is appropriate as long as children are not expected to participate in them continuously for long duration. More appropriate are intermittent aerobic activities such as recreational swimming, family walking, or aerobic activities that are included in the lifestyle activity category such as walking or riding a bicycle to school or in the neighborhood. Participation in continuous aerobic activities of long duration is not recommended for this age group.

LEVEL 2: ACTIVE SPORTS AND RECREATIONAL ACTIVITIES

Also on the second level of the Physical Activity Pyramid are active sports and recreational activities. Some examples of active sports are basketball, tennis, soccer, and hiking. Like active aerobics, this type of activity is typically more vigorous than lifestyle physical activity. Sports often involve vigorous bursts of activity with brief rest periods. Though they are often not truly aerobic in nature, when they are done without long rest periods, they have many of the same benefits as aerobic activities.

When young children choose to be involved in sports, it is necessary for the sports to be modified to meet their developmental level. In general, active sports should not comprise the major proportion of activity for Developmental Levels I and II children. It is important that children at Developmental Levels I and II have time to learn basic skills that are prerequisite to performing sports and other recreational activities, such as catching, throwing, walking, jumping, running, and striking objects.

Developmental Level III youngsters are often involved in active sports. For this reason, a greater amount of time may be dedicated to this type of activity. Lead-up games and emphasis on skill development are necessary to make the activities suitable for this age. An emphasis on conditioning for sports is unnecessary for this age group. Most of the time spent in this type of activity will be dedicated to skill learning and playing games rather than conditioning. Age-appropriate recreational activities that have a lifetime emphasis or that can be done with family and friends are encouraged.

LEVEL 3: FLEXIBILITY EXERCISES

Physical activity is a term that describes virtually all types of games, sports, and exercises. The word *exercise* is most commonly used to describe the type of physical activity done especially to build physical fitness. Flexibility exercises are included at the third level of the pyramid. They are referred to as "exercises" because they are done specifically to build the part of physical fitness called "flexibility." Flexibility is the ability to use joints through a full range of motion as a result of having long muscles and elastic connective tissues. There are, no doubt, some activities from the first two levels of the pyramid that help build flexibility to some extent. Still, to develop this part of fitness, it is necessary to do special flexibility exercises that involve stretching the muscles and using the joints through their full range of normal motion. For this purpose, stretching exercises are best.

In general, the amount of time spent on flexibility exercises for Developmental Levels I and II children should be minimal. Children are more flexible than adults. For this reason, this type of exercise is relatively easy for most children. Teaching some stretching exercises is important for illustrating the importance of flexibility. Active play activities such as tumbling and climbing are encouraged for flexibility development. More time should be spent teaching and performing flexibility exercises at Developmental Level III. Children, especially boys, begin to lose flexibility at this age. Some regular stretching is recommended either in the form of age-appropriate flexibility exercises or activities that promote flexibility such as tumbling and stunts.

LEVEL 3: STRENGTH AND MUSCULAR DEVELOPMENT EXERCISES

Exercises and physical activities designed and performed specifically to increase strength (the amount of weight one can lift) and muscular endurance (the ability to persist in muscular effort) are included in this category. Some activities at lower levels in the pyramid may contribute to the development of these parts of muscle fitness, but extra exercises are often necessary to build strength and muscular endurance, even for the most active people.

Participation in some strength exercises as part of a physical education class or a regular family fitness program is appropriate. However, as long as children are accumulating adequate daily amounts of the activities from lower levels in the pyramid, it is not necessary for them to spend large amounts of time performing organized calisthenics on a regular basis. Modified fitness activities (see pages 265–268) are an excellent way to help youngsters learn about exercises in a positive manner. Formal resistance training is usually not recommended, particularly in a group setting.

Youngsters at Developmental Level III participate in strength development activities that require them to move and lift their body weight. Participation in active play and games and sports that require muscle overload are desirable for these youngsters. Exercises using body weight are appropriate when alternative exercises are offered to allow all children to be successful. It is important to show children the relevance of these exercises. Formal exercises and conditioning programs as part of youth sports or other activity programs should not typically constitute a major part of activity periods, though highly motivated children may benefit from exposure to these activities. Children of this age can develop modest gains in strength and muscular endurance using resistance training (see Chapter 2). However, other activities are generally better suited to the needs of most children, particularly in a class setting.

LEVEL 4: REST AND INACTIVITY

At the top of the pyramid are rest and inactivity. Some types of inactivity are not necessarily detrimental to health. For example, adequate amounts of sleep are needed, and rest is important after vigorous exercise. Also, there are benefits associated with activities that are sedentary such as classroom learning. Nevertheless, the Physical Activity Pyramid is designed to provide information about the benefits of regular physical activity. Sedentary living as a lifestyle is discouraged. Long periods of inactivity during the daylight hours should be limited. Youth who sit and watch television or spend their free time playing video games are not getting the activity they need for good health. Children at this level need some private time to be involved in play of types other than in activities using the large muscles. However, long periods of sedentary living (not typically characteristic of young children) should be discouraged.

USING PEDOMETERS TO MONITOR PHYSICAL ACTIVITY

Pedometers are a natural fit in a chapter on monitoring and promoting physical activity because they measure the daily amount of physical activity a person accumulates. Pedometers do not measure the intensity of physical activity, only the quantity of physical activity. Early pedometers were mechanical and used a moving lever arm to count steps. Electronic pedometers now detect movement through a spring-loaded, counterbalanced mechanism that records vertical acceleration at the hip. Pedometers are small, unobtrusive, and easily fastened to a belt or waistband. In their most basic form, pedometers measure the number of steps a person takes. Counting steps is an effective way to measure how active a person is throughout the day even though pedometers can't measure all types of activity. Because pedometers are not waterproof, they can't measure swimming activity. Also, pedometers don't accurately measure activities on wheels such as bicycling, skateboarding, and Rollerblading. However, most of the physical activity people accumulate is overland (about 90 percent), so pedometers are still one of the best ways to measure physical activity for young and old alike. Using pedometers to measure the physical activity levels of youth is now an accepted instructional and research methodology (Beighle, Pangrazi, & Vincent, 2001; Crouter et al., 2003; Kilanowski et al., 1999).

There are a number of pedometers on the market that have features other than counting steps. Some of the more common measures include distance covered and caloric expenditure. To measure distance covered, the length of the step must be entered into the pedometer. The pedometer then calculates distance covered by multiplying the step length times the number of steps. To measure energy expenditure, a number of factors must be entered into the pedometer such as weight and stride length. Based on the number of steps taken, pedometers calculate the number of kilocalories expended. Walk4Life pedometers (www.walk4life.com) have a function that measures activity time as well. Every time a person moves, the pedometer starts accumulating time. When the person stops moving, the timing function stops. This function shows the total hours and minutes of exercise time accumulated throughout the day.

The Accuracy of Pedometers

Activity recommendations in terms of daily minutes of physical activity for youth (NASPE, 2004) and adults (USDHHS, 2000) have created an interest in accurately measuring personal movement. When people are asked to recall and self-report the amount of activity they performed throughout the previous day, most find it difficult to quantify how active they were. Additionally, it may be that recall was done on a day that is not typical, resulting in an under-or overestimation of physical activity (Sallis, 1991). With children, some type of objective measuring tool is helpful for documenting activity levels because it avoids depending on recollection and reading of questionnaires. The pedometer is an objective way to measure physical activity, and its validity and reliability have been studied by a number of researchers. A recent study (Crouter et al., 2003) evaluated the validity of ten different electronic pedometers and found them to be "most accurate." A similar study (Schneider et al., 2003) examined the reliability and accuracy of ten pedometers over a 400-meter walk with similar results.

A limitation of pedometers is that they are less accurate when people move slowly (less than four km/h) or walk with an uneven gait (Crouter et al., 2003). Pedometers depend on a fairly consistent up-and-down motion with each step, and an uneven or slow gait may not create enough movement for the pedometer to measure. Pedometers overestimate distance covered at slower speeds and underestimate actual distance at higher speeds. Caloric expenditure is most often overestimated (Crouter et al., 2003). These errors in distance and energy expenditure are not surprising since they are all based on consistency of step length and walking speed. Throughout a day of activities, it is most likely that both step length and walking speed will vary. Another factor that contributes to the error is that some pedometers require the stride length to be entered in three-inch intervals, thus resulting in over-or underestimating distance covered.

Undercounting errors may also occur with overweight students because of the placement of the pedometer. On these students, the orientation of the pedometer is often turned away from the vertical plane and moved toward the horizontal plane by excess body fat around the waist. If the pedometer is not parallel with the upright plane of the body, its accuracy is affected, and it will stop counting if the angle is too far from vertical. The next section explains how to find an accurate placement point for difficult cases. In spite of these limitations, pedometers are still one of the most

accurate and reasonably priced tools for measuring physical activity.

Teaching Students about Pedometer Placement and Accuracy

Pedometers are designed to be worn at the waistline directly in line with the midpoint of the front of the thigh and kneecap. This positioning is accurate for the majority of users. However, it is not always the best placement for 20 to 30 percent of users. Therefore, the first thing that students need to learn is a placement point where the pedometer measures most accurately. Using the following protocol will help to ensure that the pedometer measures accurately.

1. Place the pedometer on the waistband in line with the midpoint of the thigh and kneecap. The pedometer must be parallel with the body and upright. If it is angled in any direction, it will not measure accurately. Teach students to open their pedometer (without removing it from the waistband) and reset it to zero steps. Have them walk at their normal cadence while counting the number of steps they are taking. Ask them to stop immediately when 30 steps are reached. Open the pedometer and check the step count. If the step count is within plus or minus two steps of 30, this placement is an accurate location for the pedometer. If the step count is less accurate, try Step 2.

2. Move the pedometer on the waistband until an accurate position is found. Adjust the pedometer so it is positioned slightly closer to the belly button or the hip. Open the pedometer, clear it, and have the students take 30 steps as described in Step 1. Again, if the step count is within plus or minus two steps of 30, this new placement is accurate and the user should always position the pedometer in that position. If not, try another placement and repeat the step test.

3. If it is difficult to find an accurate measuring position, consider the following: Pedometers must remain in an upright plane (with the pedometer display perpendicular to the floor and parallel to the body) in order to accurately register step counts. Loose-fitting clothing will impact accuracy because the clothing absorbs the slight vertical force that occurs with each step. Excess body fat may also tilt the pedometer away from the body and negate accuracy. In these cases, placement at waist level behind the hip and on the back may offer an accurate measurement. Another alternative is to use a Velcro belt to ensure that the pedometer is maintained in an upright position. Placing the Velcro belt above the waist may be necessary to find a position where the

pedometer remains in the vertical plane. Repeat the 30-step process until an accurate placement has been identified. One caveat here: If Velcro belts are used, they will probably have to be used on all students in the class to avoid embarrassing any youngster. Walk4Life and Gopher Sport (www.gophersport.com) offer Velcro belts in different colors that can serve a double purpose as team belts. These belts can be used to hold pedometers and designate teams for games and sports.

Pedometers and Personal Goal Setting

A common approach in physical education is to use the "one standard fits all" approach. It is based on a single standard with the assumption that it is possible to set one goal that fits all types of youngsters regardless of age, gender, or health. This practice of mass prescription often turns off students who need activity the most. For example, an often-referenced standard is 10,000 steps per day (Hatano, 1993). This was intended for cardiovascular disease prevention but has grown to be an oft-quoted standard for pedometer-measured activity. A goal for youth that is often mentioned is 11,000 steps/day for girls and 13,000 steps/day for boys. This standard is used for the Presidential Active Lifestyle Award (President's Council on Physical Fitness and Sports, 2005), which is awarded to students who meet these daily standards over a six-week period.

The problem with a **single-standard goal** is that it doesn't take into account the substantial individual differences among people of all ages and gender. A predisposition to be active may make it much easier for some students to reach the step criteria while others may find it next to impossible because they are naturally less active. How many steps *should* be set as a standard? Should it be set high so that only those already-active individuals can reach it? Should it be set low so that the majority of people are able to reach the goal? Should it be set high enough to provide a proved health-related benefit? If you accumulate more than 11,000 steps, is there any point in moving beyond the 11,000-step threshold? If you accumulate 4,000 steps each day, does 11,000 steps seem an impossible goal? When all is said and done, setting one goal that applies with equivalent efficacy to a large population is a difficult proposition at best.

The approach recommended here is the **baseline and goal-setting** technique (Pangrazi, Beighle, & Sidman, 2003). This method requires that each individual identify his or her average daily activity (baseline) level. For preadolescent youth, four days of monitoring step counts (or activity time) are required to establish an average activity level (Trost et al., 2000). Baseline data can be entered in a chart similar to the one shown in Figure 12.2.

After the baseline level of activity has been established, each individual has a reference point for setting a personal goal. The personal goal is established by taking the baseline activity level and adding 10 percent more steps (or time in whole minutes) to that level. For example, assume a baseline of 6,000 steps per day. The personal goal would be 6,000 steps plus 600 more steps for a total of 6,600 steps. This will be the personal goal for the next two weeks. If the goal is reached for a majority of the days during this two-week period, another 10 percent (600 steps) is added to the goal and the process repeated. For most people, a top goal of 4,000 to 6,000 steps above their baseline level is a reasonable expectation. Using the example of 6,000 baseline steps here, a final goal of 10,000 to 12,000 steps would be the goal.

This baseline and goal-setting approach takes into consideration the fact that all individuals are unique. It gradually increases personal goals so that they seem achievable to even inactive individuals. Most individuals are interested in establishing their baseline levels of activity and this can be a good way to motivate students to increase their current activity levels.

A third way to establish step levels for youth is to define a **healthy activity zone** (HAZ). In this method, there is no one standard that each youngster has to reach. This approach has been utilized by the Fitnessgram (Cooper Institute, 2004) for specifying a range of scores (the healthy fitness zone) where students should score on fitness test items. Some of the Fitnessgram test items (e.g. PACER run and skinfolds) are based on health-related criteria, while others are based on improvement due to training. Applied to physical activity, a range of steps (or activity time) can be established for each gender that would serve as the HAZ. This method requires further research, but may be an acceptable way to establish a range of scores that apply to the vast majority of children and adults. It is also possible that a combination of methods such as baseline/goal setting and HAZ standards will ultimately be the best solution.

Using Pedometers in a Class Setting

There are a number of things to work through when the decision to use pedometers has been made. The first step is to get a set of pedometers to use in physical education classes. A set of 36 pedometers will cost in the area of four to eight hundred dollars depending on the type and accompanying materials. Many schools have been successful in asking parent-teacher groups to fund pedometers. Interest can be created by making a presentation to the group and asking for support. Another approach is a "shareware" program where pedometer companies sell to schools at a reduced price. Schools, in turn, sell the pedometers to parents and others to

Step 1: Calculate Your Baseline Step Counts

Name: _____

Date: _____

Day 1 Step Count: _____

Day 2 Step Count: _____

Day 3 Step Count: _____

Day 4 Step Count: _____

Total Step Count: _____ divided by 4 equals _____. This number is your average **baseline step count** and will be used to determine your personal activity goal.

Step 2: Calculate Your Step Count Goal

The next step is to calculate your personal step count goal. A couple of examples are shown below. The first person discovered that she had a baseline step count of 4,000 steps. After ten weeks her step count goal increases to 6,000 steps. For the person who has a baseline of 6,000 steps, her step count goal will increase to 9,000 steps by the final weeks. Thus, both individuals will increase their number of steps by one-third.

Baseline	Personal Goal (10 percent of your baseline plus your baseline)	Weeks	Total Step Counts
4,000 steps	$4,000 \times 0.10 = 400$; $400 + 4,000 = 4,400$ Every two weeks thereafter, the goal will be increased by 400 steps.	1 & 2	4,400
		3 & 4	4,800
		5 & 6	5,200
		7 & 8	5,600
		9 & 10	6,000
6,000	$6,000 \times 0.10 = 600$; plus $6,000 = 6,600$ Every two weeks thereafter, the goal will be increased by 600 steps.	1 & 2	6,600
		3 & 4	7,200
		5 & 6	7,800
		7 & 8	8,400
		9 & 10	9,000
	_____ $\times 0.10 =$ _____; plus _____ = _____ Every two weeks thereafter, the goal will be increased by _____ steps.	1 & 2	
		3 & 4	
		5 & 6	
		7 & 8	
		9 & 10	

FIGURE 12.2 Setting personal activity goals using pedometers.

raise money. Selling pedometers is a much healthier fund-raising activity than selling candy or cookie dough.

Using pedometers in physical education requires teaching proper protocol to students. Teachers quickly become frustrated with students fussing with their pedometers if they don't set standard procedures that students are to follow. Here is an example of a procedure that seems to minimize pedometer handling time, resulting in maximum instructional time. Number each of the pedometers and store no more than six pedometers in

each container (Figure 12.3, page 248). Make sure that you have the same number of pedometers in each container so it is easy to see when a pedometer is missing (and which student has it).

The process of teaching students to secure, fasten, and put away the pedometers is critical to successful integration of pedometers into the program. Students should be taught to enter the teaching area, pick up their assigned pedometer, and put it on while moving around the area. When all students have their pedometers on,

F I G U R E 1 2 . 3   A method of storing pedometers.

freeze the class and have students reset their pedometers (Figure 12.4). Class then begins as usual. At the end of class, students remove their pedometers, put them back into the proper container, record their steps or activity time on the sheet next to their container, and prepare to exit class. A couple of basic rules that help maintain minimal disruptions when using pedometers are: (1) "You shake it, we take it" and (2) "You take it off your waist, we take it." When a student takes his pedometer off, the privilege to use it that day is removed. It becomes a source of irritation if students are taking off the pedometers and opening them during the normal routine. Also, the odds of pedometers being dropped and broken increase dramatically when they are removed from the waistband.

F I G U R E 1 2 . 4   Students resetting their pedometers.

Another important thing to consider when using pedometers is the novelty phase. If the pedometers are not carefully monitored, there will be a high rate of loss in the introduction phase. A recommendation is to use the following schedule to overcome the high-interest/novelty period. For the first six to eight weeks of school, use the pedometers in physical education classes only. From that point up to the winter break, use the pedometers to evaluate how much activity students get during the school day. Students put the pedometers on in the morning and return them at the end of the school day. After winter break, the pedometers can be used to carry out 24-hour monitoring. The pedometers are put on each morning and cleared. The next morning, in class, students record their activity and reset the pedometers. Recording is only conducted Monday through Friday morning because it is difficult to get accurate readings on the weekend. The chance of pedometers being lost increases if they are allowed to leave school over the weekends. Once the pedometers become a regular part of each student's lifestyle, fewer pedometers will be lost or misplaced. Many schools have a replacement policy in place before giving students the freedom to take the pedometers out of the school environment. A letter is sent home explaining the activity program and the use of pedometers. If a pedometer is lost, it must be replaced for a fee.

Teachers find pedometers to be valuable tools for hypothesis testing. Students can be challenged to answer questions such as, "Are students more active than parents?" or "Do you take more steps during a football class or an ultimate Frisbee class?" A further idea is to have students modify or invent a game based on pedometer-determined steps. Another use for the pedometer is helping students determine their leisure-time physical activity with an aim toward establishing personal goals (as described above) or engaging in daily physical activity.

The following activities illustrate a number of ways to use pedometers in a school setting. They are explained in greater detail in the resource book *Pedometer Power* (Pangrazi, Beighle, & Sidman, 2003).

▶ MOVING ACROSS THE STATE OR UNITED STATES

Students accumulate steps and measure their stride length so they can figure out how far they have traveled across a state or U.S. map. As they reach different checkpoints, class discussions about foods, art, and various cultural sites can be conducted. An interesting interactive Web-based program to promote physical activity is offered by Walk4Life. It is called *WalkSmart! Active Schools*© and is designed so that youth can log their steps on a daily basis. As they log their steps, they also learn about fitness, nutrition, geography, history, and social studies. The walks have up to one hundred milestones and last three to four months. Teachers can access the site to monitor the activity time, steps, and goals for students, classes, or grades. Standard reports can be printed out to document the overall student activity levels. The program also can be used to allow parents to monitor their student's physical activity. For more information, check the Website at www.walk4life.com.

ACTIVE OR INACTIVE

Students can participate in a variety of physical education lessons and try to predict which lessons are high activity and which are low activity. An enjoyable related activity is to have students try to guess how many steps they will take in the activity. Over time, they will begin to understand the activity value of different sports and games.

A SAFE WALK TO SCHOOL

Walking to school can add 1,000 to 2,000 steps each day to a student's activity level. This is a good activity for teaching students about walks that are safe, walks that increase in distance (and steps), and walks that avoid traffic.

SCHOOL STEPS CONTEST

This is a school-wide contest with all classes participating. The step counts of all students in each class, and the teacher, are added and then divided by the number of students. Finding the average number of steps for the entire class makes this a group competition and avoids putting down students who are less active. A gentle reminder here is that students should not have to reveal their step count unless they choose to do so. A sensitive approach is to have the students place their step counts anonymously on a tally sheet.

The President's Council on Physical Fitness and Sports sponsors the Presidential Active Lifestyle Award (PALA) (www.presidentschallenge.org). This Website allows students to log their activity time or steps. If they accumulate 60 minutes or 11,000 (girls) to 13,000 steps (boys) for most of the days of the week for six weeks, they can earn the PALA. This award is similar to the Presidential Fitness Award patch except that it is square instead of round. If 35 percent of the students in a school earn the PALA two or more times during the year, the school can become an "Active Lifestyle Model School." Such schools receive a certificate and are recognized on the Website.

ESTIMATION, OR HOW MANY STEPS DOES IT TAKE?

Measure off a distance that is exactly one-eighth or one-quarter mile in length. Students put on their pedometers, clear them at the starting line, and walk at a normal pace to the end of the distance. Depending on the distance they walked, they multiply the number of steps they accumulated by 8 or 4. That is the number of steps it takes them to walk one mile.

Pedometers and Program Accountability

A common issue for physical education teachers is finding criteria for which they can be held accountable. Many teachers have chosen fitness or skill development as an outcome they are willing to use as a measure of their success. There are a number of issues that teachers might want to consider before choosing fitness or skill development as their success criterion. Fitness is most commonly used because tests have long been used in the school setting. However, such tests may not be a good choice because the increase in obesity among today's youth decreases fitness test performance. Common sense indicates that aerobic endurance and various strength measures are directly impacted by the increase in body fat among youth. In addition, children's ability to respond to training is strongly affected by genetics (Bouchard, 1999), with some individuals showing little or no improvement with training. Another problem in using fitness as an outcome is that the amount of time currently available for physical activity during the school day limits students' chances of improving their fitness to an extent measurable by fitness testing. Although many students will improve their fitness test scores purely as a result of maturation, this is not an accurate representation of the teacher's contribution to student fitness. Using fitness as the focal indicator of actual teaching success may be inviting failure.

Skill development is an important assessment outcome for physical education. However, a large part of skill performance is genetically endowed in much the same way that some students are born better artists or musicians. Additionally, physical skills can be difficult to evaluate due to time constraints and the overall number of students seen by the physical education teacher. Perfection is never reached in the performance of physical skills. For example, even the best basketball and soccer players in the world miss as many shots as they make. Baseball players make an "out" three times out of ten at bat. Rugby players fumble the ball and miss kicks. This does not imply that skills should not be emphasized or assessed, but since the nature of physical skill performance is one of imperfection, it is asking a lot of teachers to base the success of their programs on the skill performance of students. Also, when evaluating skill development, there are few instruments available that are valid, reliable, and easy to administer in a limited time environment. Teachers are also aware of the catch: If they take a lot of time to assess skill performance, they will have little time left to teach those same skills to students.

Why not base program success on a school increase in physical activity? What could be more important for health and wellness than increasing the amount of activity students accumulate on a daily basis? All students can move and be physically active both in and out of school. Unless there is some type of physical disability, all students can monitor their physical activity levels using pedometers. Most parents would be delighted if their youngsters were taught to live an active lifestyle. That might be one of the best legacies a physical education program could leave students.

Pedometers can be used to evaluate the baseline activity levels of students at or near the start of the school year. This can be followed with regular monitoring several times throughout the school year. Goals for increasing daily physical activity can be increased by all students regardless of genetic predisposition. Physical education teachers can establish goals for a number of subgroups including classes, grade levels, and gender. School administrators might accept a 2 percent increase in physical activity accumulated as a school-wide goal over an 18-week period. Activity levels both in and out of school could be used as separate outcomes. Out-of-school activity can be regarded as physical education homework. A program designed to increase the amount of physical activity students accumulate on a daily basis makes a valuable contribution to all students.

WALKING: THE "REAL" LIFETIME ACTIVITY

Walking is an activity that almost all people can do. In fact, it forms the basis for all lifestyle physical activity. If one has a hard time walking, the quality of life is dramatically impacted. Therefore, a strong focus of physical education should be to teach the joy of moving and walking and trying to accumulate physical activity. Students can be taught to maximize the number of steps they take rather than try to accomplish movement tasks in the fewest possible steps. Allied to this goal should be teaching the many benefits of being a walker. Walking has so many health-related benefits that if it could be put into the form of a pill to be swallowed, it would immediately become a best seller on the drug market. Walking has few side effects and the benefits are many:

- *Weight management.* When combined with a healthy approach to eating, walking is a lifetime approach to weight management. Proper weight management decreases the risks of many hypokinetic diseases such as type 2 diabetes, heart disease, stroke, cancer, and osteoarthritis.

- *Blood pressure management.* Physical activity strengthens the heart and makes it more efficient so that it pumps more blood with less effort. This results in less pressure on the arteries and vital organs. Walking appears to be as effective as some medications in reducing high blood pressure.

- *Boosting high-density lipoproteins (HDL).* HDL helps reduce low-density lipoproteins (LDL) or "destructive cholesterol." LDL increases plaque buildup in the arteries, which is a major cause of heart attacks.

- *Reducing the risk of type 2 diabetes.* Type 2 diabetes is increasing at an alarming rate among young people. People at high risk of diabetes can cut their risk in half by combining walking with lower fat intake and a 5–7 percent decrease in weight.

- *Decreasing the risk of heart disease.* Three hours of walking a week is associated with a 30–40 percent lower risk of heart disease in women.

Walking has the advantages of not requiring any special equipment and of having a low injury rate. Walking, probably more than any other activity, will be done by students when they reach adulthood. One of the things that makes walking such a valuable skill for health maintenance is its simplicity. To receive the best health results, walking should be done at least five times per week for 30 minutes or more per session. Certainly, any amount of time for walking is beneficial. The 30 minutes can be accumulated in three bouts of at least 10 minutes, but a 30-minute walk is recommended for children. There are only a few things that students need to remember to achieve maximum benefit:

1. They should walk at a brisk pace with a comfortable stride and a good arm swing.

2. Their walking pace should allow them to carry on a conversation without difficulty. If students find they can't walk and talk at the same time, encourage them to slow the pace slightly. For most youth in school, this will not be a problem and the opportunity to socialize may be more important than the walk itself. The most important outcome is that they enjoy the experience and realize the benefits of walking.

3. The walking program in school is a great place to coordinate pedometer use. Students can begin to see how many steps they typically gather in a specified amount of time. The Walk4Life pedometers can measure both walking time and steps. All things being equal, the more steps gathered in a specified time, the higher the intensity of the walk.

Walking and Weight Management

Currently, it is estimated that nearly 16 percent of youth are overweight. Another 15 percent are at risk for becoming overweight (Beals, 2003). It is estimated that 70 percent of overweight adolescents grow up to be overweight adults, making it important that activity be increased in the elementary school years. Unfortunately, over the last ten years energy expenditure through physical activity has decreased while energy intake (calories) has increased. The large servings of fast-food meals and high-fat foods have certainly contributed to this increase in caloric consumption. Weight management always deals with both caloric intake and expenditure, and people who are successful in maintaining proper body weight have usually learned to manage the balance between their food intake and physical activity. A number of studies show that if only diet is managed for weight control, pounds lost in the treatment program will usually be regained as soon as the intervention stops. There is no question that restricting diet in a highly controlled setting will result in weight loss. However, if this weight loss is not coupled with a new and more active lifestyle, success in weight management will be short lived.

Walking is probably the activity of choice for overweight students. It is easy on the joints, doesn't overly stress the cardiovascular system, and is not painful to perform. The old adage "No pain, no gain" makes no sense for overweight students. Many of these students have already been turned off of physical activity because of negative past experiences. Students who have been forced to be active when young will push back to a sedentary lifestyle when they become old enough to make personal decisions. Rekindling the joy of activity for these students must take an encouraging and kind approach. Walking is usually their choice of activity, and when coupled with pedometers, a new interest in being active can be ignited.

A question often asked is, "Does walking really make a difference in weight management?" The answer is yes, it makes a difference, but it is always possible to outeat the number of calories expended. Consider the following: The number of calories burned during exercise depends on a number of factors, the speed of walking and body size being two of the more important.

TABLE 12.3	Approximate calories burned in 30 minutes of walking
Body Weight in Pounds	**Approximate Calories Burned**
40	43
50	54
60	64
70	75
80	86
90	96
100	107
110	118
120	129
130	139
140	150
150	161
160	172

Table 12.3 shows the number of calories burned during a 30-minute walk based on body weight.

Assume an 80-pound student takes a 30-minute walk at a moderate pace and burns about 86 calories. Wanting to reward himself, this student decides to eat a typical-size candy bar. Without looking at the nutrition label, the student eats the candy bar and quickly ingests 300 to 350 calories—a net gain of over 200 calories. In general terms, about 3,500 calories equals a pound of weight gained or lost, depending on the energy intake and expenditure balance. Within two to three weeks, if this student continues to walk 30 minutes a day but adds a candy bar to his normal food intake, he will gain a pound of weight. This shows why it is necessary to keep an eye on both physical activity and diet. It also illustrates how easy it is to gain weight even when a person is adding physical activity to his day. One thing about increasing physical activity and decreasing sedentary behavior is that most people don't eat when they are active. Just being active may make it easier to decrease caloric expenditure.

Recently, walking (or trekking) poles (similar to ski poles) have come in vogue, and they may be a boon for Developmental Level III students who are overweight. They have been used for years in the Scandinavian countries and research has shown that 25–30 percent more calories are burned compared to walking without poles (Church et al., 2002). The poles increase heart rate by 10 to 15 beats and put more than 90 percent of the body's muscle mass to work. Additionally, they help absorb some of the impact on the knees and ankles, which results in an increase in upper body strength and a decrease in hip, knee, and foot injuries. Adding walking poles to a physical education program is another way to motivate students, reduce joint injuries in overweight children, and help students realize greater results from their walking. Excellent Websites on using and purchasing walking poles can be found at www.walkingpoles.com or www.trekkingpoles.com.

Implementing a School Walking Program

Safety is always a key issue. When initiating a walking program, the walking should be done where all students are in view of the teacher. However, most people will want more variety than just walking around a track or field. If approved by the administration, walking courses around the school neighborhood can be established so that students become familiar with many different walking paths and the time required to complete the circuit. All walking paths should be designed and mapped by the teacher prior to allowing students to follow them. Driving along each pathway will allow an opportunity to write directions and map the mileage for each trail. Set up safety guidelines that are integrated into each path. Some safety guidelines to consider are:

- Make sure students always use the sidewalk. If a sidewalk is not available, they should walk on the left side of the roadway facing traffic.

- Stipulate that students must walk with another person or in a small group. If someone is injured or needs help, one member of the group can return to the school for help.

- Because running from aggressive dogs only makes the problem worse, teach students to stop, face them, and give them a stern, "No!"

- Have students sign out, listing which path they will be walking. If someone is missing, it will be much easier to track such students.

- If students have a serious health problem, make sure the school nurse clears them. Also, they should be required to wear a "medical tag" in case of an accident requiring emergency care.

- Encourage parents to purchase walking or running shoes for their youngsters with reflective tape built into them. This can make it much easier for automobile drivers to see them.

- Have students warm up before the walk and teach them to cool down when they have finished walking. They should walk a short distance, stop, and stretch the arms, legs, and back (see Chapter 13 for suggested stretches). When they have finished the walk, they should stretch one more time.

- Make sure students drink plenty of water, whether it is cold or hot. They should drink eight ounces of water 15 minutes before the walk. If it is hot and dry, they should drink six ounces every 15 to 20 minutes during the walk. At the end of the walk, they should drink another 8 to 16 ounces of water. Waiting for the thirst signal as a reminder to drink may be too late. The sensation of thirstiness usually comes after the body is in need of water.

- In cold weather, teach students about layering clothing so that a layer can be removed if it gets too hot. Layers of lighter clothing are much more useful than one heavy layer. Students should wear a hat, gloves, and scarf if necessary. In hot weather, they should wear loose, light-colored clothing, a hat, and sunglasses. Emphasize that sunscreen should always be applied when students will be outside for more than a few minutes whether it is hot or cold out because ultraviolet light from the sun can quickly cause skin damage.

Suggested Walking Activities

▶ I SPY

Students take a scorecard with them on their walk that has a challenge on it. For example, "Identify as many different makes of cars as possible." Or, "List as many different birds and animals as you can." Different cards can be designed to create varying challenges. When the students complete their walks, the items they have identified can be discussed.

▶ MIXED-UP WALKS

For limited amounts of time add some walking variations (e.g., backward; sideways slide with a left shoulder lead, then a right shoulder lead; skipping; galloping). For example, have students start with backward walking for one minute, then regular walking for one minute, then skipping for one minute, then regular walking, and so on. Tasks assigned can be different types of movement or varying challenges like, "Complete your walk by making ten left turns on your route." The location of where students make a turn must be documented.

▶ INTERVAL WALK

Set up a walking circuit that includes stretching and strength activities at each corner of the football field. For example, instruct students to walk a lap, then do a standing stretch for 30 seconds, then walk half a lap to a sitting stretch, then walk another lap, then do some abdominal activities, then walk to a push-up station.

► CROSS-COUNTRY WALKING

Set up a cross-country walking race with teams from the class. Have a map set up for the walking course so there is a nice variety of walking areas. Students try to walk as quickly as possible and receive a number at the finish line. The team with the lowest number of points is the winner. This is a competitive activity, but it can be approached in a positive and fun manner.

► WALKING GOLF

Set up a walking "golf" tournament around your teaching space with hula-hoops for holes, cones for the tees, and a tennis ball for each student to throw. Students throw the ball and then walk with their group to the hoop. Students use a scorecard to keep track of the number of throws needed at each hole.

► TREASURE HUNT

Set up a walking course with a set of clues to follow to get to ten sites. At the sites you can tape a set of words that can later be arranged in a particular order to spell a popular saying or jingle. Examples of the clues to follow could include "a place for extra points on the south side"; "a place for H_2O"; "fans sit here on the west side"; "long jumpers take off here"; "stand under this for the score of the game"; "a place for trash."

► POKER WALK

Set out several decks of cards at various locations around the teaching area. Students walk to the areas and pick up one card at each without looking at it. They walk to as many areas as possible within a time limit and then add up the points. Give a prize for high- and low-point totals. Set it up so that anyone can win by just walking to the card areas, picking up the cards, and then adding up the points at the end of the time limit.

► KNOW YOUR COMMUNITY

Have the class take different walks and identify different types of businesses and professional offices along their route. Different challenges can be listed that ask students to find different businesses or locations.

► WEEKLY WALKING CALENDAR

Each week give students a five-day calendar that stipulates different types of things to do on their walk. For example: Monday: Walk with a friend. Tuesday: Walk with walking poles. Wednesday: Walk, stop, and stretch periodically. Thursday: Walk 15 minutes in one direction

and return to the starting spot by retracing your path. Friday: Walk and use a pedometer to count your steps.

► LEARN ABOUT YOUR FRIEND

Give students a series of questions on a card that will help them get to know a friend better. The goal is for them to walk and discover new things about a friend while moving.

► OFF-CAMPUS WALKS

Students can gain extra credit by taking walks outside of the school day. This can be an excellent opportunity for them to use pedometers to track their walks. They can record their steps and activity time and report back to class on both measures.

REFLECTION AND REVIEW QUESTIONS

How and Why

1. Why is walking often called the "real" lifetime activity?
2. How can walking play an important role in weight management?
3. What are the basic steps to follow when implementing a walking program in physical education?
4. What can be done to encourage students' physical activity outside of the school environment?

Content Review

1. What is the impact of adding at least 60 minutes of daily physical activity to your lifestyle?
2. What are the levels of the Physical Activity Pyramid? How much time should be spent on each of the components on a weekly basis?
3. What level in the Physical Activity Pyramid forms the foundation for good health? How can students be taught to change their activity habits to meet the minimum activity requirements?
4. What can pedometers measure? Which of the measurements is most accurate and useful for the majority of students? Why?
5. What are the steps to follow when teaching students to develop personal goals? When should the goals be reset?
6. What are the three most common areas physical educators use to establish the accountability of their programs? Which of the three might be most meaningful to choose as a program outcome?
7. What are three walking activities that can be assigned to students for after-school physical activity?

FOR MORE INFORMATION

References and Suggested Readings

American College of Sports Medicine. (2000). *ACSM's guidelines for exercise testing and prescription.* 6th ed. Philadelphia: Lippincott, Williams, & Wilkins.

Beals, K. A. (2003). Addressing an epidemic: Treatment strategies for youth obesity. *ACSM Fit Society Page,* Spring 2003, 9–11.

Beighle, A., Pangrazi, R. P., & Vincent, S. D. (2001). Pedometers, physical activity, and accountability. *JOPERD,* 72(9), 16–19.

Bouchard, C. (1999). Heredity and health related fitness. In C. B. Corbin & R. P. Pangrazi, (Eds.), *Toward a better understanding of physical fitness and activity.* Scottsdale, AZ: Holcomb Hathaway Publishers.

Church, T. S., Earnest, C. P., & Morss, G. M. (2002). Field testing of physiological responses associated with Nordic walking. *Research Quarterly for Exercise and Sport,* 73(3), 296–300.

Cooper Institute. (2004). *Fitnessgram/Activitygram test administration manual.* 3rd ed. Champaign, IL: Human Kinetics.

Corbin, C. B., & Pangrazi, R. P. (1992). Are American children and youth fit? *Research Quarterly for Exercise and Sport,* 63(2), 96–106.

Crouter, S. C., Schneider, P. L., Karabulut, M., & Bassett, D. R., Jr. (2003). Validity of 10 electronic pedometers for measuring steps, distance, and energy cost. *Medicine and Science in Sports and Exercise,* 35(8), 1455–1460.

Decker, J., & Mize, M. (2002). *Walking games and activities.* Champaign, IL: Human Kinetics.

Epstein, L. H., Valoski, A. M., Vara, L. S., McCurley, J., Wisniewski, L., Kalarchian, M. A., Klein, K. R., & Shrager, L. R. (1995). Effects of decreasing sedentary behavior and increasing activity on weight change in obese children. *Health Psychology,* 14(2), 109–115.

Gordon-Larsen, P., McMurray, R. G., & Popkin, B. M. (2000). Determinants of adolescent physical activity and inactivity patterns. *Pediatrics,* 105, E83.

Harrell, J. S., McMurray, R. G., Baggett, C. D., Pennell, M. L., Pearce, P. F., & Bangdiwala, S. I. (2005). Energy costs of physical activities in children and adolescents. *Medicine and Science in Sports and Exercise,* 37(2), 329–336.

Hatano, Y. (1993). Use of the pedometer for promoting daily walking exercise. *International Council for Health, Physical Education and Recreation,* 29, 4–28.

Kilanowski, C. K., Consalvi, A. R., & Epstein, L. H. (1999). Validation of an electronic pedometer for measurement of physical activity in children. *Pediatric Exercise Science,* 11, 63–68.

Morgan, C. F., Jr., Pangrazi, R. P. & Beighle, A. (2003). Using pedometers to promote physical activity in physical education. *JOPERD,* 74(7), 33–38.

National Association for Sport and Physical Education. (2004). *Physical activity for children: A statement of guidelines.* 2nd ed. Reston, VA: Author.

Pangrazi, R. P., Beighle, A., & Sidman, C. L. (2003). *Pedometer power: 67 lessons for K–12.* Champaign, IL: Human Kinetics.

Pate, R. R., Pratt, M., Blair, S. N., Haskell, W. L., Macera, C. A., Bouchard, C., Buchner, D., Ettinger, W., Heath, G. W., & King, A. C. (1995). Physical activity and public health. *Journal of the American Medical Association,* 273(5), 402–407.

Plowman, S. A. (1993). Physical fitness and healthy low back function. *Physical Activity and Fitness Research Digest,* 1(3), 1–8.

President's Council on Physical Fitness and Sports. (2005). *The president's challenge handbook.* Washington, DC: Author.

Sallis, J. F. (1991). Self-report measures of children's physical activity. *Journal of School Health,* 61, 215–219.

Sallis, J. F., and Patrick, K. (1994). Physical activity guidelines for adolescents: Consensus statement. *Pediatric Exercise Science,* 6(4), 302–314.

Schneider, P. L., Crouter, S. E., Lukajic, O., & Bassett, D. R., Jr. (2003). Accuracy and reliability of 10 pedometers for measuring steps over a 400-m walk. *Medicine and Science in Sports and Exercise,* 35(10), 1779–1784.

Shaw, J. M., & Snow-Harter, C. (1995). Osteoporosis and physical activity. *Physical Activity and Fitness Research Digest,* 2(3), 1–8.

Trost, S. G., Pate, R. R., Freedson, P. S., Sallis, J. F., & Taylor, W. C. (2000). Using objective physical activity measures with youth: How many days of monitoring are needed? *Medicine and Science in Sports and Exercise,* 32(2), 426–431.

U.S. Department of Health and Human Services. (1996). *Physical activity and health: A report of the Surgeon General.* Atlanta, GA: Centers for Disease Control and Prevention, National Center for Chronic Disease Prevention and Health Promotion.

U.S. Department of Health and Human Services. (2000). *Healthy people 2010. National health promotion and disease objectives.* Washington, DC: U.S. Government Printing Office.

U.S. Department of Health and Human Services. (2002). *Prevalence of overweight among children and adolescents: United States, 1999.* Atlanta, GA: Centers for Disease Control and Prevention, National Center for Health Statistics.

Vincent, S. D., & Pangrazi, R. P. (2002). Does reactivity exist in children when measuring activity levels with pedometers? *Pediatric Exercise Science,* 14(1), 56–63.

Websites

Pedometers

http://walking.about.com/cs/measure/bb/bybpedometer.htm
http://walking.about.com/cs/measure/tp/pedometer.htm
www.pecentral.org/pedometry
www.walk4life.com

Videos and Instructional Materials

www.walkingpoles.com
www.trekkingpoles.com

Walking Programs

www.walksmartactiveschools.com
www.accustep10000.org
www.americaonthemove.org
www.steptracker.com
www.10k-steps.com

13

Physical Fitness

ESSENTIAL COMPONENTS OF QUALITY PROGRAMS

▶ **I. Organized around content standards**

▶ **II. Student-centered and developmentally appropriate**

III. Physical activity and motor skill development form the core of the program

IV. Teaches management skills and self-discipline

▶ **V. Promotes inclusion of all students**

▶ **VI. Focuses on process over product**

▶ **VII. Promotes lifetime personal health and wellness**

VIII. Teaches cooperation and responsibility and promotes sensitivity to diversity

NATIONAL STANDARDS FOR PHYSICAL EDUCATION*

1. Demonstrates competency in motor skills and movement patterns needed to perform a variety of physical activities.

2. Demonstrates understanding of movement concepts, principles, and tactics as they apply to the learning and performance of physical activities.

▶ **3. Participates regularly in physical activity.**

▶ **4. Achieves and maintains a health-enhancing level of physical fitness.**

5. Exhibits responsible personal and social behavior that respects self and others in physical activity.

▶ **6. Values physical activity for health, enjoyment, challenge, self-expression, and/or social interaction.**

*National Association for Sport and Physical Education (NASPE), 2004.

SUMMARY

The value and the importance of teaching lifetime physical fitness is discussed in this chapter. An understanding of the difference between health-related and skill-related fitness helps clarify the need for emphasizing lifetime activity. High-level fitness performance is no longer an objective for the majority of children. Instead, the goal is to increase the activity and general fitness level of all students in order to improve their health status. Fitness activities for children can be moderate in intensity and still offer many health benefits. Suggestions for developing a fitness module, motivating children to maintain fitness, and developing positive attitudes toward activities are included. A variety of exercises and proper performance techniques are described so a health-related program that meets the needs of all students can be offered.

OUTCOMES

- Differentiate between skill-related and health-related physical fitness.

- Describe the fitness status of youth in the United States.

- Explain the role that a broad program of physical fitness and activity plays in the elementary school curriculum.

- Identify the various components of health-related versus skill-related physical fitness.

- List guidelines for developing and maintaining physical fitness.

- Develop a fitness module.

- Cite strategies and techniques to motivate children to maintain physical fitness.

- Discuss the importance of fitness testing and cite several tests that could be used to measure fitness in children.

- Categorize various exercises by the muscle group involved.

- Characterize isotonic, isometric, and isokinetic exercises.

- Identify harmful physical activities and exercises.

- Plan and demonstrate numerous activities and exercises that can improve the physical fitness of children.

DEFINITIONS OF PHYSICAL FITNESS

Physical activity is a process that involves accumulating a wide variety of movement. Many experts believe that if there is enough physical activity accumulated, then physical fitness will take care of itself. Physical fitness is a product that is often measured to see if there is an adequate standard in place to ensure good health. The general definition of physical fitness is "a set of attributes that people have or achieve relating to their ability to perform physical activity" (U.S. Department of Health and Human Services [USDHHS], 1996). An alternative definition of physical fitness is "a state of well-being with a low risk of premature health problems and energy to participate in a variety of physical activities" (Howley & Franks, 2003).

The two types of physical fitness most often identified are health-related physical fitness and skill-related physical fitness. The differentiation between *physical fitness related to functional health* (health related) and *physical performance related to athletic ability* (skill related) makes it easier to develop proper fitness objectives and goals for youngsters. The components of health-related physical fitness are a subset of skill-related fitness components (Figure 13.1).

Health-related fitness is characterized by moderate and regular physical activity as discussed in Chapter 12. People who are generally unwilling to exercise at high intensities should aim for health-related fitness. Health-related fitness activities can be integrated into everyday activities that are often characterized as lifetime activities.

In contrast, skill-related physical fitness includes the health-related components, but also covers components that are related to genetic limitations that control physical performance. Skill-related fitness is the right choice for people who *can* and *want* to perform at a high level, but is less acceptable to the majority of people because it requires training and exercising at high intensities.

Health-Related Physical Fitness

Teaching health-related fitness should be a priority in physical education. The benefit of health-related fitness is that all students can improve their health status through daily physical activity. Health-related fitness is one of the few areas where all students can succeed regardless of ability level and genetic limitations. Students can be assured that if they are willing to be active, they will enhance their health status. This contrasts with skill-related fitness, which is performance oriented and influenced by genetic traits and abilities. A primary reason for teaching health-related fitness is that it leaves students with positive lifetime activity habits.

Health-related physical fitness includes those aspects of physiological function that offer protection from diseases related to a sedentary lifestyle. It can be improved and/or maintained through regular physical activity. Specific components include cardiovascular endurance, body composition (ratio of leanness to fatness), flexibility, and muscular strength and endurance, and flexibility. These components are all measured in the Fitnessgram test (Cooper Institute, 2004) as described in Chapter 8. When measuring health-related fitness, criterion standards are used to indicate levels of good health. The Fitnessgram (Cooper Institute, 2004) uses criterion-referenced health standards that represent good health instead of the traditional percentile rankings often found in skill-related fitness tests. These standards represent a level of fitness that offers some degree of protection against diseases resulting from sedentary living. The Fitnessgram uses an approach that classifies fitness performance into two categories: needs improvement and healthy fitness zone (HFZ). All students are encouraged to score in the HFZ; however, there is little advantage to scoring beyond the healthy fitness zone. Criterion-referenced health standards do not compare students against each other. The goal is for all students to achieve and move their personal performance into the HFZ. The following are the major components of health-related fitness.

CARDIOVASCULAR ENDURANCE

Aerobic fitness offers many health benefits and is often seen as the most important element of fitness. *Cardiovascular endurance* is the ability of the heart, the blood vessels,

FIGURE 13.1 Components of physical fitness.

and the respiratory system to deliver oxygen efficiently over an extended period of time. To develop cardiovascular endurance, activity must be aerobic in nature. Activities that are continuous and rhythmic in nature require that a continuous supply of oxygen be delivered to the muscle cells. Activities that stimulate development in this area are paced walking, jogging, biking, rope-jumping, aerobics, and swimming.

BODY COMPOSITION

Body composition is an integral part of health-related fitness. Body composition is the proportion of body fat to lean body mass. After the thickness of selected skinfolds has been measured, the percentage of lean body mass can be calculated by using formulas that have been developed using other, more accurate methods of measuring body composition. The conversion of skinfold thickness to the percent of lean body mass is easier to communicate to parents than the more involved methods.

FLEXIBILITY

Flexibility is the range of movement through which a joint or sequence of joints can move. Inactive individuals lose flexibility, whereas frequent movement helps retain the range of movement. Through stretching activities, the length of muscles, tendons, and ligaments is increased. The ligaments and tendons retain their elasticity through constant use. Flexibility is important to fitness; a lack of flexibility can create health problems for individuals. People who are flexible usually have good posture and may have less low-back pain. Many physical activities demand a range of motion to generate maximum force, such as serving a tennis ball or kicking a soccer ball.

MUSCULAR STRENGTH AND ENDURANCE

Muscular strength is the ability of muscles to exert force. Most activities do not build strength in areas where it is needed—the arm-shoulder girdle and the abdominal-trunk region. *Muscular endurance* is the ability to exert force over an extended period. Endurance postpones the onset of fatigue so that activity can be performed for lengthy periods. Sport activities require muscular endurance, because throwing, kicking, and striking skills have to be performed many times without fatigue.

Skill-Related Physical Fitness Components

Skill-related fitness includes those physical qualities that enable a person to perform in sport activities. For years, the primary fitness test for teachers was the AAHPERD

Youth Fitness Test (AAHPERD, 1987). Today this test is known as the President's Challenge Youth Fitness Test (President's Council on Physical Fitness and Sports [PCPFS], 2005). Skill-related fitness is closely related to athletic ability. The traits of speed, agility, coordination, and so on, form the basis of the ability to excel in sports. Because skill-related fitness is strongly influenced by one's natural or inherited traits, it is difficult for the majority of students to achieve. In contrast to health-related tests, skill-related fitness tests often use norm-referenced standards where students are compared in terms of where they rank compared to their peers. For some students, the goal becomes trying to do better than other students rather than learning to do the best they can regardless of peer scores.

Skill-related fitness components are useful for performing motor tasks related to sport and athletics. The ability to perform well depends largely on the genetic endowment of the individual. Whereas it is possible for all students to perform adequately in health-related fitness activities, it is difficult, if not impossible, for a large number of youngsters to excel in this area of fitness. Asking students to "try harder" only adds to their frustration if they lack natural ability, because they see their more skilled friends perform well without effort. When skill-related fitness is taught, it should be accompanied by an explanation of why some students can perform well with a minimum of effort while others, no matter how hard they try, never excel. There are many examples that can be used to illustrate genetic differences such as speed, jumping ability, strength, and physical size in individuals. The bottom line for teachers is to understand that some students will want to work hard to improve their fitness performance while a majority will probably be satisfied to play, be active, and enjoy their bodies in a less demanding manner. For these students, health-related fitness will be an important outcome.

Skill-related physical fitness includes the health-related items listed above plus the following:

AGILITY

Agility is the ability of the body to change position rapidly and accurately while moving in space. Wrestling and football are examples of sports that require agility.

BALANCE

Balance refers to the body's ability to maintain a state of equilibrium while remaining stationary or moving. Maintaining balance is essential to all sports but is especially important in the performance of gymnastic activities.

COORDINATION

Coordination is the ability of the body to perform smoothly and successfully more than one motor task at a time. Needed for football, baseball, tennis, soccer, and other sports that require hand-eye and foot-eye skills, coordination can be developed by practicing over and over the skill to be learned.

POWER

Power is the ability to transfer energy explosively into force. To develop power, a person must practice activities that are required to improve strength, but at a faster rate, and involve sudden bursts of energy. Skills requiring power include high jumping, long jumping, shot putting, throwing, and kicking.

SPEED

Speed is the ability of the body to perform movement in a short period of time. Usually associated with running forward, speed is essential for the successful performance of most sports and general locomotor movement skills.

ARE TODAY'S CHILDREN FIT?

A popular point of view among physical education teachers is that youth today are less fit than they were in the past. This opinion is often used as a justification for more physical education time in the schools. Comparative research (Corbin & Pangrazi, 1992) suggests that the fitness of today's youngsters has not degenerated and that they perform at a level similar to students 40 years ago. When data from the last four national surveys (1957 to 1985) of youth fitness conducted by AAHPERD and/or the President's Council on Physical Fitness and Sports were compared, the only items used in all four surveys were pull-ups and the flexed-arm hang. Youngsters, both boys and girls, showed an increase in upper body strength when these two items were compared over four decades. Unfortunately, it is difficult to compare in other areas of fitness because the test items were changed on a regular basis. The area where youth have shown a serious and documented decline is body composition. As of 1999–2002, 16 percent of youth ages 6 through 19 years are overweight and another 31 percent are at risk for overweight (85th percentile of sex-specific BMI-for-age growth charts) (Hedley et al., 2004). This large increase in obesity takes its toll on fitness scores. Common sense would dictate that if someone can do 50 push-ups at normal weight, putting 20 pounds of sand on her back will decrease the number of push-ups she is able to perform. Body fat is dead weight and does not

contribute to muscular or cardiovascular performance. Thus, all strength and aerobic performance scores decrease as obesity increases at a rapid rate among youth.

Why Can't All Children Meet Established Standards of Fitness?

Is it realistic to expect all children to reach specified standards of fitness? What factors control fitness performance, and how much control do youngsters have over their fitness accomplishments? Payne and Morrow (1993) reviewed 28 studies examining training and aerobic performance in children and concluded that improvement is small to moderate in prepubescent children. They found that the relatively small-to-moderate increase in pre- to post-aerobic improvement and the weak relationship between type of training program and size of effect lead to questions concerning traditional practices when dealing with children and their fitness. Are we expecting too much from traditional physical education or fitness programs? Have award structures, designed to motivate children within these programs or test batteries, been appropriately designed when children appear to elicit only small improvements in aerobic capacity? Clearly, curriculum planners, teachers, fitness directors, exercise physiologists, and physicians need to consider carefully the ramifications of these findings.

A significant amount of fitness test performance is explained by heredity (Bouchard, 1999; Bouchard, Dionne, Simoneau, & Boulay, 1992). Other factors such as environment, nutrition, and maturation affect fitness performance as well, as reflected in physical fitness test scores. Research shows that heredity and maturation strongly impact fitness scores (Bouchard, 1999; Bouchard et al., 1992; Pangrazi & Corbin, 1990). These factors may have more to do with youth fitness scores than does activity level. Lifestyle and environmental factors also make a difference. For example, nutrition is a lifestyle factor that can influence test scores, and environmental conditions (heat, humidity, and pollution) strongly modify test performances. Some youngsters have a definite advantage on tests because of the types of muscle fibers they inherit (see Chapter 2). Even in an untrained state these children score better because of heredity.

Beyond heredity lies another factor that predisposes some youngsters to high (or low) performance. Recent research has shown that differences in "trainability" are strongly influenced by genetic predisposition (Bouchard, 1999; Bouchard et al., 1992). Trainability means that some individuals receive more benefit from training (regular physical activity) than do others. For example, assume two youngsters perform the same amount of activity (workload) throughout a semester. Child A shows dramatic improvement immediately while child B does not. Child A simply responds more favorably to training than does child B; child A inherited a system that is responsive to exercise. Child A not only improves her fitness and scores well on the test but also gets feedback that says, "The activity works—it makes me fit." Child B scores poorly, receives negative or no feedback, and concludes that "activity doesn't improve my fitness, so why bother?" The truth is that child B may improve in fitness (to a lesser degree than child A), but it will take longer to show improvement. Child B will probably never achieve the fitness level attained by child A because of genetic limitations.

Another factor that impacts fitness performance is physical maturation. Teachers know that some youngsters mature faster than others. If two youngsters are the same age and sex, but one is physiologically older (advanced skeletal maturation), the more mature youngster usually performs better on tests than does the less mature child. Examining fitness norms shows that performance levels increase as children grow older. Because age does not accurately reflect physical maturity, an immature, active child might score lower than a more mature, less active youngster even though they are the same age. Maturation can override the effects of activity among young children. Age also plays a role in fitness performance (Pangrazi & Corbin, 1990). As little as three months' difference in age helps youngsters perform better than younger children, regardless of training. Expect older students in the same class with younger children to perform better.

Many teachers and parents believe that fitness in youngsters is primarily a reflection of the amount of activity (workload) children perform on a regular basis. They assume that youngsters who score high on fitness tests are active and those who score low are inactive. This assumption is often wrong. Physical activity is an important variable in fitness development for adults, but for children and youth, other factors are of equal or greater importance. Studies have shown that the relationship between physical fitness and physical activity among children is low (Pate, Dowda, & Ross, 1990; Pate & Ross, 1987; Ross, Pate, Caspersen, Damberg, & Svilar, 1987). When teachers make the mistake of assuming that a child is inactive because of low scores on a fitness test, they create unforeseen problems.

Youngsters want to be successful. They try to behave in ways that please the teacher and impress their friends. When youngsters are told that they will improve their fitness scores if they work hard each day, most take this challenge seriously. When fitness tests are given, students expect to perform well on the tests if they have been exercising regularly, and, of course, teachers expect the same. If, however, they receive scores that are lower than expected, students become disappointed. They are

especially discouraged if the teacher concludes that their low fitness scores are a reflection of inactivity and lack of exercise. Such conclusions as, "You weren't as fit as some of your peers, therefore you must not have been working hard enough" can be destructive and often untrue statements. It may cause a loss of self-esteem and a loss of respect between student and teacher. On the flip side, assuming that youngsters who make high scores on fitness tests are active can also be incorrect. Youngsters who are genetically gifted may be inactive, yet still perform well on fitness tests because of their genetic traits. If teachers do not teach otherwise, these youngsters incorrectly develop the belief that it is possible to be fit and healthy without being active.

Why Are the Majority of Children Labeled Unfit?

For years, the only available fitness test for teachers was the Youth Fitness Test (AAHPER, 1976; AAHPERD, 1987), which is currently available as one component of The President's Challenge (PCPFS, 2005). This test measures skill-related fitness and awards the Presidential fitness award to youngsters performing at the 85th percentile or better in all test items. Data from the National School Population Fitness Survey (Reiff et al., 1987), funded by the President's Council on Physical Fitness and Sports, showed that only one-tenth of 1 percent of boys and three-tenths of 1 percent of girls could pass a battery of six tests at the 85th percentile. Why are the standards so high? A probable explanation is that it compares with academic standards, and test developers felt that physical education standards should be set at a similar level.

Because many physical educators and parents felt that the 85th percentile standard was unrealistically high, a second award was created—the National Fitness Award. To earn this award, youngsters must pass the same battery of test items at the 50th percentile or better. Unfortunately, when using a battery of tests, the overwhelming majority of students fail at least one item, causing them to lose the award and be identified as unfit. Only 15 percent of boys and 19 percent of girls are able to pass the 50th percentile standard. Using a battery of tests to define fitness is a sure way to fail the majority of children. Even at this lowered standard, over 80 percent of youngsters are failures. Common sense suggests that if youngsters pass five of six test items, they should be declared fit rather than unfit. As teachers, it is important to discuss the successes of children on fitness test items, rather than declare them unfit because they failed one item.

Another reason people believe that youngsters are unfit is because the definition of physical fitness has changed over the years. Newer fitness tests are focusing on health-related fitness and its relationship to good health and feelings of well-being. High performance on fitness test items is not necessary for good health. Evidence shows that moderate amounts of health-related physical fitness also contribute to good health (Blair et al., 1989; USDHHS, 1996). When health-related fitness test items are used to evaluate fitness, many children perform as well as those in years past.

Finally, it is likely that many physical education teachers have chosen to believe that youngsters are unfit in order to make a strong case for physical education. This belief is counterproductive because the fitness of children has been measured for over 40 years and the fitness levels of youth have neither substantially improved nor declined over the last four decades (Corbin & Pangrazi, 1992). A better approach is to accept the fact that preadolescent youth are nonresponders to training and unlikely to show fitness improvement even with training regimens. What has become an important issue to deal with is increasing problems with body weight (BMI) increases. To manage weight issues, an increase in volume of physical activity accumulated each day is critical for success. The important issues are to teach youth about fitness concepts, what type of effort they require, and the need to increase the volume of physical activity, and to leave them with a positive feeling toward physical activity and fitness.

FITNESS TESTING ISSUES

If you consider fitness testing children, the overriding consideration is to be sure the testing experience is positive and educational. Children can learn about their personal fitness and how to develop a lifestyle that maintains good health without being turned off by the testing experience. Imagine the number of children who have been embarrassed when their fitness test results are announced to the class. Many schools have tested children twice a year throughout their school careers with the result that some have been labeled unfit for an entire school career. How could this practice possibly encourage inactive children who require the most motivation?

Skill-Related or Health-Related Fitness Test?

Students should understand the difference between the types of fitness so they understand the purposes of each. Skill-related fitness helps improve performance in motor tasks related to sport and athletics. The ability to perform well on skill-related tests is strongly influenced by predetermined genetic skills. If skill-related fitness is encouraged in elementary school, it should be accompanied with an explanation about why some people perform well whereas others, no matter how hard they try, never reach high levels of performance. Many obvious examples such as individual differences in speed, jumping ability, strength, and physical size illustrate genetic differences.

In contrast, health-related physical fitness focuses on how much activity is required for good health. Emphasis is placed on the processes of activity and participation rather than on the product of high-level physical skill performance. Usually, health-related fitness batteries use criterion-referenced health standards (see page 256) in contrast to skill-related fitness tests that use percentile scores standards. Criterion-referenced standards relate to the minimum amount of activity required for good health. Performance in excess of the minimum is laudable but not required for good health. This approach teaches students the importance of maintaining a personal level of fitness through regular activity rather than comparing one's fitness level with others.

Should Performance Recognition Awards Be Used?

For years, award systems have been used to recognize students who demonstrate high levels of fitness performance. The original intent of the award systems was to motivate youngsters to improve their level of fitness. However, research shows that performance awards usually only motivate youngsters who feel they have the ability to earn them (Corbin, Lovejoy, Steingard, & Emerson, 1990; Corbin, Lovejoy, & Whitehead, 1988). Many students find it impossible to earn such awards and often feel as though there is no use in making the effort only to fail again. Fitness awards focus on a single episode of accomplishment, making the act of participating in daily activity less important than earning an award. Students learn that the only thing that counts with fitness is performance on the yearly test.

Reward systems that focus on improvement look at short-term changes. Fitness award systems ask students to look at their immediate health status. There is evidence to show that youngsters who achieve at an elite level do so because they are genetically gifted (Bouchard et al., 1992). If gifted students can pass the test without training, it leads them to believe they do not have to exercise regularly. If awards are used, it is best to reward participation in regular activity (behavior) rather than fitness performance. The role of the physical education teacher is to encourage behavior that lasts a lifetime. When the focus is on long-term behaviors, instruction is focused on participation in regular and moderate activity.

Awards are not recommended because they are extrinsic rewards that are not available to all children, and children should be taught in a way that does not undermine their intrinsic motivation. However, if for whatever reason awards are used, try to consider and incorporate the following points:

1. Base awards on achievement of goals that are challenging, yet attainable (Locke & Lathan, 1985). Goals that are difficult to attain fail to elicit effort from students (Harter, 1978). Students who are least likely to make an effort to earn an award are those with low self-esteem; these are probably the students who most need to achieve such goals.

2. If fitness goals do not seem attainable to youngsters, "learned helplessness" sets in (Harter, 1978). This phenomenon occurs when children believe there is no use trying to reach the goals and their efforts are in vain. Learned helplessness often occurs when performance rather than participation or effort is rewarded. Difficult-to-achieve goals teach youngsters who need to be motivated that there is no use in trying.

3. If an award system is used to motivate children's activity, the system should be phased out as soon as possible. Awards do motivate primary-grade children; however, by the age of nine or ten years, children start to see the rewards as bribery to do something (Whitehead & Corbin, 1991). Other children find achievement of the awards to be hopeless; they are not motivated but instead discouraged by the rewards being given to others. Gradually removing awards helps students learn that participation should be done for intrinsic and personal reasons.

4. An alternative and long-term approach that focuses on behavior rather than a single outcome is giving awards to recognize students for regular participation in activity. This places the rewards in reach of all youngsters and helps establish activity habits that last a lifetime. In addition, this approach supports the research cited in the report of the Surgeon General on the benefits of moderate-to-vigorous physical activity (USDHHS, 1996).

CREATE POSITIVE ATTITUDES TOWARD FITNESS

Teachers can do a number of things to increase the possibility of students being "turned on" to activity. Fitness activity is neither good nor bad. Rather, how fitness activities are taught determines how youngsters feel about making fitness a part of their lifestyles. The following strategies help make physical activity a positive learning experience.

Personalize Fitness Activities

Students who find themselves unable to perform exercises are not likely to develop a positive attitude toward physical activity. Fitness experiences should allow children to determine their personal workloads. Use time as the workload variable and ask children to do the best they can within a time limit. People dislike and fear experiences they perceive to be forced on them from an external source. Voluntary long-term exercise is more probable when individuals are internally driven to do their best. Fitness experiences that allow children to control the intensity of their workouts offer better opportunities for development of positive attitudes toward activity. See the Fitness Activities sections later in this chapter about offering abdominal and upper body strength activities that allow all youngsters to be successful.

Expose Youngsters to a Variety of Fitness Activities

Presenting a variety of fitness opportunities decreases the monotony of doing the same routines week after week and increases the likelihood that students will experience fitness activities that are personally enjoyable. Youngsters are willing to accept activities they dislike if they know there will be a chance in the near future to experience routines they enjoy. A yearlong routine of calisthenics and one-mile runs forces children, regardless of ability and interest, to participate in the same routine whether they like it or not. Avoiding potential boredom by systematically changing fitness activities is a significant way to help students perceive fitness in a positive light.

Give Students Positive Feedback about Their Effort

Teacher feedback contributes to the way children view fitness activities. Immediate, accurate, and specific feedback regarding effort encourages continued participation. Provided in a positive manner, this feedback can stimulate children to extend their participation habits outside the confines of the gymnasium. Reinforce all children, not just those who perform at high levels. All youngsters need feedback and reinforcement even if they are incapable of performing at an elite level.

Teach Physical Skills and Fitness

Physical education programs should concentrate on skill development as well as fitness. Some states mandate fitness testing, which causes teachers to worry that their students will not pass. Unfortunately, the skill development portion of physical education is often sacrificed to allow for an increased emphasis on teaching fitness. Physical education has two major objectives: fitness and skill development. Skills are the tools that many adults use to maintain personal fitness. These individuals maintain fitness through various skill-based activities such as tennis, badminton, swimming, golf, basketball, aerobics, bicycling, and the like. People have a much greater propensity to participate as adults if they feel competent in an activity. School programs must graduate students with requisite entry skills in a variety of activities.

Be a Role Model

Appearance, attitude, and actions speak loudly about teachers and their values regarding fitness. Teachers who display physical vitality, take pride in being active, participate in activities with children, and are physically fit will positively influence youngsters to maintain an active lifestyle. It is unreasonable to expect teachers to complete fitness routines nine times a day and five days a week. However, teachers must exercise with a class periodically to assure students that they are willing to do what they ask others to do.

Care about the Attitudes of Children

Attitudes dictate how youngsters participate in activity. Too often, adults want to force fitness on children in an effort to make them all physically fit. This results in insensitivity to the feelings of participants. Training does not equate to lifetime fitness. When youngsters are trained without concern for their feelings, the result will be fit children who may hate physical activity. Once a negative attitude is developed, it is difficult to change. This does not mean that youngsters should avoid fitness activity but that fitness participation must be a positive experience. Youngsters should not all be funneled into one type of fitness activity. For example, running may be detrimental to the health of obese children, and lean, uncoordinated students may not enjoy contact activities. The fitness experience works best when it is a challenge rather than a threat. A *challenge* is an experience that participants feel they can accomplish. In contrast, a *threat* appears to be an impossible undertaking, one in which there is no use trying. Keep fitness goals within the realm of challenge. A final note: Whether an activity is a challenge or a threat depends on the perceptions of the learner, not the instructor. Listen carefully to students rather than tell them they "should do it for their own good."

Start Easy and Progress Slowly

Fitness development is a journey, not a destination. No teacher wants students to become fit and then quit being active. A rule of thumb is to allow students to start at a level that they can *accomplish* successfully. This usually means self-directed workloads within a specified time frame. Don't force students into heavy workloads too soon. Start easy, ensure success, and gradually increase the workload. This avoids the discouragement of failure and excessive muscle soreness. When students successfully accomplish activities, they develop a system of self-talk that looks at their exercise behavior in a positive light. This minimizes the practice of self-criticism where students fail to live up to their own or others' standards.

Use Low-Intensity Activity

Make activity appropriate for the developmental level of the youngster. The amount of activity needed for good health is dictated by two variables—the intensity of the activity and the duration of the activity. Most children participate in high-volume–low-intensity activity because they have opportunities for activity sporadically all day. This naturally occurring activity is consistent with the developmental level of children. In contrast, most adults are involved in high-intensity–low-volume activity because they have little time throughout the day to be active. This contrast of activity styles leads adults to believe that children need to participate in high-intensity activities to receive health benefits. They often view children as unfit because youngsters don't like to participate in high-intensity fitness activities. This focus on high-intensity activity causes some children to become discouraged and burned out at an early age. Youngsters are the most active segment of society (Rowland, 1990), and it is important to maintain and encourage this trait. When regular activity is reinforced, fitness follows to the extent possible for each child, given heredity and maturation level.

DEVELOP AN UNDERSTANDING OF PHYSICAL FITNESS PRINCIPLES

Physical education instruction should teach habits that carry over to out-of-school activities. Regardless of how often youngsters participate in physical education, time spent learning physical fitness knowledge and physical activities is necessary. When youngsters are not taught fitness activities, they learn that such activities are unimportant or not valued by teachers and the school. Youngsters are experiential; that is, they learn from participation and develop perceptions based on those experiences. If physical activities are taught in school, youngsters begin to learn that daily activity is an important habit for a healthy lifestyle. Children are taught at a tender age how to brush their teeth so that they learn the habit and protect their teeth for a lifetime. In similar fashion, it is just as important to teach children to be active so their physical health will not decay.

Teaching students different ways to develop and maintain fitness (even if only one day per week) demonstrates that the school values health and exercise as part of a balanced lifestyle. What better outcome than to teach youngsters how to maintain a balanced fitness program for life? Consider the following for integrating knowledge of fitness into the physical education program.

1. Provide basic explanations of rudimentary anatomy and kinesiology. Children can learn the names and locations of major bones and muscle groups, including how they function in relation to selected joint action.

2. Provide an understanding of how fitness is developed. Explain the value of the procedures followed in class sessions so children understand the purpose of all fitness development tasks. In addition, teach children the basic components of a personal fitness program for life.

3. Bring the class together at the end of a lesson to discuss key fitness points in order to promote a clear understanding of why fitness is important. Learning the values of being physically fit, how to apply the principles of exercise, and how fitness can become part of one's lifestyle can positively alter students' views of physical activity. To share cognitive information, establish a muscle of the week, construct educational bulletin boards to illustrate fitness concepts, or send home handouts explaining principles of fitness development.

4. Develop cognition of the importance of fitness for wellness. Help students understand how to perform fitness activities and why these activities should be performed. They need to know the values derived from maintaining a minimal fitness level.

5. Place bulletin boards in the teaching area to explain components of the physical education program to parents and students. Bulletin boards can feature skill techniques, motivational reminders, and fitness activities that will be upcoming in class. Classroom teachers are required to develop bulletin boards for their classes; in similar fashion, when physical education teachers design visual aids for the gymnasium, credibility is enhanced.

6. Exploit the use of audiovisual aids. Audiotapes of fitness routines increase the motivation of youngsters.

Exercise videotapes are an excellent medium for beginning a new fitness activity.

7. Help children understand the values of physical fitness and the physiology of its development and maintenance. Homework dealing with the cognitive aspects of fitness development communicates to parents that their children are gaining knowledge for a lifetime.

8. Emphasize self-testing programs that teach children to evaluate their personal fitness levels (see page 151). In self-evaluation programs, children assess their fitness without concern for others judging them. Fitness and activity are personal for most adults and should be considered a personal matter for youngsters as well.

AVOID HARMFUL PRACTICES AND EXERCISES

The following points contraindicate certain exercise practices and should be considered when offering fitness instruction. For in-depth coverage of contraindicated exercises, see Lindsey and Corbin (1989) or Corbin, Lindsey, and Welk (2000).

1. The following techniques (Macfarlane, 1993) should be avoided when performing abdominal exercises that lift the head and trunk off the floor:
   - Avoid placing the hands behind the head or high on the neck. This may cause hyperflexion and injury to the discs when the elbows swing forward to help pull the body up.
   - Keep the knees bent. Straight legs cause the hip flexor muscles to be used earlier and more forcefully, making it difficult to maintain proper pelvic tilt.
   - Don't hold the feet on the floor. Having another student secure the feet places more force on the lumbar vertebrae and may lead to lumbar hyperextension.
   - Don't lift the buttocks and lumbar region off the floor. This also causes the hip flexor muscles to contract vigorously.

2. Two types of stretching activity have been used to develop flexibility. Ballistic stretching (strong bouncing movements) formerly was the most common stretching used, but this has been discouraged for many years because it was thought to increase delayed-onset muscle soreness. The other flexibility activity, static stretching, involves increasing the stretch to the point of discomfort, backing off slightly to where the position can be held comfortably, and maintaining the

stretch for an extended time. Static stretching has been advocated because it was thought to reduce muscle soreness and prevent injury. One study (Smith et al., 1993) disputed the muscle soreness and tissue damage theory with findings that showed ballistic and static stretching both produced increases in muscle soreness. In fact, static stretching actually induced significantly more soreness than did ballistic stretching. Static stretching is an excellent choice, but ballistic stretching is probably not as harmful as once thought.

3. If forward flexion is done from a sitting position in an effort to touch the toes, the bend should be from the hips, not from the waist, and should be done with one leg flexed. To conform to this concern, the Fitnessgram backsaver sit-and-reach test item is now performed with one leg flexed to reduce stress on the lower back.

4. Straight-leg raises from a supine position should be avoided because they may strain the lower back. The problem can be somewhat alleviated by placing the hands under the small of the back, but it is probably best to avoid such exercises altogether.

5. Deep knee bends (full squats) and the duck walk should be avoided. They may cause damage to the knee joints and have little developmental value. Much more beneficial is flexing the knee joint to 90 degrees and returning to a standing position.

6. When students do stretching exercises from a standing position, the knees should not be hyperextended. The knee joint should be relaxed rather than locked. It is often effective to have students do their stretching with bent knees; this will remind them not to hyperextend the joint. In all stretching activities, participants should be allowed to judge their range of motion. Expecting all students to be able to touch their toes is an unrealistic goal. If you are concerned about touching the toes from this position, have them do so from a sitting position with one leg flexed.

7. Activities that place stress on the neck should be avoided. Examples of activities in which caution should be used are the Inverted Bicycle, Wrestler's Bridge, and abdominal exercises with the hands behind the head.

8. The so-called "hurdler's stretch" should be avoided. This activity is done in the sitting position with one leg forward and the other leg bent and to the rear. Using this stretch places undue pressure on the knee joint of the bent leg. Substitute a stretch using a similar position with one leg straight in front and the other leg bent with the foot placed in the crotch area.

9. Stretches that demand excessive back arching should be avoided. An example: While lying in prone position, the student reaches back and grabs the ankles. By pulling and arching, the exerciser can hyperextend the lower back. This places stress on the discs and stretches the abdominal muscles (not needed by most people).

IMPLEMENT A YEARLONG FITNESS PLAN

Developing a yearlong plan of fitness instruction helps ensure that a variety of experiences is offered to learners. It also allows for progression and ensures that youngsters receive a well-rounded program of instruction. Plan physical fitness instruction in a manner similar to skill development sequences. The *Dynamic Physical Education Curriculum Guide: Lesson Plans for Implementation* (Pangrazi, 2007) offers a yearlong sequence of fitness units for all three developmental levels.

When organizing a yearlong plan for fitness instruction, consider the following. Fitness units should vary in length depending on the age of the youngsters. Children need to experience a variety of routines that maintain a high level of motivation. During the elementary school years, exposure to different types of activities is more important than progressive and demanding fitness routines. Adhere to one principle: *There are many methods for developing fitness, none of which is best for all children.* Offer a variety of routines and activities so youngsters learn that fitness is not lockstep and unbending. The yearlong plan should offer activities that allow all types of youngsters to find success at one time or another during the school year.

The yearlong plan reveals that routines contain more structured activities as youngsters grow older. Most of the activities listed for Developmental Level I children are unstructured and allow for wide variation of performance. For children in Developmental Levels II and III, emphasis on proper technique and performance increases. However, this is not to imply that every student must do every activity exactly the same. It is unrealistic to think that an obese youngster will be able to perform at a level similar to that of a lean child. Allow for variation in performance while emphasizing the importance of "doing your best."

IMPLEMENTING FITNESS ROUTINES

Fitness routines are exclusively dedicated to the presentation of a variety of fitness activities. The following are suggestions for successful implementation of the fitness routines.

1. Precede fitness instruction with a two- to three-minute warm-up period. Introductory activities are useful for this purpose because they allow youngsters an opportunity to prepare for strenuous activity.

2. Be sure the fitness portion of the daily lesson, including warm-up, does not extend beyond 10 to 13 minutes. Some might argue that more time is needed to develop adequate fitness. However, the reality is that most teachers are only allowed a 20- to 30-minute period of instruction. Because skill instruction is part of a balanced physical education program, compromise is necessary to ensure that all phases of the program are covered.

3. Use activities that exercise all body parts and cover the major components of fitness. Children are capable performers when workloads are geared to their age, fitness level, and abilities.

4. Use a variety of fitness routines comprising sequential exercises for total body development as a recommended alternative to a yearlong program of regimented calisthenics. Use a diverse array of activities that appeal to the interests and fitness levels of children to replace the traditional approach of doing the same routine day in and day out.

5. Assume an active role in fitness instruction. Children respond positively to role modeling. When you actively exercise with children, hustle to assist those youngsters having difficulty, and make exercise fun, your actions instill in children the value of an active lifestyle.

6. When determining workloads for children, keep in mind that the available alternatives are time or repetitions. Base the workload on time rather than on a specified number of repetitions so that youngsters can adjust their workload within personal limits. Beginning dosages for exercises should start at a level at which *all* children will succeed. The best way to ensure success is to allow students to adjust the workload to suit their capabilities. Using a specified amount of time per exercise allows less gifted children to perform successfully. All children should not be expected to perform exactly the same workload.

7. Take advantage of interval training with youngsters. Alternate stretching and strength development exercises with aerobic exercises. This gives youngsters a chance to recover from an aerobic activity while stretching. It also allows time for recovery from strength development activities. Most routines are effective in 30-second intervals. Beyond this length of time, students will start to fatigue or become bored and go off-task.

8. Use audiotapes to time fitness activity segments so you are free to move throughout the area and offer individualized instruction. The easiest way to time segments is to alternate 30-second intervals of music and silence. When music is playing, it signals that students are to perform an aerobic activity. When the silence interval is on, it signals stretching or strength development activity.

9. *Never* use fitness activities as punishment. Such a practice teaches students that push-ups and running are things you do when you misbehave. The opportunity to exercise should be a privilege as well as an enjoyable experience. Think of the money adults spend to exercise. Take a positive approach and offer students a chance to jog with a friend when they do something well. This allows them the opportunity not only to visit, but also to exercise with a positive feeling. Be an effective salesperson; sell the joy of activity and the benefits of physical fitness to youngsters.

FITNESS ACTIVITIES FOR DEVELOPMENTAL LEVEL I

Fitness activities for young children have the potential to teach components of physical fitness and to exercise various body areas. All the fitness routines that follow alternate strength and flexibility activities with cardiovascular activity. For most routines, strength and flexibility activities are listed. Together, the introductory and fitness activity provide broad coverage by including activities for each of these five areas: arm-shoulder girdle, trunk, abdomen, legs and cardiorespiratory system, and flexibility.

Modified Fitness Activities that Ensure a Successful Experience

Too often youngsters are asked to perform a fitness load that is impossible for them to accomplish. For example, look at the developmental characteristics of five-through eight-year-old children. Their heads are about 90 percent of adult size and their trunks are 50 percent of adult size. They have short legs (30–40 percent of adult size) so, in effect, they are top-heavy, short-legged little people. There is no way they could be successful at doing push-ups and sit-ups because they are top heavy. Yet, time and again, teachers ask children of this age to try and do these important exercises only to see them fail. Small wonder that the majority of children enter the intermediate grades hating push-ups and sit-ups. The following fitness activities are modifications that can help ensure a successful experience. The activity should be presented early in the year to students in all grades. Then, when push-ups or abdominal activities are assigned, students select any of the modified activities they feel they can perform successfully.

Youngsters must be given the opportunity to select activities they enjoy. The workload must be dictated by the student, not the teacher. No teacher knows how many repetitions of an activity a youngster can perform. Better that they allow each student to do his or her best. Fitness is not effective if it is something that is forced down a student's throat. Most will avoid activity in the future if they feel pressured and unsuccessful in their early experiences with fitness activities.

Stretching and flexibility activities should be alternated with aerobic activities to avoid excessively fatiguing youngsters. When youngsters are pushed too hard aerobically, they will express their fatigue in many different manners (i.e., complaining, quitting, misbehaving, or sitting out). Be aware of how far to push and when to ease up.

ARM-SHOULDER GIRDLE STRENGTH ACTIVITIES

The following are examples of challenges that can be used to help youngsters develop arm-shoulder girdle strength. They precede the push-up activities and should be practiced first. All the challenges encourage youngsters to support their body weight with the arms and shoulders.

1. Practice taking the weight completely on your hands.
2. In crab position, keep your feet in place and make your body go in a big circle. Do the same from the push-up position.
3. In crab position, go forward, backward, and to the side. Turn around, move very slowly, and so on.
4. Successively from standing, supine, and hands-knees positions: Swing one limb (arm or leg) at a time, in different directions and at different levels.
5. Combine two limb movements (arm-arm, leg-leg, or arm-leg combinations) in the same direction and in opposite directions. Vary the levels.
6. Swing the arms or legs back and forth and go into giant circles. In supine position, make giant circles with the feet.
7. In a bent-over position, swing the arms as if swimming. Try a backstroke or a breaststroke. What does a sidestroke look like?
8. Make the arms go like a windmill. Turn the arms in different directions. Accelerate and decelerate.
9. Show how else you can circle your arms.
10. Pretend that a swarm of bees is around your head. Brush them off and keep them away.

FIGURE 13.2   Push-up position.

PUSH-UP LEAD-UP ACTIVITIES

The push-up (Figure 13.2) and crab positions are excellent for developing upper body strength. Allow students to rest with one knee on the floor in the up position rather than lie on the floor. Let students select a challenge they feel able to accomplish rather than being forced to fail trying to do push-ups. Many of the directives listed for the push-up position can also be done in the crab position. As youngsters develop strength, they make a controlled descent to the floor from the up position. The following are examples that can be done with one knee down (beginning) or in the regular push-up (more challenging) position.

1. Hold your body off the floor (i.e., push-up position).
2. Wave at a friend. Wave with the other arm. Shake a leg at someone. Do these challenges in the crab position.
3. Lift one foot high. Now lift the other foot.
4. Bounce both feet up and down. Move the feet out from each other while bouncing.
5. Inch the feet up to the hands and go back again. Inch the feet up to the hands and then inch the hands out to return to the push-up position.
6. Reach up with one hand and touch the other shoulder behind the back.
7. Lift both hands from the floor. Try clapping the hands.
8. Turn over so that your back is to the floor. Now complete the turn to push-up position.
9. Walk on your hands and feet. Try two hands and one foot. Walk in the crab position (tummy toward the ceiling).
10. With one knee on the ground, touch your nose to the floor between your hands. As you get stronger, move your head forward a little and touch your nose to the floor. (The farther the nose touches the floor in front of the hands, the greater the strength demanded.)

11. Lower your body an inch at a time until your chest touches the floor. Return to the up position any way possible.

12. Pretend you are a tire going flat. Gradually lower yourself to the floor.

▶ ABDOMINAL STRENGTH LEAD-UP ACTIVITIES

The basic position for exercising the abdominal muscles is supine on the floor or on a mat. Challenges should lift the upper and lower portions of the body from the floor, either singly or together. Since young children are top heavy (large head, small body), they find it difficult to perform most abdominal exercises. Therefore, begin early abdominal development with youngsters lying on the floor and lifting the head. Progress to a sitting position and gradually lowering (with head tucked) the upper body backward to the floor.

1. Lift your head from the floor and look at your toes. Wink your right eye and wiggle your left foot. Reverse.

2. In a supine position, "wave" a leg at a friend. Use the other leg. Use both legs.

3. Lift your knees up slowly, an inch at a time.

4. Pick your heels up about six inches off the floor and swing them back and forth. Cross them and twist them.

5. Sit up any way you can and touch both sets of toes with your hands.

6. Sit up any possible way and touch your right toes with your left hand. Do it the other way.

7. In a sitting position, lean the upper body backward without falling. How long can you hold this position?

8. From a sitting position, lower your body slowly to the floor. Vary the positions of your arms (across the tummy, the chest, and above the head).

9. From a supine position, curl up by pulling up on your legs.

10. From a supine position, hold your shoulders off the floor.

11. From a supine position, lift your legs and head off the floor.

▶ TRUNK DEVELOPMENT ACTIVITIES

Movements that include bending, stretching, swaying, twisting, reaching, and forming shapes help develop trunk strength. No particular continuity exists, except that a specified approach should move from simple to more complex. Vary the position the child is to take: standing, lying down, kneeling, or sitting.

Bending

1. Bend in different ways.

2. Bend as many parts of your body as you can.

3. Make different shapes by bending two, three, and four parts of your body.

4. Bend the arms and knees in different ways and on different levels.

5. Try different ways of bending your fingers and wrist of one hand with the other. Use some resistance. (Explain resistance.) Add body bends.

Stretching

1. Keep one foot in place and stretch your arms in different directions; move with the free foot. Stretch at different levels.

2. Lie on the floor; stretch one leg different ways in space. Stretch one leg in one direction and the other in another direction.

3. Stretch as slowly as you can and then snap back to original position.

4. Stretch with different arm-leg combinations in several directions.

5. See how much space on the floor you can cover by stretching.

6. Combine bending and stretching movements.

Swaying and Twisting

1. Sway your body back and forth in different directions. Change the position of your arms.

2. Sway your body, bending over.

3. Sway your head from side to side.

4. Select a part of your body and twist it as far as you can in one direction and then in the opposite direction.

5. Twist your body at different levels.

6. Twist two or more parts of your body at the same time.

7. Twist one part of your body while untwisting another.

8. Twist your head to see as far back as you can.

9. Twist like a spring. Twist like a screwdriver.

10. Stand on one foot and twist your body. Untwist.

11. From a seated position, make different shapes by twisting.

▶ LEG AND CARDIORESPIRATORY DEVELOPMENT ACTIVITIES

Leg and cardiorespiratory development activities include a range of movement challenges in general space

13

or in place. Youngsters fatigue and recover quickly. Take advantage of this trait by alternating cardiorespiratory activities with strength and flexibility exercises.

Running Patterns

Running in different directions

Running in place

Ponies in the Stable (page 340)

Tortoise and Hare (page 340)

European Rhythmic Running (pages 342–343)

Running and stopping

Running and changing direction on signal

Jumping and Hopping Patterns

Jumping in different directions back and forth over a spot

Jumping or hopping in, out, over, and around hoops, individual mats, or jump ropes laid on the floor

Jumping or hopping back and forth over lines, or hopping down the lines

Rope-Jumping

Individual rope-jumping—allow choice

Combinations

Many combinations of locomotor movements can be used to motivate youngsters. Following are possible challenges that might be used.

1. Run in place. Do some running steps in place without stopping.
2. Skip or gallop for 30 seconds.
3. Slide all the way around the gymnasium.
4. Alternate hopping or jumping for 30 seconds with 30 seconds of rest.
5. Jump in place while twisting your arms and upper body.
6. Do ten skips, ten gallops, and finish with 30 running steps.
7. Hold hands with a friend and do 100 jumps.
8. Jump rope as many times as possible without missing.
9. Hop back and forth over a line from one end of the gym to the other.
10. Try to run as fast as you can. How long can you keep going?

Animal Movements

Animal movements are enjoyable for Developmental Level I children because they can mimic the sounds and movements of the animals. Most of the animal movements are done with the body weight on all four limbs, which helps develop the arms and shoulders. Challenge youngsters to move randomly throughout the area, across the gymnasium, or between cones delineating a specific distance. Increase the distance or the amount of time each walk is performed to increase the workload. To avoid excessive fatigue, alternate the animal movements with stretching activities. The following are examples of animal movements that can be used. See Chapter 20 for descriptions of more animal movements.

- *Puppy Walk:* Move on all fours (not the knees). Keep the head up and move lightly.
- *Lion Walk:* Move on all fours while keeping the back arched. Move deliberately and lift the "paws" to simulate moving without sound.
- *Elephant Walk:* Move heavily throughout the area, swinging the head back and forth like an elephant's trunk.
- *Seal Walk:* Move using the arms to propel the body. Allow the legs to drag along the floor much as a seal would move.
- *Injured Coyote:* Move using only three limbs. Hold the injured limb off the floor. Vary the walk by specifying which limb is injured.
- *Crab Walk:* Move on all fours with the tummy facing the ceiling. Try to keep the back as straight as possible.
- *Rabbit Jump:* Start in a squatting position with the hands on the floor. Reach forward with the hands and support the body weight. Jump both feet toward the hands. Repeat the sequence.

Fitness Games

Fitness games are excellent for cardiovascular endurance and create a high degree of motivation. Place emphasis on all students moving. One of the best ways to be sure this occurs is to play games that do not eliminate players. A player who tags someone is no longer *it* and the person tagged becomes *it*. This makes it difficult for players to tell who is *it,* which is desirable since it ensures that players cannot stop and stand when the *it* player is a significant distance from them. If various games stipulate a "safe" position, allow players to maintain this position for a maximum of five seconds. Because fitness games primarily focus on cardiovascular fitness, alternate the games with strength and flexibility activities. The following are examples of games that can be played.

- *Stoop tag:* Players cannot be tagged when they stoop.
- *Back-to-back tag:* Players are safe when they stand back to back to one another. Other positions can be designated such as toe to toe, knee to knee, and so on.
- *Train tag:* Form groups of three or four and make a train by holding the hips of the other players. Three or four players are designated as *it* and try to hook onto the rear of the train. If they are successful, the player at the front of the train becomes the new *it*.
- *Color tag:* Players are safe when they stand on a specified color. The "safe" color may be changed by the leader at any time.
- *Elbow swing tag:* Players cannot be tagged as long as they are performing an elbow swing with another player.
- *Balance tag:* Players are safe when they are balanced on one body part.
- *Push-up tag:* Players are safe when they are in push-up position. Other exercise positions, such as bent knee curl-up, V-up, and crab position, can be used.
- *Group tag:* The only time a player is safe is when all are in a group (stipulated by the leader) holding hands. For example, the number might be "4," which means that students must be holding hands in groups of four to be safe.

Miniature Challenge Courses

Miniature challenge courses (Figure 13.3) can be set up indoors or outdoors. The distance between the start and finish lines depends on the type of activity. A good starting point is a distance of about 30 feet, but this can be adjusted. Mark the course boundaries with cones.

Each child performs the stipulated locomotor movement from the start to the finish line, then turns and jogs back to the start. Movement is continuous. Give directions in advance so that no delay occurs. The number of children on each course should be limited to normal squad size or fewer. The following movements can be stipulated:

- All types of locomotor movements: running, jumping, hopping, sliding, and so on
- Movements on the floor: crawling, Bear Walk, Seal Crawl, and the like
- Movements over and under obstacles or through tires or hoops

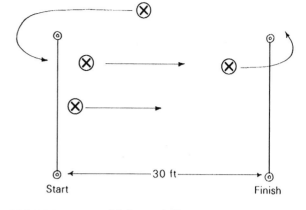

FIGURE 13.3 Miniature challenge course.

Sample Routine

1. Crawl under a wand set on two cones.
2. Roll down an inclined mat.
3. Logroll up an inclined mat.
4. Move up and down on jumping boxes. Climb on the last box, jump, and roll.
5. Crawl through hoops or bicycle tires held by individual mats.
6. Walk a balance beam.
7. Pull the body down a bench in prone position.
8. Leap over five carpet squares.
9. Move through a tunnel created by four jumping boxes (or benches) covered with a tumbling mat.
10. Hang on a climbing rope for ten seconds.
11. Crab walk from one cone to another and back.
12. Run and weave around a series of five cones.

Parachute Fitness Activities

The parachute has been a popular item in elementary physical education for many years. Usually used to promote teamwork, provide maximum participation, stimulate interest, or play games, the parachute can be used as a tool to develop physical fitness. By combining vigorous shaking movements, locomotor circular movement, and selected exercises while holding onto the chute, exciting fitness routines can be developed.

▶ **PARACHUTE FITNESS ACTIVITIES**

1. Jog while holding the chute in the left hand. (music)
2. Shake the chute. (no music)
3. Slide while holding the chute with both hands. (music)
4. Sit and perform curl-ups. (no music)

5. Skip. (music)

6. Freeze, face the center, and stretch the chute tightly. Hold for 8 to 12 seconds. Repeat five to six times. (no music)

7. Run in place while holding the chute taut at different levels. (music)

8. Sit with legs under the chute. Do a seat walk toward the center. Return to the perimeter. Repeat four to six times. (no music)

9. Place the chute on the ground. Jog away from the chute and return on signal. Repeat. (music)

10. Move into push-up position holding the chute with one hand. Shake the chute. (no music)

11. Shake the chute and jump in place. (music)

12. Lie on back with feet under the chute. Shake the chute with the feet. (no music)

13. Hop to the center of the chute and return. Repeat. (music)

14. Sit with feet under the chute. Stretch by touching the toes with the chute. Relax with other stretches while sitting. (no music)

✓ **TEACHING TIP**

Tape alternating segments (20 seconds in length) of silence and music to signal duration of exercise. Music segments indicate aerobic activity with the parachute while intervals of silence announce using the chute to enhance flexibility and strength development.

Space youngsters evenly around the chute.

Have them use different hand grips (palms up, down, mixed).

Make sure all movements are done under control. Some of the faster and stronger students will have to moderate their performance.

Walk, Trot, and Jog

Four cones outline a square or rectangular area 30 to 40 yards on a side. (Indoors, the circumference of the gymnasium is used.) Children are scattered around the perimeter, all facing in the same direction. Signals are given with a whistle. On the first whistle, children begin to walk. On the next whistle, they change to a trot. On the third whistle, they jog faster, but still under control. Finally, on the fourth whistle, they walk again. The cycle is repeated with faster-moving youngsters passing on the outside of the area.

Another way to signal change is by drumbeat. One drumbeat signals walk, two beats signals trot, and three means run. The three movements can be presented in a random order. Different locomotor movements such as

running, skipping, galloping, and sliding can be used for variation. At regular intervals, stop students and have them perform various stretching activities and strength development exercises. This allows short rest periods between bouts of activity. Examples of activities are one-leg balance, push-ups, curl-ups, touching the toes, and any other challenges.

▶ **WALK, TROT, AND JOG**

Move to the following signals:

1. One drumbeat—walk.
2. Two drumbeats—trot.
3. Three drumbeats—jog.
4. Whistle—freeze and perform exercises.

Perform various strength and flexibility exercises between bouts of walking, trotting, and jogging. Examples of exercises are:

1. Bend and Twist
2. Sitting Stretch
3. Push-Up Challenges
4. Abdominal Challenges
5. Body Twist
6. Standing Hip Bend

✓ **TEACHING TIP**

Tape alternating segments (30 seconds in length) of silence and music to signal duration of exercise. Music segments indicate walking, trotting, and jogging activities. Intervals of silence signal performance of the strength and flexibility exercises.

Any exercises can be substituted. Try to maintain a balance of exercising all body parts.

Jump Rope Exercises

Jump ropes can be used in a number of exercises and aerobic activities. Playing music with taped intervals of silence is an excellent method for alternating periods of rope-jumping and exercises. During the periods of silence, youngsters perform an exercise; during the music, children pick up their ropes and begin jumping.

▶ **JUMP ROPE ROUTINE**

1. Jump rope—30 seconds. If unable to jump, practice swinging the rope to the side while jumping.
2. Place the rope on the floor and perform locomotor movements around and over the rope. Make different shapes and letters with the rope.

3. Hold the folded rope overhead. Sway from side to side. Twist right and left.

4. Jump rope—30 seconds.

5. Lie on your back with the rope held with outstretched arms toward ceiling. Bring up one leg at a time and touch the rope with your toes. Lift both legs together. Sit up and try to hook the rope over your feet. Release and repeat.

6. Touch your toes with the folded rope.

7. Jump rope—30 seconds.

8. Place the rope on the floor and do various Animal Walks along or over the rope.

9. Do push-up variations with the rope folded and held between your hands.

10. Jump rope—30 seconds.

✔ **TEACHING TIP**

Tape alternating segments (30 seconds in length) of silence and music to signal duration of exercise. Music segments indicate aerobic activity with the jump ropes while intervals of silence announce using the jump ropes to enhance flexibility and strength development.

Teach youngsters to space themselves so they don't hit others with their rope.

Encourage nonjumpers. They will learn sooner or later. Give praise and keep them motivated.

Four-Corners Movement

Delineate a rectangle with four cones. Youngsters move around the perimeter of the rectangle. Each time they pass a corner, they change their movement pattern. On long sides, rapid movement such as running, skipping, or sliding are designated. Moving along short sides, students hop, jump, or do animal walks. Have students vary clockwise and counterclockwise directions. On signal, they should stop and perform flexibility and strength development challenges in place.

Using the four-corners ideas as a basis, other combinations can be devised. For example, the pattern in Figure 13.4 requires running along one of the long sides and sliding along the other. One of the short sides has mats and requires three forward rolls, and the other short side requires an animal walk on all fours. Another variation that stimulates children is to place different equipment around the perimeter of the area. On signal, youngsters stop and pick up a piece of equipment and manipulate it for a specified time. By interspersing four-corners movement (aerobic movement) with equipment handling (resting), teachers implement interval training.

FIGURE 13.4 Four-corners movement formation.

Equipment that can be used might be beanbags, scooters, balance beams, benches, balls, and hoops.

FITNESS ACTIVITIES FOR DEVELOPMENTAL LEVELS II AND III

In contrast to the program of Developmental Level I activities, emphasis shifts to more structured exercises and routines for Developmental Levels II and III. Starting off the year with teacher-leader exercises is suggested, as these are the basic exercises that can be used in other routines.

Exercises for Fitness Routines

The exercises in this section fall into the following categories: (a) flexibility, (b) arm-shoulder girdle, (c) abdominal, (d) leg and agility, and (e) trunk twisting and bending. Recommended exercises are presented under each of the five categories. Stress points, modifications, variations, and teaching suggestions are presented when appropriate. Include six to ten exercises in a fitness routine, with two exercises from the arm-shoulder girdle group and at least one from each of the other categories. A note to remember is that many youngsters will not be able to perform some abdominal and arm-shoulder girdle exercises. Allow them to select some of the modified fitness activities (push-ups and abdominal modifications) described in the Developmental Level I section of this chapter (pages 265–267).

FLEXIBILITY EXERCISES

▶ **BEND AND TWIST**

Starting position: Stand with the arms crossed, hands on opposite shoulders, knees slightly flexed, and feet shoulder width apart.

FIGURE 13.5   Sitting stretch position.

Movement: Bend forward at the waist (count 1). Twist the trunk and touch the right elbow to the left knee (count 2). Twist in the opposite direction and touch the left elbow to the right knee (count 3). Return to the starting position (count 4). Knees can be flexed.

▶ SITTING STRETCH

Starting position: Sit on the floor with one leg extended forward and the other bent at the knee. The foot is placed in the area of the crotch. The toes of the extended foot are touched with the fingertips of both hands as the chest gradually moves forward (Figure 13.5).

Movement: Gradually bend forward, taking three counts to bend fully. Recover to sitting position on the fourth count.

Important point: Bend from the hips.

▶ PARTNER ROWING

Starting position: Partners sit facing each other, holding hands with palms touching and fingers locked. The legs are spread and extended to touch the soles of partner's feet.

Movement: One partner bends forward, with the help of the other pulling backward, to try to bring the chest as close to the floor as possible (Figure 13.6). Reverse direction.

> **Variation:** *Steam Engine.* With both partners in the sitting position, alternate pulling hands back and forth like a pair of steam engine pistons. Do eight sets, right and left combined twists.

▶ LOWER LEG STRETCH

Starting position: Stand facing a wall with the feet about shoulder width apart. Place the palms of the hands on the wall at eye level (Figure 13.7).

FIGURE 13.6   Partner rowing.

Movement: Slowly walk away from the wall, keeping the body straight, until the stretch is felt in the lower portion of the calf. The feet should remain flat on the floor during the stretch.

▶ ACHILLES TENDON STRETCH

Starting position: Stand facing a wall with the forearms on it. Place the forehead on the back of the hands. Back two to three feet away from the wall, bend, and move one leg closer to the wall.

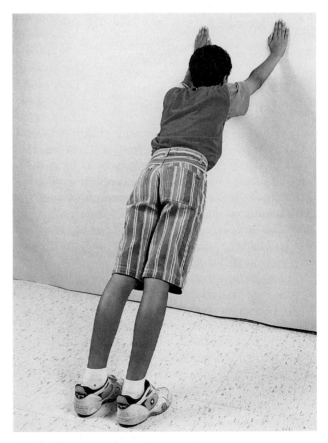

FIGURE 13.7   Lower leg stretch.

FIGURE 13.8   Body twist.

Movement: Flex the bent leg with the foot on the floor until the stretch is felt in the Achilles tendon area. The feet should remain flat on the floor as the leg closer to the wall is flexed. Repeat, flexing the other leg.

BODY TWIST

Starting position: Sit on the floor with the left leg straight. Lift the right leg over the left leg and place it on the floor outside the left knee (Figure 13.8). Move the left elbow outside the upper right thigh and use it to maintain pressure on the leg. Lean back and support the upper body with the right hand.

Movement: Rotate the upper body toward the right hand and arm. Reverse the position and stretch the other side of the body.

STANDING HIP BEND

Starting position: Stand with the knees slightly flexed, one hand on the hip and the other arm overhead.

Movement: Bend to the side with the hand resting on the hip. The arm overhead should point and move in the direction of the stretch with a slight bend at the elbow. Reverse and stretch the opposite side.

ARM-SHOULDER GIRDLE EXERCISES

Arm-shoulder girdle exercises for this age group include both arm-support and free-arm types.

PUSH-UPS

Starting position: Assume the push-up position (see Figure 13.2), with the body straight from head to heels.

Movement: Keeping the body straight, bend the elbows and touch the chest to the ground; then straighten the elbows, raising the body in a straight line.

Important points: The movement should be in the arms. The head is up, with the eyes looking ahead. The chest should touch the floor lightly, without receiving the weight of the body. The body remains in a straight line throughout, without sagging or humping.

> *Variation:* Some youngsters develop a dislike for push-ups because they are asked to perform them without any modification. Allow youngsters to judge their strength and choose a push-up challenge (page 266) they feel able to accomplish. Instead of asking an entire class to perform a specified number of push-ups, personalize the workload by allowing each youngster to accomplish as many repetitions as possible of a self-selected push-up challenge in a specified amount of time.

✓ **TEACHING TIP**

Controlled movement is a goal; speed is not desirable. Push-ups should be done at will, allowing each child to achieve individually within a specified time limit.

RECLINING PULL-UPS

Starting position: One pupil lies in supine position. Her partner is astride, with feet alongside the reclining partner's chest. Partners grasp hands with interlocking fingers, with some other suitable grip, or with an interlocked wrist grip.

Movement: The pupil on the floor pulls up with her arms until her chest touches the partner's thighs. The body remains straight, with weight resting on the heels (Figure 13.9, page 274). Then she returns to position.

Important points: The supporting student should keep the center of gravity well over the feet by maintaining a lifted chest and proper head position. The lower student should maintain a straight body during the pull-up and move only the arms.

> *Variation:* Raise as directed (count 1), hold the high position isometrically (counts 2 and 3), return to position (count 4).

TRICEPS PUSH-UP

Starting position: Assume the inverted push-up position with the arms and body held straight.

Movement: Keeping the body straight, bend the elbows and touch the seat to the ground, then straighten the elbows and raise the body.

FIGURE 13.9   Reclining pull-ups.

Important points: The fingers should point toward the toes or be turned in slightly. The body should be held firm with movement restricted to the arms.

 ARM CIRCLES

Starting position: Stand erect, with feet apart and arms straight out to the side (Figure 13.10).

Movement: Do forward and backward circles with palms facing forward, moving arms simultaneously. The number of circles executed before changing can be varied.

Important points: Avoid doing arm circles with palms down (particularly backward circles) as it stresses the shoulder joint. Correct posture should be maintained, with the abdominal wall flat and the head and shoulders held back.

 CRAB KICK

Starting position: Crab position, with the body supported on the hands and feet and the back parallel to the floor. The knees are bent at right angles. On all crab positions, keep the seat up and avoid body sag.

Movement: Kick the right leg up and down (counts 1 and 2) (Figure 13.11). Repeat with the left leg (counts 3 and 4).

CRAB ALTERNATE-LEG EXTENSION

Starting position: Assume crab position.

Movement: On count 1, extend the right leg forward so that it rests on the heel. On count 2, extend the left leg forward and bring the right leg back. Continue alternating.

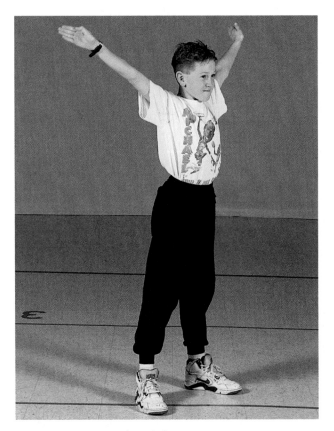

FIGURE 13.10   Arm circles.

CRAB FULL-LEG EXTENSION

Starting position: Assume crab position.

Movement: On count 1, extend both legs forward so that the weight rests on the heels. On count 2, bring both feet back to crab position.

FIGURE 13.11   Crab kick.

CRAB WALK

Starting position: Assume crab position.

Movement: Move forward, backward, sideways, and turn in a small circle right and left.

FLYING ANGEL

Starting position: Stand erect, with feet together and arms at sides.

Movement: In a smooth, slow, continuous motion, raise the arms forward with elbows extended and then upward, at the same time rising up on the toes and lifting the chest, with eyes following the hands (Figure 13.12). Lower the arms sideways in a flying motion and return to starting position.

Important points: The abdominal wall must be kept flat throughout to minimize lower back curvature. The head should be back and well up. The exercise should be done slowly and smoothly, under control.

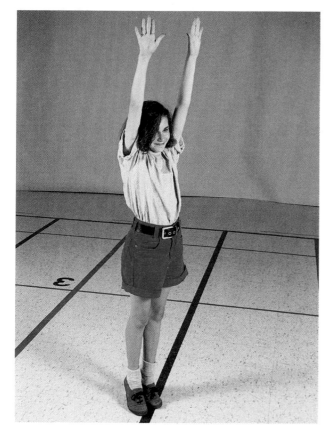

FIGURE 13.12 Flying Angel.

Variation: Move the arms forward as if doing a breast-stroke. The arms are then raised slowly, with hands in front of the chest and elbows out, to full overhead extension. Otherwise, the movement is the same as the Flying Angel.

ABDOMINAL EXERCISES

For most exercises stressing abdominal development, start from the supine position on the floor or on a mat. When lifting the upper body, begin with a roll-up (curling) action, moving the head first so that the chin makes contact or near contact with the chest, thus flattening and stabilizing the lower back curve. The bent knee position better isolates the abdominal muscles and avoids stressing the lower back region. When doing abdominal exercises, avoid moving the trunk up to the sitting position (past 45 degrees) since it may cause pain and exacerbate back injury in susceptible individuals (Macfarlane, 1993).

Some youngsters develop a dislike for abdominal work in the early school years. This occurs because they are top heavy (large head, short legs) and unable to successfully lift their upper body off the floor. To ensure success, allow students to choose an abdominal challenge they feel able to accomplish. Instead of asking an entire class to perform a specified number of curl-ups, personalize the workload by allowing youngsters to accomplish as many repetitions as possible in a specified amount of time using a self-selected abdominal challenge.

REVERSE CURL

Starting position: Lie on the back with the hands on the floor and to the sides of the body.

Movement: Curl the knees to the chest. The upper body remains on the floor. As abdominal strength increases, the child should lift the buttocks and lower back off the floor.

Important points: Roll the knees to the chest and return the feet to the floor after each repetition. The movement should be controlled, with emphasis on the abdominal contraction.

Variations:

1. Hold the head off the floor and bring the knees to the chin.

2. Instead of returning the feet to the floor after each repetition, move them one or two inches off the floor. This activity requires greater abdominal strength as there is no resting period (feet on floor).

PELVIS TILTER

Starting position: Lie on the back with feet flat on the floor, knees bent, arms out in wing position, and palms up.

FIGURE 13.13 Knee touch curl-up.

Movement: Flatten the lower back, bringing it closer to the floor by tensing the lower abdominals and lifting up on the pelvis. Hold for 8 to 12 counts. Tense slowly and release slowly.

▶ **KNEE TOUCH CURL-UP**

Starting position: Lie on the back, with feet flat and knees bent, and with hands flat on top of thighs.

Movement: Leading with the chin, slide the hands forward until the fingers touch the kneecaps and gradually curl the head and shoulders until the shoulder blades are lifted off the floor (Figure 13.13). Hold for 8 counts and return to position. To avoid stress on the lower back, do not curl up to the sitting position.

▶ **CURL-UP**

Starting position: Lie on the back with feet flat, knees bent, and arms on the floor at the side of the body with palms down.

Movement: Lift the head and shoulders (Figure 13.14) to a 45-degree angle and then back in a 2-count pattern. The hands should slide forward on the floor three to four inches. The curl-up can also be done as an 8-count exercise, moving up on count 1, holding for 6 counts, and moving down on the last count.

Important points: Roll up, with the chin first. Do not lift the hands off the floor.

▶ **CURL-UP WITH TWIST**

Starting position: Lie on the back with feet flat and knees bent. Arms are folded and placed across the chest with hands on shoulders.

Movement: Do a partial curl-up and twist the chest to the left. Repeat, turning the chest to the right (Figure 13.15).

FIGURE 13.14 Curl-up.

Variations:

1. Touch the outside of the knee with the elbow.
2. Touch both knees in succession. The sequence is up, touch left, touch right, and down.

▶ **LEG EXTENSION**

Starting position: Sit on the floor with legs extended and hands on hips.

Movement: With a quick, vigorous action, raise the knees and bring both heels as close to the seat as possible (Figure 13.16). The movement is a drag with the toes touching lightly. Return to position.

Variation: Alternate bringing the knees to the right and left of the head.

▶ **ABDOMINAL CRUNCHER**

Starting position: Lie in supine position with feet flat, knees bent, and palms of hands cupped over the ears

FIGURE 13.15 Curl-up with twist.

FIGURE 13.16   Leg extension.

(not behind the head). An alternate position is to fold the arms across the chest and place the hands on the shoulders.

Movement: Tuck the chin and curl upward until the shoulder blades leave the floor. Return to the floor with a slow uncurling.

> *Variation:* Lift the feet off the floor and bring the knees to waist level. Try to touch the right elbow to the left knee and vice versa while in the crunch position.

LEG AND AGILITY EXERCISES

▶ RUNNING IN PLACE

Starting position: Stand with arms bent at the elbows.

Movement: Run in place. Begin slowly, counting only the left foot. Speed up somewhat, raising the knees to hip height. Then run at full speed, raising the knees hard. Finally, slow down. The run should be on the toes.

> *Variations:*
> 1. Tortoise and Hare. Jog slowly in place. On the command "Hare," double the speed. On the command "Tortoise," slow the tempo to the original slow jogging pace.
> 2. March in place, lifting the knees high and swinging the arms up. Turn right and left on command while marching. Turn completely around to the right and then to the left while marching.
> 3. Fast Stepping. Step in place for ten seconds as rapidly as possible. Rest for ten seconds and repeat five or more times.

▶ JUMPING JACK

Starting position: Stand at attention.

Movement: On count 1, jump to a straddle position with arms overhead. On count 2, recover to starting position.

Variations:
1. Begin with the feet in a stride position (forward and back). Change feet with the overhead movement.
2. Instead of bringing the feet together when the arms come down, cross the feet each time, alternating the cross.
3. On the completion of each set of 8 counts, do a quarter-turn right. (After four sets, the child is facing in the original direction.) Do the same to the left.
4. Modified Jumping Jack. On count 1, jump to a straddle position with arms out to the sides, parallel to the floor, and palms down. On count 2, return to position.

▶ TREADMILL

Starting position: Assume push-up position, except that one leg is brought forward so that the knee is under the chest (Figure 13.17).

Movement: Reverse the position of the feet, bringing the extended leg forward. Change back again so that the original foot is forward. Continue rhythmically alternating feet.

Important points: The head should be kept up. A full exchange of the legs should be made, with the forward knee coming well under the chest each time.

▶ POWER JUMPER

Starting position: Begin in a semicrouched position, with knees flexed and arms extended backward.

Movement: Jump as high as possible and extend the arms upward and overhead.

FIGURE 13.17   Treadmill.

Variations:

1. Jump and perform different turns (quarter, half, and full).

2. Jump and perform different tasks (such as click heels, slap heels, clap hands, catch an imaginary pass, snare a rebound).

TRUNK-TWISTING AND BENDING EXERCISES

▶ TRUNK TWISTER

Starting position: Stand with feet shoulder width apart and pointed forward. The hands are cupped and placed loosely over the shoulders, with the elbows out and the chin tucked.

Movement: Bend downward, keeping the knees relaxed. Recover slightly. Bend downward again and simultaneously rotate the trunk to the left and then to the right (Figure 13.18). Return to original position, pulling the head back, with chin in.

▶ BEAR HUG

Starting position: Stand with feet comfortably spread and hands on hips.

Movement: Take a long step diagonally right, keeping the left foot anchored in place. Tackle the right leg around the

FIGURE 13.19   Bear Hug.

thigh by encircling the thigh with both arms. Squeeze and stretch (Figure 13.19). Return to position. Tackle the left leg. Return to position.

Important point: The bent leg should not exceed a right angle.

▶ SIDE FLEX

Starting position: Lie on one side with lower arm extended overhead. The head rests on the lower arm. The legs are extended fully, one on top of the other.

Movement: Raise the upper arm and leg diagonally (Figure 13.20). Repeat for several counts and change to the other side.

> *Variation:* Side Flex, supported. Similar to the regular Side Flex but more demanding. A side-leaning rest position is maintained throughout (Figure 13.21).

FIGURE 13.18   Trunk Twister.

FIGURE 13.20   Side Flex.

FIGURE 13.21 Side Flex, supported.

▶ BODY CIRCLES

Starting position: Stand with feet shoulder width apart, hands on hips, and body bent forward.

Movement: Make a complete circle with the upper body. A specified number of circles should be made to the right and the same number to the left.

Variations:

1. Circle in one direction until told to stop, then reverse direction.
2. Change to a position in which the hands are on the shoulders and the elbows are kept wide. Otherwise, the exercise is the same.

▶ WINDMILL

Starting position: Stand with feet shoulder width apart and arms extended sideways with palms down.

Movement: Bend and twist at the trunk, bringing the right hand down to the left toes. Recover to starting position. Bend and twist again, but bring the left hand to the right toes. Recover to starting position.

PARTNER RESISTANCE EXERCISES

Partner resistance exercises are used in conjunction with activities that demand considerable endurance such as aerobic fitness routines, jogging, or Astronaut Exercises. The exercises are simple and enjoyable; children can do them as homework with parents or friends. Partners should be roughly matched in size and strength so that they can challenge each other. The exercises are performed throughout the full range of motion at each joint and should take 8 to 12 seconds to complete.

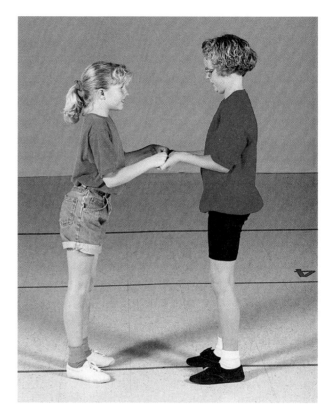

FIGURE 13.22 Arm curl-up.

The partner providing the resistance counts the duration of the exercise; positions are then reversed.

▶ ARM CURL-UP

The exerciser keeps the upper arms against the sides with the forearms and palms forward. The partner's fists are put in the exerciser's palms (Figure 13.22). The exerciser attempts to curl the forearms upward to the shoulders. To develop the opposite set of muscles, partners reverse hand positions. They push down in the opposite direction, starting at shoulder level.

▶ FOREARM FLEX

The exerciser extends the arms and places the hands, palms down, on the partner's shoulders. The exerciser attempts to push the partner into the floor. The partner may slowly stoop lower to allow the exerciser movement through the range of motion. Then they try with the palms upward.

▶ FIST PULL-APART

The exerciser places the fists together in front of the body at shoulder level. The exerciser attempts to pull the hands apart while the partner forces them together with pressure on the elbows. As a variation, with fists apart, the exerciser tries to push them together. The partner applies pressure by grasping the wrists and holding the exerciser's fists apart.

▶ BUTTERFLY

The exerciser starts with arms straight and at the sides. The partner, from the back, attempts to hold the arms down while the exerciser lifts with straight arms to the sides. Then they try with arms above the head (partner holding) to move them down to the sides.

▶ CAMELBACK

The exerciser is on all fours with head up. The partner pushes on the exerciser's back, while the exerciser attempts to arch the back like a camel's hump.

▶ BACK BUILDER

The exerciser spreads the legs and bends forward at the waist with head up. The partner faces the exerciser and places the hands on top of the shoulders. The exerciser attempts to stand upright while the partner pushes downward (Figure 13.23).

FIGURE 13.23 Back builder.

▶ SCISSORS

The exerciser lies on one side, while the partner straddles the exerciser and holds the upper leg down. The exerciser attempts to raise the top leg. Then the exerciser reverses sides and lifts the other leg.

▶ BEAR TRAP

Starting from a supine position on the floor, the exerciser spreads the legs and then attempts to move them together. Resistance is provided by the partner, who tries to keep the legs apart.

▶ KNEE BENDER

The exerciser lies in prone position with legs straight and arms pointing ahead on the floor. The partner places the hands on the back of the exerciser's ankles. The exerciser attempts to flex the knees while the partner applies pressure (Figure 13.24). Then they try in the opposite direction, starting with the knee joint at a 90-degree angle.

▶ PUSH-UP WITH RESISTANCE

The exerciser is in push-up position with arms bent, so that the body is about halfway up from the floor. The partner straddles or stands alongside the exerciser's head and puts pressure on the top of the shoulders by pushing down (Figure 13.25). The amount of pressure takes judgment by the partner. Too much causes the exerciser to collapse.

Examples of Fitness Routines

When planning fitness routines, establish variety in activities and include different approaches. This minimizes the inherent weaknesses of any single routine. The routines should exercise all major parts of the body. Additionally, when sequencing fitness activities into a routine, try not to overload the same body part with two sequential exercises.

FIGURE 13.24 Knee bender.

FIGURE 13.25 Push-up with resistance.

For example, if push-ups are being performed, the next exercise should not be crab walking, as it also stresses the arm-shoulder girdle.

Measure exercise dosage for youngsters in time rather than repetitions. It is unreasonable to expect all youngsters to perform the same number of exercise repetitions. Fitness performance is controlled by a number of factors, including genetics and trainability, making it impossible for all children to do the same workload. When time is used to determine the workload, each child can personalize the amount of activity performed within the time constraints. It is reasonable to expect a gifted youngster to be able to perform more repetitions in a certain amount of time than a less genetically endowed child. An obese youngster may not be able to perform as many push-ups as a leaner peer. Develop positive attitudes toward activity by asking youngsters to do the best they can within the time allotted.

STUDENT LEADER EXERCISES

Students enjoy leading their peers in single exercises or an entire routine. Students need prior practice if they are to lead their peers effectively in a stimulating exercise session. Don't force children to lead because this can result in failure for both the child and the class. The following routine is an example of student leader exercises.

 STUDENT LEADER EXERCISES

Encourage youngsters to do the best they can within the specified time limit.

Arm circles	30 seconds
Push-up challenges	30 seconds
Bend and twist	30 seconds
Treadmill	30 seconds
Sit-up challenges	30 seconds
Single-Leg Crab Kick	30 seconds
Knee to Chest Curl	30 seconds
Run in place	30 seconds
Standing Hip Bend	30 seconds

Conclude the routine with two to four minutes of jogging, rope-jumping, or other aerobic activity.

SQUAD LEADER EXERCISES

Squad leader exercises give students an opportunity to lead exercises in a small group. This approach is an effective method for teaching students how to lead others and to help them learn to put together a well-balanced fitness routine. A student within each squad is given a task card that has exercises and activities grouped by how they impact different parts of the body (see the example below). After the first student has led the exercise for the desired amount of time, the card is passed to another member of the squad, who becomes the leader. To ensure a balanced routine, each new leader must select an exercise from a different group. The following is an example of how exercises and activities are grouped for the squad leader exercise routine.

If there is a delay in starting an exercise, advise the squad to walk or jog rather than stand in place.

Sample Task Card for Squad Leader Exercises	
Aerobic Activities	**Abdominal Strength Exercises**
Running in Place	Reverse Curls
Jumping Jacks	Pelvis Tilters
Treadmill	Knee touch curl-ups
Power Jumper	Curl-ups
Rhythmic Jumping	Curl-ups with Twist
	Leg Extension
Flexibility Activities	**Upper Body Strength Exercises**
Bend and Twist	Push-up variations
Sitting Stretch	Reclining pull-ups
Partner Rowing	Triceps push-ups
Lower leg stretch	Arm circles
Achilles tendon stretch	Crab Kicks
Body Twist	Crab Full-leg Extensions
Standing Hip Bend	Crab Walk

✓ **TEACHING TIPS**

The class is divided into groups of four to five students. Each group is given a task card that lists eight to ten exercises. One of the group members begins as the leader and leads the group through an exercise. Each time an exercise is completed, the card is passed to a new leader.

Use alternating intervals of music to signal exercising (30 seconds) and silence (5 to 8 seconds) to indicate passing the card.

EXERCISES TO MUSIC

Exercises to music add another dimension to developmental experiences. Many commercial CD sets with exercise programs are available. Using a homemade tape with alternating intervals of silence and music signals time for exercises and aerobic activity. For example, if doing Random Moving, students could run/walk as long as the music is playing and stretch when the silent interval occurs. Having the music pretaped frees you from having to keep an eye on a stopwatch. Many exercise modules work well with music including Circuit Training, Aerobic Fitness Routines, Continuity Exercises, Astronaut Exercises, Squad Leader Exercises, and Rope-Jumping Exercises. A set of prerecorded music intervals on CD is available from Human Kinetics, P.O. Box 5076, Champaign, IL 61825-5076 (800-747-4457) or www.humankinetics.com. The CDs are titled *Physical Education Soundtracks, Vol. 1 and Vol. 2*. A routine using music follows.

Sample Routine

Crab Kicks	25 seconds
Rope-Jumping	30 seconds
Windmills	25 seconds
Walk and do arm circles	30 seconds
Abdominal Crunchers	25 seconds
Jumping Jack variations	30 seconds
Side Flex	25 seconds
Two-Step or Gallop	30 seconds
Triceps Push-ups	25 seconds
Aerobic Jumping	30 seconds
Push-Up Challenges	25 seconds
Leg Extensions	30 seconds
Walking to cool down	30 seconds

✓ **TEACHING TIPS**

Select music with a strong rhythm and easy-to-hear beat. When the music is on, students perform aerobic activities (for 30 seconds). When the silent interval is playing, students perform the strength development and flexibility exercises (for 25 seconds).

Use scatter formation.

CIRCUIT TRAINING

Circuit Training incorporates several stations, each with a designated fitness task. Students move from station to station, generally in a prescribed order, completing the designated fitness task at each station. Exercises for the circuit should contribute to the development of all parts of the body. In addition, activities should contribute to the various components of physical fitness (strength, power, endurance, agility, and flexibility).

Instructional Procedures

1. Each station provides an exercise task to perform without the aid of another child. Exercises that directly follow each other should make demands on different parts of the body. This ensures that performance at any one station does not cause fatigue that could affect the ability to perform the next task.

2. An equal number of youngsters should be placed at each station. This keeps demands on equipment low and activity high. For example, if there are 30 children for a circuit of six stations, place 5 children at each spot.

3. Music, whistle signals, and even verbal directions can be prerecorded to signal students to the next station. The tape provides time control and gives a measure of consistency to the circuit. Using tapes also allows you to help youngsters without worrying about timing each interval.

4. The number of stations can vary but probably should be no fewer than six and no more than nine. (Figures 13.26 and 13.27 show a six- and a nine-station course, respectively.)

Signs at the different stations can include the name of the activity and any necessary cautions or stress points for execution. When children move between lines as limits (as in the Agility Run), traffic cones or beanbags can be used to mark the designated boundaries.

Timing and Dosage

A fixed time limit at each station is the easiest way to administer Circuit Training. Children do their personal best during the time allotted at each station. A ten-second interval should be established to allow children to move from one station to the next. Later, this can be lowered to five seconds. Students start at any station, as designated, but follow the established station order. A second method of timing is to sound only one signal for the change to the next station. With this plan, the class ceases activity at their station, moves to the next, and immediately begins the task at that station without waiting for another signal.

The activity demands of the circuit can be increased by changing the exercises to more strenuous ones. For example, a station could specify knee or bench push-ups

Six-station course

1 Running in place	2 Curl-ups	3 Arm circles
6 Crab Walk	5 Trunk Twister	4 Agility Run

Supplies and equipment: Mats for Curl-ups (to hook toes)
Time needed: 4 minutes—based on 30-second activity limit,
10 seconds to move between stations

FIGURE 13.26 Sample six-station circuit training course.

and later change to regular push-ups, a more demanding exercise. Another method of increasing intensity is to have each child run a lap around the circuit area between station changes. Cardiovascular endurance can be enhanced by dividing the class into halves. One half exercises on the circuit while the other runs lightly around the area. On signal to change, the runners go to the circuit and the others run.

Another method of organizing a circuit is to list several activities at each station. The circuit can be performed more than once so students do a different exercise each time they return to the same station. If the circuit is to be done only once, children can perform their favorite exercise. Exercises at each station should emphasize development of the same body part. An example of a circuit training routine follows.

Sample Routine

Ask students to do the best they can for 30 seconds at each station. This implies that youngsters will not perform similar workloads. Fitness is a personal challenge.

Rope-Jumping

Triceps Push-ups

Agility Run

Body Circles

Hula-Hooping

Reverse Curls

Crab Walk

Tortoise and Hare

Bend and Twist

Conclude circuit training with two to four minutes of walking, jogging, rope-jumping, or other self-paced aerobic activity.

✓ **TEACHING TIP**

Tape alternating segments of silence and music to signal duration of exercise. Music segments (begin at 30 seconds) indicate activity at each station; intervals of silence (10 seconds) announce it is time to stop and move to the next station.

Use signals such as start, stop, and move up to ensure rapid movement to the next station.

Ask students to do their personal best. Expect workloads to differ.

Nine-station course

1 Rope-Jumping	2 Push-ups	3 Agility Run	4 Arm circles
8 Windmill	7 Treadmill	6 Crab Walk	5 Reverse Curl

9 Hula-Hooping (or any relaxing "fun" activity)

Supplies and equipment: Jumping ropes, mats for knee push-ups (if used), hoops (if used)
Time needed: 6 minutes—based on 30-second activity limit, 10 seconds to move between stations

FIGURE 13.27 Sample nine-station circuit training course.

▶ ALTERNATE TOE TOUCHING

Begin on the back with arms extended overhead. Alternate by touching the right toes with the left hand and vice versa. Bring the foot and the arm up at the same time and return to the flat position each time.

CONTINUITY EXERCISES

Children are scattered, each with a jump rope. They alternate between rope-jumping and exercises. A specified time period governs the length of the rope-jumping episode. At the signal to stop rope-jumping, children drop the ropes and take the beginning position for the exercise selected. Many of the exercises use a 2-count rhythm. When children are positioned for the exercise, the leader says, "Ready!" The class completes one repetition of the exercise and responds, "One, two!" This repeats for each repetition. To increase the enjoyment, the leader can say, "P.E.!" and the class will perform the exercise and respond with "is fun!" A number of brief phrases can be used such as "Work hard; keep fit." To enable a successful experience for children, modify the push-up and abdominal challenges (pages 265–267). An example of a routine of continuity exercises follows.

Sample Routine

Rope-jumping—forward	25 seconds
Double Crab Kick	30 seconds
Rope-jumping—backward	25 seconds
Knee touch curl-up	30 seconds
Jump and turn body	25 seconds
Push-ups	30 seconds
Rocker Step	25 seconds
Bend and Twist	30 seconds
Swing-Step forward	25 seconds
Side Flex	30 seconds
Free jumping	25 seconds

Relax and stretch for a short time.

✓ TEACHING TIP

Make a tape with music segments (25 seconds) alternated with silence segments (30 seconds). When the music is playing, students jump rope; when silence occurs, students do a flexibility and strength development exercise.

Exercises can be done in 2-count fashion. Exercises are done when the leader says, "Ready." The class answers, "One, two" and performs a repetition.

Allow students to adjust the workload to their level. This implies resting if the rope-jumping is too strenuous.

▶ HEXAGON HUSTLE

A large hexagon is formed using six cones. Students perform the "hustle" by moving around the hexagon, changing their movement patterns every time they reach one of the six points in the hexagon. On signal, the "hustle" stops and selected exercises are performed.

Instructional Procedures

1. To create a safer environment, children should move in the same direction around the hexagon.
2. Laminated posters with colorful illustrations should be placed by the cones to inform children of the new activity to be performed.
3. Faster children should pass to the outside of slower children.
4. The direction of the "hustle" should be changed after every exercise segment.

Sample Routine

Tape alternating segments of silence and music to signal duration of exercise. Music segments (25 seconds) indicate moving around the hexagon; intervals of silence (30 seconds) announce flexibility and strength development activities.

Hustle	25 seconds
Push-up from knees	30 seconds
Hustle	25 seconds
Bend and Twist (8 counts)	30 seconds
Hustle	25 seconds
Jumping Jacks (4 counts)	30 seconds
Hustle	25 seconds
Curl-ups (2 counts)	30 seconds
Hustle	25 seconds
Crab Kick (2 counts)	30 seconds
Hustle	25 seconds
Sit and stretch (8 counts)	30 seconds
Hustle	25 seconds
Power Jumper	30 seconds
Hustle	25 seconds
Squat Thrust (4 counts)	30 seconds

Conclude the Hexagon Hustle with a slow jog or walk.

TEACHING TIP

Outline a large hexagon with six cones. Place signs with locomotor movements on both sides of the cones. Locomotor movements to use include jogging, skipping, galloping, hopping, jumping, sliding, leaping, and animal movements. Sport movements such as defensive sliding, running backward, and running and shooting jump shots can also be used. The signs identify the hustle activity students are to perform as they approach a cone.

During the hustle, faster-moving students should pass on the outside of the hexagon.

Change directions at times to keep students properly spaced.

ASTRONAUT EXERCISES

Astronaut Exercises are performed in circular or scatter formation. Routines are developed by moving using various locomotor movements, alternated with stopping and performing exercises in place. The following movements and tasks can be incorporated into the routine.

1. Various locomotor movements such as hopping, jumping, running, sliding, skipping, taking giant steps, and walking high on the toes.

2. Movement on all fours—forward, backward, or sideways—with respect to the direction of walking. Repeat backward and forward using the Crab Walk.

3. Stunt movements such as the Seal Walk, Gorilla Walk, and Rabbit Jump.

4. Upper torso movements and exercises that can be done while walking such as Arm Circles, bending right and left, and body twists.

5. Various exercises performed in place when the music stops. A balance of arm-shoulder girdle and abdominal exercises should be included.

Astronaut Exercises can be adapted successfully to any developmental level. The type of movements selected will determine the intensity of the routine. More active children pass on the outside. Enjoyment comes from being challenged by a variety of movements.

Sample Routine

Walk, do arm circles	35 seconds
Crab Full-Leg Extension	30 seconds
Skip sideways	35 seconds
Body Twist	30 seconds
Slide; change lead leg	35 seconds
Jumping Jack variations	30 seconds
Crab Walk	35 seconds
Curl-ups with Twist	30 seconds
Hop to center and back	35 seconds
Four-count push-ups	30 seconds
Gallop Backward	35 seconds
Bear Hugs	30 seconds
Grapevine Step (Carioca)	35 seconds
Trunk Twisters	30 seconds
Power Jumper	35 seconds

Cool down with stretching and walking or jogging for one to two minutes.

TEACHING TIP

Tape alternating segments of music and silence to signal duration of exercise. Music segments indicate aerobic activity; intervals of silence announce flexibility and strength development activities.

Use scatter formation; ask students to change directions from time to time in order to keep spacing.

Allow students to adjust the workload pace. They should be allowed to move at a pace that is consistent with their ability level.

CHALLENGE COURSES

Challenge Courses are popular as a tool for fitness development in the elementary schools. Students move through the course with proper form rather than run against a time standard. The course is designed to exercise all parts of the body through a variety of activities. Equipment such as mats, parallel bars, horizontal ladders, high-jump standards, benches, and vaulting boxes can make effective challenge courses. A variety of courses can be designed, depending on the length of the course and the tasks included. Some schools have established permanent courses. A sample indoor course, including a climbing rope, is illustrated in Figure 13.28 on page 286.

The total equipment list for this course is as follows:

- Three benches (16 to 18 in. high)
- Four tumbling mats (4 by 8 ft)
- Four hoops
- One pair of high-jump standards with magic rope
- One climbing rope
- One jumping box
- Five chairs or cones

AEROBIC FITNESS ROUTINES

Aerobics is a fitness activity for people of all ages that develops cardiorespiratory fitness plus strength and flexibility. A leader is designated who performs a series of movements that the other students follow. There are few limits to the

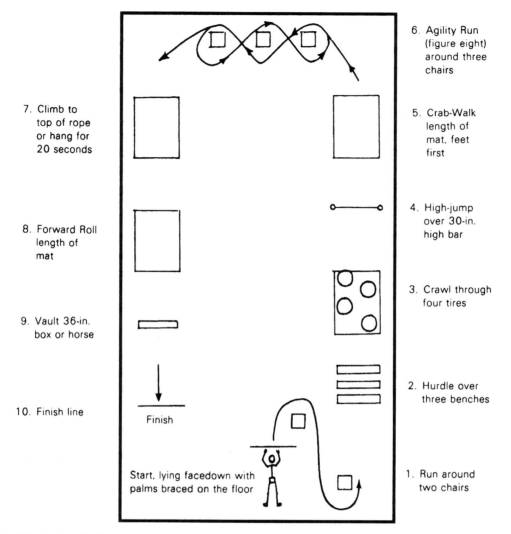

FIGURE 13.28 Indoor challenge course.

6. Agility Run (figure eight) around three chairs

7. Climb to top of rope or hang for 20 seconds

5. Crab-Walk length of mat, feet first

4. High-jump over 30-in. high bar

8. Forward Roll length of mat

3. Crawl through four tires

9. Vault 36-in. box or horse

2. Hurdle over three benches

10. Finish line

Finish

Start, lying facedown with palms braced on the floor

1. Run around two chairs

range of activities a leader can present. The leader may integrate manipulative equipment (including balls, jump ropes, hoops, and wands) with the movement activities.

Instructional Procedures

1. Use movement patterns that are organized by units of 4, 8, or 16 counts.

2. Vary movements so stretching and flowing movements are alternated with the more strenuous aerobic activities.

3. Keep steps relatively simple. Focus on activity rather than developing competent rhythmic performers. Stress continuous movement (moving with the flow) rather than perfection of routines. Running and bouncing steps are easily followed and motivating.

4. Remember that routines are best when they are not rigid. Youngsters shouldn't have to worry about being out of step.

5. Establish cue words to aid youngsters in following routines. Examples are "Bounce," "Step," "Reach," and "Jump."

Basic Steps

The following are examples of basic steps and movements that can be used to develop a variety of routines. The majority are performed to 4 counts, although this can be varied.

▶ **RUNNING AND WALKING STEPS**

1. *Directional runs*—forward, backward, diagonal, sideways, and turning.

2. *Rhythmic runs with a specific movement on the fourth beat.* Examples are knee lift, clap, jump, jump-turn, and hop.

3. *Runs with variations.* Run while lifting the knees, kicking up the heels, or slapping the thighs or heels; or run with legs extended as in the goose step.

4. *Runs with arms in various positions*—on the hips, in the air above the head, and straight down.

▶ MOVEMENTS ON THE FLOOR

1. *Side leg raises.* Do these with a straight leg while lying on the side of the body.

2. *Alternate leg raises.* While on the back, raise one leg to meet the opposite hand. Repeat, using the opposite leg or both legs.

3. *Rhythmic push-ups.* Do these in 2- or 4-count movements. A 4 count would be as follows: halfway down (count 1), nose touched to the floor (count 2), halfway up (count 3), and arms fully extended (count 4).

4. *Crab Kicks and Treadmills.* Do these to 4 counts.

▶ UPRIGHT RHYTHMIC MOVEMENTS

1. *Lunge variations.* Perform a lunge, stepping forward on the right foot while bending at the knee, and extending the arms forward and diagonally upward (counts 1 and 2). Return to starting position by bringing the right foot back and pulling the arms into a jogging position (counts 3 and 4). The lunge can be varied by changing the direction of the move and the depth and speed of the lunge.

2. *Side bends.* Begin with the feet apart. Reach overhead while bending to the side. This movement is usually done to four beats: bend (count 1), hold (counts 2 and 3), and return (count 4).

3. *Reaches.* Reach upward alternately with each arm. Reaches can be done sideways also and are usually 2-count movements. Fast alternating 1-count movements can be done, too.

4. *Arm and shoulder circles.* Make arm circles with either one or both arms. Vary the size and speed of the circles. Shoulder shrugs can be done in a similar fashion.

▶ JUMPING JACK VARIATIONS

1. *Jump with arm movements.* Alternately extend upward and then pull in toward the chest.

2. *Side Jumping Jacks.* Use regular arm action while the feet jump from side to side or forward and backward together.

3. *Feet variations.* Try different variations such as forward stride alternating, forward and side stride alternating, kicks or knee lifts added, feet crossed, or heel-toe movements (turning on every fourth or eighth count).

▶ BOUNCE STEPS

1. *Bounce and clap.* This is similar to a slow-time jump rope step. Clap on every other bounce.

2. *Bounce, turn, and clap.* Turn a quarter or halfway with each jump.

3. *Three bounces and clap.* Bounce three times and bounce and clap on the fourth beat. Turns can be performed.

4. *Bounce and rock side to side.* Transfer the weight from side to side, or forward and backward. Add clapping or arm swinging.

5. *Bounce with body twist.* Hold the arms at shoulder level and twist the lower body back and forth on each bounce.

6. *Bounce with floor patterns.* Bounce and make different floor patterns such as a box, diagonal, or triangle.

7. *Bounce with kick variations.* Perform different kicks such as knee lift and kick; double kicks; knee lift and knee slap; and kick and clap under knees. Combine the kicks with 2- or 4-count turns.

▶ ACTIVITIES WITH MANIPULATIVE EQUIPMENT

1. *Jump ropes.* Perform basic steps such as forward and backward with slow and fast time. Jump on one foot, cross the arms, and while jogging, swing the rope from side to side with the handles in one hand.

2. *Beanbags.* Toss and catch while performing various locomotor movements. Use different tosses for a challenge.

3. *Hula-hoops.* Rhythmically swing the hoop around different body parts. Perform different locomotor movements around and over hoops.

4. *Balls.* Bounce, toss, and dribble, and add locomotor movements while performing tasks.

Sample Routine

The following aerobic movements are suggestions only. When youngsters begin to fatigue, stop the aerobic fitness movements and perform flexibility and

13

strength development. This allows students time to recover aerobically.

Rhythmic run with clap

Bounce turn and clap

Rhythmic 4-count curl-ups (knees, toes, knees, back)

Rhythmic Crab Kicks (slow time)

Jumping Jack combination

Double knee lifts

Lunges (right, left, forward) with single-arm circles (on the side lunges) and double-arm circles (on the forward lunge)

Rhythmic trunk twists

Directional run (forward, backward, side, turning)

Rock side to side with clap

Side leg raises (alternate legs)

Rhythmic 4-count push-ups (If these are too difficult for students, substitute single-arm circles in the push-up position.)

✓ TEACHING TIPS

Use music to stimulate effort. Any combination of movements can be used.

Keep the steps simple and easy to perform. Some students will become frustrated if the learning curve is steep.

Signs that explain the aerobic activities will help students remember performance cues.

Don't stress or expect perfection. Allow students to perform the activities as best they can.

Alternate bouncing and running movements with flexibility and strength development movements.

PARTNER RESISTANCE AND AEROBIC FITNESS EXERCISES

Partner resistance exercises combined with aerobic fitness routines make an excellent fitness activity. Partner resistance exercises develop strength but offer little aerobic benefit. Combining them with aerobic fitness routines offers a well-balanced program. The exercises listed below refer to partner resistance exercises (pages 279–280). Enough time should be allotted so that each partner has the opportunity to resist and exercise.

Sample Routine

Students find a partner and lead each other in aerobic activities. Partners switch leader and follower roles after each partner resistance exercise. See the aerobic fitness section for descriptions of activities.

Bounce and Clap	25 seconds
Arm curl-up	45 seconds
Jumping Jack variations	25 seconds
Camelback	45 seconds
Lunge variations	25 seconds
Fist Pull-Apart	45 seconds
Directional Runs	25 seconds
Scissors	45 seconds
Rhythmic Running	25 seconds
Butterfly	45 seconds
Bounce with Body Twist	25 seconds
Push-Up with Resistance	45 seconds

Walk, stretch, and relax for a minute or two.

✓ TEACHING TIP

Tape alternating segments of music and silence to signal duration of exercise. Music segments indicate aerobic activity (25 seconds); intervals of silence announce partner resistance exercises (45 seconds).

Teach the exercises first. A sign with aerobic activities on one side and partner resistance exercises on the other helps students remember the activities. The signs can be held upright by cones and shared by two to four students.

Take 6 to 10 seconds to complete a resistance exercise.

SPORT-RELATED FITNESS ACTIVITIES

Many sport drills can be modified to place fitness demands on students. An advantage of sport-related fitness activities is that many children are highly motivated by sport activities. Thoughtful preplanning and creative thinking can result in drills that teach sport skills as well as provide fitness benefits. The following are some examples of fitness adaptations of sport skills.

▶ BASEBALL/SOFTBALL

1. *Base running.* Set up several diamonds on a grass field. Space the class evenly around the base paths. On signal, students run to the next base, round the base, take a lead, then run to the next base. Faster runners may pass on the outside.

2. *Most lead-up games.* Children waiting on deck to bat and those in the field perform selected activities (skill or fitness related) while waiting for the batter to hit.

3. *Position responsibility.* Start children at various positions on the field. On command, children are free to move quickly to any other position. Upon reaching that position, the child is to display the movement most frequently practiced at that position (for instance, shortstop fields ball and throws to first base). Continue until all players have moved to each position.

▶ BASKETBALL

1. *Dribbling.* Each child has a basketball or playground ball. Assign one or more people to be *it*. On command, everyone begins dribbling the ball and avoids being tagged by those who are *it*. If tagged, that child becomes the new *it*. A variation would be for the *its* to begin the game without a ball. Their objective would be to steal a ball from classmates.

2. *Dribbling, passing, rebounding, shooting, and defense.* Using the concept of a circuit, assign selected basketball skills to be performed at each station. Be sure that there is ample equipment at each station to keep all youngsters active. Movement from one station to another should be vigorous and may include a stop for exercise.

3. *Game play.* Divide the class into four teams. Two teams take the court and play a game of basketball. The other teams assume a position along respective sidelines, and practice a series of exercises. The playing and exercising teams change positions at the conclusion of the exercise sequence.

▶ FOOTBALL

1. *Ball carrying.* Divide the class into four to six squads. The first person in line carries the ball while zigzagging through preplaced boundary cones. The remainder of the squad performs a specific exercise. Upon completing the zigzag course, the first person hands off to the next person in line. This handoff signifies a change in exercise for the remainder of the squad.

2. *Punting.* With partners, one child punts the ball to the other. After the receiver has the ball, the object is to see which child can get to the partner's starting position first. Repeat, with the receiver becoming the punter.

3. *Forward passing.* Divide the children into groups of no more than four. Children practice running pass patterns. Rotate the passing responsibility after every six throws.

▶ VOLLEYBALL

1. *Rotating.* Place youngsters in the various court positions. Teach them the rotational sequence. As they reach a new court position, have them complete several repetitions of a specific exercise. On command, they rotate to the next position. Select activities that exercise components of fitness to enhance volleyball skill development.

2. *Serving.* Divide the class evenly among available volleyball courts. Starting with an equal number of children and a number of balls on each side of the net, have them begin practicing the serve. At the conclusion of each successful serve, the children run around the net standard to the other side of the net and retrieve a ball and serve.

3. *Bumping and setting.* Using the concept of the circuit, establish several stations for practicing the bump and set. Movement from station to station should be vigorous and may contain a special stop for exercise.

▶ SOCCER

1. *Dribbling.* Working with a partner, one child dribbles the ball around the playground with the partner following close behind. On signal, the children reverse roles.

2. *Passing and trapping.* Devise routines that cause the players to move continuously (e.g., jogging, running in place, performing selected exercises while waiting to trap and pass the soccer ball) while working with partners or small groups.

3. *Game play.* Divide the class into teams of three or four players each. Organize the playground area to accommodate as many soccer fields as necessary to allow all teams to play. Make the fields as large as possible.

Sample Routine

Instructional Activities	Teaching Hints
Station 1: Soccer Lines Drill— Working with a beach ball, dribble the ball back and forth between two lines as quickly as possible. Use only dribbling skills—long kicks not allowed.	Place even numbers of students at each station so they can partner up for the sport activities.
Station 2: Push-Up Challenges	
Station 3: Basketball Chest Pass—With a partner, practice the chest and bounce pass. If medicine balls are available, use them for strength development.	Use intervals of music and silence to signal changes to the next station. Begin this routine with 60 seconds at the sport-related activities and 30 seconds at the strength and flexibility stations. Ask students to replace the equipment where they found it.
Station 4: Flexibility Activities	
Station 5: Volleyball Passing— Using a beach ball, practice passing and setting with a partner(s).Keep the ball in the air as long as possible using two-handed passes and sets.	
Station 6: Abdominal Challenges	
Station 7: Hockey Circle Passing— One partner is stationary while the other circles around and passes to his partner. Change roles after five passes.	
Station 8: Trunk Challenges	

13

WALKING AND JOGGING

Jogging and walking, fitness activities for all ages, can lead to regular activity habits and to a lifelong exercise program. *Jogging* is defined as easy, relaxed running at a pace that can be maintained for long distances without undue fatigue or strain. It is the first level of locomotion above walking. Jogging and walking are unique in that they require no special equipment, can be done almost anywhere, are individual activities, consume relatively little time, and are not geared to a particular time of day. For most people, this type of regular activity is an exercise in personal discipline that can enhance their self-image and raise their confidence level.

Instructional Procedures

1. Let youngsters find a friend with whom they want to jog or walk. This is usually a friend of similar ability level. A way to judge correct pace is to talk with a friend without undue stress. If students are too winded to talk, they are probably running too fast. The selected friend helps ensure that the experience is positive and within the student's aerobic capacity.

2. Allow children to jog and walk in any direction so that they are unable to keep track of the distance covered. Doing laps on a track is one of the surest ways to discourage less able youngsters. They always finish last and are open to chiding by the rest of the class.

3. Have children jog and walk for a specified time rather than a specified distance. Why should all youngsters have to run the same distance? This goes against the philosophy of accommodating individual differences and varying aerobic capacities. Running or walking for a set amount of time will allow less able children to move without fear of ridicule.

4. Don't be concerned about foot action, since children select the most comfortable gait. Arm movement should be easy and natural, with elbows bent. The head and upper body should be held up and back. The eyes should look ahead. The general body position in walking and jogging should be erect but relaxed. Jogging on the toes should be avoided.

5. Don't make jogging and walking into competitive, timed activities. Each youngster should move at a self-determined pace. Racing belongs in the track program. Another reason to avoid speed is that racing negates learning to pace during a run. For developing endurance and gaining health benefits, children should move for a longer time at a slower speed instead of run at top speed for a shorter distance.

RACETRACK FITNESS

Arrange five or six fitness activities in the center (the Pit) of a large circle outlined with marking spots (the racetrack).

If desired, tumbling mats can be placed in the center of the racetrack to delineate the pit stop area. Students work with a partner and alternate running (or doing other locomotor movements) around the racetrack and going to the pit to perform a strength or flexibility exercise. A different exercise should be performed each time so students ensure variety in their workout. Intervals of 30 seconds of music with 10 seconds of silence are used to signal role changes. The student who was running the track now goes to the pit to exercise and vice versa.

Sample Routine

Instructional Activities	**Teaching Hints**
The follow are some examples of exercises that can be used for Pit exercises.	Exercise descriptions should be placed on signs in the Pit area so students can easily see the sequence of activities and know how to perform the exercises.
1. Arm circles	Mats can be placed in the Pit area to mark where students are to perform their exercises.
2. Bend and Twist	
3. Abdominal challenges	
4. Knee to Chest Curl	Different locomotor movements can be placed at the corner of the track to encourage students to perform a variety of racetrack activities. For example, use activities such as jogging, sliding, skipping, and grapevine movements. Rope-jumping can also be offered as an alternative to running around the track.
5. Push-up challenges	
6. Trunk Twister	

FITNESS ORIENTEERING

Students work together as members of a team. Eight to ten stations are placed around the area in random fashion. Each squad is given a laminated "map" card of exercise stations. Each of the maps has the stations in different order so that there is only one squad at a "landmark." The team members exercise together (each member performing at their own pace) and "hunt" for the next exercise station listed on their map card when signaled. When they complete the station activity, one member of the squad picks up a letter from the "checkpoint" and the team moves to the next station. The goal is to complete the fitness orienteering stations, pick up a letter at each station, and return to the original starting point to unscramble "the secret word." Intervals of music (30 seconds) and silence (15 seconds) signal when to exercise and when to change to a new station.

Examples of checkpoint stations on the exercise map card are:

1. Run to the northwest corner of the gym and pick up your letter now. When the music starts, continue to run to a different corner until the music stops.

2. Move to the individual mats and perform push-up challenges until the music stops.

3. Run to the benches and perform step-ups until the music stops. The count should be "up, up, down, down" with your steps.

4. Move to the red marking spots and perform two different stretches until the music stops.

5. Run and find the jump ropes. When the music starts, pick up the ropes and do some jump rope tricks you learned earlier.

6. Skip to the tumbling mats. When the music starts, perform abdominal challenges.

7. As a group, jog to the three green marking spots and pick up your letter. Jog and try to touch at least five walls, two different red lines, and three different black lines. Stay together with your group.

8. Jog to the "jumping jacks" sign and perform jumping jacks with at least four different variations in arm or foot patterns.

ALL-AROUND JACKPOT FITNESS

Three different "jackpots" (boxes) filled with fitness exercises and activities are placed around the teaching area. One jackpot is filled with a variety of strength development activities written on small index cards. A second jackpot is filled with flexibility activities. The third jackpot contains aerobic activities. Students can work individually or with a partner. They begin at one of the jackpots of choice and randomly pick out an activity to perform. If with a partner, they take turns selecting the card from the box. The only stipulations are that they must rotate to a different box each time and that they cannot select an activity they previously performed. If they pick an activity they performed on a previous stop, they return it to the jackpot and select another. A music interval of 30 seconds signals the duration of fitness activity followed by a 10- to 15-second interval used for selecting a new activity from a different jackpot. Students are expected to perform as many repetitions as possible while the music is playing.

Examples of activities for the jackpot include the following:

Aerobic Jackpot

1. Perform Carioca around the basketball court.

2. Perform a "mirror drill" with your partner for 30 seconds.

3. Jump rope using both slow and fast time.

4. Do Tortoise and Hare/Running in Place.

5. March with high steps around the area.

Strength Jackpot

1. Perform abdominal challenges.

2. Perform push-up challenges.

3. Do the Treadmill exercise.

4. Do as many Power Jumps as possible.

5. Perform as many Crab Kicks as possible.

Flexibility Jackpot

1. Perform the Bend and Twist exercise.

2. Stretch using the sitting stretch.

3. Stretch using the lower leg stretch.

4. Do the Standing Hip Bend.

5. Improve your flexibility performing the Body Twist.

PARTNER INTERVAL FITNESS

Students pair up with a partner and perform the activities below. The activities are designed so that one partner performs aerobic activity while the other is stretching or doing strength development activities. Use timed intervals of 30 seconds of music and 10 seconds of silence to signal changing positions (or activity). All the activities below should be performed.

1. *High Fives.* One partner runs around the area and gives as many "high fives" as possible to others who are running. The other partner remains stationary and performs Push-Up Challenges. On signal, they switch roles. Various locomotor movements can be used as well as different styles of the "high five."

2. *Over and Around.* One partner makes a bridge on the floor while the other moves over and around the bridges of other students. This continues until a signal is given to change positions. This ensures that one child is moving (working), while the other is resting. Students should try different types of bridges and movements to offer variety to the activity.

3. *Jump Rope and Exercise.* Each partner has a jump rope. One partner jumps the rope while the other partner folds the rope and performs strength or stretching activities. On signal, partners switch roles. An example of a stretching activity is to fold the rope in half and hold it overhead while stretching from side to side and to the toes. See pages 375–388 for other rope exercises.

4. *Stick and Stretch.* One partner tries to stick like glue to her partner, who tries to move as far away as possible. All movement should be done under control.

On signal, the other partner leads a stretching or strength development (resting) activity. On the next signal, the roles are reversed.

5. *Partner Swing and Exercise.* Partners swing each other under control while the first music interval is playing. On the next music interval, one partner leads the other in a stretching or strength development activity. The partners swing again followed by the other partner leading a stretching or strength development activity.

INTERVAL TRAINING

All fitness routines in this chapter take advantage of interval training principles. Interval training is effective with elementary school children because they fatigue and recover quickly. Interval training involves alternating work and recovery intervals. Intervals of work (large-muscle movement dominated by locomotor movements) and recovery (dominated by nonlocomotor activity or walking) are alternated at regular timed intervals. The following are examples of motivating activities that can be alternated with recovery activities.

► HIGH FIVES

Youngsters run around the area and, on signal, run to a partner, jump, and give a "high five." Various locomotor movements can be used as well as different styles of the "high five."

► OVER AND AROUND

Students find a partner. One partner makes a bridge on the floor while the other moves over and around the bridge. This continues until a signal is given to change positions. This ensures that one child is moving (working), while the other is resting. Students should try different types of bridges and movements to offer variety to the activity.

► JUMP ROPE AND STRETCH

Each student has a jump rope and is jumping it during the work interval. On signal, the student performs a stretch using the jump rope. For example, the student folds the rope in half and holds it overhead while stretching from side to side and to the toes.

► STICK AND STRETCH

Working with a partner, one partner is *it* and tries to stick like glue to the partner, who attempts to escape. Students should move under control. Upon signal, *it* leads the other person in a stretching (resting) activity. On the next signal, the roles are reversed.

► RUBBER BAND

Students move throughout the area. On signal, they time a move to the center of the area. Upon reaching the center simultaneously, they jump upward and let out a loud "yea!" or similar exhortation and resume running throughout the area. The key to the activity is to synchronize the move to the center. After a number of runs, students take a rest and stretch, or walk.

Each of these activities is used for work intervals. Recovery intervals are characterized by strength development or stretching activities. Using timed intervals of music is an effective approach for motivating youngsters. For a start, tape 30 seconds of music followed by 30 seconds of silence, taping a series of these alternating music and silent intervals. The music sequence signals youngsters to perform the work interval, and the silent interval is time for performing stretching or strength development activities.

PARTNER FITNESS CHALLENGES

Partner challenges are fitness activities that can be used with intermediate-grade youngsters. They can be used to develop aerobic endurance, strength, and flexibility. Another advantage of partner challenges is that they can be performed indoors as a rainy-day activity. It is best if youngsters are paired with someone of similar ability and size. Telling youngsters to pair up with a friend usually means they will select a partner who is caring and understanding. Emphasis should be placed on continuous movement and activity. The following are examples of partner activities that are both challenging and enjoyable.

► CIRCLE FIVE

Partner 1 stands stationary in the center of the circle with one palm up. Partner 2 runs in a circle around 1 and "gives a high five" when passing the upturned palm. Students should see how many touches can be made in 15 seconds. They reverse roles on signal.

► KNEE TAG

Partners stand facing each other. On signal, they try to tag the other person's knees. Each time a tag is made, a point is scored. Have them play for a designated amount of time.

► MINI MERRY-GO-ROUND

Partners face each other with their feet nearly touching and their hands grasped in a double-wrist grip. Partners slowly lean backward while keeping the feet in place until the arms are straight. Then they spin around as quickly as possible. It is important that partners be of similar size.

 ### AROUND AND UNDER

One partner stands with the feet spread shoulder width apart and hands held overhead. The other partner goes between the standing partner's legs, stands up, and slaps the partner's hands. They continue the pattern for a designated time.

 ### BALL WRESTLE

Both partners grasp an eight-inch playground ball and try to wrestle it away from each other.

SITTING WRESTLE

Partners sit on the floor facing each other with their legs bent, feet flat on the floor, with toes touching and hands grasped. The goal of the activity is to pull the other's buttocks off the floor.

UPSET THE ALLIGATOR

One partner lies facedown on the floor. On signal, the other opponent tries to turn the "alligator" over. The alligator tries to avoid being turned over.

SEAT BALANCE WRESTLE

Partners sit on the floor facing each other with their knees raised and feet off the floor. If desired, they place their hands under their thighs to help support their legs. They start with the toes touching. Each tries to tip the other person backward using the toes.

HEAD WRESTLE

Partners hold each other's left wrists with their right hands. On signal, they try to touch their partners' heads with their left hands, then switch the handhold and try to touch with the opposite hand.

PULL APART

One partner stands with the feet spread, arms bent at the elbows in front of the chest, with the fingertips touching. Partner 2 holds the wrists of the other and tries to pull the fingertips apart. Jerking is not allowed; the pull must be smooth and controlled.

PIN DANCE

Partners hold hands facing each other with a bowling pin (spot or cone) placed between them. On signal, each tries to cause the other person to touch the pin.

FINGER FENCING

Partners face each other with their feet one in front of the other in a straight line. The toes on the front foot of each partner should touch. Partners lock index fingers and attempt to cause the other to move either foot from the beginning position.

REFLECTION AND REVIEW QUESTIONS

How and Why

1. Why are America's youth perceived as being unfit and inactive?
2. Why must physical education teachers understand various concepts related to physical fitness?
3. Should fitness testing awards be used?
4. Why do so many students fail fitness tests? Defend your answer.
5. How can teachers make fitness fun?
6. Should physical education teachers be physically fit? Explain.

Content Review

1. Discuss several major conclusions of the Surgeon General's report on physical activity and health.
2. Differentiate between health-related fitness and skill-related fitness and identify the components of each.
3. Indicate whether American children are fit. Explain your answer.
5. Identify the purpose of physical fitness testing and the steps to implementing a fitness test battery. Include descriptions of several fitness tests and the fitness component each measures.
6. Describe methods for fostering positive attitudes toward physical fitness.
7. Discuss guidelines for promoting fitness for children.
8. Cite several harmful exercises.
9. Create a developmentally appropriate fitness routine. Be sure to identify the developmental level that will use the routine.
10. Describe or demonstrate numerous activities and exercises designed to improve the fitness of children.

FOR MORE INFORMATION

References and Suggested Readings

AAHPER. (1976). *AAHPER youth fitness test manual.* Reston, VA: Author.

AAHPERD. (1987). *Youth fitness test manual.* Reston, VA: Author.

American Academy of Pediatrics. (1991). *Sports medicine: Health care for young athletes.* Elk Grove Village, IL: Author.

American College of Sports Medicine. (1995). *ACSM's guidelines for exercise testing and prescription.* 5th ed. Baltimore: Williams & Wilkins.

Bailey, R. C., Olson, J., Pepper, S. L., Porszaz, J., Barstow, T. J., & Cooper, D. M. (1995). The level and tempo of children's physical activities: An observational study. *Medicine and Science in Sport and Exercise, 27*(7), 1033–1041.

Bar-Or, O. (1983). *Pediatric sports medicine for the practitioner.* New York: Springer-Verlag.

Blair, S. N., Kohl, H. W., Paffenbarger, R. S., Clark, D. G., Cooper, K. H., & Gibbons, L. W. (1989). Physical fitness and all-cause mortality: A prospective study of healthy men and women. *Journal of the American Medical Association, 17,* 2395–2401.

Bouchard, C. (1999). Heredity and health related fitness. In C. B. Corbin & R. P. Pangrazi (Eds.), *Toward a better understanding of physical fitness & activity.* Scottsdale, AZ: Holcomb Hathaway Publishers.

Bouchard, C., Dionne, F. T., Simoneau, J., & Boulay, M. (1992). Genetics of aerobic and anaerobic performances. *Exercise and Sport Sciences Reviews, 20,* 27–58.

Cooper Institute. (2002). *Fitnessgram test administration manual.* 2nd ed. Champaign, IL: Human Kinetics.

Corbin, C. B., & Lindsey, R. (1996). *Fitness for life teacher's resource manual.* 4th ed. Glenview, IL: Scott, Foresman.

Corbin, C. B., Lindsey, R., & Welk, G. (2000). *Concepts of physical fitness and wellness: A comprehensive lifestyle approach.* Boston: McGraw-Hill.

Corbin, C. B., Lovejoy, P. Y., Steingard, P., & Emerson, R. (1990). Fitness awards: Do they accomplish their intended objectives? *American Journal of Health Promotion, 4,* 345–351.

Corbin, C. B., Lovejoy, P. Y., & Whitehead, J. R. (1988). Youth physical fitness awards. *Quest, 40,* 200–218.

Corbin, C. B., & Pangrazi, R. P. (1992). Are American children and youth fit? *Research Quarterly for Exercise and Sport, 63*(2), 96–106.

Corbin, C. B., & Pangrazi, R. P. (1998). Physical activity pyramid rebuffs peak experience. *ACSM's Health & Fitness Journal, 2*(1), 12–17.

Erickson, D. M. (1980). *The effect of a random running program on cardiorespiratory endurance at the fourth, fifth, and sixth grade levels.* Unpublished master's thesis, Department of Health and Physical Education, Arizona State University.

Glasser, W. (1976). *Positive addiction.* New York: Harper & Row.

Gortmaker, S. L., Dietz, W. H., Sobol, A. N., & Wehler, C. A. (1987). Increasing pediatric obesity in the U.S. *American Journal of Diseases in Children, 14,* 535–540.

Harter, S. (1978). Effectance motivation revisited. *Child Development, 21,* 34–64.

Hedley, A. A., Ogden, C. L., Johnson, C. L., Carroll, M. D., Curtin, L. R., & Flegal, K. M. (2004). Prevalence of overweight and obesity among U.S. children, adolescents, and adults, 1999–2002. *Journal of the American Medical Association, 291*(23), 2847–2850.

Howley, E. T., & Franks, B. D. (2003). *Health fitness instructor's handbook.* 4th ed. Champaign, IL: Human Kinetics.

Lindsey, R., & Corbin, C. (1989). Questionable exercises— Some safer alternatives. *Journal of Physical Education, Recreation, and Dance, 60*(8), 26–32.

Locke, E. A., & Lathan, G. P. (1985). The application of goal setting to sports. *Journal of Sport Psychology, 7,* 205–222.

Lohman, T. G. (1992). *Advances in body composition.* Champaign, IL: Human Kinetics.

Macfarlane, P. A. (1993). Out with the sit-up, in with the curl-up. *Journal of Physical Education, Recreation, and Dance, 64*(6), 62–66.

National Association for Sport and Physical Education. (2004). *Physical activity for children: A statement of guidelines.* 2nd ed. Reston, VA: Author.

National Association for Sport and Physical Education. (2005a). *Physical best activity guide.* 2nd ed. Champaign, IL: Human Kinetics.

National Association for Sport and Physical Education. (2005b). *Physical education for lifelong fitness.* 2nd ed. Champaign, IL: Human Kinetics.

Pangrazi, R. P. (2007). *Dynamic physical education curriculum guide: Lesson plans for implementation.* 15th ed. San Francisco: Benjamin Cummings.

Pangrazi, R. P., & Corbin, C. B. (1990). Age as a factor relating to physical fitness test performance. *Research Quarterly for Exercise and Sport, 61*(4), 410–414.

Pangrazi, R. P., & Hastad, D. N. (1989). *Fitness in the elementary schools.* 2nd ed. Reston, VA: AAHPERD.

Pate, R., Corbin, C. B., & Pangrazi, R. P. (1998). Physical activity for young people. *Physical Fitness and Sports Research Digest, 3*(3), 1–8.

Pate, R. R., Dowda, M., & Ross, J. G. (1990). Association between physical activity and physical fitness in American children. *American Journal of Diseases of Children, 144,* 1123–1129.

Pate, R. R., & Ross, J. G. (1987). Factors associated with health-related fitness. *Journal of Physical Education, Recreation, and Dance, 58*(9), 93–96.

Payne, V. G., & Morrow, J. R., Jr. (1993). Exercise and VO_2 max in children: A meta-analysis. *Research Quarterly for Exercise and Sport, 64*(3), 305–313.

Plowman, S. A. (1993). Physical fitness and healthy low back function. *Physical Activity and Fitness Research Digest, 1*(3), 1–8.

President's Council on Physical Fitness and Sports. (2005). *The President's Challenge handbook.* Washington, DC: Author.

Reiff, G. G., Dixon, W. R., Jacoby, D., Ye, X. Y., Spain, C. G., & Hunsicker, P. A. (1987). *The President's Council on Physical Fitness and Sports 1985 national school population fitness survey.* Washington, DC: U.S. Department of Health and Human Services.

Ross, J. G., & Gilbert, G. G. (1985). The national children and youth fitness study: A summary of findings. *Journal of Physical Education, Recreation, and Dance, 56*(1), 45–50.

Ross, J. G., Pate, R. R., Caspersen, C. J., Damberg, C. L., & Svilar, M. (1987). Home and community in children's exercise habits. *Journal of Physical Education, Recreation, and Dance, 58*(9), 85–92.

Rowland, T. W. (1990). *Exercise and children's health.* Champaign, IL: Human Kinetics.

Shaw, J. M., & Snow-Harter, C. (1995). Osteoporosis and physical activity. *Physical Activity and Fitness Research Digest, 2*(3), 1–8.

Slaughter, M. H., Lohman, T. G., Boileau, R. A., Horswill, C. A., Stillman, R. J., Van Loan, M. D., & Benben, D. A. (1988). Skinfold equations for estimation of body fatness in children and youth. *Human Biology, 60,* 709–723.

Smith, L. L., Brunetz, M. H., Chenier, T. C., McCammon, M. R., Hourmard, J. A., Franklin, M. E., & Israel, R. G. (1993). The effects of static and ballistic stretching on delayed onset muscle soreness and creatine kinase. *Research Quarterly for Exercise and Sport, 64*(1), 103–107.

U.S. Department of Health and Human Services. (1996). *Physical activity and health: A report of the Surgeon General.* Atlanta, GA: Centers for Disease Control and Prevention, National Center for Chronic Disease Prevention and Health Promotion.

U.S. Department of Health and Human Services. (2002). *Prevalence of overweight among children and adolescents: United States, 1999.* Centers for Disease Control and Prevention, National Center for Health Statistics.

Whitehead, J. R., & Corbin, C. B. (1991). Effects of fitness test type, teacher, and gender on exercise, intrinsic motivation, and physical self-worth. *Journal of School Health, 61,* 11–16.

Wilcox, R. R. (1980). *RRP: An approach to cardiorespiratory fitness of primary school children, grades one, two, and three.* Unpublished master's thesis, Department of Health and Physical Education, Arizona State University.

Williams, D. P., Going, S. B., Lohman, T. G., Harsha, D. W., Webber, L. S., & Bereson, G. S. (1992). Body fatness and the risk of elevated blood pressure, total cholesterol and serum lipoprotein ratios in children and youth. *American Journal of Public Health, 82,* 358–363.

Websites

Physical Activity and Fitness Assessment
www.cooperinst.org/ftgmain.asp
www.presidentschallenge.org/home_kids.aspx

Physical Activity, Fitness, and Children
www.americanheart.org
www.cdc.gov/HealthyYouth/publications/index.htm
www.nlm.nih.gov/medlineplus/exerciseforchildren.html

Physical Activity Reports
www.cdc.gov/nccdphp/dnpa/physical/recommendations/index.htm
www.healthypeople.gov
www.actionforhealthykids.org

Teaching Fitness Concepts
http://pe4life.com

13

C H A P T E R

14

Active and Healthy Schools

SUMMARY

Weight management problems have increased rapidly over the past two decades. The need to promote active and healthy behaviors in youth led to the new MyPyramid for Kids and also to passage of the Child Nutrition and WIC Reauthorization Act of 2004. This act highlights the importance of developing solutions that increase the physical activity of children, provide nutrition education, and ultimately teach youth healthy eating and activity habits that last a lifetime. A sound physical education program is a necessity in schools; however, it is not enough. Even in a daily physical education program, children receive only a 30-minute period of instruction that offers about 15 minutes of daily physical activity. The total environment of the school must be changed in a way that encourages children to be active and to develop nutritional eating habits. This chapter will show how to change the structure of a typical school and create an active and healthy school.

OUTCOMES

■ Discuss the recommendations of the Child Nutrition and WIC Reauthorization Act of 2004.

■ Explain the importance of schools in promoting active, healthy behaviors.

■ Discuss each component of an Active and Healthy School Program.

■ Explain how to implement ideas in schools to increase the activity level of students.

■ Describe the requirements for implementing and maintaining an Active and Healthy School Program.

It's 7:00 A.M. on a cold Wednesday morning. School does not start until eight o'clock, but already the gym has 15 youngsters jumping rope and playing basketball while a third-grade teacher supervises. At 7:45, students in the "walking to school" program start arriving at school, led by a parent. During the day, the classroom teachers take a quick activity break every hour. Integrated into the physical education lessons are nutrition concepts. Today, the physical education teacher is teaching students about "sometimes" foods and "everyday" foods. Several other classroom teachers are teaching students phonics through movement. Immediately after school, several parents, the physical education teacher, and a county health agent meet in the physical education office to discuss an upcoming Health Festival planned for the end of the month. Right outside the door, children enrolled in the after-school program are learning to estimate their steps using pedometers. At 6:30 P.M. the physical education teacher starts the second of four physical education demonstration nights held throughout the year. This one is for first graders, who get to show off what they are learning in physical education. The event ends at 7:30 and so does another day at an active and healthy elementary school.

What you have just read is an example of the many opportunities that are available for increasing the activity of children. Note that the school environment has been modified in an attempt to ensure that students receive an adequate amount of activity to promote health and active learning. This chapter will show you the many possibilities for changing the environment of a school so that children have the opportunity to accumulate adequate activity and learn about nutrition, proper eating habits, and sun safety.

The health of youth (and adults) in the United States is a national matter of concern. Of particular worry are data showing that youth in the United States are more overweight now than ever and that the problem is growing rapidly. In an effort to abate the childhood obesity epidemic and improve programs for children, the Child Nutrition and WIC Reauthorization Act of 2004 was passed into law. This Act highlights the importance of developing solutions that increase the physical activity of children, provide nutrition education, and ultimately teach youth healthy eating and activity habits that last a lifetime. In short, the law requires all school districts with a federally funded school meals program (which is nearly all public schools) to develop and implement wellness policies that address nutrition and physical activity. The policy must be in place by the start of the 2006–07 academic school year. Once the wellness policy is in place, it is hoped that most districts will continually evaluate and revise their program each year. The Reauthorization Act recommends (but does not mandate) that schools implement some of the following points in an effort to meet the wellness policy plan:

- Make recess and lunchtime active settings for all students.
- Offer regularly scheduled activity breaks in the classroom. These breaks last three to five minutes and give students a respite from long periods of sitting.
- Design school walking programs that are buddy based or small group based.

- Develop activity contracts for students that teach students to monitor their daily activity patterns.
- Facilitate programs for parents; share information with parents through newsletters and school-based programs.
- Place point-of-decision prompts in classrooms to encourage healthy eating, physical activity, and other healthy behaviors.
- Encourage students to participate in after-school activities.
- Maintain and strengthen nutritional service programs.

Another important emphasis of the Reauthorization Act is to balance the impact of childhood obesity while maintaining local control for the states and schools. This means that the federal government does not dictate or tell the local school district what the wellness policy must contain. The government does, however, recommend that wellness policies address issues that impact childhood obesity such as physical activity and nutrition. Since each school district has the latitude to develop its own policy, it is likely districts will use local personnel to assist in the development of the wellness plan.

When school districts review the requirements made by the federal government, they see numerous suggestions related to physical activity, many of which are identified in the bulleted list above. It is hoped that they will seek assistance from their local physical activity experts, the physical education teachers. If the physical educators are not sought, they should ask to be a part of the wellness policy committee. As members of the committee, it is paramount that physical education teachers be familiar with the requirements of the law. In addition, physical education teachers need a plan of action that meets the requirements and serves to address the childhood obesity issues in their districts. The development of an Active and Healthy School Program (AHSP) is an approach that can be coordinated and directed by the physical education teacher. The primary purpose of an AHSP is to impact the health and wellness of youngsters through a variety of strategies that modify the overall school environment. Because every school is different, the AHSP focuses on changing the environment of the school so that students are naturally encouraged to increase their physical activity levels and make healthy choices such as healthy eating habits and sunscreen use. The remainder of this chapter presents suggested components of an AHSP and numerous strategies for implementing these components. Again, these are simply recommended strategies. It is probable that not all strategies will be effective at a particular school. However, by selecting and implementing effective strategies, reflecting on their effectiveness, and making alterations, a living AHSP that evolves over time can be created.

COMPONENTS OF AN ACTIVE AND HEALTHY SCHOOL

Quality Physical Education

In most cases, physical education teachers should serve as the physical activity coordinators in a school, specifically in an AHSP. Although they may not actively participate in an event or strategy, it is likely that they will have input into virtually every physical activity-based strategy in an AHSP. For example, a physical education teacher may organize and teach an after-school aerobics class for teachers. In addition, he may coordinate a group of teachers who supervise a before-school physical activity club for students. Without a physical education teacher, it is highly unlikely that physical activity will be an integral part of the school day. Thus, the physical education teacher is essential.

One note here: If the physical educator chooses not to be involved in the AHSP, it is important to identify another person to assume the responsibility. This may be a classroom teacher or other specialist. The point is that someone must take an active role in ensuring that her school promotes active and healthy behaviors. In the model school program created in the Mesa (Arizona) public schools, the physical education teacher is released a half-day a week to carry out administrative duties related to the AHSP program. As with most effective programs, positive things happen when quality people direct them.

A quality physical education program is important for maintaining and increasing student involvement. If physical education is not enjoyable to students, it is difficult to imagine them wanting to participate in AHSP activities. For example, if a typical physical education lesson consists of calisthenics and sitting on the sidelines while half the class plays soccer, it will be difficult to recruit students to come to an after-school program. Children might be thinking, "You want me to stay after school for more of the same?" Thus, to increase participation and ensure that a quality physical education program is present, a physical activity coordinator is the foundational component of an AHSP.

Active Learning in the Classroom

An often-heard saying is that we remember 10 percent of what we read, 20 percent of what we hear, 20 percent of what we see, and 90 percent of what we say and do. Elementary classrooms are full of students who learn by doing or experiencing. In addition, as discussed in Chapter 11, there is evidence that physical activity may be at least indirectly related to the learning process. With this in mind it follows that, when possible, teaching

through movement is beneficial in the classroom. This does not suggest that every classroom lesson, or even a majority of the lessons, has to be movement based; however, when possible, integrating movement into instruction can offer another medium for learning and promote the activity levels of students. Successful implementation of this principle requires overcoming two major barriers: Classroom teachers often do not feel comfortable teaching students in an active setting, and they do not know how to integrate movement into their lessons.

When developing strategies for integrating physical activity into a classroom lesson, there are factors that must be taken into consideration. First, how much space is available? In most classrooms, space is at a premium. Strategies for addressing this barrier are: (1) If of appropriate age, students can move their desks to the perimeter or (2) Activities that can be performed while students are in the same position (e.g., behind their desks) must be used. Second, consideration must be given to neighboring teachers—i.e., what is happening next door. In some activities, noise can become an issue. Although children can be reminded to keep their voices down, a classroom full of students making a reasonable amount of noise while being active can irritate next-door neighbors. Physical education teachers have the luxury of using a large open space for movement and must consider the issue of noise when designing activities for classroom teachers to implement.

In order to design effective activities for classroom teachers, there is pertinent information to consider as a physical educator. One, develop an understanding of what standards, objectives, or concepts the classroom teachers are teaching. In an era of accountability, most teachers will not implement an activity unless it is aligned with a specific state standard. Next, ask how the concept is being taught. If a classroom teacher is using a particular strategy, an activity that uses another strategy may confuse students. Finally, learn what the "comfort zone" of each classroom teacher is. Would she be willing to do a dance with students? Is he an outdoors person? Does she like team sports? With this information, physical educators can work with classroom teachers to generate effective and active classroom-based learning experiences for students.

Developing activities from scratch can be a difficult task, especially because physical educators have their own lessons to develop. Fortunately, many teachers and curriculum developers have created and marketed programs designed for classroom teachers that integrate physical activity into lessons that are aligned with standards. Many of the programs can be found online, and they include materials such as sample videotapes, lesson plans, equipment needed, and teaching strategies. When choosing a program and discussing options with classroom teachers, it is important that they understand that activity in the classroom is not a physical education program. Rather, the goal is to offer classroom-based strategies that teach some academic concepts through movement.

Before- and After-School Programs

Because of the sedentary nature of the school day, it is no surprise that students receive most of their physical activity outside of the school hours (Morgan, Pangrazi, & Beighle, 2003; Tudor-Locke, et al., in press). Usually, after-school hours offer the most opportunity for students to be active. In many schools, the YMCA or local recreation department uses the gymnasium for after-school programs. These programs are usually activity-based with students playing in the gymnasium, on the playground, or in a grassy space. After-school programs offer an excellent opportunity to teach students about healthy foods and other healthy behaviors. They can also provide tutoring for students who require extra assistance. Before-school hours also offer an opportunity for students to be active. Opening the school grounds and offering activities for students who arrive before school has great potential. At many schools, parents drop students off early in an effort to get to work on time. Without before-school programs, these students are left to just sit and wait outside the school.

Implementing effective extracurricular activities often requires overcoming barriers. The most prevalent barrier is cost. With the emphasis on standardized testing and childhood obesity, funding for programs that offer tutoring for physical activity and nutrition education is often available if teachers just ask. Other sources include private businesses, the PTA, and external grant sources. Most districts have resources that assist teachers who are seeking grants. Another barrier is transportation. Often the success of a program, particularly an after-school program, is strongly influenced by the availability of transportation for students (Jago & Baranowski, 2004). Attendance in such programs can be limited because students who are bused to school have to leave immediately after school. Also, if parents feel the additional transportation is a burden, they may not allow their child to participate. Ideas for eliminating this barrier vary from school to school. Some school districts provide transportation in the form of an after-school bus for students participating in district-sponsored after-school activities. Lastly, liability is sometimes a barrier to after-school activities. Districts are often reticent to allow students in the gymnasium outside of school hours due to increased insurance costs. Many schools are developing community-school programs. Parks are built next to schools so the two public institutions can work together to provide maximum use of both facilities.

Regardless of the roadblocks, they must be overcome for the good of all students.

Activity Breaks

In elementary schools, activity breaks are offered in three forms: recess, lunchtime activity time, and mini-breaks offered throughout the school day. Students should be provided with at least two 15-minute activity breaks (recess) per day. *Note that there is strong emphasis on renaming recess an* "activity break." This indicates that it has an educational purpose (to promote activity) rather than takes a recess from learning. During this time, students should be encouraged to be active. Providing equipment and organized games supervised by the playground attendant have been shown to increase physical activity during activity breaks (Jago & Baranowski, 2004). One study found that girls average almost 1,200 steps and boys 1,400 steps during a 15-minute activity break (Tudor-Locke, et al., in press). In just 15 minutes, children can accumulate approximately 10 percent of the daily physical activity award threshold for the President's Active Lifestyle Award (PCPFS, 2005).

Lunchtime also offers an excellent opportunity for physical activity. This time differs from activity breaks because the allotted time is used for eating and activity. Tudor-Locke and colleagues (in press) found that during a 40-minute lunch break, boys averaged 2,521 steps and girls 1,913 steps each day. No data are available regarding how much time was spent eating and how much was spent on the playground; however, the study clearly indicates that children also use lunchtime to be active. Just as with activity breaks, it is important that students be encouraged to be active during the lunch break. Nutritionists recommend that students be active first and then eat lunch so that they do not eat as fast as possible in order to have more time for play. There is some evidence that there is less wasted food as well. However, it is a controversial issue because it lengthens the lunch hour (cutting down time in the facility room for the physical education teacher). Also, some question whether having less playtime and eating more food is the direction we want children to pursue.

Mini-activity breaks in the classroom allow students to accumulate physical activity in small bouts throughout the day. Typically, a mini-break lasts three to five minutes and may or may not involve leaving the classroom. Pellegrini, Huberty, and Jones (1995) found that offering activity breaks every hour decreased behavior issues and problems with inattentive students. Other research has found that providing activity breaks, along with journaling activity from the previous day, is effective in increasing the daily physical activity levels of children, particularly girls (Ernst & Pangrazi, 1999; Pangrazi, Beighle, Vehige, & Vack, 2003). The uniqueness

14

of mini-breaks is the frequency with which they are offered. Unlike activity and lunch breaks, which occur once per day, mini-breaks, because they are short, are offered much more frequently (as many as six times per day). These short breaks provide a great source of physical activity with minimal long disruptions to classroom activities. With a few practice rounds, students can become quick and efficient at starting mini-breaks and immediately resuming class work following the mini-breaks. Just as is the case with other routines, this procedure must be practiced to minimize disruption.

Sun Safety Program

One method of getting students to be more active is to increase the amount of time they spend outdoors (because children are more active when outdoors). However, with this strategy comes an additional risk, that of skin damage caused by the sun. In the United States, one in five people will develop skin cancer. Children are of particular concern because overexposure to the sun at a young age puts individuals at an increased risk of skin cancer throughout life. An estimated 80 percent of a person's sun exposure occurs before age 18 (Stern et al., 1986). Blistering sunburns during childhood significantly increase the risk of developing skin cancer later in life (American Academy of Pediatrics, 1999). Arizona is the first state in the United States to mandate a course for teachers related to sun safety. For these reasons, when promoting physical activity for children, an important component of the program is to teach sun safety. Children should learn about the sun, the risks associated with exposure to the sun, and how they can be protected from the sun.

Schools can improve their sun safety in a variety of ways. Children can be encouraged or required to wear long-sleeve clothes, hats, and sunglasses when playing outside. If children do not have their own sunscreen, it can be provided before students move outside. This strategy requires collaboration with the school nurse in case of allergies. Activity breaks can be scheduled around peak sun hours of 10:00 A.M. and 2:00 P.M. Newsletters can be sent home notifying parents of the measures being taken at school and encouraging them to take similar precautions at home. Lastly, classroom lessons discussing the importance of sun safety, risks of sun exposure, and strategies for maximizing sun safety should be presented as a part of health education. The U.S. Environmental Protection Agency sponsors The Sunwise School Program, designed for educators. Sunwise is a comprehensive program that includes lesson plans, brochures, and letters for parents and workbooks for students. Included in the materials are a number of active games that can be played to teach concepts about sun safety and information on how to

become a Sunwise school. All the materials can be accessed on the Web at www.epa.gov/sunwise.

Another issue related to sun safety is that of shade from the sun. It is obvious that children are going to be exposed to the sun. However, an examination of playgrounds often reveals a lack of shade for play. In Arizona, sun shades are becoming increasingly common on playgrounds. Additionally, these structures provide protection for teachers and students during physical education classes. Hats, sunglasses, and sunscreen should also be encouraged. Teachers must allow students to wear hats (full brimmed, not baseball), even if they are only worn during outdoor activity. To send youngsters outside during the peak sun hours of the day without sunscreen, hats, and dark glasses (to protect against future cataracts) is a practice that needs to stop sooner rather than later.

Point-of-Decision Prompts

Point-of-decision prompts are simply signs placed in areas around the school where students and faculty will be making choices regarding healthy behaviors. This approach has been shown to be an effective strategy for increasing physical activity behavior in communities (Heath, 2003). A classic example is placing a sign directly above the "up" button on an elevator in an office building. The sign provides the elevator rider with the health benefits of taking the nearby stairs rather than taking the elevator. For an elementary school, signs can be posted on the playground to encourage students to be active—signs as simple as "Be Active" or that provide a list of activities that can be played during activity breaks (Figure 14.1). Nutrition-based point-of-decision prompts can be located in the cafeteria. For example, signs reminding students of healthy food choices can be used (Figure 14.2). Reminders to be sun safe, active, and to make healthy food choices can be hung on walls around the school or even made into large bulletin boards. Making signs can be a classroom project or an art project with the final work posted throughout the school.

Teacher Involvement

Encouraging faculty to improve their own health through school-based activities is another strategy to consider when developing an AHSP. Students see teachers as models. If they see their teacher eating healthier foods and being active during activity breaks, the potential impact these seemingly small acts may have is tremendous. Physical educators can coordinate walking clubs, after-school aerobics, brief nutrition education presentations at faculty meetings, or even a friendly "steps" competition among teachers. In fact, this latter approach is an effective way to introduce pedometers, particularly if a school has only five or six pedometers. A few teachers

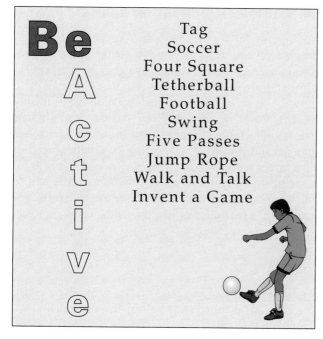

FIGURE 14.1 Example of a point-of-decision prompt sign for the playground.

wearing pedometers and discussing their steps often piques the curiosity of other teachers, who then want a pedometer. Also, youngsters begin asking about pedometers and become intrigued. Some companies sell pedometers at a discounted price for the school to resell

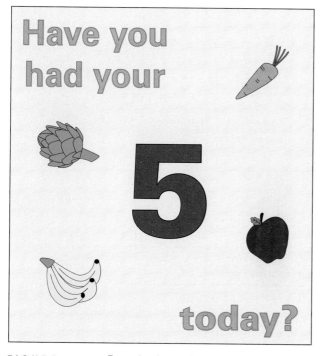

FIGURE 14.2 Example of a nutrition point-of-decision prompt sign for the school cafeteria.

for profit. This profit can then be used to purchase class sets of pedometers for use during physical education. For an example of a shareware program, see www.walk4life.com. Selling pedometers is a much healthier way to generate school funding than selling candies, cookie dough, and the like.

Walking-to-School Events

Walking-to-school programs are becoming more and more popular, with local, state, and national events held throughout the country. Even more importantly, these programs offer a safe, active, and enjoyable source of physical activity for students. The steps needed to develop a walking-to-school program are similar to the steps needed to design any program. For more in-depth coverage of this topic, see the Centers for Disease Control and Prevention Website (www.cdc.gov/nccdphp/dnpa/kidswalk).

1. **Generate interest**—Newsletters, conversations with parents, parent surveys, and discussions with local agencies such as the fire department, police department, or health department will help garner interest and provide helpful feedback during the initial planning phase of the program.

2. **Organize**—During this phase of the program, volunteers are recruited and meetings are held to work out details and logistics of the program. It is always helpful to have important personnel such as the principal, crossing guards, key district administrators, parent volunteers, and representatives from the police department to serve on the planning committee. Topics that need to be covered include:
   a. Safe, practical routes for students to walk to school
   b. Traffic management
   c. Collection of contact information and addresses of families who are interested in participating. Also, parental consent will need to be obtained.
   d. Location and scheduling of personnel during the event
   e. Time line of the event
   f. Media contacts and marketing of the event

3. **Implement and reflect**
   a. After carrying out the plan and holding a walking-to-school event, it is important that a meeting of the planning committee be held.
   b. At this meeting, members can talk openly about what they found successful and what they felt needs to be modified for the next event.
   c. If members cannot be present, they should be encouraged to present their ideas in writing.

Parental Involvement

For elementary students, parents/guardians are the most significant adults in their lives. With respect to physical activity, parents have a substantial impact on their child's attitude toward physical activity and their physical activity level (Welk, Wood, & Morss, 2003). Thus, programs that involve parents and encourage parents to be active with their children can be effective in promoting physical activity, not just for children but for an entire family. The following are a few of the ideas that foster parental involvement and that can be included in an AHSP.

ACTIVITY CALENDARS

An activity calendar can challenge youngsters and their families to participate in activities listed by day (see Figure 14.3). Families that reach a certain goal (e.g., active 75 percent of the days) get their name on the Active Family Wall of Fame posted in the gymnasium.

PE NIGHTS/DEMONSTRATION NIGHTS

PE nights consist of students and parents participating in physical education activities together. This approach shows parents what is being learned in physical education and provides them with activities they can do at home with their children. Demonstration nights involve parents watching their children participate in physical education activities. Typically the grand finale involves parents and students participating in activities together. In a larger school, these events will need to be held for specific grade levels to prevent overcrowding and to allow for safe activity. Most parents leave these programs thinking, "I wish PE was like that when I was younger" or "PE sure has changed."

FUN DAYS

Sometimes called Field Days or Play Days, these events are generally planned as an end-of-the-year celebration. However, they can also be held in September to kick off

February

Sunday	Monday	Tuesday	Wednesday	Thursday	Friday	Saturday
1 *Active Families stay healthy*	2	3 Play football with a friend	4	5 Play basketball for 10 minutes	6	7
8	9 Make a snowman	10 How many times can you jump rope without stopping?	11	12 Create a dance and practice it for 20 minutes	13 NO SCHOOL! BE ACTIVE ALL DAY!	14 Be kind to your heart . . . be active. ♥
15 *Children should be active at least 60 minutes per day*	16 Teach someone your favorite stretch	17 Teach a family member a PE game	18 Do extra chores as a favor to your parents	19 Jump rope for a total of 10 minutes	20 Invent a new exercise	21 Shovel snow
22	23 Do your favorite fitness challenge	24 Play a new game at recess	25	26	27 Start a game of tag in your neighborhood	28

If you want to do an activity other than the one on the calendar, GREAT! Write the new activity on your calendar. Mrs. Panko may even put your activity on the calendar as an activity next month.

How many minutes of activity should you do a day? _____

What types of activities are cardiovascular activities? _____

Name three lifetime activities. _____ _____ _____

What is a locomotor skill? _____

FIGURE 14.3 Example of a family physical activity calendar.

the school year. Typically, several stations are organized and classes move from station to station participating in the activities. Stations can be activities that are taught during physical education or novel activities that are simply safe and fun. Parents are great resources to serve as station attendants and as planning committee members to help coordinate the event. For primary-age student activities, upper-level elementary students can also serve on the committee to plan and set up the event as well as supervise the stations.

CHARITY EVENTS

Charity events offer an opportunity for families to be active together. Events can vary from a walk/run race, a walkathon, Chores for Change, or even a Physical Activity Festival where all proceeds go to a charity. The charity can be an outside organization or a local family, or support for the physical education program. As with any event, extensive planning and coordination will be necessary. Collaborating with the school's parent organization or other school-based organizations may help divide the labor needed for planning.

Community Involvement

Every community is full of resources that are of value to an AHSP. These resources may have experience planning events, working with other community organizations, collaborating with schools, or simply generating funding for programs. Physical educators should constantly seek collaborative, creative involvement from the community. If an organization does not have money to donate, it may have a program that encourages employees to volunteer in the community or some other resource that could prove useful. Also, members of the AHSP committee should be open to volunteering for events held by other community organizations. Building these types of relationships can have considerable benefit over the long term.

Early on in the process of developing an AHSP, potential community resources must be identified. Below is a list of organizations that may be interested in partnering with physical education teachers. Personnel from these organizations should be invited to participate in the AHSP.

- **YMCAs, recreation centers, Boys and Girls Clubs**—These organizations are all interested in physical activity and youth. In addition, they all are involved in before-school, after-school, and even during-school programs. One strategy is for the physical education teacher to offer training for their program staff. This allows the physical education teacher to teach the staff what is happening during physical education. Physical education teachers can also offer strategies that are effective and activities that youngsters enjoy.

- **County health agencies**—Many county health departments and agents are already involved with health-related programs in the schools. This makes them an excellent resource and potential collaboration partner in the development of an AHSP. County health agents may provide sun safety, nutrition education, tobacco education, and other lessons. In addition, some departments, along with the physical education teacher, can work with classroom teachers in an effort to increase classroom physical activity.

- **Businesses**—Most businesses surrounding a school or within a school district have a vested interest in contributing to the lives of youth in their community, particularly health-related businesses such as hospitals, insurance companies, bicycle shops, fitness centers, and doctor clinics. Businesses may also be willing to donate funds to purchase physical education equipment in exchange for posting a banner in the gym or having their logo on physical education newsletters.

- **Youth sports**—Youth sports offer an excellent opportunity for youngsters to be active. In order to maximize this experience, it is important that parents and coaches receive training so that all parties involved are on the same page with respect to what is good for children. Physical education teachers can provide these trainings. Being a coach or being highly skilled in a sport is not a requirement for conducting these trainings. Physical educators are the experts at teaching skills and motivating youth in a fun environment. Why not share that knowledge with coaches? One Saturday morning per season could be set aside so that parents and coaches can come together to learn how to teach skills and gain an understanding of how all adults must work together for the good of the children.

School Nutrition Environment

When developing an AHSP, physical educators should emphasize the importance of the physical activity side of weight management; after all, physical activity is what they are trained to do. However, they must not lose sight of the other side of the equation: calories consumed, or diet. Although physical education teachers are not trained to make decisions regarding school food services, they most certainly can become involved and influence the school nutrition environment.

Schools realize that to keep children healthy, youngsters must have access to ample amounts of nutritious food (Anspaugh & Ezell, 2004). For this reason, many students consume both breakfast and lunch at school. Thus, at least 67 percent of their meals are provided by the school. These foods are essential for healthy growth and development. Also motivating schools to provide two meals per day is the knowledge that healthy students perform better academically (Hanson, Muller, Austin, & Lee-Bayha, 2005). To this end, it is important that schools not only provide food, but also offer quality food. In addition, schools must provide students with nutrition education to ensure that they learn to make healthy food choices.

Physical educators can play a supportive role in enhancing the quality of nutrition in the schools. For example, the USDA recently released the new children's food guide pyramid, called MyPyramid for Kids, which also has accompanying tips, lesson plans, and coloring sheets designed to explain healthful eating to children (www.MyPyramid.gov/kids/index.html). It can be posted where youngsters will see it on a daily basis. The advanced version (Figure 14.4) contains the basic principles of nutrition and physical activity. The following are other strategies that physical education teachers can advocate to improve the school nutrition environment.

1. All students must have access to nutritious foods. Hungry children cannot perform well academically. For this reason, programs that ensure students receive a nutrient-dense breakfast and lunch should be developed.

2. If vending machines are on campus, they must serve only nutritious, healthy choices.

3. In the classrooms, foods should not be given as a reward. Many teachers hand out candy bars, gum, or other sweet treats as rewards for correct answers, good behavior, etc. To prevent this practice, policies must be developed by the principal. Stickers, pencils, and other items can be used in place of food rewards. Another alternative is to ensure that when teachers give food to students, it is nutritious. Think of the positive message sent to children about eating healthy foods if an apple is the reward for a correct answer. An apple would be viewed as a treat. This method is particularly effective if implemented during the students' first few years of school.

4. Children should be provided nutrient-dense meals. This means the empty calories of French fries and cupcakes should not make up even a small portion of the calories. Recommendations for nutrition standards and instructional materials are available from the U.S. Department of Agriculture (USDA) at www.nutrition.gov.

5. School club sales should be limited to nutritious foods.

6. The eating environment should be clean, safe, and attractive.

7. Lunch should be served as close to noon as possible. More and more schools are serving lunch to students as early as 10 A.M.

8. Bulletin boards and signs in the cafeteria can be used to complement the nutrition education, sun safety, and physical activity promotion that is occurring throughout the school.

9. Nutrition education content should be integrated into physical education activities. See the following activities for examples of nutrition games.

10. Feedback should be gathered from parents and other community members regarding their feelings about the nutrition environment at the school or the changes being made.

EXAMPLES OF NUTRITION GAMES

▶ GRAB A MEAL

Health Concept: The importance of a balanced diet

PE Concepts: Game skills, locomotor skills, cooperation

PE Lesson Part: Game activity

Supplies: Plastic food and hoops

This game is played in a similar way to Barker's Hoopla (page 569) with a few alterations. In this game the hoop is the team's plate, and rather than using beanbags, they use plastic food, which can be purchased at most toy stores. The first challenge for the teams is to accumulate as much food as possible on their plates. On signal, students move to another team's plate and pick up a single piece of food. They then return to their plate and place the food in the hoop. The process continues until you give the signal to stop. It is important that students do not "guard" their plates and that all food be placed on the plates, not tossed or thrown. The game can be further modified with the following challenges:

- Accumulate the least amount of food.
- Gather a balanced meal.
- Gather an unhealthful meal.
- Accumulate only fruits (or some other type of food) on your plate.

▶ ANYTIME AND SOMETIMES

Health Concept: The difference between healthful and unhealthful foods

PE Concepts: Chasing, fleeing, simple game skills, locomotor skills

PE Lesson Part: Game activity

Supplies: Pictures of healthful and unhealthful foods

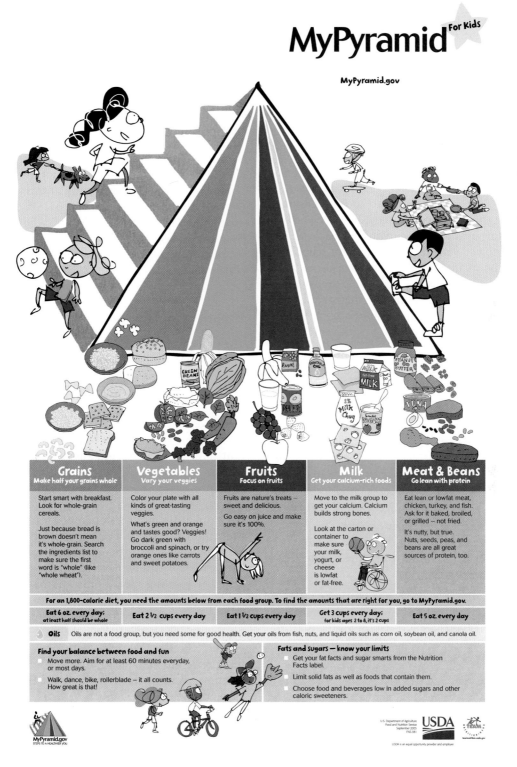

FIGURE 14.4 MyPyramid for Kids.

The game is played in the same manner as Crows and Cranes (page 561) with "anytime" and "sometimes" used as the chase words. *Anytime* foods are foods such as fruits, vegetables, whole grains, etc., that students can eat anytime. *Sometimes* foods are foods like candy, cake, soda, and potato chips that students should limit to eating only sometimes. For added challenge and to test students' understanding of the terms, rather than saying the type of food, call out a specific food (e.g., strawberries or candy bars) as the chase word. The students must determine if the food is a sometimes food or an anytime food and then move in the appropriate direction.

GETTING STARTED

As with most professionals initiating a project, one of the toughest tasks for physical educators is getting started. Often great ideas get lost because teachers do not know where to begin and end up letting the idea fall by the wayside. Also, many projects are looked at as one huge task that cannot be accomplished. This perspective also causes many great ideas to remain on the shelf. The key with any project, whether it is a paper for school or the organization of an AHSP, is to see the process as a series of manageable tasks. The following are suggestions that can help make creating and maintaining an AHSP a series of small pieces that can be accomplished in a systematic manner.

- ■ *Network.* Talk to other teachers, administrators, parents, friends, and family. One person cannot have all of the appropriate contacts. People who are not able to provide what is needed may be able to give you names of those who can.

- ■ *Introduce Yourself.* Be sure to introduce yourself to as many people in the school community as possible. When meeting people for the first time, take the time to get to know them if time permits. The first meeting is generally not an appropriate time to seek resources. Let the individual know about the AHSP.

- ■ *Get Involved.* Parent organizations, youth sports, and local youth clubs are always looking for volunteers. Offer to help or ask someone on the AHSP committee to help out at an event held by these organizations. The best way to get others to help you is to help them.

- ■ *Be Persistent.* During the process of starting an AHSP and seeking resources, you will hear "No" or "Not right now" regularly. Keep moving forward, knowing that what you are working toward is what is best for kids.

- ■ *Ask Others to Help.* When one person agrees to get involved, ask him for names of anyone else who may be interested in helping. Find out his background. He may have excellent suggestions for getting others involved or may have great contacts.

FIGURE 14.5 Tips for recruiting an Active and Healthy School Program committee.

Form an AHSP Committee

The physical educator should take on the role of the AHSP coordinator. However, without the support of others, an AHSP is difficult to achieve. When forming the committee it is important to consider key personnel in the program. Teachers, school administrators, district administrators, parents, students, university faculty, fire department representatives, local business owners, community leaders, and community organizations are just the start of a list of potential partners. All of these should be considered key personnel and invited to attend. Also, at the initial meeting of this group it is important that members of the AHSP committee be encouraged to invite other people who may not have been considered. Figure 14.5 provides a list of strategies for recruiting potential AHSP committee members and collaborators.

Develop an Implementation Plan

The first charge of the AHSP committee is to develop a plan. As the coordinator, the physical education teacher should provide the committee with some background information, the components of an AHSP, and a larger vision for the school. After brainstorming for ideas, the committee needs to prioritize the ideas and develop short-term and long-term objectives. Lastly, it is important that the AHSP begin small. This prevents overwhelming teachers, students, and communities. For example, the committee may decide that their first activity will be to give a short presentation about the program at the school's open house. Also at the open house they will set up a booth at the front door to provide fliers and survey parents. After surveying parents, the next steps can be developed. Another school may begin by sending fliers home and handing them out during school drop-off and pick-up hours while the physical education teacher begins using pedometers in his lessons. The key is to keep the tasks manageable and aligned with the goals. Over time, the AHSP will evolve into numerous activities with subcommittees that have their own set of objectives related to the original purpose of the AHSP.

Reflect, Evaluate, and Progress

The AHSP should be viewed as an evolving program that will continue to progress and become more effective. However, without reflection and evaluation, progress and improvement are difficult. The committee must meet, examine where they have been and where they are going, and adjust the program. For instance, some events may have low attendance. Was it because the event was not attractive to children and families? Was the event marketed well? Was the event on the same day as Little League opening day? Without thoughtful reflection and honest evaluation, an AHSP runs the risk of becoming stale, dormant, and, possibly, nonexistent. With quality reflection, programs can continue to evolve to meet the needs of the school and community.

Meet with Other Schools

Another strategy to help generate and maintain a quality AHSP is to meet with other schools with similar programs. The phrase "No sense reinventing the wheel" is true here. Learning what has been successful at other schools may be helpful to the committee. Keep in mind that the demographics of the school may play into the success of some activities. Therefore, an activity that wasn't effective at Franklin Elementary may be effective at Monroe Elementary and vice versa. While working with other schools, it is important to keep an open mind, collect as much information as possible, and allow the committee to discuss future directions based on the experiences of other schools.

When all is said and done, an AHSP demands a total approach to the school environment. The saying "It takes a village to raise a child" could not be truer if we are going to create a setting that not only educates children in academics but also physically educates them. No longer can we afford to make children sit for long periods in an attempt to improve their academic performance. Most adults know only too well that they can sit and concentrate for only a finite amount of time. After that, the process becomes nonproductive. Let's make sure our schools excel in activity promotion and academic performance. The old saying "A healthy mind lives in a healthy body" is a truism that must drive the environment of today's schools.

REFLECTION AND REVIEW QUESTIONS

How and Why

1. Why are Active and Healthy Schools important?

2. How can physical educators contribute to an active, healthy school?

3. How can community involvement impact the effectiveness of an AHSP?

4. Why is it important to develop an AHSP committee?

Content Review

1. Explain what the Child Nutrition and WIC Reauthorization Act means to physical education teachers.

2. Present several recommendations made by the Child Nutrition and WIC Reauthorization Act.

3. Discuss the purpose of an AHSP.

4. List and describe the components of an Active and Healthy School Program.

5. Describe how a physical education teacher can go about starting an AHSP.

FOR MORE INFORMATION

References and Suggested Readings

American Academy of Pediatrics. (1999). Ultraviolet light: A hazard to children. *Pediatrics, 104,* 328–333.

Anspaugh, D. J. & Ezell, G. (2004). *Teaching today's health.* San Francisco: Benjamin Cummings.

Ernst, M. P., & Pangrazi, R. P. (1999). Effects of a physical activity program on children's activity levels and attraction to physical activity. *Pediatric Exercise Science, 11,* 393–405.

Hanson, T. L., Muller, C., Austin, G., & Lee-Bayha, J. (2005). Research findings about the relationship between student health and academic achievement. In California Department of Education, *Getting results: Developing safe and healthy kids update 5.* Sacramento: CDE Press.

Heath, G. W. (2003). Increasing physical activity in communities: What really works? *President's Council on Physical Fitness and Sports Research Digest, 4*(4), 1–8.

Jago, R., & Baranowski, T. (2004). Non-curricular approaches for increasing physical activity in youth: A review. *Preventive Medicine, 39*(1), 157–163.

Morgan, C. F., Pangrazi, R. P., & Beighle, A. (2003). Using pedometers to promote physical activity in physical education. *Journal of Physical Education, Recreation, and Dance, 74*(7), 33–38.

Pangrazi, R. P., Beighle, A., Vehige, T., & Vack, C. (2003). Evaluating the effectiveness of the State of Arizona's Promoting Lifestyle Activity for Youth program. *Journal of School Health, 73*(8), 317–321.

Pellegrini, A. D., Huberty, P. D., & Jones, I. (1995). The effects of recess timing on children's playground and classroom behaviors. *American Educational Research Journal, 32*(4), 845–864.

President's Council on Physical Fitness and Sports. (2005). *The President's Challenge handbook.* Washington, DC: Author.

Stern, R. S., Weinstein, M. C., & Baker, S. G. (1986). Risk reduction for nonmelanoma skin cancer with childhood sunscreen use. *Archives of Dermatology, 122,* 537–545.

Tudor-Locke, C., Lee, S. M., Morgan, C. F., Beighle, A., & Pangrazi, R. P. (in press). Children's pedometer-determined physical activity patterns during the segmented school day. *Medicine and Science in Sports and Exercise.*

Welk, G. J., Wood, K., & Morss, G. (2003). Parental influences on physical activity in children: An exploration of the potential mechanisms. *Pediatric Exercise Science, 15*(1), 19–33.

14

Websites

Arizona Sunwise Program
www.azdhs.gov/phs/sunwise/pdf/activities_k-2.pdf

Centers for Disease Control Walk to School Program
www.cdc.gov/nccdphp/dnpa/kidswalk

Children's Food Pyramid
www.MyPyramid.gov/kids/index.html

Environmental Protection Agency Sunwise Program
www.epa.gov/sunwise

Gopher Sports Active and Healthy School Program
www.gophersport.com

Nutrition.gov
www.nutrition.gov

School Nutrition Association
www.asfsa.org

U.S. Department of Agriculture
www.usda.gov

U.S. Department of Health and Human Services
www.os.hhs.gov

Walk 4 Life
www.walk4life.com

Motor Skills

Young children arrive at school with little competency in fundamental motor skills. Physical education is unique because fundamental motor skills are seldom taught anywhere else in the school curriculum. Youngsters need to learn how to speak the language of movement (movement concepts) and be able to tie movement to vocabulary (movement themes). Locomotor and nonlocomotor movements form the foundation for skills that will be used throughout the life span. Introductory activities incorporate locomotor and nonlocomotor skills into enjoyable activities that warm up and prepare students for a lesson of activity. Manipulative skills become the tools that youth and adults use to participate in lifetime activities. Throwing, catching, kicking, and striking are skills used in many activities of choice later in life. Learning to control the body on different types of apparatus teaches youngsters how to manage their bodies in a variety of settings.

After reading this section, you will know how to teach basic motor skills to young people. You will understand the basic mechanics of motor skills and be able to design lessons that give students a foundation for learning specialized and sport skills.

Movement Concepts and Themes

SUMMARY

This chapter is designed to help teachers and students understand movement concepts—the classification and vocabulary of movement. Teachers learn the classification of movement concepts, including body awareness, space awareness, qualities of movement, and relationships. Emphasis at this level is placed on the process of moving rather than on the product of correct performance of a skill. Students' creativity is rewarded and ingenuity is reinforced. Movement themes are designed to integrate the concepts into actual activities on the floor.

OUTCOMES

- Explain how movement themes are used to develop an understanding of movement concepts.

- Define how human movement concepts are classified into four major categories.

- Explain the purpose of movement themes.

- Define the qualities of movement.

- Teach a variety of movement themes.

- Design a unique movement theme using the four-step approach.

- Specify individual cooperative partner activities and group activities to develop educational movement.

Physical education places emphasis on skill development in the elementary school years. It is important to learn fundamental skills in the early years because they are the building blocks for more sophisticated skills. This chapter explains the vocabulary and classification of human movement and offers teachers a framework for designing lessons that help students understand the relationship between their bodies and movement. There are three major components to learning movement concepts:

1. Know the classification scheme for movement.

2. Understand how to design effective movement themes for instruction.

3. Use movement themes to bring the concepts of movement to life. This step integrates concepts and activities for the purpose of developing a "movement educated" youngster.

Chapters 15 through 18 cover development of fundamental motor skills. This section forms the foundation for the development of a physically educated youngster. The chapters explore movement concepts, fundamental motor skills, manipulative skills, and body management skills. Even though all the skills and concepts are learned simultaneously, for the sake of organization and reference, they are listed in separate chapters. Figure 15.1 shows the movement concepts and skills addressed in each chapter.

With Developmental Level I children (ages 4 to 9), emphasis is placed on developing an understanding of movement concepts. Less emphasis is placed on skill technique and correct performance of skills. Children are taught skill techniques, but greater emphasis is placed on learning the vocabulary of movement. Lessons are designed to help students understand and physically experience the classification of movement concepts, which includes body awareness, space awareness, qualities of movement, and relationships. Instructional objectives are to show children how movements are classified and how movement themes can turn concepts into concrete movements. Emphasis is placed on the process of moving rather than on the product of correctly performing a skill.

Motor Skills

Chapter 16
Locomotor Skills: Walking, Hopping, Jumping, Sliding, Running, Leaping, Skipping, Galloping
Nonlocomotor Skills: Bending, Turning, Balancing, Pushing, Twisting, Rocking, Stretching, Pulling

Movement Concepts and Themes

Chapter 15
Space Awareness, Direction, Level, Pathways, Planes

The Foundation Skills

Manipulative Skills

Chapter 17
Striking, Throwing, Kicking, Catching, Dribbling, Volleying, Punting, Rolling, Trapping

Body Management Skills

Chapter 18
Strength, Balance, Agility, Flexibility, Coordination

FIGURE 15.1 The components of movement concepts and fundamental motor skills.

Movement themes form the foundation of movement experiences necessary for developing more specific fundamental skills. Through this process, children develop an increased awareness and understanding of the body as a vehicle for movement, and acquire a personal vocabulary of movement skills. Movement themes in this text are categorized in the major classifications of space awareness, body awareness, qualities of movement, and relationships.

CLASSIFICATION OF HUMAN MOVEMENT CONCEPTS

The movement concept categories of body awareness, space awareness, qualities of movement, and relationships offer structure and direction for planning new movement experiences. As youngsters experience movement, they learn the vocabulary of movement so they are able to discuss and understand the unlimited possibilities for creative and productive movement.

Body Awareness

This category defines *what* the body can perform; the shapes it can make, how it can balance, and the transfer of weight to different body parts. Using these categories to develop challenges can add variety to movement.

1. *Shapes the body makes.* Many shapes can be formed with the body, such as long or short, wide or narrow, straight or twisted, stretched or curled, symmetrical or asymmetrical.

2. *Balance or weight bearing.* Balance demands that different parts of the body support the weight or receive the weight. Different numbers of body parts can be involved in the movements and used as body supports.

3. *Transfer of body weight.* Many skills demand moving the body weight from one body part to another, such as walking, leaping, rolling, and so on.

4. *Flight.* This category differs from transfer of body weight in that it is explosive movement and involves lifting the body weight from the floor or apparatus for an extended period of time. The amount of time off the floor distinguishes flight from transfer of weight. Examples include running, jumping onto a climbing rope, and hanging.

Space Awareness

Space awareness defines *where* the body can move. The spatial qualities of movement related to moving in different directions and at different levels are the focus.

Teach youngsters to use space effectively when moving. The following elements describe how space can be modified and used in movement experiences.

1. *General or personal space.* Personal space is the limited area individual children can use around them, and in most cases is reserved for that individual only. General space is the total space that is used by all youngsters.

2. *Direction.* This refers to the desired route of movement, whether straight, zigzag, circular, curved, forward, backward, sideways, upward, or downward.

3. *Level.* This defines the relationship of the body to the floor or apparatus, whether low, high, or in between.

4. *Pathways.* This trait describes the path a movement takes through space. Examples are squares, diamonds, triangles, circles, figure eights, and others.

5. *Planes.* Planes are somewhat specific pathways defined as circular, vertical, and horizontal. The concept of planes is usually restricted in elementary school to performing simple activities in a specified plane.

Qualities of Movement

These constructs classify *how* the body moves. The qualities of movement define how the movement will be conducted. Rather than dealing with specific movements, the focus is on how movements are performed, for example, with speed or great force or lightly. These qualities can be applied to many different skills and activities.

1. *Time or speed.* This quality deals with the speed and duration of movement. Children learn to move with varying speeds and to control speed throughout a variety of movements. They should learn the relationship between body shape and speed and be able to use body parts to generate speed. The time factor may be varied by using different speeds—moving to a constant rhythm, accelerating, and decelerating.

2. *Force.* Force is the effort or tension generated in movement. Force can be used effectively to aid in executing skills. Learning how to generate, absorb, and direct force is an important outcome. Force qualities may be explored by using words such as *light, heavy, strong, weak, rough,* and *gentle.*

3. *Flow.* This factor establishes how movements are purposefully sequenced to create continuity of movement. Most often this quality is discussed in terms of interrupted (bound) or sustained (free) flow. *Interrupted flow* stops at the end of a movement or part of a movement. *Sustained flow* involves smoothly linking different movements or parts of a movement.

Relationship

This element defines with whom and/or to what the body relates. A *relationship* is defined as the position of the performer to a piece of apparatus or to other performers. Examples of relationships are near–far, above–below, over–under, in front–behind, on–off, and together–apart. When done with other people, relationships such as leading–following, mirroring–matching, unison–opposites can be explored. Additionally, relationships can define the body parts of a single performer, such as arms together–apart or symmetrical–asymmetrical.

TEACHING MOVEMENT SKILLS AND CONCEPTS

Four steps are suggested for creating lessons that teach movement skills and concepts incorporating the problem-solving style. The problem-solving style is effective because it allows for multiple solutions to problems and encourages creativity among students. The following steps include many specific ideas for developing the problem and increasing the diversity of responses.

Step One: Set and Define the Problem

Define a problem for students so they know what to solve. The problem should include one or more of the following:

1. *What to do.* An action word directs the activity. Are children to move a certain way, go over and under, explore alternatives, or experiment with some non-locomotor movement? Direct them to run, jump, or use a fundamental skill.

2. *Where to move.* What space is to be used—personal or general? What directional factors are to be employed—path or level?

3. *How to move.* What are the force factors (light–heavy)? What elements of time are involved (even–uneven, acceleration–deceleration, sudden–sustained)? What are the relationships (over–under–across, in front of–behind)? What body parts are involved for support? For locomotion?

4. *With whom or what to move.* With whom are children to work—by themselves, with a partner, or as a member of a group? Is there a choice involved? With what equipment or on what apparatus are they to perform?

When initiating movement patterns, the following partial sentences can be used to frame the problem. There are unlimited problems that can be developed for students to solve.

DEVELOP A PROBLEM TO SOLVE

1. Show me how a . . . moves. (Show me how an alligator moves.)

2. Have you seen a . . . ? (Have you seen a kangaroo jump?)

3. What ways can you . . . ? (What ways can you hop over the jump rope?)

4. How would you . . . ? How can you . . . ? (How would you dribble a ball, changing hands frequently?)

5. See how many different ways you can . . . . (See how many different ways you can hang from a ladder.)

6. What can you do with a . . . ? What kinds of things can you . . . ? (What can you do with a hoop?)

7. Can you portray a . . . ? (Can you portray an automobile with a flat tire?)

8. Discover different ways you can . . . . (Discover different ways you can volley a ball against a wall.)

9. Can you . . . ? (Can you keep one foot up while you bounce the ball?)

10. Who can . . . a . . . in such a way that . . . ? (Who can bounce a ball in such a way that it keeps time with the tom-tom?)

11. What does a . . . ? (What does a cat do when it is wet?)

12. Show . . . different ways to . . . . (Show four different ways to move across the floor.)

Step Two: Experiment and Explore

After the problem has been defined, encourage youngsters to solve the problem through experimentation and exploration. Variety can also be achieved by setting limitations and by asking youngsters to solve the problem in a different manner. Present problems in the form of questions or statements that elicit and encourage variety, depth, and extent of movement. Using contrasting terms is another way to increase the depth and variety of movement. A number of examples follow.

PHRASES THAT ENCOURAGE EXPLORATION AND VARIETY

1. Try it again another way. Try to . . . . (Try to jump higher.)

2. See how far (many times, high, close, low) . . . . (See how far you can reach with your arms.)

3. Find a way to . . . or find a new way to . . . . (Find a new way to jump over the bench.)

4. Apply . . . to . . . . (Apply a heavy movement to your run.)

5. How else can you . . . ? (How else can you roll your hoop?)

15

6. Make up a sequence . . . . (Make up a sequence of previous movements, changing smoothly from one movement to the next.)

7. Now try to combine a . . . with . . . . (Now try to combine a locomotor movement with your catching.)

8. Alternate . . . and . . . . (Alternate walking and hopping.)

9. Repeat the last movement and add . . . . (Repeat the last movement and add a body twist as you move.)

10. See if you can . . . . (See if you can do the movement with a partner.)

11. Trace (draw) a . . . with . . . . (Trace a circle with your hopping partner.)

12. Find another part of the body to . . . . Find other ways to . . . . (Find another part of the body to take the weight.)

13. Combine the . . . with . . . . (Combine the hopping with a body movement.)

14. In how many different positions can you . . . ? (In how many different positions can you carry your arms while walking the balance beam?)

15. How do you think the . . . would change if . . . ? (How do you think the balance exercise we are doing would change if our eyes were closed?)

16. On signal, ... (On signal, speed up your movements.)

CONTRASTING TERMS TO STIMULATE VARIETY

Another way to increase the variety of movement responses is to employ terms that stress contrasts. Contrasting terms provide a way to stimulate variety of movement. Instead of challenging children to move quickly, ask them to contrast a quick movement with a slow movement. The following list includes many common sets of contrasting terms that express relationships between movements or descriptions of ways to move.

- Above–below, beneath, under
- Across–around, under
- Around clockwise–around counterclockwise
- Before–after
- Between–alongside of
- Big–little, small
- Close–far
- Crooked–straight
- Curved–flat, straight
- Diagonal–straight
- Fast–slow
- Forward–back, backward
- Front–back, behind
- Graceful–awkward
- Heavy–light
- High–low
- In–out
- In front of–behind, in back of
- Inside–outside
- Into–out of
- Large–small
- Near–far
- On–off
- On top of–under, underneath
- Over–under, through
- Reach down–reach up
- Right–left
- Round–straight
- Separate–together
- Short–long, tall
- Sideways–forward, backward
- Smooth–rough
- Standing upright–inverted
- Sudden–sustained
- Swift–slow
- Tight–loose
- Tiny–big, large
- Top–bottom
- To the right of–to the left of
- Up–down
- Upper–lower
- Upside down–right side up
- Upward–downward
- Wide–narrow, thin
- Zigzag–straight

Some of the terms may be grouped more logically in sets of three contrasts (such as forward–sideways–backward, up–down–in between, or over–under– through). Word meanings also can be emphasized according to rank or degree (as in near–nearer–nearest, or low–lower–lowest).

Step Three: Observe and Discuss Various Solutions

In this step, allow youngsters to observe some of the patterns that others have created. Achievement demonstrations stimulate effort because children enjoy showing what they have put together. Focus discussions on how to put together different movements into flow and continuity. Also, this can be a time to discuss that there are many ways to solve problems. Justifying and explaining solutions can help other students understand how to solve future problems.

Step Four: Refine and Expand Solutions to the Problem

The final step involves integrating various ideas students have observed and expanding their ideas. This step encourages integration of ideas and thoughts into new solutions. Students can work together to develop cooperative partner and small-group skills. Make problems realistic and allow opportunity for discussion and decision making between partners. The following are examples of activities that can be cooperatively developed:

1. One child is an obstacle, and the partner devises ways of moving around the position the "obstacle" takes (Figure 15.2). Additional challenge can be added by having one partner hold a piece of equipment such as a wand or hoop to expand movements.

2. One partner partially supports the weight of the other, or the two work together to form different kinds of figures or shapes.

3. One child does a movement, and the other copies or provides a contrasting movement.

4. One child moves, and the other attempts to shadow (do the same movements). Do it slowly with uninterrupted flow predominating.

5. One partner does a movement. The other person repeats the movement and adds another. The first child repeats both movements and adds a third, and so on. Some limit on the number of movements can be set.

FIGURE 15.2 Going around a partner.

6. Children form letters or figures with their bodies on the floor or in erect positions.

7. Children practice copying activities. One child sets a movement pattern and the rest copy the actions.

MOVEMENT SKILLS AND CONCEPTS LESSON PLANS

The accompanying text, *Dynamic Physical Education: Lesson Plans for Implementation,* 15th ed. (Pangrazi, 2007), contains lesson plans for teaching movement skills and concepts. Each of the lesson plans contains four or five parts that present a variety of experiences in movement concepts and skills. This variety of activities offers children a broad spectrum of challenges and ensures a balance of experiences. Each movement lesson plan contains the following sections:

1. *Movement themes.* Two or more themes are developed to focus on teaching the concepts of movements. Locomotor and nonlocomotor movements are used as the medium for developing a movement vocabulary. Movement themes focus on a movement quality around which children build patterns and sequences. Exploration is emphasized so children develop body awareness and an understanding of movement concepts.

2. *Fundamental skills.* This section presents a wide variety of experiences of fundamental skills. Locomotor skills covered include walking, running, galloping, skipping, sliding, leaping, hopping, and jumping. Nonlocomotor skills covered are bending, rocking, swinging, turning, twisting, stretching, pushing, and pulling. Emphasis is placed on developing proper technique and using the skill in novel situations.

3. *Manipulative skills.* Manipulative skills are presented in each lesson using a variety of equipment. Skills practiced include throwing, kicking, striking, catching, bowling, and rolling.

TEACHING MOVEMENT THEMES

Movement themes are used to apply movement concepts and help students learn by moving. Movement themes focus on a movement concept that children use to create movement patterns and sequences. The purposes are to explore and experiment with the concept through movement. Some themes involve only a single principle or factor, while others involve two or more. Themes in this chapter focus on exploring different concepts of movement, but in actuality, isolating a particular factor is difficult. For example, in exploring balance, movement possibilities are expanded through the application

15

of body shape, level, and time factors. The following themes are classified into four major groups or concepts of human movement: body awareness, space awareness, qualities of movement, and relationships.

Body Awareness Themes

▶ **BODY SHAPES (FIGURE 15.3)**

"Let's try making shapes and see whether we can name them. Make any shape you wish and hold it. What is the name of your shape, John? [Wide.] Try to make different kinds of wide shapes. Show me other shapes you can make. What is the name of your shape, Susie? [Crooked.] Show me different kinds of shapes that are crooked. Make yourself as crooked as possible."

"Make yourself wide and then narrow. Now tall and then small. How about tall and wide, small and narrow, tall and narrow, and small and wide? Work out other combinations."

"Select three different kinds of shapes and move smoothly from one to another. This time I will clap my hands as a signal to change to a different shape."

"Select four different letters of the alphabet. On the floor, make your body shape successively like these letters. Try with numbers. Make up a movement sequence that spells a word of three letters. Show us a problem in addition or subtraction."

"Use your jump rope and make a shape on the floor. Make a shape with your body alongside the rope."

"Pretend to be as narrow as an arrow or telephone pole. Pretend to be as wide as a house, store, or hippopotamus."

"Squeeze into a tiny shape; now grow slowly into the biggest shape you can imagine. Travel to a different spot on the floor, maintaining the big shape. Quickly assume the tiny shape again."

"Move around the room in groups of three. On signal, form a shape with one standing, one kneeling, and one sitting."

"Pretend you are at a farm. Make a barn with your body."

"Jump upward, making a shape in the air. Land, holding that shape. Begin with a shape, jump upward with a half turn, and land in another shape."

"What body shapes can you assume standing on one foot?"

"Show me what body shapes can be made with your stomach in contact with the floor."

"Look to see where your personal space is in relation to general space. When I say 'Go,' run in general space. On the next signal, return to your space and sit down."

▶ **BALANCING: SUPPORTING BODY WEIGHT (FIGURE 15.4)**

"Explore different ways you can balance on different surfaces of your body. Can you balance on three different parts of your body? On two? On one? Put together sequences of three or four balance positions by using different body parts or different numbers of body parts."

"Can you balance on a flat body surface? What is the smallest part of the body you can balance on? Support the body on two dissimilar parts. On three dissimilar parts. Support the body on different combinations of body flats and body points."

"Use two parts of the body far away from each other to balance. Shift smoothly to another two parts."

"Who can balance on one foot with the arms stretched overhead? Out to the side?"

"Stand with feet together and eyes closed. Maintain balance while using different arm positions. Balance on one foot for ten counts."

"From a standing position, raise one leg, straighten the leg in front of you, swing the leg to side and back without losing your balance."

"Move from a narrow, unstable base to a wide, stable base."

"Balance on parts of the body forming a tripod." (Explain the term.)

FIGURE 15.3   Forming different shapes.

FIGURE 15.4   Balancing on different body parts.

"Show different balance positions with part of the weight supported by the head."

"In a hands-and-knees position, and later in a crab position, balance on the right arm and right leg, the left arm and left leg, the right arm and left leg, the left arm and right leg."

"Stand on your toes and balance, using different arm positions."

"Place a beanbag on the floor. How many different ways can you balance over it? Try with a hoop. How many different ways can you balance inside the hoop?"

"When I call out a body part or parts, you balance for five seconds on that part or part combination." (Use knees, hands, heels, flats, points, and a variety of combinations.)

"Keep your feet together and sway in different directions without losing your balance. Can you balance on one foot with your eyes closed? Bend forward while balancing on one foot? Lift both sets of toes from the floor and balance on your heels? Now sit on the floor. Can you lift your feet and balance on your seat without hand support? Can you balance on your tummy without your feet or hands touching the floor?"

"In a standing position, thrust one leg out sideways and balance on the other foot."

"Make a sequence by balancing on a narrow surface, change to a wide surface, and back again to a different narrow surface."

▶ BRIDGES (FIGURE 15.5)

"Show me a bridge made by using your hands and feet. What other kinds of bridges can you make? Can you make a bridge using only three body parts? Only two?"

"Show me a wide bridge. A narrow one. A short bridge. A long one. How about a high bridge? A low one? Can you make a bridge that opens when a boat goes through? Get a partner to be the boat and you be the bridge. If you are the boat, choose three ways of traveling under a bridge. Each time the boat goes under the bridge, change the bridge to another means of support."

"As I touch you, go under a bridge and make another bridge."

FIGURE 15.5   Making bridges.

"Show how you would make London Bridge fall down."

"With a partner, alternate going under a high bridge and going over a low bridge."

"Can you move one end of the bridge, keeping the other end still?"

"Make a bridge with one side of the body held upward. Change to the other side."

"Show me a twisted bridge. A curved bridge."

"Be an inchworm and start with a long, low bridge. Walk the feet to the hands. Walk the hands forward while the feet are fixed."

"Make a bridge with three points of contact."

"Show me a bridge at a high level. At a low level. In between."

"Work up a sequence of bridge positions, going smoothly from one to the next."

▶ FLIGHT

"Show me three different ways you can go through space. Try again, using different levels. Lead with different parts of your body."

"See how high you can go as you move through space. What helps you get height?"

"Practice various combinations for takeoff and landing. See if you can work out five different possibilities for taking off and landing, using one or both feet." (Possibilities are same to same [hop]; one foot to the opposite [leap]; one-foot takeoff, two-foot landing; two-foot takeoff, two-foot landing [jump]; two-foot takeoff, one-foot landing.)

"Run and jump or leap through the air with your legs bent. With your legs straight. With one leg bent and the other straight. Try it with your legs spread wide. With your whole body wide. With your whole body long and thin through the air."

"Project yourself upward beginning with the feet together and landing with the feet apart. Run, take off, and land in a forward stride position. Repeat, landing with the other foot forward."

"With a partner, find ways to jump over the partner as he or she changes shape."

"Using your arms to help you, run and project yourself as high as possible. Practice landing with bent knees."

▶ MOVING WITH THE WEIGHT SUPPORTED ON THE HANDS AND FEET (FIGURE 15.6)

"Pick a spot away from your personal space and travel to and from that spot on your hands and feet. Try moving with your hands close to your feet. Far away from your feet. Show me bilateral, unilateral, and cross-lateral movements. Build up a sequence."

FIGURE 15.6 Taking the weight on hands and feet.

"Move from your personal space for eight counts. Do a jump turn (180 degrees) and return to your space using a different movement."

"Lie on your stomach. Move using only your hands."

"Experiment with different hand–foot positions. Begin with a narrow shape and with hands and feet as close together as possible. Extend your hands from head to toe until they are as far apart as possible. Extend the hands and feet as wide as possible and move. Now try with the hands wide and the feet together. Reverse."

"Practice traveling so that both hands and feet are off the ground at the same time. Go forward, backward, sideways."

"With your body straight and supported on the hands and feet [push-up position], turn the body over smoothly and face the ceiling. The body should remain straight throughout. Turn to the right and left. Recover to your original position."

"What kinds of animal movements can you imitate? Move with springing types of jumps. What shapes can you assume while you move?"

▶ RECEIVING AND TRANSFERRING WEIGHT

"Support the weight on two different body parts and then transfer the weight smoothly to another pair of parts. Add another pair of unlike parts if you can."

"Take a deep breath, let the air out, relax, and drop to the floor, transferring the weight from a standing position to a position on the floor. Can you reverse the process?"

"Show in walking how the weight transfers from the heel to the ball of the foot with a push-off from the toes. In a standing position, transfer the weight from the toes, to the outside of the foot, to the heel, and back to the toes. Reverse the order."

"Using three different parts, transfer weight from one to another in a sequence."

"Travel with a jump or a leap and then lower yourself gently to your back after landing. Repeat, only lower yourself smoothly to your seat."

"From a standing position, bend forward slowly and transfer the weight partially to both hands. Lift one foot into the air. Return it to the ground gently. Repeat with the other foot. Lift a hand and a foot at the same time and return them smoothly."

"Lower yourself in a controlled manner to take the weight on your tummy. Can you turn over and take the weight on your seat with your hands and feet touching the floor?"

"Move from a supine position (on your back) to a standing position without using your arms."

"Select a shape. See if you can lower yourself to the ground and return to your original position, retaining the shape."

"Try some jump turns, quarter and half. What is needed to maintain stability as you land?"

"Project yourself into the air and practice receiving your weight in different ways. Try landing without any noise. What do you have to do? See how high you can jump and still land lightly."

"See how many different ways you can transfer weight smoothly from one part of your body to another. Work up a sequence of three or four movements and go smoothly from one to another, returning to your original position."

▶ STRETCHING AND CURLING

"In your own space, stretch out and curl. What different ways can you find to do this? Let's go slowly from a stretch to a curl and back to a stretch in a smooth, controlled movement. Curl your upper body and stretch your lower body. Now curl your lower body and stretch your upper body. Work out a smooth sequence between the two combinations."

"Show different curled and stretched positions on body points and on body flats. Go from a curled position on a flat surface to a stretched position supported on body points. Explore how many different ways you can support your body in a curled position."

"Stand in your personal space and stretch your arms at different levels. Lift one leg up and stretch it to the front, side, and back. Repeat with the other leg."

"Stretch with an arm and a leg until it pulls you over."

"In a sitting position, put your legs out in front. Bend your toes forward as far as possible. Bend them backward so that your heels are ahead of your toes. Turn both toes as far as you can inward. Turn them outward."

"Lie on the floor on your back. Stretch one leg at a time in different ways in space."

"Stand. Stretch to reach as far as you can with your hand. Try reaching as far as possible with your toe."

"Show how you can travel on different body parts, sometimes stretched, sometimes curled."

"Jump and stretch as high as possible. Now curl and roll on the floor." Repeat several times.

► TAKING THE WEIGHT ON THE HANDS (FIGURE 15.7)

Establishing proper hand positioning for taking the weight on the hands (and later for the headstand) is important.

"Put your hands about shoulder width apart, with fingers spread and pointed forward. With knees bent, alternate lifting the feet silently into the air, one foot at a time. Pick a point ahead of your hands (two feet or so), and watch it with your eyes. Keep from ducking your head between your arms."

"Place both hands on the floor. Kick up like a mule. Can you kick twice before coming down?"

"Take the weight on your hands. Make one foot go past the other while in the air."

"Do as many movements as you can while keeping your hands on the floor."

"See whether you can take the weight on your hands for a brief time. How do you get your body into the air? What different movements can you make with your feet while your weight is on your hands? See how long you can keep your feet off the ground. Repeat, and try to get your hips above your hands. Now add a twist at the waist to return your feet to the floor at a different spot."

"Try again, but shift the weight to one hand and land both feet at a different spot."

"Begin in a standing position and try to keep your feet over your head for as long as possible. Begin with the arms and hands stretched overhead, and repeat. Kick up one leg and then the other."

Space Awareness Themes (Where the Body Moves)

► MOVING IN GENERAL SPACE

Goals in these movement experiences, in addition to developing movement competence, should enhance the ability to (a) share space with other children, (b) move through space without bumping anyone, and (c) develop consideration for the safety of others.

"Run lightly in the area, changing direction without bumping or touching anyone until I call 'Stop.' Raise your hand if you were able to do this without bumping into anyone."

"Let's try running zigzag fashion in the area without touching anyone. This time, when I blow the whistle, change direction abruptly and change the type of movement."

"Run lightly in general space and pretend you are dodging someone. Can you run toward another runner and change direction to dodge?"

FIGURE 15.7 Taking the weight on the hands.

"Get a beanbag and drop it to mark your personal space. See how lightly, while under control, you can run throughout the area. When the signal is given, run to your spot, pick up your beanbag, put it on your head, and sit down [or give some other challenge]. Try this skipping."

"We are going to practice orienteering. [Explain the term.] Point to a spot on the wall, and see whether you can run directly to it in a straight line. You may have to stop and wait for others to pass so as not to bump into anyone, but you cannot change direction. Stay in a straight line. When you get to your spot, pick another spot, and repeat."

"What happens when general space is decreased? You had no problem running without touching anyone in the large space. Now let's divide the area in half with cones. Run lightly within this area so as not to touch or bump anyone. Now it's going to get more difficult. I'm going to divide the space in half once more, but first let's try walking in the new area. Now, run lightly." (Decrease the area as feasible.)

"Get a beanbag and mark your personal space. Run around the beanbag until you hear a 'Bang,' and then explode in a straight direction until I call 'Stop.' Return to your personal space."

"From your beanbag, take five [or more] jumps [hops, skips, gallops, slides] and stop. Turn to face home, and return with the same number of movements. Take the longest steps you can away from home, and then return home with tiny steps."

"Show me how well you can move with these combinations in general space: run-jump-roll, skip-spin-collapse. Now you devise a series of any three movements and practice them."

"Today our magic number is five. Can you move in any direction with five repetitions of a movement? Change direction and pick another movement to do five times. Continue."

"Blow yourself up like a soap bubble. Can you huff and puff? Think of yourself as a big bubble that is floating around. When I touch you, the bubble breaks, and you collapse to the ground. This time, blow up your bubble and float around. When you are ready, say, 'Pop,' so the bubble bursts."

"I am going to challenge you on right and left movements. Show me how you can change to the correct direction when I say either 'Right' or 'Left.' Now begin running lightly."

"This time, see whether you can run rapidly toward another child, stop, and bow to each other. Instead of bowing, shake hands, and say, 'How do you do!'"

"From your personal space, pick a spot on a wall. See whether you can run to the spot, touch it, and return without bumping anyone. This time, it's more difficult. Pick spots on two different walls, touch these in turn, and return."

EXPLORING PERSONAL SPACE

Personal space is space that can be reached from a fixed base. Youngsters can take this personal space with them when they are moving in general space. A graphic way to illustrate personal space is to have youngsters take an individual jump rope and double it. From a kneeling position, they swing it in a full arc along the floor. It should not touch another child or rope.

"Show us how big your space is. Keeping one foot in place, outline how much space you can occupy. Sit cross-legged and outline your space. Support your weight on different parts of your body and outline your space."

"Make yourself as wide [narrow, small, large, low, high] as possible. Try these from different positions—kneeling, balancing on the seat, and others. Show us what kinds of body positions you can assume while you stand on one foot. While you lie on your stomach. On your seat. Try the same with one foot and one hand touching the floor."

"Stand tall in your space. To the beat of a drum, move in increments to a squat position. Reverse."

"Move from a lying position to a standing position without using your arms or hands. Return to lying."

"Can you stay in one place and move your whole self but not your feet? Sway back and forth with your feet together and then with your feet apart. Which is better?"

"Sitting in your personal space, bend your toes forward; now backward. Bend your feet so that the heels move ahead of your toes."

"In a supine position (on your back) move your arms and legs from one position slowly and then move them back quickly to where you started. Explore other positions."

"Keeping one part of your body in place, make as big a circle as you can with the rest of your body."

"Explore different positions while you keep one leg [foot] higher than the rest of your body. Work out a smooth sequence of three different positions."

"Pump yourself up like a balloon, getting bigger and bigger. Hold until I say, 'Bang!'"

"In your personal space, show me how a top spins. Keep your feet together in place. With your arms wide to the sides, twist and make your feet turn."

▶ CIRCLES AND THE BODY (FIGURE 15.8)

"Can you form full circles with your hands and arms at different joints—wrist, elbow, and shoulder? Now what circle can you make with your legs and feet? Try this lying on your back. Use other body joints to make circles."

"Travel in general space by skipping [running, hopping, sliding]. Stop on signal and make moving, horizontal [vertical, inclined] circles with an arm. Repeat, but on signal lie down immediately on your back and make the specified circle with one foot."

"Show how a swimmer makes circles with the arms when doing the backstroke. Alternate arms and also move them together. Reverse the arm direction to make the crawl stroke. Make vertical circles with one arm and both arms across the body."

"Make a circle with one hand on your tummy and pat yourself on the top of the head with the other hand at the same time. Reverse hands."

"Keep one foot fixed and make a circle with the other foot by turning completely around."

"Select a partner. Match the arm circles the partner makes."

"Can you keep two different circles going at the same time? Make a circle turning one way, and another circle turning the other way. Repeat, using twisting actions of the body parts making the circles."

F I G U R E 1 5 . 8   Forming circles.

▶ PLANES OF MOVEMENT

"Show me a variety of movements in a horizontal plane. In a vertical plane. In a diagonal plane. Put together combinations so that you go in sequence from one type of movement to another."

"Here is a challenge. When I call out a plane of movement, respond with one that is correct. Ready?" (Specify the plane of movement.)

"Using a jump rope doubled in one hand, make circles in the different planes. Try the same with a hula hoop."

"Crouch at a low level, spin upward toward the ceiling, then back to the floor. Spin in the other direction."

▶ LEVELS

"Choose one way of traveling at a high level and another at a low level. Again, move at a high level and stop at a low level. Move at a low level and stop at a high level. Choose one way of traveling at a medium level and add this somewhere in your sequence—beginning, middle, or end."

"Select three different kinds of traveling movement with the arms at a high, medium, and low level. Link these movements together in a smooth sequence."

"Travel around the room raising your arms as high as possible. Travel on your tiptoes. Repeat with your arms as low as possible."

"Run at different levels. Run as high as you can. Run as low as possible. Run at a medium level."

"When I clap my hands, change direction and level."

"Move on all fours with your body at a high level, a medium level, and then as low as possible. Try these movements with your face turned to the ceiling."

"Use a jump rope or a line or board in the floor as your path to follow. Begin at the far end. Show me a slow, low-level movement down and back. What other ways can you go down and back slowly and at a low level? Change to a fast, high-level movement. On what other levels can you move?"

"Combine a low, fast movement down with a high, slow movement on the way back. Explore other combinations. Make different movements by leading with different parts of your body."

▶ MOVING IN DIFFERENT WAYS

"Discover different ways you can make progress along the floor without using your hands and feet. See whether you can walk with your seat. Let your heels help you."

"What ways can you move sideways or backward? What rolling movements can you make? Look carefully before you move to make sure you have a clear space."

"Use large movements and travel through general space. Make your body into a straight line and move in straight lines, changing direction abruptly. With your body in a curved shape, move in a curved pathway."

"Each time you change direction, alternate a straight body and a straight path with a curved body shape and a curved path."

"Find ways of moving close to the floor with your legs stretched. Now move with your legs bent, keeping at a low level."

"As you travel forward, move up and down. As you travel backward, sway from side to side."

"Travel, keeping high in the air. Change direction and travel at a low level. Continue to alternate."

"Counting the four limbs [two arms, two legs], travel first on all four, then on three, next on an arm and a leg, and then on one leg. Now reverse the order."

"With your hands fixed on the floor, move your feet in different ways. Cover as much space as possible. With your feet fixed, move your hands around in different ways as far away from the body as you can. Move around general space the way a skater does. The way a person on a pogo stick does. Choose other ways. Change body direction as you move, but keep facing in the original direction."

Qualities of Movement Themes (How the Body Moves)

▶ TIME (SPEED)

Speed involves the pace of action, which can be slow, fast, or any degree in between. Speed involves acceleration and deceleration; that is, the time factor either can be constant or can speed up or slow down. Time also can be even or uneven.

"With your arms, do a selected movement slowly and then quickly. Move your feet slowly and then as rapidly as you can. Change your support base and repeat."

"In turn, stretch a part of your body slowly and then return it to place quickly, like a rubber band snapping. Stretch the entire body as wide as possible and snap it back to a narrow shape."

"Travel through the area without touching anyone. Speed up when there is an open area and slow down when it is crowded."

"Choose a way of traveling across the floor quickly and then do the same movement slowly. Do a fast movement in one direction and, on signal, change to a slow movement in another direction."

"Select a magic number between 10 and 20. Do that many slow movements and repeat with fast movements of the same count."

15

"Choose a partner. With your partner a little bit away from you, begin moving rapidly toward your partner and decelerate as you draw close. Move away by beginning slowly and accelerate until you return to where you started. Repeat. Select the kinds of movement you wish to use together."

"Staying in your own personal space, begin with some kind of movement and accelerate until you are moving as fast as you can. Reverse by beginning with a fast movement and then slow down until you are barely moving. Put together a sequence of two movements by beginning with one and accelerating, then changing to another movement and decelerating. Try doing two different body movements at the same time—one that accelerates and one that decelerates."

► **CONTRASTING MOVEMENTS**

Contrasting movements have wide and frequent application in the development of other themes. See page 314 for examples of contrasting words.

"Show me a fast movement. Now a slow one. Show me a smooth movement. Now a rough, jerky movement."

"Find three ways to rise from the floor and three ways to sink to the floor. Choose one way to rise and one way to sink. Try to do this three times very smoothly."

"Make yourself as tall as possible. Now, as short as you can."

"Move with a small and delicate skip. Change to a large skip."

"Show me a wide shape. Now, an opposite one. A crooked shape. Now, its opposite. Show me a high-level movement and its contrast. Can you do a balanced movement? What is its opposite?" (Use light–heavy and other contrasts as well.)

"Pick two contrasting movements. When I clap my hands, do one, and change to the other when I clap again. What are the movements you did?"

► **FORCE**

"Show me different kinds of sudden movements. Do a sudden movement and repeat it slowly. Put together a series of sudden movements. Put together a series of sustained movements. Mix sudden and sustained movements."

"Pick a partner and do a quick, strong movement followed by a quick, light movement."

"Take five strong, slow jumps, changing your body for each jump."

"When the drum beat is loud, walk heavily. When the drum beat is soft, walk lightly."

"Reach in different directions with a forceful movement. Crouch down as low as you can and explode upward. Try again, exploding forward. Move as if you were pushing something very heavy. Pretend you are punching a heavy punching bag."

"What kinds of movements can you do that are light movements? Can you make movements light and sustained? Light and sudden? Heavy and sustained? Heavy and sudden? Which is easier? Why?"

"Try making thunder [big noise with hands and feet] and then lightning [same movements without any noise], timing each with five slow counts."

"Can you combine heavy movements in a sequence of sudden and sustained movements? Can you make one part of your body move lightly and another part heavily?"

► **TENSION AND RELAXATION**

"Make yourself as tense as possible. Now slowly relax. Take a deep breath and hold it tight. Expel the air and relax."

"Hug yourself hard! Now, harder. Follow this with the body relaxed. Shake the hands."

"Reach as high as possible with both hands, relax slowly, and drop to the floor. Tense one part of your body and relax another. Slowly shift the tension to the relaxed part, and vice versa."

"Run forward, stop suddenly in a tensed position, and then relax. Run in a tensed manner, change direction, and then run in a relaxed manner."

"Walk forward with tight, jerky movements. Change direction and walk with loose, floppy movements. Pretend that you are a boxer by using short, tense movements. Now move your arms like a floppy rag doll."

Relationship Themes (To Whom and What the Body Relates)

► **MOVING OVER, UNDER, AROUND, AND THROUGH THINGS**

This theme is flexible and can use any available equipment as obstacles to go over, under, around, and through. It can be used effectively in a rotating station system. Equipment can be already arranged, or the children can set it up themselves.

"Using the equipment, explore different ways you can go over, under, around, or through what you have set up. Lead with different parts of the body."

"Three youngsters with jump ropes form a triangle, square, and rectangle, respectively, on the floor. Move in, out, and around the figures."

"Toss your beanbag in the air. When I call out a body part, sit down quickly, and put the beanbag on that part, or on one of the parts named."

SYMMETRICAL AND ASYMMETRICAL MOVEMENTS

Symmetrical movements are identical movements using similar body parts on opposite sides of the body. Asymmetrical movements are different movements using similar body parts on opposite sides of the body. Symmetry increases stability because of the counterbalance effect of the two body halves. Asymmetry, with its weight distributed unequally, leads to quick starts and easier sequential flow due to the unequal weight distribution throughout the body. An example of a symmetrical movement is balancing on a balance beam with both arms to the side. The arms are extended symmetrically to increase stability and balance. An example of an asymmetrical movement is running where the legs are alternately flexed and extended.

"Show me different kinds of symmetrical movements. Now asymmetrical movements. Put together sequences of symmetrical and asymmetrical movements."

"Taking the weight on your hands, show symmetrical and asymmetrical movements of your legs."

"Run and jump high in the air, and place your limbs symmetrically in flight."

"Perform different movements like throwing, skipping, running, long jumping, and leaping and identify whether they are symmetrical or asymmetrical movements."

RELATIVE LOCATION OF BODY PARTS

"We are going to try some special ways of touching. Raise your right hand as high as you can—now down. Raise your left hand as high as you can—now down. Touch your left [or right] shoulder [elbow, knee, hip, ankle] with the right [or left] hand." (Try many combinations.)

"Now, point to a door [window, ceiling, basket] with an elbow [thumb, toe, knee, nose]. Let's see if you can remember right and left. Point your left [or right] elbow to the window." (Try different combinations.)

"When I name a body part, let's see if you can make this the highest part of your body without moving from your place."

"Now, the next task is a little more difficult. Move in a straight line for a short distance and keep the body part named above all the other body parts. What body parts would be difficult to keep above all the others?" (Possibilities are the eyes, both ears, both hips.)

"Touch the highest part of your body with your right hand. Touch the lowest part of your body with your left hand."

"Let's see if you can locate some of the bones in your body. When I name a bone, hold that bone, move and touch a wall, and return to your spot." (These challenges depend on bones that the children can identify. The same procedure can be used to identify selected muscles.)

FIGURE 15.9 Leading with a foot.

"Now move around the room, traveling any way you wish." (The movement can also be limited.) "The signal to stop will be a word describing a body part. Can you stop and immediately put both hands on that part or parts?" (Or, "On 'Stop,' hide the body part.") "You are to move around the room again. When I call out a body part, find a partner and place the body parts together."

"This time, when I call out a body part, you are to move around the room as you wish, while holding with one hand a named body part. When I call out another name, change the type of movement and hold the part with the other hand as you move. Now I will call out two body parts. Have the parts touch each other."

LEADING WITH DIFFERENT PARTS OF THE BODY (FIGURE 15.9)

"As you move between your beanbags [lines, markers], explore ways that different parts of your body can lead movements. Add different means of locomotion. Work at different levels."

"Have a partner make a bridge and you go under, leading with different parts of the body. Can you find five different ways to go under with different body parts leading? Now try finding five ways to go over or around."

"What body parts are difficult to lead with?"

FOR MORE INFORMATION

References and Suggested Readings

Cone, T. P., & Cone, S. (2005). *Teaching children dance.* 2nd ed. Champaign, IL: Human Kinetics.

Gabbard, C. (1994). *Physical education for children: Building the foundation.* 2nd ed. Boston: Allyn and Bacon.

15

Gallahue, D. L. (1995). *Developmental physical education for today's elementary school children.* 3rd ed. New York: McGraw-Hill.

Gilbert, A. G. (1992). *Creative dance for all ages: A conceptual approach.* Reston, VA: AAHPERD.

Graham, G., Holt/Hale, S. A., & Parker, M. (2004). *Children moving,* 6th ed. Boston: McGraw Hill.

Joyce, M. (1994). *First steps in teaching creative dance to children.* 3rd ed. Mountain View, CA: Mayfield.

Laban, R., & Lawrence, F. (1947). *Effort.* London: Union Brothers.

Logsdon, B. J., Barrett, K. R., Ammons, M., Broer, M. R., Halverson, L. E., McGee, R., & Robertson, M. A. (1984). *Physical education for children: A focus on the teaching process.* Philadelphia: Lea & Febiger.

McGreevy-Nichols, S., & Scheff, H. (1995). *Building dances: A guide to putting movements together.* Champaign, IL: Human Kinetics.

Pangrazi, R. P. (2007). *Lesson plans for dynamic physical education.* 15th ed. San Francisco: Benjamin Cummings.

Thompson, M. A. (1993). *Jump for joy!: Over 375 creative movement activities for young children.* Englewood Cliffs, NJ: Prentice Hall.

Weikert, P. S. (1993). *Teaching movement and dance.* 3rd ed. Ypsilanti, MI: High Scope Press.

Websites
Movement Activities for Young Children
www.happalmer.com/articlepg1.htm
www.cfc-efc.ca/docs/cccf/00013_en.htm
www.arepublish.com/BCM.html
http://niusi.edreform.net/subject/movementeducation
www.southernearlychildhood.org/position_arts.html

General Physical Education
www.pelinks4u.org/index.htm
www.pecentral.org
http://reach.ucf.edu/~pezone
http://pe4life.com

16

Fundamental Motor Skills and Introductory Activities

ESSENTIAL COMPONENTS OF QUALITY PROGRAMS

➤ **I. Organized around content standards**

➤ **II. Student-centered and developmentally appropriate**

➤ **III. Physical activity and motor skill development form the core of the program**

IV. Teaches management skills and self-discipline

V. Promotes inclusion of all students

➤ **VI. Focuses on process over product**

VII. Promotes lifetime personal health and wellness

VIII. Teaches cooperation and responsibility and promotes sensitivity to diversity

NATIONAL STANDARDS FOR PHYSICAL EDUCATION*

➤ **1. Demonstrates competency in motor skills and movement patterns needed to perform a variety of physical activities.**

➤ **2. Demonstrates understanding of movement concepts, principles, and tactics as they apply to the learning and performance of physical activities.**

➤ **3. Participates regularly in physical activity.**

4. Achieves and maintains a health-enhancing level of physical fitness.

5. Exhibits responsible personal and social behavior that respects self and others in physical activity.

6. Values physical activity for health, enjoyment, challenge, self-expression, and/or social interaction.

*National Association for Sport and Physical Education (NASPE), 2004.

SUMMARY

This chapter contains two major parts, fundamental skills and introductory activities.

Fundamental skills in this chapter include two major categories: locomotor and nonlocomotor skills. These skills form the foundation for nearly all physical activities students will choose to participate in throughout life. Locomotor skills define the many ways the body can be moved throughout space. Nonlocomotor movements are generally performed without the requirement of movement throughout space; these skills are learned through repetition and refinement with many variations offered to keep students motivated.

The second part of the chapter focuses on introductory activities. The foundation of introductory activities is locomotor movement. These activities are used to start a lesson. They require little instruction and immediately immerse students in large muscle activities. Beginning a lesson with introductory activities will assure students are warmed up and motivated for the rest of the lesson.

OUTCOMES

▪ Understand that teaching fundamental movement is synonymous with providing instruction toward the acquisition of a specific skill.

▪ Describe the differences between locomotor and nonlocomotor skills.

▪ Cite stress points, instructional cues, and suggested movement patterns to enhance the learning of locomotor and nonlocomotor skills.

▪ Specify activities designed to develop locomotor and nonlocomotor motor skills.

▪ Describe the rationale for including introductory activities in the lesson plan.

▪ Characterize various features of the opening phase of the lesson.

- Develop an introductory activity that meets established criteria for preparing children physiologically and psychologically.
- Describe the type of fundamental skills used in introductory activities.

FUNDAMENTAL SKILLS

Fundamental skills are those utilitarian skills that people need for living and being. This group of skills is sometimes labeled *basic* or *functional.* The designation *fundamental skills* is used because the skills are necessary for children to function effectively in the environment. *Fundamental skills* form the foundation of human movement and are usually identified by a single verb, such as walking, twisting, running, jumping, or stretching. (Most of the fundamental skills end in the suffix *-ing.*) Learning physical skills develops in a general to specific manner. This chapter focuses on general motor skills that involve large muscle movements. Fundamental skills are the tools that most adults use to participate in leisure activities. Without a learned set of fundamental skills and a positive feeling about being able to perform in activity settings, many people will relegate themselves to a lifetime of inactivity.

Learning fundamental skills requires practicing the basic locomotor and nonlocomotor skills through an unlimited number of repetitions. Repeating these skills under a wide range of conditions and constantly refining their performance helps assure that the skills will be able to be performed in varying conditions. To help you teach these skills in an efficient manner, important stress points and instructional cues are listed. These are points of emphasis that will help students learn the skills correctly and quickly. The locomotor movement activities also include a section on rhythmic activities since all locomotor movements are rhythmic in nature. The following skills are grouped for ease of teaching and ease of comprehension by students. Although the skills are presented here individually, they are most often performed in a seemingly infinite number of combinations, depending on the sport or activity.

Locomotor Skills

Locomotor skills are used to move the body from one place to another or to project the body upward. They include walking, running, skipping, galloping, leaping, sliding, jumping, and hopping. They form the foundation of gross motor coordination and involve large muscle movement.

Nonlocomotor Skills

Nonlocomotor skills are performed without appreciable movement from place to place. These skills are not as well-defined as locomotor skills. They include bending and stretching, pushing and pulling, twisting and turning, rocking, swaying, and balancing, among others.

LOCOMOTOR SKILLS

In the descriptions that follow, stress points emphasizing correct technique are listed for each of the locomotor skills. Instructional cues listed are short, concise phrases that remind students how to perform activities correctly. Suggested learning activities fall into two categories. The first, suggested movement patterns, consists of movement-oriented sequences that do not require rhythm. The second category, rhythmic activities, consists of sequences that use rhythmic background. A drum or appropriate recorded music is effective for reinforcing and expanding rhythmic possibilities.

Walking

When walking, each foot moves alternately, with one foot always in contact with the ground or floor. The stepping foot is placed on the ground before the other foot is lifted. The weight of the body is transferred from the heel to the ball of the foot and then to the toes for push-off. The toes are pointed straight ahead and the arms swing freely from the shoulders in opposition to the feet. The body is erect, with the eyes focused straight ahead and slightly below eye level. The legs swing smoothly from the hips, with knees bent enough to clear the feet from the ground. Marching is a precise type of walk, accompanied by lifted knees and swinging arms.

Stress Points

1. The toes should be pointed reasonably straight ahead.
2. The arm movement should feel natural. The arms should not swing too far.
3. The head should be kept up and the eyes focused ahead.
4. The stride length should not be excessive. Unnecessary up-and-down motion is to be avoided.

Instructional Cues

1. Head up, eyes forward.
2. Point toes straight ahead.
3. Nice, easy, relaxed arm swing.
4. Walk quietly.
5. Hold tummy in, chest up.
6. Push off from the floor with the toes.

Directives for Suggested Movement Patterns

1. Walk in different directions, changing direction on signal.
2. While walking, bring the knees up and slap with the hands on each step.
3. Walk on the heels, toes, and sides of feet.
4. Gradually lower the body while walking (going downstairs) and raise yourself again slowly (going upstairs).
5. Walk with a smooth, gliding step.
6. Walk with a wide base on the tiptoes, rocking from side to side.
7. Clap the hands alternately in front and behind. Clap the hands under the thighs while walking.
8. Walk slowly, and then increase the speed gradually. Reverse the process.
9. Take long strides. Take tiny steps.
10. On signal, change levels.
11. Walk quickly and quietly. Walk heavily and slowly.
12. Change direction on signal, but keep facing the same way.
13. Walk gaily, angrily, happily. Show other moods.
14. Hold the arms in different positions. Make an arm movement each time you step.
15. Walk in different patterns—circle, square, triangle, figure eight.
16. Walk through heavy mud. On ice or a slick floor. Walk on a rainy day. Walk in heavy snow.
17. Walk like a soldier on parade, a giant, a dwarf, a robot.
18. Duck under trees or railings while walking.
19. Point your toes in different directions—in, forward, and out.
20. Walk with high knees. Stiff knees. One stiff knee. A sore ankle.
21. Walk to a spot, turn in place while stepping, and take off in another direction.
22. Practice changing steps while walking.
23. Walk with a military goose step.
24. Walk and change direction after taking the magic number of steps. (One child picks a magic number.)
25. Tiptoe around the area and through puddles of water.
26. Walk as if you are on a balance beam. Walk across a tightrope.
27. Walk as if you are sneaking up on someone.
28. Walk with funny steps as if you are a clown.
29. Take heel-and-toe steps forward. Without turning around, walk heel-and-toe backwards.

RHYTHMIC ACTIVITIES

When using recorded music, teach youngsters to hear the phrasing in the selection. Have children walk one way during a phrase and then change to another type of walk during the next phrase.

1. Walk forward one phrase (8 counts) and change direction. Continue to change at the end of each phrase.
2. Use high steps during one phrase and low steps during the next.
3. Walk forward for one phrase and sideward during the next. The side step can be a draw step, or it can be of the grapevine type. To do a grapevine step to the left, lead with the left foot, stepping directly to the side. Cross the right foot behind the left, and then in front of the left on the next step with that foot. The pattern is a step left, cross right (behind), step left, cross right (in front), and so on.
4. Find a partner. Face each other and join hands. Pull your partner by walking backward as your partner resists somewhat (8 counts). Reverse roles. Now stand behind your partner and place the palms of your hands on your partner's shoulders. Push your partner by walking forward as your partner resists (8 counts). Reverse roles.
5. Walk slowly, then gradually increase the tempo. Now begin fast and decrease. (Use a drum for this activity.)
6. Walk in various directions while clapping your hands alternately in front and behind. Try clapping the hands under a thigh at each step, or clap the hands above the head in time with the beat.
7. Walk forward four steps, and turn completely around in four steps. Repeat, but turn the other way the next time.
8. While walking, bring the knees up and slap with the hands on each step in time with the beat.
9. On any one phrase, take four fast steps (1 count to each step) and two slow steps (2 counts to each step).
10. Walk on the heels or toes or with a heavy tramp. Change every four or eight beats.
11. Walk with a smooth, gliding step, or walk silently to the beat.
12. Walk to the music, accenting the first beat of each measure. Now sway your body to the first beat of the measure. (Use a waltz with a strong beat.)

16

FIGURE 16.1   Running.

Running

Running (Figure 16.1), in contrast to walking, is moving rapidly so that for a brief moment, both feet are off the ground. Running varies from trotting (a slow run) to sprinting (a fast run for speed). The heels can take some weight in distance running and jogging. Running should be done with a slight body lean. The knees are flexed and lifted while the arms swing back and forth from the shoulders with a bend at the elbows. Additional pointers for sprinting are found in the track, field, and cross-country running unit (Chapter 29).

Stress Points

1. The balls of the feet should be used for sprinting.
2. The faster one desires to run, the higher the knees must be lifted. For fast running, the knees also must be bent more.
3. For distance running, less arm swing is used compared with sprinting for speed. Less body lean is used in distance running, with comfort being the key. The weight is absorbed on the heels and transferred to the toes.

Instructional Cues

1. Run on the balls of the feet when sprinting.
2. Head up, eyes forward.
3. Bend your knees.
4. Relax your upper body.
5. Breathe naturally.
6. Swing the arms forward and backward, not sideways.

Directives for Suggested Movement Patterns

1. Run lightly throughout the area, changing direction as you wish. Avoid bumping anyone. Run zigzag throughout the area.

2. Run and stop on signal. Change direction on signal.
3. Run, turn around with running steps on signal, and continue in a new direction. Alternate turning direction.
4. Pick a spot away from you, run to it, and return without touching or bumping anyone.
5. Run low, gradually increasing the height. Reverse.
6. Run in patterns. Run between and around objects.
7. Run with high knee action. Slap the knees while running.
8. Run with different steps—tiny, long, light, heavy, crisscross, wide, and others.
9. Run with your arms in different positions—circling, overhead, stiff at your sides.
10. Run free, concentrating on good knee lift.
11. Run at different speeds.
12. Touch the ground at times with either hand while running.
13. Run backward, sideways.
14. Run with exaggerated arm movements. Run with a high bounce.
15. Run forward ten steps and backward five steps. Repeat in another direction. (Other tasks can be imposed after the ten steps.)
16. Run forward, then make a jump turn in the air to face in a new direction. Repeat. Be sure to use both right and left turns. Make a full reverse (180-degree) turn.
17. Run the Tortoise and Hare sequence (page 340) and Ponies in the Stable (page 340). These are interesting patterns.
18. Run with knees turned outward. Run high on your toes.
19. Show how quietly you can run. Pretend that you are running through high weeds.
20. Run to a wall and back to place. Run and touch two walls.
21. Run lightly twice around your spot. Then explode (run quickly) to another spot.

RHYTHMIC ACTIVITIES

Many of the suggested movements for walking are equally applicable to running patterns. Some additional suggestions for running include the following.

1. Walk during a phrase of music and then run for an equal length of time.
2. Run in different directions, changing direction on the sound of a heavy beat (or on a signal).

3. Lift the knees as high as possible while running, keeping time to the beat.

4. Do European Rhythmic Running (pages 342–343) to supplement the running patterns described previously.

Hopping

Hopping involves propelling the body up and down on the same foot. The body lean, the other foot, and the arms serve to balance the movement. Hopping can be practiced in place or as a locomotor movement.

Stress Points

1. To increase the height of the hop, the arms must be swung rapidly upward.

2. Hopping should be performed on the ball of the foot.

3. Small hops should be used to start, with a gradual increase in height and distance of the hop.

Instructional Cues

1. Hop with good forward motion.

2. Stay on your toes.

3. Use your arms for balance.

4. Reach for the sky when you hop.

5. Land lightly.

Directives for Suggested Movement Patterns

1. Hop on one foot and then on the other, using numbered sequences such as 1–1, 2–2, 3–3, 4–4, 5–5, 2–1, 1–2, 3–2, 2–3, and so on. The first figure of a series indicates the number of hops on the right foot, and the second specifies the number of hops on the left foot. Combinations should be maintained for 10 to 20 seconds.

2. Hop, increasing height. Reverse.

3. See how much space you can cover in two, three, or four hops.

4. Hop on one foot and do a heel-and-toe pattern with the other. Now change to the other foot. See whether a consistent pattern can be set up.

5. Make a hopping sequence by combining hopping in place with hopping ahead.

6. Hop forward, backward, sideways.

7. Hop in different patterns on the floor.

8. Hop while holding the free foot in different hand positions.

9. Hold the free foot forward or sideward while hopping. Explore other positions.

10. Hop with the body in different positions—with a forward lean, a backward lean, a sideward balance.

11. Hop lightly. Heavily.

12. While hopping, touch the floor with the hands—first one and then both.

13. Hop back and forth over a line, moving down the line as you hop.

14. Trace out numbers or letters by hopping.

15. Turn around while hopping in place.

16. Hop forward and then backward according to a magic number (selected by a student). Repeat in another direction. Now add sideward hopping instead of going backward.

17. Hop softly so that no one can hear you.

RHYTHMIC ACTIVITIES

Combining rhythm with hopping patterns is more difficult than walking, running, or skipping to rhythm because students fatigue rapidly. The suggested patterns combine other locomotor movements with hopping.

1. Walk four steps, hop three times, rest 1 count.

2. Walk four steps, then hop four times as you turn in place. Repeat in a new direction.

3. Hop eight times on one foot (8 counts) and then eight times on the other.

4. Hop forward and backward over a line to the rhythm, changing feet each phrase (8 counts).

5. Combine skipping, sliding, or galloping with hopping.

6. Practice the step-hop to music. (The child takes a step followed by a hop on the same foot. This is a 2-count movement.)

Jumping

Jumping requires taking off with both feet and landing on both feet (Figure 16.2, page 330). The arms move forward with an upswing, and the movement of the body combined with the force of the feet helps lift the weight. A jumper lands lightly on the balls of the feet with the knees bent. Jumping can be done in place or as a locomotor activity to cover ground.

Stress Points

1. The knees and ankles should be bent before takeoff to achieve more force from muscle extension.

2. The landing should be on the balls of the feet, with the knees bent to absorb the impact.

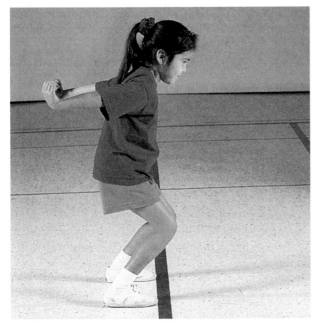

F I G U R E 1 6 . 2   Jumping.

3. The arms should swing forward and upward at takeoff to add momentum to the jump and to gain distance and height.

4. The legs must be bent after takeoff or the feet will touch the ground prematurely.

Instructional Cues

1. Swing your arms forward as fast as possible.
2. Bend your knees.
3. On your toes.
4. Land lightly with bent knees.
5. Jump up and try to touch the ceiling.

Directives for Suggested Movement Patterns

1. Jump up and down, trying for height. Try small and high jumps. Mix in patterns.
2. Choose a spot on the floor. Jump forward over the spot. Now backward and then sideways.
3. Jump with your body stiff and arms held at your sides. Jump like a pogo stick.
4. Practice jump turns in place—quarter, half, three-quarter, and full.
5. Increase and decrease your jumping speed. Increase and decrease the height of the jump.
6. Land with the feet apart and then together. Alternate with one foot forward and one backward.
7. Jump and land quietly. How is this done?

8. Jump, crossing and uncrossing the feet.
9. See how far you can go in two, three, and four consecutive jumps. Run lightly back to place.
10. Pretend that you are a bouncing ball.
11. Clap the hands or slap the thighs while in the air. Try different arm positions.
12. Begin a jump with your hands contacting the floor.
13. Jump in various patterns on the floor.
14. Pretend that you are a basketball center jumping at a jump ball. Jump as high as you can. Jump from a crouched position.
15. Combine a jump for distance with one for height.
16. Jump and click the heels in the air. Can you do two clicks?
17. Jump like a kangaroo. A rabbit. A frog.
18. Combine contrasting jumps: forward and backward. Big and little. Right and left. Light and heavy.
19. Explore different ways a jumping jack can be performed.
20. Jump and clap hands in front. Behind you. Overhead.
21. Give three preliminary swings of arms and then jump forward.
22. Jump. While in the air, touch your heels. Touch both knees. Touch both toes in front.
23. One half of the class is on the floor in selected positions. The other half jumps over those on the floor. Exchange position.

RHYTHMIC ACTIVITIES

Most of the activities suggested for hopping to rhythm are suitable for jumping. Other suggestions follow.

1. Begin jumping slowly to the drumbeat and then accelerate. Begin jumping fast and decelerate to the beat.
2. Toss a ball upward and jump in time to the bounce. (The ball must be a lively one.)
3. Do varieties of the jumping jack. First, move your feet without any arm movement. Now add an arm lift to shoulder height, then lift the arm to a full overhead position. Finally, add body turns and different foot patterns.
4. Take a forward stride position. Change the feet back and forth to the rhythm.

Sliding

Sliding is done to the side. It is a 1-count movement, with the leading foot stepping to the side and the other foot following quickly. Since the same foot always leads, practice the movement in both directions. Sliding is done on the balls of the feet with the weight shifted from the leading foot to the trailing foot. Body bounce during the slide should be minimal.

Stress Points

1. Emphasize the sideways movement. Often, students move forward or backward, which is actually galloping.
2. Both directions should be used, so that each leg has a chance to lead as well as to trail.
3. The slide is a smooth, graceful, and controlled movement.

Instructional Cues

1. Move sideways.
2. Do not bounce.
3. Slide your feet.

Directives for Suggested Movement Patterns

1. Lead in one direction with a definite number of slides, do a half turn in the air, and continue the slide leading with the other leg in the same direction. (A four-plus-four combination is excellent.)
2. Begin with short slides and increase length. Reverse.
3. Slide in a figure-eight pattern.
4. Change levels while sliding. Slide so that the hands can touch the floor with each slide.
5. Slide quietly and smoothly.
6. Pretend to be a basketball defensive player and slide with good basketball position.
7. Slide with a partner.
8. Try sliding individually in a circle.
9. Do three slides and a pause. Change the leading foot and repeat.
10. In circle formation, facing in, the whole class does ten slides one way followed by a pause. Repeat going in the other direction.

RHYTHMIC ACTIVITIES

With appropriate music, many of the above movement patterns can be set to rhythm. Use music phrases to signal a change of direction or to insert another challenge.

Galloping

Galloping is similar to sliding, but progress is in a forward direction. One foot leads and the other is brought rapidly forward to it. There is more upward motion of the body than in sliding. A way to teach the gallop is to have children hold hands and slide in a circle, either to verbal cues or to a drumbeat. Gradually ask the class to face the direction the circle is moving. This takes them naturally from a slide into a gallop. Finally, drop hands and permit free movement in general space.

Stress Points

1. The movement should be smooth and graceful.
2. Each foot should have a chance to lead.

Instructional Cues

1. Keep one foot in front of the other.
2. Now lead with the other foot.
3. Make high gallops.

Directives for Suggested Movement Patterns

1. Do a series of eight gallops with the same foot leading, then change to the other foot. Change after four gallops. Change after two gallops. (Later in the rhythmic program, the gallop is used to teach the polka, so it is important for children to learn to change the leading foot.)
2. Change the size of the gallops.
3. Gallop in a circle with a small group.
4. Pretend to hold reins and use a riding crop.
5. Gallop backward.
6. Gallop like a spirited pony. Like a heavy draft horse.

RHYTHMIC ACTIVITIES

Because galloping is essentially a rhythmic movement, many of the patterns described above should be done to rhythm. Use music phrases to signal a change in the lead foot. Check previous sections on locomotor movements for other rhythmic movement suggestions.

Leaping

Leaping is an elongated step designed to cover distance or move over a low obstacle. It is usually combined with running, since a series of leaps is difficult to maintain alone (Figure 16.3, page 332). The suggested movement patterns use combinations of running and leaping.

Stress Points

1. Height and graceful flight are goals for which to strive.
2. Landing should be light and relaxed.

FIGURE 16.3   Leaping.

Instructional Cues

1. Push off and reach.
2. Up and over, land lightly.
3. Use your arms to help you gain height.

Directives for Suggested Movement Patterns

1. Leap in different directions.
2. See how high you can leap.
3. Leap and land softly.
4. Vary your arm position when you leap. Clap your hands as you leap.
5. Leap with the same arm and leg forward. Try the other way.
6. Show a leap in slow motion.
7. Leap and turn backward.
8. Leap over objects or across a specified space.
9. Practice by playing Leap the Brook (page 550).
10. Leap and move into a balanced position.

RHYTHMIC ACTIVITIES

Because a leap is essentially an explosive movement through space, it is difficult to apply rhythm to the movement. Children must gather themselves in preparation for the leap, which makes the movement non-rhythmic in nature.

Skipping

Skipping is a series of step-hops done with alternate feet. To teach skipping, first teach youngsters to do a step and small hop on the same foot. A step followed by a hop is then performed on the other foot. Skipping is done on the balls of the feet with the arms swinging to shoulder height in opposition with the feet. Another way to teach skipping is to have youngsters hold a large ball (nine inches or more) in front at waist height. A step is taken

with one foot followed by raising the other knee to touch the ball. This stimulates the hop. Repeat with the other foot and the opposite knee.

Stress Points

1. Smoothness and rhythm are goals in skipping. Speed and distance are not.
2. The weight must be transferred from one foot to the other on the hop.
3. The arms swing in opposition to the legs.

Instructional Cues

1. Step-hop.
2. Swing your arms.
3. Skip smoothly.
4. On your toes.

Directives for Suggested Movement Patterns

Many of the suggested movement patterns for walking and running can be applied to skipping, particularly those that refer to changing direction, stopping, making floor patterns, and moving at different speeds.

1. Skip with exaggerated arm action and lifted knees.
2. Skip backward.
3. Clap as you skip.
4. Skip with a side-to-side motion.
5. Skip twice on one side (double skip).
6. Skip as slowly as possible. Skip as fast as possible.
7. Skip so lightly that the movement cannot be heard by your partner.
8. Take as few skips as you can to get to a selected spot.

RHYTHMIC ACTIVITIES

Almost all the combinations suggested for walking and running are useful for skipping movements, and many combinations of skipping, walking, and running can be devised. The piece "Pop Goes the Weasel" is excellent music for skipping. On the "Pop," some movement challenge can be specified.

NONLOCOMOTOR SKILLS

Nonlocomotor skills include bending, twisting, turning (in place), moving toward and away from the center of the body, raising and lowering the parts of the body, and other body movements done in place. Body control, flexibility, balance, and a variety of movements that lead to effective body management are important goals.

FIGURE 16.4 Bending movements.

Bending

Bending is movement at a joint. Teach how the body bends, why it needs to bend, and how bends are combined in various movements (Figure 16.4).

Stress Points

1. Bending as far as possible to increase flexibility and range of movement is a key goal.
2. The bending possibilities of many joints should be explored.
3. Time factors can be introduced in slow and rapid bending.

Instructional Cues

1. Bend as far as possible.
2. Bend one part while holding others steady.

Directives for Suggested Movement Patterns

1. Bend your body down and up.
2. Bend forward and backward, left and right, north and south.
3. Bend as many ways as possible.
4. Bend as many body parts as you can below your waist. Above your waist. Bend with your whole body.

5. Sit down and see whether you can bend differently from the ways you bent in a standing position.
6. Try to bend one body part quickly while you bend another part slowly.
7. Lie down and bend six body parts. Can you bend more than six? Now bend fewer.
8. Make a familiar shape by bending two body parts. Add two more parts.
9. Think of a toy that bends; see whether you can bend in a similar fashion.
10. Find a partner and bend together. Have your partner make big bends while you make tiny bends.
11. Show how you would bend to look funny. To look happy or sad. Bend slowly or quickly.
12. Bend your largest part. Your smallest part.
13. Begin by bending one body part. As you return this part to its original position, bend another part.
14. Bend your fingers. Bend all ten of them.
15. Bend your knees in standing position. In sitting position. In lying position. What other joint must be bent in standing position?

Rocking and Swaying

Rocking occurs when the center of gravity is fluidly transferred from one body part to another. In rocking, the body is in a rounded position where it touches the floor.

The term *swaying* implies a slower movement than rocking and is somewhat more controlled than rocking. The base of support is unchanged in swaying movements.

Stress Points

1. Rocking is done best on a body surface that has been rounded. Arm movements and movements of other body parts can facilitate the rocking motion.
2. Rocking should be done smoothly and in a steady rhythm.
3. Rocking can be started with small movements and increased in extent, or vice versa.
4. Rocking and swaying should be done to the full range of movement.
5. Swaying maintains a stable base.

Instructional Cues

1. Rock smoothly.
2. Rock in different directions. At varying speeds.
3. Rock higher (farther).
4. Sway until you almost lose your balance.

Directives for Suggested Movement Patterns

1. Rock in as many different ways as you can (Figure 16.5).
2. Show how you can rock slowly. Quickly. Smoothly.
3. Sit cross-legged with arms outstretched to the sides, palms facing the floor. Rock from side to side until the hands touch the floor.
4. Lie on your back and rock. Now point your arms and legs toward the ceiling as you rock.
5. Lie on your tummy with arms stretched overhead and rock. Hold your ankles and make giant rocks.
6. Try to rock in a standing position.
7. Rock and twist at the same time.
8. Lie on your back with knees up and rock from side to side.
9. Show me two ways to have a partner rock you.
10. From a standing position, sway back and forth. Right and left. Experiment with different foot positions. Sway slowly and rapidly. What effect does rapid swaying have?
11. Repeat swaying movements from a kneeling position.
12. Start with a small rocking motion and make it progressively bigger.
13. Choose three (or more) ways of rocking and see if you can change smoothly from one to the next.
14. Rock like a cradle. A rocking horse.
15. Sway like a tree in a heavy wind.

F I G U R E 1 6 . 5   Rocking variations.

Swinging

Swinging involves the movement of body parts in a motion that resembles a swinging rope or pendulum of a clock. Most swinging movements are confined to the arms and legs.

Stress Points

1. Swinging should be a smooth, rhythmic action.
2. The body parts involved in swinging should be relaxed and loose.
3. The extent of the swing movement should be the same on both sides of the swing.
4. Swinging movements should be as full as possible.

Instructional Cues

1. Loosen up; swing easy.
2. Swing fully; make a full movement.
3. Swing in rhythm.

Directives for Suggested Movement Patterns

1. Explore different ways to swing your arms and legs.
2. Work out swinging patterns with the arms. Combine them with a step pattern, forward and back.
3. Swing the arms back and forth, and go into full circles at times.
4. With a partner, work out different swinging movements (Figure 16.6). Add circles.
5. Develop swinging patterns and combinations. Form sequences with swinging and full-circle movements. (This activity is best done to waltz music with a slow or moderate tempo.)
6. Swing like a clock pendulum. A cow's tail.

Turning

Turning is rotation around the long axis of the body. The terms *turning* and *twisting* are sometimes used interchangeably to designate the movements of body parts. However, turning refers to movements of the body as a whole. Most turns are initiated by a twist. In the movement experiences suggested here, action involves movement of the entire body. Movements of body parts are discussed in the Twisting section.

Stress Points

1. Maintaining balance and body control is important.
2. Turning should be tried in both directions, right and left.
3. Turns in standing position can be made by jumping, hopping, or shuffling with the feet.

FIGURE 16.6   Partner swinging.

4. Most turns are made in increments or multiples of quarter turns. Multiples should be practiced.
5. Turns should be practiced in body positions other than standing—seated, on the tummy or the back, and so on.

Instructional Cues

1. Keep your balance.
2. In jump turns, land in a relaxed way with the knees relaxed.
3. Be precise in your movement, whether it is a quarter, half, or full turn.

Directives for Suggested Movement Patterns

1. In standing position, turn your body to the left and right, clockwise and counterclockwise.
2. Turn to face north, east, south, and west. (Post directions on the wall.)
3. Stand on one foot and turn around slowly. Now turn around quickly. Now turn with a series of small hops. Try to keep good balance.
4. Show me how you can cross your legs with a turn and sit down. Can you get up again in one movement?

5. Every time you hear the signal, see whether you can turn around once, moving slowly. Can you turn two, three, or four times slowly on signal?

6. Lie on your tummy on the floor and turn your body slowly in an arc. Turn over so that you are on your back. Turn back to your tummy again.

7. Find a friend and see how many different ways you can turn each other. Take turns.

8. Play Follow the Leader with your friend. You make a turn and your partner follows.

9. Begin with a short run, jump into the air, and turn to land facing in a new direction. Practice both right and left turns. Can you make a full reverse (180-degree) turn?

10. Lying on your back, turn and rest on your side. Return. Repeat on the other side.

11. Lying on your back, turn so that you are resting on your stomach. Return. Turn over the opposite way.

12. Find a partner and see how many ways you can rotate each other.

13. Walk in general space and turn completely around on signal.

14. With your hands outstretched to the sides, pretend you are a helicopter.

Twisting

Twisting is the rotation of a selected body part around its own long axis (Figure 16.7). The joints of different body parts can be used for twisting: spine, neck, shoulders, hips, ankles, and wrists. *Twisting* involves movement around the body part itself whereas *turning* focuses on the space in which the entire body turns.

Stress Points

1. Twisting should be extended as far as possible with good control.

2. The body parts on which the twist is based should be stabilized.

3. A twist in one direction should be countered by a reverse twist.

4. Some joints are better for twisting than others. (Explain why this is so.)

Instructional Cues

1. Twist far (fully).

2. Twist the other way.

3. Hold the supporting parts firm.

F I G U R E   1 6 . 7   Twisting movements.

Directives for Suggested Movement Patterns

1. Glue your feet to the floor. Can you twist your body to the left and to the right? Can you twist your body slowly? Quickly? Can you bend and twist at the same time? How far can you turn your hands back and forth?

2. Twist two or more parts of your body at the same time.

3. Twist one body part in one direction and another in the opposite direction.

4. Try twisting the lower half of your body without twisting the upper half.

5. See what parts you can twist while sitting on the floor.

6. Try to twist one body part around another part. Is it possible to twist together even more parts?

7. Balance on one foot and twist your body. Can you bend and twist at the same time?

8. Show me some different shapes that you can make by twisting your body.

9. Try to twist like a spring. Like a cord on a telephone.

10. Try to move and twist at the same time.

11. With the weight on your feet, twist as far as you can in one direction. Now take the weight on your hands and move your feet.

12. Twist like a pretzel. Like a licorice stick.

13. Twist like you are hitting a home run with a baseball bat.

14. Twist like you are hitting a golf ball.

Stretching

Stretching is a movement that moves body parts away from the body center. Stretching sometimes involves moving a joint through the range of movement. Stretching is necessary for maintaining and increasing flexibility.

Stress Points

1. Stretching should be extended to the full range of movement.
2. Stretching exploration should involve many body parts.
3. Stretching should be done in many positions.
4. Stretching can be combined with opposite movements, such as curling.
5. Stretching is done slowly and smoothly.
6. Hold full stretching position for ten seconds.

Instructional Cues

1. Stretch as far as possible. Make it hurt a little.
2. Find other ways to stretch the body part (joint).
3. Keep it smooth. Do not jerk.

Directives for Suggested Movement Patterns

1. Stretch as many body parts as you can.
2. Stretch your arms, legs, and feet in as many different directions as possible.
3. Try to stretch a body part quickly. Slowly. Smoothly.
4. Bend a body part and say which muscle or muscles are being stretched.
5. See how many ways you can stretch while sitting on the floor.
6. Lie on the floor and see whether you can stretch two, three, four, or five body parts at once.
7. Try to stretch one body part quickly while you stretch another part slowly.
8. From a kneeling position, see whether you can stretch to a mark on the floor without losing your balance.
9. Stretch your right arm while you curl your left arm.
10. Find a friend and show how many ways you can help each other stretch.
11. Try to stretch and become as tall as a giraffe. (Name other animals.)
12. Stretch and make a wide bridge. Find a partner to go under, around, and over your bridge.
13. Bend at the waist and touch your toes with your fingers. See whether you can keep your legs straight while you are stretching to touch the toes.
14. Combine stretching with curling. With bending.
15. Stretch the muscles in your chest, back, tummy, ankles, wrists, and fingers.
16. Make a shape with your body. Now stretch the shape so that it is larger.
17. As you move at a low level, curl and stretch your fingers.
18. Find a position in which you can stretch one side of the body.
19. Find a position in which you can stretch both legs far apart in the air. Now make the legs as narrow as possible.
20. Stretch like a rubber band. When I say "Snap!" move the part quickly back to original position.

Pushing

Pushing is a controlled and forceful action performed against an object to move the body away from the object or to move the object in a desired direction by applying force to it (Figure 16.8).

Stress Points

1. A forward stride position should be used to broaden the base of support.
2. The body's center of gravity should be lowered.
3. The line of force is directed toward the object.
4. The back is kept in reasonable alignment, and the body forces gathered for a forceful push. Do not bend the waist.
5. The push should be controlled and steady.

FIGURE 16.8 Pushing.

Instructional Cues

1. Broaden your foot base.
2. Use all your body forces.
3. Push steadily and evenly.
4. Lower yourself for a better push.

Directives for Suggested Movement Patterns

1. Stand near a wall and push it from an erect position, then push with the knees bent and one foot behind the other. In which position can you push with more force?
2. Push an imaginary object that is very light. Now imagine that you are pushing a heavy object.
3. Try to push a partner who is sitting on a jumping box, then try to push a partner who is sitting on a scooter. What changes must you make in your body position?
4. Push an object with your feet without using your arms or hands.
5. Sit down and push a heavy object with your feet. Can you put your back against the object and push it?
6. See how many different ways you can find to push the object.
7. Find a friend and try to push each other over a line in turn.
8. Sit back to back with your partner and see whether you can push each other backward in turn.
9. See if it is possible to lie on the floor and push.
10. Lie on the floor and push your body forward, backward, and sideward.
11. Lie on the floor and push yourself with one foot and one arm.
12. Put a beanbag on the floor and push it with your elbow, shoulder, nose, or other body part.
13. Move in crab position and push a beanbag.
14. Show how you can push a ball to a friend.

Pulling

Pulling is a controlled and forceful action that moves an object closer to the body or the body closer to an object. If the body moves and an object is being pulled, pulling causes the object to follow the body.

Stress Points

1. For forceful pulling, the base of support must be broadened and the body's center of gravity must be lowered.

2. The vertical axis of the body should provide a line of force away from the object.
3. Pulling should be a controlled movement with a minimum of jerking and tugging.
4. The hand grips must be comfortable if pulling is to be efficient. Gloves or other padding can help.
5. Pulling movements can be isolated in the body, with one part of the body pulling against the other.

Instructional Cues

1. Get your body in line with the pull. Lower yourself.
2. Widen your base of support.
3. Gather your body forces and pull steadily.

Directives for Suggested Movement Patterns

1. Reach for the ceiling and pull an imaginary object toward you quickly. Slowly and smoothly.
2. Use an individual tug-of-war rope and practice pulling against a partner. Do this with your hands and arms at different levels.
3. From a kneeling position, pull an object.
4. Try to pull with your feet while you sit on the floor.
5. Pretend to pull a heavy object while you are lying on the floor.
6. Clasp your hands together and pull as hard as you can.
7. Try pulling an object while you stand on one foot.
8. Hold hands with a partner, and pull slowly as hard as you can.
9. Have your partner sit down, and then see how slowly you can pull each other. Take turns.
10. With your partner sitting on the floor, see whether you can pull each other to your feet. Take turns.
11. Pull with different body parts.
12. Pull your partner by the feet as your partner sits on a rug square.
13. Reach for the stars with both hands and pull one back to you.
14. Balance on one foot. Try to pull something. What happens?

Pushing and Pulling Combinations

Combinations of pulling and pushing movements should be arranged in sequence. Musical phrases can signal changes from one movement to the other. Balance-beam benches are excellent for practicing pulling and pushing techniques. Partner tug-of-war ropes provide effective pulling experiences. Partner resistance exercises (pages 279–281) are also useful pulling and pushing experiences.

Fleeing, Chasing, and Tagging

Many physical education games involve fleeing, chasing, and tagging. Speed and reaction are essential for dodging by the person being chased and the response of the chaser to the movements of the target child.

Stress Points

1. Run under control.
2. The fleeing child should be in a moderate crouch position with the feet wider than usual. This position enables moving laterally in either direction quickly.
3. The fleeing child should become adept at faking, which means making a preliminary movement in one direction before determining the final path to take.
4. All runners should move on the balls of their feet.
5. The chaser should maneuver the fleeing youngster into a confined area to facilitate tagging.
6. Eyes should be focused on the center of the dodger's body to negate the effectiveness of the fake.
7. The tag should be made between the knees and shoulders in a gentle but firm manner.

Instructional Cues (Chaser)

1. Run under control.
2. Move on the balls of the feet and maintain a slightly crouched position when approaching the dodger.
3. Focus on the waistline of the dodger.
4. Tag gently but firmly.

Directives for Suggested Movement Patterns

1. Run in general space with the stipulation to run toward other classmates and dodge at the last moment. Avoid contact. To vary the activity, change direction on signal.
2. In general space, run and stop on signal.
3. In partners, have one person run and the other shadow (follow closely). The runner should change direction often. Change roles.
4. Move into squads, with the leader ten yards away from and facing the rest of the squad column. All members of the squad take turns running and dodging around a passive captain. Replace the squad captain regularly.
5. Partners mark a small area (12 by 12 feet) with cones. Chase and dodge within this area. Try with two chasers and one dodger.

INTRODUCTORY ACTIVITIES

Introductory activities represent the first activity youngsters experience when entering the activity area. Such activities incorporate vigorous fundamental motor skills and require minimal instruction. Introductory activities are used during the first two or three minutes of the lesson. They are used to warm children up physiologically and to prepare them for the physical activity that follows. It is a truism in teaching that a lesson that starts well, ends well. Introductory activities allow an opportunity for practicing management skills and focusing on the objectives of the lesson.

Regardless of the introductory activity used, it is most important to be sure a class begins in a well-managed and attentive manner. An excellent "rule of three freezes" can be used to check the disposition of a class and to get children ready for instruction. Have the class enter the teaching area on the move and then freeze on signal. Move the youngsters a second time and privately correct off-task behavior (while students are on the move). Freeze the class two more times to correct off-task behavior and to see if students are ready to learn. If the class is still not with you after three corrective episodes, don't teach an introductory activity; rather focus on a management activity such as moving and freezing on signal. Introductory activities, by their nature, are upbeat and active. They will overly arouse a poorly managed class. Use the highly active and enjoyable activities to reinforce a class that exhibits well-managed behavior.

Introductory activities are used for a number of reasons:

1. To offer youngsters immediate activity when entering the gym. This satisfies their desire to move and offers you an opportunity to establish a positive learning attitude (purposive movement performed under control) for the class.
2. To warm children up physiologically and prepare them for the activity to follow.
3. To focus youngsters on the objectives of the lesson. Focus students on learning objectives by telling them the "what and why" of activities in the upcoming lesson.

16

Perform introductory activities at a slow pace in the initial stages for safety reasons and to warm up students. For example, if using Rhythmic Running as an introductory activity, begin by walking. As the class warms up, pick up the pace to a run. If using Curl and Around (see page 345), begin by asking students to moderately move around each other. After a short period of warming up, perform the activity at full speed.

Introductory Activities Using Locomotor Movements

The movements should involve the body as a whole and provide abrupt change from one movement pattern to another. A routine can begin with running and then change to another movement pattern that is either specified by the teacher or determined by youngsters. Signals for change can be supplied with a voice command, whistle, drumbeat, or handclap. Children enjoy being challenged by having to change with the signal. Each part of a routine should be continued long enough for good body challenge and involvement, but not so long that it becomes wearisome.

Running provides much of the basis for gross movement activities, but other activities of a vigorous nature can be used. The suggested activities are classified roughly according to type and whether they are individual, partner, or group oriented.

▶ FREE RUNNING

Students run in any direction, changing direction at will.

▶ RUNNING AND CHANGING DIRECTION

Children run in any direction, changing direction on signal. As a progression, specify the type of angle (right, obtuse, 45-degree, or 180-degree). Alternate right and left turns.

▶ RUNNING AND CHANGING LEVEL

Children run high on their toes and change to a lower level on signal. Require runners to touch the floor sometimes when at the lower level.

▶ RUNNING AND CHANGING THE TYPE OF LOCOMOTION

On signal, runners change from running to free choice or to a specified type of locomotion (such as walking, jumping, hopping, skipping, sliding, or galloping).

▶ RUNNING AND STOPPING

Students run in various directions and, on signal, freeze. Stress stopping techniques and an immobilized position.

▶ MOVE AND PERFORM ATHLETIC MOVEMENTS

Students move and stop on signal. They then perform an athletic skill move, such as a basketball jump shot, leaping football pass catch, volleyball spike, or soccer kick. Students should place emphasis on correct form and timing. A variation of the activity is for students to move with a partner and throw a pass on signal, punt a ball, or shoot a basket. The partner catches the ball or rebounds the shot.

▶ RUN AND ASSUME A POSE

Pupils run and, on signal, assume a statue pose. Allow choice or specify a limitation.

▶ TORTOISE AND HARE

When the teacher calls out "Tortoise," the children run slowly in general space. On the command "Hare," they change to a rapid, circular run. During the latter, stress good knee lift.

▶ PONIES IN THE STABLE

Each child has a stable, his or her spot or place on the floor. This can be marked with a beanbag or a hoop. On the initial signal, children gallop lightly (like ponies) in general space. The next signal tells them to trot lightly to their stable and to continue trotting lightly in place.

▶ HIGH FIVES

Students move in different directions throughout the area. On signal, they are challenged to run toward a partner, jump, and give a "high five" (slap hands) while moving. Emphasis should be placed on timing so that the "high five" is given at the top of the jump. Combinations of changing the level as well as changing the speed of the movement can be developed.

▶ MOVE AND PERFORM A TASK ON SIGNAL

Youngsters move and perform a task on signal. During a signaled stop, a number of fitness challenges can be performed. Another variation is to perform individual or partner activities. Examples are Seat Circles, Balances, Wring the Dishrag, Partner Hopping, Twister, and Back-to-Back Get-Up (see Chapter 20).

RUN, STOP, AND PIVOT

Students run, stop, and then pivot. This is an excellent activity for game skill development. Youngsters enjoy it especially when they are told to imagine that they are basketball or football players.

TRIPLE S ROUTINE

The triple S's are *speed, style,* and *stop.* Children are in scatter formation throughout the area. On the command "Speed," they run in general space rapidly while avoiding contact with others. On "Style," all run with style (easy, light, loose running) in a large, circular, counterclockwise path. On the command "Stop," all freeze quickly under control. Repeat as necessary.

AGILITY RUN

Pick two lines or markers five to ten yards apart. Students run (or use other locomotor movements) back and forth between the lines for a specified time (10, 15, or 20 seconds). Students can add a personal challenge by seeing how many times they can move back and forth within the given time limit.

MOVING ON TWOS AND FOURS

Youngsters begin with a movement in upright position and change to one on all fours.

SECRET MOVEMENT

The teacher has written a number of movements on cards and selects one. Direction is given by saying, "I want you to show me the secret movement." Students select a movement and continue that movement without change until they are signaled to stop, whereupon the teacher identifies those who performed the movement on the card. The movement is then demonstrated by those who chanced upon it, and all perform it together. If no one comes up with the movement pattern on the card, repeat the activity by asking the children to change their responses.

AIRPLANES

The class pretends to be airplanes. When told to take off, they zoom with arms out, swooping, turning, and gliding (Figure 16.9). When they are commanded to land, they drop to the floor in prone position, simulating a plane at rest. To start their engines and take off, they can perform a series of push-ups and move up and down while simulating engine noise.

COMBINATION MOVEMENTS

Directives for combination movements can establish specified movements or allow some choice. The limitation might be to run, skip, and roll, or to jump, twist, and shake. Another approach is to set a number for the

FIGURE 16.9 *Performing airplanes.*

sequence and let the children select the activities. Say, "Put three different kinds of movement together in a smooth pattern."

COUNTDOWN

The teacher and class begin a countdown to blastoff: "Ten, nine, eight, seven, six, five, four, three, two, one—blastoff!" The children are scattered, and each makes an abrupt, jerky movement on each count. On the word blastoff, they jump up in the air and run in different directions until the stop signal is given.

MAGIC-NUMBER CHALLENGES

A challenge can be issued like this: "Ten, ten, and ten." Children then put together three movements, doing ten repetitions of each. Or the teacher could say, "Today we are going to play our version of Twenty-One." Twenty-one becomes the magic number that is to be fulfilled with three movements, each of which is done seven times.

CROSSING THE RIVER

A river can be set up as the space between two parallel lines about 40 feet apart, or it can be the crosswise area in a gymnasium. Each time the children cross the river, they use a different type of locomotor movement. Children should be encouraged not to repeat a movement. Play is continuous over a minute or so.

FOUR-CORNERS MOVEMENT

Lay out a square with a cone at each corner. As the student passes each corner, he or she changes to a different locomotor movement with an agility emphasis. Challenge students with some of the following sport agility movements: backward running, leaps, grapevine step, front crossover, back crossover, high knees, and slide steps. Add variation by changing the qualities of movement (i.e., soft, heavy, slow, fast, etc.). Students can pass to the outside of the area if they are doing a faster-moving movement.

JUMPING AND HOPPING PATTERNS

Each child has a home spot. The teacher provides jumping and hopping sequences to take children away from and back to their spot. The teacher could say, "Move with three jumps, two hops, and a half turn. Return to place the same way." The teacher should have on hand a number of sequences. Action can extend beyond simply jumping and hopping.

LEADING WITH BODY PARTS

Students move throughout the area with some body part leading. Try using various body parts, such as elbow, fingers, head, shoulder, knees, and toes. Try the same exercise with different body parts trailing. Try moving and leading with two different body parts. Try with three. Try also with combinations of body parts trailing the body. Children can jog with some body part leading or trailing. On signal, tell them to make a different body part lead or trail the body.

MOVE, ROCK, AND ROLL

Each youngster procures an individual mat and places it on the floor. Students are challenged to move around, over, and on the mats. When a signal is given, children move to a mat and try different ways of rocking and rolling. Rocking on different parts of the body can be specified, and different body rolls can be suggested. As another challenge, tell the children to do a rock or a roll or both on a mat, get up and run to another mat, and repeat the sequence. Older children enjoy seeing how many mats they can move to within a certain amount of time.

Rhythmic Introductory Activities

EUROPEAN RHYTHMIC RUNNING

Rhythmic Running is used in many European countries to open the daily lesson. The European style is light, rhythmic running to the accompaniment of some type of percussion, usually a drum or tambourine. Skilled runners do not need accompaniment but merely keep time with a leader. Much of the running follows a circular path (Figure 16.10), but it can be done in scatter formation. To introduce a group of children to Rhythmic Running, have them clap to the beat of the drum. Next, as they clap, have them shuffle their feet in place, keeping time. Following this, have them run in place, omitting the clapping. Finally, the class can run in single-file formation, if desired. The running should be light, bouncy, and rhythmic in time with the beat. When running in single file, youngsters should stay behind the person in front, maintain proper spacing, and lift the knees in a light, prancing step.

A number of movement ideas can be combined with the rhythmic running pattern.

1. On signal (a whistle or a double beat on the drum), runners freeze in place. They resume running when the regular beat begins again.
2. On signal, runners make a full turn in four running steps, lifting the knees high while turning.

FIGURE 16.10   European running.

3. Children clap hands every fourth beat as they run. Instead of clapping, runners sound a brisk "Hey!" on the fourth beat, raising one arm with a fist at the same time.

4. Children run in squad formation, following the path set by the squad leader.

5. On signal, children run in general space, exercising care not to bump into each other. They return to a circular running formation on the next signal.

6. Students alternate between running with high knee action and regular running.

7. Runners change to a light, soundless run and back to a heavier run. The tone of the drum can control the quality of the movement.

8. Students use Rhythmic Running while handling a parachute.

9. On the command "Center," children run four steps toward the center, turn around (four steps), and run outward four steps to resume the original circular running pattern.

10. On signal, runners go backward, changing the direction of the circle.

11. Students carry a beanbag or a ball. Every fourth step, they toss the item up and catch it while running.

12. A leader moves the class through various formations. A task that is enjoyable and challenging is crossing lines of children while they alternate one child from one line in front of one youngster from another line.

13. The class moves into various shapes on signal. Possible shapes might be a square, rectangle, triangle, or pentagon. The Rhythmic Running must be continued while the youngsters move into position.

14. When a signal is given, each class member changes position with another student and then resumes the activity. An example might be to change position with the student opposite in the circle.

15. Because the movement is rhythmic, students can practice certain skills, such as a full turn. The turn can be done to a four-count rhythm and should be more deliberate than a quick turning movement that lacks definition.

16. When the drum stops, children scatter and run in random fashion. When the beat resumes, they return to circular formation and proper rhythm.

▶ MUSICAL RELAXATION

Musical relaxation can be conducted with a drum or appropriate recorded music. Children run in time to the rhythm. When the rhythm stops, each child reclines on the back, closes the eyes, and remains relaxed until the music begins again.

▶ MOVING TO RHYTHM

The possibilities with rhythm are many. Rhythm can guide locomotor movements, with changes in tempo being part of the activity. The intensity of the sound can be translated into light or heavy movements.

▶ MOVING TO MUSIC

Pieces such as the Bleking song (pages 431–432) and Pop Goes the Weasel (pages 436–437) can provide a basis for creative movement. These are two-part pieces, so a nonlocomotor movement can be done to the first part and a locomotor movement to the second.

▶ FOLK DANCE MOVEMENT

Use a CD or tape recording to stimulate different types of rhythmic movement such as polka, schottische, and two-step. Youngsters can move around the room practicing the steps dictated by the music.

Introductory Activities with Equipment

▶ INDIVIDUAL ROPE JUMPING

Each child runs with rope in hand. On the signal to change, the child stops and begins to jump rope.

▶ HOOP ACTIVITIES

Each child runs holding a hoop. When the signal is given to stop, the child either does hula-hooping or lays the hoop on the floor and uses it for hopping and jumping patterns.

16

▶ **WAND ACTIVITIES**

Movements similar to those done with jump ropes and hoops can be performed with wands. After they run and stop, the children do wand stunts.

▶ **MILK CARTON FUN**

Each child has a milk carton stuffed with crumpled newspapers and secured with cellophane tape. The children kick the cartons in different directions for 1 minute.

▶ **BALL ACTIVITIES**

Youngsters dribble balls as in basketball or (outside) as in soccer. When a change is signaled, they stop, balance on one leg, and pass the ball under the other leg, around the back, and overhead, keeping both control and balance. Other challenges can be supplied that involve both movement with the ball and manipulative actions performed in place.

▶ **BEANBAG TOUCH AND GO**

Beanbags are spread throughout the area. On signal, youngsters move and touch as many different beanbags as possible with their hands. Different body parts can be specified for children to use for touching. Different colors of beanbags can be selected, and the command might be "Touch as many blue beanbags as possible with your elbow."

Children can also move to and around a beanbag. The type of movement can be varied; for example, they might skip around the yellow beanbags with the left side leading. Change the movement as well as the direction and leading side of the body. Another enjoyable activity for youngsters is to trace out a shape (e.g., triangle, circle, square) as they move from beanbag to beanbag.

> ***Variation:*** *Vanishing Beanbags.* Students move around the beanbags as described above. While they are moving, the teacher or a designated student picks up one or two of the bags. On signal, students move to a beanbag and sit on it. The goal is not to be left out. The activity is repeated with all students participating each time.

▶ **LONG-ROPE ROUTINE**

Students begin in a loose column composed of four people holding a long jump rope in their right hands at waist level. A series of four signals is given. On the first signal, youngsters jog lightly in a column. On the second signal, the group shifts the rope overhead from the right side to the left side of the body while jogging. At the third signal, the two inside students release the rope and begin jumping as soon as the two students at the end of the rope start turning the rope. On the fourth signal, the turners become jumpers and vice versa. The sequence is repeated a number of times.

▶ **DISAPPEARING HOOPS**

Each child gets a hoop and places it somewhere on the floor. Offer challenges such as "Move through five blue hoops, jump over four yellow hoops, and skip around six green hoops." On signal, the children move to find a hoop and balance inside it. As youngsters are moving, take away two or three hoops. At the signal, some students will not find a hoop. Those left out then offer the class the next movement challenge. Different challenges and stunts inside the hoops can be specified.

Partner and Small Group Introductory Activities

▶ **MARKING**

Each child has a partner who is somewhat equal in ability. Under control, one partner runs, dodges, and tries to lose the other, who must stay within three feet of the runner.

On signal, both stop. Chasers must be able to touch their partners to say that they have marked them. Partners then change roles.

▶ **FOLLOWING ACTIVITY**

One partner leads and performs various kinds of movements. The other partner must move in the same fashion. This idea can be extended to squad organization.

▶ **FASTEST TAG IN THE WEST**

Every player is a tagger. The object is to tag other players without being tagged. Players who are tagged must sit or kneel and await the next game. (Start new games frequently.) If two or more players tag each other simultaneously, they are both (all) "out."

▶ **MEDIC TAG**

Three or four students are designated as "taggers." They try to tag other students; when tagged, a student kneels as if injured. Another student (not one of the taggers) can "rehabilitate" the injured player with a touch, enabling the student to resume play.

HOSPITAL TAG

Every player is a tagger. Any player who is tagged must cover with one hand the body area that was touched. Students may be tagged twice but must be able to hold both tagged spots and keep moving. A student who is tagged three times must freeze. Restart the game when most of the students have been frozen.

CURL AND AROUND

Half of the children are scattered. Each is in a curled position, face down. The other half of the class moves around the curled children (Figure 16.11). On signal, reverse the groups quickly. Instead of being curled, challenge the youngsters to form arches or bridges, with the moving children going around them. A further extension is to have the children on the floor alternate between curled and bridge positions. If a moving child goes around the curled position, the floor child changes immediately to a bridge. Another challenge is to ask the moving half of the class to move backward and sideways using different locomotor movements.

LIVING OBSTACLES

This activity is similar to Group Over and Around except that the youngsters on the floor are in a bridged position and moving. The children moving over and around must move quickly, as the obstacles are moving. Change positions after a designated amount of time.

POPCORN

Half the class is scattered throughout the area and assumes the push-up position. The other half of the class will move and "pop the popcorn." This is done by moving over and around the students who are in push-up

FIGURE 16.11 Curl and around.

position. When a student moves around a student, that youngster lowers to the floor. When a student moves over a student lying on the floor, that student raises to the push-up position. Moving students should exchange places with those on the floor after a designated time.

PYRAMID POWER

Students move throughout the area. On signal, they find a partner and build a simple pyramid or partner stand. Examples are the hip-shoulder stand, double-crab stand, double-dog stand, and shoulder stand. Students should be cautioned to select a partner of similar size and to stand on the proper points of support.

BRIDGES BY THREES

Three children in a group can set up an interesting movement sequence using bridges. Two of the children make bridges, and the third child goes under both bridges and sets up a bridge. Each child in turn goes under the bridges of the other two. Different kinds of bridges can be specified, and the bridges can be arranged so that a change in direction is made. An over-and-under sequence also provides interest. The child vaults or jumps over the first bridge and then goes under the next bridge before setting up the third bridge.

RUBBER BAND

Students gather around the teacher in the center of the area. On signal, students move away from the teacher with a designated movement such as run, hop sideways, skip backward, double-lame dog, or grapevine step. On signal, they sprint back to the central point, jump, and give a shout.

NEW LEADER MOVEMENTS

Squads or small groups run around the area, following a leader. When the change is signaled, the last person goes to the head of the line to lead. Groups of three are ideal for this activity.

MANIPULATIVE ACTIVITIES

Each child has a beanbag. The children move around the area, tossing the bags upward and catching them as they move. On signal, they drop the bags to the floor and jump, hop, or leap over as many bags as possible. On the next signal, they pick up any convenient bag and resume tossing to themselves. Having one fewer beanbag than children adds to the fun. Hoops can also be used in this manner. Children begin by using hoops in rope-jumping style or for hula-hooping. On signal, the hoops are placed on the floor, and the children jump in and out of as many hoops as they can. Next, they pick up a nearby hoop and resume the original movement pattern. The activity also can be done with jump ropes.

▶ BODY PART IDENTIFICATION

Enough beanbags for the whole class are scattered on the floor. The children either run between or jump over the beanbags. When a body part is called out, the children place that body part on the nearest beanbag.

▶ DRILL SERGEANT

The drill sergeant leads the squad marching and in line. When desired, the drill sergeant gives these kinds of commands for the movement sequence to be performed: "Walk, jump twice, land, and roll." "Run, jump-turn, and freeze (pose)." "Shake, jump-turn, land, and roll." "Seal Walk, Log Roll, and jump." The squad leader can be given cards with suggested patterns written on them. To add a realistic flavor, the sergeant can call the squad members to attention, give them the directions, and then call, "March!"

Creative Introductory Activities

Another approach of interest to children is providing creative and exploratory opportunities at the beginning of a lesson. Some examples follow.

1. Put out a variety of equipment (hoops, balls, wands, beanbags) so that all children have a piece of equipment with which to explore. This can be open exploration, or the movement can follow the trend of a prior lesson, thus supplying extension to the progression.

2. Have available a number of manipulative items. The children select any item they wish and decide whether to play alone, with a partner, or as a member of a small group.

3. Make available a range of apparatus, such as climbing ropes, climbing apparatus, mats, boxes, balance beams, balance boards, and similar items. Manipulative items also can be a part of the package. The children choose the area in which they want to participate.

Tambourine-Directed Activities

The tambourine can signal changes of movement, because it can produce two different kinds of sound: the tinny noise made by vigorous shaking and the percussive sound made by striking the instrument. Movement changes are signaled by changing from one sound to the other.

▶ SHAKING SOUND

1. The children remain in one spot but shake all over. These should be gross movements.
2. The children shake and gradually drop to the floor.
3. The children scurry in every direction.
4. The children run lightly with tiny steps.

▶ DRUM SOUND

1. Students make jerky movements to the percussive beat.
2. They jump in place or through space.
3. Youngsters do locomotor movements in keeping with the beat.
4. Responding to three beats, the children collapse on the first beat, roll on the second, and form a shape on the third.

▶ COMBINATIONS

To form a combination of movements, select one from each category (shaking or percussive). When the shaking sound is made, the children perform that movement. When the sound is changed to the drum sound, the children react accordingly.

GAMES AND MISCELLANEOUS ACTIVITIES

Selected games are quite suitable for introductory activities, provided that they keep all children active, are simple, and require little teaching. Usually, a familiar game is used so that little organizational time is needed. Some appropriate games are:

- Addition Tag (page 557)
- Back to Back Tag (page 556)
- Barker's Hoopla (page 569)
- Circle Touch (page 570)
- Couple Tag (page 561)
- Loose Caboose (page 564)
- One, Two, Button My Shoe (page 552)
- Squad Tag (page 566)
- Touchdown (page 576)
- Whistle Mixer (page 568)
- European Rhythmic Running (pages 342–343)
- Airplanes (page 341)
- Curl and Around (page 345)

FOR MORE INFORMATION

References and Suggested Readings

Gabbard, C. P. (2004). *Lifelong motor development.* 4th ed. San Francisco, CA: Benjamin Cummings.

Gallahue, D. L., & Donnelly, F. C. (2003). *Developmental physical education for all children.* 4th ed. Champaign, IL: Human Kinetics.

Gallahue, D. L., & Ozmun, J. C. (2002). *Understanding motor development: Infants, children, adolescents, adults.* 5th ed. Dubuque, IA: McGraw-Hill.

Haubenstricker, J. L., & Seefeldt, V. D. (1986). *Acquisition of motor skills during childhood.* In V. D. Seefeldt (Ed.), *Physical activity and well-being.* Reston, VA: AAHPERD.

Haywood, K. H. (2005). *Lifespan motor development.* 4th ed. Champaign, IL: Human Kinetics.

Magill, R.A. (2004). *Motor learning: Concepts and applications.* 7th ed. Boston, MA: McGraw-Hill.

Payne, G. V., & Isaacs, L. D. (2005). *Human motor development: A lifespan approach.* 6th ed. Boston, MA: McGraw-Hill.

Wickstrom, R. L. (1983). *Fundamental movement patterns.* Philadelphia: Lea & Febiger.

Websites

General Physical Education
www.pelinks4u.org/index.htm
www.pecentral.org
http://reach.ucf.edu/~pezone
http://pe4life.com

Fundamental Motor Skills
www.ptsd.k12.pa.us/motor_skills.htm
www.learning.gov.ab.ca/physicaleducationonline
http://rubistar.4teachers.org/index.php

16

C H A P T E R

17

Manipulative Skills

SUMMARY

Activities in this chapter develop manipulative skills. A manipulative skill is one in which a child handles an object with the hands, feet, or other body parts. Development of sport skills results from repeating and refining activities in this chapter. Jump rope activities develop specialized motor skills, particularly visual-tactile coordination. Rope-jumping activities in this chapter progress from individual movements using rope patterns, to long-rope jumping with turners, to individual rope-jumping challenges. Rhythmic gymnastic activities combine rhythmic and manipulative skills using a particular piece of manipulative equipment while moving to accompaniment.

OUTCOMES

■ Demonstrate the various stages of development associated with throwing, catching, kicking, and striking.

■ Identify instructional procedures related to different types of manipulative skills.

■ Identify objects that can be used to help youngsters succeed in manipulative skills.

■ Outline skill progressions, activities, and instructional hints associated with using balloons, beanbags, balls, paddles, Frisbees, hoops, jump ropes, parachutes, and other objects to teach manipulative skills.

■ Identify beginning, intermediate, and advanced rope-jumping skills and routines using individual and long ropes.

■ List progressions to use when teaching rope-jumping.

Manipulative skills are characterized by the use of some type of implement, often with the hands but also with the feet or other body parts. Manipulative activities develop both hand-eye and foot-eye coordination as well as dexterity. Many different pieces of equipment are used to focus on the development of manipulative activities in different settings. Equipment such as balloons, hoops, wands, beanbags, balls of various types, tug-of-war ropes, Lummi sticks,

Frisbees, and scoops gives youngsters the opportunity to learn skills in many different settings. Activities with jump ropes are important in the program because they offer numerous possibilities for practicing multiple skills such as manipulative skills, rhythmic skills, and locomotor movements.

Balloons, beanbags, and yarn balls are used to teach throwing and catching activities for younger children. A soft and slow moving object reduces the fear younger children have of being hurt while catching an object. Start children with a challenge that allows all to achieve success, and then expand the skills and experiences from that base. Concern for progression usually dictates that most activities begin with individual practice and then move later to partner activity.

MANIPULATIVE SKILLS

Manipulative skills are basic to a number of specialized sport skills—catching, throwing, striking, and kicking, among others. These are complex motor patterns and general stages of development have been identified, from initial stages through mature patterns of performance. Most complex skills should be practiced at near-normal speed. Whereas locomotor skills can be dramatically slowed down to promote learning, doing so with complex skills such as throwing, striking, or kicking will destroy the rhythm of the skills. This implies that the proper type of equipment and enough space be allowed to help youngsters perform these skills with maximum force. Analysis of the following skills is listed by developmental stages rather than age because of the wide maturity differences among children of similar ages. Major manipulative skills are described here followed by a large number of instructional activities organized by equipment type later in the chapter.

Throwing

In throwing, an object is thrust into space and is accelerated using movement of the arm and the total coordination of the body to generate force. Young children often go through two preliminary tossing stages before entering the stages of throwing. The first toss is a two-handed underhand throw that involves little foot movement. A large ball, such as a beach ball, is best for teaching this type of throw, which begins with the ball held in front of the body at waist level. The toss is completed using only the arms. Youngsters often have difficulty maintaining balance when encouraged to throw the ball for any distance. The second preliminary toss is a one-handed underhand throw. In this toss, which resembles pitching a softball, body torque is generated and weight shifted from the rear to the front foot. This toss

requires a smaller object such as beanbags, fleece balls, and small sponge balls.

The following skill analysis considers overhand throwing only. Teach proper form before concentrating on distance or accuracy. Velocity, not accuracy, is the primary goal when trying to develop mature patterns characterized by a full range of motion and speed. Throwing for accuracy is only practiced after a mature form of the skill is in place.

STAGE ONE

Stage one throwing is generally observed between the ages of two and three years. This stage is basically restricted to arm movement from the rear toward the front of the body. The feet remain stationary and positioned at shoulder width, with little or no trunk rotation occurring (Figure 17.1). Most of the movement force originates from flexing the hip, moving the shoulder forward, and extending the elbow.

STAGE TWO

Stage two throwing develops between the ages of three and five years. Some rotary motion is developed in an attempt to increase the amount of force. This stage is characterized by a lateral fling of the arm, with rotation occurring in the trunk (Figure 17.2). Often, children

FIGURE 17.1 Throwing form, stage one.

FIGURE 17.2   Throwing form, stage two.

FIGURE 17.3   Throwing pattern, stage four.

step in the direction of the throw, although many keep their feet stationary. This throwing style sometimes looks like a discus throw rather than a baseball throw.

STAGE THREE

Typically, stage three is found among children ages five and six years. The starting position is similar to that of stages one and two in that the body is facing the target area, the feet are parallel, and the body erect. In this stage, however, a step is made toward the target with the foot on the same side of the body as the throwing arm. This allows rotation of the body and shifting of the body weight forward as the step occurs. The arm action is nearer to the overhand style of throwing than is the fling of stage two, and there is an increase in hip flexion. Unfortunately, the throwing pattern of many students never matures beyond this stage.

STAGE FOUR

Stage four is a mature form of throwing, and more force is applied to the object being accelerated. The thrower uses the rule of opposition in this stage, taking a step in the direction of the throw with the leg opposite the throwing arm. This develops maximum body torque. The target is addressed with the nonthrowing side of the body and strides toward the target to shift body weight. Beginning with the weight on the back leg, the movement sequence is as follows: (a) step toward the target, (b) rotate the upper body, and (c) throw with the arm (Figure 17.3). The cue phrase used is, "Step, turn, and throw." The elbow should lead the way in the arm movement, followed by forearm extension, and a final snapping of the wrist. This pattern must be practiced many times to develop total body coordination. Through a combination of sound instruction and practice, the majority of youngsters are able to develop a mature pattern of throwing by age eight or nine years.

Stress Points

1. Stand with the nonthrowing side of the body facing the target. The throwing arm side of the body should be away from the target.

2. Step toward the target with the foot opposite the throwing hand.

3. Rotate the hips as the throwing arm moves forward.

4. Bend the arm at the elbow. The elbow should lead the forward movement of the arm.

5. Body weight remains on the rear foot (away from the target) during early phases of the throw. Just prior to the forward motion of the arm, the weight is shifted from the rear foot to the forward foot (nearer the target).

✓ **TEACHING TIPS**

1. Offer a variety of projectiles during throwing practice so that youngsters understand how varying the weight and diameter can regulate throwing distance and speed.

2. When youngsters are learning to throw, they should throw for distance and velocity. Throwing for accuracy will discourage the development of a mature throwing form. Youngsters must be encouraged to "throw as hard as possible." Stress distance and velocity before introducing accuracy.

3. It is ineffective to work on throwing and catching at the same time. If learning to throw is the objective, youngsters will throw inaccurately and with velocity. This makes it difficult for a partner to catch the throw. Throwing should be practiced against a wall (velocity) or on a large field (distance).

4. Carpet squares or circles drawn on the floor can be used to teach youngsters proper foot movement (stepping forward).

5. Beanbags and yarn balls are excellent for developing throwing velocity since they do not rebound throughout the area.

Catching

Catching uses the hands to stop and control a moving object. Catching is more difficult to learn than throwing, because the object must be tracked and the body moved into the path of the object simultaneously. Another factor that makes catching difficult to master is the fear of being hurt by an oncoming object. When teaching the early stages of catching, use objects that cannot hurt the receiver. Balloons, fleece balls, and beach balls move slowly, make tracking easier, and do not hurt if they hit a child in the face.

STAGE ONE

In stage one of catching, hold the arms in front of the body, with elbows extended and palms up, until the ball makes contact. Then bend the arms at the elbows (Figure 17.4). The catch is actually more of a trapping movement, since the arms press the ball against the chest. Children often turn their heads away or close their eyes because of the fear response. Eliminate the fear of being hurt by a hard object and encourage them to watch the object rather than the person throwing the object.

STAGE TWO

In stage two, much of the same behavior from stage one is repeated. Rather than waiting for the ball to contact the arms, however, an anticipatory movement is made and the ball is cradled somewhat.

STAGE THREE

In stage three, the catch is prepared for by lifting the arms and bending them slightly. The chest is used as a backstop for the ball. During this stage, contact is made with the hands first, and then the object is guided to the chest (Figure 17.5).

STAGE FOUR

The fourth and final stage of catching, which occurs at approximately age nine years, is characterized by catching with the hands. Encourage catching with the hands by

FIGURE 17.4 Catching form, stage one.

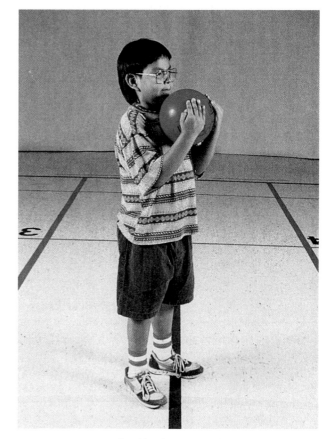

FIGURE 17.5 Catching form, stage three.

decreasing the size of the ball to be caught. Teach giving with the arms (absorbing force) while catching. The legs bend, and the feet are moved in anticipation of the catch.

Stress Points

1. Maintain visual contact with the projectile.

2. Reach for the projectile and absorb its force by bringing the hands into the body. This "giving" makes catching easier by reducing the chance for the object to rebound out of the hands.

3. Place the feet in a stride position rather than a straddle position. A fast-moving object will cause a loss of balance if feet are in the straddle position.

4. Place the body in line with the object rather than reaching to the side of the body to make the catch.

✓ **TEACHING TIPS**

1. Remove the fear factor by using projectiles that will not hurt the youngster. It is a normal reaction to dodge an object when one feels it could cause harm. The use of foam balls, yarn balls, beach balls, and balloons will facilitate learning to "keep your eye on the ball."

2. The size of the projectile should get smaller as youngsters improve their catching skills. Larger objects move more slowly and are easier than smaller projectiles to track visually.

3. Prepare youngsters for a catch by asking them to focus on the ball while it is in the thrower's hand. Use a verbal cue such as "Look (focus), ready (for the throw), catch (toss the ball)."

4. Balls and background colors should strongly contrast to facilitate visual perception.

5. If the trajectory of the projectile is raised, it will offer the youngster more opportunity for successful tracking. Beach balls will move slowly throughout a high trajectory, giving children time to focus and move into the path of the oncoming object.

6. Bounce objects off the floor so that youngsters learn to judge the rebound angle of a projectile.

Kicking

Kicking is a striking action executed with the feet. There are different types of kicking. Punting (in which the ball is dropped from the hands and kicked before it touches the ground) and placekicking (kicking the ball in a stationary position on the ground) are two. A third type is soccer kicking, which is probably the most difficult of all kicking skills because the ball is moving before the kick is executed.

STAGE ONE

In stage one, the body is stationary, and the kicking foot is flexed in preparation for the kick. The kicking motion is carried out with a straight leg and with little or no flexing at the knee. There is minimal movement of the arms and trunk, and concentration is on the ball.

STAGE TWO

In the second stage of kicking, the kicking foot is lifted backward by flexing at the knee. Usually, the child displays opposition of the limbs. When the kicking leg goes forward, the opposite arm moves forward. In stage two, the kicking leg moves farther forward in the follow-through motion compared to stage one.

STAGE THREE

In stage three, movement toward the object to be kicked is added. There is an increase in the distance the leg is moved, coupled with a movement of the upper body to counterbalance the leg movement.

STAGE FOUR

Mature displays of kicking involve a preparatory extension of the hip to increase the range of motion. A run to the ball and a small leap to get the kicking foot in position are made. As the kicking foot is carried forward, the trunk leans backward, and a small step forward is made on the support foot to regain balance (Figure 17.6).

Stress Points

1. Youngsters need to step forward with the nonkicking leg. Stand behind and slightly to the side of the ball. Eyes should be kept on the ball (head down) throughout the kick.

2. Practice kicking with both feet.

FIGURE 17.6 Kicking a soccer ball, stage four.

3. Use objects that will not hurt youngsters. For example, regulation soccer balls hurt young children's feet because they are heavy and hard-covered. Foam balls and beach balls are excellent projectiles that can be used for kicking practice.

4. Encourage kickers to move their leg backward in preparation for the kick. Beginners often fail to move the leg backward, making it difficult for them to generate kicking force.

5. Arms should move in opposition to the legs during the kick.

6. After speed and velocity of the kick have been developed, focus on altering the force of the kick. Many youngsters learn to kick only with velocity; activities like soccer demand both soft "touch" kicks and kicks of maximum velocity.

✓ **TEACHING TIPS**

1. When teaching kicking skills, focus on velocity and distance rather than accuracy. If youngsters are asked to kick accurately, they will poke at the ball rather than develop a full kicking style.

2. Kicking is similar to throwing in that all youngsters should have a ball to kick. Beach balls (for primary grades) and foam balls are excellent as they do not travel a long distance and the youngster can kick and retrieve the ball quickly.

3. Stationary balls are easier to kick than moving balls. Use this progression when teaching beginners to kick.

4. Teach various types of kicks: the toe kick, instep kick, and the side-of-the-foot kick.

Striking

Striking occurs when an object is hit with an implement. The most common forms of striking are hitting a softball with a bat, using a racket for striking in tennis and racquetball, and striking a ball with the hand as in volleyball.

STAGE ONE

In this stage, the feet are stationary and the trunk faces the direction of the tossed ball (or ball on a tee). The elbows are fully flexed, and the force is generated by extending the flexed joints in a downward plane. Little body force is generated because there is no trunk rotation and the motion developed is back to front. The total body does not play a role in generation of forces; rather, it comes from the arms and wrists.

STAGE TWO

In stage two, the upper body begins to generate force. The trunk is turned to the side in anticipation of the ball. The weight shifts from the rear foot to the forward foot prior to contacting the ball. The trunk and hips are rotated into the ball as the swing takes place. The elbows are less flexed, and force is generated by extending the flexed joints. Trunk rotation and forward movement are in an oblique plane.

STAGE THREE

When performing mature striking skills, the performer stands sideways to the path of the oncoming object. Shift the weight to the rear foot and rotate the hips, followed by a shift of weight toward the ball as it approaches the hitter. Striking occurs with the arms extended in a long arc. The swing ends with weight on the forward foot. Mature striking is characterized by a swing through the full range of motion and a sequential transfer of weight from the rear to the front plane of the body.

Stress Points

1. Track the ball as soon as possible and keep tracking until it is hit. Even though it is impossible to see the racket hit the ball, it is an excellent teaching hint and encourages tracking the object as long as possible.

2. Grip the bat with the hands together. If batting right handed, the left hand should be on the bottom (near the small end of the bat).

3. Keep the elbows away from the body. Emphasis should be placed on making a large swing with the elbows extended as the ball is hit.

4. Swing the bat in a horizontal (parallel to the ground) plane. Beginners have a tendency to strike downward in a chopping motion.

✓ **TEACHING TIPS**

1. Striking should be done with maximum force and bat velocity when the focus of instruction is on developing a mature striking form.

2. Practice hitting stationary objects before progressing to moving objects. Batting tees and balls suspended on a string are useful for beginners.

3. Use slow-moving objects such as balloons and beach balls in the early stages of striking practice. This helps the child track the moving projectile.

4. As skill in striking increases, the size of the projectile and bat (or racket) can be decreased.

5. Ensure that there is contrast between the ball and the background to enhance visual perception.
6. Use rubber footprints to help children learn to stride (step) into the ball.

MANIPULATIVE SKILL ACTIVITIES

Manipulative skills come into play when children handle an object. Most of these skills involve the hands and feet, but other parts of the body can also be used. The manipulation of objects leads to better hand-eye and foot-eye coordination, which are particularly important for tracking items in space. Manipulative skills form the foundation for many game skills. Propulsion (throwing, batting, kicking) and receipt (catching) of objects are important skills that can be taught by using beanbags and various balls. Rebounding or redirecting an object in flight (such as a volleyball) is another useful manipulative skill. Continuous control of an object, such as a wand or hoop, is also a manipulative activity.

Progression of Instructional Activities

Instructional activities within each unit in this chapter are presented in progression and are organized into major skill groups. Grouping the activities and placing them in a progression of easy to most difficult helps teachers instruct toward desired objectives. For example, the first group of skills to practice in beanbag activities is Tossing to Self in Place. As a teacher, you can take either of two approaches: Develop this group in depth, exhausting all of the possibilities, or select two or more activities from a number of groups. In the latter case, when the lesson is repeated the following day, use the same groups of activities, but pose different challenges. By working within groups of activities, youngsters are focused on the same type of skill, but they stay motivated because of the many different challenges (novelty) being offered. This results in random practice opportunities (see pages 51–52). Random practice results in better retention because students are mentally generating solutions and have less chance of boredom. Students have to think because each task is different.

Some teachers ask why activities are grouped around equipment rather than skills. It would certainly be possible to create random practice sessions by using different types of equipment to practice the same skills. However, this makes most lessons equipment intensive. The single factor that keeps most teachers from teaching certain skills and units is the amount of equipment that is required. Some teachers will avoid units that demand too much equipment because of the difficulty of

moving it in and out to the instructional area. For example, if a teacher is working with a first grade and a sixth grade during the same time period and has to move equipment outside, it can mean a great deal of equipment will have to be moved. The same goal can be accomplished (random practice sessions) by bringing out one type of equipment and offering variety by changing the activities that focus on a single skill. The result will be effective and challenging random practice sessions.

Reinforce Skills with Student-Developed Games

Skills can be reinforced and enhanced through games that students create. Children can be given a brief outline of a game situation on which they can structure a game applying the skills just learned. Specification of the game situation can range from open choice to creativity within guidelines. In either case, the focus is on using the skills just learned. As an example, the teacher might tell youngsters to create a game embodying a certain skill in which they are to select the equipment needed, outline the game space, specify number of participants, and set the rules, including scoring. More specifically, the teacher might outline certain conditions, such as use of two hoops and two bowling pins, space limitations of two lines 20 to 30 feet apart, and competing sides of two against two. Within those parameters, students would then create a game.

Creative games can be oriented toward individuals, partners, or small groups. Groups should be kept small, or individual input becomes minimal. Different kinds of equipment can be specified (such as mats, wands, goals, or benches). After a period of time, different games can be demonstrated. Remember the games should focus on applying the skills rather than serious competition when students are in the learning phase of skill development. Competition may reduce the level of performance because students focus on winning the game rather than correctly performing the skill.

ACTIVITIES WITH BALLOONS AND BEACH BALLS

Balloons provide interesting movement experiences and emphasize hand-eye coordination. Success can be achieved with balloons when students are not ready for faster-moving ball skills. Keeping a balloon afloat is within the capability of young children and special education students. Beach balls are larger, move slowly, and are more predictable in movement. Both objects are harmless and allow youngsters to learn to catch without fear of being hurt by the projectile. Emphasis should be placed on proper footwork. Because these objects move slowly, there is ample time for students to learn proper footwork—preparing for a volley, catching, and striking, for example.

Balloons are inexpensive and readily available. Extras are needed, as there is always breakage. The balloons should be of good quality and spherical in shape. At times, however, oddly shaped balloons can provide a change of pace. Balloons should be inflated only moderately, because high inflation increases the chance of breakage. Beach balls should be inflated with a ball pump. When they are no longer needed for instruction, they can be deflated and stored.

Instructional Procedures

1. Use the following instructional cues when teaching balloon and beach ball skills:
   a. Catch and control with the fingertips.
   b. Keep your eyes on the object.
   c. Move your body into the path of the oncoming object.
   d. Reach, catch, and move the object to the body (giving).

2. After blowing up each balloon, twist the neck of the balloon and fix it with a twist tie of the type used to close plastic bags. This permits the balloon to be deflated easily and reused. Tying a knot in the neck makes deflating difficult.

3. Beach balls should not be overinflated. They will last longer and be easier to control if they are a bit underinflated. Beach balls that are 16 to 20 inches in diameter are best for most youngsters and can also be used with older students for lead-up games in volleyball and soccer.

Recommended Progression

1. Begin with free exploration, having children play under control with their balloon (Figure 17.7). The objective is to have the children gain a sense of the balloon's flight.

2. Introduce specific hand, finger, and arm contacts. Include using alternate hands; contacting at different levels (low, high, in between); jumping and making high contact; using different hand contacts (palm, back, side, and different fist positions); using different finger combinations (two fingers, index finger, thumb only, others); and using arms, elbows, and shoulders.

3. Expand the activity to use other body parts. Establish contact sequences with three or four body parts.

FIGURE 17.7 Batting balloons from different body positions.

Use various levels and body shapes. Make some visual cards with names of body parts. Students must take their eye off the balloon to see the named body part. This is an excellent challenge to help young children learn to track a moving object.

4. Bat from various body positions—kneeling, sitting, lying.

5. Use an object to control the balloon (a Lummi stick, a ball, a stocking paddle).

6. Restrict movement. Keep one foot in place. Keep one or both feet within a hoop or on a mat or carpet square.

7. Work with a partner by alternating turns, batting the beach ball back and forth, employing follow-the-leader patterns, and so on.

8. Introduce some aspects of volleyball technique, including the overhand pass, the underhand pass, and the dig pass. Begin with a volleyball serve. Make this informal and on a "let's pretend" basis. Check the volleyball unit (Chapter 30) for technique suggestions.

9. Propel a balloon upward. Pick up a hoop from the floor, pass it around the balloon, replace the hoop on the floor, and keep the balloon from touching the ground.

10. Have four to six children seated on the floor in a small circle. Each circle gets two balloons to be kept

in the air. Children's seats are "glued" to the floor. Once a balloon hits the floor, it is out of play. Play for a specified time (30 to 60 seconds). Increase the challenge by using beach balls.

ACTIVITIES WITH BEANBAGS

Activities with beanbags provide valuable learning experiences for elementary school children at all levels. All parts of the body can be brought into play. For tossing and catching, though, the beanbag encourages manipulation with the hands; playground balls lead to arm and body catching. Beanbag activities can be used with older youngsters provided that the activities are carefully selected to challenge students. The more challenging partner activities—juggling, different and unique methods of propulsion, and the Split-Vision Drill (page 358)—are examples of suitable activities.

Instructional Procedures

1. Use the following instructional cues when teaching beanbag activities:
   a. Stress a soft receipt of the beanbag by giving with the hands, arms, and legs. "Giving" involves the hands going out toward the incoming beanbag and bringing it in for a soft landing.
   b. Keep your eyes on the beanbag when catching.
   c. When tossing and catching, toss slightly above eye level.
2. Make sure that beanbags are at least six inches square. This size balances well and can be controlled on various parts of the body, thus offering greater challenge to intermediate-level children.
3. Throwing and catching skills involve many intricate elements. Emphasize the principles of opposition, eye focus, weight transfer, and follow-through. It is important that children track the object being caught and focus on the target when throwing.
4. Stress laterality and directionality when teaching throwing and catching skills. Children should be taught to throw, catch, and balance beanbags with both the left and right sides of their body. They should learn to catch and throw at different levels.
5. Children should throw at chest height to a partner, unless a different type of throw is specified. Teach all types of return: low, medium, high, left, and right.

6. In partner work, keep distances between partners reasonable, especially in introductory phases. Fifteen feet or so is a reasonable starting distance.
7. In partner work, emphasize skillful and varied throwing, catching, and handling of the beanbag. Throwing too hard or out of range, to cause the partner to miss, should be avoided.

Most activities are classified as individual or partner activities. A few activities are for groups of three or more.

Individual Activities

▶ TOSSING TO SELF IN PLACE

1. Toss with both hands, with right hand only, and with left hand only. Catch the same way. Catch with the back of the hands.
2. Toss the beanbag progressively higher, then progressively lower.
3. Hold the beanbag in one hand and make large arm circles (imitating a windmill). Release the bag so that it flies upward, and then catch it.
4. Toss from side to side, right to left (reverse), front to back (reverse), and around various body parts in different combinations.
5. Toss upward and catch with hands behind the back. Toss upward from behind the body and catch in front. Toss upward and catch on the back, on the knees, on the toes, and on other body parts.
6. Hold the bag at arm's length in front of the body, with palms up. Withdraw hands quickly from under the bag, and catch it from on top in a palms-down stroke before it falls to the floor.
7. Toss upward and catch as high as possible. As low as possible. Work out a sequence of high, low, and in between.
8. Toss upward and catch with the body off the floor. Try tossing as well as catching with the body off the ground.
9. Toss in various fashions while seated and while lying.
10. Toss two beanbags upward and catch a bag in each hand.

▶ ADDING STUNTS IN PLACE

1. Toss overhead to the rear, turn around, and catch. Toss, do a full turn, and catch.
2. Toss, clap the hands, and catch. Clap the hands more than once. Clap the hands around different body parts.

3. Toss, do pretend activities (e.g., comb hair, wash face, brush teeth, shine shoes), and catch.

4. Toss, touch different body parts with both hands, and catch. Touch two different body parts, calling out the name of the parts. Touch two body parts, clap hands, and catch.

5. Toss, kneel on one knee, and catch. Try this going to a sitting or lying position. Reverse the position order, coming from a lying or sitting position to a standing position to catch.

6. Toss, touch the floor, and catch. Explore with other challenges. Use heel clicks or balance positions.

7. Bend forward, reach between the legs, and toss the bag onto the back or shoulders.

8. Reach one hand over the shoulder, drop the beanbag, and catch it with the other hand behind the back. Reverse the hands. Drop the beanbag from one hand behind the back and catch it with the other hand between the legs. Put the beanbag on the head, lean back, and catch it with both hands behind the back. Catch it with one hand.

LOCOMOTOR MOVEMENTS

1. Toss to self, moving to another spot to catch. Toss forward, run, and catch. Move from side to side. Toss overhead to the rear, run back, and catch.

2. Add various stunts and challenges described previously. Vary with different locomotor movements.

BALANCING THE BEANBAG ON VARIOUS BODY PARTS

1. Balance the beanbag on the head. Move around, keeping the beanbag in place. Sit down, lie down, turn around, and so on.

2. Balance the beanbag on other parts of the body and move around. Balance on top of the instep, between the knees, on the shoulders, on the elbows, under the chin. Use more than one beanbag.

PROPELLING WITH VARIOUS BODY PARTS

1. Toss to self from various parts of the body: the elbow, the instep, the knees, the shoulders, between the feet, between the heels.

2. Sit and toss the bag from the feet to the hands. Practice tossing in a supine position. From a supine position, pick up the bag between the toes and place it behind the head, using a full curl position. Go back and pick it up, returning it to place.

JUGGLING

1. Begin with two bags and juggle them in the air. (See pages 363–367 for instructions on juggling.)

2. Juggle three bags.

OTHER ACTIVITIES

1. From a standing wide-straddle position, place the beanbag on the floor and push it between the legs as far back as possible. Jump in place with a half turn and repeat.

2. Take the same position as above. Push the bag back as far as possible between the legs, bending the knees. Without moving the legs, turn to the right and pick up the bag. Repeat to the left.

3. Stand with feet apart and hold the beanbag with both hands. Reach as high as possible (with both hands), bend backward, and drop the bag. Reach between the legs, and pick up the bag.

4. On all fours, put the bag in the small of the back. Wiggle and force the bag off the back without moving the hands or knees from place.

5. In crab position, place the beanbag on the stomach, and try to shake it off. On all fours, put it on the back and do a Mule Kick (Figure 20.45 on page 488).

6. Push the beanbag across the floor with different body parts, such as the nose, shoulder, or knee.

7. Each student drops a beanbag on the floor. See how many different ways students can move over, around, and between the beanbags. As an example, jump three bags, crab-walk around two others, and cartwheel over one more.

8. Spread the legs about shoulder width. Bend over and throw the beanbag between the legs and onto the back. Next, throw the beanbag all the way over the head, and catch it.

Partner Activities

TOSSING BACK AND FORTH

1. Begin with various kinds of two-handed throws: underhand, overhead, side, and over the shoulder. Change to one-handed tossing and throwing.

2. Throw at different levels, at different targets, right and left.

3. Throw under the leg, around the body. Center as in football. Try imitating the shot put and the discus throw. Try the softball (full arc) throw.

4. Have partners sit cross-legged about ten feet apart. Throw and catch in various styles.

5. Use follow activities, in which one partner leads with a throw and the other follows with the same kind of throw.

6. Jump, turn in the air, and pass to partner.

7. Toss to partner from unexpected positions and from around and under different body parts.

8. Stand back to back and pass the bag around both partners from hand to hand as quickly as possible. Also try moving the bag around and through various body parts.

9. Toss in various directions to make partner move and catch.

10. Run around partner in a circle, tossing the bag back and forth.

11. Propel two beanbags back and forth. Each partner has a bag, and the bags go in opposite directions at the same time. Try having one partner toss both bags at once in the same direction, using various types of throws. Try to keep three bags going at once.

▶ PROPELLING BACK AND FORTH WITH DIFFERENT BODY PARTS

1. From a sitting position, toss the bag to partner with foot or toes, from on top of the feet, and from between the feet, with elbow, shoulder, head, and any other body part.

2. With back to partner, take a bunny-jump position. With the bag held between the feet, kick the bag back to partner. Try kicking with both feet from a standing position.

3. Partners lie supine on the floor with heads pointing toward each other, about six inches apart. One partner has a beanbag between the feet and deposits it in between the partners' heads. The other partner picks up the bag with the feet (reaching over the head) and places it on the floor by the feet after returning to a lying position. With both partners in backward curl position, try to transfer the bag directly from one partner to the other with the feet.

Group Activities and Games

▶ SPLIT-VISION DRILL

A split-vision drill from basketball can be adapted to beanbags. An active player faces two partners about 15 feet away. They are standing side by side, a short distance apart. Two beanbags, one in the hands of the active player and the other with one of the partners, are

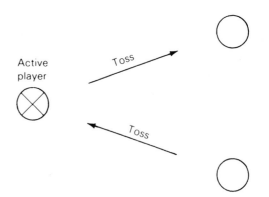

FIGURE 17.8 Split-vision drill for beanbags.

needed for the drill. The active player tosses to the open partner and at the same time receives the bag from the other partner. The two bags move back and forth between the active player and the other two, alternately (Figure 17.8). After a period of time, change positions.

▶ TARGET GAMES

Wastebaskets, hoops, circles drawn on the floor, and other objects can be used as targets for beanbag tossing. Target boards with holes cut out are available from commercial sources. Holes can be triangles, circles, squares, and rectangles, thus stressing form concepts.

▶ BEANBAG QUOITS

The game is played in the same way as horseshoes. A court is drawn with two spots on the floor about 20 feet apart. Spots can be made with masking tape and should be one inch in diameter. Each competitor has two bags, a different color for each player. Tosses are made from behind one spot to the other spot. The object is to get one or both bags closer to the mark than the opponents do. If a bag completely blocks out the spot, as viewed from directly overhead, the player scores 3 points. Otherwise, the bag nearest the spot scores 1 point. Games are played to 11, 15, or 21 points. In each round, the player winning the previous point tosses first.

▶ OTHER GAMES

Children enjoy playing One Step (page 565). Teacher Ball (page 556) is also readily adaptable to beanbags.

ACTIVITIES WITH BALLS

Included in this section are the ball skills in which the child handles balls without the aid of other equipment, such as a bat or paddle. Ball skills are mostly of two types:

(a) hand-eye skills, including throwing, catching, bouncing, dribbling (as in basketball), batting (as in volleyball), and rolling (as in bowling); and (b) foot-eye skills, including kicking, trapping, and dribbling (as in soccer).

Types of Balls

For younger children, sponge rubber, yarn, and fleece balls are all excellent for introductory throwing and catching, because they help overcome the fear factor. (See Chapter 10 for instructions on how to make balls from yarn.) The innovative teacher can probably develop other suitable objects, such as crumpled-up newspaper balls wrapped with cellophane tape, papier-mâché balls, stitched rolls of socks, and stuffed balloons.

The whiffle ball, a hollow plastic ball with holes cut in the surface, is also useful. Scoops, either commercial or home constructed, provide an extension of whiffle ball activities. Another type of ball that has value is a soft softball, a much softer version of the regular softball. It is suitable for catching and throwing but does not hold up well if batted.

The inflated rubber playground ball (8.5-inch size) should be the ball used for most ball-handling experiences. Balls should be inflated moderately so that they bounce well, but not overinflated, which makes them difficult to catch. Overinflation can also distort the ball's spherical shape.

Balls that last longer and have more utility for youngsters are the 8-inch foam balls. The foam balls are easier to catch and pass and will not hurt if youngsters are accidentally hit by one. There are many different types of foam used to make these balls and it is important to make sure that the balls are dense and that they have adequate bounce. Many of the cheaper styles are extremely light and will not bounce. An even better (but more expensive) alternative are the foam "tough-skin" balls. These are foam balls that are covered with a tough plastic coating. This skin causes the balls to bounce better and to resist damage to the soft foam. In the long run, these "tough-skin" balls may be the most economical as they will not leak or develop punctures like the standard playground ball.

Some attention should be given to the color of the balls. In a study comparing blue, yellow, and white balls against a black background and a white background, "blue and yellow balls produced significantly higher catching scores than did a white ball" (Morris, 1976). However, no data were provided for the common playground balls of red color.

Types of Organization

Instruction with younger children should begin with individual work and progress to partner and group activities.

After the children have acquired some skill, a lesson can include both individual and partner activities. In propelling the ball back and forth between partners, the children can progress from rolling the ball, to throwing with one bounce, to throwing on the fly. Be sure that a disparity in skill level between partners does not cause a problem for either.

Distance between partners should be short at first and then lengthened gradually. The concept of targets is introduced by directing the children to throw the ball to specified points. Later, a change from a stationary target to a moving target maintains progression. Relays are useful for reinforcing learning, but the skills should be learned reasonably well before application in a relay.

Group work should be confined to small groups (of three to six), so that each child can be active, and should include activities not possible in individual or partner activity.

Instructional Procedures

1. Use the following instructional cues when teaching ball skills.
   a. Keep your eyes on the ball.
   b. Catch and dribble the ball with the pads of the fingers.
   c. Use opposition and weight transfer when passing the ball.

2. In catching, soft receipt of the ball is achieved by "giving" with the hands and arms. The hands should reach out somewhat to receive the ball and then cushion the impact by bringing the ball in toward the body in a relaxed way.

3. To catch a throw above the waist, the hands should be positioned so that the thumbs are together. To receive a throw below the waist, the little fingers should be kept toward each other and the thumbs kept out.

4. In throwing to a partner, unless otherwise specified, the throw should reach the partner at about chest height. At times, different target points should be specified—high, low, right, left, at the knee, and so on.

5. A lesson should begin with basic skills within the reach of all and progress to more challenging activities.

6. Laterality is an important consideration. Right and left members of the body should be given practice in turn.

7. Split-vision should be incorporated in bouncing and dribbling. Children should learn to look forward, rather than at the ball, when bouncing and dribbling.

8. Tactile senses can be enhanced by having children dribble or bounce the ball with eyes closed.

9. Rhythmic accompaniment, particularly for bouncing and dribbling activities, adds another dimension to ball skills.

10. Enough balls should be available so that each child has one.

11. The problem of uncontrolled balls can be solved by telling children to ignore stray balls, as someone is sure to be coming after them.

Activities with balls are presented with an 8.5-inch ball in mind. Some modification is needed if the balls used are smaller or are of the type that does not bounce.

INDIVIDUAL ACTIVITIES

Each child has a ball and practices alone. In the first group of individual activities, the child remains in the same spot. Next, the child rebounds the ball against a wall. (The wall should be reasonably free of projections and irregular surfaces so that the ball can return directly to the student.) In the third group of activities, the child performs alone while on the move.

▶ CONTROLLED ROLLING AND HANDLING IN PLACE

1. In a wide straddle position (other possible positions are seated with legs crossed or outstretched, and push-up position), place the ball on the floor, and roll it with constant finger guidance between and around the legs.

2. Roll the ball in a figure-eight path in and out of the legs.

3. Reach as far to the left as possible with the ball and roll it in front of you to the other side. Catch it as far to the right of the body as possible.

4. Turn in place and roll the ball around with one hand in a large circle.

5. Roll the ball around while lying on top of it. Roll the ball around the floor while on all fours, guiding it with the nose and forehead.

6. With the back moderately bent, release the ball behind the head, let it roll down the back, and catch it with both hands.

7. Make different kinds of bridges over the ball while using the ball as partial support for the bridge.

8. Starting with one arm above the head, roll the ball down that arm, behind the back, and down the other arm, and then catch it.

▶ BOUNCING AND CATCHING IN PLACE

1. Beginning with two hands, bounce and catch the ball. Bounce a given number of times. Bounce at different levels. Bounce one-handed in a variety of ways. Bounce under the legs. Close the eyes and bounce and catch.

2. Bounce, perform various stunts (a heel click, body turn, or handclap), and catch.

3. Bounce the ball around, under, and over the body.

4. Practice various kinds of bounces, catching all with the eyes closed.

5. Bounce the ball with various body parts, such as the head, elbow, or knee.

6. Bounce the ball, using consecutive body parts (such as the elbow and then the knee), and catch.

▶ TOSSING AND CATCHING IN PLACE

1. Toss and catch, increasing height gradually. Toss from side to side. Toss underneath the legs, around the body, and from behind. Add challenges while tossing and catching. Clap the hands one or more times, make body turns (quarter, half, or full), touch the floor, click the heels, sit down, lie down, and so on.

2. To enhance body part identification, toss and perform some of the following challenges: Touch the back with both hands, touch the back with both hands by reaching over both shoulders, touch both elbows, touch both knees with crossed hands, touch both heels with a heel slap, and touch the toes. Be sure to catch the ball after completing each challenge. The teacher or a leader can quickly call out the body part, and the class must respond with a toss, touch, and catch.

3. Toss upward and catch the descending ball as high as possible. As low as possible. Work out other levels and create combinations. Catch with crossed arms.

4. From a seated position, toss the ball to self from various directions. Lie down and do the same. Toss with the feet.

5. Practice catching by looking away after the ball is tossed upward. Experiment with different ways of catching with the eyes closed.

▶ BATTING TO SELF IN PLACE

1. Bat the ball as in volleyball by using the fist, an open hand, or the side of the hand.

2. Bat and let the ball bounce. Catch in different ways.

3. Rebound the ball upward, using different parts of the body. Let it bounce. Practice serving to self.

4. Bat and rebound the ball so that it does not touch the ground. Change position while doing this.

5. Bat the ball, perform a stunt, and bat again.

► FOOT SKILLS IN PLACE

1. Put the toes on top of the ball. Roll the ball in different directions, keeping the other foot in place but retaining control.

2. Use a two-foot pickup, front and back. This is done by putting the ball between the feet and hoisting it to the hands.

3. From a seated position with legs extended, toss the ball with the feet to the hands.

4. Try doing a full curl with the ball between the feet, retaining control until the ball is again placed on the floor. Try bringing the ball between the feet to a point directly over the body. With the arms outstretched for support, lower the feet with the ball to the right and left.

5. In a supine position, hold the ball on the floor above the head. Do a curl-up, bring the ball forward, touch the toes with it, and return to supine position.

6. Drop the ball, and immediately trap it against the floor with one foot. Try to bounce it with one foot.

► DRIBBLING SKILLS IN PLACE

1. Dribble the ball first with both hands and then with the right and the left. (Emphasize that the dribble is a push with good wrist action. Children should not bat the ball downward.) Use various number combinations with the right and left hands. Dribble under the legs in turn and back around the body. Kneel and dribble. Go from standing to lying, maintaining a dribble. Return to standing position. Dribble the ball at different levels and at various tempos.

2. Dribble without looking at the ball. Dribble and change hands without stopping the dribble. Dribble with the eyes closed. Dribble the way the Harlem Globetrotters do.

► THROWING AGAINST A WALL (CATCHING ON THE FIRST BOUNCE)

1. Throw the ball against the wall, and catch the return after one bounce. Practice various kinds of throws: two-handed, one-handed, overhead, side, baseball, chest pass.

2. Throw at a target mounted on the wall.

► THROWING AGAINST A WALL (CATCHING ON THE FLY)

Repeat the throws used in the previous activity, but catch the return on the fly. It may be necessary to move closer and to have the ball contact the wall higher.

► BATTING AGAINST A WALL (HANDBALL SKILLS)

1. Drop the ball, and bat it after it bounces. Keep the ball going as in handball.

2. Serve the ball against the wall as in volleyball. Experiment with different ways to serve.

► KICKING AGAINST A WALL AND TRAPPING (FOOT-EYE SKILLS)

1. Practice different ways to control kicking against the wall and stopping (trapping) the ball on the return. Try using the foot to keep returning the ball against the wall on the bounce.

2. Put some targets on the wall and kick the ball at a target. See how many points are scored after ten kicks.

► ROLLING ON THE MOVE

1. Roll the ball, run alongside it, and guide it with the hands in different directions.

2. Roll the ball forward, then run and catch up with it.

► TOSSING AND CATCHING ON THE MOVE

1. Toss the ball upward and forward. Run forward and catch it after one bounce. Toss the ball upward in various directions (forward, sideward, backward), run under it, turn, and catch it on the fly.

2. Add various stunts and challenges, such as touching the floor, clicking the heels, or turning around.

► BATTING ON THE MOVE

With first the right and then the left hand, bat the ball upward in different directions, and catch it on the first bounce or on the fly.

► PRACTICING FOOT SKILLS ON THE MOVE

Dribble the ball (soccer style) forward and in other directions. Dribble around an imaginary point. Make various patterns while dribbling, such as a circle, square, triangle, or figure eight.

17

DRIBBLING ON THE MOVE

1. Dribble (basketball style) forward using one hand, and dribble back to place with the other. Change direction on a signal. Dribble in various directions, describing different pathways. Dribble around cones, milk cartons, or chairs.

2. Place a hoop on the floor. Dribble inside the hoop until a signal is sounded, then dribble to another hoop and continue the dribble inside that hoop. Avoid dribbling on the hoop itself.

PRACTICING LOCOMOTOR MOVEMENTS WHILE HOLDING THE BALL

1. Hold the ball between the legs and perform various locomotor movements.

2. Try holding the ball in various positions with different body parts.

Partner Activities

ROLLING IN PLACE

Roll the ball back and forth to partner. Begin with two-handed rolls and proceed to one-handed rolls. When partner rolls the ball, pick it up with the toes and snap it up into the hands.

THROWING AND CATCHING IN PLACE

1. Toss the ball to partner with one bounce, using various kinds of tosses. Practice various kinds of throws and passes to partner.

2. Throw to specific levels and points: high, low, right, left, at the knee, and so on. Try various throws: from under the leg, around the body, backward tosses, and centering as in football.

3. Throw and catch over a volleyball net.

4. Work in a threesome, with one person holding a hoop between the two partners playing catch. Throw the ball through the hoop held at various levels. Try throwing through a moving hoop.

BATTING IN PLACE (VOLLEYBALL SKILLS)

1. Toss the ball upward to self, bat it two-handed to partner, who catches and returns it in the same manner. Serve as in volleyball to partner. Partner makes a return serve. Toss the ball to partner, who makes a volleyball return. Keep distances short and keep the ball under control. Try to keep the ball going back and forth as in volleyball.

2. Bat the ball back and forth on one bounce. Bat it back and forth over a line, wand, jump rope, or bench.

KICKING IN PLACE

1. Practice different ways of controlled kicking between partners and different ways of stopping the ball (trapping).

2. Practice a controlled punt, preceding the kick with a step on the nonkicking foot. Place the ball between the feet and propel it forward or backward to partner.

3. Practice foot pickups. One partner rolls the ball, and the other hoists it to self with extended toes.

THROWING IN PLACE FROM VARIOUS POSITIONS

Practice different throws from a kneeling, sitting, or lying position. (Allow the children to be creative in selecting positions.)

TWO-BALL ACTIVITIES IN PLACE

Using two balls, pass back and forth, with balls going in opposite directions.

FOLLOW ACTIVITIES IN PLACE

Throw or propel the ball in any manner desired. Partner returns the ball in the same fashion.

THROWING AND CATCHING AGAINST A WALL

Alternate throwing and catching against a wall. Alternate returning the ball after a bounce, as in handball.

THROWING ON THE MOVE

1. One child remains in place and tosses to the other child, who is moving. The moving child can trace different patterns, such as back and forth between two spots or in a circle around the stationary child. (Spatial judgments must be good to anticipate where the moving child should be to receive the ball. Moderate distances should be maintained between children.)

2. Practice different kinds of throws and passes as both children move in different patterns. (Considerable space is needed for this type of work.) Practice foot skills of dribbling and passing.

3. Partners hold the ball between their bodies without using the hands or arms. Experiment with different ways to move together.

4. Carrying a ball, run in different directions while partner follows. On signal, toss the ball upward so that the child following can catch it. Now change places and repeat the activity.

JUGGLING

Juggling is a novel task that is exciting to elementary school youngsters. It is a challenging task that demands practice and repetition to learn. An excellent medium for teaching beginners is sheer, lightweight scarves that measure 18 to 24 inches square. These move slowly, allowing children to track them visually. Juggling with scarves teaches children correct patterns of object movement; however, it does not transfer easily to juggling with faster-moving objects such as fleece balls, tennis balls, rings, and hoops. Therefore, two distinct sections for juggling are offered: a section dealing with learning to juggle with scarves and a second discussion explaining juggling with balls. Juggling with scarves will bring success to a majority of the class. Youngsters who have mastered the scarves can move to balls and other objects.

Juggling lessons should allow opportunity for children to move, at will, between scarves and faster-moving objects. This will allow them to find an acceptable balance between success and frustration. Much practice is necessary to learn to juggle, and there will be a lot of misses during the acquisition of this skill. Because youngsters tire quickly if they are not having success, it may be desirable to play a game and then return to juggling practice.

Juggling with Scarves

Scarves are held by the fingertips near the center. To throw the scarf, it should be lifted and pulled into the air above eye level. Scarves are caught by clawing, a downward motion of the hand, and grabbing the scarf from above as it is falling. Scarf juggling should teach proper habits (for example, tossing the scarves straight up in line with the body rather than forward or backward). Many instructors remind children to imagine that they are in a phone booth or large refrigerator box—to emphasize tossing and catching without moving.

> ▶ **CASCADING**

Cascading is the easiest pattern for juggling three objects. The following sequence can be used to learn this basic technique.

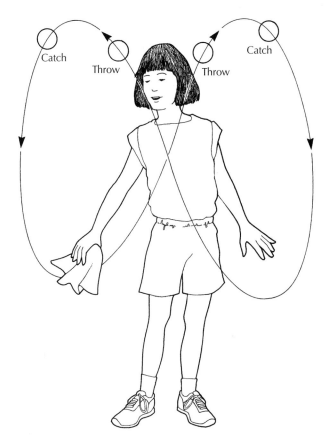

FIGURE 17.9   Clawing a scarf.

1. *One scarf.* Hold the scarf in the center. Quickly move the arm across the chest and toss the scarf with the palm out. Reach out with the other hand and catch the scarf in a straight-down motion (clawing). Toss the scarf with this hand using the motion and claw it with the opposite hand. Continue the tossing and clawing sequence over and over. The scarf should move in a figure-eight pattern as shown in Figure 17.9.

2. *Two scarves—two hands.* Hold a scarf with the fingertips in each hand. Toss the first one across the body as described in step 1. When it reaches its peak, look at it, and toss the second scarf across the body in the opposite direction. The first scarf thrown is caught (clawed) by the hand throwing the second scarf and vice versa (Figure 17.10, page 364). Verbal cues such as "Toss, claw, toss, claw" are helpful.

3. *Two scarves—one hand.* This sequence is a requisite if youngsters are going to juggle three scarves. Start with both scarves in one hand (hold them as described below in three-scarf cascading). The important skill to learn is to toss the first scarf, then the

FIGURE 17.10 Tossing and clawing with two scarves.

FIGURE 17.11 Three-scarf cascading.

second scarf, and then catch the first and the second. Verbal cues to use are toss, toss, catch, catch. If youngsters cannot toss two scarves before catching one, they will not be able to master juggling with three scarves. Practice tossing skills with both hands.

4. *Three-scarf cascading.* A scarf is held in each hand by the fingertips as described in step 2. The third scarf is held with the ring and little fingers against the palm of one hand. The first scarf to be thrown will be from the hand that is holding two scarves. Toss this scarf from the fingertips across the chest as learned earlier. When scarf one reaches its peak, scarf two from the other hand is thrown across the body. As this hand starts to come down, it catches scarf one. When scarf two reaches its peak, scarf three is thrown in the same path as that of scarf one. To complete the cycle, as the hand comes down from throwing scarf three, it catches scarf two. The cycle is started over by throwing scarf one with the opposite hand. Figure 17.11 illustrates the figure-eight motion that is used in cascading. Tosses are always alternated between left and right hands with a smooth, even rhythm.

▶ **REVERSE CASCADING**

Reverse cascading involves tossing the scarves from waist level to the outside of the body and allowing the scarves to drop down the midline of the body (Figure 17.12).

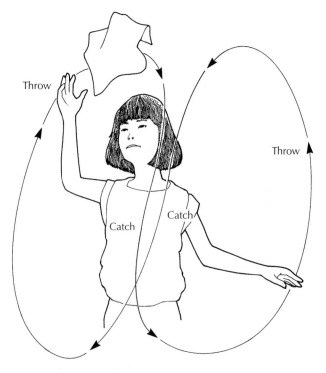

FIGURE 17.12 Reverse cascading.

1. *One scarf.* Begin by holding the scarf as described previously. The throw goes away from the midline of the body over the top, releasing the scarf so that it falls down the center of the body. Catch it with the opposite hand and toss it in similar fashion on the opposite side of the body.

2. *Two scarves.* Begin with a scarf in each hand. Toss the first as described in step 1. When it begins its descent, toss the second scarf. Catch the first scarf, then the second, and repeat the pattern in a toss, toss, catch, catch manner.

3. *Reverse cascading with three scarves.* Think of a large funnel fixed at eye level directly in front of the juggler. The goal is to drop all scarves through this funnel so that they drop straight down the center of the body. Begin with three scarves as described previously for three-scarf cascading. Toss the first scarf from the hand holding two scarves.

▶ **COLUMN JUGGLING**

Column juggling is so named because the scarves move straight up and down as though they were inside a large pipe or column and do not cross the body. To perform three-scarf column juggling, begin with two scarves in one hand and one in the other hand. Begin with a scarf from the hand that has two scarves, and toss it straight up the midline of the body overhead. When this scarf reaches its peak, toss the other two scarves upward along the sides of the body (Figure 17.13). Catch the first scarf with either hand and toss it upward again. Catch the other two scarves and toss them upward, continuing the pattern.

▶ **SHOWERING**

Showering is more difficult than cascading because of the rapid movement of the hands. There is less time allowed for catching and tossing. The scarves move in a circle following each other. It should be practiced in both directions for maximum challenge.

Start with two scarves in the right hand and one in the left. Begin by throwing the first two scarves from the right hand. Toss the scarves in a large circle away from the midline of the body and overhead as high as possible. As soon as the second scarf is released, toss the scarf across from the left hand to the right and then toss the scarf in the opposite hand and catch the first scarf with this hand also. Finish by tossing the last scarf (Figure 17.14). All scarves are caught with the left hand and passed to the right hand.

▶ **JUGGLING CHALLENGES**

1. While cascading, toss a scarf under one leg.
2. While cascading, toss a scarf from behind the back.

FIGURE 17.13   Column juggling.

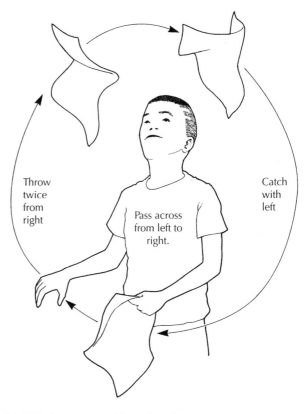

Throw twice from right

Pass across from left to right.

Catch with left

FIGURE 17.14   Showering with scarves.

3. Instead of catching one of the scarves, blow it upward with a strong breath of air.

4. Begin cascading by tossing the first scarf into the air with a foot. Lay the scarf across the foot and kick it into the air.

5. Try juggling three scarves with one hand. Do not worry about establishing a pattern, just catch the lowest scarf each time. Try both regular and reverse cascading as well as column juggling.

6. While doing column juggling, toss up one scarf, hold the other two, and make a full turn. Resume juggling.

7. Juggle three scarves while standing alongside a partner with inside arms around each other. This is actually easy to do, because it is regular three-scarf cascading.

8. Try juggling more than three scarves (up to six) with a partner.

Juggling with Balls

Two balls can be juggled with one hand, and three balls can be juggled with two hands. Juggling can be done in a crisscross fashion, which is called *cascading,* or it can be done in a circular fashion, called *showering.* Cascading is considered the easier of the two styles and should be the first one attempted.

INSTRUCTIONAL PROCEDURES

1. Juggling requires accurate, consistent tossing, and this should be the first emphasis. The tosses should be thrown to the same height on both sides of the body, about two to two and a half feet upward and across the body, since the ball is tossed from one hand to the other. Practice tossing the ball parallel to the body; the most common problem in juggling is that the balls are tossed forward and the juggler has to move forward to catch them.

2. The fingers, not the palms, should be used in tossing and catching. Stress relaxed wrist action.

3. The student should look upward to watch the balls at the peak of their flight, rather than watching the hands. Focus on where the ball peaks, not on the hands.

4. The balls should be caught about waist height and released a little above this level.

5. Two balls must be carried in the starting hand, and the art of releasing only one must be mastered.

6. Progression should be working successively with first one ball, then two balls, and finally three balls (Figure 17.15).

FIGURE 17.15   Cascading with three balls.

RECOMMENDED PROGRESSION FOR CASCADING

1. Using one ball and one hand only, toss the ball upward (two to two and a half feet), and catch it with the same hand. Begin with the dominant hand, and later practice with the other. Toss quickly, with wrist action. Then handle the ball alternately with right and left hands, tossing from one hand to the other.

2. Now, with one ball in each hand, alternate tossing a ball upward and catching it in the same hand so that one ball is always in the air. Begin again with a ball in each hand. Toss across the body to the other hand. To keep the balls from colliding, toss under the incoming ball. After some expertise has been acquired, alternate the two kinds of tosses by doing a set number (four to six) of each before shifting to the other.

3. Hold two balls in the starting hand and one in the other. Toss one of the balls in the starting hand, toss the ball from the other hand, and then toss the third ball.

RECOMMENDED PROGRESSION FOR SHOWERING

1. The showering motion is usually counterclockwise. Hold one ball in each hand. Begin by tossing with the right hand on an inward path and then immediately toss the other ball from the left directly across the body to the right hand. Continue this until the action is smooth.

2. Now, hold two balls in the right hand and one in the left. Toss the first ball from the right hand on an inward path and immediately toss the second on the same path. At about the same time, toss the ball from the left hand directly across the body to the right hand (Figure 17.16).

3. A few children may be able to change from cascading to showering and vice versa. This is a skill of considerable challenge.

FIGURE 17.16   Showering with three balls.

ACTIVITIES WITH SCOOPS AND BALLS

Scoops can be purchased (Figure 17.17) or made with bleach bottles or similar containers (see Chapter 10). They are excellent for practicing catching and tossing skills using an implement rather than the hands. The following activities are recommended.

Individual Activities

1. Put the ball on the floor and pick it up with the scoop. Toss the ball upward and catch it with the scoop. Throw the ball against a wall and catch it in the scoop. Put the ball in the scoop, throw it in the

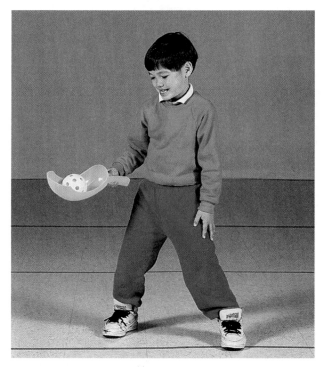

FIGURE 17.17   Catching a whiffle ball with a scoop.

air, and catch it. Throw the ball against a wall with the scoop and catch it with the scoop.
2. Throw the ball, switch the scoop to the opposite hand, and catch in the scoop. Toss the ball upward from the scoop, perform a stunt, such as a heel click or a body turn, and catch the ball in the scoop.
3. Toss the ball upward and catch it as low as possible. As high as possible. Toss it a little higher each time, and catch it in the scoop. Tell students to toss the ball so that they have to stretch to catch it. (Most activities should begin with a toss from the free hand and later employ a toss from the scoop.)

Partner Activities

1. One partner rolls the ball on the floor, and the other catches it in the scoop. Partners throw the ball back and forth and catch it in the scoop. Play One Step (page 565) while playing catch to add some challenge to the activity.
2. One partner tosses the ball from the scoop and the other partner catches. Throw the ball from the scoop at different levels and catch it at different levels. Throw and catch from various positions, such as sitting, back to back, prone, and kneeling.
3. Work with more than one partner, with more than one ball, and with a scoop in each hand.

Games and Relays

Many games and relays can be played using scoops. Modified lacrosse can be played using the scoops and a whiffle ball. Set up a lesson in which children devise games for themselves that use the scoop and a ball.

BOWLING ACTIVITIES

Younger children should practice informal rolling. As they mature, the emphasis should change from informal rolling to bowling skills. Bowling skills begin with a two-handed roll and progress to one-handed rolls, alternating between the right and left hand. Various targets can be used, including bowling pins, milk cartons, small cones, blocks, and even people.

The 8.5-inch foam or playground ball is excellent for teaching bowling skills. Volleyballs and soccer balls also can be used. Stress moderate speed in the motion of the ball. The ball should roll off the tips of the fingers with good follow-through action.

The four-step approach is the accepted form for ten-pin bowling, and its basis can be set in class work.

The technique, in brief form, for a right-handed bowler follows:

Starting position: Stand with the feet together and the ball held comfortably in both hands in front of the body.

Step one: Step forward with the right foot, pushing the ball forward with both hands and a little to the right.

Step two: Step with the left foot, allowing the ball to swing down alongside the leg on its way into the backswing.

Step three: Step with the right foot. The ball reaches the height of the backswing with this step.

Step four: Step with the left foot and bowl the ball forward.

For instructional cues, the teacher can call out the following sequence for the four steps: "Out," "Down," "Back," and "Roll."

Bowling activities are organized mostly as partner or group work. When targets are being used, having two children on the target end is desirable. One child resets the target, while the other recovers the ball. The following are partner activities unless otherwise noted. A fine game for rounding off the activities is Bowling One Step (page 566).

▶ **RECOMMENDED ACTIVITIES**

1. Use a wide straddle stance, and begin with two-handed rolls from between the legs.

2. Roll the ball first with the right and then with the left hand. The receiver can use the foot pickup, done by hoisting the ball to the hands with the extended toes.

3. Practice putting different kinds of spin (English) on the ball. (For a right-handed bowler, a curve to the left is called a hook ball, and a curve to the right is a backup ball.)

4. Get into groups of three (Figure 17.18) and use human straddle targets. Using a stick two feet long, make marks on the floor for the target child, who is in the middle between the two bowlers. The target child stands so that the inside edges of the shoes are on the marks, thus standardizing the target spread. (Targets must keep their legs straight and motionless during the bowling. Otherwise, they can make or avoid contact with the ball and upset the scoring system.) Start from a moderate distance (15 to 20 feet) at first, and adjust as proficiency increases. Scoring can be two points for a ball that goes through the legs without touching and one point for a ball that goes through but touches the leg.

FIGURE 17.18 Bowling through a human straddle target.

5. Use milk cartons or bowling pins as targets. Begin with one and progress to two or three. (Plastic bowling pins are available. Other targets might be a wastebasket lying on its side—the ball is rolled into it—or a three-pound coffee can for a smaller ball.)

ACTIVITIES WITH WANDS

Wands have been used in physical education programs for many years, but only recently have a wide variety of interesting and challenging activities been developed. Wands can be made from three-quarter-inch maple dowels or from a variety of broom and mop handles. If two lengths are chosen, make them 36 and 42 inches. If only one size is to be used, a length of one meter is recommended. Wands are more interesting when they are painted with imaginative designs, a chore that can be a class project. Wands are noisy when they hit the floor. Putting rubber crutch tips on the ends of a wand alleviates most of the noise and makes it easier to pick up. The tips should be put on with mucilage.

Instructional Procedures

1. Because wands are noisy when dropped, the children should hold their wands with both hands or put them on the floor during instruction.

2. Many wand activities require great flexibility, which means that not all children are able to do them. Girls usually perform better than boys at flexibility stunts.

3. An adequate amount of space is needed for each individual, because wand stunts demand room.

4. Wands are not to be used as fencing foils. Children may easily be injured using wands improperly. Teach children proper use of wands. Emphasize the need to use care when handling wands to avoid injury to self and others. Do not allow any improper use of wands (or other potentially dangerous equipment).

▶ **RECOMMENDED ACTIVITIES**

Wands can be used for challenge activities that offer a relatively unstructured approach. The following are some of the many possible challenges.

1. Can you reach down and pick up your wand without bending your knees?

2. Try to balance your wand on different body parts. Watch the top of the wand to get cues on how to retain the balance.

3. Can you hold your stick against the wall and move over and under it?

4. Let's see whether you can hold the stick at both ends and move through the gap.

5. Can you spin the wand and keep it going like a windmill?

6. Let's see how many different ways you can move over and around your wand when it is on the floor.

7. Put one end of the wand on the floor and hold the other end. How many times can you run around your wand without getting dizzy?

8. Place one end of the wand against a wall. Holding the other end and keeping the wand against the wall, duck underneath. Place the wand lower and lower on the wall and go under.

9. Place the wand between your feet and hop around as though you are on a pogo stick.

10. Throw your wand into the air and catch it.

11. Hold the wand vertically near the middle. Can you release your grip and catch the wand before it falls to the floor?

12. Have a partner hold a wand horizontally above the floor. Jump, leap, and hop over the wand. Gradually raise the height of the wand.

13. Put your wand on the floor and try making different kinds of bridges over it.

14. Place the wand on the floor. Curl alongside it, just touching it. Curl at one end of the wand.

15. Balance the wand vertically on the floor. Release the wand and try to complete different stunts—clapping the hands, doing a heel click, touching different body parts—before the wand falls to the floor.

16. Put the wand on the floor and see how many ways you can push it, using different body parts.

Individual Wand Stunts

▶ **WAND CATCH**

Stand a wand on one end and hold it in place with the fingers on the tip. Loop the foot quickly over the stick, letting go of the wand briefly but catching it with the fingers before it falls. Do this with the right and left hand for a complete set. Try to catch the wand with just the index finger.

▶ **THREAD THE NEEDLE (V-SEAT)**

Maintaining a V-seat position, with the wand held in front of the body with both hands, bend the knees between the arms and pass the wand over them and return, without touching the wand to the legs. Try with the ankles crossed.

▶ THREAD THE NEEDLE (STANDING)

Holding the wand in both hands, step through the space, one leg at a time, and return without touching. Step through again, but this time bring the wand up behind the back, over the head, and down in front. Reverse. Try from side to side with the stick held front and back.

▶ GRAPEVINE

Holding the wand near the ends, step with the right foot around the right arm and over the wand inward, toward the body (Figure 17.19). Pass the wand backward over the head and right shoulder (Figure 17.20), and continue sliding the wand down the body until you are standing erect with the wand between the legs. Reverse the process back to original position. Try with the left foot leading.

▶ BACK SCRATCHER

Hold the wand with an underhand grip (palms up), arms crossed in front of the body (Figure 17.21). Bend the elbows so that the wand can go over and behind the head. Attempt to pass the wand down the length of the

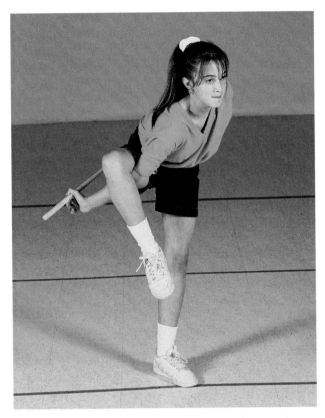

FIGURE 17.20   Grapevine, second stage (head ducks under, and wand is pressed down the back).

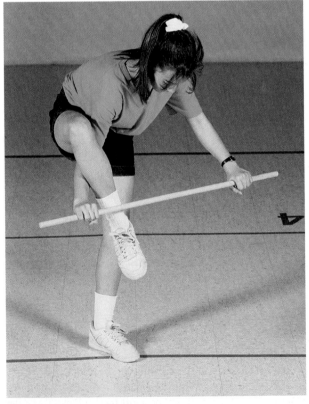

FIGURE 17.19   Beginning the Grapevine.

body from the back of the shoulders to the heels. Do not release the grip on the wand. The wand is worked down behind the back while the arms stay in front of the body.

▶ WAND WHIRL

Stand the wand upright in front of the body. Turn around quickly and grasp the wand before it falls. Do the movement both right and left. Try making two full turns and still catching the wand before it falls.

▶ TWIST UNDER

Grasp the upright wand with the right hand. Twist around under the right arm without letting go of the wand, taking it off the floor, or touching the knee to the floor. Repeat, using the left arm.

▶ JUMP WAND

Holding the wand in front of the feet with the fingertips of both hands, jump over it. Jumping back is not recommended, because the wand can hit the heels and cause an awkward fall. (A rope or a towel can be substituted for the wand if children are having difficulty.)

FIGURE 17.21 Back Scratcher (wand has been passed overhead and is now being forced down the back).

BALANCING THE WAND

Balance the wand vertically with one hand. Experiment with different hand and finger positions. Walk forward, backward, and sideward. Sit down, lie down, and move into other positions while keeping the wand balanced. Keep the eyes on the top of the wand. Balance the wand horizontally on the hands, arms, feet, and thighs. Balance it across the back of the neck. In crab position, balance it across the tummy.

THE SPRINTER

Get into a sprinter's position, with the wand on the floor, between the feet, and perpendicular to the direction of the sprint. Change the feet rapidly, alternating over the wand. Try moving both feet together forward and backward over the wand.

CRAB LEAP

Place the wand on the floor. Get into crab position and attempt to move the feet back and forth over the wand without touching it. Try this with alternating feet.

LONG REACH

Stand with legs extended and feet spread about 12 inches apart. Hold a wand in the left hand, and use it like a third limb. With a piece of chalk in the right hand, reach forward as far as possible and make a mark. Use the wand as a support and see whether the mark can be bettered.

WAND BRIDGE

On a mat, start in a straddle stance with legs straight. Hold a wand near one end, with the other end above the head and pointed toward the ceiling. Bend backward, place the wand on the mat behind you, and walk the hands down the wand. Return to standing position.

WAND TWIRL

Children in the class who have baton-twirling experience can show the class some points of technique.

Partner Wand Stunts

PARTNER CATCH

Partners face each other a short distance (5 feet) apart, each holding a wand in the right hand. On signal, each throws the wand to the partner with the right hand and catches the incoming wand with the left. Distances can be increased somewhat.

PARTNER CHANGE

Partners face each other a short distance (5 feet) apart. Each has a wand standing upright, held on top by the right hand. On signal, each runs to the other's wand and tries to catch it before it falls. This can also be done in the same way as the Wand Whirl, with each whirling to the other's wand. Try with a small group of five or six. On signal, all move to the next wand.

TURN THE DISHRAG

Partners face each other and grasp a wand. When ready, they perform a dishrag turn (see Figure 20.38 in Chapter 20).

JUMP THE WAND

One partner moves the wand back and forth along the floor, while the other partner jumps over it. To add challenge, partners should change the tempo of movement and raise the level of the wand.

▶ **WAND REACTION**

One partner holds the wand horizontally. The other partner places one hand directly above the wand, palm down. When the first partner drops the wand, the second partner tries to catch it before it strikes the floor.

▶ **COOPERATIVE MOVEMENTS**

Holding a wand between them, partners stand toe to toe and circle either way with light foot movements. Together, partners squat down and stand up. Sit down and come up. Kneel and hold the wand overhead as they face each other. Bend sideways and touch the wand to the floor.

Isometric Exercises with Wands

The isometric exercises with wands presented here are mainly grip exercises. A variety of grips should be used. With the wand horizontal, use either the overhand or underhand grip. With the wand in vertical position, grip with the thumbs pointed up, down, or toward each other. Repeat each exercise with a different grip. Exercises can also be repeated with the wand in different positions: in front of the body (either horizontal or vertical), overhead, or behind the back. Hold each exercise for 8 to 12 seconds.

▶ **PULL THE WAND APART**

Place the hands 6 inches apart near the center of the wand. With a tight grip to prevent slippage and with arms extended, pull the hands apart. Change grip and position.

▶ **PUSH THE WAND TOGETHER**

Hold the wand as previously, except push the hands together.

▶ **WAND TWIST**

Hold the wand with both hands about six inches apart. Twist the hands in opposite directions.

▶ **BICYCLE**

Holding the wand horizontally using an overhand grip, extend the wand outward and downward. Bring it upward near the body, completing a circular movement. On the downward movement, push the wand together, and on the upward movement, pull the wand apart.

▶ **ARM SPREADER**

Hold the wand overhead with hands spread wide. Attempt to compress the stick. Reverse force, and attempt to pull the stick apart.

▶ **DEAD LIFT**

Partially squat and place the wand under the thighs. Place the hands between the legs and try to lift. Try also with hands on the outside of the legs.

▶ **ABDOMINAL TIGHTENER**

From a standing position, place the wand behind the buttocks. With hands on the ends of the wand, pull forward and resist with the abdominal muscles.

Stretching Exercises with Wands

Wands are useful for stretching, bending, and twisting movements.

▶ **SIDE BENDER**

Grip the wand and extend the arms overhead with feet apart. Bend sideways as far as possible, maintaining straight arms and legs. Recover, and bend to the other side.

▶ **BODY TWIST**

Place the wand behind the neck, with arms draped over the wand from behind. Rotate the upper body first to the right as far as possible and then to the left. The feet and hips should remain in position. The twist is at the waist.

▶ **BODY TWIST TO KNEE**

Assume body twist position. Bend the trunk forward and twist so that the right end of the wand touches the left knee (Figure 17.22). Recover, and touch the left end to the right knee.

▶ **SHOULDER STRETCHER**

Grip the wand at the ends in a regular grip. Extend the arms overhead and rotate the wand, arms, and shoulders backward until the stick touches the back of the legs. The arms should be kept straight. Those who find the stretch too easy should move their hands closer to the center of the wand.

▶ **TOE TOUCH**

Grip the wand with the hands about shoulder width apart. Bend forward, reaching down as far as possible

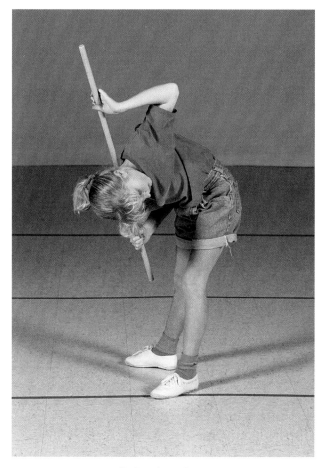

FIGURE 17.22   Body twist to knee.

without bending the knees. The movement should be slow and controlled. Try the same activity from a sitting position.

▶ **OVER THE TOES**

Sit down, flex the knees, pass the wand over the toes, and rest it against the middle of the arch on the bottoms of the feet. Grip the stick with the fingers at the outside edge of the feet. Slowly extend the legs forward, pushing against the stick and trying for a full extension of the legs.

ACTIVITIES WITH HOOPS

Most hoops manufactured in the United States are plastic, but Europeans sometimes use wooden ones. The plastic variety is less durable but more versatile. Extra hoops are needed because some breakage will occur. The standard hoop is 42 inches in diameter, but it is desirable to have smaller hoops (36 inches) for primary-grade children.

Instructional Procedures

1. Hoops produce noisy activity. The teacher may find it helpful to have the children lay their hoops on the floor when they are to listen.

2. Hoops can be a creative medium for children. Allow them free time to explore their own ideas.

3. Give the children an adequate amount of space in which to perform, for hoops require much movement.

4. In activities that require children to jump through hoops, instruct the holder to grasp the hoop lightly, so as not to cause an awkward fall if a performer hits it.

5. Hoops can serve as a "home" for various activities. For instance, the children might leave their hoops to gallop in all directions and then return quickly to the hoop on command.

6. Hoops are good targets. A hoop can be made to stand by placing an individual mat over its base.

7. When teaching the reverse spin with hoops, have the students throw the hoop up, in place, rather than forward along the floor. After they learn the upward throw, they can progress to the forward throw for distance.

RECOMMENDED ACTIVITIES

▶ **HOOPS AS FLOOR TARGETS**

Each child has a hoop, which is placed on the floor. A number of movement challenges can give direction to the activity.

1. Show the different patterns you can make by jumping or hopping in and out of the hoop.

2. Do a Bunny Jump and a Frog Jump into the center and out the other side.

3. Show the ways you can cross from one side of the hoop to the other by taking the weight on your hands inside the hoop.

4. What kinds of animal walks can you do around your hoop?

5. On all fours, show the kinds of movements you can do, with your feet inside the hoop and your hands outside. With your hands inside the hoop and your feet outside. With one foot and one hand inside, and one foot and one hand outside.

6. (Set a time limit of 15 to 30 seconds.) See how many times you can jump in and out of your hoop during this time. Now try hopping.

7. Balance on and walk around the hoop. Try to keep your feet from touching the floor.

17

8. Curl your body inside the hoop. Bridge over your hoop. Stretch across your hoop. See how many different ways you can move around the hoop.

9. Pick up your hoop and see how many different machines you can invent. Let your hoop be the steering wheel of a car. What could it be on a train or a boat?

10. Jump in and out of the hoop, using the alphabet. Jump in on the vowels and out on the consonants. Use odd and even numbers in the same way. Vary the locomotor movements.

11. Get into the hoop by using two different body parts. Move out by using three parts. Vary the number of body parts used.

12. Get organized in squads or comparable groups, and divide the hoops. Arrange the hoops in various formations, and try different locomotor movements, animal walks, and other ways of maneuvering through the maze. (After the children have gained some experience, this can become a follow-the-leader activity.)

▶ **HOOP HANDLING**

1. Spin the hoop like a top. See how long you can make it spin. Spin it again, and see how many times you can run around it before it falls to the floor.

2. Hula-hoop using various body parts such as the waist, legs, arms, and fingers. While hula-hooping on the arms, try to change the hoop from one arm to the other. Lie on the back with one or both legs pointed toward the ceiling and explore different ways the legs can twirl the hula hoop. Hula-hoop with two or more hoops.

3. Jump or hop through a hoop held by a partner. Further challenge can be added by varying the height and angle of the hoop.

4. Roll the hoop and run alongside it. Change direction when a command is given.

5. Hula-hoop on one arm. Throw the hoop in the air and catch it on the other arm.

6. Hold the hoop and swing it like a pendulum. Jump and hop in and out of the hoop.

7. Use the hoop like a jump rope. Jump forward, backward, and sideward. Do a crossover with the hands.

8. Roll the hoop with a reverse spin to make it return to you. The key to the reverse spin is to pull down (toward the floor) on the hoop as it is released. Roll the hoop with a reverse spin, jump over it, and catch it as it returns. Roll the hoop with a reverse spin, and as it returns, hoist it with the foot and catch it. Roll the hoop with a reverse spin, kick it up with the toe, and go through the hoop. Roll the hoop with a reverse spin, run around it, and catch it. Roll the hoop with a reverse spin, pick it up, and begin hooping on the arm—all in one motion.

9. Play catch with a partner. Try with two or more hoops.

10. Hula-hoop. Attempt to change hoops with a partner.

11. Have one partner roll the hoop with a reverse spin and the other attempt to crawl through the hoop. (This is done most easily just after the hoop reverses direction and begins to return to the spinner. Some children can go in and out of the hoop twice.)

12. Tell partners to spin the hoops like tops and see who can keep theirs spinning longer.

Games with Hoops

▶ **COOPERATIVE MUSICAL HOOPS**

Hoops, one per student, are placed on the floor. Players are given a locomotor movement to do. On signal, they cease the movement, find a hoop, and sit cross-legged in the center of it. Music can be used, with the children moving to the music and seeking a hoop when the music stops. Hoops can be removed by the teacher, challenging students to share hoops with each other. This can continue until all students are in three or four hoops.

▶ **AROUND THE HOOP**

The class is divided into groups of three, with children in each group numbered 1, 2, and 3. Each threesome sits back to back inside a hoop. Their heels may need to be outside the hoop. The leader calls out a direction (right or left) and names one of the numbers. The child with that number immediately gets up, runs in the stipulated direction around the hoop, then runs back to place and sits down. The winner is the first group sitting in good position after the child returns to place.

▶ **HULA-HOOP CIRCLE**

Four to six children hold hands in a circle, facing in, with a hoop dangling on one pair of joined hands. They move the hoop around the circle and back to the starting point. This requires all bodies to go through the hoop. Hands can help the hoop move, but grips cannot be released.

▶ **HULA-HOOP RELAY**

Relay teams of four to six players, each with a hoop, are placed in line or circle formation. The hoop must be held upright with the bottom of the hoop touching the floor. On signal, designated starters drop their hoops and move through the hoops held by squad members. The sequence repeats until every player has moved through the hoops.

▶ BUMPER CAR TAG

The class is divided into partners. The partners stand inside a hoop held at waist level. Three or more sets of partners are declared to be it. The object is to tag other partners, who are also moving inside a "bumper car." The game can also be played with three players in a hoop. This is challenging, as players will want to move in different directions.

▶ HOOP ADDITION RELAY

Divide the class into relay teams of four. On signal, the first person moves to the end marker (a hoop), returns, and takes the next person to the marker and so on, until all four players are in the hoop. Players must sit down in the hoop when the relay is completed.

ACTIVITIES WITH JUMP ROPES

Rope jumping is an excellent activity for conditioning all parts of the body. It increases coordination, rhythm, and timing, while offering a wide range of challenges. Rope jumping is regarded as an excellent medium for fitness development. It can be designed to suit the activity needs of all individuals regardless of age or condition. Workloads can easily be measured and modified by changing the amount of time jumped or the number of turns. It is a useful activity to teach children, because it offers carryover value for activity in later life.

Rope jumping has increased in popularity during the past decade, with the Jump Rope for Heart program offering national leadership. The program is sponsored by the American Alliance for Health, Physical Education, Recreation, and Dance as a fund-raising activity for the American Heart Association (Jump Rope for Heart materials can be obtained by contacting your local affiliate of the American Heart Association or by contacting AAHPERD at 800-213-7193, x429 or www.aapherd.org). This nationwide movement has spawned school teams, exhibitions, and competition in the form of state and national tournaments. It is a creative medium with an incredible number of variations possible. Rope-jumping skills presented in this chapter are those deemed suitable for inclusion in an elementary school physical education program. Not included are highly advanced and complex activities that are often used in competitive settings. The difficulty of advanced activities makes them less suitable for bringing success to all youngsters in physical education programs. For more information about advanced activities, review the references at the

end of the chapter. Rope-jumping activities in this chapter are grouped into three categories: (a) movements guided by rope patterns, (b) long-rope jumping, and (c) individual rope jumping.

PRE–ROPE JUMPING SKILLS

Learning to move over a rope that is placed on the floor is a prelude to rope-jumping skills. Ropes can be placed on the floor in various fashions to serve as stimuli for different locomotor and nonlocomotor movements. The educational movement factors of space, time, force, and flow can be interwoven in the activity. Youngsters can perform the challenges as individuals, with partners, or in a small group. Generally, a rope is placed in a straight line or in a circle. Geometric figures can also be formed and numbers or letters of the alphabet featured.

Rope Forming a Straight Line

When the rope is placed in a straight line, one approach is for children to begin at one end and perform the activities along the length of the rope. Many of the movements are based on hopping or jumping. The children then return to the starting point and prepare for another activity. The following are examples of pre–rope-jumping activities.

1. Jog around the rope forward and backward. Try other locomotor skills such as hopping, jumping, skipping, and sliding. Crab Walk down and back. Use various animal walks such as Bear Walk or Lame Dog Walk.
2. Hop back and forth across the rope, moving down the line. Return, using the other foot.
3. Jump lightly back and forth down the line. Return.
4. Hop slowly, under control, down the line. Hop rapidly back.
5. Jump so that the rope is between the feet each time, alternately crossing and uncrossing the feet.
6. Move on all fours, leading with different body parts.
7. Do Crouch Jumps back and forth across the rope. Vary with three points and then two points of contact.
8. Jump as high as possible going down the line and as low as possible coming back.
9. Hop with a narrow shape down and a different shape back.
10. Walk the rope like a tightrope.
11. Begin with a bridge and move the bridge down the line. Return with a different bridge.
12. Lie across the rope, holding one end. Roll down the line, causing the rope to roll around the body. Unroll the rope back to position.

13. Do a movement with the rhythm slow-slow, fast-fast-fast, going down the line, and repeat coming back.

14. "Pull" yourself down the line and "push" yourself back.

For the following movements, the child is positioned close to the center of the line and simply moves back and forth across it without materially changing the relative position.

1. Hop back and forth across the line. Jump back and forth.

2. Go over with a high movement. Come back with a low one.

3. Do a Bunny Jump across and back. A Frog Jump. A Crouch Jump.

4. Lead with different parts of the body back and forth. Propel with different parts.

5. Get into a moderately crouched position over the rope. Jump the feet back and forth over the rope.

6. Take a sprinter's position with the rope between the feet. Alternate the feet back and forth over the rope.

7. Jump back and forth lightly on the tiptoes.

8. Go back and forth, using different shapes.

9. With toes touching the rope, drop the body forward across the rope, taking the weight on both hands. Walk the hands forward, out to the limit.

10. Pretend that the rope is a river. Show different kinds of bridges that you can make over the river.

11. Stand straddling the rope. Jump up, perform a heel click (or two), and return to original position.

Rope Forming a Circle

With the rope in a circle, children can do movements around the outside clockwise and counterclockwise—walking, skipping, hopping, sliding (facing toward and away from the circle), jumping, running, and galloping. The following activities can be done with hoops also.

1. Hop in and out of the circle, moving around. Jump.

2. Jump directly in and then across. Jump backward.

3. Jump in, collapse, and jump out, without touching the rope.

4. Begin in the center of the circle. Jump forward, backward, and sideways, each time returning to the center.

5. Place the feet in the circle and walk the hands all around the outside of the circle. Place the hands inside and the feet outside. Face the floor, the ceiling, and to the side.

6. Inside the circle, make a small shape. Make a large shape so that you are touching all sides of the circle.

7. Try different balance stunts inside the circle. Close your eyes and balance.

8. Make a bridge over the circle. How many types of bridges can you make?

9. Do a Pogo Stick Jump in and out of the rope circle.

10. Do a Tightrope Walk clockwise and counterclockwise.

11. Jump and click the heels, landing inside the circle. Repeat, going out.

12. Do jump turns inside the circle without touching the rope: quarter turns, half turns, and full turns.

13. Jump in with a Bunny Jump. Jump out. Try with a Frog Jump.

14. Take the weight on the hands inside the circle so that the feet land on the other side. Try a cartwheel.

Rope Forming Various Figures

Have the rope form different figures, such as geometric shapes, letters, and numbers. In addition to the following challenges, many of the previous ones can be applied here, too.

1. With the rope and your body, form a triangle, a square, a rectangle, a diamond shape, and a figure eight.

2. With the rope and your body, form a two-letter word. Form other words.

3. Get a second rope and make your own patterns for hopping and jumping.

4. Toss the rope in the air and let it fall to the floor. Try to shape your body into the same figure that the rope made on the floor.

Partner Activity

Partner activity with ropes is excellent. Partners can work with one or two ropes, and can do matching, following, or contrasting movements. Add-On is an interesting game: One partner does an activity and the other adds on an activity to form a sequence. Using the suggested rope forms (multiple ropes) in Figure 17.23, one partner makes a series of movements. The other partner has to try to duplicate the movements.

Group Activity

Group activity with jump ropes also has good possibilities. Each child brings a rope to the group. Patterns for hopping, jumping, and other locomotor movements

FIGURE 17.23   Suggested rope forms.

can be arranged with the ropes. An achievement demonstration after a period of practice allows each group to show the patterns that they have arranged and the movements that can be done in the patterns. A further extension is to leave the patterns where they are and to rotate the groups to different locations.

LONG-ROPE JUMPING

Long-rope jumping is an excellent activity for beginning jumpers. Youngsters can concentrate on jumping the rope without learning the skill of turning. Many activities with two or more long ropes add a great deal of variety to long-rope jumping and can make it challenging for the most skilled jumpers. Long jump ropes should be 9 to 14 feet in length, with 12 to 14 feet the most commonly used. The exact length depends on the age and skill of the children; the longer the rope, the more difficult it is to turn. For primary-grade children, individual jump ropes can be used to teach beginning skills as they are shorter, making it easier for young children to turn. Another alternative is to fasten one end of the rope with a snap to an eye bolt fixed on a post or to the side of a wall. This eases the task of turning and allows more children to be actively jumping.

Chants are suggested for many of the jumping sequences. Rope-jumping chants represent a cultural heritage. In many cases, children have their own favorites. Traditionally, many chants used girls' names, because rope jumping was considered a feminine activity. Today, however, this has changed, and both sexes participate in rope-jumping activities with equal vigor and success. Several of the chants included have been modified to reflect this change.

Instructional Procedures

1. Four or five children is an appropriate group size for practicing long-rope skills. Two members of the group turn the rope while the others practice jumping. A plan for rotating turners is important so that all children receive similar amounts of practice jumping.

2. Turning the rope is a difficult skill for young children. It must be practiced regularly until children can maintain an even, steady rhythm. Effective turning is one key to successful jumping. If turning is not rhythmic, even skilled jumpers will have problems. Youngsters must be taught: Learn to turn first, then learn to jump.

3. When learning to turn the rope, incorporate the following points:
   a. Keep the elbow close to the body and concentrate on turning the rope with the forearm.
   b. The thumb should stay up during the turning motion of the hands. This will emphasize turning with the forearm.
   c. Hold the rope in front of the body at waist level. Keep the body perpendicular to the rope.

4. To practice turning, youngsters are motivated by turning the rope under a lively bouncing ball. Turners stand ready, and a third child tosses a ball upward so that it will remain in one spot while bouncing. Turners adjust the speed of the turning as the bounces become smaller and more rapid. A count can be kept of the number of successful turns before the ball ceases bouncing.

5. Children of all ages can perform long-rope jumping. To check the readiness of the children, see if they are capable of jumping in place with both feet leaving the ground simultaneously. They should be able to jump at least 2 to 3 inches off the ground, be well balanced, and land lightly with reasonably straight knees.

6. Children should understand the terms used to describe entry into the long jump rope. Front door means entering from the side where the rope is turning forward and toward the jumper after it reaches its peak. Back door means entering from the side where the rope is turning backward and away from the jumper. To enter front door, the jumper follows the rope in and jumps when it completes the turn. To enter back door, the jumper waits until the rope reaches its peak and moves in as the rope moves downward. Learning to enter at an angle is usually easier, but any path that is comfortable is acceptable.

7. Introducing and teaching youngsters long-rope jumping skills can be accomplished with the following steps:
   a. Use a shorter long rope (8 to 12 foot). Lay the rope on the floor and have youngsters jump back and forth across the rope. Emphasis should be on small, continuous jumps and learning how to jump back and forth continuously without stopping. Jumps should not be high, just enough to clear the rope.

b. Turners slowly move the rope back and forth along the floor while the jumper moves over the rope each time it moves near. The speed of the rope moving along the floor should be increased gradually. The jumper should be encouraged to jump up and down with as little forward-backward-sideways movement as possible. If necessary, use white shoe polish to mark an "X" on the floor and encourage the child to stay on target.

c. The jumper stands near the center of the rope. The rope is now moved in pendulum fashion back and forth while the jumper clears the rope each time it hits the floor. Typically, this activity is called Blue Bells.

d. The jumper starts by facing the center of the stationary rope. Use three pendulum swings followed by a full turn of the rope rotating from the jumper's back to the front. Continue jumping until a miss occurs. Verbal cueing helps most beginners find success; each time the rope hits the floor, say "Jump." If youngsters are having difficulty, have them stand behind a turner and jump (without the rope) each time the rope hits the floor.

e. When jumpers have difficulty with the rhythm, they can practice off to one side without actually jumping over the rope. A drumbeat can reinforce the rhythm with alternating heavy (jump) and light (rebound) beats.

f. Teach front-door and back-door entry, making sure that the jumper enters at an angle rather than perpendicular to the rope.

8. Instructional cues to teach long-rope jumping skills are:

a. Turn the rope with the forearm.

b. Lock the wrist and keep the thumb up while turning.

c. Stand perpendicular to the rope.

d. Barely touch the floor with the turning rope.

e. Don't cross the midline of the body with the forearm while turning the rope.

f. Jump on the balls of the feet.

g. To enter, stand near the turner and move to the center of the rope.

Introductory Skills

Some introductory skills and routines follow.

1. Holders hold the rope in a stationary position six inches above the ground. Jumpers jump over, back and forth. Raise the rope a little each time. Be sure to hold the rope loosely in the hands. This is called Building a House.

2. Ocean Wave is another stationary jumping activity. Turners make waves in the rope by moving the arms up and down. Jumpers try to time it so that they jump over a low part of the wave.

3. Holders stoop down and wiggle the rope back and forth on the floor. Jumpers try to jump over the rope and not touch it as it moves. This activity is called Snake in the Grass.

4. The jumper stands in the center between the turners, who carefully turn the rope in a complete arc over the jumper's head. As the rope completes the turn, the jumper jumps over it and exits immediately in the direction in which the rope is turned.

5. Children run through the turning rope (front door) without jumping, following the rope through.

6. While the rope is being turned, the jumper runs in (front door), jumps once, and runs out immediately.

7. Children can play school and go through the following sequence, trying to pass to the sixth grade. To pass kindergarten, run through the turning rope. To pass first grade, run in, take one jump, and run out. For the second through sixth grades, increase the number of jumps by one for each grade. A jumper who misses becomes a turner.

8. When children can jump a number of times consecutively, add motivation by using some of the chants that follow.

Intermediate Skills, Routines, and Chants

Intermediate routines require the jumper to be able to go in front door, jump, and exit front door, and to do the same sequence back door. Enough practice in the simple jumping skills and exits should be held so that confidence is fortified; students then can turn to more intricate routines. Entries and exits should be varied in the following routines.

1. Jumpers run in, jump a specified number of times, and exit.

2. Children can add chants that dictate the number of jumps, which are followed by an exit. Here are some examples.

Tick tock, tick tock,
What's the time by the clock?
It's one, two, [up to midnight].
I like coffee, I like tea,
How many people can jump like me?
One, two, three, [up to a certain number].
Hippity hop to the butcher shop,
How many times before I stop?
One, two, three, [and so on].

Bulldog, poodle, bow wow wow,
How many doggies have we now?
One, two, three, [and so on].
Michael, Michael (student's name) at the gate,
Eating cherries from a plate.
How many cherries did he (she) eat?
One, two, three, [and so on].

3. Children can label their first jump "kindergarten" and exit at any "grade." To graduate from high school, the exit would be at the twelfth grade. Each grade should be sounded crisply in succession.

4. Kangaroo (or White Horse) gets its name from the jump required for back-door entry, in which the jumper resembles a kangaroo or a leaping horse. The jumper calls out "Kangaroo!," takes the entry jump through the back door, and exits. Next time, the same jumper calls out "Kangaroo one!" and adds a jump. Successive jumps are called and added until a designated number is reached.

5. An interesting challenge is to turn the rope over a line parallel to it and have the jumper jump back and forth over the line. The jumper can vary foot position: feet together, feet apart, stride forward and back.

6. Jumpers can vary the pattern with turns. Make four quarter turns until facing the original direction. Reverse the direction of the turns.

7. Youngsters can add stunts as directed by selected chants.

Teddy Bear, Teddy Bear, turn around.
Teddy Bear, Teddy Bear, touch the ground.
Teddy Bear, Teddy Bear, show your shoe.
Teddy Bear, Teddy Bear, you better skidoo.
Teddy Bear, Teddy Bear, go upstairs.
Teddy Bear, Teddy Bear, say your prayers.
Teddy Bear, Teddy Bear, turn out the light.
Teddy Bear, Teddy Bear, say good night.
Daddy, daddy (mommy, mommy), I am sick.
Get the doctor quick, quick, quick.
Daddy, daddy, turn around.
Daddy, daddy, touch the ground.
Daddy, daddy, are you through?
Daddy, daddy, spell your name.

8. In Hot Pepper, turners turn the rope faster and faster, while the jumper tries to keep up with the increased speed. The following chants are good for Hot Pepper.

Charlie, Charlie (student's name), set the table.
Bring the plates if you are able.
Don't forget the salt and
Red hot pepper!

(On the words "Red hot pepper," the rope is turned as fast as possible until the jumper misses.)

Pease porridge hot, pease porridge cold,
Pease porridge in a pot, nine days old.
Some like it hot, hot, hot!
Ice cream, ginger ale, soda water, pop.
You get ready 'cause we're gonna turn hot!

9. In Calling In, the first player enters the rope and calls in a second player by name. Both jump three times holding hands, and then the first runs out. The second player then calls in a third player by name. Both jump three times holding hands, and the second player exits. Players should be in an informal line, since the fun comes from not knowing when one is to enter.

10. Children can enter and exit according to the call in the following chants.

In the shade and under a tree,
I'd like _____ to come in with me.
She's (he's) too fast and I'm too slow.
He stays in and I must go.
Calling in and calling out,
I call (student's name) in and I'm getting out.
House for rent,
Inquire within.
When I move out,
Let (student's name) move in.

11. In High Water, the rope is turned so that it becomes gradually higher and higher off the ground.

At the beach, at the sea,
The waves come almost to the knee.
Higher, higher, [and so forth].

12. In Stopping the Rope, the jumper (a) stops and lets the rope hit the feet, (b) stops the rope by straddling it, (c) stops with the legs crossed and the rope between the feet, or (d) stops the rope by stamping on it. The following chant works well, with accompanying action as indicated.

Junior, Junior, climb the tree.
Junior, Junior, slap your knee.
Junior, Junior, throw a kiss.
Junior, Junior, time to miss.

13. Two, three, or four children can jump at a time. After some skill has been achieved, children in combination can run in, jump a specified number of times, and run out, keeping hands joined all the time.

14. Two, three, or four children can start as a small moving circle. They run in and jump in a circle, keeping the circle moving in one direction. They run out as a circle.

15. The jumper takes in a ball or other object. Bounce the ball while jumping. Try balancing a beanbag on a body part while jumping.

17

16. A partner stands ready with a ball and tosses it back and forth to the jumper.

17. For Chase the Rabbit, four or five jumpers are in single file with a leader, the Rabbit, at the head. The Rabbit jumps in any manner he or she may wish, and all of the others must match the movements. Anyone who misses must go to the end of the line. A Rabbit who misses or stops the rope, goes to the end of the line, and the next child becomes the new Rabbit. Set a limit on how long a Rabbit can stay at the head of the line.

18. In On Four Cylinders, the challenge is to do activities in a series of fours—four of one kind of jump, four of another, and so on. The number of series can be specified, and the children may choose what they wish to include. (Tell the children that their "engines are running on four cylinders.")

19. In Begging, a jumper runs in and works his way up the rope toward one of the turners. As he jumps, he says, "Father, Father, give me a dollar." The turner replies, "Go see your mother." The jumper works his way toward the other turner and says, "Mother, Mother, give me a dollar." The turner replies, "Go to your father." This continues until a miss occurs or until one of the turners says in reply, "Get out" or "Get lost," at which time the jumper exits.

20. In Setting the Table, a jumper enters and starts jumping. A partner stands ready with at least four beanbags. While the following verse is recited, the partner tosses in the beanbags one at a time, and the jumper catches and places them in a row on the side (with the upward swing of the rope) and then exits.

> Debbie, Debbie (student's name), set the table (toss in one bag),
> Bring the plates if you are able (toss in another bag),
> Don't forget the bread and butter (toss in the other two bags).

21. Partners can go in and perform a number of stunts, such as Bouncing Ball (Figure 20.37), Wring the Dishrag (Figure 20.38), or Partner Hopping (Figure 20.81). Examine the partner stunts for other selections.

22. Children can enter and begin with a hop (one foot), then make a jump (two feet), add a hand touch next (two feet, one hand), and then jump with both hands and feet (two feet, two hands). Selected movements on hands and feet, such as Rabbit Jumps or Push-Ups, can be executed.

23. For jumping with the eyes closed, single or multiple jumpers enter and begin jumping to this chant.

> Peanuts, popcorn, soda pop,
> How many jumps before you stop?
> Close your eyes and you will see
> How many jumps that this will be!

The eyes remain closed during the jumping, which continues to a target number or a miss.

24. One or both holders can go inside and jump, turning with their outside hands. First attempts should begin with a pendulum swing and proceed to a full turn.

DOUBLE DUTCH (TWO-ROPE) JUMPING

Double Dutch rope jumping (Figure 17.24) is popular on playgrounds and in gymnasiums across the country. This type of jumping requires two rope turners using two long ropes that are turned in opposite directions. Turning two ropes simultaneously requires practice, and time must be allotted for this. Handling two ropes is tiring, so turners should be rotated frequently.

Instructional Procedures

1. Arm positions and turning motions are similar to turning a single long rope. In short, keep the upper arm stationary, rotate at the elbow with locked wrist, and keep the thumb up. Avoid crossing the midline of the body, and establish an even cadence. Rotate the hands inward toward the midline of the body (right forearm counterclockwise and left forearm clockwise). Students should concentrate on the sound of the ropes hitting the floor so that they make an even and rhythmic beat.

2. Double Dutch turning takes considerable practice. Take time to teach it as a skill that is necessary for successful jumping experiences.

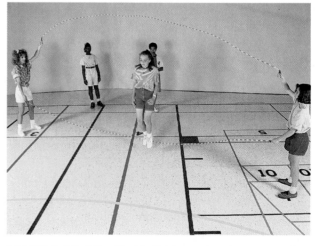

FIGURE 17.24 Double Dutch rope jumping.

3. When entering, stand beside a turner and run into the ropes when the back rope (farther from the jumper) touches the floor. Turners should be taught to say "Go" each time the back rope touches the floor.

4. Concentrate on jumping in the center of the ropes facing a turner. Use white shoe polish to mark a jumping target.

5. Exit the ropes by facing and jumping toward one turner and exiting immediately after jumping. The exit should be made as close to the turner's shoulder as possible.

6. Practice many of the skills listed in the long-rope jumping section (pages 377–380). Many of the chants and stunts provide challenge and variety to the unit.

▶ DOUBLE DUTCH SKILLS

1. *Basic jump on both feet.* Land on the balls of the feet, keeping ankles and knees together with hands across the stomach.

2. *Turnaround.* Circle left or right using the basic jump. Begin circling slowly at first and then increase speed. To increase the challenge, try the turnaround on one foot.

3. *Straddle Jump.* Jump to the straddle position and return to closed position. Try a Straddle Cross Jump by crossing the legs on return to the closed position. The straddle jumps should be performed facing away from the turners.

4. *Scissors Jump.* Jump to a stride position with the left foot forward and the right foot back about 8 inches apart. Each jump requires reversing the position of the feet.

5. *Jogging Step.* Run in place with a jogging step. Increase the challenge by circling while jogging.

6. *Hot Peppers.* Use the Jogging Step and gradually increase the speed of the ropes.

7. *Half turn.* Perform a half turn with each jump. Remember to lead the turn with the head and shoulders.

8. *Ball tossing.* Toss and catch a beanbag or playground ball while jumping.

9. *Individual rope jumping.* Enter double dutch with an individual rope and jump. Face the turner and decrease the length of the individual jump rope.

10. The following activities are interesting variations for reviving motivation:

    a. *Double Irish.* Two ropes are turned in the reverse directions used in Double Dutch. The left hand turns counterclockwise and the right hand clockwise. Entry is made when the near rope hits the floor. Jumpers should time their entry by following the near rope on its downward swing.

    b. *Egg Beater.* Two long ropes are turned at right angles simultaneously by four turners (Figure 17.25). Entry is made at the quadrant where both ropes are turning front doors. The number of ropes

FIGURE 17.25 Egg Beater.

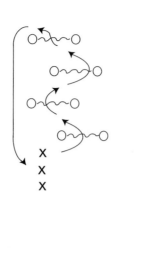

FIGURE 17.26   Formations for jumping rope.

being turned can be increased to three or four. This activity is easier than jumping Double Dutch since the jumping action is similar to single-rope jumping. It is an excellent activity for building confidence in jumping more than one long rope.

Formation Jumping

For formation jumping, four to six long ropes with turners can be placed in various patterns, with tasks specified for each rope. Ropes can be turned in the same direction, or the turning directions can be mixed. Several formations are illustrated in Figure 17.26.

INDIVIDUAL ROPE JUMPING

Individual rope jumping should place emphasis on establishing basic turning skills and letting children create personal routines. Individual rope jumping is particularly valuable as part of the conditioning process for certain sports. It lends itself to prescribed doses based on number of turns, length of participation, speed of the turning rope, and various steps. Because rope jumping is of a rhythmic nature, the addition of music is a natural progression. Music adds much to the activity and enables the jumper to create and organize routines to be performed to the musical pieces. The most effective approach is probably a combination of experiences with and without music.

There are a number of types of jump ropes on the market, all of which are satisfactory, depending on the likes and dislikes of the instructor. The most popular appear to be the solid plastic speed (often called licorice) ropes and the beaded or segmented ropes. The speed rope is excellent for rapid turning and doing tricks. It does not

maintain momentum as well as the segmented ropes, which can be important for beginners. Sash cord is economical but doesn't wear well on blacktop or cement. In addition, without handles, it is a second-rate jump rope.

Instructional Procedures

1. The length of the rope is dependent on the height of the jumper. It should be long enough so that the ends reach to the armpits (Figure 17.27) or slightly higher when the child stands on its center. Preschool children generally use 6-foot ropes, and the primary-level group needs mostly 7-foot ropes, with a few 6- and 8-foot lengths. Grades 3 through 6 need a mixture of 7-, 8-, and 9-foot ropes. A 9- or 10-foot rope serves well for tall students and most instructors. Ropes or handles can be color-coded for length.

   Two types of ropes are available—the beaded (plastic segment) and the plastic (licorice) rope. The beaded ropes are heavier and seem easier to turn for beginning jumpers. The drawback to the beaded ropes is that they hurt when they hit another student. Also, if the segments are made round, the rope will roll easily on the floor and cause children to fall when they step on it. The plastic licorice ropes are lighter and give less wind resistance. For experienced jumpers more speed and control can be gained with this type of rope. An ideal situation would be to have a set of each type.

2. Posture is an important consideration in rope jumping. The body should be in good alignment, with the head up and the eyes looking straight ahead. The jump is made with the body in an erect position. A slight straightening of the knees provides the lift

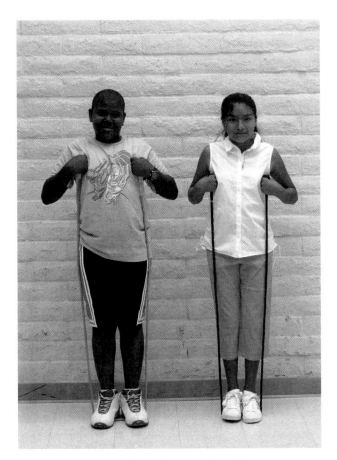

FIGURE 17.27   Correct jump rope length.

for the jump, which should be of minimal height (about one inch). The wrists supply the force to turn the rope, with the elbows kept close to the body and extended at a 90-degree angle. A pumping action and lifting of the arms is unnecessary. The landing should be made on the balls of the feet, with the knees bent slightly to cushion the shock. Usually, the feet, ankles, and legs are kept together, except when a specific step calls for a different position.

3. The rope should be held by the index finger and thumb on each side with the hands making a small circle. The elbows should be held near the sides to avoid making large arm circles with the rope.

4. Introducing and teaching youngsters individual rope jumping skills can be accomplished with the following steps:

   a. Students should first jump without the rope until they learn the correct rhythm and footwork. For slow time, this would be a jump and then a rebound step. Children can pretend that they are turning the rope. Remember that rope jumping involves learning two separate skills:

jumping a rope and turning a rope. Youngsters who have a problem need to practice the parts separately before they are put together as a whole.

   b. Turn the rope over the head of the jumper and catch it with the toes.

   c. The jumper holds the rope stationary in front of the body. Jump forward and backward over the rope. To increase the challenge, swing the rope slightly. Gradually increase the swing until a full turn of the rope is made.

   d. Hold the rope to one side with both hands, swing the rope forward, and jump each time the rope hits the floor. If swinging the rope is a problem, practice without jumping first.

5. Music can be added when jumpers have learned the first stages of jumping. Music provides a challenge for continued jumping.

6. In the primary-level group, some children cannot jump, but by the third grade, all children who have had some experience should be able to jump. Children who cannot jump may be helped by the pendulum swing of the long rope, or another student jumping with the child inside an individual rope. Cues such as "Jump" or "Ready-jump" should be used.

7. Most steps can be done with either rhythm: slow time or fast time. In slow-time rhythm, the performer jumps over the rope, rebounds, and then executes the second step (or repeats the original step) on the second jump. The rebound is simply a hop in place as the rope passes over the head. Better jumpers bend the knees only slightly, without actually leaving the floor on rebound. The object of the rebound is to carry the rhythm between steps. The rope is rotating slowly, passing under the feet on every other beat, and the feet also move slowly, since there is rebound between each jump.

   In fast-time rhythm, the rope rotates in time with the music, one turn per beat (120 to 180 turns per minute, depending on the tune's tempo), and the performer executes a step only when the rope is passing under the feet.

8. Instructional cues to use for improving jumping technique are as follows:

   a. Keep the arms at the side of the body while turning. (Many children lift the arms to shoulder level trying to move the rope overhead. This makes it impossible for the youngster to jump over the elevated rope.)

   b. Turn the rope by making small circles with the wrists.

17

FIGURE 17.28 Collecting the ropes.

c. Jump on the balls of the feet.

d. Bend the knees slightly to absorb the force of the jump.

e. Make a small jump over the rope.

9. To collect ropes at the completion of a rope-jumping activity, have two or three children act as monitors. They put both arms out to the front or to the side at shoulder level. The other children then drape the ropes over their arms (Figure 17.28). The monitors return the ropes to the correct storage area.

Basic Steps

The basic steps presented here can be done in slow or fast time. After youngsters have mastered the first six steps in slow time, fast time can be introduced. The Alternate-Foot Basic Step and Spread Legs Forward and Backward are two steps that work well for introducing fast-time jumping.

▶ SIDE SWING

Swing the rope, held with both hands to one side of the body. Switch and swing the rope on the other side of the body.

▶ DOUBLE SIDE SWING AND JUMP

Swing the rope once on each side of the body. Follow the second swing with a jump over the rope. The sequence should be swing, swing, jump.

▶ TWO-FOOT BASIC STEP

In the Two-Foot Basic Step, jump over the rope with feet together as it passes under the feet, then take a preparatory rebound while the rope is over the head.

▶ ALTERNATE-FOOT BASIC STEP

In the Alternate-Foot Basic Step, as the rope passes under the feet, the weight is shifted alternately from one foot to the other, raising the unweighted foot in a running position.

▶ BIRD JUMPS

Jump with the toes pointed in (pigeon walk) and with the toes pointed out (duck walk). Alternate toes in and toes out.

▶ SWING-STEP FORWARD

The Swing-Step Forward is the same as the Alternate-Foot Basic Step, except that the free leg swings forward. The knee is kept loose, and the foot swings naturally.

▶ SWING-STEP SIDEWAYS

The Swing-Step Sideways is the same as the Swing-Step Forward, except that the free leg is swung to the side. The knee should be kept stiff. The sideways swing is about 12 inches.

▶ ROCKER STEP

In executing the Rocker Step, one leg is always forward in a walking-stride position. As the rope passes under the feet, the weight is shifted from the back foot to the forward foot. The rebound is taken on the forward foot while the rope is above the head. On the next turn of the rope, the weight is shifted from the forward foot to the back foot, repeating the rebound on the back foot.

▶ SPREAD LEGS FORWARD AND BACKWARD

For Spread Legs Forward and Backward, start in a stride position (as in the Rocker) with weight equally distributed on both feet. As the rope passes under the feet, jump into the air and reverse the position of the feet.

▶ STRADDLE JUMP

Alternate a regular jump with a straddle jump. The straddle jump is performed with the feet spread to shoulder width.

▶ CROSS LEGS SIDEWAYS

In Cross Legs Sideways, as the rope passes under the feet, spread the legs in a straddle position (sideways) to take the rebound. As the rope passes under the feet on the next turn, jump into the air and cross the feet with the right foot forward. Then repeat with the left foot forward and continue this alternation.

▶ TOE-TOUCH FORWARD

To do the Toe-Touch Forward, swing the right foot forward as the rope passes under the feet and touch the right toes on the next count. Then alternate, landing on the right foot and touching the left toes forward.

▶ TOE-TOUCH BACKWARD

The Toe-Touch Backward is similar to the Swing-Step Sideways, except that the toes of the free foot touch to the back at the end of the swing.

▶ SHUFFLE STEP

The Shuffle Step involves pushing off with the right foot and sidestepping to the left as the rope passes under the feet. Land with the weight on the left foot and touch the right toes beside the left heel. Repeat the step in the opposite direction.

▶ SKIER

The Skier is a double-foot jump similar to a technique used by skiers. A chalked or painted line is needed. The jumper stands on both feet to one side of the line. Jumping is done sideways back and forth over the line. Children should try it in a forward and backward direction also.

▶ HEEL-TOE

In the Heel-Toe, as the rope passes under the feet, jump with the weight landing on the right foot while touching the left heel forward. On the next turn of the rope, jump, land on the same foot, and touch the left toes beside the right heel. This pattern is then repeated with the opposite foot bearing the weight.

▶ LEG FLING

On the first jump, bring the right leg up so that it is parallel to the floor with the knee bent. On the second jump, kick the same leg out and up as high as possible. Try with the other leg.

▶ HEEL CLICK

Do two or three Swing-Steps Sideways, in slow time, in preparation for the Heel Click. When the right foot swings sideways, instead of a hop or rebound when the rope is above the head, raise the left foot to click the heel of the right foot. Repeat on the left side.

▶ STEP-TAP

In the Step-Tap, as the rope passes under the feet, push off with the right foot and land on the left. While the rope is turning above the head, brush the sole of the right foot forward and then backward. As the rope passes under the feet for the second turn, push off with the left foot, land on the right, and repeat.

▶ SKIPPING

Do a step-hop (skip) over the rope. Start slowly and gradually increase the speed of the rope.

▶ SCHOTTISCHE STEP

The Schottische Step can be done to double-time rhythm, or it can be done with a varied rhythm. The pattern is step, step, step, hop (repeat), followed by four step-hops. In varied rhythm, three quick turns in fast time are made for the first three steps and then double-time rhythm prevails. The step should be practiced first in place and then in general space. Schottische music should be introduced.

▶ BLEKING STEP

The Bleking Step has the pattern slow-slow, fast-fast-fast. The rope should turn to conform to this pattern. The step begins with a hop on the left foot with the right heel forward, followed by a hop on the right with the left heel forward. This action is repeated with three quick changes: right, left, right. The whole pattern is then repeated, beginning with a hop on the right foot with the left heel extended. If done to the music for the bleking dance (page 431), four bleking steps of slow-slow, fast-fast-fast are done. The second part of the music (the chorus) allows the children to organize a routine of their own. They must listen for changes in the music.

Crossing Arms

Once the basic steps are mastered, crossing the arms while turning the rope provides an interesting variation. Crossing the arms during forward turning is easier than crossing behind the back during backward turning. During crossing, the hands exchange places. This means that for forward crossing, the elbows are close to each other. This is not possible during backward crossing. Crossing and uncrossing can be done at predetermined points after a stipulated number of turns. Crossing can be accomplished during any of the routines.

17

Double Turning

The double turn of the rope is also interesting. The jumper does a few basic steps in preparation for the double turn. As the rope approaches the feet, the child gives an extremely hard flip of the rope from the wrists, jumps from 6 to 8 inches in height, and allows the rope to pass under the feet twice before landing. The jumper must bend forward at the waist somewhat, which increases the speed of the turn. A substantial challenge for advanced rope jumpers is to see how many consecutive double-turn jumps they can do.

Shifting from Forward to Backward Jumping

To switch from forward to backward jumping without stopping the rope, any of the following techniques can be used.

1. As the rope starts downward in forward jumping, rather than allowing it to pass under the feet, the performer swings both arms to the left (or right) and makes a half turn of the body in that direction (i.e., facing the rope). On the next downward swing, the jumper spreads the arms and starts turning in the opposite direction. This method also works for shifting from backward to forward jumping.

2. When the rope is directly above the head, the performer extends both arms, causing the rope to hesitate momentarily, at the same time making a half-turn in either direction and continuing to skip with the rope turning in the opposite direction.

3. From a crossed-arm position, as the rope is going above the performer's head, the jumper may uncross the arms and turn simultaneously. This starts the rope turning and the performer jumping in the opposite direction.

Sideways Skipping

In sideways skipping, the rope is turned laterally with one hand held high and the other extended downward. The rope is swung around the body sideways. To accomplish this, the jumper starts with the right hand held high overhead and the left hand extended down the center of the body. Swing the rope to the left, at the same time raising the left leg sideways. Usually the speed is slow time, with the rebound taken on each leg in turn. Later, better jumpers may progress to fast-time speed. The rope passes under the left leg, and the jumper then is straddling the rope as it moves around his body behind him. Take the weight on the left foot, raising the right foot sideways. A rebound step on the left as the

rope moves to the front brings the jumper back to the original position.

Combination Possibilities

Numerous combinations of steps and rope tricks are possible in rope jumping. Some ideas are:

1. Changes in the speed of the turn—slow time and fast time—can be made. Children should be able to shift from one speed to another, particularly when the music changes.

2. Developing expertise in various foot patterns and steps is important. Children should practice changing from one foot pattern to another.

3. The crossed-hands position should be tried both forward and backward. Many of the basic steps can be combined with crossed-hands position to add challenge.

4. Moving from a forward to a backward turn and returning should be practiced. Perform the turn while doing a number of different basic steps.

5. Double turns combined with basic steps look impressive and are challenging. A few children may be able to do a triple turn.

6. Children should try to move forward, backward, and sideways, employing a variety of the basic steps.

7. Backward jumping is exciting as it is a different skill than forward jumping. Most basic steps can be done backward or modified for the backward turn.

8. Speedy turns (Hot Peppers) can be practiced. Have children see how fast they can turn the rope for 15 or 30 seconds.

Individual Rope Jumping with Partners

Many interesting combinations are possible when one child turns the individual rope and one or more children jump it. For those routines in which the directions call for a child to run into a jumping pattern, it may be more effective to begin with the child already in position, before proceeding to the run-in stage.

1. The first child turns the rope and the other stands in front, ready to enter.
    a. Run in and face partner, and both jump (Figure 17.29).
    b. Run in and turn back to partner, and both jump.
    c. Decide which steps are to be done; then run in and match steps.
    d. Repeat with the rope turning backward.
    e. Run in with a ball and bounce it during the jumping.

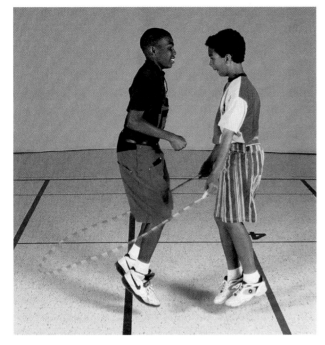

FIGURE 17.29   Rope jumping with a partner.

2. Partners stand side by side, clasp inside hands, and turn the rope with outside hands.

   a.   Face the same direction and turn the rope.

   b.   Face opposite directions, clasp left hands, and turn the rope.

   c.   Face opposite directions, clasp right hands, and turn the rope.

   d.   Repeat routines with inside knees raised.

   e.   Repeat routines with elbows locked. Try other arm positions.

3. The first child turns the rope while the second is to the rear ready to run in. The second child runs in and grasps the first child's waist or shoulders, and they jump together (engine and caboose).

4. The children stand back to back, holding a single rope in the right hand.

   a.   Turn in one direction—forward for one and backward for the other.

   b.   Reverse direction.

   c.   Change to left hands, and repeat.

5. Three children jump. One turns the rope forward; one runs in, in front; and one runs in behind. All three jump. Try with the rope turning backward.

6. Two jumpers, each with a rope, face each other and turn both ropes together, forward for one and backward for the other, jumping over both ropes at once. Turn the ropes alternately, jumping each rope in turn.

7. One partner jumps in a usual individual rope pattern. The other is positioned to the side. The turning partner hands over one end of the rope, and the other maintains the turning rhythm and then hands the rope back.

   a.   Try from the other side.

   b.   Turn the rope backward.

8. Using a single rope held in the right hand, partners face each other and turn the rope in slow time. With the rope overhead, one partner makes a turn to the left (turning in) and jumps inside the rope, exiting by turning either way. See if both can turn inside.

Movement Sequences to Music

The opportunities for creative movement sequences performed to music are unlimited. Music must have a definite beat and a bouncy quality. Pieces with a two-part format, usually labeled the verse and the chorus, are excellent. The change from the verse to the chorus signals changes in rope-jumping pattern. Many of the recordings listed in Chapter 19 can be used quite successfully for rope jumping to music. Schottisches, marches, and polkas provide good background. Popular rock music can be used to motivate youngsters if it has a strong and even rhythm. In addition, special selections for rope jumping are available from commercial sources. Suggested recordings include:

   The Muffin Man (page 426)

   Looby Loo (page 425)

   Bleking (page 431)

   Pop Goes the Weasel (page 436)

   Schottische (page 458)

   Polka (page 454)

DEVISING SEQUENCES TO MUSIC

Devising jumping sequences is a good opportunity for children to create their own routines to selected music. Simple changes from slow time to fast time can introduce this activity. Later, different steps can be incorporated, crossing and uncrossing arms can be included, and then the turning direction can be varied. Partner rope-jumping stunts can also be adapted to music. Suggestions for incorporating different steps in the sequences follow.

1. "Pop Goes the Weasel" has a definite verse and chorus change. The children can switch from slow-time jumping to fast-time jumping on the chorus.

2. Bleking offers an interesting change in rope speed. The rhythm is slow-slow, fast-fast-fast (four times). The rope should be turned in keeping with the beat. Later, the bleking step can be added.

17

3. Using schottische music, children can do the schottische step in place twice and four moving step-hops in different directions during the chorus.

4. To "Little Brown Jug," a four-part routine can be done to four rounds of the music.

   First verse: Two-Foot Basic Step (slow time)

   Chorus: Two-Foot Basic Step (fast time)

   Second verse: Alternate-Foot Basic Step (slow time)

   Chorus: Alternate-Foot Basic Step (fast time)

   Third verse: Swing-Step Forward (slow time)

   Chorus: Swing-Step Forward (fast time)

   Fourth verse: Swing-Step Sideways (slow time)

   Chorus: Swing-Step Sideways (fast time)

Assessment of Individual Rope Jumping

Individual rope-jumping stunts, because of their specificity and individuality, can be adapted easily to learning packages and contract teaching. Skill assessment can be based on the accomplishment of a stated maneuver in so many turns of the rope. The assessment can be organized progressively, or can be grouped by beginning, intermediate, and advanced tests. An example of a beginning test follows. All test items are done first in slow time and then in fast time.

1. *Two-Foot Basic Step:* 10 turns

2. *Alternate-Foot Basic Step:* 10 turns

3. *Turning rope backward:* 10 turns

4. *Alternate crossing arms:* 10 turns

5. *Running forward:* 20 turns

Intermediate and advanced tests can be organized similarly.

FOOTBAG ACTIVITIES

A footbag is a specific object used for footbag skills and games. The construction varies with the manufacturer, although most footbags are spheres constructed of leather and are stitched internally for durability. Normal size is about two inches in diameter, and the weight is a little over one ounce. The object of the activities is to keep the bag in the air by means of foot contact.

The kicking motion used for footbag activities is new to most participants because of the lift, which is performed by lifting the foot upward, not away from the body. The lifting motion enables the footbag flight to be directed upward for controlled consecutive kicks and passes. The ball is soft and flexible, with no bounce. It must be designed specifically as a footbag.

Several points contribute to successful footbag work. The basic athletic stance (ready position) is used with the feet at approximately shoulder width and pointed straight ahead. Knees are bent slightly, with the weight lowered.

There should be equal use of both feet for lifting and kicking. The support (nonkicking) foot is important for maintaining balance and keeping the body in a crouched position. Eye focus on the footbag is essential. Kicking speed should be slow; most beginners tend to kick too quickly. The kicking speed should be about that of the descending footbag. "Slow" and "low" are the key words in kicking.

The arms and upper body are used for balance and control. For the outside and back kicks, an outstretched arm, opposite to the kicking foot and in line with it, aids in maintaining balance. The near arm is carried behind the body so as not to restrict the player's vision. For inside kicks, the arms are relaxed and in balanced position.

To begin, start with a hand toss to self or with a courtesy toss from another player. A restriction is made that touching the footbag with any part of the body above the waist is a foul and interrupts any sequence of kicks. Three basic kicks are recommended.

1. *Inside kick.* This kick is used when the footbag falls low and directly in front of both shoulders. Use the inside of the foot for contact by turning the instep and the ankle upward to create a flat striking surface. Curling the toes under aids in creating a flat striking surface. Contact with the footbag is made at about knee level.

2. *Outside kick.* This kick is used when the footbag falls outside of either shoulder. The outside of the foot is used by turning the ankle and knee in to create a flat striking surface. With the kicking foot now parallel to the playing surface, use a smooth lifting motion, striking the footbag at approximately knee level. Pointing the toes up aids in creating a flat surface.

3. *Back kick.* This kick is somewhat similar to the outside kick and serves when the footbag goes directly overhead or is approaching the upper body directly. The hips and body must rotate parallel to the flight direction to enable the footbag to pass while still maintaining constant eye contact. Lean forward in the direction of the footbag's flight and allow it to pass by before executing the kick.

Play can take different forms.

1. *Individual play.* Individuals attempt to see how many consecutive times they can keep the footbag in play. One point is scored for each kick.

2. *Partner play.* Partners alternate kicking the footbag. Score one point for each alternate successful kick.

3. *Group play.* A circle of four or five individuals is the basic formation. Rules governing consecutive kicks

are (a) all members of the circle must have kicked the footbag for a consecutive run to count, and (b) return kicks are prohibited; that is, kickers may not receive return kicks from the person to whom they kicked the footbag.

Footbag play is an enjoyable activity, but the skills are not easily learned. Persistence and patience are needed. There will be many misses before students slowly gain control. Many physical education suppliers carry footbags, but if sources are needed and information is desired, write to: World Footbag Association, P.O. Box 775208, Steamboat Springs, CO 80477; 1-800-878-8797, http://worldfootbag.com.

RHYTHMIC GYMNASTICS

Rhythmic gymnastics became popular in the United States during the 1970s and was then accepted as an official sport competition in the 1984 Olympic Games. The activities are broad in scope and merit much more explanation than can be presented in this context. Essentially, activities in rhythmic gymnastics are routines done to music by a performer using a particular type of manipulative equipment. The routine can be either individual, partner, or team competition. Equipment used are balls, jump ropes, hoops, ribbons, and clubs. Wands, flags, and scarves are sometimes included, but not in national or international competition. The elements of competition will not be discussed in this presentation.

Many movement qualities, such as balance, poise, grace, flow of body movement, coordination, rhythm, and kinesthetic sense, grow out of serious participation in rhythmic gymnastics. Fitness qualities of agility, flexibility, and proper posture are also developed. Furthermore, skill in handling the various pieces of manipulative equipment is enhanced, because these skills must be mastered before they can be organized into a routine set to music.

Participants, after initial practice in skill development, should work with music. In competitive situations the music is restricted to one instrument. In the school setting the music should be instrumental, light, lively, and enjoyable to the gymnast. Most companies dealing in music for physical education stock specialized recordings for gymnastic movement, with different selections specified for various pieces of equipment. Most of these contain directions for suggested routines. There is no substitute, however, for teacher ingenuity in helping children expand and create their routines.

This is an excellent unit for developing group routines in which a class works together. Routines can be used for physical education demonstrations, back-to-school presentations, and at halftimes of athletic events. The routines are impressive and do not require a high level of skill. All youngsters are capable of participating and will enjoy the opportunity to be involved in a "team" event.

Organizing the Program

The activities presented here focus on balls, jump ropes, hoops, and ribbons, all of which ordinarily are covered in the elementary program. The club is one of the most difficult of the hand apparatus to use and is therefore not an item for instruction in elementary school programs.

The goal of rhythmic gymnastics is continuous body movement with the selected piece of equipment. Composition goals are originality, variety of movement, use of the performing area, performance presentation, and smoothness of transition. Harmony of movement with the music, the apparatus, and execution factors are also important. The length of an individual competitive routine is one minute to one minute and 30 seconds, but performing time should be shortened for youngsters. Group routines last two to three minutes and may involve one or two types of equipment. The primary goal is the personal satisfaction that students receive from participating in the program. Offering students an introduction to these activities is more important than the competitive aspect.

Probably the most practical way to include rhythmic gymnastics in the curriculum is a dual approach. The basic skills are taught to all children in physical education classes, allowing opportunity for expression through the composition of creative routines. More refined work can take place through the intramural program or a sport club. Students can choose on an elective basis to participate in competition. Instructors often lack background in these activities. This problem may be solved by bringing in dance instructors from private clubs to introduce the activities.

Developing Routines

Routines for the elementary level should be uncomplicated and based on learned skills. Aesthetics, although important as skill develops, should be of secondary emphasis. Ballet, jazz, and modern dance movements, along with basic dance steps, are normally included in high-level competition.

In developing routines to music, children need to remember that most music is based on units of 8 or 16 counts. Movements are performed in the sagittal, frontal, and horizontal planes. This is the terminology used when developing routines and should be learned by youngsters. The sagittal plane is an imaginary division of the body into right and left halves. Movements "in the sagittal" are performed parallel to this plane on either side of the body. The horizontal plane involves movements that are parallel to the floor. The frontal plane divides the body into front and rear halves. Movements in this plane are performed parallel to this plane either in front of or in back of the body.

An effective way to form a routine is to teach the beginning of a routine and then let youngsters create the remainder. For example, perform the following movements using ribbons. End each series with the hands in front of the waist.

Sagittal forward circles on the right side (6 counts)

Sagittal forward circles on the left side (6 counts)

Elevator (page 482) (4 counts)

In this fashion the routine could consist of a number of 16-count units, each of which is concluded with the Elevator (four counts). Students could develop additional units. For any one piece of apparatus, certain skill areas can be specified. It is then up to the participant to include these at some point in the routine.

▶ RHYTHMIC GYMNASTIC BALL SKILLS

The ball should be of sufficient size that it cannot be grasped by the hand but must rest in the hand and be controlled by balance. For elementary school children, use either a 6-inch or an 8.5-inch ball. Balls should be moderately inflated.

In handling the ball, the fingers should be closed and slightly bent, with the ball resting in the palm. In throwing, the ball can roll from the fingertips. After catching, the ball returns immediately to the palm.

The following ball skills are representative of activities that can be combined to develop a routine:

1. Rolling. In a sitting position, try the following activities: Roll under the legs and around the back; around the body; down the legs; down the arms; down the legs, lift legs and toss the ball off the toes into the air and catch.

2. Bouncing. Combine basketball dribbling drills with graceful body movements; execute locomotor dance-type movements while bouncing.

3. Toss and catch the ball employing different body positions.

4. Add locomotor movements to tosses and catches.

5. Perform body waves with the ball.

6. Throw and/or bounce the ball in a variety of ways.

7. Execute swinging movements (also circular movements). Swinging movements are more difficult than they first appear. The ball must be retained in the palm while the movements are performed.

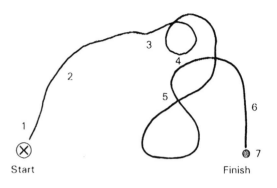

FIGURE 17.30 Floor pattern for routine using balls.

8. Try different balancing movements. These are spirals, curls, and other balances that are inherent to rhythmic gymnastics.

9. Allow opportunity for student exploration combining a number of these activities.

Figure 17.30 is an example of a simple routine using balls. The numbers refer to the floor area in the figure where each activity should be performed.

1. Bounce the ball in place.

2. Bounce the ball while moving forward slowly.

3. Run forward while making swing tosses from side to side.

4. Bounce the ball and make a full turn.

5. Run in a figure-eight pattern.

6. Toss the ball up and catch it with one hand.

7. Finish with a toss and catch behind the back.

▶ RHYTHMIC GYMNASTIC ROPE ROUTINES

As with ball routines, jump rope routines can be categorized in a number of areas. Most important is that the participant be able to do the basic jumps with consummate skill. Ropes can be used full length, folded in half, or folded in fourths. Knotting the end of the rope makes it easier to handle. Proper length is determined by standing on the center of the rope with one foot and extending the rope ends to the outstretched hands at shoulder level. Handles are not appropriate. Most rope jumping is done with the hands far apart. The rope should not touch the floor, but should pass slightly above it. The jumping techniques used for rhythmic gymnastics obviously differ from those taught in the physical education class. The following are examples of movements that can be performed using jump ropes.

1. Try single and double jumps forward and backward.
2. Circle the rope on each side of the body holding both ends of the rope.
3. Make figure-eight swings by holding both ends of the rope; or, holding the center of the rope and swinging the ends.
4. Swing the rope in pendulum fashion and jump it.
5. Run or skip over a turning rope. Try forward and backward.
6. Do a schottische step over a turning rope.
7. Holding the ends and center of the rope, kneel and horizontally circle the rope close to the floor. Stand and circle the rope overhead.
8. Perform a body wrap with the rope. (Hold one end on the hip, wrap the rope around the body with the other hand.)
9. Upon completion of a jump over a backward-turning rope, toss the rope with both ends into the air and catch.
10. Run while holding both ends of the rope in one hand and circling the rope sagittally backward at the side of the body. Toss the rope and catch it while running.
11. While performing a dance step, toss and catch the rope.
12. Hold both ends of the rope and swing it around the body like a cape.
13. Perform leaps while circling the rope sagittally at one side of the body.
14. Try different balance movements. Balance movements add variety and permit the performer to catch his breath. These involve held body positions, with the rope underneath the foot or hooked around a foot.
15. Hold the rope around the foot and make shapes with the body and foot-rope connection.
16. Explore and combine a number of the activities described.

▶ RHYTHMIC GYMNASTIC HOOP MOVEMENTS

The basic hoop stunts and challenges (pages 373–375) should first be mastered. The same hoop used in physical education classes is suitable for these routines. The hoop may be held, tossed, or caught in one or both hands and with a variety of different grips (Figure 17.31). Hoops may turn forward or backward. Some suggested rhythmic movements with hoops follow.

FIGURE 17.31 Rhythmic gymnastic movements using hoops.

1. *Swinging movements.* A variety of swinging movements are possible. The swinging movement should be very large. Good alignment between body and hoop is important. Hoops can be swung in a frontal, sagittal, or horizontal plane. The movements can be done in place or involve locomotion. Examples include the following:
   a. across the body
   b. with body lean
   c. around the body, changing hands
   d. across the body, changing hands
   e. overhead, changing hands, and swinging downward
   f. swinging in a figure-eight pattern
2. *Spinning movements.* This movement entails turning the hoop, usually with both hands but sometimes with one. The hoop also can be spun on the ground. Examples include the following:
   a. Spin in front of the body.
   b. Spin on the floor.
   c. Spin and kick one leg over the hoop. Add a full body turn after the kickover.
3. *Circling movements.* These are the movements most characteristic of hoop activities. Hoops can be twirled by the hand, wrist, arm, leg, or body (hula-hooping). Changes are made from one hand or wrist to the other. Examples of possible activities include the following:
   a. Extend the arm in front of the body. Circle on the hand between the thumb and first finger in the frontal plane.
   b. Circle the hoop while swaying from side to side.

c. Circle the hoop horizontally overhead.

d. Hold both sides of the hoop and circle it in front of the body.

e. Circle the hoop around different parts of the body.

4. *Tossing and catching movements.* The hoop can be tossed high in the air with one or both hands. The catch should be one-handed, between the thumb and index finger. Most tosses grow out of swinging or circling movements. Examples include the following:

a. Try with one- and two-handed catches.

b. Toss the hoop in different directions.

c. Toss overhead from hand to hand.

d. Circle the hoop on the hand, toss into the air, and catch.

5. *Rolling movements.* The hoop can be rolled on the floor—either forward or reverse (return) rolling—or can be rolled on the body in diverse ways. If rolled along the floor, various jumps can be executed over the rolling hoop. The hoop can be rolled along one arm to the other, on the front or the back of the body. Specific rolling activities include the following:

a. Roll the hoop and run alongside it.

b. Roll the hoop and move through it.

c. Roll the hoop and jump over it.

6. *Jumping movements.* The hoop, turned forward or backward, can be used in a manner similar to a jump rope.

▶ RHYTHMIC GYMNASTIC RIBBON MOVEMENTS

Ribbon movements are spectacular and make effective demonstrations. Official ribbon length is around 21 feet with the first 3 feet doubled, but for practical purposes, shorter lengths are used at the elementary school level.

Ribbons can be made easily in a variety of colors. A rhythmic flow of movement is desired, featuring circular, oval, spiral, and wavelike shapes. A light flowing movement is the goal, with total body involvement. The dowel or wand to which the ribbon is attached should be an extension of the hand and arm. Laterality is also a consideration. The following are basic ribbon movements.

1. *Swinging movements.* The entire body should coordinate with these large, swinging motions:

a. Swing the ribbon forward and backward in the sagittal plane.

b. Swing the ribbon across and in front of the body in the frontal plane.

c. Swing the ribbon overhead from side to side.

d. Swing the ribbon upward and catch the end of it.

e. While holding both ends of the ribbon, swing it upward, around, and over the body.

2. *Circling movements.* Large circles should involve the whole arm; smaller circles involve the wrist. Circles are made in different planes: frontal, sagittal, and horizontal.

a. Circle the ribbon at different levels.

b. Circle the ribbon horizontally, vertically, or diagonally.

c. Circle the ribbon in front of the body, around the body, and behind the body.

d. Run while circling the ribbon overhead; leap as the ribbon is circled downward and under the legs.

e. Add dance steps and turns while circling the ribbon.

3. *Figure-eight movements.* Figure eights are also made in the three planes. The two halves of the figure eight should be the same size and on the same plane level. The figure can be made with long arm movements or with movements of the lower arm or wrist. While performing a figure eight, hop through the loop when the ribbon passes the side of the body.

4. *Zigzag movements.* Zigzag movements can be made in the air or on the floor. These are done with continuous up-and-down hand movements, using primarily wrist action. The following are suggested:

a. Execute the zigzag in the air in front, around, and behind the body.

b. Run backward while zigzagging the ribbon in front of the body. Perform at different levels.

c. Run forward while zigzagging behind the body at different levels.

5. *Spiral movements.* The circles in the spiral can be of the same size or of an increasing or decreasing progression. Spirals can be made from left to right or the reverse.

a. Execute spirals around, in front of, or beside the body while performing locomotor dance steps.

b. Execute spirals while performing forward and backward rolls.

6. Throwing and catching movements. These skills are usually combined with swinging, circling, or figure-eight movements. The ribbon is tossed with one hand and is caught with the same hand or with the other hand. Throwing and catching is a difficult maneuver.

7. *Exchanges.* During group routines, the ribbon is handed or tossed to a partner.

FOR MORE INFORMATION

References and Suggested Readings

Cassidy, J., & Rimbeaux, B. C. (2002). *Juggling for the complete klutz.* Palo Alto, CA: Klutz Press.

Fujimoto, M. (1996). *Rhythmic gymnastics.* Los Angeles: Price Stern Sloan.

Hackett, P., & Owen, P. (1997). *The juggling book.* New York: Lyons & Burford.

Lee, B. (2003). *Jump rope training.* Champaign, IL: Human Kinetics.

Loredo, E. (1996). *The jump rope book (classic games).* New York: Workman Publishers.

Marrott, B. (1997). *Getting a jump on fitness.* New York: Barricade Books.

Mauer, T. (1997). *Rhythmic gymnastics.* Vero Beach, FL: Rourke Press.

Mitchelson, M. (1997). *The most excellent book of how to be a juggler.* Brookfield, CT: Copper Beech Books.

Morris, G. S. (1976). Effects ball and background color have upon the catching performance of elementary school children. *Research Quarterly, 47,* 409–415.

Poppen, J. D. (1989). *Action packet on jumping rope.* Puyallup, WA: Action Productions.

Robertson-Williams, J. (1994). *So, you want to learn how to double dutch?* Pittsburgh: Dorrance Publishers.

Websites

General Physical Education Sites
www.pelinks4u.org/index.htm
www.pecentral.org
http://reach.ucf.edu/~pezone

Footbag
http://worldfootbag.com

Frisbees
www.ukultimate.com/Links/default.aspx
www2.upa.org/index.php
www.ultimatehandbook.com/uh

Jump Rope
www.worldofropejumping.com
www.aahperd.org

17

Body Management Skills

ESSENTIAL COMPONENTS OF QUALITY PROGRAMS

➤ **I. Organized around content standards**

➤ **II. Student-centered and developmentally appropriate**

➤ **III. Physical activity and motor skill development form the core of the program**

IV. Teaches management skills and self-discipline

➤ **V. Promotes inclusion of all students**

➤ **VI. Focuses on process over product**

VII. Promotes lifetime personal health and wellness

VIII. Teaches cooperation and responsibility and promotes sensitivity to diversity

NATIONAL STANDARDS FOR PHYSICAL EDUCATION*

➤ **1. Demonstrates competency in motor skills and movement patterns needed to perform a variety of physical activities.**

➤ **2. Demonstrates understanding of movement concepts, principles, and tactics as they apply to the learning and performance of physical activities.**

➤ **3. Participates regularly in physical activity.**

4. Achieves and maintains a health-enhancing level of physical fitness.

5. Exhibits responsible personal and social behavior that respects self and others in physical activity.

6. Values physical activity for health, enjoyment, challenge, self-expression, and/or social interaction.

*National Association for Sport and Physical Education (NASPE), 2004.

SUMMARY

Body management skills are required for control of the body in a variety of situations. Body management skills require an integration of agility, coordination, strength, balance, and flexibility. Activities in this chapter help students learn to control their bodies while using a wide variety of apparatus. This chapter offers organizational hints, instructional strategies, and activities for helping youngsters develop body management skills.

OUTCOMES

▪ Know how to help students develop body management skills using large and small apparatus.

▪ Apply proper instructional procedures to a wide variety of apparatus activities.

▪ Design a safe environment when teaching large apparatus activities.

▪ Teach a variety of activities on large apparatus, including climbing ropes, benches, balance beams, and jumping boxes.

▪ Teach activities using small apparatus, including magic ropes, individual mats, tug-of-war ropes, and gym scooters.

Body management skills are an important component of movement competency. Efficient movement demands integration of a number of physical traits, including agility, balance, strength, flexibility, and coordination. In addition, youngsters must develop an understanding of how to control their bodies while on large apparatus, such as beams, benches, and jumping boxes. A basic understanding of movement concepts and mechanical principles used in skill performance is necessary for quality movement.

The focus of this chapter is on developing body management skills using large and small apparatus. Children have an innate desire to run, jump, swing, and climb. The first half of this chapter includes large apparatus activities, including climbing ropes, benches, balance beams, and jumping boxes. Large apparatus activities offer an opportunity to learn body management skills while free of ground support. The second half of the chapter contains small apparatus activities, including magic ropes, individual mats, and gym scooters. Small apparatus activities help develop body control in space and on the ground.

SAFE AND EFFECTIVE USE OF APPARATUS

Apparatus often has to be placed in position before a class arrives. Youngsters should understand they are not to use the equipment until instructor approval has been given. Establish instructional procedures for setup, storage, and safe use of apparatus and mats. The following are guidelines for using apparatus in the instructional setting.

1. Placement of tumbling mats for shock absorption is critical. Tumbling mats should be positioned for safety in dismounting and where falls are possible. Tumbling mats should be placed directly under all climbing ropes.

2. Apparatus should be carried, not dragged, across the floor. For particular pieces that need cooperation among the children, designate the number of children and the means of carrying. Teach children how to lift and carry the apparatus properly. Proper setup and storage of apparatus should be discussed and practiced by students.

3. Activity on apparatus should occur only when it is directed by teachers. Youngsters should be instructed to stay away from all apparatus in the area that has been prearranged for later use.

4. Because improper use of apparatus can result in injury, instruction should precede apparatus activity. Signs emphasizing proper use of apparatus can be placed on cones near individual pieces of equipment.

5. Use return activities to increase the movement potential of apparatus. Return activity requires children to perform a movement task (jumping, hopping, skipping, animal walks, etc.) after they have performed on the apparatus. This reduces the time children stand in line waiting for another turn after completion of their task on the apparatus. To increase the amount of time youngsters are actively engaged, increase the distance children have to travel. Return activities demand little supervision. An example of a return activity to use when teaching balance beam activities would be the following: Walk across the beam, do a straddle dismount, and crab walk (the return activity) to a cone and back to place.

6. Speed of movement is never expected when working on apparatus. Many of the activities require balance and agility. Controlled and sustained movements are the expectations teachers should have of students.

ACTIVITIES WITH CLIMBING ROPES

Climbing ropes offer high-level developmental possibilities for the upper trunk and arms as well as training in coordination of different body parts (Figure 18.1). Adequate grip and arm strength are prerequisites for climbing. Becoming accustomed to the rope and gaining confidence are important early goals. Climbing rope sets can be purchased from Gopher Sport, 220 24th Avenue NW, P.O. Box 998, Owatonna, MN 55060-0998 (1-800-533-0446 or www.gophersport.com).

Instructional Procedures

1. Mats should be placed under all ropes.

2. The hand-over-hand method should be used for climbing and the hand-under-hand method for descending.

FIGURE 18.1 Rope-climbing on an eight-rope set.

3. Caution the children not to slide; sliding can cause rope burns on the hands and legs.

4. A climber who becomes tired should stop and rest. Proper rest stops should be taught as part of the climbing procedure.

5. Children also should be taught to leave enough margin for a safe descent. No children should go higher than their strength allows.

6. Spotters should be used initially for activities in which the body is inverted.

7. Rosin in powdered form and magnesium chalk aid in gripping. It is particularly important that they be used when the rope becomes slippery.

8. Children swinging on the ropes should be instructed to make sure that other children are out of the way.

9. Marks to limit the climb can be put on the rope with adhesive tape. A height of 8 to 10 feet above the floor is reasonable until a child demonstrates proficiency.

10. If the ceiling is higher than 15 or 16 feet, a wooden stop (circle) positioned on the rope to limit climbing beyond that height is suggested.

Preliminary Activities

Progression is important in rope climbing, and the fundamental skill progressions should be followed.

▶ SUPPORTED PULL-UPS

In supported pull-up activities, a part of the body remains in contact with the floor. The pull-up is hand-over-hand and the return is hand-under-hand.

1. Kneel directly under the rope. Pull up to the tiptoes and return to kneeling position.

2. Start in sitting position under the rope. Pull up; legs are supported on the heels. Return to sitting position.

3. Start in a standing position. Grasp the rope, rock back on the heels, and lower the body to the floor. Keep a straight body. Return to standing position.

▶ HANGS

In a hang, the body is pulled up in one motion and held up for a length of time (5, 10, or 20 seconds). Progression is important.

1. From a seated position, reach up as high as possible and pull the body from the floor, except for the heels. Hold.

2. Same as the previous stunt, but pull the body completely free of the floor. Hold.

3. From a standing position, jump up, grasp the rope, and hang. This should be a Bent-Arm Hang, with the hands about even with the mouth. Hold.

4. Repeat the previous stunt, but add leg movements—one or both knees up, bicycling movement, Half Lever (one or both legs up, parallel to the floor), Full Lever (feet up to the face).

▶ PULL-UPS

In the Pull-Up, the body is raised and lowered repeatedly. The initial challenge should be to accomplish one Pull-Up in the defined position. The number of repetitions should be increased with care. All of the activities described for hangs are adaptable to Pull-Ups. The chin should touch the hands on each Pull-Up.

▶ INVERTED HANG

For the Inverted Hang, both hands reach up high. The rope is kept to one side. The performer jumps to a bent-arm position, and at the same time brings the knees up to the nose to invert the body, which is now in a curled position. In a continuation of the motion, the feet are brought up higher than the hands, and the legs are locked around the rope. The body should now be straight and upside down. In the learning phase, teachers should spot.

▶ SWINGING AND JUMPING

For swinging and jumping, a bench, box, or stool can serve as a takeoff point. To take off, the child reaches high and jumps to a bent-arm position. Landing should be with bent knees.

1. Swing and jump. Add half turns and full turns.

2. Swing and return to the perch. Add single- and double-knee bends.

3. Jump for distance, over a high-jump bar or through a hoop.

4. Swing and pick up a bowling pin and return to the perch.

5. Carry objects (beanbags, balls, or deck tennis rings). A partner, standing to the side away from the takeoff bench, can put articles to be carried back on the takeoff perch by placing each article between the knees or feet.

6. Not using a takeoff device, run toward a swinging rope, grasp it, and gain momentum for swinging.

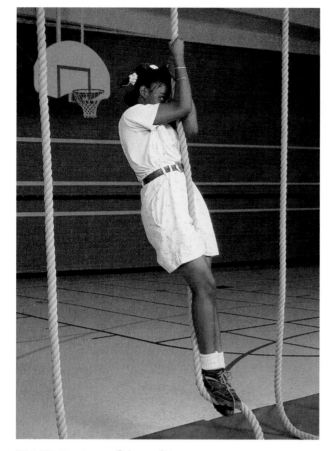

FIGURE 18.2   Scissors Grip.

CLIMBING THE ROPE

▶ **SCISSORS GRIP**

For the Scissors Grip, approach the rope and reach as high as possible, standing with the right leg forward of the left. Raise the back leg, bend at the knee, and place the rope inside the knee and outside the foot. Cross the forward leg over the back leg, and straighten the legs with the toes pointed down (Figure 18.2). This should give a secure hold. The teacher can check the position.

To climb using the Scissors Grip, raise the knees up close to the chest, the rope sliding between them, while supporting the body with the hand grip. Lock the rope between the legs and climb up, using the hand-over-hand method and stretching as high as the hands can reach. Bring the knees up to the chest and repeat the process until you have climbed halfway. Later, strive for a higher climb.

▶ **LEG-AROUND REST**

To do the Leg-Around Rest (Figure 18.3), wrap the left leg completely around the rope, keeping the rope between the thighs. The bottom of the rope then crosses

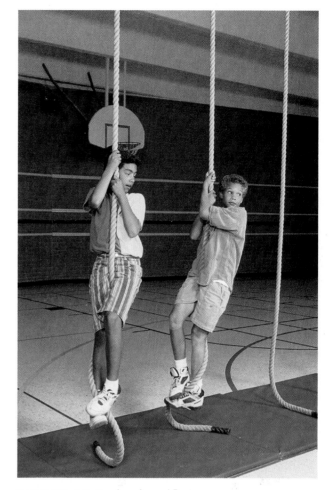

FIGURE 18.3   Leg-Around Rest.

over the instep of the left foot from the outside. The right foot stands on the rope as it crosses over the in-step, providing pressure to prevent slippage. To provide additional pressure, release the hands and wrap the arms around the rope, leaning away from the rope at the same time.

To climb using the Leg-Around Rest, proceed as in climbing with the Scissors Grip, but loosen the grip each time and re-form higher up on the rope.

Descending the Rope

There are four methods to descend the rope. The only differences are in the use of the leg locks, as the hand-under-hand is used for all descents.

▶ **SCISSORS GRIP DESCENT**

From an extended Scissors Grip position, lock the legs and lower the body with the hands until the knees are against the chest. Hold with the hands, and lower the legs to a new position.

▶ **LEG-AROUND REST DESCENT**

From the Leg-Around Rest position, lower the body until the knees are against the chest. Lift the top foot, and let the feet slide to a lower position (see Figure 18.3, page 397). Secure with the top foot and repeat.

▶ **INSTEP SQUEEZE DESCENT**

Squeeze the rope between the insteps by keeping the heels together. Lower the body while the rope slides against the instep.

▶ **STIRRUP DESCENT**

Have the rope on the outside of the right foot and carry it over the instep of the left. Pressure from the left foot holds the position. To get into position, let the rope trail along the right leg, reach under, and hook it with the left instep. When the pressure from the left leg is reduced, the rope slides smoothly while the descent is made with the hands.

Other Climbing Activities

▶ **CLIMBING FOR TIME**

To climb for time, a stopwatch and a definite mark on the rope are needed. The height of the mark depends on the children's skill and capacity. Each child should have three trials (not in succession, however), with the best time recorded. Children should start from a standing position with hands reaching as high as desired. The descent should not be included in the timing, because too much emphasis on speed in descent may incite the children to drop or may promote rope burns.

▶ **CLIMBING WITHOUT USING THE FEET**

The strenuous activity of climbing without using the feet should be attempted only by the more skilled. During early sessions, the mark should not be set too high. Climbers start from a sitting position. The activity can be timed.

▶ **ORGANIZING A TARZAN CLUB**

The teacher can put a marker at the top limit of the rope. Each child who climbs to and touches the marker becomes a member of the Tarzan Club. A Super-Tarzan Club can be formed for those who can climb to the marker without using their feet. The climber must start from a sitting position on the floor.

Stunts Using Two Ropes

Two ropes hanging close together are needed for the following activities.

▶ **STRAIGHT-ARM HANG**

To do the Straight-Arm Hang, jump up, grasp one rope with each hand, and hang with the arms straight.

▶ **BENT-ARM HANG**

Perform as for the Straight-Arm Hang, but bend the arms at the elbows.

▶ **ARM HANGS WITH DIFFERENT LEG POSITIONS**

1. Do single- and double-knee lifts.
2. Do a Half Lever. Bring the legs up parallel to the floor and point the toes.
3. Do a Full Lever. Bring the feet up to the face and keep the knees straight.
4. Do a Bicycle. Pedal as on a bicycle.

▶ **PULL-UPS**

The Pull-Up is the same as on a single rope, except that each hand grasps a rope.

▶ **INVERTED HANGS**

1. Hang with the feet wrapped around the ropes.
2. Hang with the feet against the inside of the ropes.
3. Hang with the toes pointed and the feet not touching the ropes (Figure 18.4).

▶ **SKIN THE CAT**

From a bent-arm position, kick the feet overhead and continue the roll until the feet touch the mat. Return to the starting position. A more difficult stunt is to start from a higher position so that the feet do not touch the mat. Reverse to original position.

▶ **CLIMBING**

1. Climb up one rope, transfer to another, and descend.
2. Climb halfway up one rope, cross over to another rope, and continue to climb to the top.
3. Climb both ropes together without using the legs. This is difficult and requires the climber to slide one hand at a time up the ropes without completely releasing the grip.
4. Climb as on a single rope, with hands on one rope and feet on the other rope.

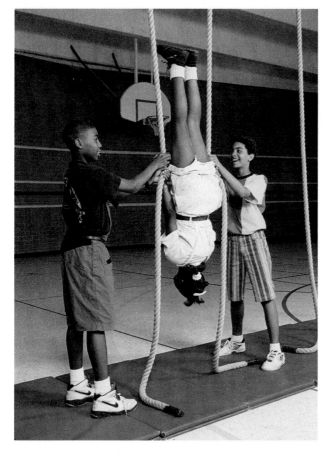

FIGURE 18.4 Spotting an Inverted Hang on two ropes. (Holding the performer's hands ensures confidence and safety.)

Activity Sequences

Rope-climbing activities are conducive to forming sequences through which the child can progress. The following sequence represents the kind of progressive challenges that can be met.

1. Jump and hang (10 seconds).
2. Pull up and hold (10 seconds).
3. Scissors climb to blue mark (10 feet).
4. Scissors climb to top (15 feet).
5. Demonstrate Leg-Around Rest (10 feet).
6. Do an Inverted Hang, with body straight (5 seconds).

Teachers can structure three achievement levels from the activities included in this chapter. Each level could be given a characteristic name and organized as a task card or a contract project.

ACTIVITIES ON BALANCE BEAMS

Balance-beam activities contribute to control in both static and dynamic balance situations (Figure 18.5). The balance-beam side of a balance beam bench is ideal for such activities, with its 2-inch-wide and 12-foot-long beam. Balance-beam benches can be purchased from Gopher Sport, 220 24th Avenue NW, P.O. Box 998, Owatonna, MN 55060-0998 (1-800-533-0446 or www.gophersport.com). Balance beams come in many other sizes, however, and can be constructed from common lumber materials (see Chapter 10). Some teachers prefer a wider beam for kindergarten and first-grade children and, in particular, for special education children. Students should graduate to the narrower beam as soon as the activities on the wider beam no longer seem to challenge them.

Other ideas for balance equipment are also interesting. A pole with ends shaped to fit the supports can be substituted for the flat balance beam. The pole is more challenging. Another idea is constructing a beam that begins with a two-inch width and narrows to a one-inch width at the other end. Beams of varying widths (from one to four inches) can also be used. Children progress from the wider to the narrower beams. A variety of widths is preferable for children with disabilities.

Instructional Procedures

1. Children should move with controlled, deliberate movements. Speed is not a goal. The teacher should advise performers to recover their balance before taking another step or making another movement.

2. In keeping with the principle of control, children should step slowly on the beam, pause momentarily in good balance at the end of the activity, and dismount with a small, controlled jump from the end of the beam when the routine is completed.

18

FIGURE 18.5 Walking on a balance beam bench.

3. Mats can be placed at the end of the bench to cushion the dismount and to allow for rolls and stunts after the dismount.

4. Visual fixation is important. Children should look straight ahead rather than down at the feet. Eye targets can be marked on or attached to walls to assist in visual fixation. This fixation allows balance controls other than vision to function more effectively. From time to time, movements can be done with the eyes closed, entirely eliminating visual control of balance.

5. Children should be told to step off the beam when they lose their balance, rather than teetering and falling off awkwardly. Allow the performer to step back on the beam and to continue the routine.

6. Success in a balance-beam activity can be based on two levels. The lower level allows the performer to step off the beam once during the routine. The higher level demands that the student remain on the beam throughout. For both levels, the children should pause in good balance at the end of the beam before dismounting.

7. Both laterality and directionality are important. Right and left feet should be given reasonably equal treatment. For example, if a performer does steps leading with the right foot, the next effort should be made leading with the left foot. Directions right and left should be given equal weight. A child naturally uses the dominant side and direction but must be encouraged to perform with both sides.

8. The child next in line should begin when the performer ahead is about three-quarters of the distance across the beam.

9. Return activities (see page 395) are a consideration for enhancing the breadth of activity.

10. A child or the teacher can assist the performer. The assistant holds the hand palm up, ready to help the performer if and when help is needed.

Activity Sequences

Activities for the balance beam are presented as a progression of movement themes. The teacher can develop fully all of the activities and possibilities within a theme before proceeding to the next theme, or can take a few activities from each theme and cover more territory.

► ACTIVITIES ON PARALLEL BEAMS

Activities on two parallel beams are presented first as lead-up practice for the single-beam tasks. The beams should be placed about 10 to 30 inches apart. The parallel-beam activities can be done alone or with a partner when more security is desired.

1. With a partner, join inside hands and walk forward, backward, and sideways. Walk sideways, using a grapevine step. Hold a beanbag in the free hand.

2. Without a partner, perform various animal walks, such as the Crab Walk, Bear Walk, Measuring Worm, and Elephant Walk.

3. With one foot on each beam, walk forward, backward, and sideways.

4. Step to the opposite beam with each step taken.

5. Progress the length of the beams with hands on one beam and feet on the other.

6. Progress to the middle of the beams and perform various turns and stunts, such as picking up a beanbag, moving through a hoop, and stepping over a wand.

► MOVEMENTS ACROSS THE FULL LENGTH OF A SINGLE BEAM

1. Perform various locomotor tasks, such as walking, follow steps, heel-and-toe steps, side steps, tiptoe steps, the grapevine step (step behind, step across), and so on.

2. Follow different directions—forward, backward, sideways.

3. Use different arm and hand positions—on the hips, on the head, behind the back, out to the sides, pointing to the ceiling, folded across the chest.

4. Move across the beam as you assume different shapes.

5. Balance an object (beanbag or eraser) on various body parts—on the head, on the back of the hands, on the shoulders. Try balancing two or three objects at once.

► HALF-AND-HALF MOVEMENTS

Half-and-half movements repeat the movements, arm positions, and balancing stunts described previously, except that the performer goes halfway across the beam using a selected movement and then changes to another type of movement on the second half of the beam.

► CHALLENGE TASKS OR STUNTS

For challenge tasks, the performer moves halfway across the beam with a selected movement, performs a particular challenge or stunt at the center, and finishes the movements on the second half of the beam. Examples of challenges or stunts that can be performed at the center of the beam include the following:

1. Balances: Forward Balance (page 481), Backward Balance (page 481), Stork Stand (page 480), Seat Balance (page 494).

2. Stunts: Leg Dip (page 493), Finger Touch (pages 494–495).

3. Challenges: Make a full turn, pick up a beanbag at the center, pick up some paper at the center with the teeth, do a push-up.

MORE DIFFICULT MOVEMENTS ACROSS THE BEAM

1. Hop the length of the beam—forward, sideways, and backward.

2. Do the Cat Walk (page 475), Rabbit Jump (page 475), Lame Dog Walk (page 476), Seal Crawl (page 487), or Crab Walk (page 476).

3. Do various locomotor movements with the eyes closed.

4. Walk to the center of the beam and do a Side-Leaning Rest. Try on the other side as well.

5. Walk to the center and do a complete body turn on one foot only.

ACTIVITIES WITH WANDS AND HOOPS

1. Carry a wand or hoop. Step over the wand or through the hoop in various fashions.

2. Step over or go under wands or hoops held by a partner.

3. Twirl a hula-hoop on the arms or around the body while moving across the beam.

4. Balance a wand on various body parts while moving across the beam.

5. Balance a wand in one hand and twirl a hoop on the other hand and proceed across the beam.

MANIPULATIVE ACTIVITIES WITH SELF

1. Using one or two beanbags, toss to self in various fashions—over the head, around the body, under the legs.

2. Using a ball, toss to self. Circle the ball around the body, under the legs.

3. Bounce a ball on the floor. On the beam. Dribble on the floor.

4. Roll a ball along the beam.

MANIPULATIVE ACTIVITIES WITH A PARTNER

With a partner standing beyond the far end of the beam, throw a beanbag or ball back and forth. Have partner toss for a volleyball return. Bat the ball (as in a volleyball serve) to partner.

STUNTS WITH A PARTNER

1. Do a Wheelbarrow (page 502) with the supporting performer keeping the feet on the floor.

2. Partners start on opposite ends of the beam and move toward each other with the same kind of movement, do a balance pose together in the center, and return to their respective ends of the beam.

3. Partners start on opposite ends of the beam and attempt to pass each other without losing their balance and without touching the floor. Find different ways to pass.

ACTIVITIES ON BENCHES

The balance-beam bench is effective in developing strength and balance. Bench activities are challenging to children and offer a variety of movement possibilities.

Instructional Procedures

1. All activities on the benches should be broken down into three distinct parts: the approach to and mounting of the bench, the actual activity on the bench, and the dismount from the bench.

2. Mats should be placed at the ends of the bench to facilitate the dismount and various rolls and stunts executed after the dismount.

3. Benches can be positioned horizontally or inclined. They can also be combined with other equipment for variation and greater challenge.

4. Four to five children is the maximum number that should be assigned to one bench.

5. The child next in turn should begin when the performer ahead is about three-quarters of the way across the bench.

6. Return activities add to the activity potential.

7. Speed is not a goal in bench activities. Movements should be done deliberately and carefully, with attention given to body control and body management.

8. Attention also should be paid to laterality and directionality. For example, if a child hops on the right foot, the next effort should be made on the left foot. In jump turns, both right and left movements should be used.

Activity Sequences

ANIMAL WALKS

Perform various animal walks on the bench, such as the Seal Crawl (page 487), Cat Walk (page 475), Lame Dog Walk (page 476), and Rabbit Jump (page 475).

FIGURE 18.6 Prone movements, head first.

▶ LOCOMOTOR MOVEMENTS

Perform various locomotor movements along the length of the bench, such as stepping or jumping on and off the side of the bench, hopping on and off the side of the bench, or skipping and galloping on the bench.

▶ PULLS

Pull the body along the bench, using different combinations of body parts. Use the arms only, the legs only, the right leg and the left arm, or the left leg and the right arm. Pull along the bench, using the following positions.

1. Prone position (head first and feet first) (Figure 18.6)
2. Supine position (head first and feet first) (Figure 18.7)
3. Side position (head first and feet first)

Various leg positions (such as legs up in a half-lever position, knees bent, and so on) should be used in performing pulls and pushes. Those body parts not being used to pull can be used to carry a piece of manipulative equipment, such as a beanbag, ball, or wand. Employ

FIGURE 18.7 Supine movements, feet first.

different body shapes. Try the Submarine (one foot in the air like a periscope).

▶ PUSHES

Push the body along the bench, using different parts of the body as discussed for pulls. Push the body, using the following positions.

1. Prone position (head first and feet first)
2. Supine position (head first and feet first)
3. Side position (head first and feet first)

▶ MOVEMENTS ALONG THE SIDE OF THE BENCH

Proceed alongside the bench in the following positions with the hands on the bench and the feet on the floor as far from the bench as possible.

1. Prone position
2. Supine position
3. Turn-over (Proceed along the bench, changing from prone to supine position.)

Repeat these positions with the feet on the bench and the hands on the floor as far from the bench as possible.

▶ SCOOTER MOVEMENTS

Sit on the bench and proceed along it without using the hands in the following ways.

1. Do a Scooter. Proceed with the feet leading the body. Try to pull the body along with the feet.
2. Do a Reverse Scooter. Proceed as for the Scooter but with the legs trailing and pushing the body along the bench.
3. Do a Seat Walk. Proceed forward by walking on the buttocks. Use the legs as little as possible.

▶ CROUCH JUMPS

Place both hands on the bench and jump back and forth over it. Progress the length of the bench by moving the hands forward a few inches after each jump.

1. Do a regular Crouch Jump (Figure 18.8). Use both hands and both feet. Jump as high as possible.
2. Do a Straddle Jump. Straddle the bench with the legs, take the weight on the hands, and jump with the legs as high as possible.
3. Use one hand and two feet. Do a Crouch Jump, but eliminate the use of one hand.
4. Use one hand and one foot. Perform the Crouch Jump, using only one hand and one foot.

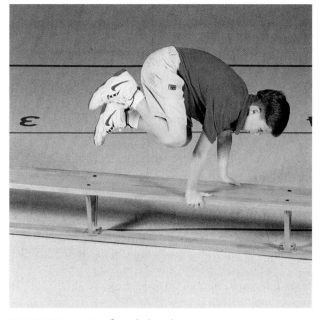

FIGURE 18.8   Crouch Jumping.

5. Stand to one side, facing the bench, with both hands on it. With stiff arms, try to send the seat as high as possible into the air. Add the Mule Kick (page 488) before coming down.

▶ **BASIC TUMBLING STUNTS**

Basic tumbling stunts can be incorporated into bench activities: the Back Roller (page 478), Backward Curl (page 478), Forward Roll (page 478) (Figure 18.9), Backward Roll (pages 478–479), and Cartwheel (page 492).

▶ **DISMOUNTS**

All bench activities in which the child moves from one end of the bench to the other should end with a dismount. The following dismounts are suggested. Many other stunts can be used.

1. Single jump (forward or backward) (Figure 18.10).
2. Jump with turns (half turn, three-quarter turn, or full turn).
3. Jackknife. Jump, kick the legs up, and touch the toes with the fingertips. Keep the feet together.
4. Jackknife Split. Same as the Jackknife, but spread the legs as far as possible.
5. Jump to a Forward Roll.
6. Backward jump to a Backward Roll.
7. Side jump to a Side Roll (page 477).
8. Judo Roll.
9. Jump with combinations of the stunts noted in this list.

FIGURE 18.9   Preparing to do a Forward Roll on the bench.

Additional Experiences on Benches

1. The range of activities can be extended with the addition of balls, beanbags, hoops, and wands. Wands and hoops can be used as obstacles to go over, under, around, or through. Basic balance and manipulative skills can be incorporated into the activity with balls and beanbags.
2. Two can perform at one time, each child near an opposite end of the bench, doing different balance positions on the bench.

FIGURE 18.10   Dismounting from a bench.

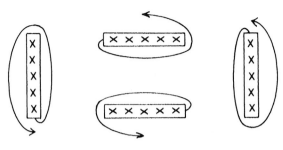

FIGURE 18.11 Rectangular bench activities.

3. Children like to go over and under a row of benches arranged in a kind of obstacle course. Some of the benches can be supported by jumping boxes, making them excellent for vaulting activities.

4. A bench can be supported by two jumping boxes and used as a vaulting box. Each bench is long enough to accommodate three children. They can jump off it, Mule Kick on it, and vault over it.

5. Four benches can be placed in a large rectangle (Figure 18.11), with a squad standing at attention on top of each bench. On signal, each squad gets off its bench, runs around the outside of the other three benches, and then runs back to its own bench. The first squad back and at attention on the bench is the winner.

6. Benches can be placed in a square formation, with children moving around the square and doing a different movement on each bench.

7. One end of the bench can be placed on a jumping box or on another bench. Children receive jumping practice by running up the incline and striving for jump height at the end of the bench.

8. Benches are appropriate for some partner activities. Partners can start on each end and pass through or around each other, reversing original positions. Wheelbarrow Walks are also suitable.

9. Another enjoyable activity is arranging the benches in a course as illustrated in Figure 18.12. A student is chosen to lead the squad or class through the challenge course. A different activity must be performed at each bench.

ACTIVITIES WITH JUMPING BOXES

Jumping boxes can be constructed or purchased. They provide opportunities for children to jump from a height and propel the body through space. Activities with jumping boxes are generally confined to the primary grades. Boxes can be of varying heights; 8 inches and 16 inches are suggested. A rubber floor pad can be placed under the box to protect the floor and to prevent sliding. Plans for constructing boxes are given in Chapter 10.

Instructional Procedures

1. Attention should be given to landing in proper form. Lightness, bent-knee action, balance, and body control should be stressed.

2. Mats should be used to cushion the landing.

3. The exploratory and creative approach is important; there are few standard stunts in jumping box activities.

4. No more than four or five children should be assigned to each series of boxes.

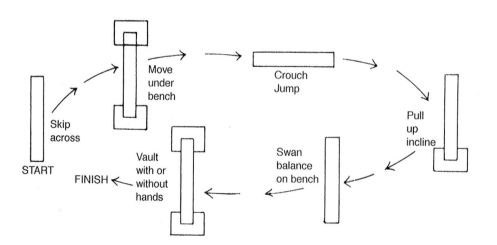

FIGURE 18.12 Challenge course using benches.

5. Additional challenges can be incorporated by the use of hoops, wands, balls, and the like. Rolling stunts after the dismount extend the movement possibilities.

6. Return activities work well with boxes.

7. Children should strive for height and learn to relax as they go through space.

Activity Sequences

The activities that follow can be augmented easily. Let the children help expand the activity.

 VARIOUS APPROACHES TO THE BOXES

The approach to the boxes can be varied by performing movements such as these.

1. Fundamental locomotor movements: run, gallop, skip, and hop

2. Animal walks: Bear Walk, Crab Walk, and so on

3. Moving over and under various obstacles: jumping over a bench, moving through a hoop held upright by a mat, doing a Backward Roll on the mat

4. Rope-jumping to the box: students try to continue jumping while mounting and dismounting the box

MOUNTING THE BOX

Many different combinations can be used to get onto the box.

1. Practice stepping onto the box (mounting) by taking the full weight on the stepping foot and holding it for a few seconds. This develops a sense of balance and tends to stabilize the support foot.

2. Mount the box, using locomotor movements such as a step, jump, leap, or hop. Perform various turns—quarter, half, three-quarter, and full—while jumping onto the box.

3. Use a Crouch Jump to get onto the box.

4. Back up to the box and mount it without looking at it.

5. Mount the box while a partner tosses you a beanbag.

6. Make various targets on top of the box with a piece of chalk, and try to land on the spot when mounting.

DISMOUNTING THE BOX

The following dismounts can be used to develop body control.

1. Jump off with a quarter turn, half turn, or full turn.

2. Jump off with different body shapes: stretching, curling up in a ball, jackknifing.

FIGURE 18.13 Jump dismounting.

3. Jump over a wand or through a hoop.

4. Jump off, and do a Forward Roll or a Backward Roll.

5. Change the foregoing dismounts by substituting a hop or a leap in place of the jump.

6. Increase the height and distance of the dismount.

7. Dismount in various directions, such as forward (Figure 18.13), backward, sideways, northward, and southward.

8. Jump off using a jackknife or wide straddle dismount.

9. Perform a balance stunt on the box and then dismount.

After the class has learned the basic movements used with jumping boxes, continuous squad motion can be incorporated. The squad captain is responsible for leading the group through different approaches, mounts, and dismounts. The same activity cannot be used twice in succession.

ADDITION OF EQUIPMENT

Various pieces of equipment enhance box activities. Some suggestions follow.

1. Toss beanbags up while dismounting, or try to keep one on your head while mounting or dismounting the box.

2. Try to dribble a playground ball while performing the box routine.

3. Jump through a stationary hoop held by a partner while dismounting, or use the hoop as a jump rope and see how many times you can jump through it while dismounting.

4. Jump over or go under a wand.

▶ **BOX COMBINATIONS**

Boxes can be arranged in a straight line and in other patterns. Children do a different movement over each box as though running a challenge course.

ACTIVITIES WITH INDIVIDUAL MATS

Individual mats have an English origin and are the basis for many exploratory and creative movements. Essentially, the mat serves as a base of operation or as an obstacle to go over or around. Mats vary in size, with the most popular being 24 by 48 inches. Standard thickness is three-quarters of an inch, but this also varies. The mat should have rubber backing to prevent slipping. Rubber-backed indoor-outdoor carpeting makes excellent mats; however commercial models are available.

Instructional Procedures

1. Educational movement techniques are very important in mat work.
2. Body management and basic skills of locomotor and nonlocomotor movement should be emphasized.
3. Mats should be far enough apart to allow free movement around them.
4. Each child should have a mat.

Activity Sequences

Rigid adherence to the sequence presented below is not necessary. The activities are quite flexible and require only fundamental skills.

COMMAND MOVEMENTS

In command movements, children change movement on command. The commands used include the following:

- *Stretch:* Stretch your body out in all directions as wide as possible.
- *Curl:* Curl into a tight little ball (Figure 18.14).
- *Balance:* Form some kind of balanced position.
- *Bridge:* Make a bridge over the mat.
- *Reach:* Keeping the toes of one foot on the mat, reach out as far as possible across the floor in a chosen direction.
- *Rock:* Rock on any part of the body.
- *Roll:* Do some kind of roll on the mat.
- *Twist:* Make a shape with a part of the body twisted.
- *Prone:* Lie prone on the mat.
- *Melt:* Sink down slowly into a little puddle of water on the mat.

FIGURE 18.14 Curl activities on individual mats.

- *Shake:* Shake all over, or shake whatever parts of the body are designated.
- *Fall:* Fall to the mat.
- *Collapse:* The movement is similar to a fall but follows nicely after a bridge.

Sequencing can be established in several ways. The children can emphasize flow factors by moving at will from one movement to another, or changes can be made on a verbal signal or on the beat of a drum. Magic number challenges can be used, too.

Another means of exploration is selecting one of the movement challenges—say, Stretch—and changing from one type of stretch position to another. If Balance is selected, the movement sequence can begin with a balance on six body parts; then the number can be reduced by one on each signal until the child is balancing on one body part. Different kinds of shapes can be explored.

▶ **MOVEMENTS ON AND OFF THE MAT**

Children do different locomotor movements on and off the mat in different directions. Turns and shapes can be added (Figure 18.15).

1. Take the weight on the hands as you go across the mat.
2. Lead with different body parts as you go on and off the mat. Move on and off the mat with a specified number of body parts (one, two, three, four, five) used for landing.
3. Jump backward, forward, sideways. Make up a rhythmic sequence. Move around the area, jumping from mat to mat.

▶ **MOVEMENTS OVER THE MAT**

Movements over the mat are similar to the preceding movements, but the child goes completely over the mat each time.

FIGURE 18.15   Movements on and off the mat.

▶ MOVEMENTS AROUND THE MAT

Locomotor movements around the mat are done both clockwise and counterclockwise.

1. Do movements around the mat, keeping the hands on the mat. Now do movements around, keeping the feet on the mat.

2. Change to one foot and one hand on the mat. Vary with the Crab position.

3. Work out combinations of stunt movements and locomotor activities, going around the mats. Reverse direction often.

4. Move throughout the area, running between the mats, and on signal jump over a specified number of mats.

▶ ACTIVITIES USING MATS AS A BASE

1. Stretch and reach in different directions to show how big the space is.

2. Do combination movements away from and back to the mat. For example, do two jumps and two hops or six steps and two jumps.

3. Use the magic-number concept.

4. See how many letters you can make. Find a partner, put your mats together, and make your bodies into different letters and numbers.

▶ MAT GAMES

Each child is seated on a mat. On signal, each rises and jumps over as many different mats as possible. On the next signal, each child takes a seat on the nearest mat.

The last child to be seated can pay a penalty. The game can also be played by eliminating one or two mats so that one or two children are left without a home base. The teacher can stand on a mat or turn over mats to put them out of the game. To control roughness, the rule should be that the first child to touch a mat gets to sit on it.

A variation of this game is to have each child touch at least ten mats and then sit cross-legged on the eleventh, or a child can be required to alternate touching a mat and jumping over the next mat until a total of ten is reached. "See how many mats you can cartwheel or jump over in ten seconds." Change the challenge and try again.

▶ DEVELOPMENTAL CHALLENGES

1. Experiment with curl-ups (partial or full). (This can be done informally and on a challenge basis.)

2. From a sitting position on the mat, pick up the short sides of the mat and raise the feet and upper body off the floor. Try variations of the V-Up (page 508).

▶ MANIPULATIVE ACTIVITIES

Keeping one foot on the mat, maintain control of a balloon in the air, either with a hand, a nylon-stocking paddle, or a Lummi stick. Try the same activity with a stocking paddle and a paper ball. The number of touches, or strokes, can be counted. Try with both feet on the mat.

ACTIVITIES WITH MAGIC ROPES

Magic rope activities originated in Germany. Each rope is similar to a long rubber band. Magic ropes can be made by knitting wide rubber bands together, or they can be constructed from ordinary three-quarter-inch elastic tape available in most clothing stores. Children place their hands through loops on each end and grasp the rope. Ropes should be long enough to stretch to between 30 and 40 feet (see Chapter 10). A major advantage of the magic rope is its flexibility; children have no fear of hitting it or tripping on it while performing. Ropes should be stretched tight, with little slack.

Instructional Procedures

1. Two or more children are rope holders while the others are jumping. The teacher should develop some type of rotation plan so that all children participate as holders.

2. Many variations can be achieved with the magic ropes by changing the height or by raising and lowering opposite ends of the ropes.

3. The jumping activities are strenuous and should be alternated with activities that involve crawling under the ropes.

4. The class should concentrate on not touching the rope. The magic rope can help develop body perception in space if the rope is regarded as an obstacle to be avoided.

5. Better use can be made of the rope by using an angled approach, which involves starting at one end of the rope and progressing to the other end by using jumping and hopping activities. In comparison, the straight-on approach allows the child to jump the rope only once.

6. A total of 8 to 12 ropes are needed for a class, 2 for each squad. Squads are excellent groups for this activity because the leader can control the rotation of the rope holders.

7. The child next in turn begins when the child ahead is almost to the end of the rope.

Activity Sequences

▶ ACTIVITIES WITH SINGLE ROPES

Start the ropes at a six-inch height and raise them progressively to add challenge.

1. Jump over the rope (Figure 18.16).
2. Hop over the rope.
3. Jump and perform various body turns while jumping.
4. Make different body shapes and change body size while jumping.

5. Crawl or slide under the rope.
6. Crouch-jump over the rope.
7. Hold the rope overhead and have others jump up and touch it with their foreheads.
8. Gradually lower the rope, and do the limbo under it without touching the floor with the hands.
9. Jump over the rope backward without looking at it.
10. Perform a Scissors Jump over the rope.

▶ ACTIVITIES WITH DOUBLE ROPES

Vary the height and spread of the ropes.

1. Do these activities with the ropes parallel to each other.
   a. Jump in one side and out the other (Figure 18.17).
   b. Hop in one side and out the other.
   c. Crouch-jump in and out.
   d. Perform various animal walks in and out of the ropes.
   e. Do a long jump over both of the ropes.
   f. Perform a stunt while jumping in between the two ropes. Possible stunts are the Heel Click, body turn, handclap, and Straddle Jump.
   g. Jump or leap over one rope and land on the other rope.

2. With the ropes crossed at right angles to each other, do these activities:
   a. Perform various movements from one area to the next.
   b. Jump into one area and crawl out of that area into another.

FIGURE 18.16   Jumping over a single magic rope.

FIGURE 18.17   Jumping in and out of two magic ropes.

3. With one rope above the other to resemble a barbed-wire fence, do these activities. Vary the height of the ropes and their distance apart. This adds much excitement to the activity because the children are challenged not to touch the ropes.

   a. Step through the ropes without touching.

   b. Crouch-jump through.

> ### MISCELLANEOUS ACTIVITIES WITH MAGIC ROPES

These miscellaneous activities are useful, too. The class should be given time to create their own ideas with the ropes and other pieces of equipment.

1. Perform the various activities with a beanbag balanced on the head. Perform while bouncing a ball.

2. Use four or more ropes to create various floor patterns.

3. Use a follow-the-leader plan to add variety to the activity.

4. Create a challenge course with many ropes for a relay.

ACTIVITIES WITH PARTNER TUG-OF-WAR ROPES

A partner tug-of-war rope is about six feet long with a loop on each end. (See Chapter 10 for instructions on making partner tug-of-war ropes.) Tug-of-war ropes help in the development of strength, because contestants must use maximum or near-maximum strength in the contests. These strength demands may continue over a short period of time.

Instructional Procedures

1. The most important procedure is to start and stop the tugging with clear signals. Tugging bouts should last no more than five to seven seconds. Problems occur when students become tired and one partner gets pulled around. The point is not to pull until someone loses their equilibrium, but to have a good tug and stop.

2. Contests should be between partners of comparable ability. Each child should have a chance to win.

3. Plan a system of rotation so that children meet different partners. If students stay with the same partner, the outcome will be that the same person continues to win.

4. Caution students to not let go of the rope. If the grip is slipping, they should inform the other student to stop pulling, renew the grip, and start over.

5. Individual ropes are excellent for partner resistance activities. A few of these activities should be practiced each time the children use the ropes.

6. A line on the floor perpendicular to the direction of the rope makes a satisfactory goal for determining a win. One child pulls the other forward until the second child is over the line. Another criterion for a win could be for children to pick up objects placed behind them.

Partner Activities

Children should try the following ways of pulling. The tug-of-war rope offers good possibilities in movement exploration. Let students try to devise ways other than those mentioned by which they can pull against each other.

1. Pull with the right hand only, the left hand only, both hands.

2. Grasp with the right hand, with the body supported on three points (the left hand and the feet). Change hands.

3. Pull with backs toward each other, with the rope between the legs, holding with one hand only.

4. Partners get down on all fours, with feet toward each other. Hook the loops around one foot of each partner. For each contestant, the force is provided by both hands and the foot that remains on the floor.

5. Partners get into Crab position and pull the rope by hooking a foot through the loop (Figure 18.18).

6. Partners face each other and stand on one foot only. Contestants try to pull each other off balance without losing their own balance. If the raised foot touches the floor, the other person is declared the winner.

FIGURE 18.18 Pulling in Crab position.

7. Contestants stand with opposite sides toward each other. They hold a tug-of-war rope with opposite hands and move apart until the rope is taut. The goal is to make the other person move the feet by pulling and giving on the rope. The legs must be kept straight, and only the arms can be used in the contest.

8. Students stand 10 feet away from the rope, which is on the floor. On signal, they run to the rope, pick it up, and have a tug-of-war. Contestants can start from different positions, such as push-up, curl-up, or Crab.

9. Instead of partners pulling each other across a line, each tries to pull the other toward a peg or bowling pin placed behind them so that they can pick up the objects.

10. Two individual ropes are tied together at the center so that four loops are available for pulling. Four cones form a square, and four children compete to see who can pick up a cone first.

11. Two children pull against two others. The rope loops should be made big enough so that both can secure handholds on each end. They can use right hands only or left hands only.

12. For Frozen Tug-of-War, two children take hold of a rope, each with both hands on a loop. The children are positioned close enough together so that there is some slack in the rope. A third child grasps the rope to make a six-inch bend at the center, and the contestants then pull the rope taut so that there is no slack (Figure 18.19). On the signal "Go," the third child drops the loop, and the opponents try to pull each other off balance. The feet are "frozen" to the floor; if the position of either foot is moved, that player loses.

13. Hawaiian Tug-of-War involves two parallel lines drawn about 20 feet apart. The game is between two people, but as many pairs as are in a class can play. A partner tug-of-war rope is laid on the floor at right angles to, and midway between, the two parallel lines. The players position themselves so that each is standing about one foot from one of the loops of the rope. They are in position to pick up the rope and pull against each other on signal. The object of the game is to pull the other child far enough to be able to touch the line behind. The magic word is "Hula." This is the signal to pick up the rope and begin to pull. Children must not reach down and pick up the rope until "Hula" is called. The teacher can use other commands, such as "Go" and "Begin," to deceive the children.

14. Group contests are possible. (See Figure 10.28 for a diagram of rope arrangements suitable for groups.)

Partner Resistance Activities

Children should follow exercise principles, exerting sufficient force (near maximum), maintaining resistance through the full range of motion for eight to ten seconds, and stabilizing the base so that the selected part of the body can be exercised. The force is a controlled pull, not a tug. The partner should not be compelled to move out of position. Much of the exercise centers on the hands and arms, but other parts of the body come into play as braces. Partners work together, both in the same position.

As in other activities, grip can be varied. The upper grip (palms away from performer) and the lower grip (palms toward performer) are usually used. Occasionally, a mixed grip, with one hand in upper position and one hand in lower position, can be used. Laterality must be kept in mind so that the right and left sides of the body receive equal treatment.

► PARTNERS STANDING WITH SIDES TOWARD EACH OTHER

1. Use a lower grip. Do a flexed-arm pull, with elbows at right angles.

2. Use an upper grip. Extend the arm from the side at a 45-degree angle. Pull toward the side.

3. Use a lower grip. Extend the arm completely overhead. Pull overhead.

4. Loop the rope around one ankle. Stand with feet apart. Pull with the closer foot.

► PARTNERS STANDING, FACING EACH OTHER

1. Use a lower grip. Do a flexed-arm pull, with one and then both hands.

2. Use an upper grip. Extend the arms at the side or down. Pull toward the rear.

3. Use an upper grip. Pull both hands straight toward chest.

4. Use an upper grip. Extend the arms overhead. Pull backward.

FIGURE 18.19 Frozen Tug-of-War.

FIGURE 18.20 Partner resistance activity in sitting position.

▶ PARTNERS SITTING, FACING EACH OTHER

1. Repeat the activities described for standing position (Figure 18.20).
2. Hook the rope with both feet. Pull.

▶ PARTNERS PRONE, FACING EACH OTHER

1. Use an upper grip. Pull directly toward the chest.
2. Use a lower grip. Do a flexed-arm pull.

▶ PARTNERS PRONE, FEET TOWARD EACH OTHER

1. Hook the rope around one ankle. With knee joint at a right angle, pull.
2. Try with both feet together.

Pulling Resistance Activities

Using mostly the standing positions, work out resistance exercises such as the following: One child pulls and makes progress with eight steps. The other child then pulls the first back for eight counts. The addition of music makes this an interesting activity. The child being pulled must provide enough resistance to make the puller work reasonably hard.

ACTIVITIES WITH GYM SCOOTERS

Gym scooters make excellent devices for developmental activity when used properly. The minimum number is one scooter for two children, unless the scooters are used for relays only. In that case, four or six scooters will suffice for an average-sized class. Two rules are important in the use of scooters. First, children are not to stand on scooters as they would on skateboards. Second, scooters, with or without passengers, must not be used as missiles.

Children can work individually or in pairs. A child working alone can do many different combinations by varying the method of propulsion and the method of supporting the body. Children can propel the scooter with their feet, their hands, or both. The body position can be kneeling, sitting, prone, supine, or even sideways. The body weight can be wholly or partially supported on the scooter. The variation of space factors, particularly direction, adds interest.

When children work in pairs, one child rides and the other pushes or pulls. The rider's weight may be wholly supported by the scooter or partially supported by the scooter and partially supported by the partner. Educational movement methodology is applicable to scooter work, but care should be exercised so that the scooter activities are developmental and not just a free play session.

FOR MORE INFORMATION

Websites

General Physical Education
www.pelinks4u.org/index.htm
www.pecentral.org
http://reach.ucf.edu/~pezone
http://pe4life.com

Body Management Skills
www.learning.gov.ab.ca/physicaleducationonline
http://rubistar.4teachers.org/index.php
www.extension.iastate.edu/Publications/PM1359B.pdf
www.uen.org/Lessonplan/preview.cgi?LPid=945
www.mpsaz.org/tafttest/programdescrip.html

18

Specialized Motor Skills

Skills developed in this section are much more refined, and related to activities that many youth will use in adulthood. Rhythmic movement skills include activities that are varied and attractive to youth in all grades. There are different types of rhythmic activities, but the core of these activities pursues a single goal: learning to move in a rhythmic manner. Gymnastic skills are skills that have less utility, but are often attractive to students because they are individual in nature. These skills range from simple balances to tumbling activities and challenging stunts. Cooperative skills focus on teaching youth how to work with peers toward a common goal. The activities are designed so students will find it difficult to be successful if they don't cooperate closely with peers. Game skills are honed in loosely-organized games that maximize physical activity. These games usually focus on one or two specialized skills so youngsters can participate in a successful climate.

After reading this section, you will be able to teach youngsters a wide variety of specialized motor skills. You will teach them to work together toward common goals and how to compete fairly in loosely organized games. The joy of moving rhythmically will be shared with students through a wide variety of rhythmic movement activities.

Rhythmic Movement Skills

I. Organized around content standards

▷ **II. Student-centered and developmentally appropriate**

▷ **III. Physical activity and motor skill development form the core of the program**

IV. Teaches management skills and self-discipline

▷ **V. Promotes inclusion of all students**

VI. Focuses on process over product

VII. Promotes lifetime personal health and wellness

▷ **VIII. Teaches cooperation and responsibility and promotes sensitivity to diversity**

NATIONAL STANDARDS
FOR PHYSICAL EDUCATION*

▷ **1. Demonstrates competency in motor skills and movement patterns needed to perform a variety of physical activities.**

2. Demonstrates understanding of movement concepts, principles, and tactics as they apply to the learning and performance of physical activities.

▷ **3. Participates regularly in physical activity.**

▷ **4. Achieves and maintains a health-enhancing level of physical fitness.**

5. Exhibits responsible personal and social behavior that respects self and others in physical activity.

▷ **6. Values physical activity for health, enjoyment, challenge, self-expression, and/or social interaction.**

*National Association for Sport and Physical Education (NASPE), 2004.

SUMMARY

Activities in this chapter are selected for the purpose of developing rhythmic movement skills. The activities are listed in progression of easy to more complex and also by developmental level. The development of social skills and a positive self-concept occur when rhythmic activities are taught in a sensitive and educational manner. Rhythmic activities should be scheduled in the same manner as other phases of the yearly physical education program. Most dances use skills and steps that are learned in a sequential manner.

OUTCOMES

- Know where to find sources of rhythmic accompaniment.

- Understand the inherent rhythmic nature of all physical activity.

- Outline components of the yearly rhythmic movement program and identify accompanying activities and skill progressions.

- Describe instructional procedures and ideas to facilitate implementation of rhythmic movements into the yearly program.

- Cite creative rhythms, movement songs, folk dances, and other dance activities that are used as learning experiences in physical education.

- Describe dance progressions that are appropriate for the various levels of development that children exhibit.

Rhythm is the basis of music and dance. Rhythm in dance is simply expressive movement made with or without music. All body movements tend to be rhythmic—the beating of the heart, swinging a tennis racket, wielding a hammer, throwing a ball. Most movements that take place in physical education class contain elements of rhythm. Movement to rhythm begins early in the child's school career and continues throughout. Rhythmic activities are particularly appropriate for younger children. A sizable portion of the Developmental Level I program is devoted to such activities. One problem in incorporating rhythmic activities in the program is the vast amount of material available, which requires judicious selection to present a broad, progressive program. Another problem is that many teachers are hesitant about the subject area. If you prepare properly, you will become comfortable with rhythms and find that these activities are a favorite among children.

Early experiences center on functional and creative movement forms. Locomotor skills are inherently rhythmic in execution, and the addition of rhythm can enhance development of these skills. An important component of children's dance is fundamental rhythms. Instruction begins with and capitalizes on locomotor skills that children already possess—walking, running, hopping, and jumping. Rhythmic activities provide a vehicle for expressive movement. These activities offer opportunity for broad participation and personal satisfaction for all, as children personalize their responses within the framework of the idea. Youngsters have a chance to create unique rhythmic responses within action songs and dances.

IMPLEMENTING THE RHYTHMIC MOVEMENT PROGRAM

The rhythmic program should be balanced and should include activities from each of the categories of rhythmic movement. Table 19.1 shows recommended types of rhythmic activities for each developmental level.

TABLE 19.1 Types of Rhythmic Activity			
	Developmental Level		
Activity	**I**	**II**	**III**
Creative rhythms	X		
Folk dances	X	X	X
Line dances		X	X
Mixers	X	X	X
Aerobic dancing		X	X
Square dancing			X
Rope jumping to music	S	X	X
Musical games	S	S	S
Rhythmic gymnastics (refer to Chapter 17)			

Note: X means that the activity is an integral part of the program. S means that the activity is given only minor emphasis.

Skill Progressions

Another factor in program construction is the progression of basic and specific dance steps. Dances employing the following skills and steps appear in each of the respective developmental level programs.

DEVELOPMENTAL LEVEL I

Youngsters in Developmental Level I focus on creative rhythms and movement songs. Simple folk dances and mixers are learned with a focus on one or two locomotor movements. Simple mixers are used to help children learn to find new partners and move rhythmically. The focus at this level is to offer activities that require a minimum of instruction while giving students a positive experience with rhythms.

DEVELOPMENTAL LEVEL II

At this level, greater practice on folk dances and line dances includes combinations of locomotor skills, such as the step-hop, and the grand right and left. Marching, basic tinikling steps, and introductory square dancing steps are taught as skill improves. All the activities are taught with an emphasis on mastering simple locomotor skills rather than performing the dances with perfection.

DEVELOPMENTAL LEVEL III

Developmental Level III students begin to learn some of the more difficult steps such as the grapevine step, schottische, polka, intermediate tinikling steps, two-step, advanced tinikling steps, square dancing, and all steps introduced at earlier levels. Developmentally, these students are not comfortable moving with partners of the opposite sex, so activities are modified to allow for individual activity.

Understanding Rhythmic Accompaniment

Music has essential characteristics that children should recognize, understand, and appreciate. These characteristics are also present to varying degrees in other purely percussive accompaniment.

Tempo is the speed of the music. It can be constant, show a gradual increase (acceleration), or decrease (deceleration).

Beat is the underlying rhythm of the music. Some musicians refer to the beat as the pulse of the music. The beat can be even or uneven. Music with a pronounced beat is easier to follow.

Certain notes or beats in a rhythmic pattern receive more force than others, and this defines *accent*. Accent is generally expressed by a more forceful movement in a sequence of movements.

A *measure* is a group of beats made by the regular occurrence of a heavy accent. Usually the accent is applied to the first beat of a measure. A measure represents the underlying beat enclosed between two adjacent bars on a musical staff.

The *intensity* of music can be loud, soft, light, or heavy. Mood is related to intensity but carries the concept deeper into human feelings. Music can reflect many moods—happiness, sadness, gaiety, fear, or stateliness, for example.

A *phrase* is a natural grouping of measures. Phrases of music are put together into rhythmic *patterns*. Children should learn to recognize when a pattern repeats or changes.

Sources of Rhythmic Accompaniment

Essential to any rhythmic program is accompaniment that encourages desired motor patterns and expressive movement. If children are to move to a rhythm, it must be stimulating, appropriate for the expected responses, and appealing to the learners. Skillful use of a drum or tambourine adds much to rhythmic experiences. A major use of the drumbeat is to guide the movement from one pattern to another by signaling tiny increments of change with light beats that control the flow. The motion in striking is essentially a wrist action, not an arm movement.

Each school and teacher should build a collection of recorded music. Sets created especially for physical education movement patterns and dance are available from a number of sources (See information on Wagon Wheel Records on page 464.) Physical education CDs or tapes should be stored in the physical education facility rather than in the school library. Storage should be arranged so that each recording has its assigned place and is readily available.

CREATIVE RHYTHMS

Creativity should be part of all dance and rhythmic activities, with the scope of the activity determining the degree of freedom. Creative rhythms, however, provide a special program area in which creativity is the goal and functional movement is secondary. The emphasis is on the process and not on the movement outcomes.

Creativity manifests itself in the opportunity for each child to respond expressively within the scope of the movement idea, which can range from total freedom to stated limits. Children's judgment should be respected, and teachers should look for original interpretations. Stimulation should be positive in nature, guiding the movement patterns by suggestions, questions, encouragement, and challenges that help children structure their ideas and add variety. Careful guidance is necessary to fan the spark of self-direction, because freedom in itself does not automatically develop creativity.

Instructional Procedures

1. Appropriate music or rhythmic background is important; otherwise, movement can become stilted. An atmosphere of creative freedom must be established. The class should be comfortable and relaxed.

2. When analyzing the setting, ask, "What is the basic idea? What expressive movements can be expected? What are the guidelines or boundaries of movement? What space are the children to use?"

3. Listening is an important element, because children must understand the mood or sense of the rhythmic background. Some questions that can be posed to children are, "What does the music make us think of?" and "What does the music tell us to do?" If the movement or interpretation is preselected, little time need be wasted in getting under way. Provide enough music so children can grasp the impact. Have them clap the beat if necessary and then move into action.

4. Use action-directing statements such as, "Let's pretend we are . . . ," "Let's try being like . . . ," "Try to feel like a . . . ," and "Make believe you are. . . . "

5. In some lessons, the initial focus may be on the selection of appropriate rhythmic background. In this instance children formulate a creative rhythm of the dramatic type and then seek suitable music for their dance.

6. Give children time to develop and try their ideas. This is an open-ended process that has a variety of solutions. Coaching and guidance are important aspects at this stage. Application of time, space, force, flow, and body factors is essential. Encourage large, free movement of all body parts. Use the entire area and fill in the empty places in general space. Allow time for exploration.

Expressive Movement

Children can express moods and feelings and show reactions to colors and sounds by improvising dances or movements that demonstrate different aspects of force, or gestures that depict different feelings. A piece of music is played and is followed by a discussion of its qualities and how it makes the children feel. Children may interpret the music differently. Moods can be described as happy, lighthearted, sad, brave, fearful, cheerful, angry, solemn, silly, stately, sleepy, funny, cautious, bold, or nonchalant.

IDENTIFICATION

There are endless subject sources for identification and interpretation. Children can take on the identity of a familiar character, creature, or object. The following ideas should be useful.

1. Animals—elephants, ducks, seals, chickens, dogs, rabbits, lions, and others

2. People—soldiers, firefighters, sailors, nurses, various kinds of workers, forest rangers, teachers, cowboys and cowgirls, and so on

3. Play objects—seesaws, swings, rowboats, balls, various toys, and many other common articles with which children play

4. Make-believe creatures—giants, dwarfs, gnomes, witches, trolls, dragons, pixies, fairies, and so on

5. Machines—trains, planes, jets, rockets, automobiles, bicycles, motorcycles, tractors, elevators, and the like

6. Circus characters—clowns, various trained animals, trapeze artists, tightrope performers, jugglers, acrobats, and bands

7. Natural phenomena—fluttering leaves, grain, flowers, rain, snow, clouds, wind, tornadoes, hurricanes, volcanoes, and others

DRAMATIZATION

Dramatization and rhythm are useful vehicles for group activity. Suitable background music or rhythmic accompaniment is a necessary ingredient. Excellent recordings are available, from short numbers lasting a minute or two to more elaborate productions such as those found in the Dance-a-Story series (RCA Victor).

Here are some useful ideas for dramatic rhythms.

1. Build a house, garage, or other structure.

2. Make a snowman, throw snowballs, go skiing.

3. Fly a kite, go hunting or fishing, go camping.

4. Act out stories about astronauts, cowboys and cowgirls, firefighters, explorers.

5. Interpret familiar stories, such as "Sleeping Beauty," "The Three Bears," or "Little Red Riding Hood."

6. Do household tasks such as chopping wood, picking fruit, mowing the lawn, cleaning the yard, washing dishes, and vacuuming.

7. Celebrate holidays such as Halloween, the Fourth of July, Thanksgiving, or Christmas, or dramatize the seasons.

8. Play sports such as football, basketball, baseball, track and field, swimming, tennis, and golf.

9. Divide the class in groups of three or four, and assign each group a sport other than one of the major sports.

Have them develop a series of movements dramatizing that sport to the class. Have the remaining groups guess which sport is being presented. Slow-motion movements add to this activity.

10. Plan a trip through a haunted house. A recording by Hap Palmer ("Movin'," Kimbo EA 546) has an excellent sequence about being in a haunted house.

11. Have the children make a motor. One student starts by getting into a position of choice in the middle of the floor and by putting one body part in motion. The motion should be a steady, rhythmic movement. The remaining students, one at a time, attach onto the first person, and each person puts one body part in motion. After all are attached, a machine with many moving parts is the result.

12. Act out the children's favorite parts in popular movies. Having the children perform to the original soundtrack brings more realism to the performance.

13. Select a favorite poem ("Old Mother Hubbard," "Pat-a-Cake," "The Giant") and design a sequence of activities to fit the meaning of the poem. Stories have excellent appeal.

An example that shows how an idea can be exploited for a lesson on creative rhythm is called "The Wind and the Leaves." One or more children are chosen to be the wind, and the remaining children are the leaves. Two kinds of rhythm are needed; a tambourine can be used. The first rhythm should be high, fast, and shrill, indicating the blowing of the wind. The intensity and tempo should illustrate the speed and force of the wind. The second rhythm should be slow, measured, and light, to represent the leaves fluttering in the still air and finally coming to rest at various positions on the ground. During the first rhythm, children representing the wind act out a heavy gust. While this is going on, the leaves show what it is like to be blown about. During the second rhythm, the wind is still and the leaves flutter to the ground. Other characterizations can be added. For example, street sweepers can come along and sweep up the leaves.

Another lesson strategy is to divide the class into groups and to give each group the task of acting out an idea with percussive accompaniment. Each group puts on a performance for the others. At completion, the other groups guess what the interpretation was. In this game, the interpretations should not last too long.

FOLK DANCES

A *folk dance* is defined as a traditional dance of a particular culture. In this concept, a definite pattern or dance routine is usually specified and followed. Folk dancing is one phase of a child's education that can assist in bringing about international understanding. A country's way of life and many other habits are often reflected in its folk music. From these dances, children gain an understanding of why people from certain countries act and live as they do, even though modern times may have changed their lifestyle from that of days gone by.

Folk dances in Developmental Level I consist of simple fundamental locomotor skills, either singly or in combination. Dances such as the two-step, polka, and schottische, with more specialized steps, are found in Developmental Levels II and III. The first consideration when teaching folk dance is to determine whether children know the basic skills required for the dance. If a skill needs to be taught, it can be handled in one of two ways. The first way is to teach the skill separately, before teaching the dance. The second is to teach the dance in its normal sequence, giving specific instruction at the time when the skill appears. The first method is often best, because children can concentrate solely on learning the skill.

Teaching New Dances Successfully

The underlying goal of folk dancing is to learn to move rhythmically. Unfortunately, many students (often boys) develop negative attitudes and feelings of failure about rhythmic activities. Effective teachers have long recognized the need to modify sport activities to ensure that students learn skills correctly and experience success. Modifications, such as using smaller balls, lower baskets, and slower-moving objects, are now commonplace in most elementary school physical education activities. Interestingly, when teaching rhythmic activities the same approach is often discarded. Dances are taught with precision and emphasis on "doing it right," instead of making modifications so they are appealing and easier to learn. The following steps offer guidelines for modifying rhythmic activities to increase the probability of success.

1. *Slow down the music.* The first contact with the activity must be a successful one. No student wants to be embarrassed because he or she is out of step. If it appears that students are still not doing well, stop the music and walk them through it. If there is difficult footwork, repeat the sequence a number of times. Start from the beginning each time so students who are lost can begin anew.

2. *As a general rule, if the dance is short, use the whole-teaching approach.* If it is a longer dance with several different parts, use the part–whole method and teach one part at a time. For example, have children learn half of a two-part dance or one-third of a three-part dance and then put that part to music. After all the parts are learned, put them together in a complete dance.

3. *Introduce a new dance with students placed in scattered formation.* Circles and formations cause some students to feel others are looking directly at them.

If they are self-conscious about their ability, a circle formation may be intimidating. A scattered formation allows them to move near the rear of the area where fewer peers can see them perform.

4. *Avoid the use of partners when teaching a new activity.* Partners add a degree of complexity to many dances and should be added only after the basic steps have been mastered. In addition, avoid forcing intermediate grade students to pair up with a partner of the opposite sex unless they choose to do so. Students who do not want to dance with a partner should be allowed to perform the steps without one.

5. *Avoid the left-right and clockwise-counterclockwise orientation when introducing a new dance.* Anytime students are asked to move in a specified direction, it increases the possibility of error. Allow students to choose the direction they would like to move when learning new steps. Later, after the steps have been mastered, left-right and clockwise-counterclockwise orientations and formations can be added.

6. *To avoid stressing students, perform a dance once or twice in a daily lesson.* Presenting a number of dances, rather than one or two in depth, gives students who are having difficulty a chance to start with a clean slate on a new dance. Come back to a difficult dance and practice it in a later lesson. Some students panic when they experience difficulty, and the increased stress limits their ability to learn. Not staying on any one dance for too long keeps students from becoming frustrated.

7. *Teach rhythmic activities in the same way sport skills are taught.* Teachers expect that students will make mistakes regardless of their ability level; baskets are missed and passes are dropped. Treat rhythmic activities like sport skills and expect that perfection is virtually impossible to reach. The purpose of teaching rhythmic activities is to learn to move rhythmically, not to showcase one or two dances learned perfectly. If student errors are accepted, students soon learn that rhythms are fun and worth trying.

8. *Dances that emphasize strong movements such as hand clapping and foot stomping appeal to boys.* Since boys are often "hard to sell" on rhythmic activities, it makes sense to introduce them to some activities that include strong and bold physical movements.

Modifying Rhythmic Activities

Folk dances are traditional rhythmic activities that have been done for generations. However, the traditional music and style may not appeal to some youngsters in a school setting. With a few modifications, the dances can become easier to learn. Table 19.2 shows how some common folk dances can be modified to increase student interest and increase the ease of learning.

TABLE 19.2	Examples of Dance Modifications		
Dance	**Skills**	**Modifications**	**Formation**
The Bird Dance	Skipping or walking, elbow swing or star	Good introductory dance for all levels	Scattered
Shortnin' Bread	Sliding, turning with a partner, clapping	Slow music Practice without partner	Scattered first, then with partner
Jump Jim Jo	Jumping, running, draw step	No partner Move in any direction	Scattered
Eins Zwie Drie	Walking, heel-toe step, sliding	No partner, no numbering Slide any direction Play giant cymbals	Scattered, then facing center of area
Wild Turkey Mixer	Walking, elbow swing	Groups of three—scattered Center person with pinnie Don't mix when learning	Scattered first, then circle formation
Irish Washerwoman	Walking, swinging, promenade position	No partners Swing and promenade the closest partner or move to the center for a partner Emphasize clapping and stomping	Facing center
Oh Susanna	Walking, promenade, grand right and left	Half of class with pinnies Use a wild grand right and left Go to center and find partner if left without one	Facing center
Jessie Polka	Step and touch, two-step or polka	Slow down music No partners Practice step and touch first	Scattered, students can hook on if they desire
Limbo Rock	Touch step, swivel step, jump clap clap	Slow down music Teach steps and add together	Scattered
Inside Out Mixer	Wring the dishrag, walk, change partners	Practice without music No mixing until learned	Groups of three
Teton Mountain Stomp	Walking, two-step	Do individually Emphasize clapping Move in any direction No side car or banjo position	Scattered

Another way to motivate students is to use current music and change traditional dances into line dances. Line dances can motivate students to learn new steps without worrying about a partner. The following are examples of folk and popular dances that can be done as line dances.

- Popcorn, page 445
- Jiffy Mixer, page 446
- Cotton-Eyed Joe, page 453
- Jessie Polka, page 456
- Teton Mountain Stomp, page 453
- Alley Cat, page 455

Arranging for Partners

Arranging for partners can be a source of deep hurt or embarrassment for some children. To be acceptable, a method of arranging for partners must avoid the situation in which children are looked over and overlooked. Some suggestions follow.

1. Dancing boy-girl fashion in the traditional mode is not necessary. When starting a dance program with students who are uncomfortable with each other, allow students to dance with a partner of their choice. If this places boys with boys and girls with

girls, allow that arrangement. Partners can be referred to as number 1 and number 2 or colored pinnies can be placed on one of the partners. Instead of giving directions for the girls or for the boys, call it out as "The people in red on the outside of the circle do. . . . " Be careful not to label one group as playing the role of boys or girls. Change partners frequently; sooner or later the members of both sexes will dance with members of the opposite sex. In this chapter we use the designations "Partner A" and "Partner B" for the leading and following positions respectively. Gender references, where they appear, will alternate by example.

2. In a follow-the-leader approach, put on some brisk marching music and begin walking among the students, who are scattered in general space. As you pass students, tap them on the shoulder, and ask them to "fall in" behind you. Subsequent students go to the end of the line when tagged until all students are chosen. This allows you to either arrange students as desired, or just to separate children who do not work well together.

3. Boys join hands in a circle formation, and each girl steps behind a boy. Reverse the procedure, and have girls make the circle, or have half of the class wear red pinnies and form the circle.

4. Girls stand in a circle facing counterclockwise, while boys form a circle around them facing clockwise. Both circles move in the direction in which they are facing and stop on signal. The girl takes the boy nearest her as her partner.

5. For square dances, take the first four couples from any of the previous formations to form a set. Continue until all sets are formed.

CDs and Cassette Tapes for Folk Dances

Quality recordings are difficult to find. Wagon Wheel Records is a reliable source for obtaining music accompaniment for all the dances included in this chapter. You can order compact discs (CDs), cassette tapes, and a catalog from the following address:

Wagon Wheel Records
16812 Pembrook Lane
Huntington Beach, CA 92649
Phone/Fax:(714) 846-8169
Website: www.wagonwheelrecords.net
E-mail: info@wagonwheelrecords.net

In this chapter, a code is listed for each dance that identifies whether it is in CD or cassette format and a catalog number to identify the source for ordering.

WWCD indicates it is available in CD format while WWC signifies cassette tape format.

Formations for Folk Dances

Figure 19.1 illustrates the formations that are used with folk dances that follow in this chapter. Each folk dance description begins with a listing of records, skills, and the formation to be used. If teachers are unsure about how the class should be arranged, the figure should be consulted. The formations are grouped into categories of single-circle, double-circle, triple-circle, and others.

Dance Positions

In most dance positions, Partner A holds a hand or hands palms up and Partner B joins the grip with a palms-down position. The following dance positions or partner positions are common to many dances.

PARTNERS FACING POSITION

In partners facing position, as the name suggests, the partners are facing. Partner A extends hands forward with palms up and elbows slightly bent. Partner B places hands in A's hands.

SIDE-BY-SIDE POSITION

In side-by-side position (Figure 19.2, page 422), Partner A always has Partner B to the right. Partner A offers the right hand, held above the waist, palm up. B places the left hand in A's raised hand.

CLOSED POSITION

Closed position is the social dance position. Partners stand facing each other, shoulders parallel, and toes pointed forward. Partner A holds Partner B's right hand in A's left hand out to the side, at about shoulder level, with elbows bent. Partner A places the right hand on B's back, just below the left shoulder blade. B's left arm rests on A's upper arm, and B's left hand is on A's right shoulder.

OPEN POSITION

To get to open position from closed position, Partner A turns to the left and Partner B to the right, with their arms remaining in about the same position. Both face in the same direction and are side by side.

PROMENADE POSITION

Promenade position (Figure 19.3, page 422) is the crossed-arm position in which dancers stand side by side, facing the same direction, with the right hand held by partner's right and the left by partner's left.

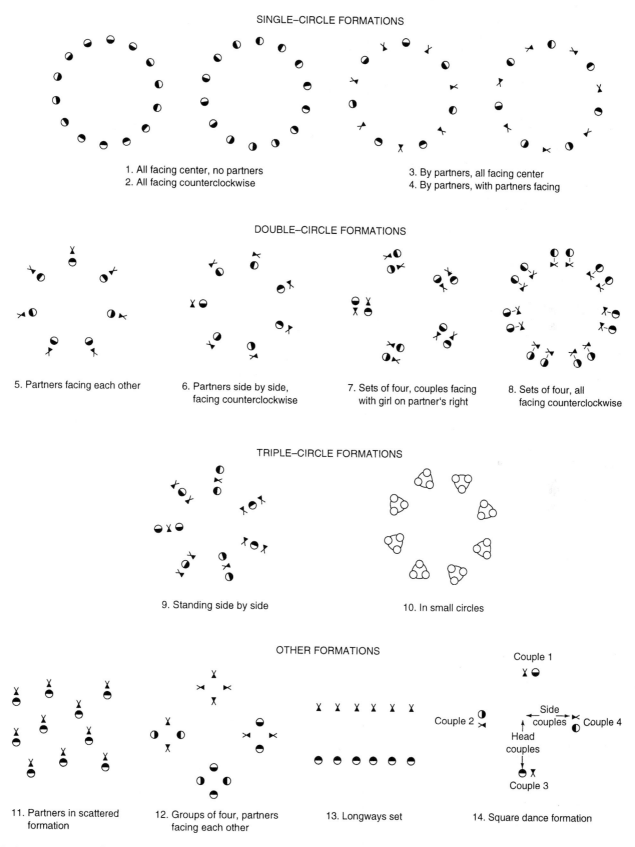

SINGLE–CIRCLE FORMATIONS

1. All facing center, no partners
2. All facing counterclockwise

3. By partners, all facing center
4. By partners, with partners facing

DOUBLE–CIRCLE FORMATIONS

5. Partners facing each other

6. Partners side by side, facing counterclockwise

7. Sets of four, couples facing with girl on partner's right

8. Sets of four, all facing counterclockwise

TRIPLE–CIRCLE FORMATIONS

9. Standing side by side

10. In small circles

OTHER FORMATIONS

11. Partners in scattered formation

12. Groups of four, partners facing each other

13. Longways set

14. Square dance formation

Couple 1
Couple 2
Side couples
Couple 4
Head couples
Couple 3

FIGURE 19.1 Dance formations.

FIGURE 19.2 Side-by-side position.

FIGURE 19.3 Promenade position.

VARSOUVIENNE POSITION

Partners stand side by side and face the same direction. Partner B is slightly in front and to the right of Partner A. A holds B's left hand in his or her left hand in front and at about shoulder height. B brings the right hand directly back over the right shoulder, and A reaches behind B at shoulder height and grasps that hand with his or her right hand.

PROGRESSION OF FOLK DANCES

The dances in this section are listed in progression beginning with the easiest and progressing to the most difficult dance. Three developmental levels are listed to give you the widest possible latitude in selecting dances that fit the maturity and skill of the youngsters. Table 19.3 (pages 423–424) lists all dances in alphabetical order by developmental level and lists skills required for the

dance. Dances throughout the chapter can be found easily by referring to the page number in the table. This table gives instructors a quick and clear overview of the total dance program.

Regarding level of difficulty, teachers must keep in mind that if a group of students is lacking in rhythmic background, the dances in the progression may be too difficult. For example, a sixth-grade class, lacking in dance skills, may need to begin with Developmental Level II dances. On the other hand, avoid boring a class by starting children on material below their maturity level.

DEVELOPMENTAL LEVEL I DANCES

Dances in this section contain movement songs and folk dances that are introductory in nature and involve simple formations and uncomplicated changes. The movements are primarily basic locomotor skills

TABLE 19.3	Alphabetical Listing of Folk Dances by Developmental Level	

Dance	Skills	Page
	Developmental Level I	
Ach Ja	Walking, sliding	427
Ballin' the Jack	Sliding, Do-sa-do	426
Bleking	Bleking step, step-hop	431
Bombay Bounce	Hesitation step, side step	431
Carousel	Draw step, sliding	431
Children's Polka	Step-draw	429
Chimes of Dunkirk (Var. 1)	Turning in a small circle with a partner, changing partners	428
Chimes of Dunkirk (Var. 2)	Turning with a partner, skipping	430
Circassian Circle	Walking, skipping, promenade	434
Clapping Out	Rhythmic clapping	426
Danish Dance of Greeting	Running or sliding, bowing	427
Did You Ever See a Lassie?	Walking at $^3/_4$ time, creativity	425
Eins Zwei Drei	Walking, sliding	430
Hitch Hiker, The	Chug step, skipping	433
Hokey Pokey	Body identification, nonlocomotor movements	425
How D'Ye Do, My Partner?	Bowing, curtsying, skipping	427
Jingle Bells (Var. 1)	Elbow swing, skipping, sliding	433
Jolly Is the Miller	Marching	431
Jump Jim Jo	Jumping, running, draw step	429
Little Liza Jane	Marching, rope jumping, galloping	425
Looby Loo	Skipping or running, body identification	425
Movin' Madness	Keeping time, creativity	425
Muffin Man, The	Jumping, skipping	426
Nixie Polka	Bleking step	432
Patty Cake Polka	Heel and the polka step, sliding, elbow swing, skipping	433
Rhythm Sticks (It's a Small, Small World)	Rhythmic tapping and manipulation of sticks	435
Seven Jumps	Step-hop, balance, control	428
Seven Steps	Running, hopping	434
Shoemaker's Dance	Skipping, heel and toe	429
Shortnin' Bread	Sliding, turning with a partner	428
Skip to My Lou	Skipping, changing partners	426
Turn the Glasses Over	Walking, wring the dishrag	432
Yankee Doodle	Walking, galloping, sliding, bowing	430
	Developmental Level II	
Apat Apat	Walking, star hold	443
Bingo	Walking, right-and-left grand	438
Bird Dance, The (Chicken Dance)	Skipping or walking, elbow swing or star	435
Crested Hen	Step-hop, turning under	441
Csebogar (Csehbogar)	Skipping, sliding, draw step, elbow swing	436
E-Z Mixer	Walking, elbow swing, or swing in closed position	440
Grand March	Controlled walking, marching, grand march figures	438
Green Sleeves	Walking, star formation, over and under	439

19

(continued)

TABLE 19.3	Alphabetical Listing of Folk Dances by Developmental Level (*continued*)	
Developmental Level II		
Gustaf's Skoal	Walking (stately), skipping, turning	442
Irish Washerwoman	Walking, elbow swing, promenade	441
Jiffy Mixer	Heel-and-toe step, chug step	446
Jingle Bells (Var. 2)	Skipping, promenade position, sliding, elbow swing	440
La Raspa	Bleking step, running, elbow swing	437
Los Machetes	Marching, rhythmic clapping	444
Lummi Sticks	Rhythmic movements	447
Oh, Susanna	Walking, promenade position, grand right and left	441
Pata Pata	Toe touches, knee lifts, quarter turns	444
Polly Wolly Doodle	Sliding, turning, walking	437
Pop Goes the Weasel	Walking, skipping, turning under	436
Popcorn	Toe touches, knee lifts, jumps	445
Red River Valley	Walk, buzz swing	445
Savila Se Bela Loza	Running step, crossover step, hop	444
Shoo Fly	Walking	443
Sicilian Circle	Walking, two-hand swing, wheel turn	446
Tinikling	Tinikling steps	447
Troika	Running step, turning under	442
Ve David	Walking, pivoting, buzz-step turn	440
Wild Turkey Mixer	Walking, elbow swing, partner change	437
Developmental Level III		
Alley Cat	Grapevine step, touch step, knee lifts	455
Alunelul	Step behind step, grapevine step, stomping	458
Big Sombrero Circle Mixer	Circling, Do-sa-do, swing	460
Circle Virginia Reel	Star, swing, Do-sa-do, promenade	461
Cotton-Eyed Joe	Heel-toe, two-step	453
D'Hammerschmiedsgselln	Clapping routine, step-hops	456
Doudlebska Polka	Polka step, walking, clapping pattern	457
Hora	Stepping sideways, step-swing	451
Horse and Buggy Schottische	Schottische step	458
Inside-Out Mixer	Wring the dishrag, walking, changing partners	456
Jessie Polka	Step and touch, two-step or polka step	456
Jugglehead Mixer	Two-step, elbow turn (forearm grasp)	452
Kalvelis	Polka step, swing, clapping pattern, grand right and left	457
Klumpakojis	Walking, starts, polka step	454
Korobushka	Schottische step, balance step, cross-out-together step, walking step	459
Limbo Rock	Touch step, swivel step, jump clap step	455
Oh Johnny	Shuffle step, swing, allemande left, Do-sa-do, promenade	459
Shindig in the Barn	Walking, Do-sa-do, swinging, sliding	460
Ten Pretty Girls	Walking, grapevine	455
Teton Mountain Stomp	Walking, banjo position, sidecar position, two-step	453
Trio Fun Mixer	Walking, Do-sa-do, star	460
Virginia Reel	Skipping, arm turn, Do-sa-do, sliding (sashay), reeling	451

and hand gestures or clapping sequences. There are dances both with and without partners. As the difficulty of the dances increases, patterns become more definite, and more folk dances are included. The movements are still primarily of the simple locomotor type, with additional and varied emphasis on more complicated movement patterns.

▶ MOVIN' MADNESS (AMERICAN)

Music Source: WWCD-1044

Skills: Keeping time, creativity

Formation: Scattered

Directions: The music is in two parts.

Part I: The tempo is slow, slow, fast-fast-fast. The children do any series of movements of their choice to fit this pattern, repeated four times. The movements should be large, gross motor movements.

Part II: During the second part (chorus) of the music, the children do any locomotor movement in keeping with the tempo. The step-hop or a light run can be used with the tempo of Part II.

✓ TEACHING TIP

Have the youngsters clap the rhythm. They should pay particular attention to the tempo in Part I. The music is Bleking, a dance presented later. The music for "I See You" is also suitable, but note that the movements in Part I are repeated twice instead of four times. The Part II music is suitable for skipping, sliding, or galloping.

▶ DID YOU EVER SEE A LASSIE? (SCOTTISH)

Music Source: WWCD-7054; WWC-7054

Skills: Walking at three-quarters time, creativity

Formation: Single circle, facing halfway left, with hands joined; one child in the center

Directions:

Measures	Action
1–8	All walk (one step per measure) to the left in a circle with hands joined. (Walk, 2, 3, 4, 5, 6, 7, 8.) The child in the center gets ready to demonstrate some type of movement.
9–16	All stop and copy the movement suggested by the child in the center.

As the verse starts over, the center child selects another to do some action in the center and changes places with him or her.

▶ LOOBY LOO (ENGLISH)

Music Source: WWCD-7054; WWC-7054

Skills: Skipping or running, body identification

Formation: Single circle, facing center, hands joined

Directions: The chorus is repeated before each verse. During the chorus, all children skip around the circle to the right. On the verse part of the dance, the children stand still, face the center, and follow the directions of the words. On the words "and turn myself about," they make a complete turn in place and get ready to skip around the circle again. The movements should be definite and vigorous. On the last verse, they jump forward and then backward, shake vigorously, and then turn about.

The dance can be made more fun and more vigorous by changing the tasks in the song. Try these tasks: Right side or hip, left side or hip, big belly, backside.

▶ HOKEY POKEY (AMERICAN)

Music Source: WWC-9126

Skills: Body identification, nonlocomotor movements

Formation: Single circle, facing center

Directions: During the first four lines, the children act out the words. During lines five and six, they hold their hands overhead with palms forward and do a kind of hula while turning around in place. During line seven, they stand in place and clap their hands three times.

The basic verse is repeated by substituting, successively, the left foot, right arm, left arm, right elbow, left elbow, head, right hip, left hip, whole self, and backside.

✓ TEACHING TIP

Encourage the youngsters to make large and vigorous motions during the Hokey Pokey portions and during the turn around. This adds to the fun. The children should sing lightly as they follow the directions given in the song.

▶ LITTLE LIZA JANE (AMERICAN)

Music Source: WWCD-FFD

Skills: Marching, rope jumping, galloping

Formation: Single circle, facing center

Directions: Students do a different movement every 32 counts. After each movement, they perform the chorus.

Measures	Action
1–4	Introduction: Listen to the rhythm.
1–16	Feet together and bend the knees up and down.
17–32	Swing arm over head like swinging a lasso (16 counts in each hand).
33–48	March eight steps to the center and eight steps back (repeat).
49–64	Jump rope for 32 counts.
65–80	Do arm circles (16 forward and 16 backward).
81–96	Gallop around the circle (16 gallops in each direction).
97–112	Join hands an circle (16 steps in each direction).

Chorus: After each movement above, the chorus is performed. Roll the hands four times in front, then touch both hands to the knees, clap hands together, and push palms forward. Sing, "Roll Little Liza, Little Liza Jane" while performing the hand pattern. Perform this movement in eight counts (roll, 2, 3, 4, knees, clap, palms for 2). Repeat the chorus four times.

▶ THE MUFFIN MAN (AMERICAN)

Music Source: WWCD-YR002; WWC-YR002

Skills: Jumping, skipping

Formation: Single circle, facing center, hands at sides. One child, the Muffin Man, stands in front of another child of the opposite gender.

Directions:

Verse 1: The children stand still and clap their hands lightly, with the exception of the Muffin Man and his partner. These two join hands and jump lightly in place while keeping time to the music. On the first beat of each measure, a normal jump is taken, followed by a bounce in place (rebound) on the second beat.

Verse 2: The Muffin Man and his partner then skip around the inside of the circle individually and, near the end of the verse, each stands in front of a child, thus choosing a new partner.

Verse 1 is then repeated, with two sets of partners doing the jumping. During the repetition of verse 2, four children skip around the inside of the circle and choose partners. This procedure continues until all children have been chosen.

The children choose the name of a street to put in the verses.

▶ CLAPPING OUT (AMERICAN)

Music Source: WWCD-FFD

Skills: Clapping hands rhythmically

Formation: Single circle facing center

Directions:

Measures	Action
	Short introduction (8 counts).
1–4	Hand pattern number one: Two hands touch own thighs, then touch knees of the person on the right, clap own knees, then touch knees of the person on the left. Repeat four times for 16 counts.
5–8	Hand pattern number two: Clap own knees; cross hands and clap own knees; uncross hands and clap own knees; clap out hands to the right and left of the person next to you at the same time. Other person's hands can pass over or underneath. Repeat four times for 16 counts.
9–12	Hand pattern number three: Clap own knees; clap own hands; snap fingers twice while bumping hips from side to side. Repeat four times.
13–16	Hand pattern number four: Clap own knees; clap own hands; snap fingers twice while bumping hips from side to side. Repeat four times.
17–32	Repeat entire dance with only the rhythm section of the music playing.
33–48	Repeat entire dance again. This time there will be no music for hand patterns one through three. The group continues clapping without accompaniment. On hand pattern number four, the music will start and if the group has maintained the correct rhythm, they will be right in time with the music.

▶ SKIP TO MY LOU (AMERICAN)

Music Source: WWCD-7054; WWC-7054

Skills: Skipping, changing partners

Formation: Scattered with a partner

Directions: During the chorus, partners skip around the area. At the verse, everyone finds a new partner and continues skipping.

▶ BALLIN' THE JACK (AMERICAN)

Music Source: WWCD-FFD

Skills: Sliding, Do-sa-do

Formation: Double circle, partners facing each other

Directions:

Measures	Action
1	Each person slaps own thighs twice.
2	Each person claps hands twice.
3	Each person does a scissors movement with hands twice (with palms down, slide right hand over left, then left hand over right).
4	Each person touches partner's hands twice.
5–16	Repeat the sequence above three more times.
17–18	Holding hands, slide four steps (step-close) to the outside circle person's right.
19–20	Slide four steps (step-close) and return to the original position.
21	Slide two steps (step-close) to the outside circle person's right.
22	Slide two steps (step-close) and return to the original position.
23–26	Drop hands and Do-sa-do, passing right shoulders for eight counts back to the original position or partner.

Variation: To change partners after the Do-sa-do, outside people return to their original position. Inside circle partners move one space to the right after the Do-sa-do. On the last two beats of the Do-sa-do, move to the right diagonally to face a new partner.

▶ HOW D'YE DO, MY PARTNER? (SWEDISH)

Music Source: WWCD-1041; WWC-07042

Skills: Bowing, curtsying, skipping

Formation: Double circle, partners facing, Partner A on inside

Directions:

Measures	Action
1–2	Partners A bow to their partner. (Bow)
3–4	Partners B bow. (Bow)
5–6	A offers the right hand to B, who takes it with the right hand. (Join right hands) Both turn to face counterclockwise. (Face counterclockwise)
7–8	Couples join left hands in promenade position in preparation to skip when the music changes. (Join left hands)
9–16	Partners skip counterclockwise in the circle, slowing down on measure 15. (Skip)

On measure 16, Bs stop and As move ahead to secure a new partner. (New partner)

▶ DANISH DANCE OF GREETING (DANISH)

Music Source: WWCD-1041; WWC-07042

Skills: Running or sliding, bowing

Formation: Single circle, all face center. Partner A stands to the left of Partner B.

Directions:

Measures	Action
1	All clap twice and bow to partner. (Clap, clap, bow)
2	Repeat but turn back to the partner and bow to the neighbor. (Clap, clap, bow)
3	Stamp right, stamp left. (Stamp, stamp)
4	Turn around in four running steps. (Turn, 2, 3, 4)
5–8	Repeat the action of measures 1–4.
9–12	All join hands and run to the left for four measures. (Run, 2, 3, 4, . . . 16)
13–16	Repeat the action of measures 9–12, taking light running steps in the opposite direction. (Run, 2, 3, 4, . . . 16)

Variation: Instead of a running step, use a light slide.

▶ ACH JA (GERMAN)

Music Source: WWCD-0860; WWC-0860

Skills: Walking, sliding

Formation: Double circle, partners facing counterclockwise, Partners A on the inside, inside hands joined

Directions: Explain that "Ach Ja" means "Oh yes."

Measures	Action
1–2	Partners walk eight steps in the line of direction. (Walk, 2, 3, 4, 5, 6, 7, 8)
3	Partners drop hands and bow to each other. (Bow)
4	Each A then bows to the B on the left, who returns the bow. (Bow)
5–8	Measures 1–4 are repeated.
9–10	Partners face each other, join hands, and take four slides in the line of direction. (Slide, 2, 3, 4)

19

11–12	Four slides are taken clockwise. (Slide, 2, 3, 4)
13	Partners bow to each other. (Bow)
14	A bows to the B on the left, who returns the bow. (Bow) To start the next dance, A moves quickly toward this B, who is the next partner.

▶ **SEVEN JUMPS (DANISH)**

Music Source: WWCD-1043; WWC-3528

Skills: Step-hop, balance, control

Formation: Single circle, hands joined

Directions: There are seven jumps to the dance. Each jump is preceded by the following action.

Measures	Action
1–8	The circle moves to the right with seven step-hops, one to each measure. On the eighth measure, all jump high in the air and reverse direction. (Step-hop, 2-hop, 3-hop, . . . 7-hop, change direction)
9–16	Circle to the left with seven step-hops. Stop on measure 16 and face the center. (Step-hop, 2-hop, 3-hop, . . . 7-hop, face center)
17	All drop hands, place their hands on hips, and lift the right knee upward with the toes pointed downward. (Knee up)
18	All stamp the right foot to the ground on the signal note, then join hands on the next note. (Stamp)
1–18	Repeat measures 1–18, but do not join hands.
19	Lift the left knee, stamp, and join hands.
1–19	Repeat measures 1–19, but do not join hands.
20	Put the right toe backward and kneel on the right knee. Stand and join hands.
1–20	Repeat measures 1–20; do not join hands.
21	Kneel on the left knee. Stand and join hands.
1–21	Repeat measures 1–21; do not join hands.
22	Put the right elbow to the floor with the cheek on the fist. Stand and join hands.
1–22	Repeat measures 1–22; do not join hands.
23	Put the left elbow to the floor with the cheek on the fist. Stand and join hands.
1–23	Repeat measures 1–23; do not join hands.
24	Put forehead on the floor. Stand, join hands.
1–16	Repeat the first measures.

✓ **TEACHING TIP**

This dance was performed originally in Denmark by men as a control-elimination competition. Those who made unnecessary movements or mistakes were eliminated.

Variation: To increase motivation, the dance can be done with a parachute. The dancers hold the parachute taut with one hand during the step-hops. The chute is kept taut with both hands for all jumps except the last, during which the forehead touches the chute on the floor.

▶ **CHIMES OF DUNKIRK, VAR. 1 (FRENCH-BELGIAN)**

Music Source: WWCD-1042; WWC-07042

Skills: Turning in a small circle with a partner, changing partners

Formation: Double circle, partners facing

Directions:

Measures	Action
1–2	Stamp three times in place, right-left-right. (Stamp, 2, 3)
3–4	Clap hands three times above the head (chimes in the steeple). (Clap, 2, 3)
5–8	Partner A places both hands on Partner B's hips; B places both hands on A's shoulders. Taking four steps, they turn around in place. (Turn, 2, 3, 4) On the next four counts, Partner B (on the outside) moves one person to the left with four steps. (Change, 2, 3, 4) Repeat the sequence from the beginning.

Variation: An alternative to the turn described is to do an elbow turn by linking right elbows.

▶ **SHORTNIN' BREAD (AMERICAN)**

Music Source: WWCD-7050; WWC-7050

Skills: Sliding, turning with a partner

Formation: Scattered with partner

Directions:

Measures	Action
1–2	Clap own hands.
3–4	Slap partner's hands, palms together.
5–6	Clap own hands.
7–8	Slap own thighs.
9–16	Repeat measures 1–8.
17–20	Couples slide to the right holding hands.
21–24	Circle holding hands.
25–32	Repeat measures 17–24 moving to the left.

▶ **CHILDREN'S POLKA (GERMAN)**

Music Source: WWCD-07042; WWC-07042

Formation: Single circle of couples, partners facing

Skills: Step-draw

Directions:

Measures	Action
1–2	Take two step-draw steps toward the center of the circle, ending with three steps in place. (Draw, draw, step, 2, 3)
3–4	Take two step-draw steps away from the center, ending with three steps in place. (Draw, draw, step, 2, 3)
5–8	Repeat the pattern of measures 1–4.
9	Slap own knees once with both hands; clap own hands once. (Slap, clap)
10	Clap both hands with partner three times. (Clap, 2, 3)
11–12	Repeat the pattern of measures 9 and 10.
13	Hop, placing one heel forward, and shake the forefinger at partner three times. (Scold, 2, 3)
14	Repeat the "scolding" pattern with the other foot and hand. (Scold, 2, 3)
15–16	Turn once around in place with four running steps and stamp three times in place. (Turn, 2, 3, 4; Stamp, 2, 3)

▶ **SHOEMAKER'S DANCE (DANISH)**

Music Source: WWCD-1042; WWC-07042

Skills: Skipping, heel and toe

Formation: Double circle, partners facing, with Partner A's back to the center of the circle

Directions:

Measures	Part I Action
1	With arms bent and at shoulder height, and with hands clenched to form fists, circle one fist over the other in front of the chest. (Wind the thread)
2	Reverse the circular motion and wind the thread in the opposite direction. (Reverse direction)
3	Pull the elbows back vigorously twice. (Pull and tighten the thread)
4	Clap own hands three times. (Clap, 2, 3)
5–7	Repeat the pattern of measures 1–3.
8	Tap own fists together three times to drive the nails. (Tap, 2, 3)

	Part II Action
9–16	Partners face counterclockwise, inside hands joined. Skip counterclockwise, ending with a bow. (Skip, 2, 3, . . . 15, bow)

Variation: Variation of Part II Action

Measures	Action
9	Place the heel of the outside foot forward (counts 1 and), and point the toe of the outside foot in back (2 and).
10	Take three running steps forward, starting with the outside foot and pausing on the last count.
11–12	Repeat the pattern of measures 9–10, starting with the inside foot.
13–16	Repeat the pattern of measures 9–12, entire "heel and toe and run, run, run" pattern dance, four times singing Part II verse.

▶ **JUMP JIM JO (AMERICAN)**

Music Source: WWCD-1041

Skills: Jumping, running, draw step

Formation: Double circle, partners facing, both hands joined

Directions:

Measures	Action
1–2	Do two jumps sideways, progressing counterclockwise, followed by three quick jumps in place. (Slow, slow, fast, fast, fast)
3–4	Release hands and turn once around in place with four jumps (two jumps per measure). Finish facing partner and rejoin hands. (Jump, turn, 3, 4)
5	Take two sliding steps sideways, progressing counterclockwise. (Slide, slide)

6	Partners face counterclockwise with inside hands joined and tap three times with the toe of the outside foot. (Tap, tap, tap)
7–8	Take four running steps forward, then face partner, join both hands, and end with three jumps in place. (Run, 2, 3, 4; Jump, 2, 3)

▶ **YANKEE DOODLE (AMERICAN)**

Music Source: WWCD-FDN

Skills: Walking, galloping, sliding, bowing

Formation: Scattered or open circle facing counterclockwise

Directions:

Measures	Action
1–4	All gallop eight steps. (Gallop, 2, . . . 8)
5–8	All stop, face center, point to cap and bow on word "macaroni." (Stop, point, bow)
9–12	All join hands and take six slides to the right and stamp feet two times on word "dandy." (Slide, 2, 3, . . . 6; Stamp, stamp)
13–16	All slide six times to the left and clap hands two times on the word "candy." (Slide, 2, 3, . . . 6; Clap, clap)

Variation: Change the locomotor movements to fit the age and interest of the group. Have the class create new movement patterns.

▶ **EINS ZWEI DREI (GERMAN)**

Music Source: WWCD-1042

Skills: Walking, sliding

Formation: Single circle of couples (Partner B to Partner A's right) facing the center and numbered alternately couple 1, 2, 1, 2

Directions: Explain that "Eins, Zwei, Drei" means "one, two, three" in German.

Measures	Part I Action
1–2	Couples 1 take three steps toward the center of the circle as they clap their hands by brushing them vertically like cymbals. (Forward, 2, 3, pause)
3–4	Couples 1 repeat measures 1–2, walking backward to place. (Back, 2, 3, pause)
5–8	Couples 1 face, join both hands, and take four slides toward the center of the circle and four slides back to place. Partner A starts with the left foot, Partner B with the right. (Slide, 2, 3, 4)
9–16	Couples 2 repeat measures 1–8.

Measures	Part II Action
17	Partner A turns and touches the right heel sideways while shaking the right index finger at partner. Partner B does the same with the left heel and left index finger. (Scold, 2, 3)
18	Repeat measure 17 with the corner, reversing footwork and hands. (Scold, 2, 3)
19–20	Repeat measures 17 and 18.
21–24	All join hands and circle left with eight slides. (Slide, 2, 3, . . . 8)
25–32	Repeat measures 17–24, reversing the direction of the slides. (Slide, 2, 3, . . . 8)

Variation: To facilitate learning, practice all steps individually in a scattered formation.

▶ **CHIMES OF DUNKIRK, VAR. 2 (FRENCH-BELGIAN)**

Music Source: WWCD-1042

Skills: Turning with a partner, skipping

Formation: Single circle of couples, partners facing

Directions:

Measures	Action
1–2	Stamp three times in place. (Stamp, 2, 3)
3–4	Clap own hands three times. (Clap, 2, 3)
5–8	Do a two-hand swing with partner. Join both hands with partner and turn once clockwise with eight running or skipping steps. (Swing, 2, 3, . . . 8)

	Chorus Action
1–8	Circle left, singing, "Tra, la, la, la, la, . . ." All join hands and circle left with 16 running or skipping steps, ending with a bow. (Run, 2, 3, . . . 15, bow)

✓ **TEACHING TIP**

The dance can also be used as a mixer by Partner B's advancing one partner to the left. Also, instead of a two-hand swing with partner, substitute the shoulder-waist position. A places a hand on B's waist, and B places both hands on A's shoulders.

To facilitate forming the circle for the chorus, make a four-step turn instead of an eight-step turn on measures 5–8. This gives the children four counts to get ready for the circle formation and four counts to make the circle.

BOMBAY BOUNCE

Music Source: Any music with a definite and moderately fast beat

Skills: Hesitation step, side step

Formation: Scattered, all facing forward

Directions:

Part I (16 counts): A hesitation step to the left is performed by taking a short step to the left followed by touching the right foot near the left while the weight remains on the left foot. A hesitation step to the right is similar except it begins with a step to the right. To begin the dance, eight hesitation steps are performed in place with a hand clap on each touch. (Left, touch and clap; right, touch and clap.) Repeat four times.

Part II (16 counts): Take two side steps to the left, then two to the right. Clap on counts 4 and 8. (Left, close; Left, close and clap; Right, close; Right, close and clap). Repeat the pattern.

Part III (16 counts): Take four side steps left and four side steps right. Clap only on count 8. (Left, close, left, close, left, close, left, close and clap.) Repeat to the right.

Part IV (16 counts): Take four steps forward and four steps backward, four steps forward and four steps backward. Clap on counts 4, 8, 12, and 16. (Forward, 2, 3, 4 and clap; Backward, 2, 3, 4 and clap; Forward, 2, 3, 4 and clap; Backward 2, 3, 4 and clap.)

> **Variation:** Variations are possible (e.g., in Part IV, instead of four steps, use three steps and a kick [swing]).

CAROUSEL (SWEDISH)

Music Source: WWCD-1041

Skills: Draw step, sliding

Formation: Double circle, facing center. The inner circle, representing a merry-go-round, joins hands. The outer players, representing the riders, place their hands on the hips of the partner in front.

Directions:

Measures	Verse Action
1–16	Moving to the left, children take 12 slow draw steps and stamp on the last 3 steps. (Step, together, 2, 3, . . . 12, stamp, stamp, stamp, rest)

Measures	Chorus Action
17–24	Moving left, speed up the draw step until it becomes a slide or gallop. Sing the chorus. (Slide, 2, 3, . . . 8)
25–32	Repeat measures 17–24 while moving to the right. (Slide, 2, 3, . . . 8)

During the chorus, the tempo is increased, and the movement is changed to a slide. Children should take short, light slides to prevent the circle from moving out of control.

> **Variation:** The dance can also be done with youngsters holding the perimeter of a parachute.

JOLLY IS THE MILLER (AMERICAN)

Music Source: WWC-317

Skills: Marching

Formation: Double circle, partners facing counterclockwise, the A partners on the inside, with inside hands joined. A "miller" is in the center of the circle.

Directions: All sing. Youngsters march counterclockwise, with inside hands joined. During the second line when "the wheel goes round," the dancers turn their outside arm in a circle to form a wheel. Children change partners at the words "right steps forward and the left steps back." The miller then has a chance to get a partner. The child left without a partner becomes the next miller.

BLEKING (SWEDISH)

Music Source: WWCD-1044; WWC-07042

Skills: Bleking step, step-hop

Formation: Single circle, partners facing, both hands joined. Partners A face counterclockwise and Partners B clockwise.

Directions:

Part I—The Bleking Step: Cue by calling "Slow-slow, fast-fast-fast."

Measures	Action
1	Hop on the left foot and extend the right heel forward with the right leg straight. At the same time, thrust the right hand forward. Hop on the right foot, reversing the arm action and extending the left foot to rest on the heel. (Slow, slow)
2	Repeat the action with three quick changes—left, right, left. (Fast, fast, fast)
3–4	Beginning on the right foot, repeat the movements of measures 1 and 2. (Slow, slow, fast, fast, fast)
5–8	Repeat measures 1–4.

Part II—The Windmills: Partners extend their joined hands sideways at shoulder height.

Measures	Action
9–16	Partners turn in place with a repeated step-hop. At the same time, the arms move up and down like a windmill. The turning is done clockwise, with A starting on the right foot and B on the left. At the completion of the step-hops (16), the partners should be in their original places ready for Part I again. (Step-hop, 2-hop, 3-hop, . . . 16-hop)

Variations:

1. Change from original positions to a double circle, partners facing, A partners with back to the center. Part I is as described. For Part II, all face counterclockwise, and partners join inside hands. Partners do the basic schottische of "step, step, step, hop" throughout Part II (page 458).

2. Another excellent variation is to do the dance with partners scattered in general space. Part I is as described. For Part II, the children leave their partners and step-hop in various directions around the dancing area. When the music is about to change back to Part I, performers find a partner wherever they can, and the dance is repeated.

3. Bleking is excellent music for creative dance, with the stipulation that the children maintain individually the bleking rhythm of "slow-slow, fast-fast-fast" during Part I and do any kind of movement in place that they wish. During Part II, they may do any locomotor or other movement that they choose.

▶ NIXIE POLKA (NIGAREPOLSKA) (SWEDISH)

Music Source: WWCD-1041; WWC-572

Skills: Bleking step

Formation: Single circle, all facing center, with one or more children scattered inside the circle

Measures	Part I Action
1–4	With hands joined, all spring lightly onto the left foot and extend the right foot forward, heel to ground, toe up. Next, spring lightly onto the right foot and extend the left foot forward. Repeat this action until four slow Bleking steps are completed. (Slow, slow, slow, slow)
5–8	All clap hands once and shout "Hey!" The center child then runs around the inside of the circle, looking for a partner, finally

selecting one. They join both hands and run lightly in place until the music is finished. This refrain is repeated, so the children have time to get back to the center of the circle. (Clap, run)

Part II Action

1–4	The center dancer and partner, with both hands joined, repeat the action of measures 1–4. All dancers in the circle also repeat the action of measures 1–4. (Slow, slow, slow, slow)
5–8	On the first count, all clap hands, shouting "Hey!" The center dancer then about-faces and places both hands on the shoulders of partner, who now becomes the new leader. In this position, both shuffle around the inside of the circle, looking for a third person to dance with. The music is repeated again to allow ample time to return to the center. (Clap, run)

Part III Action

1–4	The action of measures 1–4 is repeated, with the new dancer facing the circle and the two others facing the new dancer. (Slow, slow, slow, slow)
5–8	On the first count, all clap hands, shouting "Hey!" The two people in the center then about-face. All three now face the center to form a line of three dancers with a new leader, who looks for a fourth dancer. The music is repeated. (Clap, run)

The entire dance is thus repeated, accumulating dancers with each repetition. There should be one center dancer for each dozen dancers in the circle.

▶ TURN THE GLASSES OVER (AMERICAN-ENGLISH)

Music Source: WWCD-W0F1

Skills: Walking, wring the dishrag

Formation: Single circle of couples in promenade position. Extra students are in the center.

Directions:

Measures	Verse Action
1–16	The couples walk forward singing the verse. At the words "turn the glasses over," they raise their arms, keeping the hands joined, and turn under the raised arms, making one complete outward "dishrag" turn. Youngsters must anticipate the turn

and be prepared to start in time to complete the movement by the end of the phrase.

Measures	Chorus Action
1–16	Youngsters in the outer circle continue walking while those in the inner circle turn and walk in the opposite direction. An extra player(s) joins one of the circles and continues with the group. At the words "girl in the ocean," youngsters take the nearest person for a new partner. Those without a partner move to the center.

▶ JINGLE BELLS, VAR. 1 (DUTCH)

Music Source: Any version of Jingle Bells or WWCD-FFD

Skills: Elbow swing, skipping, sliding

Formation: Double circle, partners facing, with both hands joined

Directions:

Measures	Action
1–2	Partners take eight slides counter-clockwise. (Slide, 2, 3, . . . 8)
3–4	Partners turn so they are standing back to back, and take eight more slides in the line of direction. This move is best made by dropping the front hands and swinging the back hands forward until the dancers are standing back to back. They rejoin the hands that are now in back. Make this move with no loss of rhythm. (Slide, 2, 3, . . . 8)
5–6	Repeat the action of measures 1 and 2. To get back to the face-to-face position, let go of the back hands and swing the front hands backward, allowing the bodies to pivot and face again. (Slide, 2, 3, . . . 8)
7–8	Repeat measures 3 and 4. (Slide, 2, 3, . . . 8)
	Chorus Action
1	Clap own hands three times. (Clap own, 2, 3)
2	Clap both hands with partner three times. (Clap both, 2, 3)
3	Clap own hands four times. (Clap own, 2, 3, 4)
4	Clap both hands with partner once. (Clap both)
5–8	Right elbow swing with partner. Partners hook right elbows and swing clockwise with eight skips. (Swing, 2, 3, 4, 5, 6, 7, 8)
9–12	Repeat clapping sequence of measures 1–4.
13–16	Left elbow swing with partner for eight skips, finishing in the original starting position, ready to repeat the entire dance with the same partner; or do a left elbow swing with partner for four skips, which is once around, then all children in the inner circle skip forward to the outer dancer ahead and repeat the entire dance from the beginning with a new partner. (Swing, 2, 3, 4, 5, 6, 7, 8)

▶ THE HITCH HIKER (AMERICAN)

Music Source: WWCD-FDN

Skills: Chug step (a short backward jump with the feet together on the floor), skipping

Formation: Double circle, partners facing each other with boys inside facing out

Directions:

Measures	Action
1–2	Introduction
1–2	Take two chugs away from partner and clap hands on each step. Jerk right thumb over right shoulder while twisting right foot with heel on the floor. Repeat. (Chug chug, right, right)
3–4	Same as measures 1–2 except use left thumb and foot. (Chug, chug, left, left)
5–6	Same as measures 1–2 except use both thumbs and feet. (Chug, chug, both, both)
7–8	Skip diagonally forward and to the right toward a new partner with four skips; continue with four more skips around your new partner with right hands joined and get ready to repeat the dance. (Skip, 2, 3, 4, around, 2, 3, 4)

The sequence repeats eight times.

▶ PATTY CAKE (HEEL AND TOE) POLKA (INTERNATIONAL)

Music Source: WWCD-FDN

Skills: Heel and toe polka step, sliding, elbow swing, skipping

Formation: Double circle, partners facing, A in the inner circle with back to the center. Both hands are joined with partner. A's left foot and B's right foot are free.

19

Directions:

Measures	Part I Action
1–2	Heel-toe twice with A's left and B's right foot. (Heel, toe, heel, toe)
3–4	Take four slides sideways to A's left, progressing counterclockwise. Do not transfer the weight on the last count. Finish with A's right and B's left foot free. (Slide, 2, 3, 4)
5–8	Repeat the pattern of measures 1–4, starting with A's right and B's left foot, progressing clockwise. Finish with the partners separated and facing. (Heel, toe, heel, toe; Slide, 2, 3, 4)
	Part II Action
9	Clap right hands with partner three times. (Right, 2, 3)
10	Clap left hands with partner three times. (Left, 2, 3)
11	Clap both hands with partner three times. (Both, 2, 3)
12	Slap own knees three times. (Knees, 2, 3)
13–14	Right elbow swing with partner. Partners hook right elbows and swing once around with four walking steps, finishing with A's back to center. (Swing, 2, 3, 4)
15–16	Progress left to a new partner with four walking steps. (Left, 2, 3, 4)

Repeat the entire dance with the new partner.

▶ **CIRCASSIAN CIRCLE (ENGLISH)**

Music Source: WWCD-FDN

Skills: Walking, skipping, promenade

Formation: Large single circle of couples facing center with all hands joined

Directions:

Measures	Action
1–2	Introduction
1–2	All walk four steps toward center and back four steps to place. (Walk 2, 3, 4; back, 2, 3, 4)
3–4	Repeat measures 1 and 2. (Walk 2, 3, 4; back, 2, 3, 4)
5–6	Girls walk four steps toward center and back four steps. (Girls, 2, 3, 4; back, 2, 3, 4)
7–8	Boys walk four steps toward center, then turn a half-turn left and walk diagonally

clockwise four steps to a new partner. (Boys, 2, 3, 4; move to new partner)

| 9–10 | Using a cross-arm grip, new partners lean away from each other and skip eight steps clockwise once around each other. (Skip, 2, 3, 4, 5, 6, 7, 8) |
| 11–12 | Without dropping hands, couples promenade counterclockwise for eight steps. Take the last two steps to stop and face the center to do the dance again. (Promenade, 2, 3, 4, 5, 6, face center) |

The dance is performed four times.

▶ **SEVEN STEPS (AUSTRIAN)**

Music Source: WWCD-FDN

Skills: Running, hopping

Formation: Double circle with couples facing counter-clockwise with inside hands joined

Directions:

Measures	Action
1–2	Introduction
1–2	Start with outside foot and run seven steps forward counterclockwise, and then pause with weight on outside foot on eighth count. (Run, 2, 3, 4, 5, 6, 7, pause)
3–4	Start with inside foot and run seven steps backward (clockwise), and then pause with weight on inside foot on eighth count. (Run, back, 3, 4, 5, 6, 7, pause)
5	Release hands, turn away from partner and starting with the outside foot, run three steps away from partner and hop on the outside foot on the fourth count. (Away, 2, 3, hop)
6	Turn and face partner and starting with the inside foot, run three steps toward partner and then hop on the inside foot on the fourth count. (Back, 2, 3, hop)
7–8	Partners with right hands joined run once around each other with eight running steps clockwise to the right. (Swing, 2, 3, 4, 5, 6, 7, 8)
9	Release hands, turn away from partner and starting with the outside foot, run three steps away from partner; on the fourth count hop and turn on the outside foot to face diagonally toward new partner. (Apart, 2, 3, hop)

| 10 | Take three running steps to a new partner (inside partner moves counterclockwise forward diagonally toward new partner and outside partner moves clockwise backward diagonally to next partner). Then hop on the fourth count. |
| 11–12 | New partners run once around each other with eight running steps counterclockwise with left hands joined. Finish in starting position with inside hands joined. |

Perform the dance a total of five times.

▶ RHYTHM STICKS—IT'S A SMALL, SMALL WORLD (AMERICAN)

Rhythm sticks or Lummi sticks are 12 to 15 inches in length. Activities may be done individually or in partners. This routine is done individually. The sticks are held in the thumb and the forefinger at about the bottom third of the stick.

Music Source: WWCD-2015; WWC-2015

Skills: Rhythmic tapping and manipulation of sticks

Formation: Children sitting cross-legged individually scattered around the area

Directions:

Measures	Call	Action
1–2	Down, cross, down, cross	Tap ends of both sticks on the floor, and then cross the arms over, tapping the sticks on the floor again.
3–4	Down, cross, down, cross	Repeat.
5–6	Down, cross, down, cross	Repeat.
7–8	Chorus: It's a small, small world.	Lean forward touching head to knees (curl forward).
9–10	Tap, tap, knees, knees.	Tap sticks two times in front of the chest, and then lightly tap the knees twice.
11–12	Tap, tap, knees, knees	Repeat
13–14	Tap, tap, knees, knees	Repeat
15–16	Chorus: It's a small, small world.	Lean forward touching head to knees (curl forward).

The sequence above repeats a number of times with touches to the toes, shoulders, head, and nose.

As a variation, youngsters can face a partner and tap both of their sticks to their partner's sticks.

DEVELOPMENTAL LEVEL II DANCES

Developmental Level II activities focus clearly on folk dance. Locomotor skills are still the basis of the movement patterns, but in most of the dances, the patterns are more difficult than those in Developmental Level I. At this level, each dance always has at least two parts and may have three or more. Because the movement patterns are longer, the part-whole teaching method is used more often with this age group. These dances are vigorous and fast moving, which makes them exciting for youngsters to perform.

Tinikling and Lummi sticks add challenge and novelty to the progression. Emphasis should be on participation and enjoyment without excessive concern for perfection. Normal progress through the rhythms program will assure that adequate quality will result.

▶ THE BIRD DANCE (CHICKEN DANCE)

Music Source: WWC-9126

Skills: Skipping or walking, elbow swing or star

Formation: Circle or scatter formation, partners facing

Directions:

Measures	Part I Action
1	Four snaps—thumb and fingers, hands up.
2	Four flaps—arms up and down, elbows bent.
3	Four wiggles—hips, knees bent low.
4	Four claps.
5–16	Repeat action of measures 1–4 three times.

Measures	Part II Action
1–8	With a partner, either do a right-hand star with 16 skips or 16 walking steps, or do an elbow swing. (Skip, 2, 3, . . . 15, change hands)
9–16	Repeat with the left hand. On the last four counts of the last swing, everyone changes partners. If dancing in a circle formation, partners B advance forward counterclockwise to the next partner A. If dancing in a scattered formation, everyone scrambles to find a new partner. (Skip, 2, 3, . . . 12, change partners)

19

✓ **TEACHING TIP**

Perform the dance individually, with everyone moving to find a new partner on the skipping sequence. The locomotor movements can be varied to include sliding or galloping.

▶ **CSEBOGAR (HUNGARIAN)**

Music Source: WWCD-1042

Skills: Skipping, sliding, draw step, elbow swing

Formation: Single circle, partners facing center, hands joined with partners B on the right

Directions:

Part I:

Measures	Action
1–4	Take seven slides to the left. (Slide, 2, 3, 4, 5, 6, 7, change)
5–8	Take seven slides to the right. (Back, 2, 3, 4, 5, 6, 7, stop)
9–12	Take three skips to the center and stamp on the fourth beat. Take three skips backward to place and stamp on the eighth beat. (Forward, 2, 3, stamp; backward, 2, 3, stamp)
13–16	Hook right elbows with partner and turn around twice in place, skipping. (Swing, 2, 3, 4, 5, 6, 7, 8)

Part II: Partners face each other in a single circle with hands joined.

Measures	Action
17–20	Holding both of partner's hands, take four draw steps (step, close) toward the center of the circle. (Step-close, 2-close, 3-close, 4-close)
21–24	Take four draw steps back to place. (Step-close, 2-close, 3-close, 4-close)
25–26	Go toward the center of the circle with two draw steps. (In-close, 2-close)
27–28	Take two draw steps back to place. (Out-close, 2-close)
29–32	Hook elbows and repeat the elbow swing, finishing with a shout and facing the center of the circle in the original formation. (Swing, 2, 3, 4, 5, "Csebogar")

✓ **TEACHING TIP**

Instead of an elbow swing, partners can use the Hungarian turn. Partners stand side by side, put the right arm around the partner's waist, and lean away from partner. The left arm is held out to the side, with the elbow bent, the hand pointing up, and the palm facing the dancer.

▶ **POP GOES THE WEASEL (AMERICAN)**

Music Source: WWCD-1043; WWCD-FDN

Skills: Walking, skipping, turning under

Formation: Double circle of sets of four; couples facing with Partner B on Partner A's right. Couples facing clockwise are number 1 couples; couples facing counterclockwise are number 2 couples.

Directions:

Measures	Action
1–4	Join hands in a circle of four and circle left, once around, with eight skipping or sliding steps. (Circle, 2, 3, 4, 5, 6, 7, 8)
5–6	Take two steps forward, raising the joined hands, and two steps backward, lowering the hands. (Forward, 2; back, 2)
7–8	"Ones" pop the "Twos" under (i.e., couples number 1 raise their joined hands to form an arch and pass the number 2 couples under). All walk ahead to meet a new couple. (Forward, and pop through)

Repeat as desired.

Variations:

1. Dancers are in sets of three, all facing counterclockwise. Each forms a triangle with one child in front and the other two with joined hands forming the base. The front dancer reaches back and holds the outside hands of the other two dancers. The groups of three are in a large circle formation.

Measures	Action
1–2	Sets of three dancers skip forward four times. (Forward, 2, 3, 4)
3–4	Sets of three skip backward four times. (Backward, 2, 3, 4)
5–6	Sets of three skip forward four times. (Forward, 2, 3, 4)
7–8	On "Pop goes the weasel," the two back dancers raise their joined hands, and the front dancer backs up underneath to the next set. This set, in the meantime, has "popped" its front dancer back to the set behind it. (Raise and pop under)

2. "Pop Goes the Weasel" is excellent for stimulating creative movement. The music actually consists of a verse and a chorus part. During the verse part, the children can slide, gallop, or skip until the "Pop" line, at which time they make a half or full turn in the air. During the chorus, they can do jerky nonlocomotor movements.

Other options include ball routines, in which the children dribble in time to the music during the verse and pass the ball around various parts of the body during the chorus. Another variation involves ropes. The children carry a jump rope while skipping, sliding, or galloping. During the chorus, they jump in time to the music, and on the word "Pop," they try to do a double jump.

▶ WILD TURKEY MIXER

Music Source: WWC-FFD or any music with a definite rhythm

Skills: Walking, elbow swing, partner change

Formation: Trios abreast facing counterclockwise around the circle

Directions:

Measures	Action
1–8	In lines of three, with the right and left person holding the near hand of the center person, all walk 16 steps forward. (Walk, 2, 3, . . . 16)
9–12	The center person (Wild Turkey) turns the right-hand person once around with the right elbow. (Turn, 2, 3, 4, 5, 6, 7, 8)
13–16	The Wild Turkey turns the left-hand person with the left elbow, and then moves forward to repeat the dance with the two new people ahead. (Turn, 2, 3, 4; forward, 2, 3, 4)

The same dance can be adapted to other pieces of music. With a faster tempo, the elbow swings are done with a skip instead of a walk.

▶ LA RASPA (MEXICAN)

Music Source: WWCD-05117

Skills: Bleking step, running, elbow swing

Formation: Partners facing, couples scattered around room

Directions: La raspa means "the rasp" or "the file," and the dance movements are supposed to represent a rasp or file in action. Directions are the same for both partners.

Part I: To begin, the partners face each other, Partner B with hands at sides and Partner A with hands behind the back.

Measures	Action
1–4	Beginning right, take one bleking step (page 431). (Slow, slow, fast, fast, fast)
5–8	Turn slightly counterclockwise away from partner (right shoulder to right shoulder) and, beginning with a jump on the left foot, repeat measures 1–4. (Slow, slow, fast, fast, fast)
9–12	Repeat action of measures 1–4, facing opposite direction (left shoulder to left shoulder). (Slow, slow, fast, fast, fast)
13–16	Repeat action of measures 1–4, facing partner. (Slow, slow, fast, fast, fast)

Part II: Partners hook right elbows; left elbows are bent and left hands are pointed toward the ceiling.

Measures	Action
1–4	Do a right elbow swing, using eight running or skipping steps. Release and clap the hands on the eighth count. (Swing, 2, 3, 4, 5, 6, 7, clap)
5–8	Do a left elbow swing, using eight running or skipping steps. Release and clap the hands on the eighth count. (Swing, 2, 3, 4, 5, 6, 7, clap)
9–16	Repeat the actions of measures 1–8.

Variations:

1. Face partner (all should be in a single-circle formation for this version) and do a grand right and left around the circle. Repeat Part I with a new partner.

2. All face center or face a partner and do the Bleking or raspa step. On each pause, clap own hands twice.

▶ POLLY WOLLY DOODLE (AMERICAN)

Music Source: WWCD-1041

Skills: Sliding, turning, walking

Formation: Double circle of dancers, partners facing with both hands joined, Partner A with back to the center of the circle

Directions:

Measures	Part I Action
1–4	All slide four steps—A partners to left, Bs to right, counterclockwise. (Slide, 2, 3, 4)
5–8	Drop hands and all turn solo circle, A partners to left, Bs to right, with five stamps in this rhythm: 1-2-1, 2, 3. (Stamp on the word "Polly," stamp on the other foot on the word "doodle," and take three quick stamps on the word "day.") (Turn, 2, stamp, 2, 3)
9–16	Repeat measures 1–8, but in the opposite direction, A partners moving to right and Bs to left. (Slide, 2, 3, 4; turn, 2, stamp 2, 3)

19

Part II Action

1–4   Both bow to each other, A partners with hands on hips, Bs with hands at sides. (A bows; B bows)

5–8   With four walking steps (or skipping steps), both move backward, away from each other. (Back, 2, 3, 4)

9–12   Both move diagonally forward to own left to meet a new partner. (Diagonal, 2, 3, 4)

13–16 With the new partner, elbow swing in place using a skipping step. (Swing, 2, 3, 4) Repeat the dance from the beginning with the new partner.

▶ BINGO (AMERICAN)

Music Source: WWCD-FDN

Skills: Walking, right-and-left grand

Formation: Double circle, partners side by side and facing counterclockwise, Partners A on the inside and inside hands joined.

Note: "Bingo" is a favorite of young people. The singing must be brisk and loud. The dance is in three parts.

Directions:

Part I: Partners walk counterclockwise around the circle, singing the refrain. (Walk, 2, 3, . . . 15, face center)

Part II: All join hands to form a single circle, Partner B on Partner A's right. They sing (spelling out) with these actions.

Action:

All take four steps into the center.

All take four steps backward.

All take four steps forward again.

Take four steps backward, drop hands, and face partner.

Part III: Shake right hands with the partner, calling out B on the first heavy note. All walk forward, passing their partner, to meet the oncoming person with a left handshake, calling out I on the next chord. Continue to the third person with a right handshake, sounding out the N. Pass on to the fourth person, giving a left handshake and a G. Instead of a handshake with the fifth person, face each other, raise the arms high above the head, shake all over, and sound out a long, drawn-out O. The fifth person becomes the new partner, and the dance is repeated.

✓ TEACHING TIP

The dance can be adapted to the use of a parachute. At the end of Part II (the end of the line "And Bingo was his name") Partners A face the chute and hold it with both hands, lifting it to shoulder level. Partners B drop their hands from the parachute and get ready to move clockwise. On each of the letters B-I-N-G-O, they move inside the first A, outside the next, and so on, for five changes. They then take a new place as indicated and get ready to repeat the dance. The next sequence can have Partners B remaining in place, holding the chute, while Partners A move counterclockwise.

▶ GRAND MARCH (AMERICAN)

Music Source: WWCD-W0F-2 or any good march or square dance music

Skills: Controlled walking, marching, grand march figures

Formation: Partners B are on the left side of the room, facing the end, and Partners A are on the right side, facing the same end. This is the foot of the hall. The teacher or caller stands at the other end of the room, the head of the hall. An alternative formation is to put half of the class on each side of the room and to designate each half with different colored pinnies.

Directions:

Call	Action
Down the center by twos.	The lines march forward to the foot of the hall, turn the corner, meet at the center of the foot of the hall, and march in couples toward the caller (Figure 19.4), with

FIGURE 19.4 Formation and action for Grand March.

inside hands joined. The Bs' line should be on the proper side so that, when the couples come down the center, A is on B's left. Odd couples are numbered 1, 3, 5, and so on. Even couples are numbered 2, 4, 6, and so on.

Twos left and right.	The odd couples go left and the even couples go right around the room and meet at the foot of the hall.
Down the center by fours.	The couples walk down the center, four abreast.
Separate by twos.	When they approach the caller, odd couples go left and even couples right. They meet again at the foot of the hall.
Form arches.	Instead of coming down the center, odd couples form arches and even couples tunnel under. Each continues around the sides of the hall to meet at the head.
Other couples arch.	Even couples arch, and odd couples tunnel under. Each continues around the sides of the room to the foot.
Over and under.	The first odd couple arches over the first even couple, then ducks under the second even couple's arch. Each couple goes over the first couple and under the next. Continue around to the head of the hall.
Pass right through.	As the lines come toward each other, they mesh and pass through each other in the following fashion: All drop handholds. Each B walks between the A and B of the opposite couple and continues walking to the foot of the hall.
Down the center by fours.	Go down the center four abreast.
Fours left and right.	The first four go left around the room, and the second four go right. The fours meet at the foot of the hall.
Down the center by eights.	Go eight abreast down the center.
Grapevine.	All persons in each line join hands and keep them joined. The leader takes either end of the first line and starts around the room with the line trailing. The other lines hook on to form one long line.
Wind it up.	The leader winds up the group in a spiral formation, like a clock spring. The leader makes the circles smaller and smaller until he or she is in the center.
Reverse (unwind).	The leader turns and faces in the opposite direction and walks between the lines of winding dancers. The leader unwinds the line and leads it around the room.
Everybody swing.	After the line is unwound, everybody does a square dance swing.

✓ **TEACHING TIP**

The leaders (couples 1 and 2) should maintain an even, steady pace and not hurry, or the march becomes a race. When one set of couples forms arches (as in movements 5 and 6) for the other set of couples to tunnel under, the arches should be made with the inside arms, and the couples should continue marching while they form the arches.

▶ **GREEN SLEEVES (ENGLISH)**

Music Source: WWCD-1042

Skills: Walking, star formation, over and under

Formation: Double circle with couples in sets of four, facing counterclockwise. Two couples form a set and are numbered 1 and 2. Inside hands of each couple are joined.

Directions:

Measures	Call	Action
1–8	Walk	Walk forward 16 steps.
9–12	Right-hand star	Each member of couple 1 turns individually to face the couple behind. All join right hands and circle clockwise (star) for eight steps.
13–16	Left-hand star	Reverse direction and form a left-hand star. This should bring couple 1 back to place facing in the original direction.
17–20	Over and under	Couple 2 arches and couple 1 backs under four steps while couple 2 moves forward four steps. Couple 1 then arches and couple 2 backs under (four steps for each).
21–24	Over and under	Repeat the action of measures 17–20.

▶ **JINGLE BELLS, VAR. 2 (DUTCH)**

Music Source: Any version of Jingle Bells or WWCD-FFD

Skills: Skipping, promenade position, sliding, elbow swing

Formation: Circle of couples facing counterclockwise, Partner B on Partner A's right. Promenade position, hands crossed in front, right hands joined over left, right foot free.

Directions:

Measures	Part I Action
1–2	Take four skips forward and four skips backward, starting with the right foot free. (Forward, 2, 3, 4; back, 2, 3, 4)
3–4	Repeat the pattern of measures 1 and 2. (Forward 2, 3, 4; back, 2, 3, 4)
5	Do four slides to the right, away from the center of the circle. (Out, 2, 3, 4)
6	Now do four slides left, toward the center. (In, 2, 3, 4)
7–8	Execute eight skips, making one turn counterclockwise, with Partner A pivoting backward and Partner B moving forward. Finish in a double circle, partners facing, with A's back to the center. (Skip, 2, 3, 4, 5, 6, 7, 8)
	Part II Action
1	Clap own hands three times. (Clap, 2, 3)
2	Clap both hands with partner three times. (Both, 2, 3)
3	Clap own hands four times. (Clap, 2, 3, 4)
4	Clap both hands with partner once. (Both)
5–8	Right elbow swing with partner. Partners hook right elbows and swing clockwise for eight skips. (Swing, 2, 3, 4, 5, 6, 7, 8)
9–12	Repeat clapping pattern of measures 1–4.
13–16	Left elbow swing with partner using eight skips and finishing in the original starting position to repeat the entire dance with the same partner; or left elbow swing with partner once around, then all of the children in the inner circle skip forward to the outer dancer ahead and repeat the entire dance with a new partner. (Swing, 2, 3, 4, 5, 6, 7, 8)

▶ **E-Z MIXER**

Music Source: WWC-FFD or any music with a definite rhythm

Skills: Walking, elbow swing or swing in closed position

Formation: Circle formation with couples in promenade position, inside hands joined, facing counterclockwise

Directions:

Measures	Action
1–2	With Partner B on the right, walk forward four steps. (Forward, 2, 3, 4) Back out to face center in a single circle. (Circle, 2, 3, 4)
3–4	Partners B walk to the center. (In, 2, 3, 4) Back out of the center. (Out, 2, 3, 4)
5–6	Partners A take four steps to the center, turning one-half left face on the fourth step. (In, 2, 3, turn left face) They take four steps toward the corner. (Out, 2, 3, 4)
7–8	Partners A swing the corner B twice around, opening up to face counterclockwise, back in starting position, to begin the dance again. (Swing, 2, 3, open)

Any piece of music with a moderate 4/4 rhythm is appropriate for this basic mixer.

▶ **VE DAVID (ISRAELI)**

Music Source: WWCD-FFD; WWC-RM3

Skills: Walking, pivoting, buzz-step turn

Formation: Double circle, couples facing counterclockwise, Partner B on Partner A's right. Inside hands joined, right foot free.

Directions:

Measures	Part I Action
1–2	All walk forward and form a ring. Take four walking steps forward, starting with the right foot and progressing counterclockwise, then back out, taking four walking steps to form a single circle, facing center, with all hands joined. (Walk, 2, 3, 4; single, circle, 3, 4)
3–4	All forward and back. Four steps forward to center and four steps backward, starting with the right foot. (Forward, 2, 3, 4; back, 2, 3, 4)
	Part II Action
1–2	B partners forward and back; A partners clap. Partners B, starting with the right foot, walk four steps forward to the center and four steps backward to place while Partners A clap. (Bs in, 2, 3, 4; out 2, 3, 4)

Part III Action

1–2 Partners A forward, circle to the right, and progress to a new partner; all clap. A partners, clapping hands, walk four steps forward to the center, starting with the right foot. They turn right about on the last "and" count and walk forward four steps, passing their original partner and progressing ahead to the next. (A partners in, 2, 3, 4; turn to new partner)

3–4 Swing the new partner. The A and the new Partner B swing clockwise with right shoulders adjacent, right arms around each other across in front, and left arms raised—pivoting with right foot for an eight count "buzz-step" swing. (Swing, 2, 3, 4, 5, 6, 7, 8)

Repeat the entire dance.

▶ IRISH WASHERWOMAN (IRISH)

Music Source: WWCD-1043

Skills: Walking, elbow swing, promenade

Formation: Single circle, couples facing center, Partner B to the right, hands joined

Directions: Dancers follow the call.

Action:

Beginning left, take four steps to the center. (Center, 2, 3, 4)
Stamp four times in place. (Stamp, 2, 3, 4)
Take four steps backward to place. (Back, 2, 3, 4)
Swing the corner and promenade in the line of direction. (Swing, 2, 3, promenade)
Dancers keep promenading until they hear the call again to repeat the pattern.

▶ OH, SUSANNA (AMERICAN)

Music Source: WWCD-1043

Skills: Walking, promenade position, grand right and left

Formation: Single circle, all facing center, Partner B on the right

Directions:

Measures	Part I Action
1–4	Partners B walk forward four steps and back four, as Partners A clap hands. (Forward, 2, 3, 4; back, 2, 3, 4)
5–8	Reverse, with A walking forward and back, and B clapping time. (Forward, 2, 3, 4; back, 2, 3, 4)

Part II Action

1–8 Partners face each other, and all do a grand right and left by grasping the partner's right hand, then passing to the next person with a left-hand hold. Continue until reaching the seventh person, who becomes the new partner. (Face, 2, 3, 4, 5, 6, 7, 8)

Chorus

1–16 All join hands in promenade position with the new partner and walk counterclockwise around the circle for two full choruses. (Promenade, 2, 3, . . . 16)

Repeat the dance from the beginning, each time with a new partner. For variety in the chorus, skip instead of walk, or walk during the first chorus and swing one's partner in place during the second chorus.

▶ CRESTED HEN (DANISH)

Music Source: WWCD-1042

Skills: Step-hop, turning under

Formation: Sets of three. One child is designated the center child.

Directions:

Part I:

Measures	Action
1–4	Dancers in each set form a circle. Starting with a stamp with the left foot, each set circles to the left, using step-hops. (Stamp and, 2 and, 3 and, 4 and, 5 and, 6 and, 7 and, stop)
5–8	The figure is repeated. Dancers reverse direction, beginning again with a stamp with the left foot and following with step-hops. The change of direction should be vigorous and definite, with the left foot crossing over the right. At the end of the sequence, two dancers release each other's hands to break the circle and stand on either side of the center person, forming a line of three while retaining joined hands with the center dancer. (Stamp and, 2 and, 3 and, 4 and, 5 and, 6 and, 7 and, line)

Part II: During this part, the dancers use the step-hop continuously while making the pattern figures.

Measures	Action
9–10	The dancer on the right moves forward in an arc to the left and dances under the arch formed by the other two. (Under and, 2 and 3 and 4 and)

11–12   After the right dancer has gone through, the two forming the arch turn under (dishrag), to form once again a line of three. (Turn and, 2 and, 3 and, 4 and)

13–16   The dancer on the left then repeats the pattern, moving forward in an arc under the arch formed by the other two, who turn under to unravel the line. (Under and, 2 and, 3 and, 4 and; turn and, 2 and, 3 and, circle)

As soon as Part II is completed, dancers again join hands in a small circle. The entire dance is repeated. Another of the three can be designated the center dancer.

▶ TROIKA (RUSSIAN)

Music Source: WWCD-3528; WWC-3528

Skills: Running step, turning under

Formation: Trios face counterclockwise. Start with hands joined in a line of three. The body weight is on the left foot; the right foot is free.

Directions:

Measures	Part I Action
1	Take four running steps diagonally forward right, starting with the right foot. (Forward, 2, 3, 4)
2	Take four running steps diagonally forward left, starting with the right foot. (Diagonal, 2, 3, 4)
3–4	Take eight running steps in a forward direction, starting with the right foot. (Forward, 2, 3, 4, 5, 6, 7, 8)
5–6	The center dancer and the left-hand partner raise joined hands to form an arch and run in place. Meanwhile, the right-hand partner moves counterclockwise around the center dancer with eight running steps, goes under the arch, and back to place. The center dancer unwinds by turning under the arch. (Under, 2, 3, 4; turn, 2, 3, 4)
7–8	Repeat the pattern of measures 5 and 6, with the left-hand partner running under the arch formed by the center dancer and the right-hand partner. (Under, 2, 3, 4; turn, 2, 3, circle)

Part II Action

| 9–11 | The trio joins hands and circles left with 12 running steps. (Run, 2, 3, 4, 5, 6, 7, 8, 9, 10, 11, 12) |

12	Three stamps in place (counts 1–3), pause (count 4). (Stamp, 2, 3, pause)
13–15	The trio circles right with 12 running steps, opening out at the end to re-form in lines of three facing counterclockwise. (Run, 2, 3, 4, 5, 6, 7, 8, open, 10, 11, 12)
16	The center dancer releases each partner's hand and runs under the opposite arch of joined hands to advance to a new pair ahead. Right- and left-hand partners run in place while waiting for a new center dancer to join them in a new trio. (Stamp, 2, line, pause)

✓ **TEACHING TIP**

Practice the running steps in groups of three. Then introduce turning under the arch and finish by practicing the running circle with accent stamps.

▶ GUSTAF'S SKOAL (SWEDISH)

Music Source: WWCD-1044CD; WWCD-FDN

Skills: Walking (stately), skipping, turning

Formation: The formation is similar to a square dance set of four couples, each facing center. Partner A is to the left of Partner B. Couples join inside hands; the outside hand is on the hip. Two of the couples facing each other are designated the head couples. The other two couples, also facing each other, are the side couples.

Directions: The dance is in two parts. In Part I, the music is slow and stately. The dancers perform with great dignity. The music for Part II is light and represents fun.

Measures	Part I Action
1–2	The head couples, inside hands joined, walk forward three steps and bow to the opposite couple. (Forward, 2, 3, bow)
3–4	The head couples take three steps backward to place and bow to each other. (The side couples hold their places during this action.) (Back, 2, 3, bow)
5–8	The side couples repeat action of measures 1–4 while the head couples hold their places. (Forward, 2, 3, bow; back, 2, 3, bow)
9–16	The dancers repeat measures 1–8.

Part II Action

| 17–22 | The side couples raise joined hands to form an arch. Head couples skip forward four steps, release partners' hands, join inside hands with opposite person, and |

skip under the nearest arch with new partner. After going under the arch, they drop hands and head back home to their original partner. (Head couples: Skip, 2, 3, 4; under, 2, 3, 4; around, 2, 3, 4)

23–24   All couples join both hands with partners and swing once around with four skipping steps. (Swing, 2, 3, 4)

25–30   Head couples form arches while side couples repeat the action of measures 17–22. (Side couples: Skip, 2, 3, 4; under, 2, 3, 4; around, 2, 3, 4)

31–32   All couples then repeat the movements in measures 23–24. (Swing, 2, 3, 4)

✓ TEACHING TIP

During the first action sequence of Part I (in which the dancers take three steps and bow), a shout of "Skoal" and raising the right fist high above the head as a salute can be substituted for the bow. The word *skoal* is a toast. (Note that the dancers' hands are not joined.)

▶ SHOO FLY (AMERICAN)

Music Source: WWCD-FDN

Skills: Walking

Formation: Single circle of couples facing the center with all hands joined; approximately six couples to a circle

Directions:

Measures	Part I Action
4	Introduction
1–4	All walk four steps to the center and four steps back to place. (Center, 2, 3, 4; back, 2, 3, 4)
5–8	Repeat action of measures 1–4. (Center, 2, 3, 4; back, 2, 3, 4)
9–12	Partners turn each other clockwise with a right forearm grasp using eight walking steps. (Turn, partner, 3, 4, 5, 6, 7, 8)
13–16	Partners turn each other counterclockwise with a left forearm grasp using eight walking steps. (Turn, partner, 3, 4, 5, 6, 7, 8)

Part II Action

1–8   Repeat action of measures 1–8 in Part I.

9–12   Keep hands joined. The leading couple (must be designated) forms an arch by lifting inside joined hands and moves toward the center of the circle. The couple opposite the leading couple pulls the

continuous circle through the arch using eight steps. (Through, arch, 3, 4, 5, 6, 7, 8)

13–16   When all have passed through the arch and are facing out, the leading couple turns under their joined arms turning the circle inside-out. (Inside, out, 3, 4, 5, 6, 7, 8)

Part III Action

1–8   Repeat the action of measures 1–8 in Part I except that all walk backward four steps to the center and then forward four steps back to place. Repeat. (Backward, 2, 3, 4, forward, 6, 7 8; repeat)

9–12   Leading couple release joined hands (others keep joined hands) and separate, pulling dancers attached to them by joined hands around the circle with eight walking steps. (Release, 2, 3, 4, 5, 6, 7, 8)

13–16   Continue following leaders with 8 walking steps until in original places facing the center. Lead couple joins hands to form a circle again. (Circle, 2, 3, 4, 5, 6, 7, 8)

Perform the dance twice.

▶ APAT APAT (PHILIPPINES)

Music Source: WWCD-572; WWC-572

Skills: Walking; star hold

Formation: Double circle of partners facing counterclockwise with inside hands joined

Directions:

Measures	Action
	Introduction
1	All face counterclockwise with inside hands joined and walk forward four steps. On count four, release hands and execute a half turn right to face clockwise. (Walk, 2, 3, turn)
2	Take four walking steps forward clockwise. Release hands on the fourth step and face partner. (Walk, 2, 3, face)
3	Walk four steps backward away from partner. (Away, 2, 3, 4)
4	Walk four steps forward toward partner with each partner taking a quarter turn to the right on the fourth count. Partners will be facing in opposite directions. (Forward, 2, 3, right turn)
5	Walk forward four steps with partners moving in opposite directions. (Forward, 2, 3, 4)
6	Walk backward four steps to meet partner. (Backward, 2, 3, 4)

19

7 Face partner. With right hand star (join right hands with elbows bent) walk clockwise around partner four steps in place. (Star, 2, 3, 4)

8 Release hands; inside circle youngsters walk forward four steps counterclockwise to meet next partner. Outside circle youngsters turn a half turn in place to wait for new partner.

Repeat the dance.

PATA PATA (AFRICAN)

Music Source: WWCD-3528; WWC-3528

Skills: Toe touches, knee lift, quarter turns

Formation: Single lines facing in one direction

Directions:

Measures	Action
1–2	Start with feet together; touch right foot sideways right and return next to left foot. (Right touch, together)
3–4	Same as above with left foot. (Left touch, together)
5	With feet together, move toes out, keeping heels on the ground. (Toes out)
6	Turn heels out, keeping toes on the ground. (Heels out)
7	Turn heels in, keeping toes on the ground. (Heels in)
8	Turn toes in, keeping heels on the ground. The feet should now be together. (Toes in)
9–12	Raise right knee diagonally in front of the body and then touch right foot next to left foot. Repeat for counts 11–12. (Lift, touch, lift, touch)
13–16	Kick left foot forward while turning a quarter turn to the right with weight on the right foot. Step backward left, right, left. Feet should be together at the end of count 16. (Kick, left, right, left)

Repeat the dance.

✓ TEACHING TIP

When youngsters learn the footwork, it is enjoyable to add some arm movements to the dance. At count 5, with elbows close to the body, raise hands up and straight out, palms up. Count 6, turn palms down with elbows out. Count 7, turn palms up. Count 8, turn palms down.

SAVILA SE BELA LOZA (SERBIAN)

Music Source: WWCD-572; WWC-572

Skills: Running step, crossover step, hop

Formation: Broken circle or line; joined hands held down

Directions: Explain Savila Se Bela Loza (pronounced SAH-vee-lah say BAY-lah LOH-zah) means a "grapevine entwined in itself."

Measures	Part I Action
	Introduction
1–20	Face slightly to right; move right starting with the right foot, taking 18 small running steps forward. Do a step-hop on steps 19 and 20. (Run, 2, 3, . . . 18, step, hop)
21–40	Face slightly left and repeat above action starting with the left foot. Finish with a step-hop on the left foot. (Run, 2, 3, . . . 18, step, hop)
	Part II Action
41–44	Beginning with right, take one schottische step moving right. Translated, this is a step to the right sideways on the right foot, a step with the left foot behind the right followed by a step-hop on the right foot. (Right, left, right, hop)
45–48	Beginning with left, take one schottische step moving left. This is done with a step to the left sideways on left foot, a step with the right foot behind the left followed by a step-hop on the left foot. (Left, right, left, hop)
49–64	Repeat the action of counts 41–48 two more times.

Repeat the dance. During the music for Part I, the leaders on the ends of the lines may lead the line anywhere, winding or coiling the line like a grapevine.

LOS MACHETES (MEXICO)

Central America and parts of Mexico are largely covered with dense jungle and the workers (macheteros), both men and women, must clear the trails with machetes. At fiestas, the macheteros often perform this dance.

Music Source: WWCD-FFD

Skills: Marching, rhythmic clapping

Formation: Two lines of partners facing forward

Directions:

Measures	Action
Introduction	No movement
1–4	March forward 16 steps clapping or clicking sticks.
5–8	Youngsters make an about face and march back 16 steps.
9–12	The two lines face each other. Partners walk backward four steps and bow on the fourth beat (1, 2, 3, bow). An alternative to the bow is to click Lummi sticks on the fourth beat. Walk forward to original position and clap on the fourth beat.
13–16	Repeat measures 9–12.
17–18	Clapping sequence facing partner. Clap own hands once (1); clap right hand to partner's right hand (2); clap own hands once (3); clap left hand to partner's left hand (4); clap own hands once (5); clap both hands to partner's hands (6); clap own hands together three times fast (7–8).
19–20	Repeat clapping sequence (measures 17–18).
21–28	With partner, do a right-hand star for eight counts; do a left-hand star for eight counts. Repeat.
29–84	Repeat the entire dance two more times.

▶ POPCORN (AMERICAN)

Music Source: WWCD-RM7; WWC-RM7

Skills: Toe touches, knee lifts, jumps, quarter turns

Formation: Single lines of students; no partners

Directions:

Counts	Action
1–24	Wait 24 counts; gently bounce up and down by bending the knees during the introduction
1–4	Touch right toe in front and return; repeat. (Right, together, right, together)
5–8	Touch left toe in front and return; repeat. (Left, together, left, together)
9–12	Touch right toe in back and return; repeat. (Back, together, back, together)
13–16	Touch left toe in front and return; repeat. (Back, together, back, together)

17–20	Lift right knee up in front of left knee and return; repeat. (Knee up, return, knee up, return)
21–24	Lift left knee up in front of right knee and return; repeat. (Knee up, return, knee up, return)
25–26	Lift right knee up in front of left knee and return. (Knee up, return)
27–28	Lift left knee up in front of right knee and return. (Knee up, return)
29–30	Clap both hands together once. (clap)
31–32	Jump and turn a quarter turn to the right. (Jump and turn)

Repeat entire dance to the end of the music.

▶ RED RIVER VALLEY (AMERICAN)

Music Source: WWCD-FDN

Skills: Walk, buzz swing, Do-sa-do

Formation: Triple circle with three dancers side by side in sets of six dancers—two trios facing each other. Half the trios face counterclockwise and half face clockwise.

Directions:

Measures	Part I Action
1–4	Introduction
1–4	Middle person of each trio leads partners forward to right to meet oncoming trio using eight walking steps. (Walk, 2, 3, . . . 8)
5–8	Join hands with oncoming trio and circle to the left (clockwise) four walking steps; reverse direction and circle right using four walking steps. (Circle, left, 3, 4; Circle, right, 3, 4)
9–12	Middle person swings around with person on left using eight buzz (shuffling) steps. (Swing, 2, 3, . . . 8)
13–16	Middle person swings around with person on right using eight buzz (shuffling) steps. (Swing, 2, 3, . . . 8)
	Part II Action
1–8	Repeat action of measures 1–8 in Part I. (Walk, 2, 3, . . . 8)
9–12	The four outside youngsters form a right-hand star in the center of the set and walk around once to starting point using eight walking steps. (Star, 2, 3, . . . 8)
13–16	The two middle youngsters Do-sa-do around each other, returning to own place using eight walking steps. (Do-sa-do, 2, 3, . . . 8)

Part III Action

1–8   Repeat action of measures 1–8 in Part I. (Walk, 2, 3, . . . 8)

9–12   The two left-hand outside youngsters change places diagonally across using eight walking steps. (Left, diagonal, 3, . . . 8)

13–16 The two right-hand outside youngsters change places diagonally across using eight walking steps. The middle person now has different partners. (Right, diagonal, 3, . . . 8)

The entire dance is repeated twice.

JIFFY MIXER (AMERICAN)

Music Source: WWCD-FDN

Skills: Heel-and-toe step, chug step

Formation: Double circle, partners facing

Directions: The music includes an introduction. Directions are for Partners A; B's actions are opposite.

Measures   Introduction

1–4   Wait, wait, balance apart (push away on the left foot and touch the right). Balance together (forward on the right and touch the left).

       Action

1–4   Strike the left heel diagonally out and return to touch the toe near the right foot. Repeat. Do a side step left with a touch. (Heel, toe; heel, toe; side, close; side, touch)

5–8   Repeat while moving in the opposite direction, beginning with the right foot. (Heel, toe; heel, toe; side, close; side, touch)

9–12   Take four chug steps backward, clapping on the up beat. (Chug, clap, chug, clap, chug, clap, chug, clap)

13–16 Starting with the left foot, take four slow, swaggering steps diagonally to the right, progressing to a new partner. (Walk, 2, 3, 4)

The chug step is done by jumping and dragging both feet backward. The body is bent slightly forward.

✓ TEACHING TIP

The dance can be introduced by having all join hands in a single circle, facing inward. There are no partners and no progressions to new partners.

SICILIAN CIRCLE (AMERICAN)

Music Source: WWCD-FDN

Skills: Walking, two-hand swing (either walking or buzz turn), wheel turn

Formation: Double circle composed of groups of two couples facing each other with partners side by side. Couples are numbered 1 and 2 with number 1 couples moving counterclockwise and number 2 couples clockwise.

Directions:

Measures   Part I Action

1–4   Introduction

1–4   The sets of two couples join hands and walk eight steps to the left, ending where they started, and drop hands. (Circle, left, 2, 3, 4, . . . 8)

5–8   Partners join both hands and swing once around to the left using eight walking or buzz steps. (Swing, left, 2, 3, 4, . . . 8)

9–12   Couples advance toward each other and pass right shoulders through to opposite's place using four walking steps. As soon as they are across, couples do a wheel-turn around with partner on the left walking backward four steps and moving into place on partner's left, who turns in place using four steps. If desired, left partner can hold left hand with partner's left hand and right hand around back of partner's waist. Hands are dropped. (Pass, through, 3, 4; wheel, turn, 3, 4)

13–16 Couples pass through again as described in measures 9–12. (Back, through, 3, 4; wheel, turn, 3, 4)

17–20 Right-hand partners advance toward each other, join right hands briefly, pass each other by right shoulders, drop hands, and join left hand with opposite left partner using four steps. The opposite left partner does a wheel turn as described in measures 9–12 using four steps. (Right partner, chain, 3, 4; wheel, turn, 3, 4)

21–24 Right-hand partners chain back again and turn as in measures 17–20 using eight steps and end with left hands joined with partner. (Chain, back, 3, 4; wheel, turn, 3, 4)

25–28 Partners join hands in promenade position and advance four steps toward opposite and four steps backward to place. (Forward, 2, 3, 4; back, 2, 3, 4)

29–32   Each couple with hands in promenade position advances to the left of the opposite couple to the next couple using eight steps. (New couple, 2, 3, . . . 8)

Dance is repeated three times.

▶ LUMMI STICKS

Music Source: WWCD-2015 or 2014; WWC-2000

Skills: Rhythmic tapping, flipping, and catching of sticks

Formation: Couples scattered throughout the area

Lummi sticks are smaller versions of wands; they are 12 to 15 inches long. Some believe that lummi sticks were a part of the culture of the Lummi Indians in northwest Washington. Others give credit to South Pacific cultures for the origin of the sticks. Their actual origin remains obscure.

Most lummi stick activities are done by partners, although some can be done individually. Each child sits cross-legged, facing a partner at a distance of 18 to 20 inches. Children adjust this distance as the activities demand. The sticks are held in the thumb and fingers (not the fist) at about the bottom third of the stick.

Routines are based on sets of six movements; each movement is completed in one count. Many different routines are possible. Only the basic ones are presented here. The following one-count movements are used to make up routines.

Vertical tap: Tap both sticks upright on the floor.

Partner tap: Tap partner's stick (right stick to right stick, or left to left).

End tap: Tilt the sticks forward or sideways and tap the ends on the floor.

Cross-tap: Cross hands and tap the upper ends to the floor.

Side tap: Tap the upper ends to the side.

Flip: Toss the stick in air, giving it a half turn, and catch other end.

Tap together: Hold the sticks parallel and tap them together.

Toss right (or left): Toss the right-hand stick to partner's right hand, at the same time receiving partner's right-hand stick.

Pass: Lay the stick on the floor and pick up partner's stick.

Toss right and left: Toss quickly right to right and left to left, all in the time of one count.

A number of routines, incorporating the movements described, are presented here in sequence of difficulty.

Each routine is to be done four times to complete the 24 beats of the chant.

1. Vertical tap, tap together, partner tap right, vertical tap, tap together, partner tap left.
2. Vertical tap, tap together, pass right stick, vertical tap, tap together, pass left stick.
3. Vertical tap, tap together, toss right stick, vertical tap, tap together, toss left stick.
4. Repeat numbers 1, 2, and 3, but substitute an end tap and flip for the vertical tap and tap together. Perform the stated third movement (that is, end tap, flip, partner tap right, end tap, flip, partner tap left).
5. Vertical tap, tap together, toss right and left quickly, end tap, flip, toss right and left quickly.
6. Cross-tap, cross-flip, vertical tap (uncross arms), cross-tap, cross-flip, vertical tap (uncross arms).
7. Right flip side—left flip in front, vertical tap in place, partner tap right. Left flip side—right flip in front, vertical tap in place, partner tap left.
8. End tap in front, flip, vertical tap, tap together, toss right, toss left.
9. Vertical tap, tap together, right stick to partner's left hand, toss own left stick to own right hand. Repeat. This is the circle throw.
10. Same as in number 9, but reverse the circle.

The activity can be done by four children with a change in the timing. One set of partners begins at the start, and the other two start on the third beat. All sing together. In this way, the sticks are flying alternately.

▶ TINIKLING (PHILIPPINE ISLANDS)

Music Source: WWC/CD-8095; WWC/CD-9015

Skills: Tinikling steps

Formation: Sets of fours scattered around the room. Each set has two strikers and two dancers (Figure 19.5 on page 448).

Note: The dance represents a rice bird as it steps, with its long legs, from one rice paddy to another. The dance is popular in many countries in Southeast Asia, where different versions have arisen.

Directions: Two eight-foot bamboo poles and two crossbars on which the poles rest are needed for the dance. A striker kneels at each end of the poles; both strikers hold the end of a pole in each hand. The music is in waltz meter, three-quarters time, with an accent on the first beat. The strikers slide and strike the poles together on count 1. On the other two beats of the waltz measure, the poles are opened about 15 inches apart, lifted an inch or so, and tapped twice on the crossbars in time to counts 2 and 3. The rhythm "close, tap, tap" is continued

FIGURE 19.5 Tinikling set.

throughout the dance, each sequence constituting a measure.

Basically, the dance requires that a step be done outside the poles on the close (count 1) and that two steps be done inside the poles (counts 2 and 3) when the poles are tapped on the crossbars. Many step combinations have been devised.

The basic tinikling step should be practiced until it is mastered. The step is done singly, although two dancers are performing. Each dancer takes a position at an opposite end and on the opposite side so that the dancer's right side is to the bamboo poles.

Count 1: Step slightly forward with the left foot.

Count 2: Step with the right foot between the poles.

Count 3: Step with the left foot between the poles.

Count 4: Step with the right outside to dancer's own right.

Count 5: Step with the left between the poles.

Count 6: Step with the right between the poles.

Count 7: Step with the left outside to the original position.

The initial step (count 1) is used only to get the dance under way. The last step (count 7) to original position is actually the beginning of a new series (7, 8, 9, 10, 11, 12).

Some tinikling dances and records guide the dancers with a different type of rhythm (tap, tap, close),

necessitating adjustment of the steps and patterns in these descriptions.

Tinikling steps also can be adjusted to four-quarters rhythm (close, close, tap, tap), which requires the poles to be closed on two counts and open on the other two. The basic foot pattern is two steps outside the poles and two inside. For the sake of conformity, we present all routines in the original three-quarters time (close, tap, tap). If other rhythms are used, adjust accordingly.

Dancers can go from side to side, or can return to the side from which they entered. The dance can be done singly, with the two dancers moving in opposite directions from side to side, or the dancers can enter from and leave toward the same side. Dancers can do the same step patterns or do different movements. They can dance as partners, moving side by side with inside hands joined, or facing each other with both hands joined.

✓ **TEACHING TIP**

Steps should be practiced first with stationary poles or with lines drawn on the floor. Jump ropes can be used as stationary objects over which to practice. Students handling the poles should concentrate on watching each other rather than the dancer to avoid becoming confused by the dancer's feet.

To gain a sense of the movement pattern for three-quarters time, slap both thighs with the hands on the "close," and clap the hands twice for movements inside the poles. For four-quarters time, slap the right thigh with the right hand, then the left thigh with the left hand, followed by two claps. This routine should be done to music, with the poles closing and opening as indicated. Getting the feel of the rhythm is important.

▶ OTHER TINIKLING STEPS AND ROUTINES

Straddle step: Dancers do a straddle jump outside the poles on count 1 and execute two movements inside the poles on counts 2 and 3. Let the dancers explore the different combinations. Jump turns are possible.

Jump step: Dancers begin the side jump with their side toward the poles. They can execute the jump from either side.

Measure 1:

Count 1: Jump lightly in place.

Counts 2 and 3: Jump twice between the poles.

Measure 2:

Count 1: Jump lightly in place (other side).

Counts 2 and 3: Jump twice between the poles.

The feet should be kept close together to fit between the poles. Dancers can exit to the same side from which they entered, or can alternate sides. Another way to enter and exit is by facing the poles and jumping forward and backward rather than sideways. When jumping sideways, one foot can be kept ahead of the other in a stride position. This position can be reversed on the second jump inside the poles.

Rocker step: For the rocker step, dancers face the poles and begin with either foot. As they step in and out (forward and backward), they make a rocking motion with the body.

Crossover step: The crossover step is similar to the basic tinikling step, except that the dancer begins with the right foot (forward step) and steps inside the poles with the left foot, using a cross-foot step. Each time, the dancer must step in or out using a cross-step.

Circling poles: For circling the poles, dancers position themselves as in the basic tinikling step (Figure 19.6) and execute the following movements:

Measure 1:

Count 1: Step slightly forward with the left foot.

Count 2: Step with the right foot between the poles.

Count 3: Step with the left foot between the poles.

Measure 2:

Count 1: Step with the right foot outside the poles to the right.

Counts 2 and 3: With light running steps, make a half circle to a position for the return movement.

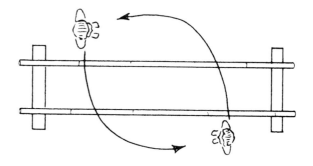

FIGURE 19.6 Circling poles for tinikling.

Measures 3 and 4:

Dancers return to their original position using the same movements as in measures 1 and 2.

Fast tinikling trot: The fast tinikling trot is similar to circling the poles, except that the step goes twice as fast and thus requires only two sets of three counts. Instead of having the side of the body to the poles, as in the basic tinikling step, the dancers face the poles. The following steps are taken:

Measure 1:

Count 1: Shift the weight to the left foot and raise the right foot.

Count 2: Step with the right foot between the poles.

Count 3: Step with the left foot outside the poles and begin turning to the left.

Measure 2:

Count 1: Step with the right foot outside the poles, completing the left turn to face the poles again.

Count 2: Step with the left foot inside the poles.

Count 3: Step outside with the right foot.

The next step is done with the left foot to begin a new cycle. The movement is a light trot with quick turns. Note that the step outside the poles on count 3 in each measure is made with the poles apart.

Cross-step: To do the cross-step, the dancer begins with the basic tinikling position, and uses the following sequence:

Measure 1:

Count 1: Cross-step across both poles with the left foot, hopping on the right side.

Counts 2 and 3: Hop twice on the right foot between the poles.

Measure 2:

Count 1: Hop on the left foot outside the poles to the left.

Counts 2 and 3: Hop twice again on the right foot between the poles.

19

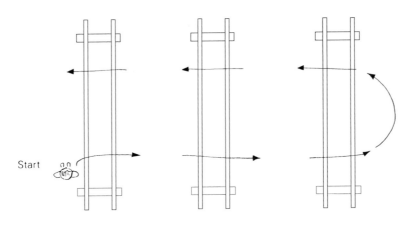

FIGURE 19.7 Movement through line of poles for tinikling.

Line of poles: Three or more sets of poles are about six feet apart. The object is to dance down the sets, make a circling movement (as in Circling Poles), and return down the line in the opposite direction (Figure 19.7). The dancer keeps his or her right side toward the poles throughout.

During measure 1 (three counts), the dancer does a basic tinikling step, finishing on the right side of the first set of poles. During measure 2 (three counts), he uses three light running steps to position himself for the tinikling step at the next set of poles. When he gets to the end, he circles with three steps to get in position for the return journey.

Square formation: Four sets of poles can be placed in a square formation for an interesting dance sequence (Figure 19.8). Four dancers are positioned as shown. The movements are as follows: During measure 1, each dancer does a tinikling step, crossing to the outside of the square. On measure 2, the dancers circle to position for a

return tinikling step. During measure 3, the dancers do a tinikling step, returning to the inside of the square. On measure 4, they rotate counterclockwise to the next set of poles with three running steps.

The basic tinikling step must be mastered if children are to enjoy the activity. Tell them to look ahead (not at the poles), so they learn by thinking and doing and not by gauging the pole distances visually.

Four-pole set: This arrangement features two longer crossbars, on which two sets of poles rest, leaving a small space between the poles when the sets are open. Four clappers control the poles. Two dancers begin by each straddling a set of poles on opposite ends, so the dancers face each other. Changes in foot pattern should be made every 16 measures, which for most selections is a full pattern of music. The following steps and routines are suggested.

1. Straddle, jump, jump, exiting on measure 16 to the left.

2. Do the basic tinikling step, exiting on the left foot.

3. Do the basic tinikling step, first on one's own set of poles and then on the other set of poles. As the dancer comes out of the first set of poles with the right foot, she makes a half turn to do the tinikling step through the other poles. On the return, she makes another half turn in the middle to face and return to her original position. Repeat the sequence twice.

4. Do the same routine as in number 3, but move diagonally, passing the oncoming dancer with right shoulder to right shoulder, in effect changing places. (Do not use half turns.) Turn around in six steps and return to position. Repeat.

5. Jump to a straddle position with one foot in each of the pole openings. On "close," jump to the space between the sets. On measure 16, the dancer jumps out to the left on both feet.

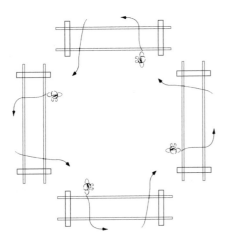

FIGURE 19.8 Square formation for tinikling.

6. Two-footed step: Jump twice with both feet inside the first set of poles, to the space between, twice inside the second set, and out. Return. Repeat twice.

DEVELOPMENTAL LEVEL III DANCES

At this level, children should be adept dancers, especially if they have participated in rhythmic activities for several years. If students do not have a well-developed dance background, it is recommended that they first learn dances from Developmental Levels I and II. Developmental Level III dances include dance patterns that must be performed with skill and finesse. At this level, patterns become longer, requiring more concentration and memorization. The schottische, polka, and two-step make their first appearance in these dances. The progression ranges from a dance that is performed in a circle and introduces square dance moves, to dances that feature the two-step, polka step, and schottische.

▶ HORA (HAVA NAGILA) (ISRAELI)

Music Source: WWCD-3528; WWC-3528

Skills: Stepping sideways, step-swing

Formation: Single circle, facing center, hands joined. The circle can be partial.

Note: The hora is regarded as the national dance of Israel. It is a simple dance that expresses joy. The traditional hora is done in circle formation, with the arms extended sideways and the hands on the neighbors' shoulders. It is easiest to introduce the dance step individually. Once the step is learned, youngsters can join hands and practice the circle formation counterclockwise or clockwise. The clockwise version is presented here.

There are an old and a new hora, as done in Israel. The new hora is more energetic, with the dancers springing high in the air and whirling around with shouts of ecstasy. The hora can be done to many tunes, but the melody of "Hava Nagila" is the favorite.

Directions—Old Hora:

Measures	Action
1–3	Step left on the left foot. Cross the right foot in back of the left, with the weight on the right. Step left on the left foot and hop on it, swinging the right foot forward. Step-hop on the right foot and swing the left foot forward. The same step is repeated over and over. (Side, behind, side, swing; side, swing)

The circle may move to the right also, in which case the same step is used, but the dancers begin with the right foot.

Directions—New Hora:

Measures	Action
1–3	Face left and run two steps. Jump in place. Hop on the left foot, swinging the right foot forward. Take three quick steps in place. Continue in the same manner, moving to the left. (Run, run, jump, hop-swing, step, step, step)

The hora often begins with the dancers swaying in place from left to right as the music builds. Gradually, the dance increases in pace and intensity. Shouts accompany the dance as the participants call to each other across the circle. The words Hava Nagila mean "Come, let us be happy!"

▶ VIRGINIA REEL (AMERICAN)

Music Source: WWCD-05114

Skills: Skipping, arm turn, Do-sa-do, sliding (sashay), reeling

Formation: Six couples in a longways set of two lines facing. Partners on one end of the set are designated the head couple.

Directions:

Measures	Call	Action
1–4	All go forward and back.	Take three steps forward, curtsy or bow. Take three steps back and close.
5–8	Right hands around.	Move forward to partner, turn once in place using a right forearm grasp and return to position.
9–12	Left hands around.	Repeat measures 5–8 with a left forearm grasp.
13–16	Both hands around.	Partners join both hands, turn once in a clockwise direction, and move backward to place.
17–20	Do-sa-do your partner.	Partners pass each other right shoulder to right shoulder and then back to back and move backward to place.
21–24	All go forward and back.	Repeat the action of measures 1–4.
25–32	Head couple sashay.	The head couple, with hands joined, takes eight

19

		slides down to the foot of the set and eight slides back to place.
33–64	Head couple reel.	The head couple begins the reel with linked right elbows and turns one and one-half times to face the next couple in line. Each member in the head couple then links left elbows with the person facing and turns once in place. The head couple meets again in the center and turns once with a right elbow swing. The next dancers down the line are turned with a left elbow swing and then the head couple returns to the center for another right elbow turn. The head couple thus progresses down the line, turning each dancer in order. After the head couple has turned the last dancers, they meet with a right elbow swing, turn halfway around, and sashay (slide) back to the head of the set.
65–96	Everybody march.	All couples face toward the head of the set with the head couple in front. The person on the right turns to the right while the person on the left turns to the left and goes behind the line followed by the other dancers. When the head couple reaches the foot of the set, they join hands and make an arch, under which all other couples pass. The head couple is now at the foot of the set and the dance is repeated with a new head couple.

The dance is repeated until each couple has had a chance to be the head couple.

✓ **TEACHING TIP**

Versions of this dance vary. Some allow time at the beginning for a Do-sa-do after the "both hands around" (measures 13–16) while others do not. Check the music for phrasing before presenting the dance to the class.

Technically, the dance is written for eight couples in each set. For the head couple to reel all couples in the set, they must not miss one beat of the music or they will be behind the phrasing for the reel section. When introducing the dance to a class for the first time, having only six couples in each set is helpful. Then, if a couple gets behind the music for the reeling section, they still can stay in time to the music and finish before the "casting off" section begins.

Teaching the Two-Step

Children can be taught the forward two-step simply by moving forward on the cue "Step, close, step," starting on the left foot and alternating thereafter. The close-step is made by bringing the toe of the closing foot to a point even with the instep of the other foot. All steps are almost slides, a kind of shuffle step.

The two-step just described is nothing more than a slow gallop, alternating the lead foot. One way to help students learn the step-close-step pattern is to put them in a single circle and have them gallop forward. They should all start on the left foot and move forward eight slow gallops. Stop the class and have them put their right foot forward and repeat the gallops. Continue this pattern, and have the students make the change from galloping with their left foot forward to galloping with their right foot forward without stopping. When they make this transition, they should bring the right foot forward in a walking step—the weight being on the left foot. Reverse the procedure when moving the left foot forward. The movement should be very smooth. When the students master this pattern, repeat the sequence, but do four gallops with each foot forward. After this pattern is mastered, repeat the pattern with two gallops on each foot. When students can do this, they are performing the forward two-step.

Next, arrange the children by couples in a circle formation, Partners A on the inside, all facing counterclockwise. Repeat the instruction, with both partners beginning on the left foot. Practice the two-step with a partner, with Partner A beginning on the left foot and Partner B starting on the right. In the next progression, the children move face to face and back to back.

▶ **JUGGLEHEAD MIXER (AMERICAN)**

Music Source: Any music with a definite and steady beat

Skills: Two-step, elbow turn (forearm grasp)

Formation: Double circle facing counterclockwise in promenade position

Directions: Actions described are for the inside partner; directions are opposite for the partner on the outside of the circle.

Measures	Call	Action
1–4	Two-step left and two-step right, walk-2-3-4.	Do a two-step left and a two-step right and take four walking steps forward.
5–8	Two-step left and two-step right, walk-2-3-4.	Repeat measures 1–4.
9–10	Turn your partner with the right.	Inside partner takes the outside partner's right hand and walks around to face the person behind.
11–12	Now your corner with your left.	Inside partner turns the person behind with the left hand.
13–14	Turn your partner all the way around.	Inside partner turns partner with the right hand going all the way around.
15–16	And pick up the forward lady.	Inside partner steps up one place to the outside person ahead, who becomes the new partner.

▶ **TETON MOUNTAIN STOMP (AMERICAN)**

Music Source: WWCD-FDN

Skills: Walking, banjo position, sidecar position, two-step

Formation: Form single circle of partners in closed dance position, Partners A facing counterclockwise, Partners B facing clockwise.

Directions:

Measures	Action
1–4	Step to the left toward the center of the circle on the left foot, close right foot to the left, step again to the left on the left foot, stomp right foot beside the left but leave the weight on the left foot. Repeat this action, but start on the right foot and move away from the center. (Side, close; side, stomp; side, close; side, stomp)
5–8	Step to the left toward the center on the left foot; stomp the right foot beside the left. Step to the right away from the center on the right foot, and stomp the left foot beside the right. In "banjo" position (modified closed position with right hips adjacent), Partner A takes four walking steps forward while Partner B takes four steps backward, starting on the right foot. (Side, stomp, side, stomp; walk, 2, 3, 4)
9–12	Partners change to sidecar position (modified closed position with left hips adjacent) by each making a one-half turn to the right in place, A remaining on the inside and B on the outside. A walks backward while B walks four steps forward. Partners change back to banjo position with right hips adjacent by each making a left-face one-half turn; then they immediately release from each other. A walks forward four steps to meet the second B approaching, while B walks forward four steps to meet the second A approaching. (Change, 2, 3, 4; new partner, 2, 3, 4)
13–16	New partners join inside hands and do four two-steps forward, beginning with A's right foot and B's left. (Step, close, step; repeat four times)

✓ **TEACHING TIP**

If the dancers are skillful enough, use the following action for measures 13–16: New partners take the closed dance position and do four turning two-steps, starting on A's left (B's right) and make one complete right-face turn while progressing in the line of direction.

▶ **COTTON-EYED JOE (AMERICAN)**

Music Source: WWCD-FDN

Skills: Heel-toe, two-step

Formation: Double circle of couples with Partner B on the right, holding inside hands and facing counterclockwise. Varsouvienne position can also be used.

Directions:

Measures	Action
1–2	Starting with the left foot, cross the left foot in front of the right foot, kick the left foot forward. (Cross, kick)

3–4	Take one two-step backward. (Left, close, left)
5–6	Cross the right foot in front of the left foot; kick the right foot forward. (Cross, kick)
7–8	Do one two-step backward. (Right, close, right)
9–16	Repeat measures 1–8.
17–32	Perform eight two-steps counterclockwise beginning with the left foot. (Step, close, step; repeat eight times)

✓ **TEACHING TIP**

During measures 17–32, the last four two-steps may be done in a circle.

Teaching the Polka Step

The polka and the two-step are much alike. They both have a step-close-step pattern. The two-step is simply step-close-step, but the polka is step-close-step-hop. Technically, the polka is usually described as hop-step-close-step (or hop-step-together-step). However, the first description is probably more helpful when working with beginning students.

The polka step can be broken down into four movements: (1) step forward left, (2) close the right foot to the left, bringing the toe up and even with the left instep, (3) step forward left, and (4) hop on the left foot. The series begins with the weight on the right foot.

Several methods can be used to teach the polka:

1. *Step-by-step rhythm approach.* Analyzing the dance slowly, have the class walk through the steps together in even rhythm. The cue is "Step, close, step, hop." Accelerate the tempo to normal polka time and add the music.

2. *Gallop approach.* A method preferred by many elementary instructors is the gallop approach. (Review the previous section on teaching the two-step, which uses the gallop.) The approach is the same, but add the polka hop and speed up the tempo. When moving the right foot forward, a hop must be taken on the left foot. When moving the left foot forward, the hop is on the right foot.

3. *Two-step approach.* Beginning with the left foot, two-step with the music, moving forward in the line of direction in a single circle. Accelerate the tempo gradually to a fast two-step and take smaller steps. Without stopping, change to a polka rhythm by following each two-step with a hop. Use polka music for the two-step, but slow it down considerably to start.

4. *Partner approach.* After the polka step has been learned individually by one of the three methods, the step can be practiced with partners in a double-circle formation, Partners A on the inside and all facing counterclockwise, with inside hands joined. Partners A begin with the left foot and Partners B with the right.

▶ **KLUMPAKOJIS (SWEDISH)**

Music Source: WWCD-1042

Skills: Walking, stars, polka step

Formation: Couples in a circle, side by side, all facing counterclockwise, with Partner B to the right

Directions:

Measures	Part I Action
1–4	With inside hands joined, free hand on hip, all walk briskly around the circle for eight steps counterclockwise. (Walk, 2, 3, 4, 5, 6, 7, turn)
5–8	Turn individually to the left, reverse direction, change hands, and walk eight steps clockwise. (Walk, 2, 3, 4, 5, 6, 7, turn)
	Part II Action
9–12	Face partner and make a star by joining right hands (making certain that the right elbow is bent). The left hand is on the hip. With partner, walk around clockwise for eight walking steps. Change hands and repeat the eight steps, reversing direction. (Star, 2, 3, 4, 5, 6, 7, 8; reverse, 2, 3, 4, 5, 6, 7, 8)
	Part III Action
13–16	Listen to the musical phrase, then stamp three times on the last two counts. Listen to the phrase again, then clap own hands three times. (Listen, listen, stamp, 2, 3; listen, listen, clap, 2, 3)
17–20	Shake the right finger in a scolding motion at partner. (Scold, 2, 3) Shake the left finger. (Scold, 2, 3)
21–24	Turn solo to the left, clapping partner's right hand once during the turn. Use two walking steps to make the turn, and finish facing partner. (Turn, 2, stamp, 2, 3)
25–32	Repeat the action of measures 13–24.
	Part IV Action
33–40	With inside hands joined, do 16 polka steps (or two-steps) forward, moving

counterclockwise. (Later, as the dance is learned, change to the promenade position.) On polka steps 15 and 16, Partner A moves forward to take a new Partner B while handing the original Partner B to the A in back. New couple joins inside hands. (Step, close, step, hop; step, close, step, hop; repeat for a total of 16 polka steps)

▶ **ALLEY CAT (AMERICAN)**

Music Source: WWCD-9126; WWC-RM3

Skills: Grapevine step, touch step, knee lifts

Formation: None, although all should face the same direction during instruction

Directions:

Measures	Action
1–2	Do a grapevine left and kick: Step sideways left, step right behind left, step left again, and kick. Repeat to the right. (Left, behind, left, kick; right, behind, right, kick)
3–4	Touch the left toe backward, bring the left foot to the right, touch the left toe backward again, bring the left foot to the right, taking the weight. Repeat, beginning with the right toe. (Left and, left and; right and, right and)
5–6	Raise the left knee up in front of the right knee and repeat. Raise the right knee up twice, similarly. (Left and, left and; right and, right and)
7–8	Raise the left knee and then the right knee. Clap the hands once and make a jump quarter turn to the left. (Left and, right and, clap and, jump)

After the routine is repeated three times, the dancer should be facing in the original direction.

▶ **TEN PRETTY GIRLS (AMERICAN)**

Music Source: WWCD-1042

Skills: Walking, grapevine

Formation: Circle of groups of any number, with arms linked or hands joined, all facing counterclockwise

Directions:

Measures	Action
1–2	Starting with the weight on the right foot, touch the left foot in front, swing the left

foot to the left and touch, swing the left foot behind the right foot and put the weight on the left foot, step to the right, close the left foot to the right. (Front, side, back-side, together)

3–4	Repeat, starting with the weight on the left foot and moving to the right. (Front, side, back-side, together)
5–6	Take four walking or strutting steps forward, starting on the left foot. (Walk, 2, 3, 4)
7–8	Swing the left foot forward with a kicking motion; swing the left foot backward with a kicking motion; stamp left, right, left, in place. (Swing, swing, stamp, stamp, stamp)

Repeat the entire dance 11 times, starting each time with the alternate foot. The dance can be used as a mixer when performed in a circle by groups of three. On measures 7–8, have the middle person move forward to the next group during the three stamps.

▶ **LIMBO ROCK**

Music Source: WWCD-9126

Skills: Touch step, swivel step, jump clap step

Formation: Single circle or scattered

Directions:

Measures	Part I Action
1–2	Touch left foot in. Touch left foot out. Three steps in place. (In, out, left, right, left)
3–4	Repeat measures 1 and 2 beginning with opposite foot. (In, out, right, left, right)
5–8	Repeat measures 1–4.
	Part II Action
9–10	Swivel toes right, swivel heels right. Repeat and straighten feet. (Swivel, 2, 3, straighten)
11–12	Repeat beats 1 and 2 beginning with swivel toes left.
13–14	Jump in, clap; jump out, clap. (Jump, clap, jump, clap)
15–16	Repeat measures 13 and 14.

✓ **TEACHING TIP**

An easier version involves walking eight steps right during measures 9–16.

19

▶ **JESSIE POLKA (AMERICAN)**

Music Source: WWCD-RM8

Skills: Step and touch, two-step, or polka step

Formation: Circle, couples facing counterclockwise with inside arms around each other's waist

Directions:

Measures	Part I Action
1	Beginning left, touch the heel in front, then step left in place. (Left heel, together)
2	Touch the right toe behind. Then touch the right toe in place, or swing it forward, keeping the weight on the left foot. (Right toe, touch)
3	Touch the right heel in front, then step right in place. (Right heel, together)
4	Touch the left heel to the left side, sweep the left foot across in front of the right. Keep the weight on the right. (Left heel, crossover)
	Part II Action
5–8	Take four two-steps or polka steps forward in the line of direction. (Step, close, step; step, close, step; step, close, step; step, close, step)

✓ **TEACHING TIP**

The dance may be done as a mixer by having Partner B turn out to the right on the last two two-steps and come back to the A behind her. Partners A continue to move forward on the last two two-steps, to make it easier to meet the B coming toward them. Another variation is to perform this activity as a line dance. Youngsters place their hands on the waist or shoulders of the dancer in front of them.

▶ **INSIDE-OUT MIXER**

Music Source: Any music with a pronounced beat suitable for walking at a moderate speed

Skills: Walking, wring the dishrag, change partners

Formation: Triple circle (three children standing side by side), facing counterclockwise, inside hands joined. A pinnie can be worn by the center person for identification.

Directions:

Measures	Action
1–4	Take eight walking steps forward. (Forward, 2, 3, 4, 5, 6, 7, 8)
5–8	Form a small circle and circle left in eight steps back to place. (Circle, 2, 3, 4, 5, 6, 7, 8)
9–12	The center person walks forward under the raised arms opposite, pulling the other two under to turn the circle inside out. (Inside-out, 2, 3, 4, 5, 6, 7, 8)
13–16	The trio circles left in eight steps, returning to place. When almost back to place, drop hands. The center person walks forward counterclockwise, and the other two walk clockwise (the way they are facing) to the nearest trio for a change of partners. (Circle, 2, 3, 4, mix, 6, 7, 8)

▶ **D'HAMMERSCHMIEDSGSELLN (BAVARIAN)**

Music Source: WWCD-FFD; WWC-TC1

Skills: Clapping routine, step-hops

Formation: Circle of four

Directions: Translated, the title of the dance means "The Journey Blacksmith."

Measures	Action
1–16	First opposites do a clapping pattern beginning on the first count of measure 1, while the other pair does a clapping pattern beginning on the first count of measure 2. The six-count pattern is performed as follows: With both hands, slap own thighs (count 1), slap own chest (count 2), clap own hands (count 3), clap right hands (count 4), clap left hands (count 5), and clap opposite's hands (count 6). (Thighs, chest, together, right, left, both) Repeat the six-count pattern seven additional times.
	Part I
17–24	Join hands and circle left with eight step-hops. (Step-hop, 2-hop, . . . 8-hop)
25–32	Circle right in the same manner. (Step-hop, 2-hop, . . . 8-hop)
33–48	Repeat the chorus action.
	Part II—Star
49–56	Right-hand star with eight step-hops. (Step-hop, 2-hop, . . . 8-hop)
57–64	Left-hand star in the same manner. (Step-hop, 2-hop, . . . 8-hop)
65–80	Repeat the chorus action.
	Part III—Big Circle
81–88	Circles of four open to form one large circle, and circle left with eight step-hops. (Step-hop, 2-hop, . . . 8-hop)
89–96	Reverse direction, continuing with eight step-hops. (Step-hop, 2-hop, . . . 8-hop)

Variation: As a mixer, try the following sequence.

Measures	Action
1–16	Use the chorus clapping pattern described.
17–24	As in Part I or II, circle left, or do a right-hand star with step-hops (or simple walking steps).
25–32	Do eight step-hops with the corner in general space or in any comfortable position, progressing anywhere.

Repeat the entire sequence with a new foursome.

▶ KALVELIS (LITTLE BLACKSMITH) (LITHUANIAN)

Music Source: WWCD-WOF3

Skills: Polka step, swing, clapping pattern, grand right and left

Formation: Single circle of couples facing center, Partner B on Partner A's right, all hands joined in a single circle with the right foot free.

Directions:

Measures	Part I Action
1–8	Circle right with seven polka steps, ending with three stamps. (Circle and, 2 and, 3 and, 4 and, 5 and, 6 and, 7 and, stamp, stamp, stamp)
9–16	Circle left with seven polka steps, ending with three stamps. (Circle and, 2 and, 3 and, 4 and, 5 and, 6 and, 7 and, stamp, stamp, stamp)

	Chorus
1–2	Clap own hands four times, alternating, left hand onto own right, then right hand onto own left. (Clap, 2, 3, 4)
3–4	Right elbow swing with four skips. (Swing, 2, 3, 4)
5–6	Repeat the clapping pattern of measures 1 and 2. (Clap, 2, 3, 4)
7–8	Left elbow swing with four skips. (Swing, 2, 3, 4)
9–16	Repeat the pattern of measures 1–8.

	Part II Action
1–8	Partners B dance three polka steps forward toward the center, ending with three stamps. They then turn to face their partner and return to place with three polka steps forward, ending with three

stamps, facing center again. (Step-close-step-hop; step-close-step-hop; step-close-step-hop; stamp, stamp, stamp)

Measures	Action
9–16	Partners A repeat the pattern of measures 1–8, but dance more vigorously, stamping on the first beat of each measure. (Step-close-step-hop; step-close-step-hop; step-close-step-hop; stamp, stamp, stamp)

	Chorus
1–16	As described.

	Part III Action
1–16	Grand right and left around the circle with 16 polka steps, meeting a new partner on the last measure. (Step-close-step-hop; repeat 16 times)

	Chorus
1–16	As described, but with a new partner.

▶ DOUDLEBSKA POLKA (CZECHOSLOVAKIAN)

Music Source: WWCD-572; WWC-572

Skills: Polka step, walking, clapping pattern

Formation: Make either one large circle or several smaller circles scattered around the floor. The following description is for one large circle.

Directions:

Measures	Part I Action
1–16	Partners assume the varsouvienne position and do 16 polka steps around the circle, one couple following another. (Polka, 2, 3, . . . 16)

	Part II Action
17–32	Partner A puts the right arm around Partner B's waist as they stand side by side, while B puts the left hand on A's right shoulder. A puts the left hand on the shoulder of the A in front. This closes the circle. Partners A move sideways to the center to catch up with the A ahead. In this position, all march forward counterclockwise and sing loudly, "La, la, la," and so forth. This takes 32 walking steps. (Walk, 2, 3, . . . 32)

	Part III Action
33–48	Partners A face the center, and Partners B drop behind their partner. Bs turn to face the other way, clockwise, and polka around the circle (around the A partners) with their hands on hips. At the same time,

19

A partners, who face center, clap a rhythm as follows: Clap hands twice, then extend both hands, palms outward, toward the neighbor on each side, and clap hands once with the neighbor. Repeat this pattern over and over. For variation, A partners may slap a thigh occasionally, or duck down, or cross their arms when clapping the neighbor's hand. (A: Clap, clap, out; repeat 16 times) (B: Polka, 2, 3, . . . 16)

At the end of Part III, Partners A turn around, take whichever Partner B is behind them, and resume the dance from the beginning. If some children are without a partner, they move to the center and thus find a partner.

Extra children can enter the dance during the clapping part for Partners A, and some can join the ring to polka around the outside. Those left without a partner wait for the next turn. When the group is large, several circles can be made, and it is perfectly proper for unpartnered children to steal into another circle. The polka in this case is done anywhere around the room. During the march, make circles of any number of people.

Teaching the Schottische Step

The schottische is actually a light run, but when students are learning, it should be practiced as a walking step. (This is also true in polka instruction.) Lively music will quicken the step later. The cue is "Step, step, step, hop; step, step, step, hop; step-hop, step-hop, step-hop, step-hop." A full pattern of the schottische, then, is three steps and a hop, repeated once, followed by four step-hops. Partner A starts on the left foot and Partner B on the right. The step can be learned first in scattered formation, then a single circle, and practiced later by couples in a double circle. An effective way to introduce the schottische is with the "Horse and Buggy Schottische."

 HORSE AND BUGGY SCHOTTISCHE (AMERICAN)

Music Source: WWCD-1046

Skills: Schottische step

Formation: Couples in sets of four in a double circle, facing counterclockwise. Couples join inside hands and give outside hands to the other couple (Figure 19.9).

Directions:

Measures	Action
1–2	Moving forward, perform two schottische steps. (Step, step, step, hop; step, step, step, hop)
3–4	Progress in line of direction performing four step-hops. (Step-hop, 2-hop, 3-hop, 4-hop)

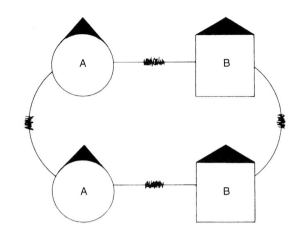

F I G U R E 1 9 . 9 Horse and Buggy Schottische formation.

During the four step-hops, one of three movement patterns can be done.

1. The lead couple drops inside hands and step-hops around the outside of the back couple, who move forward during the step-hops. The lead couple then joins hands behind the other couple, and the positions are reversed.

2. The lead couple continues to hold hands and move backward under the upraised hands of the back couple, who untwist by turning away from each other.

3. Alternate 1 and 2.

▶ **ALUNELUL (ROMANIAN)**

Music Source: WWCD-FFD; WWC-TC1

Skills: Step behind step, grapevine step, stomping

Formation: Single circle, hands on shoulders to both sides, arms straight ("T" position)

Directions: The Romanians are famous for rugged dances. This dance is called "Little Hazelnut." The stomping action represents the breaking of the hazelnuts. The title is pronounced "ah-loo-NAY-loo."

Measures	Part I Action
1–2	Sidestep right, step left behind right, sidestep right, step left behind right, sidestep right, stomp left foot twice. (Side, back, side, back, side, stomp, stomp)
3–4	Beginning with the left foot, repeat the action but with reverse footwork. (Side, back, side, back, side, stomp, stomp)
5–8	Repeat the action of measures 1–4.
	Part II Action
9–10	Sidestep right, left behind right, sidestep right, stomp. (Side, back, side, stomp)

11–12   Sidestep left, right behind left, sidestep left, stomp. (Side, back, side, stomp)

13–16   Repeat the action of measures 9–12.

Part III Action

17–18   In place, step right, stomp left; step left, stomp right; step right, stomp left twice. (Side, stomp, side, stomp, side, stomp, stomp)

19–20   In place, step left, stomp right; step right, stomp left; step left, stomp right twice. (Side, stomp, side, stomp, side, stomp, stomp)

21–24   Repeat action of measures 17–20.

✓ **TEACHING TIP**

The stomps should be made close to the supporting foot. In teaching the dance, scatter the dancers in general space so they can move individually.

▶ **KOROBUSHKA (RUSSIAN)**

Music Source: WWCD-572; WWC-572

Skills: Schottische step, balance step, cross-out-together step, walking step

Formation: Double circle, Partner A's back to the center, with partners facing and both hands joined. A's left and B's right foot are free.

Directions:

Measures	Part I Action

1–2   Take one schottische step away from the center (Partner A moving forward, Partner B backward) starting with A's left and B's right foot. (Out, 2, 3, hop)

3–4   Repeat the pattern of measures 1 and 2, reversing direction and footwork. (In, 2, 3, hop)

5–6   Repeat the pattern of measures 1 and 2, ending on the last count with a jump on both feet in place. (Out, 2, 3, jump)

7–8   Hop on the left foot, touching the right toes across in front of the left foot (count 1). Hop on the left foot, touching the right toes diagonally forward to the right (count 2). Jump on both feet in place, clicking the heels together (count 1), pause, and release the hands (count 2). (Across, apart, together)

Part II Action

9–10   Facing partner and beginning with the right foot, take one schottische step right, moving sideways away from partner. (Side, back, side, hop)

11–12   Facing partner and beginning with the left foot, take one schottische step left, returning to partner. (Side, back, side, hop)

13–14   Joining right hands with partner, balance forward and back: Step forward on the right foot (count 1), pause (count 2), rock back on the left foot in place (count 3), pause (count 4). (Forward, hop, back, hop)

15–16   Take four walking steps forward, starting with the right foot, and change places with partner. (Walk, 2, 3, 4)

17–24   Repeat the pattern of measures 9–16, returning to place.

✓ **TEACHING TIP**

To use the dance as a mixer, during measures 19 and 20, move left to the person just before partner and continue with this new partner. Practice the schottische steps in different directions prior to introducing the dance as a whole.

▶ **OH JOHNNY (AMERICAN)**

Music Source: WWCD-05114; WWC-57

Skills: Shuffle step, swing, allemande left, Do-sa-do, promenade

Formation: Single circle of couples facing inward with Partner B on the right

Directions: A shuffle step is used throughout this dance.
Action

All join hands and circle for eight steps.

All stop and swing with partner.

A partners turn to their left and swing the corner B.

Swing with partner again.

A partners turn to their left and do an allemande left with their corner.

A partners turn to their right and do a Do-sa-do with their partner.

A partners promenade with the corner B, who becomes the new partner for the next repetition.

✓ **TEACHING TIP**

To simplify the dance, begin in scattered formation and teach each call with students changing from partner to corner using any nearby person. Since this is a fast-moving dance, the music should be slowed down until students can successfully complete the dance.

▶ SHINDIG IN THE BARN (AMERICAN)

Music Source: WWC-FFD

Skills: Walking, Do-sa-do, swinging, sliding

Formation: Contra Style (two lines with partners facing each other). Seven couples will fit the music.

Directions:

Measures	Action
2 (8 counts total)	Introduction
1–2	Everybody walk forward four steps and back four steps. (Forward, 2, 3, 4; back, 2, 3, 4)
3–4	All pass through to the other side by walking forward four steps toward partner, do a half turn while passing right shoulder of partner, and walk four steps backward. (Walk, 2, 3, 4, turn, 6, 7, 8)
5–6	Everybody forward and back— repeat measures 1–2 above. (Forward, 2, 3, 4; back, 2, 3, 4)
7–8	Everybody pass through to the other side with eight steps— repeat measures 3–4 above. (Walk, 2, 3, 4, turn, 6, 7, 8)
9–10	All couples Do-sa-do by passing right shoulders and back. (Do-sa-do, 2, 3, . . . 8)
11–12	All couples do a two-hand swing one time around to the left using eight steps. After the swing, all couples except the head couple go back to their original position. The head couples remain in the middle with their hands joined facing each other. (Swing, 2, 3, . . . 8)
13–14	The head couple takes eight sliding (sashay) or skipping steps to the foot of the line. All the other couples clap to the beat and watch. (Slide, 2, 3, . . . 8)
15–16	Head couple does a right elbow swing at the foot of the line for 8 counts and remains at the foot of the line creating a new head couple. (Swing, 2, 3, . . . 8)

Repeat dance to the end of the music.

▶ BIG SOMBRERO CIRCLE MIXER (AMERICAN)

Music Source: WWC-FFD

Skills: Circling, Do-sa-do, star, swing

Formation: Sicilian Circle. Couples facing couples clockwise and counterclockwise around the circle.

Directions:

Measures	Action
2 (8 counts total)	Introduction
1–2	Join hands with the facing couple and circle left using eight walking steps. (Circle, 2, 3, . . . 8)
3–4	Keeping hands joined, circle right using eight walking steps. (Circle right, 2, 3, . . . 8)
5–6	Face partner and Do-sa-do using eight walking steps. (Do-sa-do, 2, 3, . . . 8)
7–8	Face opposite and Do-sa-do using eight walking steps. (Opposite, 2, 3, . . . 8)
9–10	All four circle while doing a right-hand star using eight walking steps. (Star, 2, 3, . . . 8)
11–12	All four circle while doing a left-hand star using eight walking steps. (Star, 2, 3, . . . 8)
13–14	Swing partner by linking right elbows and swinging once or twice. (Swing, 2, 3, . . . 8)
15–16	Pass through the opposite couple passing right shoulders and walk to the next couple using eight steps. (Pass, through, 3, 4, . . . 8)

Repeat the dance to the end of the music. Youngsters should always return back to their starting position after every 8-count movement.

▶ TRIO FUN MIXER (AMERICAN)

Music Source: WWC-FFD

Skills: Walking, Do-sa-do, star

Formation: Lines of three facing lines of three in a large circle

Directions:

Measures	Action
1–4	Facing threesomes (six dancers) join hands and circle left one time around back to place. (Circle, 2, 3, . . . 16)

5–6	Center students in each threesome do a Do-sa-do with each other. (Do-sa-do, 2, 3, . . . 8)
7–8	Right youngsters in each threesome move diagonally to Do-sa-do with each other. (Do-sa-do, 2, 3, . . . 8)
9–10	Left youngsters in each threesome move diagonally to Do-sa-do with each other. (Do-sa-do, 2, 3, . . . 8)
11–12	Center person in each threesome faces the person on the right and turns that person with a right-hand star and then turns the person on the left with a left-hand star and goes back to place. (Star, 2, 3, 4; left, 2, 3, 4)
13–14	Lines of three go forward 4 counts and back 4 counts. (Forward, 2, 3, 4; back, 2, 3, 4)
15–16	Lines of three walk forward passing right shoulders and move forward to the next group of three. (Forward pass, 2, 3, . . . 8)

Repeat to the end of the music.

▶ CIRCLE VIRGINIA REEL (AMERICAN)

Music Source: WWCD-57; WWC-57

Skills: Star, swing, Do-sa-do, swing, promenade

Formation: Couples facing in a double circle with dancers about 4 feet apart

Directions:

Measures	Action
1–4	Partners walk forward four and backward four steps; repeat. (Forward, 2, 3, 4; back, 2, 3, 4; forward, 2, 3, 4; back, 2, 3, 4)
5–8	Partners make a start by joining right hands (with bent elbows) and circling around once clockwise in eight steps. Reverse direction and star with left hands back to place in eight steps. (Right star, 2, 3, . . . 8; left star, 2, 3, . . . 8)
9–10	Partners join hands with bent elbows held chest high and circle clockwise back to place in eight steps. (Circle, 2, 3, . . . 8)
11–12	Partners walk forward and Do-sa-do passing right shoulders and stepping to the right when passing back to back. After passing, each partner moves diagonally (veers) to the right to end in front of a new partner. (Do-sa-do, 2, 3, 4; veer, 2, 3, 4)
13–16	Facing a new partner and joining hands, inside circle partner begins with left foot and outside circle begins with right foot doing two heel-toe steps and four slide

	steps counterclockwise. Repeat to the other side sliding clockwise. (Heel, toe, heel, toe, slide, slide, slide, slide; heel, toe, heel, toe, slide, slide, slide, slide)
17–20	Partners do a right elbow swing in place for 12 counts using a walking step and use four counts to end in promenade position. (Swing, 2, 3, . . . 12; promenade position 15, 16)
21–24	In promenade position, partners walk forward counterclockwise 16 steps and end facing each other. (Promenade, 2, 3, . . . 16)

INTRODUCTORY SQUARE DANCE

Introductory square dance should be just that—introductory. In no case should the goal be finished, accomplished square dancing. The emphases should be on enjoyment and learning the basics within the maturity capabilities of elementary school children. This can involve, however, considerable skill and polish. Square dancing is a broad and colorful activity with numerous figures, patterns, and dances. The large quantity of materials (introductory, intermediate, and advanced) poses a selection problem given the limited amount of program time that can be allocated to the activity.

Square dance fun begins with an effective caller, and calling takes practice. In a few instances, youngsters can develop into satisfactory callers. One solution is to select square dance music that includes some selections with calls and some with the music only. Directions are usually supplied with the CDs. Singing calls should be used that can be done by one individual, by a group, or by the entire class. Singing calls are fun to dance to, because youngsters know what is coming next.

Square dance instruction should begin modestly in the fourth grade, with the impetus increasing in the fifth and sixth grades. This does not rule out the use of square dance–related figures in folk dances taught earlier. Square dance as a specialized dance activity requires the application of appropriate methodology. Some teaching suggestions follow.

1. In early figure practice or patter calls, pairing off by gender is not important. Let boys dance with boys and girls with girls if necessary. Avoid labeling one position for boys and one for girls. In a couple, one partner becomes the left partner and the other the right. The goal is, however, to have boys dance with girls, and vice versa. In the following section, calls will be given in their traditional forms, and gender references, where they appear, will correspond with the traditional calls.

2. The shuffle step should be used, rather than the skipping or running step that beginners usually tend to use. The shuffle step makes a smoother and more graceful dance, has better carryover to other dancing, and conserves energy. It is a quick walk, almost a half glide, in time to the music and is done by reaching out with the toes in a gliding motion. The body should be in good posture position and should not bounce up and down on each step.

3. Teach the children to listen to the call. Equally important is that they know what the call means. They should have fun, but they must be quiet enough to hear the call.

4. It is important to follow the caller's directions and not move too soon. The children should be ready for the call and then move at the proper time.

5. Generally, the caller explains the figures, has the children walk through the patterns, and then calls the figures.

6. The teacher should remember that there are many different ways to do different turns, swings, hand positions, and so on, and as many opinions on how these should be done. Settle on good principles and stick with them.

7. When a set becomes confused, each couple should return to its home position and try to pick up from that point. Otherwise, the choice is to wait until the dance is over or a new sequence has started.

8. Change partners at different times during the dancing. Have each Partner A move one place to the right and take a new partner, or have all of the A partners (or Bs) keep their positions and have their partners change to another set.

The Individual Approach to Square Dance

Many square dance terms can be taught using an individual approach. Students are scattered in general space. A piece of country and western music with a strong beat is played. Anytime students hear the call, they perform the same task with the person nearest to them. Note that there are no boy or girl roles. The two-handed swing is to be used instead of the regular buzz-step swing.

Two calls are basic. "Hit the lonesome trail" directs students to promenade individually in general space in diverse directions. This call can be inserted at any time to move the students in new directions. The other basic call is "Stop where you are and keep time to the music." Students stop and beat time to the music with light claps. Other calls can be selected from the following list.

1. *Right (or left) arm round.* With a forearm grasp, turn your partner once around and return to place.

2. *Honor your partner, honor your corner.* Bow to one person, then bow to another.

3. *Do-sa-do your partner, Do-sa-do your corner.* Pass around one person, right shoulder to right shoulder, and back to place. Repeat with another person.

4. *Right- (or left-) hand star.* Place indicated hands (palm to palm with fingers pointed upward) about shoulder height with elbow somewhat bent. The next call will indicate how far to turn the star.

5. *Two-hand swing.* Partners grasp both hands, lean away from each other, and circle clockwise once around.

6. *Go forward and back.* Move forward with three steps and a touch toward another person, who is moving similarly toward you. Move back to place with three steps and a touch.

The next teaching strategy is to divide the class into groups of four. Use a call such as, "Circle up, four hands round." Groups of four circle clockwise. There usually will be extras. If there are three extras, one person can pretend to have a partner. Rotate the extras in and out.

Circle fours until all groups are formed. With the call, "Break and swing," the fours separate into pairs within the foursome. Position the pairs so they face each other. Use the terms "left partner" and "right partner" instead of boy and girl. If convenient, when there are mixed pairs put the girl on the right.

The following figures can be practiced in fours.

1. *Circle to the left (or right).* Join hands and circle once around as indicated.

2. *Form a right- (or left-) hand star.* Hold right hands at about shoulder height and turn clockwise. A left-hand star reverses the direction.

3. *Swing your opposite and swing your partner.* Left partners walk toward their right partner opposite and swing. They walk back to their own partner and swing. The call can be reversed.

4. *Birdie in the cage and three hands round.* One child (the birdie) goes to the center, while the other three join hands and circle left once around.

5. *The birdie hops out and the crow hops in.* The birdie joins the circle and another child goes in the center.

6. *Go into the middle and come back out; go into the middle and give a little shout.* This is done from a circle-right or circle-left formation. The dancers face center

and come together. Repeat again, but with a light shout.

7. *Round and round in a single file; round and round in frontier style.* Circle left (or right), drop hands and move into a single file.

8. *Dive for the oyster—dig for the clam.* Usually after circling left once around, one couple goes partially under the raised joined hands of the other couple. The other couple repeats the same maneuver. Stepping should be: In, 2, 3, touch; out, 2, 3, touch.

The caller can use the "Hit the lonesome trail" call at any time to break up the makeup of the fours, and then reorganize later with different combinations of students.

Square Dance Formation

Each couple is numbered around the set in a counterclockwise direction. It is important that the couples know their position. The couple with their backs to the music is generally couple 1, or the head couple. The couple to the right of them is number 2, and so on. While the head couple is number 1, the term head couples includes both couples 1 and 3; couples 2 and 4 are the side couples.

With respect to any one left-hand partner (gent), the following terms are used in traditional calls (adjust references to gender as necessary):

Partner: The other (right-hand) dancer of the couple

Corner or corner lady: The right-hand partner on the left

Right-hand lady: The right-hand partner in the couple to the right

Opposite or opposite lady: The right-hand partner directly across the set

Other terms that are used include these:

Home: The couple's original or starting position

Active or leading couple: The couple leading or visiting the other couples for different figures

Once the square dance formation has been introduced, the figures and patter calls discussed previously should be practiced in the full formation of four couples. Although there is some repetition of material already presented in the movement approach section, the following figures merit discussion with the square dance formation as the background.

American Square Dance Figures

Some common square dance figures are the following:

1. *Honor your partner.* Partners bow to each other.

2. *Honor your corner.* Left-hand dancer bows to corner, who returns the bow.

3. *Shuffle step.* A light walking step on the ball of the foot. The body is upright and movement is in time with the music.

4. *Do-sa-do your partner (or corner).* Partners face and pass each other right shoulder to right shoulder, move around each other back to back, and return to the original position facing their partner.

5. *Promenade.* The couple walks side by side, right hand joined to right hand and left to left in a crossed-arm promenade position. They walk around the square once and return to home position.

6. *Circle right (or left).* All eight dancers join hands and circle. The caller can add "Into the center with a great big yell." The circle can be broken with a swing at home place.

7. *Right-and-left grand.* All face their partner, join right hands, walk past the partner, and join left hands with the next person in the ring, and so on down the line. This causes left-hand partners to go in one direction (counterclockwise) around the circle and right-hand partners to go in the other direction, alternately touching right and left hands until partners meet again. Right-and-left grand starts with your partner and ends with your partner, at which time another call is needed.

8. *Allemande left.* Left-hand dancer faces corner, grasps corner with a left-forearm grip, walks around corner, and returns to partner.

9. *Arm swing.* Left-hand dancer turns partner with a right-arm swing, using a forearm grasp.

10. *Swing your partner (or corner).* Partners stand side by side with right hip against right hip. The dancers are almost in social dance position, except that the left-hand partner's right arm is more around to the side than back at the shoulder blade. The dancers walk around each other with a slight lean away from each other until they reach their starting position.

11. *Do paso.* Starting position is a circle of two or more couples. Partners face, take a left forearm grasp, and turn each other counterclockwise until facing the corner. Turn corner with right forearm grasp until facing partner. Take partner with the left hand; left-hand partner turns the other with a courtesy turn.

12. *All around your left-hand lady, seesaw your pretty little taw.* Corners move one time around each other in a loop pattern, left-hand dancer starting behind the corner, on around corner and back to place, right-hand dancer starting in front of corner and around back to place. Repeat with partner to complete the other half of the loop.

19

13. *Ladies chain.* From a position with two couples facing each other, the girls cross over to the opposite boy, touching right hands as they pass each other. When they reach the opposite boy, they join left hands with him. At the same time, each boy places his right arm around the girl's waist and turns her once around to face the other couple. On "Chain right back," the girls cross back to their partner in a similar figure.

14. *Right-and-left through (and back).* Two couples face each other. Dancers join right hands and pull past opposite, passing right shoulder to right shoulder. Couples have backs to each other. Courtesy turn to face again and repeat to original place.

Selecting Square Dances and Music

In past years, the types of square dances suggested for elementary students were traditional square dances using a patter call. Today, square dancing is a popular form of adult recreation. The singing call and use of modern music has helped in adult popularity, but more important is the difference in traditional calls versus modern calls. In traditional square dancing everyone knew what call was coming next. In modern square dancing nobody knows what the next call will be and nobody wants to know.

Two popular series of albums with different developmental levels and proper progression are the Wagon Wheel Fundamentals of Square Dancing, Levels 1, 2, and 3, and Square Dance Party for the New Dancer, No. 1 and No. 2. Both series feature the calling of Bob Ruff. They can be ordered from the following source:

Wagon Wheel Records
16812 Pembrook Lane
Huntington Beach, CA 92649
Phone/Fax: (714) 846-8169
Website: wagonwheelrecords.net
E-mail: info@wagonwheelrecords.net

CULMINATING EVENTS FOR THE RHYTHMS UNIT

Country-Western Day

After all of the grade levels have reached a specified performance level in square dancing, a country-western day can be sponsored by the school. Teachers and students should be encouraged to wear country-western-style clothing all day, and then during the last hour of the school day, the student body can have a square dance. It is important to include activities that everyone, from third-grade students to sixth graders, can do together. The movement approach presented previously can help achieve this goal.

May Festival

In the spring when the rhythm program is drawing to a close, it is exciting to feature in a May festival all of the dances learned. To have this activity include everyone, each class or grade level should make a dance presentation. The announcer should describe the history and background of each dance (consult specialty dance books for a description of the various dances), and the festival should end with the entire school performing the Maypole Dance.

FOR MORE INFORMATION

Websites
Dance Ideas
 www.pecentral.org
Dances of Mexico
 www.alegria.org/rgndance.html
Multicultural Dances
 www.activevideos.com/multicultural.htm
 www.centralhome.com/ballroomcountry/video_store.htm
Music Sources
 www.wagonwheelrecords.net
Square Dancing
 www.dosado.com

20

Gymnastic Skills

ESSENTIAL COMPONENTS OF QUALITY PROGRAMS

▷ **I. Organized around content standards**

▷ **II. Student-centered and developmentally appropriate**

▷ **III. Physical activity and motor skill development form the core of the program**

   IV. Teaches management skills and self-discipline

   V. Promotes inclusion of all students

▷ **VI. Focuses on process over product**

▷ **VII. Promotes lifetime personal health and wellness**

   VIII. Teaches cooperation and responsibility and promotes sensitivity to diversity

NATIONAL STANDARDS FOR PHYSICAL EDUCATION*

▷ **1. Demonstrates competency in motor skills and movement patterns needed to perform a variety of physical activities.**

   2. Demonstrates understanding of movement concepts, principles, and tactics as they apply to the learning and performance of physical activities.

▷ **3. Participates regularly in physical activity.**

▷ **4. Achieves and maintains a health-enhancing level of physical fitness.**

   5. Exhibits responsible personal and social behavior that respects self and others in physical activity.

▷ **6. Values physical activity for health, enjoyment, challenge, self-expression, and/or social interaction.**

*National Association for Sport and Physical Education (NASPE), 2004.

Gymnastic activities make a significant contribution to the overall physical education experience for children in elementary schools. Gymnastic activities develop body management skills without the need for equipment and apparatus. Flexibility, agility, balance, strength, and body control are outcomes that are enhanced through participation in gymnastics. Specialized motor skills such as body rolling, balance skills, inverted balances, and tumbling skills are learned through these activities. Various partner and group activities offer opportunity for social interaction and cooperation. Positive learning experiences in gymnastic activities are dependent on progression. Enjoyable teaching activities, developing a positive attitude, and overcoming students' personal limitations are more important than stressing performance with perfect technique. Safety is foremost in the gymnastic program.

- List progressions and developmental level placements for gymnastic activities.

- Understand the techniques of spotting when teaching gymnastic activities.

- Organize a comprehensive lesson of gymnastic activities that includes the six basic groups: (a) animal movements; (b) tumbling and inverted balances; (c) balance stunts; (d) individual stunts; (e) partner and group stunts; and (f) partner support activities.

- Identify effective management techniques when teaching gymnastic activities.

- Cite safety considerations essential to the gymnastic program.

- Describe tumbling activities that are appropriate for elementary school children.

Gymnastic activities are an important part of every child's overall experience in physical education, and they can make a significant contribution to the goals of physical education. Through the gymnastics program, such personal characteristics as dedication and perseverance can be furthered, for stunts are seldom mastered quickly. Because much of the work is individual, children face challenges and have the opportunity to develop resourcefulness, self-confidence, and courage. When a challenging stunt is mastered, satisfaction, pride of achievement, and a sense of accomplishment contribute to improved self-esteem. Social interplay is provided through various partner and group stunts requiring cooperative effort. The social attributes of tolerance, helpfulness, courtesy, and appreciation for the ability of others grow out of the lessons when the methodology is educationally sound.

Important physical values emerge from a gymnastics program. Body management opportunities are presented, and coordination, flexibility, and agility are enhanced. The opportunity to practice balance is present in many activities. The demands of holding positions and executing stunts contribute to the development of strength and power in diverse parts of the body. Many stunts demand support, wholly or in part, by the arms, thus providing development of the often weak musculature of the arm-shoulder girdle.

PROGRESSION AND DEVELOPMENTAL LEVEL PLACEMENT

Progression is important in the gymnastics program. In this book, activities are listed in progression within the three developmental levels. To avoid safety problems, the order of these activities should be reasonably maintained. Adherence to developmental level is secondary to the principle of progression. If children have little or no experience in these activities, start them on activities specified in a lower developmental level.

Activities in this chapter are divided into six basic groups: (1) animal movements; (2) tumbling and inverted balances; (3) balance stunts; (4) individual stunts; (5) partner and group stunts; and (6) partner support activities. This arrangement allows the individual to pick activities from each group for a well-balanced lesson. Often, too much time is spent on tumbling activities, causing children to become bored and fatigued. In addition, for children who do not like tumbling activities, choosing activities from all the categories will help them find something they enjoy. At the heart of a gymnastic program are the standard tumbling activities, such as rolls, stands, springs, and related stunts. In performing the activities, emphasis should be placed on exposure and overcoming fear. Perfect technique is less important than developing positive approach behaviors. The suggested progression of the basic activities for each development level is presented in the following lists.

Developmental Level I

- Rolling Log
- Side Roll
- Forward Roll (Tuck Position)
- Back Roller
- Forward Roll (Straddle Position)
- Backward Curl
- Backward Roll (Handclasp Position)
- Climb-Up
- Three-Point Tip-Up
- Mountain Climber—Handstand Lead-Up Activity
- Switcheroo—Handstand Lead-Up Activity

Developmental Level II

- Forward Roll (Pike Position)
- Backward Roll (Regular)
- Frog Handstand (Tip-Up)
- Half Teeter-Totter—Handstand Lead-Up Activity
- Cartwheel
- Forward Roll to a Walkout
- Forward Roll Combinations
- Backward Roll Combinations
- Headstand Practice and Variations
- Teeter-Totter—Handstand Lead-Up Activity
- Handstand

Developmental Level III

- Forward and Backward Roll Combinations
- Back Extension
- Headstand Variations
- Handstand against a Wall
- Freestanding Handstand
- Cartwheel and Round-Off
- Judo Roll
- Forward and Backward Roll Combinations
- Developing Gymnastic Routines
- Straddle Press to Headstand
- Headspring
- Walking on the Hands
- Walk-Over

The Developmental Level I program relies on simple stunts, with a gradual introduction to tumbling stunts classified as lead-ups or preliminaries to more advanced stunts. Stunts requiring exceptional body control, critical balancing, or substantial strength should be left for higher levels of development. The Developmental Level II and III programs are built on activities and progressions developed earlier. Emphasis is placed on learning more standard gymnastic activities. Most stunts at Developmental Level I can be performed with a wide range of performance being acceptable, whereas at Developmental Levels II and III increasing conformance to correct technique is desirable. In general, the upper developmental level activities place higher demands on strength, control, form, agility, balance, and flexibility.

Most activities at Developmental Level I can be done—at least in some fashion—by most students; but certain activities at Developmental Levels II and III may be too challenging for some students. Arrange lessons that include a variety of activities: stunts that everyone can do, stunts that are moderately challenging, and stunts that are more challenging.

INSTRUCTIONAL METHODOLOGY FOR GYMNASTICS

Warm-Up and Flexibility Activity

Normal introductory activity and fitness development activity usually supply sufficient warm-up for the gymnastics lesson. If additional stretching seems warranted, take a wide straddle position with the feet about 3 feet apart and the toes pointed ahead. With arms out to the sides, bend, twist, and generally stretch in all directions. Next, touch the floor with the hands to the front, sides, and back, with some bending of the knees.

Extra flexibility may be required in the wrists, ankles, and neck. The following activities can be used prior to participating in the gymnastic activities.

▶ WRISTS

1. Extend one arm forward. With the other hand, push the extended hand down, thus stretching the top of the wrist and forearm muscles. Hold the position for eight counts. Next, pull the hand backward and hold for eight counts to stretch the wrist flexor muscles.

2. Clasp the fingers of both hands in front of the chest. Make circles with both hands and stretch the wrists.

▶ ANKLES AND QUADRICEPS

1. Kneel and sit on both feet. Smoothly and gently lean backward over the feet, using the arms to support the body.

2. In a sitting position, cross one leg over the other. Use the hands to help rotate each foot through its full range of motion. Reverse legs and repeat.

▶ NECK

1. In a sitting position, slowly circle the head in both directions through the full range of motion.

2. In the same position, hold the chin against the chest for eight counts. Repeat with the head looking backward as far as possible. Look to each side and hold for eight counts.

▶ LOWER BACK AND SHOULDERS

Begin in a supine position. Place the hands back over the head on the mat so that the fingers point toward the toes. Bridge up by extending the arms and legs. While in the bridge position, slowly rock back and forth.

Effective Class Management

A commonly heard criticism of gymnastics lessons is that children must wait in line for turns on the mat. Waiting can be controlled so that everyone is reasonably active. How children are arranged depends on the activities selected and whether mats are required. The following ideas help establish priorities.

1. Whenever possible, all children should be active and performing. When mats are not required for the activities, there is little problem. Individual mats can be used for many of the simple balances and rolling stunts, particularly at Developmental Level I. When larger mats are required, be more ingenious. Ideally, each group of three students should have a mat. When return activities are used in conjunction with groups as small as three, there is little standing around. Small groups also work well when spotting and other types of cooperation are needed.

2. When the number of mats is limited, perform across the mats sideways. An 8-foot-long mat can be used by three performers at the same time. With this arrangement, the focus is on single rolls, but an occasional series of rolls lengthwise on the mat is not ruled out. The ends of the mats can be used for various stands, as long as children are aligned so they do not fall toward each other.

3. Consider station teaching if equipment is limited. Make plans that ensure the experience stresses progress and diligence. A few tumbling and inverted balance stations can be included, with other stations featuring less demanding activities. Wall charts listing the activities in progression provide excellent guidance.

Formations for Teaching

1. *Squad Formation.* Mats are placed in a line, with squads lined up behind the mats. Each child takes a turn and then goes to the end of the squad line, with the others moving up. An alternative method is for each child to perform and then return to a seated position.

2. *Semicircular Formation.* Students are positioned in a semicircular arrangement. This formation directs attention toward the teacher, who stands in the center.

3. *U-shaped Formation.* The mats are placed in the shape of a large U. This formation offers an excellent view for the teacher, and children are able to see what their classmates are doing.

4. *Demonstration Mat.* One mat is placed in a central position and is used exclusively for demonstrations. Little movement is necessary to see demonstrations.

Description and Demonstration of New Gymnastic Activities

To enhance student learning when presenting an activity, the following sequence may be helpful.

1. *Significance of the Name.* Most activities have a characteristic name which should be learned. If the stunt is of an imitative type, the animal or character represented should be described and discussed.

2. *Description of the Activity.* Stunts can be approached in terms of three parts: starting position, execution, and finishing position. Most stunts have a defined starting position which must be performed properly. Explain the position to assume as the first step. Next, key movements for proper execution of the activity are presented. Such factors as how far to travel, how long to balance, and how many times a movement should be done can be clarified. In some gymnastic activities, a definite finishing position or action is part of the stunt. In balancing stunts try to return to a standing (or some other) position without losing balance and moving the feet.

3. *Demonstration of the Activity.* Three levels of demonstration are recognized: (a) minimal demonstration in the form of the starting position; (b) slow, step-by-step demonstration of the entire stunt, with an explanation of what is involved; and (c) execution of the stunt as it is normally done. Keep in mind that children need to analyze and solve problems. Too much demonstration defeats this goal. Explanation and demonstration should cover only one or two points. Show points necessary to get the activity under way. Add further details and refinements as the instruction progresses. Demonstrations at the end of a unit can show what has been achieved. Allow each squad or group to demonstrate its achievements in turn.

OPPORTUNITIES FOR PRACTICE AND IMPROVEMENT

The character of each stunt determines the amount of practice needed and the number of times the stunt should be performed. Analyze the stunt thoroughly enough so you can verbalize the points necessary for proper performance. Practice and repetition are essential in establishing effective movement patterns. To maximize activity and minimize standing in line, allow the class to practice the activity a desired number of times. On the command or whistle to "freeze," the class stops whatever they are doing without returning to formation. Directions are given for the next activity, and the class resumes practicing. This method decreases the amount of management time spent waiting for each squad to finish and return to formation.

SAFETY CONSIDERATIONS

Safety is a foremost consideration in the gymnastic program. The inherent hazards of an activity and how to avoid them must be included in the instructional procedures.

Spotting

The purpose of spotting is twofold. First and most important is the performer's safety and the prevention of injury. Of secondary importance is guiding the performer through the stunt to help develop proper body awareness. When spotting for safety, the goals are to assist the performer, help support the body weight, and prevent a hazardous fall. A particularly difficult problem is working with obese children in tumbling activities.

You will have to decide whether to teach activities that require spotting. If you lack confidence in this area or lack adequate knowledge about proper presentation of the activities, it is probably best to avoid tumbling and inverted balance activities. Because tumbling and inverted balance activities make up only about 10 percent of the activities in this chapter, there are many other stunts and balance activities that can be offered to teach youngsters body management skills. Above all, do not force youngsters to participate in tumbling and inverted balance activities. Specific spotting techniques for competent teachers are offered in this chapter for activities that demand spotting.

Two major questions are related to spotting.

1. *Should teachers spot youngsters?* The answer is grounded in your expertise and experience. Many teachers have little, if any, gymnastics background. This makes spotting correctly a difficult task. In addition,

obese youngsters may actually weigh more than you, making spotting next to impossible. If this is the case, it is probably best to avoid activities that involve spotting. Also, remember that you can only spot one child at a time, which minimizes the opportunity for youngsters to be actively involved and increases standing in line.

2. *Should students spot their peers?* In many situations, it is difficult to get all students to take spotting responsibilities seriously. Additionally, if many students are spotting in the class, how do you assure quality control? If an accident were to occur while a student was spotting, who would be liable? Legal authorities might try to show that you were not supervising the spotting carefully or that students are too young and not responsible enough to fulfill the duties of correct spotting. If your only recourse is to have students spot each other, avoid teaching those activities. Rarely are students able to perform quality spotting.

INSTRUCTIONAL PROCEDURES

1. Although mats are not necessary for some stunts, it is wise to include stunts requiring mats in every lesson. Children like to perform on mats, and rolling stunts using mats are vital to the gymnastic program.

2. Many partner stunts work best when partners are about the same size. If the stunt requires partner support, the support child should be strong enough to hold the weight of the other.

3. No two children are alike. Respect individual differences, and allow for different levels of success.

4. Relating new activities to those learned previously is important. An effective approach is to review the lead-up stunt for an activity.

5. When a stunt calls for a position to be held for a number of counts, use a standard counting system (e.g., "One thousand one, one thousand two, . . . ").

6. When appropriate, have children work in pairs, with one child performing and the second providing a critique.

7. Shifting of mats should not be necessary during the course of instruction. When arranging a gymnastic routine for a day's lesson, group the mat stunts. The tumbling mats should be bordered with Velcro so that, once fastened, they stay fastened together.

Start-and-Expand Technique

The start-and-expand technique should be applied to stunts when feasible. Consider someone teaching a simple Heel Click (page 483). The instructor begins by saying, "Let's see all of you jump high in the air and click your heels together before you come down." (This is the start.) "Now, to do the stunt properly, you should jump into the air, click your heels, and land with your feet apart with a nice bent-knee action to absorb the shock." (This is the expansion.) Further expansion could be adding a quarter or half turn before landing, clapping the hands overhead while clicking the heels, or clicking the heels twice before landing. In general, the start is made simple, so that all children can experience a measure of success. The instruction then expands to other elements of the stunt, with variations and movement factors added and refined as indicated.

Basic Mechanical Principles

Certain mechanical principles should be established as the foundation of an effective gymnastic program. If children can build on these basic principles, instruction is facilitated.

1. Momentum needs to be developed and applied, particularly for rolls. Tucking, starting from a higher point, and preliminary raising of the arms are examples of ways to increase momentum.

2. The center of weight must be positioned over the center of support in balance stunts, particularly in the inverted stands.

3. In certain stunts, such as the Headspring, the hips should be projected upward and forward to raise the center of gravity for better execution.

4. In stunts in which the body is wholly or partially supported by the hands, proper positioning of the hands is essential for effective performance. The hands should be approximately shoulder width apart, and the fingers should be spread and pointed forward.

Basic Gymnastic Positions

Students should be able to recognize and demonstrate basic positions that are unique to gymnastics. Emphasis at the elementary level should be placed on a rough estimation of how the positions are performed, rather than on pure technique.

TUCK POSITION

The tuck position is performed with the legs bent and the chin tucked to the chest. Students can be cued to "curl up like a ball." There are three different tuck positions, and students should know all of them: the Sitting Tuck (Figure 20.1 on page 470), the Standing Tuck, and the Lying Tuck.

PIKE POSITION

The pike position is performed by bending forward at the hips and keeping the legs straight. The three basic pike positions are the Sitting Pike (Figure 20.2, page 470), the Standing Pike, and the Lying Pike.

FIGURE 20.1   Tuck position.

STRADDLE POSITION

The straddle position is accomplished by bending forward at the hips and spreading the legs apart to the sides as far as possible. The legs should be kept straight. Variations of the straddle position are the Sitting Piked Straddle (Figure 20.3), the Standing Piked Straddle, and the Lying Piked Straddle.

FRONT-SUPPORT POSITION

This position is similar to the push-up position. The body is straight with the head up (Figure 20.4).

BACK-SUPPORT POSITION

The back-support position is an inverted push-up position. The body is kept as straight as possible (Figure 20.5).

Gymnastic Dance Positions

ATTITUDE

An attitude is a position in which the body weight is supported on one leg while the other leg is lifted and

FIGURE 20.2   Pike position.

FIGURE 20.3   Straddle position.

bent at the knee. The arm on the side of the lifted leg is usually bent over the head, and the other arm is extended at the side (Figure 20.6).

LUNGE POSITION

In lunge position, the nonsupporting rear leg is straight while the forward, supporting leg is bent at the hip and knee. Most of the weight is placed on the forward leg. The arms are extended, and the head is up with the eyes forward (Figure 20.7).

PLIÉ

A plié is the bending of the knees. Both knees are bent, the arms are extended at right angles to the sides, and the seat is tucked to maintain a flat abdominal wall. The plié teaches children how to absorb the force of the landing. There are different plié positions, but the basic purpose of the plié in gymnastic instruction is to teach landing with grace and control.

FIGURE 20.4   Front-support position.

FIGURE 20.5 Back-support position.

RELEVÉ

The relevé is an extension movement from the plié position. The movement goes from the plié (knees bent) position to the extended position. Extension should be complete through all of the joints, stretching upward from the balls of the feet.

ARABESQUE

In the arabesque position, the weight is supported on one leg while the other leg is extended to the rear. The extended leg is kept straight with the toe pointed, and the chest is kept erect (Figure 20.8 on page 474). The Back Extension and the Cartwheel are often brought to completion with an Arabesque.

FIGURE 20.6 Attitude.

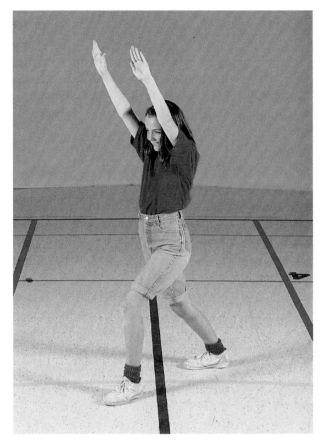

FIGURE 20.7 Lunge position.

JUMPS

Three jump variations are used commonly in gymnastic dance. They are the Tuck Jump, the Pike Jump, and the Straddle Jump. These jumps are simply a jump with the prescribed position added. The arms are raised in a lifting motion to increase the height of the jump and to enhance balance. The impact of the landing is absorbed at the ankles and knee joints.

CHASSÉ

The chassé is a slide. This basic locomotor movement involves one leg chasing the other out of position. It is done close to the floor with a light spring in the step.

Stunts and Tumbling Activities

The stunts and tumbling activities are organized in order of difficulty into three developmental levels. Table 20.1 (pages 472–474) lists all the activities in each of the levels and offers a page reference for rapid access to descriptions of each activity. A brief discussion of each of the developmental levels follows.

TABLE 20.1   Stunts and Tumbling Activities

TABLE 20.1   Stunts and Tumbling Activities (*continued*)

20

(*continued*)

TABLE 20.1	Stunts and Tumbling Activities *(continued)*
Individual Stunts	
Wall Walk-Up	510
Skier's Sit	510
Rocking Horse	510
Heel Click (Side)	511
Walk-Through	511
Jump-Through	511
Circular Rope Jump	511
Bouncer	512
Pretzel	512
Jackknife	512
Heel-and-Toe Spring	512
Single-Leg Circle (Pinwheel)	512
Partner and Group Stunts	
Double Scooter	513
Double Roll	513
Tandem Bicycle	513
Circle High Jump	513
Stick Carries	513
Two-Way Wheelbarrow	514
Partner Rising Sun	514
Triple Roll	515
Quintuplet Roll	515
Dead Person Lift	515
Injured Person Carry	515
Merry-Go-Round	515
Partner Support Stunts	
Front Sit	516
Flying Dutchman	516
All-Fours Support	517
Angel	517
Side Stand	517
Pyramids	517

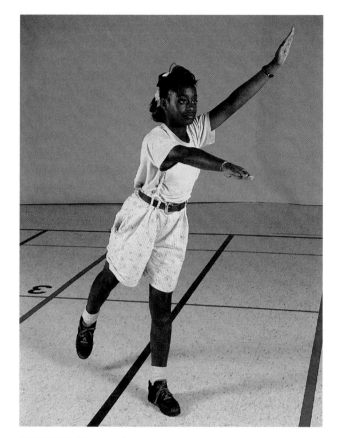

FIGURE 20.8   Arabesque.

DEVELOPMENTAL LEVEL I ACTIVITIES

Developmental Level I activities consist primarily of imitative walks and movements, plus selected balance stunts and rolls. The Forward Roll is practiced, but its refinement is left to later levels. The Back Roller is practiced as a prelude to the Backward Roll.

Emphasis should be placed on the creative aspects of the activities as well as on performance standards.

Children at this level tend to do stunts in different ways because of their different interpretations of what is required. Directional concepts and a basic understanding of common movement terminology should have a prominent place in the instruction.

Animal Movements

▶ **ALLIGATOR CRAWL**

Lie facedown on the floor with elbows bent. Move along the floor in alligator fashion, keeping the hands close to the body and the feet pointed out (Figure 20.9). First, use unilateral movements—that is, right arm and leg moving together—then change to cross-lateral movements.

▶ **KANGAROO JUMP**

Carry the arms close to the chest with the palms facing forward. Place a beanbag or ball between the knees. Move in different directions by taking small jumps without dropping the object.

FIGURE 20.9   Alligator Crawl.

PUPPY DOG RUN

Place the hands on the floor, bending the arms and legs slightly. Walk and run like a happy puppy. Look straight ahead. Keeping the head up, in good position, strengthens the neck muscles (Figure 20.10). Go sideways, backward, and so on. Turn around in place.

Variations:

1. *Cat Walk.* Use the same position to imitate a cat. Walk softly. Stretch at times like a cat. Be smooth and deliberate.

2. *Monkey Run.* Turn the hands and feet so that the fingers and toes point in (toward each other).

FIGURE 20.10   Puppy Dog Run.

FIGURE 20.11   Bear Walk.

BEAR WALK

Bend forward and touch the ground with both hands. Travel forward slowly by moving the hand and foot on the same side together (that is, first the right hand and foot, then the left hand and foot) (Figure 20.11). Make deliberate movements.

Variation: Lift the free foot and arm high while the support is on the other side.

GORILLA WALK

Bend the knees and carry the trunk forward. Let the arms hang at the sides. Touch the fingers to the ground while walking.

Variation: Stop and beat on the chest like a gorilla. Bounce up and down on all fours with hands and feet touching the floor simultaneously.

RABBIT JUMP

Crouch with knees apart and hands placed on the floor. Move forward by reaching out with both hands and then bringing both feet up to the hands. The eyes look ahead.

The teacher should emphasize that this is a jump rather than a hop because both feet move at once. Note that the jump is a bilateral movement.

Variations:

1. Try with knees together and arms on the outside. Try alternating with knees together and apart on successive jumps. Go over a low hurdle or through a hoop.

2. Experiment with taking considerable weight on the hands before the feet move forward. To do this, raise the seat higher in the air when the hands move forward.

ELEPHANT WALK

Bend well forward, clasping the hands together to form a trunk. The end of the trunk should swing close to the

20

FIGURE 20.12   Elephant Walk.

ground. Walk in a slow, deliberate, dignified manner, keeping the legs straight and swinging the trunk from side to side (Figure 20.12). Stop and throw water over the back with the trunk. Recite the following verse while walking, and move the trunk appropriately.

> The elephant's walk is steady and slow,
>
> His trunk like a pendulum swings to and fro.
>
> But when there are children with peanuts around
>
> He swings it up and he swings it down.

Variation: With a partner, decide who will be the mahout (the elephant keeper) and who will be the elephant. The mahout walks to the side and a little in front of the elephant, with one hand touching the elephant's shoulder. Lead the elephant around during the first two lines of the poem, and then during the last two lines release the touch, walk to a spot in front of the elephant, and toss the elephant a peanut when the trunk is swept up. Return to the elephant's side and repeat the action.

▶ **SIAMESE TWIN WALK**

Stand back to back with a partner. Lock elbows (Figure 20.13). Walk forward, backward, and sideways in unison.

▶ **TIGHTROPE WALK**

Select a line, board, or chalked line on the floor as the high wire. Pretend to be on the high wire and do various tasks with exaggerated loss and control of balance. Add tasks such as jumping rope, juggling balls, and riding a bicycle. Pretend to hold a parasol or a balancing pole

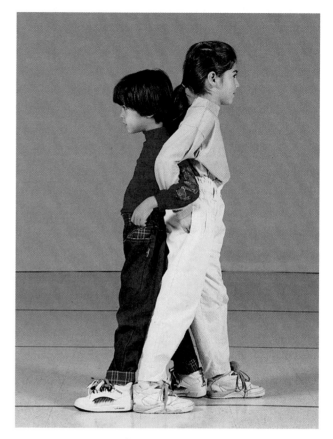

FIGURE 20.13   Siamese Twin Walk.

while performing. Children should give good play to the imagination. The teacher can set the stage by discussing what a circus performer on the high wire might do.

▶ **LAME DOG WALK**

Walk on both hands and one foot. Hold the other foot in the air as if injured. Walk a distance and change feet. The eyes should look forward. Move backward also and in other combinations. Try to move with an injured front leg.

▶ **CRAB WALK**

Squat down and reach back, putting both hands on the floor without sitting down. With head, neck, and body level, walk forward, backward, and sideways (Figure 20.14). Children have a tendency to lower the hips. The teacher should emphasize that the body is kept in a straight line.

Variations:

1. As each step is taken with one hand, slap the chest or seat with the other.
2. Move the hand and foot on the same side simultaneously.
3. Try balancing on one leg and the opposite hand for five seconds.

FIGURE 20.14 Crab Walk.

Tumbling and Inverted Balances

ROLLING LOG

Lie on the back with arms stretched overhead (Figure 20.15). Roll sideways the length of the mat. The next time, roll with the hands pointed toward the other side of the mat. To roll in a straight line, keep the feet slightly apart.

Variation: Alternately curl and stretch while rolling.

FIGURE 20.15 Rolling Log.

FIGURE 20.16 Forward Roll.

SIDE ROLL

Start on the hands and knees, with one side toward the direction of the roll. Drop the shoulder, tuck both the elbow and the knee under, and roll over completely, returning to the hands-and-knees position. Momentum is needed to return to the original position. Practice rolling back and forth from one hand-and-knee position to another.

FORWARD ROLL

Stand facing forward, with the feet apart. Squat and place the hands on the mat, shoulder width apart, with elbows against the insides of the thighs. Tuck the chin to the chest and make a rounded back. A push-off with the hands and feet provides the force for the roll (Figure 20.16). Carry the weight on the hands, with the elbows bearing the weight of the thighs. If the elbows are kept against the thighs and the weight is assumed there, the force of the roll is transferred easily to the rounded back. Try to roll forward to the feet. Later, try with the knees together and no weight on the elbows.

Spotting: The spotter should kneel alongside the child and place one hand on the back of the child's head and the other under the thigh (Figure 20.17). As the child

FIGURE 20.17 Spotting the Forward Roll. (One hand is on the back of the head and one is under the thigh.)

FIGURE 20.18   Back Roller.

FIGURE 20.19   Backward Curl (Handclasp Position).

moves through the roll, give an upward lift on the back of the neck to assure the neck does not absorb the weight of the body. This technique should be used for all forward roll variations.

 BACK ROLLER

Begin in a crouched position with knees together and hands resting lightly on the floor. Roll backward, securing momentum by bringing the knees to the chest and clasping them with the arms (Figure 20.18). Roll back and forth rhythmically. On the backward movement, go well back on the neck and head. Try to roll forward to original position. If you have difficulty rolling back to original position, cross the legs and roll to a crossed-leg standing position. (This stunt is a lead-up to the Backward Roll.)

 FORWARD ROLL (STRADDLE POSITION)

Start with the legs spread in the straddle position. Bend forward at the hips, tuck the head, place the hands on the mat, and roll forward. The performer must push with the hands at the end of the roll to return to the standing position.

FORWARD ROLL PRACTICE AND VARIATIONS

Review the Forward Roll (tucked), with spotting and assistance as necessary. Work on coming out of the roll to the feet. Grasping the knees at the end of the roll will help.

Variations:

1. Roll to the feet with ankles crossed.
2. Try to roll with knees together.

BACKWARD CURL

Approach this activity in three stages. For the first stage, begin in a sitting position, with the knees drawn up to the chest and the chin tucked. The hands are clasped and placed behind the head with the elbows held out as far

as possible. Gently roll backward until the weight is on the elbows (Figure 20.19). Roll back to starting position.

In stage two, perform the same action as before, but place the hands alongside the head on the mat while rolling back. The fingers are pointed in the direction of the roll, with palms down on the mat. (A good cue is, "Point your thumbs toward your ears and keep your elbows close to your body.")

For stage three, perform the same action as in stage two, but start in a crouched position on the feet with the back facing the direction of the roll. Momentum is secured by sitting down quickly and bringing the knees to the chest. This, like the Back Roller, is a lead-up to the Backward Roll. Teach children to push against the floor to take pressure off the back of the neck.

BACKWARD ROLL (HANDCLASP POSITION)

Clasp the fingers behind the neck, with elbows held out to the sides (Figure 20.20). From a crouched position, sit down rapidly, bringing the knees to the chest for a tuck to secure momentum. Roll completely over backward, taking much of the weight on the forearms (Figure 20.21). With this method, the neck is protected.

Spotting: Spotting is not necessary for this lead-up activity. Youngsters can have early success in learning

FIGURE 20.20   Handclasp Position.

FIGURE 20.21 Backward Roll.

the backward roll by using this approach. Children should be reminded to keep their elbows back and out to the sides to ensure maximum support and minimal neck pressure. This is a lead-up activity to the regular backward roll. If youngsters cannot roll over, allow them to practice rocking back and forth with the elbows out. In no case should force be applied to the hips by another individual in an attempt to force the child over.

▶ CLIMB-UP

Begin on a mat in a kneeling position, with hands placed about shoulder width apart and the fingers spread and pointed forward. Place the head forward of the hands, so that the head and hands form a triangle on the mat. Walk the body weight forward so that most of it rests on the hands and head. Climb the knees to the top of the elbows. (This stunt is a lead-up to the Headstand.)

Spotting: In the Climb-Up as well as in the Three-Point Tip-Up, overweight or weak children may need spotting. This is done by placing one hand on the child's shoulder and the other on the back of the thigh.

Variation: Raise the knees off the elbows.

▶ THREE-POINT TIP-UP

Squat down on the mat, placing the hands flat with fingers pointing forward. The elbows should be inside and pressed against the inner part of the lower thighs. Lean forward, slowly transferring body weight to the bent elbows and hands until the forehead touches the mat (Figure 20.22). Return to starting position.

FIGURE 20.22 Three Point Tip-Up.

The Three-Point Tip-Up ends in the same general position as the Climb-Up, but with the elbows on the inside of the thighs. Some children may have better success by turning the fingers in slightly, thus causing the elbows to point outward more and offering better support at the thigh contact point. This stunt is a lead-up to the Headstand and the Handstand done at later levels.

Spotting: Same as for the Climb-Up.

Variation: Tuck the head and do a Forward Roll as an alternative finishing act.

▶ MOUNTAIN CLIMBER

This activity is similar to the exercise known as the Treadmill. The weight is taken on the hands with one foot forward and one foot extended back, similar to a sprinter's start. When ready, the performer switches foot position with both feet moving simultaneously. This activity is a lead-up to the Handstand and teaches children to support the body weight briefly with the arms.

▶ SWITCHEROO

This Handstand lead-up activity begins in the front lunge position with the arms overhead. In one continuous movement, bend forward at the hips, place the hands on the mat, and invert the legs over the head. Scissor the legs in the air, and then reverse the position of the feet on the mat. Repeat in a smooth and continuous motion.

Balance Stunts

▶ ONE-LEG BALANCE

Lift one leg from the floor. Later, bring the knee up. The arms should be free at first and then assume specified positions: folded across the chest, on the hips, on the head, or behind the back.

▶ DOUBLE-KNEE BALANCE

Kneel on both knees, with the feet pointed to the rear. Lift the feet from the ground and balance on the knees. Vary the position of the arms. Experiment with different arm positions.

▶ HEAD TOUCH

On a mat, kneel on both knees, with feet pointed backward and arms outstretched backward for balance. Lean forward slowly and touch the forehead to the mat. Recover to position (Figure 20.23). Vary the arm position.

FIGURE 20.23 Head Touch.

HEAD BALANCE

Place a beanbag, block, or book on the head (Figure 20.24). Walk, stoop, turn around, sit down, get up, and so on. The object should be balanced so that the upper body is in good posture. Keep the hands out to the sides for balance. Later, vary the position of the arms—folded across the chest or placed behind the back or down the sides. Link together a series of movements.

ONE-LEG BALANCE STUNTS

Each of the following stands should be done with different arm positions, starting with the arms out to the sides and then folded across the chest. Have children devise other arm positions.

FIGURE 20.24 Head Balance.

FIGURE 20.25 Stork Stand.

Each stunt can be held first for three seconds and then for five seconds. Later, the eyes can be closed during the count. The child should recover to original position without loss of balance or excessive movement. Stunts should be repeated, using the other leg.

1. *Kimbo Stand.* With the left foot kept flat on the ground, cross the right leg over the left to a position in which the right foot is pointed partially down and the toe is touching the ground.
2. *Knee-Lift Stand.* From a standing position, lift one knee up so that the thigh is parallel to the ground and the toe is pointed down. Hold. Return to starting position.
3. *Stork Stand.* From a standing position, shift all of the weight to one foot. Place the other foot so that the sole is against the inside of the knee and thigh of the standing leg (Figure 20.25). Hold. Recover to standing position.

BALANCE TOUCH

Place an object (eraser, block, or beanbag) a yard away from a line. Balancing on the line on one foot, reach out with the other foot, touch the object (no weight should be placed on it) (Figure 20.26), and recover to the starting position. Reach sideways, backward.

Variation: Try placing the object at various distances. On a gymnasium floor, count the number of boards to establish the distance for the touch.

FIGURE 20.26   Balance Touch.

▶ SINGLE-LEG BALANCES

1. *Forward Balance.* Extend one leg backward until it is parallel to the floor. Keeping the eyes forward and the arms out to the sides, bend forward, balancing on the other leg (Figure 20.27). Hold for 5 seconds without moving. Reverse legs. (This is also called a Forward Scale.)

2. *Backward Balance.* With knee straight, extend one leg forward, with toes pointed. Keep the arms out to the sides for balance. Lean back as far as possible. The bend should be far enough back so that the eyes are looking at the ceiling.

FIGURE 20.28   Hand-and-Knee Balance.

3. *Side Balance.* Stand on the left foot with enough side bend to the left so that the right (top) side of the body is parallel to the floor. Put the right arm alongside the head and in line with the rest of the body. Reverse, using the right leg for support. (Support may be needed momentarily to get into position.)

▶ HAND-AND-KNEE BALANCE

Get down on all fours, taking the weight on the hands, knees, and feet, with toes pointed backward. Lift one hand and the opposite knee (Figure 20.28). Keep the free foot and hand from touching during the hold. Reverse hand and knee positions.

▶ SINGLE-KNEE BALANCE

Perform the same action as in the previous stunt, but balance on one knee (and leg), with both arms outstretched to the sides (Figure 20.29). Use the other knee.

FIGURE 20.27   Forward Balance.

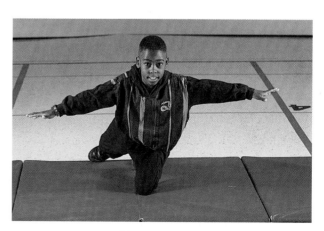

FIGURE 20.29   Single-Knee Balance.

Individual Stunts

▶ DIRECTIONAL WALK

For a left movement, begin in standing position. Do all of the following simultaneously: Take a step to the left, raise the left arm and point left, turn the head to the left, and state crisply "Left." Close with the right foot back to standing position. Take several steps left and then reverse. The Directional Walk is designed to aid in establishing right-left concepts. Definite and forceful simultaneous movements of the arm, head (turn), and leg (step) coupled with a crisp enunciation of the direction are the ingredients of this stunt.

▶ LINE WALKING

Use a line on the floor, a chalked line, or a board. Walk forward and backward on the line as follows. First, take regular steps. Next, try follow steps—the front foot moving forward and the back foot moving up. The same foot always leads. Then do heel-and-toe steps, bringing the back toe up against the front heel on each step. Finally, hop along the line on one foot. Change to the other foot. The eyes should be focused ahead.

▶ FLUTTERING LEAF

Keeping the feet in place and the body relaxed, flutter to the ground slowly, just as a leaf would do in autumn. Swing the arms back and forth loosely to accentuate the fluttering.

▶ ELEVATOR

With the arms out level at the sides, pretend to be an elevator going down. Lower the body a little at a time by bending the knees, but keep the upper body erect and the eyes forward. Return to position. Add a body twist to the downward movement. (A drum can be used.)

▶ CROSS-LEGGED STAND

Sit with the legs crossed and the body bent partially forward. Respond appropriately to these six commands.

"Touch the right foot with the right hand."
"Touch the left foot with the right hand."
"Touch the right foot with the left hand."
"Touch the left foot with the left hand."
"Touch both feet with the hands."
"Touch the feet with crossed hands."

The commands should be given in varied sequences. The child must interpret that his right foot is on the left side, and vice versa. If this seems too difficult, have children start with the feet in normal position (uncrossed).

Variation: Do the stunt with a partner, one child giving the commands and the other responding as directed.

▶ WALKING IN PLACE

Pretend to walk vigorously by using the same movements as in walking but without making any progress. This is done by sliding the feet back and forth. Exaggerated arm movement should be made. (Children can gain or lose a little ground. Two children can walk alongside each other, with first one and then the other going ahead.)

▶ JUMP TURNS

Do jump turns (use quarter turns and half turns) right and left, as directed. The arms should be kept outstretched to the sides. Land lightly without a second movement. Jump turns reinforce directional concepts. Number concepts can also be developed with jump turns. The teacher calls out the number as a preparatory command and then says, "Move." Number signals are: "One" for a left quarter turn, "Two" for a right quarter turn, "Three" for a left half turn, and "Four" for a right half turn. Give children a moment after the number is called and before the "Move" command.

▶ RUBBER BAND

Get down in a squat position with the hands and arms clasped around the knees. On the command "Stretch, stretch, stretch," stretch as tall and as wide as possible. On the command "Snap," snap back to original position.

Variation: *Pumping Up the Balloon.* One child, the pumper, is in front of the other children, who are the balloons. The pumper pretends to use a bicycle pump to inflate the balloons. The balloons get larger and larger until the pumper shouts, "Bang," whereupon the balloons collapse to the floor. The pumper should give a "shoosh" sound every time a pumping motion is made.

▶ RISING SUN

Lie on the back. Using the arms for balance only, rise to a standing position.

Variation: Fold the arms over the chest. Experiment with different positions of the feet. The feet can be crossed, spread wide, both to one side, and so on.

FIGURE 20.30   Heel Click.

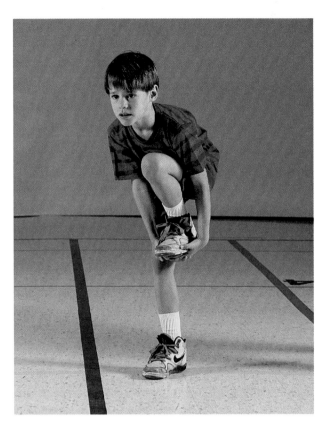

FIGURE 20.31   Thread the Needle.

▶ HEEL CLICK

Stand with the feet slightly apart, jump up, and click the heels, coming down with the feet apart (Figure 20.30). Try with a quarter turn right and left.

Variations:

1. Clap the hands overhead as the heels are clicked.
2. Join hands with one or more children. Count, "One, two, THREE," jumping on the third count.
3. Begin with a cross-step to the side, then click the heels. Try both right and left.
4. Try to click the heels twice before landing. Land with the feet apart.

▶ LOWERING THE BOOM

Start in push-up (front-leaning rest) position. Lower the body slowly to the floor. The movement should be controlled so that the body remains rigid.

Variations:

1. Pause halfway down.
2. Go down in stages, inch by inch. (Be sure that children understand the concept of an inch as a measure of distance.)
3. Go down slowly to the accompaniment of noise simulating air escaping from a punctured tire. Try representing a blowout, initiated by an appropriate noise.
4. Go down in stages by alternating lowering movements of the right and left arms.
5. Vary the stunt with different hand-base positions, such as fingers pointed in, thumbs touching, and others.

▶ TURN-OVER

From a front-leaning rest position, turn over so that the back is to the floor. The body should not touch the floor. Continue the turn until the original position is reassumed. Reverse the direction. Turn back and forth several times. The body should be kept as rigid as possible throughout the turn.

▶ THREAD THE NEEDLE

Touch the fingertips together in front of the body. Step through with one foot at a time while keeping the tips in contact (Figure 20.31). Step back to the original position. Next, lock the fingers in front of the body, and repeat the stunt. Finally, step through the clasped hands without touching the hands.

▶ HEEL SLAP

From an erect position with hands at the sides, jump upward and slap both heels with the hands (Figure 20.32).

Variation: Use a one-two-three rhythm with small preliminary jumps on the first and second counts. Make a quarter or half turn in the air. During a jump, slap the heels twice before landing.

20

F I G U R E 2 0 . 3 2   Heel Slap.

▶ **POGO STICK**

Pretend to be on a pogo stick by keeping a stiff body and jumping on the toes. Hold the hands in front as if grasping the stick (Figure 20.33). Progress in various directions. (The teacher should stress upward propelling action by the ankles and toes, with the body kept stiff, particularly at the knee joints.)

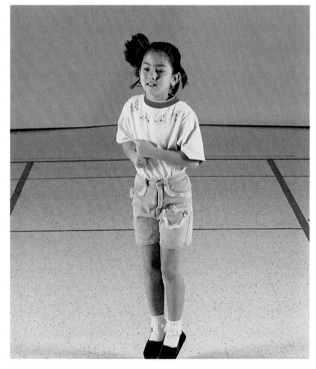

F I G U R E 2 0 . 3 3   Pogo Stick.

▶ **TOP**

From a standing position with arms at the sides, try jumping and turning to face the opposite direction, turning three-quarters of the way around, or making a full turn to face the original direction. Land in good balance with hands near the sides. No movement of the feet should occur after landing. Turn both right and left. (Number concepts can be stressed in having children do half turns, three-quarter turns, and full turns.)

Variation: Fold the arms across the chest.

▶ **SITTING STAND**

Stand with feet apart and arms folded in front. Pivot on the balls of both feet, and face the opposite direction. The legs are now crossed. Sit down in this position. Reverse the process. Get up without using the hands for aid, and uncross the legs with a pivot to face in the original direction. Little change should occur in foot position (Figure 20.34).

▶ **PUSH-UP**

From a front-leaning rest position, lower the body and push up, back to original position. Be sure that the only movement is in the arms, with the body kept rigid. (Because the Push-Up is used in many exercises and testing programs, it is important for children to learn proper execution early.)

Variation: Stop halfway down and halfway up. Go up and down by inches.

F I G U R E 2 0 . 3 4   Sitting Stand.

FIGURE 20.35   Crazy Walk.

FIGURE 20.36   Seat Circle.

body erect, imitate the ball by beginning with a high bounce and gradually lowering the height of the jump to simulate the ball coming to rest. Children should push off from the floor with the hands to gain additional height and should absorb part of the body weight with their hands as well. Toss a real ball into the air and move with the ball.

> *Variation:*   Try this with a partner, one partner serving as the bouncer and the other as the ball (Figure 20.37). Reverse positions. Try having one partner dribble the ball in various positions.

▶ CRAZY WALK

Progress forward in an erect position by bringing one foot behind and around the other to gain a little ground each time (Figure 20.35). (The teacher can set a specified distance and see which children cover the distance in the fewest steps.)

> *Variation:*   Reverse the movements and go backward. This means bringing the foot in front and around to gain distance in back.

▶ SEAT CIRCLE

Sit on the floor, with knees bent and hands braced behind. Lift the feet off the floor and push with the hands, so that the body spins in a circle with the seat as a pivot (Figure 20.36). Spin right and left.

> *Variation:*   Place a beanbag between the knees or on the toes and spin without dropping it.

Partner and Group Stunts

▶ BOUNCING BALL

Toss a lively utility ball into the air and watch how it bounces lower and lower until it finally comes to rest on the floor. From a bent-knee position with the upper

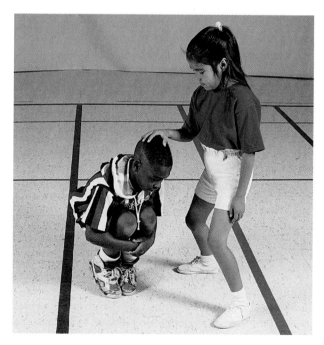

FIGURE 20.37   Bouncing Ball.

20

FIGURE 20.38   Wring the Dishrag.

FIGURE 20.39   Partner Toe Toucher.

high shoulder position, as this is the point of most difficulty. (Partners should be of about the same height.)

> *Variation:*   One child carries a beanbag, a ball, or some other article between the feet, and transfers the object to the partner, who lowers it to the floor.

▶ DOUBLE TOP

Face partner and join hands. Experiment to see which type of grip works best. With straight arms, lean away from each other and at the same time move the toes close to partner's (Figure 20.40). Spin around slowly in either direction, taking tiny steps. Increase speed.

▶ SEESAW

Face and join hands with a partner. Move the seesaw up and down, one child stooping while the other rises. Recite the words to this version of "Seesaw, Margery Daw."

> Seesaw, Margery Daw,
>
> Maw and Paw, like a saw,
>
> Seesaw, Margery Daw.

> *Variation:*   Jump upward at the end of the rise each time.

▶ WRING THE DISHRAG

Face and join hands with a partner. Raise one pair of arms (right for one and left for the other) and turn under, continuing a full turn until back to original position (Figure 20.38). Take care not to bump heads. Reverse.

> *Variation:*   Try the stunt at a lower level, using a crouched position.

▶ PARTNER TOE TOUCHER

Partners lie on their backs with heads near each other and feet in opposite directions. Join arms with partner using a hand-wrist grip, and bring the legs up so that the toes touch partner's toes. Keep high on the shoulders and touch the feet high (Figure 20.39). Strive to attain the

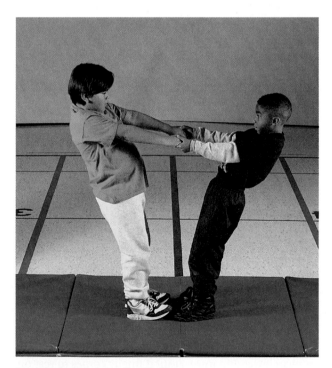

FIGURE 20.40   Double Top.

Variations:

1. Use a stooped position.
2. Instead of holding hands, hold a wand and increase the body lean backward. Try the stunt standing right side to right side.

▶ ROLY POLY

Review the Rolling Log. Four or five children lie facedown on the floor, side by side. The last child does a Rolling Log over the others and then takes a place at the end. Continue until all have rolled twice.

DEVELOPMENTAL LEVEL II ACTIVITIES

In Developmental Level II, more emphasis is placed on form and quality of performance than at the previous level. Stunts such as the Frog Handstand, Mule Kick, Teeter-Totter, and Handstand give children experience in taking the weight totally on the hands. Partner support stunts are introduced. Flops or falls are another addition.

Animal Movements

▶ CRICKET WALK

Squat. Spread the knees. Put the arms between the knees and grasp the outside of the ankles with the hands. Walk forward or backward. Chirp like a cricket. Turn around right and left. See what happens when both feet are moved at once!

▶ FROG JUMP

From a squatting position, with hands on the floor slightly in front of the feet, jump forward a short distance, landing on the hands and feet simultaneously (Figure 20.41). Note the difference between this stunt and the Rabbit Jump. Emphasis eventually should be on both height and distance. The hands and arms absorb part of the landing impact to prevent excessive strain on the knees.

FIGURE 20.41   Frog Jump.

FIGURE 20.42   Seal Crawl.

▶ SEAL CRAWL

Start in the front-leaning rest position, the weight supported on straightened arms and toes. Keeping the body straight, walk forward, using the hands for propelling force and dragging the feet (Figure 20.42). Keep the body straight and the head up.

Variations:

1. Crawl forward a short distance and then roll over on the back, clapping the hands like a seal, with appropriate seal barks.
2. Crawl with the fingers pointed in different directions, out and in.
3. *Reverse Seal Crawl.* Turn over and attempt the crawl, dragging the heels.
4. *Elbow Crawl.* Assume the original position but with weight on the elbows. Crawl forward on the elbows (Figure 20.43).
5. Use the crossed-arm position for a more challenging stunt.

▶ MEASURING WORM

From a front-leaning rest position, keeping the knees stiff, inch the feet up as close as possible to the hands.

20

FIGURE 20.43   Elbow Crawl.

FIGURE 20.44 Measuring Worm.

Regain position by inching forward with the hands. Keep the knees straight, with the necessary bending occurring at the hips (Figure 20.44).

► MULE KICK

Stoop down and place the hands on the floor in front of the feet. The arms are the front legs of the mule. Kick out with the legs while the weight is supported momentarily on the arms (Figure 20.45). Taking the weight on the hands is important. The stunt can be learned in two stages. First, practice taking the weight momentarily on the hands. Next, add the kick.

Variation: Make two kicks before the feet return to the ground.

► WALRUS WALK

Begin in a front-leaning rest position, with fingers pointed outward. Make progress by moving both hands forward at the same time (Figure 20.46). Try to clap the hands with each step. (Before doing this stunt,

review the similar Seal Crawl [Figure 20.42] and its variations.)

Variation: Move sideways so that the upper part of the body describes an arc while the feet hold position.

► DOUBLE-LAME DOG

Support the body on one hand and one leg (Figure 20.47). Move forward in this position, maintaining balance. The distance should be short (5 to 10 feet), as this stunt is strenuous. Different leg-arm combinations should be employed such as cross-lateral movements (right arm with left leg and left arm with right leg).

Variation: Keep the free arm on the hip.

► TURTLE

Hold the body in a wide push-up position with the feet apart and the hands widely spread (Figure 20.48). From this position, move in various directions, keeping the plane of the body always about the same distance from

FIGURE 20.45 Mule Kick.

FIGURE 20.46   Walrus Walk.

FIGURE 20.48   Turtle.

Tumbling and Inverted Balances

▶ FORWARD ROLL TO A WALKOUT

Perform the Forward Roll as described previously, except walk out to a standing position. The key to the Walkout is to develop enough momentum to allow a return to the feet. The leg that first absorbs the weight is bent while the other leg is kept straight.

Spotting: Same as the Forward Roll (Figure 20.17).

▶ BACKWARD ROLL (REGULAR)

In the same squat position as for the Forward Roll, but with the back to the direction of the roll, push off quickly with the hands, sit down, and start rolling over onto the back. The knees are brought to the chest, so that the body is tucked and momentum is increased. Quickly bring the hands up over the shoulders, with palms up and fingers pointed backward. Continue rolling backward with knees close to the chest. The hands touch the mat at about the same time as the head. It is necessary at this point to push hard with the hands to release pressure on the neck. Continue to roll over and to push off the mat until the roll is completed (Figure 20.49). Emphasize proper hand position by telling children to point their thumbs toward their ears and spread their fingers for better push-off control.

Spotting: Rather than spotting the youngster who is having trouble doing the Backward Roll, it may be wise to substitute a different activity such as the Log Roll. If you choose to spot this activity, care must be taken never

the floor. Movements of the hands and feet should occur in small increments only.

▶ WALRUS SLAP

From the front-leaning rest position, push the body up in the air quickly by force of the arms, clap the hands together, and recover to position. Before doing this stunt, review the Seal Crawl and the Walrus Walk.

Variations:

1. Try clapping the hands more than once.
2. Move forward while clapping the hands.
3. *Reverse Walrus Slap.* Turn over and do a Walrus Walk while facing the ceiling. Clapping the hands is quite difficult in this position and should be attempted only by the more skilled. Work on a mat.

FIGURE 20.47   Double-Lame Dog.

FIGURE 20.49   Regular Backward Roll.

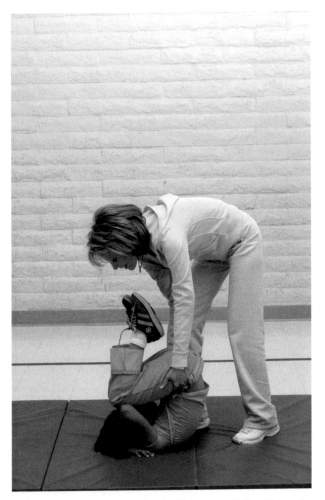

FIGURE 20.50   Spotting the Backward Roll. (The lift is at the hips of the roller. The performer should be lifted, not forced, over.)

FIGURE 20.51   Headstand based on the Climb-Up.

maintaining the triangle position of the hands and the head is essential.

In the final inverted position, the feet should be together, with legs straight and toes pointed. The weight is evenly distributed among the three points—the two hands and the forward part of the head. The body should be aligned as straight as possible.

The safest way to come down from the inverted position is to return to the mat in the direction that was used in going up. Recovery is helped by bending at both the waist and the knees. The child should be instructed, in the case of overbalancing, to tuck his or her head under and go into a Forward Roll. Both methods of recovery from the inverted position should be included in the instructional sequences early in the presentation.

▶ HEADSTAND CLIMB-UP

Take the inverted position of the Climb-Up (page 479) and move the feet slowly upward to the headstand position (Figure 20.51).

Spotting: The spotter is stationed directly in front of the performer and steadies the performer as needed. The spotter must be alert to moving out of the way when the performer goes into a Forward Roll to come out of the inverted position.

▶ HEADSTAND KICK-UP

Keeping the weight on the forward part of the head and maintaining the triangle base, walk the feet forward until the hips are high over the body, somewhat similar to the Climb-Up position. Keep one foot on the mat, with the knee of that leg bent, and the other leg extended somewhat backward. Kick the back leg up to the inverted position, following quickly with a push by the other leg, thus bringing the two legs together in the inverted position (Figure 20.52). The timing is a quick one-two movement.

to push a child at the hips or buttocks, thus forcing the roll. This puts undue pressure on the back of the neck. The proper way to aid a child who has difficulty with the stunt is as follows: The spotter stands in a straddle position, with the near foot alongside the spot where the performer's hands and head will make contact with the mat (Figure 20.50). The other foot is one stride in the direction of the roll. The critical point is for the spotter to lift the hips just as the head and hands of the performer make contact with the mat. This is accomplished by taking the back hand and reaching across to the far hip of the performer, getting under the other hip with the near hand. The lift is applied on the front of the hips just below the beltline to assure pressure on the neck is released.

▶ HEADSTAND

Two approaches are suggested for the Headstand. The first is to relate the Headstand to the Climb-Up, and the second is to go directly into a Headstand, using a kick-up to achieve the inverted position. With either method,

FIGURE 20.52   Headstand based on the Kick-Up.

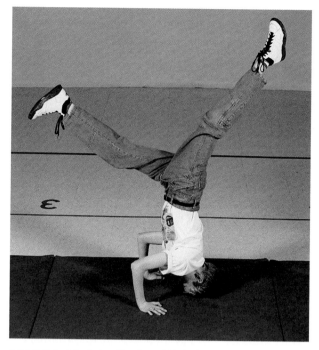

FIGURE 20.54   Headstand Variation.

Emphasize the importance of the triangle formed by the hands and the head and the importance of having the weight centered on the forward part of the head. Most difficulties with the Headstand come from an incorrect head-hand relationship. The correct positioning has the head placed the length of the performer's forearm from the knees and the hands placed at the knees. A useful technique to aid children in finding the proper triangle is to mark the three spots on the mat with chalk. (More lasting spots can be made with paint.)

Spotting: When learning, youngsters can attempt the stunt with a spotter on each side. Each spotter kneels, placing the near hand under the shoulder of the performer. The performer then walks the weight above the head and kicks up to position. The spotter on each side supports by grasping a leg (Figure 20.53). Most of the

responsibility for getting into the inverted position should rest with the performer.

HEADSTAND PRACTICE AND VARIATIONS

Continue work on the Headstand. Try the following variations. (Spot as needed.)

1. Clap the hands and recover. The weight must be shifted momentarily to the head for the clap. (Some children will be able to clap the hands twice before recovery.)

2. Use different leg positions (Figure 20.54)—legs split sideways, legs split forward and backward, and knees bent.

3. Holding a utility ball or a beanbag between the legs, go into the Headstand, retaining control of the ball.

FROG HANDSTAND (TIP-UP)

Squat down on the mat, placing the hands flat, with fingers pointing forward and elbows inside and pressed against the inner part of the knees. Lean forward, using the leverage of the elbows against the knees, and balance on the hands (Figure 20.55). Hold for 5 seconds. Return to position. The head does not touch the mat at any time. The hands may be turned in slightly if this makes better contact between the elbows and the insides of the thighs. (This stunt follows from the Three-Point Tip-Up.)

FIGURE 20.53   Spotting the Headstand.

20

HALF TEETER-TOTTER

This comprises continued lead-up activity for the Handstand. Begin in the lunge position and shift the weight to the hands. Kick the legs up in the air to a 135-degree angle, then return to the feet. This activity is similar to the Switcheroo, except that the feet are kicked higher without switching foot position.

CARTWHEEL

Start with the body in an erect position, arms outspread and legs shoulder width apart. Bend the body to the right and place the right hand on the floor. Follow this, in sequence, by the left hand, the left foot, and the right foot (Figure 20.56). Perform with a steady rhythm. Each body part should touch the floor at evenly spaced intervals. The body should be straight and extended when in the inverted position. The entire body must be in the same plane throughout the stunt, and the feet must pass directly over the head.

Children who have difficulty with the Cartwheel should be instructed to concentrate on taking the weight of the body on the hands in succession. They need to

F I G U R E   2 0 . 5 6   Cartwheel.

learn to support their weight and later concentrate on getting the body into proper position. After the class has had some practice in doing Cartwheels, a running approach with a skip can be added before takeoff.

FORWARD ROLL (PIKE POSITION)

Begin the piked Forward Roll in a standing pike position. Keep the legs straight and bend forward at the hips. Place the hands on the mat, bend the elbows, and lower the head to the mat. Keep the legs straight until nearing the end of the roll. Bend at the knees to facilitate returning to the feet.

FORWARD ROLL COMBINATIONS

Review the Forward Roll, with increased emphasis on proper form. Combinations such as the following can be introduced.

1. Do a Forward Roll preceded by a short run.
2. Do two Forward Rolls in succession.
3. Do a Leapfrog (page 501) plus a Forward Roll.
4. Do a Forward Roll to a vertical jump in the air, and repeat.
5. Do a Rabbit Jump plus a Forward Roll.
6. Hold the toes while doing a Forward Roll.

BACKWARD ROLL COMBINATIONS

Review the Backward Roll. Continue emphasis on the Push-Off with the hands. Combinations to be taught are these:

1. Do a Backward Roll to a standing position. A strong push by the hands is necessary to provide enough momentum to land on the feet.
2. Do two Backward Rolls in succession.
3. Do a Crab Walk into a Backward Roll.
4. Add a jump in the air at the completion of a Backward Roll.

TEETER-TOTTER

The Teeter-Totter is the final lead-up activity for the Handstand. It is performed in a manner similar to the Half Teeter-Totter, except that the feet are held together for a moment in the handstand position before returning to the standing position.

HANDSTAND

Start in the lunge position. Do a Teeter-Totter to the inverted position. The body, which is extended in a line from the shoulders through the feet, should be kept

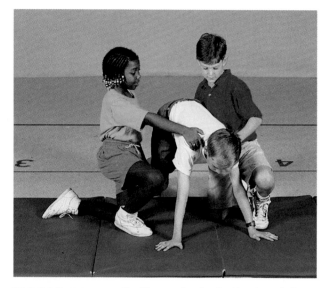

FIGURE 20.57   Double spotting for the Handstand, first stage. (Note the hand support under the shoulders.)

FIGURE 20.58   Double spotting for the Handstand, second stage.

straight with the head down. It is helpful to teach the correct position first in a standing position with the arms overhead and the ears between the arms.

Spotting: The Handstand can be done with double or single spotting. In double spotting, the spotters are stationed on both sides of the performer. Each spotter should have a firm grip with one hand beneath the performer's shoulder. The other hand can assist the lift by upward pressure on the thigh (Figure 20.57). The performer walks the hips forward until they are over the hands and then kicks up with one foot, pushing off with the other and raising that leg to join the first in the inverted position (Figure 20.58). The rhythm is a one-two count.

In single spotting, the spotter takes a stride position, with the forward knee bent somewhat (Figure 20.59 on page 494). The performer's weight is transferred over the hands, and the body goes into the handstand position with a one-two kick-up. The spotter catches the legs and holds the performer in an inverted position (Figure 20.60 on page 494).

Balance Stunts

▶ ONE-LEG BALANCE REVERSE

Assume a forward balance position (page 481). In a quick movement, to give momentum, swing the free leg down and change to the same forward balance position facing in the opposite direction (a 180-degree turn) (Figure 20.61 on page 494). No unnecessary movement of the supporting foot should be made after the turn is completed. The swinging foot should not touch the floor.

▶ TUMMY BALANCE

Lie prone on the floor with arms outstretched forward or to the sides, with palms down. Raise the arms, head, chest, and legs from the floor and balance on the tummy (Figure 20.62 on page 494). The knees should be kept straight.

▶ LEG DIP

Extend both hands and one leg forward, balancing on the other leg. Lower the body to sit on the heel and return without losing the balance or touching the floor with any part of the body. Try with the other foot. (Another child can assist from the back by applying upward pressure to the elbows.)

▶ BALANCE JUMP

With hands and arms out to the sides and body parallel to the ground, extend one leg back and balance the weight on the other leg (Figure 20.63 on page 495).

20

FIGURE 20.59 Single spotting for the Handstand, first stage. (The performer's shoulder is against the spotter's leg.)

Quickly change balance to the other foot, maintaining the initial position but with the feet exchanged (Figure 20.64). Keep the body parallel to the ground during the change of legs. Try with arms outstretched forward. Working in pairs might be helpful. One student critiques the other's performance to make sure that the arms and body are straight and parallel to the floor.

FIGURE 20.60 Single spotting for the Handstand, second stage. (Note knee pressure against performer's shoulder.)

FIGURE 20.61 One-Leg Balance Reverse.

SEAT BALANCE

Sit on the floor, holding the ankles in front, with elbows inside the knees. The feet are flat on the floor, and the knees are bent at approximately a right angle. Raise the legs (toes pointed) so that the knees are straight (Figure 20.65), and balance on the seat for five seconds.

FACE-TO-KNEE TOUCH

Begin in a standing position with feet together. Placing the hands on the hips, balance on one foot, with the other leg extended backward. Bend the trunk forward and touch the knee of the supporting leg with the forehead (Figure 20.66). Recover to original position.

Teachers can have children begin by keeping the arms away from the sides for balance and then stipulate the hands-on-hips position later. In the learning stages, assistance can be given from behind by supporting the leg extended backward, or the child can place one hand against a wall.

FINGER TOUCH

Put the right hand behind the back with the index finger straight and pointed down. Grasp the right wrist with the left hand. From an erect position with the feet about six inches apart, squat down and touch the floor with the index finger (Figure 20.67 on page 496). Regain the erect

FIGURE 20.62 Tummy Balance.

FIGURE 20.63   Balance Jump, starting position.

position without losing balance. Reverse hands. (In the learning stages, the teacher can use a book or the corner of a mat to decrease the distance and make the touch easier.)

Individual Stunts

▶ REACH-UNDER

Take a position with the feet pointed ahead (spaced about two feet apart) and toes against a line or a floor board. Place a beanbag two boards in front of, and midway between, the feet. Without changing the position of the feet, reach one hand behind and between the legs to pick up the beanbag. Now pick up with the other hand. Repeat, moving the beanbag a board farther away each time.

   Variation: Allow the heels to lift off the floor. Use the other hand.

FIGURE 20.64   Balance Jump.

FIGURE 20.65   Seat Balance.

▶ STIFF PERSON BEND

Place the feet about shoulder width apart and pointed forward. Place a beanbag a few inches behind the right heel. Grasp the left toes with the left hand, thumb on top. Without bending the knees, reach the right hand outside the right leg and pick up the beanbag without releasing the hold on the left toes. Gradually increase the distance of the reach. Reverse sides (Figure 20.68).

▶ COFFEE GRINDER

Put one hand on the floor and extend the body to the floor on that side in a side-leaning rest position. Walk around the hand, making a complete circle and keeping the body straight (Figure 20.69). The stunt should be done slowly, with controlled movements. The body should remain straight throughout the circle movement.

▶ SCOOTER

Sit on the floor with legs extended, arms folded in front of the chest, and chin held high. To scoot, pull the seat

FIGURE 20.66   Face-to-Knee Touch.

F I G U R E   2 0 . 6 7   Finger Touch.

toward the heels, using heel pressure and lifting the seat slightly (Figure 20.70). Extend the legs forward again and repeat the process. (This is an excellent activity for abdominal development.)

▶ HIP WALK

Sit in the same position as for the Scooter, but with arms in thrust position and hands making a partial fist. Progress forward by alternate leg-seat movements. The arm-leg coordination is unilateral.

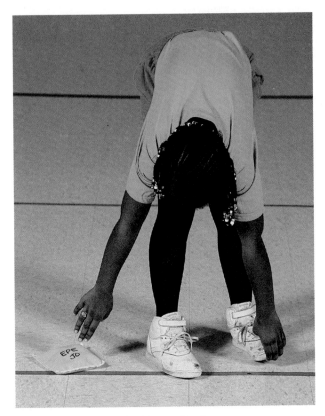

F I G U R E   2 0 . 6 8   Stiff Person Bend.

F I G U R E   2 0 . 6 9   Coffee Grinder.

▶ LONG BRIDGE

Begin in a crouched position with hands on the floor and knees between the arms. Push the hands forward a little at a time until an extended push-up position is reached (Figure 20.71). Return to original position. (The teacher should challenge children to extend as far forward as they can and still retain the support.)

Variations:

1. Begin with a forward movement, then change to a sideways movement, establishing as wide a spread as possible.

2. Work from a crossed-hands position.

▶ HEELSTAND

Begin in a full-squat position with the arms dangling at the sides. Jump upward to full leg extension with the weight on both heels and fling the arms out diagonally. Hold momentarily, then return to position (Figure 20.72 on page 498). Several movements can be done rhythmically in succession.

▶ WICKET WALK

Bend over and touch the floor with the weight evenly distributed on the hands and feet, thus forming a wicket. Walk the wicket forward, backward, and sideways. Keep the arms and legs as nearly vertical as possible (Figure 20.73 on page 498). Be sure that the knees are reasonably straight, for the stunt loses much of its flexibility value if the knees are bent too much. A common error in the

FIGURE 20.70   Scooter.

execution of this stunt is to keep the hands positioned too far forward of the feet. (The stunt gets its name from the child's position, which resembles a wicket in a croquet game.)

▶ KNEE JUMP TO STANDING

Kneel, with seat touching the heels and toes pointing backward (shoelaces against the floor). Jump to a standing position with a vigorous upward swing of the arms (Figure 20.74 on page 498). It is easier to jump from a smooth floor than from a mat, because the toes slide more readily on the floor.

> *Variation:* Jump to a standing position, doing a quarter turn in the air in one quick motion. Try a half turn.

INDIVIDUAL DROPS OR FALLS

Drops, or falls, can challenge children to achieve good body control. Mats should be used. The impact of a forward fall is absorbed by the hands and arms. During the fall, the body should maintain a straight-line position. Make sure that little change in body angles occurs, particularly at the knees and waist.

▶ KNEE DROP

Kneel on a mat, with the body upright. Raise the feet up, off the floor, and fall forward, breaking the fall with the hands and arms (Figure 20.75 on page 498).

▶ FORWARD DROP

From a forward balance position on one leg with the other leg extended backward and the arms extended forward and up, lean forward slowly, bringing the arms toward the floor. Continue to drop forward slowly until overbalanced, then let the hands and arms break the fall (Figure 20.76 on page 498). The head is up and the extended leg is raised high, with knee joints kept reasonably straight. Repeat, changing position of the legs.

▶ DEAD BODY FALL

Fall forward from an erect position to a down push-up position (Figure 20.77 on page 499). A slight bend at the waist is permissible, but the knees should be kept straight, and there should be no forward movement of the feet.

▶ STOOP AND STRETCH

Hold a beanbag with both hands. Stand with heels against a line and feet about shoulder width apart. Keeping the knees straight, reach between the legs with the beanbag and place it as far back as possible. Reach back and pick it up with both hands.

> *Variations:*
> 1. Bend at the knees, using more of a squatting position during the reach.
> 2. Use a piece of chalk instead of a beanbag. Reach back and make a mark on the floor. Try writing a number or drawing a small circle or some other figure.

20

FIGURE 20.71   Long Bridge.

FIGURE 20.72 Heelstand.

FIGURE 20.73 Wicket Walk.

FIGURE 20.74 Knee Jump to Standing.

FIGURE 20.75 Knee Drop.

▶ TANGLEFOOT

Stand with heels together and toes pointed out. Bend the trunk forward and extend both arms down between the knees and around behind the ankles. Bring the hands around the outside of the ankles from behind and touch the fingers to each other (Figure 20.78). Hold for a 5-second count.

> ***Variation:*** Instead of touching, clasp the fingers in front of the ankles. Hold this position in good balance for 5 seconds without releasing the handclasp.

▶ EGG ROLL

In a sitting position, assume the same clasped-hands position as for Tanglefoot. Roll sideways over one shoulder, then to the back, then to the other shoulder, and finally back up to the sitting position (Figure 20.79). The movements are repeated in turn to make a full circle back to place. The secret is a vigorous sideways movement to secure initial momentum. If mats are used, two should be placed side by side to cover the extent of the roll.

FIGURE 20.76 Forward Drop.

FIGURE 20.77 Dead Body Fall.

(Some children can do this stunt better from a crossed-ankle position.)

▶ TOE TOUCH NOSE

From a sitting position on the floor, touch the toes of either foot to the nose with the help of both hands. Do first one foot and then the other. More flexible youngsters will be able to place the foot on top of the head or even behind the neck. Although this is a flexibility exercise, caution should be used; the leg can be forced too far.

FIGURE 20.79 Egg Roll.

Variation: Perform from a standing position. Touch the toes to the nose and return the foot to original position without losing balance. Try the standing version with eyes closed.

▶ TOE TUG WALK

Bend over and grasp the toes with thumbs on top (Figure 20.80). Keep the knees bent slightly and the eyes

FIGURE 20.78 Tanglefoot.

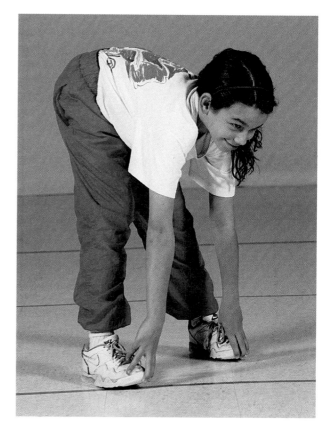

FIGURE 20.80 Toe Tug Walk.

forward. Walk forward without losing the grip on the toes. Walk backward and sideways to provide more challenge. Walk in various geometric patterns, such as a circle, triangle, or square. (This stunt can be introduced in an easier version by having children grasp the ankles, thumbs on the insides, and perform the desired movements.)

Variation: Try doing the walk with the right hand grasping the left foot, and vice versa.

Partner and Group Stunts

Depending on the maturity and nature of the class, it may be more effective to separate boys and girls for some of the partner and group stunts. These activities are enjoyable for youngsters, but some of the requisite touching may cause problems for some classes.

▶ PARTNER HOPPING

Partners coordinate hopping movements for short distances and in different directions and turns. Three combinations are suggested.

1. Stand facing each other. Extend the right leg forward to be grasped at the ankle by partner's left hand. Hold right hands and hop on the left leg (Figure 20.81).

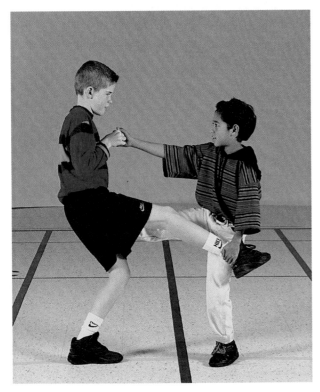

FIGURE 20.81   Partner Hopping.

2. Stand back to back. Lift the leg backward, bending the knee, and have partner grasp the ankle. Hop as before.

3. Stand side by side with inside arms around each other's waist. Lift the inside foot from the floor and make progress by hopping on the outside foot.

If either partner begins to fall, the other should release the leg immediately. Reverse foot positions.

▶ PARTNER TWISTER

Partners face and grasp right hands as if shaking hands. One partner swings the left leg over the head of the other and turns around, taking a straddle position over partner's arm (Figure 20.82). The other swings the right leg over the first partner, who has bent over, and the partners are now back to back. First partner continues with the right leg and faces in the original direction. Second partner swings the left leg over the partner's back to return to the original face-to-face position. Partners need to duck to avoid being kicked by each other's feet as the legs are swung over.

Variation: The stunt can be introduced by grasping a wand instead of holding hands.

▶ PARTNER PULL-UP

Partners sit facing each other in a bent-knee position, with heels on the floor and toes touching. Pulling cooperatively, they come to a standing position (Figure 20.83).

Variation: Try with feet flat on the floor.

▶ BACK-TO-BACK GET-UP

Partners sit back to back and lock arms. From this position, they try to stand by pushing against each other's

FIGURE 20.82   Partner Twister.

FIGURE 20.83   Partner Pull-Up.

FIGURE 20.85   High, medium, and low Leapfrog positions.

back (Figure 20.84). Sit down again. If the feet are sliding, do the stunt on a mat.

Variations:

1.   Try with three or four children.

2.   Try from a halfway-down position, and move like a spider.

► ROWBOAT

Partners sit on the floor or on a mat, facing each other with legs apart and feet touching. Both grasp a wand

FIGURE 20.84   Back-to-Back Get-Up.

with both hands. Pretend to row a boat. Seek a wide range of movement in the forward-backward rowing motion. (The stunt can be done without a wand by having children grasp hands.)

► LEAPFROG

One student forms a back. A leaper takes a running start, lays hands flat on the back at the shoulders, and vaults over the low student. Backs are formed at various heights (Figure 20.85). To form a low back, crouch down on the knees, curling into a tight ball with the head tucked well down. To form a medium back, reach down the outside of the legs from a standing position and grasp the ankles. The feet should be reasonably spread and the knees straight. The position must be stable in order to absorb the shock of the leaper. To form a high back, stand stiff-legged, bend over, and brace arms against the knees. The feet should be spread, the head down, and the body braced to absorb the vault.

Leapfrog is a traditional physical education activity, but the movement is actually a jump-and-vault pattern. The takeoff must be made with both feet. At the height of the jump, the chest and head must be held erect to avoid a forward fall. The teacher should emphasize a forceful jump to achieve height, coordinated with light hand pressure to vault over the back. Landing should be done lightly and under good control, with a bent-knee action.

Variations:

1.   Work in pairs. Alternate leaping and forming the back while progressing around the room.

2.   Have more than one back for a series of jumps.

3.   Using the medium back, vault from the side rather than from the front. The vaulter's legs must be well spread, and the back must keep the head well tucked down.

4.   Following the Leapfrog, do a Forward Roll on a mat.

20

FIGURE 20.86   Wheelbarrow.

▶ WHEELBARROW

One partner gets down on the hands with feet extended to the rear and legs apart. The other partner (the pusher) grasps partner's legs about halfway between the ankles and the knees. The wheelbarrow walks forward on the hands, supported by the pusher (Figure 20.86). Movements should be under good control.

Children have a tendency to grasp the legs too near the feet. The pusher must not push too fast. The wheelbarrow should have the head up and look forward. Fingers should be pointed forward and well spread, with the pads of the fingers supporting much of the weight. The pusher should carry the legs low and keep the arms extended.

▶ WHEELBARROW LIFTING

Partners assume the wheelbarrow position. The pusher lifts partner's legs as high as possible without changing the hand position. The pusher should be able to lift the legs enough so that the lower child's body is at an angle of about 45 degrees to the floor.

Variation: The pusher brings the legs up to the level described, changes the handgrip to a pushing one, and continues to raise the lower child toward a handstand position. The lower child keeps arms and body straight.

▶ CAMEL LIFT AND WALK

In the wheelbarrow position, the wheelbarrow raises the seat as high as possible, forming a camel. Camels can lower themselves or walk in the raised position.

▶ DUMP THE WHEELBARROW

Get into the wheelbarrow position. Walk the wheelbarrow over to a mat. The lower child ducks the head (chin to waist), raises the seat (bending at the waist), and exits from the stunt with a Forward Roll. The pusher gives a little push and a lift of the feet to help supply momentum.

▶ DROMEDARY WALK

One child (the support) gets down on the hands and knees. The other child sits on the support, facing the rear, and fixes the legs around the support's chest. The top child leans forward, to grasp the back of the support's ankles. The top child's arms are reasonably extended (Figure 20.87). The support takes the weight off the knees and walks forward with the top child's help.

▶ CENTIPEDE

One child, the stronger and larger individual, gets down on the hands and knees. The other child faces the same direction, places the hands about two feet in front of the support's, then places the legs and body on top of the support. The knees should be spread apart and the heels locked together. The centipede walks with the top child using hands only and the supporting child using both hands and feet. The support should gather the legs well under while walking and not be on the knees.

Variation: More than two can do this stunt (Figure 20.88). After getting into position, the players should keep step by calling "Right" and "Left" out loud.

FIGURE 20.87   Dromedary Walk.

FIGURE 20.88 Centipede.

DOUBLE WHEELBARROW

Two children assume the same position as for the Centipede, except that the under child has the legs extended to the rear and the feet apart. A third child stands between the legs of the under child, reaches down, and picks up the legs of the lower child (Figure 20.89). The Double Wheelbarrow moves forward with right and left arms moving together.

An easy way to get into position for this activity is to form the front of the wheelbarrow first and then to pick up the legs of the second child. This stunt usually is done by three children but can be done by more.

Partner Support Stunts

Several considerations are important in the conducting of partner support stunts at this level. The lower child (the support) should keep the body as level as possible. This means widening the hand base so that the shoulders are more nearly level with the hips. The support performer must be strong enough to handle the support chores. Spotters are needed, particularly when the top position involves a final erect or inverted pose. The top child should avoid stepping on the small of the lower child's back. In the Lighthouse and the Hip-Shoulder Stand, the top performer can remove his or her shoes, making the standing position more comfortable for the support. When holding the final pose, the top child should fix the gaze forward and relax as much as possible while maintaining the position.

Another consideration regards the size of students. Obvious mismatches should be avoided and an attempt should be made to see that students of somewhat equal size are partnered. Some students may be designated as bases only, since their size restricts their ability to be supported by others. Also, in some settings, it is best to pair students of the same sex when performing these activities to avoid the touching issues.

DOUBLE BEAR

The bottom child gets down on the hands and knees. The top child assumes the same position directly above the support, with hands on the shoulders and knees on the hips of the support (Figure 20.90).

FIGURE 20.89 Double Wheelbarrow.

FIGURE 20.90 Double Bear.

FIGURE 20.91   Table.

Touch up the final position by holding heads up and backs straight.

▶ TABLE

The bottom performer assumes a crab position. The top performer straddles this base, facing the rear, and positions the hands on the base's shoulders, fingers pointing toward the ground. The top child then places the feet on top of base's knees, forming one crab position on top of another (Figure 20.91). As a final touch, the heads are positioned so that the eyes look up toward the ceiling, and the seats are lifted so that the backs are straight.

▶ STATUE

The first child gets down in crab position. The second child straddles either foot, facing the child in crab position. With the help of a third person, the second child mounts each knee of the base child so that the statue is standing erect (Figure 20.92). Hold the position for a few seconds. Partners should be facing each other. The top child should not mount with back toward the base child. (Spotters are important and must not be eliminated until the stunt is mastered.)

▶ LIGHTHOUSE

The support gets down on the hands and knees. The top child completes the figure by standing on the support's

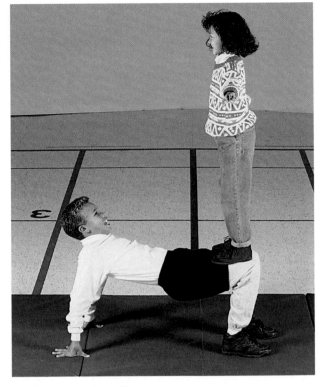

FIGURE 20.92   Statue.

shoulders and facing in the same direction. The lighthouse stands erect with hands out to the sides (Figure 20.93).

> *Variation:*   The support turns around in a small circle, while the partner keeps the standing balance.

▶ HIP-SHOULDER STAND

The support is on the hands and knees, with hands positioned out somewhat so that the back is level. The top child faces to the side and steps up, first with one foot on support's hips and then with the other on the shoulders (Figure 20.94). A spotter should stand on the opposite side and aid in the mounting. Care must be taken to avoid stepping on the small of the support's back.

DEVELOPMENTAL LEVEL III ACTIVITIES

It is unrealistic to expect all children to accomplish the entire list of stunts at this level. In fact, it is unrealistic to think some children will ever become outstanding at the tumbling and inverted stunts. These types of activities are difficult for heavier and less strong students.

FIGURE 20.93   Lighthouse.

FIGURE 20.94   Hip-Shoulder Stand.

Some children at this level will become skillful at both the Forward and the Backward Rolls. The Judo Roll, Cartwheel with Round-Off, and Double Roll continue the tumbling activities. Improvement in the Headstand is expected. Such stunts as the Headspring, Front Seat Support, Elbow Balance, Straddle Press to Headstand, and Walk-Over provide sufficient breadth for even the most skilled.

Tumbling and Inverted Balances

▶ FORWARD AND BACKWARD ROLL COMBINATIONS

Combinations from Developmental Level II should be reviewed. The following routines can be added.

1. Begin with a Forward Roll, coming to a standing position with feet crossed. Pivot the body to uncross the feet and to bring the back in the line of direction for a Backward Roll (Figure 20.95 on page 506).

2. Hold the toes, heels, ankles, or a wand while rolling. Use different arm positions, such as out to the sides or folded across the chest. Use a wide straddle position for both the Forward Roll and the Backward Roll.

▶ BACK EXTENSION

Carry the Backward Roll to the point where the feet are above and over the head. Push off vigorously with the hands, shoot the feet into the air, and land on the feet.

▶ HEADSTAND VARIATIONS

Review the various aspects of the Headstand, using the single-spotter technique as needed. Vary with different leg positions. Add the two-foot recovery. After the stand has been held, recover by bending at the waist and knees, pushing off with the hands, and landing on the feet back in the original position.

▶ HANDSTAND AGAINST A WALL

Using a wall as support, do a Handstand. The arms must be kept straight, with the head between the arms

FIGURE 20.95 Alternating Forward and Backward Rolls.

(Figure 20.96). Some performers like to bend the knees so that the soles of the feet are against the wall.

A critical point in the Handstand against a Wall is to position the hands the correct distance from the wall. It is better to be too close than too far. Being too far can cause the performer to collapse before the feet gain the support of the wall. A mat should be used in the preliminary stages.

 FREESTANDING HANDSTAND

Perform a Handstand without support. Students must learn to turn the body when a fall is imminent, so that they land on the feet. (Spotters can be used to prevent an awkward fall.) Move the hands to help control the balance.

 CARTWHEEL AND ROUND-OFF

Practice the Cartwheel, adding a light run with a skip for a takeoff. To change to a Round-Off, place the hands somewhat closer together during the early Cartwheel action. Bring the feet together and make a quarter turn to land on both feet, with the body facing the starting point. The Round-Off can be followed by a Backward Roll.

 JUDO ROLL

For a left Judo Roll, stand facing the mat with the feet well apart and the left arm extended at shoulder height. Bring the arm down and throw the left shoulder toward the mat in a rolling motion, with the roll made on the shoulder and the upper part of the back (Figure 20.97).

Reverse for a right Judo Roll. Both right and left Judo Rolls should be practiced. Later, a short run and a double-foot takeoff should precede the roll. The Judo Roll is a basic safety device to prevent injury from tripping and falling. Rolling and taking the fall lessen the chances of injury. The Judo Roll is essentially a Forward Roll with the head turned to one side. The point of impact is the back of one shoulder and the finish is a return to the standing position.

Variations:

1. Roll to the feet and to a ready position.
2. Place a beanbag about 3 feet in front of the toes and go beyond the bag to start the roll.

 ADVANCED FORWARD AND BACKWARD ROLL COMBINATIONS

Put together different combinations of Forward Rolls and Backward Rolls. The emphasis should be on choice, exploration, and self-discovery. Variations can involve different approaches, execution acts, and finishes. Try the following variations of the Forward Roll.

1. Roll while holding the toes, heels, ankles, or a wand.
2. As above, but cross the hands.
3. Roll with hands on the knees or with a ball between the knees.
4. Roll with arms at the sides, folded across the chest, or on the back of the thighs.
5. Press forward from a front-leaning rest position and go into the roll.

Try the following suggestions with the Backward Roll.

FIGURE 20.97   Judo Roll.

to a straddle position and finish with the legs brought together in regular Headstand position. All movement is done as a slow, controlled action. (This is a more difficult stunt than the regular Headstand.)

▶ **HANDSTAND VARIATIONS**

The first two stages of the Handstand, done with double spotting and then single spotting with knee support (pages 492–493), should be reviewed. Progression can then follow this order.

1. Single spotting, without knee support
2. Handstand against a wall
3. Freestanding Handstand
4. Walking on the hands
5. Stunts against a wall

Spotting: For single spotting without knee support, the performer and the spotter face each other four or five feet apart. The performer lifts both arms and the left leg upward as a preliminary move, with the weight shifted to the right leg. The lifted arms and forward leg come down forcefully to the ground, with the weight shifted in succession to the left leg and then to the arms. The right leg is kicked backward and upward for initial momentum and is followed quickly by the left leg. The downward thrust of the arms, coupled with the upward thrust of the legs, inverts the body to the handstand position. The placement of the hands should be about two feet in front of the spotter, who reaches forward and catches the performer between the knees and the ankles (Figure 20.98).

▶ **HEADSPRING**

With forehead and hands on the mat and knees bent, lean forward until almost overbalanced. As the weight begins to overbalance, raise the feet sharply and snap forward, pushing with the hands. As the feet begin to touch the ground, snap the body to a bent-knee position

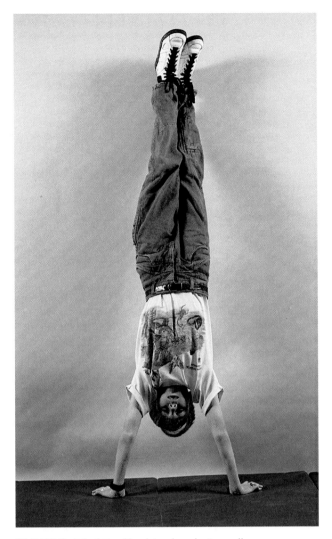

FIGURE 20.96   Handstand against a wall.

1. Begin with a Stiff-Legged Sitdown and go into the roll.
2. Push off into a Back Extension, landing on the feet.
3. Roll to a finish on one foot only.
4. Roll with hands clasped behind the neck.
5. Roll with a ball between the knees.
6. Walk backward using a Crab Walk and then roll.

In addition to these, combine Forward Rolls with Backward Rolls in various ways.

▶ **STRADDLE PRESS TO HEADSTAND**

Begin by placing the hands and head in the Triangular Headstand position. The feet are in a wide straddle position and the hips are up. Raise the hips slowly by pressing to a point over the base of support. Slowly raise the legs

FIGURE 20.98 Single spotting for the Handstand.

(Figure 20.99). Keep control of balance and rise to a standing position.

Spotting: Two spotters should be used, one on each side of the performer. Each spotter places one hand under the performer's back and the other hand under a shoulder. The spotters should give the performer a slight lift under the shoulders to help in snapping to the standing position.

▶ WALKING ON THE HANDS

Walk on the hands in a forward direction, bending the knees slightly, if desired, for balance. (Walking can be done first with a spotter supporting, but this support should be minimal.)

Variation: Walk on the hands, using a partner. The performer does a Handstand and the partner catches the feet. The performer then walks the hands forward until they are on the partner's feet. The two walk cooperatively.

FIGURE 20.99 Headspring.

FIGURE 20.100 V-Up.

▶ WALK-OVER

Do preliminary movements as if for the Handstand. Let the legs continue beyond the handstand position and contact the floor with a one-two rhythm. The body must be well arched as the leading foot touches the floor. Push off with the hands and walk out.

Spotting: The spotter gives support under the small of the back.

Balance Stunts

▶ V-UP

Lie on the back, with arms overhead and extended. Keeping the knees straight and the feet pointed, bring the legs and the upper body up at the same time to form a V shape. The entire weight is balanced on the seat (Figure 20.100). Hold the position for 5 seconds. This exercise, like the Curl-Up, is excellent for development of the abdominal muscles. It is quite similar to the Seat Balance except for the starting position.

Variation: Place the hands on the floor in back for support. (This makes the stunt easier for those students having trouble.)

▶ PUSH-UP VARIATIONS

Begin the development of Push-Up variations by reviewing proper Push-Up techniques. The only movement is in the arms. The body should come close to, but not touch, the floor. Explore the following variations.

Monkey Push-Up. Point the fingers toward each other. Next, bring the hands close enough for the fingertips to touch.

Circle-O Push-Up. Form a circle with each thumb and forefinger.

FIGURE 20.101 Flip-Flop.

Fingertip Push-Up. Get up high on the fingertips.

Different Finger Combinations. Do a Push-Up using the thumb and three or two fingers only.

Extended Push-Up. Extend the position of the hands progressively forward or to the sides.

Crossed Push-Up. Cross the arms. Cross the legs. Cross both.

One-Legged Push-Up. Lift one leg from the floor.

One-Handed Push-Up. Use only one hand, with the other outstretched or on the hip.

Exploratory Approach. See what other types of Push-Ups or combinations can be created.

FLIP-FLOP

From a push-up position, propel the body upward with the hands and feet, doing a Turn-Over (Figure 20.101). Flip back. The stunt should be done on a mat. (Review the Turn-Over [page 483] before having students try this stunt.)

LONG REACH

Place a beanbag about three feet in front of a line. Keeping the toes behind the line, lean forward on one hand and reach out with the other hand to touch the beanbag (Figure 20.102). Recover in one clean, quick movement to the original position, lifting the supporting hand off the floor. Increase the distance of the bag from the line.

FIGURE 20.102 Long Reach.

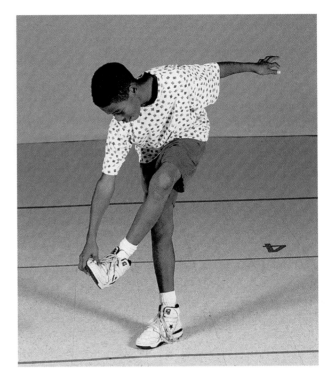

FIGURE 20.103 Toe Jump.

TOE JUMP

Hold the left toes with the right hand (Figure 20.103). Jump the right foot through without losing the grip on the toes. Try with the other foot. (Teachers should not be discouraged if only a few can do this stunt; it is quite difficult.)

HANDSTAND STUNTS

Try these challenging activities from the handstand position against a wall.

1. Turn the body in a complete circle, maintaining foot contact with the wall throughout.
2. Shift the support to one hand and hold for a moment.
3. Do an Inverted Push-Up, lowering the body by bending the elbows and then returning to handstand position by straightening the elbows.

FRONT SEAT SUPPORT

Sit on the floor, with the legs together and forward. Place the hands flat on the floor, somewhat between the hips and the knees, with fingers pointed forward. Push down so the hips come off the floor, with the weight supported on the hands and heels. Next, lift the heels and support the entire weight of the body on the hands for three to five seconds. (Someone can help the performer get into position by giving slight support under the heels.)

FIGURE 20.104   Elbow Balance.

▶ **ELBOW BALANCE**

Balance the body facedown horizontally on two hands, with elbows supporting the body in the hip area. To get into position, support the arched body with the toes and forehead. Work the forearms underneath the body for support, with fingers spread and pointed to the back. Try to support the body completely on the hands for three seconds, with elbows providing the leverage under the body (Figure 20.104). (Slight support under the toes can be provided.) The Elbow Balance presents a considerable challenge. The teacher should take time to discuss the location of the center of gravity. The elbow support point should divide the upper and lower body mass.

Individual Stunts

▶ **WALL WALK-UP**

From a push-up position with feet against a wall, walk up the wall backward to a handstand position (Figure 20.105). Walk down again.

▶ **SKIER'S SIT**

Assume a sitting position against a wall with the thighs parallel to the floor and the knee joints at right angles. (The position is the same as if sitting in a chair, but, of course, there is no chair.) The hands are placed on the

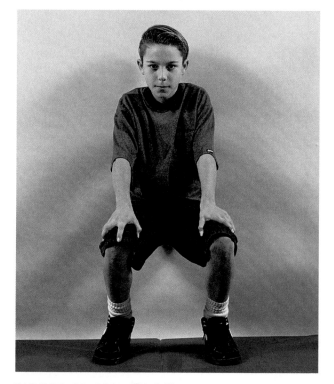

FIGURE 20.106   Skier's Sit.

thighs with the feet flat on the floor and the lower legs straight up and down (see Figure 20.106). Try to sit for 30 seconds, 45 seconds, and one minute. The Skier's Sit is an isometric type of activity and is excellent for developing the knee extensor muscles. It is done by skiers to develop the muscles used in skiing.

> ***Variation:***   Support the body with crossed legs. A more difficult stunt is to support the body on one leg, with the other leg extended forward.

▶ **ROCKING HORSE**

Lie facedown on a mat with arms extended overhead, palms down. With back arched, rock back and forth (Figure 20.107). (Some children may need to have someone start them rocking.)

FIGURE 20.105   Wall Walk-Up.

FIGURE 20.107   Rocking Horse.

Variation: Reach back and grasp the insteps with the hands. (The body arch is more difficult to maintain in this position.) Also try rocking from a side position.

▶ HEEL CLICK (SIDE)

Balance on one foot, with the other out to the side. Hop on the supporting foot, click the heels, and return to balance. Try with the other foot. Good form dictates recovering to the one-foot balance position without excessive foot movement.

Variations:

1. Take a short step with the right foot leading. Follow with a cross-step with the left and then a hop on the left foot. During the hop, click the heels together. To hop on the right foot, reverse these directions.
2. Jump as high as possible before clicking the heels.
3. Combine right and left clicks.

▶ WALK-THROUGH

From a front-leaning rest position, walk the feet through the hands, using tiny steps, until the body is fully extended with the back to the floor (Figure 20.108). Reverse the body to original position. The hands stay in contact with the floor throughout.

▶ JUMP-THROUGH

Starting in a front-leaning rest position, jump the feet through the arms in one motion. Reverse with another jump and return to original position. The hands must push off sharply from the floor, so the body is high enough off the floor to allow the legs to jump under. (The child may find it easier to swing a little to the side with one leg, going under the lifted hand, as indicated in Figure 20.109.)

▶ CIRCULAR ROPE JUMP

Crouch down in a three-quarter knee bend, holding a folded jump rope in one hand. Swing the rope under

FIGURE 20.108 Walk-Through.

FIGURE 20.109 Jump-Through.

the feet in a circular fashion, jumping it each time (Figure 20.110). Reverse the direction of the rope. Work from both right and left sides with either a counterclockwise or clockwise turn of the rope.

Variations:

1. Perform the rope jump with a partner.
2. Jump using different foot patterns (one foot or alternate feet) and using slow and fast time.
3. Establish standards for declaring a class champion in different areas. Some categories could be maximum number of turns in 30 seconds, most unique routine, and most jumps without a miss.

FIGURE 20.110 Circular Rope Jump.

20

FIGURE 20.111 Pretzel.

▶ **BOUNCER**

Start in a push-up position. Bounce up and down with the hands and feet leaving the ground at the same time. Try clapping while doing this. Move in various directions. Turn around.

▶ **PRETZEL**

Touch the back of the head with the toes by raising the head and trunk and bringing the feet to the back of the head. Try first to bring the toes close enough to the head so the head-to-toe distance can be measured by another child with a handspan (the distance between the thumb and little finger when spread) (Figure 20.111). If this distance is met, then try touching one or both feet to the back of the head.

▶ **JACKKNIFE**

Stand erect with hands out level to the front and a little to the side. Jump up and bring the feet up quickly to touch the hands. Vary by starting with a short run. Be sure the feet come up to the hands, rather than the hands moving down to the feet (Figure 20.112). Do several Jackknives in succession. The takeoff must be with both feet, and good height must be achieved.

▶ **HEEL-AND-TOE SPRING**

Place the heels against a line. Jump backward over the line while bent over and grasping the toes. (Lean forward slightly to allow for impetus and then jump backward over the line.) Try jumping forward to original position. To be successful, the child should retain the grasp on the toes. The teacher can introduce the stunt

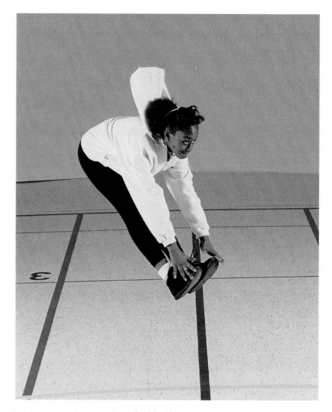

FIGURE 20.112 Jackknife.

by first having children grasp their ankles when making the jumps. This is less difficult.

▶ **SINGLE-LEG CIRCLE (PINWHEEL)**

Assume a squatting position, with both hands on the floor, left knee between the arms and right leg extended to the side. Swing the right leg forward and under the lifted right arm, under the left leg and arm, and back to starting position (Figure 20.113). Several circles should be made in succession. Reverse position and try with the left leg.

Partner and Group Stunts

Depending on the maturity and nature of the class, it may be more effective to separate boys and girls for

FIGURE 20.113 Single-Leg Circle.

FIGURE 20.114   Double Scooter.

some of the partner and group stunts. These activities are enjoyable for youngsters, but some of the requisite touching may cause problems for some students.

▶ DOUBLE SCOOTER

Two children about the same size face each other, sitting on each other's feet (Figure 20.114). With arms joined, scoot forward or backward with cooperative movements. When one child moves the seat, the other child should help by lifting with the feet. Progress is made by alternately flexing and extending the knees and hips. (Review the Scooter [Figure 20.70] before doing this stunt.)

▶ DOUBLE ROLL

One child lies on a mat with his feet in the direction of the roll. The other takes a position with feet on either side of the first child's head. The first child reaches back and grasps the other's ankles with thumbs on the inside and then raises his own feet, so that the other child can similarly grasp his ankles. The second child propels her hunched body forward, while the first sits up and takes the position originally held by the other (Figure 20.115). Positions are then reversed and the roll continues.

Be sure that the top child hunches well and ducks the head to cushion the roll on the back of the neck and shoulders. Also, when the top child propels herself forward, bent arms should momentarily take the weight. It is important that the underneath child keep the knees bent.

▶ TANDEM BICYCLE

One child forms a bicycle position, with back against a wall and knees bent, as if sitting. The feet should be placed under the body. The second child backs up and sits down lightly on the first child's knees. Other children may be added in the same fashion, their hands around the waist of the player immediately in front for support (Figure 20.116 on page 514). Forward progress is made by moving the feet on the same side together.

▶ CIRCLE HIGH JUMP

Stand in circles of three, each circle having children of somewhat equal height. Join hands. One child tries to jump over the opposite pair of joined hands (Figure 20.117 on page 514). To be completely successful, each circle must have each child jump forward in turn over the opposite pair of joined hands. (Jumping backward is not recommended.) To reach good height, an upward lift is necessary. Try two small preliminary jumps before exploding into the jump over the joined hands.

> ***Variation:*** Precede the jump with a short run by the group. A signal can be sounded so that all know when the jump is to occur during the run.

▶ STICK CARRIES

Children of similar weight stand in groups of three, each group having a sturdy broom handle about four feet long. Using movement exploration techniques, two of the children carry the third with the broom handle (Figure 20.118 on page 514). The child who is carried may be partially or wholly supported by the handle. Exchange

FIGURE 20.115   Double Roll.

FIGURE 20.116   Tandem Bicycle.

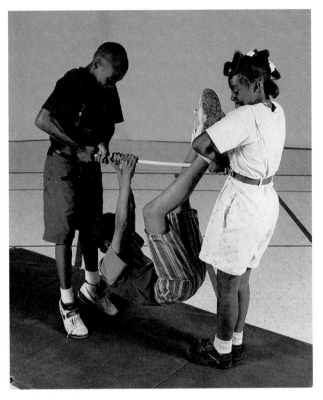

FIGURE 20.118   Stick Carry.

positions. (It is better to use special sticks for this purpose because ordinary wands may break.)

TWO-WAY WHEELBARROW

One child holds two wheelbarrows, but with one in front and one behind. The child secures the front wheelbarrow first in a normal wheelbarrow position. The back wheelbarrow assumes position by placing the ankles

over the already established hand position of the holder (Figure 20.119). (Review the various wheelbarrow activities [pages 502–503] before doing this stunt.)

PARTNER RISING SUN

Partners lie facedown on the floor, with heads together and feet in opposite directions. They hold a volleyball or a basketball (or a ball of similar size) between their heads (Figure 20.120). Working together, they stand up and return to position while retaining control of the ball. Do not touch the ball with the hands. A slightly deflated

FIGURE 20.117   Circle High Jump.

FIGURE 20.119   Two-Way Wheelbarrow.

FIGURE 20.120 Partner Rising Sun.

FIGURE 20.122 Quintuplet Roll.

The upward projection of the body to allow the rolling child to go under is important.

QUINTUPLET ROLL

Five children can make up a roll series. They are numbered 1 through 5, as shown in Figure 20.122. Numbers 3 and 5 begin by going over numbers 2 and 4, respectively, who roll under. Number 1 goes over number 3 as soon as possible. Each then continues to go alternately over and under.

DEAD PERSON LIFT

One child lies facing the ceiling, with body stiff and arms at the sides. Two helpers stand, one on each side of the "dead" person, with hands at the back of the neck and fingers touching. Working together, they lift the child, who remains rigid, to a standing position (Figure 20.123 on page 516). From this position, the child is released and falls forward in a Dead Body Fall.

INJURED PERSON CARRY

The "injured" child lies on the back. Six children, three on each side, kneel down to do the carry. The lifters work their hands, palms upward, under the person to form a human stretcher, then lift up (Figure 20.124 on page 516). (The "injured" child must maintain a stiff position.) They walk a short distance and set the person down carefully.

MERRY-GO-ROUND

From 8 to 12 children are needed. Half of the children form a circle with joined hands, using a wrist grip. The remaining children, the riders, stand within the circle and each one leans back against a pair of joined hands. The riders stretch out their bodies, faces up, toward the center of the circle, with the weight on the heels. Each rider then connects hands, behind the circle of standing children, with the riders on either side. There are two sets of joined hands—the first circle, or merry-go-round, and the riders (Figure 20.125, page 516). The movement of the Merry-Go-Round is counterclockwise. The circle children, who provide the support, use sidesteps. The riders keep pace, taking small steps with their heels.

ball works best. Some caution is necessary to prevent bumping heads if the ball is suddenly squeezed out.

TRIPLE ROLL

Three children get down on their hands and knees on a mat, with heads all in the same direction to one of the sides. The performers are about 4 feet apart. Each is numbered—1, 2, or 3—with the number 1 child in the center. Number 2 is on the right and number 3 is on the left. Number 1 starts rolling toward and under number 2, who projects upward and over number 1. Number 2 is then in the center and rolls toward number 3, who projects upward and over number 2. Number 3, in the center, rolls toward and under number 1, who, after clearing number 3, is back in the center. Each performer in the center thus rolls toward and under the outside performer (Figure 20.121). (Review the Side Roll [page 477] before doing this stunt.)

Children should be taught that as soon as they roll to the outside, they must get ready to go over the oncoming child from the center. There is no time for delay.

FIGURE 20.121 Triple Roll.

FIGURE 20.123   Dead Person Lift.

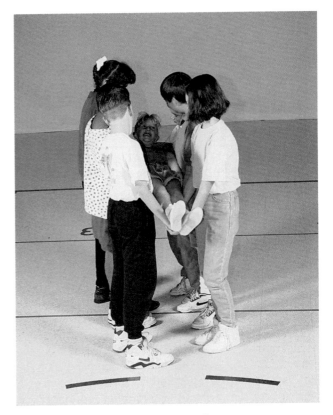

FIGURE 20.124   Injured Person Carry.

Partner Support Stunts

Instructional procedures that assure safety and proper class organization for partner support stunts (page 503) should be reviewed.

▶ FRONT SIT

The support gets down in the same position as for the Back Layout. The top partner straddles the support so that the support and the top partner are looking at each other. The top partner backs up to sit on the support's feet. As the support raises the top partner into a seated position, the top partner extends the legs forward so that the support can reach up and grasp them to stabilize the seated position (Figure 20.126). (Spotting should be done from behind.)

▶ FLYING DUTCHMAN

The support takes a position as for the Back Layout. The top child takes a position facing the support, grasping

FIGURE 20.125   Merry-Go-Round.

FIGURE 20.126   Front Sit.

FIGURE 20.128   All-Fours Support.

support's hands and at the same time bending over support's feet. The support then raises the top partner from the floor by extending the knees. The top child arches the back and can then release the grip and put the arms out level to the sides in a flying position (Figure 20.127). A little experimentation determines the best place for the foot support. (Spotting should be available for getting into position and for safety.)

ALL-FOURS SUPPORT

The bottom performer lies on the back with legs apart and knees up. The hands are positioned close to the shoulders with palms up. The top performer stands on the partner's palms and leans forward, placing the hands on the support performer's knees. The support raises the top performer by lifting with the arms. The top performer is then in an all-fours position, with feet supported by the bottom performer's extended arms and

hands supported by the bottom performer's knees (Figure 20.128).

ANGEL

The top performer stands in front of the support partner. Both face the same direction. The support squats down, placing the head between the legs of the top performer. Support rises, so that the top partner is sitting on support's shoulders. The top performer then proceeds to take a position on support's knees. Support must lean well back for balance, removing the head from between the top performer's legs. The top performer stands erect on support's knees, with arms held level out to the side. The bottom performer takes hold of the top's thighs and leans back to place the pose in balance (Figure 20.129 on page 518). Hold for 5 seconds. (Children need to experiment to determine the best way to achieve the final position.)

SIDE STAND

The support partner gets down on the hands and knees to form a rigid base. The top performer stands to the side, bends over the support's back, and hooks the hands, palms up, well underneath the support's chest and waist. The top child leans across, steadying with the hands, and kicks up to an inverted stand (Figure 20.130 on page 518). (Spotters are needed on the far side.)

> *Variation:*   The top performer, instead of hooking hands underneath, grasps the bottom performer's arm and leg.

PYRAMIDS

Making pyramids is a pleasurable activity for children and uses skills learned in the gymnastics program. Emphasis in this section is on smaller pyramid groups. Pyramids provide an opportunity for creativity, since a variety of figures can be made. Stunts using only one performer or pair should be practiced as a preliminary

FIGURE 20.127   Flying Dutchman.

FIGURE 20.129 Angel.

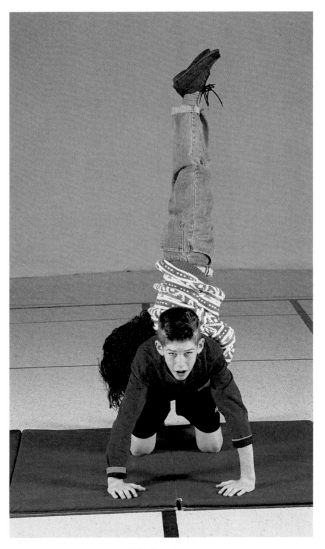

FIGURE 20.130 Side Stand.

to pyramid building with three students. The example presented in Figure 20.131 is composed of three performers; groups larger than this are not recommended as they increase the potential for accidents.

Developing Gymnastic Routines

The teacher can put together in sequence various stunts and other movements. The problems might be structured like the following.

1. Specify the number and kind of stunts and movements to be done and the sequence to be followed. For example, tell the child to do a balance stunt, a locomotor movement, and a rolling stunt.

2. Arrange the mats in some prescribed order so that they become the key to the movement problems. Two or three might be placed in succession, three or four in a U shape, or four in a hollow-square formation. There should be some space between mats, depending on the conditions stated in the problem. The problem could be presented like this: "On the first mat, do a Forward Roll variation and then a movement to the next mat on all fours. On the second mat,

FIGURE 20.131 Pyramid Formations.

do some kind of balance stunt, and then proceed to the next mat with a jumping or hopping movement. On the third mat, you have a choice of activity." The problem can also be stated in more general terms, and children can do a different stunt or variation on each mat and a different movement between mats.

3. Have partners work out a series of stunts. The paired children should be of equal size and strength, so that they can alternate as the support. If children are of different sizes, the larger child can provide support for the smaller, and a third child may act as a spotter to take care of safety factors. After children have practiced for a period of time, each partnership can demonstrate the routines they have developed.

FOR MORE INFORMATION

References and Suggested Readings

Bizley, K. (1999). *Gymnastics.* Des Plaines, IL: Heineman Library.

Mitchell, D., Davis, B., & Lopez, R. (2002). *Teaching fundamental gymnastic skills.* Champaign, IL: Human Kinetics.

Malmberg, E. (contributor), Nance, J. (contributor), & Hacker, P. (1996). *Gymnastics Fun & Games.* Champaign, IL: Human Kinetics Publishers.

Malmburg, E. (2003). *Kidnastics: A child-centered approach to teaching gymnastics.* Champaign, IL: Human Kinetics Publishers.

Mattern, J. (1999). *Gymnastics.* Vero Beach, FL: Rourke Corporation.

Readhead, L. (1997). *The fantastic book of gymnastics.* Brookfield, CT: Copper Beech Books.

Werner, P. H. (1992). *Teaching children gymnastics: Becoming a master teacher.* Champaign, IL: Human Kinetics Publishers.

Websites

www.usa-gymnastics.org/publications/technique/2000/8/specialneeds.html

www.onlinesports.com/pages/I,HK-0-87322-708-5.html

www.geocities.com/Colosseum/Stadium/7261/DEVGYM6.HTM

www.usa-gymnastics.org/publications/technique/2004/4/stretch.pdf

www.usa-gymnastics.org/publications/technique/2004/10/recreational.pdf

www.usa-gymnastics.org

20

Cooperative Skills

SUMMARY

Cooperative activities teach students to work together for the common good of the group. The activities in this chapter provide students with the opportunity to learn skills associated with cooperation and apply those skills in a rewarding activity. Through participation in these activities, students learn cooperative skills such as listening, discussing, thinking as a group, group decision making, and sacrificing individual wants for the good of the group. In addition, cooperative activities provide students with unique challenges. Parachute activities were moved to this chapter because they demand that an entire class work together to accomplish desired outcomes with the parachute. The parachute provides numerous opportunities to teach cooperative skills while students are performing many fundamental motor and fitness skills.

ESSENTIAL COMPONENTS OF QUALITY PROGRAMS

I. Organized around content standards

▷ II. Student-centered and developmentally appropriate

▷ III. Physical activity and motor skill development form the core of the program

▷ IV. Teaches management skills and self-discipline

▷ V. Promotes inclusion of all students

▷ VI. Focuses on process over product

▷ VII. Promotes lifetime personal health and wellness

▷ VIII. Teaches cooperation and responsibility and promotes sensitivity to diversity

NATIONAL STANDARDS FOR PHYSICAL EDUCATION*

▷ 1. Demonstrates competency in motor skills and movement patterns needed to perform a variety of physical activities.

2. Demonstrates understanding of movement concepts, principles, and tactics as they apply to the learning and performance of physical activities.

▷ 3. Participates regularly in physical activity.

▷ 4. Achieves and maintains a health-enhancing level of physical fitness.

▷ 5. Exhibits responsible personal and social behavior that respects self and others in physical activity.

▷ 6. Values physical activity for health, enjoyment, challenge, self-expression, and/or social interaction.

*National Association for Sport and Physical Education (NASPE), 2004.

OUTCOMES

▪ Understand the role of cooperative activities in physical education.

▪ Understand the steps that should be taken when teaching cooperative activities.

▪ Communicate the importance of questioning and discussion following cooperative activities.

▪ Describe several group challenges appropriate for elementary school children.

▪ Present various parachute activities and explain their role as cooperative activities.

THE ROLE OF COOPERATIVE ACTIVITIES

In physical education terms such as *team building, cooperative learning, cooperative,* and *adventured education* are used interchangeably to describe a variety of activities. Although each term has subtle differences, regardless of the label, the primary focus of most of these activities is to teach cooperation. For the purpose of this chapter the term *cooperative activities* is used to describe such activities.

Two primary objectives guide the teaching of cooperative activities. First, cooperative activities provide students with the opportunity to apply a variety of fundamental motor skills in a unique setting. Students are typically asked to perform motor skills in a preset fashion, such as "skip in general space" or "balance on one foot and one elbow." However, rarely are students asked to skip with their hands on the shoulders of someone in front of them, or walk with big steps while placing their feet on small spots, or walk across an area blindfolded while someone directs their moves. Cooperative activities allow students to apply their skills in new and unique situations. Due to this uniqueness, cooperative activities are also enjoyable for youngsters.

Second, cooperative activities teach children personal and social skills necessary to function in daily life. Often, cooperation is thought of as conforming to the norms of the group. For example: Scott doesn't speak out in class unless he is asked; therefore he is cooperative. Although this is a form of cooperation and it is apparent in cooperative activities, a more advanced form of cooperation is also apparent. The more advanced cooperation occurs in activities in which students must outwardly cooperate for the good of the group. This type of cooperation may require students to sacrifice what they want to do in order to help the group. This is best exemplified with an example of a simple parachute activity. The challenge for the class is to get a tennis ball to fall through the hole in the center of the chute. After many different approaches have been tried, the first grade class decides to have everyone raise the chute above their heads. Barbara would rather make waves with the chute by her waist. However, when she did that before, the ball rolled to her and did not go in the hole. This time, she decides to raise her hands above her head so the class can see the ball fall through from the bottom of the chute. This is a simple concept for adults because we have learned that, at times, cooperation—in this case sacrificing individual desires for the good of the group—is necessary to reach class outcomes. Youngsters, however, do not always understand this and thus such activities provide a method of teaching these concepts.

Cooperative activities also teach other social skills. Students are often required to work with classmates they may have never worked with before. In many classes, students become members of cliques and rarely interact with other students, even in their own class. Effectively implemented cooperative activities will require all students to work together. Working together allows students to learn that all students are important, that everyone has similarities and differences, and that all students can assume a role that contributes to the group's effort to accomplish the common goal. Obvious roles include leader and follower, but other student roles, such as being responsible for organizing a plan, keeping the group focused, and remembering specific rules, will emerge. With the variety of roles and the uniqueness of the activities, most cooperative activities offer an opportunity for all students to contribute and experience success. This is especially helpful for less physically skilled students who often benefit greatly from enhanced self-confidence. In summary, cooperative activities teach social skills such as teamwork, communication, decision making, and conflict resolution while using fundamental motor skills in unique situations.

TEACHING COOPERATIVE ACTIVITIES

It is a common misconception that teaching cooperative activities and skills simply means providing students with the appropriate activities. In fact, providing the activities without appropriate introduction and summary can be do more harm than good. Without a series of concluding questions or effective teacher monitoring, negative outcomes may emerge. Quiet, less skilled students may have their usual role of "stay in the back and don't be embarrassed" reinforced while dominant students continue to dominate the activities while learning nothing about group dynamics and cooperation. Explaining what cooperative skills the group will be using before the activity can also limit the effectiveness of the activity. By doing so, you may cause students to begin focusing on specific skills, which prevents them from learning other skills that may present themselves. Students that are told the activity will require them to communicate will focus on listening and talking, but may lose sight of the different roles other students are assuming to help accomplish the goal. Similarly, telling the group what they learned after the activity will diminish the effectiveness of the cooperative activity. For example, after students have participated in an activity that requires discussion about methods of accomplishing a task the teacher says, "In that activity you had to think and explain your ideas to your teammates. That is communication, which is important in cooperation." It could very well be that one student figured out that he had to listen to his group more or that he realized that he did not explain himself clearly. Just as is the case with all education, it is important to remember all children are individuals and they will all approach challenges differently. To encourage individuality and maximize the effectiveness of cooperative activities in teaching cooperative skills, the following steps can be used.

21

Steps to Teaching Cooperative Activities

1. **Set the Stage**   During this first step it is the teacher's job to sell the activity with the following information:

What is the challenge?

What are the rules?

What are the consequences for breaking the rules?

Are there any safety issues that need to be addressed?

During this step, only the essential information to get the group going is provided. This information is best presented in the form of a descriptive and often imaginary story. For example, rather than framing a challenge as getting the entire group through a hoop hanging from a basketball basket, instead place the students in an imaginary jungle where they just found a time-traveling cell. They are lost and their only way out of the jungle is to get everyone in the group through the cell. However, if anyone touches the cell it will push everyone that is already through out and they will have to start over. These types of stories work to pique student interest and allow imagination and creativity to be expressed.

2. **Facilitate**   Once the stage has been set, the teacher's role is to step back and let the students work. For many teachers this is a difficult task because they want to tell students how to accomplish the task or at least give them a few hints. During this step, it is best to simply answer questions and monitor the group for safety. Often, teachers will answer questions vaguely so as to not give too much information that may provide too much of a hint. This forces students to improve their questioning skills to get the answer they need. While monitoring the class, physical and emotional safety are the highest priorities. If youngsters get frustrated and begin making disrespectful remarks, stop or refocus the activity immediately and offer a fresh beginning. During this step, it is not critical that the group accomplish the task. Often, time may run out before the class has time to complete the challenge. In cooperative activities, success does not always mean the task is accomplished; learning to cooperate is more important than completing the task. Much can be learned and gained from simply working on the task. It is critical that teachers allow time for the final step.

3. **Debrief**   Debriefing may be the most important component in effectively implementing cooperative activities. Up to this point, little has been said about cooperation. This step of the cooperative activity process allows for students to share their experiences and affords teachers the opportunity to meet their own objectives (e.g., to discuss listening) and to connect what was learned to daily living.

The foundation of debriefing is open-ended questions. Question such as, "Did that work?" or "Would you do that again?" require a yes or no response and do not foster discussion. The following are examples of open-ended questions:

- What did you have to do in order to accomplish the goal?
- What does "communicate" mean?
- What happened that was positive?
- What happened that could have been better?
- How could you have changed things?
- What does it mean to be patient?
- How can you compromise?
- What would you have done differently? The same?

At some point during the debriefing, it is important to tie in how the skills learned in the activity can be used outside of PE. Again, open-ended questions such as, "When would you have to be patient outside of PE?" or "How would good communication skills help you at home?" will lead into discussion of these ideas.

GROUP CHALLENGES

Group challenges are designed to place students in an unfamiliar situation that requires some form of cooperation. The activities and rules are created in such a manner that the task cannot be accomplished alone. Students must cooperate in an effort to meet the challenge. Many of these activities are most effective with small groups and can be taught in one of three ways. The first method is for the entire class to be working on the same task or activity, such as Pig Ball. Another method is for all groups to be working independently on the same task. For example, Group A could work on Group Juggling in one area, while Group B works on Group Juggling in another space. With this approach it is important that the activities do not become races. This is best accomplished by deemphasizing the speed and emphasizing cooperation. Furthermore, when a team accomplishes the task they should have an additional task to challenge them. For example, if they were able to Group Juggle five times without dropping the ball, they should then try to better their own record. This allows for continuous challenge for all groups. Many of the teaching tips for the group challenge activities are designed for this purpose.

Another method for teaching these activities is through stations. The number of stations depends on the number of groups. Each team reports to a station and begins the challenge by reading the task card. Task cards allow teachers to integrate reading into physical education without sacrificing physical education time. Also, task cards allow for a more efficient and thus active lesson because all of the challenges do not have to be explained. For challenges that may seem too difficult, after getting the class engaged, quickly stop the entire class and explain the activity. Depending on the challenge, place groups at each station for 5 to 10 minutes and then rotate. Not all groups will get to all challenges, but students can be encouraged to work on the challenges at recess, particularly those activities that require few pieces of equipment.

The following group challenges are intended for Developmental Levels II and III. For Developmental Level I, basic cooperative skills such as sharing, listening, and individual or partner decision-making are taught throughout the curriculum. Although these skills are taught and reinforced throughout the curriculum for the older children, these cooperative activities provide a specific vehicle for focusing on those skills and more advanced skills such as group decision-making and group communication.

LIFEBOATS

Formation: Groups of 8 to 12 students

Supplies: Two to three individual mats or hoops, two scooters, and one long jump rope per group

The group is positioned on one side of the gym (a slow sinking ship) and given a scooter (lifeboat) and a long jump rope. The objective is to get the entire group from the sinking ship to the mainland (the other side of the gym) using only their lifeboats. Spaced randomly between the starting and stopping points are three individual mats (or hoops), which are islands in the ocean. Any students that touch the gym floor (water) must return to the starting point or island they were on (if hoops are used as islands, inside the hoop does not count as water). Thus, all students must remain on a mat at all times unless they are traveling across the ocean in a lifeboat (scooter). Students may be pulled with the jump rope but they may not be pushed. Students who are transported across the ocean must remain on the mainland and cannot return to the island or lifeboats; however, if they step into the "water" trying to rescue a teammate, they must return to the final island. Figure 21.1 shows a sign that you can post at a lifeboat station.

MAT FOLDING

Formation: Groups of four to five students

Supplies: One tumbling mat for each group

The group is given one tumbling mat and instructed to stand on it. While keeping their feet on the mat at all times, teams are given the following challenges:

1. Rotate the mat 360 degrees.
2. Move the mat 15 feet.
3. Without using any hands, fold the mat into fourths.
4. Unfold the mat without using any hands.

✓ TEACHING TIP

This is an enjoyable activity to use at the end of a gymnastics lesson.

Lifeboats

The Challenge
Save the entire group by getting everyone to the
mainland using only the lifeboats, islands, and tug rope

Your Equipment:
Lifeboats–Scooters
Tug rope–Long Jump Rope
Islands–Tumbling Mats

Rules:
1. Anyone that touches the ocean (gym floor) must return to the starting point.
2. Lifeboats may only be pulled.
3. Once you make it to the mainland you must stay there unless you step in the water
4. Only one person on the lifeboat at a time.

FIGURE 21.1   Station sign for Lifeboats.

▶ ATTACHED AT THE . . .

Formation: Partners

Supplies: One beanbag or ball for each set of partners

Partners stand on one side of the activity area. The challenge is to get to the other sideline or end line while attached at the hip, head, back, ankle, elbow, hamstring, etc. Locomotor movements can be specified for moving across the area. For a more difficult activity, provide a beanbag or ball for the students to put between the "attached" body parts.

✓ TEACHING TIPS

To add difficulty, after completing tasks with a partner, challenge students to work in groups of three, four, or more.

▶ MOVING TOGETHER

Formation: Groups of four students

Supplies: None

Groups of four students form teams on the sidelines of the teaching area. The objective is for the team to move to the other sideline with the following stipulations:

1. Six feet touching the floor and all team members touching an ankle.
2. Eight body parts (no heads) touching the ground at all times.
3. Half of the team at a high level and half the team at a low level.
4. Every foot touching one other foot.
5. Only four feet can touch the ground.
6. Four feet and one hand must be on the ground.
7. Move with the fewest number of feet possible touching the floor.
8. Move with the most hands and fewest feet touching the floor.

✓ TEACHING TIP

Additional challenges can be made by providing the teams with different pieces of equipment to carry while attempting the challenges. To minimize competition provide each group with a list of challenges. Once they have completed one challenge, they choose their next challenge from the list. This provides continuous activity for all groups.

▶ BALANCE BEAM MIXER

Formation: Groups of 8 to 10 students

Supplies: One low balance beam or bench per group

Students stand shoulder to shoulder on a low balance beam or bench (for younger students) with mats alongside the beam for safety (Figure 21.2). While remaining on the balance beam or bench, students are challenged to get in order based on the following criteria:

1. Alphabetical order by first name from left to right.
2. Alphabetical order by first name from right to left.
3. Tallest to shortest.
4. Month of birth date (January to December or vice versa).

▶ QUIET COOPERATION

Formation: Groups of 10 to 12 students

Supplies: One marking spot for each student

Students stand in a line shoulder to shoulder with a marking spot under their feet. Without talking, making any noise, or touching the gym floor, students get in order using these criteria:

1. Number of pets (fewest to most).
2. Alphabetical by first name (father's, mother's, or pet name can also be used).
3. Alphabetical by last name.
4. Month of birthday (January to December or vice versa).
5. Shortest to tallest.

F I G U R E   2 1 . 2   Balance Beam Mixer.

FIGURE 21.3   Moving the World.

ALL ABOARD

Formation: Entire class scattered with hoops spread through area

Supplies: 15 hoops

Students are challenged to get as many students as possible into one hoop placed on the ground. In order for a person to be considered "on board," one foot must be touching the ground inside of the hoop and no body parts touching the floor outside the hoop. One technique to lead up to this activity is to play **Musical Hoops.** Hoops are scattered throughout the gym and music is playing. When the music stops students move to a hoop, placing at least one foot inside the hoop. More than one student can be in a hoop. Each time the music plays the teacher removes one or two hoops until only enough hoops remain for all students to be aboard.

HUMAN SPELLING BEE

Formation: Squads of five to six players

Supplies: None

Groups of five to six students are challenged with spelling out words, letter by letter, with their bodies while lying on the floor. All team members must be in the letter and the team must identify the bottom of the letter. Physical education terms or spelling words may be used. Also, students can spell out answers to questions asked by the teacher. Mathematical equations could also be written (i.e., $7 \times 7 = 49$), one number and symbol at a time.

MOVING THE WORLD

Formation: Entire class scattered throughout area

Supplies: One large cageball

Using a cageball or other large ball as the world, the world is transported to different locations in the gym. The ball may not be kicked, thrown, or struck, and all class members must be involved:

1. No hands can touch the world.
2. Only feet can touch the ball.
3. Half of the team must be lying on their backs.
4. Only backs can touch the ball.
5. Only elbows can touch the ball and no talking is allowed (Figure 21.3).
6. Students must crabwalk.

TEACHING TIP

Directions such as "move the ball 30 feet northwest" or "move the world 25 feet in the same direction you would travel from Arcanum to Pittsburgh" can be used.

GROUP JUGGLING

Formation: Squads of five to six students

Supplies: One ball or beanbag for each student

Teams of five to six students are formed and each student has a ball or beanbag. A variety of types of balls will add to the excitement of this activity. On signal (e.g. "one, two, ready, toss"), each team member tosses his ball to another teammate and then catches a ball tossed to him (Figure 21.4). The objective is to see how many successful tosses can be made in unison. Typically students will toss to the same person each time. A successful toss occurs when all team members catch the ball tossed to them. After several tosses, the teacher gives each group the responsibility of selecting one team to give the signal for their group.

21

FIGURE 21.4   Group Juggling.

▶ STRANDED

Formation: Squads of five to six students

Supplies: One tumbling mat, three hoops (or volleyball standards), two scooters, and one long jump rope per team

The objective of this challenge is to get all team members from a capsized, but floating, boat (represented by a tumbling mat), across the river via three islands in the river, to the shore. Each island (represented by a hoop) is approximately 15 feet apart from the others and has two team members on it. The remainder of the team is positioned on a boat, or mat. The students on the boat have two scooters and a 16- to 20-foot-long jump rope. While on the scooters students may not be pushed by other students or pulled using the rope; they must find a way to move without touching the "water." Any student touching the water must return to the boat.

▶ SCOOP BALL

Formation: Squads of six to eight students

Supplies: Four basketballs, one hoop, four tinikling poles (or 10- to 15-foot sections of PVC pipe), and two scoops for every team

Teams of six to eight students attempt to move four basketballs approximately 50 feet, without touching the basketballs with any body parts, and place the balls into a hoop. Four tinikling poles and two scoops are provided. The following rules apply:

1. If a ball touches the floor or a student, the ball must be retuned to the starting point.
2. Players may not walk with the balls.
3. The balls may not be thrown, kicked, or passed.
4. Balls that roll or bounce out of the hoop must be returned to the starting point.
5. Students are only permitted to hold one scoop at a time.

▶ CENTIPEDE

Formation: Entire class shoulder to shoulder

Supplies: None

All students stand shoulder to shoulder on a sideline, facing the same direction, with feet touching the person next to them. The entire class must move to the other sideline without breaking the chain of touching feet. If the chain breaks, the group must take three steps back. Students may put their arms around each other if desired.

✓ TEACHING TIP

Some classes may require a progression starting with partners, then small groups, and finally the entire class.

▶ FLIPPERS

Formation: Entire class divided into two teams

Supplies: 30–40 flying disks

The flying disks are spread throughout the teaching area and two teams formed. One team is charged with flipping the disks so they are face up, while the other team attempts to flip the disks to a face-down position. After a practice game, the following stipulations can be used.

1. No hands.
2. Feet only.
3. Students must crabwalk or bear crawl.
4. Feet only, and only one foot can touch the disk at a time.
5. Knees only.
6. Heel only.

▶ CIRCLE UP

Formation: Groups of six to eight students in circle formation

Supplies: Three to four hoops per group

All students join hands or wrists to close the circle. Two students release hands and the teacher places a hoop between them. The students then rejoin hands inside the hoop. Without releasing hands, the hoop must be passed around the circle. That is, each student must pass through the hoop without letting go of their neighbors' hands. Once the students get the hang of going through the hoop, additional hoops are added. If a slightly smaller hoop is available, this hoop can be added going in the opposite direction.

✓ TEACHING TIP

Using one or two hoops, the groups can be timed to see how long it takes to get the hoop around the circle. The team will then get a chance to briefly discuss how to move the hoop faster and then attempt to beat their record. This activity is not a race between groups, but rather an attempt for each group to beat their own best record.

▶ IS IT RAINING?

Formation: Entire class in a circle

Supplies: None

This activity works well at the end of a vigorous lesson. Standing in a circle, the teacher initiates a movement that makes a sound and then the child immediately to her right starts the movement and so on in the fashion of a wave at a stadium. When the "wave" gets back to the teacher another movement is started. The students keep the previous sound until the next one gets around to them. The movements can be any sounds that mimic those heard in nature during a storm. The following are examples:

- Clapping
- Snapping
- Patting quadriceps
- Stamping
- Patting the chest
- Rubbing the hands on the legs
- Rubbing the hands together
- Clucking the tongue
- Making hollow whistles
- Making "Shhhhh" sounds

✓ TEACHING TIPS

Allow students to create movements and lead the changes. Instruct students to close their eyes and rely on their hearing to not only listen for the sound to come around, but to also see if they can figure out what the new movement is.

▶ BE CAREFUL

Formation: Groups of six to eight students

Supplies: For each set of eight students: four blindfolds, 10 beanbags, 10 yarn balls, eight poly spots, eight cones, and three jump ropes

Mark off a 10-foot-by-10-foot area with four cones. Next, scatter the beanbags, yarn balls, poly spots, jump ropes, and remaining cones inside the area in a manner as to not have any straight paths from any one side to another. In partners, students decide who will be the walker and who will be the driver. Roles will be reversed later. The walker is blindfolded and attempts to get from one side of the area to the opposite side without touching any of the equipment. The driver will be standing on the opposite side giving directions such as, "Walk forward" to the walker (Figure 21.5). Thus, the walker must trust the driver and follow strict directions. For each piece of equipment that is touched the team gets one point. The goal is to get to the other side with zero points. As students experiment with the activity, directions will become more specific.

FIGURE 21.5 Be Careful.

✓ TEACHING TIPS

For an advanced activity start one walker on each side of the square and add one point for each walker who is touched. To motivate each set of partners to move faster, allow them to time how long it takes to cross. Then add their time in seconds to the number of points they accumulate multiplied by ten. For example, if a team takes 30 seconds to cross and touches two items, their score is 50. These partners would then attempt to cross and achieve a better score.

▶ ZAP

Formation: Groups of 4 to 10 students

Supplies: One tumbling mat, one magic rope or jump rope, two volleyball standards or device to attach the ropes

The rope is attached on either side of the mat and approximately 3 to 4 feet off the ground, depending on the age of the children. For this activity the challenge is to get the entire group over the rope and to the other side without touching, or getting "zapped," by the rope. However, to enhance the challenge and keep it safe, jumping over the rope is not allowed. In addition, to start, the group forms a circle and joins hands to form a "closed chain." This chain must remain closed throughout the challenge. If anyone is zapped by the rope or the chain is broken (two people let go hands), the entire group must go back to the other side and start over.

▶ KEEP IT FLOATING

Formation: Groups of four to eight students

Supplies: For each group, two balloons, one beach ball, and one hoop for every two youngsters

FIGURE 21.6   Keep It Floating.

Students form a circle and join hands. Their challenge is to keep a balloon up for as many hits as possible without letting go of hands (Figure 21.6). After a few rounds, another balloon is added to increase the difficulty. Finally, a beach ball and one balloon are used.

Variation: For advanced classes, place one hoop between each set of students. Students must keep one foot in each hoop on either side of them. This advanced challenge is best with only one balloon. To integrate other academic content, have the students do the following while participating in the initial version of the challenge:

1. State a different fruit or vegetable with each hit.
2. Count in a foreign language.
3. Count by twos, threes, fours, etc.
4. Attempt to strike the balloon with a different bone or muscle each time and call out the name of that body part.
5. Call out a different lifetime activity with each hit.

▶ SHOE TYING

Formation: Partners

Supplies: Shoes with shoelaces

This is a great activity for the end of a highly active lesson. Partners sit side by side and untie one shoe. That is, of the four shoes, only one should be untied. Each partner then puts one hand behind his/her back. Using both remaining hands cooperatively, they must then tie the shoe. Once completed, instruct the partners to attempt using the other hand. Finally, using only one hand, have them attempt to tie the shoe with their eyes closed.

✓ TEACHING TIP

There are several different ways of tying shoes, and many students do not tie their shoes the same way. For this reason, some partners may become frustrated simply because their method of tying shoes is different. This is a great teachable moment for dealing with frustration and the importance of communication.

▶ PIG BALL

Formation: Two equal teams

Supplies: A rubber pig. If not available, a deflated playground ball will work.

This activity is a continuous version of Alaskan Baseball. Team A stands in a single-file line with the last person in line holding the pig. To start the game, the pig is thrown anywhere in the teaching area. The teacher will have to delineate this area. Team B then hustles to the pig and stands in a single-file line behind the first person to reach the pig. They then hand the pig to the back of the line, alternating between passing it over the head and between the legs. This is best described as "Over and Under, Over and Under." While Team B is doing this, the person who threw the pig is hustling around her team, which is still standing in a single-file line. Each time an end of the line is passed, the team receives a point. This allows all children to score at least one run for their team. When the pig gets to the last person on Team B, the team yells, "PIG," and the pig is thrown anywhere in the teaching area. At this time the person who threw the pig begins running around his teammates, who remain in a single-file line. At the same time, Team A is hustling to the pig and beginning the over-and-under passing. The game continues in this fashion for as long as desired.

✓ TEACHING TIPS

This game is very rigorous. For this reason, after three to four rounds the game should be stopped and some type of instruction given. The instruction could be about cardiovascular health and why the heart is beating faster, why Pig Ball is cooperative, or strategy for the game. However, after a short bout of instruction and rest, students will be ready for more. Also, the teacher can identify a specific locomotor movement or animal movement that all students must use.

▶ PRETZEL

Formation: Groups of 6 to 10 students

Supplies: None

Students stand shoulder to shoulder in a circle with arms extended in front. Each student must grasp two other hands, one in each hand. The hands that each student grasps cannot be of the same person, and they cannot be of the person beside them. The group must then undo the pretzel they have just created to form a circle without letting go of hands. Once unraveled, some people may be facing towards the center and some away from the center. Figure 21.7 shows a sign that you could place at a Pretzel station.

▶ WHO'S LEADING?

Formation: Entire class in a circle
Supplies: None

The entire class stands shoulder to shoulder in a circle. One student volunteers to go in the middle and cover her eyes. The teacher then selects a volunteer to lead the class in movements while remaining in the circle. This must be done quietly so the person in the middle does not know who the leader is. The teacher will need to provide the leader with examples of movements such as jogging or skipping in place, bicep curls, jumping jacks, etc. The leader will also be instructed to change activities every few seconds. The person in the middle then opens her eyes and watches the movements. She must stay in the middle but may scan the entire class in an effort to find the leader as he changes movements.

✓ TEACHING TIPS

To add difficulty, encourage the leader to make small changes in movements. For example, start with normal jumping jacks and then move to skier jacks, and then to skiers with no arm movements and finally walking in place. Also, provide the guesser with the idea of watching one-half of the circle. If the activity changes and they don't see anyone do it first, the leader is probably in the other half of the circle. Remind followers to not give the leader away by staring at her.

▶ HOW ARE WE ALIKE?

Formation: Partners
Supplies: None

This activity is a great one for the physical education orientation held at the beginning of the school year, when students are getting to know each other and the teacher. Students join with a partner and discuss, "How are we alike?" The teacher should give a few categories, such as appearance, family, favorite activities, and birthdays, and then let the students talk. Before grouping students with a different partner or a group of four to repeat the activity, allow volunteers to share their findings.

✓ TEACHING TIPS

After "How are we alike?" have students find out "How are we different?" This sets the tone for a physical education setting in which children understand that we all have similarities and we all have differences and that is okay. It is important for students to understand early on that respecting similarities and differences is an important component of working with others.

FIGURE 21.7   Station sign for the Pretzel.

▶ **LILY PADS**

Formation: Groups of 6–15 students

Supplies: One poly spot per child

Students will begin standing on their poly spots, or lily pads, in a straight line. Each lily pad should be about 12 inches apart. The team's challenge is to reverse their order so that the two youngsters on the end switch places, the second to last switch places, etc. See below for a visual explanation. The catch is that each member of the team must have at least one foot on a lily pad at all times. If either of these rules is broken, the teams must start over in the original order.

START	FINISH
1 2 3 4 5 6 7 8	8 7 6 5 4 3 2 1

✓ **TEACHING TIPS**

If poly spots are not available, this activity can also be done using a line or a long piece of tape. Simply make the rule that one foot must be on the tape at all times.

▶ **THE CELL**

Formation: Groups of five to six students

Supplies: One tumbling mat and one hula hoop suspended from a basketball hoop. The hoop should be about 2 to 4 feet off of the mat at its lowest point.

Students are charged with the task of getting everyone on the team through the hoop, or cell. No team member may touch the hoop. Jumping through the hoop is not allowed. Students may step through or the group may "hand" team members through.

✓ **TEACHING TIP**

The height of the hoop will determine the difficulty of the challenge. For an additional challenge, require that all team members hold hands throughout the challenge.

▶ **DOT BRIDGE**

Formation: Groups of five to six students

Supplies: One rubber dot per player plus one additional dot

The challenge is for students to get from one side of the river (teaching area) to the other, but they can't touch the water (the floor). The only tools they have are their floating dots. If anyone touches the water the entire team must start over

> **Variations:** To add difficulty, place hazards (hoops, cones, etc.) that the students must avoid throughout the river to prevent the group from moving straight across the river. Also, add the rule that if at any time a dot is not being touched, it sinks and can no longer be used.

ACTIVITIES WITH PARACHUTES

Parachute play can be enjoyed by children of all ages while teaching them a variety of skills, including cooperation skills. Without all students working together, many of the tasks are difficult to accomplish. Activities must be selected carefully for younger children, since some of the skills presented would be difficult for them. One parachute is generally sufficient for a class of 30 children. Parachutes come in different sizes, but those with diameters ranging from 24 to 32 feet are suitable for a regular class. The size with most utility is the 28-foot parachute. Each parachute has an opening near the top to allow trapped air to escape and to keep the parachute shaped properly. Most parachutes are constructed of nylon. A parachute should stretch tight and not sag in the middle when it is pulled on by children spaced around it. One that does not do so has limited usefulness.

Values of Parachute Play

For most adults and children, parachute activities rank very high on the all-time enjoyable physical education activities. In addition to being enjoyable, parachute play holds many educational opportunities as well. Movement concepts and fundamental motor skills can be learned and reinforced through parachute play. Levels of movement, speed, weight transfer, force, direction, balancing, pulling, bending, twisting, and all locomotor movements can all be incorporated and taught while using the parachute.

Parachutes provide an interesting means of accomplishing physical fitness goals as well: a good development of strength, agility, coordination, and endurance. Strength development is focused especially on the arms, hands, and shoulder girdle. At times, however, strength demands are made on the entire body. A variety of movement possibilities, some of which are rhythmic, can be used in parachute play. Locomotor skills can be practiced while manipulating the parachute. Rhythmic beats of the tom-tom or appropriate music can guide locomotor movements. Lastly, parachute play can also be used to teach cooperation. The success and enjoyment gained from many parachute activities are dependent on group and individual cooperation. Without every student working together, the tasks cannot be completed. If one child decides to not sit on his part of the chute to make the dome, the air will escape and the dome will collapse.

Grips

The grips used in handling the parachute are comparable to those employed in hanging activities on an apparatus. Grips can be with one or two hands, overhand (palms facing away), underhand (palms facing toward), or mixed (one hand underhand and the other overhand). The grips should be varied.

Instructional Procedures

1. Certain terms peculiar to parachute activity must be explained carefully. Terms such as *inflate, deflate, float, dome,* and *mushroom* need to be clarified when they are introduced.

2. For preliminary explanations, the parachute can be stretched out on the ground in its circular pattern, with the children seated just far enough away so that they cannot touch the parachute during instructions. When the children hold the parachute during later explanations, they should retain their hold lightly, letting the center of the parachute drop to the ground. Children must be taught to exercise control and not to manipulate the parachute while explanations are in progress.

3. The teacher explains the activity, demonstrating as needed. If there are no questions, the activity is initiated with a command such as "Ready—begin!"

4. Squads can be used to form the parachute circle, with each squad occupying a quarter of the chute's circumference. Squads are useful for competitive units in game activity.

5. The teacher must watch for fatigue, particularly with younger children.

Activities are presented according to type, with variations and suggestions for supplementary activities included. Unless otherwise specified, activities begin and halt on signal. Pupils' suggestions can broaden the scope of activity.

Exercise Activities

Exercises should be done vigorously and with enough repetitions to challenge the children. In addition to the exercises presented, others can be adapted to parachute play.

▶ TOE TOUCHER

Sit with feet extended under the parachute and hold the chute taut with a two-hand grip, drawing it up to the chin. Bend forward and touch the grip to the toes. Return parachute to stretched position.

▶ ABDOMINAL CURL-UP (GOOD MORNING AND GOOD NIGHT)

Extend the body in supine position under the parachute in curl-up position, so that the chute comes up to the chin when held taut. Do Curl-Ups, returning each time to the stretched chute position. Students say "Good morning!" when they rise to the sitting position and "Good night!" when they return to the supine position.

▶ DORSAL LIFT

Lie prone, with head toward the parachute and feet pointed back, away from it. Grip the chute and slide toward the feet until there is some tension on the chute. Raise the chute off the ground with a vigorous lift of the arms, until head and chest rise off the ground. Return.

▶ V-SIT

Lie supine, with head toward the chute. Do V-Sits by raising the upper and lower parts of the body simultaneously into a V-shaped position. The knees should be kept straight.

▶ BACKWARD PULL

Face the parachute and pull back, away from its center. Pulls can be made from a sitting, kneeling, or standing position.

▶ OTHER PULLS

With arm flexed, do Side Pulls with either arm. Other variations of pulling can be devised.

▶ HIP WALK AND SCOOTER

Begin with the parachute taut. Move forward with the Scooter (page 495) or Hip Walk (page 496). Move back to place with the same movement until the chute is taut again.

▶ ELEVATOR

Begin with the chute taut and at ground level. On the command "Elevator up," lift the chute overhead while keeping it stretched tight. On the command "Elevator down," lower the chute to starting position. Lowering and raising can be done quickly or in increments.

21

Levels can also bring in body part identification, with children holding the chute even with their head, nose, chin, shoulders, chest, waist, thighs, knees, ankles, and toes.

► RUNNING IN PLACE

Run in place while holding the chute at different levels.

► ISOMETRICS

Hold the chute taut at shoulder level and try to stretch it for 10 seconds. Many other isometric exercises can be performed with the parachute to develop all body parts.

Dome Activities

To make a dome, children begin with the parachute on the floor, holding with two hands and kneeling on one knee. To trap air under the chute, children stand up quickly, thrusting their arms above the head (Figure 21.8), and then return to starting position (Figure 21.9). Some or all of the children can change to the inside of the chute on the down movement. Domes can also be made while moving in a circle.

► STUDENTS UNDER THE CHUTE

Tasks for under the chute can be specified, such as turning a certain number of turns with a jump rope, throwing and catching a beanbag, or bouncing a ball a number of times. The needed objects should be under the chute before the dome is made.

► NUMBER EXCHANGE

Children are numbered from one to four. The teacher calls a number as the dome is made, and those with the number called must change position to be under the dome before the chute comes down. Locomotor movements can be varied.

► PUNCHING BAG

Children make a dome and stand on the edges. They then punch at the chute while slowly and gently walking the edges of the chute toward the center.

► TIDAL WAVE OR BUBBLE

Youngsters create a dome and then stand on the edges. The teacher then pushes the chute to the left while still

FIGURE 21.8 Making a dome.

FIGURE 21.9 Holding the air inside a dome.

standing on the edges. The person to the teacher's left follows and pushes the parachute to the left. Each person then continues pushing the parachute in the same direction immediately after the person before them while keeping his feet on the edges. After a few rounds a bubble, or wave, of air will begin quickly circulating around the chute.

 BLOOMING FLOWER

Children make a dome and kneel with both knees on the edge of the chute. Youngsters hold hands around the chute and lean in and out to represent a blooming flower opening.

LIGHTS OUT

While making a dome, the children take two steps toward the center and sit inside the chute. The chute can be held with the hands at the side or by sitting on it.

CLASS PICTURE

After making a dome, students carefully move to their knees and then to their stomach. While lying on their

stomach and with the parachute in their hands, students bring their hands to their shoulders. This leaves only their head inside the chute.

MUSHROOM ACTIVITIES

To form a mushroom, students begin with the chute on the ground, kneeling on one knee and holding with two hands. They stand up quickly, thrusting the arms overhead. Keeping the arms overhead, each walks forward three or four steps toward the center. The arms are held overhead until the chute is deflated.

MUSHROOM RELEASE

All children release at the peak of inflation and either run out from under the chute or move to the center and sit down, with the chute descending on top of them.

MUSHROOM RUN

Children make a mushroom. As soon as they move into the center, they release holds and run once around the inside of the chute, counterclockwise, back to place.

21

Activities with Equipment

▶ **BALL CIRCLE**

Place a basketball or a cageball on the raised chute. Make the ball roll around the chute in a large circle, controlling it by raising or lowering the chute. Try the same with two balls. A beach ball is also excellent.

▶ **POPCORN**

Place a number of beanbags (from 6 to 10) on the chute. Shake the chute to make them rise like corn popping (Figure 21.10).

▶ **CAGEBALL ELEVATOR**

A two-foot cageball is placed on the chute. On signal, the class elevates the chute and allows it to make a mushroom. Just before the chute with the ball on it reaches its apex, youngsters snap the chute to the floor. Done correctly, the cageball should be elevated to the ceiling.

▶ **TEAM BALL**

Divide the class in half, each team defending half of the chute. Using from two to six balls of any variety, try to

bounce the balls off the opponents' side, scoring one point for each ball.

▶ **POISON SNAKE**

Divide into teams. Place from 6 to 10 jump ropes on the chute. Shake the chute and try to make the ropes hit players on the other side. For each rope that touches one team member, that team has a point scored against it. The team with the lower score is the winner.

▶ **CIRCULAR DRIBBLE**

Each child has a ball suitable for dribbling. The object is to run in circular fashion counterclockwise, holding onto the chute with the left hand and dribbling with the right hand, retaining control of the ball. As an equalizer for left-handers, try the dribbling clockwise. The dribble should be started first, and then, on signal, children start to run. A child who loses a ball must recover it and try to hook on at his or her original place.

▶ **HOLE IN ONE**

Use four or more plastic whiffle balls the size of golf balls. The balls should be of two different colors. The class is

 FIGURE 21.10   Popping popcorn.

divided into two teams on opposite sides of the chute. The object is to shake the other team's balls into the hole in the center of the chute.

Other Activities

▶ MERRY-GO-ROUND MOVEMENTS

Merry-go-round movements, in which children rotate the chute while keeping the center hole over the same spot, offer many opportunities for locomotor movements, either free or to the beat of a tom-tom. European Rhythmic Running is particularly appropriate. Also appropriate are fundamental movements, such as walking, running, hopping, skipping, galloping, sliding, draw steps, and grapevine steps. The parachute can be held at different levels. Holds can be one- or two-handed.

▶ SHAKING THE RUG AND MAKING WAVES

Shaking the Rug involves rapid movements of the parachute, either light or heavy. Making Waves involves large movements to send billows of cloth up and down. Waves can be small, medium, or high. Different types of waves can be made by having children alternate their up-and-down motions, or by having the class work in small groups around the chute. These small groups take turns showing what they can do. For a more demanding activity, children can perform locomotor movements while they shake the rug.

▶ CHUTE CRAWL

Half the class, either standing or kneeling, stretches the chute at waist level parallel to the ground. The remaining children crawl under the chute to the opposite side from their starting position.

▶ KITE RUN

The class holds the chute on one side with one hand. The leader points in the direction they are to run while holding the chute aloft like a kite.

▶ RUNNING NUMBER GAME

The children around the chute count off by fours; then they run lightly, holding the chute in one hand. The teacher calls out one of the numbers. Children with that number immediately release their grip on the chute and run forward to the next place vacated. They must put on a burst of speed to move ahead.

▶ ROUTINES TO MUSIC

Like other routines, parachute activities can be adapted to music. A sequence should be based on eight counts, with the routine composed of an appropriate number of sequences.

▶ TUG-OF-WAR

For team tug-of-war, divide the class in halves. On signal, teams pull against each other and try to reach a line located behind them (Figure 21.11). Another approach

FIGURE 21.11   Parachute Tug-of-War.

that is often more enjoyable for primary-age children is an individual tug, in which all children pull in any direction they desire.

► ### ACTION SONGS AND DANCES

A number of action songs, games, and dances can be performed while children hold on to a parachute. The following are suggested: Carousel (page 431), Bingo (page 438), and Seven Jumps (page 428).

FOR MORE INFORMATION

References and Suggested Readings

Dyson, B., & Rubin, A. (2003). Implementing cooperative learning in elementary physical education. *JOPERD, 74*(1), 48–53.

Gabbei, R. (2004). Generating effective facilitation questions for team-building/personal-challenge activities. *JOPERD, 75*(9), 20–24, 49.

Glover, D.R., & Midura, D.W. (1992). *Team building through physical challenges.* Champaign, IL: Human Kinetics.

Grineski, S. (1996). *Cooperative learning in physical education.* Champaign, IL: Human Kinetics.

Hall, H. (2002). Team building made easy. *Strategies,* 15(6), 27–29.

Le Fevre, D.N. (2002). *Best new games.* Champaign, IL: Human Kinetics.

Midura, D.W., & Glover, D.R. (1995). *More team building challenges.* Champaign, IL: Human Kinetics.

Rogers, K. (2004). Team building for young students. *Strategies,* 17(4), 17–19.

Rohnke, K. & Butler, S. (1995). *Quicksilver: Adventure games, initiative problems, trust activities and a guide to effective leadership.* Dubuque, IA: Kendall/Hunt Publishing Co.

Websites

Project Adventure
www.pa.org

PE Central Cooperative Lessons
www.pecentral.org/lessonideas/searchresults.asp?subcategory=cooperative+learning

Team-Building Activities
www.corporategames.com
www.wilderdom.com/games/InitiativeGames.html
www.teachingideas.co.uk/pe/contents.htm

C H A P T E R

22

Game Skills

SUMMARY

Games are excellent activities for developing social skills. Students can be taught to display appropriate interactive skills, such as leading, following, and making decisions. Cooperative skills that include following directions, accepting individual differences, and participating in a teamwork situation are necessary for reaching common goals. Game situations offer many scenarios for teaching sportsmanship behavior. Games that involve only a few children, allow some children to dominate, or offer little opportunity for skill development should not be part of the program. Children should be allowed the opportunity to create and modify games to meet their needs. Safety is a primary concern in the selection and presentation of game activities.

ESSENTIAL COMPONENTS OF QUALITY PROGRAMS

▷ **I. Organized around content standards**

▷ **II. Student-centered and developmentally appropriate**

▷ **III. Physical activity and motor skill development form the core of the program**

▷ **IV. Teaches management skills and self-discipline**

▷ **V. Promotes inclusion of all students**

▷ **VI. Focuses on process over product**

VII. Promotes lifetime personal health and wellness

▷ **VIII. Teaches cooperation and responsibility and promotes sensitivity to diversity**

NATIONAL STANDARDS FOR PHYSICAL EDUCATION*

▷ 1. **Demonstrates competency in motor skills and movement patterns needed to perform a variety of physical activities.**

▷ 2. **Demonstrates understanding of movement concepts, principles, and tactics as they apply to the learning and performance of physical activities.**

▷ 3. **Participates regularly in physical activity.**

▷ 4. **Achieves and maintains a health-enhancing level of physical fitness.**

▷ 5. **Exhibits responsible personal and social behavior that respects self and others in physical activity.**

▷ 6. **Values physical activity for health, enjoyment, challenge, self-expression, and/or social interaction.**

*National Association for Sport and Physical Education (NASPE), 2004.

OUTCOMES

▪ Explain various ways in which games can be created or modified.

▪ Understand safety precautions associated with the teaching of games.

▪ Cite various ways to teach games effectively.

▪ Identify games that provide maximum participation and afford an opportunity for skill development.

▪ List games that can be explained quickly and can be implemented quickly.

▪ Classify various games according to developmental levels.

Games make a valuable contribution to the growth and development of youngsters. Through games, children receive an opportunity to experience success and accomplishment. Some social objectives that can be accomplished through games are the development of interpersonal skills, understanding rules and limitations, and learning how to behave in a variety of competitive and cooperative situations. Games are a laboratory where children can apply physical skills in a game-like setting. Many games help develop large-muscle groups and enhance the child's ability to run, dodge, start, and stop under control while sharing space with others. By applying strategy in games, children learn the importance of alertness and the mental aspect of participation.

As an important part of the physical education program, games should be scrutinized and evaluated in terms of what they offer children. Many traditional games can be modified so they make a meaningful contribution to the program. Offering youngsters a chance to create and modify games fosters an understanding that game components can be changed to make the play experience beneficial for all.

EVALUATING GAMES

A number of factors impact the worth of games including the physical skills required, the number of participants, the complexity of rules, and the amount of strategy involved. Successful participation demands that youngsters have learned requisite skills in a practice setting. If skills are not learned, it will be difficult for players to apply the skills in a game setting. For example, children may be able to throw with proper form, but unable to throw accurately in a game setting. They may be able to hit a stationary object but not a moving target.

Youngsters also have to learn how to cooperate with teammates and compete against peers. The greater the number of teammates and competitors, the more difficult the game becomes. Cooperating with teammates is just as difficult as competing in a meaningful fashion. Moving from partner, to small-group, to team games is a natural progression and a formula for success. A number of games are more effective when played in small groups, because the participants handle objects more often and have more chances to be an active contributor.

The number of rules and the amount of strategy required increase the difficulty of a game. Developmental Level I children find it difficult (and uninteresting) to play a game that has many rules. If cognitive strategy is required, requisite physical skills should be learned previously (overlearned) so concentration can be applied to the mental aspect of the game rather than the skill. Most elementary school children are not able to concentrate on skill performance and strategy simultaneously. Complex games require team members to play specific roles, and some of these roles (such as goalkeeper or line positions) may not appeal to many youngsters. In contrast, many of the more popular games are spontaneous in nature and demand little concentration on strategy.

Be sure that children receive positive feedback from game experiences. The younger children are, the less willing they are to wait for the outcome; feedback must be immediate. Children become bored and tire of playing long games. Fatigue is also a factor in the interest level of children; watch carefully for such signs.

Games require a combination of skills. A game in which children must sequence many skills may result in failure or frustration for many. Lead-up games are developed for the express purpose of limiting the number of skills needed for successful participation. Evaluate the number of skills required and build a progression of games that gradually increases the use of skill combinations.

CREATING OR MODIFYING GAMES

Games can be modified and new variations created by you or students or by both together. For example, you may observe that a specific game is not meeting the desired objectives and may decide to modify or change the game to facilitate skill development. Stop the class and ask them to think of a way to make the game better. Alternatives can be implemented and the newly created activity tested to see whether it is indeed more effective. With Developmental Level II and III students, you can offer some parameters for developing a game and then allow time for the class to create and to implement the activity. Establish ground rules that facilitate group dynamics. For example, suggest voting on a rule change or specify a maximum number of changes allowed per period.

If students and teachers are to make meaningful modifications, they must understand how to analyze a game. The most recognized elements of game structure are desired outcomes, skills, equipment, rules or restrictions, number of players, and scheme of organization. Morris and Stiehl (1999) provide an approach to game analysis that may be helpful if you are interested in game modification. Youngsters need to learn how and what to modify and they need to practice the process. Some suggestions to start youngsters thinking include the following:

1. Change the distance to be run by decreasing or increasing it. For example, in Star Wars, go around once instead of twice.

2. Change the means of locomotion. Use hopping, walking, skipping, or galloping instead of running.

3. Play the game with one or more partners. The partners can move and act as if they were a single person.

4. Change the method of tagging in simple tag games. Call out "Reverse" to signal that the chaser is to become the tagger and vice versa.

5. Make goals or restricted areas larger or smaller. In Over the Wall, the restraining area can be made larger or smaller or its shape can be changed.

6. Vary the boundaries of the game by making them larger or smaller, as dictated by the number of players.

7. Change the formation in which the game is played. For example, Circle Kickball could be played in a square or triangular shape.

8. Change the requirements necessary for scoring. In Hand Hockey, players might be required to make four passes before a shot is taken.

9. Increase the number of players, taggers, or runners. The amount of equipment used can also be increased. For example, in Nine Lives, the more fleece balls used, the more practice youngsters get in throwing at a moving target.

10. Change the rules or penalties of the game. For example, allow players a maximum of three dribbles or to hold the ball for no more than 3 seconds.

COOPERATION AND COMPETITION

Without cooperation there would be no game activities. If participants chose not to follow the rules and play with teammates, it would be impossible to structure games. Clearly, games require cooperation before competition can be an outgrowth of an activity. *Cooperation* involves two or more children working together to achieve a common goal. *Competition* is characterized by opponents working against each other as each tries to reach a goal or reward. Since cooperation precedes competition and is more difficult for youngsters to learn, emphasis should be placed on this phase of game activity. Through games, players can develop a spirit of working together, a concern for teammates, and an appreciation for the collective skills of the group.

Achieving a balance between offense and defense helps participants understand that both phases are important. In tag and capture games, offer opportunities to remain safe as well as a challenge to be at risk and elude capture. Evaluate game components continually and modify them in the interest of retaining an enjoyable environment. Teams should be somewhat equal so all participants have an opportunity to find success. There is little motivation when there is no opportunity to win. Emphasizing cooperation reinforces the need to play with all classmates regardless of ability level. It is the teacher's responsibility to assure that teams offer youngsters a chance to be successful. Rotate students regularly so they have a chance to play with different classmates and to play on a winning team. Include youngsters with disabilities in all rotation plans.

SAFETY

Safety is a primary consideration in game situations. Check the play area for dangerous objects and hazards. Tables, chairs, equipment, and apparatus can become dangerous when a high-speed game is under way. Teach children to move in a controlled fashion and to use the entire playing area to avoid collisions. Learning to stop play immediately when a signal is given conditions youngsters to games with referees and assures safety. This is an important prerequisite for later sports experiences.

TEACHING GAMES EFFECTIVELY

1. *Put youngsters in the formation they are going to use prior to presenting a new game to a class.* If they can sit in game formation, that will make it easier to understand instructions. Make directions as brief as possible and implement the game quickly. Get the game under way with minimal instruction and gradually implement more subtle rules. Try the game first before answering any questions students may have. This ensures they have some perception of the game and how it is to proceed, so many questions are answered without using additional time and boring students who already understand.

2. *Use a trial period (no scoring) during the first stages of learning a game.* This avoids the possibility of children feeling resentful about losing a point or being caught off guard because they did not understand the activity.

3. *Do not use games that isolate one child.* This may create a negative experience for youngsters who have low self-esteem. Instead, place two to four youngsters in isolated position so the team can share the credit and blame. An example of a common game where this happens is "Birdie in the Cage." This sport lead-up game traditionally puts one youngster in the center of the circle to try and intercept or touch passes made by circle players. A youngster who doesn't have quick reactions or is overweight may never be successful and might bear the brunt of failure. Placing a couple of other students in the center makes it a team game and passes the responsibility to all center players.

4. *Develop a rotation plan that allows all children to play for an equal amount of time.* Avoid a situation where winners stay on the court and losers sit out, receiving much less practice than the better players. By the same token, do not play elimination games until one or two children remain. The least skilled youngsters will be eliminated early and have to sit the most. Keep in mind that the purpose of games is to keep youngsters involved in physical activity. Sitting out does not contribute to the goals of physical education.

5. *Assure that all children have an equal chance to participate in games that require taking turns.* When using games where numbers are called, write the

numbers on a card so no one is left out. Use caution with games that eliminate children. If children are eliminated, do so for one or two turns only, and allow them back in the game quickly.

6. *Do some careful planning before attempting to teach a new game.* Identify safety hazards, anticipate difficult concepts, and adapt the game to the class and the situation. Make physical preparations prior to teaching. Establish boundaries and have equipment ready for distribution. The size of the playing area is usually dictated by the skill and age of the participants. If you plan to do some instruction during a game, decrease the size of the playing area so students are closer to you.

7. *When playing low-organized and sport lead-up games, try to avoid using the out-of-bounds rule.* Instead, make a rule that whoever gets to the ball first gains possession. This speeds up the pace of the game and offers a strong incentive for quickly getting the ball back into play. If playing a game that uses a goal line or running to a line, establish a safety zone. Instead of using the wall or a line near the wall as the goal, draw safety lines 10 feet from the wall to allow for deceleration. Cones or spots can be used to mark the deceleration zone. Try to play as many games as possible.

8. *Change the makeup of the teams often and play relatively short games.* Nobody likes to lose all the time. Playing games for short periods of time means more games can be played, so more winners can be identified. If a team wins twice in a row, that is usually a signal to scramble the students into new teams. This gives everybody a fresh start and keeps a greater number of students motivated.

9. *To identify teams, use pinnies, crepe paper armbands, colored shoulder loops, or team belts worn around the waist.* Have a standing rule that the team that puts on the pinnies gets to have the ball out of bounds first. Youngsters usually don't like to wear pinnies and this gives them some incentive.

10. *Games are an excellent platform for learning social skills.* Encourage children to call infractions or penalties on each other and on themselves. Teach youngsters to accept calls made by officials as an integral part of any game situation. When disagreements occur, adopt the role of arbitrator, rather than taking one side or the other. Encourage players to learn negotiation skills and to resolve differences among themselves rather than having a teacher decide each issue.

11. *Help youngsters understand that learning to perform skills correctly is more important than the outcome of the game.* Continue instruction throughout the early phases of a game. Look for opportunities to stop the game briefly and offer instruction or correction. Offer coaching hints to improve skill techniques.

12. *Use the "rule of three" as a way of simplifying rules.* For example, the "rule of three" means you can only hold the ball for three seconds, take three steps, or miss three catches, etc. This reduces the number of rules youngsters have to remember and makes games easier to play. It also seems to diminish the disagreements youngsters have about rules.

SELECTION OF GAMES

Games in this chapter were selected because they require minimal skill and offer activity for all children. Analyze the skills children must practice before playing. Drills and skill practice become more meaningful when children comprehend that the skill will be used in a game situation. Games have been sorted by difficulty and placed into three developmental levels. Table 22.1 (pages 541–543) lists each of the games alphabetically by developmental level. Also listed in Table 22.1 are the skills required for successful play and the page in the text where the description of the game is listed. Games in Developmental Level I do not require competency in sport skills. Most use basic locomotor skills and offer an environment in which children can practice and participate successfully. These games can be modified easily to allow all children to have enjoyable experiences.

Specialized sport skills are required in many of the games in Developmental Levels II and III. Ball-handling and movement skills, with emphasis on agility, are important for success in many of these games. Offer opportunities for children to practice requisite game skills prior to being placed in a competitive situation.

SPORT LEAD-UP GAMES

Games in Developmental Levels II and III fall into two categories: sport lead-up games and low-organization games. This chapter includes low-organization games only; however, sport lead-up games can also be integrated into the games program. Sport lead-up games limit the number of skills required for successful participation in order to help children experience success in a sport setting. For example, Five Passes is a game designed to develop passing skills. Children do not have to perform other skills (such as dribbling or shooting) required by the regulation sport to achieve success. Table 22.2 (pages 544–545) lists all sport-related lead-up games presented in Chapters 24 to 30. If you are teaching soccer skills and want to finish the lesson with a lead-up game, consult this chart to find an appropriate activity. Many of the lead-up games are excellent choices for skill development, particularly with Developmental Level III youngsters.

TABLE 22.1	Alphabetical Listing of Games by Developmental Level	
Games	**Skills**	**Page**
	Developmental Level I Games	
Animal Tag	Imagery, running, dodging	545
Aviator	Running, locomotor movements, stopping	545
Ball Passing	Object handling	546
Blindfolded Duck	Fundamental locomotor movements	546
Bottle Bat Ball	Batting, retrieving balls	546
Bottle Kick Ball	Kicking, trapping	546
Cat and Mice	Running, dodging	547
Change Sides	Body management	547
Charlie over the Water	Skipping, running, stopping, bowling (rolling)	547
Circle Stoop	Moving to rhythm	547
Circle Straddle Ball	Ball rolling, catching	548
Colors	Color or other perceptual concepts, running	548
Corner Spry	Light, silent walking	548
Firefighter	Running	548
Flowers and Wind	Running	549
Forest Ranger	Running	549
Freeze	Locomotor movements to rhythm	549
Hill Dill	Running, dodging	550
Hot Potatoes	Object handling	550
Jack Frost and Jane Thaw	Running, dodging, holding position	550
Leap the Brook	Leaping, jumping, hopping, turning	550
Marching Ponies	Marching, running	551
May I Chase You?	Running, dodging	551
Midnight (Lame Wolf)	Running, dodging	551
Mix and Match	Fundamental locomotor movements	551
Mousetrap	Skipping, running, dodging	552
Musical Ball Pass	Passing and handling	552
One, Two, Button My Shoe	Running	552
Popcorn	Curling, stretching, jumping	553
Red Light	Fundamental locomotor movements, stopping	553
Right Angle	Rhythmic movement, body management	553
Rollee Pollee	Ball rolling, dodging	554
Scarecrow and the Crows, The	Dodging, running	554
Sneak Attack	Marching, running	554
Soap Bubbles	Body management	554
Squirrel in the Trees	Fundamental locomotor movements	555
Statues	Body management, applying force, balance	555
Stop Ball	Tossing, catching	555
Tag Games (Simple)	Fundamental locomotor movements, dodging	555
Back-to-Back		556
Bowing		556
Frozen		556

(continued)

TABLE 22.1	Alphabetical Listing of Games by Developmental Level (*continued*)	

Games	Skills	Page
One Step	Throwing, catching	565
Partner Stoop	Marching rhythmically	566
Ricochet	Rolling	566
Squad Tag	Running, dodging	566
Steal the Treasure	Dodging	567
Trades	Imagery, running, dodging	567
Trees	Running, dodging	567
Whistle March	Moving rhythmically	568
Whistle Mixer	All basic locomotor movements	568
Wolfe's Beanbag Exchange	Running, dodging, tossing, catching	568
Developmental Level III Games		
Air Raid	Throwing	568
Barker's Hoopla	Running	569
Cageball Target Throw	Throwing	569
Chain Tag	Running, dodging	569
Circle Touch	Dodging, body management	570
Clean-Up	Throwing	570
Fast Pass	Passing, catching, moving to an open area	570
Flag Chase	Running, dodging	570
Four Square	Batting a ball	577
Galactic Empire and Rebels	Chasing, fleeing, dodging	571
Guess the Leader	Body management	571
Jolly Ball	Kicking	571
Jump-the-Shot Variations	Rope jumping	572
Mushrooms	Rolling and throwing	572
Octopus	Maneuvering, problem solving	572
One-Base Tagball	Running, dodging, throwing	572
Over the Wall	Running, dodging	573
Pacman	Fleeing, reaction time	573
Partner Dog and Cat	Chasing, fleeing, dodging	573
Pin Knockout	Rolling, dodging	573
Right Face, Left Face (Streets and Alleys)	Running, dodging	574
Scooter Kickball	Striking with various body parts	574
Star Wars	Running	575
Strike the Pins	Throwing	575
Sunday	Running, dodging	575
Team Handball	Running, dribbling, passing, throwing, catching	577
Tetherball	Batting a ball	578
Touchdown	Running, dodging	576
Triplet Stoop	Moving rhythmically	576
Two Square	Batting a ball	579
Volley Tennis	Most volleyball skills	579
Whistle Ball	Passing, catching	576

22

TABLE 22.2   Lead-Up Games from Sport Chapters 24 to 30*

Basketball (Chapter 24)	
Developmental Level II	**Page**
Circle Guard and Pass	622
Basketball Tag	623
Birdie in the Cage	623
Captain Ball	623
Dribblerama	623
Around the Key	624
Five Passes	625
Captain Basketball	625
Developmental Level III	**Page**
Quadrant Basketball	625
Sideline Basketball	626
Twenty-One	626
Lane Basketball	627
Freeze Out	627
Flag Dribble	627
Through the Maze	627
One-Goal Basketball	628
Basketball Snatch Ball	628
Three-on-Three	628
Basketrama	628

Football (Chapter 25)	
Developmental Level II	**Page**
Football End Ball	638
Five Passes	639
Speed Football	639
Developmental Level III	**Page**
Kick-Over	639
Fourth Down	640
Football Box Ball	640
Flag Football	641
Pass Ball	642

Hockey (Chapter 26)	
Developmental Level II	**Page**
Stick Handle Competition	651
Circle Keep-Away	651
Star Wars Hockey	652
Lane Hockey	652
Modified Hockey	652

Developmental Level III	Page
Goalkeeper Hockey	653
Sideline Hockey	653
Regulation Elementary Hockey	653

Soccer (Chapter 27)	
Developmental Level II	**Page**
Circle Kickball	668
Soccer Touch Ball	668
Diagonal Soccer	668
Dribblerama	669
Bull's-Eye	669
Pin Kickball	669
Sideline Soccer	669
Kick Bowling	670
Soccer Golf	670
Developmental Level III	**Page**
Manyball Soccer	670
Addition Soccer	670
Over the Top	671
Lane Soccer	671
Line Soccer	671
Mini-Soccer	672
Six-Spot Keepaway	673
Regulation Soccer	673

Softball (Chapter 28)	
Developmental Level II	**Page**
Throw-It-and-Run Softball	687
Two-Pitch Softball	687
Hit and Run	688
Kick Softball	688
In a Pickle	689
Beat Ball	689
Steal a Base	689
Developmental Level III	**Page**
Five Hundred	689
Batter Ball	670
Home Run	670
Tee Ball	691
Scrub (Work-Up)	691
Slow-Pitch Softball	692
Babe Ruth Ball	692
Hurry Baseball (One Pitch)	693
Three-Team Softball	693

TABLE 22.2	Lead-Up Games from Sport Chapters 24 to 30* (*continued*)		
Volleyball (Chapter 30)		**Developmental Level III**	**Page**
		Pass and Dig	715
Developmental Level II	**Page**	Mini-Volleyball	715
		Rotation Mini-Volleyball	715
Beach Ball Volleyball	714	Regulation Volleyball	716
Informal Volleyball	714	Three-and-Over Volleyball	716
Shower Service Ball	714	Rotation Volleyball	716
		Four-Square Volleyball	716
		Wheelchair Volleyball	717

*Many of these games are used as culminating activities with sport lesson plans.

DEVELOPMENTAL LEVEL I

Games in the early part of Developmental Level I feature individual games and creative play. Little emphasis is placed on team play or on games that have a scoring system. The games are simple, easily taught, and not demanding of skills. Dramatic elements are present in many of the games, and others help establish number concepts and symbol recognition. As children mature, they enjoy participation in running, tag, and ball games. Few team activities are included, and the ball games require the skills of throwing and catching.

ANIMAL TAG

Supplies: None
Skills: Imagery, running, dodging
Formation:

```
X |              | O
X |              | O
X |              | O
X |              | O
X |              | O
X |              | O
X |              | O
X |              | O
X |              | O
X |              | O
```

Two parallel lines are drawn about 40 feet apart. Children are divided into two groups, each of which takes a position on one of the lines. Children in one group get together with their leader and decide what animal they wish to imitate. Having selected the animal, they move over to within five feet or so of the other line.

There they imitate the animal, and the other group tries to guess the animal correctly. If the guess is correct, they chase the first group back to its line, trying to tag as many as possible. Those caught must go over to the other team. The second group then selects an animal, and the roles are reversed. If the guessing team cannot guess the animal, however, the performing team gets another try. To avoid confusion, children must raise their hands to take turns at naming the animal. Otherwise, many false chases will occur. If children have trouble guessing, the leader of the performing team can give the initial of the animal.

AVIATOR

Supplies: None
Skills: Running, locomotor movements, stopping
Formation:

```
        |              | O
        |              | O
        |              | O
        |              | O
        | ATC          | O
        |              | O
        |              | O
        |              | O
        |              | O
        |              | O
```

Players are parked (in push-up position) at one end of the playing area. The air traffic controller (ATC) is in front of the players and calls out, "Aviators aviators, take off!" Youngsters take off and move like airplanes to the opposite side of the area. The first person to move to the other side and land the plane (get into push-up position facing the ATC) is declared the new ATC.

If the ATC yells out some type of stormy weather, all planes must return to the starting line and resume the parked position. Examples of stormy weather commands are lightning, thunder, hurricane, and tornado. Each ATC is allowed to give stormy weather warnings once.

▶ BALL PASSING

Supplies: Five or six different kinds of balls for each circle

Skill: Object handling

Formation: Circles with 15 or fewer in each circle

The class is divided into two or more circles, with no more than 15 children in any one circle. Each circle consists of two or more squads, but squad members need not stand together.

The teacher starts a ball around the circle; it is passed from player to player in the same direction. The teacher introduces more balls until five or six are moving around the circle at the same time and in the same direction. If a child drops a ball, he must retrieve it, and a point is scored against his squad. After a period of time, a whistle is blown, and the points against each squad are totaled. The squad with the lowest score wins. Beanbags, large blocks, or softballs can be substituted for balls.

▶ BLINDFOLDED DUCK

Supplies: A wand, broomstick, cane, or yardstick

Skills: Fundamental locomotor movements

Formation:

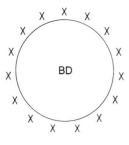

One child, designated the duck (Daisy if a girl, Donald if a boy), stands blindfolded in the center of a circle and holds a wand or similar article. She taps on the floor and tells children to hop (or perform some other locomotor movement). Children in the circle act accordingly, all moving in the same direction. Daisy then taps the wand twice on the floor, which signals all children to stop. Daisy moves forward with her wand, still blindfolded, to find a child in the circle. She asks, "Who are you?" The child responds, "Quack, quack." Daisy tries to identify this person. If the guess

is correct, the identified child becomes the new duck. If the guess is wrong, Daisy must take another turn. After two unsuccessful turns, another child is chosen to be the duck.

▶ BOTTLE BAT BALL

Supplies: A plastic bottle bat, whiffle ball, batting tee (optional), home plate, base marker

Skills: Batting, retrieving balls

Formation: Scattered

Batters get three pitches (or swings if a batting tee is used) to hit a fair ball, or they are out. The pitches are easy (as in slow-pitch softball), so that the batter has a chance to hit the ball. The batter hits the ball and runs around the base marker and back to home. If the ball is returned to the pitcher's mound before the batter reaches home, the batter is out. (A marker should designate the pitcher's mound.) Otherwise, the batter has a home run and bats again. One fielder other than the pitcher is needed, but another can be used. The running distance to first base is critical. It can remain fixed or can be made progressively (one step) longer, until it reaches such a point that the fielders are heavily favored.

✓ TEACHING TIP

Use a plastic bottle bat and whiffle ball. A rotation system should be established when an out is made. Limit the number of home runs per at bat to three.

▶ BOTTLE KICK BALL

Supplies: Plastic gallon jugs (bleach or milk containers) and 8-inch foam balls

Skills: Kicking, trapping

Formation:

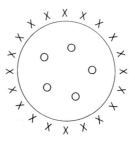

Players form a large circle around 10 to 12 plastic gallon jugs (bowling pins) standing in the middle of the circle. Students kick the balls and try to knock over the

bottles. Use as many foam balls as necessary to keep all children active. If the group is large, make more than one circle of players.

▶ CAT AND MICE

Supplies: None
Skills: Running, dodging
Formation:

Form a large circle. Two or three children are the cats and four others are the mice. The cats and mice cannot leave the circle. On signal, the cats chase the mice inside the circle. As they are caught, the mice join the circle. The last three mice caught become the cats for the next round. Start at one point in the circle and go around the circle selecting mice so that each child gets a chance to be in the center. Sometimes, children have difficulty catching the last mouse or any of the mice. If this is the case, children forming the circle can take a step toward the center, thus constricting the running area. Regardless, cut off any prolonged chase sequence.

▶ CHANGE SIDES

Supplies: None
Skill: Body management
Formation:

Establish two parallel lines 30 feet apart with half of the class on each line. On signal, all players cross through to the other line, face the center, and stand at attention. The first group to do all three things correctly wins a point. Children must be cautioned to use care when passing through the opposite group. They should be spaced well along each line; this allows room for them to move through each group. Vary the locomotor movements used by specifying skipping, hopping, long steps, sliding, and other varieties of movement. The position to be assumed at the finish can be varied also.

▶ CHARLIE OVER THE WATER

Supplies: A volleyball or playground ball
Skills: Skipping, running, stopping, bowling (rolling)
Formation: Scattered

Place the class in circle formation. Two or more children are placed in the center of the circle, holding a ball. One of the center players is designated as Charlie (or Sally). The class skips around the circle to the following chant.

Charlie over the water,
Charlie over the sea,
Charlie caught a bluebird,
But can't catch me!

On the word *me*, the center players toss their balls in the air while the rest of the class runs and scatters throughout the area. When Charlie catches his ball, he shouts, "Stop!" All of the children stop immediately and must not move their feet. All of the center players roll their ball in an attempt to hit one of their scattered classmates. If a ball is rolled into a scattered player, that child becomes a new Charlie. If center players miss, they remain in the center, and the game is repeated. If a center player misses twice, however, he or she joins the circle and picks another person as a replacement.

▶ CIRCLE STOOP

Supplies: Music or tom-tom
Skills: Moving to rhythm
Formation:

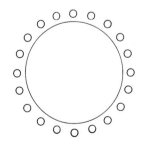

Children are in a single circle, facing counterclockwise. A march or similar music, or a tom-tom beat, can be used to signal movement. The class marches until the music stops, at which point they stoop and touch both hands to the ground without losing balance. The last child to touch both hands to the ground and those children who lost balance pay a penalty by going into the mush pot (the center of the circle) for one turn. The duration of the music should be varied so youngsters don't anticipate the signal.

Variations:

1. Using suitable music, have children employ different locomotor movements, such as skipping, hopping, or galloping.

2. Vary the stopping position. Instead of stooping, use positions such as the push-up, Crab, or Lame Dog, balancing on one foot, or touching with one hand and one foot.

► CIRCLE STRADDLE BALL

Supplies: Two or more eight-inch foam balls
Skills: Ball rolling, catching
Formation: Circles of 10–15 students

Children are in circle formation, facing in. Each player stands in a wide straddle stance with the side of each foot against their neighbors'. Their hands are on the knees. Two or more balls are used. The object of the game is to roll a ball between the legs of another player before that player can get hands down to stop the ball. Keep the circles small so students have more opportunities to handle the ball. Players must catch and roll the ball, rather than batting it. Children must keep their hands on their knees until a ball is rolled at them. After some practice, the following variation can be played.

Variation: Two or more children are in the center, each with a ball. The other children are in the same formation as before. The center players try to roll the ball through the legs of any child, masking intent by using feints and changes of direction. Any child allowing the ball to go through becomes it.

► COLORS

Supplies: Colored paper (construction paper) cut in circles, squares, or triangles for markers
Skills: Color or other perceptual concepts, running
Formation:

Use five or six different-colored markers, with a number of children having the same color. Children are standing or seated in a circle with a marker in front of each child. The teacher (or another player) calls out a color. Everyone having that color runs counterclockwise around the circle and back to place. The first player seated upright and motionless is declared the winner. Different kinds of locomotor movement can be specified, such as skipping, galloping, walking, and so on. After a period of play, the children leave the markers on the floor and move one place to the left.

Variation: Shapes (circles, triangles, squares, rectangles, stars, and diamonds) can be used instead of colors, as can numbers or other articles or categories, such as animals, birds, or fish.

► CORNER SPRY

Supplies: Blindfold
Skills: Light, silent walking
Formation:

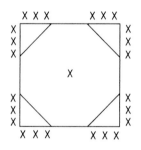

One person is blindfolded and stands in the center of the square. The other players are scattered in the corner areas. On signal they travel as quietly as possible from corner area to corner area. The blindfolded person, when ready (less than 20 seconds), calls out "Corner Spry!" All players finish their trips to the corner nearest them. The blindfolded person then picks (by pointing) a corner, trying to select the one with the most players. A new player is then selected to be blindfolded.

Variation: The corners can be numbered 1, 2, 3, and 4, and the blindfolded person can call out the corner number. The leader can also start class movement by naming the locomotor movement to be used.

► FIREFIGHTER

Supplies: None
Skill: Running

Formation:

A fire chief runs around the outside of a circle of children and taps a number of them on the back, saying "Firefighter" each time. After making the round of the circle, the chief goes to the center. When the chief says "Fire," the firefighters run counterclockwise around the circle and back to place. The one who returns first and is able to stand in place motionless is declared the winner and the new chief.

The chief can use other words to fool children, but they run only on the word Fire. This merely provides some fun, since there is no penalty for a false start. The circle children can sound the siren as the firefighters run.

> *Variation:* Have children stand while the chief is circling. All children not tapped drop to their knees as they would if there was a fire.

▶ FLOWERS AND WIND

Supplies: None
Skill: Running
Formation:

X		O
X		O
X		O
X		O
X		O
X		O
X		O
X		O
X		O
X		O
X		O
X		O

Two parallel lines long enough to accommodate the children are drawn about 30 feet apart. Children are divided into two groups. One is the flowers and the other the wind. Each of the teams takes a position on one of the lines and faces the other team. The flowers secretly select the name of a common flower. When ready, they walk over to the other line and stand about three feet away from the wind. The players on the wind team begin to call out flower names—trying to guess the flower chosen. When the flower has been guessed, the flowers run to their goal line, chased by the players of the other team. Any player caught must join the other side. The roles are reversed and the game is repeated. If one side has trouble guessing, a clue can be given to the color or size of the flower or the first letter of its name.

> *Variation:* Change the object that students choose to integrate other academic areas, i.e., trees, spelling words, math functions.

▶ FOREST RANGER

Supplies: None
Skill: Running
Formation:

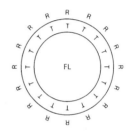

Half of the class forms a circle and faces the center. These are the trees. The other half of the class stands behind the trees as forest rangers. An extra child, the forest lookout, is in the center. The forest lookout starts the game by calling, "Fire in the forest. Run, run, run!" Immediately, the forest rangers run around the outside of the circle to the right. After a few moments, the lookout steps in front of one of the trees. This is the signal for each of the rangers to step in front of a tree. One player is left out, who then becomes the new forest lookout. The trees become rangers and the rangers become trees. Each time the game is played, the circle must be moved out somewhat, because the formation narrows when the rangers step in front of the trees.

▶ FREEZE

Supplies: Music or tom-tom
Skills: Locomotor movements to rhythm
Formation: Scattered

Scatter the class throughout the room. When the music starts, players move throughout the area, guided by the music. They walk, run, jump, or use other locomotor movements, depending on the selected music or beat. When the music is stopped, they freeze and do not move. Any child caught moving after the cessation of the rhythm receives a point. The object is to not accumulate points. A tom-tom or a piano is a fine accompaniment for this game, because the rhythmic beat can be varied easily and the rhythm can be stopped at any time.

This game is useful for practicing management skills because it reinforces freezing on a stop signal.

Variations:

1. Specify the level at which children must freeze.
2. Have children fall to the ground or balance or go into a different position, such as the push-up, Crab, Lame Dog, or some other defined position.

▶ HILL DILL

Supplies: None
Skills: Running, dodging
Formation:

Two parallel lines are established 50 feet apart. Two or more players are chosen to be it and stand in the center between the lines. The other children stand on one of the parallel lines. One of the center players calls,

> Hill Dill! Come over the hill,
> Or else I'll catch you standing still!

Children run across the open space to the other line, while the one in the center tries to tag them. Anyone caught helps the tagger in the center. When children cross over to the other line, they must await the next call. Start a new game when a majority of youngsters have been tagged.

▶ HOT POTATOES

Supplies: One to three balls or beanbags for each group
Skill: Object handling
Formation: Circles with 8 to 12 players

Group players in small circles (8 to 12 per circle) so objects can be passed from one to another around the circle. Balls or beanbags or both are passed around the circle. The teacher or a selected student, who is standing with his or her back to the class, randomly shouts,

"Stop!" The point of the game is to avoid being the person who passes the object to the person who caught it when the signal occurs. If this happens, the player(s) who passed the object gets up and moves to the next circle. Begin the game with one object and gradually add objects if the class is capable. Call out "Reverse" to signal a change in the direction the object is passed.

▶ JACK FROST AND JANE THAW

Supplies: Blue streamers or pinnies for Jack Frosts and red ones for Jane Thaws
Skills: Running, dodging, holding position
Formation: Scattered

The class is scattered and moves to avoid being frozen (tagged) by two or three Jack Frosts, who carry a blue pinnie or streamer in one hand. Frozen children remain immobile until touched (thawed) by the Jane Thaws who are identified by a red streamer or pinnie.

▶ LEAP THE BROOK

Supplies: None
Skills: Leaping, jumping, hopping, turning
Formation:

Mark off a brook across the floor. For the first third of the brook, it is about 3 feet wide; for the next third, about 4 feet wide; and for the last third, it is 5 feet wide. Youngsters line up on one side of the area. On the signal, "Cross the Brook!" players pick a challenge and try to jump across the brook. The wider the brook, the greater the challenge. Use different styles of locomotor movements such as hopping, jumping, and leaping over the brook. The selection of the distances is arbitrary and can be changed if they seem unsuitable for any particular group of children.

> *Variation:* Use different types of turns while jumping the brook, such as right or left; quarter, half, three-quarter, or full. Use different body shapes, different arm positions, and so on.

> ▶ **MARCHING PONIES**

Supplies: None

Skills: Marching, running

Formation:

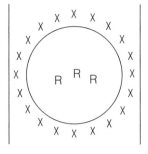

Two or three children are ringmasters and crouch in the center of a circle of ponies formed by the rest of the class. Two goal lines on opposite sides of the circle are established as safe areas. The ponies march around the circle in step, counting as they do so. At a predetermined number (whispered to the ringmasters by the teacher), the ringmasters jump up and attempt to tag the others before they can reach the safety lines. Anyone tagged joins the ringmasters in the center and helps catch others. Reorganize the game after six to eight children have been caught. Try other characterizations, such as lumbering elephants, jumping kangaroos, and the like.

> ▶ **MAY I CHASE YOU?**

Supplies: None

Skills: Running, dodging

Formation:

The class stands behind a line long enough to accommodate all. Two or three runners stand about 5 feet in front of the line. The class asks, "May I chase you?" One of the runners (designated by teacher) replies, "Yes, if you are wearing . . . " and names a color, an article of clothing, or a combination of the two. All who qualify immediately chase the runners until one is tagged. New runners are chosen and the game is repeated. Encourage players to think of other ways to identify those who run.

> ▶ **MIDNIGHT**

Supplies: None

Skills: Running, dodging

Formation:

A safety line is established about 40 feet from a den in which two or three players, the foxes, are standing. The others stand behind the safety line and ask, "What time is it, Mr. Fox?" One of the foxes is designated to answer in various fashions, such as "one o' clock," "four o' clock," etc. When the fox says a certain time, the class walks forward that number of steps. For example, if the fox says, "six o'clock" the class has to move forward six steps. The fox continues to draw the players toward him. At some point, the fox answers the question by saying "Midnight," and chases the others back to the safety line. Any player who is caught becomes a fox in the den and helps to catch others.

> *Variation:* *Lame Wolf.* The wolf is lame and advances in a series of three running steps and a hop. Other children taunt, "Lame Wolf, can't catch me!" or "Lame Wolf, tame wolf, can't catch me!" The wolf may give chase at any time. Children who are caught join the wolf and must also move as if lame.

> ▶ **MIX AND MATCH**

Supplies: None

Skills: Fundamental locomotor movements

Formation:

A line is established through the middle of the area. Half of the children are on one side and half are on the other. Two or three extra persons are on one side of the area. The teacher gives a signal for children to move as directed on their side of the line. They can be told to run, hop, skip, or make some other movement. On signal, players run to the dividing line and reach across to join hands with a player on the opposite side. The goal is to find a partner and not be left out. Children may reach over but may not cross the line. The players left out move to the opposite side so that players left out come from alternating sides of the area. Encourage students to raise their hands if they don't have a partner. That will speed up the partner-finding process.

Variation: The game also can be done with music or a drumbeat, with the players rushing to the centerline to find partners when the rhythm stops.

▶ MOUSETRAP

Supplies: None

Skills: Skipping, running, dodging

Formation:

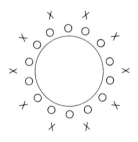

Half of the class forms a circle with hands joined and face the center. This is the trap. The other children are on the outside of the circle. These are the mice. Three signals are given for the game. These can be word cues or other signals. On the first signal, the mice skip around, outside the circle, playing happily. On the second signal, the trap is opened. (The circle players raise their joined hands to form arches.) The mice run in and out of the trap. On the third signal, the trap snaps shut. (The arms come down.) All mice caught inside join the circle. The game is repeated until most of the mice are caught. The players then exchange places, and the game begins anew.

▶ MUSICAL BALL PASS

Supplies: One or two playground balls per group, music

Skills: Passing and handling

Formation:

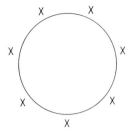

Break the class into a number of small groups (six to seven players) in circle formation facing the center. One ball is given to a player in each circle and is passed around the circle when the music starts. When the music stops, the player with the ball (or the last player to touch the ball) takes the ball and moves to another circle. To avoid arguments, a player must move to the next circle if the ball is in her hands or on the way to her. More than one ball may be used.

▶ ONE, TWO, BUTTON MY SHOE

Supplies: None

Skill: Running

Formation:

Two parallel lines are drawn on opposite sides of the playing area. Two or three players are selected as leaders and stand in front of the class. The rest of the class is behind one of the lines. The leaders say "Ready." The following dialogue takes place between the leaders and the children.

Children:	One, two.
Leader:	Button my shoe.
Children:	Three, four.
Leader:	Close the door.
Children:	Five, six.
Leader:	Pick up sticks.
Children:	Seven, eight.
Leader:	Run, or you'll be late!

As children carry on the conversation with the leaders, they toe the line, ready to run. When the leaders say the word "late," players run to the other line and return. New leaders are chosen after each run. The leaders can give the last response ("Run, or you'll be late!") in any timing desired—pausing or dragging out the words. No player can leave before the word "late" is uttered.

▶ POPCORN

Supplies: None
Skills: Curling, stretching, jumping
Formation:

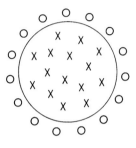

Half of the class is designated as popcorn; they crouch down in the center of the circle formed by the rest of the class. The circle children, also crouching, represent the heat. One of them is designated the leader whose actions serve as a guide to the other children. The circle children gradually rise to a standing position, extend their arms overhead, and shake them vigorously to indicate the intensifying heat. In the meantime, the popcorn in the center starts to pop. This should begin at a slow pace and increase in speed and height as the heat is applied. In the final stages, children are popping up rapidly. After a time, the groups change places and the action is repeated.

▶ RED LIGHT

Supplies: None
Skills: Fundamental locomotor movements, stopping
Formation:

```
X |
X |
X |
X |            O
X |
X |
X |            O
X |
X |
X |            O
X |
```

A goal line is established at one end of the area. The object of the game is to move across the area successfully without getting caught. Two or three players are leaders and stand on the goal line. The leaders turn away from the players. One of the leaders claps five times. All leaders turn around on the fifth clap. In the meantime, the players move toward the goal line, timing their movements to end on the fifth clap. If any of the leaders catch any movement by any person, that person is required to return to the starting line and begin anew. After the clapper turns away, she can turn back immediately to catch any movement. Once she begins clapping, however, five claps must be completed before she turns around. The first child to reach the goal line successfully without being caught in an illegal movement is the winner. New leaders are chosen for the next game.

Variations:

1. An excellent variation of the game is to have the leaders face the oncoming players. The designated leader calls out "Green light" for them to move and "Red light" for them to stop. When the leader calls other colors, the players should not move.

2. Different types of locomotion can be explored. The leader names the type of movement (e.g., hop, crawl, skip) before turning her back to the group.

3. The leader can specify how those caught must go back to place—walk, hop, skip, slide, crawl.

4. Divide the area into quadrants and have four games with one or two leaders.

✓ TEACHING TIP

In the original game of Red Light, the leader counts rapidly, "One, two, three, four, five, six, seven, eight, nine, ten—red light," instead of clapping five times. This has proved impractical in most gymnasiums, however, because children moving forward cannot hear the counting. Clapping, which provides both a visual and an auditory signal, is preferable.

▶ RIGHT ANGLE

Supplies: Music
Skills: Rhythmic movement, body management
Formation: Scattered

A tom-tom can be used to provide the rhythm for this activity. Children quickly change direction at right angles on each heavy beat or change of music. The object of the game is to make the right-angle change on signal and not to bump into other players.

22

ROLLEE POLLEE

Supplies: Many 8-inch foam balls
Skills: Ball rolling, dodging
Formation:

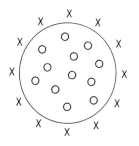

Half of the class forms a circle; the other half is in the center. Balls are given to the circle players. The circle players roll the balls at the feet and shoes of the center players, trying to touch them with a ball. The center players move around to avoid the balls. A center player who is touched leaves the center and joins the circle. After a period of time or when all of the children have been touched, the teams trade places.

✓ TEACHING TIP

The instructor can have the children practice rolling a ball first. Balls that stop in the center are dead and must be taken back to the circle before being put into play again. The preferable procedure is to have players who recover balls roll them to a teammate rather than return to place with the ball.

THE SCARECROW AND THE CROWS

Supplies: None
Skills: Dodging, running
Formation:

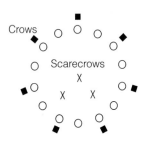

Children form a large circle representing the garden that is guarded by two or three players who are designated as scarecrows. Six to eight crows scatter on the outside of the circle, and the scarecrows assume a characteristic pose inside the circle. Players in the circle raise their joined hands and let the crows run through, into the garden, where they pretend to eat. The scarecrows try to tag the crows. The circle children help the crows by raising their joined hands and allowing them to leave the circle, but they try to hinder the scarecrows. If the scarecrows run out of the circle, all the crows immediately run into the garden and start to nibble at the vegetables while the circle children hinder the scarecrows' reentry.

When the scarecrows have caught one or two crows, new players are selected. If, after a reasonable period of time, the scarecrows have failed to catch any crows, change players.

SNEAK ATTACK

Supplies: None
Skills: Running
Formation:

```
O        |        X
O        |        X
O        |        X
O        |        X
O        |        X
O →      |        X
O        |        X
O        |        X
O        |        X
O        |        X
O        |        X
```

Two parallel lines are drawn about 60 feet apart. The class is divided into two teams. One team takes a position on one of the lines, with their backs to the area. These are the chasers. The other team is on the other line, facing the area. This is the sneak team. The sneak team moves forward on signal, moving toward the chasers. When they get reasonably close, a signal is given, and the sneak team turns and runs back to their line, chased by the other team. Anyone tagged before reaching the line changes to the chase team. The game is then repeated, with the roles exchanged.

SOAP BUBBLES

Supplies: Cones to delineate space, music
Skills: Body management
Formation: Scattered

Four cones are used to delineate the movement area. Each player is a soap bubble floating throughout the area. A locomotor movement is called out and youngsters perform it, moving within the four cones. As the game progresses, the cones are moved toward the center of the area to decrease the size of the area. The object of the game is not to touch or collide with another bubble. When this occurs, both bubbles burst and sink to the floor, making themselves as small as possible. The space is made smaller until only a few have not been touched. Players who are broken bubbles can go to the area outside of the cones and move. This game teaches the concept of moving in general space without touching.

▶ SQUIRREL IN THE TREES

Supplies: None
Skills: Fundamental locomotor movements
Formation:

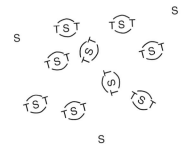

A number of trees are formed by two players facing each other and holding hands or putting hands on each other's shoulders. A squirrel is in the center of each tree, and one or two extra squirrels are outside. On signal, the trees open up and let the squirrels move around the area. The trees stay together and also move throughout the area. On signal, the trees freeze in place and the squirrels find any available tree. Only one squirrel is allowed in a tree. Quickly begin another game to avoid drawing attention to those who did not find a tree.

✓ TEACHING TIP

Rotation is necessary so all students get to be a squirrel. Once the squirrels are in a tree, ask them to face one of the tree players. The person they are facing becomes their partner for a tree and the other person becomes a new squirrel.

▶ STATUES

Supplies: None
Skills: Body management, applying force, balance
Formation: Scattered in pairs

Children are scattered in pairs around the area. One partner is the swinger and the other the statue. The teacher voices a directive, such as "Pretty," "Funny," "Happy," "Angry," or "Ugly." The swinger takes the statue by one or both hands, swings it around in a small circle two or three times (the teacher should specify), and releases it. The statue then takes a pose in keeping with the directive, and the swinger sits down on the floor.

A committee of children can determine which children are the best statues. The statue must hold the position without moving or be disqualified. After the winners are announced, the partners reverse positions. Children should be cautioned that the swinging must be controlled.

Variation: In the original game, the swinging is done until the directive is called. The swinger then immediately releases the statue, who takes the pose as called. This gives little time for the statue to react. More creative statues are possible if the directive is given earlier.

▶ STOP BALL

Supplies: A ball
Skills: Tossing, catching
Formation:

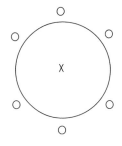

Divide the class into small circles of five to seven players. One player, with hands over the eyes, stands in the center of each circle. A ball is tossed clockwise or counterclockwise from player to player around the circle. At a time of her own selection, the center player calls, "Stop." The player caught with the ball (or the ball coming to her) takes the ball to the next circle and plays with a new team. The center player should be allowed three or four turns and then be changed.

▶ TAG GAMES (SIMPLE)

Supplies: None
Skills: Fundamental locomotor movements, dodging
Formation: Scattered

Tag has many variations. The following are "give up the tag" games because a player is no longer it when she tags another person, who then becomes it. Children are scattered throughout the area. A number of players are designated as it. When a tag is made, that player states, "You're it." The new it can chase any player other than the person who tagged him (no tagbacks). Eliminating tagbacks keeps students from always being it because they aren't as quick as the person that tagged them.

22

Variations:

1. Touching a specified type of object (such as wood or iron) or the floor or an object of a specified color can make a runner safe.

2. Children can be safe by doing a particular action or by striking a certain pose.

   a. *Stoop Tag.* Players touch both hands to the ground.

   b. *Stork Tag.* Players stand on one foot. (The other cannot touch.)

   c. *Turtle Tag.* Players get on their backs, feet pointed toward the ceiling.

   d. *Bowing Tag.* Players make an obeisance with forehead to the ground.

   e. *Nose-and-Toe Tag.* Players touch the nose to the toe.

   f. *Back-to-Back Tag.* Players stand back to back with any other child.

   g. *Skunk Tag.* Players reach an arm under one knee and hold the nose.

3. *Locomotor Tag.* The child who is it specifies how the others should move—skipping, hopping, jumping. The tagger must use the same kind of movement.

4. *Frozen Tag.* Two children are it. The rest are scattered over the area. When caught, they are "frozen" and must keep both feet in place. Any free player can tag a frozen player and thus release her. The goal of the tagger is to freeze all players. Frozen players can be required to hop in place until released.

▶ TEACHER BALL (LEADER BALL)

Supplies: A volleyball or rubber playground ball
Skills: Throwing, catching
Formation:

One child is the leader and stands about 10 feet in front of three other students, who are lined up facing the leader. The object of the game is to move up to the teacher's spot by avoiding making bad throws or missing catches. The leader throws to each child in turn, beginning with the child on the left, who must catch and return the ball. Any child making a throwing or catching error goes to the end of the line, on the leader's right. Those in the line move up, filling the vacated space.

A leader who makes a mistake must go to the end of the line and the child at the head of the line becomes the new leader. The leader scores a point by remaining in position for three rounds (three throws to each child). After scoring a point, the leader takes a position at the end of the line, and another child becomes the leader.

> *Variation:* The leader can suggest specific methods of throwing and catching, such as "Catch with the right hand only" or "Catch with one hand and don't let the ball touch your body."

▶ TOE TO TOE

Supplies: None
Skills: Fundamental locomotor movements
Formation: Scattered

Youngsters perform a locomotor movement around the area. On signal, each child must find a partner and stand toe to toe (one foot only) with that person. An important skill is to take the nearest person for a partner instead of searching for a particular friend. Youngsters who can't find a partner within their immediate area must run quickly to the center of the area (use a marking spot or cone) to find a partner. The goal is to find a nearby partner as quickly as possible and avoid being the last pair formed. If the number of youngsters playing is uneven, the teacher can join in and play. Change locomotor movements often.

▶ TOMMY TUCKER'S LAND

Supplies: About 10 beanbags for each game
Skills: Dodging, running
Formation:

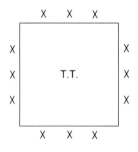

Two or three youngsters, Tommy and Tammy Tucker, stand in the center of a 15-foot square, within which the beanbags are scattered. The Tuckers are guarding their land and treasure. The other children chant,

> I'm on Tommy Tucker's land,
> Picking up gold and silver.

Children attempt to pick up as much of the treasure as they can while avoiding being tagged by the Tuckers.

Any child who is tagged must return the treasure and retire from the game. The game is over when only one child is left or when all of the beanbags have been successfully filched. The teacher may wish to call a halt to the game earlier if a stalemate is reached. In this case, new Tuckers are selected.

▶ TWINS (TRIPLETS)

Supplies: None

Skills: Body management, running

Formation: Scattered with partner

Youngsters are scattered throughout the area with a partner (twin). The teacher gives commands such as "Take three hops and two leaps" or "Walk backward four steps and three skips." When the pairs are separated, the teacher says, "Find your twin!" Players find their twin and stand frozen toe to toe. The goal is to not be the last pair to find each other and assume the frozen position. Make sure students move away from each other during the movements. One alternative is to find a new twin each time. Another variation is to separate twins in opposite ends of the playing area.

> ***Variation:*** The game becomes more challenging when played in groups of three (triplets). When using this variation, new partners should be selected each time.

▶ UP PERISCOPE

Supplies: None

Skills: Fundamental locomotor movements

Formation: Scattered

While in scattered formation, children move around the area pretending to be ships. Remind the ships to not contact another ship and to keep as much space as possible. When the teacher says "Submarines," players quickly lower their bodies and move at a low level. When the teacher says "Up periscope," students move to their backs and put one leg in the air to imitate a periscope. On "Double periscope," both legs are raised to imitate two periscopes. While the students are in Double periscope position, the teacher can quickly give the previous commands to keep students moving. When the teacher says "Surface," the students resume moving through the area as ships.

▶ WHERE'S MY PARTNER?

Supplies: None

Skills: Fundamental locomotor movements

Formation:

Children are in a double circle by couples, with partners facing. The inside circle has two or three more players than the outside. When the signal is given, the circles skip (or walk, run, hop, or gallop) to the right. This means that they are skipping in opposite directions. On the command "Halt," the circles face each other to find partners. The players left without a partner go to the mush pot (the center area of the circle) for one turn. The circles should be reversed after a time.

> ***Variation:*** The game can also be played with music or a drumbeat. When the music stops, the players seek partners.

DEVELOPMENTAL LEVEL II

Compared with the games in Developmental Level I, the games program undergoes a definite change. Chase and tag games become more complex and demand more maneuvering. Introductory lead-up games make an appearance. Children become more interested in games that have a sport slant, and kicking, throwing, catching, batting, and other sport skills are beginning to mature.

▶ ADDITION TAG

Supplies: None

Skills: Running, dodging

Formation:

Two or more couples are it, and each stands with inside hands joined. These are the taggers. The other children run individually. The couples move around the area, trying to tag with the free hands. The first person tagged joins the couple, making a trio. The three then chase until they catch a fourth. Once a fourth person is caught, the four divide and form two couples, adding another set of taggers to the game. This continues until the majority of players are tagged.

✓ **TEACHING TIP**

Some area restrictions can be established if couples are having problems catching the runners. The game moves faster if started with more couples. A tag is legal only when the couple or group of three keeps their hands joined.

▶ **ALASKA BASEBALL**

Supplies: A volleyball or soccer ball

Skills: Kicking, batting, running, ball handling

Formation:

Players are organized in two teams; one is at bat while the other is in the field. A straight line provides the only out-of-bounds line, and the team at bat is behind this line at about the middle. The other team is scattered around the fair territory. One player propels the ball, either batting a volleyball or kicking a stationary soccer ball. Teammates are in a close file behind the batter. As soon as the batter sends the ball into the playing area, he or she starts to run around the line of teammates. Each time the runner passes the head of the file, the team gives a loud count.

There are no outs. The first fielder to get the ball stands still and starts to pass the ball back overhead to the nearest teammate, who moves directly behind to receive it. The remainder of the team in the field must run to the ball and form a file behind it. The ball is passed back overhead, with each player handling the ball. When the last field player in line has a firm grip on it, she shouts "Stop." At this signal, a count is made of the number of times the batter ran around her team. To score more sharply, half rounds should be counted. Five batters or half of the team should bat; then the teams should change places. This is better than allowing an entire team to bat before changing to the field, because players in the field tire from many consecutive runs.

Variation: Regular bases can be set up, and the batter can run the bases. Scoring can be in terms of a home run made or not; or the batter can continue around the bases, getting a point for each base.

▶ **ARCHES**

Supplies: Music

Skills: Moving rhythmically

Formation:

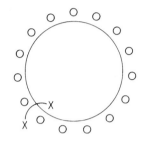

The game is similar to London Bridge. An arch is placed in the playing area. (To form an arch, two players stand facing one another with hands joined and arms raised.) When the music starts, the other players move in a circle, passing under the arch. Suddenly, the music stops, and the arch is brought down by dropping the hands. All players caught in an arch immediately pair off to form other arches, keeping in a general circle formation. If a caught player does not have a partner, he waits in the center of the circle until one is available. The last players caught (or left) form arches for the next game. The arches should be warned not to bring down their hands and arms so forcefully that children passing under are pummeled.

Variation: Different types of music can be used, and children can move according to the pattern of the music.

▶ **BAT BALL**

Supplies: An 8-inch foam ball

Skills: Batting, running, catching, throwing

Formation:

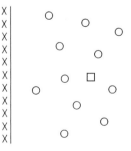

A serving line is drawn across one end of the field, and a 3-by-3-foot base is established about 50 feet from the serving line. Children are divided into two teams. One team is scattered over the playing area. The other team is behind the serving line, with one player at bat. The batter puts the ball into play by batting it with a hand into the playing area. To be counted as a fair ball, the ball must land in the playing area or be touched by a member of the fielding team. As soon as the ball is hit, the batter runs to the base and back across the serving line. In the meantime, the fielding team fields the ball and attempts to complete five passes before the runner gets back across the line.

Fielders may not run with the ball. It must be passed from fielder to fielder. A pass may not be returned to the fielder from whom it was received. Violation of any of these rules constitutes a foul.

A run is scored each time the batter hits a fair ball, touches the base, and gets back to the serving line. A run is also scored if the fielding team commits a foul.

The batter is out when the ball is caught on the fly. Two consecutive foul balls also put the batter out. The batter is out when hit by a thrown ball in the field of play. Sides change when three outs are made.

BEACH BALL BAT BALL

Supplies: Four to six beach balls
Skills: Batting, tactile handling
Formation:

To begin the game, the balls are placed on the centerline dividing the court area. Four to six beach balls are in play at the same time. A score occurs when the beach ball is batted over the end line. Once the ball moves across the end line it is dead. Players concentrate on the remaining balls in play. If a ball is on the floor, it is picked up and batted into play. At no time may a ball be carried. After all four balls are scored, the game ends. A new game is started after teams switch goals.

BIRD CATCHER

Supplies: Hoops or cones
Skills: Chasing, fleeing, dodging
Formation: Class in line formation with two to four players in the bird nest

Two to four players are designated bird catchers and stand in the center of the teaching area. One child is chosen as the mother/father bird and stands on an end line or other predetermined line. An area around the mother/father bird can be established with cones and called a nest. The remainder of the class stands on the other end line. Students on the end line quickly choose the type of bird they will be for the game. On signal, the mother/father bird commands a specific type of bird to fly, for example, "Cardinals fly." All students that chose to be cardinals then attempt to get to the mother/father bird's nest without being tagged by the bird catchers. If tagged by the bird catchers, students begin helping the bird catcher until a new game is started.

✓ **TEACHING TIP**

Specific types of birds may need to be given to expedite the game.

BOUNCE BALL

Supplies: Volleyballs or rubber playground balls of about the same size
Skills: Throwing, ball rolling
Formation:

The court is divided into halves. Children form two teams. Each team occupies one-half of the court and is given a number of balls. Two players from each team are assigned to retrieve balls behind their own end lines. The object of the game is to bounce or roll the ball over the opponents' end line. A ball thrown across the line on a fly does not count. Two scorers are needed, one at each end line. Players can move wherever they wish in their own area but cannot cross the centerline. After the starting signal, the balls are thrown back and forth at will.

BOX BALL

Supplies: A sturdy box, 2 feet square and about 12 inches deep; four volleyballs (or similar balls)
Skills: Running, ball handling

Formation:

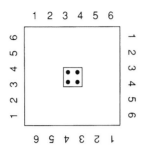

The class is divided into four even teams, with six to ten players per team. Each team occupies one side of a hollow square at an equal distance from the center. Players face inward and each team numbers off consecutively from right to left. A box containing four balls is put in the center. The instructor calls a number, and the player from each team who has that number runs forward to the box, takes a ball, and runs to the head of her line, taking the place of Player 1. In the meantime, the players in the line have moved to the left just enough to fill in the space left by the runner. On reaching the head of the line, the runner passes the ball to the next person and so on down the line to the end child. The last child runs forward and returns the ball to the box. The first team to return the ball to the box scores a point.

The runner must not pass the ball down the line until she is in place at the head of the line. The ball must be caught and passed by each child. Failure to conform to these rules results in team disqualification. Runners stay at the head of the line, retaining their original number. The lines are not kept in consecutive number sequence.

▶ BUSY BEE

Supplies: None
Skills: Fundamental locomotor movements
Formation:

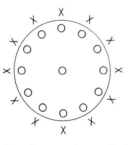

Half of the class forms a large circle, facing in, and is designated the stationary players. The other players seek partners from this group, and stand in front of the stationary players. An extra child in the center is the busy bee. The bee calls out directions such as "Toe to toe," "Face to face," "Shake hands," "Kneel on one knee [or both]," and "Hop on one foot." All the children in the double circle follow these directions. The center child then calls out, "Busy bee." Stationary players stand still, and their partners seek new partners while the center player also tries to get a partner. The child without a partner becomes the new busy bee.

✓ TEACHING TIP

Teach youngsters a variety of movements they can do if they become the busy bee. When changing partners, children must select a partner other than the stationary player next to them. After a period of time, the active and stationary players are rotated.

▶ CAGEBALL KICK-OVER

Supplies: A cageball, 18-, 24-, or 30-inch size
Skill: Kicking
Formation:

```
O |  | X
O |  | X
O |  | X
O |  | X
O |  | X
O |  | X
O |  | X
O |  | X
O |  | X
O |  | X
O |  | X
```

Players are divided into two teams and sit facing each other, with legs outstretched and soles of the feet about 6 to 12 feet apart. While maintaining the sitting position, each player supports his weight on the hands, which are placed slightly to the rear. The teacher rolls the cageball between the two teams. The object of the game is to kick the ball over the other team, thereby scoring a point. After a point is scored, the teacher rolls the ball into play again. Rotate players by having a player on the left side of the line take a place on the right side after a point is scored, thus moving all the players one position to the left. When the ball is kicked out at either end, no score results, and the ball is put into play again by the teacher.

✓ TEACHING TIP

Children can be allowed to use their hands to stop the ball from going over them.

▶ CLUB GUARD

Supplies: A juggling club or bowling pin and foam-rubber ball
Skill: Throwing

Formation:

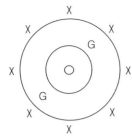

A circle about 15 feet in diameter is drawn. Inside the circle at the center, an 18-inch circle is drawn. The club is put in the center of the small circle. Two or three youngsters guard the club. The other players stand outside the large circle, which is the restraining line for them. The circle players throw the ball at the club and try to knock it down. The guards try to block the throws with the legs and body but must stay out of the small inner circle. The outer circle players pass the ball around rapidly so that one of the players can get an opening to throw as the guards maneuver to protect the club. Rotate in new guards after a short period of time (15–20 seconds). The guards are disqualified if they step into the small circle.

✓ TEACHING TIPS

1. More than one club can be placed in the center.
2. Play multiple games to increase the activity level for all players.

▶ COMPETITIVE CIRCLE CONTESTS

Supplies: Volleyballs or 8-inch foam rubber balls, two bowling pins

Skills: Throwing, catching

Formation: Two circles with the same number of students in each

Two teams arranged in independent circles compete against each other. The circles should be of the same diameter; lines can be drawn on the floor to ensure this. The players of each team are numbered consecutively so that each player in one circle corresponds to a player in the other circle. Two numbered players, in sequence, go to the center of the opponents' circle to compete for their team in either of the following activities.

1. *Circle Club Guard.* The two center players guard a bowling pin. The circle that knocks down the club first wins a point. The ball should be rolled at the club.
2. *Touch Ball.* The circle players pass the ball from one to another while the two center players try to touch it. The center player who touches the ball first wins a point for the respective team. In case neither player is able to touch the ball in a reasonable

period of time, the action should be cut off without awarding a point.

After all players have competed, the team with the most points wins. For Circle Club Guard, there must be three passes to different people before the ball can be rolled at the club. Establishing circle lines may be necessary to regulate throwing distance.

▶ COUPLE TAG

Supplies: None

Skills: Running, dodging

Formation:

Two goal lines are established on opposite sides of an area. Players run in pairs, with inside hands joined. All pairs, except two, line up on one of the goal lines. The pairs in the center are it. They call "Come," and the children, keeping hands joined, run to the other goal line. The pairs in the center, also retaining joined hands, try to tag any other pair. As soon as a couple is caught, they help the center couples. The game continues until all are caught. The last two couples caught are it for the next game.

> *Variation:* *Triplet Tag.* The game can be played with sets of threes. Tagging is done with any pair of joined hands. If a triplet breaks joined hands, it is considered caught.

▶ CROWS AND CRANES

Supplies: None

Skills: Running, dodging

Formation:

```
X | O
X | O
X | O
X | O
X | O
X | O
X | O
X | O
X | O
X | O
X | O
```

22

Establish two goal lines on opposite sides of an area. The class is divided into two groups—the crows and the cranes. The groups face each other at the center of the area, about 5 feet apart. The leader calls out either "Crows" or "Cranes," using a cr-r-r-r-r sound at the start of either word to mask the result. If "Crows" is the call, the crows chase the cranes to the goal line. If "Cranes" is the call, then the cranes chase. Any player caught goes over to the other side and becomes a member of that group. The goal is to try and capture the most players.

Variations:

1. *Toe to Toe.* Instead of facing each other, children stand back to back, about a foot apart, in the center.

2. *Red and Blue.* A piece of cardboard painted red on one side and blue on the other can be thrown into the air between the teams, instead of having someone give calls. If red comes up, the red team chases, and vice versa.

3. *Nouns and Verbs.* When the leader calls out any verb, the nouns team chases and vice versa.

4. *Odd and Even.* Large foam rubber dice can be thrown in the air. If they come up even, the even team chases. If they come up odd, the odd team chases.

5. *Blue, black, and baloney.* On the command "Blue" or "Black," the game proceeds as described. On the command "Baloney," no one is to move. The caller should draw out the bl-l-l-l sound before ending with one of the three commands.

6. Have a leader tell a story using as many words beginning with cr- as possible. Words that can be incorporated into a story might be *crazy, crunch, crust, crown, crude, crowd, crouch, cross, croak, critter.* Each time one of these words is spoken, the beginning of the word is lengthened with a drawn out *cr-r-r-r* sound. No one may move on any of the words except crows or cranes.

▶ FLY TRAP

Supplies: None
Skills: Fundamental locomotor movements
Formation:

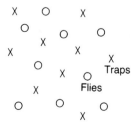

Half of the class is scattered around the playing area, sitting on the floor in cross-legged fashion. These children form the trap. The rest of the players are the flies, and they buzz around the seated children. When a whistle is blown, the flies must freeze where they are. If any of the trappers can touch a fly, that fly sits down at that spot and becomes a trapper. The trappers must keep their seats glued to the floor. The game continues until all of the flies are caught. Some realism is given to the game if the flies make buzzing sounds and move their arms as wings.

✓ TEACHING TIP

Some experience with the game enables the teacher to determine how far apart to place the seated children. After most of the flies have been caught, the groups trade places. The method of locomotion should be changed occasionally.

▶ FOLLOW ME

Supplies: A marker for each child (squares of cardboard or plywood can be used; individual mats or beanbags work well)
Skills: All locomotor movements, stopping
Formation:

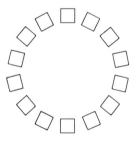

The class is arranged in a rough circle, each youngster standing or sitting with one foot on a marker. Two extra players are guides. They move around the circle, pointing at different players and asking them to follow until all players are selected. Each player chosen falls in behind the guide that pointed at him or her. The guides then take the groups on a tour, and the members of each group perform just as the guide does. The guide may hop, skip, do stunts, or execute other movements, and children following must do likewise. At the signal "Home," all run for places with a marker. Two players will be left without a marker. They can become guides or choose other guides.

▶ FOX HUNT

Supplies: None
Skills: Running, dodging

Formation:

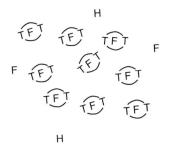

Pairs of players form trees by facing each other and holding hands. A third member of each group is a fox and stands between the hands of the trees. Three players are identified as foxes without trees and three players are designated as hounds. The hounds try to tag foxes who are not in trees. The extra foxes may move to a tree and displace the fox who is standing in the tree. In addition, the foxes in trees may leave the safety of their trees at any time. If the hound tags a fox, their roles are reversed immediately, the fox becoming the hound.

The game should be stopped at regular intervals to allow the players who are trees to change places with the foxes and hounds. Different locomotor movements can be specified to add variety to the game.

▶ GALLOPING LIZZIE

Supplies: A beanbag or fleece ball

Skills: Throwing, dodging, running

Formation: Scattered

Two or more players are it and have fleece balls. The other players are scattered around the playground. The players with the balls run after the others and attempt to hit other players below the waist with the fleeceball. The person hit becomes it, and the game continues. The tagger must throw the ball, not merely touch another person with it.

▶ HAND HOCKEY

Supplies: 8-inch gray foam balls

Skills: Striking, volleying

Formation:

```
X  X        O   O
X  X     X  O       O
X  X       O   O    O
X     X       O     O
X  X       O     O  O
X     X      O      O
X  X        O    O
```

Players are divided into two teams. Half of the players on each team are guards and are stationed on the goal line as defenders. The other half are active players and are scattered throughout the playing area in front of their goal line.

The object of the game is to bat or push the ball with either hand so that it crosses the goal line that the other team is defending. Players may move the ball as in hockey but may not throw, hoist, or kick it. The defensive goal line players are limited to one step into the playing field when playing the ball. The ball is put into play by being rolled into the center of the field. After a goal has been scored or after a specified period, guards become active players, and vice versa. An out-of-bounds ball goes to the opposite team and is put into play by being rolled from the sidelines into the playing area. If the ball becomes entrapped among players, play is stopped, and the ball is put into play again by a roll from the referee.

Players must play the ball and not resort to rough tactics. A player who is called for unnecessary roughness or for illegally handling the ball must go to the sidelines (as in hockey) and remain in the penalty area until the players change positions. Players should scatter and attempt to pass to each other rather than bunch around the ball. Once youngsters learn the game, introduce more than one ball to increase the amount of activity.

Variation: *Scooter Hockey.* The active center players from each team are on gym scooters. The position that each child takes on the gym scooter can be specified or can be a free choice. Possible positions are kneeling, sitting, or balancing on the tummy. A hard surface is needed. This game version is usually played indoors on a basketball court.

▶ HOME BASE

Supplies: Cones to delineate the area, four pinnies

Skills: Reaction time, locomotor movements, body management

Place a number of marking spots on the floor throughout the area. Divide the class into groups of five or six. Ask each group to quickly line up with one person on a marking spot and the rest of the players behind in single file. The person on the spot is designated as the team captain. A locomotor movement is called and all players do this movement throughout the area. When "Home base" is called, the captains quickly find the closest spot and their respective squad members line up behind them. The first team to return to proper position (standing in a straight line) is declared the winner.

22

✓ **TEACHING TIP**

Avoid calling "Home base" until the students are thoroughly mixed. A number of different formations can be specified that students must assume upon return to their home base.

▶ **INDIANAPOLIS 500**

Supplies: None
Skills: Running, tagging
Formation:

Children start in a large circle and are numbered off in threes or fours. A race starter says "Start your engines," and then calls out a number. Those children with the corresponding number run the same way around the circle and try to tag players in front of them. If the leader yells "Pit stop," all runners have to stop and return to their original position. If "Car wreck" is called by the leader, all runners change direction and continue running until "Pit stop" is called. Change the starter often.

▶ **JUMP THE SHOT**

Supplies: Jump-the-shot ropes
Skill: Rope jumping
Formation:

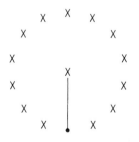

Divide the class into four or five small circles. One player with a long rope stands in the center. A soft object is tied to the free end of the rope to give it some weight. An old, deflated ball or beanbag makes a good weight (tie the rope to it and use duct tape to keep it from becoming untied). The center player turns the rope under the feet of

the circle players, who must jump over it. A player who touches the rope with the feet must move up to the next group.

Variations:

1. Change the center player after one or two misses. The center player should be cautioned to keep the rope along the ground. The rope speed can be varied. A good way to turn the rope is to sit cross-legged and turn it over the head. Different tasks can be performed such as hopping, jumping and turning, or jumping and clapping.

2. Squads line up in spoke formation. Each member does a specified number of jumps (from three to five) and then exits. The next squad member in line must come in immediately without missing a turn of the rope. A player scores a point for the squad by coming in on time, jumping the prescribed number of turns, and exiting successfully. The squad with the most points wins.

3. Couples line up in the same formation. They join inside hands and stand side by side when jumping.

▶ **KEEP 'EM MOVIN'**

Supplies: Tennis balls, whiffle balls, foam balls
Skills: Body management
Formation: Scattered throughout the teaching area

Numerous tennis balls and/or whiffle balls (10–15 more than there are students) are scattered throughout the teaching area. Students are in scattered formation. On signal, students begin tapping the tennis balls with their feet or hands to get them moving or "alive." Balls may not be picked up or kicked. While the students try to keep all balls moving, the teacher looks for balls that are stationary. Once three different balls are seen not moving the teacher yells, "Dead bugs," and all students move to their backs with their arms and legs up and moving like a bug. After several seconds, the teacher gives the start signal and the game begins again.

▶ **LOOSE CABOOSE**

Supplies: None
Skills: Running, dodging
Formation:

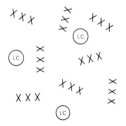

Two or three children are designated as loose cabooses that try to hook onto a train. Trains are formed by three or four children standing in column formation with their hands placed on the shoulders of the child immediately in front. The trains, by twisting and turning, endeavor to keep the caboose from hooking onto the back. Should the caboose manage to hook on, the front child in the train becomes the new caboose. Each train should attempt to keep together. If a train breaks while being chased, they go to the side and count to 25 before reentering.

▶ **NINE LIVES**

Supplies: Fleece balls

Skills: Throwing, dodging

Formation: Scattered

Any number of fleece balls can be used—the more the better. At a signal, players get a ball and hit as many people below waist level as possible. When a player counts that she has been hit nine times, she leaves the game and stands out of bounds until she has counted to 25. A player may run anywhere with a ball or to get a ball, but may possess only one ball at a time. Players must not be hit in the head. This puts the thrower out.

✓ **TEACHING TIP**

Children often cheat about the number of times they have been hit. A few words about fair play may be necessary, but a high degree of activity is the important game element.

Variations:

1. For a ball caught on the fly, a designated number of hits may be taken away.

2. Either left- or right-hand throwing can be specified.

▶ **NONDA'S CAR LOT**

Supplies: None

Skills: Running, dodging

Formation:

Two or three players are it and stand in the center of the area between two lines established at opposite ends of the playing area. The class selects four brands of cars (e.g., Honda, Corvette, Toyota, Cadillac). Each student then selects a car from the four but does not tell anyone what it is.

One of the taggers calls out a car name. All students who selected that name attempt to run to the other line without getting tagged. The tagger calls out the cars until all students have run. When a child (car) gets tagged, he must sit down at the spot of the tag. He cannot move but may tag other students who run too near. When the one who is it calls out "Car lot," all of the cars must go. Change taggers often.

▶ **ONE BEHIND**

Supplies: None

Skills: All locomotor and nonlocomotor movements

Formation: Scattered formation

Students are instructed to watch the leader's activities and stay one move behind. As the leader begins an activity, the children watch. After 10–15 seconds the leader changes movements and the students begin the first leader movement. Each time the leader changes movements, the students stay "one behind." The leader can attempt to trick students by doing an activity with her eyes closed. Thus, when the students begin this activity, they have no way of knowing when to change activities or what the preceding leader activity was.

✓ **TEACHING TIP**

This activity can be done for any skills or with any piece of equipment.

▶ **ONE STEP**

Supplies: A ball or beanbag for each pair of children

Skills: Throwing, catching

Formation:

Two children stand facing each other about 3 feet apart. One has a ball or a beanbag. The object of the game is to throw or toss the item in the stipulated manner so that the partner can catch it without moving the feet on or from the ground. When the throw is completed successfully, the thrower takes one step backward and waits for the throw from her partner. Children can try to increase their distance to an established line, or the two children who move the greatest distance apart can be declared the winners. When either child misses, moves the feet, or fails to follow directions, the partners move forward and start over. Variables to provide interest and challenge are type of throw, type of catch, and kind of step. Throwing can be underhand, overhand, two-handed, under one leg, around the back, and so on. Catching can be two-handed, left-handed, right-handed, to the side, and so on. The step can be a giant step, a tiny step, a hop, a jump, or a similar movement.

Variation: *Bowling One Step.* In groups of 4 to 6, each of the players in turn gets a chance to roll the ball at a bowling pin. A minimal distance (5 to 10 feet) is established, so that most bowlers can hit the pin on the first try. The player takes a step backward each time the pin is knocked down, and keeps rolling until he misses. The winner is the child who has moved the farthest from the pin.

▶ PARTNER STOOP

Supplies: Music

Skills: Marching rhythmically

Formation:

The game follows the same basic principle of stooping as in Circle Stoop, but is played with partners. The group forms a double circle, with partners facing counterclockwise; one partner is on the inside, and one is on the outside. When the music begins, all march in the line of direction. After a short period of marching, a signal (whistle) is sounded, and the inside circle reverses direction and marches the other way—clockwise. The partners are thus separated. When the music stops, the outer circle stands still, and the partners making up the inner circle walk to rejoin their respective outer circle partners. As soon as children reach their partner, they join inside hands and stoop without losing balance. The last couple to stoop and those who have lost balance go to the center of the circle and wait out the next round. Start the game walking and gradually increase the speed of movements when the class moves under control.

▶ RICOCHET

Supplies: Foam balls, fleece balls

Skills: Ball rolling

Formation: Circle

Several foam balls are placed in the center of a large circle of students. The class is also given a number of fleece balls. On signal, the class begins rolling the fleece balls in an attempt to hit the foam balls and move them out of the circle. Children may move outside of the circle to retrieve fleece balls, but may not enter the circle. The game is over when all or most of the foam balls are out of the circle.

✓ TEACHING TIPS

1. Time the students and challenge them to beat their best class time.
2. Have several games at one time.
3. Use beach balls rather than foam balls.

▶ SQUAD TAG

Supplies: Pinnies or markers for one squad, stopwatch

Skills: Running, dodging

Formation:

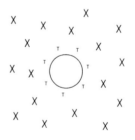

Delineate the running area with cones. An entire squad acts as taggers. The object is to see which squad can tag the remaining class members in the shorter time. The tagging squad should be marked. They stand in a football huddle formation in the center of the area with their heads down. The remainder of the class scatters as they wish throughout the area. On signal, the tagging squad scatters and tags the other class members. A class member who is tagged stops in place and remains there. Time is recorded when the last person is tagged. Each squad gets a turn at tagging.

✓ **TEACHING TIP**

Children should be cautioned to move under control, because there is much chasing and dodging in different directions. Definite boundaries are needed.

▶ **STEAL THE TREASURE**

Supplies: A bowling pin
Skill: Dodging
Formation:

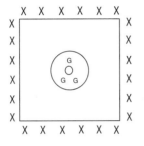

A playing area about 20 feet square is outlined, with a small circle in the center. A bowling pin placed in the small circle (hula hoop) is the treasure. Two or more guards are selected to protect the treasure. The guards can move as far from the treasure as they like to tag a player. Anyone tagged must retire and wait for the next game. To successfully steal the treasure, a player must pick it up cleanly without getting tagged. The guards tag them when they come too near. If the treasure is knocked over by a player trying to steal it, that player must also wait out a turn. There is a delicate balance for the guards between being too far from the treasure and staying too near the treasure and never tagging anyone. If the guards tag all players, they are declared billionaires.

Variation: *Bear and Keeper.* Instead of a treasure, a bear (seated cross-legged on the ground) is protected by two keepers. Anyone who touches the bear without being tagged becomes the new keeper.

▶ **TRADES**

Supplies: None
Skills: Imagery, running, dodging

Formation:

The class is divided into two teams of equal number, each of which has a goal line on opposite sides of the area. One team, the chasers, remains behind its goal line. The other team, the runners, approaches from its goal line, marching to the following dialogue:

Runners:	Here we come.
Chasers:	Where from?
Runners:	New Orleans.
Chasers:	What's your trade?
Runners:	Lemonade.
Chasers:	Show us some.

Runners move up close to the other team's goal line and proceed to act out an occupation or a specific task that they have chosen previously. The opponents try to guess what the pantomime represents. On a correct guess, the running team must run back to its goal line chased by the others. Any runner tagged must join the chasers. The game is repeated with roles reversed. The team ending with the greater number of players is the winner.

✓ **TEACHING TIP**

If a team has trouble guessing the pantomime, the other team should provide hints. Teams also should be encouraged to have a number of activities selected so that little time is consumed in choosing the next activity to be pantomimed.

▶ **TREES**

Supplies: None
Skills: Running, dodging
Formation:

22

Two parallel lines are drawn at opposite ends of the playing area. All players, except two or three taggers, are on one side of the area. On the signal "Trees," the players run to the other side of the court. The taggers try to tag as many as possible. Any player tagged becomes a tree, stopping where tagged and keeping both feet in place. Trees cannot move their feet but can tag any runners who come close enough. The taggers continue to chase the players as they cross on signal until a few are left. New players are selected to be taggers.

▶ **WHISTLE MARCH**

Supplies: Music
Skill: Moving rhythmically
Formation: Scattered

Brisk marching music is used with this game. Children are scattered around the room, walking in various directions and keeping time to the music. A whistle is blown a number of times. At this signal, lines are formed of that precise number of children, no more and no fewer. To form the lines, children stand side by side with locked elbows. As soon as a line of the proper number is formed, it begins to march to the music counterclockwise around the room. Any children left over go to the center of the room and remain there until the next signal. On the next whistle signal (a single blast), the lines break up, and all walk individually around the room in various directions.

When forming a new line, stipulate that children may not form the same combinations as in the previous line.

▶ **WHISTLE MIXER**

Supplies: A whistle
Skills: All basic locomotor movements
Formation: Scattered

Children are scattered throughout the area. To begin, they walk around in any direction they wish. The teacher blows a whistle a number of times in succession with short, sharp blasts. Children then form small circles with the number in the circles equal to the number of whistle blasts. If there are four blasts, children form circles of four—no more, no less. The goal is not to be left out or caught in a circle with the incorrect number of students. Encourage players to move to the center of the area and raise their hands to facilitate finding others without a group. After the circles are formed, the teacher calls "Walk," and the game continues.

Variation: Another version of this game is done with the aid of a tom-tom. Different beats indicate different locomotor movements—skipping, galloping, slow walking, normal walking, running. The whistle is still used to set the number for each circle.

▶ **WOLFE'S BEANBAG EXCHANGE**

Supplies: One beanbag per child
Skills: Running, dodging, tossing, catching
Formation: Scattered

Five or six children are identified as taggers. The remaining children start scattered throughout the area, each with a beanbag in hand. The taggers chase the players with beanbags. When a tag is made, the tagged player must freeze, keeping her feet still and beanbag in hand. To unfreeze a player, a non-frozen player can exchange his beanbag for a beanbag held by a frozen player. If two frozen players are within tossing distance, they can thaw each other by exchanging their beanbags through the air using a toss and catch. Both tosses have to be caught or the beanbags must be retrieved and tried again.

Variation: After students have learned the game, tell the taggers that they may interfere with the tossing of beanbags between two frozen players by batting them to the floor. This forces the toss to be tried again and the players remain frozen until successful catches are made by both players.

DEVELOPMENTAL LEVEL III

Games at this level become more complex and organized. A great deal more cooperation is needed to make the activities enjoyable. In addition, an opportunity to use strategy exists, thus encouraging cognitive development. Strategy is important for successful play at this level.

▶ **AIR RAID**

Supplies: Four to eight tumbling mats, fleece balls, foam balls
Skills: Throwing
Formation: Class divided into two teams

Two teams are placed on opposite halves of the teaching area. Each team is given two tumbling mats that are fastened together and set on end to form an upright cylinder or target. The target is then placed near the back wall in the center of the gym (if baskets are obstructing the flight of balls the cylinder may need to be moved).

Teams are also given fleece balls and foam balls to throw. On signal, teams attempt to throw as many balls into the target as possible. The team with the most balls in at the end of the game wins.

Variations:

1. Use two targets for each side.
2. Place the target in a corner and have balls that ricochet in count as two points.
3. Allow the students to decide where to place the target.
4. Allow students to guard their target. This may require cones around the target to keep guards from colliding with the target.

▶ BARKER'S HOOPLA

Supplies: Hoops, beanbags
Skill: Running
Formation:

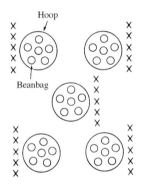

Five hoops are arranged with one in each corner and the other in the center of the playing area. Any distance between hoops can be used, but 25 to 30 feet is a challenging distance. Five to six beanbags are placed in each hoop. The class is divided into five equal teams, one group near each hoop. This is their home base. The object of the game is to steal beanbags from other hoops and return them to the hoop that is home base for each respective team. The following rules are in effect:

1. A player can take only one beanbag at a time. That player must take the beanbag to the home base before returning for another one.
2. Beanbags cannot be thrown or tossed to the home base, but must be placed on the floor in the hoop before being released.
3. No player can protect the home base or its beanbags with any defensive maneuver.

4. Beanbags may be taken from any hoop.
5. When the stop signal is given, every player must freeze immediately and release any beanbags in possession. Any follow-through of activities to get a better score is penalized.

The team with the most beanbags in their home-base hoop is declared the winner.

▶ CAGEBALL TARGET THROW

Supplies: A cageball (18- to 30-inch), 12 to 15 smaller balls of various sizes
Skill: Throwing
Formation:

An area about 20 feet wide is marked across the center of the playing area, with a cageball in the center. The object of the game is to throw the smaller balls against the cageball, thus forcing it across the line in front of the other team. Players may come up to the line to throw, but they may not throw while inside the cageball area. A player may enter the area, however, to recover a ball. No one is to touch the cageball at any time, nor may the cageball be pushed by a ball in the hands of a player. If the cageball seems to roll too easily, it should be deflated slightly. The throwing balls can be of almost any size—soccer balls, volleyballs, playground balls, for example.

▶ CHAIN TAG

Supplies: None
Skills: Running, dodging
Formation:

Two parallel lines are established at opposite ends of the playing area. Two groups of three players form a chain with joined hands and occupy the center. The players with free hands on either end of the chain do the tagging. All other players line up on one of the parallel lines. The players in the center call "Come on over," and children cross from one line to the other. The chains try to tag the runners. Anyone caught joins the chain. When the chain grows to six players, it divides into two groups of three players.

> **Variation:**   *Catch of Fish.* The chain catches runners by surrounding them like a fishing net. The runners cannot run under or through the links of the net.

▶ CIRCLE TOUCH

Supplies: Yarnballs and marking spots

Skills: Dodging, body management

Formation:

One child plays against three others, who form a small circle with joined hands. The object of the game is for the lone child to touch a designated child (on the shoulders) in the circle with a yarnball. The other two children in the circle, by moving side to side, attempt to keep the tagger away from the third member of the circle. The circle players may circle in any direction but must not release hand grips. The circle is not allowed to move across the floor; they must circle back and forth around a marking spot. The tagger, in attempting to touch the protected circle player, must go around the outside of the circle. He is not permitted to go underneath or through the joined hands of the circle players. To avoid roughness, the game should be played in short, seven-second bouts and then a new tagger rotated in.

> **Variation:**   *Grab the Flag.* A piece of cloth, a handkerchief, or a flag is tucked into the belt in back of the protected child. The fourth child, the tagger, tries to pull the flag from the belt.

▶ CLEAN-UP

Supplies: Volleyball net or magic rope, fleece balls, and/or foam balls

Skill: Throwing

Formation: Scatter formation with the class in two large groups

The gym is divided in half by a volleyball net with one team placed on each side of the net. Numerous fleece balls are scattered around each side of the gym (the more balls the better). On signal, students begin throwing balls over the net one at a time. After throwing one ball, students quickly find another ball and throw it over the net. This process continues until the game is stopped. The team with the fewest number of balls on their side of the gym is declared the winner.

> **Variation:**   Scoring can be tracked individually, with children getting one point for each ball thrown over the net. Balls that hit the back wall are worth two points.

▶ FAST PASS

Supplies: One 8-inch foam rubber ball, pinnies

Skills: Passing, catching, moving to an open area

Formation: Scattered

One team begins with the ball. The object is to complete five consecutive passes without the ball touching the floor. The team without the ball attempts to intercept the ball or recover an incomplete pass. Each time a pass is caught, the team shouts the number of consecutive passes completed. Each time a ball touches the floor or is intercepted, the count starts over.

Players may not contact each other. Emphasis should be placed on spreading out and using the entire court area. If players do not spread out, the area can be broken into quadrants and players restricted to one quadrant.

▶ FLAG CHASE

Supplies: Flags, stopwatch

Skills: Running, dodging

Formation: Scattered

One team wears flags positioned in the back of the belt. The flag team scatters throughout the area. On signal, the object is for the chasing team to capture as many flags as possible in a designated amount of time. The flags are brought to the teacher or placed in a box. Players cannot use their hands to ward off a chaser. Roles are reversed. The team pulling the most flags is declared the winner.

▶ **GALACTIC EMPIRE AND REBELS**

Supplies: None

Skills: Chasing, fleeing, dodging

Court markings:

This game can be played indoors or outdoors in a square that is approximately 100 feet on each side. Each team's spaceport is behind the end line, where the single space fighters are stationed, waiting to issue against the enemy. To begin, one or more space fighters from either team move from their spaceport to entice enemy flyers for possible capture. A flyer leaving the spaceport may capture only opposing flyers who previously have left their respective spaceport. This is the basic rule of the game. A flyer may go back to her spaceport and be eligible immediately to issue again to capture an opponent who was already in general space. The technique of the game is to entice enemy flyers close to the spaceport so that fellow flyers can issue and capture (tag) an opposing flyer.

As an illustration of how the game proceeds: Rebel flyer 1 moves into general space to entice Empire flyer 1 so that he can be captured. Rebel flyer 1 turns back and heads for her spaceport, chased by Empire flyer 1. Rebel flyer 2 now leaves her spaceport and tags Empire flyer 1 before the Empire flyer can tag Rebel flyer 1. The Empire flyer is now a prisoner.

A player captured by an opposing flyer is taken to the tagger's prison—both captor and captive are given free passage to the prison. In prison, the captives form a chain gang, holding hands and extending the prisoners' line toward their own spaceport. The last captive is always at the end of the prisoners' line with one foot in the prison. Captives can be released if a teammate can get to them without being tagged. The released prisoner (only the end one) is escorted back to her own spaceport, and both players are given free passage.

The game becomes one of capturing opposing flyers and securing the release of captured teammates. Flyers stepping over the sideline automatically become prisoners. One or two players in the spaceport should be assigned to guard the prison. Set a time limit of 10 minutes, and declare the team with the most prisoners the winner.

▶ **GUESS THE LEADER**

Supplies: None

Skills: Body management

Formation:

The class forms a large circle and two to three people, the guessers, are chosen to be in the middle. While the guessers have their eyes closed, a leader in the circle is chosen. This person leads the class in an exercise and the guessers open their eyes and attempt to guess who the leader is. As the guessers watch the class, the leader continues to lead the class in various exercises. The guessers are watching for the student that changes first (the leader). The guessers are allowed three guesses before the leader is identified. A new leader is then identified.

▶ **JOLLY BALL**

Supplies: A cageball 24 inches or larger (or a 36- to 48-inch pushball)

Skill: Kicking

Formation:

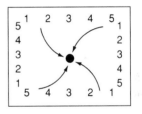

Four teams are organized, each of which forms one side of a hollow square. Children sit down, facing in, with hands braced behind them (Crab position). The members of each team are numbered consecutively. Children wait until their number is called. Four active players (one from each team) move in Crab position and try to kick the cageball over any one of the three opposing teams. The sideline players can also kick the ball. Ordinarily, the hands are not used, but this could be allowed in the learning stages of the game.

A point is scored against a team that allows the ball to go over its line. A ball that goes out at the corner between teams is dead and must be replayed. When a point is scored, the active children retire to their teams and another number is called. The team with the fewest points wins the game. This game is quite strenuous for the active players, so they should be rotated after a reasonable length of time when there is no score.

Variation: Two children from each team can be active at once.

22

▶ JUMP-THE-SHOT VARIATIONS

Supplies: A jump-the-shot rope

Skill: Rope jumping

Formation:

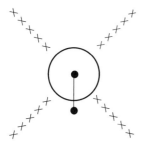

Before the following variations are tried, the jump-the-shot routines and variations listed previously (page 564) should be reviewed.

1. Two or more squads are in file formation facing the rope turner. Each player runs clockwise (against the turn of the rope), jumping the rope as often as necessary to return to the squad.

2. Each player runs counterclockwise and tries to run around the circle before the rope can catch up with him. If this happens, he must jump to allow the rope to go under him. The best time for a player to start his run is just after the rope has passed.

3. Players can try some of the stunts in which the hands and feet are on the ground, to see whether they can have the rope pass under them. The Rabbit Jump, push-up position, Lame Dog, and others are possibilities.

▶ MUSHROOMS

Supplies: 10–16 cones, 10–16 Frisbees, fleece balls (or foam balls)

Skill: Rolling, throwing

Formation: Class divided into two equal teams; scattered formation

Two teams are formed with each occupying one-half of the gym. On the end line of each half are five to eight cones with a Frisbee balanced on top of the cone (these resemble mushrooms). Each team is also given enough foam balls for each child to have one. On signal, team members try to roll (or throw) their balls and knock off the Frisbees. Students may not guard the cones and any Frisbee knocked off has to stay off, even if touched by a team's member. When all Frisbees have been knocked off, the game is over.

▶ OCTOPUS

Supplies: None

Skills: Maneuvering, problem solving

Formation: Groups of six to nine, holding hands, tangled

Octopus is a game that gets its name from the many hands joined together in the activity. Children stand shoulder to shoulder in a tight circle. Everyone thrusts the hands forward and reaches through the group of hands to grasp the hands across the circle. Players must make sure that they do not hold both hands of the same player. Players also may not hold the hand of an adjacent player. The object is to untangle the mess created by the joined hands by going under, over, or through fellow players. No one is permitted to release a hand grip during the unraveling. What is the end result? Perhaps one large circle or two smaller connected circles.

✓ TEACHING TIP

If, after a period of time, the knotted hands do not seem to unravel, call a halt and administer first aid. The teacher and group can decide where the difficulty is and allow a change in position of those hands until the knot is dissolved. This is a cooperative game that demands teamwork.

▶ ONE-BASE TAGBALL

Supplies: A base (or standard), a volleyball (8-inch foam ball for younger children)

Skills: Running, dodging, throwing

Formation:

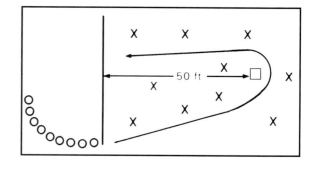

A home line is drawn at one end of the playing space. A base or standard is placed about 50 feet in front of the home line. Two teams are formed. One team is scattered around the fielding area, the boundaries of which are determined by the number of children. The other team is lined up in single file behind the home line. The object of the game is for the fielding team to tag the runners with the ball. Two runners at a time try to round the base and head back for the home line without being tagged. The game is continuous, meaning that as soon as a running team player is tagged or crosses the home line, another player starts immediately.

The fielding team may run with the ball and pass it from player to player, trying to tag one of the runners. The running team scores a point for each player who runs successfully around the base and back to the home line. At the start of the game, the running team has two players ready at the right side of the home line. The others on the team are in line, waiting for a turn. The teacher throws the ball anywhere in the field, and the first two runners start toward the base. They must run around the base from the right side. After all of the players have run, the teams exchange places. The team scoring the most points wins.

✔ TEACHING TIP

To facilitate tagging a runner, players on the fielding team should make passes to a person close to the runner. They must be alert, because two children at a time are running. The next player on the running team must watch carefully in order to start the instant one of the two preceding runners is back safely behind the line or has been hit.

▶ OVER THE WALL

Supplies: None
Skills: Running, dodging
Formation:

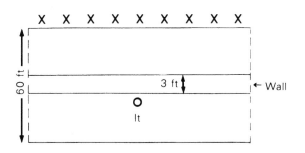

Two parallel goal lines are drawn about 60 feet apart. Two additional parallel lines about 3 feet apart are laid out parallel to the goal lines in the middle of the game area. This is the wall. Two or three players are it and stand on, or behind, the wall. All of the other players are behind one of the goal lines. One of the taggers calls "Over the wall." All of the players must then run across the wall to the other goal line. The taggers try to tag any crossing players. Anyone caught helps catch the others. Players also are considered caught when they step on the wall. They must clear it with a leap or a jump and cannot step on it anywhere, including on the lines. After crossing over to the other side safely, players wait for the next call. The game can be made more difficult by increasing the width of the wall. Taggers can step on or run through the wall at will.

▶ PACMAN

Supplies: Markers in the shape of Pacman
Skills: Fleeing, reaction time
Formation:

Three students are it and carry the Pacman marker. The remainder of the class is scattered throughout the area, standing on a floor line. Movement can only be made on a line. Begin the game by placing the three taggers at the corners of the perimeter lines. Play is continuous; a player who is tagged takes the marker and becomes a new tagger. If a player leaves a line to escape being tagged, that player must secure a marker and become an additional tagger. Tagbacks are not allowed; that is, players may not tag the person who tagged them.

▶ PARTNER DOG AND CAT

Supplies: None
Skills: Chasing, fleeing, dodging
Formation: Partners

Partners stand toe to toe on a line in the center of the gym. Partner A begins the game by saying "Dog." Partner B can then say "Dog" or "Cat." If Partner B says "Cat," she is chased to a designated line by Partner A. If Partner A tags Partner B, Partner A gets a point and the game starts over.

✔ TEACHING TIP

Try varying the number of "dogs" that must be said before "cat" can be called out. Usually four or five "dogs" will make the game more enjoyable for partners.

▶ PIN KNOCKOUT

Supplies: Many playground balls, 12 bowling pins
Skills: Rolling, dodging

Formation:

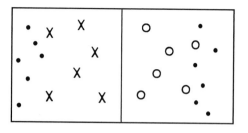

Two teams of equal number play the game. Each team is given many playground balls and six bowling pins. A court 30 by 60 feet or larger with a centerline is needed. The size of the court depends on the number of children in the game. The object of the game is to knock down all of the opponents' bowling pins. The balls are used for rolling at the opposing team's pins. Each team stays in its half of the court.

A player is eliminated if any of the following occurs:

1. He is touched by any ball at any time, regardless of the situation (other than picking up a ball).

2. She steps over the centerline to roll or retrieve a ball. (Any opposing team member hit as a result of such a roll is not eliminated.)

3. He attempts to block a rolling ball with a ball in his hands and the rolling ball touches him in any manner.

A foul is called when a player holds a ball longer than ten seconds without rolling at the opposing team. Play stops, and the ball is given to the opposing team.

The bowling pins are put anywhere in the team's area. Players may guard the pins, but must not touch them. When a pin is down, even though it might have been knocked over unintentionally by a member of the defending team, it is removed immediately from the game. The game is over when all pins on one side have been knocked down.

▶ RIGHT FACE, LEFT FACE (STREETS AND ALLEYS)

Supplies: None
Skills: Running, dodging
Formation:

```
X   X   X   X
X   X   X   X
X   X   X   X
X   X   X   X
```

Children stand in rows that are aligned both from front to rear and from side to side. Two runners and two chasers are chosen. Players all face the same way and join

hands with the players on each side. The chasers try to tag the runners, who run between the rows with the restriction that they cannot break through or under the arms. The teacher can help the runners by calling "Right face" or "Left face" at the proper time. On command, the children drop hands, face the new direction, and grasp hands with those who are then on each side, thus making new passages available. When the runner is caught or when children become tired, new runners and chasers are chosen.

Variations:

1. Directions (north, south, east, west) can be used instead of the facing commands.

2. *Streets and Alleys.* The teacher calls, "Streets," and the children face in one direction. The call "Alleys" causes them to face at right angles.

3. The command "Air raid" can be given, and children drop to their knees and make themselves into small balls, tucking their heads and seats down. This allows unlimited movement by the taggers and runners.

▶ SCOOTER KICKBALL

Supplies: A cageball, gym scooters for active players
Skill: Striking with various body parts
Formation:

```
X   X        O   O
X  X            O  O
X                  O
   X  X ● O  O     O
X                  O
X  X          O  O
X   X        O   O
```

Divide each team into active players (on scooters) and goal defenders. The active players are seated on the scooters, and the goal defenders are seated on the goal line, with feet extended. The object of the game is to kick the cageball over the goal line defended by the opposite team. The players are positioned as shown above. The game starts with a face-off of two opposing players on scooters at the center of the court. The face-off is also used after a goal is scored. The active players on scooters propel the ball mainly with their feet. Touching the ball with the hands is a foul and results in a free kick by the opposition at the spot of the foul. A player also may use the head and body to stop and propel the ball.

The players defending the goal are seated on the goal line. They may not use their hands either, but use of the feet, body, and head is permitted. (If scoring seems too easy, then the defenders can be allowed to use their hands.) Defenders should be restricted to the seated position at the goal line and are not permitted to enter the field of play to propel or stop the ball.

✓ TEACHING TIP

The number of scooters determines the number of active players. The game works well if half of the players from each team are in the center on scooters and the other half are goal defenders. After a goal or after a stipulated time period, active players and goal defenders exchange places. Any active player who falls off a scooter should be required to sit again on the scooter before becoming eligible to propel the ball.

Variation: If there are enough scooters for everyone, the game can be played with rules similar to soccer. A more restricted goal (perhaps half of the end line) can be marked with standards. A goalie defends this area. All other players are active and can move to any spot on the floor. The floor space should be large enough to allow some freedom of play.

▶ STAR WARS

Supplies: Four bowling pins
Skill: Running
Formation:

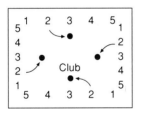

Four teams, each of which occupies one side facing in, form a hollow square, about 10 yards on each side. Members of each team are numbered consecutively from right to left. This means that one person on each team has the same number as one player on each of the other three teams. At the center of the square, place four bowling pins, one in front of each team and placed apart so as to avoid collisions of players.

When a number is called, the four children with that number run to the right, around the square, and through their own vacated space to the center of the square. The first child to lay the team bowling pin down on the floor is the winner.

Scoring is kept by letters in the words *Star Wars*. The player who puts the pin down first receives two letters while the second player gets one letter. The first team to spell Star Wars is the winner and a new game begins. Since numbers are not called in order, keep a tally to make sure every number is called.

▶ STRIKE THE PINS

Supplies: 8 to 12 bowling pins per team, 15 to 20 foam-rubber balls
Skill: Throwing
Formation:

A line is drawn across the center of the floor wall to wall. This divides the floor into two courts, each of which is occupied by one team. Another line is drawn 25 feet from the centerline in each court. This is the line where each team spaces its bowling pins. Each team has at least five balls. The object of the game is to knock over the other team's pins by rolling the balls. Players roll the balls back and forth, but cannot cross the centerline. Whenever a pin is knocked over by a ball or player (accidentally or not), that pin is removed. The team with the most pins standing at the end of the game is declared the winner. Out-of-bounds balls can be recovered but must be rolled from inside the court.

Variation: Pins can be reset instead of removed. Two scorers, one for each pin line, are needed.

▶ SUNDAY

Supplies: None
Skills: Running, dodging
Formation:

Two parallel lines are drawn at each end of the playing area. Three or more players are it and stand in the center of the area between the two lines. The rest of the class is on one of the two lines. The object is to cross to the other line without being tagged or making a false start.

All line players stand with their front foot on the line. The line players must run across the line immediately when the tagger calls "Sunday." Anyone who does not run immediately is considered caught. The tagger can call other days of the week to confuse the runners. No player may make a start if another day of the week is called.

✓ **TEACHING TIP**

"Making a start" must be defined clearly. To begin, it can be defined as a player moving either foot. Later, when children get better at the game, any forward movement of the body can constitute a start.

▶ **TOUCHDOWN**

Supplies: A small object (coin, thimble) that can be concealed in the hand

Skills: Running, dodging

Formation:

```
X |          | O
X |          | O
X |          | O
X |          | O
X |          | O
X |          | O
X |          | O
X |          | O
X |          | O
X |          | O
X |          | O
```

Two parallel lines are placed at each end of the playing area. Two teams face each other, each standing on one of the parallel lines. One team (offensive) huddles and the members decide which player is to carry an object to the opponents' goal line. The offensive team moves out of the huddle and spreads out along the line. On the signal "Hike," the offensive players move toward the opponents' goal line, each player holding the hands closed as if carrying the object. On the charge signal, the opponents (defense) also run forward and try to tag the players. On being tagged, players must stop immediately and open both hands to show whether or not they have the object. If the player carrying the object reaches the goal line without being tagged, that player calls "Touchdown," and scores six points. The defensive team now goes on the offense.

▶ **TRIPLET STOOP**

Supplies: Music

Skill: Moving rhythmically

Formation:

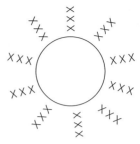

The game is played in groups of three with the three youngsters marching abreast in the same direction. On signal, the outside player of the three continues marching in the same direction. The middle player stops and marches in place. The inside player reverses direction. When the music stops, the groups of three attempt to reunite at the spot where the middle player stopped. The last three to join hands and stoop move to the center to wait out one turn.

▶ **WHISTLE BALL**

Supplies: A ball for each group of six to eight players

Skills: Passing, catching

Formation: Circles of six to eight

Eight or fewer children stand in circle formation. A ball is passed rapidly back and forth among them in any order. The object is to stay in the game as long as possible. A player sits down in place after making any of the following errors:

1. A player has the ball or the ball is on the way when the signal occurs. (Time intervals can be signaled with music on—music off, taped in segments of 5 to 15 seconds.)

2. A poor throw is made or a catch is not made after a catchable throw.

3. A pass is made back to the person from whom it was received.

✓ **TEACHING TIP**

Another way to control the time periods is to appoint a child as timer and to give her a list of the time periods, a whistle, and a stopwatch. The timer should be cautioned not to give any advance indication of when the stop signal will be blown. Restart the game when there are four or five players left standing so no one sits out for too long.

MISCELLANEOUS PLAYGROUND GAMES

The following games are useful only for small groups, but children do enjoy playing them on the playground.

▶ FOUR SQUARE

(Developmental Levels II and III)

Supplies: 8-inch playground ball or volleyball

Skill: Batting a ball

Court markings:

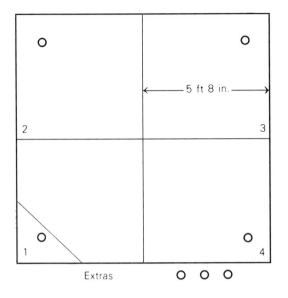

Lines are drawn as shown above. The squares should be numbered 1, 2, 3, and 4. A service line is drawn diagonally across the far corner of square 1. The player in this square always serves and must stay behind the line when serving.

The ball is served by dropping and serving it underhanded from the bounce. If the serve hits a line, the server is out. The server can hit the ball after it has bounced once in his square. The receiver directs it to any other square with an underhand hit. Play continues until one player fails to return the ball or commits a fault. Any of the following constitutes a fault:

1. Hitting the ball sidearm or overhand
2. Landing a ball on a line between the squares (A ball landing on an outer boundary is considered good.)
3. Stepping into another square to play the ball
4. Catching or carrying a return volley
5. Allowing the ball to touch any part of the body except the hands

A player who misses or commits a fault goes to the end of the waiting line and all players move up. The player at the head of the waiting line moves into square 4.

Variations:

1. A 2-foot circle can be drawn at the center of the area. Hitting the ball into the circle constitutes a fault.

2. The game can be changed by varying the method of propelling the ball. The server sets the method. The ball can be hit with a partially closed fist, the back of the hand, or the elbow. A foot or knee also can be used to return the ball. The server calls "Fisties," "Elbows," "Footsies," or "Kneesies" to set the pattern.

3. *Chain Spelling.* The server names a word, and each player returning the ball must add the next letter in the sequence.

4. Hula hoops can be used so that all students can play at one time.

5. Cooperative scoring can be used with Developmental Level I students to see how many consecutive hits they can make without missing.

▶ TEAM HANDBALL

Supplies: Team handball, foam rubber ball, or volleyball; cones; pinnies

Skills: Running, dribbling, passing, throwing, catching

Court markings:

Outdoor field markings

The court is marked with a 6-meter goal area, a 7-meter penalty line, and a 9-meter free-throw line. The goal is 2 by 3 meters. The goal area inside the six-meter line is only for the goalie. Other players are not allowed in this area. The 7-meter line is used for a major penalty shot, and the 9-meter line is used for a minor penalty shot. A regulation court is 20 by 40 meters. Boundary cones, tape on the wall, rope through a chain-link fence, soccer goals, or field hockey goals can be substituted for actual team handball goals. For indoor play, a basketball court can be modified for team handball by running a line from the corners of the court to top of the key.

The object of the game is to move a small soccer ball down the field by passing and dribbling and then to throw the ball into a goal area that is three meters wide and two meters high. In regulation play, each team has six court players and one goalie. The six court players cover the entire court. A player is allowed three steps before and

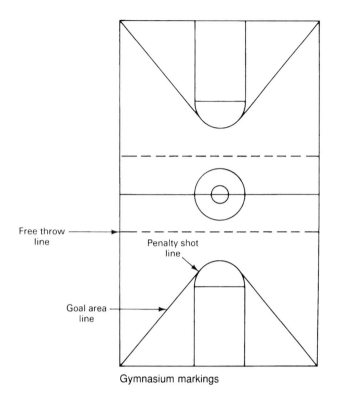

Gymnasium markings

after dribbling the ball. There is no limit on the number of dribbles. Dribbling is, however, discouraged because passing is more effective. A double dribble is a violation. A player can hold the ball for 3 seconds only before passing, dribbling, or shooting. Players cannot kick the ball in any way, except the goalie.

One point is awarded for a goal. Violations and penalties are similar to basketball. A free throw is taken from the point of the violation, and defense must remain three meters away while protecting the goal. A penalty throw is awarded from the seven-meter line for a major violation. A major violation occurs when an offensive player who is inside the nine-meter line in a good shooting position is fouled. During a penalty throw, all players must be behind the nine-meter line.

For more in-depth coverage of rules, a teaching resource kit can be secured from USA Team Handball, One Olympic Plaza, Colorado Springs, CO 80909 or www.usateamhandball.org

The offensive team starts the game with a throw-on from the center line. A throw-on also initiates play after each goal. All six offensive players line up at the centerline, and a teammate throws the ball to a teammate. The defense is in position, using either a zone or person-to-person defense. Offensive strategy is similar to basketball with picks, screens, rolls, and movement

to open up shots on the goal. With a zone defense, short, quick passes are made in an overloaded portion of the zone.

The defensive strategy is similar to basketball, with person-to-person and zone defense being popular. Beginning players should start with the person-to-person defense and learn how to stay with an offensive player. The back players in the zone are back against the goal line, while the front players are just inside the 9-meter line. The zone rotates with the ball as passes are made around the court.

✓ TEACHING TIPS

Learning stations can be set up for passing, shooting, goal tending, dribbling, and defensive work. Performance objectives are useful for structuring practice time at each station. Students can play with nerf balls, playground balls, and volleyballs to get more practice attempts and to help beginning goalies perfect their skills. Group drills from basketball are applicable to team handball defense, offense, passing, and dribbling. Various instructional devices can be included for targets in passing, timing for dribbling through cones, or narrowing the goal area for shots to the corners. Penalty shots should be practiced. Competitive-type drills are enjoyable and motivating for most students.

Variation: *Sideline Team Handball.* This game can be played when space is limited and too many students are in a class. Extra team members spread out along each sideline. These sideline players can receive passes from teammates and can help pass the ball down the court. Sideline members can only pass the ball, however, and the three-second rule applies to them. One sideline can be one team, and the other sideline the other team. A challenging variation might have different team members on each sideline. This distribution forces the active players to sharpen their passing skills.

▶ TETHERBALL

(Developmental Levels II and III)

Supplies: A tetherball assembly (pole, rope, and ball)

Skill: Batting a ball

Court markings:

The first server is picked by lot. One player stands on each side of the pole. The server puts the ball into play by tossing it into the air and hitting in the direction he chooses. The opponent must not strike the ball on the first swing around the pole. On its second swing around the pole, she hits the ball back in the opposite direction. As the ball is hit back and forth, each player tries to hit it so that the rope winds completely around the pole in the direction in which he is hitting the ball. The game is won by the player who succeeds in doing this or whose opponent forfeits the game by making a foul. A foul is any of the following:

1. Hitting the ball with any part of the body other than the hands or forearms
2. Catching or holding the ball during play
3. Touching the pole
4. Hitting the rope with the forearms or hands
5. Throwing the ball
6. Winding the ball around the pole below the 5-foot mark

After the opening game, the winner of the preceding game serves. Winning four games wins the set.

▶ TWO SQUARE

(Developmental Levels II and III)

Supplies: A playground ball or volleyball

Skill: Batting a ball

The basic rules and lines are the same as for Four Square, except that only two squares are used. If there are players waiting for a turn, the active player who misses or fouls can be eliminated as in Four Square. If only two players wish to play, score can be kept. The ball must be served from behind the baseline.

▶ VOLLEY TENNIS

Supplies: A volleyball

Skills: Most volleyball skills

Formation: Scattered

The game can be played as a combination of volleyball and tennis. The net is put on the ground, as in tennis, and the ball is put into play with a serve. It may bounce once or can be passed directly to a teammate. The ball must be hit three times before going over the net. Spiking is common because of the low net. A point is scored when the ball cannot be returned over the net to the opposing team.

FOR MORE INFORMATION

References and Suggested Readings

Barbarash, L. (1997). *Multicultural games.* Champaign, IL: Human Kinetics.

Kasser, S.L. (1995). *Inclusive Games: Movement fun for everyone.* Champaign, IL: Human Kinetics.

Le Fevre, D.N. (2002). *Best new games.* Champaign, IL: Human Kinetics.

Lichtman, B. (1999). *More innovative games.* Champaign, IL: Human Kinetics.

Morris, G. S. D., & Stiel, J. (1999). *Changing kids' games* (2nd ed.). Champaign, IL: Human Kinetics.

Lifetime Activities and Sport Skills

Having a wide range of physical skills is desired by most people. In many cases, participating in a wide range of lifetime and sport activities leaves one with a better understanding and appreciation of sport activities. The focus of this section is to teach the basic skills of the activities and to expose youngsters to a variety of activities to help them learn their personal likes and dislikes. Part of being physically educated is learning one's individual strengths and weaknesses. In these chapters future teachers will learn to teach basic skills, drills for practicing the skills, and lead-up game activities that give children the opportunity to apply skills they have learned. Lead-up games are designed to restrict focus to one or two types of skills so it is easier to be successful.

After reading this section, you will be able to teach common sport and lifetime activities. The chapters are organized to simplify the presentation of common sport activities. You will know how to modify the activities so all youngsters can successfully participate.

23

Lifetime Activities

ESSENTIAL COMPONENTS OF QUALITY PROGRAMS

▶ I. Organized around content standards

▶ II. Student-centered and developmentally appropriate

▶ III. Physical activity and motor skill development form the core of the program

▶ IV. Teaches management skills and self-discipline

▶ V. Promotes inclusion of all students

▶ VI. Focuses on process over product

▶ VII. Promotes lifetime personal health and wellness

▶ VIII. Teaches cooperation and responsibility and promotes sensitivity to diversity

NATIONAL STANDARDS FOR PHYSICAL EDUCATION*

▶ 1. Demonstrates competency in motor skills and movement patterns needed to perform a variety of physical activities.

▶ 2. Demonstrates understanding of movement concepts, principles, and tactics as they apply to the learning and performance of physical activities.

▶ 3. Participates regularly in physical activity.

▶ 4. Achieves and maintains a health-enhancing level of physical fitness.

▶ 5. Exhibits responsible personal and social behavior that respects self and others in physical activity.

▶ 6. Values physical activity for health, enjoyment, challenge, self-expression, and/or social interaction.

*National Association for Sport and Physical Education (NASPE), 2004.

SUMMARY

Lifetime activities can be used to maintain an active lifestyle throughout the life span. Too often, curriculums are limited in scope and don't offer activities that students can use as they become mature adults. This chapter is designed to introduce students to a number of activities that can be performed alone or in small groups. These activities can be played in highly competitive situations or can be enjoyed in recreational settings. Rather than creating outstanding performers, the focus of this chapter will be to introduce students to activities that are not always found in elementary school settings.

OUTCOMES

▪ Provide an explanation as to why lifetime physical activities should be taught in physical education.

▪ Identify characteristics of lifetime physical activities.

▪ Discuss the importance of teaching walking in elementary schools.

▪ Design an orienteering course for students and list the necessary skills students will need to know before completing the course.

▪ List a variety of racquet skills and lead-up games involving racquets.

▪ Discuss a variety of Frisbee activities that can be taught in the elementary schools.

L ifetime physical activities are activities that can be participated in throughout the life span. A primary role of physical education is to promote lifetime physical activity for all students. For this reason, it is important that physical education teachers have a firm understanding of what is being promoted. When most people think of lifetime activities, they immediately envision activities for the elderly. After all, by definition, the activity must be one that can be participated in throughout life, including when elderly. Since the elderly typically engage in less intense activities, the thought process might go something like this: "An 80-year-old grandmother can walk for exercise; therefore, walking is a lifetime activity"; or "Basketball requires large amounts of intense running, so you probably can't play if you are in your seventies; therefore it's not a lifetime activity." Although this is logical thinking, it is not entirely accurate. For an activity to be regarded as a lifetime activity it usually meets all or most of the following criteria:

- The activity offers opportunity for participation at various intensities, including low and vigorous.

- The activity can be noncompetitive; it is an activity that is enjoyable even if competition is not the focus of participation.

- The activity can be done alone or with a partner or teammates.

- The activity can contribute to the overall health of the participant.

For most people, as age increases, the desire and ability to engage in intense physical activity decrease. Thus as people age, the physical activities they find enjoyable will change. At the age of 20, football and rugby may be desirable activities; however, football and rugby are not typically an activity of choice beyond the age of 25. In fact, most traditional team sports, because they are usually vigorous in nature, are not thought of as lifetime activities. In addition, team sports, in their purest form, do not meet the criteria of being a lifetime activity. Traditionally, physical education has focused on team sports. However, new data suggest that the types of activities adults participate in are not team sports. The National Sporting Goods Association (2003) reports that of the top 20 activities participated in by adults, only two (basketball is number 10 and baseball is number 19) are team sports. As Table 23.1 shows, not all of the top 20 activities are appropriate for elementary children or the physical education setting. Also, the data do not suggest that these activities are the only activities that should be included in physical education. They merely state that these are the most popular.

The feasibility of including physical activity in a typical day also plays a role in lifetime activity. Most adults work an eight-hour day, care for children, and run errands, leaving little time for physical activity. Those people who deem physical activity important must work it into their schedules when time permits. Thus, trying to find a group of six to eight adults who are able to work physical activity into their schedules at the same time and on the same day is difficult, although it can be done; for example, at universities small groups of faculty and staff often participate in sports during lunch on a regular basis. However, it is important to remember most adults do not work on a campus that has access to facilities such as gyms and fields. For these reasons, the majority of lifetime physical activities only require one or two people

TABLE 23.1	Top 20 Physical Activities for Adults
1. Exercise Walking	
2. Camping	
3. Exercising with Equipment	
4. Swimming	
5. Bowling	
6. Fishing	
7. Bicycle Riding	
8. Billiards/Pool	
9. Aerobic Exercising	
10. Basketball	
11. Weight Lifting	
12. Golf	
13. Hiking	
14. Boating	
15. Running/Jogging	
16. Hunting	
17. Target Shooting	
18. Roller Skating	
19. Baseball	
20. Backpacking	

Source: Data from the National Sporting Goods Association's Sport Participation in 2003: Series I.

for participation, since it is easier to coordinate schedules when the number of participants is limited.

The role of physical education is to promote lifetime physical activity for all students. Because all students have unique needs and desires, it is important to offer a variety of activities. Using the four criteria listed earlier in the chapter, virtually all activities, with a few modifications, can be participated in throughout life. Thus, a variety of activities, including gymnastics, rhythms, traditional sports, and lifetime activities, should be taught via a balanced curriculum.

WALKING

Walking is by far the most popular physical activity for adults (National Sporting Goods Association, 2003). It requires minimal equipment, results in very few injuries, and can be done alone or in small groups. For these reasons, walking is likely the activity most physical education students will engage in as adults. Walking is an often overlooked, but important, component of any physical education curriculum designed to promote lifetime physical activity.

Instructional Procedures

1. Delineate the walking route with cones.
2. Emphasize appropriate posture and technique: head up, eyes forward, and smooth arm swing.
3. Check the course before student use.
4. If an outside course is used emphasize safety.
   a. Always know where the person behind you is.
   b. Use crosswalks.
   c. Watch for irregular sidewalks.
   d. Walk on the left, looking toward oncoming traffic.
5. During the walking lessons, emphasize the excellent health benefits gained from walking.
6. Walking activities can be done alone, with a partner, or with small groups. For most activities, students should be encouraged to walk with a friend. Being able to socialize is a great motivator for children.
7. Teach "Pace, don't race." Many students will want to start out fast, even jogging, only to tire out quickly. Pacing is a difficult concept for some students to grasp and thus it must be taught.
8. Avoid using laps and having children walk in the same direction. Counting laps and having all students moving in the same direction conveys the message that winning, finishing last, and lap counting are important.
9. Use a course delineated by cones and allow students to walk in any direction they choose.
10. Use time as the workload rather than laps. Have students walk for a set number of minutes. This helps minimize the ridicule many slower students face.
11. Some students may enjoy walking with a piece of equipment. Bean bags, hoops, jump ropes, and basketballs can be used while walking.
12. Following the walking portion of the lesson, provide students with choices of activities such as basketball, hopscotch, jump rope, or four square.

Walking Activities

▶ **MOVE TO THE BEAT**

Playing Area: Gymnasium and/or outside teaching area

Players: Individuals

Supplies: Cones and one tambourine

Skills: Walking, pacing

Begin with students walking in general space to the beat of the drum. When the drumbeat is fast students

F I G U R E 2 3 . 1   Move to the Beat.

walk fast; when the drumbeat slows, students move accordingly. Pacing is introduced as moving at fast, medium, or slow rate. Also, students should be taught that a fast pace is harder to maintain for long distances. Next, have students walk around the perimeter (marked by cones) of the teaching area to the beat of the drum (Figure 23.1). Directions such as "Take a step with each beat" will help students learn to move with the pace of the drum. Once students have grasped the concept of fast, medium, and slow paced walking, introduce the concept of pacing. Explain that the goal is to get from one cone to the next in a designated number of steps. The student's goal is to not reach the cone before or after the last beat, but "just in time." The teacher says "Go" and begins a steady beat, stopping on the designated beat. Students should be right at the next cone. If not, they move to the closest cone and another set of beats begins. Many students will take one step per beat, which may or may not be the correct pace. For some students, it will take time to adjust. Once students learn this pacing, the tempo can be increased or decreased. Each time the teacher asks, "Is this a slower beat (tempo) or a faster beat (tempo)?" Finally, students can be taken outside on a larger trail. The walking path does not have to be symmetrical and does not have to be on a track. Start students at different places on a track marked by cones and present the activity as described above.

✓ **TEACHING TIP**

Teachers can use a beat per second, ultimately removing the beat, to challenge students to move from cone to cone in a specific amount of time. Progressively increase the distance students move by increasing the number of cones they have to pass.

FIGURE 23.2   Walking Interviews.

▶ WALKING INTERVIEWS

Playing Area: Gymnasium or outside walking course

Players: Partners

Supplies: 4- by 6-inch index cards with interview questions

Skills: Walking, communication, pacing

Children choose a partner. Each set of partners is given an index card with a series of questions. For this activity, students simply walk with their partner and interview them using the questions provided (Figure 23.2). Once all of the questions are asked, the partners switch roles using the questions on the back side of the card. Examples of interview questions include:

- What is your favorite physical activity? Why?
- What is your favorite movie and why?
- How many people are in your family?
- What do you usually do after school?
- What is your favorite subject in school?
- Who was your teacher last year?
- What is your favorite fruit or vegetable?

✓ TEACHING TIP

Minimize the number of questions to ask so students have to change partners often. This increases the number of peers students will get to know. Another motivating idea is to allow students to create their own questions.

▶ BANK WALK

Playing Area: Gymnasium or outside walking trail

Players: Individuals or partners

Supplies: Cones and fake money or other tokens

Skills: Walking, pacing, counting money, communication

Students choose a partner and begin walking a predesignated route. The teacher begins walking the route in the opposite direction of the students. Each time the students pass the teacher they receive money. After a set amount of time, students then count their money. Next, they give the money back to the teacher and begin again, this time trying to beat the income they earned the first time.

✓ TEACHING TIP

To promote politeness, students who are polite (e.g., say "please" and "thank you") get extra pay. To prevent students from saying, "Thank you" just to get money, keep this bonus a secret by *not* telling the class what the bonus money is for until after the lesson.

▶ GIANT MAP CONSTRUCTION

Playing Area: Gymnasium or defined teaching area

Players: Groups of two to three students

Supplies: One sheet of paper and a pencil for each set of partners

Skills: Walking, map reading, cooperation

In an activity setting defined by cones, each set of partners maps a route they will walk together. Shapes, words, or letters, can be used as routes. They then walk the route with their partner. For example, a spelling word for the week may be "intensity." Using the entire activity area as their "mapping area," the partners walk and spell out the word "intensity" from left to right.

✓ TEACHING TIP

The key to this activity is to get students to use the entire designated area for the trail they will map and walk. If pedometers are used, have students guess the number of steps it will take one or both partners to finish the route. Sets of partners can test the number of steps or amount of activity time it takes to walk the route and then swap maps with another group.

▶ NEW ENGINEER

Playing Area: Gymnasium or defined activity area

Players: Groups of six to eight students

Supplies: A small piece of equipment (beanbag or baton) for a group of four to six students

Skills: Walking, pacing

Groups of four to six students stand in a single-file line and begin walking with the leader (engineer) holding the piece of equipment and leading the group throughout the teaching area. On signal, the leader hands

23

the piece of equipment to the second person, who hands it to the third and so on. This is all done while the line is still walking. When the equipment gets back to the last person (the caboose), the caboose begins speed walking to the front of the line to become the "new engineer."

✓ **TEACHING TIP**

Challenge students to move with a brisk walk. At different intervals, stop and change the makeup of the teams to provide renewed interest.

▶ **JUST WALK**

Playing Area: Outside walking area
Players: Groups of one to four students
Supplies: Cones
Skills: Walking, pacing

A walking course is set up using cones. If desired, a map can be drawn to provide path directions to students. If a map is used, this activity serves as a precursor to an orienteering lesson presented below. Students can walk alone, with a partner, or in groups. The only rule is that they have to be moving and remain on the course for a predetermined time. This activity is not intended to take an entire period. In fact, 10–15 minutes is sufficient. This offers an excellent opportunity for teachers to walk with students and get to know them as individuals.

▶ **WALKING CLUB**

Walking clubs offer great avenues for getting youth moving both in school and out of the school setting. Following a motivating walking unit, students should be excited to start walking whenever possible. When starting a walking club, it is important to emphasize safety. Figure 23.3 offers walking safety tips for children. Walking courses on campus can be created by the physical education teacher. These courses can be changed often to add excitement. The beauty of walking clubs is that they can be conducted before school, after school, and even during recess. This provides more opportunities for participation. To make a walking club most effective, great care must be given to the planning and organization of the club. Programs that are hastily put together tend to disappear quickly. The following is a list of steps that can be used to implement a walking club.

1. Envision what a walking club should look like at the elementary level.
   a. How many students will participate?
   b. What grades will be invited?
   c. When will the club meet?
   d. Who will be responsible for administering the program?
2. Discuss the possibilities and options with the principal.
3. Recruit other teachers that may be interested in co-supervising the club.
4. Develop an inclement weather plan. Most schools have hallways or a gym/cafeteria that could be used for walking in case of rain, snow, or other weather not conducive to outside physical activity. It is important that the club function even during long stretches of poor weather.
5. Create and post a schedule. The schedule will depend on the number of supervisors and the number

Walking Safety Tips for Children
- Always tell an adult or teacher where you will be walking
- Always walk with a friend or small group
- Use the sidewalk
- Only cross the street where there is a sidewalk
- Obey the traffic signs
- Avoid crowded areas
- Wear bright colored clothes with safety reflective materials
- Look left, right, left, right, before crossing
- Avoid dangerous areas such as construction sites

FIGURE 23.3   Walking safety tips.

of participants. It may be necessary to have one or two grades participate per day and rotate grades each day, especially for before-school and after-school clubs. Starting with one grade level, or even one classroom, may also help alleviate unanticipated problems before taking the club schoolwide.

6. Advertise the club with school announcements, during physical education lessons, in a physical education newsletter to parents, and at a booth at open houses. As the implementation of the club approaches, letters home inviting parents to participate will help in recruiting participants.

7. Design a system for tracking participation. Sheets can be designed to track laps or minutes of participation. Given the number of laps that equal one mile, students can track their progress on a map of their city, state, or country. A similar system can be devised for minutes of movement. For example, 12 minutes of walking equals one mile. Granted, the pace at which a youngster moves will impact this formula, but the idea is to get students moving, regardless of the pace.

8. Consider calling your club a "Physical Activity Club," or PAC for short, and include a variety of activities, either structured or unstructured. This allows you to address the interests of a variety of students, especially those that may not find walking enjoyable.

9. Approach local businesses about helping sponsor the club. Money can also be raised by hosting a Family Walk-a-Thon. Not only will this allow for fund-raising, but it is great public relations for the physical education program.

10. If funds are available, pedometers can be purchased to be used during the club. Also, funds can be used to purchase walking club T-shirts for all club members. Local sporting good stores may be willing to help with T-shirts.

11. Using activities from the following section, teachers and students can create challenging orienteering courses.

ORIENTEERING

Orienteering is a navigation and sport activity that incorporates walking or jogging, determining directions, and map reading. The object of the activity is to use a map and compass to locate specific points in a given area. Competitive orienteering can involve skills such as skiing, mountain biking, compass readings, and point tracking, while navigating a wilderness course designed to test the skills of participants. At the elementary level, the focus of orienteering is to teach students fundamental concepts such as recognizing directions (north, south, east, and west) and map reading. Orienteering can also be integrated with walking, Frisbee golf, challenge courses or other activities that involve map reading. Students will actively learn the skills necessary to navigate an area such as the gymnasium, a classroom, the school, the playground, or a local park.

Instructional Procedures

1. Introduce map directions by placing a large N, S, E, and W on the appropriate walls.

2. Refer to the walls as the east wall or the north wall when giving directions. For example, "When I say *go*, hustle to the red line closest to the east wall."

3. To introduce directional travel, use small instructional bouts such as, "If we run from this wall (pointing to the east wall) to that wall (pointing to the west wall) what direction are we moving?" Presenting this information in a variety of lessons leading up to orienteering will help set the stage for those lessons. For example, if working on basketball passing with a partner, you might say, "When I say *go*, work on your overhead pass with one partner facing north and one facing south."

4. Introduce students to basic symbols used to designate landmarks and controls. Controls refer to the specific locations students are challenged to find on an orienteering course. See Figures 23.4 and 23.5 on page 588 for examples of maps with symbols.

5. If pencils are needed, for safety reasons provide students with a pencil box or folder to carry all of their materials (maps, pencils, etc.).

Orienteering Skills

DETERMINING DIRECTIONS

For many students, learning directions is difficult. One strategy is to mark the walls in the gymnasium with an N, S, E, or W to identify compass directions. This allows students to learn the relationship of each direction. For example, when facing east, north is to the left. Another strategy is to mark landmarks on the school grounds. The slide on the south side of the playground could have an "S" painted on it. Similarly, the fence on the east side of the school grounds could have an "E" painted, or hung, on it. These strategies allow teachers to teach directions inside and outside. Older children can be taught to determine directions by looking at the sun. The sun always rises in the east. Thus, if students are looking at the sun in the morning, west is always behind them. Another way to teach this concept is to know that

FIGURE 23.4   Gymnasium orienteering map.

in the morning one's shadow points west. Next, students can transfer what was learned in the gym and know that if they are facing east, to the left is north and to the right is south. Conversely, in the afternoon, when students look at the sun, their shadow points east; to the right is north and to the left is south. This will take time for students to process and understand. Since most physical education classes occur at the same time each day, students will be able to learn one method before another is presented.

READING A MAP

Most students have seen a map and relate to it as a drawing of an area. Most classrooms have maps and globes that help students understand the idea of map reading. Reading a map involves determining landmarks and directions. For elementary students in a gymnasium, this could be recognizing doors, the clock, or posters on a wall when shown a map of the gymnasium. This will involve students recognizing symbols. Figure 23.4 shows a gymnasium

FIGURE 23.5   School grounds orienteering map.

map with symbols. Students will ultimately read the map in order to find specific locations called "controls."

In order to read a map, students must orient the map. This involves turning the map until what is in front of the student in the gymnasium is in front of the student on the map. For example, using Figure 23.4, students may be standing in the southeast corner of the gym facing the side door on the west wall. They would then turn the map until the southeast corner of the gym on the map is closest to them and the west wall is farthest away. Teachers can give instruction such as "Standing where you are, orient your map to the clock." Students can also be taught to keep their thumb where they are on the map and move their thumb as they move. This is called "thumbing."

Orienteering Activities

▶ **GYMNASIUM ORIENTEERING**

Playing Area: Gymnasium or designated teaching area

Players: Individuals, partners, or small groups (three or four students)

Supplies: Map of the gymnasium, cones, and poly spots

Skills: Map reading, problem solving, cooperation

Orienteering will likely be a novel activity for most students. For this reason, it is best to begin map reading and learning to find controls in a controlled environment like the gymnasium. It is also important that concepts such as map reading and directions be introduced in short pieces leading up to orienteering activities. For example, when teaching circuit training, students could be given a simple map of the stations and instructed to find their next stations when prompted. Another option is to use poster board and draw a large map that students can see from a distance. The objective of this activity is to introduce students to map reading while searching for controls. The following steps will aid in planning for this activity.

1. Using a drawing of the gymnasium, lay out an orienteering course on paper. (See Figure 23.4 for an example.) It is important that N, S, E, and W be marked on the map. In Figure 23.4, circles with numbers are used to designate control points and triangles with numbers written in them are used to designate cones, or landmarks. If a gymnasium does not have an abundance of landmarks, numbered cones can be used to supplement already existing landmarks. Poly spots represent controls and should be numbered as well.

2. Next develop a set of instructions that students will follow in order to get to the next control point. (See Figure 23.6 for a set of gymnasium orienteering instructions.) Each instruction will be printed, cut

At Control:	Instructions:
1	Move directly east to find Control 2.
2	To find Control 3, go to the southwest corner of the gym.
3	Control 4 is close to Landmark 6.
4	Find Control 5 in the middle of the south wall.
5	Control 6 is just north of Landmark 4.
6	To find Control 7, walk directly north of Control 6.
7	You will find Control 8 directly south of Landmark 5.
8	Control 8 is in the southeast corner of the gym.
9	Walk directly north of Control 9 to find Control 10.
10	To find Control 10, go to the northeast corner of the gym.
11	Control 12 is in the middle of the gym.
12	Control 1 can be found by walking northwest from Control 12.

FIGURE 23.6 Gym orienteering instructions.

into individual instructions, and taped to the appropriate control marker or poly spot. For example, instructions how to find control number 2 will be on control number 1.

3. Once instructions are written, it is a good idea to walk through them using the map to ensure they are accurate.

4. On the day of instruction be sure to have the appropriate number of cones with numbers on them and the appropriate number of poly spots, or controls, with numbers on them. Using the map, set the cones and control points in their appropriate location.

Divide the class into groups of two or three students. Give each group a map and instruct them to report to any numbered control. Review the concepts that have been taught leading up to this lesson. For example, ask "If I am walking from the south wall to the north wall, what direction am I traveling?" Also a refresher on map orienting may be helpful as well. After this quick review, let the groups begin, starting with the instructions on the control where they are. This will have all groups searching for a different control.

✓ **TEACHING TIP**

To add difficulty, remove the control numbers from the map. This will force students to use the directions on the control and the map, rather than just the map. Also, at each control, place a pencil box. After finding each control and before moving on to the next, students draw a line from the previous control to the current cone. With some extra planning these lines could draw an object, make a letter, or spell a short word. Also, each control could have a trivia question, a skill to perform, or fitness challenge. This allows orienteering to be integrated with other physical education lessons.

23

▶ SCHOOL GROUNDS ORIENTEERING

Playing Area: School grounds

Players: Groups of one, two, three, or four students

Supplies: Map of school grounds with landmarks and controls

Skills: Map reading, cooperation

This activity is a follow-up, or progression, from Gymnasium Orienteering. Thus, the process of planning is identical. Depending on the classes' familiarity with finding N, S, E, and W outside, the instructions may have to change. For example, rather than an instruction of, "Move northwest from control number 7 to find control number 8," the instruction may read, "From control number 7, move towards the slide to find control number 8." Figure 23.5 on page 588 is an example of a school grounds orienteering map. Notice that regardless of where the teacher is standing, all controls are visible. This allows the teachers to keep all students in sight. Prior to this activity students should be given instructions regarding what area they will use. For example, if using the map in Figure 23.5, students could be told that there will be no controls on the K–2 playground, or in front of the school.

✓ TEACHING TIP

For additional challenge, remove the numbers from each control. Just as with Gymnasium Orienteering, students will have to use the instructions and their map reading skills to find the controls.

▶ SCAVENGER HUNT

Playing Area: Entire gymnasium or designated teaching area

Players: Individuals, partners, or small groups of three to four students

Supplies: An orienteering map, instructions, an envelope for each control, a clue for each control

Skills: Map reading, problem solving

An orienteering course is set up similar to those presented above. The activity is taught and participated in just as an orienteering course. The only exception is that at each control, youngsters collect a clue that is part of a series of clues to be collected at each control. At the conclusion of the course, each team must then use the clues to solve the puzzle. The following is a list of possible puzzles to be solved.

- At each control, students collect an index card with a single letter. All of the letters together spell out O-R-I-E-N-T-E-E-R-I-N-G.

- A picture is cut into the same number of pieces as there are controls and pasted onto an index card. At each control, groups collect a piece of the puzzle that they will assemble into a picture after completing the course.

- At each control, students collect an index card with one word. When put together, the words form a question, such as, "What is an important part of a healthy lifestyle?" Each group will probably come up with a different answer, such as "physical activity," "a balanced diet," or "not smoking."

- The letters to two or three of a class's spelling words could be used as well. This will require students to unscramble the letters to spell the words. This is also an excellent method of reinforcing classroom content without sacrificing physical education objectives.

TENNIS

Tennis is a popular activity throughout the world. Because it can be played at varying levels and intensities, it is also a lifetime activity that many older adults enjoy. It can be played on concrete, grass, clay, and synthetic flooring. Figure 23.7 offers a diagram of a regulation tennis court. At the elementary level, most students have not experienced many racquet activities and their skill levels

FIGURE 23.7 Regulation tennis court.

FIGURE 23.8 Shake hands grip.

will be rudimentary. Thus, the role of physical education is to expose them to using a tennis racquet to strike the ball using modified activities. Again, the purpose of these activities is to allow children to explore the game of tennis and provide them with a chance to be successful while using a racquet. Practice in tennis should move from individual to partner as quickly as is feasible. Partner work is the basis for tennis activities.

Tennis Skills

GRIP

Proper grip must be emphasized, and seeing that children maintain this is a constant battle. The easiest method to teach the proper grip is to have the student hold the paddle perpendicular to the floor and "shake hands" with it (Figure 23.8). Young people tend to revert to the inefficient hammer grip, so named because it is similar to the grip used on a hammer. Students should practice picking up their racquet using a shake hands grip. Spinning the racquet and stopping in a "shake hands" grip can also be used as a challenge. Early activities such as the grip can be attempted with both the right and the left hand, but the dominant hand should be developed in critical skills.

READY POSITION

Getting ready to hit is the first step to a successful tennis stroke. This is an often overlooked skill because it is usually missed by spectators who are watching the other player hit the ball. Preparing to hit involves being in a solid athletic position with heels slightly raised (just enough to get a piece of paper under the heels) and ready to move. The racquet is gripped in the "shake hands" grip with the other hand placed just below the strings. This position enables youngsters to move quickly to the ball. The following instructional cues will aid skill development:

1. Athletic position.
2. Paper under your heels.
3. Racquet in front.
4. Little jump.

FOREHAND

The forehand shot is the most frequently used tennis shot. It is the stroke that most people think of when they think of a tennis shot, and it is often the easiest to learn. For this reason, many students will want to make every shot a forehand. It is important that as instruction progresses students be encouraged to try other shots. For the forehand stroke, the body is turned sideways; for a right-handed player, the left side points in the direction of the hit. Contact is made with the ball slightly before the ball reaches the body. Instructional cues for a proper forehand shot are as follows:

1. Ready position.
2. Opposite side to target.
3. Racquet back.
4. Watch the ball.
5. Step and swing through the ball with a stiff wrist.
6. Ready position.

BACKHAND

The backhand is often a difficult stroke for children. While the forehand is somewhat similar to other motions youngsters often perform, such as throwing and swinging a baseball bat, the backhand is just the opposite. For this reason, it feels unnatural and must be practiced in order for it to feel comfortable. For the backhand stroke, the thumb is placed against the handle of the racquet for added support and force, and the body is turned sideways so the shoulder on the side of the racquet hand points in the direction of the stroke. The racquet strikes the ball even with or slightly before it reaches the front leg (Figure 23.9).

1. Ready position.
2. Same side to target.
3. Both hands back.
4. Watch the ball.
5. Step and swing through the ball.
6. Follow through high.
7. Ready position.

23

FIGURE 23.9   Tennis backhand sequence.

SERVE

The serve, which is used to get the ball into play, is often a difficult skill for children to perform accurately. For this reason, most serves do not result in a ball that can be returned. If serving, begin by allowing any serve that crosses the net to be played, regardless of location. In the elementary school, the goal of playing activities is to maximize repetitions and refinement. For this reason, the ball is put into play with a bounce and forehand or backhand stroke.

VOLLEY

A volley is made with a sort of punch stroke. The hitter faces in the direction of the hit, and the racquet is pushed forward rather than being stroked. When using modified courts and activities this is a very common stroke for children. For many, it will be their primary stroke. The following skill cues will help development of the volley:

1. Ready position.
2. Step and push the racquet toward the ball.
3. Ready position.

Tennis Drills

INDIVIDUAL DRILLS

▶ RACQUET SPIN

Stand the racquet on its frame with the grip up. On signal, spin the racquet like a top and quickly grab the racquet and turn it until it is in a "shake hands" grip.

▶ BOUNCE DOWNS

In scattered formation, each youngster has a racquet and a tennis ball. The racquet is used to dribble the ball on the ground. Emphasis is placed on bouncing the ball waist high. This is similar to dribbling a basketball with a tennis racquet. Instruct students to switch hands periodically. Bouncing the ball and catching can also be allowed.

▶ BOUNCE UPS

As the name suggests, this activity is the opposite of bounce downs. Each student has a ball and bounces the ball into the air. Students are instructed to keep the ball "eye high." After a short time, students switch hands. Challenge students to bounce the ball up several times and then catch the ball on their racquet.

▶ EDGIES

In scattered formation, each child has a ball and racquet. On signal, they begin bouncing the ball, either up or down, using the edge of the racquet. Switching hands is encouraged as is using different edges of the racquet.

▶ FLIP-FLOPS

Every student starts with a racquet and a ball in scattered formation. Using bounce ups, students rally the ball with alternating sides of the racquet. Notice the positioning of the hand in Figures 23.10 and 23.11. If necessary, the ball can bounce on the floor. Students should be instructed to switch hands often.

FIGURE 23.10 Tennis flip.

FIGURE 23.11 Tennis flop.

INVENT-A-BOUNCE

Once comfortable with basic bouncing, encourage players to invent different methods of bouncing the ball. Initially, examples may be offered such as around the back, under the leg, using the handle, or balancing on one foot. To modify an activity, students develop a dribbling routine such as two bounce downs, two bounce ups, two edgies, and two flip-flops.

SELF-RALLY

With a ball and racquet, students attempt to rally the ball for as many times as possible. Bounce ups, bounce downs, edgies, and flip-flops can be used. Youngsters can also choose if they want to allow a bounce. The primary goal is for students to develop personal challenges and try to better previous self-rally scores.

PICK IT UP

All students start with the racquet in the hand and the ball on the floor. The challenge is get the ball on the racquet without touching it with the other hand. One strategy is to scoop the ball up with the racquet. An easier alternative is to get the ball rolling by tapping it with the racquet and scooping it up. Students may also choose to trap the ball between the outside of their foot and the racquet. They then lift the foot and racquet, raising the ball to a level where it can be dropped. The ball then bounces and they attempt to balance it on the racquet.

Lastly, students can start dribbling the ball, gradually bouncing it higher and higher. The ball can then be caught on the racquet by placing the racquet under the ball and "giving" with the knees as the ball touches the racquet.

WALL RALLY

Introducing the forehand and backhand by using Wall Rally allows students many repetitions. Standing with her opposite side to the wall, the student bounces the ball with the "other" hand, and lightly taps the ball to the wall. The teacher then stops the class periodically to introduce the next cue. For example, the instruction might be "If you want to continue working on bringing your racquet back that's great. If you are ready, go ahead and work on stepping toward the wall when you hit the ball. Remember, watch the ball. Go." Wall Rally can be used to teach every tennis stroke with instruction progressing to students counting the number of times they can rally the ball without missing. A controlled soft racquet is emphasized.

PARTNER DRILLS

RACQUET GRAB

Partners stand about three feet apart with their racquet on its frame with the grip standing up. On the teacher's signal each partner lets go of his racquet and moves forward toward her partner's racquet. The goal is to grab the partner's racquet before it hits the ground and quickly take a "shake hands" grip. With each success, partners take one step back.

▶ PARTNER TOSS

One partner has a racquet and the other partner stands approximately 8 feet away with the ball. The partner with the racquet begins in ready position. The partner with the ball lightly tosses the ball to the other partner's forehand side. The racquet partner quickly turns so the opposite side is to the target and lightly hits the ball back to the partner. Be sure to emphasize the importance of the toss. After five hits, partners switch roles. Each group of partners is challenged to see how many times they can execute a toss to the forehand side followed by correct forehand hit. This activity can be used for backhand and volley strokes as well. As the skills of students progress, increase the distance and use a line in the area as the net.

▶ PARTNER RALLY

Players are paired up, each with a racquet and one ball. The person with the ball bounces it and hits a forehand or backhand shot. After striking the ball, the player returns to the ready position. In the meantime, the receiving partner moves from the ready position to a striking position and hits either a forehand or backhand shot. The purpose of the activity is to learn to return to the ready position after stroking the ball. For an increased challenge, have students find a line on the floor and use it as a net.

▶ STEP BACK

This drill is similar to Partner Rally with one exception. For every four consecutive hits, each player takes one step back. Thus, all students must be in a formation that allows students to step back without getting in the way of others. Figure 23.12 shows how students might look in the middle of a Step Back game.

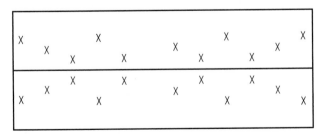

FIGURE 23.12   Step back formation. Each X represents a student. Partners are across the line from each other and should each be the same distance from the line.

▶ JUGGLE RALLY

Each set of partners needs two racquets and one ball. The partner with the ball starts the rally with two individual drills. This could be two bounce downs, or an edgie and a bounce up. After the two hits, the third hit is to her partner. The partner then receives the ball with one hit, executes another individual activity, and then hits it back to his partner. Children may choose to use floor bounces, the wall, or any other creative idea they choose. The only rule is that they hit the ball three times during each rally.

▶ TOSS AND CATCH

Partners stand approximately 8 feet apart, one with a racquet and one with a ball. The partner with the ball tosses the ball to the partner with the racquet, who uses his hand and racquet to catch the ball against the racquet strings. The ball is then tossed back to the tosser and the drill repeated. The object of this activity is to teach students to move to the ball. The tosser attempts to move the catcher forward, backward, left, and right.

▶ TOSS, HIT, CATCH

One partner starts with a ball and the other with a racquet. The partner with the ball tosses the ball to the partner with the racquet, who hits it back; the tosser then attempts to catch the ball. As a variation, the tosser can have a racquet and attempt to trap the ball against the racquet with the nondominant hand. The game can also be changed to Hit, Hit, Catch, or ultimately Hit, Hit, Hit, which is essentially a tennis rally.

Tennis Activities

▶ TENNIS VOLLEYBALL

Playing Area: Volleyball court

Players: Two teams of 8 to 10 students

Supplies: One training ball, one racquet per child, and a net

Skills: Forehand, backhand, volley, and score keeping

Two teams are formed. A player from Team A puts the ball in play by hitting onto Team B's half of the court. After the ball hits the floor on Team B's side, anyone from Team B can hit the ball. Team B players can hit the ball to their teammates or directly over the net to Team A's side. There is no limit to the number of times a team can hit the ball before hitting it back over the net. Also, there is no limit to bounces. The ball is considered dead when it rolls. No boundaries, other than the net, are used. Games are played to 11 points and then started over. As with most games, the makeup of teams should be changed often.

▶ TENNIS OVER THE LINE

Playing Area: Teaching area divided into 5-by-10-foot squares with masking tape

Players: Partners

Supplies: One training ball, one racquet for each student, one line, strips of masking tape

Skills: Forehand, backhand, volley

Prior to class, mark off 5-by-10-feet segments of line throughout the teaching area using masking tape and existing lines. This will make two 5-feet squares with a common middle line. One youngster stands in one square and her opponent stands in the other. The game is a combination of two square and tennis. Only underhand shots are permitted. Player A puts the ball in play by dropping the ball and hitting a forehand or backhand off of the bounce into Player B's square. Before the ball bounces twice, Player B must return the ball, again using only an underhand stroke, to Player A's square. If a player cannot return the ball into her opponent's square or does not hit the ball before it bounces twice, a point is scored. Player A serves five times in a row, regardless of scoring, and then Player B serves.

▶ USA SCHOOL TENNIS

Playing Area: Gymnasium divided into enough courts so there is one court per six students

Players: Three students per team

Supplies: One racquet per student; one training ball per group of six; tumbling mats, stretched magic rope or other equipment to use as a net for each court (see Figure 23.13)

Skills: Forehand, backhand, volley, score keeping

This is a team game of tennis with no more than three players on a side. The focus of the game is controlled swings. All balls must have an upward movement when leaving the racquet, and no spiking is allowed. Again, racquet control is important. Each game is played to five points by ones. A point is lost

- If the ball rolls. Once the ball rolls it is dead, and the point goes to the other team.
- If the first bounce after the ball crosses the net is not inbounds; the point goes to the other team.
- If the ball is spiked; the point goes to the other team.

Play is started with a drop serve, which means one player drops the ball and hits a forehand or backhand over the net. If players are having difficulty with spacing

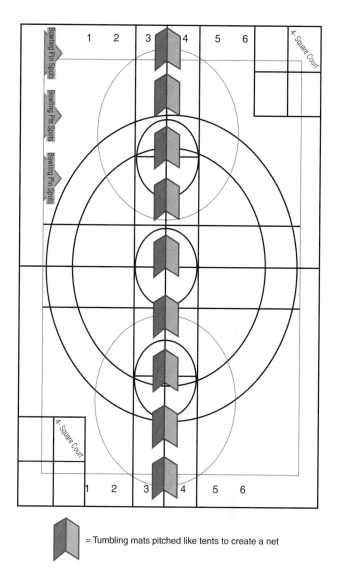

= Tumbling mats pitched like tents to create a net

FIGURE 23.13 USA School Tennis diagram.

and staying in their own area, the halves of the court can be divided into three equal areas, with each player instructed to stay in his or her area. There is no limit on the number of times one team can hit the ball before sending it back to the other side. Similarly there are not limits on the number of bounces allowed. A modification of the game allows a rolling ball to be in play. This requires students to scoop the ball up and continue play. In this version, the only dead ball is one that is not moving.

RACQUETBALL

Racquetball is a popular racquet activity played in clubs throughout the world. A game is typically played on a four-walled court with a ceiling. (See Figure 23.14 on page 596 for a diagram of a regulation racquetball court.) However, there are three-walled courts in some

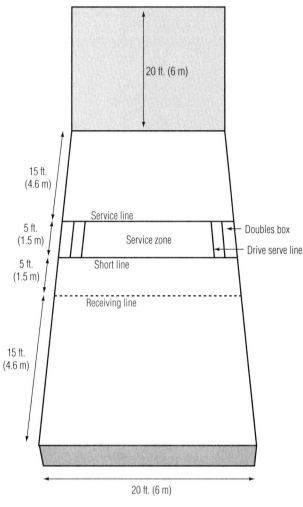

20 ft. (6 m)

15 ft.
(4.6 m)

Service line

5 ft.
(1.5 m)

Service zone — Doubles box

— Drive serve line

5 ft.
(1.5 m)

Short line

Receiving line

15 ft.
(4.6 m)

20 ft. (6 m)

FIGURE 23.14   Regulation racquetball court.

parts of the country, and the game can be played on one wall as well. In elementary schools, three-walled and four-walled courts are rarely available; thus at the elementary level, racquetball skills are taught using one wall. Similar to tennis, the grip, the forehand, and the backhand are the primary skills emphasized. If racquetball racquets are not available, wooden or plastic paddles with safety strings can also be used. For safety, racquetball is typically played with goggles. To increase the success of students and provide more enjoyment, foam balls or whiffle balls can be used. Racquetballs are too lively for elementary-age students.

Racquetball Skills

GRIP

The "shake hands" grip is the best beginning grip for students. This grip is taught by asking students to

hold the racquet perpendicular to the floor with their nondominant hand and the grip closest to them. They then simply shake hands with the racquet. The "meaty" part of the hand between the thumb and forefinger should form a "V" just slightly off the top of the grip away from the center of the body.

READY POSITION

The ready position in racquetball is the same as the ready position in virtually every activity. Feet are shoulder width apart, knees slightly bent, weight shifted forward, and the racquet in front. As the opponent strikes the ball, the receiving player jumps forward slightly to initiate movement toward the ball. This is sometimes called a "ready jump" or a "rock step." It is important that students are taught to return to the ready position, in the middle of the court, after each shot.

FOREHAND

The forehand is the most commonly used shot in racquetball and also the easiest to learn. The racquetball forehand is a sidearm motion, similar to the motion used when skipping a rock across a pond or swinging a baseball bat with one hand. When striking a racquetball forehand, the racquet starts back and high with the elbow and shoulder at the same height. This is accomplished by making the arm into an "L" with the racquet high. The knees are then bent and the forearm comes through level, striking the ball when it is in the middle of the body. This will result in the shot going straight. Figure 23.15 is a series of drawings depicting the entire racquetball forehand shot. The follow-through is level as well with the racquet ending up waist high. The following cues are helpful for teaching the forehand shot.

1. Ready position.
2. Opposite side to target.
3. "L" with racquet high.
4. Bend your knees.
5. Level swing through the ball.
6. Ready position.

BACKHAND

As with most racquet activities, the backhand in racquetball is more difficult than the forehand shot, especially for beginners. As the ball approaches, the player's first move is from the ready position to the dominant side-to-wall position. Next, the body is twisted away from the ball and the racquet positioned about shoulder height with the feet planted and knees bent. The swinging

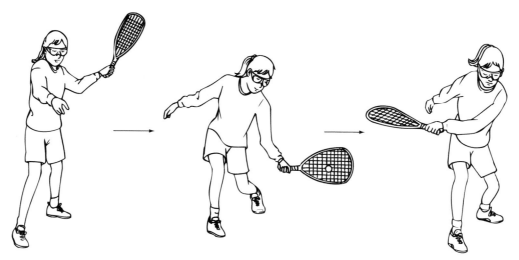

FIGURE 23.15   Racquetball forehand sequence.

motion is very similar to the motion of throwing a Frisbee. The ball is struck in the middle of the body and the follow-through is level. See Figure 23.16 for an illustration of this motion. Cues such as the following will be helpful when teaching youngsters this stroke.

1. Ready position.
2. Dominant side to target.
3. Twist away from the ball and racquet up.
4. Throw the Frisbee.
5. Follow-through level.
6. Ready position.

Racquetball Drills

▶ RACQUET ROLL

All students place a ball on their racquet. When signaled, they begin rolling the ball around the racquet. The challenge is for the ball to touch every hole on the racquet. This can be done seated, standing, or walking. After a short time, allow students to let the ball bounce off the floor once and catch it on the other side of the racquet. If the ball falls, they simply catch it, turn the racquet over so the other side of the hand is up, and place the ball on the racquet.

FIGURE 23.16   Racquetball backhand sequence.

DRIBBLING

Each student bounces or dribbles his ball off the floor using the racquet. Controlled dribbling is emphasized. This activity starts with students stationary and progresses to students walking, skipping, and jogging while dribbling. Students should be allowed to choose the locomotor skill that provides the appropriate challenge. For example, if walking is too easy students may choose walking or skipping. Also, students should be encouraged to alternate hands and use both sides of the racquet.

AIR DRIBBLING

Each child has a ball and a racquet. On signal, children begin with little bounces in the air. As time progresses, they may attempt higher bounces; however, bounces should not be higher than the eyes. Youngsters can be challenged to turn the racquet over (so the back of the hand is facing up) while the ball is in the air. To move back to Racquet Roll, have students make their dribbles smaller and smaller until the ball is rolling on the racquet. "Give with the ball to absorb the bounce" may be a helpful cue for students having difficulty.

RACQUETBALL RALLY

With a racquet and ball, challenge students to keep their ball bouncing, either off the floor or into the air as many times as possible. If the ball bounces on the floor twice between hits the streak is over and the count starts over. Students can even use the wall to see how many times they can rally against the wall with no bounces or one bounce.

RACQUETBALL STUNTS

Each student has a ball and racquet. When instructed, they hit the ball into the air and attempt to touch the floor, do a heel click, clap their hands, or turn around, before the ball hits the floor. Controlled racquets and bounces must be emphasized. For this activity, beanbags can be used rather than balls. If balls are used, once the ball hits the floor, have students attempt to absorb the force of the bounce by dribbling the ball back down until it is rolling on the racquet. Once the ball is rolling, have them try another stunt.

Racquetball Activities

RACQUET ROLL TAG

Playing Area: Gymnasium or specified playing area
Players: Entire class

Supplies: One racquet and ball per student
Skills: Racquet awareness, dodging, fleeing

Every player has a racquet with a ball balanced on it. Two to four students are designated taggers. All players must move with the ball balanced on their racquet. If tagged by a tagger, that person becomes "it," and the previous tagger is no longer "it." If the ball falls off, the child quickly grabs the ball, places it on the racquet, and continues. In order to tag someone, the tagger's ball must be on his racquet. The game should be stopped and restarted often to prevent students from getting frustrated if they are not able to tag someone or if they keep getting tagged.

RACQUETBALL RED LIGHT

Playing Area: Gymnasium or specified playing area
Players: Entire class
Supplies: One racquet and ball per student
Skills: Racquet awareness, cooperation

This game is played in the same fashion as regular Red Light (see page 553) with two twists. The traffic controller holds a red piece of paper and a green piece of paper. Rather than yell "red light" to stop students' movement or "green light" to start them, pieces of paper are held up as commands. This forces students to keep their eyes up and not focused on the ball. If this is too challenging, the traditional method of calling out commands can be used. Also, all players must have their ball balanced on their racquet. If the ball falls off, they must return to the starting line. Just as in the original game, the first person to reach the line the traffic controller is standing on becomes the traffic controller.

WALL RALLY

Playing Area: Gymnasium or playing area with wall sections of 5 to 6 feet for every group of two to four
Players: Groups of two to four students
Supplies: One racquet per youngster, one ball for groups of two to four, masking tape to mark off wall space
Skills: Forehand, backhand, court movement

Groups of two to four are assigned a section of wall designated with tape. A 5- to 6-foot section of wall works best. For this activity, all students on the court are working together as a team to see how many times they can consecutively rally without the ball being called dead. One player puts the ball in play by bouncing it and hitting a forehand or backhand (Figure 23.17). After the ball hits the wall, the second player must return the ball to the same section. However, there is no limit to the number of

FIGURE 23.17 Rallying against the wall.

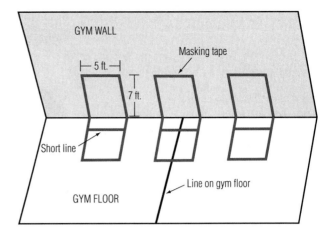

FIGURE 23.18 One-wall racquetball setup.

hits or the number of bounces allowed before the ball is hit back to the wall. Students should be encouraged to hit it back after the first bounce. To keep the rally going, even rolls are allowed. Also, the order in which players hit the ball to the wall must be maintained: first player, second player, third player, etc. However, players should be reminded that they are all a team and they can help each other. For example, Player 1 hits the ball off the wall and Player 2 is unable to reach it, but Player 3 can. Player 3 can stop the ball with his racquet and set it up for Player 2. The only thing Player 3 cannot do is hit it to the wall until after Player 2 does. The rally is over if:

1. The ball stops rolling.
2. The ball is hit toward the wall and is not between the tape lines.
3. The ball is hit to the wall but not in the correct order of players.

▶ **ONE-WALL RACQUETBALL**

Playing Area: Gymnasium or playing area with wall sections of 5 to 6 feet for every group of two to four (See Figure 23.18 for setup.)

Players: Groups of two to four students

Supplies: One racquet per youngster, one ball for groups of two to four, masking tape to mark off wall space

Skills: Forehand, backhand, score keeping, court movement

Player A serves the ball to the wall. The ball must hit the wall and come off the wall past the short line. The short line is three feet from the wall. Player B then has to return the ball to the wall before it bounces twice and before her third hit. Thus, after Player A hits it off the wall, Player B can let it bounce once, hit it in the air, let it bounce again, and then hit it to the wall. Short strokes should be emphasized. Spiking and hitting the ball downward are not permitted. Points are scored as follows:

- If the ball bounces more than twice before being returned to the wall.
- If the ball is hit more than twice before returning to the wall.
- If the ball hits the wall, but not in the space designated by tape.
- If the ball hits the wall, but does not come back past the short line.

BADMINTON

Badminton is a popular sport throughout the world. Although not as popular in the United States as in other countries, it is still ranked as one of students' most popular activities in many physical education programs. The game is played with shuttlecock, or birdie, racquets (see Figure 23.19 on page 600) and a net on a regulation court unique to badminton (see Figure 23.20 on page 600). Badminton is considered a lifetime activity because it can be played at a fast pace, which it is at competitive levels, or it can be played at a slower pace as a recreation or leisure activity. The basic badminton strategy is not necessarily

23

FIGURE 23.19 Birdie and badminton racquet.

hitting the birdie as hard as possible. In fact, finesse and moving the opponent up, back, and side-to-side is an effective strategy. At the elementary level, the focus is exposing students to striking a birdie with a badminton racket. For this reason, emphasis is placed on skills and strokes that will enable students to successfully participate in modified badminton games. To increase success, large birdies are now available from several equipment manufacturers. Also, smaller paddles or racquets can be used initially and then students can progress to the longer badminton racquets. Once this skill is learned students will experience greater success in other skills, and badminton can be an enjoyable lifetime activity.

FIGURE 23.20 Regulation badminton court.

Badminton Skills

SERVE

At the elementary level, the most appropriate serve is the underhand forehand serve. This serve can be used for a long serve or a short serve. It is useful to teach this skill first for two reasons. One, for children to have success early on and to learn the basic underhand motion, they must drop the birdie to themselves. In essence, this is the underhand serve (see Figure 23.21). Also, in order to progress to partner rallying, students must be able to get the birdie started. The easiest way to do this is the underhand serve. For the underhand serve, the child begins with the opposite foot forward; the dominant foot is back with the weight shifted to the back foot. The birdie is held by the tip in front of the body by the nondominant hand. The racquet goes straight back in the backswing. As the racquet comes forward, the weight is shifted to the front foot, the birdie is dropped, and contact is made about knee level. Hit through the birdie and stop when the arm is parallel to the ground. Instructional cues for the serve include the following:

1. Favorite foot back with weight on back foot.
2. Birdie by tip and out in front.
3. Backswing, shift weight, drop, swing.
4. Racquet follows birdie.

FOREHAND UNDERHAND CLEAR

The underhand clear on the forehand side is a very common shot in badminton and is one of the easier strokes to learn. The major difference in this forehand and forehands in other racquet activities is the step. For the forehand underhand clear, the player reaches with the dominant foot and the dominant hand, which has the racquet in it. This allows for a greater reach for the birdie. The shot begins with the student in ready position. After seeing that the birdie will fall in front on the dominant side, the student quickly steps toward the birdie. If necessary, a few shuffles or slide steps may be used. The player then swings with an upward motion with the palm of the hand up. Cues for introducing the forehand underhand clear are as follows:

1. Ready position.
2. Move toward birdie with dominant side.
3. Reach with dominant hand and foot.
4. Swing low to high.
5. Ready position.

FIGURE 23.21 Badminton serve sequence.

FOREHAND OVERHEAD CLEAR

The forehand overhead clear uses a similar motion to throwing. When the player sees that the birdie is a high shot that he can move in line with, he moves into position as if to make a throw with the nonstriking side closest to the net. The racquet is then brought back as if scratching the back. Next, the player swings forward trying to contact the birdie as high as possible. The follow-through is down to the waist. The trajectory of this shot is either straight or upward. The following instructional cues will help in skill development:

1. Ready position.
2. Opposite side to net.
3. Scratch your back.
4. Swing high to low.
5. Ready position.

BACKHAND UNDERHAND CLEAR

The backhand underhand clear shot is executed when the birdie is on the nondominant side and cannot be hit above the head. The shot will start with the player stepping with the dominant foot toward the birdie and placing his side or back to the net. As this is taking place, the thumb is shifted from the "shake hands" grip to on top of the racquet. Next, the player reaches back and swings to strike the birdie using an upward motion. Useful cues for teaching this skill include the following:

1. Ready position.
2. Step with dominant foot towards birdie.
3. Back to net.

4. Swing low to high.
5. Ready position.

BACKHAND OVERHEAD CLEAR

The backhand overhead clear is the most difficult shot taught at the elementary level. Much of this difficulty is due to the uniqueness of the movement. The shot begins much like the underhand backhand clear. However, once the player gets his back to the net, the dominant elbow is raised and the racquet comes down toward the nondominant hip. The player then looks up and over his dominant shoulder. The swing is actually a lean or shift of weight onto the "tippy toes" and a snapping of the racquet up so the arm is straight in an effort to contact the birdie as high as possible. The arm then follows around and down to the player's side. Cues for this skill include the following:

1. Ready position.
2. Step with dominant foot toward birdie.
3. Back to net.
4. Elbow high, racquet on stomach.
5. Climb to tiptoes and racquet snaps high.
6. Racquet down to side.
7. Ready position.

Individual Drills

▶ **CRADLE THE BIRDIE**

Beginning with the racquet in hand and the birdie on the ground, each student attempts to scoop the birdie up off the ground without using anything but the racquet. The goal is to get the birdie on the racquet and balanced. Once this happens, the birdie is dropped, and the child attempts this activity again. This activity can be combined with Birdie Balance and Bird Bounce below.

▶ BIRDIE BALANCE

Each student has a badminton racquet and a birdie. When instructed, the birdie is placed on the racquet, and the students move around the instructional area using various locomotor skills. Initially most students will place the birdie on the racquet, feathers down. Next, instruct students to put the birdie on its side and continue moving. For added challenges, add jumping, jumping while turning, sitting down, lying down, standing up, and other movements while balancing the birdie.

▶ BIRD BOUNCE

Each student begins with a racquet and birdie. When signaled, they begin bouncing the birdie with their racquet. This activity can begin stationary and progress to moving. Students can also be challenged to hit with opposite sides of the racquet after every hit. In addition, students should also be encouraged to use their nondominant hand as well. Switching hands between hits can also be offered as a challenge. As a lead-up to other activities, after every third hit the youngster is asked to catch the birdie with the nondominant hand.

▶ FLIP AND CATCH

With a birdie and a racquet, students balance the birdie on the racquet by standing it on its feathers. Next they toss the birdie into the air with the racquet and catch it with the other hand. This skill is practiced with the racquet in the nondominant hand as well. Next, toss the birdie in the air and catch it on the racquet. Students should be reminded that "giving" with the birdie, by bending their knees, will create a "soft" racquet and help with catching. Also, high flips are not encouraged and make it more difficult to catch. Have students stand in hoops to emphasize safe, controlled flips.

▶ FLIP AND HIT

This drill is a continuation of Flip and Catch. Rather than catch the birdie, the student attempts to hit the birdie using the appropriate stroke. This is an excellent opportunity to review which situations call for which strokes. It is important that ample spacing be provided and students be reminded of the importance of safe, low tosses. To facilitate this, students could be given a hoop to stand in while flipping and hitting.

Partner Drills

▶ HIT AND CATCH

The trajectory and path of the birdie are unlike those of a ball because birdies tend to drop at a steeper angle. For this reason, players must learn to track the flight of a birdie. For this activity one partner has a birdie and a racquet. Using the underhand serve, she hits it to her partner, who then tracks the birdie and catches it with her hands. The serving partner is encouraged to hit high shots, low shots, short shots, and long shots. After five to ten serves, partners reverse roles. Next, the receiving partner is given a racquet and is instructed to trap the birdie with one hand and the racquet. Finally, the receiver is challenged to catch the birdie with just the racquet.

▶ BOUNCE, BOUNCE, HIT

Each partner has a racquet and the partners have one birdie between them. The first partner bounces the birdie twice on his racquet just as in Birdie Bounce. After the second bounce, he then hits it to his partner. The partner receives the birdie by attempting to do two consecutive bounces before returning it. The goal of the partners is to see how many times they can hit the birdie back and forth in this fashion.

▶ PARTNER RALLY

Partners begin with a racquet each and one birdie. The partner with the birdie begins the rally with an underhand serve. The receiving partner sends the birdie back to her partner with one stroke. The partners attempt to see how many times they can hit it back and forth, or rally, without a mistake. A net can be used or a line used to simulate a net. The birdie must also pass over the line in order to count. Once teams reach 20–25 times, they can be challenged to use two birdies. With the challenge, each partner starts with a birdie and serves at the same time. From then on, each partner will strike the birdie at approximately the same time and then quickly find the returning birdie.

Badminton Activities

▶ BADMINTON CONVEYER

Playing Area: Gymnasium or designated teaching area
Players: 8 to 10 students
Supplies: One racquet per student, one birdie, one cone
Skills: Racquet awareness, cooperation

Students begin in a line on one end of the teaching area. With racquet in hand, they are challenged to get the birdie to the other end of the teaching area and set it on the cone. The following limitations apply:

1. The birdie must be touching a racquet at all times.
2. The birdie cannot be touching more than two racquets at a time.
3. The birdie may only touch racquets until it is set on a cone.
4. If the birdie is on your racquet, your feet may not move.

If students pick up on this activity quickly, the cone can be moved as the group moves. Also, encourage students to experiment by putting the racquet in their non-dominant hand or even blindfold them and require them to communicate to move the birdie.

▶ **SHUTTLE SHUTTLE**

Playing Area: Courts, 20 feet by 8 feet

Players: Six per court

Supplies: One racquet per student, one birdie per court, nets or lines, lines or tape for boundaries

Skills: Forehand strokes, backhand strokes, serving, court movement

Six players are assigned per court with three players on each side. One player from each side is in bounds while the others wait by the back line. The first player puts the birdie in play by serving to the other side. Immediately after striking the birdie, he quickly runs out of bounds, around the net or line, and to the other side, quickly getting in line behind the two players out of bounds. The receiving player returns the birdie and hustles to the side he just hit it to in the same fashion as the server. See Figure 23.22 for a diagram of this activity. All players on the court are working together to see how many times they can rally the birdie in this manner. The rally is over if the birdie hits the ground. Double hits are allowed.

▶ **BADMINTON 500**

Playing Area: Gymnasium or designated teaching area

Players: Two to four students

Supplies: One racquet per student, one birdie

Skills: Serving, tracking

One student is the server and the other students scatter out approximately 20 feet in front of him. The server serves the birdie toward the other students, who are attempting to catch the birdie with their racquet for points. To provide safety and order, students either

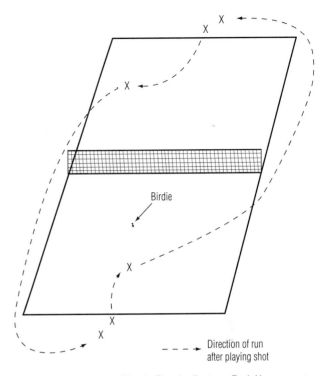

FIGURE 23.22 Shuttle Shuttle diagram. Each X represents a student.

alternate turns catching or the first player to call it gets to attempt the catch. Scoring goes as follows:

- Clean catch with the racquet with no hands and no bounces = 100 pts.
- Catch with no hands and one bounce = 75 pts.
- Catch with no hands and two bounces = 50 pts.
- Catch using racquet and the other hand or more than two bounces = 25 pts.

After each catch, the catcher quickly serves the birdie back to the server for another round. The first player to earn 500 points becomes the server.

FRISBEES

Frisbee activities are popular with children of all ages. These skills can be used for Frisbee Golf, Frisbee Bowling, and Ultimate Frisbee, which is a popular sport. However, manipulating a Frisbee is a novel skill for elementary school children and they will require considerable guidance to develop skills.

Instructional Procedures

1. Allow students to individually toss and catch the Frisbee first. Otherwise students spend more time chasing than they do throwing and catching.

2. Use the following instructional cues:

    a. Release the disk parallel to the ground. If it is tilted, a curved throw results.

    b. Step toward the target and follow through on release of the disk.

    c. Snap open the wrist and make the Frisbee spin.

3. If space is limited, all Frisbees should be thrown in the same direction. Students can line up on either side of the area and throw across to each other.

4. Each child should have a disk so that practice time can be maximized. However, most activities are best practiced by pairs of students using one disk.

5. Youngsters can develop both sides of the body by learning to throw and catch the disk with either hand. The teacher should design the activities so that youngsters get both right-hand and left-hand practice.

6. Because a Frisbee is somewhat different from the other implements that children usually throw, devote some time to teaching form and style in throwing and catching. Avoid drills that reward speed in throwing and catching.

Frisbee Skills

BACKHAND THROW

The backhand grip (Figure 23.23) is used most often. The thumb is on top of the disk, the index finger along the rim, and the other fingers underneath. To throw the Frisbee with the right hand, stand in a sideways position with the right foot toward the target. Step toward the target and throw the Frisbee in a sideways motion across the body, snapping the wrist and trying to keep the disk flat on release.

UNDERHAND THROW

The underhand throw uses the same grip as in the backhand throw, but the thrower faces the target and holds the disk at the side of the body. Step forward with the leg opposite the throwing arm while bringing the Frisbee forward. When the throwing arm is out in the front of the body, release the Frisbee. The trick to this throw is learning to release the disk so that it is parallel to the ground.

THUMB-DOWN CATCH

The thumb-down catch is used for catching when the disk is received at waist level or above. The hand is shaped like a "C" with the thumb pointing toward the ground. The Frisbee should be tracked from the thrower's hand. This clues the catcher about any tilt on the disk that may cause it to curve.

THUMB-UP CATCH

The thumb-up catch is used when the Frisbee is received below waist level. The thumb points up, and the fingers are spread. As with the thumb-down catch, the hand forms a "C" and then clamps the disk (Figure 23.24).

SANDWICH CATCH

In preparation for making the catch, one hand is placed around the chin and the other around the stomach. As the disk approaches and the location of the arrival of the disk becomes apparent, the hands move closer to that location. To catch the disk, one hand is on the top and one is on the bottom with the disk in the middle, thus forming a disk sandwich.

FIGURE 23.23 Frisbee backhand throw.

FIGURE 23.24 Thumb-up catch.

TRICK CATCHES

The disk can be caught in different positions. The two most popular trick-catch positions are behind the back and between the legs. In the behind-the-back catch, the thumb-up technique is used, and the disk is caught with the arm that is farthest away from the thrower. For the between-the-legs catch, the thumb-up catch is also used, and one leg can be lifted to facilitate the catch.

Frisbee Drills
INDIVIDUAL DRILLS

▶ THROW AND CATCH

Each with a Frisbee, all students practice the appropriate throws and catches individually. The Frisbee is tossed into the air using the backhand grip and the underhand throw. The disk must be released at a sharp angle to get it to "boomerang" back to the thrower. This offers an excellent chance to try the thumb-up, thumb-down, and sandwich catches as well. Students can also be challenged to throw and catch the Frisbee with their nondominant hand. To add difficulty, students can perform stunts such as throwing the disk under their leg or behind their back, doing a trick while the disk is in the air, and catching the disk under the leg, on the foot, or some other creative way. Throughout this activity, controlled throwing is emphasized.

▶ THROW TO A WALL

Each student has a disk and practices a soft underhand throw to a wall that is approximately three feet away. This activity allows students lots of repetitions and prevents them from having to spend most of their time chasing the Frisbee. Early on, lots of repetitions in throwing are important.

▶ OUTSIDE THROWING AND CATCHING

If outside, students can move through the Throw and Catch progression described above, and then try other drills. Youngsters can make the disk respond like a boomerang, by throwing the disk into the wind at a steep angle. Also, challenge students to throw the Frisbee into the air and then run and catch it. Each time, they try to increase the throwing distance and still make the catch before the disk touches the ground.

PARTNER/SMALL GROUP DRILLS

▶ TOSSING AND CATCHING

After practicing the grips and catches individually, these drills allow students to practice the skills more authentically. Each set of partners has one disk and is about 15 to 20 feet apart. The following challenges can be given.

- Throw the Frisbee at different levels to a partner.
- Catch the Frisbee, using various catching styles and hand positions.
- Throw a curve by tilting the disk. Try curving it to the left, the right, and upward. Throw a slow curve and then a fast slider.
- Throw a bounce pass to a partner. Throw a low, fast bounce. Throw a high, slow bounce.
- As the catcher, do various stunts after the disk has left the partner's hand. Examples are a full turn, heel click, handclap, or touching the ground.
- Throw the disk with the nondominant hand. Try to throw for accuracy first, and then strive for distance.
- Have the partner hold a hoop as a target. See how many times you can throw the Frisbee through the hoop. Play a game of One Step, in which you move back a step each time you throw the disk through the hoop. When you make two misses in a row, your partner gets a chance to try.
- Place a series of hoops on the ground. Different colored hoops can signify different point values. Have a contest with your partner to see who can earn more points in five throws.
- Play catch while both partners are moving. Try to throw the disk so that your partner does not have to break stride to catch it.
- Throw for distance. Try to throw farther than your partner by using a series of four throws.
- Throw for both distance and accuracy. Using a series of four or more throws, try to reach a goal that is a specified distance away. Many different objects can be used as goals, such as basket standards, fence posts, and trees. (This could be the start of playing Frisbee Golf, which is becoming a popular recreational sport.)
- Set a time limit of 30 seconds. Within this time, see how many successful throws and catches can be made. A certain distance apart must be set for all pairs, and missed catches do not count as throws.

23

- Working in groups of three, try to keep the disk away from the person in the middle. The children can establish their own rules as to when someone else must move to the middle.

- In groups of three, with one person in the middle, try to throw the Frisbee through the middle person's legs. A point is scored each time the disk is thrown through the legs without touching. Legs must be spread to shoulder width.

Frisbee Activities

▶ FRISBEE KEEPAWAY

Playing Area: Gymnasium, 10 by 10 feet

Players: Groups of four to five students

Supplies: One Frisbee per group

Skills: Throwing and catching

Two players start on defense. The remaining players spread out around the designated area and are the offense. Cones can be used to establish boundaries if necessary. The players on offense attempt to make three consecutive throws. Defensive players attempt to break up the consecutive throws by knocking the disk down or catching it. Once the disk is caught, it cannot be taken away or knocked to the ground. If the disk is caught or knocked from the air to the ground, the person that threw the disk becomes a member of the defense, and the defensive player that knocked the disk down or caught it is on offense. If three consecutive throws are made, two players from offense switch with the defensive players and the game continues.

▶ STEP BACK

Playing Area: Gymnasium or designated activity area

Players: Partners

Supplies: One Frisbee per set of partners

Skills: Throwing and catching

Partners begin standing one to two feet apart with the gym's center line between them. With each successful catch, one partner steps back. If the disk is dropped, the partners return to the center line and begin again.

▶ FRISBEE BOWLING

Playing Area: Gymnasium or outside, in 8-by-15-foot lanes

Players: Groups of three students

Supplies: Two Frisbees and six to ten bowling pins (rectangular blocks or plastic two-liter soda bottles will work)

Skills: Throwing

Each group is assigned an 8-by-15-foot lane with 6 to 10 bowling pins. Two students take on the role of pin setters and stand beside the pins. The other student is the bowler. The bowler stands 15 feet from the pins and has two throws to knock down as many pins as possible. After the first throw the setters only remove the Frisbee. All pins are left as they are. After the second throw, the setters quickly tell the bowler how many pins were knocked down. One setter then collects both Frisbees and reports to the bowling line while the other setter sets the pins up. Initially a triangular shape can be used; however, ultimately the students can choose how they want to set up the pins. The only stipulation is they have to be set up the same way each time. After the pins are set, the next bowler begins. This process then continues with every student rotating to each role. The setters can also retrieve errant throws when they see they are not going to hit the pins. Safety reminders will be needed throughout this activity. Primarily, students will need to be reminded to look before throwing and before stepping in front of someone on the bowler's end of the lane.

▶ FRISBEE GOLF

Playing Area: Large outside playing area

Players: Groups of two to four students

Supplies: One Frisbee per child, 8 to 10 hoops, 8 to 10 cones

Skills: Throwing

Frisbee Golf is played exactly like golf except the disk is thrown rather than a ball hit with a club. Prior to playing, an overview of golf is given. Students are informed that the idea is to get their Frisbee from the cone, which is called the tee, to the hole, or hoop, in the fewest number of steps. To begin, each group is assigned a starting tee. This will minimize waiting after each hole. Each person in the group throws his Frisbee, one at a time. Students then hustle to their Frisbee for the second throw. The person farthest from the hole goes first. For safety reasons, all members of the group should watch the throw. This process continues until all players have thrown the Frisbee into the hoop. The next tee is located close to the previous hole. Students should be taught that after they play hole 5, they move to hole 6. If they start on hole 6, they will be finished when they play hole 5. Also, students can track their own score or use a scorecard (see Figure 23.25). Rather than having students carry pencils, which creates

Player	Hole										Total
	1	2	3	4	5	6	7	8	9	10	
1											
2											
3											
4											

1. After each hole, record each member of your group's number of throws. Pencils are found at the next tee. DO NOT TAKE THE PENCILS WITH YOU.
2. After all 10 holes have been completed, each player adds their total number of throws.
3. The person with the fewest number of throws wins.

FIGURE 23.25   Frisbee Golf score card.

a safety hazard, pencils can be placed at each tee. Before starting the next hole, they first record their score from the previous hole. Also, before beginning the hole, students must wait until the group in front of them is finished and has moved on to the next hole. If desired, inexpensive flags (see Figure 23.26) can be created with one-inch PVC pipe or wands and plastic triangles and then placed in cones. This will help students locate the hole. Providing students with a map of the course (Figure 23.27).

FIGURE 23.26   Frisbee Golf tees and flags.

will allow integration of orienteering with Frisbee activities. It may be easiest to print the scorecard on the back of the map.

ULTIMATE FRISBEE

Playing Area: Gymnasium or outside area 40 by 50 feet

Players: 8 to 10 students per team

Supplies: One Frisbee, cones to mark boundaries, pinnies

Skills: Throwing, catching, moving to open spaces, cooperation

Ultimate Frisbee is a combination of basketball, soccer, and football, played with a Frisbee. At the elementary school level, rules are minimized and activity emphasized. Teams attempt to move the Frisbee down the field or court by throwing it to teammates. The following rules apply:

1. The disk can only be stolen when it is in the air. Thus, the disk can not be taken from someone's hands.
2. The player with the Frisbee can only take three steps.
3. The player with the Frisbee can only hold it for five seconds.
4. If the Frisbee is dropped or hits the ground after a throw, it goes to the other team.
5. A point is scored when a team throws the Frisbee across the other team's end line and it is caught.

Following each score, the scoring team quickly throws the Frisbee down the field and the opposing

23

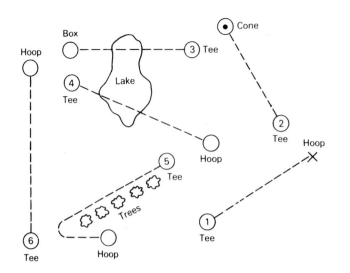

F I G U R E 2 3 . 2 7 Frisbee Golf course.

team either catches it or picks it up and begins moving the Frisbee downfield in an effort to score.

FOR MORE INFORMATION

References and Suggested Readings

Curtis, J. M. (1998). *Pickle-ball for player and teacher.* 3rd ed. Belmont, CA: Thomson Wadsworth.

Darst, P.W., & Pangrazi, R.P. (2006). *Dynamic physical education for secondary school students.* 5th ed. San Francisco, CA: Pearson Benjamin Cummings.

Decker, J., & Mize, M. (2002). *Walking games and activities: 40 new ways to make fitness fun.* Champaign, IL: Human Kinetics.

Fronske, H. (2005). *Teaching cues for sport skills.* 3rd ed. San Francisco: Benjamin Cummings.

Grice, T. (1996). *Badminton: Steps to success.* Champaign, IL: Human Kinetics.

McNeill, C., Cory-Wright, J., & Renfrew, T. (1998). *Teaching orienteering.* 2nd ed. Champaign, IL: Human Kinetics.

Mood, D. P., Musker, F. F., and Rink, J. E. (2003). *Sports and recreational activities.* 13th ed. Boston: McGraw-Hill.

National Sporting Goods Association. (2003). *Sports participation in 2003: Series I.* Mt. Prospect, IL: National Sporting Goods Association.

Schmottlach, N., and McManama, J. (2002). *The physical education handbook.* 10th ed. San Francisco: Benjamin Cummings.

United States Tennis Association. (2000). *USA school tennis curriculum.* 8th ed. White Plains, NY: United States Tennis Association, Inc.

United States Tennis Association. (2003). *Learn to rally and play: A coach's guide.* White Plains, NY: United States Tennis Association, Inc.

Websites

Walking

http://walking.about.com
www.dshs.state.tx.us/wellness/wolt2.shtm
www.walksmartvirginia.com
www.walktoschool-usa.org

Orienteering

www.us.orienteering.org
www.pelinks4u.org
www.eduref.org
www.orienteering.org
www.4orienteering.com
www.orienteeringunlimited.com

Tennis

www.usta.com
www.tennisone.com
www.tennisserver.com

Racquetball

www.racquetball.org
www.surfermall.com/rball
www.rbdepot.com

Badminton

www.worldbadminton.com
www.badmintoncentral.com
www.northwestbadminton.org
www.pier55.com/Sports-Recreation/Play-Badminton.shtml

Frisbees

www.discgolf.com
www.pdga.com
www.whatisultimate.com
http://freestyledisc.org
www.frisbee.com

24

Basketball

SUMMARY

Skills instruction for basketball is introduced primarily during the intermediate grades after youngsters have mastered the basic prerequisite skills. The teaching of rules and strategies for basketball should be an integral part of the instructional process. Using proper progression is a key to success when teaching fundamental skills and lead-up games associated with basketball. Lead-up games provide an opportunity to emphasize development of selected basketball skills in a setting that is compatible with the ability of participants.

ESSENTIAL COMPONENTS OF QUALITY PROGRAMS

▶ **I. Organized around content standards**

▶ **II. Student-centered and developmentally appropriate**

▶ **III. Physical activity and motor skill development form the core of the program**

▶ **IV. Teaches management skills and self-discipline**

▶ **V. Promotes inclusion of all students**

▶ **VI. Focuses on process over product**

VII. Promotes lifetime personal health and wellness

▶ **VIII. Teaches cooperation and responsibility and promotes sensitivity to diversity**

NATIONAL STANDARDS FOR PHYSICAL EDUCATION*

▶ **1. Demonstrates competency in motor skills and movement patterns needed to perform a variety of physical activities.**

▶ **2. Demonstrates understanding of movement concepts, principles, and tactics as they apply to the learning and performance of physical activities.**

▶ **3. Participates regularly in physical activity.**

4. Achieves and maintains a health-enhancing level of physical fitness.

▶ **5. Exhibits responsible personal and social behavior that respects self and others in physical activity.**

▶ **6. Values physical activity for health, enjoyment, challenge, self-expression, and/or social interaction.**

*National Association for Sport and Physical Education (NASPE), 2004.

OUTCOMES

▪ Structure learning experiences efficiently with respect to appropriate formations, progressions, and coaching techniques.

▪ Know the basic rules of basketball.

▪ Develop a unit plan and lesson focus for basketball.

▪ Identify safety precautions associated with teaching basketball.

▪ Describe essential elements for a successful lead-up game.

▪ Cite assessment procedures for evaluating basketball skills.

Basketball is an activity enjoyed by many American boys and girls. The reinforcement offered when a basket is made renders it an attractive game, and this, when coupled with the impact that basketball has on the participants' cardiorespiratory system, makes it a strong contributor to the total curriculum. Basketball instruction in the elementary school focuses on developing skills and competence so students can participate later in life. Often, elementary basketball programs have sought to develop future high school stars with little concern for less talented youngsters. Place emphasis on lead-up games that allow all students to experience success and enjoyment.

With emphasis on instruction and skill development in the physical education setting, little time is available for regulation basketball during school hours. More skilled and interested students should be given additional opportunities through intramural programs, recreational leagues (such as the Youth Basketball Association), or an educationally sound interschool competitive league.

Modifying equipment used by elementary school children is important. Smaller balls and lower baskets help develop technically correct patterns, increase the success of the participants, and maintain motivation. It is impossible for youngsters to practice the ball control drills if the ball is too large for their hands.

INSTRUCTIONAL EMPHASIS AND SEQUENCE

Table 24.1 shows the sequence of basketball activities divided into two developmental levels. In most cases,

youngsters are not ready to participate in the activities in this chapter until the age of eight.

Developmental Level II

Little emphasis is placed on regulation basketball at this level. Concentration is placed on the fundamental skills of passing, catching, shooting, and dribbling. Lead-up games such as Birdies in the Cage, Circle Guard and Pass, and Basketball Tag allow participants to learn skills in a setting that offers both enjoyment and success. Movement of players is somewhat limited, which increases the opportunity for a positive experience. As children mature at this level, a goal should be to develop a range of skills, including passing, catching, dribbling, and shooting.

TABLE 24.1   Suggested Basketball Program

Developmental Level II	Developmental Level III	Developmental Level II	Developmental Level III
Skills		**Knowledge**	
Passing		Dribbling	Held ball
Chest pass	All passes to moving targets	Violations	Personal fouls
One-hand push pass	Two-hand overhead pass	Traveling	Holding
Bounce pass	Long passes	Out-of-bounds	Hacking
Two-hand overhead pass	Three-player weave	Double dribbling	Charging
			Blocking
Catching			Pushing
Above the waist	While moving		Conducting the game
Below the waist			Officiating
Dribbling		**Activities**	
Standing and moving	Figure eight	Circle Guard and Pass	Quadrant Basketball
Down and back	Pivoting	Basketball Tag	Sideline Basketball
Right and left hands	Individual dribbling skills	Dribblerama	Twenty-One
		Birdies in the Cage	Lane Basketball
Shooting		Captain Ball	Freeze Out
One-hand (set) push shot	Free-throw shot	Around the Key	Flag Dribble
Lay-up, right and left	Jump shot	Five Passes	Through the Maze
		Captain Basketball	One-Goal Basketball
Defending and stopping			Basketball Snatch Ball
Pivoting	Parallel stop		Three-on-Three
Feinting	Stride stop		Basketrama
			Paper Clip Basketball
		Skill Tests	
		Straight Dribble	Figure-eight dribble
			Wall pass test
			Baskets per minute
			Free throws

The layup shot and the one-hand push shot should receive instructional attention. Captain Ball adds elements of simple defense, jump balls, and accurate passing.

Developmental Level III

A number of lead-up activities are introduced at this level. Shooting games, such as Twenty-One and Freeze Out, become favorites. Sideline Basketball and Captain Basketball offer meaningful competition. Continued practice on fundamental skills is necessary to ensure a good base of motor development. Drills to enhance skill performance are used, and rules for regulation basketball are presented. Teach officiating so youngsters can learn to appreciate the importance and difficulty of refereeing. Allow players to conduct some games through self-officiating.

FIGURE 24.1 Chest pass.

BASKETBALL SKILLS

Basketball skills at the elementary level are divided into the following categories: passing, catching, dribbling, shooting, defending, stopping, and pivoting. Feinting should be taught as part of the passing, dribbling, and offensive maneuvers.

Passing

Certain factors are common to all passes regardless of which pass is used. For firm control, the ball should be handled with the thumb and finger pads, not with the palms of the hands. The passer should step forward in the direction of the receiver. Passes should be made with a quick arm extension and a snap of the wrists, with thumbs and fingers providing momentum. After the pass is released, the palms should be facing the floor.

The following are instructional cues that can be used to help students focus on proper performance of passing.

1. Fingers spread with thumbs behind the ball.
2. Elbows in; extend through the ball.
3. Step forward, extend arms, and rotate hands slightly inward.
4. Throw at chest level to the receiver.
5. For bounce passes, bounce the ball past the halfway point closer to the receiver.

CHEST (OR TWO-HAND) PASS

For the chest, or two-hand, pass, one foot is ahead of the other, with the knees flexed slightly. The ball is released at chest level, with the fingers spread on each side of the ball. Pass the ball by extending the arms and snapping the wrists as one foot moves toward the receiver (Figure 24.1).

ONE-HAND PUSH PASS

For a one-hand push pass, the passer holds the ball with both hands but supports the ball more with the left than with the right, which is a little back of the ball. The ball is pushed forward, with a quick wrist snap, by the right hand.

BOUNCE PASS

Any of the preceding passes can be adapted to a bounce pass. The object is to get the pass to the receiver on the first bounce, with the ball coming to the receiver's outstretched hands at about waist height. Some experimentation determines the distance. The ball should be bounced a little more than halfway between the two players to make it come efficiently to the receiver.

TWO-HAND OVERHEAD PASS

The two-hand overhead pass is effective against a shorter opponent. The passer is in a short stride position, with the ball held overhead (Figure 24.2 on page 612). The momentum of the pass comes from a forceful wrist and finger snap. The pass should take a slightly downward path.

Catching

Receiving the ball is a fundamental skill. Many turnovers involve failure to handle a pass properly. The receiver

24

FIGURE 24.2   Two-hand overhead pass.

FIGURE 24.3   Dribbling.

Instructional cues for dribbling include the following:

1. Push the ball to the floor. Don't slap it.
2. Push the ball forward when moving.
3. Keep the hand on top of the ball. (Carrying the ball is illegal.)
4. Eyes forward and head up.

Shooting

Shooting is an intricate skill, and students need to develop consistent and proper technique rather than be satisfied when the ball happens to drop into the basket.

1. Good body position is important. Both the toes and the shoulders should face the basket. The weight should be evenly distributed on both feet. When preparing to shoot, the ball is held between shoulder and eye level.
2. A comfortable grip, with fingers well spread and the ball resting on the pads of the fingers, is essential. One should be able to see daylight between the palm of the hand and the ball. The shooting elbow is held near the side so that the hand moves up through the ball toward the basket.
3. As soon as the decision is made to shoot, the eye is fixed on the front of the rim for the rest of the shot.
4. As the shot starts, the wrist is cocked.
5. The follow-through imparts a slight backspin to the ball. The arms are fully extended, the wrist is completely flexed, and the hand drops down toward the floor ("make a swan's neck"). The arc should be 45 degrees or a little higher.

The following instructional cues aid skill development:

1. Use the pads of the fingers. Keep the fingers spread.
2. Keep the shooting elbow in (near the body).
3. Extend through the ball.
4. Bend the knees and use the legs for more force.
5. Release the ball off the fingertips.

should move toward the pass with the fingers spread and relaxed, reaching for the ball with elbows bent and wrists relaxed. The hands should give as the ball comes in.

Instructional cues for catching include the following:

1. Move to the ball.
2. Spread the fingers and catch with the fingertips.
3. Reach for the ball.
4. Give with the ball (absorb the force of the ball by reaching and bringing the ball to the chest).

Dribbling

Dribbling is used to advance the ball, break for a basket, or maneuver out of a difficult situation. The dribbler's knees and trunk should be slightly flexed (Figure 24.3), with hands and eyes forward. Peripheral vision is important. The dribbler should look beyond the ball and see it in the lower part of the visual area. The ball is propelled by the fingertips with downward wrist action. Younger children tend to slap at the ball rather than push it. The dribbling hand should be alternated, and practice in changing hands is essential.

ONE-HAND SHOT

The one-hand shot is usually a jump shot at short distances and a set shot at longer distances for young children. Most youngsters in elementary school are not capable of shooting a jump shot. The one-hand set shot can serve as a prelude to the jump shot as students mature. The ball is held at shoulder-eye level with both hands; the body is erect, and the knees are flexed slightly in preparation for a jump. For a jump shot, the shooter executes a vertical jump, leaving the floor slightly (Figure 24.4). (In a set shot, the shooter rises on the toes.) The supporting (nonshooting) hand remains in contact with the ball until the top of the jump is reached. The shooting hand then takes over with fingertip control, and the ball rolls off the center three fingers. The hand and wrist follow through. Visual concentration on the target is maintained throughout. Proper technique should be emphasized rather than accuracy.

LAY-UP SHOT

The lay-up is a short shot taken when going in toward the basket either after receiving a pass or at the end of a dribble. In a shot from the right side, the takeoff is with the left foot, and vice versa. The ball is carried with both hands early in the shot and then shifted to one hand for the final push. The ball, guided by the fingertips, should be laid against the backboard with a minimum of spin.

FREE-THROW SHOT

The one-hand set shot is the shot of choice for free throws. Complete concentration, relaxation, and a rhythmic, consistent delivery are needed. Some players find it helpful to bounce the ball several times before shooting. Others like to take a deep breath and exhale

completely just before shooting. The mechanics of the shot do not differ materially from those of any shot at a comparable distance. Smoothness and consistency are most important.

JUMP SHOT

The jump shot has the same upper-body mechanics as the one-hand shot described above. The primary difference is the height of the jump. The jump should be straight up, rather than at a forward or backward angle. The ball should be released at the height of the jump (Figure 24.5). Because the legs cannot be used to increase the force applied to the ball, the jump shot is difficult for the majority of elementary school youngsters. It may be best to avoid teaching the shot to youngsters who lack enough strength to shoot the ball correctly and resort to

FIGURE 24.4   One-hand push shot.

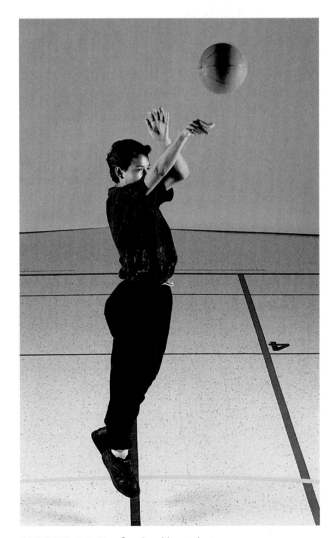

FIGURE 24.5   One-hand jump shot.

throwing it. If the jump shot is presented, the basket should be at the lowest level available and a junior-sized basketball used to develop proper shooting habits.

Another way to practice proper form with the jump shot is to use gray foam balls and cardboard boxes or garbage cans for goals. The balls are light and can be shot easily by children. Concentrate on proper form rather than on making baskets. Reinforce students who use proper technique.

Defending

Defending involves a characteristic stance. The defender, with knees bent slightly and feet comfortably spread (Figure 24.6), faces the opponent at a distance of about three feet. The weight should be distributed evenly on both feet to allow for movement in any direction. Sideways movement is done with a sliding motion. The defender should wave one hand to distract the opponent and to block passes and shots. A defensive player needs to learn to move quickly and not be caught flatfooted.

Instructional cues for proper defending are as follows.

1. Keep the knees bent.
2. Keep the hands up.
3. Don't cross the feet when moving.

FIGURE 24.6   The defensive position.

FIGURE 24.7   Stopping.

Stopping

To stop quickly, the weight of the body is dropped to lower the center of gravity and the feet are applied as brakes (Figure 24.7). In the parallel stop, the body turns sideways and both feet brake simultaneously. The stride stop comes from a forward movement and is done in a one-two count. On the first count, one foot hits the ground with a braking action; the other foot is planted firmly ahead on the second count. The knees are bent, and the center of gravity is lowered. From a stride stop, the player can move into a pivot by picking up the front foot and carrying it to the rear and, at the same time, fading to the rear.

Pivoting

Pivoting is a maneuver that protects the ball by keeping the body between the ball and the defensive player. The ball is held firmly in both hands, with elbows out to protect it. One foot, the pivot foot, must always be in contact with the floor. Turning on that foot is permitted, but it must not be dragged away from the pivot spot. The lead foot may, however, step in any direction (Figure 24.8).

If a player has received the ball in a stationary position or during a jump in which both feet hit the ground simultaneously, either foot may become the pivot foot. If a player stops after a dribble on a one-two count, the pivot foot is the foot that made contact on the first count.

Feinting

Feinting (faking) masks the intent of a maneuver or pass and is essential to basketball. Feinting is faking motion in

FIGURE 24.8 Pivoting.

one direction when the intent is to move in another direction. It can be done with the eyes, the head, a foot, or the whole body. In passing, feinting means faking a pass in one manner or direction and then passing in another.

INSTRUCTIONAL PROCEDURES

1. Many basketball skills do not require the use of basketballs. Other balls, such as volleyballs or rubber balls, can be used successfully.

2. Many skills can be practiced individually or in pairs with playground balls. This allows all children to develop at their own pace, regardless of skill level. Dribbling, passing, and catching skills receive more practice when many balls are used.

3. Baskets should be lowered to seven, eight, or nine feet, depending on the size of the youngsters. If the facility is also used for community purposes, adjustable baskets—preferably power-driven—are the key. Baskets of 5- or 6-foot height are good for children in wheelchairs. This height also allows for experimentation by younger children. These lower baskets can be mounted directly on a wall and set up and removed as needed. No backboard is necessary. When the baskets are mounted to one side, children with disabilities can shoot baskets even though they may not be able to participate in other basketball activities.

4. The program should concentrate on skills and include many drills. Basketball offers endless possibilities, and using many drills gives variety and breadth to the instructional program. Each child should have an opportunity to practice all skills. This is not possible when a considerable portion of class time

is devoted to playing regulation basketball on a full-length court.

BASIC BASKETBALL RULES

The game of basketball played at the elementary school level is similar to the official game played in the junior and senior high schools, but is modified to assure the opportunity for success and for proper skill development. A team is made up of five players, including two guards, one center, and two forwards. The game is divided into four quarters, each 6 minutes in length. The game is under the control of two or three referees, all of whom have an equal right to call violations and fouls. The following rules apply to the game for elementary school children. A caveat here: the rules are seldom followed to the letter in physical education or intramural settings with young children. When modifying the rules makes for more activity and enjoyment, the rules should be adapted to the needs of the players.

Putting the Ball into Play

Each quarter is started with a jump ball at the center circle. Throughout the game, the jump ball is called when the ball is tied up between two players or when it is uncertain which team caused the ball to go out-of-bounds. Even though these situations are called a jump ball, the ball is alternately awarded to each team rather than jumped off between the two players. In other words, the first called jump ball goes to Team A and the second called jump ball goes to Team B, etc. After each successful basket or free throw, the ball is put into play at the end of the court under the basket by the team against whom the score was made.

Violations

The penalty for a violation is to award the ball to the opponents near the out-of-bounds point. The following are violations.

1. Traveling, that is, taking more than one step with the ball without passing, dribbling, or shooting (sometimes called *walking* or *steps*).

2. Stepping out-of-bounds with the ball or causing the ball to go out-of-bounds.

3. Taking more than 10 seconds to cross the centerline from the back to the front court. (Once in the forward court, the ball may not be returned to the back court by the team in control.)

4. Double dribbling, which is taking a second series of dribbles without another player's having handled

24

the ball; palming (carrying) the ball; or dribbling the ball with both hands at once.

5. Stepping on or over a restraining line during a jump ball or free throw.

6. Kicking the ball intentionally.

7. Remaining more than three seconds in the area under the offensive basket, which is bounded by the two sides of the free-throw lane, the free-throw line, and the end of the court. This area is called the lane or key, i.e., "three seconds in the key."

8. To equalize scoring opportunities, a time limit (30 seconds) may be established during which the offensive team must score or give up the ball.

Fouls

Personal fouls are holding, pushing, hacking (striking), tripping, charging, blocking, and unnecessary roughness. When a foul is called, the ball is awarded to the team that was fouled. After five fouls in a half, one shot and a bonus shot (if the first foul shot was made) is awarded to the team that was fouled. If fouled in the act of shooting and the basket was missed, the fouled player receives two shots. If, despite the foul, the basket was made, the basket counts and one free throw is awarded. A player who has five personal fouls is out of the game and must go to the sidelines.

Scoring

A basket from the field scores two points and a free throw one point. In most cases, the three-point goal is not a consideration due to the distance of the shot. If desired, teachers could create a three-point line to simulate the game played by older students. The team that is ahead at the end of the game is declared the winner. If the score is tied, an overtime period of 2 minutes is played. If the score is still tied after this period, the next team to score (one or two points) is declared the winner. Some teachers alter the rules to offer more scoring opportunities. If the backboard is hit, the team scores one point. If it hits the basket (rim) the team scores two points, and if the ball goes in the basket, it is a three pointer.

Substitutes

Substitutes must report to the official scorer and await a signal from the referee or umpire before entering the game. The scorer will sound the signal at a time when the ball is not in play so that the official on the floor can signal for the player to enter the game. In physical education classes, all students should be involved in multiple games so they all have equal opportunity to learn.

BASKETBALL DRILLS

Drills should emulate actual game situations. Youngsters should understand that practice is ineffective unless it is purposeful and correct. When using drills, instructors should use the technique suggestions for the skill being practiced and apply movement principles. The drills presented here cover both single skills and combinations of skills.

Ball-Handling Drills

These drills are practiced continuously for about 30 seconds. The ball is handled with the pads of the fingers. The drills are listed in order of difficulty.

▶ **AROUND THE BODY DRILLS**

1. *Around the waist.* Hold the ball in the right hand, circle it behind the back, and transfer to the left hand. The left hand carries it to the front of the body for a transfer to the right hand. Start with the left hand and move the ball in the opposite direction.

2. *Around the head.* With shoulders back, send the ball around the head in much the same manner described above. Perform in both directions.

3. *Triple play.* Begin by circling around the head; move to waist level and follow by knee level circles. Move the ball in the opposite direction.

▶ **FIGURE EIGHT**

1. Begin in a squatting position with the ball in the right hand. Move the ball around the leg to the right and bounce the ball between the legs to the left hand. Circle the ball around the left leg, through the legs to the right hand.

2. Bounce the ball through the legs front to back followed by the figure-eight motion.

▶ **SPEED DRILL**

Feet are placed shoulder width apart. The ball is held between the legs with one hand in front and the other behind the back in contact with the ball. In a quick motion, flip the ball slightly upward and reverse the hand positions. Using a quick exchange of the hands, make a series of rapid exchanges. The ball will appear to be suspended between the legs (Figure 24.9).

FIGURE 24.9   Speed drill.

DOUBLE CIRCLE DRILL

Beginning with the ball in the right hand, go around both legs, with an assist from the left hand. When the ball returns to the right hand, move the left foot away from the right foot. With the ball moving in the same direction, circle the right leg. Move the leg back to the starting position and circle both legs, followed by moving the legs apart and circling the left leg (Figure 24.10). In short, circle both legs, circle the right leg, circle both legs, circle the left leg. Try moving the ball in the opposite direction.

TWO-HAND CONTROL DRILL

Start from a semicrouched position with the feet shoulder width apart. The ball is held with both hands between the legs in front of the body (Figure 24.11 on page 618). Let go of the ball, move the hands behind the body, and catch it before the ball hits the floor. It may be helpful to give the ball a slight upward flip to facilitate the catch. Reverse the action, moving the hands to the front of the body. Perform continuously.

CHANGING HANDS CONTROL DRILL

Begin with the ball in the right hand; move it around the back of the right leg and catch with both hands. The right hand should be in front and the left hand behind. Drop the ball and quickly change position of the hands on the ball after it has bounced once (Figure 24.12). Immediately after the catch, bring the ball to the front of the body with the left hand and switch the ball to the right hand. Repeat continuously. Try moving the ball in the opposite direction.

Individual Dribbling Drills

HOOP DRIBBLING DRILL

Each youngster has a ball and hula hoop. Place the hoop on the floor and practice dribbling the ball inside the hoop while walking outside the hoop. Dribble counterclockwise using the left hand and clockwise using the right hand. Repeat with the dribbler inside the hoop and the ball dribbled outside the hoop.

RANDOM DRIBBLING

Each child has a ball. Dribbling is done in place, varied by using left and right hands. Develop a sequence of body positions (standing, kneeling, lying on the side, on two feet and one hand). Encourage players to develop a sequence by dribbling a certain number of times in each selected position. Dribble with each hand.

ONE-HAND CONTROL DRILL

Begin with the right hand holding the ball. Make a half circle around the right leg to the back. Bounce the ball between the legs (back to front) and catch it with the right hand and move it around the body again (Figure 24.13 on page 619). After continuing for a short time, switch to the left hand.

FIGURE 24.10   Double circle drill.

FIGURE 24.11   Two-hand control drill.

 FIGURE-EIGHT DRIBBLING DRILL (SPEED)

Start with the right or left hand. Dribble outside the respective leg, between the feet, and continue in front with the opposite hand in figure-eight fashion. Begin slowly and gradually increase the speed of the dribble.

 FIGURE-EIGHT DRIBBLING DRILL (ONE BOUNCE)

Assume a semicrouched position with the feet shoulder width apart. Start with the ball in the right hand and bounce it from the front of the body between the legs. Catch it with the left hand behind the legs (Figure 24.14). Bring the ball to the front of the body with the left hand and start the sequence over with that hand.

FIGURE-EIGHT DRIBBLING DRILL (TWO BOUNCES)

Begin in the same position as described in the preceding drill. Using the right hand, take one dribble outside the right leg (angled toward the back) and a second dribble between the legs to the left hand in front of the body (Figure 24.15). Repeat, starting with the left hand.

Group Dribbling Drills

Dribbling can be practiced as a single skill or in combination with others.

FILE DRIBBLING

In file dribbling, players dribble forward around an obstacle (such as a bowling pin, a cone, or a chair) and back to the line, where the next player repeats (Figure 24.16). A variation has each player dribbling down with one hand and back with the other.

SHUTTLE DRIBBLING

Shuttle dribbling begins at the head of a file. The head player dribbles across to another file and hands the ball off to the player at the head of the second file. The first player then takes a place at the end of that file (Figure 24.17). The player receiving the ball dribbles back to the first file. A number of shuttles can be arranged for dribbling crossways over a basketball court.

OBSTACLE, OR FIGURE-EIGHT, DRIBBLING

For obstacle, or figure-eight, dribbling, three or more obstacles are positioned about five feet apart. The first player at the head of each file dribbles in and around each obstacle, changing hands so that the hand opposite the obstacle is the one always used (Figure 24.18).

Dribbling and Pivoting Drills

In dribbling and pivoting drills, the emphases are on stopping and pivoting.

FILE DRILL

For the file drill, each player in turn dribbles forward to a designated line, stops, pivots, faces the file, passes back

FIGURE 24.12   Changing hands control drill.

FIGURE 24.13   One-hand control drill.

FIGURE 24.14   Figure-eight dribbling drill (one bounce).

FIGURE 24.15   Figure-eight dribbling drill (two bounces).

FIGURE 24.16   File dribbling.

FIGURE 24.17   Shuttle dribbling.

FIGURE 24.18   Obstacle, or figure-eight, dribbling.

to the next player, and runs to a place at the end of the line (Figure 24.19). The next player repeats the pattern.

▶ **DRIBBLE-AND-PIVOT DRILL**

For the dribble-and-pivot drill, players are scattered by pairs around the floor (Figure 24.20 on page 620). One ball is required for each pair. On the first whistle, the front player of the pair dribbles in any direction and fashion on the court. On the second whistle, the player stops and pivots back and forth, and on the third whistle, dribbles back and passes to the partner, who immediately dribbles forward, repeating the routine.

Passing Drills

In passing practice, regular use should be made of the various movement formations (Chapter 3), including two-line, circle, circle-and-leader, line-and-leader, shuttle turn-back, and regular shuttle formations. A number of other drills should be considered.

▶ **SLIDE CIRCLE DRILL**

In the slide circle drill, a circle of four to six players slides around a person in the center. The center person passes to and receives from the sliding players. After the ball has gone around the circle twice, another player takes the center position.

▶ **CIRCLE-STAR DRILL**

With only five players, a circle-star drill is particularly effective. Players pass to every other player, and the path of the ball forms a star (Figure 24.21 on page 620). The star drill works well as a relay. Any odd number of players will cause the ball to go to all participants, assuring that all receive equal practice.

FIGURE 24.19   File drill.

24

FIGURE 24.20   Dribble-and-pivot drill.

▶ TRIANGLE DRILL

Four to eight players can participate in the triangle drill. The ball begins at the head of a line and is passed forward to a player away from the line. This player then passes to a teammate out at a corner, who then passes back to the head of the line (Figure 24.22). Each player passes and then moves to the spot to which he passed the ball, thus making a continual change of positions.

▶ SQUAD SPLIT-VISION DRILL

This drill requires two basketballs. The center player holds one ball, while Player 1 (Figure 24.23) has the other. The center player passes the ball to Player 2, while receiving the other ball from Player 1. The center player now passes to Player 3 and receives the other ball from Player 2 until the balls move completely around the semicircle. To rotate to a new center player, the center player becomes Player 1 while the player with the ball moves to the center spot. All players adjust one space to the right.

▶ THREE-LANE RUSH

This is a lead-up to the three-player weave, which is difficult for elementary school youngsters to learn. Youngsters

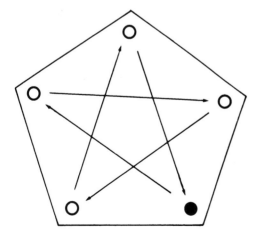

FIGURE 24.21   Circle-star drill formation.

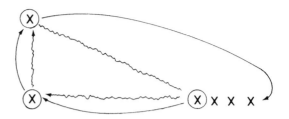

FIGURE 24.22   Triangle drill formation.

are in three lines across one end of the area. The first three players move parallel down the court while passing the ball back and forth to each other. A layup shot can be taken as players near the basket.

▶ THREE-PLAYER WEAVE

This drill requires practice and should be learned at slow speed. Walking students through the drill can sometimes help. If it is too difficult for a class, it should be avoided. The player in the center always starts the drill. She passes to another player coming across in front and then goes behind that player. Just as soon as she goes behind and around the player, she heads diagonally across the floor until she receives the ball again. The pass from the center player can start to either side.

Shooting Drills

Shooting drills may involve just shooting or a combination of shooting and other skills.

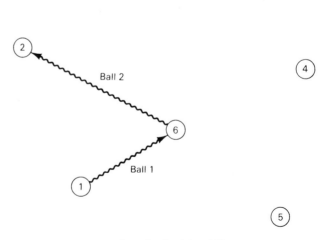

FIGURE 24.23   Squad split-vision drill.

FIGURE 24.24 File-and-leader drill.

FIGURE 24.26 Layup drill.

▶ SIMPLE SHOOTING DRILL

In one simple shooting drill, players form files of no more than four people and take turns shooting a long and then a short shot or some other prescribed series of shots.

▶ FILE-AND-LEADER DRILL

For a file-and-leader drill, the first player in each file has a ball and is the shooter. He passes the ball to the leader, who returns the ball to the spot that the shooter has selected for the shot (Figure 24.24).

▶ DRIBBLE-AND-SHOOT DRILL

For the dribble-and-shoot drill, two files are established on one end of the floor. One file has a ball. The first player dribbles in and shoots a layup. A member of the other file recovers the ball and passes it to the next player (Figure 24.25). As each person in turn either shoots or retrieves, she goes to the rear of the other file. After some proficiency in the drill has been developed, two balls can be used, allowing for more shooting opportunities.

▶ SHOOT AND REBOUND DRILL

In the shoot and rebound drill, players are scattered an equal distance around the basket in a semicircle. Players should begin close enough to the basket so that they can shoot accurately. All shooters have a ball and must

rebound their own shots. A bit of competition can be injected by allowing a successful shooter to take one step back for the next shot.

▶ LAY-UP DRILL

The lay-up drill is a favorite. One line passes to the other line for layup shots (Figure 24.26). Shooters come in from the right side first (this is easier), then from the left, and finally from the center. Each player goes to the end of the other line.

▶ JUMP-SHOT DRILL

The jump-shot drill is similar to the layup drill, except that the incoming shooter receives the ball, stops, and takes a jump shot. The line of shooters should move back so that there is room for forward movement to the shooting spot. As soon as the passer releases the ball to the shooter, he moves to the end of the shooter's line. The shooter goes to the passer's line after shooting (Figure 24.27).

One extension of this drill is to allow a second jump shot when the shooter makes the first. In this case, the incoming passer passes to the shooter taking a second shot as well as to the next shooter. Another extension, which creates a gamelike situation, is having both the shooter and the incoming passer follow up the shot when the basket has not been made. As soon as the follow-up shot is made or there are three misses by the followers, the passer passes the ball to the new shooter. The avenues

FIGURE 24.25 Dribble-and-shoot drill.

FIGURE 24.27 Jump-shot drill.

FIGURE 24.28   Group defensive drill.

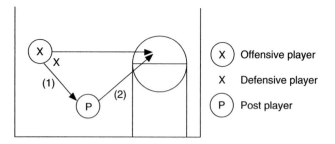

FIGURE 24.29   Offensive-defensive drill with post.

by which the shooters approach should be varied, so that children practice shooting from different spots.

Offensive and Defensive Drills

▶ GROUP DEFENSIVE DRILL

For the group defensive drill, the entire class is scattered on a basketball floor, facing one of the sides (Figure 24.28). The instructor or the student leader stands on the side, near the center. The drill can be done in a number of ways.

1. The leader points in one direction (forward, backward, or to one side) and gives the command "Move." When the students have moved a short distance, the leader commands, "Stop." Players keep good defensive position throughout.

2. Commands can be changed so that movement is continuous. Commands are "Right," "Left," "Forward," "Backward," and "Stop." The leader must watch that movement is not so far in any one direction that it causes players to run into obstructions. Commands can be given in order, and pointing can accompany commands.

3. The leader is a dribbler with a ball, who moves forward, backward, or to either side, with the defensive players reacting accordingly.

It is important to stress good defensive position and movement. Movement from side to side should be a slide. Movement forward and backward is a two-step, with one foot always leading.

▶ OFFENSIVE-DEFENSIVE DRILL WITH A POST

The offensive-defensive drill with a post consists of an offensive player, a defensive player, and another player who acts as a passing post. The post player generally remains stationary and receives the ball from and passes to the offensive player. The player on offense tries to maneuver around or past the defensive player to secure a good shot (Figure 24.29). Plays can be confined to one side of an offensive basket area, thus allowing two drills to go on at the same time on one end of the basketball floor. If there are side baskets, many drills can be operated at the same time. After a basket has been attempted, a rotation of players, including any waiting player, is made.

The defensive player's job is to cover well enough to prevent shots in front of her. Some matching of ability must occur or the drill is nonproductive.

BASKETBALL ACTIVITIES

Developmental Level II

▶ CIRCLE GUARD AND PASS

Playing Area: Any smooth surface with circle markings

Players: Eight to ten per team

Supplies: A basketball or playground ball

Skills: Passing, catching, guarding

The offensive team is placed in formation around a large (30-foot diameter) circle. Two or more offensive players move into the center. The defensive team is in position around a smaller (20-foot) circle inside the larger circle. On signal, the offensive team tries to pass the ball to the center players. They may pass the ball around the circle to each other before making an attempt to the center. The defensive team tries to bat the ball away but cannot catch it. After a stipulated time (one minute), offensive and defensive teams trade positions. If score is kept, two points are awarded for each successful pass.

> **Variation:** More than one ball can be used, and different types of passes can be stipulated. The defensive team also can earn points for each time a team member touches the ball.

▶ **BASKETBALL TAG**

Playing Area: Gymnasium or playground area, 30 by 50 feet

Players: Eight to ten per team

Supplies: A foam rubber basketball, pinnies

Skills: Catching, passing, dribbling, guarding

There are two versions of this game. The simpler version is to designate three to five students to be "it" and wear a pinnie. The rest of the class may only pass the ball and try to tag one of the students who is "it" with the ball. Players may move wherever they desire when they don't have the ball. However, when they have the ball in their control they may not move or dribble. If desired, more than one ball can be used.

A more difficult version of the game allows dribbling and tagging with the hands. Two or more players from each team are designated to be "its" and they wear pinnies. The object of the game is to tag the "its" with a hand when they have the ball. The players who are "it" may move only by walking. The rest of the players can only move when they are dribbling or do not have the ball. The players who are "it" try to avoid moving near the ball, while other players try to pass and dribble in an attempt to get close enough to tag the roving "its."

✓ **TEACHING TIPS**

1. Play two or more games simultaneously so students get more opportunity to handle the ball.

2. Designate two teams to play each other. Both teams have "its" who wear different colored pinnies. They are "it" when their team does not have the ball. When their team has the ball, they play offense with their teammates.

▶ **DRIBBLERAMA**

Playing Area: Any smooth surface with a large circle or square, clearly outlined

Players: Entire class

Supplies: One basketball for each player

Skills: Dribbling and protecting the ball

The playing area is a large circle or square. Dribblerama can be played at three levels of difficulty.

Level 1: All players dribble throughout the area, controlling their ball so that it does not touch another ball. If a touch occurs, both players go outside the area and dribble around the area. Once youngsters have completed dribbling around the area, they reenter the game.

Level 2: The area is divided in half and all players move to one of the halves. While dribbling and controlling

a ball, each player attempts to cause another player to lose control of his ball. When control is lost, that player takes his/her ball and moves to the opposite half of the area. Play continues against other players who have lost control. When five or six players remain, bring all players back into the game and start over.

Level 3: The class is divided into four teams and the area is divided into equal quadrants. Each of the four teams goes to one of the quadrants in the teaching area. When control of the ball is lost, that player moves to the next quadrant and begins play. This variation is more controlled and keeps youngsters involved continuously.

▶ **BIRDIES IN THE CAGE**

Playing Area: Any smooth surface with circle marking

Players: 8 to 15 per team

Supplies: A soccer ball, basketball, or volleyball

Skills: Passing, catching, intercepting

Players are placed in circle formation with two or more children in the center of the circle. The object of the game is for the center players to try to touch the ball while circle players are passing it. After a brief time (15–20 seconds) choose new players to enter the circle. If scoring is desired, center players can count the number of touches they made. The ball should move rapidly. Passing to a neighboring player is not allowed. Play can be limited to a specific type of pass (bounce, two-hand, push).

▶ **CAPTAIN BALL**

Playing Area: Playground or gymnasium area, about 30 by 40 feet

Players: Seven or more on each team

Supplies: A basketball, pinnies, mats or spots

Skills: Passing, catching, guarding

Two games can be played crosswise on a basketball court. A centerline is needed (Figure 24.30); otherwise, normal boundary lines are used. Marking spots delineate where forwards and the captains must stay. A team is composed of a captain, three or more forwards, and three or more guards. The guards are free to move in their half of the playing area and try to keep the ball from being thrown to the opposing captain. The captain and forwards are each assigned to their respective spots and must always keep one foot on their assigned marking spot.

The game is started by a jump at the centerline with two guards from opposing teams. The guards can roam in their half of the court but may not touch the opposing forwards. Once points are scored by getting the ball

24

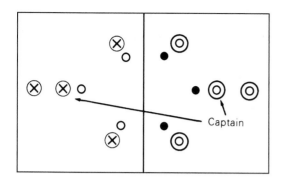

FIGURE 24.30 Formation for Captain Ball.

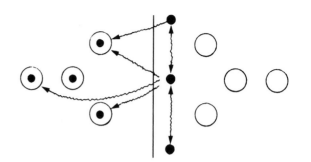

FIGURE 24.31 An effective offensive formation in Captain Ball.

to the captain, an opposing guard immediately puts the ball into play with an inbounds throw. Guards try to throw the ball to their forwards, who maneuver to be open while keeping a foot on their spot. The forwards can throw the ball to their guards and forwards or to the captain. Three points are scored when two forwards handle the ball and it is passed to the captain. Two points are scored when the ball is passed to the captain but has not been handled by two forwards. No points are scored when a guard throws the ball to the captain.

Stepping over the centerline is a foul. It is also a foul if a guard steps on a forward's marking spot or makes personal contact with a player on a spot. The penalty for a foul is a free throw. For a free throw, the ball is given to an unguarded forward, who has five seconds to get the ball successfully to the guarded captain. If the throw is successful, one point is scored. If it is not successful, the ball is in play. Rotate free-throw shooting among all the forwards.

As in basketball, when the ball goes out-of-bounds, it is awarded to the team that did not cause it to go out. If a forward or a captain catches a ball without a foot touching her spot, the ball is taken out-of-bounds by the opposing guard. For violations such as traveling or kicking the ball, the ball is awarded to an opposing guard out-of-bounds. No score may be made from a ball that is thrown in directly from out-of-bounds.

✓ **TEACHING TIP**

An effective offensive formation places guards spaced along the centerline (Figure 24.31—only the offensive team is diagrammed). By passing the ball back and forth among the guards, the forwards have more opportunity to be open, since the passing makes the guards shift position. The guards may dribble, but are restricted to three dribbles for the purpose of advancing the ball. The forwards and captain should shift back and forth to become open for passes. They must keep one foot on the spot. Short and accurate passing uses both chest and bounce passes. Forwards and

centers may jump for the ball but must come down with one foot on their spot.

Variations:

1. A five-spot formation like that on a die can be used. Nine players are needed on each team: four forwards, four guards, and one captain. Depending on space and the size of the courts, even more players can be utilized.

2. Use more than one captain on each side to make scoring easier.

▶ **AROUND THE KEY**

Playing Area: One end of a basketball floor
Players: Three to eight
Supplies: A basketball
Skills: Shooting

Spots are arranged for shooting as indicated in Figure 24.32. A player begins at the first spot and continues around the key, shooting from each spot. When a

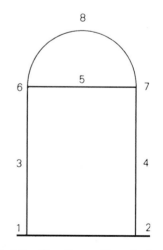

FIGURE 24.32 Shooting positions for Around the Key.

miss occurs, the player can stop and wait for the next opportunity and begin from the point at which the miss occurred. The alternative to waiting is to risk it and try another shot immediately from the point at which the first try was missed. If the shot is made, the player continues. If the shot is missed, the player must start over from the beginning spot on the next turn. The winner is the player who completes the key first or who makes the most progress.

Variations:

1. Each child shoots from each spot until a basket is made. A limit of three shots from any one spot should be set. The child finishing the round of eight spots with the lowest number of shots taken is the winner.

2. The order of the spots can be changed. A player can start on one side of the key and continue back along the line, around the free-throw circle, and back down the other side of the key.

▶ FIVE PASSES

Playing Area: Half of a basketball floor

Players: Five or more on each team

Supplies: A basketball, pinnies

Skills: Passing, guarding

Two teams play. Divide the area into smaller areas so many teams can play simultaneously. The object of the game is to complete five consecutive passes, which scores a point. The game is started with a jump ball at the free-throw line. The teams observe regular basketball rules in ball handling and with regard to traveling and fouling. The team with the ball counts out loud as a pass is completed.

The ball may not be passed back to the person from whom it was received. No dribbling is allowed. If for any reason the ball is fumbled and recovered or improperly passed, a new count is started. After a successful score, the ball is immediately turned over to the other team. A foul draws a free throw, which can score a point. Teams should be well marked to avoid confusion.

Variations:

1. After each successful point (five passes), the team is awarded a free throw, which can score an additional point.

2. After a team has scored a point, the ball can be given to the other team out-of-bounds to start play again.

▶ CAPTAIN BASKETBALL

Playing Area: A basketball court with centerline

Players: Six or more on each team

Supplies: Basketballs, pinnies

Skills: All basketball skills except shooting

A captain's area is laid out by drawing a line (or placing a tumbling mat) between the two foul restraining lines four feet out from the end line. The captain must keep one foot in this area. Captain Basketball is more like regulation basketball than Captain Ball. Captain Ball limits the movements of the forwards. Captain Basketball brings in more natural passing and guarding situations without the movement restrictions on the forwards.

A team typically is composed of three forwards, one captain, and four guards. The captain must keep one foot in the area under the basket. The game is started with a jump ball, after which the players advance the ball as in basketball. No player may cross the centerline, however. The guards must bring the ball up to the centerline and throw it to one of their forwards. The forwards maneuver and attempt to pass successfully to the captain. A throw by one of the forwards to the captain scores two points; a free throw scores one point.

Fouls are the same as in basketball. In addition, stepping over the centerline or a guard stepping into the captain's area draws a foul. In the case of a foul, the ball is given to a forward at the free-throw line. The player is unguarded and has five seconds to pass successfully to the captain, who is guarded by one player. The ball is in play if the free throw is unsuccessful.

✓ TEACHING TIP

Using a folding tumbling mat to designate the captain's area at each end of the court discourages intrusion by guards. Even though players are required to remain in their own half of the court, they should be taught to move freely within that area. Short, quick passes should be stressed, because long passes are often ineffective. Captain Basketball offers the chance for practicing proper guarding techniques.

Developmental Level III

▶ QUADRANT BASKETBALL

Playing Area: Basketball court divided into four equal areas

Players: At least eight per team with a minimum of two placed in each area

Supplies: Basketball, pinnies

Skills: Passing, catching, dribbling, guarding, shooting

Divide the court by its length and width into four equal areas with markers. Play can be started with a jump ball or by giving the ball to one team. Two offensive and two defensive players are placed in each quadrant. Players may not leave the quadrant during the course of play. Normal rules of basketball are used, with the exception of limiting the number of dribbles to three. The purpose of this game is to teach youngsters to remain spaced throughout the area. Rotate players to different quadrants so that they have the opportunity to play offense and defense.

> *Variation:* Limit the number of passes that may be made consecutively in one quadrant to encourage passing to other areas. Reduce amount of time a player may hold the ball to five seconds to encourage passing.

▶ SIDELINE BASKETBALL

Playing Area: Basketball court
Players: Entire class
Supplies: A basketball, pinnies
Skills: All basketball skills

Divide the class into two teams, each lined up along one side of the court, facing the other. Three or four active players from each team enter the floor to play regulation basketball. The remainder of the players, who stand on the sideline, can catch and pass the ball to the active players. Sideline players may not shoot, nor may they enter the playing floor. They must keep one foot completely out of bounds at all times.

The active players play regulation basketball, with the additional rule that they must pass and receive the ball three times from sideline players before they can attempt a goal. Sideline players may pass to each other but must pass back to an active player after three sideline passes. The game starts with active players occupying their half of the court. The ball is taken out of bounds under its own basket by the team that was scored on. Play continues until a period of time (i.e., 30 seconds to 1 minute) elapses. Teams do not change after a score; only after the time has elapsed. The active players then go to the end of their line and three new active players come out from the right. All other players move down and adjust to fill the space left by the new players.

No official out-of-bounds on the sides is called. The players on that side of the floor simply recover the ball and put it into play with a pass to an active player without delay. Out-of-bounds on the ends is the same as in regular basketball. If one of the sideline players enters the court and touches the ball, it is a violation, and the ball is awarded out-of-bounds on the other side to a sideline player of the other team. Free throws are awarded when a player is fouled.

✓ TEACHING TIP

A modified scoring system is an excellent idea that allows all students to contribute to the game. Hitting the backboard is one point, hitting the rim is two points, and making a basket is worth three points.

▶ TWENTY-ONE

Playing Area: One end of a basketball court
Players: Three to eight in each game
Supplies: A basketball
Skills: Shooting

Players are in file formation by teams. Each player is permitted a long shot (from a specified distance) and a follow-up shot. The long shot, if made, counts two points and the short shot counts one point. The follow-up shot must be made from the spot where the ball was recovered from the first shot. The normal one- to two-step rhythm is permitted on the short shot from the place where the ball was recovered. The first player scoring a total of 21 points is the winner. If the ball misses the backboard and basket altogether on the first shot, the second shot must be taken from the corner.

✓ TEACHING TIP

The rules above are for regulation Twenty-One. A modified version is an excellent idea that allows for more activity time and practice on rebounding skills. The scoring modification gives one point for hitting the backboard, two points for hitting the rim, and three points for a made basket. If a player makes the basket or hits the rim he or she gets a free long shot that must go through the basket to count. If the long shot is missed, the player that gets the rebound attempts to score. If the shot is not made but hits the backboard or rim, the shooter gets one point or two points, respectively, and play continues. Because players are learning these skills, standing and waiting for long shots will not happen frequently.

Variations:

1. Start with a simpler game that allows dribbling before the second shot.
2. Allow players to shoot as long as every shot is made. This means that if both the long and the short shot are made, the player goes back to the original position for a third shot. All shots made count and the shooter can continue until a miss.
3. Use various combinations and types of shots.

LANE BASKETBALL

Playing Area: Basketball court divided into six or more lanes

Players: Five per team

Supplies: Basketball, pinnies, cones to mark zones

Skills: All basketball skills

The court is divided into six lanes as shown in Figure 24.33. Players must stay in their lane and cannot cross the midcourt line. Regular basketball rules prevail, with the exception that players cannot dribble more than three times. Play is started with a jump ball. At regular intervals, youngsters rotate to the next lane to assure they get to play offense and defense.

A number of rule changes can be implemented to change the focus of the game. For example, three passes may be required before shooting may occur. Also, to increase the amount of activity, youngsters can move the entire length of the floor within their lane.

FREEZE OUT

Playing Area: One end of the basketball court

Players: Four to eight

Supplies: A basketball

Skills: Shooting under pressure

There are many types of freeze-out shooting games. This version is an interesting shooting game that culminates quickly and allows players back into the game with minimal wait time. Each player can have three misses before being out. After the first miss, the player gets an O; after the second, a U; and after the third, a T. This spells OUT and puts the player out. The last player remaining is the winner.

The first player shoots a basket from any spot desired. If the basket is missed, there is no penalty and the next player shoots. If the basket is made, the following player must make a basket from the same spot or it is scored as a miss (and a letter). If the player ahead of him misses, she may shoot from any spot she chooses without penalty.

FLAG DRIBBLE

Playing Area: One end of a basketball floor or a hard-surfaced area outside with boundaries

Players: 10 to 20

Supplies: A basketball and a flag for each player

Skills: Dribbling

The object is to eliminate other players and avoid being eliminated. Players are eliminated if they lose control of the ball, if their flag is pulled, or if they go out-of-bounds. Keeping control of the ball by dribbling is interpreted to mean continuous dribbling without missing a bounce. A double dribble (both hands) is regarded as a loss of control.

Start the game with players scattered around the area near the sidelines. Each has a ball, and all have flags tucked in the back of their belts. On signal, all players begin to dribble in the area. While keeping control of the dribble and staying in bounds, they attempt to pull a flag from any other player's back. When players lose control, they move to the perimeter of the area and practice their dribbling skills. As soon as the game is down to a few players, start the game over. Sometimes two players lose control of their basketball at about the same time. In this case, both are eliminated.

Variations:

1. If using flags is impractical, the game can be played without this feature. The objective then becomes to knock aside or deflect the other basketballs while retaining control of one's own ball.

2. Flag Dribble can be played with teams or squads. In this case, each squad or team is clearly marked.

THROUGH THE MAZE

Playing Area: Basketball court

Players: Two teams of five to seven

Supplies: Each player on offense has a ball

Skills: Dribbling, ball control, guarding, tackling

One team is on offense and one on defense, placed according to Figure 24.34. Defensive players stay in their assigned areas. On signal, all offensive players try to dribble through the three areas without losing their ball. A player is eliminated if her ball is recovered by a defensive player or goes out-of-bounds. The offensive team scores one point for each ball dribbled across the opposite end line.

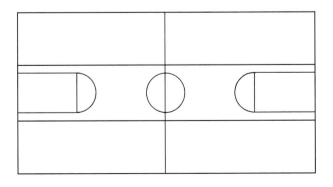

FIGURE 24.33 Court markings for Lane Basketball.

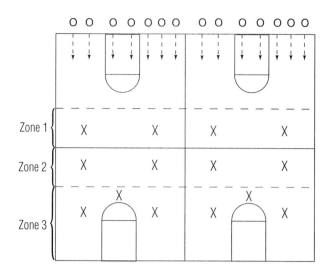

FIGURE 24.34   Through the Maze.

Reverse roles and give the other team a chance to score. Use a number of marking spots to identify the areas where the defensive players must stay. A variation is to put neutral zones between the active zones.

ONE-GOAL BASKETBALL

Playing Area: An area with one basketball goal

Players: Two to four on each team

Supplies: A basketball, pinnies (optional)

Skills: All basketball skills

This is an excellent class activity if four or more baskets are available. The game is played by two teams according to the rules of basketball but with the following exceptions.

1. When a defensive player recovers the ball, either from the backboard or on an interception, the ball must be taken out beyond the foul-line circle before offensive play is started and an attempt at a goal is made.

2. After a basket is made, the ball is taken in the same fashion away from the basket to the center of the floor, where the other team starts offensive play.

3. Regular free-throw shooting can be observed after a foul, or some use can be made of the rule whereby the offended team takes the ball out-of-bounds.

4. An offensive player who is tied up in a jump ball loses the ball to the other team.

5. Individuals are responsible for calling fouls on themselves.

BASKETBALL SNATCH BALL

Playing Area: Basketball court

Players: Six to twenty on each team

Supplies: Two basketballs, two hoops

Skills: Passing, dribbling, shooting

Each of two teams occupies one side of a basketball floor. The players on each team are numbered consecutively from the right-hand end of the line. Two balls are placed inside two hoops, one hoop on each side of the centerline. When the teacher calls three or more numbers, players from each team whose numbers were called run to the ball assigned to them. These players pass and dribble to the basket on their right and try to make a basket. Three passes must be made and all players must handle the ball before a basket can be shot. As soon as a basket is made, the players pass and dribble back and place the ball in the hoop. The first team to return the ball after making a basket scores a point for that team. Use a system to keep track of the numbers so that all children have a turn. Numbers are called in any order.

THREE-ON-THREE

Playing Area: Half of a basketball court

Players: Many teams of three players each

Supplies: Basketballs

Skills: All basketball skills

Three teams of three are assigned to a basket. The offensive team stands at the top of the key facing the basket. The defensive team starts at the free throw line. The remaining team waits for their turn beyond the end line. Regular basketball rules are used. The offensive team tries to score. The offensive team plays until they score or the ball is stolen by the defense. In either case, the defensive team moves to the center of the floor and becomes the offensive unit. The waiting team moves onto the floor and plays defense. The previous offensive team goes to the rear of the line of waiting players. Each of the teams keeps its own score. Many games can be carried on at the same time depending on the number of available baskets. A team wins when they score three points. Winning teams can be rotated to games at other baskets.

BASKETRAMA

Playing Area: Area around one basket

Players: Usually two

Supplies: A basketball for each player

Skills: Shooting under pressure

On signal, two players, each with a basketball, begin to shoot individually as rapidly as possible, taking any kind of shots they wish, until one scores ten baskets to become the winner. Each player must handle her own basketball and must not impede or interfere with the other's ball. Naturally, the balls do collide at times, but deliberate interference by knocking the other ball out of the way or kicking it means disqualification.

Balls should be marked so that there is no argument as to ownership. This can be done by using different types of basketballs or by marking with chalk or tape. Each player can count out loud each basket he makes, or another student can keep score for each contestant.

▶ **PAPER CLIP BASKETBALL**

Playing Area: Basketball court
Players: Entire class
Supplies: Basketballs, hoops, paper clips, Frisbees
Skills: Shooting, passing, dribbling

Four equal teams are formed and each team stands on the sideline of one quadrant of the basketball floor (see Figure 24.35). Each team has a basketball and a hoop that has been placed near the center of the gym. Allow enough room between the hoops so players do not collide. On signal, the first three players for each team must hustle for their ball, then pass and dribble toward one basket. Each team member must receive the

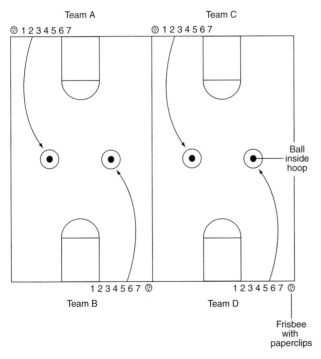

FIGURE 24.35 Paper Clip Basketball.

ball before a shot can be attempted. Once a shot is made or after three shots, the players return the ball to their team's hoop and return to their team and give a "high five" to the next three players. These three players repeat the process toward the other basket. On the sideline each team also has a Frisbee and several paper clips. If any of the three players makes a basket the team places one paper clip into the Frisbee upon returning to the sideline. The game continues for several minutes and the team with the most paper clips in their Frisbee at the conclusion is declared the winner. In order to have different combinations of players working together, it is best if the team number is not divisible by three.

BASKETBALL SKILL TESTS

Tests in basketball cover dribbling, passing, shooting, and making free throws. For each of the first four tests presented here, a stopwatch is needed.

Straight Dribble

A marker is placed 15 yards down the floor from the starting point. The dribbler must dribble around the marker and back to the starting position, where he finishes by crossing the starting line. The marker must remain standing or disqualification results. The teacher should allow two or three trials and take the best time.

Figure-Eight Dribble

Four obstacles (bowling pins, bases, or cones) are placed five feet apart in a straight line beginning 5 feet from the starting line. The player must dribble in and out of the markers in the path of a figure eight, finishing at the point where she started. The teacher can allow two or three trials and take the best time.

Wall Pass Test

A player stands 5 feet from a smooth wall. He is given 30 seconds to make as many catches as he can from throws or passes against the wall. The two-hand or chest pass is generally used. Balls must be caught on the fly to count. Another student should do the counting. Only one trial is allowed. A board or mat provides a definite restraining line.

Baskets Made in Thirty Seconds

A player stands near the basket in any position she wishes. On signal, she shoots and continues shooting for a period of 30 seconds. Her score is the number of baskets she makes during the time period. Another student should do the counting. Only one trial is allowed.

24

Free Throws

Score is kept of the number of free throws made out of ten attempts. The player should get three or four warm-up trials and announce when he is ready. Score should be kept by another student with pencil and paper. An X is marked for a basket made, and an O for a miss.

FOR MORE INFORMATION

References and Suggested Readings

American Sport Education Program. (2001). *Coaching youth basketball.* 3rd ed. Champaign, IL: Human Kinetics.

Fronske, H. (2005). *Teaching cues for sport skills.* 3rd ed. San Francisco: Benjamin Cummings.

Head-Summitt, P. H., & Jennings, D. (1996). *Basketball.* 2nd ed. Dubuque, IA: McGraw-Hill.

Krause, J. (2000). *Basketball skills and drills.* 2nd ed. Champaign, IL: Human Kinetics.

Mood, D. P., Musker, F. F., and Rink, J. E. (2003). *Sports and recreational activities.* 13th ed. Boston: McGraw-Hill.

Nix, C. (2000). *Skills, drills and strategies for basketball.* Scottsdale, AZ: Holcomb Hathaway Publishers.

Paye, B. (2001). *Youth basketball drills.* Champaign, IL: Human Kinetics.

Schmottlach, N., and McManama, J. (2002). *The physical education handbook.* 10th ed. San Francisco: Benjamin Cummings.

Wilkes, G. (1998). *Basketball.* 7th ed. Dubuque, IA: McGraw-Hill.

Wissel, H. (1994). *Basketball: Steps to success.* Champaign, IL: Human Kinetics.

Websites

American Youth Basketball Tour
www.aybtour.com

Basketball Congress International
www.bcibasketball.org

FB Basketball
www.fbbasketball.com/youthbasketball

Youth Basketball of America
www.yboa.org

CHAPTER

25

Football

ESSENTIAL COMPONENTS OF QUALITY PROGRAMS

▶ **I. Organized around content standards**

▶ **II. Student-centered and developmentally appropriate**

▶ **III. Physical activity and motor skill development form the core of the program**

▶ **IV. Teaches management skills and self-discipline**

▶ **V. Promotes inclusion of all students**

▶ **VI. Focuses on process over product**

VII. Promotes lifetime personal health and wellness

▶ **VIII. Teaches cooperation and responsibility and promotes sensitivity to diversity**

NATIONAL STANDARDS FOR PHYSICAL EDUCATION*

▶ **1. Demonstrates competency in motor skills and movement patterns needed to perform a variety of physical activities.**

▶ **2. Demonstrates understanding of movement concepts, principles, and tactics as they apply to the learning and performance of physical activities.**

▶ **3. Participates regularly in physical activity.**

4. Achieves and maintains a health-enhancing level of physical fitness.

▶ **5. Exhibits responsible personal and social behavior that respects self and others in physical activity.**

▶ **6. Values physical activity for health, enjoyment, challenge, self-expression, and/or social interaction.**

*National Association for Sport and Physical Education (NASPE) 2004.

SUMMARY

Skills instruction for football is introduced during the intermediate grades after youngsters have mastered the basic prerequisite skills. The teaching of rules and strategies for football is an integral part of the instructional process. Using proper progression is a key to success when teaching fundamental skills and lead-up games associated with football. Lead-up games provide an opportunity to emphasize development of selected football skills in a setting that is compatible with the abilities of participants.

OUTCOMES

- Structure learning experiences efficiently with respect to appropriate formations, progressions, and coaching techniques.

- Develop a unit plan and lesson focus for football.

- Identify safety precautions associated with teaching football.

- Describe instructional procedures for implementing a successful lead-up game.

- Cite assessment procedures for evaluating football skills.

The shape of the football makes throwing and catching more difficult than with a round ball. Specialized skills are needed, which means that time must be spent on football skills if children are to enjoy participating. Touch and Flag Football are modifications of the game of American football. A ball carrier usually is considered down in Touch Football when touched by one hand. In Flag Football, a player wears one or two flags, which opponents must seize to down the ball carrier; hence the name Flag Football. Flag Football has advantages over Touch Football in that there is more twisting and dodging, which makes the game more interesting and challenging. In addition, in Flag Football, argument over whether the ball carrier was downed is less likely.

INSTRUCTIONAL EMPHASIS AND SEQUENCE

Table 25.1 shows the sequence of football activities divided into two developmental levels. Regular and junior-sized footballs are difficult to throw and catch. The ends of the football are hard and can hurt children who haven't mastered catching skills. For this reason, the use of foam footballs is encouraged. A number of companies manufacture the balls in sizes that are suitable for youngsters. Youngsters will show a greater tendency to participate when they know the projectile is harmless.

Developmental Level II

Passing, centering, and catching receive the majority of focus at this level. Most of the instructional time should be spent on skills. The lead-up games of Five Passes and Football End Ball make use of the skills listed.

TABLE 25.1	Suggested Football Program
Developmental Level II	**Developmental Level III**
Skills	
Forward pass	Stance
Centering	Pass receiving
Catching	Punting
	Blocking
	Carrying the ball
	Running and dodging
	Handing off the ball
	Lateral pass
Knowledge	
Football rules	Plays and formations
Activities	
Football End Ball	Kick-Over
Five Passes	Fourth Down
Speed Football	Football Box Ball
	Flag Football
	Pass Ball
Skill Tests	
Passing for distance	Kicking for distance
Centering	Passing for distance
	Passing for accuracy

Developmental Level III

At this level, emphasis shifts to passing skills, with moving receivers in football drills. Punting and kicking games are introduced. More specialized skills, such as blocking, carrying the ball, exchanging the ball, and football agility skills, provide lead-up work for the game of Flag Football.

FOOTBALL SKILLS

Forward Pass

Skillful forward passing is needed in Flag Football and in the lead-up games; passing is a potent weapon. The ball should be gripped lightly behind the middle with the fingers on the lace. The thumbs and fingers should be relaxed (Figure 25.1).

In throwing, the opposing foot should point in the direction of the pass, with the body turned sideways. In preparation for the pass, the ball is raised up and held over the shoulders. The ball is delivered directly forward with an overhand movement of the arm and with the

FIGURE 25.1   Preparing to pass.

FIGURE 25.2   Passing (left-handed thrower).

index finger pointing toward the line of flight. A left-hander is illustrated in Figure 25.2.

The following instructional cues will help students improve their throwing technique:

1. Turn the nonthrowing side toward the direction of the throw.
2. Grasp the ball with the pads of the fingers.
3. Throw the ball with an overhand motion.
4. Step toward the pass receiver.
5. Follow through with the arm after releasing the ball.

Lateral Pass

Lateral passing is a simple underhand toss of the ball to a teammate (Figure 25.3). The ball must be tossed sideways or backward to qualify as a lateral. It should be tossed with an easy motion, and no attempt should be made to make it spiral like a forward pass.

Catching

In catching, the receiver should keep both eyes on the ball and catch it in the hands with a slight give (Figure 25.4 on page 634). As soon as the ball is caught, it should be tucked into the carrying position. The little fingers are together for most catches.

The following instructional cues will help students focus on catching technique:

1. Keep eyes on the ball.
2. Thumbs together for a high pass (above shoulder level).
3. Thumbs apart for a low pass (below shoulder level).
4. Reach for the ball, give, and bring the ball to the body.

FIGURE 25.3   Preparing for a lateral pass.

Handing Off the Ball

Children enjoy working plays in which the ball is exchanged from one player to another, as for a reverse. In a reverse, the object is to start the play in one direction and then give the ball to another player heading in the opposite direction. The ball can be handed backward or forward. The player with the ball always makes the exchange with the inside hand, the one near the receiving player. The ball is held with both hands until the receiver is about 6 feet away. The ball then is shifted to the hand on that side, with the elbow bent partially away from the body. The receiver comes toward the exchange player with the near arm bent and carried in front of the chest, the palm down. The other arm is carried about waist height, with the palm up (Figure 25.5 on page 634). As the ball is handed off (not tossed), the receiver clamps down on the ball to secure it. As quickly as possible, the receiver then changes to a normal carrying position.

A fake reverse, sometimes called a bootleg, is made when the ball carrier pretends to make the exchange but keeps the ball instead and hides it momentarily behind one leg.

25

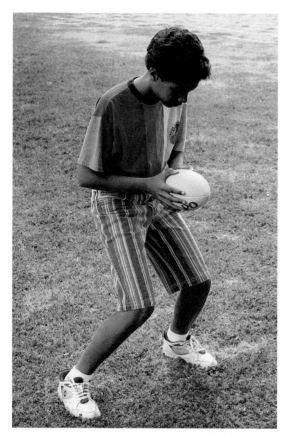

FIGURE 25.4 Catching a pass.

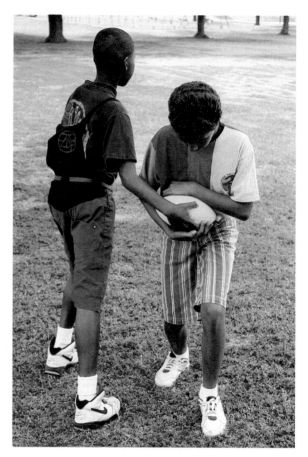

FIGURE 25.5 Handing off the ball.

Carrying the Ball

The ball should be carried with the arm on the outside and the end of the ball tucked into the notch formed by the elbow and arm. The fingers add support for the carry (Figure 25.6).

Centering

Centering involves transferring the ball, on a signal, to the quarterback. In elementary school, the shotgun formation is most often used. This requires snapping the ball a few yards backward to the quarterback. A direct snap involves placing the hands under the buttocks of the center. The ball is then lifted, rotated a quarter turn, and snapped into the hands of the quarterback.

The centering player takes a position with the feet well spread and toes pointed straight ahead. Knees are bent and close enough to the ball to reach it with a slight stretch. The right hand takes about the same grip as is used in passing. The other hand is on the side near the back of the ball and merely acts as a guide (Figure 25.7). On signal from the quarterback, the center extends the arms backward through the legs and centers the ball to the quarterback.

Instructional cues for centering include the following:

1. Keep legs spread and toes straight ahead.
2. Reach forward for the ball.
3. Snap the ball with the dominant hand.
4. Guide the ball with the nondominant hand.

Stance

The three-point stance is the offensive stance most generally used in Flag Football. The feet are about shoulder width apart and the toes point straight ahead, with the toes of one foot even with the heel of the other. The hand on the side of the foot that is back is used for support; the knuckles rest on the ground. The player should look straight ahead and always take the same stance (Figure 25.8).

Some players prefer the parallel stance, in which the feet, instead of being in the heel-and-toe position, are lined up evenly. In this case, either hand can be placed down for support. Some defensive players like to use a four-point stance, as shown. Both hands are in contact with the ground (Figure 25.9 on page 636).

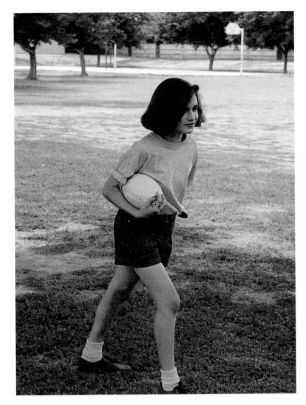

FIGURE 25.6   Carrying the ball securely.

The following instructional cues will help students learn proper stance:

1. Bend the knees; keep the back parallel to the ground.
2. Keep the majority of the weight on the legs.
3. Don't lean forward or backward.

Blocking

When blocking, the blocker must maintain balance and not fall to the knees. The elbows are out, and the hands are held near the chest. The block should be more of an obstruction than a takeout and should be set with the shoulder against the opponent's shoulder or upper body (Figure 25.10 on page 636). Making contact from the rear in any direction not only is a penalty but also could cause injury.

The following instructional cues will help students learn the blocking technique:

1. Keep feet spread and knees bent.
2. Keep head up.
3. Stay in front of the defensive player.
4. Move your feet; stay on the balls of the feet.

FIGURE 25.7   Centering (note the hand and finger positions).

Punting

The kicker stands with the kicking foot slightly forward. The fingers are extended in the direction of the center. The eyes should be on the ball from the time it is centered until it is kicked, and the kicker should actually see the foot kick the ball. After receiving the ball, the kicker takes a short step with the kicking foot and then a second step with the other foot. The kicking leg is swung

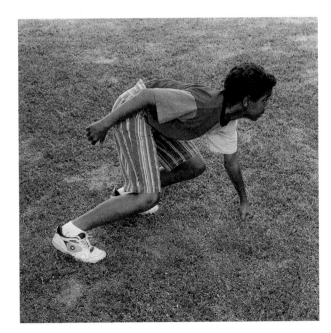

FIGURE 25.8   Offensive three-point stance.

25

FIGURE 25.9   Defensive four-point stance.

FIGURE 25.11   Punting.

forward and, at impact, the leg is straightened to provide maximum force. The toes are pointed, and the long axis of the ball makes contact on the top of the instep. The leg should follow through well after the kick (Figure 25.11). Emphasis should be placed on dropping the ball properly. Beginners have a tendency to throw it in the air, making the punt more difficult.

The following instructional cues will help students learn punting techniques:

1. Drop the football; don't toss it upward.
2. Keep the eyes focused on the ball.
3. Kick upward and through the ball.
4. Contact the ball on the outer side of the instep.

INSTRUCTIONAL PROCEDURES

1. All children need the opportunity to practice all skills, and a system of rotation should be set up to ensure this.
2. Drills should be performed with attention to proper form, and they should approximate game conditions. For example, when going out for passes is being practiced, start the pattern using the proper stance.
3. Junior-sized or foam footballs should be used. At least six to eight footballs should be available for football drills. The best teaching situation is to have one football for each pair of children.
4. Roughness and unfair play must be controlled by supervision and strict enforcement of the rules.

FOOTBALL DRILLS

▶ **BALL CARRYING**

Formation: Scattered

Players: Four to six students

Supplies: A football, a flag for each player, cones to mark the zones

The ball carrier stands on the goal line ready to run. Three defensive players wait at 20-yard intervals, each one stationed on a zone line of a regular Flag Football field, facing the ball carrier (Figure 25.12). Each defender is assigned to the zone that she is facing and must down the ball carrier by pulling a flag while the carrier is still in the zone. The ball carrier runs and dodges, trying to get by each defender in turn without having her flag pulled. If the flag is pulled, the runner continues, and the last defender uses a two-handed touch to down the ball carrier. After the runner has completed the run, she goes to the end of the defender's line and rotates to a defending position.

FIGURE 25.10   Blocking position.

FIGURE 25.12   Ball carrying drill.

▶ **BALL EXCHANGE**

Formation: Shuttle, with the halves about 15 yards apart

Players: Four to ten students

Supplies: A football

The two halves of the shuttle face each other across the 15-yard distance. A player at the head of one of the files has a ball and carries it over to the other file, where he makes an exchange with the player at the front of that file (Figure 25.13). The ball is carried back and forth between the shuttle files. The receiving player should not start until the ball carrier is almost up to him. A player, after handing the ball to the front player of the other file, continues around and joins that file. A simpler way to practice ball exchanges is to use scatter formation where half the class has a ball and the other half doesn't. On signal, students without the ball run toward those who have a ball. Handoffs continue as students alternate handing off with taking the handoff.

▶ **COMBINATION**

Formation: Regular offensive formation with passer, center, end, and ball chaser

Players: Four to eight students

Supplies: A football

Passing, centering, and receiving skills are combined in one drill. Each player, after her turn, rotates to the next spot. A minimum of four players is needed. The center player centers the ball to the passer; the passer passes the ball to the end; the end receives the pass; and the ball chaser retrieves the ball if missed by the end, or takes a pass from the end (if she caught the ball) and carries the ball to the center spot, which is her next assignment (Figure 25.14).

FIGURE 25.13   Ball exchange drill.

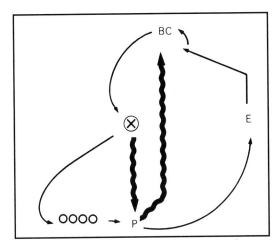

FIGURE 25.14   Combination drill.

The rotation follows the path of the ball. This means that the rotation system moves from center to passer to end to ball chaser to center. Extra players should be stationed behind the passer for their turns.

▶ **ONE-ON-ONE DEFENSIVE DRILL**

Formation: Center, passer, end, defender

Players: Eight to ten students

Supplies: A football

The one-on-one defensive drill is as old as football itself. A defensive player stands about eight yards back, waiting for an approaching end. The passer tries to complete the pass to the end while the defender tries to break up the pass or intercept the ball. One defender should practice against all the players and then rotate (Figure 25.15). The passer must be able to pass well or this drill has little value.

Variation: The drill can be played with two ends and two defenders. The passer throws to the end who appears to be most unguarded.

FIGURE 25.15   One-on-one defensive drill.

25

▶ **PUNT RETURN**

Formation: Center, kicker, two lines of ends, receivers

Players: 10 to 20 students

Supplies: A football, a flag for each player

The object of the drill is for the receiver to catch a punted ball and return it to the line of scrimmage while two ends attempt to pull a flag or make a tag. Two ends are ready to run downfield. The center snaps the ball to the kicker, who punts the ball downfield to the punt receiver. The ends cannot cross the line of scrimmage until the ball has been kicked. Each end makes two trips downfield as a "tackler" before rotating to the punt-receiving position.

✓ **TEACHING TIP**

An effective punter is necessary for this drill. Only children with the degree of skill required to punt far enough downfield should be permitted to kick. It is also important for the ends to wait until the ball is kicked, or they will be downfield too soon for the receiver to have a fair chance of making a return run.

▶ **STANCE**

Formation: Squads in extended file formation

Players: Six to eight students in each file

Supplies: None

The first person in each file performs and when finished with his chores, goes to the end of his file. On the command "Ready," the first person in each file assumes a football stance. The teacher can correct and make observations. On the command "Hike," the players charge forward for about five yards (Figure 25.16). The new player at the head of each line gets ready.

FOOTBALL ACTIVITIES

Developmental Level II

▶ **FOOTBALL END BALL**

Playing Area: A 20-by-40-foot-court

Players: 9 to 12 students on each team

Supplies: Footballs

Skills: Passing, catching

The court is divided in half by a centerline. End zones are marked 3 feet wide, completely across the court at each end. Players on each team are divided into three

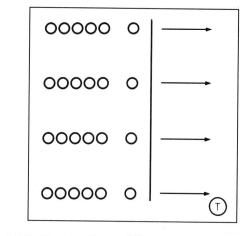

FIGURE 25.16   Stance drill.

groups: forwards, guards, and ends. The object is for a forward to throw successfully to one of the end-zone players. The players from each team are positioned as diagrammed in Figure 25.17. End-zone players take positions in one of the end zones. Their forwards and guards then occupy the half of the court farthest from this end zone. The forwards are near the centerline, and the guards are back near the end zone of their half of the court.

When a team gets the ball, the forwards try to throw over the heads of the opposing team to an end-zone player. To score, a player with both of her feet inside the end zone must catch the ball. No moving with the ball is permitted by any player. After each score, play is resumed by a jump ball at the centerline.

A penalty results in loss of the ball to the other team. Penalties are assessed for the following.

1. Holding a ball for more than 5 seconds.
2. Stepping over the end line or stepping over the centerline into the opponent's territory.
3. Pushing or holding another player.

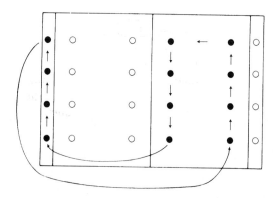

FIGURE 25.17   Player positions for Football End Ball.

In case of an out-of-bounds ball, the ball belongs to the team that did not cause it to go out. The nearest player retrieves the ball at the sideline and returns it to a player of the proper team.

> *Variation:* Using more than one ball increases activity and throwing repetitions. However, more than one ball requires a different rotation system. When a throw is completed to an end, he or she switches with the forward that threw the ball. Throughout the game, play is stopped, and forwards/ends quickly become guards and guards assume the role of forwards and ends.

Fast, accurate passing is to be encouraged. Players in the end zones must practice jumping high to catch the ball while still landing with both feet inside the end-zone area. A system of rotation is desirable. Each time a score is made, players on that team can rotate one person (see Figure 25.17).

To outline the end zones, some instructors use folding mats (4 by 7 feet or 4 by 8 feet). Three or four mats forming each end zone makes a definite area and eliminates the problem of defensive players (guards) stepping into the end zone.

▶ FIVE PASSES (FOOTBALL)

Playing Area: Football field or other defined area

Players: Six to ten students on each team

Supplies: A football, pinnies, or other identification

Skills: Passing, catching

Players scatter on the field. The object of the game is for one team to make five consecutive passes to five different players without losing control of the ball. This scores one point. The defense may play the ball only and may not make personal contact with opposing players. No player can take more than three steps when in possession of the ball. More than three steps is called traveling, and the ball is awarded to the other team.

The ball is given to the opponents at the nearest out-of-bounds line for traveling, minor contact fouls, after a point has been scored, and for causing the ball to go out of bounds. No penalty is assigned when the ball hits the ground. It remains in play, but the five-pass sequence is interrupted and must start again. Jump balls are called when the ball is tied up or when there is a pileup. Players should call out the pass sequence.

▶ SPEED FOOTBALL

Playing Area: Football field 30 by 60 yards divided into three equal sections

Players: Entire class divided into two teams

Supplies: Football, flag for each player

Skills: Passing, catching, running with ball

The ball is kicked off or started at the 20-yard line. The object is to move the ball across the opponent's goal by running or passing. If the ball drops to the ground or if a player's flag is pulled when carrying the ball, it is a turnover and the ball is set into play at that spot. Interceptions are turnovers and the intercepting team moves on offense. Teams must make at least four complete passes before they are eligible to move across the opponent's goal line. No blocking is allowed. To speed up the game, as soon as a team scores, the team can immediately (without waiting for the opponents to set up) kick or throw off. This provides incentive for all players to hustle after a score.

> *Variation:* Playing more than one game at a time on smaller fields allows more students to be actively involved in the game. This is also an enjoyable game when played with Frisbees.

Developmental Level III

▶ KICK-OVER

Playing Area: Football field with a 10-yard end zone

Players: Six to ten students on each team

Supplies: A football

Skills: Kicking, catching

Teams are scattered on opposite ends of the field. The object is to punt the ball over the other team's goal line. If the ball is caught in the end zone, no score results. A ball kicked into the end zone and not caught scores a goal. If the ball is kicked beyond the end zone on the fly, a score is made regardless of whether the ball is caught.

Play is started by one team with a punt from a point 20 to 30 feet in front of its own goal line. On a punt, if the ball is not caught, the team must kick from the spot of recovery. If the ball is caught, three long strides are allowed to advance the ball for a kick.

✓ TEACHING TIP

The player kicking next should move quickly to the area from which the ball is to be kicked. Players are numbered and kick in rotation. If the players do not kick in rotation, one or two aggressive players will dominate the game.

25

FOURTH DOWN

Playing Area: Half of a football field or equivalent space

Players: Six to eight students on each team

Supplies: A football, pinnies

Skills: Most football skills, except kicking and blocking

Every play is a fourth down, which means that the play must score or the team loses the ball. No kicking is permitted, but players may pass at any time from any spot and in any direction. There can be a series of passes on any play, either from behind or beyond the line of scrimmage.

The teams line up in an offensive football formation. To start the game, the ball is placed into the center of the field, and the team that wins the coin toss has the chance to put the ball into play. The ball is put into play by centering. The back receiving the ball runs or passes to any of his teammates. The one receiving the ball has the same privilege. No blocking is permitted. After each touchdown, the ball is brought to the center of the field, and the team against which the score was made puts the ball into play.

To down a runner or pass receiver, a two-handed touch above the waist is made. The back first receiving the ball from the center has immunity from tagging, provided that he does not try to run. All defensive players must stay ten feet away unless he runs. The referee should wait for a reasonable length of time for the back to pass or run. If the ball is still held beyond that time, the referee should call out, "Ten seconds." The back must then throw or run within ten seconds or be rushed by the defense.

The defensive players scatter to cover the receivers. They can use a one-on-one defense, with each player covering an offensive player, or a zone defense.

Because the team with the ball loses possession after each play, the following rules are used to determine where the ball should be placed when the other team takes possession.

1. If a ball carrier is tagged with two hands above the waist, the ball goes to the other team at that spot.

2. If an incomplete pass is made from behind the line of scrimmage, the ball is given to the other team at the spot where the ball was put into play.

3. Should an incomplete pass be made by a player beyond the line of scrimmage, the ball is brought to the spot from which it was thrown.

TEACHING TIP

The team in possession must pass by the count of ten, because children tire from running around to become free for a pass. The defensive team can score by intercepting a pass.

Because passes can be made at any time, on interception the player should look down the field for a pass to a teammate.

Variation: The game can be called Third Down, with the offensive team having two chances to score.

FOOTBALL BOX BALL

Playing Area: Football field 50 yards long

Players: 8 to 16 students on each team

Supplies: A football, pinnies

Skills: Passing, catching

Five yards beyond each goal is a 6-by-6-foot square, which is the box. Teams are marked so they can be distinguished. The game is similar to End Ball in that the teams try to make a successful pass to the captain in the box.

To begin the play, players are onside, which means that they are on opposite ends of the field. One team, losing the toss, kicks off from its own 10-yard line to the other team. The game then becomes a kind of keep-away, with either team trying to secure or retain possession of the ball until a successful pass can be made to the captain in the box. The captain must catch the ball on the fly and still keep both feet in the box. This scores a touchdown.

A player may run sideways or backward when in possession of the ball. Players may not run forward but are allowed momentum (two steps) if receiving or intercepting a ball. The penalty for illegal forward movement while in possession of the ball is loss of the ball to the opponents, who take it and immediately begin play.

The captain is allowed only three attempts to score or one goal. If either occurs, another player is rotated into the box. On any incomplete pass or failed attempt to get the ball to the captain, the team loses the ball. If a touchdown is made, the team brings the ball back to its ten-yard line and kicks off to the other team. If the touchdown attempt is not successful, the ball is given out-of-bounds on the end line to the other team.

Any out-of-bounds ball is put into play by the team that did not cause the ball to go out-of-bounds. No team can score from a throw-in from out-of-bounds.

In case of a tie ball, a jump ball is called at the spot. The players face off as in a jump ball in basketball.

Players must play the ball and not the individual. For unnecessary roughness, the player is sidelined until a pass is thrown to the other team's captain. The ball is awarded to the offended team out-of-bounds.

On the kickoff, all players must be onside, that is, behind the ball when it is kicked. If the kicking team is called offside, the ball is awarded to the other team out-of-bounds at the centerline. After the kickoff, players may move to any part of the field. On the kickoff, the ball must travel 10 yards before it can be recovered by either team. A kickoff outside or over the end line is treated as any other out-of-bounds ball.

A ball hitting the ground remains in play as long as it is inbounds. Players may not bat or kick a free ball. The penalty is loss of the ball to the other team out-of-bounds. Falling on the ball also means loss of the ball to the other team.

✓ **TEACHING TIP**

A 4-by-7-foot or a 4-by-8-foot folding tumbling mat can be used to define the box in which the captain must stand to catch the ball for a score.

▶ **FLAG FOOTBALL**

Playing Area: Field 30 by 60 yards

Players: Six to nine students on a team

Supplies: A football, two flags per player (about three inches wide and 24 inches long), pinnies

Skills: All football skills

The field is divided into three zones by lines marked off at 20-yard intervals. There also should be two end zones, from five to ten yards in width, defining the area behind the goal in which passes may be caught. Flag Football is played with two flags on each player. The flag is a length of cloth that is hung from the side at the waist of each player. To down (stop) a player with the ball, one of the flags must be pulled.

Flag Football should rarely, if ever, be played with 11 players on a side. This results in a crowded field and leaves little room to maneuver. If six or seven are on a team, four players are required to be on the line of scrimmage. For eight or nine players, five offensive players must be on the line.

The game consists of two halves. A total of 25 plays makes up each half. All plays count in the 25, except the try for the point after a touchdown and a kickoff out-of-bounds.

The game is started with a kickoff. The team winning the coin toss has the option of selecting the goal it wishes to defend or choosing to kick or receive. The loser of the toss takes the option not exercised by the first team. The kickoff is from the goal line, and all players on the kicking team must be onside. The kick must cross the first zone line or it does not count as a play. A kick that is kicked out-of-bounds (and is not touched by the receiving team) must be kicked again. A second consecutive kick out-of-bounds gives the ball to the receiving team in the center of the field. The kickoff may not be recovered by the kicking team unless caught and then fumbled by the receivers.

A team has four downs to move the ball into the next zone or they lose the ball. If the ball is legally advanced into the last zone, then the team has four downs to score. A ball on the line between zones is considered to be in the more forward zone, and the team with the ball may continue to advance it.

Time-outs are permitted only for injuries or when called by the officials. Unlimited substitutions are permitted. Each substitute must report to the official.

The team in possession of the ball usually huddles to make up the play. After any play, the team has 30 seconds to put the ball into play after the referee gives the signal.

Blocking is done with the arms close to the body. Blocking must be done from the front or side, and blockers must stay on their feet.

A player is down if one of her flags has been pulled. The ball carrier must make an attempt to avoid the defensive player and is not permitted to run over or through the defensive player. The tackler must focus on making physical contact with the flags, not with the ball carrier. Good officiating is needed, because defensive players may attempt to hold or grasp the ball carrier until they are able to remove one of her flags.

All forward passes must be thrown from behind the line of scrimmage. All players on the field are eligible to receive and intercept passes.

All fumbles are dead at the spot of the fumble. The first player who touches the ball on the ground is ruled to have recovered the fumble. When the ball is centered to a back, she must gain definite possession of it before a fumble can be called. She is allowed to pick up a bad pass from the center when she does not have possession of the ball.

All punts must be announced. Neither team can cross the line of scrimmage until the ball is kicked. Kick receivers may run or use a lateral pass. They cannot make a forward pass after receiving a kick.

A pass caught in an end zone scores a touchdown. The player must have control of the ball in the end zone. A ball caught beyond the end zone is out-of-bounds and is considered an incomplete pass.

A touchdown scores six points, a completed pass or run after touchdown scores one point, and a safety scores two points. A point after touchdown is made from a distance of three feet from the goal line. One play (pass or run) is allowed for the extra point. Any ball kicked over the goal line is ruled a touchback and is brought out to the 20-yard line to be put into play by the receiving team. A pass intercepted behind the goal line can be a touchback if the player does not run it out, even if she is tagged behind her own goal line.

A penalty of 5 yards is assessed for the following:

1. Being offside.
2. Delaying the game (too long in huddle).
3. Failure of substitute to report to the official.

4. Passing from a spot not behind line of scrimmage. (This also results in loss of down.)

5. Stiff-arming by the ball carrier, or not avoiding a defensive player.

6. Failing to announce intention to punt.

7. Shortening the flag in the belt, or playing without flags in proper position.

8. Faking the ball by the center, who must center the pass on the first motion.

The following infractions are assessed a 15-yard loss:

1. Holding, illegal tackling.

2. Illegal blocking.

3. Unsportsmanlike conduct. (This also can result in disqualification.)

✓ **TEACHING TIP**

Specifying 25 plays per half eliminates the need for timing and lessens arguments about a team's taking too much time in the huddle. Using the zone system makes the first-down yardage point definite and eliminates the need for a chain to mark off the 10 yards needed for a first down.

▶ **PASS BALL**

Playing Area: Field 30 by 60 yards

Players: Six to nine students on a team

Supplies: A football, flags (optional), pinnies

Skills: All football skills, especially passing and catching

Pass Ball is a more open game than Flag Football. The game is similar to Flag Football with these differences.

1. The ball may be passed at any time. It can be thrown at any time beyond the line of scrimmage, immediately after an interception, during a kickoff, or during a received kick.

2. Four downs are given to score a touchdown.

3. A two-handed touch on the back is used instead of pulling a flag. Flags can be used, however.

4. If the ball is thrown from behind the line of scrimmage and results in an incomplete pass, the ball is down at the previous spot on the line of scrimmage. If the pass originates otherwise and is incomplete, the ball is placed at the spot from which this pass was thrown.

5. Because the ball can be passed at any time, no downfield blocking is permitted. A player may screen the ball carrier but cannot make a block. Screening is defined as running between the ball carrier and the defense.

FOOTBALL SKILL TESTS

Tests for football skills cover centering, passing, and kicking (punting).

Centering

Each player is given five trials to center at a target. The target should be stationed 6 yards behind the center. Some suggestions for targets follow.

1. An old tire can be suspended so that the bottom of the tire is about 2 feet above the ground. For centering the ball through the tire, two points are scored. For hitting the tire but not going through it, one point is scored. The possible total is ten points.

2. A baseball pitching target from the softball program can be used. Scoring is the same as with the tire target.

3. A 2-by-3-foot piece of plywood is held by a player at the target line in front of his body, with the upper edge even with the shoulders. The target is held stationary and is not to be moved during the centering. For hitting the target, one point is scored. The possible total is five points.

Passing for Accuracy

To test accuracy in passing, each player is given five throws from a minimum distance of 15 yards at a tire suspended at about shoulder height. (To make the tire fairly stable, it can be suspended from goal posts or from volleyball standards.) As skill increases, increase the distance.

For throwing through the tire, two points are scored. For hitting the tire but not passing through, one point is scored. The possible total for each player is ten points.

Passing for Distance

Each player is allotted three passes to determine how far she can throw a football. The longest throw is measured to the nearest foot. Reserve the test for a relatively calm day, because the wind can be quite a factor (for or against the player) in this test.

The passes should be made on a field marked off in 5-yard intervals. Use markers made from tongue depressors to indicate the first pass distance. If a later throw is longer, the marker should be moved to that point. When individual markers are used, the members of a squad can complete the passing turns before measuring.

Balanced (tight ends):

    E O X O E

Unbalanced right (tight ends):

    E X O O E

Line over right (tight end):

    X E O O E

Right end out (can be one or both):

    E O X O (5 yards) E

Right end wide (can be one or both):

    E O X O (15 yards) E

Right end wide, left end out (can be reversed):

    E (5 yards) O X O (15 yards) E

Spread (3 to 5 yards between each line position):

    E O X O E

FIGURE 25.18 Offensive line formations.

Kicking for Distance

Punting, place kicking, and drop kicking can be measured for distance by using techniques similar to those described for passing for distance.

FLAG FOOTBALL FORMATIONS

A variety of offensive formations are shown in Figures 25.18 and 25.19, including the T-formation. The T-formation has limited use in Flag Football, because the passer (the quarterback) is handicapped by being too close to the center. Emphasis should be on using a variety of formations and on spread formations, with flankers and ends positioned out beyond normal placement.

The following formations are based on a nine-player team, with four in the backfield and five on the line. The formations will vary if the number on each team is decreased. Presenting a variety of formations to players makes the game more interesting. Backfield formations can be right or left (Figure 25.19).

Offensive Line Formations

Only formations to the right are presented in Figure 25.18. The center is indicated by an X, backs by B, ends by E, and line positions by O.

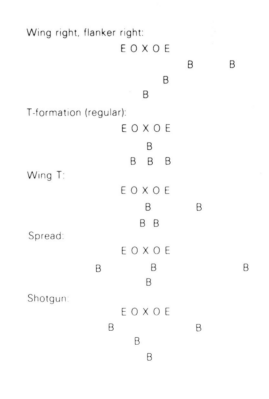

FIGURE 25.19 Offensive backfield formations.

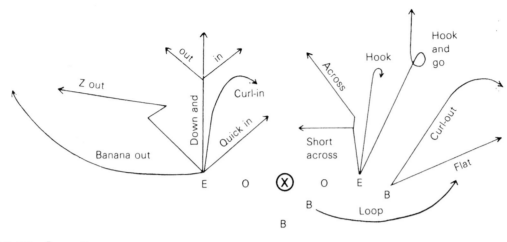

FIGURE 25.20 Pass patterns.

Offensive Backfield Formations

The formations diagrammed in Figure 25.19 can be combined with any of the offensive line formations. For purposes of clarity, however, the illustrations for all formations show a balanced line with tight ends.

Pass Patterns

The pass patterns illustrated in Figure 25.20 may be run by the individual pass catcher, whether he occupies a line position or is a back. They are particularly valuable in practice, when the pass receiver informs the passer of his pattern.

FOR MORE INFORMATION

References and Suggested Readings

Domitrovitz, M. (2002). Flag football. In N. Dougherty (Ed.), *Physical activity and sport for the secondary school student.* 5th ed. Reston, VA: NASPE and AAHPERD.

Fronske, H. (2005). *Teaching cues for sport skills.* 3rd ed. San Francisco: Benjamin Cummings.

Mood, D. P., Musker, F. F., and Rink, J. E. (2003). *Sports and recreational activities.* 13th ed. Boston: McGraw-Hill.

Schmottlach, N., and McManama, J. (2002). *The physical education handbook.* 10th ed. San Francisco: Benjamin Cummings.

The United States Flag and Touch Football League. Current ed. The United States flag and touch football rules. Mentor, OH: USFT Football League. (Available from NIRSA, 850 SW 15th St., Corvallis, OR 97333)

Websites

American Flag and Touch Football League
www.aftfl.com

Flag Football **Magazine**
www.flagmag.com

Go Flag Football
www.goflagfootball.com

International Women's Flag Football Association
www.iwffa.com

United States Flag and Touch Football League
www.usftl.com

26

Hockey

SUMMARY

Skills instruction for hockey is introduced during the intermediate grades after youngsters have mastered basic prerequisite skills. Teaching the rules and strategies for hockey is an integral part of the instructional process. Using proper progression is a key to success when teaching fundamental skills and lead-up games associated with hockey. Lead-up games provide an opportunity to emphasize development of selected hockey skills in a setting that is compatible with the abilities of participants.

OUTCOMES

- Structure learning experiences efficiently using appropriate formations, progressions, and coaching techniques.
- Develop a unit plan and lesson focus for hockey.
- Identify safety precautions associated with teaching hockey.
- Describe instructional procedures used for implementing a successful lead-up game.
- Cite assessment procedures used for evaluating hockey skills.

Hockey is a fast-moving game that can be adapted for use in the elementary school. Hockey at the elementary level is a lead-up to ice hockey as well as field hockey. With a plastic puck or yarn ball, hockey can be played indoors (Figure 26.1). Outdoors, a plastic whiffle ball is used. Success at hockey demands much running and team play. Teach fundamental skills and position play rather than the disorganized "everyone chase the puck" style of hockey.

INSTRUCTIONAL EMPHASIS AND SEQUENCE

Table 26.1 shows the sequence of hockey activities divided into two developmental levels. The actual presentation of activities is dictated by the maturity and past experience of participants.

ESSENTIAL COMPONENTS OF QUALITY PROGRAMS

▶ I. Organized around content standards

▶ II. Student-centered and developmentally appropriate

▶ III. Physical activity and motor skill development form the core of the program

▶ IV. Teaches management skills and self-discipline

▶ V. Promotes inclusion of all students

▶ VI. Focuses on process over product

   VII. Promotes lifetime personal health and wellness

▶ VIII. Teaches cooperation and responsibility and promotes sensitivity to diversity

NATIONAL STANDARDS FOR PHYSICAL EDUCATION*

▶ 1. Demonstrates competency in motor skills and movement patterns needed to perform a variety of physical activities.

▶ 2. Demonstrates understanding of movement concepts, principles, and tactics as they apply to the learning and performance of physical activities.

▶ 3. Participates regularly in physical activity.

   4. Achieves and maintains a health-enhancing level of physical fitness.

▶ 5. Exhibits responsible personal and social behavior that respects self and others in physical activity.

▶ 6. Values physical activity for health, enjoyment, challenge, self-expression, and/or social interaction.

*National Association for Sport and Physical Education (NASPE) 2004.

FIGURE 26.1   Hockey equipment.

TABLE 26.1	Suggested Hockey Program
Developmental Level II	**Developmental Level III**
Skills	
Gripping and carrying the stick	Controlled dribble
Loose dribble	Side field
Passing	Tackle
Front field	Dodging
Goalkeeping	Face-off
	Driving
	Jab shot
Knowledge	
Hockey rules	Ball handling and passing
	The game of hockey
	Team play and strategy
Activities	
Circle Keep-Away	Goalkeeper Hockey
Star Wars Hockey	Sideline Hockey
Lane Hockey	Regulation Elementary
Modified Hockey	Hockey
Skill Tests	
Passing for accuracy	Dribbling for speed
Fielding	Driving for distance

Developmental Level II

At this level, little strategy is introduced. Drills are used to develop fundamental skills. Learning to carry the ball loosely, receive the ball, and make short passes should receive the most attention.

Developmental Level III

At Developmental Level III, skill development continues, with more emphasis on ball control and passing accuracy. Lead-up games using skills involved in regulation hockey are played. The drills presented are designed to foster team play. Lead-up games are used to introduce strategy and field positioning. The rules of regulation hockey are introduced, and the actual game is played. Skills should be reviewed and practiced through the use of selected drills and lead-up games.

HOCKEY SKILLS

Gripping and Carrying the Stick

The hockey stick should be held with both hands and carried as low to the ground as possible. The basic grip puts the left hand at the top of the stick and the right hand 6–12 inches below the left (Figure 26.2). The player should learn to carry the stick to the right of the body, with the blade close to the ground, while running. To ensure accuracy as well as safety, the stick must not be swung above waist height.

Passing

Regardless of which pass is used, the manner in which the stick is carried and gripped will remain constant. For a right-handed player, the basic grip has the left hand at the top of the stick and the right hand 6–12 inches below

FIGURE 26.2 Gripping and carrying.

FIGURE 26.3 Forehand pass.

Receiving

Receiving and controlling the ball is referred to as receiving and is an important fundamental skill. Many turnovers involve failure to handle a pass properly.

Instructional cues for fielding include the following:

1. Keep soft hands/stick.
2. Give as the puck hits the stick. Receive the pass; don't just stop it.
3. Maintain the carrying grip.

RECEIVING A PASS FROM THE FRONT

In order to receive a pass from the front, the player must first move to a point in line with the path of the puck. The flat part of the blade is then extended out toward the puck. The puck should be received in front of the player (Figure 26.4).

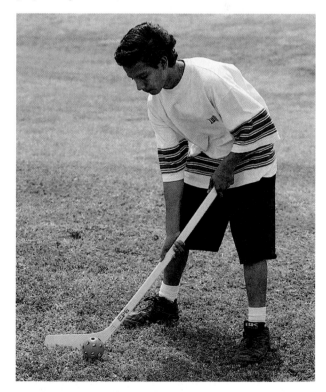

FIGURE 26.4 Receiving a pass from the front.

the left. The stick is carried with both hands and low to the ground at all times. Passers should avoid telegraphing the direction of the pass. They should learn to use peripheral vision and keep their eyes moving from place to place to develop an awareness of their teammates' positions. At the same time, they should anticipate the spot toward which a teammate will be moving to receive the pass.

The following are instructional cues that can be used to help players focus on proper performance of passing.

1. When first learning to pass keep the eyes and head down looking toward the puck.
2. Keep the stick below the waist at all times.
3. Transfer the weight from the back foot to the front foot.
4. Drive through the puck.
5. Keep the stick on the ground until the puck is struck.

Forehand Pass

The forehand pass is the pass most often used and typically occurs while stick handling. It is a short, accurate pass. The puck is approached with the stick low. The stick is then pulled back in line with the desired direction of the pass and no higher than waist level. The hands remain in the carrying position as the right hand guides the stick through the puck. Following contact with the puck, a small follow-through occurs (Figure 26.3).

FIGURE 26.5 Receiving a pass from the side.

FIGURE 26.6 Controlled stick handling.

RECEIVING A PASS FROM THE SIDE

A pass coming from the side is a more difficult skill. In order to field a puck from the side, the player must field the puck on her stick side (Figure 26.5). Thus, a right-handed player fielding the puck from the left must allow the puck to pass in front of him prior to controlling it with the stick. The player's body and feet should remain facing the direction she wishes to move after controlling the pass.

Stick Handling

Stick handling is used to advance the puck, break for the goal, or maneuver out of a difficult situation.

Instructional cues for stick handling include the following:

1. Keep the puck under control (within a stick length).
2. Move under control.
3. Keep the head up.
4. Keep the elbows out (away from the body).

LOOSE STICK HANDLING

Loose stick handling is the easiest type of stick handling. Typically used in open field play with no defenders around, loose stick handling involves the player pushing the puck 10–15 feet ahead and then "chasing" after the puck. However, it is important to stress controlled taps and not "slap and chase" hockey. Loose stick handling allows players to move at a faster speed.

CONTROLLED STICK HANDLING

Controlled stick handling (Figure 26.6) consists of a series of soft taps in the desired direction of movement.

The puck should be kept far enough away from the feet but less than one stride ahead to allow for control.

Shooting

There are three basic shots in hockey: the wrist shot, the slap shot, and the one-timer.

WRIST SHOT

Wrist shots are similar to the forehand pass. The following are instructional cues that can be used to help players focus on proper performance of the wrist shot:

1. Keep the stick below the waist; there is no backswing on a wrist shot.
2. Transfer weight from back foot to front foot as you carry the puck forward.
3. Release the puck from the toe of the stick. The higher the stick blade when the puck is released, the higher the shot will go.

SLAP SHOT

The following are instructional cues that can be used to help players focus on proper performance of the slap shot:

1. Stand with feet shoulder width apart, with the non-dominant side of the body facing the net. Puck placement should be approximately 1–2 feet in front (board side) of your front foot.
2. Keep the backswing below waist level.

3. Transfer weight from back to front foot as you swing, making contact with the playing surface 1–2 inches behind the puck. Follow through the puck, slapping it toward the net.

4. Hitting the playing surface before the puck causes the stick to whip, creating a harder shot.

ONE-TIMER

The one-timer is simply a redirection of an existing pass. It is a very fast shot meant to catch the goalie by surprise. During a one-timer, the player receiving a pass doesn't actually receive it but, instead, shoots it immediately on net. Basically it is a slap shot with a shorter back-swing designed to redirect the puck. The following are instructional cues that can be used to help players focus on proper performance of the one-timer:

1. Take a short knee- to waist-level backswing.

2. Time your swing to arrive when the puck arrives to the spot you want to shoot from.

3. Just concentrate on making contact and sending it to the goal. This is typically an inaccurate shot so don't worry about aiming it.

4. Fire through the puck, releasing it quickly.

Defense

STICK CHECK

In hockey, stick checking refers to a means of taking the puck away from an opponent. As the player moves toward the opponent with the puck, the check is timed so the stick makes contact with the puck when the opponent's stick is off the puck. After knocking the puck away, the player quickly stick handles or passes the puck in the desired direction. Throwing the stick or slapping at the puck carelessly should be discouraged. Note: The stick can also be used to lift an opponent's stick off the ground to take the puck from him.

POKE CHECK

This attempt to steal the puck from the opponent involves a quick poke toward the puck (Figure 26.7). Just as in the case of stick checking, careless swinging and jabbing with the stick should be discouraged.

Face-Off

The face-off is used at the start of the game, after a goal, or when the ball is stopped from further play by opposing players. The face-off is taken by two players, each facing a sideline, with their right sides facing the goal that

FIGURE 26.7   Poke check.

their team is defending. Players simultaneously hit the ground three times with their sticks (on their side of the base). After the third hit on the ground, the ball is played, and each player attempts to control the ball or to pass it to a teammate. The right hand can be moved down the stick to facilitate a quick, powerful movement. An alternate means of starting action is for a referee to drop the ball between the players' sticks.

Goalkeeping

The goalie may kick the ball, stop it with any part of the body, or allow it to rebound off the body or hand. He may not, however, hold the ball or throw it toward the other end of the playing area. The goalkeeper is positioned in front of the goal line and moves between the goal posts. When a ball is hit toward the goal, the goalie should attempt to move in front of the ball and to keep the feet together. This allows the body to block the ball should the stick miss it. After the block, the ball is passed immediately to a teammate.

INSTRUCTIONAL PROCEDURES

1. For many children, hockey is a new experience. Few have played the game, and many may never have seen a game. Showing a film of a hockey game as an introduction may be helpful.

2. Since few children have had the opportunity to develop skills elsewhere, it is necessary to teach the basic skills in a sequential manner and to allow ample time in practice sessions for development.

26

3. Hockey is a rough game if children are not taught the proper methods of stick handling. They need to be reminded often to use caution and good judgment when handling hockey sticks.

4. Ample equipment increases individual practice time and facilitates skill development. A stick and a ball or puck for each child are desirable.

5. If hockey is played on a gym floor, a plastic puck or yarn ball should be used. If played on a carpeted area or outdoors, a whiffle ball is used. An eight-foot folding mat set on end makes a satisfactory goal.

6. Hockey is a team game that is more enjoyable for all when the players pass to open teammates. Excessive control of the ball by one person should be discouraged.

7. An individual who is restricted to limited activity can be designated as a goalie. This is an opportunity for children with disabilities to participate and receive reinforcement from peers. An asthmatic child, for example, might serve as a goalkeeper.

8. Fatigue may be a problem, for hockey is a running game that demands agility and endurance. Children should be in reasonably good physical condition to participate. Frequent rotation and rest periods help prevent fatigue.

HOCKEY DRILLS

Stick Handling Drills

1. *Phantom Stick Handling.* Successful hockey play demands good footwork and proper stick handling. To develop these skills, spread players on the field, carrying the stick in proper position, in a group mimetic drill. On command, players move forward, backward, and to either side. Quick reactions and footwork are the focus.

2. *Direction Stick Handling.* Each player with a ball practices handling it individually. Practice first at controlled speeds and then at faster speeds as skill develops. On signal, players change direction while maintaining control of the ball.

3. *Change of Direction Stick Handling.* Players are spread out on the field, each with a ball. On command, they carry the ball left, right, forward, and backward. On the command "Change direction," the players move away from an imaginary tackler. Players should concentrate on ball control and dodging in all directions.

4. *Down, Around, and Pass.* Players can practice in pairs, with partners standing about 20 feet apart. One player carries the ball toward a partner, goes

FIGURE 26.8   Down, Around, and Pass drill.

around the partner, and returns to the starting spot (Figure 26.8). The ball is then passed to the partner, who moves in a similar manner. A shuttle type of formation can be used with three players.

Passing and Receiving Drills

1. *Partner Passing.* In pairs, about 20 feet apart, players pass the ball quickly back and forth. Emphasis should be on passing immediately after receiving the ball. The cue phrase might be "Receive and pass."

2. *Pass and Carry.* One player passes the ball to a partner, who carries the ball a few steps to the left or right, and passes back to the other. Passes should be received from various angles and from the right and left sides.

3. *Sliding Circle Drill.* In this drill, a circle of four to six players skates around a person in the center. The center person passes to and receives from the skating players. After the puck has gone around the circle twice, another player takes the center position.

4. *Triangle Drill.* Four to eight players can participate in the triangle drill. The puck begins at the head of a line and is passed forward to a player off to one side of the line. This player then passes to a teammate out at a corner, who then passes back to the head of the line. Each player passes and then moves to the spot to where he passed the puck, thus making a continual change of positions. Note: This drill replicates the motion of cycling the puck.

5. *Circle Star Drill.* With only five players, a circle-star drill is particularly effective. Players pass to every other player, and the path of the puck forms a star. Any odd number of players will cause the puck to go to all participants, assuring that all receive equal practice.

6. *Downfield Drill.* This drill is useful for polishing passing and receiving skills while moving. Three files of players start at one end of the field. One player from each file proceeds downfield, passing to and fielding from the others until the other end of the field is reached. A goal shot can be made at this point. The players should remain close together for short passes until a high level of skill is reached.

7. Practice driving for distance and accuracy with a partner.

FIGURE 26.9 Cone Dodge drill.

Dodging and Checking Drills

1. *Cone Dodge.* Three players form the drill configuration as diagrammed in Figure 26.9. Player 1 has the puck in front, approaches the cone (which represents a defensive player), dodges around the cone, and passes to Player 2, who repeats the dodging maneuver in the opposite direction. Player 2 passes to Player 3, and the drill continues in that manner.

2. *Partner Stick Checks.* Players work in pairs. One partner dribbles toward the other, who attempts to make a stick check. Reverse the roles at regular intervals. This drill should be practiced at moderate speeds in the early stages of skill development.

3. *Three on Three.* A three-on-three drill affords practice in many skill areas. Three players are on offense and three are on defense. The offense can concentrate on passing, stick handling, and dodging, while the defense concentrates on checking. A point is given to the offense when they reach the opposite side of the field. Reverse offensive and defensive roles on a timed basis.

Shooting Drills

1. *Give and Go Drill.* For the give and go drill, each player has a partner. The first partner has a puck and is the shooter. He passes the puck to the wing (partner), who passes the puck to the spot where the shooter has selected for the shot. Note: To increase difficulty, have players try one-timers.

2. *Three Person Rush.* In this drill, three lines are established on one end of the ice. One line has a puck. One player from each line moves down the ice, passing to the other two players. As the players near the goal, one of the players shoots on goal. The other players retrieve the puck and all three players hustle back to the starting point to begin the process again.

HOCKEY ACTIVITIES

Developmental Level II

▶ STICK HANDLE COMPETITION

Playing Area: Any clearly defined area

Players: Entire team

Supplies: One stick and puck (or ball) for each player

Skills: Stick handling and protecting the puck

Stick handle battle can be played at two levels of difficulty.

Level 1: All players stick handle throughout half of the area, controlling their puck so that it does not touch another puck. If a touch occurs, both players go outside the area and stick handle around the perimeter of the other area. Once youngsters have completed stick handling around the second area, they reenter the game.

Level 2: The area is divided in half and all players move to one of the halves. While stick handling and controlling a puck, each player attempts to cause another player to lose control of his puck. When control is lost, that player takes his/her puck and moves to the opposite half of the area. Play continues against other players who have lost control. When five or six players remain, bring all players back into the game and start over.

▶ CIRCLE KEEPAWAY

Playing Area: A 20- to 25-foot circle

Players: Eight to ten students

Supplies: One stick per person, a puck or ball

Skills: Passing, receiving

Players are spaced evenly around the circle, with two or more players in the center. The object of the game is to keep the players in the center from touching the puck. The puck is passed back and forth, with emphasis on accurate passing and receiving. Center players see how many touches they can make during their turn. Change the center players after a time limit so all youngsters have an opportunity to be center players.

▶ FIVE PASSES

Playing Area: Any defined area

Players: Five or more students on each team

Supplies: One puck (or ball) and a stick for each player, pinnies

Skills: Passing, guarding

Two teams play. Divide the area into smaller areas so many teams can play simultaneously. The object of the game is to complete five consecutive passes and score a point. The game is started with a face-off in the center of the area. The teams observe regular hockey rules. The team with the puck counts out loud as a pass is completed. The puck may not be passed back to the person from whom it was received. No stick handling is allowed. If for any reason the puck is fumbled and recovered or improperly passed, a new count is started. After a successful score, the puck is immediately turned over to the other team. A foul draws a penalty shot, which can score a point. Teams should be well marked to avoid confusion.

Variations:

1. After each successful point (five passes), the team is awarded a penalty shot, which can score an additional point.

2. After a team has scored a point, the puck can be given to the other team out-of-bounds to start play again.

▶ **STAR WARS HOCKEY**

Playing Area: Playground or gymnasium

Players: Four teams of equal size

Supplies: One stick per player, four pucks or balls

Skills: Stick handling

Each team forms one side of a square formation. The game is similar to Star Wars (page 575), with the following exceptions:

1. Four pucks (or balls) are used. When a number is called, all players with that number go to a puck and stick handle it out of the square through the spot previously occupied, around the square counterclockwise, and back to the original spot. Circles 12 inches in diameter are drawn on the floor to provide a definite place to which the puck must be returned. If the game is played outdoors, hoops can mark the spot to which the puck must be returned.

2. No player is permitted to use anything other than the stick in making the circuit and returning the puck to the inside of the hoop. The penalty for infractions is disqualification.

▶ **LANE HOCKEY**

Playing Area: Hockey field or gymnasium, 60 by 100 feet

Players: Nine students on each team

Supplies: Hockey stick per player, puck, two goals

Skills: All hockey skills

The field is divided into eight lanes as illustrated in Figure 26.10. A defensive and an offensive player are placed in each of the eight lanes. A goalkeeper for each team is also positioned in front of the goal area. Players may not leave their lane during play. A shot on goal may not be taken until a minimum of two passes have been completed. This rule encourages looking for teammates

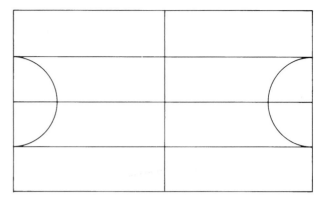

FIGURE 26.10 Field markings for Lane Hockey.

and passing to someone in a better position before taking a shot on goal.

Players should be encouraged to maintain their spacing during play. The purpose of the lanes is to force them to play within a zone rather than rushing to the puck. Rules used for regulation hockey enforce situations not described here. A free shot (unguarded) is awarded a team if a foul occurs. Players should be rotated after a goal is scored or at regular time intervals.

Variation: Increase the number of lanes by five or six. This involves a larger number of players. On a large playing area, the lanes may be broken into thirds rather than halves. Increase the number of passes that should be made prior to a shot on goal. To add more activity to Lane Hockey, use more than one puck or add one or two more goals and goalies.

▶ **MODIFIED HOCKEY**

Playing Area: Hockey field or gymnasium

Players: 7 to 11 on each team

Supplies: One stick per person, a puck or ball

Skills: Stick handling, passing, dodging, checking, face-off

The teams may take any position on the field as long as they remain inside the boundaries. The object of the game is to hit the puck through the opponent's goal. No goalies are used. At the start of the game and after each score, play begins with a face-off. Each goal is worth one point.

✓ **TEACHING TIP**

The distance between goal lines is flexible but should be on the long side. If making goals is too easy or too difficult, the width of the goals can be adjusted accordingly.

FIGURE 26.11   Team positions for Goalkeeper Hockey.

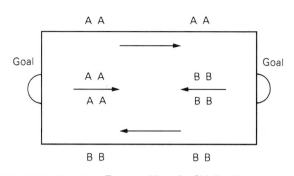

FIGURE 26.12   Team positions for Sideline Hockey.

Developmental Level III

▶ GOALKEEPER HOCKEY

Playing Area: A square about 40 by 40 feet

Players: Two teams of equal size

Supplies: One stick per player, a puck or ball

Skills: Passing, receiving, goalkeeping

Each team occupies two adjacent sides of the square (Figure 26.11). Team members are numbered consecutively from left to right. Two or three numbers are called by the instructor. These players enter the playing area and attempt to capture the ball, which is placed in the center of the square, and to pass it through the opposing team. A point is scored when the ball goes through the opponent's side. Sideline players are goalies and should concentrate on goalkeeping skills. After a short period of time (one minute), the active players return to their positions, and new players are called.

✓ TEACHING TIP

Keep track of the numbers called so that all players have an equal opportunity to play. Different combinations can be called.

▶ SIDELINE HOCKEY

Playing Area: Hockey field or gymnasium area, 60 by 100 feet

Players: 6 to 12 players on each team

Supplies: One hockey stick per player, a puck or ball, two 4-by-8-foot folding tumbling mats

Skills: Most hockey skills, except goaltending

Each team is divided into two groups. They are positioned as indicated in Figure 26.12, which shows eight players on each team. Three to six players from each team move onto the court; these are the active players. The others will actively participate on the sidelines. No goalkeeper is used. A face-off at the center starts the game and puts the ball into play after each score. Each team on the field, aided by sideline players, attempts to score a goal. The sideline players help keep the ball inbounds and can pass it onto the court to the active players. Sideline players may pass to an active player or to each other.

Any puck that goes out-of-bounds on a sideline belongs to the team guarding that sideline and is immediately put into play with a pass. An out-of-bounds shot over the end line that does not score a goal is put into play by the team defending the goal. The group of players on the field changes places with the sideline players on their team as soon as a goal is scored or after a specified time period.

Illegal touching, sideline violations, and other minor fouls result in loss of the ball to the opposition. Roughing fouls and illegal striking should result in banishment to the sideline for the remainder of the competitive period.

✓ TEACHING TIP

Try to encourage team play and passing strategies rather than having all players charge and swarm the puck. An effective rule is to require active players to make three passes to their sideline teammates before taking a shot on goal. This makes all players an important part of the game.

▶ REGULATION ELEMENTARY HOCKEY

Playing Area: Hockey field or gymnasium area, approximately 40 to 50 feet by 75 to 90 feet

Players: Six or more students on each team

Supplies: One stick per player, a puck or ball

Skills: All hockey skills

In a small gymnasium, the walls can serve as the boundaries. In a large gymnasium or on an outdoor field, the playing area should be delineated with traffic cones. The area should be divided in half, with a 12-foot restraining circle centered on the midline. This is where play begins at the start of the periods, after goals, or after foul shots. The official goal is 2 feet high by 6 feet wide, with a restraining area 4 by 8 feet around the goal to protect the goalie (Figure 26.13). Each team has a goal-keeper, who stops shots with her hands, feet, or stick; a center, who is the only player allowed to move full court and who leads offensive play (the center has her stick striped with black tape); two guards, who cannot go beyond the centerline into the offensive area and who are responsible for keeping the puck out of their defensive half of the field; and two forwards, who work with the center on offensive play and who cannot go back over the centerline into the defensive area.

A game consists of three periods of eight minutes each, with a three-minute rest between periods. Play is started with a face-off by the centers at midcourt. Other players cannot enter the restraining circle until the ball has been hit by the centers. The clock starts when the puck is put into play and runs continuously until a goal is scored or a foul is called. Substitutions can be made only when the clock is stopped. If the ball goes out-of-bounds, it is put back into play by the team that did not hit it last.

Whenever the ball passes through the goal on the ground, one point is scored. If, however, the ball crosses the goal line while in the air, it must strike against the mat or back wall to count for a score. Under no circumstances can a goal be scored on a foul. The puck can deflect off a player or equipment to score, but it cannot be kicked into the goal.

The goalkeeper may use her hands to clear the puck away from the goal, but she may not hold it or throw it toward the other end of the playing area. She is charged with a foul for holding the puck. The goalkeeper may be pulled from the goal area but cannot go beyond the centerline. No other player may enter the restraining area without being charged with a foul.

FIGURE 26.13 Regulation elementary hockey playing field.

The following are fouls and are penalized by loss of the puck at the spot of the foul.

1. Illegally touching the puck with the hands.
2. Swinging the stick above waist height (called "high sticking").
3. Guards or forwards moving across the centerline.
4. Player other than the goalie entering the restraining area.
5. Goalie throwing the puck.
6. Holding, stepping on, or lying on the puck.

Defenders must be 5 yards back when the puck is put into play after a foul. If the spot where the foul occurred is closer than 5 yards to the goal, only the goalkeeper may defend. The puck is then put into play 5 yards directly out from the goal.

Personal fouls include any action or rough play that endangers other players. A player committing a personal foul must retire to the sidelines for two minutes. The following are personal fouls:

1. Hacking or striking with a stick.
2. Tripping with either the foot or the stick.
3. Pushing or blocking.

HOCKEY SKILL TESTS

Passing for Accuracy

In passing for accuracy, the player has five attempts to pass the puck or ball into a 3-by-3-foot target. The target can be drawn or taped on the wall, or a three-foot square of cardboard can be used. The player must pass from a distance of 30 feet. He can approach the 30-foot restraining line in whatever fashion he chooses. Two points are awarded for each successful pass.

Receiving

Three players are designated as passers and pass from different angles to a person being tested for receiving. The puck must be definitely stopped and controlled. The instructor can judge whether the pass was a fair opportunity for the player to field. Six passes, two from each angle, are given, and one point is awarded for each successful field.

Stick Handling for Speed

To test carrying for speed, three cones are placed in line 8 feet apart. The first cone is 16 feet from the starting line. The player carries the puck around the cones in a figure-eight fashion to finish at the original starting line.

A stopwatch is used for timing, and the score is recorded to the nearest tenth of a second. Two trials are given, and the faster trial is recorded as the score.

Shooting for Distance

Shooting for distance should be tested outdoors only. A restraining line can be used as a starting point. Each player is given five trials to see how many goals can be scored from an established distance. The distance to the goal can be increased or decreased depending on the ability level of the players. Players can be lined up in four or five squads behind the restraining line. After players have taken their five trials, they can exchange places with someone who is returning pucks.

FOR MORE INFORMATION

References and Suggested Readings

American Sports Education Program. (2001). *Coaching youth hockey.* Champaign, IL: Human Kinetics.

Anders, E. (1999). *Field hockey: Steps to success.* Champaign, IL: Human Kinetics.

Chambers, D. (1995) *The incredible hockey drill book.* New York: McGrawHill.

Fronske, H. (2005). *Teaching cues for sport skills.* 3rd ed. San Francisco: Benjamin Cummings.

Mood, D. P., Musker, F. F., & Rink, J. E. (2003). *Sports and recreational activities.* 13th ed. New York: McGraw-Hill.

Rulebook for outdoor and indoor hockey. Current edition. Colorado Springs: United States Field Hockey Association.

Schmottlach, N., and McManama, J. (2002). *The physical education handbook.* 10th ed. San Francisco: Benjamin Cummings.

Trimble, R. M. (1997). *The ultimate hockey drill book.* Indianapolis: Masters Press.

Whitney, M. G. (Ed.). *Eagle, Official Publication of the United States Field Hockey Association Inc.* USFHA: Colorado Springs, CO (periodical).

Websites

Field Hockey Information
www.fieldhockey.com

Hockey Guidebook.com
www.hockeyguidebook.com

International Field Hockey
www.planetfieldhockey.com

United States Hockey
www.usahockey.com

United States Field Hockey Association
www.usfieldhockey.com

26

Soccer

SUMMARY

Skills instruction for soccer is introduced during the intermediate grades after youngsters have mastered basic prerequisite skills. Teaching the rules and strategies for soccer is an integral part of the instructional process. Using proper progression is key to successfully teaching fundamental skills and lead-up games associated with soccer. Lead-up games provide an opportunity to emphasize development of selected soccer skills in a setting that is compatible with the abilities of participants.

OUTCOMES

- Structure learning experiences efficiently using appropriate formations, progressions, and coaching techniques.

- Develop a unit plan and a lesson focus for soccer.

- Identify safety precautions associated with teaching soccer.

- Describe instructional procedures needed to implement a successful lead-up game.

- Cite assessment procedures used for evaluating soccer skills.

Soccer is the most popular and, probably, the most active sport in America for youth. Effective soccer instruction stresses position play, in contrast to a group of children chasing the ball. If players are to improve their playing ability, organized practice that emphasizes handling the ball as often as possible is essential. Offer students frequent opportunities on offense to kick, control, dribble, volley, and shoot the ball and frequent opportunities on defense to mark, guard, tackle, and recover the ball. Success in soccer depends on how well individual skills are coordinated in team play.

MODIFICATIONS OF SOCCER FOR CHILDREN

A regulation soccer ball is too large and too heavy for young soccer players who want to learn the sport. Many youngsters avoid contact with the regulation ball for fear of getting hurt. There are a number of manufacturers

---

ESSENTIAL COMPONENTS OF QUALITY PROGRAMS

▶ I. Organized around content standards

▶ II. Student-centered and developmentally appropriate

▶ III. Physical activity and motor skill development form the core of the program

▶ IV. Teaches management skills and self-discipline

▶ V. Promotes inclusion of all students

▶ VI. Focuses on process over product

VII. Promotes lifetime personal health and wellness

▶ VIII. Teaches cooperation and responsibility and promotes sensitivity to diversity

NATIONAL STANDARDS FOR PHYSICAL EDUCATION*

▶ 1. Demonstrates competency in motor skills and movement patterns needed to perform a variety of physical activities.

▶ 2. Demonstrates understanding of movement concepts, principles, and tactics as they apply to the learning and performance of physical activities.

▶ 3. Participates regularly in physical activity.

▶ 4. Achieves and maintains a health-enhancing level of physical fitness.

▶ 5. Exhibits responsible personal and social behavior that respects self and others in physical activity.

▶ 6. Values physical activity for health, enjoyment, challenge, self-expression, and/or social interaction.

*National Association for Sport and Physical Education (NASPE), 2004.

who produce smaller-sized soccer balls that move and rebound in a manner identical to regulation balls. Foam balls covered with a tough plastic skin that simulates the appearance of a soccer ball can negate players' fear of being hurt. Beach balls are excellent for teaching beginning skills because they move slowly and don't hurt when they strike someone. If heading skills are taught, a beach ball should be the only type of ball used.

Decrease the number of players in games to ensure more opportunity for students to practice skills. When learning soccer, the 11-person team is not suitable. Mini-Soccer is an excellent game with six or seven players on a team. Two games can be played crosswise on a regulation soccer field. With the exception of a penalty area and the out-of-bounds lines, the field does not have to be marked. The official regulation soccer goal, 24 feet wide and 8 feet high, is too large for elementary school play. The size should be such that teams have a reasonable chance of scoring as well as preventing a score. The suggested size is from 18 to 21 feet in width and 6 to 7 feet in height. The size can be further scaled down as determined by the character of the game.

INSTRUCTIONAL EMPHASIS AND SEQUENCE

Table 27.1 shows the sequence of soccer activities divided into developmental levels. Depending on the amount of experience children have received through community sports programs, the actual sequence may differ in certain areas and communities.

Developmental Level II

The two basic skills in soccer are (1) controlling or stopping the ball with the foot so that the ball is in a position to be kicked and (2) passing the ball with the foot to another player or to a target. Activities at this level should stress games and drills that facilitate practice and use of fundamental skills. To maximize involvement, one ball for every two players should be available.

Developmental Level III

To enhance control of the ball, dribbling skills are introduced and students are taught to control the ball with other body parts, such as the thigh and chest. Passing continues to receive major emphasis so that games with two to five players per team can be introduced. The basic goalkeeping skills of catching low and high balls are taught. Further development of basic skills is recommended, along with the introduction of shooting, tackling, heading, jockeying, and the concept of two-touch soccer for more advanced players. Fundamentals of team and positional play are taught, along with the

TABLE 27.1 Suggested Soccer Program	
Developmental Level II	**Developmental Level III**
Skills	
Dribbling	Dribbling
Inside-of-the-foot pass	Outside-of-the-foot pass
Long pass	Ball control (trapping)
Foot trap	Passing
Passing	Tackling
Goalkeeping	Kicking goals
Defensive maneuvers	Kickoff (placekicking)
	Punting
	Volleying
	Heading with beach balls
Knowledge	
Soccer rules	Ball control and passing
	The game of soccer
	Team play and strategy
Activities	
Circle Kickball	Manyball Soccer
Soccer Touch Ball	Addition Soccer
Diagonal Soccer	Over the Top
Dribblerama	Lane Soccer
Bull's-Eye	Line Soccer
Pin Kickball	Mini-Soccer
Sideline Soccer	Six-Spot Keepaway
Kick Bowling	Regulation Soccer
Soccer Golf	
Skill Tests	
Controlled passing	Figure-eight dribbling
Kicking for accuracy	Controlling (three types)
Placekicking	Punting for distance
	Penalty kicking

rules of the regular game. A unit of study focusing on soccer as an international game is valuable because few children in the United States realize how important this game is in other countries.

SOCCER SKILLS

Offensive skills taught in the elementary grades are passing, kicking, controlling, dribbling, volleying (including heading), and shooting. *Shooting* is defined as taking a shot at the goal with the intent to score. Defensive skills include marking, guarding, jockeying, tackling, and recovering the ball.

Dribbling

Dribbling involves moving the ball with a series of taps or pushes to cover ground while still retaining control. It allows a player to change direction quickly and to avoid opponents. The best contact point is the inside of the foot, but the outside of the foot will be used at faster running speeds. The player should keep the ball close to maintain control. The following instructional cues can be used to emphasize proper form:

1. Keep the head up in order to see the field.
2. Move on the balls of the feet.
3. Contact the ball with the inside, outside, or instep of the foot.
4. Keep the ball near the body so it can be controlled. (Don't kick it too far in front of the body.)
5. Dribble the ball with a controlled tap.

Passing

Balance and timing provide the keys to accurate passing. The basic purposes of passing are to advance the ball to a teammate and to shoot on goal. Occasionally, a pass is used to send the ball downfield so that a team has a chance to regroup, with their opponents having an equal chance to recover the ball.

The following are instructional cues to enhance accurate passing:

1. Place the nonkicking foot alongside the ball.
2. Keep the head down and the eyes focused on the ball during contact.
3. Spread the arms for balance.
4. Follow through with the kicking leg in the intended direction of the ball.
5. Make contact with the outside or inside of the foot rather than with the toe.
6. Practice kicking with both the left and the right foot.

INSIDE-OF-THE-FOOT PASS (PUSH PASS)

The inside-of-the-foot pass is used for accurate passing over distances of up to 15 yards. Because of the technique used, this pass is sometimes referred to as the *push pass*. The nonkicking foot is placed well up alongside the ball. As the kicking foot is drawn back, the toe is turned out. During the kick, the toe remains turned out so that the inside of the foot is perpendicular to the line of flight. The sole is kept parallel to the ground. At contact, the knee of the kicking leg should be well forward,

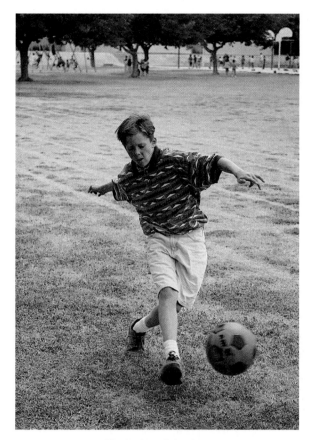

FIGURE 27.1   The inside-of-the-foot pass.

over the ball, and both knees should be slightly bent (Figure 27.1).

OUTSIDE-OF-THE-FOOT PASS (FLICK PASS)

The nonkicking foot is placed more to the side of the ball than it is for the inside-of-the-foot kick, and the kicking leg approaches directly behind the ball. The kicking foot is fully extended, and contact with the ball is on the outside of the foot between laces and sole-line. This pass can be used effectively while running without breaking stride, or for flicking the ball to the side.

THE LONG PASS (SHOELACE KICK)

The long pass is the power pass in soccer. It is used for kicking for distance or for power when kicking the ball past a goalie. Beginners often use the toes instead of the top of the foot (shoelace) area, which can result in injury or an inaccurate kick. The ball is approached at an angle to the line of flight in a full running stride. The nonkicking foot is placed alongside the ball, with the kicking leg cocked in the backswing. Just before contact, the ankle of the kicking foot is fixed with the toes pointed down. As with all passes, the head is kept down with the eyes focused on the ball. Contact is made with the shoelaces on the top of the foot. The passer gives the lower leg a good forward snap at the knee. A normal follow-through in the intended direction of the pass completes the action. To lift the ball, contact is made below the midline of the ball, close to the ground, with the body leaning slightly backward. The nonkicking leg is placed to the side and slightly behind the ball so that the kicking foot makes contact just on the start of the upswing of the leg. The lofted pass is aimed over the heads of opposing players.

Ball Control (Trapping)

Learning to receive a ball and place it into the ideal position for making a pass or shot is vital. In fact, one of the best measures of skilled players is how quickly they can bring the ball under control with the feet, legs, or torso. Advanced players are able to achieve this in one smooth movement with one touch of the ball. The second touch occurs when the pass is made.

For efficient control, a large surface of the body should be presented to the ball. On contact, the surface should be momentarily withdrawn to produce a sponge-like or shock-absorbing action, which decelerates the ball and allows it to drop into an ideal position about a yard in front of the body. The pass or shot can then be made. The following instructional cues will help students develop ball control skills:

1. Move in line with the path of the ball.
2. Reach to meet the ball and give with the contact.
3. Stay on the balls of the feet.
4. Keep the eyes on the ball.

INSIDE-OF-THE-FOOT TRAP

This is the most common method of control; it is used when the ball is either rolling along the ground or bouncing up to knee height. The full surface of the foot, from heel to toe, should be presented alongside the ball (Figure 27.2).

CHEST AND THIGH TRAPS

The chest and the inside of the thigh also are used to deflect the ball downward when it is bouncing high. The chest trap requires that the chest be lined up squarely with the direction from which the ball is traveling (Figure 27.3 on page 660). On contact, the chest and waist are drawn back, resulting in a forward body lean that causes the ball to drop directly to the ground in front of the player. The thigh trap demands that the player turn the body sideways to the flight of the ball. The ball is contacted with the inside of the thigh, which is then relaxed and drawn backward. This action absorbs the force of the ball and causes it to drop to the ground ready to be played.

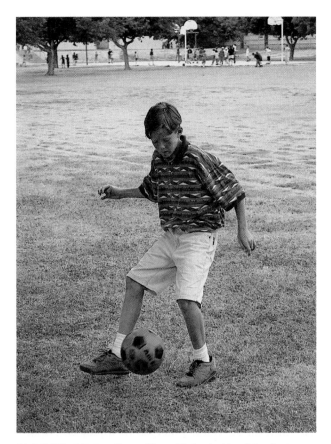

FIGURE 27.2   Controlling with the inside-of-the-foot.

SOLE-OF-THE-FOOT TRAP

This method of control, sometimes called trapping the ball, is used occasionally to stop the ball. For beginners, it is not as successful a method as the inside-of-the-foot trap, because the ball can roll easily under the foot. The sole is also used to roll the ball from side to side in dribbling and to adjust for a better passing position.

Heading

Heading is a special kind of volleying in which the direction of flight of the ball is changed through an impact with the head. Recent research has shown that heading might cause some brain damage. With this in mind, beach balls should be used in place of soccer balls if heading skills are going to be practiced. Since beach balls move slowly, they offer beginners time to get into proper position. Heading with a regulation ball should be avoided with elementary school youngsters.

In heading, the neck muscles are used to aid in reducing the impact of the blow. The eye must be kept on the ball until the moment of impact. The point of contact is the top of the forehead at the hairline. In preparing to contact the ball with the head, the player stands in stride position, with knees relaxed and trunk bent backward at the hips. At the moment of contact, the trunk

27

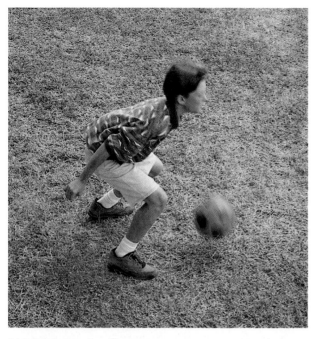

FIGURE 27.3 Chest trap.

moves forward abruptly, driving the forehead into the ball. Advanced heading is achieved in midair, and is especially useful in beating other players to the ball. Midair heading can be done by a running one-footed takeoff or a standing two-footed jump.

Defensive Maneuvers

Tackling is a move to take possession of the ball away from an opponent who is dribbling. The most common tackle is the front block, which involves contacting the ball with the inside of the foot just as the opponent touches it. The tackler presents a firm instep to the ball, with his weight behind it. The stronger the contact with the ball, the greater the chance of controlling it. Body contact should be avoided, as this may constitute a foul. Other tackles may be made when running alongside the player with the ball.

How much tackling to teach in elementary school programs is a question of concern. In most cases, it is probably best to teach tackling skills that involve the defensive player remaining upright. Methods like the hook slide and split slide are of little value in elementary school instructional programs.

Jockeying

Knowing when to make a tackle, and when not to, is one of the most difficult skills to learn. A failed tackle may mean that an attacker breaks through with a free shot on goal. Often, defenders should jockey until defensive support arrives. This means backing off while staying close enough to pressure the advancing player. The defender should stay on the toes, watching the ball rather than the opponent's feet and keeping within one to two yards of the ball.

Throw-Ins

The throw-in is the only time field players can handle the ball with their hands. The throw-in is guided by rules that must be followed closely or the result will be a turnover to the other team. The rules are as follows:

1. Both hands must be on the ball.
2. The ball must be released from over the thrower's head.
3. The thrower must face the field.
4. The thrower may not step onto the field until the throw is released.
5. Both feet must remain in contact with the ground until the ball is released.
6. The thrower cannot play the ball until it has been touched by another player on the field.

The throw-in from out-of-bounds (see Figure 27.20 on page 667) may be executed from a standing or running position. Beginning players should learn how to make the throw without a running start. The feet often are placed one behind the other, with the rear toe trailing along the ground. Delivery of the ball should be from behind the head, using both arms equally. Release should be in front of the forehead with arms outstretched. Instructional cues to help students perform correctly are "Drag your back foot" and "Follow through with both hands pointing toward the target."

Shooting

Scoring is the purpose of the game, and shooting skills should be practiced both while stationary and while on the run. As with passing, the inside, outside, and top of the foot can be used.

Goalkeeping

Goalkeeping involves blocking shots by catching, stopping, or otherwise deflecting the ball. Goalkeepers should become adept at catching low rolling balls, diving on rolling balls, catching airborne balls at waist level and below (Figure 27.4), and catching airborne balls at waist height and above.

Youngsters should practice catching low rolling balls in much the same manner as a baseball outfielder does. The goalie gets down on one knee, with her body behind the ball to act as a backstop, and catches the ball with both hands, fingers pointing toward the ground.

When catching a ball below the waist, the thumbs should point outward as the arms reach for the ball, with body and arms giving and bringing the ball into

FIGURE 27.4 Goalie catching a ball below waist level.

FIGURE 27.5 Punt.

the abdomen. For balls above waist level, the thumbs should be turned inward, arms reaching to meet the ball and giving to guide it to the midsection. If the goalie must dive for the ball, he should throw his body behind it and cradle it with his hands. A goalie should always try to get his body behind the ball. Drills for goalies should offer opportunities to catch the different shots described. All students should receive goaltending practice.

Punting

Used by the goalkeeper only, the punt can be stationary or done on the run. The ball is held in both hands at waist height in front of the body and directly over the kicking leg. For the stationary punt, the kicking foot is forward. A short step is taken with the kicking foot, followed by a full step with the other foot. With the knee bent and the toe extended, the kicking foot swings forward and upward. As contact is made with the ball at the instep, the knee straightens, and additional power is secured from the other leg through a coordinated rising on the toes or a hop (Figure 27.5).

The goalkeeper who can develop a strong placekick has an advantage. Distance and accuracy are important in setting up the next attack. Over shorter distances,

throwing underhand or overhand can be more accurate than kicking. In those cases, a straight arm should be used for rolling or throwing the ball to players.

Instructional Procedures

1. Soccer skills must be practiced if children are to participate successfully in the sport. Controlling the ball and passing should predominate in practices. Organize drills and activities to maximize the involvement of all children. One ball is needed per two children.

2. Many combination drills featuring both offense and defense should be included. Enjoyment is the key to continued learning. Drills and lead-up activities can be used to make the skills challenging, but all activities should be appropriate to the developmental level of players.

3. Small-group games (with two to five players per team) should be used to ensure maximum activity. The number of team members can be increased as skill improves.

4. Lead-up games are designed to encourage the use of the skills practiced in drills. For example, if long passing is the skill of the day, lead-up games requiring and rewarding long passing should be played. In the early stages of learning soccer, it may be best not to allow tackling.

5. The grid system is useful when organizing drills, activities, and small-sized games. Using cones or chalk, mark a grid system of 10-yard squares on the playing field. The number of squares needed depends on the size of the class, but at least one square for every three students is recommended. Possible layouts are shown in Figure 27.6 on page 662. The squares are used as boundaries for tackling, keeping possession, and passing diagonally or sideways. Drill and game areas can be defined easily, so that a number of small-sized games can be played simultaneously.

6. Balls smaller and lighter than the regulation soccer ball should be used. Partially deflated 8-inch rubber playground balls can be used, provided their quality is

27

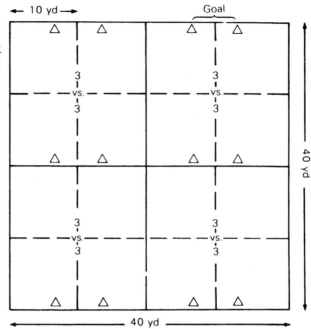

FIGURE 27.6 Examples of grid layouts and usage.

good enough to withstand kicking. A better alternative for novices is the toughskin foam-rubber training ball. It withstands heavy usage and does not hurt youngsters on impact. Another alternative is a beach ball. They are light and move slowly, making them an excellent choice for unskilled players. The key to soccer practice is to have plenty of balls available. Rubber balls mean more fun, because they can be kicked far, controlled easily, and even headed without discomfort. Junior-sized soccer balls (number 4) are also excellent but are more expensive.

7. Soccer, with its attack and defense, can be a rough game. Rough play such as pushing, shoving, kicking, and tripping must be controlled. Rules need to be strictly enforced.

8. Modified scoring can be used to make the activity more enjoyable for more children. Scoring must be a challenge—neither too easy nor too difficult. To avoid arguments in situations in which the ball is to be kicked through a line of children, limit the height of the kick to shoulder level or below. Cones and designated spots can be used to mark goal outlines. Regulation soccer goals are not necessary for the elementary school program.

SOCCER DRILLS

In soccer drills, two approaches are most often used. The first is to practice technique with no opposition from any

defense. The second is the skill approach, which involves both offensive and defensive players and perhaps a target. In drills using the skill approach, the goal is to outmaneuver the opponent. Some drills begin with the technique approach and then move to the skill approach. Individual practice is excellent, particularly with dribbling techniques, but most practice is best accomplished with combinations of two or three students and small groups.

The type of surface has a marked effect on the quality of soccer practice. Grass is the most desirable practice surface, but some schools have only hard-top surfaces. In this case, balls should be deflated slightly to approximate how they travel on grass. When space is restricted, outline areas with cones, beanbags, jugs, or boundary boards.

▶ INDIVIDUAL WORK

Dribbling practice is best done individually. Activity can begin by having youngsters dribble in various directions and signaling them to make right and left turns. As a variation, children can react to signals: One whistle means turn left, two means turn right, and three means reverse direction. A number of cones can be scattered around the area, and players then dribble around one cone clockwise and around the next cone counterclockwise.

Have youngsters practice heading skills by tossing a beach ball overhead and heading it. Alternate heading with a short period of dribbling practice. To teach trapping skills, drop a ball and show students how to smother it with a foot. Another drill is to have youngsters toss the ball into the air, let it bounce, and then kick it to themselves with an instep or inside-of-the-foot pass. Yet another activity is to toss the ball high and use the instep kick to control the ball.

Rebounding to oneself continuously, although not actually used in the game of soccer, is an excellent way to learn ball control. (This is sometimes called foot juggling.) Students begin by dropping the ball so that it bounces to waist height, and then practice the following skills:

1. Rebound the ball with alternating feet, letting it bounce between contacts.

2. Play the ball twice with one foot, let it bounce, and then play it twice with the other foot.

3. Toss the ball so it can be handled with the thigh and then catch it. Add successive rebounds with the thigh.

4. Play ball with the foot, thigh, head, thigh, foot, and catch it.

The foot pickup is another skill that can be taught in two ways. The first is to have students put the ball between their feet, jump up, and hoist the ball so it can be caught. The second is the toe pickup. Students put a toe on top of the ball and pull the toe back and down so that the ball spins up the instep, from which it can be hoisted to the hands. Another bit of individual work is toe changing on top of the ball. Students put the ball of the foot on top of the ball. On signal, they change feet.

▶ DRILLS FOR TWO PLAYERS

Many introductory drills can be practiced best with a partner. One of the best ways to organize partner drills is to use the grid system mentioned earlier in this chapter. The distance between the grid lines depends on the skills to be practiced. Partners position themselves opposite each other so that two lines of players are formed, which gives the teacher a clear view of the class in action (Figure 27.7). This approach is recommended for introducing all new skills, such as passing with both sides of the foot and ball control. Skill combinations can be used, such as throw-ins by one partner and control-and-pass by the other. Within the grids, partners can work on passing, dribbling, keepaway, and one-on-one games.

The following are examples of drills that can be used in partner formation.

1. *Dribbling, marking, and ball recovery.* Pairs are scattered, with one player in each pair having a soccer ball. That player dribbles in various directions, and the second player attempts to stay close to the first (marking). As skill improves, the defensive player attempts to recover the ball from the dribbler. If successful, roles are reversed.

2. *Dribbling.* One player of the pair has a ball and dribbles in different directions. On signal, she passes to her partner, who repeats the dribbling, continuing until another signal is given.

3. *Dribbling, moving, and passing.* Two lines of paired children face each other across a 40-to-60-foot distance, as illustrated in the Figure 27.8 diagram on page 664. Each child in one of the lines has a ball and works with his partner directly across from him. A player with a ball from line A moves forward according to the challenges listed below. When he moves near his partner, he passes to him, and the partner (line B) repeats the same maneuver back to line A. Repeating the maneuver immediately results in both players returning to their starting place.

   a. Dribble across to partner, using the outside of either foot.

   b. Gallop across, handling the ball with the front foot only. On return, lead with the other foot.

   c. Skip across, dribbling at the same time.

   d. Slide across, handling the ball with the back foot. On return, lead with the other foot.

   e. Hop across, using the lifted foot to handle the ball. Be sure to change feet halfway across.

   f. Dribble the ball to a point halfway across. Stop the ball with the sole of the foot and leave it there. Continue to the other line. In the meantime, the partner from line B moves forward to dribble the ball back to line A.

   g. Player A dribbles to the center and passes to Player B. Player A now returns to line A. Player B repeats and returns to line B.

4. *Volleying and controlling.* Pairs of players are scattered. One player in each pair has a ball and acts as a feeder, tossing the ball to practice various receptive skills including different kinds of volleying and controlling balls in flight. Controlled tossing is essential to this drill.

Position 2	XXX	XXX	XXX	XXX	
	ııı ııı	ııı ııı	ııı ııı	ııı ııı	Teacher
Position 1	XXX	XXX	XXX	XXX	

FIGURE 27.7 Class organized along grid lines.

Line A **X X X X X X X X X X X X X**

40–60 ft

Line B **X X X X X X X X X X X X X**

FIGURE 27.8   Dribbling, moving, and passing.

▶ DRILLS FOR THREE PLAYERS

With one ball for three players, many of the possibilities suggested for pair practice are still possible. An advantage of drills for three players is that fewer balls are needed.

1. *Passing and controlling.* The trio of players sets up a triangle with players about 10 yards apart. Controlled passing and practice in ball control should occur.

2. *Volleying and controlling.* One player acts as a feeder, tossing to the other two players, who practice volleying and controlling in-flight balls.

3. *Dribbling and passing.* A shuttle-type drill can be structured as shown in Figure 27.9. Players keep going back and forth continuously. Player 1 has the ball and dribbles to Player 2, who dribbles the ball back to Player 3, who in turn dribbles to Player 1. Players can dribble the entire distance or dribble a portion of the distance and then pass the ball to the end player. Obstacles can be set up to challenge players to dribble through or around each obstacle.

4. *Dribbling and stopping the ball.* Three dribblers are in line, each with a ball. The leader moves in various directions, followed by the other two players. On signal, each player controls her ball. The leader circles around to the back ball, and the other two move one ball forward. The dribbling continues for another stop. A third stop puts the players back in their original positions.

5. *Passing.* Players stand in three corners of a 10-yard square. After a player passes, he must move to the empty corner of the square, which is sometimes a diagonal movement (Figure 27.10).

6. *Passing and defense.* One player is the feeder and rolls the ball to either player. As soon as she rolls the ball, she attempts to block or tackle the player

receiving the ball to prevent a pass to the third player, who, if the pass is completed, attempts to pass back (Figure 27.11).

▶ DRILLS FOR FOUR OR MORE PLAYERS

Drills for four or more players should be organized so that a rotation gives all players an equal opportunity to practice skills.

1. *Dribbling.* Four players are in line as diagrammed in Figure 27.12. Each player in front has a ball. Both front players dribble to the center, where they exchange balls and continue dribbling to the other side. The next players perform similarly. A variation is to have the two players meet at the center, exchange balls, and dribble back to their starting point. Action should be continuous.

2. *Passing, guarding, and tackling.* Four players occupy the four corners of a square respectively (Figure 27.13). One player has a ball. Practice begins with one player rolling the ball to the player in the opposite corner, who, in turn, passes to either of the other two players. There should be two attempts each round so

FIGURE 27.10   Passing drill.

Note: The following symbols are used in soccer game formation diagrams:

✕	Defensive player
○	Offensive player
──────▶	Player moving without the ball
------▶	Player dribbling
∿∿∿∿▶	Pass, kick, or shot on goal

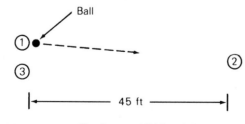

Ball

① ━ ━ ━ ━ ━ ━ ▶

③   ②

|◀────── 45 ft ──────▶|

FIGURE 27.9   Shuttle-type dribbling drill.

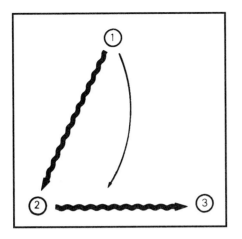

FIGURE 27.11   Passing and defense drill.

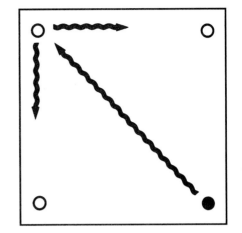

FIGURE 27.13   Passing, guarding, and tackling drill.

that kicks are possible both ways. The next progression calls for the player who rolled the ball to move forward rapidly to block the pass to either side. Several tries should occur before another player takes over the rolling duties.

3. *Shooting, goalkeeping, and defense.* A shooting drill against defense can be coordinated with four players and a 15-foot goal set off with cones or other markers (Figure 27.14). One player has the ball. He advances and attempts to maneuver around a second player so that he can shoot past the goalkeeper guarding the goal. A fourth player acts as the retriever. Rotate positions.

4. *Dribbling.* Four or five players, each with a ball, form a line. A "coach" stands about 15 yards in front of the line. Each player, in turn, dribbles up to the coach, who indicates with a thumb in which direction the player should dribble. The coach should give the direction at the last possible moment.

5. *Passing, controlling, and defense.* Four players stand in the four corners of a square, ten yards on a side. Two defensive players are inside the square. The corner players stay in place within the square and attempt to pass the ball among themselves, while the two defenders attempt to recover the ball (Figure 27.15 on page 666). After a period of time, another two players take over as defenders.

6. *Shooting.* For two-way goal practice, two to six players are divided, half on each side of the goal. The width of the goal can vary, depending on the skill of the players. Two types of shooting should be practiced: (a) kicking a stationary ball from 10 to 20 yards out and (b) preceding a kick with a dribble. In the second type, a restraining line 12 to 15 yards out is needed. This line can be marked by cones, as illustrated (Figure 27.16 on page 666). Use at least four balls for this two-way drill. After a period of kicking, the groups should change sides. Ball chasers are the players at the end of each line.

7. *Shooting and goalkeeping.* Scoring can also be practiced with a goalkeeper (Figure 27.17, page 667). Practice should be done with a stationary ball from 12 yards out (penalty distance) and with kicks preceded by a dribble. The goalie and the chaser should remain for one complete round and then rotate. Having a second ball to play with saves time because play can continue while the chaser is recovering the previous ball.

8. *Kicking and trapping.* This is an excellent squad drill. Approximately eight players form a circle 15 yards in diameter. Two balls are passed back and forth independently. Passes should be kept low, using primarily the side-of-the-foot kick. Using three balls can be tried also.

9. *Passing and shooting.* The drill can be done with four to six players. Two balls are needed. A passer is stationed about 15 yards from the goal, and a retriever is behind the goal. The shooters are in line, 20 yards from the goal and to the right. The first shooter passes to the passer, and then runs forward.

FIGURE 27.12   Dribble exchange drill.

FIGURE 27.14   Shooting, goalkeeping, and defense.

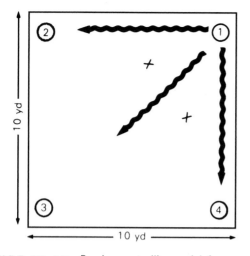

FIGURE 27.15   Passing, controlling, and defense.

his place at the other side of the field. Player 2 repeats the routine, passing the ball off to the next player in the line. If the ball goes out of control or is stopped by the defender, it is rolled to the player whose turn is next. Play is continuous, with the defender maintaining his position for several rounds.

BASIC SOCCER RULES FOR LEAD-UP GAMES

The ball may not be played deliberately with the hands or arms, but incidental or unintentional handling of the ball should be disregarded in the early stages. Eventually, a violation leads to a direct free kick in which the ball is placed on the ground with the opposition a specified distance away (ten yards on a full-sized field). A goal can be scored directly from this type of kick.

The goalkeeper is allowed to handle the ball within her area by catching, batting, or deflecting with the hands. If the goalie has caught the ball, she may not be charged by the opponents. While the goalie is holding the ball, official rules limit her to four steps. In elementary school play, the teacher should insist on the goalkeeper getting rid of the ball immediately by throwing or kicking. This removes the temptation to rough up the goalie. In some lead-up games, a number of students may have the same ball-handling privileges as the goalie. The rules need to be clear, and ball handling should be done within a specified area.

All serious fouls, such as tripping, kicking a player, holding, or pushing, result in a direct free kick. If a defender commits one of these fouls or a handles a ball in his own penalty area, a penalty kick is awarded. Only the goalkeeper may defend against this kick, which is shot from 12 yards out. All other players must be outside the penalty area until

The passer returns the ball to the shooter. The shooter tries to time her run forward so that she successfully shoots the pass through the goal. Both the passer and the retriever should stay in position for several rounds of shooting and then rotate to become shooters. The first pass can be from a stationary ball. Later, however, the kicker can be allowed to dribble forward a short distance before making the first pass. Reverse the field and practice from the left, shooting with the nondominant leg (Figure 27.18).

10. *Tackling and ball handling.* A defender is restricted to tackling in the area between two parallel lines, which are one yard apart. The field is 20 by 40 yards (Figure 27.19). Four to six players can practice this drill. Player 1 advances the ball by dribbling and attempts to maneuver past the defender. After he has evaded the defender, he passes to Player 2 and takes

FIGURE 27.16   Shooting drill.

FIGURE 27.17 Shooting and goalkeeping.

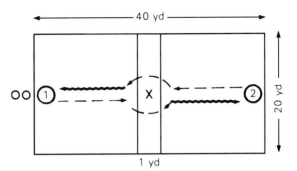

FIGURE 27.19 Tackling and ball-handling drill.

the ball is kicked. In lead-up games, consideration should be given to penalty fouls committed in a limited area near the goal by the defensive team. A kick can be awarded or an automatic goal can be scored for the attacking team.

The ball is out of play and the whistle blown when the ball crosses any of the boundaries, when a goal is scored, or when a foul is called. The team that last touched the ball or caused it to go out-of-bounds on the side of the field loses possession. The ball is put into play with an overhead throw-in using both hands (Figure 27.20).

If the attacking team causes the ball to go over the end line, the defending team is awarded a kick from any point chosen near the end line of that half of the field. If the defense last touched the ball going over the end line, then the attacking team is awarded a corner kick. The ball is taken to the corner on the side where the ball went over the end line, and a direct free kick is executed. A goal may be scored from this kick.

The game is normally started by a kickoff with both teams onside. In lead-up games, the ball can be dropped for a free ball. In some games, the teacher may find it advisable simply to award the ball for a free kick in the backcourt to the team not making the score.

Lead-up games can continue for a set length of time (by halves) or until a predetermined score is attained. In a regular soccer game, the play is timed.

When the ball is ensnarled among a number of players or when someone has fallen, a quick whistle is needed. The ball can be put into play by dropping it between players of the opposing teams.

Even though implementation of the offside rule is of little value in elementary school play, children should understand the rule and the reasons for it. Its purpose is to prevent the "cheap" goal (i.e., a player on offense waits near the goal to take a pass behind the defenders and to score easily against the goalkeeper). Although the concept of *offsides* involves a number of details, it essentially

FIGURE 27.18 Passing and shooting.

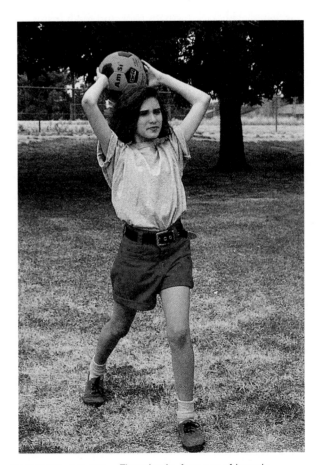

FIGURE 27.20 Throwing in, from out-of-bounds.

means that a player on offense who is ahead of the ball must have two defensive players between her and the goal when the ball is kicked forward. One of these players is, of course, the goalie. The offside rule does not apply when the player receives the ball directly from an attempted goal kick or from an opponent, on a throw-in or corner kick, or when the player is in her own half.

Players should not raise their feet high or show the soles or cleats of their shoes when other players are in the vicinity. This constitutes dangerous play, and an *indirect free kick* is awarded.

SOCCER ACTIVITIES

Developmental Level II

▶ CIRCLE KICKBALL

Playing Area: Playground or gymnasium
Players: 10 to 20 students
Supplies: Two beach balls or 8-inch foam-rubber balls
Skills: Blocking (goalie skills), kicking

Players are in circle formation. Using the sides of their feet, players kick the balls back and forth inside the circle. The object is to kick the ball out of the circle beneath the shoulder level of the other players. Circle players can use their hands and feet to block the ball since they are goalies. A point is scored against each of the players if a ball leaves the circle between them. If, however, a lost ball is clearly the fault of a single player, then the point is scored against that player only. Any player who kicks a ball higher than the shoulders of the circle players has a point scored against her. Players with the fewest points scored against them win. A player is not penalized if she leaves the circle to recover a ball and the second ball goes through the vacated spot.

✓ TEACHING TIP

Specify the types of kicks players may use.

▶ SOCCER TOUCH BALL

Playing Area: Playground or gymnasium
Players: Eight to ten students
Supplies: Soccer balls, beach balls, or 8-inch foam-rubber balls
Skills: Kicking, controlling

Players are spaced around a circle 10 yards in diameter with two players in the center. The object of the game is to keep the players in the center from touching the ball.

The ball is passed back and forth as in soccer. If a center player touches the ball with a foot, he is awarded a point. To keep the game moving, implement a rule that no player may contain or hold the ball longer than 3 seconds. Rotate two new players into the center after 15 to 30 seconds.

▶ DIAGONAL SOCCER

Playing Area: A square about 60 by 60 feet
Players: 20 to 30 students
Supplies: Soccer ball, beach ball, or 8-inch foam-rubber ball and pinnies (optional)
Skills: Kicking, passing, dribbling, some controlling, defending, blocking shots

Two corners are marked off with cones 5 feet from the corners on both sides, outlining triangular dead areas. Each team lines up as illustrated in Figure 27.21 and tries to protect two adjacent sides of the square. To begin competition, three players from each team move into the playing area in their own half of the space. These are the active players who may roam anywhere in the square. The other players act as goalkeepers.

The object of the game is for active players to kick the ball through the opposing team's line (beneath shoulder height) to score. After 30 to 45 seconds, active players rotate to the sidelines and new players take their place. Players on the sidelines may block the ball with their bodies and use their hands. The team against whom the point was scored starts the ball for the next point. Only active players may score. Scoring is much the same as in Circle Kickball in that a point is awarded for the opponents when any of the following occur:

1. A team allows the ball to go through its line below the shoulders.
2. A team touches the ball illegally.
3. A team kicks the ball over the other team above shoulder height.

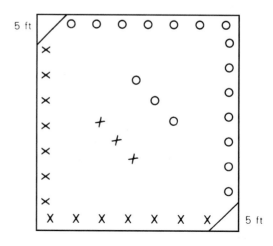

FIGURE 27.21 Formation for Diagonal Soccer.

DRIBBLERAMA

Playing Area: Playground

Players: 10 to 20 students

Supplies: Soccer ball or 8-inch foam-rubber ball for each player

Skills: Dribbling, protecting the ball

The playing area is a large circle or square, clearly outlined. All players dribble within the area. The game is played on two levels.

Level 1: Each player dribbles throughout the area, controlling the ball so that it does not touch another ball. If a touch occurs, both players go outside the area and dribble around the area. Once youngsters have completed dribbling one lap, they may reenter the game.

Level 2: Two equal playing areas are delineated. All players start in one of the areas. While dribbling and controlling the ball, each player attempts to kick any other ball out of the area. When a ball is kicked out, the player owning that ball takes it to the other area and dribbles. As more players move to the second area, a second game ensues. Players in this area move back to the opposite side. This keeps all players actively involved in the games.

Level 3: Start with one game on each half of the teaching area. When a person is out, he moves to the other game. Or he takes one lap dribbling and then joins the other game. Also, the area can be divided into quadrants and four games played with players choosing another game to move to when ousted from a game.

BULL'S-EYE

Playing Area: Playground

Players: Six to ten students

Supplies: Soccer ball or 8-inch foam-rubber ball for each player

Skills: Dribbling, protecting the ball

The playing area is a large outlined area—circle, square, or rectangle. One player holds a ball in her hands, which serves as the bull's-eye. The other players dribble within the area. The player with the bull's-eye attempts to throw her ball (basketball push shot) at any other ball. The player whose ball is hit now becomes the new bull's-eye player. The old bull's-eye player becomes one of the dribblers. A new bull's-eye cannot hit back immediately at the old bull's-eye. If the group is large, have two bull's-eyes. No score is kept and no one is eliminated.

✓ TEACHING TIP

Specify that the bull's-eye must keep one foot on a marking spot.

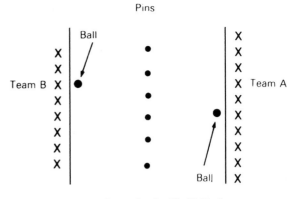

FIGURE 27.22 Formation for Pin Kickball.

PIN KICKBALL

Playing Area: Playground or gymnasium

Players: Seven to ten students on each team

Supplies: Ten or more pins (cones or bowling pins) and many soccer or foam-rubber balls

Skills: Kicking, controlling

Two teams start about 20 yards apart, facing each other. At least ten pins are placed between the two lines of players. A number of balls are given to each team at the start of the kicking (Figure 27.22). Kicks must be made from the line behind which the team is standing. Each knocked-down pin scores a point for that team. After all of the pins have been knocked down, they are reset, and the game resumes.

✓ TEACHING TIP

This is a flexible game; the number of pins, balls, and players can be varied easily. The type of kick can be specified, or it can be left up to the players to choose. As accuracy improves, the distance between the teams can be increased.

SIDELINE SOCCER

Playing Area: Rectangle about 60 by 100 feet

Players: 10 to 12 students on each team

Supplies: A soccer or foam-rubber ball, four cones, and pinnies (optional)

Skills: Most soccer skills, competitive play

Teams line up on the sidelines of the rectangle. Three or four active players from each team are called from the end of the team line (Figure 27.23 on page 670). These players remain active until a point is scored; then they rotate to the other end of the line. The object is to kick the ball between cones (goals) that define the scoring area. The active players on each team compete against each other, aided by their teammates on the sidelines.

FIGURE 27.23   Formation for Sideline Soccer.

To start play, the ball can be given to one team or dropped between two opposing players at the center of the field. To score, the ball must be kicked last by an active player and must go through the goal at or below shoulder height. A goal counts as one point. Sideline players can pass to other sideline players or an active teammate, but a sideline kick cannot score a goal.

Regular soccer rules generally prevail, with special attention to restricting pushing, holding, tripping, or other rough play. Rough play is a foul and causes a point to be awarded to the other team. For an out-of-bounds ball, the team on the side of the field where the ball went out-of-bounds is awarded a free kick near that spot. No score can result from a free kick. Violation of the touch rule also results in a free kick.

✓ TEACHING TIP

Rotate in a new set of players after 30 to 45 seconds. More active players can be added when the class is large. A number of passes to sideline players can be mandated before a shot on goal can be taken. After some expertise is acquired, the cones should be moved in to narrow the goal area. If the ball goes over the end line but not through the goal area, the ball is put into play by a defender with a kick.

▶ KICK BOWLING

Playing Area: Playground or soccer field

Players: Groups of four students

Supplies: Soccer balls or 8-inch foam-rubber balls and bowling pins

Skills: Kicking

Kick bowling is played similarly to bowling with the exception that students kick rather than roll the ball at pins. Place students in groups of four. One student is the kicker, one is the pinsetter, and the other two are ball retrievers.

▶ SOCCER GOLF

Playing Area: Playground or soccer field

Players: Groups of three or four students

Supplies: One soccer ball per student, hoops to mark each hole, and cones to mark tees

Skills: Kicking, knowledge of golf rules

This game is played like golf, with the exception that students kick a soccer ball rather than hit a golf ball. A course similar to a Frisbee golf course (pages 606–607) can be set up prior to the lesson with trees, boxes, and other equipment as obstacles.

Developmental Level III

▶ MANYBALL SOCCER

Playing Area: Soccer field

Players: Entire class

Supplies: Six foam-rubber or soccer balls, cones, and pinnies

Skills: All soccer skills

Players are divided into two teams and begin in the defensive half of the field. Players are free to roam the entire field with the exception of the goalie boxes, which are delineated with cones. Only the goalie is allowed in the goalie box, and goalies are the only players who can touch the ball with their hands. The goalie tries to keep the balls from going between the cones and can return the ball to play by punting or throwing. More than one goalie can be used to increase the difficulty of scoring.

The object is to kick one of the six balls through the goal. If a ball goes through the goal, the player who scored (not the goalie) retrieves the ball and returns it to the midline for play. All balls are in play simultaneously except when being returned after a goal. Basic soccer rules (pages 666–668) are used to control the game.

▶ ADDITION SOCCER

Playing Area: Playground

Players: 10 to 15 students

Supplies: One soccer ball per player

Skills: Dribbling, ball control

Five or more players are designated to defend against the other players. The remainder of the players dribble throughout the area, trying to keep the defenders from touching any ball with their feet. When a player touches a ball, that player rolls the ball to the side of the playing area and joins hands with the defender to become his partner. They operate as a twosome and must keep their hands joined as they try to touch other balls. When another ball is touched, that player takes his ball to the side and joins hands with one of the other defenders. This twosome becomes defenders also, adding their efforts to those of the first twosome. Play continues until all the defenders have touched a ball and have a partner, or for one minute, whichever occurs first. The game then starts over. If partners break joined hands in touching a ball, the touch does not count. The game is similar to Addition Tag (page 557).

▶ OVER THE TOP

Playing Area: Playground

Players: Two teams of five to seven students each

Supplies: A ball for each player on offense

Skills: Dribbling, ball control, guarding, tackling

One team is on offense and the other is on defense, placed according to Figure 27.24. Defensive players stay in their respective areas. On signal, all offensive players dribble through the three areas. A player is eliminated if her ball is recovered by a defensive player or goes out-of-bounds. The offensive team scores one point for each ball dribbled across the far end line. Have the teams reverse roles to give the other team a chance to score. Field markings need to be definite to keep the defensive players in their respective zones. A variation is to put neutral zones between the active zones.

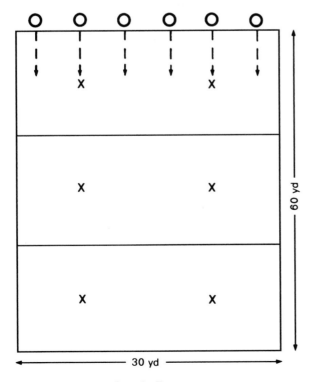

FIGURE 27.24 Over the Top.

▶ LANE SOCCER

Playing Area: Soccer field

Players: Nine students per team

Supplies: Soccer, foam-rubber, or beach balls and pinnies

Skills: All soccer skills

The field is divided into four lanes (eight equal sections) as illustrated in Figure 27.25. A defensive and an offensive player are placed in each of the eight areas. A goalkeeper guards each goal per regulation soccer rules. At least two passes must be made before a shot on goal can be taken. Basic soccer rules guide play. The goalie is the only player who can handle the ball with the hands. A free kick is given to a player who has been fouled by an opponent. Failing to stay within a lane also results in a free kick. Players must be rotated after a goal is scored or a specified amount of time has elapsed. This rotation will enable all students to play four positions: defense, midfield defense, midfield offense, and offense.

✓ TEACHING TIPS

The number of lanes can be varied depending on the number of players and the size of the field. Allow players to choose an opponent for their lane. Usually, they will choose an opponent of equal ability.

Increase the number of balls, goals, and goalies.

▶ LINE SOCCER

Playing Area: Soccer field

Players: Eight to ten students on each team

Supplies: A soccer, foam-rubber, or beach ball, four cones, and pinnies

Skills: Most soccer skills, competitive play

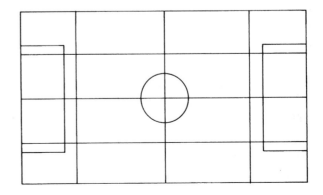

FIGURE 27.25 Field markings for Lane Soccer.

Two goal lines are drawn 80 to 120 feet apart. A re-straining line is drawn 15 feet in front of and parallel to each goal line. Field width can vary from 50 to 80 feet. Each team stands on one goal line, which it defends. The referee stands in the center of the field and holds a ball (Figure 27.26). At the whistle, three players (more if the teams are large) run from the right side of each line to the center of the field and become the six active players. The referee drops the ball to the ground, and the players try to kick it through the team defending the goal line. The players in the field may advance by kicking only.

A score is made when an active player kicks the ball through the opposing team and over the end line (pro-vided that the kick was made from outside the restrain-ing line). Cones should be put on field corners to define the goal line. One point is scored when the ball is kicked over the opponent's goal line below shoulder level. One point is also scored in the case of a personal foul involv-ing pushing, kicking, tripping, and the like.

Line players act as goalies and are permitted to catch the ball. Once caught, however, the ball must be laid down immediately and either rolled or kicked. It cannot be punted or drop-kicked.

For illegal touching by the active players, a direct free kick from a point 12 yards in front of the penalized team's goal line is given. All active players on the defend-ing team must stand to one side until the ball is kicked. Only goalies can defend. An out-of-bounds ball is awarded to the opponents of the team last touching it. The regular soccer throw-in from out-of-bounds should be used. If the ball goes over the shoulders of the de-fenders at the end line, any end-line player may retrieve the ball and put it into play with a throw or kick.

A time limit of one minute is set for any group of active players. After time is up, play is halted and the players are changed. Use a system of player rotation so that all participants get to play.

FIGURE 27.26 Line Soccer.

▶ **MINI-SOCCER**

Playing Area: Any large area 100 by 150 feet, with goals
Players: Seven students on each team
Supplies: A soccer ball, pinnies or colors to mark teams, and four cones for the corners
Skills: All soccer skills

Each end of the field has a 21-foot-wide goal marked by jumping standards. A 12-yard semicircle on each end outlines the penalty area. The center of the semicircle is at the center of the goal (Figure 27.27).

The game follows the general rules of soccer, with one goalie for each side. One new feature, the corner kick, is incorporated in this game. This kick is used when the ball, last touched by the defense, goes over the end line but not through the goal. The ball is taken to the nearest corner for a direct free kick, and a goal can be scored from the kick. In a similar situation, if the attacking team last touched the ball, the goalkeeper kick is awarded. The goalie puts the ball down and placekicks it forward.

The players are designated as center, right-forward, left-forward, right halfback, left halfback, fullback, and goalie. Players should rotate positions. The forwards play in the front half of the field, and the guards play in the back half. Neither position, however, is restricted to these areas entirely, and all may cross the centerline without penalty.

A foul by the defense within its penalty area (semi-circle) results in a penalty kick, taken from a point 12 yards distant, directly in front of the goal. Only the goalie is allowed to defend. The ball is in play, with others waiting outside the penalty area.

✓ **TEACHING TIP**

Position play should be emphasized. The lines of three should be encouraged to spread out and stay in their area. The number of players can vary, with some games using as few as three on a side in a more restricted area.

FIGURE 27.27 Formation for Mini-Soccer.

SIX-SPOT KEEPAWAY

Playing Area: Playground, gymnasium

Players: Two teams, six offensive players on one and three defensive players on the other

Supplies: One soccer ball and a stopwatch

Skills: Passing, ball control, guarding

There are six offensive and three defensive players in this activity. Five offensive players are arranged in a pentagon formation, with the sixth player in the center (Figure 27.28). The pentagon is about 20 yards across. The game begins with the ball in possession of the center player. Three defenders from the other team enter the pentagon and attempt to interrupt the offensive team's passing the ball from one to another. Offensive players should stay reasonably in position. A player may not pass the ball back to the person from whom it was received.

The object of the game is to make as many good passes as possible against the three defenders. After one minute, three offensive players become defensive players and repeat the activity. One more rotation occurs so that all players have been on defense. The threesome scoring the most points is the winner.

REGULATION SOCCER

Playing Area: Soccer field (Figure 27.29)

Players: 11 students on each team

Supplies: A soccer ball and pinnies

Skills: All soccer skills

A team usually consists of three forwards, three midfield players, four backline defenders, and one goalkeeper. More can be placed on a team depending on

FIGURE 27.29   Regulation soccer field.

class size. Forwards are the main line of attack and focus primarily on scoring. Midfield players need good passing and tackling skills as well as a high level of cardiovascular fitness. Defenders work to keep the opponent from scoring. They try to keep the ball away from their own penalty area and avoid dribbling or passing toward their own goal unless it is absolutely safe to do so. Goalkeepers are usually quick and agile and have good ball-handling skills.

After the toss of a coin, the winning team gets its choice of kicking off or selecting which goal to defend. The loser exercises the option not selected by the winner.

On the kickoff, the ball must travel forward at least about 1 yard, and the kicker cannot touch it again until another player has kicked it. The defensive team must be 10 yards away from the kicker. After each score, the team not winning the point gets to kick off. Both teams must be onside at the kickoff. The defensive team must stay onside and out of the center circle until the ball is kicked. Regular soccer rules call for scoring by counting the number of goals made.

Elementary school children usually play 6-minute quarters; however, this can be adjusted depending on the development of the players. There should be a rest period of 1 minute between quarters and 10 minutes between halves.

When the ball goes out-of-bounds on the sideline, it is put into play with a throw-in from the spot where it crossed the line. A goal may not be scored nor may the thrower play the ball a second time until another player has touched it. All opponents are to be 10 yards back at the time of the throw.

If the attacking team causes the ball to go out-of-bounds on the end line, a goal kick is awarded. The ball is placed in the goal area and kicked beyond the penalty area by a defending player, who may not touch the ball twice in succession. If a player touches the ball before it goes out of the penalty area, it is not yet in play and should be kicked again.

If the defensive team causes the ball to go out-of-bounds over the end line, a corner kick is awarded.

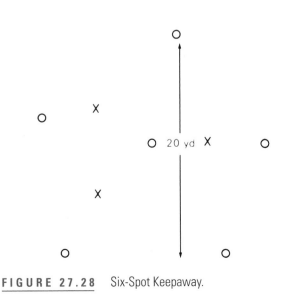

FIGURE 27.28   Six-Spot Keepaway.

27

The ball is placed 1 yard from the corner of the field and kicked into the field of play by an attacking player. The 10-yard restriction also applies to defensive players.

If the ball is touched by two opponents at the same time and caused to go out-of-bounds, a drop ball is called. The referee drops the ball between two opposing players, who cannot kick it until it touches the ground. A drop ball is also called when the ball is trapped among downed players.

If a player is closer to the opponent's goal line than to the ball at a time when the ball is played in a forward direction, it is an offside infraction. Exceptions exist, and a player is not offside when he is in his half of the playing field, when two opponents are nearer their goal line than the attacking player at the moment the ball is played, or when the ball is received directly from a corner kick, a throw-in, or a goal kick.

Personal fouls involving unnecessary roughness are penalized. Tripping, striking, charging, holding, pushing, and jumping an opponent intentionally are forbidden.

It is a foul for any player, except the goalkeeper, to handle the ball with the hands or arms. The goalkeeper is allowed only four steps and must then get rid of the ball. After the ball has left his possession, the goalkeeper may not pick it up again until another player has touched it. Players are not allowed to screen or obstruct opponents, unless they are in control of the ball.

Penalties are as follows:

1. A direct kick is awarded for all personal fouls and handled balls. A goal can be scored from a direct free kick. Examples of infringements are pushing, tripping, kicking a player, and holding.

2. A penalty kick is awarded if a defender in his penalty area commits direct free-kick infringements.

3. An indirect free kick is awarded for offsides, obstruction, dangerous play such as high kicking, a goalkeeper's taking more than four steps or repossessing the ball before another player has touched it, and playing the ball twice after a dead-ball situation. A second player must touch the ball before a goal can be scored. A referee signals if the kick is indirect by pointing one arm upward vertically.

✓ **TEACHING TIP**

Players should be encouraged to use the space on the field to the best advantage. When a team is in possession of the ball, players should attempt to find a position where they can pass either behind the player with the ball to give support, or toward the goal to be in a better position to shoot. When a team is forced into defense, the defenders should get "goalside" of attackers (between the attackers and their own goal) to prevent them from gaining an advantage.

From an early stage, players should be taught to give information to each other during the game, especially when they have possession of the ball. Valuable help can be given by shouting instructions such as "Man on," "You have time," or "Player behind," and also by calling for the ball when in position to receive a pass.

SOCCER SKILL TESTS

The tests for soccer skills cover various kinds of kicks, dribbling, and controlling. An excellent use of the skill tests is to set up self-testing stations. Signs will tell students how to test themselves. If desired, the teacher can formally test students at one of the stations. Students rotate from station to station after a designated amount of time.

Passing against a Wall

Players pass the ball from behind a line between five and ten yards away from a wall. The student should be encouraged to control the ball before kicking. The score consists of the number of passes made from behind the line in one or two minutes. This is an excellent test of general ball control and short passing skill.

Figure-Eight Dribbling

For a figure-eight dribbling test, three obstacles or markers are arranged in a line, 4 yards apart, with the first marker positioned 4 yards from the starting line. The finish line is 4 yards wide. A stopwatch is used, and the timing is done to the nearest tenth of a second.

Each player gets three trials, with the fastest trial taken as the score. On each trial, the player dribbles over the figure-eight course and finishes by kicking or dribbling the ball over the 4-yard finish line, at which time the watch is stopped. The test is best done on a grass surface, but if a hard surface must be used, the ball should be deflated somewhat so that it can be controlled.

Controlling

For the controlling test, the formation is a file plus one. A thrower stands 15 to 20 feet in front of the file and rolls or bounces the ball to the player at the head of the file. Three trials each are given for sole-of-the-foot control, foot control, and body control. The ball must be definitely stopped and controlled. A score of nine points, one for each successful control, is possible.

The thrower should adopt one type of throw for all controls and one type for all players. If the scorer judges that the roll was not a good opportunity, the trial is taken over. Five trials can be allowed.

Punting and Placekicking for Distance and Accuracy

To test punting for distance, a football field or any other field marked in gridiron fashion at 5- or 10-yard intervals is needed. One soccer ball is required, but when three are used, considerable time is saved. A measuring tape (25 or 50 feet) plus individual markers complete the supply list.

Each player is given three kicks from behind a restraining line. One child marks the kick for distance, while one or two others act as ball chasers. After three kicks, the player's marker is left at the spot of the longest kick. This is determined by marking the point at which the ball first touched the ground after the kick. Measurement is taken to the nearest foot.

Every student in the squad or small group should kick before the measurements are taken. The punt must be from a standing, not a running, start. If a child crosses the line during the kick, it counts as a trial and no measurement is taken.

Placekicking for distance is tested in the same way as punting for distance, with two exceptions. First, the ball is kicked from a stationary position and must be laid on a flat surface and not elevated by dirt, grass, or other means. Second, the child is given credit for the entire distance of the kick, including the roll. The kicking should be done on a grassy surface, because the ball will roll indefinitely on a smooth, hard surface. If the surface presents a problem, the test can be limited to the distance the ball has traveled in flight.

Penalty Kicking and Short Passing Accuracy

In the penalty-kicking test, the kicker faces a target area from a point 12 yards out, where the ball has been placed. The target area is formed by a rope stretched tight 6 feet above the ground. Four ropes, at distances 5 feet apart, are dropped from the stretched rope. This outlines three target areas 6 feet high and 5 feet wide. The center target area scores one point and the side areas score two points (Figure 27.30). (This reflects the principle that a penalty kick should be directed away from a goalkeeper and toward either corner of the goal.) Each child is allotted five kicks at the target. A score of ten points is possible.

The same target is used for kicking for accuracy, but the center area scores two points and the side areas score one point each. A chalk line is drawn about 20 feet from the target, and the child is back another 20 feet for the start. The player dribbles the ball forward and must kick the ball as it is moving and before it crosses the chalk line. Five trials are given, and a score of ten points is possible.

FOR MORE INFORMATION

References and Suggested Readings

Beswick, B. (2001). *Focused for soccer.* Champaign, IL: Human Kinetics.

Bungsbo, J., & Peitersen, B. (2000). *Soccer systems and strategies.* Champaign, IL: Human Kinetics.

Fellenbaum, J. E. (1993). Soccer. In N. Dougherty (Ed.), *Physical activity and sport for the secondary school student.* Reston, VA: NASPE and AAHPERD.

Fronske, H. (2005). *Teaching cues for sport skills.* 3rd ed. San Francisco: Benjamin Cummings.

Luxbacher, J. (1995). *Soccer practice games.* 2nd ed. Champaign, IL: Human Kinetics.

Luxbacher, J. (1996). *Teaching soccer: Steps to success.* Champaign, IL: Human Kinetics.

Luxbacher, J. (1999). *Soccer winning techniques.* 3rd ed. Champaign, IL: Human Kinetics.

Mood, D. P., Musker, F. F., & Rink, J. E. (2003). *Sports and recreational activities.* 13th ed. New York: McGraw-Hill.

National Soccer Coaches Association of America. T. Schum (Ed.). (1996). *Coaching soccer.* Indianapolis: Masters Press.

Negroesco, S. (1993). *Soccer.* Dubuque, IA: Brown & Benchmark.

Schmottlach, N., & McManama, J. (2002). *The physical education handbook.* 10th ed. San Francisco: Benjamin Cummings.

U.S. Soccer Federation. (1998). *FIFA laws of the game: A guide for referees.* Hitzigweg, Switzerland: FIFA.

Wein, H. (2000). *Developing youth soccer players.* Champaign, IL: Human Kinetics.

Wein, H. (2000). *105 practical soccer drills.* Orange, CA: Oceanprises Publications.

Websites

Soccer America Magazine
www.socceramerica.com

Soccer Coaching International
www.soccercoachinginternational.com

U.S. Soccer Federation
www.ussoccer.org

U.S. Youth Soccer Association
www.usyouthsoccer.org

Women's United Soccer Association
www.wusa.com

FIGURE 27.30 Penalty-kicking target area.

27

Softball

SUMMARY

Skills instruction for softball is introduced during the inter-mediate grades after youngsters have mastered basic prerequi-site skills. Teaching the rules and strategies for softball is an integral part of the instructional process. Using proper pro-gression is key to successful teaching of fundamental skills and lead-up games associated with softball. Lead-up games pro-vide an opportunity to emphasize development of selected softball skills in a setting that is compatible with the abilities of participants.

ESSENTIAL COMPONENTS OF QUALITY PROGRAMS

► I. Organized around content standards

► II. Student-centered and developmentally appropriate

► III. Physical activity and motor skill development form the core of the program

► IV. Teaches management skills and self-discipline

► V. Promotes inclusion of all students

► VI. Focuses on process over product

VII. Promotes lifetime personal health and wellness

► VIII. Teaches cooperation and responsibility and promotes sensitivity to diversity

NATIONAL STANDARDS FOR PHYSICAL EDUCATION*

► 1. Demonstrates competency in motor skills and movement patterns needed to perform a variety of physical activities.

► 2. Demonstrates understanding of movement concepts, principles, and tactics as they apply to the learning and performance of physical activities.

► 3. Participates regularly in physical activity.

4. Achieves and maintains a health-enhancing level of physical fitness.

► 5. Exhibits responsible personal and social behavior that respects self and others in physical activity.

► 6. Values physical activity for health, enjoyment, challenge, self-expression, and/or social interaction.

*National Association for Sport and Physical Education (NASPE), 2004.

OUTCOMES

■ Structure learning experiences efficiently using appropriate formations, progressions, and coaching techniques.

■ Develop a unit plan and lesson focus for softball.

■ Identify safety precautions associated with teaching softball.

■ Describe instructional procedures used for implementing a successful lead-up game.

■ Cite assessment procedures used for evaluating softball skills.

Youngsters enjoy softball, and a good program should make use of this drive. The emphases in softball should be on instruction and lead-up games. Chil-dren have adequate opportunity during recess, at the noon hour, and at other times to play the regulation game.

INSTRUCTIONAL EMPHASIS AND SEQUENCE

Table 28.1 shows the sequence of softball activities di-vided into two developmental levels. The activities are listed in progression. Youngsters can practice many of the skills of softball but may not be ready to participate in the activities in this chapter until the age of eight years.

TABLE 28.1	Suggested Softball Program		
Developmental Level II	**Developmental Level III**	**Developmental Level II**	**Developmental Level III**
Skills		*Pitching*	
Throwing		Simple underhand	Target pitching
Gripping the ball	Throw-in from outfield	Application of pitching rule	Slow pitches
Overhand throw		**Knowledge, Rules**	
Underhand toss		Strike zone	Pitching rule
Around the bases		Foul and fair ball	Position
Catching and Fielding		Safe and out	Illegal pitches
Catching thrown balls	Catching flies from fungo bat	Foul tip	Infield fly
Catching fly balls	Infield practice	Bunt rule	Keeping score
Grounders		When batter safe or out	Base running
Fielding grounders in infield			Situation quiz
Sure stop for outfield		**Activities**	
Batting		Throw-It-and-Run Softball	Five Hundred
Simple skills	Different positions at plate	Two-Pitch Softball	Batter Ball
Tee batting	Bunting	Hit and Run	Home Run
Fungo hitting		Kick Softball	Tee Ball
Fielding Positions		In a Pickle	Scrub (Work-Up)
Infield practice	Backing up other players	Beat Ball	Slow-Pitch Softball
How to catch	Double play	Steal a Base	Babe Ruth Ball
Base Running			Hurry Baseball (One-Pitch Softball)
To first base and turn	Fast start off base		Three-Team Softball
Circling the bases	Tagging up on fly ball	**Skill Tests**	
	Sacrifice	Throwing for distance	Pitching
		Throwing for accuracy	Circling the bases
			Fielding grounders

Developmental Levels I and II

The fundamental skills of batting, throwing, and catching are emphasized at these levels. Batting receives much attention, for softball is little fun unless children can hit. Proper form and technique in all three fundamental skills are parts of the instruction, with attention paid not only to the how but also to the why. Lead-up games provide an introduction to the basic rules of the game. As youngsters mature, specific skills for pitching, infield play, base running, and batting make up the instructional material.

Developmental Level III

Youngsters at this level develop the background to play the game of regulation softball. Tee Ball provides an

opportunity for developing all softball skills except pitching and catching. Home Run and the ever-popular Scrub (Work-Up) provide a variety of experiences, and Batter Ball stresses hitting skills. Experiences with batting, throwing, catching, and infield play are practiced. New pitching techniques, situation play, and double-play work are added. Slow-Pitch provides lots of action. Babe Ruth Ball emphasizes selective hitting.

SOFTBALL SKILLS

Children can find many ways to execute softball skills effectively by trial and error and through instruction. Do not attempt to mold every child into a prescribed form. Work toward making the most of each child's movement patterns.

FIGURE 28.1   Gripping the ball, two-finger grip.

FIGURE 28.2   Gripping the ball, full grip. (The little finger supports on the side.)

Gripping the Ball

The standard softball grip, which is difficult for elementary school children, calls for the thumb on one side, the index and middle fingers on top, and the other fingers supporting along the other side (Figure 28.1). Younger children with small hands will find it best to use a full-hand grip, in which the thumb and fingers are spaced rather evenly (Figure 28.2). Regardless of the grip used, the pads of the fingers should control the ball.

Throwing (Right-Handed)

Softball requires accurate throwing. Players must practice proper throwing technique if they are going to be able to perform well in softball. Of all the team sports, softball is probably the most difficult for youngsters because of the fine motor coordination required. The following instructional cues can be used to help students develop proper throwing technique:

1. Place the throwing-arm side of the body away from the target.
2. Step toward the target with the foot opposite the throwing hand.
3. Rotate the hips as the throwing arm moves forward.
4. Bend and raise the arm at the elbow. Lead with the elbow.
5. Shift the weight from the rear foot to the forward foot (nearest the target) prior to the forward motion of the arm.

OVERHAND THROW

In preparation for throwing, the child secures a firm grip on the ball, raises the throwing arm to shoulder height, and brings the elbow back. For the overhand throw, the hand with the ball is then brought back over the head so that it is well behind the shoulder at about shoulder height. The left side of the body is turned in the direction of the throw, and the left arm is raised in front of the body. The weight is on the back (right) foot, with the left foot advanced and the toe touching the ground. The arm comes forward with the elbow leading, and the ball is thrown with a downward snap of the wrist (Figure 28.3). The body weight is brought forward into the throw, shifting to the front foot. The child should follow through so that the palm of the throwing hand faces the ground at completion of the throw. The eyes should be on the target throughout, and the arm should be kept free and loose during the throw.

UNDERHAND THROW

For the underhand throw, the throwing hand and arm are brought back, with palm facing forward, in a pendulum swing. The elbow is bent slightly. The weight is mostly on the back foot. The arm comes forward, almost in a bowling motion, and the ball is tossed. The weight shifts to the front foot during the toss. The flight of the ball should remain low and arrive at about waist height.

Pitching

Official rules call for the pitcher to have both feet in contact with the pitcher's rubber, but few elementary schools

FIGURE 28.3   Throwing overhand.

FIGURE 28.5   Ready position for the infielder.

possess one. Instead, the pitcher can stand with both feet about even, facing the batter, and hold the ball momentarily in front with both hands. The pitcher takes one hand from the ball, extends the right arm forward, and brings it back in a pendulum swing, positioning the ball well behind the body. A normal stride taken with the left foot toward the batter begins the throwing sequence for a right-handed pitcher. The arm is brought forward with an underhanded slingshot motion, and the weight is transferred to the leading foot. Only one step is permitted. The follow-through motion is important (Figure 28.4).

The windmill is an alternate pitching motion in which the arm makes a full arc overhead, moving behind the body and then forward toward the batter. The arm goes into full extension on the downward swing in the back, gathering momentum as the forward motion begins. The pitch is otherwise the same as the normal motion. The windmill is generally a difficult style for youngsters to master. Instructional cues for pitching are as follows:

1. Face the plate.
2. Keep your eyes on the target.

FIGURE 28.4   Pitching.

3. Swing the pitching arm backward and step forward.
4. Keep the pitching arm extended.

Fielding

Infielders should assume the ready position—a semi-crouch, with legs spread shoulder width apart, knees bent slightly, and hands on or in front of the knees (Figure 28.5). As the ball is delivered, the weight is shifted to the balls of the feet. The outfielder's position is a slightly more erect semicrouch. Instructional cues for fielding are the following:

1. Move into line with the path of the ball.
2. Give when catching the ball.
3. Use the glove to absorb the force of the ball.
4. For grounders, keep the head down and watch the ball move into the glove.

FLY BALLS

There are two ways to catch a fly ball. For a low ball, the fielder keeps the fingers together and forms a basket with the hands (Figure 28.6, page 670). For a higher ball, the thumbs are together, and the ball is caught overhead (Figure 28.7, page 670). The fielder should give with the hands, and care must be taken with a spinning ball to squeeze the hands sufficiently to stop the spinning. The eye is on the ball continually until the ball hits the glove or hands. The knees are flexed slightly when receiving and aid in giving when the ball is caught.

GROUNDERS

To field a grounder, the fielder should move as quickly as possible into the path of the ball (Figure 28.8, page 670) and then move forward and play the ball on a good hop. The eyes must be kept on the ball, following it into the

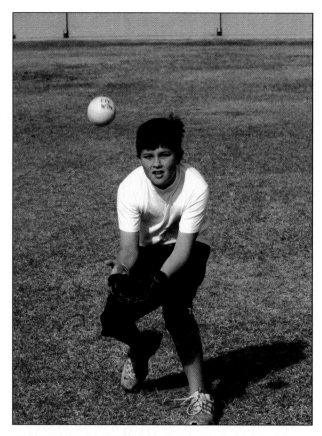

FIGURE 28.6 Catching a low fly ball.

FIGURE 28.7 Catching a high fly ball.

hands or glove. The feet are spread, the seat is kept down, and the hands are carried low and in front (Figure 28.9). The weight is on the balls of the feet or on the toes, and the knees are bent to lower the body. As the ball is caught, the fielder straightens up, takes a step in the direction of the throw, and makes the throw.

SURE STOP FOR OUTFIELD BALLS

To keep the ball from going through the hands and thus allowing extra bases, the outfielder can use the body as a barrier. The fielder turns halfway to the right and lowers one knee to the ground at the point toward which the ball is traveling (Figure 28.10). The hands catch the rolling ball, but if they miss it, the body will generally stop it.

FIRST-BASE POSITIONING

When a ball is hit to the infield, the first-base player moves to the base until the foot is touching it. The player then judges the path of the ball, stepping toward it with the left foot (if right-handed) and stretching forward. The right foot remains in contact with the base (Figure 28.11).

CATCHER'S POSITION

The catcher assumes a crouched position with the feet about shoulder width apart and the left foot slightly ahead of the right. The catcher should use a glove and wear a mask. A body protector is desirable. The catcher is positioned just beyond the range of the swing of the bat (Figure 28.12).

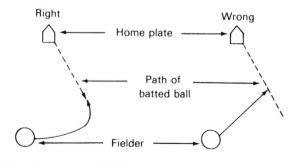

FIGURE 28.8 Fielding a grounder correctly.

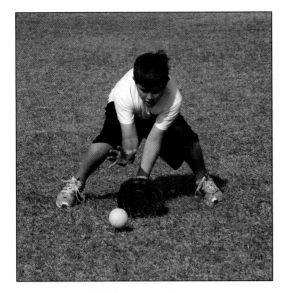

FIGURE 28.9   Fielding a grounder.

Batting (Right-Handed)

The batter stands with the left side of the body toward the pitcher. The feet are spread and the weight is on both feet. The body should be facing the plate. The bat is held with the trademark up, and the left hand grasps the bat

FIGURE 28.11   First-base player stretching for a catch.

lower than the right hand. The bat is held over the right shoulder, pointing both back and up. The elbows are away from the body (Figure 28.13). The swing begins with a hip roll and a short step forward in the direction of the pitcher. The bat is then swung level with the ground at the height of the pitch. The eyes are kept on the ball until it is hit.

The batter should avoid the following: lifting the front foot high off the ground, stepping back with the rear foot,

FIGURE 28.10   Sure stop.

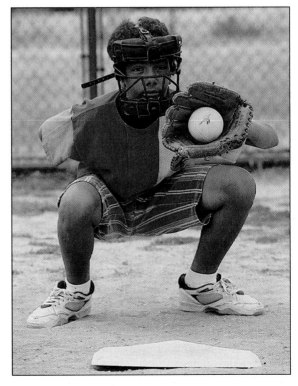

FIGURE 28.12   Catcher's position.

28

FIGURE 28.13   Batter's position.

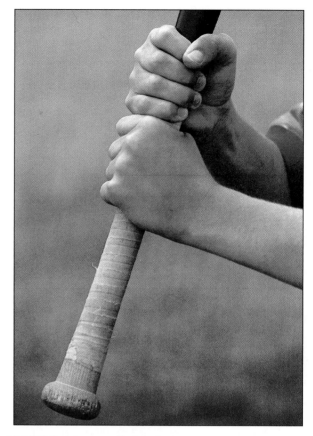

FIGURE 28.14   Choke grip.

dropping the rear shoulder, chopping down on the ball, golfing, dropping the elbows, and crouching or bending forward. Failure to keep the eyes on the ball is a serious error. Youngsters should get experience with the choke grip (Figure 28.14), the long grip (Figure 28.15), and the middle grip (Figure 28.16). Beginning batters can start with the choke grip. In all three, the grip should not be too tight. The following are instructional cues for batting:

1. Keep the hands together.
2. Swing the bat horizontally.
3. Swing through the ball.
4. Hold the bat off the shoulder.
5. Watch the ball hit the bat.

Bunting (Right-Handed)

To bunt, the batter turns to face the pitcher, the right foot alongside home plate. As the pitcher releases the ball, the batter's upper hand is run about halfway up the bat. The bunter holds the bat loosely in front of the body and parallel to the ground to meet the ball (Figure 28.17 on page 684). The ball can be directed down the first- or third-base line.

The surprise, or drag, bunt is done without squaring around to face the pitcher. The batter holds the bat in a choke grip. When the pitcher lets go of the ball, the batter runs the right hand up the bat and directs the ball down either foul line, keeping it as close as possible to the line in fair territory.

Base Running

A batter who hits the ball should run hard and purposefully toward first base, no matter what kind of hit it is. The runner should run past the bag, touching it in the process, and should step on the foul-line side of the base to avoid a collision with the first-base player.

Because a runner on base must hold the base position until the pitcher releases the ball, securing a fast start away from the base is essential. With either toe in contact with the base, the runner assumes a body lean, the weight on the ball of the leading foot and the eyes on the pitcher. After the pitch is made, the runner takes a few steps away from the base in the direction of the next base.

FIGURE 28.15 Long grip.

FIGURE 28.16 Middle grip.

Instructional Procedures

1. Safety is of the utmost importance. The following precautions should be observed:

    a. Throwing the bat is a constant danger. Members of the batting team should stand well back from the baseline, preferably behind a fence or in a dugout if available.

    b. The following are techniques that can teach the batter not to throw the bat:

    Have the batter touch the bat to the ground before dropping it.

    Call the batter out if the bat is thrown.

    Have the batter carry the bat to first base.

    Have the batter change ends of the bat before dropping it.

    Have the batter place the bat in a 3-foot circle before running.

    c. Sliding can lead to injury and destruction of clothing. With unskilled players, it is best not to permit sliding.

    d. A catcher who stands close behind the plate while catching must wear a mask. A body protector is also recommended.

    e. Colliding while running for a fly ball can be avoided by teaching players to call for the ball and to stay out of another player's area.

    f. When changing fields at the beginning of an inning, the batting team stays on the first-base side of the infield. The fielding team goes to bat via the third-base side of the infield.

    g. Soft softballs should be used, particularly in the early stages of development. Fleece balls are excellent for introductory fielding skills. Because many youngsters fear batted balls, using balls that will not hurt them is a necessity.

2. Batting skills must be stressed. There is no more ego-shattering experience for a youngster than to stand at the plate and demonstrate an ineptness that draws scorn and ridicule from peers. Make sure that youngsters know the correct stance and proper mechanics of batting. Improved hitting will come with practice.

3. The spoiler of many softball games is the pitcher-batter duel. If this becomes prolonged, the other players become justifiably bored while standing around. Having a member of the batting team pitch

28

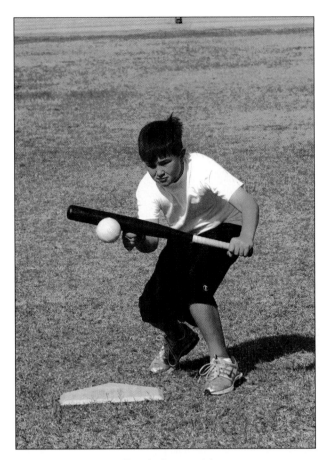

FIGURE 28.17   Regular bunt position.

or allowing two or three swings per batter are ways to eliminate the problem.

4. Players should rotate positions often. In physical education classes, everyone, including the pitcher, should rotate to another position at the start of each inning.

5. The distance between the bases greatly affects the game. The distance should be lessened or increased according to the game and the capacities of the players.

6. Umpires can be appointed, or the team at bat can umpire. A convenient rule to follow is that the person who made the last out of the previous inning will be the umpire for the next inning. Teach all students how to umpire.

7. Teachers should encourage players to recognize and give approval and support to those who are less skillful. Because there will be many differences in ability, the opportunity is present for lessons in tolerance. It is important not to let an error become a tragedy to a player.

8. Each player should run out a hit, no matter how hopeless it seems.

9. Teachers should analyze the purpose of lead-up games. The needed skills should be practiced before inclusion in a game.

10. Players must learn respect for officials and acceptance of the umpire's judgment. The disreputable practice of baiting the umpire should not be a part of children's softball experiences.

ORGANIZING FOR INSTRUCTION

It is essential that students develop skills in softball and acquire knowledge about the various phases of the game. The amount of field space and the equipment available determine the instructional organization. To cover the various phases of the game, a multiple-activity or station pattern is effective. The following guidelines offer suggestions for instruction:

1. Children must be given many opportunities to practice different skills. Even with rotation, there should be as many small groups as possible. For example, two children can practice throwing and fielding grounders.

2. Ability differences need to be addressed. Because some players have practiced more, they often have skill levels higher than those of others in the class. Skillful youngsters can be used in various phases of instruction, provided that sufficient direction for these efforts is given.

3. Activities and procedures to be stressed at each station should be carefully planned and communicated to all participants. Prior meetings with captains and other helpers are valuable. Appropriate softball rules should be covered.

4. Complete rotation of stations is not necessary at each class session. During a class session, teams may practice at one station for part of the time and then use the remainder of the time to participate in an appropriate lead-up game.

5. Directions must be listed at each station so that students can make the most of the skill development opportunities. Place signs that offer instructional strategies on cones at each station.

6. The use of the rotational station system does not rule out activities involving the class as a whole. Mimetic drills (i.e., drills without equipment) are valuable for establishing fundamental movement patterns for most skills. Have students practice such techniques as batting, pitching, throwing, and fielding without worrying about results.

7. Station teaching provides an excellent opportunity for older students to provide assistance. In some

school systems, high school students visit elementary schools on a regular basis for observation and educational experiences.

8. Moving from one station to another provides encouragement, correction, coaching, and motivation for learning.

9. A motivational factor can be introduced through comparisons of the rotational system with varsity or major league practices. This gives the activity an adult flavor.

10. Selection can be made from the list of lead-up games, particularly for activities that are suitable for squads or smaller groups.

BASIC SOFTBALL RULES

Most sporting goods establishments have copies of the official rules for softball. Although an official rule guide should be used by students when they are studying rules, a general idea of the basic rules of the game can be obtained from the following discussion.

The official diamond has 60-foot baselines and a pitching distance of 46 feet. In elementary school it is recommended that youngsters use a diamond with baselines no longer than 45 feet and a pitching distance of 35 feet or less. The nine players on a softball team are the catcher; the pitcher; first-, second-, and third-base players; the shortstop; and left, center, and right fielders. The right fielder is the outfielder nearest first base.

Batting Order

Players may bat in any order, although having them bat according to their positions in the field is at times convenient in class. Once the batting order has been established, it may not be changed, even if the player changes to another position in the field.

Pitching

The pitcher must face the batter with both feet on the pitching rubber and with the ball held in front with both hands. The pitcher is allowed one step toward the batter and must deliver the ball while taking that step. The ball must be pitched underhanded. The pitcher cannot fake a pitch or make any motion toward the plate without delivering the ball. It is illegal to roll or bounce the ball to the batter. No quick return is allowed before the batter is ready. To be called a *strike,* a pitch must be over the plate and between the knees and shoulders of the batter. A *ball* is a pitch that does not go through this area.

Batting

The bat must be a softball bat. The batter cannot cross to the other side of the plate when the pitcher is ready to pitch. If a player bats out of turn, she is out. A bunt that goes foul on the third strike is an out. A pitched ball that touches or hits the batter entitles the batter to first base, provided she does not strike or bunt at the ball.

Striking Out

A batter who misses the ball on the third strike is out. This is called striking out.

Batter Safe

A batter who reaches first base before the fielding team can field the ball and throw it to first is safe.

Fair Ball

A fair ball is any batted ball that settles on fair territory between home and first base and home and third base. A ball that rolls over a base or through the field into fair territory is a fair ball. Fly balls (including line drives) that drop into fair territory beyond the infield are fair balls. Foul lines are in fair territory.

Foul Ball

A foul ball is a batted ball that settles outside the foul lines between home and first or between home and third. A fly ball that drops into foul territory beyond the bases is a foul.

Fly Ball

Any fly ball (foul or fair), if caught, is an out. A foul fly, however, must rise over the head of the batter or it is ruled a foul tip. A foul tip caught on the third strike, then, puts the batter out.

Base Running

In base running, no leadoff is permitted. On penalty of being called out, the runner must stay on base until the ball leaves the pitcher's hand. On an overthrow when the ball goes into foul territory and out of play, runners advance one base beyond the base to which they were headed at the time of the overthrow. On an overthrow at second base by the catcher with the ball rolling into center field, the runners may advance as far as they can. The runner may try to avoid being tagged on a baseline but is limited to a three-foot distance on each side of a direct line from base to base. A runner hit by a batted ball while off the base is out. The batter, however, is entitled to first base. Base runners must touch all bases. If a runner fails to touch a base, it is an *appeal play,* which means that the fielding team must call the oversight to the attention of the umpire before she will rule on the play.

Runners may overrun first base without penalty. On all other bases, however, the runner must maintain contact with the base or will be tagged out. To score, the runner must make contact with home plate.

Scoring

A run is scored when the base runner makes the circuit of the bases (i.e., first, second, third, and home) before the batting team has three outs. If the third out is a force out, no run is scored, even if the runner crossed home plate before the out was actually made.

The situation needing the most clarification occurs when a runner is on base with one out and the batter hits a fly ball that is caught, making the second out. The runner is forced to return to the base previously occupied before the ball reaches that base, or she, too, is out. If she makes the third out as a result of her failure to return to the base in time, no run is scored.

SOFTBALL DRILLS

Softball drills lend themselves to a station setup. For a regular class of 30 students, four squads with 7 or 8 students each are suggested. Activities at each station can emphasize a single skill or a combination of skills. Situational drills can also be incorporated. Children should realize that constant repetition is necessary to develop, maintain, and sharpen softball skills.

The multitude of softball skills to be practiced allows for many different combinations and organizations. The following are examples of combinations and organizations that can be used in station teaching:

1. Batting can be organized in many ways. One key to an effective program is to ensure that each child has many opportunities to hit the ball successfully. Sufficient area is needed.

    a. Have the students use a batting tee. For each station, two tees are needed, with a bat and at least two balls for each tee. Three to five children are assigned to each tee. There should be a batter, a catcher to handle incoming balls, and fielders. When only three children are in a unit, the catcher should be eliminated. Each batter is allowed a certain number of swings before rotating to the field. The catcher becomes the next batter, and a fielder moves up to catcher.

    b. Organize informal hitting practice. A batter, a pitcher, and fielders are needed. Two batting groups should be organized at each station. A catcher is optional.

    c. Have the students practice hitting a foam-rubber ball thrown underhand. The larger ball is easier to hit.

    d. Have the students practice bunting with groups of three: a pitcher, a batter, and a fielder.

2. Throwing and catching can be practiced with the following drills:

    a. Throwing back and forth, practicing various throws.

    b. Throwing ground balls back and forth for fielding practice.

    c. A player acting as a first-base player, throwing grounders to the other infielders and receiving the put-out throw.

    d. Throwing flies back and forth.

    e. Hitting flies, with two or three fielders catching.

    f. Establishing four bases and throwing from base to base.

3. Proper pitching and catching form should be used for pitching practice.

    a. Pitch to another player over a plate.

    b. Call balls and strikes. One player is the pitcher, the second is the catcher, and the third is the umpire. A fourth player can be a stationary batter to provide a more realistic pitching target.

    c. Pitch toward pitching targets—either a wooden target (see page 694) or a similar area outlined on a wall.

4. For infield drills, children should be placed in the normal infield positions: behind the plate; at first, second, and third base; and at shortstop. One child acts as the batter and gives directions. The play should begin with practice in throwing around the bases in either direction. After this, the batter can roll the ball to the different infielders, beginning at third base and continuing in turn around the infield, with each player throwing to first to retire an imaginary runner. Various playing situations can be developed. A batter who is skillful enough can hit the ball instead of rolling it to infielders, thus making the drill more realistic. Using a second softball saves time when the ball is thrown or batted past an infielder, because players will not have to wait for the ball to be retrieved before proceeding with the next play. After the ball has been thrown to first base, other throws around the infield can take place. The drill can also be done with only a partial infield.

5. Various situations can be arranged for practicing base running.

   a. Bunt and run to first base. A pitcher, a batter, an infielder, and a first-base player are needed. The pitcher serves the ball up for a bunt, and the batter, after bunting, takes off for first base. A fielding play can be made on the runner.

   b. Bunt and run to second base. The batter bunts the ball and runs to first base and then on to second, making a proper turn at first.

6. Play Pepper. (This is one of the older skill games in baseball.) A line of three or four players is about 10 yards in front of and facing a batter. The players toss the ball to the batter, who attempts to hit controlled grounders back to them (Figure 28.18). The batter stays at bat for a period of time and then rotates to the field.

7. Some of the game-type activities, such as Batter Ball, In a Pickle, Five Hundred, and Scrub, can be scheduled at stations. Stations might be organized as follows. (Numbers and letters refer to the drills just listed. The page number refers to an activity not yet discussed.)

   Station 1: Batting (see 1a)

   Station 2: Throwing and fielding grounders (see 2c)

   Station 3: Base running—In a Pickle (see page 689)

   Station 4: Bunting and base running (see 5a)

   Another example of station arrangement is the following:

   Station 1: Batting and fielding—Pepper (see 6)

   Station 2: Pitching and umpiring (see 3b)

   Station 3: Infield practice (see 4)

   Station 4: Batting (see 1b)

   Stations might also be arranged as follows:

   Station 1: Fly ball hitting, fielding, and throwing (see 2e)

   Station 2: Bunting and fielding (see 1d)

   Station 3: Pitching to targets (see 3c)

   Station 4: Batting (see 1a and 1b)

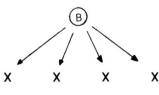

FIGURE 28.18 Play Pepper.

SOFTBALL ACTIVITIES

Developmental Level II

▶ **THROW-IT-AND-RUN SOFTBALL**

Playing Area: Softball diamond reduced in size

Players: 7 to 11 (usually 9) students on each team

Supplies: A softball or similar ball

Skills: Throwing, catching, fielding, base running

Throw-It-and-Run Softball is played like regular softball with the following exception: With one team in the field at regular positions, the pitcher throws the ball to the batter, who, instead of batting the ball, catches it and immediately throws it into the field. The ball is then treated as a batted ball, and regular softball rules prevail. No stealing is permitted, however, and runners must hold their bases until the batter throws the ball. A foul ball is an out.

Variations:

1. *Under-Leg Throw.* Instead of throwing directly, the batter can turn to the right, lift the left leg, and throw the ball under the leg into the playing field.

2. *Beat-Ball Throw.* The fielders, instead of playing by regular softball rules, throw the ball directly home to the catcher. The batter, in the meantime, runs around the bases. A point is scored for each base the batter touches before the catcher receives the ball. A ball caught on the fly means no score. Similarly, a foul ball does not score points but counts as a turn at bat.

▶ **TWO-PITCH SOFTBALL**

Playing Area: Softball diamond

Players: 7 to 11 students on each team

Supplies: A softball and a bat

Skills: Most softball skills, except regular pitching

Two-Pitch Softball is played like regular softball with the following changes:

1. A member of the team at bat pitches. A system of rotation should be set up so that every child takes a turn as pitcher.

2. The batter has only two pitches in which to hit the ball, and must hit a fair ball on one of these pitches or is out. The batter can foul the first ball, but if the second is fouled, the batter is out. There is no need to call balls or strikes.

3. The pitcher does not field the ball. A member of the team in the field acts as the fielding pitcher.

4. If the batter hits the ball, regular softball rules are followed. No stealing is permitted, however.

28

Since the pitcher is responsible for pitching a ball that can be hit, the pitching distance can be shortened to give the batter ample opportunity to hit the ball. The instructor can act as the pitcher.

Variation: *Three Strikes:* In this game, the batter is allowed three pitches (strikes) to hit the ball. Otherwise, the game proceeds as in Two-Pitch Softball.

▶ HIT AND RUN

Playing Area: Softball field or gymnasium

Players: 6 to 15 students on each team

Supplies: A volleyball, soccer ball, or playground ball; home plate; and base markers

Skills: Catching, throwing, running, dodging

One team is at bat, and the other is scattered in the field. Boundaries must be established, but the area does not have to be shaped like a baseball diamond. The batter stands at home plate with the ball. In front of the batter, 12 feet away, is a short line over which the ball must be hit to be in play. In the center of the field, about 40 feet away, is the base marker.

The batter bats the ball with the hands or fists so that it crosses the short line and lands inside the area, and then attempts to run down the field, around the base marker, and back to home plate without being hit by the ball (Figure 28.19). The members of the other team field the ball and try to tag the runner. The fielders may not run or walk with the ball but may throw to teammates who are closer to the runner.

A run is scored each time a batter runs around the marker and back to home plate without getting tagged

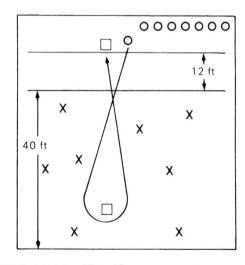

FIGURE 28.19 Hit and Run.

by the ball. A run is also scored if a foul is called on the fielding team for walking or running with the ball.

The batter is out in any of the following circumstances:

1. A fly ball is caught.
2. The ball is not hit beyond the short line.
3. The team touches home plate with the ball before the runner returns. (This out is used only when the runner stops in the field and does not continue.)

The game can be played in innings of three outs each, or a change of team positions can be made after all members of one team have batted.

The distance the batter runs around the base marker may have to be shortened or lengthened, depending on players' abilities.

Variation: *Five Passes:* The batter is out when a fly ball is caught or when the ball is passed among five different players of the team in the field, with the last pass to a player at home plate beating the runner to the plate. The passes must not touch the ground.

▶ KICK SOFTBALL

Playing Area: Regular softball field with a home base 3 feet square

Players: 7 to 11 students on each team

Supplies: A soccer ball or another ball to be kicked

Skills: Kicking a rolling ball, throwing, catching, running bases

The batter stands in the kicking area, a 3-foot-square home plate. The batter kicks the ball rolled on the ground by the pitcher. The ball should be rolled at moderate speed. An umpire calls balls and strikes. A strike is a ball that rolls over the 3-foot square. A ball rolls outside this area. Strikeouts and walks are called just as in regular softball. The number of foul balls allowed should be limited. No base stealing is permitted. Otherwise, the game is played like softball.

Variations:

1. The batter kicks a stationary ball. This saves time, as there is no pitching.
2. *Punch Ball.* The batter can hit a volleyball as in a volleyball serve or punch a ball pitched by the pitcher.

▶ IN A PICKLE

Playing Area: Any flat surface with 60 square feet of room

Players: Three or more students

Supplies: A softball and two bases 45 to 55 feet apart

Skills: Throwing, catching, running down a base runner, tagging

A base runner who gets caught between two bases and is in danger of being run down and tagged is "in a pickle." To begin, both fielders are on bases, and one has a ball. The runner is positioned in the base path 10 to 15 feet away from the fielder who has the ball. The two fielders throw the ball back and forth in an attempt to run down and tag the runner between the bases. A runner who escapes and secures a base gets to try again. Otherwise, a system of rotation is established, including any sideline (waiting) players. No sliding is permitted.

▶ BEAT BALL

Playing Area: Softball diamond, bases approximately 30 feet apart

Players: Two teams of 5 to 12 students each

Supplies: Soft softball, bat, and batting tee (optional)

Skills: All softball skills

One team is at bat, and the other team is in the field. The object of the game is to hit the ball and run around the bases before the fielding team can catch the ball, throw it to first base, and then throw it to the catcher at home plate. If the ball beats the hitter home or a fly ball is caught, it is an out. If the hitter beats the ball to home plate, a run is scored. All players on a team bat once before switching positions with the fielding team. The ball must be hit into fair territory before the hitter can run. Only three pitches are allowed per hitter.

✓ TEACHING TIPS

1. Depending on the maturity of the players, a batting tee may be used. The hitter can be allowed the option of using the batting tee or hitting a pitched ball.

2. The pitcher can be selected from the batting team. This ensures that an attempt will be made to make pitches that can be hit.

3. Vary the distance so that hitters have a fair opportunity to score. If hitters score too easily, another base can be added.

▶ STEAL A BASE

Playing Area: Any 40-by-20-foot flat area, or larger with more skilled students

Players: Six to ten students

Supplies: Hoops, softball, and gloves (optional)

Skills: Throwing, catching, tagging, running

The hoops are spaced approximately 20 feet apart in a rectangular fashion. Hoops are used as bases to prevent collisions. One player, serving as a fielder, is stationed by each hoop to begin the game. All other players are on a base; more than one runner is permitted on a base. On signal, runners begin accumulating runs by running to another base without being tagged. Fielders attempt to work together to tag as many runners as possible. Fielders may leave their base and chase runners if necessary. If a fielder leaves his base, other fielders may rotate to the vacant bag. Fielders and runners change positions every 2 to 3 minutes.

Variation: Runners may not move to an adjacent base.

Developmental Level III

▶ FIVE HUNDRED

Playing Area: Field big enough for fungo hitting

Players: 3 to 12 (or more) students

Supplies: A softball and a bat

Skills: Fungo batting, catching flies, fielding grounders

There are many versions of the old game Five Hundred. A batter stands on one side of the field and bats the ball to a number of fielders, who are scattered. The fielders attempt to become the batter by reaching a score of 500. Fielders earn 200 points for catching a ball on the fly, 100 points for catching a ball on the first bounce, and 50 points for fielding a grounder cleanly. Whenever a change of batters is made, all fielders lose their points and must start over.

✓ TEACHING TIP

The ball can be hit off a batting tee if fungo hitting is too difficult.

Variations:

1. The fielder's points must total exactly 500.

2. Points are subtracted from the fielder's score if a ball is mishandled. If a fly ball is dropped, for example, 200 points are lost.

28

▶ **BATTER BALL**

Playing Area: Softball diamond

Players: 8 to 12 students on each team

Supplies: A softball, a bat, and a mask

Skills: Slow-pitching, hitting, fielding, catching flies

Batter Ball involves batting and fielding but no base running. It is much like batting practice but adds the element of competition. A line is drawn directly from first to third base. This is the balk line over which a batted ball must travel to be fielded. Another line is drawn from a point on the foul line 3 feet behind third base to a point 5 feet behind second base and in line with home plate. Another line connects this point with a point on the other baseline 3 feet behind first base. The shaded area in the diagram is the infield (Figure 28.20).

Each batter is given three pitches by a member of his own team to hit the ball into fair territory across the balk line. The pitcher may stop any ground ball before it crosses the balk line. The batter then gets another turn at bat.

Scoring is as follows:

1. A successful grounder scores one point. A grounder is successful when an infielder fails to handle it cleanly within the infield area. Only one player may field the ball. If the ball is fielded properly, the batter is out.

2. A line drive in the infield area is worth one point if not caught. It can be handled for an out on any bounce. Any line drive caught on the fly is also an out.

3. A fly ball in the infield area scores one point if not caught. For an out, the ball must be caught legally by the first person touching it.

4. A two-bagger scores two points. Any fly ball, line drive or not, that lands fairly in the outfield area without being caught scores two points. If it is caught, the batter is out.

5. A home run scores three points. Any fly ball driven over the head of the farthest outfielder in that area scores a home run.

Three outs can constitute an inning, or all batters can be allowed one turn at bat and then the team changes to the field. A new set of infielders should be in place for each inning. The old set goes to the outfield. Pitchers should be limited to one inning. They also take a turn at bat.

✓ **TEACHING TIP**

Many games of this type require special fields, either rectangular or narrowly angled. This game was selected because it uses a regular softball field with the added lines, which can be drawn with a stick or can be marked using regular marking methods.

The pitcher has to decide whether to stop the ball. If the ball goes beyond the restraining line, it is in play even if the pitcher touched it.

Variation: Batter Ball can be modified for use as a station in rotational teaching, with the emphasis on individual batting and squad organization. One member of the squad would be at bat and would get a definite number of chances (e.g., five) to score. She keeps her own point total. The other squad members occupy the necessary game positions.

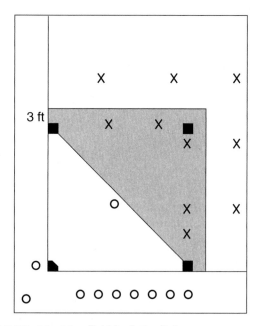

3 ft

FIGURE 28.20 Field for Batter Ball.

▶ **HOME RUN**

Playing Area: Softball diamond (only first base is used)

Players: Four to ten students

Supplies: A softball and a bat

Skills: Most softball skills, modified base running

The crucial players are a batter, a catcher, a pitcher, and one fielder. Any other players are fielders; some can take positions in the infield. The batter hits a regular pitch and on a fair ball must run to first base and back home before the ball can be returned to the catcher.

The batter is out whenever any of the following occurs:

1. A fly ball (fair or foul) is caught.
2. The batter strikes out.
3. On a fair ball, the ball beats the batter back to home plate.

✓ **TEACHING TIPS**

To keep skillful players from staying too long at bat, a rule can be made that, after a certain number of home runs, the batter automatically must take a place in the field. A rotation (work-up) system should be established. The batter should go to right field, move to center, and then go to left field. The rotation continues through third base, shortstop, second base, first base, pitcher, and catcher. The catcher is the next batter. Naturally, the number of positions depends on the number of players in the game. If there are enough players, an additional batter can be waiting to take a turn.

The game can be played with only three youngsters, eliminating the catcher. With only one fielder, the pitcher covers home plate. The first-base distance should be far enough away to be a challenge but close enough so that a well-hit ball scores a home run. The distance depends on the number playing and the capacities of players.

Variations:

1. This game can be played like softball—allowing the batter to stop at first base if another batter is up.
2. A fly ball caught by a fielder puts that player directly to bat. The batter then takes a place at the end of the rotation, and the other players rotate up to the position of the fielder who caught the ball. This rule has one drawback in that it may cause children to scramble and fight for fly balls, which is not desirable in softball. The ball belongs to the player in whose territory it falls.
3. *Triangle Ball.* First and third bases are brought in toward each other, thus narrowing the playing field. Second base is not used. The game gets its name from the triangle formed by home plate and the two bases. The batter must circle first and third bases and return home before the ball reaches home plate. This game can also be played with as few as three players, with the pitcher covering home plate.

▶ **TEE BALL**

Playing Area: Softball field
Players: 7 to 11 students on each team
Supplies: A softball, a bat, and a batting tee
Skills: Most softball skills (except pitching and stealing bases), hitting a ball from a tee

Tee Ball has many advantages. There are no strikeouts, every child hits the ball, there is no dueling between pitcher and batter, and fielding opportunities abound.

This game is played under softball rules with the following exceptions:

1. Instead of hitting a pitched ball, the batter hits the ball from a tee. The catcher places the ball on the tee. After the batter hits the ball, the play is the same as in regular softball. With no pitching, there is no stealing. A runner stays on the base until the ball is hit by the batter.
2. A fielder occupies the position normally held by the pitcher. The primary duties of this fielder are to field bunts and ground balls and to back up the infielders on throws.

Teams can play regular innings for three outs or switch to the field after each player on the batting team has had a turn at bat.

✓ **TEACHING TIP**

A tee can be purchased or made from a radiator hose. An improvised batting tee is shown in Figure 28.21 (page 692). (For another type of tee, see page 203.) If the tee is not adjustable, three different sizes should be available. The batter should take a position far enough behind the tee so that, in stepping forward to swing, the ball will be slightly in front of the midpoint of the swing.

▶ **SCRUB (WORK-UP)**

Playing Area: Softball field
Players: 7 to 15 students
Supplies: A softball and a bat
Skills: Most softball skills

The predominant feature of Scrub is the rotation of the players. The game is played with regular softball rules, with individuals more or less playing for themselves. There are at least two batters, generally three. A catcher, a pitcher, and a first-base player are essential. The remaining players assume the other positions. A batter who is out goes to a position in right field. All other players move up one position, with the catcher becoming the batter. The first-base player becomes the pitcher, the pitcher moves to catcher, and all others move up one place.

✓ **TEACHING TIP**

If a fly ball is caught, the fielder and batter exchange positions.

28

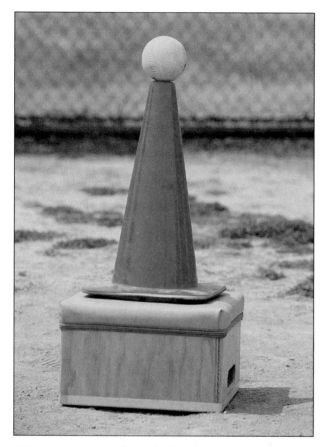

FIGURE 28.21   Improvised batting tee.

SLOW-PITCH SOFTBALL

Playing Area: Softball diamond

Players: Ten students on each team

Supplies: A softball and a bat

Skills: Most softball skills

The major difference between regular softball and Slow-Pitch Softball is in the pitching, but there are other modifications to the game as well. With slower pitching, there is more hitting and thus more action on the bases and in the field. Outfielders are an important part of the game, because many long drives are hit. Rule changes from the game of official softball are as follows:

1. The pitch must be a slow-pitch. Any other pitch is illegal and is called a ball. The pitch must be slow, with an arc of one foot. It must not rise over 10 feet from the ground, however. Its legality depends on the umpire's call.

2. There are ten players instead of nine. The extra one, called the roving fielder, plays in the outfield and handles line drives hit just over the infielders.

3. The batter must take a full swing at the ball and is out if he chops at the ball or bunts.

4. If the batter is hit by a pitched ball, she is not entitled to first base. The pitch is merely called a ball. Otherwise, balls and strikes are called as in softball.

5. The runner must stay at his base until the pitch has reached or passed home plate. No stealing is permitted.

✓ **TEACHING TIP**

Shortening the pitching distance somewhat may be desirable. Much of the success of the game depends on the pitcher's ability to get the ball over the plate.

▶ **BABE RUTH BALL**

Playing Area: Softball diamond

Players: Five students

Supplies: A bat, a ball, and four cones or other markers

Skills: Batting, pitching, fielding

The three outfield zones—left, center, and right field—are separated by four cones. It is helpful if foul lines have been drawn, but cones can define them (Figure 28.22). The batter calls the field to which he intends to hit. The pitcher throws controlled pitches so that the batter can hit easily. The batter remains in position as long as he hits to the designated field. Field choices must be rotated. The batter gets only one swing to make a successful hit. He may allow a ball to go by, but if he swings, it counts as a try. There is no base running. Players rotate.

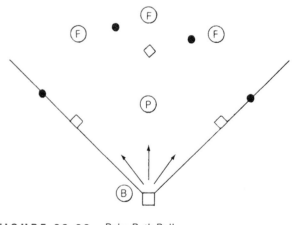

FIGURE 28.22   Babe Ruth Ball.

Children play this game informally on sandlots with a variety of rules. Some possibilities to consider are these: What happens when a fly ball is caught? What limitations should be made on hitting easy grounders? Let the players discuss these points and others not covered by the stated rules.

▶ **HURRY BASEBALL (ONE-PITCH SOFTBALL)**

Playing Area: Softball diamond

Players: 8 to 12 students on each team

Supplies: A softball and a bat

Skills: Slow-pitching, most softball skills except stealing bases and bunting

Hurry Baseball demands rapid changes from batting to fielding, and vice versa. The game is like regular softball, with the following exceptions:

1. The pitcher is from the team at bat and must not interfere with, or touch, a batted ball on penalty of the batter's being called out.

2. The team coming to bat does not wait for the fielding team to get set. Because it has its own pitcher, the pitcher gets the ball to the batter just as quickly as the batter can grab a bat and get ready. The fielding team has to hustle to get out to their places.

3. Only one pitch is allowed to a batter. The batter must hit a fair ball or she is out. The pitch is made from about two-thirds of the normal pitching distance.

4. No stealing is permitted.

5. No bunting is permitted.

The batter must take a full swing. The game provides much activity in the fast place changes that must be made after the third out. Teams in the field learn to make the next hitter a catcher, so that she can bat immediately when the third out is made. Batters must bat in order. Scoring follows regular softball rules.

▶ **THREE-TEAM SOFTBALL**

Playing Area: Softball diamond

Players: 12 to 15 students

Supplies: A mask, a ball, and a bat

Skills: All softball skills

Three-Team Softball works well with 12 players, a number considered too few to divide into two effective fielding teams. The players are instead divided into three teams. The rules of softball apply, with the following exceptions:

1. One team is at bat, one team covers the infield (including the catcher), and the third team consists of the outfielders and the pitcher.

2. The team at bat must bat in a definite order. This means that because of the small number of batters on each side, instances can occur when the person due to bat is on base. To take a turn at bat, the runner must be replaced by a player not on base.

3. After three outs, the teams rotate, with the outfield moving to the infield, the infield taking a turn at bat, and the batters going to the outfield.

4. An inning is over when all three teams have batted.

5. The pitcher should be limited to one inning only. A player may repeat as pitcher only after all members of that team have had a chance to pitch.

SOFTBALL SKILL TESTS

Throwing for Accuracy

To test accuracy in throwing, a target with three concentric circles of 54, 36, and 18 inches is drawn on a wall. Scoring is one, two, and three points, respectively, for the circles. Five trials are allowed, for a possible score of 15. Balls hitting a line score the higher number.

Instead of the suggested target, a tire can be hung. Scoring allows two points for a throw through the tire and one point for simply hitting the tire. A maximum of ten points is possible with this system.

Throwing for Distance

In the test of throwing for distance, each child is allowed three throws, and the longest throw on the fly is recorded.

Fielding Grounders

A file of players is stationed behind a restraining line. A thrower is about 30 feet in front of this line. Each player in turn attempts to field five ground balls. The score is the number of balls fielded cleanly. Inconsistencies will occur in the throw and bounce of the ground balls served up for fielding. Therefore, if the opportunity was obviously not a fair one, the child should get another chance.

Circling the Bases

Runners are timed as they circle the bases. A diamond with four bases and a stopwatch for timing are needed. Two runners can run at one time by starting from opposite corners of the diamond. Two stopwatches are needed with this system. The batter can bunt a pitched ball and run around the bases. The timing starts with the bunt and finishes when the batter touches home plate.

Pitching

Pitching is one of the easier skills to test in softball and is certainly one of the most popular with children. Two basic methods are used for testing. In the first, each child makes a certain number of pitches at a target. Scoring is on the basis of the number of strikes that are thrown. In the second, each child pitches regularly, as if to a batter, with balls and strikes being counted. Batters are either struck out or walked. The score is the number of batters the child is able to strike out from a given number at bat. This score is expressed as a percentage.

In either method, a target is needed. It should be 19 inches wide and 42 inches high. It can be outlined temporarily on a wall with chalk or paint. The lower portion of the target should be about 18 inches above the ground or floor. If the target is constructed from plywood or wood, some means of support or of hanging the target will be needed. The boundaries of the target should be counted as strikes. The pitching distance should be normal (35 feet), and regular pitching rules should be observed.

Old Woody is the name of a pitching target in the form of a stand that can be moved from school to school. The target size is shown in Figure 28.23. A sturdy frame holds the target and allows it to be used in almost any spot.

FIGURE 28.23   Old Woody pitching target.

FOR MORE INFORMATION

References and Suggested Readings

Amateur Softball Association of America. (2005). *Official rules of softball.* Oklahoma City, OK: ASA.

American Sport Education Program. (1996). *Coaching youth softball.* Champaign, IL: Human Kinetics.

Fronske, H. (2005). *Teaching cues for sport skills.* 3rd ed. San Francisco: Benjamin Cummings.

Garman, J. (2001). *Softball skills and drills.* Champaign, IL: Human Kinetics.

Kneer, M., & McCord, C. (1995). *Softball: Slow and fast pitch.* 6th ed. Dubuque, IA: Brown & Benchmark.

Mood, D. P., Musker, F. F., & Rink, J. E. (2003). *Sports and recreational activities.* 13th ed. New York: McGraw-Hill.

Potter, D. L., & Brockmeyer, G. (1999). *Softball: Steps to success.* Champaign, IL: Human Kinetics.

Schmottlach, N., and McManama, J. (2002). *The physical education handbook.* 10th ed. San Francisco: Benjamin Cummings.

U.S. Olympic Committee Sport Series. (2001). *A basic guide to softball.* Torrance, CA: Griffen Publishing Group.

Websites

Amateur Softball Association
www.softball.org

Softball Manitoba
www.softball.mb.ca

Softball Skills by Howard Kabota
www.softballskills.com

USA Softball
www.usasoftball.org

Track, Field, and Cross-Country Running

ESSENTIAL COMPONENTS OF QUALITY PROGRAMS

▶ **I. Organized around content standards**

▶ **II. Student-centered and developmentally appropriate**

▶ **III. Physical activity and motor skill development form the core of the program**

▶ **IV. Teaches management skills and self-discipline**

▶ **V. Promotes inclusion of all students**

▶ **VI. Focuses on process over product**

▶ **VII. Promotes lifetime personal health and wellness**

▶ **VIII. Teaches cooperation and responsibility and promotes sensitivity to diversity**

NATIONAL STANDARDS FOR PHYSICAL EDUCATION*

▶ **1. Demonstrates competency in motor skills and movement patterns needed to perform a variety of physical activities.**

▶ **2. Demonstrates understanding of movement concepts, principles, and tactics as they apply to the learning and performance of physical activities.**

▶ **3. Participates regularly in physical activity.**

4. Achieves and maintains a health-enhancing level of physical fitness.

▶ **5. Exhibits responsible personal and social behavior that respects self and others in physical activity.**

▶ **6. Values physical activity for health, enjoyment, challenge, self-expression, and/or social interaction.**

*National Association for Sport and Physical Education (NASPE), 2004.

SUMMARY

Skills instruction for track, field, and cross-country running is introduced during the intermediate grades after youngsters have mastered basic prerequisite skills. Teaching the rules and strategies for track, field, and cross-country running is an integral part of the instructional process. Using proper progression is key to successful teaching of fundamental skills and lead-up games associated with track, field, and cross-country running. Lead-up games provide an opportunity to emphasize development of selected track, field, and cross-country running skills in a setting that is compatible with the abilities of participants.

OUTCOMES

- Structure learning experiences efficiently using appropriate formations, progressions, and coaching techniques.

- Develop a unit plan and lesson focus for track, field, and cross-country running.

- Identify safety precautions associated with teaching track, field, and cross-country running.

- Describe instructional procedures used for implementing a successful lead-up game.

- Cite assessment procedures used for evaluating track, field, and cross-country running skills.

The elementary program in track and field consists of short sprints (40 to 100 yards); running and standing long jumps, high jumps, and hop-step-and-jumps; and relays. Jogging and distance running are encouraged throughout the program. The primary emphases are on practice and personal accomplishment, but modified competition in cross-country running is acceptable. Hurdling can be included when the equipment is available.

Children should experience the differences between walking, sprinting, running, striding (for pace), and jogging. Sprinting techniques are particularly important, with instruction centering on correct form for starting, accelerating, and sprinting. Speed and quickness are important attributes that govern the degree of success in many play and sport activities. Teach the rules for different events. Because few elementary schools have a permanent track, laying out and lining the track (see page 703) each year are valuable educational experiences.

INSTRUCTIONAL EMPHASIS AND SEQUENCE

Table 29.1 divides track and field activities into two developmental levels. The activities are listed in progression. Because many track and field skills involve locomotor movements, youngsters of all ages can enjoy and participate in these activities.

Developmental Levels I and II

Because running and jumping skills are easily mastered by children, they are introduced in Developmental Level I. Early experiences at this level stress running short distances, learning different starting positions, and participating in the two types of long jump. Some running for distance is included, and cross-country meets are introduced. Relays offer exciting experiences and involve a large number of youngsters in a quasi-team activity.

Developmental Level III

More serious efforts to achieve proper form begin at this level. The scissors style can be introduced in high jumping,

TABLE 29.1	Suggested Track, Field, and Cross-Country Program
Developmental Levels I and II	**Developmental Level III**
Track and Cross-Country Skills	
40- to 60-yard sprints	50- to 100-yard sprints
Standing start	Distance running
Sprinter's start	Relays
Jogging and cross-country running	Hurdling
	Baton passing
Field Skills	
Standing long jump	High jump
Long jump	Hop-step-and-jump

and experimentation with other styles can be encouraged. Students should begin to use check marks with the running long jump. Running for distance and cross-country activities are emphasized. Hurdling using modified hurdles is an exciting event. In the high jump, critical points of the Straddle Roll and the Western Roll are explained. Developing pace in distance running without strong elements of competition is taught. The hop-step-and-jump extends the range of jumping activities. Relays and baton passing are given increased coverage at this level.

TRACK AND FIELD SKILLS

Starting

STANDING START

The standing start should be practiced, because this type of start has a variety of uses in physical education activities. Many children find it more comfortable than the sprinter's start. As soon as is practical, however, children should accept the sprinter's start for track work.

In the standing start, the feet should be in a comfortable half-stride position. An extremely long stride is to be avoided. The body leans forward so that the center of gravity is forward. The weight is on the toes, and the knees are flexed slightly. The arms can be down or hanging slightly back (Figure 29.1).

NORWEGIAN START

The Norwegians use the standing start in a novel way. On the command "On your mark," the runner takes a position at the starting line with the right foot forward. On "Get set," the left hand is placed on the right knee and the right hand is carried back for a thrust (Figure 29.2). On "Go," the right hand comes forward, coupled with a drive by the right foot. The advantage claimed for this start is that it forces the body to lean and makes use of the forward thrust of the arm coordinated with the step off on the opposite foot.

SPRINTER'S START

There are several kinds of sprinter's starts, but teachers are advised to concentrate on a single one. The "On your mark" position places the toe of the front foot from 4 to 12 inches behind the starting line. The thumb and first finger are just behind the line, with other fingers adding support. The knee of the rear leg is placed just opposite the front foot or ankle (Figure 29.3).

For the "Get set" position, the seat is raised so that it is nearly parallel to the ground. The knee of the rear

FIGURE 29.1 Standing start.

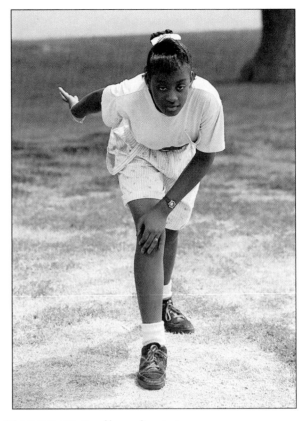

FIGURE 29.2 Norwegian start.

leg is raised off the ground, and the shoulders are moved forward over the hands. The weight is evenly distributed over the hands and feet (Figure 29.4, page 698). The head is not raised, as the runner should be looking at a spot a few feet in front of the starting line.

On the "Go" signal, the runner pushes off sharply with both feet, with the front leg straightening as the back leg comes forward for a step. The body should rise gradually rather than pop up suddenly. The instructor should watch for a stumbling action on the first few steps. This results from too much weight resting on the hands in the "Get set" position.

RUNNING

Sprinting

In proper sprinting form, the body leans forward, with the arms swinging in opposition to the legs. The arms are bent at the elbows and swing from the shoulders in a forward and backward plane, not across the body (Figure 29.5, page 698). Forceful arm action aids sprinting. The knees are lifted sharply forward and upward and are brought down with a vigorous motion, followed by a forceful push from the toes. Sprinting is a driving

and striding motion, as opposed to the inefficient pulling action displayed by some runners.

Distance Running

In distance running, as compared with sprinting, the body is more erect and the motion of the arms is less pronounced. Pace is an important consideration. Runners should try to concentrate on the qualities of lightness, ease, relaxation, and looseness. Good striding action,

FIGURE 29.3 Sprinter's start—"On your mark."

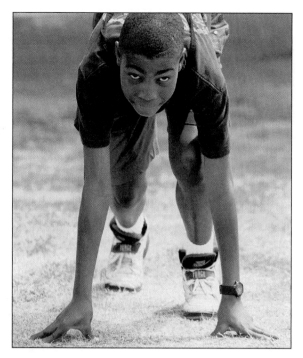

FIGURE 29.4   Sprinter's start—"Get set!"

a slight body lean, and good head position are also important. Runners should be encouraged to strike the ground with the heel first and then push off with the toes (Figure 29.6).

Relays

Two types of relays are generally included in a program of track and field for children. Instruction in baton passing should be incorporated into relay activity. Running on the track is always done in a counterclockwise direction.

CIRCULAR (PURSUIT) RELAYS

Circular relays make use of the regular circular track. The baton exchange technique is important, and practice is needed. On a 220-yard or a 200-meter track, relays

FIGURE 29.5   Proper sprinting form.

FIGURE 29.6   Proper running form.

can be organized in a number of ways, depending on how many runners are spaced for one lap. Four runners can do a lap, each running one-quarter of the way; two can do a lap, each running one-half of the distance; or each runner can complete a whole lap. In these races, each member of the relay team runs the same distance. Relays can also be organized so that members run different distances.

SHUTTLE RELAYS

Because children are running toward each other, one great difficulty in running shuttle relays is control of the exchange. In the excitement, the next runner may leave too early, and the tag or exchange is then made ahead of the restraining line. A high-jump standard or cone can be used to prevent early exchanges. The next runner awaits the tag with an arm around the standard or a hand on a cone.

BATON PASSING

Two methods of baton passing are commonly used. The first method is the right-hand-to-left-hand method and is used in longer distance relays. It is the best choice for elementary school children as it is easy and offers a consistent method for passes. This pass allows the receiver to face the inside of the track while waiting to receive the baton in the left hand. The oncoming runner holds the baton in the right hand like a candle when passing it to a teammate. The receiver reaches back with the left hand, fingers pointing down and thumb to the inside, and begins to run as the runner advances to within 3 to 5 yards. The receiver grasps the baton and shifts it from the left to the right hand while moving. If the baton is dropped, it must be picked up, or the team is disqualified. An alternative way to receive the baton is to reach back with the hand facing up; however, the fingers-down method is considered more suitable for sprint relays.

The second style of passing, the alternating hand-off, is usually used in the 400- and 800-meter relays. The first exchange is right to left, the second exchange is left to right, and the third exchange is right to left, a method that prevents the runner from having to switch the baton from hand to hand while sprinting. This method is used in high-level competition in short distances, but probably is less useful with elementary-age youngsters.

Receivers can look over their shoulders to see the oncoming runner or can look forward in the direction of the run. Looking backward is called a *visual pass* and is slower than passing while looking forward (called a *blind pass*). However, there is a greater chance for error when the receiver is not looking backward and at the baton during the pass. The visual pass is recommended for elementary school children.

Horizontal Jumping

In both the standing and the running long jump, the measurement is made from the takeoff board or line to the nearest point on the ground touched by the jumper. It is therefore important for children not to fall or step backward after making the jump.

STANDING LONG JUMP

In the standing long jump, the child toes the line with feet flat on the ground and fairly close together. The arms are brought forward in a preliminary swing and are then swung down and back (Figure 29.7). The jump is made with both feet as the arms are swung forcibly forward to

assist in lifting the body upward and forward. In the air, the knees should be brought upward and forward, with the arms held forward to sustain balance.

LONG JUMP

For the running long jump, a short run is needed. The run should be executed so that the toes of the jumping foot contact the board in a natural stride. The jumper takes off from one foot and strives for height. The landing is made on both feet after the knees have been brought forward. The landing should be in a forward direction, not sideways.

More efficient jumping is achieved when a checkpoint is used. The checkpoint can be established about halfway down the run. Competitors can help each other mark checkpoints. Each jumper should know how many steps back from the takeoff board the checkpoint is located. On the run for the jump, the student hits the mark with the appropriate foot (right or left) so as to reach the board with the correct foot in a normal stride for the jump.

The jumper should arrive at the checkpoint at full speed. The last four strides taken before the board should be relaxed in readiness for the takeoff. The last stride can be shortened somewhat (Figure 29.8).

A fair jump takes off behind the scratch line. A foul (scratch) jump is called if the jumper steps beyond the scratch line or runs into or through the pit. Each contestant is given a certain number of trials (jumps). A scratch jump counts as a trial. Measurement is from the scratch line to the nearest point of touch.

HOP-STEP-AND-JUMP

The hop-step-and-jump event is increasing in popularity, particularly because it is now included in Olympic competition. A takeoff board and a jumping pit are needed. The distance from the takeoff board to the pit should be one that even less skilled jumpers can make. The event begins with a run similar to that for the running long jump. The takeoff is with one foot, and the jumper must land on the same foot to complete the hop. He then takes a step followed by a jump. The event finishes like the long jump, with a landing on both feet

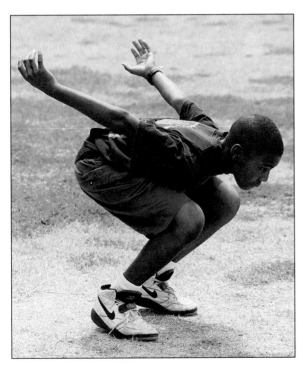

FIGURE 29.7 Standing long jump. (Note position of hands and arms.)

FIGURE 29.8 Long jump.

FIGURE 29.9   Hop-step-and-jump.

FIGURE 29.10   Straddle Roll.

(Figure 29.9). The pattern can be changed to begin with the left foot. A checkpoint should be used as for the running long jump.

The jumper must not step over the takeoff board in the first hop, under penalty of fouling. Distance is measured from the front of the takeoff board to the closest place the body touches. This is usually a mark made by one of the heels, but it could be a mark made by an arm or another part of the body if the jumper landed poorly and fell backward.

High Jumping

High-jump techniques are developed by practice. The bar should be at a height that offers challenge but allows concentration on technique rather than on height. Too much emphasis on competition for height quickly eliminates the poorer jumpers, who need the most practice. Safety is of utmost importance. Using a flexible elastic rope as a crossbar and having the students avoid any type of flop will prevent injury. Youngsters often want to emulate the Fosbury Flop, but this technique can result in a neck or back injury if not performed correctly. It should not be used in the elementary school program. A crash pad should be used to absorb the force of the landing for Straddle Roll and Western Roll techniques.

SCISSORS JUMP

For the Scissors Jump, the high-jump bar is approached from a slight angle. The takeoff is by the leg that is farther from the bar. The nearer leg is lifted and goes over, followed quickly by a looping movement of the rear leg. Students should focus on an upward kick with the front leg and an upward thrust of the arms. The knees should be straightened at the highest point of the jump. The landing is made on the lead foot followed by the rear foot.

STRADDLE ROLL

For the Straddle Roll (Figure 29.10), the approach is made from the left side at an angle of no more than 45 degrees. There are four key parts to the jump with respect to coaching:

1. *Gather.* The last three steps are fast and vigorous, with the body leaning back a bit. The takeoff is on the left foot.

2. *Kick.* The right leg is kicked vigorously as the jumping foot is planted.

3. *Arm movement.* An abrupt lift with both arms is made, with the left arm reaching over the bar and the right arm moving straight up. This puts the jumper in a straddle position while going over.

4. *Back leg clearance.* Clearance is accomplished by straightening the body, rolling the hips to the right (over the bar), or dropping the right shoulder.

WESTERN ROLL

For the Western Roll, the approach, gather, and kick are the same as for the Straddle Roll, but instead of being facedown, the jumper clears the bar by lying parallel to it on her side. The left arm is pointed down at the legs while crossing the bar and then is lowered. The head is turned toward the pit after clearance, and the landing is made on both hands and the left (takeoff) foot.

Hurdling

For safety, youngsters should use hurdles that are designed specifically for elementary schools. The hurdles should tip over easily when struck by runners. Youngsters have a tendency to want to jump hurdles in the wrong direction. This can cause a serious fall since the hurdles do not give when crossed from the wrong side. Hurdles can be made from electrical conduit pipe. (See page 205 for a diagram.) Wands supported on blocks or cones can also be used as hurdles. Hurdling should begin with hurdles set at 12 inches in height and increase to 18 inches. They should be placed about 25 feet apart. Using six hurdles, a 60-yard (180-foot) course can be established as diagrammed in Figure 29.11.

Several key points govern good hurdling technique. The runner should adjust his stepping pattern so that

Start X |25 ft|25 ft|25 ft|25 ft|25 ft|25 ft|30 ft| Finish

←———————— 180 ft ————————→

FIGURE 29.11 Hurdling course.

the takeoff foot is planted 3 to 5 feet from the hurdle. The lead foot is extended straight forward over the hurdle; the rear (trailing) leg is bent, with the knee to the side. The lead foot reaches for the ground, quickly followed by the trailing leg. A hurdler may lead with the same foot over consecutive hurdles or may alternate the leading foot. Some hurdlers like to thrust both arms instead of a single arm forward. A consistent step pattern should be developed.

INSTRUCTIONAL PROCEDURES

1. Spiked running shoes are not permitted. They create a safety problem and also give an unfair advantage to children whose parents can afford them.

2. Form should be stressed at all times, but it should be appropriate to the individual. Youngsters should be encouraged to develop good technique within their own style. Observation of any event at a track meet bears out the fact that many individual styles are successful.

3. The program should offer something for all boys and girls, the highly skilled and the less skilled, and those with physical problems. Children with weight problems need particular attention. They must be stimulated and encouraged, because their participation will be minimal if little attention is paid to them. Special goals can be set for overweight children, and special events and goals can also be established for children with disabilities.

4. The amount of activity, particularly distance work, should be increased progressively. A period of conditioning should precede any competition or all-out performance. If this procedure is followed, children will show few adverse effects.

5. Warm-up activity should precede track and field work and should include jogging as well as bending and stretching exercises.

6. Pits for the long jump and the high jump must be maintained properly. They should be filled with fresh sand of a coarse variety. For high jumping, commercial impact landing pads are necessary though expensive. If they are not available, high jumping should be restricted to the scissors style, with tumbling mats used for the landing area.

7. The metal high-jump crossbar is economical in the long run, although it will bend. A satisfactory crossbar can be made of nylon cord with a weight on each end to keep it taut while still allowing it to be displaced. Magic ropes (rubberized stretch ropes) can be adapted for low-level jumping practice.

8. The use of a track starter signal is recommended. The clapboard track starter approximates the sound of the usual starter's gun and does not have the drawback of requiring expensive ammunition. (See page 211 for a diagram showing how to construct this starting device.)

9. The goal of the program should be to allow students to develop at their own rate. Instructional sessions should be strenuous enough to ensure some overload but not so strenuous that students become discouraged or physically ill. The instructor needs to be perceptive enough to determine whether students are working too hard or too little. Special attention must be given to students who appear disinterested, dejected, emotionally upset, or withdrawn.

ORGANIZING FOR INSTRUCTION

Track, field, and cross-country running differ from other areas of the elementary school program in that considerable preparation must be made before the classes begin.

1. A track or a cross-country course must be laid out when there are no permanent courses. This can be done with marking lime. Lanes for sprinting are of value but are not an absolute requirement.

2. A hurdling area should be similarly outlined in an appropriate location.

3. Separate pits should be placed for the running long jump, the high jump, and the hop-step-and-jump. These pits should be spaced well apart to minimize interference.

4. High-jump equipment should be checked. Standards with pins, crossbars (or cord substitutes), and cushioned landing pads are needed.

5. Takeoff boards for the long jump and the hop-step-and-jump should be in place. Jumping without the use of a takeoff board is not a satisfying experience.

6. Accessory materials should be gathered, including batons, starter clapboards, watches, hurdles, and yarn for the finish line.

7. The value of starting blocks is debatable. Doubtless, they add interest to the program, but their use and adjustment are sometimes difficult for the elementary school student to master.

The organization of students is as important as the organization of equipment. Height and weight are factors affecting the degree of physical performance in

29

track, field, and cross-country activities. More efficient instruction is possible when children are grouped by height and weight. They also can be arranged by gender. The following groups may serve as a basis for instruction: (1) heavier and taller boys, (2) shorter and lighter boys, (3) heavier and taller girls, and (4) shorter and lighter girls. A simple way to form groups is to rank boys and girls separately according to the following formula, which yields a standard number: Score = 10 × age (to the nearest half-year) + weight (in pounds).

After the boys have been ranked, the upper 50 percent are assigned to group 1 and the remainder to group 2. A similar division is made with the girls. Some decisions regarding borderline cases may have to be made.

Some track and field skills can be practiced with a single-activity organization. Starting skills can be practiced with perhaps one-fourth of the children at one time. Four groups can practice baton passing skills at one time. Striding for distance can be practiced with each group running as a unit.

STATION TEACHING

The predominant plan of organization should be one of multiple activities. Four stations can make use of the selected group organization, but more stations are desirable. If eight stations are used, two stations can be assigned to each group. Stations can be selected from the following skill areas: (1) starting and sprinting, (2) baton passing, (3) standing and running long jump, (4) hop-step-and-jump, (5) high jump, (6) hurdles, (7) striding for distance and pace judgment, and (8) the Potato Shuttle Race. (See the following section.)

It is generally not sound to have children practice at all stations in any one class session. The entire circuit can be completed during additional sessions. Putting written directions at each station is helpful. The directions can state what is to be accomplished as well as offering points of technique.

In later instruction, students can select the skills that they want to practice. With guidance, the choice system could embrace the entire program, with children determining at each session those areas on which they would like to concentrate. This choice approach can be related to individualized or contract instruction.

TRACK AND FIELD DRILLS AND ACTIVITIES

POTATO SHUTTLE RACE

The Potato Shuttle Race is an adaptation of an old U.S. custom during frontier harvest celebrations. For each competitor, a number of potatoes were placed in a line

Start Box

FIGURE 29.12 Potato Shuttle Race.

at various distances. The winner was the one who brought in his potatoes first, one at a time. He won a sack of potatoes for the best effort.

The modern version of this race uses blocks instead of potatoes, and each runner runs the following course: A box is placed 15 feet in front of the starting line, with four blocks in individual circles, which are the same distance (15 feet) apart (Figure 29.12). The runner begins behind the starting line and brings the blocks, one at a time, back to the box. She can bring the blocks back in any order desired, but all blocks must be put inside the box. The box should be 12 by 12 inches, with a depth of 3 to 6 inches. Blocks must be placed or dropped, not thrown, into the box.

The most practical way to organize competition in this race is to time each individual and then award places on the basis of elapsed time, for the race is physically challenging. The competitors must understand that each person is running individually and that they should strive for their best time, regardless of position or place of finish in the race.

Timers can act as judges to see that the blocks are not thrown into the box. A block that lands outside the box must be placed inside before the student goes after another. Blocks should be about two inches square, but this can vary.

The race can be run as a relay as follows: The first runner brings all of the blocks in, one at a time, and then tags the second member of the team, who returns the blocks, one at a time, to the respective spots. The third relay member brings the blocks in again, and the fourth puts them out again. For this race, it is necessary to have pie tins, floor tiles (9 by 9 inches), or some other items in addition to the box so that when the blocks are put out by the second and fourth runners, it can be determined definitely that they rest in the proper spot. A block must be on its spot in the proper fashion before the runner delivers the next one.

RUNNING FOR PACE

Children should have some experience in running moderate distances to acquire an understanding of pace. The running should be loose and relaxed. Distances up to 1,600 meters may be part of the work. To check his time, each runner needs a partner. Someone with a stopwatch loudly counts the elapsed time second by second, and the partner notes the runner's time as he crosses the finish line.

Allowing children to estimate their pace and time can be motivating. On a circular track, at a set distance, let each runner stipulate a target time and see how close she can come to it.

INTERVAL TRAINING

Children should know the technique of interval training, which consists of running at a set speed for a specified distance and then walking back to the starting point. On the one-eighth-mile track, children can run for 110 yards and then walk to the starting point, repeating this procedure a number of times. They can also run the entire 220 yards, take a timed rest, and then repeat. Breathing should return to near normal before the next 220-yard interval is attempted.

SUGGESTED TRACK FACILITY

The presence of a track facility is a boon to any program. Few elementary schools have the funds or space for a quarter-mile track. A shorter track facility that can be installed permanently with curbs or temporarily with marking lime is suggested. Discarded fire hoses can be used to mark curbs and can be installed each spring with spikes.

The short facility is one-eighth mile (220 yards) in length and has a straightaway of 66 yards, which is ample for the 60-yard dash (Figure 29.13). It allows flexibility in relays, since relay legs of 55, 110, and 220 yards are possible. In keeping with international practice, a 200-meter track may be preferable (Figure 29.14). Running on a track is always done in a counterclockwise direction.

FIGURE 29.14   200-meter track.

CONDUCTING TRACK AND FIELD DAYS

Track and field days can range in organization from competition within a single classroom to competition among selected classes, from an all-school playday meet to a meet between neighboring schools or an areawide or all-city meet. In informal meets within a class or between a few classes, all children should participate in one or more events. Each student can be limited to two individual events plus one relay event, with no substitutions permitted. An additional condition could be imposed that competitors for individual events enter only one track event and one field event.

For larger meets, two means of qualification are suggested:

1. Qualifying times and performance standards can be set at the start of the season. Any student meeting or bettering these times or performances is qualified to compete.

2. In an all-school meet, first- and second-place winners in each class competition qualify for entry. For a district or all-city meet, first- and second-place winners from each all-school meet become eligible.

Generally, competition is organized for each event by sex and grade or age. This does not preclude mixed teams competing against mixed teams in relays. Height and weight classifications can be used to equalize competition.

Planning the Meet

The order of events should be determined by the type of competition. Relays are usually last on the program. If preliminary heats are necessary, these relays are run off first. Color-coded cards should be given to the heat qualifiers. This helps get them into the correct final race.

The local track coach can give advice about details of organizing the meet. Helpers can be secured from

FIGURE 29.13   One-eighth-mile (220-yard) track.

29

among school patrons, secondary students, teacher-training students, and service clubs. Adequate and properly instructed help is essential. A list of key officials and their duties follows.

1. *Meet director.* The meet director should be positioned at a convenient point near the finish line, with a table on which all official papers are kept.

2. *Announcer.* The announcer can be in charge of the public address system. Much of the success of the meet depends on the announcer's abilities.

3. *Clerk of the course.* The clerk of the course is in charge of all entries and places the competitors in their proper starting slots.

4. *Starter.* The starter works closely with the clerk of the course.

5. *Head and finish judges.* There should be one finish judge for each place awarded, plus one extra. The first competitor "out of the money" is identified in case there is a disqualification. The head judge can cast the deciding vote if there is doubt about the first- and second-place winners.

6. *Timers.* Three timers should time first place, although fewer can be used. Another timer, if available, can time second place. Timers report their times to the head timer, who determines the correct winning time. Accurate timing is important if records are a factor.

7. *Messenger.* A messenger takes the entry card from the clerk of the course to the finish judge, who records the correct finish places and the winner's time after the race is completed. The messenger then takes the final record of the race to the meet director's table.

8. *Field judges and officials.* Each field event should be managed by a sufficient crew, headed by a designated individual. Each crew head should be given a clipboard with the rules of the particular event fully explained.

9. *Marshals.* Several marshals should be appointed to keep general order. They are responsible for keeping noncompetitors from interfering with the events. Competitors can be kept under better control if each unit has an assigned place, either in the infield or in the stands.

Only the assigned officials and competitors should be present at the scenes of competition.

In smaller meets, first, second, and third places are usually awarded, with scoring on a five-, three-, and one-point basis, respectively. Relays, because of multiple-student participation, should count double in the place point score. For larger meets, more places can be awarded, and the individual point scores can be adjusted.

Ribbons can be awarded to winners but need not be elaborate. The name of the meet should be printed on the ribbon, with the individual event and the place designated. Blue ribbons are given for first place, red for second, and white for third. They are usually awarded after each event. Awarding ribbons at the conclusion of a large interschool meet is anticlimactic, because many spectators will have left.

An opening ceremony, including a salute to the flag, is desirable for larger meets. Competitors from each unit can be introduced as a group, with announcements and instructions emphasized or clarified at this time. Holding the event on a school morning or afternoon gives status to the affair and allows all children to participate.

It is helpful if the competitors wear numbers. Safety pins, rather than straight pins, should be used to keep the numbers in place. Numbers can be made at the individual schools prior to the meet when well-defined instructions pertaining to the materials, colors, and sizes have been delineated.

Organizing the Competition

The overriding goal of elementary school competition is to have many children take part and experience a measure of success. The determination of individual champions and of meet winners is lower in priority. Track and field competition can take many forms.

In informal competition, competitors are assigned to different races and compete only in those races. There are no heats as such, nor is there advancement to a final race. Races are chosen so that individuals on the same team usually do not run against each other. Points may or may not be given toward an overall meet score. The informal meet is more like a playday and can include nontrack events also, such as the softball throw, the football kick, and the Frisbee throw.

Track and field competition can be focused on individuals or teams. In individual competition, there is no team scoring and only individuals are declared winners. When team competition is incorporated, both individual winners and team winners are determined. Points scored by individual winners, such as five points for first place, or three points for second place, are credited to respective teams. The team with the highest score wins. Different team winners can be determined for different grades and/or levels.

Relay competition is a carnival in which a number of relays make up the program. Performances can be combined for several individuals if field events are to be included. Few, if any, uncombined scores are taken into consideration. A number of relays should be part of track and field days under any plan. Relays increase student participation. Mixed relays are another possibility.

CROSS-COUNTRY RUNNING

Many youngsters are motivated by running laps around a track. Others soon tire of these circular efforts, however, and can be motivated by cross-country running. Students can run marked or unmarked courses for enjoyment of the competition. Emphasis is on improving one's personal time rather than on winning. This enables all students to have personalized goals and an ongoing incentive for running.

Cross-country courses can be marked with a chalk line and cones so that runners follow the course as outlined. Checkpoints every 220 yards offer runners a convenient reference point so that they can gauge accurately how far they have run. Three courses of differing lengths and difficulty can be laid out. The beginning course can be one mile in length, the intermediate 1.25 miles, and the advanced 1.5 miles. Including sandy or hilly areas in the course increases the challenge. When students run cross country, they can select the course that challenges them appropriately.

It is important for students to learn the concept of pace when running long distances. One technique for teaching students how to pace themselves is to place cones at similar intervals and to challenge students to run from cone to cone at a specified rate. A student or the instructor can call out the time at each cone, and students can adjust their running to the desired pace. Another method is to break down long-distance runs into smaller segments and times, which enables youngsters to get a feel for how fast they must run the shorter distances to attain a certain cumulative time over the longer distance. Table 29.2 gives times for the 40- and 100-yard dashes.

CROSS-COUNTRY MEETS

Cross-country meets provide a culminating activity for youngsters involved in distance running. The attractiveness of cross-country competition lies in the fact that it is a team activity and all members of the team are crucial to its success. Youngsters should learn how to score a meet. Probably the easiest way to keep team scores is to assign seven (depending on class size) members to each team. Points are assigned to finishers based on their placement in the race. For example, the first-place runner receives one point, the tenth-place runner receives ten points, and so on. The points for all team members are totaled, and the team with the lowest score is declared the winner.

Teams can be equalized by having youngsters run the course prior to the meet and recording their times. Teams can then be organized by the teacher so that members are somewhat matched. As a guideline, Table 29.3 offers suggested competitive divisions and distances to be run. Divisions 5 and 6 are classed as open divisions, which any child in the elementary school may enter, even if below the age of 12. Ages are defined by birthdays; that is, a child is classified as being a certain age until the next birthday.

A primary concern is that children gauge their running pace so that they are able to finish the race. Improvement of previous times should be the focus of the activity, with place at the finish of the race a secondary goal. The timekeeper can voice the time as each runner finishes to help children evaluate their performance.

A funnel made of cones at the finish line prevents tying times (Figure 29.15). As runners go through the funnel, the meet judges and helpers can hand each one a marker with the place of finish on it. This practice simplifies scoring at the end of the meet. Each team captain can total the scores and report the result.

TABLE 29.2	Times for 40- and 100-Yard Dashes	
To run a mile in:	**Runner has to run 40-yard dash 44 times— each dash run in:**	**Runner has to run 100-yard dash 17.6 times— each dash run in:**
3:44 minutes (world record time)	5.18 seconds	12.95 seconds
5:00 minutes	6.81 seconds	17.04 seconds
6:00 minutes	8.18 seconds	20.45 seconds
7:00 minutes	9.55 seconds	23.87 seconds
8:00 minutes	10.90 seconds	27.25 seconds
10:00 minutes	13.62 seconds	34.08 seconds

TABLE 29.3	Suggested Divisions for Cross-Country Meets		
Division	**Age**	**Sex**	**Distance (in miles)**
1	8–9	M	1
2	8–9	F	1
3	10–11	M	1.25
4	10–11	F	1.25
5	12–13	M	1.5
6	12–13	F	1.5

29

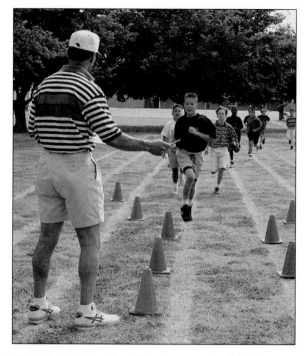

FIGURE 29.15 Funneling runners at the finish line.

Cross-country runners should learn to cool down on completion of a race. Youngsters have a tendency to fall down rather than to move. They should jog gently until they are somewhat rested. Because runners do not all finish at the same time, it is sometimes helpful to have some recreational activities set out near the track so that the youngsters can stay involved in activity.

FOR MORE INFORMATION

References and Suggested Readings

Carr, G. (1999). *Fundamentals of track and field.* 2nd ed. Champaign, IL: Human Kinetics.

Fronske, H. (2005). *Teaching cues for sport skills.* 3rd ed. San Francisco: Benjamin Cummings.

Jackson, C. (1996). *Young track and field athlete.* New York: DK Publishing.

Mood, D. P., Musker, F. F., & Rink, J. E. (2003). *Sports and recreational activities.* 13th ed. New York: McGraw-Hill.

NASPE and Hershey Corporation. (2002). *Hershey's track & field official rule book and manual.* Hershey, PA: Hershey.

Schmottlach, N., & McManama, J. (2002). *The physical education handbook.* 10th ed. San Francisco: Benjamin Cummings.

Websites

American Track and Field
www.american-trackandfield.com

Hershey Youth Track and Field Program
www.hersheys.com/trackandfield

USA Track & Field
www.usatf.org

C H A P T E R

30

Volleyball

SUMMARY

Skills instruction for volleyball is introduced during the intermediate grades after youngsters have mastered basic prerequisite skills. Teaching the rules and strategies for volleyball is an integral part of the instructional process. Using proper progression is key to successful teaching of fundamental skills and lead-up games associated with volleyball. Lead-up games provide an opportunity to emphasize development of selected volleyball skills in a setting that is compatible with the abilities of participants.

OUTCOMES

- Structure learning experiences efficiently using appropriate formations, progressions, and coaching techniques.
- Develop a unit plan and lesson focus for volleyball.
- Identify safety precautions associated with teaching volleyball.
- Describe instructional procedures used for implementing a successful lead-up game.
- Cite assessment procedures used for evaluating volleyball skills.

To play volleyball successfully on the elementary level, basic skills need to be learned properly. This requires sufficient practice in serving and passing skills and the development of hand-eye and body coordination for effective ball control. Attention to proper technique is essential. Informal practice begins with activities that mimic volleyball skills—passing, serving, and rebounding of all types. Blocking is an important skill that youngsters can perform if they anticipate correctly. Setting and spiking are skills that challenge the most skilled youngsters so little time should be devoted to this phase of the game.

ESSENTIAL COMPONENTS OF QUALITY PROGRAMS

▶ **I. Organized around content standards**

▶ **II. Student-centered and developmentally appropriate**

▶ **III. Physical activity and motor skill development form the core of the program**

▶ **IV. Teaches management skills and self-discipline**

▶ **V. Promotes inclusion of all students**

▶ **VI. Focuses on process over product**

VII. Promotes lifetime personal health and wellness

▶ **VIII. Teaches cooperation and responsibility and promotes sensitivity to diversity**

NATIONAL STANDARDS FOR PHYSICAL EDUCATION*

▶ **1. Demonstrates competency in motor skills and movement patterns needed to perform a variety of physical activities.**

▶ **2. Demonstrates understanding of movement concepts, principles, and tactics as they apply to the learning and performance of physical activities.**

▶ **3. Participates regularly in physical activity.**

4. Achieves and maintains a health-enhancing level of physical fitness.

▶ **5. Exhibits responsible personal and social behavior that respects self and others in physical activity.**

▶ **6. Values physical activity for health, enjoyment, challenge, self-expression, and/or social interaction.**

*National Association for Sport and Physical Education (NASPE), 2004.

INSTRUCTIONAL EMPHASIS AND SEQUENCE

Indoor facilities sometimes pose a problem for volleyball play. In some gymnasiums, the lack of court space means playing with 12 to 15 children on a side in a single game. This arrangement results in little activity for the majority of participants as a few skilled players on each side dominate the game. A basketball court can be divided into two volleyball courts where players play crosswise. Lowering nets to six feet or less ensures success. The nets can gradually be raised as children mature. Nets should be attached firmly so that both the upper and lower net cords are tight. A loose net does not allow for ball recovery from the net.

An adequate number of volleyballs is necessary. For individual practice, the number of balls can be supplemented with beach balls and foam balls of comparable size. Few schools have 30 to 35 volleyballs available. In larger school systems, having a rotating schedule of volleyball activities from school to school can solve the problem of volleyball supply. Few practice activities require a net, so outdoor participation is possible.

The overhand serve, setup, and spike are skills that are usually introduced when a competitive situation exists, such as intramurals or an interschool program. Normally, in physical education classes, the program dwells on keeping the ball in play, thereby increasing activity, skill development, and enjoyment. As a matter of game orientation, however, students should learn setup, spike, and blocking techniques.

In the primary grades, children can practice ball-handling activities related to volleyball skills. Rebounding and controlling balloons are excellent related experiences, particularly for younger children. These preliminary experiences in visual tracking are advantageous for volleyball skills learned in the upper grades.

Table 30.1 shows a sequence of volleyball activities divided into two developmental levels. In most cases, youngsters are not ready to participate in the activities in this chapter until the age of eight.

Developmental Level II

Experiences at this level are based on the use of the beach ball and culminate in the game of Beach Ball Volleyball. A beach ball is larger and more easily handled than a volleyball and allows a level of success not possible with a smaller and heavier ball. Simple returns and underhand serves can be practiced with beach balls. The games of Informal Volleyball and Shower Service

| TABLE 30.1 | Suggested Volleyball Program |
Developmental Level II	Developmental Level III
Skills	
Underhand serve	Overhand pass
Simple returns	Forearm pass
	Overhand serve
	Setup*
	Spike*
	Blocking*
Knowledge	
Simple rules	Basic game rules
Rotation	Game strategy
Activities	
Beach Ball Volleyball	Pass and Dig
Informal Volleyball	Mini-Volleyball
Shower Service Ball	Rotation Mini-Volleyball
	Regulation Volleyball
	Three-and-Over Volleyball
	Rotation Volleyball
	Four-Square Volleyball
Skill Tests	
Simplified serving	Serving for accuracy
	Wall volleying

*Skilled players only.

Ball are played with a beach ball or a volleyball trainer ball, which moves more slowly and is easier to handle.

Developmental Level III

Beach balls and foam balls can be used at this level of instruction, but a shift to volleyball trainer balls should be made when the maturity of the youngsters dictates. Foam-rubber and training volleyballs (8-inch) are excellent substitutes for volleyballs (Figure 30.1). They move slowly, afford an opportunity for successful play, and do not hurt youngsters. Students should exhibit basic technique in handling high and low passes. Only the most skilled students are able to learn the overhand serve, setup, spike, and blocking. Instruction focuses on the underhand serve and the overhand and forearm passes. An introduction to elementary strategy is part of the instructional approach.

FIGURE 30.1   Different balls for volleyball.

VOLLEYBALL SKILLS

Serving

The serve is used to start play. The underhand serve is easiest for elementary school children to learn even though the overhand (floater) serve is the most effective. Few youngsters will be capable of mastering the overhand serve. The following instructional cues focus on correct performance of the serve:

1. Use opposition. Place the foot opposite of the serving hand forward.
2. Transfer the weight to the forward foot.
3. Keep the eyes on the ball.
4. Decide prior to the serve where it should be placed.
5. Follow through; don't punch at the ball.

UNDERHAND SERVE

Directions are for a right-handed serve. The player stands facing the net with the left foot slightly forward and the weight on the right (rear) foot. The ball is held in the left hand with the left arm across and a little in front of the body. The ball is lined up with a straightforward swing of the right hand. The left-hand fingers are spread, and the ball rests on the pads of these fingers. On the serving motion, the server steps forward with the left foot, transferring the weight to the front foot, and at the same time brings the right arm back in a preparatory motion. The right hand now swings forward and contacts the ball just below its center. The ball can be hit with an open hand or with the fist (facing forward or sideways). An effective follow-through with the arm ensures a smooth serve (Figure 30.2). Children should explore the best way to strike the ball, with the flat of the hand or the fist. Each player can select the method that is personally most effective.

FIGURE 30.2   Underhand serve.

OVERHAND SERVE

This serve is seldom mastered by elementary school youngsters. It can be presented as an option for students who have mastered the underhand serve. For the right-handed serve, the student stands with the left foot in front and the left side of the body turned somewhat toward the net. The weight is on both feet. The server must master two difficult skills: tossing the ball and contacting the ball. The ball is held in the left hand directly in front of the face. The ball must be tossed straight up and should come down in front of the right shoulder. As the ball is tossed, the weight shifts to the back foot. The height of the toss is a matter of choice, but from three to five feet is suggested. As the ball drops, the striking arm comes forward, contacting the ball a foot or so above the shoulder. The weight is shifted to the forward foot, which can take a short step forward. The contact is made with the open palm or with the fist. An effective serve is one that has no spin—a floater.

Passing (or Returning)

The overhand pass is probably the most used skill in elementary school volleyball. Using beach balls and trainer volleyballs will allow youngsters time to move into the path of the volleyball instead of reaching for the ball. Proper footwork is critical to success in volleyball; using proper balls will help ensure that youngsters learn correctly. Instructional cues for passing include the following:

1. Move into the path of the ball; don't reach for it.
2. Bend the knees prior to making contact.
3. Contact the ball with the fingertips (overhand pass).
4. Extend the knees upon contact with the ball.
5. Follow through after striking the ball.

OVERHAND PASS (SETTING)

The overhand pass is most often used by young players to return the ball to the other team. As players become more proficient, it is used to set up other teammates. To execute

30

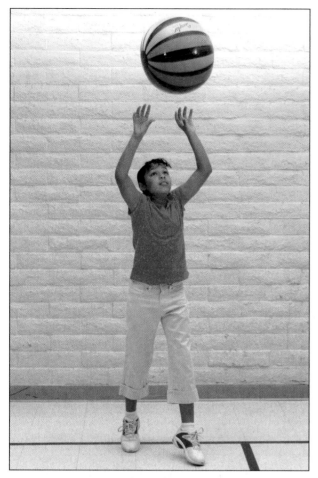

FIGURE 30.3   Completing an overhead pass.

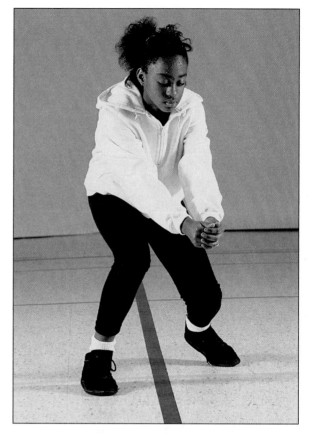

FIGURE 30.4   Forearm (underhand) pass position.

an overhand pass, the player moves underneath the ball and controls it with the fingertips. Feet should be in an easy, comfortable position, with knees bent. A cup of the fingers is made so that the thumbs and forefingers are close together and the other fingers are spread. The hands are held forehead high, with elbows out and level with the floor. The player, when in receiving position, looks ready to shout upward through his cupped hands (Figure 30.3).

The player contacts the ball above eye level and propels it with the force of spread fingers, not with the palms. At the moment of contact, the legs are straightened and the hands and arms follow through. The set should be passed high enough to allow a teammate time to move under the ball.

FOREARM PASS (UNDERHAND PASS)

The body must be in good position to ensure a proper underhand pass. The player must move rapidly to the spot where the ball is descending to prepare for the pass. Body position is important. The trunk leans forward and the back is straight, with a 90-degree angle between the thighs and the back. The legs are bent, and the body is in a partially crouched position, with the feet shoulder

width apart (Figure 30.4). The hands are clasped together so that the forearms are parallel. The clasp should be relaxed, with the type of handclasp a matter of choice. In one method, the thumbs are kept parallel and together, and the fingers of one hand make a partially cupped fist, with the fingers of the other hand overlapping the fist. In another method, both hands are cupped and turned out a little, so that the thumbs are apart. In either case, the wrists are turned downward and the elbow joints are reasonably locked. The forearms are held at the proper angle to rebound the ball, with contact made with the fists or forearms between the knees as the receiver crouches.

Advanced Volleyball Skills

The setup, the spike, and blocking are skills that are difficult for the majority of youngsters to master. Volleyball lead-up games do not require the use of these skills. Because the majority of children will not be able to master these skills, it is best to introduce them on an individual basis.

SETUP

The term "setup" applies to a pass that sets the ball for a possible spike. The object is to raise the ball with a soft, easy pass to a position 1 or 2 feet above the net and about one foot away from it. The setup is generally the second pass in a series of three. An overhand pass is used for the setup. It is important for the back line player, who has to tap to the setter, to make an accurate and easily handled pass.

SPIKE

The spike is the most effective play in volleyball, and when properly done is extremely difficult to return. Its success depends a great deal on the ability of a teammate to set up properly. At the elementary school level, spiking should be done by jumping high in the air and striking the ball above the net, driving it into the opponent's court. Experienced players may back up for a short run, but the jump must be made straight up so that the player does not touch the net and the striking hand does not go over the net.

BLOCKING

Blocking involves one or more members of the defensive (receiving) team forming a screen of arms and hands near the net to block a spike. At the elementary school level, blocking is rarely used. To block a ball, a player jumps high with arms outstretched overhead, palms facing the net, and fingers spread. The jump must be timed with that of the spiker, and the blocker must avoid touching the net. The ball is not struck but rather rebounds from the blocker's stiffened hands and arms.

INSTRUCTIONAL PROCEDURES

1. Most volleyball-type games begin with a serve, so it becomes critical that this be successful. Regular volleyball rules call for one chance to serve the ball over the net without touching the net. Three modifications can achieve more successful serving. The first is to serve from the center of the playing area instead of the back line. A second is to allow another serve if the first is not good. The third is to allow an assist by a team member to get the ball over the net.

2. To save time, players should be instructed to roll the ball back to the server. Other players should let the ball roll to its destination without interception.

3. Effective instruction is possible only when the balls can be rebounded from the hands and arms without pain. A heavy or underinflated ball takes much of the enjoyment out of the game. Beach balls are excellent for beginning players.

4. The predominant instructional pattern should be individual or partner work. For individual work, each child needs a ball.

5. An 8-inch foam-rubber training ball has much the same feel as a volleyball but does not cause pain. The foam balls should be used early in skill practice.

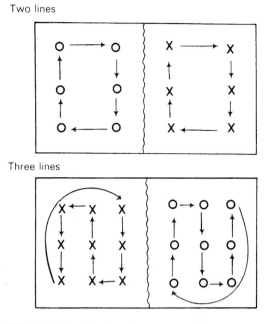

Two lines

Three lines

FIGURE 30.5 Rotation plans.

A new ball, the volleyball trainer, most closely resembles a volleyball but is larger in diameter and lighter in weight. The use of either ball helps keep children from developing a fear of the fast-moving object.

6. The use of the fist to hit balls on normal returns causes poor control and interrupts play. Both hands should be used to return the ball. Teachers should rule that hitting with the fist will result in a loss of a point if the practice persists.

7. Rotation should be introduced early and used in lead-up games. Two rotation plans are illustrated in Figure 30.5.

ORGANIZING FOR INSTRUCTION

Practice sessions can be categorized as individual play, partner work, or group work. These tasks can be prefaced by "Can you . . . " or "Let's see if you can. . . . " A skill to learn early is tossing to oneself to initiate a practice routine. This occurs when the practice directions call for a pass from one individual to oneself or to another student.

Individual Play

1. For wall rebounding, the player stands 6 feet away from a wall. He throws the ball against the wall and passes it to the wall. The player then catches and begins again. He should allow two passes against the wall before a catch is made. A further extension is for the player to pass the ball against the wall as many times as possible without making a mistake.

2. From a spot six feet in front of the wall, the player throws the ball against the wall and alternates an overhand pass with a forearm pass. The player then catches the ball.

3. In another wall-rebounding exercise, the player throws the ball to one side (right or left) and then moves to the side to pass the ball to the wall. She then catches the rebound.

4. The player passes the ball directly overhead and catches it. She should try making two passes before catching the ball. Later, she should alternate an overhand pass with a forearm pass and catch the ball. A further extension of the drill is for the player to keep the ball going five or six times with one kind of pass or with alternate passes. This is a basic drill and should be mastered before proceeding to others.

5. The player passes the ball 10 feet high and 10 feet forward, moves rapidly under the ball, and catches it. Later, he should make additional passes without the catch.

6. The player passes the ball 15 feet overhead, makes a full turn, and passes the ball again. This should vary with other stunts such as touching the floor, making a half turn, clapping the hands at two different spots, and others. Allow choice in selecting the stunt.

7. Two lines 3 feet apart are needed. The player stands in front of one line, makes a backward pass overhead, moves to the other line, and repeats the procedure.

8. The player passes 3 feet or so to one side, moves under the ball, and passes it back to the original spot. The next pass should be to the other side.

9. The player passes the ball directly overhead. On the return, he should jump as high as possible to make a second pass. Make as many passes as possible.

10. The player stands with one foot in a hoop. She passes the ball overhead and attempts to continue passing while keeping that foot in the hoop. She should then try with both feet in the hoop.

11. The player stands about 15 feet away from a basketball hoop, either in front or to the side. He passes toward the hoop in an attempt to make a basket. He scores three points if the basket is made, two points for no basket but for hitting the rim, and one point for hitting the backboard only. A further challenge would be for the player to make a pass to himself first and a second pass toward the hoop.

Partner Work (Passing)

1. Players are about 10 feet apart. Player A tosses the ball (controlled toss) to Player B, who passes the ball back to A, who catches the ball. This continues for several exchanges and then Player B becomes the change thrower. Another option is for Player B to make a pass straight overhead, catch the ball, and then toss to Player A. Yet another variation is to have one player toss the ball slightly to the side. Player B then makes a pass to Player A. Player A can make the toss in such a fashion that Player B must use a forearm return.

2. Two players are about 15 feet apart. Player A passes to herself first and then makes a second pass to Player B, who catches the ball and repeats. This can be followed with a return by Player B.

3. Players A and B try to keep the ball in the air continuously.

4. Players are about 15 feet apart. Player A remains stationary and passes in such a fashion that Player B must move from side to side. An option is to have Player B move forward and backward.

5. Players are about 10 feet apart. Both have hoops and attempt to keep one foot in the hoop while passing. Then they should try keeping both feet in the hoop.

6. Two players pass back and forth, making contact with the ball while off the ground.

7. Players are about 15 feet apart. Player B is seated. Player A attempts to pass to Player B. A second method is for both players to stand. Player A passes to Player B and then sits down quickly. Player B attempts to pass the ball back to Player A, who catches it in the seated position.

8. Player A passes to Player B and does a complete turnaround. Player B passes back to Player A and also does a full turn. Other stunts can be used.

9. Player A is stationed near a basketball hoop, with Player B in the lane. Player A passes to Player B in the lane; Player B attempts a pass to the basket. They score three points for a basket, two points for a miss that hits the rim, and one point for hitting the backboard only. Any pass from Player A that lands outside the center lane is void, and another chance is given.

10. Partners stand on opposite sides of a volleyball net. The object is to keep the ball in the air. The drill can be done by as many as six players.

Partner Work (Serving and Passing)

1. Partners are about 20 feet apart. Partner A serves to Partner B, who catches the ball and returns the serve to Partner A.

2. Partner A serves to Partner B, who makes a pass back to Partner A. Then they switch so that Partner B serves.

3. *Service One-Step.* Partners begin about 10 feet apart. Partner A serves to Partner B, who returns the serve with Partner A catching. If there is no error and if neither receiver moved the feet to catch, both players take one step back. This process is repeated each time no error or foot movement by the receivers occurs. If an error occurs or if appreciable foot movement is evident, the players revert to the original distance of ten feet and start over.

4. A player stands at the top of the key on a basketball court. The object is to serve the ball into the basket. Scoring can be as in other basket-making drills: three points for a basket, two points for hitting the rim, and one point for hitting the backboard but not the rim. The partner retrieves the ball.

Group Work

1. A leader stands in front of not more than four other players, who are arranged in a semicircle. The leader tosses to each player in sequence around the circle and they return the ball. After a round or two, another player comes forward to replace the leader.

2. For blocking, six players are positioned alongside the net, each with a ball. The players take turns on the other side of the net, practicing blocking skills. Each spiker tosses the ball to himself for spiking. A defensive player moves along the line to block a total of six spikes consecutively. The next step is to have two players move along the line to practice blocking by pairs.

3. Players can practice setup and spiking according to the drill shown in Figure 30.6. A back player tosses the ball to the setup player, who passes the ball properly for a spike. The entire group or just the spikers can rotate.

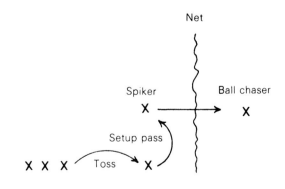

FIGURE 30.6   Setup and spiking drill.

4. Two groups of children stand on opposite sides of a net. Eight to ten balls must be available to make this a worthwhile experience. Players serve from in back of the end line and recover balls coming from the other team. The action should be informal and continuous.

BASIC VOLLEYBALL RULES

Officially, six players make up a team, but any number from six to nine makes a suitable team in the elementary school program.

To begin, captains toss a coin for the order of choices. The winner can choose to serve or to select a court. The opposing captain takes the option that the winner of the toss did not select. At the completion of a game, teams change courts, and the losing side serves.

To be in the proper position to serve, a player must have both feet behind the right one-third of the end line and must not step on the end line during the serve. The server covers the right back position. Only the serving team scores. The server retains the serve, scoring consecutive points, until that side loses a point and is put out. Members of each team take turns serving, the sequence being determined by the plan of rotation.

Official rules allow the server only one serve to get the ball completely over the net and into the opponent's court. Even if the ball touches the net (a net ball) and goes into the correct court, the serve is lost. The lines bounding the court are considered to be inbounds; that is, balls landing on the lines are counted as good. Any ball that touches or is touched by a player is considered to be inbounds, even if the player who touched the ball was clearly outside the boundaries at the time. The ball must be returned over the net by the third volley, which means that the team has a maximum of three volleys to make a good return.

The following major violations cause the loss of the point or serve:

1. Touching the net during play.
2. Not clearly batting the ball—sometimes called palming or carrying the ball.
3. Reaching over the net during play.
4. Stepping over the centerline. (Contact with the line is not a violation.)

A ball going into the net may be recovered and played, provided that no player touches the net. The first team to reach a score of 15 points wins the game if the team is at least two points ahead. If not, play continues until one team secures a two-point lead. Only players in the front line may spike, but all players may block. No player may volley the ball twice in succession.

30

VOLLEYBALL ACTIVITIES

Developmental Level II

▶ **BEACH BALL VOLLEYBALL**

Playing Area: Volleyball court

Players: Six to nine students on each team

Supplies: A beach ball 12 to 16 inches in diameter

Skills: Most passing skills, modified serving

The players of each team are in two lines on their respective sides of the net. Serving is done, as in regulation volleyball, by the player on the right side of the back line. The distance is shortened, however, because serving a beach ball successfully from the normal volleyball serving distance is difficult. The player serves from the normal playing position on the court in the right back position. Scoring is as in regulation volleyball. Play continues until the ball touches the floor.

A team loses a point to the other team when it fails to return the ball over the net by the third volley or when it returns the ball over the net but the ball hits the floor out-of-bounds without being touched by the opposing team. The server continues serving as long as that team scores. Rotation is as in regulation volleyball.

✓ **TEACHING TIP**

The server must be positioned as close to the net as possible while still remaining in the right back position on the court. Successful serving is an important component of an enjoyable game.

Variations:

1. In a simplified version of Beach Ball Volleyball, the ball is put into play by one player in the front line, who throws the ball into the air and then passes it over the net. Play continues until the ball touches the floor, but the ball may be volleyed any number of times before crossing the net. When either team has scored five points, the front and back lines of the respective teams change. When the score reaches ten for the leading team, the lines change back. The game is won at 15 points.

2. Any player in the back line may catch the ball as it comes initially from the opposing team and may immediately make a little toss and pass the ball to a teammate. The player who catches the ball and bats it cannot send it across the net before a teammate has touched it.

▶ **INFORMAL VOLLEYBALL**

Playing Area: Volleyball court, 6-foot net

Players: Six to eight students on a team

Supplies: A trainer volleyball

Skills: Passing

This game is similar to regulation volleyball, but there is no serving. Each play begins with a student on one side tossing to herself and passing the ball high over the net. Points are scored for every play, as there is no "side-out." As soon as a point is scored, the nearest player takes the ball and immediately puts it into play. Otherwise, basic volleyball rules govern the game. Rotation occurs as soon as a team has scored five points, with the front and back lines changing place. Action is fast, and the game moves rapidly, as every play scores a point for one team or the other.

▶ **SHOWER SERVICE BALL**

Playing Area: Volleyball court

Players: 6 to 12 students on each team

Supplies: Four to six trainer volleyballs

Skills: Serving, catching

A line parallel to the net is drawn through the middle of each court to define the serving area. Players are scattered in no particular formation (Figure 30.7). The game involves the skills of serving and catching. To start the game, two or three volleyballs are given to each team and are handled by players in the serving area.

Balls may be served at any time and in any order by a server, who must be in the back half of the court. Any ball served across the net is to be caught by any player near the ball. The person catching or retrieving the ball moves quickly to the serving area and serves. A point is

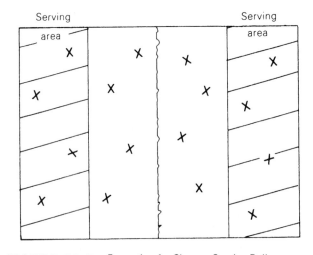

FIGURE 30.7 Formation for Shower Service Ball.

scored for a team whenever a served ball hits the floor in the other court or is dropped by a receiver. Two scorers are needed, one for each side. As children improve, all serves should be made from behind the baseline.

Developmental Level III

▶ PASS AND DIG

Playing Area: Playground or gymnasium
Players: Five to eight students on each team
Supplies: A trainer volleyball for each team
Skills: Overhand and forearm passes

Each team forms a small circle of not more than eight players. The object of the game is to see which team can make the greater number of passes in a specified time or which team can keep the ball in the air for the greater number of consecutive passes without error.

On the signal "Go," the game is started with a volley by one of the players. The following rules are in force:

1. Balls are passed back and forth with no specific order of turns, except that the ball cannot be returned to the player from whom it came.
2. A player may not pass a ball twice in succession.
3. Any ball touching the ground does not count and ends the turn.

✓ TEACHING TIP

Players should be responsible for calling illegal returns on themselves and thus interrupting the consecutive pass count. The balls used should be of equal quality, so that one team cannot claim a disadvantage. Groups should count the passes out loud, so that their progress is known.

▶ MINI-VOLLEYBALL

Playing Area: Gymnasium or badminton court
Players: Three students on each team
Supplies: A volleyball or trainer volleyball
Skills: Most volleyball skills

Mini-Volleyball is a modified activity designed to offer opportunities for successful volleyball experiences to children between the ages of 9 and 12. The playing area is 15 feet wide and 40 feet long. Many gymnasiums are marked for badminton courts that are 20 by 44 feet with a spiking line 6.5 feet from the center. This is an acceptable substitute court.

The modified rules used in Mini-Volleyball are as follows:

1. A team consists of three players. Two substitutions may be made per game.
2. Players are positioned for the serve so that there are two front line players and one back line player. After the ball is served, the back line player may not spike the ball from the attack area or hit the ball into the attack area unless the ball is below the height of the net.
3. The height of the net is 6 feet, 10 inches.
4. Players rotate positions when they receive the ball for serving. The right front line player becomes the back line player, and the left front line player becomes the right front line player.
5. A team wins a game when it scores 15 points and has a 2-point advantage over the opponent. A team wins the match when it wins two out of three games.

The back line player cannot spike and thus serves a useful function by allowing the front players to receive the serves while moving to the net to set up for the spikers.

✓ TEACHING TIP

This game can be modified to suit the needs of participants. Sponge training balls work well in the learning stages of Mini-Volleyball.

▶ ROTATION MINI-VOLLEYBALL

Playing Area: Basketball or volleyball court
Players: Three students on each team
Supplies: A volleyball or trainer volleyball
Skills: All volleyball skills

Three games, involving 18 active players, can be played at the same time crosswise, on a regular basketball court. The remaining children, organized in teams of three, wait on the sideline with teams designated in a particular order. Whenever a team is guilty of a "sideout," it vacates its place on the floor and the next team in line moves in. Each team keeps its own running score. If, during a single side-in, ten points are scored against a team, that team vacates its place. Teams in this arrangement move from one court to another and play different opponents. The one or two extra players left over from team selection by threes can be substitutes and should be rotated into play on a regular basis.

30

▶ **REGULATION VOLLEYBALL**

Playing Area: Volleyball court

Players: Six students on each team

Supplies: A volleyball or trainer volleyball

Skills: All volleyball skills

Regulation volleyball should be played with one possible rule change: In early experiences, it is suggested that the server be allowed a second chance when failing to get the first attempt over the net and into play. This should apply only to the initial serve. Some instructors like to shorten the serving distance during the introductory phases of the game. It is important for the serving to be done well enough to keep the game moving. There should be some emphasis on team play. Backcourt players should be encouraged to pass to frontcourt players rather than merely batting the ball back and forth across the net.

A referee should supervise the game. There are generally three calls:

1. *"Side-out."* The serving team fails to serve the ball successfully to the other court, fails to make a good return of a volley, or makes a rule violation.

2. *"Point."* The receiving team fails to make a legal return or is guilty of a rule violation.

3. *"Double foul."* Both teams make fouls on the same play, in which case the point is replayed. No score or side-out results.

> ***Variation:*** The receiver in the backcourt is allowed to catch the serve, toss it, and propel it to a teammate. The catch should be limited to the serve, and the pass must go to a teammate, not over the net. This counteracts the problem of children in the backcourt being unable to handle the serve to keep the ball in play if the served ball is spinning, curving, or approaching with such force that it is difficult to control.

▶ **THREE-AND-OVER VOLLEYBALL**

Playing Area: Volleyball court

Players: Six students on each team

Supplies: A volleyball or trainer volleyball

Skills: All volleyball skills

The game Three and Over emphasizes the basic offensive strategy of volleyball. The game follows regular volleyball rules with the exception that the ball must be played three times before going over the net. The team loses the serve or the point if the ball is not played three times.

▶ **ROTATION VOLLEYBALL**

Playing Area: Volleyball court

Players: Variable

Supplies: A volleyball or trainer volleyball

Skills: All volleyball skills

If four teams are playing in two contests at the same time, a system of rotation can be set up during any one class period. Divide the available class time roughly into three parts, less the time allotted for logistics. Each team plays the other three teams on a timed basis. At the end of a predetermined time period, whichever team is ahead wins the game. A team may win, lose, or tie during any time period, with the score determined at the end of the respective time period. The best win-loss record wins the overall contest.

▶ **FOUR-SQUARE VOLLEYBALL**

Playing Area: Volleyball court

Players: Two to four students on each team

Supplies: A volleyball or trainer volleyball

Skills: All volleyball skills

A second net is placed at right angles to the first net, dividing the playing area into four equal courts. The courts are numbered as in Figure 30.8. There are four teams playing, and an extra team can be waiting to rotate to court number 4. The object of the game is to force one of the teams to commit an error. Whenever a team makes an error, it moves down to court 4 or off the courts if a team is waiting. A team errs by not returning the ball to another court within the prescribed three volleys or by causing the ball to go out-of-bounds.

The ball is always put in play with a serve by a player from Team number 1, the serve being made from any point behind the end line of that team. Players must rotate for each serve. The serve is made into court 3 or 4. Play proceeds as in regular volleyball, but the ball may be volleyed into any of the other three courts. No score is kept. The object of the game is for Team 1 to retain its position.

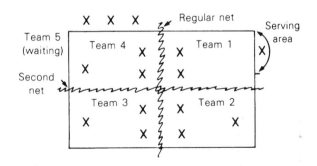

FIGURE 30.8 Four-Square Volleyball courts.

FIGURE 30.9   Court for Wheelchair Volleyball.

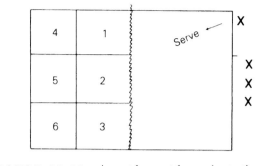

FIGURE 30.10   Layout for court for service testing.

✓ **TEACHING TIP**

The game seems to work best with five or more teams. With four teams, the team occupying court 4 is not penalized for an error, because it is already in the lowest spot.

▶ **WHEELCHAIR VOLLEYBALL**

Children in wheelchairs can participate successfully in some phases of volleyball. For example, a child confined to a wheelchair can compete against another student on a one-on-one basis when courts are laid out as illustrated in Figure 30.9. The difference in size of the playing areas equalizes the mobility factor. The net should be about 6 feet in height and a beach ball should be used. Serving by the able child is done from behind the back line and by the child in a wheelchair with the wheels on the back line. Rules should be adjusted as necessary.

VOLLEYBALL SKILL TESTS

Serving and volleying are the skills to be tested in volleyball. Serving is tested in two ways: (a) with a simple serve and (b) with an accuracy score.

Simplified Serving

In the simplified serving test, the child to be tested stands in normal serving position behind the end line on the right side and is given a specific number of trials in which to serve. The score is the number of successful serves out of ten trials. The serve must clear the net without touching and must land in the opponent's court. A ball touching a boundary line is counted as good.

Serving for Accuracy

To test serving for accuracy, a line is drawn parallel to the net through the middle of one of the courts. Each half is further subdivided into three equal areas by lines drawn parallel to the sidelines. This makes a total of six areas, which correspond to the positions of the members of a volleyball team. The areas are numbered from 1 to 6 (Figure 30.10).

Each child is allowed one attempt to serve the ball into each of the six areas in turn. Two points are scored for serving into the designated court area. One point is scored for missing the designated area but landing in an adjacent area. No points are scored otherwise.

Wall Volleying

For the wall volleying test, the player stands behind a restraining line four feet away from a wall. A line, representing the height of the net, is drawn on the wall parallel to the floor and 6.5 feet up. A player is allowed 30 seconds to make as many volleys as possible above the line while staying behind the restraining line. A counter is assigned to each testing station to count the successive volleys. To start, the child makes a short toss to herself for the first volley. If time permits, more than one 30-second period can be allowed, with the best count being taken as the score. A mat can mark the restraining line. Stepping on top of the mat makes that volley illegal.

FOR MORE INFORMATION

References and Suggested Readings

American Sport Education Program. (2003). *Coaching youth volleyball.* Champaign, IL: Human Kinetics.

American Volleyball Coaches Association, K. S. Asher (Ed.). (1997). *Coaching volleyball.* Indianapolis: Masters Press.

Fronske, H. (2005). *Teaching cues for sport skills.* 3rd ed. San Francisco: Benjamin Cummings.

30

Kluka, D. A., & Dunn, P. J. (2000). *Volleyball.* 4th ed. Dubuque, IA: McGraw-Hill.

Mood, D. P., Musker, F. F., & Rink, J. E. (2003). *Sports and recreational activities.* 13th ed. Boston: McGraw-Hill.

Pellet, T. (1999). *Volleyball.* Scottsdale, AZ: Holcomb Hathaway Publishers.

Schmottlach, N., & McManama, J. (2002). *The physical education handbook.* 10th ed. San Francisco: Benjamin Cummings.

Viera, B. L., & Ferguson, B. J. (1996). *Volleyball: Steps to success.* 2nd ed. Champaign, IL: Human Kinetics.

Wise, M. (1999). *Volleyball drills for champions.* Champaign, IL: Human Kinetics.

Websites

About Volleyball
http://volleyball.about.com/od/skillshowtosinfo

American Volleyball Coaches Association
www.avca.org

Volleyball World Wide
www.volleyball.org

Glossary

A

AAHPERD American Alliance for Health, Physical Education, Recreation and Dance

absorbing force Lessening the force of a projectile by bending the arms while catching it

accent Certain notes or beats in a rhythmic pattern that receive more force than others

act of God Defense that places the cause of injury on forces beyond the control of the teacher or the school; the defense is made that it was impossible to predict an unsafe condition, but through an act of God, the injury occurred

act of omission See *nonfeasance*

Active and Healthy School Program (AHSP) An approach that focuses on changing the environment of the school so students are naturally encouraged to increase their physical activity levels and make healthy choices, such as eating habits and sunscreen use

active listener One who convinces the speaker he/she is interested in what the speaker is saying; much of this is done through nonverbal behavior, such as eye contact, nodding the head in agreement, facial expressions, and moving toward the speaker

active sports This type of activity is typically more vigorous than lifestyle physical activity; sports often involve vigorous bursts of activity with brief rest periods; examples include basketball, tennis, soccer, and hiking

active supervision Supervision that involves moving among students and offering them personalized feedback

activity reinforcers Reinforcement that uses types of activities that children enjoy

aerobic activities Activities performed at a pace for which the body can supply adequate oxygen to meet the demands of the activity

aerobic capacity Maximum ability to use oxygen in the body for metabolic purposes

affective domain Deals with feelings, attitudes, and values; the major categories of learning in this area are receiving, responding, valuing, organization, and characterization

agility The ability of the body to change position rapidly and accurately while moving in space

anecdotal record sheet A record sheet that contains student names and has room for comments about student behavior that can be used to assess student progress

anticipatory set Pre-focuses on the skill and cognitive objectives of the lesson

arousal Level of excitement stress produces; level of arousal can have a positive or negative impact on motor performance

assessment The collection of information about student performance; traditionally directed at functions of compliance (i.e., participation, attendance, effort) and not on components that reflect student learning

asymmetrical movements Different movements using similar body parts on opposite sides of the body

attractive nuisance The legal concept of an *attractive nuisance* implies that some piece of equipment or apparatus, usually left unsupervised, was so attractive to children that they could not be expected to avoid it. When an injury occurs, even though students may have been using the apparatus incorrectly, teachers and school administration are often held liable because the attractive nuisance should have been removed from the area when unsupervised

B

balance The body's ability to maintain a state of equilibrium while remaining stationary or moving

ballistic stretching Strong bouncing movements; formerly was the most common stretching used, but this has been discouraged for many years because it was thought to increase delayed onset muscle soreness

baseline and goal-setting technique Approach that requires each individual to identify their average daily activity (baseline) level so that each individual has a reference point for setting a personal goal

basic urges An innate desire to do or accomplish something

baton passing The passing of batons during a relay race

batting Swinging at a ball that's pitched to you

beat The underlying rhythm of the music; some musicians refer to the beat as the pulse of the music

behavior contract A written statement specifying certain student behaviors that must occur to earn certain rewards or privileges; it is agreed upon and signed by the student and teacher

behavior games Strategy for changing class behavior in the areas of management, motivation, and discipline; use the shaping technique and are useful in changing whole-class behavior

blocked practice Practice where all the trials of one task are completed before moving on to the next task

body awareness Awareness of what the body can perform

body composition The proportion of body fat to lean body mass; it is an integral part of health-related fitness

body management skills Skills required for control of the body in a variety of situations; body management skills necessitate an integration of agility, coordination, strength, balance, and flexibility

breach of duty Failing to conform to the required duty; after it is established that a duty was required, it must be proved that such duty was not performed

C

cage ball A large canvas-covered ball that is 24 inches or more in diameter

cardiovascular endurance The ability of the heart, the blood vessels, and the respiratory system to deliver oxygen efficiently over an extended period of time

cardiovascular fitness Fitness that includes aspects of physiological function that promote cardiovascular endurance; activities are aerobic in nature

centering Involves transferring the football, on a signal, to the quarterback

closure Brought on by the closing activity; stressing and reinforcing skills learned, revisiting performance techniques, and checking cognitive concepts

cognitive domain Includes six major areas: knowledge, comprehension, application, analysis, synthesis, and evaluation; the focus of the cognitive domain for physical education is knowing rules, health information, safety procedures, and so on, and being able to understand and apply such knowledge

comparative negligence Under the doctrine of comparative negligence, the injured party can recover only if found to be less negligent than the defendant (the teacher). Where statutes apply, the amount of recovery is generally reduced in proportion to the injured party's participation in the circumstances leading to the injury

competition Characterized by opponents working against each other as each tries to reach a goal or reward

conceptual framework A series of statements that characterize the desired curriculum; directs the selection of activities and reflects beliefs about education and the learner

conflict resolution Cooperative approach to solving problems; can help students build positive feelings and learn to solve conflicts in a peaceful manner with no apparent losers

contrasting movements Movements that differ in their qualities, for example, smooth and jerky

contributory negligence Improper behavior by the injured party that causes the accident; harm that resulted from the injured party's contribution. This responsibility is directly related to the maturity, ability, and experience of the child

cooperation Involves two or more children working together to achieve a common goal

cooperative learning A style that focuses on the importance of people working together to accomplish common goals

coordination The ability of the body to perform smoothly and successfully more than one motor task at the same time

corrective feeedback Feedback offered with the intent of correcting a problem

criterion-referenced health standards Standards that represent a level of fitness that offers some degree of protection against diseases resulting from sedentary living; represent good health instead of traditional percentile rankings

D

deadweight Fat; has a negative impact on motor performance because it reduces relative strength

demonstration mat One mat is placed in a central position and is used exclusively for demonstrations

Developmental Levels I–III Levels used to group activities and units of instruction because it allows for greater variation of skill development among students

direct style The most teacher-controlled approach to teaching; teacher provides instruction to either the entire class or small groups and guides the pace and direction of the class

dramatization Acting out an idea with music or rhythmic accompaniment

dribbling Moving the ball with a series of taps or pushes to cover ground and still retain control

due process guidelines Guidelines required so that parents and children are informed of their rights and have the opportunity to challenge educational decisions they feel are unfair or incorrect

duration recording Used to evaluate practice time; a student or fellow teacher observes the lesson and times when students are involved in practicing skills

duty Responsibility or obligation

E

ectomorph Identified as being extremely thin, with a minimum of muscle development, and is characterized as "skinny"; may be less able in activities requiring strength and power, but able to perform well in aerobic endurance activities such as jogging, cross-country running, and track and field

endomorph Characterized as soft and round, with an excessively protruding abdomen; may perform poorly in many areas, including aerobic and anaerobic skill-oriented activities

endurance training Exercises that increase one's endurance; examples include distance running, bicycling, and swimming

equipment Items that are more or less fixed in nature; has a relatively long lifespan, needs periodic safety checks, and requires planned purchasing

exploration style/free exploration The most child-centered style of learning; guidance by the teacher is limited to the selection of the instructional materials to be used and designation of the area to be explored

expulsion The act of removing a student from the class or school setting, usually as a punishment

extinction Method of reinforcement wherein the teacher ignores performance that does not meet the predetermined criterion

extrinsic reward Rewards offered to encourage performance; examples include trophies, published league standings, ribbons, and excessive parental involvement

F

face-off Used at the start of the hockey game, after a goal, or when the ball is stopped from further play by opposing players

fast twitch (FT) fibers Fast contracting fibers in skeletal muscle tissue; capable of bursts of intense activity but are subject to rapid fatigue. These fibers are well-suited to activities demanding short-term speed and power (for example, pull-ups, standing long jump, and shuttle run)

feedback Any kind of information about a movement performance; impacts what is to be learned, what should be avoided, and how the performance can be modified

fielding Catching balls when they're hit out to the infield or outfield

Fitnessgram Test used to measure health-related physical fitness and is the recommended test for the AAHPERD. The focus of the Fitnessgram is on teaching students about the importance of activity for good health

flexibility The range of movement through which a joint or sequence of joints can move

flexibility exercises Exercises done specifically to build the part of physical fitness called flexibility

folk dance A traditional dance of a particular culture

follow through The final phase of any skill performance. In most cases, the follow through occurs after maximum force has been generated

force The effort or tension generated in movement

forearm pass Underhand pass in volleyball

foreseeability The ability to foresee potentially harmful situations; courts expect trained professionals to predict and anticipate the danger of a harmful act or situation and to take appropriate measures to prevent it from occurring

foreseeable dangers Dangers that school district personnel predict or anticipate happening (so that they can prevent such problems from occurring)

formation jumping Rope jumping where four to six ropes with turners are placed in various patterns

fundamental motor skills Locomotor and nonlocomotor skills that form the foundation for nearly all physical activities

fundamental skills Basic or functional skills; requisite for children to function fully in the environment. Fundamental skills are divided into three categories: locomotor, non-locomotor, and manipulative skills

G

galloping A movement similar to sliding, but progressing in a forward direction. One foot leads and the other is brought rapidly forward to it. There is more upward motion of the body than in sliding

game skills Games allow children to apply newly learned skills in a meaningful way; social objectives include development of interpersonal skills, acceptance of rule parameters, and a better understanding of oneself in a competitive and cooperative situation

general supervision Refers to broad coverage, when students are not under direct control of a teacher or a designated individual (for example, playground duty). A plan of supervision should be made, designating the areas to be covered and including where and how the supervisor should rotate

gross motor movements Often referred to as large muscle movements. Most often used to identify locomotor (skipping, walking, etc.) and non-locomotor movements (twisting, turning, etc.)

guided discovery Used when there is a predetermined choice or result that the teacher wants students to discover

gymnastic skills Help develop flexibility, agility, balance, strength, and body control; basic gymnastic skills include body rolling, balance skills, inverted balances, and tumbling

H

heading In soccer, a special kind of volleying in which the direction of flight of the ball is changed through an impact with the head

health-related fitness Can be integrated into regular everyday activities that are often characterized as lifetime activities; people who are generally unwilling to exercise at high intensities should aim for health-related fitness

healthy activity zone (HAZ) A suggested way to promote physical activity using pedometer step counts

healthy fitness zone (HFZ) Category that Fitnessgram uses to classify fitness performance; students are encouraged to score in the HFZ

Healthy People 2010 Document that addresses two major goals: (1) increasing the years of healthy life; and (2) eliminating health disparities; includes enabling goals concerned with promoting healthy behaviors, protecting health, achieving access to quality health care, and strengthening community prevention

hidden curriculum Implied messages sent to students through how the lesson is organized, the types of activities presented, how teachers view students who are less successful, and how children with disabilities are treated

hop-step-and-jump An event that begins with a run similar to that for the running long jump. The takeoff is with one foot, and the jumper must land on the same foot to complete the hop. He then takes a step followed by a jump. The event finishes like the long jump, with a landing on both feet

hopping Propelling the body up and down on the same foot

horizontal articulation See *scope*

human wellness An area where physical education can have a lifelong impact on students; wellness instruction teaches the principles of fitness, the importance of daily physical activity, and the benefits of physical fitness

I

IDEA Individuals with Disabilities Education Act; Public Law 105-17 has the objective of providing handicapped individuals with the least restrictive environment in the school setting—Physical education services must be made available to every child with a disability receiving a free appropriate public education

IEP Individualized Educational Program; a specific learning program for each disabled student as mandated by PL 94-142

individualized style Individualized curriculum that uses a variety of teaching strategies designed to allow students to progress at an individual rate; each student's needs are diagnosed and a program is prescribed to address those needs

indoor facilities Indoor space designated for play; gymnasium

institutional evaluation Program that involves examining the fitness levels of students to see if the institution (school) is reaching its desired objectives

instructional cues Keywords that quickly and efficiently communicate proper technique and performance of skills and movement tasks

instructional feedback Feedback given to students so that meaningful goals for improvement can be established

instructional time The amount of instruction offered to students

intensity The intensity of music can be loud, soft, light, or heavy. Mood is related to intensity but carries the concept deeper into human feelings

interrupted flow Motion that stops at the end of one movement or part of a movement before beginning another

intrinsic motivation Willingness to do something for the sake of doing it

introductory activities Activities used for starting a lesson that require little instruction and immediately immerse students in large muscle movements

J

jump shot For a jump shot, the shooter executes a vertical jump, leaving the floor slightly. The supporting (nonshooting) hand remains in contact with the ball until the top of the jump is reached. The shooting hand then takes over with fingertip control, and the ball rolls off the center three fingers. The hand and wrist follow through.

jumping box Boxes of varying heights; 8 inches and 16 inches are suggested

K

knowledge of performance Feedback that is verbal, extrinsic in nature, and occurs after the performance; relates to the process of the skill performance and refers to specific components

knowledge of results Extrinsic feedback given after a skill has been performed; usually verbal information about performance

L

large apparatus Climbing ropes, benches, balance beams, and jumping boxes; large apparatus activities offer an opportunity to learn body management skills while free of ground support

lead-up activities See *lead-up games*

lead-up games Games developed for the express purpose of limiting the number of skills needed for successful participation

leaping An elongated step designed to cover distance or move over a low obstacle

least restrictive environment Refers to the idea that not all individuals can do all of the same activities in the same environment; used to help determine the best placement arrangement of students with disabilities

liability The responsibility to perform a duty to a particular group; an obligation to perform in a particular way that is required by law and enforced by court action

lifestyle physical activities Activities that people can do as part of their regular everyday work or daily routine; examples include yard work and delivering the mail

locomotor movements Movements performed where the body travels through space

locomotor skills Skills used to move the body from one place to another or to project the body upward, as in jumping and hopping. These skills also include walking, running, skipping, leaping, sliding, and galloping

M

mainstreaming The practice of placing children with disabilities into classes with able youngsters

magic ropes Flexible ropes, similar to large rubber bands that stretch between 30 and 40 feet

malfeasance Act that occurs when a teacher does something improper by committing an act that is unlawful and wrongful, with no legal basis (often referred to as an *act of commission*)

management time Episodes that occur when students are moved into various formations, when equipment is gathered or put away, and when directions are given relative to these areas

manipulative skills Skills in which a child handles an object with the hands, feet, or other body parts

mastery learning An instructional strategy that takes a general program outcome and breaks it into smaller parts, providing a progression of skills

mental practice Involves practicing a motor skill in a quiet, relaxed environment—the experience involves thinking about the activity and its related sounds, color, and other sensations; used in combination with regular practice, not in place of it

mesomorph Characterized as having a predominance of muscle and bone and is often labeled "muscled;" in general, children who possess a mesomorphic body type perform best in activities requiring strength, speed, and agility

METS Resting metabolic rate; used to quantify activity

misfeasance Occurs when a teacher follows proper procedures but does not perform according to the required standard of conduct; based on performance of the proper action, but not up to the required standard. It is usually the sub par performance of an act that might have been otherwise lawfully done

mismatched opponents The mismatching of students on the bases of size and ability; just because the competitors are the same gender and choose to participate does not absolve the instructor of liability if an injury occurs

modeling Teachers exhibiting behaviors they expect of students

movement concepts The classification and vocabulary of movement

movement education Instruction and training in skills and concepts associated with fitness and physical education

movement themes Movements that are categorized in the major classifications of space awareness, body awareness, qualities of movement, and relationships

multicultural education Creates an educational environment in which students from a variety of backgrounds and experience come together to experience educational equality

muscular endurance The ability to exert force over an extended period; endurance postpones the onset of fatigue so that activity can be performed for lengthy periods

muscular strength The ability of muscles to exert force

MyPyramid for Kids The new children's food guide pyramid that was recently released by the USDA; it has accompanying tips, lesson plans, and coloring sheets designed to explain healthful eating to children

N

NASPE National Association for Sport and Physical Education

negative feedback Feedback that focuses on negative aspects of performance; should be avoided

negligence Defined by the courts as conduct that falls below a standard of care established to protect others from unreasonable risk or harm; several types of negligence can be categorized

nonfeasance Based on lack of action in carrying out a duty; this is usually an *act of omission* (i.e., the teacher knew the proper procedures but failed to follow them)

nonlocomotor movements Movements performed without the body traveling through space

nonlocomotor skills Skills performed in place, without appreciable spatial movement. They include bending and stretching, pushing and pulling, balancing, rolling, curling, twisting, turning, and bouncing

nonverbal behavior Another way to deliver feedback; nonverbal feedback is effective because it is easily interpreted by students and often perceived as more meaningful than words

nonverbal feedback Feedback that is given nonverbally

Norwegian Start On the command "On your mark," the runner takes a position at the starting line with the right foot forward. On "Get set," the left hand is placed on the right knee and the right hand is carried back for a thrust. On "Go," the right hand comes forward, coupled with a drive by the right foot

O

objectives Instructional goals designed and listed for the purpose of accomplishing standards

opposition Refers to throwing or kicking skills most often. For example, proper form implies stepping forward with the left foot when throwing with the right hand.

outdoor apparatus Outdoor equipment that help users develop various components of fitness; abstract in nature and can be manipulated and changed to suit the needs of users

outdoor facilities Outdoor area designated for play; the outdoor areas should include field space for games, a track, hard-surfaced areas, apparatus areas, play courts, age-group–specific play areas, covered play space, and a jogging trail

P

PACER Aerobic fitness test that can be administered indoors and does not require running to exhaustion; as a cardiovascular fitness measure, the PACER is as accurate as the mile run and produces much less emotional stress for participants

part practice Method that breaks down a skill into a series of parts and then combines the parts into the whole skill

partial mainstreaming Students participate in selected physical education experiences but do not attend on a full-time basis because they can be successful in only a few of the offerings; their developmental needs are usually met in special classes.

partner resistance activities Partner activities where each partner pulls against each other with a tug-of-war rope

partner tug-of-war ropes A rope that is about 6 feet long with a loop on each end

passing Advancing the ball to a teammate

pedometers Small devices that measure the quantity of physical activity; they are fastened to a belt or waistband

perceived competence How people feel about their ability level; becomes more specific as students mature

personal wellness Developing a personal lifestyle that is balanced in all phases with *moderation* the keyword

phrase A natural grouping of measures; phrases of music are put together into rhythmic patterns

physical activity Bodily movement that is produced by the contraction of skeletal muscle and that substantially increases energy expenditure; it is a process oriented outcome related to behavior and lifestyles

Physical Activity Pyramid A prescription model for good health that helps students understand how much and what type of activity they need

physical education Education through movement; it is an instructional program that gives attention to all learning domains: psychomotor, cognitive, and affective.

physical education specialist Teachers certified in physical education

physical fitness A set of attributes that people have or achieve relating to their ability to perform physical activity; it is a product outcome with an emphasis on achieving a higher state of being

pitching The act of throwing a softball to the catcher

placheck recording Placheck (planned activity check) recording is a technique used to observe group behavior at different times during a lesson; used to monitor behavior that is "yes or no" in nature

PL 94-142 Public Law 94-142 states that all youngsters have the right to a free and public education and must be educated in the least restrictive educational environment possible. Children with disabilities cannot be assigned to segregated classes or schools unless a separate environment is determined by due process to be in the child's best interest

point-of-decision prompts Signs placed in areas around the school where students and faculty will be making choices regarding healthy behaviors

posture Refers to the habitual or assumed alignment and balance of the body segments while the body is standing, walking, sitting, or lying

power The ability to transfer energy explosively into force

Premack principle Principle that states a highly desirable activity can be used to motivate students to learn an activity they enjoy to a lesser degree

problem solving Teaching style that involves input, reflection, choice, and response; the problem is structured so there is no one prescribed answer

process of learning outcomes Relates to the performance of movement patterns and skills with emphasis on correct technique; the form used to execute the movement is the point of assessment rather than the outcome of the skill performed

product outcomes Focus on performance in terms of measurable increments of what learners accomplish

progression Sequential presentation of skills

proximate cause Defense that attempts to prove that the accident was not caused by the negligence of the teacher

psychomotor domain This domain is the primary focus of instruction for physical educators; the seven levels in psychomotor domain taxonomy are movement vocabulary, movement of body parts, locomotor movements, moving implements and objects, patterns of movement, moving with others, and movement problem solving

punting Kicking in football

Q

qualities of movement How the body moves

R

random practice Method where the order of multiple task presentations is mixed and no task is practiced twice in succession

recreational activities Activities that involve playing games or sports for fun

reinforcement Positive behavior given when students perform acceptable behavior

relative strength Strength in relation to body size

reprimanding Approach used to decrease unacceptable behavior

resistance training The term is used here to denote the use of barbells, dumbbells, rubber bands, or machines as resistance

response latency The amount of time it takes for students to respond when commands or signals are given

responsible behavior Implies behaving in a manner that doesn't negatively impact on others; Includes behaving in an acceptable manner and assuming responsibility for the consequences of one's actions

return activities Activities that require children to perform a movement task (jumping, hopping, skipping, animal walks, etc.) after they have performed on an apparatus; this reduces the time children stand in line waiting for another turn after completion of their task on the apparatus

reverse mainstreaming Able students are brought into a special physical education class to promote intergroup peer relationships

rhythmic activities Activities performed to a rhythmic beat

rhythmic gymnastics Routines done to music by a performer using a particular type of manipulative equipment

rhythmic movement skills Skills involving motion with a regular and predictable pattern; can be attained through a rhythmic program that includes dance, rope jumping, and rhythmic gymnastics

S

scoliosis Lateral curvature in the spine

scope The yearly content of the curriculum; also referred to as the *horizontal articulation* of the curriculum

screening A process that involves all students in a school setting and is part of the "child find" process; screening tests may be administered without parental permission and are used to make initial identification of students who may need special services

self-concept A person's perception of self

self-control Level 1 of responsible behavior; the student does not participate in the day's activity or show much mastery or improvement; these students control their behavior enough so they do not interfere with other students' right to learn or the teacher's right to teach

self-responsibility Level 3 of responsible behavior; students take responsibility for their choices and for linking these choices to their own identities; they are able to work without direct supervision, eventually taking responsibility for their intentions and actions

semicircular formation Students are positioned in a semicircular arrangement; this formation directs attention toward the teacher, who stands in the center

sequence Defines the skills and activities to be covered on a year-to-year basis; also known as *vertical articulation*

shaping technique Using extinction and reinforcement to build new acceptable behavior

single standard goal Approach that is based on a single standard with the assumption that it is possible to set one goal that fits all types of youngsters regardless of age, gender, or health

skill refinement Teaching how to perform and/or refine skills properly; not synonymous with performance improvement

skill-related fitness Activities that helps improve performance in motor tasks related to sport and athletics; for people who can and want to perform at a high level because it requires training and exercising at high intensities

skipping A series of step-hops done with alternating feet

sliding A one-count movement done to the side, with the leading foot stepping to the side and the other foot following quickly; facilitate performance in the mile run or other endurance-oriented activities.

slow twitch (ST) fibers Slow contracting fibers in skeletal muscle tissue that have a rich supply of blood and related energy mechanisms; this results in a slowly contracting, fatigue-resistant muscle fiber that is well suited to endurance-type (aerobic) activities

small apparatus Magic ropes, individual mats, tug-of-war ropes, gym scooters; small apparatus activities help develop body control in space and on the ground

social reinforcers Praise, physical contact, and facial expressions to acknowledge acceptable behavior

social skills Ability to interact with others

somatotype Classification of body physique

space awareness Awareness of where the body can move

specialized motor skills Specialized skills used in various sports and other areas of physical education, including apparatus activities, tumbling, dance, and specific games; many of these skills have critical points of technique, and teaching emphasizes correct performance

specific feedback Feedback that identifies the student by name and reinforces an actual behavior; it also might be accompanied with a valuing statement

specific supervision Supervision that requires that the instructor be with a certain group of students (a class)

speed The ability of the body to perform movement in a short period of time; usually associated with running forward, speed is essential for the successful performance of most sports and general locomotor movement skills

spiking Jumping high in the air and striking the volleyball above the net, driving it into the opponent's court

sport skills Skills learned in a context of application, using an approach of teaching skills, drills, and lead-up activities

spotting A safety precaution that involves assisting a performer by helping support the body weight, and preventing a hazardous fall

squad formation Mats are placed in a line, with squads lined up behind the mats. Each child takes a turn and then goes to the end of the squad line, with the others moving up. An alternative method is for each child to perform and then return to a seated position.

static stretching Involves increasing the stretch to the point of discomfort, backing off slightly to where the position can be held comfortably, and maintaining the stretch for an extended time

strength training Weight training

striking Hitting an object with an implement, such as a bat or a hand

supplies Nondurable items that have a limited period of use

sustained flow Smoothly linking different movements or parts of a movement

symmetrical movements Identical movements using similar body parts on opposite sides of the body

T

tackling A move by a soccer player to take possession of the ball away from an opponent who is dribbling

teacher movement Moving into position to observe skill performance; enhances teacher's ability to improve student learning

tempo The speed of the music; can be constant or show a gradual increase (acceleration) or decrease (deceleration)

The Child Nutrition and WIC Reauthorization Act of 2004 This act highlights the importance of developing solutions that increase the physical activity of children, provide nutrition education, and ultimately teach youth healthy eating and activity habits that last a lifetime

time on task The amount of time students spend practicing skills that result in accomplishment of program objectives; also known as

practice time or ALT-PE (Academic Learning Time in Physical Education)

time-out Equitable technique for dealing with unacceptable behavior that occurs randomly on an individual basis; it moves youngsters out of the class setting and places them into a predesignated area when they misbehave so that they have time to reconsider and redirect their misbehavior

Title IX Title IX of the Educational Amendments Act of 1972 rules out separation of sexes and calls for all offerings to be coeducational.

token enforcers Some type of token used as a reinforcer

tort In education, a tort is concerned with the teacher–student relationship and is a legal wrong that results in direct or indirect injury to another individual or to property. *Black's Law Dictionary* defines a tort as a private or civil wrong or injury, other than breach of contract, for which the court will provide a remedy in the form of an action for damages

trainability Ability of an individual to receive more benefit from training (regular physical activity) than others

trapping Method of ball control

trekking poles See *walking poles*

twisting The rotation of a selected body part around its own long axis

U

U-shaped formation The mats are placed in the shape of a large U. This formation offers an excellent view for the teacher, and children are able to see what their classmates are doing.

V

value orientation A set of personal and professional beliefs that provides a basis for determining curricular decisions

vertical articulation See *sequence*

W

waiver forms Forms that explain the risks involved in voluntary participation and discuss briefly the types of injuries that have occurred in the past during practice and competition; participants in extracurricular activities should be required to sign a responsibility waiver form

walking poles Poles that are used in conjunction with walking or a physical education program in order to motivate students, reduce joint injuries in overweight children and realize greater results from walking

wand A sticklike piece of equipment about $^3/_4$-inch thick and between 36 and 42 inches long

Western Roll For the Western Roll, the approach, gather, and kick are the same as for the Straddle Roll, but instead of being facedown, the jumper clears the bar by lying parallel to it on her side. The left arm is pointed down at the legs while crossing the bar and then is lowered. The head is turned toward the pit after clearance, and the landing is made on both hands and the left (takeoff) foot.

whole practice Method that refers to the process of learning the entire skill or activity in one dose

General Index

A

AAHPERD, 187
AAHPERD Youth Fitness Test, 257
Abdominal strength, testing of, 158
Academic integration, 213–233
  activities in, 216–233
  benefits and limitations of, 215
  language arts and, 221–226
  mathematics and, 217–221
  process of, 214, 216
  reasons for, 214–215
  science and, 226–230
  social studies and, 230–233
  types of, 215
Academic Learning Time in Physical
  Education (ALT-PE), 164
Academic performance, physical education
  programs and, 11
Academic success, perceptual-motor
  programs and, 7
Accent, 415–416
Acceptable behavior
  behavior management to increase, 114–116
  Premack principle and, 115
  prompts for, 116
  shaping of, 116
  teaching, 110–114
Accident report, student, 186, 187
Accidents, 57
Accompaniments, for rhythmic activities,
  415–416
Accomplishment, level of successful, 262
Accountability
  assessment and, 145–146
  grading system and, 154
  pedometers and, 249–250
Active aerobics, 243
Active and Healthy School Program
  (AHSP), 297
  components of, 298–305
  initiating, 305–307
Active learning, in classroom, 298–299
Active lifestyle, standard for, 15–16
Active listening, 97
Active sports and recreational activities, 243
Active supervision, student contact and,
  170, 171
Activities. *See* Instructional activities;
  Introductory activities; Physical activity
Activity breaks, 299–300
Activity calendar, family, 302
Activity level, fitness and, 259

Activity reinforcers, acceptable behavior and,
  114–115
Act of commission, malfeasance as, 178
Act of God, *as* defense against
  negligence, 179
Act of omission, nonfeasance and, 178
Administration
  instructional responsibility and, 181
  legal levels of, 180
  responsibility for equipment and
    facilities, 183
Administrative tasks, grading on
  accomplishment of, 154
Administrators
  curriculum design and, 69
  sharing classroom rules with, 105
Adventure urges, curriculum design
  and, 72
Aerobic capacity, 30–31
  PACER fitness test and, 35
  testing of, 158
Aerobic exercise
  active, 243
  fitness routines for, 285–288
  importance of, 16
Affective domain
  characteristics and interests of children
    and, 73, 74, 75
  evaluation of skills in, 147–148, 149
  learning, 7
  student-centered objectives and, 71
Affective skills, positive, 95
After-school programs, 299
Age groups, play spaces for, 191
Aggression, conflict resolution and, 112–113
Aggressive communicator, teacher as, 101
Agility, 257
  exercises, 36
  modifications for children lacking, 135
AHSP. *See* Active and Healthy School
  Program (AHSP)
AHSP committee, 306
American Academy of Pediatrics, 34–35, 36
  report on television viewing by children, 10
American Heart Association, Jump Rope for
  Heart program, 375
American Orthopaedic Society for Sports
  Medicine (ACSSM), 36
*Analyzing Physical Education and Sport
  Instruction* (Darst, Zakrajsek, &
  Mancini), 161
Anecdotal record sheets, 149–151, 152

Animal movements, 268, 472, 474–477,
  487–489
Anticipatory set, 84
Apparatus. *See also* Equipment
  outdoor, 192–193
  safe use of, 395
Approval urges, curriculum design and,
  71–72
Arm-shoulder girdle exercises, 273–275
Arousal, in skill learning, 49
Assertive communicator, teacher as, 101–102
Assessment. *See also* Evaluation
  defined, 145
  of disabled students, 128–129
  interpretation of disability, 128
  process of learning vs. product outcomes
    in, 146
  skill refinement vs. skill performance in,
    146–147
  standards for disability, 129
  of student outcomes, 147–152
  of student performance, 145–147
Assessment tools
  anecdotal record sheets, 149–151, 152
  checklist rubrics, 148–149
  observation checklists, 149, 150
  rating scales, 149, 151
  student logs, 151
  student self-assessments, 151–152, 153
  written tests, 152
Assumption of risk, as defense against
  negligence, 179
Asymmetrical movements, 323
Attitude(s)
  caring about children's, 262
  toward fitness, 261–262
  vs. skill performance in grading, 154
Attitude development, 7
Attractiveness urges, curriculum design
  and, 72
Attractive nuisance, legal concept of, 183
Audio signal, to stop a class, 105–106
Auditorium, as gymnasium, 193, 194–195
Award systems, 160–161, 260–261

B

Backhand
  in racquetball, 596–597
  in tennis, 591
Backhand overhead clear, in badminton, 601
Backhand throw, in frisbee, 604
Backhand underhand clear, in badminton, 601

Activities Index

Photo Credits

Section 1
Section 1 opener: Bob Daemmrich/The Image Works; Chapter 1 opener: Bob Daemmrich/The Image Works; Chapter 2 opener: Bob Daemmrich/The Image Works.

Section 2
Section 2 opener: VCG/Taxi/Getty Images, Inc.; Chapter 3 opener: Elizabeth Crews/Elizabeth Crews Photography; Chapter 4 opener: Bob Daemmrich/The Image Works; Chapter 5 opener: James A. Sugar/Bettman/CORBIS; Chapter 6 opener: Myrleen Ferguson Cate/PhotoEdit Inc.; Chapter 7 opener: Bob Daemmrich/The Image Works.

Section 3
Section 3 opener: Benjamin Cummings Publishing, Pearson Education; Chapter 8 opener: Will Faller; Chapter 9 opener: David Young-Wolff/PhotoEdit Inc.; Chapter 10 opener: Cindy Charles/PhotoEdit; Chapter 11 opener: Bob Daemmrich/The Image Works.

Section 4
Section 4 opener: Ron Chapple/Taxi/Getty Images, Inc.; Chapter 12 opener: Michael Newman/PhotoEdit Inc.; Chapter 13 opener: Dennis MacDonald/PhotoEdit; Chapter 14 opener: Mary Kate Danny/Stone/Getty Images, Inc.

Section 5
Section 5 opener: Bob Daemmrich/The Image Works; Chapter 15 opener: Bob Daemmrich/The Image Works; Chapter 16 opener: Bob Daemmrich/The Image Works; Chapter 17 opener: Elizabeth Crews/Elizabeth Crews Photography; Chapter 18 opener: Bob Daemmrich/The Image Works.

Section 6
Section 6 opener: Bob Daemmrich/Stock Boston; Chapter 19 opener: Benjamin Cummings Publishing, Pearson Education; Chapter 20 opener: Frank Pedrick/The Image Works; Chapter 21 opener: Michelle D. Bridwell/PhotoEdit Inc.; Chapter 22 opener: Bob Daemmrich/Stock Boston.

Section 7
Section 7 opener: Bob Daemmrich/Stock Boston; Chapter 23 opener: Michael Newman/Photo Edit; Chapter 24 opener: Jeff Kaufman/Taxi/Getty Images, Inc.; Chapter 25 opener: Ron Chapple/Taxi/Getty Images, Inc.; Chapter 26 opener: Jim Pickerell/The Image Works; Chapter 27 opener: Nancy Richmond/The Image Works; Chapter 28 opener: David Young-Wolff/PhotoEdit Inc.; Chapter 29 opener: Bob Daemmrich/The Image Works; Chapter 30 opener: Peter Cade/Stone/Getty Images, Inc.